Second Edition

Abnormal Psychology

Brian L. Burke
Fort Lewis College

Sarah E. Trost
Cardinal Stritch University

Terri A. deRoon-Cassini
Medical College of Wisconsin

Douglas A. Bernstein
University of South Florida

Adapted from *Abnormal Psychology* by

Michael T. Nietzel, Senior Policy Advisor to Governor Jay Nixon, Missouri
(*Formerly of Missouri State University*)
Matthew L. Speltz, *University of Washington*
Elizabeth A. McCauley, *University of Washington*
Douglas A. Bernstein, *University of South Florida*

Academic Media Solutions
Affordable - Quality Textbooks, Study Aids, & Custom Publishing

Dedications

To my late father and to my father figures:
Robert Burke, who taught me why and how to think;
Gary Schwartz, who taught me how to think big;
Hal Arkowitz, who taught me how to think like a scientist-practitioner;
Jerry Phelps, who taught me how to think like a professional psychologist; and
Colin Smith, who taught me how to think like an existential human being.
And to my life partner, Leslie Goldstein, for giving new meaning to the word *support* throughout this process, as well as throughout my adult life.

—Brian Burke, March 2015

To my parents, Frederick and Louise, and to my siblings, Marianne, Margaret, Christine, and Paul, for being my role models;
To Simon and Clare, for their love and light;
And to John, for everything.

—Sarah Trost, March 2015

To my mom and dad, Corrin and Bob, for constant encouragement; to Brent, Kelley, and Adrian, for bringing joy and miracles to life; to Andy, Sophia and Cooper, for being the loves of my life; and to Andy, for your unwavering support.

—Terri deRoon-Cassini, March 2015

Cover photo: agsandrew/Shutterstock.com

MAPS icons: Medical myths (Allies Interactive/Shutterstock.com), Attempted answers (Nikitina Olga/Shutterstock.com), Prejudicial pigeonholes (El Greco/Shutterstock.com), and Superficial syndromes (Brian L. Burke).

Abnormal Psychology, 2e, Brian L. Burke, et al.

Paperback (black/white): ISBN-13: 978-1-942041-10-8
ISBN-10: 1-942041-10-1
Paperback (color): ISBN-13: 978-1-942041-11-5
ISBN-10: 1-942041-11-X
Loose-leaf version: ISBN-13: 978-1-942041-09-2
ISBN-10: 1-942041-09-8
Online version: ISBN-13: 978-1-942041-12-2
ISBN-10: 1-942041-12-8

Printed in the United States of America by Academic Media Solutions.

Brief Contents

Contents

6 Depressive Disorders

7 Anxiety Disorders 247

8 Obsessive-Compulsive and Related Disorders 281

11 Somatic Symptom and Related Disorders 363

12 Eating, Feeding, and Sleep-Wake Disorders 387

13 Sexual Dysfunctions and Gender Dysphoria 415

14 Substance-Related and Addictive Disorders 447

15 Neurocognitive Disorders 505

Preface

Overview of This Book

Abnormal Psychology, 2e, is an innovative textbook, completely organized (not just "updated") around the *DSM-5*, and built *by* and *for* teachers of psychology. It is also a student-friendly book that has been vetted and even edited by undergraduate students. The examples are fresh and modern, with references to popular culture, celebrities, and important world events. The tables and figures are easy to read, and the comics and images make the material pop. Boxes in each chapter focus on current controversies and/or prevention of mental disorders, adding a unique focus to the text; interviews with famous and working psychologists add a personal and practical dimension; and cases that start and end each chapter further bring the content to life. The text emphasizes critical thinking and looking beyond *DSM* diagnoses to understand key foundational principles of abnormal psychology. Finally, this is a text that is arranged according to how instructors teach—with only two chapters of introductory material and then detailed content regarding treatment integrated into each of the remaining 15 *DSM-5* chapters so that instructors can get into the mental disorders as quickly as possible, which is why students registered for the course in the first place.

To the Instructor

Abnormal Psychology, 2e, arose from a vision that the authors shared about a more exciting organization for an abnormal psychology textbook, as well as a new set of emphases on how disorders develop and may be prevented. This vision was focused by our experiences teaching abnormal psychology courses, by talking with other instructors about their classes, and most important, by talking with students about what *they* wanted in an abnormal psychology text. We have translated this vision into a book that students will enjoy reading and that instructors will appreciate assigning in their classes and at a fraction of the cost of competing abnormal textbooks.

Innovative Text Organization

The traditional abnormal psychology text begins with four to six chapters on the history of psychology and abnormality, an overview of theoretical approaches to abnormal behavior, a survey of classification and assessment techniques, and often, a primer on research methods. In many cases, a fourth to a third of the book is devoted to these topics. In our experience, this type of organization creates several problems, which we have tried to eliminate in *Abnormal Psychology*, 2e. First, students routinely become bored with so much background material and grow impatient, as they often put it, "to get to the interesting stuff"—the disorders themselves. Instructors frequently respond by not assigning all of the opening chapters, but this can result in an incomplete introduction to the course, inadequately explained content later, or both.

In *Abnormal Psychology*, 2e, we compress the necessary preparatory content into the first two chapters. In those chapters, we describe the basics of assessment and classification, survey major historical periods and their associated worldviews, summarize various theoretical and psychotherapeutic perspectives on abnormality, and introduce the logic of the scientific method. We confine ourselves to the fundamentals of this material, but we return to all of these issues later in the text by discussing them in the context of specific mental disorders. By the end of the book, students have been exposed to all the basic historical, psychological, and scientific concepts in a way that is more interesting and less artificial than the format of the typical abnormal psychology text.

A second major innovation in *Abnormal Psychology*, 2e, is the placement of chapters on disorders in childhood and adolescence. In the typical text, these disorders are discussed in the last third of the text, usually after all the major adult disorders have been described. This standard organization does nothing to help students understand the many important links between childhood experiences and adult problems. In *Abnormal Psychology*, 2/e, disorders of childhood and adolescence (e.g., developmental disorders) are examined before all others. This arrangement helps students learn how, in many individuals, childhood experiences are linked to adult disorders.

This special attention to developmental contributions to mental disorder is enhanced by an emphasis on *prevention*. A "Prevention" feature appears in most chapters to provide suggestions for detecting and treating disorders as they may be developing. Some "Prevention" topics include curbing adolescent suicide (Chapter 5), parenting programs and other interventions for children (Chapters 1, 2, and 3), civil commitment (Chapter 17), and preventing schizophrenia, PTSD, and personality disorders (Chapters 4, 9, and 16, respectively). Although our current knowledge of psychopathology does not yet permit the design of effective prevention programs for all disorders, there has been considerable progress in several areas. *Abnormal Psychology*, 2e, portrays what is currently known about prevention and helps students understand the importance of research in this vital area.

Abnormal Psychology, 2e, surveys a wide variety of theoretical models to explain mental disorders, but for each disorder, we emphasize the causal model that existing data best support. For most disorders, this turns out to be a *diathesis-stress model*, which emphasizes an interaction between a vulnerability or predisposition to a disorder (diathesis) and the stressors and other triggering events that translate the diathesis into a full-blown disorder. The diathesis-stress model is one example of a *biopsychosocial model* of mental disorders—a general model or approach positing that biological, psychological (thoughts, emotions, and behaviors), and social (socioeconomic, environmental, and cultural) factors all play a significant role in human functioning in the context of disorder or disease. To highlight the importance of these models, we discuss causes of each disorder in biological, psychological, and social categories, and we use carefully and consistently color-coded diagrams to depict the diatheses and stressors involved in the genesis of specific disorders.

Why do men and women differ in the frequency with which they are diagnosed with certain disorders? What is the most effective form of treatment for a given disorder? Should we devote increased resources to preventing mental disorders or to treating them once they appear? For many of these questions, the answers remain unclear. Scholars often disagree about how to interpret empirical data about such questions or even about whether the data can resolve their disagreement. To acquaint students with these inevitable—and desirable—disputes, we have included a "Controversy" feature in most chapters that focuses on an unresolved diagnostic, causal, or treatment issue. Topics include flaws in the *DSM-5* (Chapter 1), genetic influences on abnormal behavior (Chapter 2), weighing the risks of Ritalin (Chapter 3), and eating disorders in men (Chapter 12). The purpose of these "Controversy" features is to point students toward some of the "big questions" that remain unanswered in the field of abnormal psychology, while encouraging students to deepen their understanding by thinking critically about these issues. To this end, each "Controversy" feature concludes with Thinking Critically questions.

Just as childhood experiences are often linked to later problems, the symptoms, causes, and treatments of one type of disorder are often relevant to other conditions as well. Given the degree to which biological, psychological, and social factors interact with each other, this overlap should not be surprising, though it is often overlooked. One essential skill in learning about abnormal behavior is being able to see linkages between different disorders, causal factors, treatment methods, and outcomes. *Abnormal Psychology*, 2e, promotes this kind of insight by noting some of the connections among chapters. These "Connections" features appear in the margins of the text and direct readers to content in other parts of the text that is related to the current topic under discussion.

Finally, discoveries in abnormal psychology are unfolding at an astounding rate. New knowledge in the areas of diagnosis, causation, and treatment appears almost every day. To ensure that students are exposed to the most current and sophisticated thinking available, each chapter concludes with a feature called "A Conversation with . . .," which is an interview with a world-renowned expert, active researcher, or practicing clinician on a topic covered in that chapter. These experts also suggest some of the most crucial questions in need of future study. Examples include Elizabeth Loftus on repressed memory and dissociative disorders (Chapter 10), James Pennebaker on stress and health (Chapter 11), and Constance Hammen on depression (Chapter 6).

Promoting Interest and Learning

To promote student interest in the material and aid understanding, *Abnormal Psychology*, 2e, employs, in addition to the features already mentioned, a number of pedagogical devices in all chapters. In addition to brief case histories liberally distributed throughout the text, each chapter begins with a case history entitled "From the Case of . . .," which illustrates the clinical reality of a mental disorder discussed in that chapter. The case is then re-examined at the end of the chapter in "Revisiting the Case of . . .," which summarizes the course and outcome of the individual's problem. These introductory and revisited cases show how general concepts of cause and treatment operate in individuals.

Students' understanding of the material is facilitated by additional learning tools, including:

- *Section Reviews* that highlight and summarize the key points of major sections in each chapter
- *End-of-Chapter Summaries* that identify and integrate the most important subject matter in chapters
- *Key Terms*, which are boldfaced in the chapter, defined in the margin, listed at the end of each chapter with page references, and compiled alphabetically in the end-of-book Glossary

Other Special Features

Abnormal Psychology, 2e, incorporates the *DSM-5* into the chapters in two highly effective and unique ways. First, whereas most abnormal psychology texts contain "*DSM-5* updates," this entire text has been revised according to the *DSM-5*, with the chapters and order based on *DSM-5* categories and organization. Second, tables entitled "The *DSM-5* in Simple Language" in each disorder chapter explain the diagnostic criteria to students in easy-to-understand bullet points without using jargon or other murky language.

Finally, the diagnosis of mental disorders is frequently based on oversimplified medical assumptions and surface characteristics of human beings, as well as influenced by sociopolitical climate and stereotypes, rather than on a profound and real understanding of mechanism and cause. *Abnormal Psychology*, 2e, allows instructors to teach abnormal psychology from a psychological—rather than medical—perspective. The acronym MAPS, used throughout the text, stands for the four key psychological principles that pervade the field of abnormal psychology: (1) **M**edical myths (the overuse of the medical model), (2) **A**ttempted answers (the notion that many disorders are created by people's misguided attempts to solve their problems), (3) **P**rejudicial pigeonholes (the importance of multicultural considerations in the *DSM*), and (4) **S**uperficial syndromes (the *DSM* approach of listing mainly overt and easy-to-spot symptoms, rather than causal elements, in making diagnoses). Each of these four guiding principles is explained in Chapter 1 and then represented by an icon displayed in the margin throughout the text whenever that particular principle applies.

Online and in Print

Student Options: Print and Online Versions

This second edition of *Abnormal Psychology* is available in multiple versions: online, in PDF, and in print as either a paperback or loose-leaf text. The content of each version is identical.

All are sold at a fraction of the cost of leading competitors. The most affordable version is the online book, with upgrade options including the online version bundled with a print version. The print version offers you the freedom of being unplugged—away from your computer. The people at Academic Media Solutions recognize that it is difficult to read from a screen at length and that most of us read much faster from a piece of paper. The print options are particularly useful when you have extended print passages to read.

The online edition allows you to take full advantage of embedded digital features, including search and notes. Use the search feature to locate and jump to discussions anywhere in the book. Use the notes feature to add personal comments or annotations. You can move out of the book to follow Web links. You can navigate within and between chapters using a clickable table of contents. These features allow you to work at your own pace and in your own style, as you read and surf your way through the material.

Harnessing the Online Version

The online version of *Abnormal Psychology*, 2e, offers the following features to facilitate learning and to make using the book an easy, enjoyable experience:

- *Easy-to-navigate/clickable table of contents*—You can surf through the book quickly by clicking on chapter headings, or first- or second-level section headings. Plus, the table of contents can be accessed from anywhere in the book.
- *Key terms search*—Type in a term, and a search engine will return every instance of that term in the book; then jump directly to the selection of your choice with one click.
- *Notes and highlighting*—The online version includes study apps such as notes and highlighting. Each of these apps can be found in the tools icon embedded in the Academic Media Solutions/Textbook Media's online eBook reading platform (http://www.academicmediasolutions.com).
- *Upgrades*—The online version includes the ability to purchase additional study apps and functionality that enhance the learning experience.

Instructor Supplements

In addition to its student-friendly features and pedagogy, the variety of student formats available, and the uniquely affordable pricing options that are designed to provide students with a flexibility that fits any budget and/or learning style, *Abnormal Psychology*, 2e, comes with the following teaching and learning aids:

- *Test Item File*—This provides an extensive set of multiple-choice, short answer, and essay questions for every chapter for creating original quizzes and exams.
- *Instructor's Manual*—This is an enhanced version of the book offering assistance in preparing lectures, identifying learning objectives, and constructing course syllabi. The best feature in this manual is a list of 8 to 10 suggestions for teaching each chapter's material, including specific resources for classroom discussions, videos, and activities from award-winning teachers.
- *PowerPoint Presentations*—Key points in each chapter are illustrated in a set of PowerPoint files designed to assist with your instruction.

Student Supplements and Upgrades (additional purchase required)

- *Lecture Guide*—This printable lecture guide is designed for student use and is available as an in-class resource or study tool. *Note:* Instructors can request the PowerPoint version of these slides to use as developed or to customize.

- *StudyUpGrade (interactive online study guide)*—Students can turbo-charge their online version of *Abnormal Psychology*, 2e, with a unique study tool designed to "up your grade." StudyUpGrade is a software package that layers quizzes and flash cards into the online version. This inexpensive upgrade helps you improve your grades through the use of interactive content that is built into each chapter. Features include self-scoring multiple-choice quizzes, key concept reviews with fill-in-the-blank prompts, and e-flash cards comprised of key term definitions. For more on this helpful study tool, check out the flash demo at the Academic Media Solutions or Textbook Media websites.

- *Study Guide*—A printable version of the online study guide is available via downloadable PDF chapters for easy self-printing and review.

Acknowledgements

A special thank you to the authors of the original edition of this textbook, who set the tone beautifully for this second edition: Michael Nietzel, Elizabeth McCauley, Matthew Speltz, and Doug Bernstein. Other contributors who helped with the second edition of this book were: Jason Charles Levine and Rebecca Cogwell Anderson, who co-authored Chapter 11; Jennifer Hauser Kunz, who authored Chapter 3; Michelle Di Paolo, who co-authored Chapters 13 and 17; Carole Hetzel, who co-authored Chapter 13; Abbey Valvano, who co-authored Chapter 13 and Chapters 5, 6, 7, 11, and 13 of the Instructor's Resource Manual; Matthew Seipel, who co-authored Chapter 12 and authored the Test Bank; Toby Allen, who contributed his stunning artwork; Alan Light, who shared his excellent celebrity photos with us; the Lundbeck Institute, for allowing us to use their superb brain drawings; Bailey Burke, who consented to having his photos used throughout the book; and those who edited or contributed ideas to various chapters, including Katey Redmond and Emily Stout (comics), Lena Edstrom and Chris Wenzel (photographs), Sharon Sears (Chapter 2), Josh Hunt (who co-authored Chapters 4 and 9), Gary Mangel (Chapter 6), Hal Arkowitz (Chapter 8), Felicity Harl (who co-authored Chapter 10 and Chapters 9, 10, and 15 of the Instructor's Resource Manual), Kristin Anderson Franke (Chapter 11), Angela Campbell (Chapter 12), Svenja Rauchstaedt-Schneider (Chapter 13), Trina Keil (Chapter 13), and Kathleen Hazlett (who co-authored Chapter 15 and Chapters 9, 10, and 15 of the Instructor's Resource Manual). Heartfelt thanks to our diligent editors—Victoria Putman, Mary Monner, and Marilee Aschenbrenner—and to our superb designer/illustrator Craig White. Thanks also to the Fort Lewis College students who helped shape this edition of the textbook via their abnormal psychology and senior seminar classes.

In addition, we were fortunate to be able to interview and share with you the wisdom of the following leaders and practitioners in the field of abnormal psychology, and we thank them deeply: Susan Campbell, Constance Hammen, Elizabeth Loftus, Alan Frances, Alan Marlatt, James Pennebaker, Lee Sechrest, Tom Widiger, Erin Williams, Colin Smith, Tiffany O'Meara, Hal Arkowitz, Ann Marie Warren, Ted Weltzin, Meredith Leischer, Carson Smith, Mark F. Lenzenweger, and Brad Sagarin.

About the Authors

Brian Burke is a clinical psychologist whose principal academic interests include teaching, motivational interviewing, and terror management theory. Dr. Burke has a degree in college teaching and regularly attends teaching conferences, twice winning the Doug Bernstein Poster Award for innovative classroom ideas at the National Institute on the Teaching of Psychology (NITOP). Dr. Burke has won three awards in his 12-plus years at Fort Lewis College: the New Faculty Teaching Award in 2005, the Featured Scholar Award in 2011, and the Achievement Award in 2013. He has published several meta-analyses of studies evaluating the efficacy of motivational interviewing—an emerging treatment for substance use and other problem behaviors that combines the humanistic elements of client-centered therapy (Carl Rogers) with more active strategies (e.g., cognitive-behavioral therapy) designed to facilitate human change. He has also published several meta-analyses of terror management theory, which states that much of what we humans do may be a defense against our inevitable mortality. Dr. Burke originally hails from Montreal, Canada, and received his PhD from the University of Arizona in 2003, which is where he had the idea to take photographs of saguaro cacti to represent the different *DSM* disorders found in this textbook. He has been a licensed psychologist in Colorado since November 2004 and has served as assistant training director for the Student Counseling Center at Fort Lewis College. Dr. Burke lives in Durango, Colorado, with his wife, son, and Checkers the dog.

Sarah Trost is a clinical psychologist whose research and clinical interests focus on clinical health psychology. She has provided outpatient group, couples, and individual psychotherapy to adults presenting with concurrent physical and mental health concerns. She also has expertise in the psychosocial factors involved in organ transplantation and has conducted numerous psychological evaluations of potential transplant recipients and donors. Dr. Trost is an associate professor of psychology at Cardinal Stritch University in Milwaukee, Wisconsin, where she has taught abnormal psychology for over 10 years. She received her PhD in clinical psychology from the University of Arizona in 2004 and completed a postdoctorate in clinical health psychology at the Medical College of Wisconsin. She has been a licensed psychologist in Wisconsin since 2006. Dr. Trost lives with her husband, son, and daughter in Milwaukee, Wisconsin.

Terri deRoon-Cassini is a licensed psychologist and assistant professor in the Department of Surgery, Division of Trauma and Critical Care, at the Medical College of Wisconsin, where she is the primary psychologist for the Level 1 Trauma Center at Froedtert Hospital. She also has secondary appointments with the Department of Psychiatry and Behavioral Medicine and the Institute for Health and Society. She received her PhD in clinical psychology from Marquette University in 2008 and completed a postdoctoral fellowship in trauma and health psychology at the Medical College of Wisconsin. Dr. deRoon-Cassini provides clinical care to inpatient and outpatient survivors of traumatic injury, as well as to people who are adjusting to acute or chronic illness. She has been a licensed psychologist in Wisconsin since 2010. She also conducts research on the neurobiological and psychosocial risk factors for post-traumatic stress disorder. This research is funded by the National Institute of Health/National Institute of Mental Health. She lives in Delafield, Wisconsin, with her husband, daughter, and son.

Doug Bernstein received his master's and PhD degrees in clinical psychology at Northwestern University in 1966 and 1968, respectively. From 1968 to 1998, he taught graduate and undergraduate classes at the University of Illinois at Urbana-Champaign and served both as associate department head and as director of introductory psychology. From 2006 to 2008, he was visiting professor of psychology and education advisor to the School of Psychology at Southampton University, and in January 2009, he was visiting professor and education consultant at l'Institut du Psychologie at the University of Paris Descartes. He is currently professor emeritus at the University of Illinois, courtesy professor of psychology at the University of South Florida, and a teaching consultant at Ecole de Psychologues Praticiens in Paris. His teaching awards include the University of Illinois Psychology Graduate Student Association Teaching Award, the University of Illinois Psi Chi Award for Excellence in Undergraduate Teaching, the Illinois Psychology Department's Mabel Kirkpatrick Hohenboken Teaching Award, and the APA Distinguished Teaching in Psychology Award. He has co-authored textbooks on introductory psychology, abnormal psychology, clinical psychology, criminal behavior, and progressive relaxation training. With Sandra Goss Lucas, he wrote *Teaching Psychology: A Step-by-Step Guide*, now in its second edition.

About the Authors

Identifying, Detecting, and Classifying Mental Disorders: MAPS of the Territory

Chapter Outline

Source: A.R. Monko/Shutterstock.com.

After reading this chapter, you will be able to answer the following key questions:

- What are mental disorders?
- How do health professionals detect mental disorders?
- How do health professionals categorize mental disorders?
- How common are mental disorders in the United States and worldwide?
- What are four guiding principles to keep in mind when studying abnormal psychology?

From the Case of Bill

When Bill contacted the clinician, he told her that he had been constantly nervous for the past year or so. She learned that he was a 58-year-old business executive at a national computer company. Bill grew up in a working-class family, the oldest of three brothers. He was an average student through school, except for some behavior problems in the fifth grade, as well as a car accident when he first learned to drive. (Both events are discussed later in this chapter.) Bill also remembered never "having much fun" growing up. He was quiet and overweight as a teenager and always felt slighted by other boys who were more interested in and successful at sports.

Bill married his high-school girlfriend while they both were attending the same college. They have been married for 35 years and have two grown children. In addition to his salary of about $150,000 per year, Bill has reaped excellent profits from rental properties and business ventures. Despite his material success, Bill has felt restless and unhappy for the past 2 years.

Now, Bill says, his stomach is "always upset," and often he feels he can't "get his breath." According to his physician, Bill has Crohn's disease, a potentially dangerous intestinal disorder. Bill also says that he feels so agitated he can't sit still, can't concentrate at work, and has trouble remembering things. One night he drove out of the parking lot at work and left his briefcase on the pavement where he had parked his car. His success at work has begun to decline. He can't fall asleep until 3 A.M. most nights because his mind is "spinning" with constant worry about work and marital problems. He reports being sexually "impotent," a problem that has caused so much conflict with his wife that, 2 months ago, they "just gave up" trying to have sex. He describes their marriage as "extremely tense and uncomfortable"; he and his wife avoid each other as much as possible. He has been carrying on an affair with a co-worker for over a year and has kept this relationship a secret from everyone, a deception that he recognizes is beginning to take a toll on him.

Bill is also worried because his company is downsizing its workforce. Other mid-level executives have recently been fired, and Bill is sure it is just a matter of time before he gets his pink slip. At his age, he is convinced that no one else will hire him. Increasingly, when he thinks about the future, Bill feels depressed and desperate. In fact, he becomes so obsessed with the fear that he will die an early death that he sometimes wonders whether he just shouldn't kill himself and put an end to his insecurity and fear.

Bill's complaints are familiar to most clinicians. Like many clients, he complains of a mixture of anxiety, depression, physical symptoms, and marital discord. What has caused Bill's problems? Is he suffering from a **mental disorder**, or is he just going through a rough time in his life? Are Bill's problems the cause or the result of his marital difficulties? How could a clinician decide? If Bill does have a mental disorder, which diagnosis would be most accurate? What methods should a clinician use to diagnose Bill? Will his treatment differ depending on his diagnosis? These are some of the questions that mental health professionals try to answer through clinical assessment and diagnostic classification.

mental disorder: A behavioral or psychological syndrome that produces harmful dysfunction in an individual, causing objective impairment and/or subjective harm.

In this chapter, we review several definitions of mental disorders, discuss their advantages and disadvantages, and then offer a working definition to be used throughout the book. We will describe how mental health professionals assess and classify mental disorders in North America, how they distinguish disorders from nondisorders, and how they differentiate one disorder from another. We also discuss the frequency with which different mental disorders are diagnosed and how these diagnoses are affected by various real-world considerations, including financial concerns and cultural differences. We then lay out a map of the territory by describing the four guiding principles to keep in mind when studying abnormal psychology that will reappear throughout this textbook. Finally, we return to the case of Bill and see how his clinician assessed and diagnosed his problem.

Identifying Mental Disorders: What Are They?

If you decided that Bill (in the chapter-opening case) does indeed have a psychological disorder, what was it that led to your decision? Was it because you think it is unusual for someone to have such strong physical symptoms? Was it because Bill seems to be so upset by his anxious thoughts? Perhaps it was because Bill is seeking treatment for his problem. Was it because you disapprove of Bill's behavior? Maybe you concluded that Bill's behavior or emotional state could be harmful to himself and others. Or did you question whether Bill actually had a mental disorder? Each of these views reflects a different perspective on what constitutes a mental disorder.

What Is a Mental Disorder?

Mental disorder has been defined in five general ways throughout history as:

1. deviation from social expectations,
2. what mental health professionals treat,

3. a label for disliked actions,
4. subjective distress, and/or
5. a dysfunction that causes harm.

We discuss each of those five definitional approaches in more detail next.

Disorder As a Deviation From Social Expectations

Mental disorder can be defined as a deviation from social expectations. Typically, the deviation is in the negative direction from expectations. Otherwise, all unusual qualities, including high intelligence or outstanding memory abilities, for example, would be classified as disorders. Usually, a behavior that deviates from social expectations is also statistically rare. In fact, when a formerly unusual behavior becomes too frequent in society, it stops being a sign of nonconformity or a violation of expectations and starts becoming an expected behavior or norm. For example, after James Dean popularized them in the movie *Rebel Without a Cause*, wearing blue jeans became a symbol of youth rebellion during the 1950s. Because of this, jeans were sometimes banned in theaters, restaurants, and schools. During the 1960s, wearing jeans became more acceptable, and by the 1970s, it had become general fashion in the United States for casual wear (Sullivan, 2007).

Several serious problems make this social-deviation definition incomplete. First, it ignores characteristics that are not rare but are still problematic and require treatment. For example, if many people in a community suffer severe anxiety following a devastating hurricane, should the high frequency of the symptoms rule out a diagnosis of disorder? Second, how rare must a condition be before qualifying as a disorder? For schizophrenia, which affects about 1% of adults in North America, a statistical approach works fairly well because 1% is a reasonable definition of "rare." However, a deviation-based definition is less adequate for alcohol use disorder or attention-deficit/hyperactivity disorder (ADHD), each of which may affect up to 10% of American adults. Third, deviation-based definitions imply that conformity to social expectations is synonymous with mental health, but this is not necessarily the case. Not everyone who meets a society's expectations is mentally healthy, nor are those—such as jean-wearers in the 1950s or today's modern artists—who challenge those expectations necessarily mentally disordered.

Source: Mikael Damkier/Shutterstock.com.

This photo shows the city hall in Stockholm, Sweden, where the Nobel banquet occurs annually each December in recognition of cultural and/or scientific advances since 1895. The Nobel Prize in Physiology or Medicine 2013 was awarded jointly to James E. Rothman, Randy W. Schekman, and Thomas C. Südhof "for their discoveries of machinery regulating vesicle traffic, a major transport system in our cells" (Nobel Media, 2013). Many of the characteristics of such prize winners—such as high intelligence and creativity—are extremely rare, but because they are valued achievements in our culture, they are not viewed as signs of mental disorder.

epidemiology: The scientific study of the onset and frequency of disorders in certain populations.

Connections

Is schizophrenia rare in all cultures? To learn about the frequency of this disorder in different countries, see Chapter 4.

Disorder As What Mental Health Professionals Treat

A second, pragmatic definition is that mental disorders are whatever problems or symptoms clinicians treat. This definition is occasionally used in epidemiology, the scientific study of the onset and frequency of disorders in certain populations. The greatest strength of this definition is its simplicity, but it has several disadvantages. First, not everyone who consults a clinician is suffering symptoms. Many people consult mental health professionals because they want to learn how to communicate better with their spouses, to be more effective parents, or to be happier in their jobs. Obviously, people can pursue such goals without having a mental disorder. Second, this definition assumes that everyone—regardless of the disorder they suffer, the availability of treatment, or their ability to pay for it—is equally likely to seek professional treatment. However, this assumption is incorrect, so the definition of disorder on which it is based would be misleading. It would underestimate, for example, the frequency of disorders among those of low socioeconomic status, who are least likely to receive treatment.

Disorder As a Label for Disliked Actions

Some argue that most mental disorders represent nothing more than labels bestowed by mental health professionals on people whose behavior is disturbing to others. Thomas Szasz (1961) argued that mental illness should refer only to those relatively few behavioral problems that are clearly traceable to organic causes. Skeptics such as Szasz believe that labeling people who fall outside this category as mentally ill harms them by stigmatizing them. In addition, the labels often lead to the imposition of treatment, which invades people's privacy and limits their freedom.

This skeptical view has a declining influence today, mainly because it appears to trivialize the problems of people in whom no specific biological deficit has been found but whose troubles are nevertheless very real to them. It also fails to account for the fact that behavior problems often do not go away and sometimes worsen if unlabeled, and they often improve when treated. However, this definition, along with the two other definitional approaches already discussed—deviation from social expectations and what mental health professionals treat—serves to remind us of the importance of cultural factors in mental disorders.

Disorder As Subjective Distress or Unhappiness

Personal distress and unhappiness often accompany mental disorders; indeed, these feelings frequently lead people to seek treatment. Although subjective distress is a symptom of some mental disorders, distress alone cannot define disorder. People feel unhappy over many events in their lives. They worry about finances, become jealous of lovers, and get angry at bosses. In fact, *not* feeling emotionally upset in the face of a devastating loss or a callous insult might be interpreted as a sign of disorder. In addition, this definition does not distinguish between the temporary upset that accompanies stressful events and distress that may be more chronic, intense, and seemingly unrelated to external stressors. Finally, certain patterns of behavior, such as some of the personality disorders described in Chapter 16, cause little or no distress for individuals displaying them, although they create problems for other people around them. Few would argue that such behavior patterns should be disqualified as mental disorders.

Disorder As Dysfunction That Causes Harm

A useful definition is provided by Jerome Wakefield (1992), who said that mental disorders are dysfunctions that cause harm. *Dysfunction* refers to the failure of a biological or psychological mechanism to operate as it should; there is a breakdown in the way a person thinks, feels, or perceives the world. When Bill (from the chapter-opening case) experiences problems in concentration and memory, he is experiencing cognitive dysfunctions.

The concept of *harm* in this definition refers to the consequences of dysfunction that a society or an individual considers to be negative. Because not every dysfunction produces harm, not every dysfunction would be considered a disorder by this definition. Bill's cognitive lapses produced harm because they led to growing problems at work.

Defining mental disorders as harmful dysfunctions is not ideal for all circumstances and purposes, and it is not always entirely clear (Lilienfeld & Marino, 1995). For example, how much impairment must appear before it becomes a "dysfunction"? Are some psychological conditions dysfunctional in one culture, but functional in others? And when do the consequences of dysfunction cease to be merely annoying and become harmful? One parent, for example, might tolerate a child's misbehavior as "just a phase" of rambunctiousness, whereas another might see the same behavior as a symptom of a disorder requiring medication. Clearly, there is room for bias to creep into the definition. And, like all other definitions, this one can be misused and misapplied. Still, defining mental disorder as harmful dysfunction appears to be the most workable, least arbitrary definition, and the one that best captures both the objective impairment and the subjective harm that is usually associated with the concept of mental disorders.

The *DSM* Definition

The *Diagnostic and Statistical Manual of Mental Disorders* (*DSM-5*; American Psychiatric Association, 2013a) is a widely used compendium that lists all known mental disorders and that is discussed in detail later in this chapter. The *DSM-5* introduced an updated definition of a *mental disorder* when it was published in May 2013. The new definition retained the ideas already discussed of cultural context, distress/disability, and individual dysfunction found in the *DSM-IV* (American Psychiatric Association, 1994), but added the concepts of emotion regulation and developmental processes:

> A mental disorder is a syndrome characterized by clinically significant disturbance in an individual's cognition, *emotion regulation*, or behavior that reflects a dysfunction in the psychological, biological, or *developmental processes* underlying mental functioning. Mental disorders are usually associated with significant distress or disability in social, occupational, or other important activities. An expectable or culturally approved response to a common stressor or loss, such as the death of a loved one, is not a mental disorder. Socially deviant behavior (e.g., political, religious, or sexual) and conflicts that are primarily between the individual and society are not mental disorders unless the deviance or conflict results from a dysfunction in the individual, as described above. (American Psychiatric Association, 2013a, p. 20)

By including "emotion regulation" in its revised definition, the *DSM-5* affirms that mental health does not arise so much from reducing certain emotions but, rather, from adaptively managing the range of human "positive" and "negative" emotions; this reflects our rapidly growing understanding of the deep primary roles played by our affective systems (Sander, 2013; Davidson, Jackson, & Kalin, 2000). For instance, you can think about particular emotions that you find challenging when you feel them, and reflect upon how long it takes you to get "unstuck" from different emotions, as well as strategies you might use to cope with them.

The inclusion of "developmental processes" as a potential area of dysfunction emphasizes the *DSM-5*'s use of a lifespan developmental approach to classification (Klott, 2012), which you will see reflected throughout this textbook. Once you understand how mental disorders are defined, you can then think about how to detect and categorize them, as discussed in the remainder of this chapter.

Section Review

Mental disorders have been defined as:

- deviations from social expectations,
- conditions that clinicians treat,
- labels applied to unpopular behavior,
- conditions causing subjective distress and unhappiness, and
- dysfunctions or breakdowns in a biological or psychological process that lead to harm.

Assessment and Diagnosis

Imagine that nothing happens when you turn on your television set to watch your favorite show. You check to see whether the TV has been unplugged. If it hasn't, has an electric switch in the room been flipped off? If not, is a circuit breaker tripped? If the answer to all these questions is no, you check whether other electrical devices in the house are working, whether your neighbors have power, and so on. These steps are all part of **assessment**, the collection of information for the purpose of making an informed decision. In the case of the malfunctioning TV, you are assessing the situation to classify or to make a **diagnosis** of the problem. Unless you can classify the problem with your TV, it will be hard to understand or fix it. The relationship between assessment and diagnosis is the same when trying to understand mental disorders. Clinical assessment is the foundation on which accurate diagnosis of mental disorders rests.

Assessment proceeds in three steps. Clinicians first gather assessment information. Next, they organize and process this information into a description or understanding of the person they are assessing. Finally, they compare this description with what is known about various disorders to arrive at a diagnosis of the problem. This last step in diagnosis is guided by a **nosology**, a classification system containing a set of categories of disorder and rules for categorizing disorders based on the signs and symptoms that appear (Millon, 1991). As noted earlier, the *DSM-5* is the main diagnostic nosology in North America; clinicians in other parts of the world use the World Health Organization's *International Classification of Diseases (ICD-11)*.

Clinicians use a variety of sources to gather assessment information—from interviews and observations to psychological tests and personal diaries. The quality of assessment sources and the information they provide is evaluated on two dimensions: reliability and validity.

Reliability and Validity

Reliability, which refers to consistency or agreement among assessment data, can be measured in several ways. If an assessment is repeated at different times with essentially the same results, the assessment instrument is said to have high *test-retest reliability*. Another form of reliability that is especially important for psychological tests is *internal consistency*, which is judged to be high if one portion of a test provides information that is similar to that coming from other parts of the test. A third type of reliability that is especially important for diagnosis is interrater reliability. High *interrater reliability* means that different clinicians typically reach the same diagnosis, description, or conclusion about a person after using the same assessment tools. As a teenager, one of our friends was shooting Coke cans with a BB gun with a boy she had a crush on and wanted to impress. She was an excellent shooter but kept hitting just to the left side of the can without hitting the can itself. Then she realized the sight on the BB gun was off. So initially she was consistent (reliability), but not accurate (validity, as discussed next). Once she adjusted the sight, "Bam!"

The **validity** of an assessment instrument reflects the degree to which the instrument measures what it is supposed to measure. It provides an estimate of an instrument's accuracy or meaning. There are several types of validity. *Content validity* refers to the extent to which a tool measures all aspects of the domain it is supposed to measure. For example, an intelligence test that measures only math skills would be low in content validity because intelligence involves more than mathematical ability. If an assessment procedure accurately forecasts a person's behavior (e.g., grade-point average, suicide attempts), it is said to have high *predictive validity*. When the results of one procedure agree closely with the results of another assessment method that was given at about the same time, the two methods are said to have high *concurrent validity*.

A final form of validity is construct validity (Cronbach & Meehl, 1955). An assessment method has high *construct validity* when its results coincide with what a theory about some construct would predict. For example, theories of anxiety predict that people's anx-

---

assessment: The collection of information for the purpose of making an informed decision.

diagnosis: The classification of mental disorders by determining which of several possible descriptions best fits the nature of the problem(s).

nosology: A classification system containing categories of disorders and rules for categorizing disorders depending on observable signs and symptoms.

reliability: Consistency or agreement among assessment data; includes test-retest reliability, internal consistency, and interrater reliability.

validity: The degree to which an assessment instrument measures what it is supposed to measure, thereby providing an estimate of accuracy or meaning.

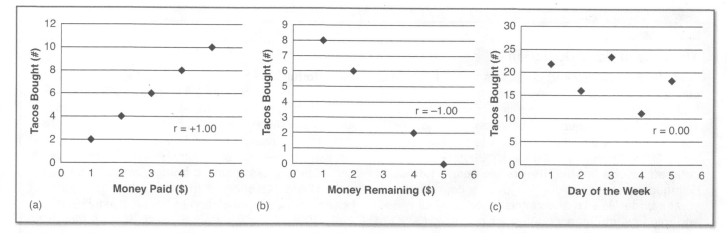

FIGURE 1.1 Correlations Showing Different Relationships Between Two Variables

(a) The cost of a taco purchase shows a *perfect positive correlation* (+1.00) with the number of tacos purchased; the more 50-cent tacos you buy, the more you pay. (b) The amount of money remaining in your wallet shows a *perfect negative correlation* (−1.00) with your purchase; the more you buy, the less cash you have left. (c) This graph illustrates a *zero correlation* in which the number of tacos purchased is unrelated to day of the week on which the purchase is made. (This last graph might change, of course, if your local taqueria has two-for-one taco Tuesdays!)

iety levels will increase under stressful circumstances. Thus, an anxiety assessment tool would have construct validity if it yields higher scores when people are in situations they fear, such as speaking in public. If not, the tool may not be measuring anxiety—that is, its construct validity is suspect. Construct validity cannot usually be established with a single experiment or demonstration; it requires a series of studies. The availability of assessment devices with good construct validity is important for identifying factors that place a person at risk for certain disorders and, in turn, for guiding the development of prevention programs, as discussed in the "Prevention" feature in this chapter. (Each chapter in the book has a "Prevention" feature covering the application of scientific methodology [see Chapter 2] that seeks to prevent or moderate mental disorders before they occur.)

The reliability and validity of assessments are typically expressed as **correlation coefficients**, which summarize the relationship between two variables. The size of a correlation, noted by the symbol r, ranges from 0.00 to +1.00 or −1.00. As Figure 1.1 illustrates, an r of 0.00 means that there is no relationship between two variables. A correlation of +1.00 or −1.00 is a perfect correlation, which means that if you know the value of one variable, you can predict the value of the second one with certainty. The larger the correlation (whether positive or negative), the stronger is the relationship between the two variables. In psychological assessment, adequate reliability is usually indicated by correlation coefficients in the .70 to .90 range. In most psychological research, validity correlations are in the .20 to .60 range, indicating that two variables are related to some less-than-perfect degree.

The validity of an assessment device can be no higher than its reliability, but it can be lower, sometimes much lower. In other words, high reliability does not guarantee validity. Consider the example provided by the popular *Harry Potter* series in literature and film. One of the main characters in the series, Professor Severus Snape, typically appears angry and mean. Most readers initially judge Snape to be evil, and this assessment would have high interrater reliability—that is, most readers (or film viewers) would have agreed. This high reliability did not ultimately make their assessment correct or valid, however.

correlation coefficient: A number that quantifies the size of relationship between two variables, noted by the symbol r, and ranging from +1.00 to −1.00. The larger the absolute value of the correlation, the stronger the relationship between the variables.

Diagnostic Errors

It is fun to be fooled in the context of entertainment, but there is nothing funny about diagnostic errors in real life. Because people's lives can be drastically affected by clinicians' diagnostic judgments, the validity of those judgments is crucial. A clinician can reach two kinds of correct diagnostic conclusions: true positives and true negatives. In the case of

The Role of Early Detection

Juvenile delinquency and crime has long been one of our society's most pressing problems. In the United States, the rate at which juveniles committed serious violent crimes changed little between 1973 and 1989, peaked in 1993, and then declined to the lowest level since 1986 (Snyder & Sickmund, 1999). Females accounted for one fourth (28%) of the nearly 1.4 million delinquency cases handled by juvenile courts in 2010, youths under age 16 accounted for 52% of all cases, and minority youths accounted for one third (36%) of all cases (OJJDP Statistical Briefing Book, 2013). The costs of these crimes is enormous, as is the fear they cause, but the declining rates in the past two decades suggests that juvenile delinquency can be prevented. An approach to further reducing juvenile delinquency depends, first, on whether we can:

- pinpoint early risk factors that lead to delinquency,
- assess which children actually possess or have been exposed to these risk factors, and
- design preventive interventions to reduce these risks.

Research by behavioral scientists has uncovered a valid set of early childhood risk factors for later aggression and chronic delinquency (Tolan, Guerra, & Kendall, 1995). Children at greatest risk are those who (1) have a difficult temperament; (2) are subject to abusive, hostile, or inconsistent parental discipline; (3) experience family adversity or other negative life events, including exposure to peer violent victimization; (4) lack self-control and do poorly at school; and (5) come from a low socioeconomic background (Yoshikawa, 1994; Jackson, Hanson, Amstadter, Saunders, & Kilpatrick, 2013). Further, family disruption and deviant behavior of friends have more influence on delinquent behavior of females, whereas the lack of self-control is more strongly related to delinquency among males (Steketee, Junger, & Junger-Tas, 2013).

Several of these risk factors can be detected during the preschool or elementary school years with special assessment techniques. These assessments include scales that measure antisocial behavior, family risk, and socioeconomic status to yield reliable and valid information about the early risk factors preceding juvenile delinquency (Zara & Farrington, 2013).

Early detection, in turn, allows interventions to be put in place before problems become entrenched. The newest delinquency prevention programs recognize that early aggression and later delinquency are caused by multiple factors arising in homes, schools, and peer systems and that changes must be achieved in each of these settings for prevention to be successful (Borduin et al., 1995; Tremblay, Pagani-Kurtz, Masse, Vitaro, & Pihl, 1995). The prevention programs that have proved most successful with early-aggression children combine extra educational assistance (such as Head Start) to improve commitment to school with training of parents to use more consistent and nurturing child-rearing methods (Yoshikawa, 1994; Zigler, Taussig, & Black, 1992).

Head Start programs began in 1965 as part of the Johnson administration's War on Poverty efforts to help reduce the gap in achievement between children from low-income families and their more advantaged peers (Resnick, 2010); they alone have resulted in improvement of about a quarter of a standard deviation across all cognitive and achievement outcomes (Shager et al., 2013). Often used together with Head Start, the Incredible Years is an evidence-based program that trains parents to relate to and discipline their children more effectively, and it has shown improvements in children's negative behaviors of anywhere from half to one-and-a-half standard deviations (Hurlburt, Nguyen, Reid, Webster-Stratton, & Zhang, 2013).

Despite these research-backed prevention programs, juvenile awareness programs based on confrontation, fear, and threat rather than empirically validated risk factors remain in operation. For instance, "Scared Straight," parodied on *Saturday Night Live* by Kenan Thompson, typically involves adult inmates describing the extremely brutal, harsh, and unpleasant conditions associated with jail or prison incarceration to delinquent or at-risk youth in a secure setting. These programs have no statistically significant effect on at-risk juveniles and in fact may even increase the likelihood of future offending (Klenowski, Bell, & Dodson, 2010).

sensitivity: The probability that a person with a mental disorder is diagnosed as having that disorder.

specificity: The probability that a person without any mental disorder will be diagnosed as having no disorder.

a *true positive*, the clinician correctly concludes that a condition is present. This is also called the **sensitivity** of diagnosis, which is the probability that a person with a mental disorder will be diagnosed as having that disorder. Conversely, a *true negative* conclusion occurs when the clinician correctly states that the person does not have the condition. This is called the **specificity** of the diagnosis, the probability that a person without any mental disorder will indeed be seen not to have one.

Unfortunately, clinicians can also make two kinds of diagnostic errors: false positives and false negatives. A *false positive* occurs when the clinician concludes that the person suffers a mental disorder when no disorder is, in fact, present. A *false negative* occurs when the clinician diagnoses no mental disorder when the person actually has one. Both kinds of errors can have severe consequences. False positives can lead to unnecessarily labeling and possibly stigmatizing people with no disorders. False negatives can keep troubled people from receiving the professional help they need. As you will see, scholars have argued that the *DSM-5* is much more concerned with avoiding false negatives and therefore raises the number of false positives—that is, people who will be diagnosed with mental disorders that they do not actually have.

Section Review

The three major steps in assessment and diagnosis are:
- gathering information,
- organizing the information into a clinical description of the person, and
- using this description and a nosology to reach a diagnosis.

The quality and utility of diagnoses depend on:
- the reliability and validity of the assessment tools used, and
- the sensitivity and specificity of the diagnoses (false positives and negatives).

Assessment Tools: How Do Health Professionals Detect Mental Disorders?

To avoid false positives and false negatives, clinicians need reliable sources of information. In practice, clinicians usually combine information from one or more assessment tools. When they use multiple channels of information, clinicians can compare the results from all sources, thus strengthening their confidence in their findings. Here we consider the reliability and validity of the five most commonly used assessment tools—life records, interviews, tests, observations, and biological measures—and how each is used by clinicians in reaching diagnoses.

Life Records

Life records are documents associated with important events and milestones in a person's life, such as school grades, court records, police reports, and medical records. This information can be helpful in determining whether, when, and how often a certain problem has occurred. Because life records are usually made for reasons other than a formal assessment, they are unlikely to be distorted by a person's attempt to create a certain impression.

> **life records:** Documents associated with important events and milestones in a person's life, such as school grades, court records, police reports, and medical histories.

Forensic psychologists generally rely heavily on life records when completing postmortem assessments following unusual death circumstances to attempt to determine whether an individual's death was related to suicide or other causes. This is called a psychological autopsy. In these cases, the psychologist does not have the opportunity to use any of the next four assessment tools (except to possibly interview friends and family members), and so they must use whatever records are at their disposal to piece together the deceased person's mental state prior to his or her death.

Interviews

Interviews are the most widely used assessment tool for classifying mental disorders. Because they resemble other forms of conversation, interviews are a natural way of gaining personal information. In addition, they are relatively inexpensive and flexible with respect to their content.

Modern diagnostic interviewing usually follows a structured format. In a **structured interview**, the interviewer asks questions in a predetermined sequence so that the procedure is essentially the same from one respondent to another. Consistent rules are provided for scoring respondents' answers or for using additional probes designed to obtain scorable responses. Usually, the interviewer is also given detailed guidelines for what to

> **structured interview:** An interview in which the interviewer asks questions in a predetermined sequence so that the procedure is essentially the same from one interview to another.

TABLE 1.1 Structured Interviews Frequently Used to Assess Clinical Conditions

Interview	Purpose
The Schedule of Affective Disorders and Schizophrenia (SADS)	Differential diagnosis of more than 20 categories of mental disorder
The Diagnostic Interview Schedule (DIS), which led to the Composite International Diagnostic Interview (CIDI)	Used by nonprofessionals in large-scale epidemiological studies of mental disorder
Structured Clinical Interview for *DSM* (SCID)	Broad-scale differential diagnoses tied to the *DSM* criteria
Diagnostic Interview Schedule for Children–Revised (DISC-R)	Parallel formats for children and parents for making differential diagnoses of childhood disorders
Anxiety Disorders Interview Schedule (ADIS)	Differential diagnoses among anxiety disorders
Personality Disorders Interview-IV	Differential diagnoses among the *DSM* personality disorders
Interdisciplinary Fitness Interview, Revised (IFI-R)	Evaluation of competence to stand trial
Rogers Criminal Responsibility Assessment Scales (R-CRAS)	Assess criminal responsibility against specific legal criteria
Psychopathy Checklist, Revised (PCL-R)	Evaluation of major dimensions of psychopathic (antisocial) behavior

ask when the respondent answers questions in a given manner (for example, "If the respondent answers 'no,' skip to question 32 and continue with the interview."). Of course, interviewers are permitted some flexibility in how they word questions and in the number of questions they ask, but they are expected to indicate such changes whenever they deviate from the standard format so that the effects of any changes can be studied.

Table 1.1 describes some of the most common of the many structured interviews in use today (see also Gross & Hersen, 2008; Rogers, 2001). Several of these interviews are coordinated with *DSM* criteria to help the interviewer arrive at a diagnosis, and most are updated/revised periodically to reflect new research or changing diagnostic criteria. The Personality Disorders Interview-IV (Widiger, Mangine, Corbitt, Ellis, & Thomas, 1995) is one example. Clinicians can use it to determine whether a given client meets criteria for any of the personality disorders in the *DSM-5*. For instance, one criterion for diagnosing someone with *borderline personality disorder* is whether the person has acted impulsively in at least two areas that could be personally damaging. An interviewer assesses this criterion with the following questions:

1. Did you ever spend so much money that you had trouble paying it off?
2. Have you ever gone on a drinking or eating binge?
3. Have you ever taken any major chances or risks with drugs?
4. Have you ever done anything impulsive that was risky or dangerous?
5. Have you ever become sexually involved with someone in a risky or dangerous way?

mental status examination (MSE): A brief, specialized, and focused interview designed to assess a person's memory, mood, orientation, thinking, and concentration.

Another type of structured interview is the **mental status examination (MSE)**, a brief, specialized, and focused interview designed to assess a person's memory, mood, orientation, thinking, and ability to concentrate. The MSE is analogous to the brief physical exam that physicians employ at the beginning of patient assessments. The questioning is direct, as suggested by the following excerpt:

Clinician: Good morning. I would like to ask you some questions. Is that all right?

Client: Fine.

Clinician: How long have you been here?

Client: Since yesterday morning.

Clinician: What are you here for?

Client: I don't know. I think my wife called the police and here I am.

Clinician: Well, what did you do to make her call the police?

Client: I don't know.

Clinician: What day is today?

Client: Tuesday, the twelfth.

Clinician: What year is it?

Client: 2015.

Clinical interviews also assess a person's **social history**, including educational achievements, occupational positions, family history, marital status, physical health, and prior contacts with mental health professionals (and this information can be augmented by life records if available). An accurate social history is crucial to the correct diagnosis of mental disorders because it helps to establish whether the person has experienced symptoms of mental disorders in the past and, if so, which of the symptoms have been most prominent.

Interrater and test-retest reliability generally exceed +.70 for structured diagnostic interviews and mental status examinations, although, as the interval between interviews becomes longer, test-retest reliability sometimes decreases (Olin & Zelinski, 1991). The validity of structured interviews has been studied less often than their reliability has, but they are generally superior to any other diagnostic assessment tool (Rogers, 2003). Occasionally, they even serve as the standard against which to judge the diagnostic validity of other assessment methods, such as tests or observations.

Unfortunately, many clinicians do not routinely use structured diagnostic interviews, preferring instead to "play their interviews by ear." In fact, clinicians reported using structured interviews, on average, with only about 15% of their clients (Bruchmüller, Margraf, Suppiger, & Schneider, 2011). Often, clinicians say that structured interviews are too bothersome to learn and that less-structured interviews increase flexibility and save time. Or they mistakenly believe that their clients will not accept the use of structured interviews, even though about 80% of clients report finding these interviews helpful (Bruchmüller, Margraf, Suppiger, & Schneider, 2011). However, unstructured interviews are almost always less reliable and less valid than structured ones (Samuel et al., 2013). Thus, what clinicians gain in flexibility and efficiency by using unstructured interviews instead of more-structured formats tends to be offset by what they lose in accurate and comprehensive information (Rogers, 1995, 2001, 2003).

Psychological Tests

A **psychological test** is a systematic procedure for observing and describing a person's behavior in a standardized situation. **Standardization** means that the test is administered and scored using uniform procedures for all test-takers. Tests require a person to respond to a set of stimuli such as inkblots, true/false statements, or multiple-choice questions. These responses are then scored and compared with **norms**, scores obtained from large numbers of people who have taken the test previously under the same conditions.

Almost all of the thousands of psychological tests now in use can be grouped into one of five categories: achievement and aptitude tests, attitude and interest tests, intelligence tests, neuropsychological tests, and personality tests. **Aptitude tests** measure the accumulated effects of educational or training experiences and attempt to forecast future performance; the Scholastic Aptitude Test (SAT), which most American high-school graduates take before applying to college, is a familiar example. **Achievement tests** measure

social history: Obtained as part of clinical interviews, it includes assessment of educational achievements, occupational positions, family history, marital status, physical health, and prior contacts with mental health professionals.

psychological test: A systematic procedure for observing and describing a person's behavior in a standardized situation.

standardization: Administering and scoring a test using uniform procedures for all respondents.

norm: A score obtained from large numbers of people who have taken a test previously under similar conditions.

aptitude test: A measure of the accumulated effects of educational or training experiences that attempts to forecast future performance. One example is the Scholastic Aptitude Test (SAT).

achievement test: A measure of how much a person has learned about a specific area. One example is the Wide Range Achievement Test–Revised (WRAT-3).

how much a person knows or can do in a specific area; the Wide Range Achievement Test–Revised (WRAT-3) is a good example. Although achievement and aptitude tests are often used in diagnosing learning disorders and, occasionally, disorders that have an organic cause, they do not play a major role in diagnosing most mental disorders. Similarly, **attitude and interest tests**—which measure the range and strength of a person's interests, attitudes, preferences, and values—are seldom used in diagnostic classification, although they can add important information to a general psychological assessment.

attitude and interest tests: Tests that measure the range and strength of a person's interests, attitudes, preferences, and values.

intelligence test: A measure of general mental ability and various specific intellectual abilities, such as verbal reasoning, quantitative skills, abstract thinking, visual recognition, and memory.

Intelligence Tests

Intelligence tests measure general mental ability and various specific intellectual abilities, such as verbal reasoning, quantitative skills, abstract thinking, visual recognition, and memory (see Figure 1.2). The Stanford-Binet Intelligence Scale (5th edition; Roid & Barram, 2004), the Wechsler Intelligence Scale for Children (WISC-IV; Wechsler, 2003), and the Wechsler Adult Intelligence Scale (WAIS-IV; Wechsler, 2008) are the best-known intelligence tests in the world today. Like structured interviews, these tests have been revised several times throughout their history. Although originally written in English, these tests have all been translated into several languages, and norms are available for many different countries. The Wechsler scales have an especially high correlation with *g*, the general factor of intelligence, also known as intelligence quotient or IQ (Reynolds, Floyd, & Niileksela, 2013). Intelligence tests are used in the assessment and classification of brain damage, intellectual disabilities, and other developmental disorders (see Chapter 3 for more on their use and limitations).

Neuropsychological Tests

neuropsychological test: A psychological assessment tool that measures deficits in behavior, cognition, or emotion known to correlate with brain dysfunction and damage, and helps to determine whether a person is suffering from brain damage or deterioration.

Neuropsychological tests measure deficits in behavior, cognition, or emotion that are known to correlate with brain dysfunction and damage. They are valuable tools for determining whether a person is suffering brain damage or deterioration, or for assessing how well a person has recovered following neurosurgery (Prigatano, Parsons, & Bortz, 1995). Neuropsychological testing often consists of a standardized set, or *battery*, of tests, but as illustrated in the continuation of the chapter-opening case that follows, it may also be individualized, beginning with a few standard tests, followed by tests selected with questions specific to the client in mind (Lezak, 1995).

When Bill, whose case opens this chapter, was 16 years old and first started driving, he was involved in a car accident and sustained a closed-head injury. About a year later, Bill's family physician referred him to a psychologist for diagnostic testing because of a variety of lingering symptoms, including sleeplessness, loss of memory and concentration, and unusual outbursts of impulsivity and anger.

FIGURE 1.2 A Sample Figure Completion Task From a Test of Cognitive Ability

Intelligence tests have started to incorporate more items that are less reliant on language and specific cultural information, such as a figure completion task like the one shown here. The item is designed to assess the ability to recognize figural series. The correct answer is *d*.

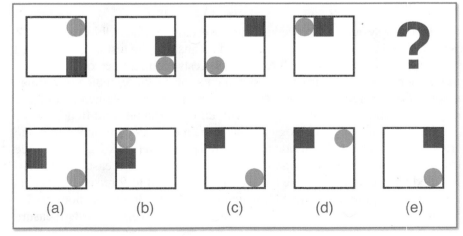

After taking a social history and learning about Bill's accident, the psychologist was especially interested in determining whether Bill might be suffering from some sort of head injury or from an anxiety disorder due to the stress of the accident. A number of neuropsychological tests were selected to measure Bill's attention, memory, perceptual accuracy, and language skills. When they all yielded normal results, the psychologist concluded that Bill's symptoms were the result of posttraumatic stress and recommended brief psychotherapy.

The most widely used neuropsychological test battery in North America is the one developed by Ward Halstead and later modified by his student, Ralph Reitan. Table 1.2 summarizes some of the tests included in the Halstead-Reitan Neuropsychological Test Battery (Reitan & Wolfson, 2009). Two additional popular batteries are the Adult Luria-Nebraska Neuropsychological Battery (Golden, 2004) and the Luria-Nebraska Neuropsychological Children's Battery (Golden, 2011). Many neuropsychologists question the validity

TABLE 1.2 Some Tests Used in the Halstead-Reitan Neuropsychological Test Battery

Test	Description
Categories test	Consists of 208 slides that require a subject to form correct categorizations of the visual stimuli in the slides. The test measures mental efficiency and the ability to form abstract concepts.
Tactual performance test	Consists of a board with spaces into which 10 blocks of various shapes can be fitted, somewhat like a large jigsaw puzzle. The subject is blindfolded and then asked to fit the blocks into the spaces as quickly as possible. This test measures such abilities as motor speed, tactile and kinesthetic perception, and incidental memory.
Rhythm test	Presents 30 pairs of rhythmic beats. The subject says whether the rhythms are the same or different. It is a measure of nonverbal auditory perception, attention, and concentration.
Speech-sounds perception test	Requires that the subject match spoken nonsense words to words on written lists. Language processing, verbal auditory perception, attention, and concentration are measured by this task.
Finger-tapping test	A simple test of motor speed in which the subject depresses a small lever with the index finger as fast as possible for 10 seconds. Several trials with each hand are performed, allowing comparison of lateralized motor speed.
Trail-making test	A kind of "connect-the-dots" task involving a set of circles that are numbered or lettered. The circles must be connected in a consecutive sequence, requiring speed, visual scanning, and the ability to use and integrate different sets.
Strength-of-grip test	A right-side versus left-side comparison of strength. The subject simply squeezes a dynamometer twice with each hand.
Sensory-perceptual exam	Assesses whether the subject can perceive tactile, auditory, and visual stimulation when presented on each side of the body.
Tactile perception tests	Various methods to assess the subject's ability to identify objects when they are placed in the right and left hand, to perceive touch in different fingers of both hands, and to decipher numbers traced on the fingertips.
Aphasia screening test	A short test that measures several aspects of language usage and recognition, as well as abilities to reproduce geometric forms and pantomime simple actions.

of the Luria-Nebraska batteries (Purisch, 2001), but their major advantage is that they can be administered in 3 to 4 hours, about half the time required for the Halstead-Reitan battery. Although these comprehensive batteries were originally designed primarily for differentiating between brain-injured and normal individuals, they have good test-retest reliabilities (Calamia, Markon, & Tranel, 2013) and continue to offer a rich array of clinical information regarding brain-behavior relations (Davis, Johnson, & D'Amato, 2005).

Personality Tests

personality test: A standardized psychological assessment of an individual's predominant personality traits and characteristics.

projective tests: Personality tests that require the person to respond to ambiguous stimuli, such as inkblots, incomplete sentences, or vague drawings. The responses are thought to reveal important characteristics about people by the way they project meaning onto the ambiguous stimuli.

Personality tests measure an individual's predominant personality traits and characteristics. There are projective and objective personality tests. **Projective tests** present ambiguous stimuli, such as inkblots, incomplete sentences, or vague drawings to which people are asked to respond in any way they choose, often by telling a story or filling in a blank. Three major projective instruments are the Rorschach Inkblot Test (see Figure 1.3), the Thematic Apperception Test (TAT), and human figure drawings. Users of projective tests assume that these responses will reflect the meaning that people "project" onto the ambiguous stimuli—that is, the way they perceive and interpret them—and thus reveal important characteristics about their personalities.

Recently developed scoring systems, such as the widely used comprehensive system for scoring Rorschach responses (e.g., Exner, 1993), are designed to provide quantitative summaries of projective tests and have increased the tests' reliability, but they are still not as reliable as the best objective personality tests (Rogers, 2001; Wood, Nezworski, & Stejskal, 1996). In addition, there is empirical support for the validity of a small number of indexes derived from the Rorschach and TAT. However, the substantial majority of Rorschach and TAT indexes, as well as human figure drawings, are not empirically valid (Lilienfeld, Wood, & Garb, 2000). The Rorschach may be especially valuable for detecting psychosis (see Chapter 4), but overall, it has not lived up to the lofty claims made in its scoring manual (Mihura, Meyer, Dumitrascu, & Bombel, 2013). Finally, utilizing the

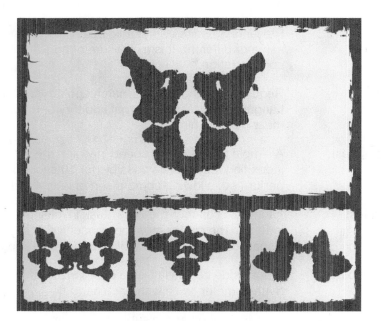

FIGURE 1.3 Inkblot Such As Those Used in the Rorschach

What do these inkblots look like to you? Your response to this question might be determined by the shape of the blot ("The top one looks like a pelvis"), the whole blot ("The bottom one on the right looks like two socks tied together"), just some part of it ("The bottom left blot has a butterfly in the center"), or even the white spaces in the middle ("The bottom middle blot has two eyes in the center"). Some people might even perceive movement taking place, such as two clowns dancing in the top blot.

Source: Dimec/Shutterstock.com.

comprehensive scoring system correctly takes extensive and ongoing training, and therefore, few practicing clinicians actually apply the system as it was intended (Hunsley & Bailey, 1999). Accordingly, projective tests tend to be less useful (and less often used) for diagnostic classification than other assessment tools.

Objective tests require answers or ratings to specific questions or statements (for example, "Have you ever felt depressed?"); the responses can be scored quantitatively. The most widely used objective test of personality is the Minnesota Multiphasic Personality Inventory (MMPI). Originally developed in the 1930s, it was revised in the 1980s and 2000s and, more recently, reconceived as the Minnesota Multiphasic Personality Inventory-2-Restructured Form (MMPI-2-RF; Ben-Porath & Tellegen, 2008/2011). A separate form of the MMPI has been developed for adolescents (the MMPI-A) (Butcher et al., 1992).

objective test: A personality test that requires answers or ratings to specific questions or statements that are scored quantitatively.

The MMPI-2-RF takes 35 to 50 minutes to complete and consists of 338 true/false statements that are included in the test because they (1) distinguish between people who do and do not display mental disorders, and (2) differentiate people with different mental disorders. For example, one group of items tends to be answered in the same way by people with schizophrenia, a different set of items tends to be answered similarly by people with depression, and a third set is answered in a typical way by people who are socially introverted. Based on these empirical differences, 9 groups of differentiating items, called *clinical scales*, were named for the groups of people with which they were originally associated. Note that the original MMPI had 10 such clinical scales, but these were empirically refined into 9 restructured clinical (RC) scales (Tellegen et al., 2003). These 9 RC scales demonstrate a moderate improvement in validity over the standard clinical scales (van der Heijden, Egger, Rossi, Grundel, & Derksen, 2013).

Table 1.3 summarizes the RC scales, along with key *validity scales*, groups of items on the MMPI-2-RF that help detect test-taking attitudes and distortions that may influence clinical scale scores. For example, the *F* (or infrequency) scale contains items that are rarely endorsed by members of any diagnostic group. High *F* scores suggest that a respondent was careless, attempted to exaggerate symptoms, or displayed a severe disorder. The MMPI validity scales can help detect *malingering*, the purposeful production of falsely or grossly exaggerated complaints with the goal of receiving a reward (Wygant et al., 2011).

To interpret a valid MMPI-2-RF, clinicians create a *scale profile* showing a client's scores, such as the one presented in Figure 1.4. They then conduct a *profile analysis* by comparing the client's scale profile with the profiles of other clients. Based on that comparison, they form hypotheses about the person's psychological condition. The comparison can be based on the clinician's own experience with the MMPI-2-RF or on published norms showing the profiles of clients with various kinds of disorders. Increasingly, clinicians rely on computerized scoring and interpretation of the MMPI-2-RF, in which a given client's profile is compared with thousands of other clients using actuarial formulas applied by a computer. The MMPI-2-RF normative sample is drawn from the MMPI-2 normative sample and consists of 2,276 men and women, 1,138 of each gender, between the ages of 18 and 80, from several regions and diverse communities in the United States (Ben-Porath, 2012).

Despite its continued widespread use, the MMPI system has been criticized for having been developed without reference to any underlying psychological theory about mental disorders (Helmes & Reddon, 1993). Items were included on the test as long as they differentiated people with different disorders, but the items themselves may not possess much construct validity or explain much about the nature of the disorders with which they correlate. Several other objective personality tests have attempted to overcome the perceived weaknesses of the MMPI system and to conform more closely to the *DSM*. Among the more influential of these tests are the Millon Clinical Multiaxial Inventory-III (Millon & Meagher, 2004) and the online Personality Inventory for the *DSM-5* (PID-5; American Psychiatric Association, 2013b). In addition, tests of normal personality, such as the California Personality Inventory (Gough, 1987; Megargee, 2009) and the NEO Personality Inventory–Revised (Costa & McCrae, 1992a), are also used to assess characteristics associated with mental disorders (Costa & McCrae, 1992b), usually as supplements to other objective measures of psychopathology (Ben-Porath & Waller, 1992).

TABLE 1.3 MMPI-2-RF Scales and Simulated Items

Key Validity (or Test-Taking Attitude) Scales	Description
CNS (Cannot Say)	Number of items left unanswered
L (Lie or Uncommon Virtues)	Items of overly good self-reports, such as "I smile at everyone I meet" (True)
F (Infrequent Responses)	Items answered in the scored direction by 10% or less of test-takers, such as "There is an international plot against me" (True)
K (Correction or Adjustment Validity)	Items reflecting defensiveness in admitting to problems, such as "I feel bad when others criticize me" (False)

Restructured Clinical (RC) Scales (With Original MMPI-2 Scale Name in Parentheses)	Description
RCd: Demoralization (New Scale)	Twenty-four items derived from clients showing general unhappiness and dissatisfaction, such as "I usually feel that life is interesting and worthwhile" (False)
RC1: Somatic Complaints (Hypochondriasis)	Twenty-seven items derived from clients showing diffuse physical health complaints, such as "I have chest pains several times a week" (True)
RC2: Low Positive Emotions (Depression)	Seventeen items from clients showing a distinctive, core vulnerability factor and depression, such as "I often feel sad" (True)
RC3: Cynicism (Hysteria)	Fifteen items from clients who show beliefs that others are bad and not to be trusted, such as "People do not usually do what they say they will" (True)
RC4: Antisocial Behavior (Psychopathic Deviate)	Twenty-two items from clients showing rule-breaking and irresponsible behavior, such as "I don't like following rules" (True)
RC6: Ideas of Persecution (Paranoia)	Seventeen items from clients showing self-referential beliefs that others pose a threat to them, such as "There are evil people trying to influence my mind" (True)
RC7: Dysfunctional Negative Emotions (Psychasthenia)	Twenty-four items from clients showing obsessions, compulsions, abnormal fears, and guilt and indecisiveness, such as "I save nearly everything I buy, even after I have no use for it" (True)
RC8: Aberrant Experiences (Schizophrenia)	Eighteen items from clients showing bizarre or unusual thoughts or behavior, who are often withdrawn and experiencing delusions and hallucinations, such as "Things around me do not seem real" (True) and "It makes me uncomfortable to have people close to me" (True)
RC9: Hypomanic Activation (Hypomania)	Twenty-eight items from clients characterized by emotional excitement, overactivity, and flight of ideas, such as "At times I feel very 'high' or very 'low' for no apparent reason" (True)

Source: Ben-Porath & Tellegen, 2008/2011.

Objective personality tests tend to have good reliability and adequate validity. For example, test-retest reliabilities for the RC scales of the MMPI-2-RF range from .67 to .88, averaging .78 (van der Heijden, Egger, & Derksen, 2008). Several studies have also demonstrated that these scales possess good construct validity for the assessment of different mental disorders and clinical conditions (Tellegen et al., 2003; Tellegen, Ben-Porath, & Sellbom, 2009).

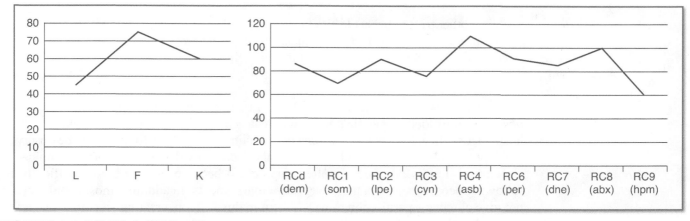

FIGURE 1.4 MMPI-2-RF Profile

This profile is based on the actual MMPI-2 taken by Jeffrey Dahmer in 1992. Jeffrey Lionel Dahmer (May 21, 1960–November 28, 1994), also known as the Milwaukee Cannibal, was an American serial killer and sex offender who raped, murdered, and dismembered 17 men and boys between 1978 and 1991, with many of his later murders also involving necrophilia, cannibalism, and the permanent preservation of body parts. Dahmer's scale would be valid despite an elevated F scale. He would be considered a 4-8 code type (based on RC scales 4 and 8 being his most elevated), which is common among violent offenders, especially sex offenders, though is not in itself diagnostic of a criminal (Fraboni, Cooper, Reed, & Saltstone, 1990) and represents only about 5% of incarcerated offenders (Wise, 2009).

Source: Based on data from Nichols, 2006.

Nonetheless, objective test results are not foolproof indicators of mental disorders. They can be distorted by clients who are motivated to appear either overly healthy or extremely disturbed. Furthermore, test publishers sometimes assert claims for the test's predictive powers that go beyond the findings of empirical research. Accordingly, most clinicians are careful not to use psychological tests in isolation. Such tests should be just one element in a comprehensive evaluation that includes several assessment methods as cross-checks.

Observations

Observational data often contribute to clinical assessment and diagnosis. Observational assessments are especially popular with clinicians who follow a behavioral model of mental disorders (discussed in Chapter 2). In combination with other methods, observations can lead to a more comprehensive view of mental disorders, particularly when other instruments produce conflicting results. Observation is also useful when it helps clinicians learn how changes in the environment might affect a problem behavior. These advantages are illustrated in the continuation of the chapter-opening case that follows:

Bill, whose case begins this chapter, was 10 when he was referred by his fifth-grade teacher to a psychologist because of behavior problems at school. According to the teacher, every time she asked Bill a question or gave him a direction, Bill talked back to her, making such statements as "I hate school, and you can't make me like it" or "You're picking on me; the other kids don't have to work so hard." Bill's mother disputed the teacher's account. She said that Bill never misbehaved at home and that the teacher did not know how to manage Bill, who was bored with school because he was "too smart" for the fifth grade. The psychologist gave Bill an intelligence test and found his IQ to be in the normal range. She then obtained permission to observe Bill at school and also arranged for Bill and his mother to come to the clinic, where she could watch them through a one-way mirror.

The classroom observation revealed that, compared with his classmates, Bill spent more time talking to other children, completed fewer tasks, and was often inattentive. During the play assessment, Bill frequently contradicted his mother or ignored her suggestions.

Bill's mother tried to persuade him to cooperate by reasoning with him or by threatening to cancel their planned trip to the mall. Based on these observations, the psychologist concluded that Bill was noncompliant in both settings, but in different ways.

Observations can be conducted in many different settings. Clinicians use *naturalistic observation* to look at people's behavior as it occurs spontaneously in a school, home, hospital, or office. In *controlled observation*, a clinician arranges for people to be observed reacting to controlled and standardized events, such as a video about a feared stimulus.

Naturalistic observations are often impractical because of the obvious difficulty of following people around in their everyday environments. In addition, most people would not give clinicians permission to watch them in this fashion, creating an ethical barrier to many observations. As a result, direct observation for the purpose of assessing or diagnosing mental disorders is used mainly with children in school, daycare, or at play, and with severely disturbed patients in mental hospitals (Paul & Lentz, 1977). With adults, **self-monitoring** may be used instead. This is a special form of observation in which clients record the frequency, duration, intensity, or quality of their own moods, thoughts, and behaviors, such as smoking and eating (Nietzel, Bernstein, & Milich, 1998).

Most modern observational approaches using well-trained observers achieve excellent interrater reliabilities. Self-monitoring clients often attain correlations in the .90s between their observations and those of external observers. Observations can also be highly valid if they meet three important criteria (Nietzel, Bernstein, & Milich, 1998). First, the observed behavior (e.g., a parent speaking in a raised voice to a child) must provide a satisfactory example of the construct being assessed (e.g., aggression). Second, the format for summarizing the observations (e.g., counting the number of voice raisings) must fairly represent the behaviors observed. Finally, the summary must provide a fair representation of the client's behavior when it is not being observed; for instance, the presence of an observer might cause a parent to be more controlled than usual.

Biological Measures

Biological methods allow a special kind of observation of changes in a client's body chemistry or other internal functioning that are almost never available to the naked eye (Tomarken, 1995) or revealed through self-reports. Biological assessment is especially important because genetic and biological factors are becoming more prominent in explaining mental disorders (see Chapter 2).

Advances in medical technology have led to the possibility of assessing several mental disorders via the measurement of the biological changes that are uniquely associated with those disorders. These *biological markers* include counting fat cells that are associated with obesity (Brownell & Wadden, 1992), monitoring elevations in liver enzymes or blood proteins (e.g., platelet monoamine oxidase B) to detect alcoholism (Allen & Litten, 1993; Snell et al., 2012), measuring changes in the immune system following exposure to stressors (Kielcolt-Glaser & Glaser, 1992), and monitoring neurochemical, endocrinological, and more recently, immunological/inflammatory changes in depression (Slavich & Irwin, 2014), bipolar disorder (Mathews et al., 2013), and schizophrenia (Hazlett, Dawson, Buchsbaum, & Nuechterlein, 1993; Bergink, Gibney, & Drexhage, 2014).

Biological measurements are also useful for assessing anxiety, mood, sexual, and other disorders that have clear physiological components. For example, in people with anxiety disorders, heart rate, respiration, blood pressure, muscle tension, and skin conductance are often measured as a way of studying the relationships between physiological arousal, subjective distress, and behavioral dysfunction (McNeil, Vrana, Melamed, Cuthbert, & Lang, 1993). Physiological measures are also important in assessing sexual arousal, especially for clients who are attracted to socially deviant stimuli. Several studies, for example, have found that rapists show more arousal to rape stimuli than to scenes of consensual sex, while nonrapists show the opposite pattern (Hall, 1990).

self-monitoring: A special form of observation in which people record the frequency, duration, intensity, or quality of their own behaviors, such as smoking, eating, moods, or thoughts.

Connections

Are measures of sexual arousal reliable enough to use in diagnosing specific sexual disorders? For the pros and cons, see Chapter 13.

TABLE 1.4 Some Neurodiagnostic Procedures

Procedure	Description
Neurological clinical exam	The physician screens the patient's sensory abilities, eye movements, cognitive and perceptual abilities, language, motor and postural irregularities, and symptom history as a preliminary investigation of brain disturbance.
Lumbar puncture	Spinal fluid is extracted from the spinal cord through a needle. Examination of the fluid can help diagnose brain infections, hemorrhages, and some tumors. It has some complications, the most common of which are headaches.
Electroencephalogram (EEG)	The EEG monitors the electrical activity of the cerebral cortex. EEGs are useful in diagnosing seizure disorders and vascular diseases affecting large blood vessels in the brain, but they yield a relatively high rate of false positives. EEG recordings as a person sleeps—*polysomnographic measures*—are used to assess sleep disorders and can be collected in a person's home (Lacks & Morin, 1992).
Other electrical tests—electromyogram (EMG), evoked potentials, and nerve conduction velocities	All three tests measure electrical activity of some sort: in muscles (EMG), in the brain when elicited by an external stimulus (evoked potentials), or in peripheral nerves (nerve conduction velocities). They are useful in the diagnosis of muscle disease, sensory deficits, serious headaches, and nerve disease caused by conditions such as diabetes (Blanchard, 1992). Evoked potentials also have shown promise as a substitute for the polygraph in lie detection (Bashore & Rapp, 1993).
Arteriography	Dye is injected into arteries, and a series of X-rays is taken of the arteries as the dye passes through them. It is used to diagnose cerebrovascular disease, especially strokes and hemorrhages. Arteriograms can be uncomfortable and sometimes dangerous.
Biopsies and exploratory surgery	Both of these procedures involve direct examination of suspect tissue. Although they are risky, they can give definite diagnoses of some neurological conditions.
Computerized topographic mapping of EEGs	This technique uses computers to synthesize EEGs more efficiently. The computer analyzes EEG signals, codes their different frequencies with different colors, and then prints a multicolored map of the brain, showing differences in EEG activity. Use of this technique has declined in recent years as other brain-imaging procedures have evolved (Figure 1.5).

The most widely used biological measures of mental disorders are techniques for studying the brain and its functions. Some direct neurodiagnostic procedures are summarized in Table 1.4; others involve brain-imaging procedures shown in Figure 1.5. These latter procedures, several of which have been introduced during the past 20 years, identify abnormalities in the structure or functioning of certain areas of the brain. For example, **computerized tomography** (CT scan) provides computer-enhanced, three-dimensional images of successive slices of the brain. CT scans are valuable in diagnosing tumors, traumatic damage, and degenerative diseases such as Alzheimer's and cerebrovascular disease (Imabayashi et al., 2013).

Positron emission tomography (PET scan) shows changes not just in the structure of the brain but also in its metabolic functioning. PET scans do this by tracking the rate at which brain cells consume radioactive glucose injected into the brain. Since diseased tissue uses glucose at a different rate than normal tissue, PET scans can reveal specific areas of abnormal brain physiology, as shown in Figure 1.5c. Before fMRI technology came online, PET scanning was the preferred method of functional (as opposed to structural) brain imaging, and it still continues to make large contributions to neuroscience (Meyer, Rijntjes, & Weiller, 2012). PET scanning is also used for diagnosis of brain disease, most notably because brain tumors, strokes, and neuron-damaging diseases that cause dementia

computerized tomography (CT): A neurodiagnostic procedure that provides computer-enhanced, three-dimensional pictures of the brain.

positron emission tomography (PET): A neurodiagnostic procedure that shows changes in the structure of the brain and in its metabolic functioning by tracking the rate at which brain cells consume injected radioactive glucose.

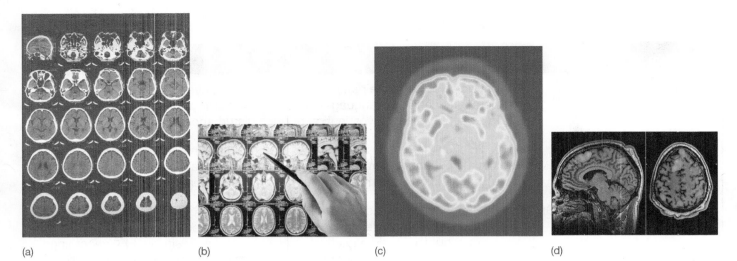

FIGURE 1.5 Mapping the Geography of the Brain

CT, MRI, PET, or fMRI? Each type of brain scan has advantages and disadvantages. (a) CT scans show detailed pictures of the brain, but they cannot distinguish a live brain from a dead one. (b) MRIs can resolve structures that are only a fraction of an inch apart, but they cannot picture the activity of these structures. (c) PET scans rely on radioactive sugar (glucose) to allow neuroscientists to watch different areas of the brain "light up" as they go about their work, but they cannot picture structure. (d) fMRI scans, which track cerebral blood flow, have largely superseded PET scans for the study of brain activation patterns. PET scans, however, retain the significant advantage of being able to identify specific brain receptors (or transporters) associated with particular neurotransmitters through their ability to image radio-labelled receptors (Kim et al., 2014).

Sources: (a) Santibhavanak P/Shutterstock.com. (b) Triff/Shutterstock.com. (c) Jens Maus (Langner) (http://www.jens-langner.de) (d) John Graner, Neuroimaging Department, National Intrepid Center of Excellence, Walter Reed National Military Medical Center, 8901 Wisconsin Avenue, Bethesda, MD 20889, USA.

single photon emission computed tomography (SPECT): Similar to positron emission tomography (PET), a SPECT scan uses a radioactive chemical that allows pictures of the brain from several angles.

magnetic resonance imaging (MRI): A neurodiagnostic procedure that tracks the activity of atoms in the body as they are "excited" by magnets in a chamber or coil placed around the patient.

functional magnetic resonance imaging (fMRI): Functional magnetic resonance imaging or functional MRI (fMRI) is a functional neuroimaging procedure using magnetic resonance imaging (MRI) technology that measures brain activity by detecting associated changes in cerebral blood flow.

(such as Alzheimer's disease) all cause great changes in brain metabolism, which in turn causes easily detectable changes in PET scans even before MRI scans (see next paragraph) can detect any damage (Scott & Poon, 2004). **Single photon emission computed tomography (SPECT)** is a similar procedure using a radioactive chemical that lasts longer than those used in PET scans. Therefore, SPECT can take pictures of the brain from several angles.

Another technique, called **magnetic resonance imaging (MRI)**, works by tracking the activity of atoms in the body as they are "excited" by magnets in a chamber or coil placed around the patient (see Figure 1.5b). MRIs do not involve X-ray exposure. A newer version of magnetic resonance imaging, called **functional magnetic resonance imaging (fMRI)**, allows the simultaneous imaging of the brain's structure and function by detecting changes in cerebral blood flow (Huettel, Song, & McCarthy, 2009). Most fMRI scanners allow subjects to press a button or move a joystick in response to different visual images, sounds, and touch stimuli. Consequently, fMRI can be used to reveal brain structures and processes associated with perception, thought, and action. The resolution of fMRI is 2 to 3 millimeters, limited by the spatial spread of the hemodynamic response to neural activity (Huettel et al., 2009). Clinicians also use fMRI to anatomically map the brain and detect the effects of tumors, stroke, head and brain injury, or diseases such as Alzheimer's, although direct clinical use of fMRI still lags behind its use in research (Rombouts, Barkhof, & Sheltens, 2007).

Diffusion MRI (or dMRI), also referred to as diffusion tensor imaging, is yet another magnetic resonance imaging (MRI) method that allows the mapping of the diffusion process of molecules, mainly water, in biological tissues, in vivo and noninvasively (Alexander, Lee, Lazar, & Field, 2007). These water molecule diffusion patterns can reveal microscopic details about the architecture of the brain—that is, how the neurons of the brain are connected to or communicating with one another. For instance, recent studies using dMRI have identified abnormal diffusion patterns in the left middle temporal region of the brains of people with schizophrenia, which correspond with functional abnormalities in the language network (Leroux et al., 2013). Because it can reveal abnormalities in white matter fiber structure and provide models of brain connectivity, dMRI is rapidly becoming a standard for white-matter disorders, such as multiple sclerosis and stroke (Hagmann et al., 2006).

The reliability of biological measures is generally good, although each is sensitive to the effects of such factors as medication, circadian cycles, smoking, and overall fitness (Tomarken, 1995). These factors can also lower the validity of biological measures by misleading the diagnostician or researcher about a client's biological functioning. For example, most people with severe mental disorders receive medication, often for months or years. The effects of such medication may make it impossible to obtain a valid assessment of the original biological factors that might have contributed to their disorder (Rombouts et al., 2007). Further, the validity of biological assessments can vary from one disorder to the next or from one population to the next. Children, for example, often display abnormal EEGs, despite the absence of any brain damage. Like other assessments, biological methods are fallible, and their relationship to psychological variables is often ambiguous. Overall, the promise of the 1990s ("the decade of the brain") for research on mental disorders has remained largely unfulfilled even several decades later. Neuroscience has shed great light on how the brain functions, but the causes of mental disorders still elude us (Paris, 2013).

Section Review

Clinicians collect assessment data from five sources, which are then usually combined to help them diagnose mental disorders. Each of these assessment sources has unique strengths:

- Life records are relatively immune to deliberate attempts by individuals to create particular impressions.
- Interviews are flexible sources of information that, when sufficiently structured, yield highly reliable diagnoses.
- Psychological tests are standardized instruments that allow accurate comparisons of a person's scores to those of others.
- Observations permit clinicians to assess the effects of situations on a person's behavior and to resolve discrepancies among other assessment sources.
- Biological measures permit assessment of internal changes that are neither observable nor reportable by clients themselves.

Diagnostic Classification: How Do Health Professionals Categorize Mental Disorders?

The ultimate purpose of the different assessment tools discussed in the previous section is to arrive at a diagnosis of the client's problem. Accurate diagnosis is a necessary first step for the treatment and scientific study of mental disorders. Diagnosing disorders helps bring order to what would otherwise be a confusing welter of individual symptoms. Classifying mental disorders makes it possible to study them, to better understand their likely course, and to look for common causal factors in the backgrounds, experiences, and other characteristics of people with similar disorders. Diagnosis also allows clinicians to describe mental disorders with a common language that is efficient and easy to understand.

A Brief History

Although efforts to classify mental disorders began as early as Hippocrates' humoral system, scientifically based classification schemes did not appear until the nineteenth century. Several European physicians in that era proposed classification systems, beginning with Wilhelm Griesinger (1817–1868), who argued that mental disorders should be understood as biological diseases of the brain. The most influential classification scheme of this era was developed by Emil Kraepelin, a German psychiatrist. Kraepelin believed that the thousands of mental patients he observed throughout the world could be placed in three categories: *dementia praecox* (now called schizophrenia), *manic-depressive*

Personification of the four temperaments—sanguine, choleric, melancholic, phlegmatic—from the title page of Adriaen Collaert: *Septem Planetae* (*The Seven Planets*, 1581). The four temperaments, first described by Hippocrates and later named by Galen, formed an early classification system. Hippocrates believed that all disorders were biologically caused, and he linked different mental disorders to body fluids, or humors: Too much blood (upper left) resulted in an optimistic or a changeable temperament, an excess of yellow bile (upper right) caused mania or irritability, too much black bile (lower left) resulted in melancholy or depression, and too much phlegm (lower right) caused sluggishness or lethargy.

Source: Adriaen Collaert.

psychosis (now called bipolar disorder), and *organic brain disorders* (now called dementia, delirium, and other neurocognitive disorders).

By 1917, a simple classification system for mental disorders was being used to gather hospital statistics in the United States. It did not prove clinically useful, however, so other classification schemes were developed in the 1930s and 1940s, including systems by the military to classify the many veterans who suffered mental disorders as a result of combat in World War II (see Widiger et al., 1991 for an historical review of this period). In 1948, the World Health Organization (WHO) published the sixth edition of the *Manual of the International Statistical Classification of Diseases, Injuries, and Causes of Death (ICD-6)* .

The First *DSM*

The *ICD-6* included some mental disorders, classified essentially in the same way as in the system used by the U.S. military. However, because the classification schemes were often in substantial disagreement with one another, the American Psychiatric Association (APA) decided to create its own system. In 1952, it published the first edition of the *Diagnostic and Statistical Manual of Mental Disorders (DSM-I)*. To make the *DSM* conform more closely to the eighth edition of the *International Classification of Diseases* (*ICD*; World Health Organization, 1968), a second version of the *DSM* (*DSM-II*) was published in 1968.

The *DSM-I* and *DSM-II* had several major weaknesses. They lacked a uniform principle for assigning diagnoses. Some diagnoses were based on theories of causation (often psychoanalytic; see Chapter 2), others concentrated on symptoms that tended to cluster, and some reflected an assortment of criteria. Many disorders were defined so vaguely that it was difficult to obtain adequate reliability for them. Low reliability, in turn, ensured low validity for many diagnoses. Furthermore, early *DSM* systems focused almost exclusively on a single label. They failed to consider background factors that influence the severity and prognosis of disorders, such as a client's medical problems, psychosocial stress, and cultural influences. Ultimately, and ironically, these systems had little effect on how different clients were treated, and they did not predict the course of disorders the way that a valid classification system should.

To correct these and other problems, the APA published the *DSM-III*, a radically revised edition of the *DSM*, in 1980, followed by another slightly revised edition, known as the *DSM-III-R* (American Psychiatric Association, 1987). The advent of the *DSM-III* and *DSM-III-R* signaled a major change in how the North American classification system was constructed. The *DSM-III* was the first edition of the *DSM* to provide specific, clearly defined criteria, some combination of which had to be present for a disorder to be diagnosed. These operational definitions uncoupled the *DSM* diagnoses from warring theoretical assumptions about the cause and nature of disorders. By focusing instead on the observable signs and symptoms of various disorders, the *DSM-III* and *DSM-III-R* greatly improved the reliability of diagnoses by clinicians, regardless of their theoretical model of psychopathology (American Psychiatric Association, 1980, 1987).

Despite their many improvements, the *DSM-III* and *DSM-III-R* continued to have serious weaknesses. Several diagnostic criteria were still too vague and sometimes inconsistent, and interrater reliabilities were low for some of the diagnoses. Furthermore, the influence of clients' gender, age, and cultural factors on diagnosis was not emphasized. In addition, many clinicians believed that too little attention was paid to the construct validity of many diagnoses (see Bellack & Hersen, 1988; Kaplan, 1983; McReynolds, 1989;

Millon & Klerman, 1986; Nathan, 1987a; and Vaillant, 1984 for these and other critiques of the *DSM-III* and *DSM-III-R*). In the *DSM-III* and *DSM-III-R*, many diagnostic criteria were based on the opinions of experts, not on empirical findings, because an insufficient number of diagnostic research studies were available at that time. Finally, the *DSM-III* and *DSM-III-R* did not clearly document the rational or empirical support for their diagnostic criteria.

One year after the publication of the *DSM-III-R*, the APA formed a task force to develop the *DSM-IV*, chaired by Allen Frances. This task force was charged with correcting many of the weaknesses in the *DSM-III-R*, but there were other reasons for the revision as well. First, WHO was ready to publish the latest edition of its *ICD (ICD-10)* in 1993, and the United States was under a treaty obligation to maintain classification systems consistent with those of WHO. Second, there was a desire to build a stronger empirical foundation for *DSM* criteria. As discussed next, these two objectives—harmonizing with WHO and improving the evidence base—also have heavily guided the most recent versions of the *DSM—DSM-5*.

Harmonizing With WHO

Between 2003 and 2008, a cooperative agreement between the APA and WHO, supported by the National Institute of Mental Health (NIMH), convened 13 international *DSM-5* research planning conferences involving 400 participants from 39 countries. These conferences reviewed the world literature in specific diagnostic areas to prepare for revisions in developing both WHO's *ICD-11* and the *DSM-5* (American Psychiatric Association, 2013a).

Diagnosis of mental disorders in the United States and Canada is guided by the *DSM*, while the *ICD* is officially used in the rest of the world as the global clinical and research standard. Like the *DSM*, the *ICD* is updated periodically, with the *ICD-11* published in 2017. In truth, the *DSM-5* has been used unofficially by clinicians around the world, many of whom believe its diagnostic criteria are better validated than those of the *ICD*.

However, since October 2015, all mental health professionals in the United States have been required to use *ICD* diagnostic codes—not *DSM* codes, though the categories are similar—for insurance reimbursement and compliance with the Health Insurance Portability and Accountability Act (HIPAA; Goodheart, 2014). As a result of WHO's decision to also use specific operational definitions of mental disorders, the two systems have moved closer in their approaches to diagnosis, making greater international cooperation possible and reducing cross-cultural variations in diagnostic practices (Sartorius, Ustiin, Korten, Cooper, & van Drimmelen, 1995; American Psychiatric Association, 2013). International contributions to classification are important, given that about 75% of psychiatric populations live in developing countries, primarily in Asia, Africa, and South America (Mezzich & von Cranach, 1988).

Improving the Evidence Base

Both the *DSM-IV* and *DSM-5* started by assembling groups of researchers and clinicians to study specific disorders and recommend the best way to diagnose them (Widiger et al., 1991; American Psychiatric Association, 1994, 2000, 2013a). For the *DSM-5*, David Kupfer chaired an overall task force of 28 members and oversaw 13 work groups generally consisting of 6 to 15 experts each in that particular disorder; these experts were mainly medical doctors, with some psychologists and other mental health professionals in the mix as well.

To resolve specific diagnostic controversies, the work groups conducted a series of field trials. A **field trial** is a research study conducted in the natural environment. For *DSM-5* field trials, diagnostic interviews using *DSM-5* criteria were conducted by 279 clinicians of varied disciplines, who received training comparable to what would be available to any clinician after publication of the *DSM-5*. Overall, 2,246 participants with various diagnoses and levels of comorbidity were enrolled in these field trials, of which over 86% were seen for two diagnostic interviews (Clarke et al., 2013). In adults, test-retest

field trial: A research study conducted in the natural environment.

The more recent *DSM-5*, stacked on top of a French version of the *DSM-IV-TR*.

reliabilities of the cross-cutting symptom items generally were good to excellent. Reliabilities were not as uniformly good for child respondents. Clinicians rated psychosis with good reliability in adult clients but were less reliable in assessing clinical domains related to psychosis in children and to suicide in all age groups (Narrow et al., 2013).

Between 2010 and 2012, the APA posted various iterations of draft diagnostic criteria and proposed changes in organization on a website dedicated to this process (www .dsm5.org) for three separate comment periods. Feedback from more than 13,000 submissions was reviewed by each of the 13 work groups before arriving at the final version of the *DSM-5* in 2013. The website remains operative today and is an excellent resource for students to learn about the process and issues surrounding the long-awaited publication of the *DSM-5*.

Why Use the *DSM-5*?

There is a critical dichotomy in the *DSM* between its value as a guide for researchers and its clinical utility—that is, how useful it is for mental health professionals in actual practice. Some scholars have even suggested the creation of two separate diagnostic manuals—one for researchers and one for clinicians—to account for the fact that these two groups use the manual quite differently (Paris, 2013). Whereas researchers may follow the algorithmic model of *DSM* diagnosis (e.g., using a structured interview to examine and check for at least five of the nine listed symptoms of major depression), clinicians rely on a prototype model, retaining a general idea of what a specific disorder looks like, rather than taking the time to count criteria (Zimmerman & Galione, 2010).

According to the *DSM-5* Task Force, improving clinical utility was among the top priorities for the latest *DSM* revision (American Psychiatric Association, 2013a). Therefore, although the *DSM* retains its high value as a research tool, its mental health classifications are also useful in helping clinicians: (1) communicate; (2) select effective interventions; (3) predict course, prognosis, and future management needs; and (4) differentiate disorder from nondisorder for the purpose of determining who might benefit from treatment (First, 2010).

In addition, the *DSM-5* opens with a cautionary statement about its use in forensic (legal) settings:

> Although the *DSM-5* diagnostic criteria and text are primarily designed to assist clinicians in conducting clinical assessment, case formulation, and treatment planning, *DSM-5* is also used as a reference for the courts and attorneys in assessing the forensic consequences of mental disorders. As a result, it is important to note that the definition of mental disorder included in *DSM-5* was developed to meet the needs of clinicians, public health professionals, and research investigators, rather than all the technical needs of the courts and legal professionals. (APA, 2013a, p. 25)

This detailed warning has been lauded by many forensic psychologists as a vital attempt to prevent misuse of the *DSM-5* in legal cases (Kocsis, 2013).

Because of their widespread acceptance and use in a multitude of settings both in the United States and worldwide, the *DSM-5* categories and criteria are followed in this textbook. We describe the general strategy for using the *DSM-5* in the next section. However, using the *DSM-5* does not mean that you should be blind to its serious shortcomings, as outlined in the final major section of this chapter ("The Four Guiding Principles: MAPS of the Territory"). As Joel Paris (2013, p. 187) advises, you should "learn the *DSM-5* but do not believe it."

Diagnoses With the *DSM-5*

The *DSM-III* first introduced **multiaxial classification**, which was continued through the *DSM-IV*; this means that a person was described along several dimensions or *axes* (the plural of *axis*), such as physical health and social and occupational functioning, as well as the presence of mental disorders. The *DSM-5*, however, has moved to a nonaxial documentation of diagnosis, combining what was formerly **Axis I**/most mental disorders, **Axis II**/Personality Disorders, and **Axis III**/General Medical Conditions onto a single axis, with separate notations for important psychosocial and contextual factors (formerly **Axis IV**) and disability (formerly **Axis V**). *DSM-5* diagnoses of mental disorders are now arranged on a single axis according to the following 20 major categories, provided here with a brief description and indication of which chapter in this textbook covers that particular category:

1. **Neurodevelopmental disorders.** These include a group of conditions with onset in the developmental period (i.e., childhood) and are covered in Chapter 3. Included here are intellectual disabilities, learning disorders, communication disorders, autism spectrum disorder, attention-deficit/hyperactivity disorder, and several other problem behaviors typically associated with childhood.

2. **Elimination disorders.** These involve the inappropriate elimination of urine or feces and are usually first diagnosed in childhood or adolescence, so they are covered in Chapter 3.

3. **Disruptive, impulse-control, and conduct disorders.** These include conditions involving problems in the self-control of emotions and behaviors. Although there is no set age limit for these disorders, they usually appear at least by adolescence and are also covered in Chapter 3.

4. **Schizophrenia spectrum and other psychotic disorders.** Covered in Chapter 4, schizophrenia and other psychoses typically involve serious disturbances in a person's perception and thinking, emotional responsiveness, and behavioral appropriateness. Several bizarre symptoms can be present in a psychosis; the most prominent usually involve distorted perceptions and thinking.

5. **Bipolar and related disorders.** These disorders, covered in Chapter 5, involve disturbances in emotion and usually entail shifts between periods of depression and periods of highly elevated mood and energy, known as *manic episodes*. These have been separated from the depressive disorders in the *DSM-5* and placed between the chapters on schizophrenia and depression in recognition of their place as a bridge between those two diagnostic classes in terms of symptomatology.

6. **Depressive disorders.** Covered in Chapter 6, these disorders involve disturbances in emotion that usually include prolonged periods of sad, empty, or irritable mood, similar to bipolar disorder. Issues of duration, timing, or presumed etiology (cause) differentiate the disorders in this category from one another.

7. **Anxiety disorders.** Strong "irrational" feelings of fear, anxiety, and panic, along with avoidance of feared situations, typify the anxiety disorders, detailed in Chapter 7. Various anxiety disorders are defined by the nature of the feared stimulus and the primary way the anxiety is expressed, such as through panic attacks, chronic worry, or avoidance of specific stimuli.

8. **Obsessive-compulsive and related disorders.** In Chapter 8, we cover disorders that involve persistent thoughts, urges, or images that are experienced as unwanted, which may also be accompanied by behaviors or mental acts that an individual may feel driven to perform.

9. **Trauma- and stressor-related disorders.** These include disorders in which exposure to a traumatic or stressful event is listed explicitly as a diagnostic criterion, ranging from posttraumatic stress disorder (PTSD) to adjustment disorders, covered in Chapter 9.

multiaxial classification: A system for diagnosing mental disorders and describing a person along several dimensions, or axes, including physical health, psychosocial and environmental problems, and global functioning.

Axis I: In *DSM-IV*, the dimension that contained 16 general groupings of major mental disorders.

Axis II: In *DSM-IV*, the dimension that consisted of 10 personality disorders and mental retardation. *DSM-5* now includes these 10 disorders with all the other (former Axis I) disorders on a single axis.

Axis III: In *DSM-IV*, the dimension where clinicians listed general medical conditions that could be relevant to understanding or treating a person's mental disorder. Using *DSM-5*, medical conditions are simply listed along with the mental disorders on the same axis.

Axis IV: In *DSM-IV*, the dimension where clinicians recorded psychosocial and environmental stressors that could affect the diagnosis, treatment, and course of a mental disorder. Using *DSM-5*, these factors may be listed along with the mental disorders on the same axis.

Axis V: In *DSM-IV*, the dimension on which clinicians rated a person's overall level of functioning at the time of the evaluation, giving a summary assessment of the person's general clinical status and providing a gauge for how well the person responded to treatment. *DSM-5* encourages use of the WHODAS system instead.

10. **Dissociative disorders.** These disorders, covered in Chapter 10, involve a disturbance or alteration in the normally integrated functions of identity, consciousness, or memory. Examples include multiple personality disorder (now called dissociative identity disorder) and psychologically caused memory disruptions.

11. **Somatic symptom and related disorders.** The central feature of these disorders is the existence of physical complaints or symptoms that suggest a physical disorder but that are, in fact, caused by psychological factors. The temporary loss of a sensory ability such as vision is a common example, to be covered in Chapter 11.

12. **Feeding and eating disorders.** Covered in Chapter 12, these disorders are characterized by a persistent disturbance of eating or eating-related behavior that results in the altered consumption or absorption of food and that significantly impairs physical health or psychosocial functioning. *Anorexia nervosa* (self-starvation) and *bulimia nervosa* (binging and purging) are the main disorders in this category.

13. **Sleep-wake disorders.** Insomnia, excessive sleepiness, recurrent nightmares and sleep terrors, and other sleep-related difficulties are included here. These problems, covered in Chapter 12, are not considered disorders when they occur only occasionally.

14. **Sexual dysfunctions.** This is a heterogeneous group of disorders, covered in Chapter 13, that are typically characterized by a clinically significant disturbance in a person's ability to respond sexually or experience sexual pleasure.

15. **Gender dysphoria.** There is only one overarching diagnosis in this category, covered in Chapter 13, which is indicated by a strong, persistent discomfort with one's gender and a preference to be the other sex.

16. **Substance-related and addictive disorders.** Included in this category are mental disorders arising from dependence on or abuse of alcohol, amphetamines, caffeine, cannabis, cocaine, hallucinogens (such as phencyclidine), inhalants, nicotine, opioids, and other drugs. Covered in Chapter 14, this category also includes gambling addiction.

17. **Neurocognitive disorders.** These disorders all involve impairment in a person's cognitive functioning. Discussed in Chapter 15, they can be the result of substance abuse, disease, trauma, or age-related deterioration.

18. **Personality disorders.** Formerly covered on Axis II, these disorders entail enduring patterns of inner experience and behavior that deviate markedly from the expectations of the individual's culture. Further, these patterns are stable over time, pervasive and inflexible, have an onset in adolescence or early adulthood, and lead to distress or impairment. They are covered in Chapter 16.

19. **Paraphilic disorders.** This category, covered in Chapter 17, involves people who derive intense and persistent sexual interest from acts or objects other than physically mature, consenting human partners.

20. **Other mental disorders.** This category includes certain mental disorders for which historical, physical, or laboratory findings point to a medical condition as the cause, along with a variety of clinical conditions that do not meet the criteria for being a mental disorder but are problematic conditions nonetheless and may be the focus of professional treatment. Examples include psychological symptoms that lead to a medical problem, that make a medical condition worse, or that delay a person's recovery from the condition; interpersonal conflicts involving romantic partners or family members; academic and occupational problems; bereavement; and other life crises.

Criteria for Diagnosis

Like the *DSM-III* and *DSM-IV*, the *DSM-5* lists specific operational criteria that must be met before a given disorder can be diagnosed. And like its predecessors, the *DSM-5* retains a **polythetic approach** to classification, meaning that, to be diagnosed with a mental disorder, a person must meet a particular number of criteria out of a larger set of possible criterion symptoms. For example, Figure 1.6 shows that even though Gollum, from *The Hobbit* and *Lord of the Rings* literature and film series, does not display all possible

Connections

How do personality disorders, which used to be listed on a separate axis during diagnosis, differ from other mental disorders? Are they simply less severe? Are they the causes or the results of some mental disorders? See Chapter 16.

polythetic approach: An approach to classification that requires a person to meet a particular number of criteria out of a larger set of criterion symptoms to be diagnosed with a specific mental disorder.

symptoms of schizotypal personality disorder, he meets enough *DSM-5* diagnostic criteria (four of the seven) to be diagnosed with the disorder (see Chapter 16). The polythetic approach contrasts with the **classical method of classification** in which every disorder is assumed to be a distinct, unique condition for which each and every attribute must be present for a diagnosis to be made.

classical method of classification: A method of classification in which every disorder is assumed to be a distinct and unique condition for which each and every attribute must be present for a diagnosis to be made.

Classical models are commonly used to diagnose physical illnesses, and they usually yield *homogeneous* categories. In other words, all individuals given the same diagnosis appear very similar to one another. Polythetic systems, on the other hand, produce greater variability among people receiving the same diagnosis. They generate *heterogeneous* categories; the same diagnosis can be given to patients who have a similar, *but not identical*, set of symptoms.

In addition, a person may be diagnosed with more than one *DSM-5* disorder at the same time if he or she meets the criteria for each disorder. In fact, there are several reasons why mental disorders are likely to coexist, a condition known as **comorbidity** (Kendall & Clarkin, 1992). First, different disorders can result from the same cause or from different, but simultaneous, causes. For example, exposure to a violent stressor, such as the 2013 bombing near the finish line of the Boston Marathon, could lead to both an anxiety disorder and to depression. Second, the appearance of one disorder can lead to the development of another disorder. Third, comorbidity may merely reflect the fact that different disorders often share similar criteria, resulting in an increased probability that diagnosis of one disorder will be accompanied by diagnosis of another disorder with overlapping criteria.

comorbidity: The co-occurrence of two or more mental disorders in the same person.

The comorbidity of mental disorders, to be discussed again later in this chapter and in several other chapters, has numerous implications for how clinicians diagnose and treat mental disorders (Clarkin & Kendall, 1992). Does each disorder require different, but simultaneous, treatment, or should the more serious disorder be treated first? Does the presence of a comorbid disorder make the targeted disorder more difficult to treat? These are some of the questions that researchers will study as comorbid mental disorders are fully investigated in the future.

The *DSM-5* also contains new supplementary material that accompanies the criteria for many disorders. For example, one special section provides descriptions on specific cultural, age, and gender features that might accompany a particular diagnosis. Another section lists physical examination or general medical findings that might be associated with a disorder. These portions of the *DSM-5* reflect two modern directions in the study of abnormal behavior—an increasing interest in discovering the biological foundations of disorders and a recognition that mental disorders need to be understood in their larger cultural and social context.

Diagnosis in the Real World

When clinicians conduct assessments and assign specific diagnoses, their decisions are affected by many factors other than a person's social history, test responses, or clinical interview. Consider again the case of Bill that opened this chapter. Based on Bill's history and current symptoms, what diagnosis do you think a clinician would give him?

FIGURE 1.6 A *DSM-5* Diagnosis of Gollum from *The Hobbit* and *Lord of the Rings* (J. R. R. Tolkien, 1937, 1954–1955)

Here is Bashir et al.'s (2004) diagnosis of the case: Sméagol (Gollum), a 587-year-old homeless male of hobbit descent, presents with antisocial behavior, increasing aggression, and preoccupation with a specific object (a ring). His criminal history consists of at least one murder and another attempted murder (of Samwise Gamgee). He has no history of a substance use disorder, although he smoked "pipe weed" in adolescence, like many of his tribe.

Several differential diagnoses need to be considered, as well as potential organic (biological) causes for his symptoms. Gollum is hypervigilant and does not seem to need much sleep. Along with his bulging eyes and weight loss, this suggests hyperthyroidism.

Psychologically, Gollum displays a pervasive pattern of detachment from social relationships and a restricted range of emotions in interpersonal settings, beginning in childhood. He fulfills four of the seven criteria for schizoid personality disorder, as per *DSM-5*: lack of desire for close relationships, almost always choosing solitary activities, lack of close friends, and showing emotional coldness.

Source: Mawardi Bahar/Shutterstock.com.

Money, Privacy, and Diagnoses

Bill's symptoms satisfy the criteria for an anxiety disorder, the amount of conflict in his marriage points to a marital problem, and the psychological stress of an impending job loss indicates the likelihood of an adjustment disorder. The clinician may assign any or all of these diagnoses, but additional factors that are distinct from, and go beyond, Bill's clinical complaints will influence the final decision.

First, like the majority of Americans, Bill has health insurance, paid for in part by his employer. His health insurance covers mental disorders according to the Mental Health Parity Act, legislation signed into U.S. law on September 26, 1996 that requires that annual or lifetime dollar limits on mental health benefits be no lower than any such dollar limits for medical and surgical benefits. So Bill's insurance policy will pay for psychotherapy for *DSM* disorders, including anxiety disorders, but it does not cover treatment of marital problems. There is thus an obvious *financial* incentive for the clinician (and Bill) to diagnose an anxiety disorder.

To make Bill's treatment financially feasible, the clinician could decide to diagnose anxiety disorder, but Bill is concerned that his insurance company will review the diagnosis and treatment before reimbursement is made. He wants assurance from the clinician that the diagnosis will be kept confidential; otherwise, he is convinced that his employer will use the anxiety disorder diagnosis to hasten his dismissal. The clinician cannot, in good conscience, provide this assurance because, if Bill's case goes to court, confidentiality may be overridden by a judge's order.

In addition to Bill's financial and social considerations, the clinician's professional interests may influence the diagnosis. Clinicians who have expertise in treating one disorder may construe ambiguous cases in a way that results in the favored diagnosis. Some clinicians try to build a reputation for specializing in specific disorders, so marketing considerations might also influence diagnoses.

Another factor that influences diagnosis is that many people with mental disorders do not go first to mental health professionals, but to a hospital emergency room, their family physician, or a health maintenance organization (HMO). Compared with mental health specialists, primary care physicians tend to underdiagnose mental disorders (Munoz, Hollon, McGrath, Rehm, & VandenBos, 1994). If Bill had first consulted his primary care physician, he might well have been diagnosed with, and treated for, a physical rather than a mental disorder.

Diversity and Assessment Measures

When you first read about Bill, how did you visualize him? If you are like most of the people who have read this case, you may have assumed that Bill was Caucasian. But, in fact, Bill is African American. Assumptions about Bill's ethnicity illustrate another major influence on the way clinical diagnosis is conducted in the real world. Human diversity affects the manifestation and diagnosis of mental disorders in several ways. For example, most psychological tests, structured interviews, and observational systems were first developed and normed on Caucasian samples. Could these measures be biased against ethnic minorities as a result?

A test can be biased in at least two ways. First, people from a certain ethnic group may do poorly on a test relative to other groups *for reasons that have nothing to do with what the test is measuring*. For example, a person whose first language is not English will probably not perform as well on an IQ test administered in English as a person who has always spoken English. Many popular IQ and personality tests have been translated into different languages to overcome this bias, but you still must be cautious that the translation does not introduce subtle differences in meaning that may distort the interpretation of test scores.

A second type of bias occurs when scores on a test lead to valid predictions for one ethnic group but invalid predictions for another group. For example, if subjects from different ethnic groups take a personality test, do their scores lead to equally accurate predictions? If not, the test is biased. In one study (Timbrook & Graham, 1994), African Americans and Caucasians completed the MMPI-2, and their spouses or partners rated them on a variety of traits and behaviors that should correlate with the test scores. No ethnic differences were found for the accuracy of MMPI-2 scores in predicting the partners' ratings. At least on the basis of this preliminary study, the MMPI-2 was therefore not biased in its ability to predict outcomes for African American and Caucasian test-takers.

Another possible problem is that members of various ethnic groups may respond differently to interviews. To take just one example, being surveyed about symptoms of a mental disorder over the telephone by a stranger probably has a unique meaning for an older Chinese woman whose traditions suggest that personal problems are matters to be kept within the family (Ying, 1989). At the same time, she might see refusing to cooperate with an interviewer as unacceptably rude. Many traditional Chinese women appear to resolve this dilemma by not acknowledging to interviewers that they have experienced certain symptoms.

Diversity and Definitions of Mental Disorders

Ethnic or cultural factors are most likely to distort diagnoses when clinicians do not understand a person's cultural or ethnic background. For example, Asian Americans may express psychological problems through physical complaints, a tendency known as **somaticizing**. This form of complaint may be less embarrassing to people from an Asian background than admitting to emotional problems. Another example is the use of culturally specific expressions of distress, such as *susto* (fright), *nervios* (nerves), and *ataque de nervios* (attack of nerves), which are widely experienced amongst Hispanic Americans and often associated with psychiatric disorders (Durà-Vilà & Hodes, 2012). Therefore, clinicians need to consider how cultural tolerance and language for different kinds of problems may affect the way clients experience and present distress.

somaticizing: A tendency to express psychological problems through physical complaints.

To foster an appreciation of how diversity affects the expression of mental disorders, the *DSM-5* includes a separate section on cultural formulation, which provides a framework for assessing information about the cultural features of an individual's mental health problem and how it relates to a social and cultural context and history (American Psychiatric Association, 2013a, p. 749). In addition, the *DSM-5* describes many **culture-bound syndromes**, patterns of abnormal behavior that appear only in certain localities or cultures. For instance, *koro*, covered in Chapter 2, appears in the *DSM-5* under Obsessive-Compulsive and Related Disorders, as well as in the special appendix called "Glossary of Cultural Concepts of Distress."

culture-bound syndrome: A pattern of abnormal behavior that appears only in certain localities or cultures.

Connections

How could social adversity and poverty contribute to the incidence of mental disorders? See Chapter 2.

Diversity and Interactions Between Clients and Clinicians

The effect of ethnic or cultural factors on diagnosis stems in part from their impact on how clinicians and clients interact. At the most obvious level, if they have difficulty understanding each other's spoken language, the clinician will have difficulty understanding the client's psychological functioning. In particular, clinicians must be cautious about how they interpret idioms, such as "My nerves are shot" or "I'm having my spells again."

Cultural values can also affect a person's willingness to disclose personal problems to a professional. The cultural background of many Hispanic Americans, for example, tends to discourage seeking help from outside professionals, so it is not surprising that Hispanic Americans use formal mental health services less than other ethnic groups (Sue, Zane, & Young, 1994).

Failure to understand the influences of clients' cultural background and experience can lead clinicians to make two fundamental mistakes (Lopez, 1989). First, clinicians can misconstrue a certain behavior as a symptom of a mental disorder when, in fact, the behavior is considered desirable in the client's culture. An example of this **overpathologizing** error is when a Hispanic American's deference to family authority figures is interpreted as a sign of anxiety or immaturity. The opposite of this tendency is the **underpathologizing** error, in which clinicians dismiss some bizarre behavior as merely the reflection of a cultural difference when, in fact, it is the symptom of a mental disorder. This mistake sometimes occurs when clinicians try too hard to prove their cultural sensitivity and can result in people being denied the treatment they clearly need.

overpathologizing: A tendency to mistakenly construe some behavior as a symptom of a mental disorder when, in fact, the behavior is culturally appropriate.

underpathologizing: A tendency for clinicians to mistakenly construe some behavior as merely reflecting a cultural difference when, in fact, it is the symptom of a mental disorder.

Scientific classification of mental disorders was first widely established in the United States with the introduction of the *DSM* in 1952. In *DSM-5* diagnoses:

■ a person's behavior is compared with a set of clearly specified criteria for each disorder;

■ the person's behavior must satisfy a predetermined number of these criteria for a disorder to be diagnosed; and

■ a person is also assessed for medical conditions, exposure to stressors, and overall functioning, as well as the presence of mental disorders.

Diagnoses of mental disorders in the real world are influenced by:

■ financial considerations,

■ concerns about privacy, and

■ ethnic and cultural factors that shape the way clinicians and clients understand and interact with each other.

The Frequency of Mental Disorders: How Common Are They?

How many people currently suffer from a mental disorder or have suffered from one at some point in their lives? These are among the questions addressed by the field of epidemiology. The total number of people who suffer from a disorder in a specific population is called the **prevalence** of a disorder. Lifetime prevalence is the percentage of people in a population who have had a disorder at any time in their lives, and point prevalence includes only those who have the disorder at one specific point in time (i.e., at the time of interview). The 1-year prevalence is a hybrid type of prevalence between lifetime prevalence and point prevalence, recording the history of the disorder within a year prior to assessment (Eaton et al., 1985). The number of people who develop a new disorder in a specific time period (usually the previous 6 or 12 months) is known as the **incidence** of a disorder.

Epidemiologists have studied the prevalence of mental disorders in the United States and other parts of the world throughout the latter half of the 20th century. Their studies are usually based on interviews with large numbers of people who have been selected to represent a larger population. For example, researchers conducting the Midtown Manhattan Study (Srole, Langner, Michael, Opler, & Rennie, 1962) interviewed more than 1,600 people in New York City. Based on these interviews, the authors estimated that about 26% of the population had a mental disorder.

The most comprehensive study of mental disorders in the United States was the Epidemiologic Catchment Area (ECA) Project sponsored by the National Institute of Mental Health (Robins & Regier, 1991). In this study, trained interviewers used a structured interview (the Diagnostic Interview Schedule [DIS], discussed in Table 1.1) to collect information about 30 major mental disorders in five large "catchment" areas: Los Angeles, California; St. Louis, Missouri; New Haven, Connecticut; Baltimore, Maryland; and Durham, North Carolina. More than 20,000 subjects were selected so that their age, gender, economic status, education, and place of residence made them as representative as possible of the U.S. population in general. Interviews were conducted not only with community residents, but with people living in prisons, nursing homes, hospitals, and other institutions.

More recently, WHO expanded its Composite International Diagnostic Interview (CIDI; Table 1.1), the interview used in almost all major psychiatric epidemiological surveys in the world over the past decade, to include detailed questions about severity (Kessler & Ustun, 2004). This expanded CIDI was used in a coordinated series of epidemiological surveys carried out under WHO auspices and known as the World Mental Health (WMH) Survey Initiative. Using similar methodology, these surveys continue to be conducted regularly worldwide (Eaton et al., 2012), as well as in the United States as the National Comorbidity Survey (NCS; Kessler, Chiu, Demler, & Walters, 2005).

prevalence: The total number of people who suffer from a disorder in a specific population.

incidence: The number of people who develop a disorder in a specific time period, usually the previous six or twelve months.

So what can these large-scale epidemiological projects tell us about national and global mental health? Note that these studies were all based on *DSM-IV* diagnostic criteria, so the precise numbers may change somewhat as surveys begin to use *DSM-5* criteria instead. In addition to being a product of the screening tool used (e.g., the *DSM*), measuring the frequency of mental disorders may also be subject to errors due to differential reporting (e.g., some people may not want to reveal that they have a disorder). However, these data still provide a vital snapshot of the approximate frequency of mental disorders. Some highlights of this ongoing research are:

1. Mental disorders are common in the United States and internationally. An estimated 26.2% of Americans ages 18 and older—about one in four adults—suffer from a diagnosable mental disorder in a given year (Kessler et al., 2005), which translates to about 60 million people. Even though mental disorders are widespread in the population, the main burden of these disorders is concentrated in a much smaller proportion—about 6%, or 1 in 17—who suffer from a serious mental illness. In addition, mental disorders are the leading cause of disability in the United States and Canada.

2. The lifetime prevalence of mental disorders is frequently related to demographic or social variables. Within the United States, higher rates of disorder are associated with being poor and not completing high school. African Americans have higher rates of mental disorder than Caucasian or Hispanic Americans. However, according to more detailed ECA and NCS results, if cognitive symptoms that are strongly correlated with social class are excluded, African Americans actually show a lower prevalence of several disorders, including mood disturbances and substance use disorders, than Caucasian Americans (Kessler et al., 1994).

3. In the United States, about 38% of people with a history of disorder are "in **remission**," defined as being free of symptoms during the year prior to the interview. Over half of the persons who had suffered drug abuse/dependence, generalized anxiety disorder, alcohol abuse, or antisocial personality disorder had been without symptoms of these disorders during the prior year.

   remission: When symptoms of a previously present disorder are no longer apparent, implying improvement or recovery.

4. In the United States, remission rates far exceed the percentage of people seeking treatment for a disorder. Indeed, only 19% of community residents with a current disorder report receiving recent treatment for it, usually from general physicians rather than mental health professionals. Children, the elderly, ethnic minorities, the poor and homeless, and people with physical disabilities are especially likely to be *underserved*, meaning that they do not receive interventions that may be needed.

5. Comorbidity of mental disorders is common in the United States. If we define comorbidity simply as having at least two different diagnoses, 18% of the ECA sample would be classified as comorbid, and 60% of people with one disorder in their lifetime had at least one additional diagnosed mental disorder. The comorbidity results from the NCS are even more striking. Among respondents with a history of at least one disorder, 56% had suffered one or more other disorders in their lifetime, and over half of all lifetime disorders occurred in the 14% of the sample having a history of three or more comorbid disorders. In other words, the major burden of mental disorders is concentrated in a group of comorbid people who constitute less than one sixth of the population.

6. In the ECA study, the first symptoms of most mental disorders occur at a surprisingly early age. Considering all disorders, the average age for noticing the first symptoms of a disorder was 16. In the NCS study, anxiety disorders and eating disorders often began in people's teenage years, and as you might expect, disorders such as ADHD and autism were typically diagnosed in childhood (Kessler, Chiu, Demler, & Walters, 2005). This finding helps explain the dual emphases throughout this book on understanding the developmental origins of mental disorders and on the need for preventive programs that focus on children and adolescents.

7. As Table 1.5 shows, the prevalence and projected lifetime risk of mental disorders varies considerably worldwide. For instance, the projected risk of a person meeting

TABLE 1.5 Worldwide Prevalence of *DSM* Disorders (Percent of Sample With Disorders in Their Lifetime and Projected Lifetime Risk As of Age 75)

Country	Any Anxiety Disorder		Any Mood Disorder		Any Substance Use Disorder		Any Mental Disorder	
	Prevalence (%)	Projected Lifetime Risk (%)	Prevalence (%)	Projected Lifetime Risk (%)	Prevalence (%)	Projected Lifetime Risk (%)	Prevalence (%)	Projected Lifetime Risk (%)
Belgium	13.1	15.7	14.1	22.8	8.3	10.5	29.1	37.1
Columbia	25.3	30.9	14.6	27.2	9.6	12.8	39.1	55.2
France	22.3	26.0	21.0	30.5	7.1	8.8	37.9	47.2
Germany	14.6	16.9	9.9	16.2	6.5	8.7	25.2	33.0
Israel	5.2	10.1	10.7	21.2	5.3	6.3	17.6	29.7
Italy	11.0	13.7	9.9	17.3	1.3	1.6	18.1	26.0
Japan	.6.9	9.2	7.6	14.1	4.8	6.2	18.0	24.4
Lebanon	16.7	20.2	12.6	20.1	2.2	—	25.8	32.9
Mexico	14.3	17.8	9.2	20.4	7.8	11.9	26.1	—
Netherlands	15.9	21.4	17.9	28.9	8.9	11.4	31.7	42.9
New Zealand	24.6	30.3	20.4	29.8	12.4	14.6	39.3	48.6
Nigeria	6.5	7.1	3.3	8.9	3.7	6.4	12.0	19.5
China	4.8	6.0	3.6	7.3	4.9	6.1	13.2	18.0
South Africa	15.8	30.1	9.8	20.0	13.3	17.5	30.3	47.5
Spain	9.9	13.3	10.6	20.8	3.6	4.6	19.4	29.0
Ukraine	10.9	17.3	15.8	25.9	15.0	18.8	36.1	48.9
United States	31.0	36.0	21.4	31.4	14.6	17.4	47.4	55.3

Source: Based on data from Kessler et al. (2007).

diagnostic criteria for any mental disorder at some point in his or her lifetime ranges from 18% in China to over 55% in the United States, with most European countries somewhere in the middle of those extremes. In addition, the specific type of disorders that are frequently diagnosed differs by nation. Anxiety disorders are most common in the United States, Columbia, and New Zealand, whereas mood disorders are most often diagnosed in the United States, New Zealand, and France. Substance use disorders are highest in the United States, the Ukraine, and South Africa.

8. Overall, the most common disorders worldwide are personality disorders and alcohol use disorders, followed by dementia for older adults, major depression, and anxiety disorders such as simple phobias (see Table 1.6).

9. Having a mental disorder in the developing world can be grim (Clay, 2014). Up to 85% of people with severe mental disorders in low- and middle-income countries receive no treatment, according to WHO. People with mental disorders often face inhumane living conditions and harmful, degrading treatment practices in healthcare facilities. They are frequently denied the right to work, go to school, and have families. That may soon change, thanks to WHO's new Comprehensive Mental Health Action Plan 2013–20 (World Health Organization, 2013). Adopted by the World Health Assembly in October 2013, the plan is a call to action that will help guide countries as they strive to ensure that all citizens with mental disorders receive the treatment they need. The plan has four specific objectives: (1) strength-

TABLE 1.6 Prevalence of Specific Mental Disorders in Adults Worldwide (Percent of Sample With Disorders in the 12 Months Prior to Interview)

Mental Disorder	Median 1-Year Prevalence	Prevalence Range	Number of Studies
Panic disorder	0.9	0.6–1.9	33
Social phobia	2.8	1.1–5.8	30
Simple phobia	4.8	3.5–7.3	25
Major depressive disorder	5.3	3.6–6.5	42
Obsessive-compulsive disorder	1.0	0.6–2.0	19
Drug use disorder	1.8	1.1–2.7	11
Alcohol use disorder	5.9	5.2–8.1	14
Personality disorders	9.1	9.0–14.4	5
Schizophrenia	0.5	0.3–0.6	23
Bipolar disorder	0.6	0.3–1.1	16
Dementia (age > 65 years)	5.4	3.2–7.1	25

Source: Based on data from Eaton et al. (2008).

ening leadership in mental health, (2) providing comprehensive mental health and social services in community-based settings, (3) implementing prevention and mental health promotion strategies, and (4) strengthening research programs and information systems for mental health fields.

The Four Guiding Principles: MAPS of the Territory

Criticisms of *DSM* Diagnoses

As we discuss in the "Controversy" feature as well as in this section, the *DSM-5* is still a target of significant criticisms (Clark, Watson, & Reynolds, 1995; Frances, 2012; Paris, 2013) despite continued improvement in the empirical foundations for diagnoses and greater sophistication in the way the diagnostic system is organized. It is all too easy to assume that the wide variety of mental disorders we describe in this textbook are real "things" (diseases) that people "have." Whereas that is sometimes true, we want you to remember that there are potential limitations to traditional notions about the nature, diagnosis, and treatment of mental disorders. To remind you of these potential limitations, we offer you the acronym MAPS, which stands for M*edical myths*, A*ttempted answers*, P*rejudicial pigeonholing*, and S*uperficial syndromes*. Each of these four guiding principles, discussed in more detail in the sections that follow, is represented by an icon that will display throughout the text whenever that particular principle applies.

M = Medical Myths

Medical myths is the notion that, despite the urgings of powerful drug companies and the potential increases in diagnosis of mental disorders in the *DSM-5* (Frances, 2012), pills are not always (or even often) the optimal first-line treatment for most of the disorders in the *DSM-5* (Heuzenroeder et al., 2004; Hofmann, Asnaani, Vonk, Sawyer, & Fang, 2012), with the exception of bipolar disorder (Smith, Cornelius, Warnock, Tacchi, & Taylor, 2007). Furthermore, the biological/medical model discussed in Chapter 2 is only

MAPS - Medical Myths

DSM-5 Is Guide Not Bible—Ignore Its Ten Worst Changes

The following was published on December 2, 2012 by Allen J. Frances, M.D., in DSM-5 in Distress blog and is reprinted with permission of the author.

Allen Frances, M.D., was chair of the DSM-IV *Task Force and of the department of psychiatry at Duke University School of Medicine, Durham, NC. He is currently professor emeritus at Duke and is the author of two recent (2013) books:* Saving Normal: An Insider's Revolt Against Out-of-Control Psychiatric Diagnosis, DSM-5, Big Pharma and the Medicalization of Ordinary Life *and* Essentials of Psychiatric Diagnosis, Revised Edition: Responding to the Challenge of DSM-5.

This is the saddest moment in my 45-year career of studying, practicing, and teaching psychiatry. The Board of Trustees of the American Psychiatric Association (APA) has given its final approval to a deeply flawed *DSM-5* containing many changes that seem clearly unsafe and scientifically unsound. My best advice to clinicians, to the press, and to the general public—be skeptical and don't follow *DSM-5* blindly down a road likely to lead to massive overdiagnosis and harmful overmedication. Just ignore the ten changes that make no sense.

Brief background. *DSM-5* got off to a bad start and was never able to establish sure footing. Its leaders initially articulated a premature and unrealizable goal—to produce a paradigm shift in psychiatry. Excessive ambition combined with disorganized execution led inevitably to many ill-conceived and risky proposals.

These were vigorously opposed. More than 50 mental health professional associations petitioned for an outside review of *DSM-5* to provide an independent judgment of its supporting evidence and to evaluate the balance between its risks and benefits. Professional journals, the press, and the public also weighed in—expressing widespread astonishment about decisions that sometimes seemed not only to lack scientific support but also to defy common sense.

The *DSM-5* has neither been able to self-correct nor willing to heed the advice of outsiders. It has instead created a mostly closed shop—circling the wagons and deaf to the repeated and widespread warnings that it would lead to massive misdiagnosis. Fortunately, some of its most egregiously risky and unsupportable proposals were eventually dropped under great external pressure (most notably "psychosis risk," mixed anxiety/depression, Internet and sex addiction, rape as a mental disorder, "hebephilia," cumbersome personality ratings, and sharply lowered thresholds for many existing disorders). But APA stubbornly refused to sponsor any independent review and has given final approval to the ten reckless and untested ideas that are summarized below.

The history of psychiatry is littered with fad diagnoses that in retrospect did far more harm than good. Yesterday's APA approval makes it likely that the *DSM-5* will start a half dozen or more new fads which will be detrimental to the misdiagnosed individuals and costly to our society. . . .

So, here is my list of *DSM-5*'s ten most potentially harmful changes. I would suggest that clinicians not follow these at all (or, at the very least, use them with extreme caution and attention to their risks); that potential patients be deeply skeptical, especially if the proposed diagnosis is being used as a rationale for prescribing medication for you or for your child; and that payers question whether some of these are suitable for reimbursement. My goal is to minimize the harm that may otherwise be done by unnecessary obedience to unwise and arbitrary *DSM-5* decisions.

1. Disruptive mood dysregulation disorder: *DSM-5* will turn temper tantrums into a mental disorder—a puzzling decision based on the work of only one research group. We have no idea whatever how this untested new diagnosis will play out in real-life practice settings, but my fear is that it will exacerbate, not relieve, the already excessive and inappropriate use of medication in young children. During the past two decades, child psychiatry has already provoked three fads—a tripling of attention deficit disorder, a more than 20-times increase in autistic disorder, and a 40-times increase in childhood bipolar disorder. The field should have felt chastened by this sorry track record and should engage itself now in the crucial task of educating practitioners and the public about the difficulty of accurately diagnosing children and the risks of overmedicating them. *DSM-5* should not be adding a new disorder likely to result in a new fad and even more inappropriate medication use in vulnerable children.

2. Normal grief will become major depressive disorder, thus medicalizing and trivializing our expectable and necessary emotional reactions to the loss of a loved one and substituting pills and superficial medical rituals for the deep consolations of family, friends, religion, and the resiliency that comes with time and the acceptance of the limitations of life.

3. The everyday forgetting characteristic of old age will now be misdiagnosed as minor neurocognitive disorder, creating a huge false positive population of people who are not at special risk for demen-

DSM-5 Is Guide Not Bible—Ignore Its Ten Worst Changes *(Continued)*

tia. Since there is no effective treatment for this "condition" (or for dementia), the label provides absolutely no benefit (while creating great anxiety) even for those at true risk for later developing dementia. It is a dead loss for the many who will be mislabeled.

4. *DSM-5* will likely trigger a fad of adult attention deficit disorder, leading to widespread misuse of stimulant drugs for performance enhancement and recreation and contributing to the already large illegal secondary market in diverted prescription drugs.

5. Excessive eating 12 times in 3 months is no longer just a manifestation of gluttony and the easy availability of really great-tasting food. *DSM-5* has instead turned it into a psychiatric illness called binge eating disorder.

6. The changes in the *DSM-5* definition of autism will result in lowered rates: 10% according to estimates by the *DSM-5* work group, perhaps 50% according to outside research groups. This reduction can be seen as beneficial in the sense that the diagnosis of autism will be more accurate and specific— but advocates understandably fear a disruption in needed school services. Here the *DSM-5* problem is not so much a bad decision, but the misleading promises that it will have no impact on rates of disorder or of service delivery. School services should be tied more to educational need, less to a controversial psychiatric diagnosis created for clinical (not educational) purposes and whose rate is so sensitive to small changes in definition and assessment.

7. First-time substance abusers will be lumped in definitionally with hard-core addicts, despite their very different treatment needs and prognosis and the stigma this will cause.

8. *DSM-5* has created a slippery slope by introducing the concept of behavioral addictions that eventually can spread to make a mental disorder of everything we like to do a lot. Watch out for careless overdiagnosis of Internet and sex addiction and the development of lucrative treatment programs to exploit these new markets.

9. *DSM-5* obscures the already fuzzy boundary around generalized anxiety disorder and the worries of everyday life. Small changes in definition can create millions of anxious new "patients" and expand the already widespread practice of inappropriately prescribing addicting antianxiety medications.

10. *DSM-5* has opened the gate even further to the already-existing problem of misdiagnosis of PTSD (posttraumatic stress disorder) in forensic settings.

DSM-5 has dropped its pretension to being a paradigm shift in psychiatric diagnosis and instead (in a dramatic 180-degree turn) now makes the equally misleading claim that it is a conservative document that will have minimal impact on the rates of psychiatric diagnosis and in the consequent provision of inappropriate treatment. This is an untenable claim that *DSM-5* cannot possibly support because, for completely unfathomable reasons, it never took the simple and inexpensive step of actually studying the impact of *DSM* on rates in real-world settings.

Except for autism, all the *DSM-5* changes loosen diagnosis and threaten to turn our current diagnostic inflation into diagnostic hyperinflation. Painful experience with previous *DSM*s teaches that if anything in the diagnostic system can be misused and turned into a fad, it will be. Many millions of people with normal grief, gluttony, distractibility, worries, reactions to stress, the temper tantrums of childhood, the forgetting of old age, and "behavioral addictions" will soon be mislabeled as psychiatrically sick and given inappropriate treatment.

People with real psychiatric problems that can be reliably diagnosed and effectively treated are already badly shortchanged. *DSM-5* will make this worse by diverting attention and scarce resources away from the really ill and toward people with the everyday problems of life who will be harmed, not helped, when they are mislabeled as mentally ill.

Our patients deserve better, society deserves better, and the mental health professions deserve better. Caring for the mentally ill is a noble and effective profession. But we have to know our limits and stay within them.

DSM-5 violates the most sacred (and most frequently ignored) tenet in medicine: First Do No Harm! That's why this is such a sad moment.

Thinking Critically

The previous article shows that, although the APA and WHO have gone to great lengths to offer national and international diagnostic systems that they believe to be of scientific value, doubt remains about the science behind these systems. Specifically, there are concerns about whether these systems might continue to create diagnostic errors and other problems. To what extent are such concerns valid? Deciding requires critical thinking, which involves asking yourself the following questions about this or any other controversial topic,

(Continued)

DSM-5 Is Guide Not Bible—Ignore Its Ten Worst Changes (Continued)

such as those featured in the "Controversy" feature present in each chapter in this text (Bernstein, 2007; Burke, Sears, Kraus, & Roberts-Cady, 2014):

1. What are you being asked to *believe or accept*?
2. What *evidence* is available to support the claim?
3. What *alternative* ways are there to interpret the evidence?
4. How would you rate all the evidence/alternatives on a 0–10 scale based on *validity/strength*?
5. What *assumptions or biases* came up when answering questions 1–4 (e.g., using intuition/emotion, authority, or personal experience rather than science)?
6. What *additional evidence* would help you evaluate the alternatives?
7. What *conclusions* are most reasonable or likely?

Regarding question 1, Allen Frances makes several key claims in his blog, including the notion that *DSM-5* will lead to increased diagnosis of depression, neurocognitive disorders, PTSD in forensic settings, and ADHD in adults. Additional critical-thinking steps you should consider are:

- What evidence would you need to be convinced that these disorders will (or will not) be overdiagnosed now that the *DSM-5* is in wide use?
- What types of research studies could psychologists design to test Frances's key claims?

This is precisely the kind of thinking that we hope you will engage in as you read this book.

one narrow lens through which we view disorders, and we currently have no disorders for which the biological/genetic underpinnings have been fully established (Paris, 2013). It is tempting to take the simplest route possible to understanding and treating mental disorders—for instance, to view depression as an illness or disease resulting merely from low serotonin levels in the brain. But viewing mental disorders as physical diseases is oversimplified and sometimes just plain wrong.

The Medical Model Stresses the Individual Above the Sociocultural Context

Especially with the removal of the multiaxial system (and Axis IV, which formerly listed psychosocial stressors), the *DSM-5* emphasizes individual dysfunction far more than the effects of harmful environments and social policies that impair people's psychological adjustment. Some critics believe that this emphasis on internal factors is one of the most harmful effects of the medical model of mental disorders around which the *DSM* is organized. By focusing diagnoses exclusively on individual problems, mental health professionals run the risk of blaming the victims of poverty, discrimination, undereducation, unemployment, and abuse. In a country such as the United States, where one in every five children lives in poverty, the potential significance of considering the external factors contributing to psychopathology is obvious. If destructive environments and social policies are the true culprits behind some mental disorders, diagnostic practices that distract mental health professionals from working on these external problems do a disservice to people with mental disorders and to society at large.

A = Attempted Answers

MAPS - Attempted Answers

Far from being medical illnesses, mental disorders are just a collection of potentially interrelated symptoms—subjective observations a person makes, indicating that something might be wrong. What is important to note is that these symptoms often arise as the person's attempted solution to a problem. For instance, delusions may create meaning for people who are depressed, compulsive behaviors (e.g., hand-washing) may reduce the anxiety caused by obsessional thoughts (e.g., worries about getting sick), children with autism may seek sameness/rituals to manage their discomfort, and children with ADHD may overstimulate themselves to "wake their brains up." Moreover, there may be adaptive advantages to certain mental disorders. For instance, depression can help people temporarily withdraw from others after losses/stressors so they can "lick their wounds" (in ancestral environments, sometimes literally!) and return to society when they are ready to reengage. Throughout this textbook, we help you understand *why* specific symptoms might emerge in specific situations and what functions they might serve for the individual who may have generated them.

P = Prejudicial Pigeonholes

We delve deeper into our history of understanding mental disorders in Chapter 2, and you will see how the historical context can change the way we view them. Even in modern times, the labels included in each version of the *DSM* and which treatments are implemented first are partly reflections of historical trends and sociocultural attitudes. For example, homosexuality was included as a mental disorder until its removal from the *DSM-III-R* in 1987, and several scholars still argue that the remaining sexual behavior categories of disorders in the *DSM*, now called paraphilic disorders in the *DSM-5* (covered in Chapter 17), should be removed as well (Silverstein, 2009). As we discuss next, pigeonholing someone, which means thinking of that individual unfairly as belonging to a particular group, can have dire consequences for that person's future.

MAPS - Prejudicial Pigeonholes

Labeling Produces Stereotypes, Prejudice, and Harm

It is easy to forget that diagnoses apply to disorders, not individuals. When people overlook this fact, diagnoses can have many adverse effects, including rejection and discrimination.

The potential dangers of labeling were suggested several decades ago by a famous study conducted by David Rosenhan (1973). Rosenhan and seven other people, *none of whom suffered from a mental disorder*, presented themselves to psychiatric hospitals in five states and asked to be admitted as patients. Each person complained of the same, single symptom: hearing voices saying the words *thud*, *empty*, and *hollow*. In almost every instance, the hospital staff admitted these people and diagnosed them with schizophrenia, a serious disorder. Following their admissions to the hospitals, these pseudopatients behaved as normally as possible. Nonetheless, their actions were often interpreted as signs of disorder. For example, the hospital staff interpreted behaviors intended to relieve boredom, such as keeping a personal journal, as symptoms of mental illness. Despite their normal behavior, the researchers were kept in the hospitals anywhere from 7 to 52 days. After being discharged, they were usually given the diagnosis "schizophrenia, in remission," suggesting that the disorder (which they never had in the first place!) might return someday.

You should be careful not to make too much of this study. As many critics have pointed out (e.g., Spitzer, 1975), hospital staff are rarely confronted by normal people who report hearing nonexistent voices and ask to be admitted. Usually, something is wrong, and the clinician's wisest and safest course is to take the complaint seriously and admit the patient to the hospital. In fact, failing to do so might well be negligent, so legal considerations make the staff's reactions appear more reasonable. Still, the Rosenhan study did dramatically demonstrate how labels can exert too much influence, distorting the interpretation of a labeled person's behavior.

Labels of mental disorders can also lead to detrimental changes in the labeled person's behavior. If a person is incorrectly diagnosed as having diabetes, this false-positive diagnosis may be frightening and could lead to additional, costly, medical procedures. But the label itself would not cause diabetes. With mental disorders, however, false labels can sometimes make the conditions they describe more likely, an outcome known as a *self-fulfilling prophecy*. This concern is particularly strong with some childhood disorders. For example, children incorrectly diagnosed as having learning disabilities may decrease their academic effort because they believe that no amount of effort can ever overcome their "disabilities." Tragically, decreased motivation might increase their risk of academic difficulties, until the diagnosis finally appears accurate.

Chapter 1 Identifying, Detecting, and Classifying Mental Disorders: MAPS of the Territory

The good news here is that abnormal psychology classes—the likely reason you are reading this textbook—can reduce students' prejudices against people with mental disorders (Barney, 2014).

Gender Bias in the *DSM*

Also under the broad umbrella of prejudicial pigeonholing is the claim that the diagnosis of mental disorders is gender biased. For example, some charge that *DSM* diagnostic criteria codify "masculine-based assumptions about what behaviors are healthy and what behaviors are crazy" (Kaplan, 1983) and that this shows up especially in diagnosis of personality disorders (Chapter 16). Others object that society encourages women to be submissive and dependent, but then labels them as mentally disordered if they show too much of these qualities. In the *DSM-5*, for example, one criterion for histrionic personality disorder (which is much more commonly diagnosed in women than men) is "consistently uses physical appearance to draw attention to self." Our male-dominated society appears to want women to be physically beautiful so they are more sexually desirable, but it then condemns them with a diagnostic label if they show what men think to be too much of this quality.

In one study (Ford & Widiger, 1989), psychologists read one of three case histories that illustrated antisocial personality disorder (APD; diagnosed more often in males), histrionic personality disorder (HPD; diagnosed more often in females), or an ambiguous mixture of the two. One third of the psychologists were told that their case involved a female client, one third were told it was a male, and one third were not informed of the client's gender. A second group of psychologists rated the extent to which each symptom presented in the cases represented a criterion for antisocial or histrionic diagnosis. For the antisocial case, the psychologists failed significantly more often to diagnose APD for the female (15%) than for the male (42%). The reverse was true for the HPD case; the psychologists significantly underdiagnosed this disorder in males (44%) compared with females (76%). The ambiguous case was not affected by the gender of the client, and the gender of the psychologists themselves made little difference to their diagnoses. This and other research suggests that the diagnosis of personality disorders in the *DSM-5* may result in prejudicial pigeonholing, using data that go beyond the relevant symptoms of each client.

S = Superficial Syndromes

The last several versions of the *DSM* (*III*, *IV*, and *5*) have had high interrater reliability in diagnoses—that is, agreement between different observers—because the diagnostic criteria are commonly based on superficial signs and symptoms. In other words, diagnosis is made typically using features that clinicians or clients can easily see/observe, such as depressed mood, restlessness, social awkwardness, or hypervigilance, rather than by any deeper understanding of cause. Many of the later chapters will have a photo or two of a specific cactus to illustrate the key caveat that the *DSM* is based on observable syndromes rather than diseases per se (Paris, 2013). The cactus icon also reappears throughout this textbook because it shows how easily we can diagnose people—and even cactus trees—with mental disorders using only what we see on the outside (e.g., droopy cactus arms = depression). In this textbook, we explore abnormality behind the cactus to get at what causes these disorders and how to treat them, and not just how to spot them based on surface characteristics.

MAPS - Superficial syndromes

Source: Taras Boichuk/Shutterstock.com.

Mental Disorders Occur on a Continuum, Not in Discrete Categories

Related to their reliance on superficial syndromes, *DSM*-based diagnoses imply that a person either does, or does not, have a disorder. This categorical, all-or-none approach to classification has been challenged by mental health professionals, who argue that mental disorders are not arranged so neatly in real life (Carson, 1991). Many argue as well that the line separating disorder from nondisorder in the *DSM*—in terms of the particular number of symptoms needed to define a disorder—tends to be rather arbitrary (Paris, 2013).

One alternative is for clinicians to think of disorders occurring along different dimensions (Widiger, Trull, Hurt, Clarkin, & Frances, 1987). In a **dimensional approach**, a person receives scores on several dimensions of personality, such as extraversion, openness to different kinds of experiences, conscientiousness, and emotional stability. When taken together, these scores produce a profile that summarizes the person's standing on those dimensions. How would Bill from the chapter-opening case be described by a dimensional system? Using the most common personality dimensions—sometimes called "The Big Five"—a clinician might describe Bill as moderately open, introverted, relatively conscientious, mildly disagreeable, and emotionally unstable.

dimensional approach: An approach to describing mental disorders in which disorders are portrayed along different personality dimensions that produce a profile summarizing the person's functioning.

The categorical approach has remained dominant in the *DSM* for several reasons: (1) the medical tradition of diagnosis emphasizes discrete illnesses (see the "Medical Myths" section earlier), (2) clinicians find it easier to use categorical systems, and (3) theorists have not been able to agree on the nature or number of personality dimensions necessary to describe psychopathology adequately (Millon, 1991).

The *DSM* Pays Too Much Attention to Reliability, Not Enough to Validity

To ensure high interrater reliability, the diagnostic criteria for *DSM* disorders were simplified and made specific enough that clinicians could agree on them. However, this simplification may have distorted the true nature of some disorders (Carson, 1991; Widiger & Trull, 1991). Imagine that you used the same approach in setting up a movie review system to help different movie critics agree on whether a particular film is good enough to earn four stars. You might require that only movies with French subtitles be rated four stars. This four-star criterion would produce excellent agreement among movie critics but would not be valid because it excludes many potentially excellent movies from consideration. Likewise, too much simplification in diagnostic criteria may enable clinicians to agree, but their diagnoses may not adequately reflect the core features or implications of many mental disorders behind the cacti.

To sum up MAPS (the four guiding principles that reappear throughout this book), the diagnosis of mental disorders is frequently based on oversimplified medical assumptions and surface characteristics of human beings, as well as influenced by sociopolitical climate and stereotypes, rather than on a profound and real understanding of mechanism and cause. As (Paris 2013) puts it:

> Thirty-odd years after the *DSM-III*, we are still in the dark about the nature of most disorders. . . . Advances in neuroscience have not succeeded in explaining ANY mental disorder. Genetics has raised more questions than it can answer. Neurochemistry turns out to be much more complex than most people believed. And the beautiful pictures of neuroimaging will be seen by future generations as, at best, suggestive and, at worst, primitive. Clinical observation and consensus from experts, rather than hard facts, are still the guiding forces behind the manual. (pp. 183–184)

Revisiting the Case of Bill

The case of Bill, which began this chapter, is typical of what clinicians encounter in their everyday practice. Bill's symptoms are common, and his concerns about being diagnosed are also familiar to most clinicians. His case illustrates how clinicians must constantly balance knowledge about disorders and official classifications with the many practical consequences of a *DSM* diagnosis.

The clinical psychologist who assessed Bill conducted a comprehensive psychological assessment that included a social history and review of Bill's medical and work records, an extensive structured interview geared to measure *DSM-5* diagnostic criteria, and psychological testing with the MMPI-2-RF and the Wechsler Adult Intelligence Scale (WAIS-IV). The clinician also conducted one session in which, after obtaining Bill's permission, she interviewed Bill's wife to gain additional information about the couple's marital problems.

Based on these assessment data, the clinician concluded that Bill was experiencing a generalized anxiety disorder, which, as discussed in Chapter 7, is a common type of disorder found somewhat more often among minority than among Caucasian populations. Bill's nervous stomach and shortness of breath are examples of the physical symptoms often associated with generalized anxiety disorder, as is the marital dissatisfaction that Bill reported. To provide a thorough diagnostic evaluation, Bill's psychologist completed his chart as follows: generalized anxiety disorder; medical conditions: Crohn's disease; stressors: threat of job loss, marital difficulties.

Before reporting the diagnosis to Bill's health insurance company, the psychologist discussed with Bill the implications of the diagnosis. She explained that she would do all that she could to protect against unnecessary disclosures of information about his condition but that she was almost certain that his diagnosis would be known to the claims manager of the insurance company. She also explained that generalized anxiety disorder can be effectively treated with cognitive-behavioral therapy (CBT) even more so than with medication, which is discussed further in Chapter 7.

Because he concluded that the risks of breaches of confidentiality were outweighed by the reimbursement offered by his insurance, Bill decided to continue in psychotherapy. Like most good clinicians, Bill's therapist took the time to explain what is known about the cause of his disorder. His treatment lasted 14 sessions, after which he reported that most of his symptoms had declined considerably, that he no longer felt suicidal, and that he was doing better at work. He said that his marital problems had not changed much but that neither he nor his wife was ready to work on them.

As Bill's case illustrates, diagnoses seldom help clients understand how or why they developed a disorder. This is both a strength and weakness of systems such as the *DSM*. Because it bases diagnoses on specific symptoms rather than on presumed causes, the *DSM* allows clinicians of different theoretical persuasions to agree on most diagnoses. However, this agreement sometimes comes at the price of not indicating enough about the origins or implications of a disorder. In the remaining chapters, we describe what clinicians know about the causes and treatment of mental disorders to get a glimpse behind the cacti.

Source: Reprinted with permission from Ted Weltzin.

Summary

Identifying Mental Disorders: What Are They?

Mental disorders have been defined in various ways, but the definition that we prefer is that mental disorders involve a dysfunction or failure of biological or psychological processes to operate as they should, resulting in some harm to the individual.

Assessment and Diagnosis

Clinical assessment is the process that clinicians follow to gather the information necessary for diagnosing mental disorders. The quality of clinical assessment is judged along two dimensions: reliability and validity.

Assessment Tools: How Do Health Professionals Detect Mental Disorders?

Clinicians use life records, interviews, psychological tests, behavioral observations, and biological measures as their primary sources of information. Data from these sources are usually then combined to help clinicians diagnose mental disorders.

Diagnostic Classification: How Do Health Professionals Categorize Mental Disorders?

Although attempts to classify mental disorders have been made from antiquity, formal nosological systems

Thomas Widiger

Dr. Thomas Widiger, professor of psychology at the University of Kentucky, is a leading expert on the diagnosis of mental disorders. Dr. Widiger has written extensively about classification issues, and he served as the research coordinator for the DSM-IV.

Diagnosis

Q *Why do we need a classification system such as the DSM?*

A The main reason is the one you discuss in this chapter. We have to have a common language so we can discuss what we are studying. Classification allows us to communicate about mental disorders. Without it, meaningful communication would be impossible. Even though diagnosis carries risks of bias and stigmatization, these risks are outweighed by the communication advantage that formal classification provides. On the other hand, careful construction of a system such as the *DSM* is crucial because, like any language, it governs how clinicians think about their clients.

Q *What is the role of psychological assessment in diagnosis?*

A Beginning with the *DSM-III*, the use of well-defined classification criteria has resulted in an increased emphasis on structured and semistructured diagnostic interviews. Although psychological testing remains an important element in assessment, its role in diagnosis is diminishing. Obviously, this trend means that students need much better training in interviewing techniques than they have typically received so that they are competent in using the new structured interviews.

Q *How prevalent are mental disorders?*

A I actually think they are much more prevalent than existing studies in fact suggest. I am convinced that all people suffer a mental disorder at some point in their lives. We recognize this to be true for our neighbors or roommates or friends, but we find it difficult to admit ourselves. If we acknowledged that mental disorders are more common in ourselves, it would have the added advantage of decreasing their stigma. People are less stigmatized by physical illnesses, in part, because we recognize they are just a part of life. Mental disorders are really no different. Nobody is entirely physically healthy, and nobody is entirely psychologically healthy.

Q *How will diagnosis change in the future?*

A The biggest change in the future will be an increasing reliance on neurochemical models of disorder. You can already see this trend in the progress and emphasis on medication treatments and in the *DSM* itself, which includes a special section for listing any lab and physical exam findings that are associated with the disorder. This emphasis is, of course, part of a larger trend within psychiatry, which is betting more and more of its money on biological horses. NIMH (National Institute of Mental Health) has, in fact, developed its own diagnostic system that is explicitly tied to neurobiological models of brain disease. However, I believe the pendulum is swinging too far in the biological direction. We are psychosocial beings as well as biochemical animals, and our understanding of mental disorders needs to reflect this fact.

I also think we will see dimensional approaches to mental disturbance becoming more accepted. This was, in fact, an explicit emphasis in *DSM-5*. Very few mental disorders will have single or specific etiologies and pathologies. Mental disorders are the result of a complex interaction of a variety of genes with an array of environmental experiences. The end result can be a complex profile of psychopathology that is not well described by a single, homogenous diagnostic category. It will be much better to recognize that many of the existing categories do not refer to distinct conditions but rather to different slices or forms of underlying dimensions that usually shade into normality.

Source: Reprinted with permission from Ted Weltzin.

are a product of the twentieth century. The two systems in widest use—the *Diagnostic and Statistical Manual of Mental Disorders (DSM)* in North America and the *International Classification of Diseases (ICD)* in the rest of the world—have been revised many times. In their most recent versions, these two nosologies base diagnoses on specific, operational criteria. The *DSM-5* also allows for evaluations of other dimensions that contribute to mental disorders.

The Frequency of Mental Disorders: How Common Are They?

According to major epidemiological surveys, about one third to almost one half of adults have experienced a mental disorder at some point in their lives, and about one quarter have suffered a disorder in the prior year. Mental disorders often coexist (are comorbid); in fact, most people with one disorder in their lifetimes have had at least one other diagnosed mental disorder. The prevalence of mental disorders is associated with various demographic factors, including age, gender, educational level, and ethnicity, and varies throughout the world.

The Four Guiding Principles: MAPS of the Territory

Criticisms of the *DSM* include concerns that official labels can have harmful effects, that disorders do not constitute clear categories that are distinct from other variations in behavior, that too much attention has been paid to the reliability of diagnoses at the expense of their validity, and that most diagnostic labels imply that mental disorders are caused by individual, internal factors, thus minimizing the role of possible social causes. Diagnoses may also be affected by such real-world factors as the reimbursement requirements of health insurance companies, clients' concerns about the confidentiality of their diagnoses, clinicians' personal preferences and interests, and the ethnic and cultural backgrounds of both clinicians and clients.

Throughout this textbook, we keep four guiding principles about the *DSM* and the nature of mental disorders in mind via the acronym MAPS—medical myths, attempted answers, prejudicial pigeonholing, and superficial syndromes. Icons representing each of these four principles appear throughout the book to signal whenever a particular principle is relevant.

Key Terms

achievement test, p. 11

aptitude test, p. 11

assessment, p. 6

attitude and interest test, p. 12

Axis I, p. 25

Axis II, p. 25

Axis III, p. 25

Axis IV, p. 25

Axis V, p. 25

classical method of classification, p. 27

comorbidity, p. 27

computerized tomography (CT), p. 19

correlation coefficient, p. 7

culture-bound syndrome, p. 29

diagnosis, p. 6

diffusion MRI (dMRI), p. 20

dimensional approach, p. 39

epidemiology, p. 4

field trial, p. 23

functional magnetic resonance imaging (fMRI), p. 20

incidence, p. 30

intelligence test, p. 12

life record, p. 9

magnetic resonance imaging (MRI), p. 20

mental disorder, p. 2

mental status examination (MSE), p. 10

multiaxial classification, p. 25

neuropsychological test, p. 12

norm, p. 11

nosology, p. 6

objective test, p. 15

overpathologizing, p. 29

personality test, p. 14

polythetic approach, p. 26

positron emission tomography (PET), p. 19

prevalence, p. 30

projective test, p. 14

psychological test, p. 11

reliability, p. 6

remission, p. 31

self-monitoring, p. 18

sensitivity, p. 8

single photon emission computed tomography (SPECT), p. 20

social history, p. 11

somaticizing, p. 29

specificity, p. 8

standardization, p. 11

structured interview, p. 9

underpathologizing, p. 29

validity, p. 6

Past and Present Understandings of Mental Disorders

CHAPTER 2

Source: Lightspring/Shutterstock.com.

Chapter Outline

From the Case of Nelson McGrath

Soon others will notice their discoloration. It's been going on for years but so slowly that only a few people are aware of it. Everyone gets a few more tiny spots every day—on their skin, their fingernails, everywhere—but they still don't see them. Lack of insight or hindsight. They are too far gone to save. Soon they will all be out of sight and out of mind.

I first noticed my own spots about five years ago, when I was 17. Little dots in the folds of my skin. I needed a magnifying glass to see them then and to study how the ink was filling up my pores. I burned my skin, salted it, rubbed myself with sand. But I couldn't stop the ink. Now I know I was looking in the wrong places. Spots come from the inside. All religions teach this lesson: Evil is our tar. Eat pure and think sure; they were the cure. My contamination was carried by the poison of cooked animals and the unclean thoughts of the young girls always around me. No one else seemed to understand. Hospitals are the worst places you can be for these contagious contaminations.

They had to be stopped despite what my parents and the doctors thought. I had undergone their procedures for years, and they did no good. I didn't get any better, only more full of light rays and sophistry. How could I be a sophist and a prophet? I knew the answer: Stay away from the young girls

After reading this chapter, you will be able to answer the following key questions:

- What causes mental disorders?
- How did people understand mental disorders at different times in history?
- What are the main models that we use today to understand mental disorders?
- How do scientists study mental disorders?

and the cooked animals. I knew the answer. My brother and John the Baptist told me just as they had told others. But I listened when others didn't. I scared the girls away—even those who didn't scare easy—but they wouldn't be missed. And I eat the right stuff. White flour and cauliflower; they're the best. They keep you bright and clean. And I stay home, away from everyone who doesn't understand. Away from everybody. I lock myself in at night, and I put chairs against the door because you never can be sure when they might try to break through on you. Try to come in and wreck you. No wonder I can't sleep. I shouldn't sleep too deep. The girls are out there, and they're nothing but a dirty bunch of grotesqueries.

I could never have faced the terrors alone. I have guides who have gone before me. They talk to me. My older brother (who isn't dead like others say) warned me of my enemies. John the Baptist does too; being next to Christ on the cross made him sadder but wiser, and a good thing, too, for me. The rest of them can go to Hell. My mother, a whore if there ever was one. And all my fathers, always nagging me that I should work and wear cotton clothes. They don't know that I do work. I'm rich. I work on my inside. And that is a lot better than those s#@! drugs they try to give me. Poking me with needles; left arm, then right. I put a stop to that. I told them I'd take the pills if they stopped the shots. Idiots. Hadn't they noticed how "well behaved and intact" the trash cans had been the last few months? Stop the spots. Stop the spots. I will stop the spots.

—*From the diary of Nelson McGrath*

You probably agree that Nelson McGrath's behavior is bizarre and that his thinking is disturbed. But what else do you think about Nelson? Would you fear him? Condemn him? Pity him? Envy his fantasy life? And how would you explain Nelson's thoughts and actions? Is he evil? Sick? Inspired? Mentally disordered?

These are just a few of the attitudes and ideas about abnormality that people have adopted in various parts of the world at different times in history. Prevailing attitudes tend to reflect a society's broader values, beliefs, and standards regarding issues such as the importance of science or religion and the degree to which people are responsible for their own problems. The specific attitudes that prevail at a given time and place strongly influence what happens to those who are labeled *abnormal*. As a result, people such as Nelson have been callously ignored, given cleansing baths, offered "talking therapy," confined in dismal cells, granted special privileges, drugged, operated on, or burned at the stake. In fact, your own background has shaped your reaction to people such as Nelson, just as it shapes your interactions with the rest of the world.

MAPS - Prejudicial Pigeonholes

Throughout time, every culture has struggled to define the forms of conduct that constitute abnormal behavior, also known as madness, mental illness, or mental disorders, which is the term used by most clinicians today. Like attitudes toward troubled people, these definitions grow out of historical and cultural contexts. As discussed in Chapter 1, in some settings, the most important criterion for defining abnormality has been whether behavior violates social expectations. In other settings, personal distress and suffering have been emphasized. Meanwhile, some people believe that the terms *crazy*, *mad*, or *ill* have always been no more than labels for behaviors that certain people dislike.

In Chapter 1, we evaluated various definitions of *abnormality* that have been prominent throughout the ages. Although none of these definitions is completely objective or universally accepted, we believe that **abnormal behavior** is best defined as a disturbance of an individual's behavioral, psychological, or physical functioning that is not culturally expected and that leads to psychological distress, behavioral disability, or impaired overall functioning. Chapter 1 covered how we define, detect, and categorize abnormal behavior as mental disorders today. In the sections that follow, we describe how societies throughout history have attempted to understand and treat such behavior.

abnormal behavior: A pattern of behavioral, psychological, or physical functioning that is not culturally expected and that leads to psychological distress, behavioral disability, or impaired overall functioning.

Definitions of abnormal behavior depend on certain characteristics of people, such as their developmental stage and maturity. An adult who behaved in the same way as these children might be considered abnormal because such behavior would violate social expectations about how "normal" adults behave.

Making Sense of Abnormality: A Brief History of Early Models of Mental Disorders

Several distinct themes appear in the way people in various cultures and historical eras have viewed and treated abnormality. To review these themes, this chapter will take a whirlwind tour through time to give you an idea of how a person such as Nelson McGrath might be received in different cultures and at different times in history.

Faraway Places, Ancient Times, and Supernatural Forces

There are no systematic, written records prior to the Egyptian and Mesopotamian cultures of around 3500–3000 B.C.E., so scholars depend on archeological discoveries and interpretations of oral myths to speculate about what our ancient ancestors would have made of someone such as Nelson McGrath. Some evidence suggests that they would have considered his behavior, and any other abnormality, as a reflection of the presence of evil spirits or other overpowering supernatural forces. Seen as an innocent victim of his affliction, Nelson might have been helped to expel his invader. This might have included *trephining*, a crude form of surgery practiced during the Stone Age in which a hole was bored through a person's skull, probably to give evil spirits a means of escape (Restak, 2000).

As ancient Chinese, Egyptian, and Hebrew civilizations developed, abnormal behavior was often blamed on evil spirits and demons, as were bad weather, earthquakes, physical illness, and other unexplainable events. For example, according to the Biblical account, Israel's first king, Saul, was said to be troubled by evil spirits and was treated with calming music. Indeed, when "David took the harp and played it. . . Saul was refreshed and was well, and the evil spirit departed from him" (I Samuel 16:14–23). However, abnormality was sometimes interpreted Biblically as divine punishment for disobedience or other misbehavior. For example, Nebuchadnezzar, King of Babylon, was said to be stricken with *lycanthropy* (the belief that one is a wolf) as divine retribution for his boastfulness (Daniel 4: 28–33). The king had to live in the wild until, after acknowledging God's power, his reason was restored, and he was reinstated.

Thus, ancient civilizations might have dealt with Nelson in many ways (Hergenhahn & Henley, 2013). Prayer and faith healing were used to treat abnormal behaviors and may have been timed to coincide with the movement of planets or stars in hopes of enhancing the treatment. Some practitioners favored exorcism rituals designed to scare, drown, pummel, or whip evil spirits out of the host body, or they concocted mixtures of animal excrement and blood to poison the evil spirits. But priests and religious healers supplemented incantations with treatments designed to correct problems in biological processes that were also seen as related to abnormality. If they had treated Nelson McGrath, they might have prescribed exercise, peaceful activities, an improved diet, and additional rest.

The Birth of the Medical Tradition: The Classical Period

The development of formal philosophy by the Greeks around 600–500 B.C.E. introduced the belief that humans were capable of understanding and taking control of themselves and their world. The Greek philosophic traditions of critical analysis and careful observation were refined during the third, fourth, and fifth centuries B.C.E. by the two greatest philosophers of the Classical period: Plato and Aristotle. Plato believed that humans gained knowledge of the world rationally, through reasoning and recollection, and that people could discover universal concepts and truths that lay behind misleading appearances. Aristotle, on the other hand, claimed that people acquired knowledge through analyzing perceived events, thus laying the groundwork for the empirical method on which psychology and other sciences are based today.

These attempts to understand and to explain events in natural (rather than supernatural) terms were compatible with the Greeks' increasing knowledge of the human body. Hippocrates (460–370 B.C.E.), the early physician known as the "father of medicine," argued that all illnesses had physical causes (Grammaticos & Diamantis, 2008). He concluded that mental disorders were also biological in nature and could be traced to imbalances among the four major fluids, or *humors*, of the body: yellow bile, black bile, blood, and phlegm. For example, excessive yellow bile was thought to cause the overexcitement of mania or Nelson McGrath's anger and impulsivity, whereas too much black bile was related to depression. Treatment consisted of efforts to restore balance among the humors, usually through special diets, laxatives, and purgatives. Hippocrates' views guided Greek and Roman physicians for several centuries. Galen, a famous Roman doctor who lived about A.D. 130–201, refined humoral theory and used it to describe human temperaments and "diseases of the soul." Galen also emphasized the role of the brain in controlling mental processes. To rebalance humors, Galen, like Hippocrates, prescribed medicine, as well as special diets and physical therapy, such as showers, sunbathing, and even sneezing bouts.

Similar ideas about the desirability of physical balance can be found in the Chinese culture of this era and the philosophy of Taoism. Normal behavior was thought to depend on the proper balance between *yin* and *yang*, the two major opposing forces in the universe. Yin is usually associated with nurturance, darkness, and femininity; yang, with power, light, and masculinity. Unifying these opposites is seen as the major task of life, requiring moderation in behavior and openness to nature's healing forces.

The Nelson McGraths of ancient times might also have received some sort of "talking cure." From antiquity, physicians, philosophers, and clerics have believed that the skillful use of words could soothe troubled minds and alter disordered behavior. In the 4th century B.C.E., for example, Stoic philosopher Epictetus argued that "men are disturbed not by things, but by the view which they take of them." Galen himself subscribed to Plato's belief that the power of reason could control emotions and argued that a physician could, through persuasion and advice, help patients overcome anger, anxiety, and other emotional problems.

To summarize, thinkers in the Classical period began to emphasize natural over supernatural causes of mental disorders, paving the way for later biological and psychological theories of abnormality. The Classical period also established in Western minds the idea that medical doctors were the experts responsible for understanding and treating mental disorders. This idea ultimately led to the rise of psychiatry as a specialty that most people in modern Western cultures recognize as an important mental health profession.

From Demons to Instincts: The European Tradition

The Greek and Roman civilizations began to decline around A.D. 200 and continued to deteriorate until the fall of the Roman Empire in A.D. 476. During the next 500 years, a period known as the *early Middle Ages*, Europe experienced great political and economic upheaval. The feudal system replaced nation states, and wars were common. Reliance on rationalism and empiricism as sources of knowledge was replaced by the belief that, through faith and meditation, God would reveal divine truths.

We concentrate on developments in Europe throughout this period because contemporary mental health fields grew largely from Western European origins. However, non-European cultures influenced the understanding and treatment of abnormal behavior as well (Shiraev, 2010). For example, in both the Middle East and Africa, beliefs about the causes of abnormal behavior vacillated between the supernatural and the physical. In both cultures, folk healers combined magic, herbal medicines, and common sense to treat the disturbed. Both also stressed the value of the local community in caring for people with mental disorders, a key notion that we return to in future chapters.

The Middle Ages and the Return of Demons

As the influence of Christian theology grew in Western Europe, science became less important. Once again, people began to believe that supernatural forces, especially the Devil and his demons and witches, were responsible for disordered behavior and that it should be treated with exorcisms or other religious rituals. Magical potions were concocted to purge evil forces. Nelson McGrath might have been given this one:

> Take a testicle of a goat that has been killed on a Tuesday midnight, during the first quarter of the moon, and the heart of a dog, mix with the excrement of a newborn babe, and after pulverizing, take an amount equivalent to half an olive twice a day. (Roback, 1961, p. 215)

Greek and Roman traditions did not disappear completely. For example, in his book *The Canon of Medicine*, the Islamic physician Avicenna described humane procedures that preserved the philosophical traditions of Aristotle and the medical practices of Galen. Beginning in the 8th century, Islamic physicians pioneered the use of hospitals in which mentally disordered people received special treatment. In Europe, numerous monasteries served as sanctuaries for the mentally disordered. By providing a place where disturbed persons could be isolated from stress and treated kindly, these facilities represented a continuation of the Greek medical tradition.

There was certainly plenty of disturbance to deal with, including a phenomenon in which entire groups of people behaved in an extremely agitated fashion. In one form of this mass madness known as *St. Vitus' Dance or tarantism*, groups of men and women would suddenly begin frenzied jumping and dancing, tearing off their clothes as they frolicked in the streets (no, this was not a frat party or college basketball game). This bizarre behavior was widely blamed on demonic possession, but others attributed it to a naturalistic cause, the bite of the tarantula. Modern scholars still cannot agree on an explanation.

In the Middle Ages, supernatural forms of intervention such as exorcism once again became a standard treatment for the mentally ill.

The late Middle Ages (from A.D. 1000 to the 14th century) saw harbingers of a new era. For one thing, the influence of the Christian Church on politics and philosophy began to weaken. However, the Church did not relinquish its dominant role in human affairs easily. As more secular worldviews gained influence, the Church intensified its use of power in a search for suspected heretics and witches. Thousands of suspects were tortured, and many were burned at the stake in the name of religious orthodoxy. Physician-priests "diagnosed" the "possessed" by looking for signs of the devil (*stigmata diaboli*) on their skin (Spanos, 1978). The search for the demon-possessed was guided by the publication of *Malleus Maleficarum*, or *Witches' Hammer*, about 1486, by the Dominican monks Heinrich Kraemer and Johan Sprenger. This book was regarded as the definitive treatise on the links between sin, demonic possession, witchcraft, and disordered behavior. It described magical methods for detecting demonic possession, as well as many gruesome methods for extracting confessions from witches, which, had he lived in the late Middle Ages, might have been used on Nelson McGrath from the chapter-opening case (though about 75% of the people prosecuted as witches were female).

The Renaissance and the Rise of Humanism

The spirit of the European Renaissance appeared as early as the thirteenth and fourteenth centuries as intellectual, cultural, and political life became more and more secular. The dawn of the Renaissance itself is generally marked as 1453, when the fall of Constantinople to the Turks ended the Byzantine Empire. The Renaissance saw a secularization of life and values known as *humanism* (Leahey, 1992). It was greatly facilitated by the advent of the printing press in 1440. As books became more accessible, people came in contact with ideas other than those authorized by the Church. For example, Copernicus's (1473–1543) theory that the sun, not the earth, was the center of the universe paved the way for later scientific discoveries that demystified all aspects of nature, from the heavens to the inner workings of human beings. People began to see the study of individuals and human nature—including behavior and social relations—not as a way to discover or honor God, but as a worthy topic in its own right. The Renaissance may have been the first era in which *psychological* concerns equaled or surpassed theological issues as the dominant questions of the day.

At the same time, physicians again came to view the human body as a biological machine to be studied empirically, not as an inviolate creation of God. The philosopher Rene Descartes (1596–1650) sought to explain a great deal of human mental activity in physical, mechanical terms. In fact, he suggested that we could learn about human minds by studying animal behavior, a view shared by many modern psychologists. The physicians Paracelsus (1493–1541) and Johann Weyer (1515–1588) championed naturalistic explanations of mental disorders that included both biological and psychological factors. Weyer is often considered the first **psychiatrist** (a medical doctor who specializes in the study and treatment of mental disorders) because of his careful descriptions of various mental disorders and his belief that treatment of these disorders required a "therapeutic relationship marked by understanding and kindness" (Brems, Thevenin, & Routh, 1991, p. 9). Weyer ridiculed beliefs in witches and condemned the brutal treatments supported by many theologians.

psychiatrist: A medical doctor who specializes in the study and treatment of mental disorders.

On the assumption that quarantine provided the best protection for both the public and the mentally disturbed, treatment of mental disorders during the Renaissance gradually took the form of confinement in hospitals and asylums, many of which had once been monasteries. If Nelson McGrath had lived in London, for example, he might have been admitted to the St. Mary of Bethlehem monastery, which had become a hospital in 1547. Local citizens referred to this "madhouse" as "Bedlam," a contraction of the word *Bethlehem*.

Unfortunately, Renaissance treatments for mental disorders were not much better than were those of the Middle Ages. Indeed, the "insane" in the hospitals of the Renaissance were usually treated as prisoners and had to endure abominable conditions. Jonathan Swift (1704), a great novelist of the period, described the condition of a Bedlam inmate this way:

> Accost the hole of another Kennel, first stopping your Nose, you will behold a surley, gloomy, nasty slovenly Mortal, raking in his own Dung and dabling in his Urine. The best part of his Diet, is the reversion of his own Ordure, which expiring into Steams, whirls perpetually about, and at last reinfunds. His Complexion is of a dirty Yellow, with a thin scattered Beard, exactly agreeable to that of his Dyet upon its first Declination; like other Insects, who having their Birth and Education in an Excrement, from thense borrow their Colour and their Smell.

The Enlightenment and the Rise of Science

In the seventeenth and eighteenth centuries, the trend toward naturalistic world views blossomed. This era, known as the *Enlightenment*, was characterized by an unshakable confidence in human reason and in science especially. During this era, Kepler (1571–1630) proposed the basic laws of planetary motion, and Newton (1642–1727) described the principle of gravity and developed calculus. It was assumed that empirical research would reveal mathematical or mechanical principles that governed all phenomena, including human behavior. This assumption made it possible, late in the 1800s, for psychology to become a scientific discipline.

Although modern science had begun, the deplorable conditions in European and North American asylums for the insane had not changed much. A group of reformers tried, in the last half of the 1700s, to improve the living conditions and treatment in asylums. Among these mental health "muckrakers" were Vincenzo Chiarugi (1759–1820) in Italy, William Tuke (1732–1822) in England, and Benjamin Rush (1745–1813) in the United States. Their work ushered in what became known as the *moral treatment era.*

The inspirational leader of the moral treatment movement was Philippe Pinel (1745–1826), a French physician. When placed in charge of the Bicêtre asylum in Paris in 1793, Pinel unchained its in-

Source: Tony Robert-Fleury [Public domain], via Wikimedia Commons.

Philippe Pinel is immortalized in paintings such as this one, where he is shown removing the chains from patients at the Paris Asylum for insane women. Pinel was known for his moral era's reformist spirit and pioneering of important methods, such as taking notes to document his observations of patients.

mates and insisted that they be treated with kindness and consideration. Pinel justified this risky, but courageous, experiment as follows: "It is my conviction that these mentally ill are intractable only because they are deprived of fresh air and liberty" (Ullmann & Krasner, 1975, p. 135). In 1795, Pinel became chief physician of the Hospice de la Salpêtrière, a post that he retained for the rest of his life. Moral treatment tried to instill in patients like Nelson McGrath the expectation that they could alter their disordered behavior, learn to manage daily stress, find useful employment, and get along better with others. After years of being treated as wild beasts and acting accordingly, many of the inmates at Bicêtre, Salpêtrière, and other moral treatment centers seemed transformed almost overnight into well-behaved human beings.

However, moral treatment all but disappeared by the late 1800s, especially in the United States. Why? Ironically, its own success was partially responsible. Many assumed that hospital care could help more patients if hospitals were larger than traditional moral treatment centers. In mid-19th-century America, this assumption fueled the *mental hygiene movement*, led by crusaders such as Dorothea Dix (1802–1887), a Boston schoolteacher, and Clifford W. Beers (1876–1943), a former mental patient who helped to form the National Committee for Mental Hygiene. Dix became a tireless agitator for the construction of large, public mental hospitals. Unfortunately, these new state hospitals were so understaffed that they could offer little more than custodial care to the large number of patients they housed.

Moral treatment approaches were also overshadowed in the late 1800s because psychiatrists and other physicians working in mental health came to believe that disordered behaviors were caused by biological rather than social factors and thus required treatment based on medicine. As one physician put it, there can be "no twisted thought without a twisted molecule" (Abood, 1960).

MAPS - Medical Myths

Indeed, even under the best circumstances, moral treatment approaches had only limited effects on severely disturbed patients—they often halted further deterioration but did not cure mental disorders. Some of these patients suffered a particularly severe disorder that involved ever-worsening delusions, muscle paralysis, and ultimately, death. In 1825, this deteriorative brain syndrome was termed *general paresis*, and throughout the remainder of the 19th century, physicians searched for its cause. By the turn of the 20th century, following basic discoveries of how bodily infections were caused, the puzzle was finally solved. The cause of general paresis turned out to be syphilitic infection of the brain. With this mental disorder traced to a biological cause, the search was on to find other links between mental disorders and physical causes. That search continues to this day, with varying and often limited success (Paris, 2013), and we describe its findings throughout this book.

Chapter 2 Past and Present Understandings of Mental Disorders

Connections

How do these early classification systems compare
with those in use today?
For a history of various
systems used to classify
mental disorders, see
Chapter 1.

The presence of thousands of mental patients in public hospitals in the United States, Canada, and Europe allowed psychiatrists to compare individual patterns of disordered behavior. By the end of the 19th century, these comparisons had led to systems for classifying mental disorders. The most prominent of these systems was developed by Emil Kraepelin (1856–1926) in Germany and Eugen Bleuler (1857–1939) in Switzerland.

Better classification of disorders often helped practitioners apply treatments that were most effective for specific problems, but effective treatments for *any* problems were still scarce. Physicians simply did not know enough about organic causes to develop treatments that were much different from those of their predecessors. For example, American psychiatrist Benjamin Rush treated mental patients like Nelson McGrath from the chapter-opening case with bleedings and purges, and physicians often sought to tranquilize agitated patients by binding them in chairs, confining them in narrow cribs, dunking them in water, or wrapping them tightly in wet sheets (Benjamin, 2007). Believing that mental health depended on proper digestion, Horace Fletcher advocated chewing each mouthful of food hundreds of times before swallowing.

The Psychoanalytic Revolution

Of all the treatments for mental disorders used during the Enlightenment, *hypnotism* is best remembered, and it is still used today. First known as *mesmerism*, hypnotism was popularized as a quasi-magical cure by a French physician, Franz Anton Mesmer (1734–1815), who believed it could realign magnetic forces in the body.

Soon, a number of reputable physicians were experimenting with hypnosis. For example, in India, James Esdaile pioneered hypnotic anesthesia during surgery. French psychiatrists such as Jean Charcot, Pierre Janet, and Hippolyte Bernheim discovered that hypnosis could be helpful in the treatment of hysteria, a disorder in which patients with normal physical abilities appear unable to see or hear or walk. This success helped to reawaken the idea that at least some mental disorders might be caused by psychological factors as well as—or even instead of—biological dysfunctions (Hergenhahn & Henley, 2013).

hysteria: A mental disorder in which patients with normal physical abilities appear unable to see or hear or walk.

Enter Sigmund Freud, a Viennese neurologist who, with his colleague Joseph Breuer, successfully used hypnosis—and other "talking cures"—to treat cases of hysteria. Late in the 1800s, Freud's clinical experience led him to conclude that many forms of abnormal behavior were caused by intense, prolonged, and largely unconscious mental struggles between instinctual desires and concern over social prohibitions against fulfilling those desires (Gay, 2006). Freud was certainly not the first to focus on unconscious processes as the basis for abnormal behavior. Philosophers such as Johann Herbart (1776–1841) and Gottfried Wilhelm Leibniz (1646–1716) had discussed the importance of the unconscious, and writers and artists of the early 19th century had suggested that our most base passions are rooted in the unconscious and revealed in our dreams. It was Freud, however, who synthesized these ideas into a coherent theory of personality and abnormal behavior that suggested *how* and *why* unconscious conflicts and other psychological processes create disordered behavior (discussed later in the chapter). Freud also applied his theory of abnormality via psychoanalysis, the first modern psychological treatment ("talking cure") of mentally disturbed people.

clinical psychology: The branch of psychology devoted to studying, assessing, diagnosing, treating, and preventing abnormal behavior.

Psychological explanations of abnormal behavior gained influence with the help of a new mental health profession known as clinical psychology, the branch of psychology devoted to scientifically studying mental disorders as well as assessing, diagnosing, and treating them. In the United States, the first psychological clinic was founded in 1896 (Nietzel, Bernstein, & Milich, 1998). When Freud came to the United States to deliver lectures at Clark University in 1909, he received a warm reception from American psychologists interested in mental disorders. Their response came partly because Freud's ideas suggested an important role for psychologists, not just psychiatrists, in assessing and treating psychological disorders (see Table 2.1). Many clinical psychologists began to apply their training in motivation, emotion, learning, social influences, and other areas to develop psychological theories about abnormal behavior that went beyond—and often conflicted with—Freud's doctrine, as we discuss further later in the chapter.

TABLE 2.1 The Mental Health Professions

Profession	Description
Psychiatrists	Psychiatrists are physicians who have completed additional years of training (called a *residency*) in the specialty of psychiatry. Psychiatrists have an MD degree like other medical doctors and can prescribe medication.
Clinical psychologists	Psychologists have earned a doctoral degree (PhD or PsyD) in psychology and specialize in applying scientific methods and psychological knowledge to the study, assessment, and treatment of mental disorders. Except for in a small number of states with a special certification, clinical psychologists cannot prescribe medication.
Psychiatric (clinical) social workers	Psychiatric social workers usually have completed a master's degree in social work (MSW) and concentrate on treating mental disorders and family problems, as well as working with communities and larger systems.
Psychiatric nurses, occupational therapists, and recreational therapists	These professionals have completed advanced training in their specialty areas (e.g., RN, OT) and offer treatment services, usually as members of a mental health team. Some nurse practitioners (NP) can prescribe medication under a physician's supervision.
Professional counselors	Counselors typically complete a master's of counseling degree (MA) and offer treatment to their clients in individual and/or group settings.
Marriage and family counselors	These professionals have usually completed postgraduate study with a specialization in marriage and family therapy (MFT). They offer treatment for couples and family problems, which sometimes also involve mental disorders.

Contemporary Approaches to Abnormality

Our historical review shows that there has always been competition among approaches or conceptual models to explain the abnormal behavior of people such as Nelson McGrath. **Models of abnormality** are comprehensive accounts of how and why mental disorders develop and how best to treat them. They provide a conceptual map to help researchers and practitioners decide which aspects of abnormal behavior are most important to study—overt behavior or accompanying thoughts, for example—and which treatment methods—exorcism, drugs, or talking—are most likely to help. The popularity of different models has waxed and waned from time to time and place to place throughout history. For example, in Western cultures today, the supernatural model of abnormality is largely overshadowed by the biological, psychological, sociocultural, and diathesis-stress models. In the following sections, we consider each of these models in more detail and how they seek to account for abnormal behavior.

model of abnormality: A comprehensive account of how and why abnormal behaviors develop and how best to treat them.

Section Review

Views of abnormal behavior are influenced by historical context, social attitudes, and cultural standards. Key figures in the history of the development of scientific approaches to abnormal behavior include:

- Hippocrates and Galen, physicians of ancient Greece and Rome who developed treatments of abnormal behavior derived from medical knowledge;
- Avicenna, an Islamic physician whose writings helped preserve Greek and Roman learning during the early Middle Ages;
- Pinel, a French physician and inspirational leader of the moral treatment movement who unchained the inmates of the *Bicêtre* asylum in Paris in 1793; and
- Sigmund Freud, who developed the first purely psychological model of abnormal behavior.

The Biological Model

The basic assumption of the **biological model** of abnormality is that the nervous system controls all thought and behavior, whether normal or abnormal. From this perspective, any event or substance that affects the functioning of the nervous system also affects thinking and behavior. The abnormal behaviors and thought patterns displayed by Nelson McGrath from the chapter-opening case—and others who are diagnosed with mental disorders—are assumed to arise from changes in neural functioning triggered by drugs, hormone imbalances, environmental toxins, head trauma, major infections, genetic defects, or other biological factors. Biological treatments attempt to change the patient's physical condition, usually through the use of therapeutic drugs.

Stemming directly from the biological model, the **medical model** of abnormal behavior considers that disturbed behavior involves *symptoms* of some underlying illness that is the result of specific causal or **etiological factors**. The person with the symptoms is considered a patient. The symptoms tend to go together in a pattern known as a *syndrome* that follows a well-recognized course, allowing professionals to diagnose a specific illness and to offer a prognosis of how the illness will likely unfold. The medical model often looks for biochemical or other physical causes of a syndrome.

Insights into the biological factors involved in abnormal behavior have expanded greatly in recent decades, thanks in large part to research in **neuroscience**, a set of disciplines that study the structure, organization, functions, and chemistry of the nervous system, especially the brain.

The Nervous System and Abnormality

The human brain has been categorized into three major regions—hindbrain, midbrain, and forebrain—each with its own interrelated specialty functions.

The Hindbrain

The **hindbrain** includes structures that maintain activities essential to life. For example, it includes the *medulla*, which maintains and regulates basic functions such as breathing, swallowing, heart rate, and blood pressure; the *reticular formation*, which controls arousal, attention, and sleep-wakefulness cycles; and the cerebellum, which maintains balance and posture and controls locomotion and finely coordinated movements such as threading a needle. Damage to parts of the hindbrain can leave a person comatose (Myers, 2011).

The Midbrain

The **midbrain** helps coordinate head and eye movements and controls gross movements of the body and limbs. The midbrain is also involved in basic responses to visual, auditory, and tactile stimuli and regulates responsiveness to rewarding stimuli.

The Forebrain

The largest part of the brain, the **forebrain**, includes structures that are responsible for a wide variety of functions, from processing sensory information and guiding the body's movements, to accomplishing the most complex aspects of thought and imagination.

The thalamus, hypothalamus, and cerebrum are key structures in the forebrain, as shown in Figure 2.1. The **thalamus** is a kind of relay station that receives, analyzes, and sends on information from all the senses (except the sense of smell). Located just below the thalamus is a small but vital structure called the **hypothalamus**, which regulates hunger (food), thirst (fluids), temperature (fever), and our sex drive, sometimes grouped together as "the 4 Fs" (think about it for a minute).

The hypothalamus receives information from the autonomic nervous system about the functioning of internal organs, and helps regulate the activity of those organs. It responds to chemical messengers called **hormones** that are secreted by the cortical (outer) portion of the adrenal glands and other parts of the **endocrine system**, a network of glands that

---

biological model: A model of abnormal behavior that explains how biological factors influence thought and behavior, both normal and abnormal.

medical model: A model that explains abnormal behavior as symptoms resulting from an underlying illness.

etiological factor: A specific cause of disorders.

neuroscience: A set of disciplines that study the structure, organization, functions, and chemistry of the nervous system, especially the brain.

hindbrain: One of the three main parts of the brain, it includes structures such as the medulla, the reticular formation, and the cerebellum, which maintain activities essential to life.

midbrain: One of the three main parts of the brain, it helps coordinate head and eye movements, controls gross body movements, and is involved in basic responses to visual, auditory, and tactile stimuli.

forebrain: The largest of the three main parts of the brain, it includes structures that are responsible for processing sensory information, guiding body movements, and thinking.

thalamus: A key structure in the forebrain that receives, analyzes, and sends on information from all the senses except smell.

hypothalamus: A key structure in the forebrain that aids in regulating hunger, thirst, sex drive, and other motivated behavior, as well as activity of various internal organs.

hormone: A chemical messenger secreted by the adrenal glands or other parts of the endocrine system.

endocrine system: A network of glands that affects organs throughout the body by releasing hormones into the bloodstream.

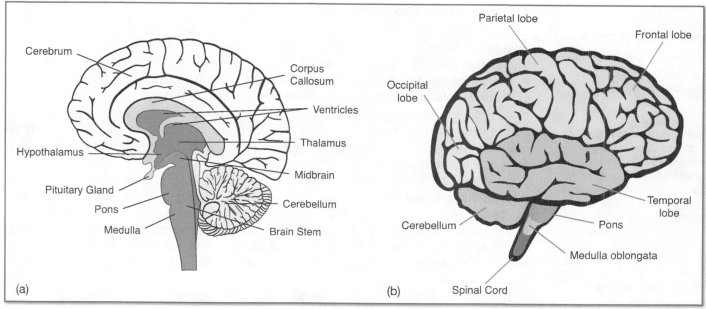

FIGURE 2.1 The Human Brain

This figure shows major regions of the human brain. (a) This side view of the human brain shows the right cerebral hemisphere (the right half of the brain), including major parts of the hindbrain, along with the thalamus and hypothalamus, which are part of the limbic system in the forebrain. (b) The second image provides a broad view of the four main lobes of the brain: frontal, parietal, occipital, and temporal.

Source: (a) udaix/Shutterstock.com. (b) Athanasia Nomikou/Shutterstock.com.

affect organs throughout the body by releasing hormones into the bloodstream. The hypothalamus connects to the **pituitary gland**, which in turn serves as the director of the endocrine system. As we discuss in later chapters (e.g., Chapter 9), activity in the hypothalamus and pituitary are key elements of our physiological responses to stressful events. The hypothalamus is also part of the *limbic system*, a group of interconnected forebrain structures that play important roles in regulating emotion and memory.

pituitary gland: A structure in the forebrain that controls the endocrine system and plays a key role in physiological responses to stressful events.

The Cerebrum and Cerebral Cortex

The **cerebrum**, and especially its outer covering, the **cerebral cortex**, is the part of the human brain that is the most distinct from the brains of other mammals and the most active in such distinctively human capabilities as abstract thought and complex language. The cortex is divided into two hemispheres, each of which is itself divided into regions, called *lobes* (see Figure 2.1). Different lobes are involved in somewhat specialized aspects of information processing. It is the cerebral cortex that allows humans to think and wonder about the world, not just react to it. We can plan, but we can also worry. As Carl Sagan (1977) noted, a "price we pay for anticipation of the future is anxiety about it."

cerebrum: Main part of human brain, covered by the cerebral cortex; responsible for integrative processes such as thought, language, and emotion. It is divided into two hemispheres, which are further divided into lobes.

Mental Disorders and the Brain

Until recently, evidence of a direct link between mental disorders and brain structures depended on autopsies or, perhaps, neurosurgery. Today, however, imaging techniques such as *computerized tomography (CT scans), magnetic resonance imaging (MRI, fMRI, and dMRI scans),* and *positron emission tomography (PET scans)* provide new ways of watching the brain at work (see Chapter 1). Imaging techniques allow the study of how brain damage or subtle problems in brain functioning might account for certain mental dysfunctions. For example, these techniques show that the mental decline in patients with Alzheimer's disease (described in Chapter 15) is related to progressive degeneration in the cerebral cortex and in a structure called the *hippocampus* (Van Hoesen & Damasio, 1987). They also indicate that some cases of schizophrenia (Chapter 4) are related to atrophy of brain tissue and to irregularities in the flow of blood to the brain (Gur & Pearlson, 1993).

cerebral cortex: The outermost layered structure of neural tissue of the cerebrum (brain) in humans and other mammals. It is referred to as "gray matter" because it consists of cell bodies and capillaries and contrasts with the underlying white matter, which consists mainly of the white myelinated sheaths of neuronal axons.

The Role of Neurotransmitters

Researchers have also investigated the possibility that disorders such as schizophrenia might be linked not only to problems in particular brain structures but also to breakdowns in communication among the brain's billions of nerve cells or **neurons**. In fact, the human brain has been found to contain an average of 86 billion neurons, with less than 20% of these located in the cerebral cortex (Azevedo et al., 2009). All normal activity, from moving an arm to thinking rationally, depends on smooth and organized communication among neurons in our brain. This communication occurs when electrochemical activity in one neuron causes it to *fire*, thus releasing chemicals called **neurotransmitters** that carry messages between neurons.

As Figure 2.2 shows, neurotransmitters are released from the end of an **axon**, a long fiber on the neuron; they flow across the **synapse**, a tiny gap between neurons, and come in contact with branchlike structures called **dendrites** on the next neuron. If the neurotransmitter binds with *receptor sites* on the dendrite, a signal is sent up the dendrite, which makes this neuron either more or less ready to fire. After affecting other neurons, neurotransmitters are reabsorbed into the neurons that released them, through a process called **reuptake**.

Bundles of axons from many neurons make up the pathways along which information travels to and from the brain and within the central nervous system (CNS; the brain plus the spinal cord). Sensory neurons bring information from all parts of the body to the CNS, where the information is processed and then sent via motor neurons to control the response of muscles and glands. The effects of communication along many of these pathways have been well established.

For example, neuron systems in the brain that communicate via the neurotransmitter **acetylcholine** (ACH) are involved in learning (Becker et al., 2013), memory (Prickaerts et al., 2012), and sleep (Platt & Riedel, 2011). The muscles involved in voluntary movement of the arms or legs contract when they receive ACH. In the parasympathetic branch of the autonomic nervous system (ANS), this same neurotransmitter acts to slow heart rate, lower blood pressure, and increase digestion. **Norepinephrine** is another important neurotransmitter. In the sympathetic branch of the ANS, it acts to increase heart rate and respiration. Systems in the brain that communicate via norepinephrine are involved in sleep and arousal (Kim, Chen, McCarley, & Strecker, 2013), attention (Kim et al., 2013), mood (Ruhé, Mason, & Schene, 2007), and eating behavior (Latagliata, Patrono, Puglisi-Allegra, & Ventura, 2010). In this model, Nelson McGrath from the chapter-opening case would be assumed to have too much of the neurotransmitter **dopamine** in his brain, which has been implicated in schizophrenia (Chapter 4). Two other vital neurotransmitters—**serotonin** and **GABA**—play roles in depression (Chapter 6) and anxiety (Chapter 7), respectively.

FIGURE 2.2 The Synapse and Communication Among Neurons

When a neuron fires, the nervous impulse is carried along the axon, which triggers release of a neurotransmitter across the synapse, where it may bind to a receptor on the dendrite of another neuron. The result is the spread of an electrical impulse on the dendrite of the second neuron. This impulse may stimulate or inhibit this neuron from firing and releasing its own neurotransmitters.

Source: Andrea Danti/Shutterstock.com.

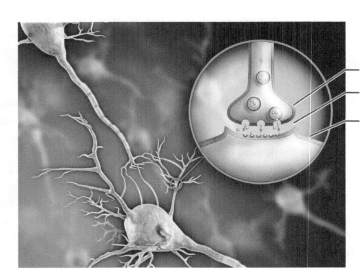

Axon

Synapse

Dendrite of next neuron

It is no wonder that drugs that alter neurotransmitters can produce complex psychological and behavioral effects. As we discuss in later chapters, most of the drugs used to treat mental disorders have a strong effect on the level or activity of some neurotransmitter, such as Prozac increasing the availability of serotonin in the brain. Nelson McGrath would likely be prescribed a drug such as Thorazine, which would reduce the level of dopamine in his brain.

Genetic Influences on Abnormality

Why would neurotransmitters operate abnormally? Why do brain structures deteriorate? In some cases, genes may hold the answer. **Genes**, the basic units of heredity, determine many aspects of who and what we are, from eye color and skin tone to body type and vulnerability to disease. At conception, the new cell formed by the fertilization of an egg by a sperm contains 23 pairs of chromosomes—half from the father and half from the mother. As the new cell divides and redivides into billions of cells, a human being is formed out of a unique combination of genes from both parents (Brooker, 2011).

What Are Genes and What Do They Do?

Human heredity is determined by an estimated 100,000 genes, each of which rests at a specific location, or *locus*, along a chromosome. Chemically, genes are strands of **deoxyribonucleic acid**, or **DNA**, which is made up of nucleotides. Each **nucleotide** consists of sugar, phosphate, and bases containing nitrogen. Through a complex series of steps, DNA directs chemical reactions that assemble amino acids into proteins. The specific proteins produced depend upon the particular order in which the nitrogen-containing bases occur in the nucleotides. Proteins, in turn, form and direct the structure of human cells. In short, DNA provides the genetic code that, during prenatal development, determines how proteins are used to build each cell in the body, including the brain (Brooker, 2011).

Note that genes affect physical features and behavior indirectly, by determining the production of proteins. However, not every gene is expressed in a person's physical characteristics or behavior. Whether a gene is expressed depends on which other genes are present. The path from genes to physical characteristics or behavior is further complicated by the fact that many genes at different locations influence most characteristics. No single gene controls height or skin color, for example; these characteristics are governed by *polygenic inheritance*, involving multiple, interacting genes. The degree to which a genetic predisposition is actually expressed in behavior or physical features is called **penetrance**, also defined as the proportion of individuals with a genetic mutation causing a particular disorder who exhibit clinical symptoms of that disorder.

A faulty gene or a problem with genetic expression can cause serious dysfunctions. For example, *phenylketonuria (PKU)* is a rare disorder that has been traced to the malfunction of a single gene. This malfunction creates a deficiency in the enzyme that metabolizes phenylalanine, an amino acid found in many foods. Unless given a special diet that excludes foods containing phenylalanine, individuals with PKU suffer a variety of physical problems and progressive mental deterioration. PKU illustrates that a person's genetic makeup, or **genotype**, interacts with the environment—in this case, a nutritional environment—to determine one's **phenotype**, the characteristics and traits actually displayed.

The expression of genetic predispositions is also influenced by such prenatal factors as hormones, drugs, maternal nutrition, and health; by childhood illnesses; by the home and school environment; and by a variety of other social experiences and relationships. In short, genetic endowment (often referred to as *nature*) is always interacting with past and present environmental factors (often called *nurture*) to shape physical and behavioral characteristics.

norepinephrine: A neurotransmitter involved in sleep and arousal, attention, mood, and eating.

dopamine: A neurotransmitter that is prominent in several areas of the brain and is linked with several types of mental disorder.

serotonin: A neurotransmitter that influences emotion, sleep, and behavioral control.

gamma-aminobutyric acid (GABA): A neurotransmitter that inhibits postsynaptic activity.

gene: Strands of DNA that are located along a chromosome and are the basic units of heredity.

deoxyribonucleic acid (DNA): The substance that is the primary component of genes.

nucleotide: Any of several biochemical compounds that make up DNA and contain sugar, phosphate, and a nitrogen base.

penetrance: The degree to which a genetic predisposition is actually expressed in behavior or physical features.

genotype: A person's genetic makeup.

phenotype: The characteristics a person displays that result from the interaction of genetic makeup and the environment.

epigenetics: The study of heritable changes in gene activity that are not caused by changes in the actual DNA sequence. Epigenetics literally means "above" or "on top of" genetics and refers to external modifications to DNA that turn genes "on" or "off."

In the past decade or so, a new area of science has blossomed. **Epigenetics** is the study of heritable changes in gene activity that are not caused by changes in the actual DNA sequence. Epigenetics literally means "above" or "on top of" genetics and refers to external modifications to DNA that turn genes "on" or "off" (Rettner, 2013). The burgeoning field of epigenetics has great relevance for abnormal psychology via its contributions to *behavioral genetics*, described in the next section. Research has identified epigenetic mechanisms mediating between environmental and psychological factors that contribute to normal and abnormal behavioral development (González-Pardo & Álvarez, 2013). In fact, it is now clear that epigenetic mechanisms promote key neurobiological processes, ranging from neural stem cell maintenance and differentiation to learning and memory (Qureshi & Mehler, 2013). As such, epigenetics plays a role in a wide range of mental disorders, including autism spectrum (Rangasamy, D'Mello, & Narayanan, 2013) and substance use disorders (Nestler, 2014). For example, there is mounting evidence that repeated exposure to drugs of abuse can cause epigenetic changes within a person's brain's reward regions, ultimately resulting in changes in his or her future addictive behavior (Nestler, 2014).

Behavioral Genetics

behavioral genetics: A scientific field that examines genetic influences on behavior and their interaction with the environment.

heritability: The proportion of observable differences among individuals in a particular trait that is due to genetic differences.

family study: A technique used by behavioral geneticists to examine patterns of a disorder in members of a family.

Scientists in the field of **behavioral genetics** use specialized research methods to study genetic—and epigenetic—influences on behavior and to understand the combined influences of nature and nurture on human behavior (e.g., Klahr & Burt, 2014). A key concept for behavioral genetics is **heritability**, the proportion of observable differences in a behavioral trait between individuals that is due to genetic differences (Gjerde et al., 2012). To determine heritability, behavioral geneticists often conduct **family studies** that examine the pattern of disorder in members of the same family. These studies capitalize on the fact that the closer the relationship between people, the more genes they share. Identical, or *monozygotic*, twins share 100% of their genes; parents and their children, as well as fraternal—or *dizygotic*—twins and other siblings, share about 50% of their genes. Nieces, nephews, aunts, and uncles who are genetically related share about 25%, first cousins about 12.5%. Thus, if a trait is based entirely on genetic heritage, we should be able to predict the likelihood that two individuals will share that trait from a knowledge of their genetic similarity. For example, *Huntington's disease*, a genetically determined disorder that causes severe behavioral and mental problems, is caused by a single dominant gene (Giles et al., 2012). Thus, the child of a parent with the Huntington's gene has a 50% likelihood of having this gene, too.

concordance rate: The rate, at which a trait or disorder is shared with close relatives, such as a twin.

However, genetic influences are seldom as clear as in Huntington's disease. For example, in the chapter-opening case, Nelson McGrath's disorder is thought to be caused by an interaction of multiple genes, rather than by a single gene. Moreover, closer kin tend to share more similar environments as well as more similar genes. Finding a high **concordance rate**—or sharing—of a trait or disorder in close relatives cannot by itself prove that the trait or disorder is inherited. Siblings might display the same disorder because they are eating the same food or living near the same toxic waste dump, not because they share genes. This possibility is gruesomely illustrated by *kuru*, a fatal disease of the central nervous system found only in cannibalistic tribes in the highlands of New Guinea. Some of the symptoms of kuru are similar to those of Huntington's disease, and because those most closely related to kuru victims are most likely to develop the disease themselves, it was long considered a genetic disorder. Recent research suggests, however, that the cause may not be genetic but biological—a virus that is transmitted when individuals eat the brains of recently deceased relatives in a respectful attempt to acquire the relative's traits. Closer family members were allowed to consume the part of the brain most likely to contain the virus. With the decline of cannibalism among these tribes, kuru has almost disappeared.

adoption study: A method of systematically examining traits and disorders in persons who were separated from their biological parents at early ages; the method compares similarities between adopted individuals and their biological and adoptive parents.

The interaction of nature and nurture can be explored more powerfully by observing results of the "natural experiments" that occur when children are adopted or when twins are separated. In **adoption studies**, researchers look at traits and disorders in people who were separated from their biological parents at very early ages. If such people's traits are more like those of their biological parents (with whom they share many genes) than like those of their adoptive parents, a genetic influence on those traits is supported. In one study, adopted children whose biological parents had an alcohol use disorder were more likely to have problems with alcohol themselves, regardless of the alcohol habits of their adoptive parents (Cloninger, Bohman, & Sigvardsson, 1981). Twin studies compare the traits of monozygotic twins who were separated soon after birth and raised in different environments with the traits of monozygotic twins reared together and dizygotic twins reared together or apart. Finding very similar traits in identical twins, even when they experienced different environments, provides evidence for a genetic influence on those traits. Several twin studies have found just such evidence in children's temperament and personality (e.g., Buss, 1995; Loehlin, 1989; Tellegen et al., 1988).

twin study: A method of systematically comparing the traits of monozygotic twins reared together or apart with the traits of dizygotic twins reared together or apart.

Adoption and twin studies can be used together to determine the heritability of a particular disorder, with heritability estimates from adoption studies typically lower than those from twin studies (Burt, 2009). For instance, twin studies suggest moderate to high heritability (i.e., ~50%–85%) of disordered eating symptoms (e.g., weight preoccupation, body dissatisfaction, and binge eating behaviors) during adolescence and adulthood (e.g., Klump, Burt, McGue, & Iacono, 2007). Similarly, adoption studies also find significant genetic influences (~50%–82%) on all forms of disordered eating, with environmental factors (nurture) accounting for the remaining variance (Klump, Suisman, Burt, McGue, & Iacono, 2009). Other recent studies have combined twin and adoption methodologies to estimate influences of both environment and genetics on personality development (Matteson, McGue, & Iacono, 2013).

The meaning of research on behavioral genetics is often misunderstood. The results cannot tell us whether any particular individual's behavior is due to genes or environment. And the research does not explain differences between groups such as men and women or African Americans and Caucasian Americans. What behavioral genetics research can do is *estimate the average influence* that genes and environment exert on *individual differences within a group of people*. For example, this research has shown that Nelson McGrath's chances of developing schizophrenia would be higher if he had a biological parent with this disorder, and higher still if he had an identical twin with schizophrenia (see Chapter 4), which would be covered in the family history section of any assessment with Nelson. We describe evidence from numerous studies of behavioral genetics in later chapters, as we examine genetic and environmental influences on a variety of abnormal behavior patterns. As this chapter's "Controversy" feature suggests, claims about genetic influences on abnormal behavior often lead to passionate debates about the relative importance of nature (genes/biology) and nurture (environment).

Section Review

The biological model explains abnormal behavior in terms of physical malfunctions of the nervous system. Of particular interest are:

- the cerebral cortex, the part of the brain that is involved in abstract thought and language;
- the hypothalamus, a structure of the forebrain that receives information from the autonomic nervous system (which determines physiological arousal); connects to the pituitary gland (which directs the endocrine system); is part of the system that responds to stress; and is part of the system that regulates emotion and memory; and
- the neurotransmitters, chemical messengers that, when released by neurons, stimulate or inhibit the firing of other neurons.

The development of the nervous system, and every other part of the body, is controlled by genes, which:

- are composed of DNA and are located on the chromosomes;
- influence an organism's characteristics by orchestrating the production of proteins; and
- interact with each other and with the environment in complex ways to produce the unique characteristics of every human being.

Should We Study Genetic Causes of Abnormality?

Genes influence many prominent physical features—weight, eye color, and whether we ultimately grow bald. Genes also help account for diseases such as high blood pressure or diabetes. Although the mechanics of how genes control physical features and processes are still not completely understood, little controversy exists about whether genes are necessary for understanding the biological qualities of people.

More controversial is the role that genetic factors play in shaping mental abilities, behavior, personality traits, and mental disorders. Although few mental disorders appear to be caused solely by genetic inheritance, research consistently suggests that some combination of genes may increase people's vulnerability to certain disorders. For example, five major mental disorders—autism, attention-deficit/hyperactivity disorder (ADHD), bipolar disorder, major depressive disorder, and schizophrenia—appear to share common genetic risk factors, according to an examination of genetic data from more than 60,000 people worldwide (Novotney, 2013). Researchers in 19 countries examined the genomes of more than 33,000 individuals with one of the disorders and nearly 28,000 controls. They found four regions of the genetic code where variation was linked to all five disorders.

When genetic factors are considered as contributors to a disorder, controversy often follows (Ossorio & Duster, 2005). For decades, attempts to study the genetics of behavior problems have been condemned or blocked because of concerns that even asking questions about genes and abnormality is risky or improper. What accounts for such controversy? Why are genetic theories of abnormality so unpopular? What makes it so difficult for some people to look objectively at the tangled issues involving the possible genetic roots of abnormal behavior? Does the problem reflect honest scientific disagreements or the pursuit of political agendas?

One concern appears to be that if scientists find that genetics plays a causal role in mental disorders, they will neglect key sociocultural and environmental factors, along with social programs designed to correct them. This concern reflects the misconception that either nature *or* nurture is responsible for disorders; in fact, they always interact. Consistent with the diathesis-stress model, inheriting a vulnerability to a disorder should increase attention to the importance of the environment. Just as the person who is genetically predisposed to high blood pressure might need to be especially cautious about diet, the person who is genetically vulnerable to schizophrenia might need extra social support and guidance to cope with environmental threats.

A second concern about studying the genetics of abnormality is that it will lead to certain people being designated as genetically "inferior." As horribly exemplified by the Nazi era in Europe, genetic research has led to awful abuses, including forced sterilization, genocide, coerced abortions, and discriminatory immigration policies—all conducted to get rid of supposedly inferior people. Although critics of contemporary genetic research often associate it with past sins, most genetic researchers are cautious not to overstate the role of genetic contributions to mental disorders and not to argue that purely biological treatments are sufficient.

A third reason for negative reactions to genetic theories is that they can imply racist or discriminatory practices. For example, Richard Herrnstein and Charles Murray's book *The Bell Curve* (1994) sparked a firestorm of criticism, not so much because of its claim that intellectual abilities were genetically influenced (a contention with which many psychologists agree), but because of its argument that genetic factors account for most of the measured IQ differences among different ethnic groups (a contention *not* endorsed by most psychologists). Another example is that, when researchers seek genetic explanations for criminal behavior, they examine a flammable triumvirate of associations among genes, crime, and race. Like the phrenology of the 19th century (interpreting bumps on the skull to predict personality), findings of genetic markers that correlate with criminalized behavior will likely be only that—correlations and not explanations of the causes of violence or crime. The many causes of crime (or any human behavior) involve a wide range of forces, including genes that encode particular proteins and prenatal development (Ossorio & Duster, 2005).

Scientists must always be concerned that a person's genotype not be used as a basis for deciding whether that person is hired for a job, given a promotion, accepted to a school, or stigmatized in any way. Behavioral genetics cannot explain whether any given individual's behavior is due to genes or environment; it can only estimate the average influence that both genes and environment exert on individual differences within a group of people. Furthermore, the average degree to which a behavior is inheritable *within one group* of people cannot explain behavioral differences *between groups*.

A simple example will illustrate this important principle. Height is clearly heritable. Assume that a large group of people are raised in a culture in which they are chronically underfed; on average, the taller parents in this culture will still have taller children. However, the children in this culture might be a few inches shorter on average than children raised in another culture where food is plentiful and diet is adequate. Height is genet-

Should We Study Genetic Causes of Abnormality? *(Continued)*

ically determined in both cultures, but the difference between children from the two cultures is not due to genetic differences. Likewise, even though height is linked to genes, a purely environmental intervention—better diet for the first culture—would be an effective treatment. Throughout this book, we often note the role of genetic influences on mental disorders, but this does not mean that environmental factors or interventions are unimportant. What factors in Nelson McGrath's environment might have contributed to his current disorder? (See Chapter 4.)

Thinking Critically

As noted later in this chapter, scientific methods have an important role to play in resolving controversies about abnormal behavior, including those about the role of genetics. The scientific method provides public, agreed-upon procedures for engaging in *critical thinking* about a dispute. You can use the seven steps to critical thinking discussed in Chapter 1 to examine the issue, and ask yourself the following questions:

- How could finding a common genetic vulnerability for various mental disorders help in the search for prevention or treatment strategies?
- What does it mean to say that genetics influence mental disorders but do not cause them?
- Should scientists continue to study the genetic causes of abnormality despite the potential pitfalls?

Psychological and Sociocultural Models

Biological factors are critical to understanding both normal and abnormal behavior, but they do not tell the whole story. Many mental disorders occur without any apparent biological reason. To understand abnormality fully, clinicians recognize that they must also consider the influence of psychological and sociocultural variables. These variables play a prominent role in psychodynamic, interpersonal, behavioral, cognitive, humanistic, and sociocultural theories of abnormality.

Psychodynamic Theories

Formal psychological models of abnormal behavior began with the work of Sigmund Freud, discussed earlier in the chapter. Freud's **psychoanalysis** is defined by the idea that both normal and abnormal behaviors are influenced by *unconscious forces*—especially sexual and aggressive instincts. From this perspective, even apparently innocent events, such as forgetting a friend's name or writing the word *date* instead of *data*, can be interpreted as expressing feelings of anger or lust of which the person is unaware. Freud believed that, because sexual or aggressive instincts often conflict with the moral demands and realistic constraints of society, each individual faces a lifelong struggle to find ways of expressing these instincts without suffering punishment, anxiety, or guilt. As a result, said Freud, a hidden war among aspects of personality that represent instinct, reason, and morality rages within us. From the Freudian perspective, Nelson McGrath's behavior problems, like all other psychological disorders, result from this war, and they are best treated by psychoanalysis, a "talking cure" that is designed to help people become aware of, understand, and resolve unconscious conflicts.

Freudian Personality Structures

Freud identified three personality structures: the id, ego, and superego. The **id** is the location of the most basic, unconscious instincts. Present at birth, the id provides the energy (which Freud called **libido**) that motivates us to satisfy our need for food, water, and other basic requirements of life. The id operates on the **pleasure principle** ("if it feels good, do it"), seeking immediate gratification of its desires and impulses. Around the age of 2, however, infants begin to learn that cultural rules place limits on their behavior and require "appropriate" patterns of eating, speaking, toileting, and the like. The child's **ego**, or "self," said Freud, begins to develop in response to these limits. The ego operates on

psychoanalysis: A theory of human behavior and a therapeutic approach based on the idea that both normal and abnormal behaviors are influenced by conflicting unconscious forces, especially sexual and aggressive instincts.

id: One of the three structures in the psychoanalytic conception of personality; it represents basic, unconscious instincts and provides the energy, or libido, to satisfy those instincts.

libido: In psychoanalytic theory, the energy that motivates people to satisfy their basic needs.

pleasure principle: In psychoanalysis, the premise that immediate gratification of desires and impulses is a primary motive for behavior.

ego: One of the three structures in the psychoanalytic conception of personality; it seeks compromise between the id and the superego by following the reality principle.

reality principle: In psychoanalysis, a process used by the ego to reach rational compromises between the instincts of the id and the moral demands the superego.

superego: One of the three structures of the psychoanalytic conception of personality; it is the repository of cultural rules, models of ideal behavior, and moral values.

defense mechanism: In psychoanalytic theory, psychological processes that operate unconsciously to minimize conflicts between the id, ego, and superego.

repression: A psychoanalytic defense mechanism that involves motivated forgetting of anxiety-arousing thoughts, images, or impulses.

Connections

Does the sexual abuse of children have links to later abnormal behavior? For contemporary answers to this question, see Chapters 10 and 16.

ego analyst: A psycho-analytically oriented theorist who differs from Freud by assigning more importance to conscious personality factors.

object relations theory: A modern variant of psychoanalytic theory that explains how adult personality is based on the nature and quality of early interactions between infants and their caregivers.

the **reality principle**. It constrains the id by seeking rational compromises between the blind demands of the id and the limits other people impose. We can see the workings of the ego when, instead of simply grabbing a cookie, a child asks permission to have one. Eventually, often by the age of 5 or so, the child begins to adopt, or *introject*, the rules taught by the culture, and young children can often be heard scolding themselves for wrongdoing. **Superego** is the name Freud gave to the part of the personality that becomes the repository of cultural rules, models of ideal behavior, and moral values. The superego is a stern taskmaster; it insists on socially acceptable, even perfect behavior.

Freud believed that the constant conflicts among the id, ego, and superego can cause anxiety, guilt, and many other unpleasant emotional problems, especially if unconscious desires reach consciousness. The ego employs a variety of **defense mechanisms** that operate mostly outside our awareness to minimize these conflicts and keep them from reaching consciousness. One of the most important defense mechanisms is **repression**, a form of motivated forgetting by which the ego keeps us unaware of threatening impulses from the id.

Because his clients reported many sexual events from their childhoods, Freud initially believed that their problems stemmed from sexual molestation by parents or other relatives. Various forms of this idea enjoy empirical support (Trickett & Putnam, 1993), but within a few years of proposing this theory, Freud abandoned it (Masson, 1983). Instead, he claimed that these sexual recollections were not memories of real events, but of taboo sexual wishes and fantasies from childhood. Freud further believed that the symptoms of mental disorders were lingering surrogates of long-repressed sexual fantasies that the id, ego, and superego continue to battle over.

More specifically, here's how Freud would have viewed the chapter-opening case of Nelson McGrath. After introducing the structural model of the mind in 1923, Freud re-envisioned schizophrenia to be the result of a primary conflict between the ego and the external world. In other words, the external world no longer governs the ego. Instead, the ego determines reality by creating a world that is driven by the impulses of the id. Moreover, the ego's break from reality is motivated by an attempt to avoid painful events in external reality (Ridenour & Moehringer, 2014).

Contemporary Psychodynamic Theories

Many of Freud's colleagues and students—not to mention the general public—have been dissatisfied with his emphasis on the unconscious, his belief in childhood sexuality, his emphasis on male rather than female sexuality, his focus on instincts as the major motivation behind human behavior, and other aspects of his work. Consequently, several theorists have suggested revisions to Freud's theory of personality development and mental disorders. Some of these revisions involved a change in emphasis; others, such as Carl Jung's (1875–1961), altered or even rejected many of Freud's main principles. **Ego analysts** assign a larger role than Freud did to conscious personality factors and see the ego as an autonomous force, not just a mediator of unconscious conflicts. Erik Erikson (1946), for example, proposed eight stages of *psychosocial* development that stress an individual's interactions with others rather than conflict over instincts. At each stage, the person faces a social crisis that is either resolved or left partly unfinished. Positive outcomes at each stage help the person deal with the crisis of the next stage, whereas unsettled problems interfere with continued development. For example, if infants do not develop the feeling that they can trust parents to take care of their needs, they are unlikely to feel secure enough to try new behaviors on their own, as is expected around the age of 2.

One of the more important modern variants on psychoanalysis is object relations theory, associated with analysts such as Ronald Fairbairn (1952), Donald Winnicott (1965), Margaret Mahler (Mahler, Pine, & Bergman, 1975), and Melanie Klein (1975). Closely related to object relations views are the theories of Otto Kernberg (1976) and Heinz Kohut (1977). The fundamental assumption of **object relations theory** is that the adult personality is based on the nature and quality of interpersonal relationships, especially in the early interactions between infant and caregiver. If these interactions do not allow infants to feel pride in themselves or to develop a secure sense of self-esteem, for example, they cannot achieve a stable sense of self; the result will be disturbed behavior and personality in childhood and adulthood.

Associated primarily with American psychiatrist Harry Stack Sullivan, **interpersonal theory** emerged from psychodynamic ideas and explains abnormal behavior as the result of interaction styles that become so rigid and extreme that they are maladaptive. Sullivan (1953) believed that psychological disorders result from these fossilized interpersonal styles, which develop in people who are too anxious to behave flexibly and thus insist on interacting the same way with everyone. According to Sullivan, people try to feel secure and prevent anxiety through repeated interpersonal ploys (Carson, 1969). They elicit, or "pull," certain behaviors from others by using a typical interpersonal style (Leary, 1957). Interpersonal theory appears to account especially well for *personality disorders*, which are extreme and inflexible behaviors that cause substantial difficulties in a person's social life (see Chapter 16).

Sigmund Freud (1856–1939) was the founder of psychoanalysis, the first comprehensive psychological theory of abnormal behavior. This is the house where Freud lived with his daughter Anna (1895–1982) after fleeing Austria to escape the Nazis during World War II.

interpersonal theory: A theory that explains personality as the result of consistent styles of interaction.

Psychodynamic Treatment

The primary goal of psychoanalysis is to help clients gain insight into the unconscious origins of their behavior so that they can eventually control their impulses through a strengthened ego. Freud believed that clients gain this insight through the therapist's skillful use of techniques such as *free association* ("say whatever comes into your mind without trying to control it") as well as the *interpretation* of dreams, slips of the tongue, and everyday mistakes that might reveal a hidden motive. The most important technique is *transference*, in which clients, responding to the therapist, relive emotional reactions that are actually reenactments of early emotional conflicts with their parents. Because transference reveals how past conflicts are still influencing their lives, clients can learn to recognize the importance of these conflicts and then gradually begin to resolve them. Therefore, the psychoanalyst first allows the transference to emerge and then helps clients understand what it means for their current lives.

Variations on Freud's psychoanalytic theories have led to variations of his treatment techniques. Because ego analysts assume that people are more capable of actively controlling their behavior than Freud believed them to be, their treatments concentrate more on exploring clients' egos and helping clients understand how they rely too heavily on defense mechanisms to cope with personal conflicts and environmental demands. Object relations therapists, on the other hand, use the therapeutic relationship to repair the psychological defects and insults that clients suffered as very young children. The goal is not so much to understand the real or imagined traumas of childhood as it is to give clients a second chance at forming the secure and healthy relationships that they missed in childhood.

From the interpersonal perspective, treatment of disordered behavior involves helping people to develop more flexible, less extreme ways of relating to others. Take, as an example, the antisocial client whose style of interaction is to be hostile and dominant toward everyone. This style "invites" others, including therapists, to be hostile and submissive in return. The interpersonal therapist would try to act in a consistently friendly and dominant manner, thereby forcing the antisocial client to give up this coercive interpersonal strategy. Interpersonal therapists also help clients try out new behaviors in the safety of therapy sessions and then encourage them to use these new behaviors with other people.

Behavioral Theories

Psychoanalytic theories of disorder grew out of 19th-century therapists' efforts to treat disturbed individuals. During the first half of the 20th century, several alternative psychological theories emerged that sought to explain abnormal behavior in terms of the laws of learning being mapped out by academic psychologists' laboratory research on human and animal behavior. These **behavioral theories** (also called **learning theories**) are based on the assumption that genetic and biological factors provide an individual's basic physical structures and tendencies but that specific behaviors—normal and abnormal—are shaped by people's experiences with the world. Behaviorists place special emphasis on how people *learn* to behave as a result of these experiences.

Behavioral theorists differ among themselves primarily in terms of the learning processes they emphasize. *Operant* theorists stress the functional relationships between behavior and its environmental consequences, especially rewards and punishments. Others concentrate on *classical* conditioning and the associations that develop between stimuli and responses (such as between being bitten by a dog and later developing a fear of dogs). *Cognitive-behavioral* theorists see behavior as guided not only by consequences and associations, but also by the thoughts and expectations people acquire as they grow. They emphasize differences in the way people process and understand information about their lives.

Operant Conditioning

Edward L. Thorndike (1874–1949) was an American psychologist who proposed that learning follows the *law of effect:* Behaviors followed by pleasurable outcomes are more likely to be repeated, whereas behaviors that lead to unpleasant effects are less likely to be repeated. Expanding on this basic idea, psychologist B. F. Skinner (1904–1990) argued that it is not necessary to focus on unconscious—or even conscious—mental activity to understand human behavior because all behavior is learned via **operant conditioning**. In this model, if we want to explain why someone does something, we need only examine the functional relationships between their behavior and what comes before (*antecedent conditions*) and after it (*consequences*). According to Skinner, the act of ordering a pizza can be explained by noting the number of hours since the person last ate and whether pizza-ordering behavior has been rewarded in the past. There is no need to invoke the mentalistic concept of "hunger."

Behavior is strengthened through **reinforcement**—that is, when positive consequences follow the behavior. Positive consequences can take two forms: the appearance of something pleasant, such as food or praise, or the disappearance of something unpleasant, such as an annoying sound. Being paid for shoveling a snowy sidewalk is an example of the first form of reinforcement, called *positive reinforcement*; getting rid of a headache after taking a pain reliever illustrates the second kind of reinforcement, called *negative reinforcement*. Any type of reinforcement makes behavior such as shoveling snow or taking aspirin *more* likely to occur on appropriate occasions in the future. Thus, some behaviorists might suggest that Nelson McGrath's aversion to young women was based on negative reinforcement because the act of avoiding them reduced his anxiety.

Behavior is *less* likely to occur when it is followed by negative consequences; this process is called **punishment**. Negative consequences can take two forms: the appearance of something unpleasant, such as pain, or the loss of something valued, such as privileges. Behavior can also be made less likely to occur through **extinction**, or the absence of *any* notable consequences. Extinction is at work when we give up calling someone on our cell phone after repeatedly getting no answer or when we continually expose ourselves to a feared situation but the event we are afraid of never happens.

Often, behavior is not reinforced or punished every time it occurs. Employees, for example, may be paid once a month, not after each task they do. Skinner noted that such *schedules of reinforcement* often hold the key to understanding certain aspects of behavior. Intermittent reinforcement results in remarkably persistent behavior. Note how long some people will gamble or play golf or video games, even though the rewards may be infrequent. Recently, changing schedules of reinforcement have been employed as part of the behavioral treatment for individuals with autism spectrum disorder (Murray & Healy, 2013).

behavioral theory: A theory of behavior that explains how normal and abnormal behaviors are shaped by people's experiences with the world, and how people learn to behave as a result of these experiences.

learning theories: Explanations of how new behaviors are acquired, retained, and used.

operant conditioning: A form of learning in which the consequences of a behavior influence the probability of its being performed in the future.

reinforcement: The operant learning process that increases the frequency of a preceding behavior.

punishment: The operant learning process that decreases the frequency of a preceding behavior.

extinction: The decrease in a behavior caused by the absence of reinforcers for that behavior.

Classical Conditioning

Another behavioral theory of abnormality has its roots in the work of Ivan Pavlov (1849–1936). Pavlov and other Russian scientists in the early 20th century believed that behavior was based on reflexes that were automatically elicited by the environment. In his famous experiments with dogs, Pavlov repeatedly paired an *unconditioned stimulus* such as food, which elicits a reflexive (or *unconditioned response*) such as salivation, with a neutral stimulus such as a tone. Eventually, the neutral stimulus became a *conditioned stimulus* that elicits salivation as a *conditioned response*; the dogs learned to salivate in response to the tone. This process of **classical conditioning** is depicted in Figure 2.3.

Behavioral psychologists soon began to apply the laws of classical conditioning to the study and treatment of abnormal behavior. The most famous early example of this work was the case of "Little Albert," first reported by John Watson and Rosalie Rayner (1920) and remerging recently when the boy was identified as possibly being Douglas Merritte (1919–1925), who died a few years after the case study from hydrocephalus (Fridlund, Beck, Goldie, and Irons, 2012). Current psychological detective work indicates that this study may actually have been more of advertisement for Watson's lab than good science and that Albert B. may, in fact, have been a composite of two different baby boys (Beck, 2014). In any case, Watson's lab work demonstrated that you could teach a child to develop a fear of a previously neutral object. "Albert" initially interacted with a white

classical conditioning: A form of learning in which a formerly neutral stimulus is able to elicit a new response. This learning occurs after repeated associations between the neutral stimulus and an unconditioned stimulus that automatically elicits a response that resembles the learned one.

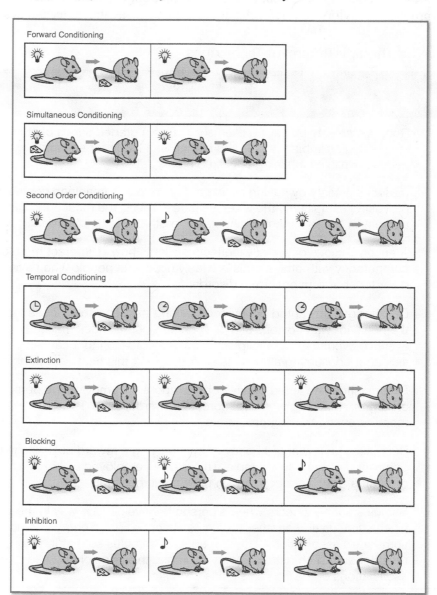

FIGURE 2.3 Pavlovian Conditioning

In forward classical conditioning, the bell or light (the neutral stimulus) is presented just before food (the unconditioned stimulus) is presented to the animal. After several pairings, the bell or light becomes a conditioned stimulus and elicits a set of responses that resemble the unconditioned responses that the food alone elicited (i.e., salivation in preparation for eating). Other classical conditioning processes are also illustrated here, such as extinction, in which the bell or light is presented without any food repeatedly so that the conditioned response is reduced. Behavioral psychologists believe that certain phobias develop through classical conditioning and can therefore be treated by learning principles such as extinction.

laboratory rat without fear, but the researchers made a loud sound behind Albert's back by striking a suspended steel bar with a hammer whenever he touched the rat. Little Albert responded to the noise by crying and showing fear. After several such pairings of the two stimuli, Albert was again presented with only the rat. After about a week, Albert did indeed show fear whenever he saw the rat.

Behavioral Treatment

A few years after the case of "Little Albert" was reported, Mary Cover Jones used classical conditioning to *reduce* children's learned fears by pairing the feared stimulus (such as a rabbit) with a pleasant activity such as eating (Jones, 1924). Researchers have applied both classical and operant conditioning methods to a wide range of problems, including phobias, substance use disorders, sexual disorders, and attention-deficit/hyperactivity disorder (e.g., Günzler & Berner, 2012; Sonuga-Barke et al., 2013). By the 1960s, an arsenal of new behavioral techniques had been developed and tested for therapeutic use (Eysenck & Rachman, 1965; Wolpe, 1958). Table 2.2 describes some of these frequently used treatments.

Behavioral treatments, also known as **behavior therapy** or **behavior modification**, are aimed at helping clients decrease specific maladaptive behaviors and increase adaptive ones (Bellack, Hersen, & Kazdin, 1990). The focus of behavior therapy is on the here and now. Less attention is paid to early psychological history than to the current skills the client does or does not have and to the environmental conditions that serve to sustain problem behaviors. In brief, behavior therapists use treatment techniques that are derived

behavior modification (behavior therapy): Behavioral treatments based on learning theory that are aimed at helping people decrease specific maladaptive behaviors and increase adaptive behaviors.

TABLE 2.2 Common Behavior Therapy Treatment Techniques

Behavior Therapy Technique	How It Is Used
Systematic desensitization	Reduces anxiety by having clients visualize a graded series of anxiety-provoking stimuli (e.g., climbing higher and higher on a ledge for someone who is afraid of heights) while maintaining a relaxed state.
Exposure	Reduces anxiety by having clients maintain real or imagined contact with anxiety-provoking stimuli until the fear dissipates. This is the most important principle to address in the treatment of phobias and other anxiety disorders.
Social skills training	Teaches anxious or socially ineffective clients how to interact more confidently and competently with others. This is widely used with people who have social anxiety disorder or autism spectrum disorder.
Aversive therapy	Discourages unwanted behavior by pairing the behavior or cues that lead to the behavior with noxious stimuli such as electric shock, nausea, or imaginary aversive events. Antabuse (disulfiram), a medication that causes people to feel sick after consuming alcohol, is an example of this treatment principle.
Time out	Extinguishes unwanted behavior by temporarily removing the person, usually a child, from a setting where reinforcers (rewards) exist. This is a key component of most parenting training programs.
Response cost	Decreases an unwanted behavior by removing a reward or privilege following the behavior; fines are an example. This is often employed within token economy programs, which are common in psychiatric hospitals.
Stimulus control therapy	Stimulus control occurs when a person behaves in one way in the presence of a given stimulus and another way in its absence. The therapy attempts to change someone's associations with that specific stimulus so that it no longer guides their behavior. For instance, with insomnia, this principle is used to break negative associations of the bed as a place of frustration.

from the same basic laws of learning that led to these problem behaviors in the first place. These interventions, which are often combined with cognitive techniques discussed in the next section, are aimed at specific changes that can be quantitatively measured, such as a reduction in anxiety. For Nelson McGrath from the chapter-opening case, behavioral treatment might focus on increasing his ability to be around young women, take his medications, and eat a variety of foods, perhaps first by systematic desensitization and later by in vivo (real-world) exposure to these feared objects.

Connections

For what mental disorders are behavioral treatments particularly useful? For a discussion of their effectiveness in treating childhood disorders, see Chapter 3.

Cognitive Theories

To many observers, operant or classical conditioning explanations of human behavior and mental disorders seem incomplete because they pay too little attention to what people *think* about the world and themselves. By the 1970s, psychologists who agreed with this critique had developed cognitive, or social learning, theories of development and behavior modification. These theories were actually part of a larger movement known as the cognitive revolution that began to sweep through all of psychology in the late 1960s and gained momentum with the invention of computers.

According to **cognitive** and **social learning theories**, learning occurs not only as a result of operant and classical conditioning, but also through the way people process information about the world—what they attend to, perceive, think about, and remember.

Important Cognitive Processes

One prominent social learning theorist, Albert Bandura, emphasized **observational learning** (Bandura, 1969, 1986, 2011), still under study today (Rak, Bellebaum, & Thoma, 2013). In Bandura's view, behavior develops not only through first-hand conditioning, but also as a result of observing other people—known as *models*—and the consequences of their behavior. For example, if a preschooler observed a parent repeatedly showing a fear of snakes, avoiding outdoor activities whenever there might be a chance of encountering snakes, and refusing to read about or view scenes containing snakes, the child might develop a phobia of snakes. According to Bandura, observational learning can stimulate new responses, inhibit or disinhibit already learned responses (as when a person violates a "Don't Walk" sign after watching someone else do so), and prompt behavior (as when people in an airport line up at an unattended check-in counter after a single prankster stands in front of it).

Expectancies also play a major role in social learning theories. For example, Julian Rotter (1954) argued that the probability that a given behavior will occur depends on (1) what the person has learned to expect will happen after the response, and (2) the value the person places on that outcome. One type of expectancy is **self-efficacy**, the belief that one can successfully perform a given behavior, such as meeting new people at a party. Bandura (1977, 1982, 1986, 2012) believes that overt behavior is controlled by an individual's perceived self-efficacy: Your chances of trying something depend directly on how confident you are in your ability to do it. Other important cognitive processes include appraisals, attributions, and long-standing beliefs or assumptions.

Appraisals are individuals' evaluations of their own behavior and the behavior of others. Appraisals often precede and influence emotional reactions automatically and outside of a person's awareness. According to psychiatrist Aaron Beck (1976), individuals who always evaluate their performance as inadequate will interpret compliments as a sign that others are merely being polite. People who see the world in such a negative light also tend to see themselves as worthless and inadequate and are predisposed to mental disorders such as depression (Ghahramanlou-Holloway, Bhar, Brown, Olsen, & Beck, 2012).

cognitive theory: A theory that explains behavior primarily in terms of the way people process information about the world—what they attend to, perceive, think about, and remember.

social learning theory: A theory that explains how behavior is learned through observation (vicarious learning), direct experiences, and cognitive processes such as expectancies.

observational learning: In social learning theory, the view that behavior develops as a result of observing other people's behavior and its consequences.

self-efficacy: A person's belief that he or she can successfully perform a given behavior.

appraisal: An evaluation of our own behavior and the behavior of others.

Across different cultures, children pay close attention to and model the behavior of their parents. They are able to imitate a wide range of behaviors precisely.

Source: Photo courtesy of Brian Burke.

attribution: An individual's explanation for behavior or other events.

Attributions are explanations for behavior and other events. They have three key characteristics: (1) internality—whether we see the cause of an event as due to something about ourselves or something about the environment; (2) stability—whether we see the cause as enduring or temporary; and (3) globalness—whether we see the cause as specific to a given situation or affecting all situations. Thus, a student who explains having failed a test by saying "it was too hard" is employing an external, temporary, and specific attribution. On the other hand, the statement "I have always been stupid" reflects an internal, stable, and global attribution, which also increases the likelihood of that person developing depression (Abramson, Seligman, & Teasdale, 1978). In addition, more "extreme" (i.e., excessively pessimistic or optimistic) attributions predict a greater likelihood of developing an episode of mood elevation (mania) in individuals with bipolar disorder (Stange et al., 2013).

Albert Ellis emphasized the role of enduring negative expectancies and especially what he calls *irrational beliefs* in the development of behavior disorders (Ellis, 1962). These irrational beliefs are often associated with "must" or "should" statements (e.g., "I must do everything right" or "everyone should like me") that create unrealistically high standards that leave a person doomed to failure or disappointment and render them vulnerable to mental disorders.

Connections

How do cognitive therapists target the distortions underlying anxiety disorders and depression? For answers, see Chapters 6–9.

Cognitive Therapies

Cognitive therapists attempt to modify maladaptive behavior by encouraging clients to consider new information and change the way they think about themselves, other people, and the world in general. They assume that psychological problems are largely caused by irrational or distorted thinking. Correcting these misconceptions should therefore be therapeutic. Cognitions about the self—about a person's abilities or the degree to which a person is liked by others—are particularly important therapy targets because such cognitions affect how people react to success and failure in their lives.

cognitive therapy: A therapy that uses learning principles to alter maladaptive thoughts and beliefs that accompany behavior problems.

For example, Beck's original version of **cognitive therapy** was developed to help depressed clients correct cognitive distortions to which they are prone—pessimistic, self-deprecating, catastrophizing beliefs about themselves and their future. Much of the research on Aaron Beck's therapy has focused on its use in the treatment of depression (Dobson, 1989; Robins & Hayes, 1993), but his methods have also been applied to many other mental disorders, including anxiety, personality disorders, substance use problems, and even schizophrenia (Beck et al., 1990; Grant, Reisweber, Luther, Brinen, & Beck, 2013; Linehan, 1993). Cognitive therapists teach clients to identify these cognitive distortions and then ask them to examine whether there is any valid evidence for their negative views. Ideally, clients discover that no such evidence exists or that they have been exaggerating the importance of negative events or the significance of potential threats—a process called *catastrophizing*, which plays a prominent role in anxiety disorders (Ghahramanlou-Holloway, Wenzel, Lou, & Beck, 2007). Clients are then helped to develop more realistic thoughts to substitute for their pessimistic beliefs. The next step is to complete "homework assignments" that require clients to practice their new thinking strategies in the situations that have led to their strongest distortions and most problematic emotional reactions (Cammin-Nowak et al., 2013).

In dealing with generalized anxiety disorder, for example, the cognitive therapist seeks to alter clients' beliefs that even relatively minor negative events are major threats, whereas cognitive treatment of obsessive-compulsive disorder might focus on exploring the belief that chaos and danger will occur unless the client performs elaborate mental or behavioral rituals (Clark & Beck, 2010).

rational emotive therapy (RET): Therapy developed by Albert Ellis based on the theory that psychological problems are caused by irrational thinking; the therapy challenges irrational beliefs and helps clients replace them with more logical beliefs.

The core principles of Albert Ellis's **rational emotive therapy (RET)** are literally as simple as ABC (Ellis, 1973; Ellis & Ellis, 2014). Ellis believes that people suffer anxiety, depression, and other psychological problems when activating events (A) are followed by upsetting emotional consequences (C). However, he says that A does not actually cause C. Instead, emotional consequences are the result of problems in how a person *thinks* about activating events—in other words, in his or her personal *belief system* (B). Specifically, Ellis says that anxiety, depression, and other problems are the result of beliefs that are extreme, irrational, and self-defeating. Rational emotive therapy challenges these irrational beliefs and helps clients replace them with more logical thoughts. Shakespeare anticipated RET when he had Hamlet say that "there is nothing either good or bad but thinking makes it so."

For Nelson McGrath in the chapter-opening case, cognitive treatment would focus on first identifying his irrational thoughts, such as "I have dots on my skin," "I must eat all white food to protect myself," and "I should not take the pills that I am being prescribed or something terrible will happen" (catastrophizing). With the help of the therapist and through homework, Nelson would begin to challenge the evidence for these beliefs, with the ultimate goal of replacing them with more accurate ones. As you will see in the coming chapters, specific types of cognitive distortions and irrational beliefs can lead to or exacerbate many different mental disorders.

Humanistic and Positive Psychology Theories

A third broad psychological approach to abnormality, known as the **humanistic model**, asserts that human behavior is determined not by instincts, conflicts, or environmental consequences, but by each person's unique perception of the world at any given moment. Either these perceptions allow the person to live an emotionally authentic and behaviorally effective life, or they constrain the person to a life that is based on false assumptions and excessive desires to meet others' expectations.

humanistic model: Any of several theories of human behavior that explain how behavior is influenced by each person's unique perception of the world, rather than by instincts, conflicts, or environmental consequences.

Carl Rogers' Self Theory

Carl Rogers (1902–1987) believed that people have an innate drive toward personal growth that he called *self-actualization*. And he saw all human behavior, normal and abnormal, as a reflection of the individual's efforts at self-actualization in the world the person perceives. Thus, aggression might be seen as seeking personal goals in a world that must be conquered, whereas speech anxiety might reflect personal growth stunted by the perceived threat of negative evaluations from others. Even Nelson McGrath's bizarre ideas would be viewed not as illness but as his attempt to cope with a world that he perceives as horribly dangerous.

According to Rogers (1951, 1962, 2007), people value the positive regard of others so highly that they will seek it even if it means thinking and acting in ways that are *incongruent* with their own experience and even if it thwarts self-actualization. This tendency is encouraged, beginning in childhood, by *conditions of worth*, circumstances in which children get positive regard from others *only if* they display certain behaviors and attitudes. These conditions, first set up by parents, family, and others, eventually become part of the person's belief system in a manner similar to Freud's concept of superego or the Beck/Ellis notion of irrational thoughts.

Rogers said that when people try to please others at the expense of personal growth, they become uncomfortable with the incongruity, and they try to reduce their discomfort by distorting reality. For example, men whose early conditions of worth made crying or fearfulness unacceptable may distort their emotional experience by denying genuine feelings of sadness or fear (and perhaps ridiculing these feelings in others). This could lead to men being diagnosed more often with substance use or anger issues than with depression. According to Rogers, the greater the discrepancy between real feelings and self-concept, the more severe the resulting problems.

Maslow and Humanistic Psychology

Like Rogers, Abraham Maslow, one of the founders of humanistic psychology, saw people as capable of self-actualization, but he suggested that people's failure to realize their full potential is caused by unmet needs. Maslow (1954, 1962) believed that human needs form a hierarchy. At the base of the hierarchy are basic physiological requirements (such as food and water); needs for safety, security, love, belongingness, self-esteem, and self-actualization appear at successively higher levels. According to Maslow, lower-level needs must be at least partially satisfied before people can focus on higher-level needs.

Thus, a starving person is unlikely to be concerned with fulfilling the need for love or belongingness. Similarly, Nelson McGrath may be unable to fulfill those higher-level needs until he gets his need for safety and security met.

The Rise of Positive Psychology

Positive psychology is the scientific study of what goes right in life, from birth to death and at all stops in between. It is a relatively new approach that emerged from humanistic psychology in the late 20th century. Everyone's life has peaks and valleys, and positive psychology does not deny the valleys. Its signature premise is more nuanced, but nonetheless important: What is good about life is as genuine as what is bad and, therefore, deserves equal attention from psychologists.

Drawing on methods effectively used to advance the science of mental disorders (discussed later in the chapter), positive psychologists have been studying mental health and well-being (Seligman, Steen, Park, & Peterson, 2005). Building on pioneering work by Rogers (1951), Maslow (1954, 1962), Erikson (1982), Deci and Ryan (1985), and Ryff and Singer (1996)—among many others—positive psychologists have enhanced our understanding of how, why, and under what conditions positive emotions, positive character, and the institutions that enable them flourish (e.g., Gardner, Csikszentmihalyi, & Damon, 2001; Kahneman, Diener, & Schwarz, 1999; Seligman, 2011). Positive psychologists do not claim to have invented the good life or to have ushered in its scientific study, but the value of the overarching term *positive psychology* lies in its uniting of what had been scattered and disparate lines of theory and research about what makes life most worth living (Peterson & Park, 2003). Positive psychology as an explicit perspective has existed only since 1998, but enough relevant theory and research now exist to fill a textbook on its own (Peterson, 2006), and entire books authored by psychological scientists have explicitly focused on the eternal question of what makes humans happy (e.g., Gilbert, 2006; Haidt, 2006).

Humanistic Therapies

Humanistic therapists view therapy as an opportunity for clients to discover how they have allowed themselves to become restricted or hemmed in by the expectations of others. As a result, they may have stopped growing and do not take full responsibility for their lives. The therapist's main task, therefore, is to create a context in which clients feel free to explore their potential and to express a full range of emotions. In Rogers' (1951, 2007) client-centered therapy, he details what he views as the "necessary and sufficient" conditions for therapeutic change, including the therapist acting in a genuine, nonjudgmental, and empathic manner toward the client so that the client can freely express her or his concerns.

In this model, clients are not diagnosed, evaluated, or given advice; rather, they are valued as unique individuals, no matter how problematic their behavior might be. Instead of judgment, the therapist strives for *empathic understanding* by trying to see the world as the client sees it. Therapists communicate **empathy** by reflecting what they perceive of the cli-

How different perspectives deal with a common childhood complaint of monsters under the bed

The cartoon demonstrates how different models might approach the problem of a child afraid of monsters: looking for a deeper cause (Freud), using operant conditioning to change the behavior (Skinner), using Socratic questioning to examine the cognitions (Beck), empathizing with the fear (Rogers), or prescribing medication (psychiatry).

Source: Cartoon by Brian L. Burke; illustrated by Katey Redmond.

ent's feelings. Often, reflection takes the form of rephrasing the client's statements in terms that show that the therapist has recognized the emotions that underlie the words. Finally, the therapist must be *genuine* in relating to the client; all actions and feelings must be *congruent*. Being congruent and genuine requires therapists to say what they feel, tactfully, but free from hypocrisy and pretense. Ideally, once clients begin to experience, perhaps for the first time, a relationship in which someone offers nonjudgmental support, empathy, and genuineness, their confidence will increase and their progress toward self-actualization should resume.

empathy: The ability to appreciate and share the feelings of another person.

Current treatment applications emerging from positive psychology specifically include the Comprehensive Soldier Fitness Program, which is designed to build **resilience** and enhance performance of U.S. military personnel and their families. The program does this by providing training and self-development tools so that members of the military are better able to cope with adversity, perform better in stressful situations, and thrive in life (Seligman & Fowler, 2011). Further, positive psychology interventions have been found to be promising for autism spectrum disorders (Zager, 2013), substance use disorders (Krentzman, 2013), and even physical diseases such as breast cancer (Casellas-Grau, Font, & Vives, 2014).

resilience: The ability to solve problems effectively, cope with stressors, and overcome adversity.

For Nelson McGrath in the chapter-opening case, his humanistic therapist would first and foremost seek to understand his worldview without judging him, and positive psychology could provide him with strategies for building on his current strengths or cultivating happiness-inducing qualities such as gratitude (e.g., by writing a letter of appreciation to someone in his life), resilience (e.g., by determining how he might be able to get through this harrowing and stressful skin dot episode), or forgiveness (e.g., by working to forgive those who may have harmed him in the past).

The Sociocultural Model

All the models discussed so far focus on internal dysfunctions, conflicts, deficits, or misuse of strengths that ultimately result in abnormal behavior. They share an assumption that something *inside* a person is disturbed and needs to be repaired or rebuilt. Without necessarily denying the role of such factors, the **sociocultural model** of abnormality emphasizes *external* factors, such as harmful environments, adverse social policies, powerlessness, and cultural traditions as causes of mental disorders. It is a perspective describing people's behavior and mental processes as shaped in part by their social and/or cultural contact, including race, gender, and nationality (Sanderson, 2010). Because it highlights the need to view people's behavior in relation to the sociocultural environment in which it occurs, this approach is sometimes referred to as the **ecological model** (Rappaport, 1977). Some proponents of this model see social and cultural forces as being so dominant that they question whether mental disorders really exist or whether they are merely a set of labels that a particular culture attaches to certain persons or behaviors that do not fit with the prevailing norms.

sociocultural model: Explanations of mental disorders that emphasize external factors, such as harmful environments, unfortunate social policies, lack of personal power, and cultural traditions; also called the *ecological model*.

ecological model: Another name for the sociocultural model.

Traces of the sociocultural model can be found throughout history, especially during the moral treatment era in the 1800s discussed earlier in the chapter, when evidence about the potentially harmful effects of living in an industrializing society began to be considered. The sociocultural model would suggest, for example, that a person such as Nelson McGrath may have developed his bizarre and dysfunctional behaviors largely as a result of living in a complex, stressful culture.

Epidemiological studies, which look at the patterns and frequency of disorders in certain populations, do suggest that the nature and frequency of abnormal behavior are related to environmental, socioeconomic, ethnic, and cultural variables. For example, in the United States, where aggressive behavior is accepted and often encouraged, particularly among boys, problems involving poor control of behavior, such as disobedience and excessive attention-seeking, are more frequent than in societies such as Thailand or Jamaica, where respect for parental authority and submissiveness are promoted. In Thailand and Jamaica, however, there are higher rates of "overcontrol" problems, such as withdrawal and physical complaints (Lambert, Weisz, & Knight, 1989; Weisz, Suwanlert, Chaiyasit, & Walter, 1987).

Because of such widespread cultural differences, even the assessment scales and measures used to detect disordered behavior (see Chapter 1) need to be different (Weisz, Weiss, Suwanlert, & Chaiyasit, 2006). Sociocultural explanations for such differences in disorder patterns include social causation or social drift, social relativism, and social labeling.

Social Causation or Social Drift

social causation theory: A theory suggesting that stress, poverty, racism, inferior education, unemployment, and social changes are sociocultural risk factors leading to mental disorders.

It could be that social, environmental, or cultural hardships put people at greater risk for a disorder, thereby increasing the rates of disorder in certain populations. This **social causation theory** suggests that stress, poverty, racism, inferior education, unemployment, and social changes are sociocultural risk factors for abnormal behavior.

A number of studies suggest, for example, that children who are chronically exposed to high levels of violence suffer higher rates of disordered behavior (Osofsky, 1995). Scientific evidence shows that early life stress in general triggers, aggravates, maintains, and increases the recurrence of psychiatric disorders (Carr, Martins, Stingel, Lemgruber, & Juruena, 2013). As an example, Helzer et al. (1990) assessed rates of alcohol addiction among adults in St. Louis, Missouri; Edmonton, Alberta (Canada); Puerto Rico; Taiwan; and Korea. Alcohol consumption tends to be more discouraged by cultural values in most Asian countries than in most Western communities. However, in contrast to Taiwan, heavy consumption is encouraged in Korea, especially among men, who often compete with one another to see who can drink the most. In Edmonton, at the time of the research, stress arising from unemployment and an unpredictable economy was especially high. As shown in Table 2.3, the results are consistent with predictions derived from social causation theory. The highest overall rate of problem drinking was in Edmonton, where economic adversity was greatest, and the lowest rate was in Taiwan, where excessive drinking is culturally discouraged.

social drift hypothesis: Also called the *social selection hypothesis*, it explains higher rates of mental disorders among lower socioeconomic groups as the consequence of disordered people sinking to lower socioeconomic levels because of their disorders.

An alternative explanation of social and cultural differences in psychological disorders is that people with certain mental disorders gravitate to certain locations or status levels within a culture. This **social drift**, or *social selection*, **hypothesis** explains higher rates of some disorders among lower socioeconomic groups as the inevitable consequence of disordered people falling to lower socioeconomic levels *because* of their disorders (Eaton, Muntaner, & Sapag, 2010). The fact that mental disorders are associated with different demographic and social factors is consistent with social causation, social drift, or an interaction between both of these explanations. Scholars continue to debate the issue of which explanation is better (e.g., Eaton et al., 2010; Faris & Dunham, 1939; Robins & Regier, 1991), generally concluding that both drift and causation interact to contribute to mental disorders.

TABLE 2.3 Lifetime Percentage Rates of Alcohol Abuse by Gender in Five Countries

	Alcohol Abuse (%)		
	Men	*Women*	*Total*
St. Louis, Missouri	16.1	3.0	9.2
Edmonton, Alberta, Canada	18.5	3.9	11.3
Puerto Rico	15.7	1.6	8.2
Taiwan 　　Metropolis 　　Townships	 2.9 3.2	 0.1 0.2	 1.5 1.8
Korea	20.4	1.0	10.4

Source: Based on Helzer et al., 1990.

Social Relativism

A third explanation of social and cultural differences in abnormality holds that disorders are defined or diagnosed in different ways in different places by different groups. This social relativism viewpoint involves the idea that the same standards and definitions of abnormal behavior do not apply in all cultures. For example, a clinician who is not sensitive to a client's cultural values and traditions can easily mistake that person's devoutly held religious beliefs or averting of the eyes for delusions, inordinate shyness, or depression.

Some forms of abnormality are found only in certain cultures and are covered as **culture-bound syndromes** in the *DSM-5* (see Chapter 1). For example, in *koro*, a condition seen only in Southeast Asia, a man believes his penis is about to retract into his stomach and kill him. *Windigo* is an anxiety disorder among North American Indians in which victims believe that monsters will possess them and turn them into homicidal cannibals. Anorexia nervosa, an eating disorder that is discussed in Chapter 12, is most common in Western societies that place a premium on thinness as a criterion for physical beauty. Immigrants to these societies appear to be at increased risk for the disorder as they adopt the Western aversion to larger body sizes (Ritenbaugh, Shisslak, Teufal, & Leonard-Green, 1996).

Even when the basic nature of a disorder is similar across cultures, its predominant symptoms may vary a great deal from one culture to another. For example, the content of hallucinations and delusions tends to vary among people with schizophrenia, depending on the society in which they live (Al-Issa, 1977). Even the pattern of course and functioning for these people differs based on where they live—for schizophrenia, the 20-year prognosis is distinctly better in developing nations than it is in more developed countries (Thara, 2004).

social relativism: The idea that the same standards and definitions of abnormal behavior do not apply in all cultures.

culture-bound syndrome: A pattern of abnormal behavior that appears only in certain localities or cultures.

Social Labeling

The most extreme version of cultural relativism suggests that mental disorders are merely labels applied to behavior that is unpopular or troubling at a given time or place, as discussed in Chapter 1. A prominent contemporary advocate of this position was Thomas Szasz (1961, 1986), an American psychiatrist who maintained that mental illness is a myth created by medical professionals to legitimize their coercive treatment of people who simply have "problems in living." According to Szasz, these problems in living are usually due to economic hardships, political oppression, or a crisis in personal values. Labelling someone like Nelson McGrath from the chapter-opening case as having an "illness" or "disorder," according to Szasz, makes things worse as it subjects the victim to the stigma of being perceived as "mentally ill" and therefore not a fully responsible member of society (see also Sarbin, 1969; Scheff, 1966).

Social labeling theory forces us to think seriously about the possible dangers of labeling problematic behavior as a disorder or illness. Labels can be demeaning, often producing prejudice and discrimination, and even making it more likely that people will behave in accordance with the label. However, most mental health professionals see social labeling theory as incomplete for two reasons: (1) it fails to explain how problematic behaviors begin, and (2) it ignores the fact that people's problems tend to persist and worsen even if they are not officially labeled and that these problems are often relieved following diagnosis and treatment.

The various versions of the sociocultural model reflect the idea that maladaptive behavior develops when people's needs and abilities are not well suited to their environment. By implication, people can be

Source: arindambanerjee/Shutterstock.com.

The symptoms of some mental disorders depend, in part, on sociocultural influences. This drawing depicts symbols that are unique to the artist's Indian background, just as a drawing by someone from another culture might focus on different images.

helped either by improving their living skills or by making their environments more supportive. Developing and studying interventions that modify environments or build individual competencies defines the field of *community psychology*, which employs various perspectives within and outside of psychology to address issues of communities, the relationships within them, and how they shape people's attitudes and behavior. Many community psychologists argue that *preventing* abnormal behavior is preferable to *treating* it. We believe that the goal of preventing mental disorders is so important that we return to it throughout this book in a special feature of each chapter called "Prevention." The "Prevention" feature that appears later in this chapter examines the notion of breaking the cycle of intergenerational cognitive disability.

Section Review

Psychological and sociocultural variables play an important role in several theories of abnormality, including:

- psychodynamic theories,
- interpersonal theories,
- behavioral theories,
- cognitive theories,
- humanistic theories, and
- the sociocultural model.

Each of these theories:

- emphasizes a different set of psychological or sociocultural factors that contribute to abnormal behavior, and
- is associated with interventions designed to change those factors the theory specifies as leading to abnormal behavior.

diathesis-stress model: A model that explains how a mental disorder can result from the interaction of a predisposition (diathesis) for a disorder with a trigger (stressor) that converts the predisposition into the actual disorder.

The Diathesis-Stress Model

The idea that abnormal behavior results from the interaction of particular people within specific environments is given the fullest expression in the **diathesis-stress model** of abnormality, first introduced in the 1960s to understand schizophrenia (Ingram & Luxton, 2005). The basic assumption of the diathesis-stress model, illustrated in Figure 2.4, is that a mental disorder results from the combined effects of two influences: (1) a *predisposition*

FIGURE 2.4 The Diathesis-Stress Model of Abnormality

According to the diathesis-stress model, mental disorders result when a predisposition to a disorder interacts with stressors. Stressors and diatheses can also influence each other. A diathesis can make people more likely to encounter stressors, and a stressor can intensify a diathesis. Here, the *x*-axis indicates quality of the environment/experiences, from negative to positive. The *y*-axis indicates the developmental outcome, from negative to positive. The lines depict two categorical groups that differ in their responsiveness to a negative environment: The "vulnerable" group shows a negative outcome when exposed to a negative environment, while the "resilient" group is not affected by it. No differences between the two groups emerge in a positive environment.

Source: By Mpluess (own work) [Public domain], via Wikimedia Commons.

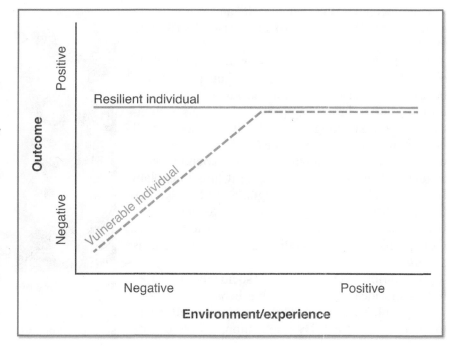

or vulnerability for that disorder—called a **diathesis**, and (2) a **stressor**, which is any event significant enough that it causes a person to have to adjust to it. According to this model, stressors are the triggers that convert a predisposition for a disorder into the actual appearance of that disorder.

diathesis: A biological or psychological predisposition for a disorder.

The specific nature of the diathesis and the particular triggering events vary according to the disorder in question. Research suggests that in the chapter-opening case regarding Nelson McGrath, for example, the predisposition may take the form of a biochemical imbalance or a defect in the brain that is probably genetically transmitted (see Chapter 4). In some forms of depression, the diathesis may be a biological problem, a psychological characteristic, or a combination of both. The triggering stressors may take the form of a harsh family environment, an abusive romantic relationship, the loss of a loved one, or chronic economic adversity.

stressor: Any event that requires a person to adjust.

The diathesis-stress model is one example of a **biopsychosocial model** (Engel, 1977) of mental disorders—a general model or approach positing that biological, psychological (which entails thoughts, emotions, and behaviors), and social (socioeconomic, environmental, and cultural) factors all play a significant role in human functioning in the context of disorder or disease. According to the diathesis-stress model, there is an ongoing interaction of ever-changing individual characteristics and ever-changing environments. Both factors, in turn, can influence each other. Thus, the loss of a loved one might be particularly stressful for a person who is predisposed to be shy and has few friends. Likewise, a tendency toward shyness might be strengthened by interpersonal rejections or conflicts. As genetic influences, emotional temperament, early adversities, emerging symptoms, and random events are woven together over time, it becomes increasingly difficult to disentangle the complex pattern of factors that cause a particular behavior disorder. Still, the diathesis-stress model provides a helpful framework for thinking about causation without assuming that there is only one cause per disorder, without prescribing exactly what the causes might be, and without automatically ruling out any of them. Biological, psychodynamic, interpersonal, behavioral, cognitive, humanistic, and sociocultural factors can all contribute. In fact, just as in trying to explain exactly why you received a particular grade—illness, a bad teacher, a chance encounter, hard work, a role model, intellectual gifts, or whatever—it may be fundamentally impossible to say *exactly* what causes some behavior disorders (Coyne & Downey, 1991).

biopsychosocial model: A view that explains illness as the outgrowth of biological vulnerability, psychological processes, and social conditions.

One relatively recent outgrowth of the diathesis-stress model's emphasis on continuing interactions between people and situations is research in the area of **developmental psychopathology**. Scientists in this field study how problems that first appear in childhood or adolescence are linked to disorders that occur later in life. This developmental view of abnormal behavior helps reveal the numerous ways in which childhood versions of behavior and behavior problems express themselves in adulthood. We discuss the developmental view of abnormal behavior in more detail when we focus on childhood and adolescent disorders in Chapter 3.

developmental psychopathology: A field of study that focuses on how problems that first appear in childhood or adolescence are linked to disorders occurring later in life.

Not surprisingly, advocates of the diathesis-stress model suggest that effective treatment of disorders must include a combination of techniques that deal with all aspects of causation. Thus, psychotherapy and exercise are often combined in the treatment of depression, whereas parenting training is often combined with individual work for children with ADHD. Similarly, people with schizophrenia are often given medication and enrolled in community support programs designed to enhance daily living skills and reduce the effects of stressful experiences. The diathesis-stress model also has implications for how best to prevent disorders, as the "Prevention" feature later in the chapter illustrates.

The major principles of the diathesis-stress model and the other models of abnormality we have discussed are summarized in Table 2.4. These models, which are used to understand and explain the causes of mental disorders, each bring with them different treatments. More details about such treatments will be covered in each subsequent chapter because these treatments are typically altered to fit what we know about each mental disorder.

To illustrate how the various models of abnormality may be complementary pieces of the same puzzle, consider the example of Sandy Hook. On December 14, 2012,

On December 14, 2012, 20-year-old Adam Lanza fatally shot 20 children and 6 adult staff members in a mass murder at Sandy Hook Elementary School in the village of Sandy Hook in Newtown, Connecticut. This was a memorial established nearby in the wake of the tragedy to commemorate those who perished.

20-year-old Adam Lanza fatally shot 20 children and 6 adult staff members in a mass murder at Sandy Hook Elementary School in the village of Sandy Hook in Newtown, Connecticut. Before driving to the school, Lanza shot and killed his mother, Nancy, at their Newtown home (Barron, 2012). As first responders arrived, he committed suicide by shooting himself in the head. It was the second-deadliest mass shooting to that point by a single person in American history, after the 2007 Virginia Tech massacre, and the second-deadliest mass murder at a U.S. elementary school, after the 1927 Bath School bombings in Michigan (Bratu, 2012).

Of course, in the aftermath of such a horrific event, we all attempt to understand why it happened. A November 2013 report issued by the Connecticut State Attorney's office concluded that the perpetrator acted alone and planned his actions, but no evidence collected provided any indication as to the specific causes of his behavior or why he targeted Sandy Hook Elementary School (Sedensky, 2013).

But each one of the models of abnormality shown in Table 2.4 might provide one potential clue or piece to the mysterious puzzle. Psychoanalysis could point to Adam's childhood, including his estranged older brother, Ryan, and his father, Peter. Interpersonally, Adam rarely connected with people and withdrew from almost everyone, beginning in the seventh grade. He did not even communicate with his mother, Nancy, with whom he lived, except via email. Behaviorally, he received rewards primarily from playing violent video games, including one called "School Shooting," and going to the shooting range with his mother, the only activity the two shared. Though he

TABLE 2.4 Major Psychosocial Theories of Abnormal Behavior

Theory	Basic Assumption About Abnormality	
Psychoanalytic	Abnormality is determined by unconscious conflicts between social rules and personal impulses. Other versions of this theory stress unconscious disturbances in early relationships between infants and caregivers that later affect adult development.	
Interpersonal	Abnormality involves extreme and rigid styles of interpersonal behavior in which a person tries to induce others to behave in ways that protect the person from anxiety.	
Behavioral	Abnormality is caused by learning experiences involving operant and classical conditioning. These same forms of learning are responsible for normal behavior and provide the basis for treatment.	
Cognitive	Abnormality results from biased or irrational thinking by which people distort their perceptions or understanding of themselves and events around them, leading to emotional disturbances.	
Humanistic	Abnormality develops from subjective perceptions that lead people to feel constrained in their ability to live authentic, freely directed lives.	
Sociocultural	Abnormality is the result of external forces, such as poverty, environmental stress, harsh family background, and cultural traditions that influence the frequency and form of disorders.	
Diathesis-Stress	Abnormality is the product of two interacting factors: a biological or psychological predisposition to disorder and stressors arising from the family, environment, or the person's own behavior that translates the diathesis into an actual disorder.	

was described by teachers as "intelligent," Adam's thoughts (cognitions) became increasingly centered on violence as early as the fifth grade, when he produced "The Big Book of Granny" for a class project. The main character had a gun in her cane and shot people (Sedensky, 2013).

Humanistic psychologists might focus on Adam's need for love and connection that he never received (except via violence), whereas sociocultural factors would point to his easy access to firearms, given U.S. laws and his mother's apparent consent to purchase weapons for him. The incident prompted renewed debate about gun control in the United States and proposals for new legislation banning the sale and manufacture of certain types of semi-automatic firearms and magazines with more than 10 rounds of ammunition.

Adam's vulnerability or diathesis may have been having a mental disorder. In 2005, he was diagnosed as being on the autism spectrum (then called Asperger's). Tutoring, desensitization, and medication were recommended, but Adam refused to take suggested medication and did not engage in suggested behavior therapies (Sedensky, 2013). Although there is no clear evidence that people with autism spectrum disorder are more likely than others to commit violent crimes, there is a subset of people with this disorder who are overrepresented in the criminal justice system (Mouridsen, 2012). Adam's social isolation resulting from his autism spectrum disorder may have been a diathesis that then interacted catastrophically with his life stress—his father and brother leaving, his mother's plan to move and her recent 3-day trip away, his difficulty eating food, and his spreadsheet detailing some of the worst massacres in American history.

As a result of such a wide array of potentially causal elements in the Sandy Hook massacre, a group of mental health professionals produced a research-based position statement. In this statement, they recommended a thoughtful approach to safer schools, guided by four key elements—balance, communication, connectedness, and support—along with strengthened attention to mental health needs in the community, structured threat assessment approaches, revised policies on youth exposure to violent media, and improved policies and practices related to commonsense gun safety (Astor et al., 2013).

Section Review

The diathesis-stress model is an example of a biopsychosocial model that integrates all different kinds of causes together in explaining the occurrence of a mental disorder. The model states that any disorder results from the combined effects of two influences:

- a diathesis, which is a predisposition or vulnerability for that disorder, and
- a stressor, any event significant enough that it causes a person to have to adjust to it. According to this model, stressors are the triggers that convert a predisposition for a disorder into the actual appearance of that disorder.

Scientific Methods and Models of Mental Disorders

So which models of abnormality combine to provide the "correct" explanation for mental disorders such as that of Nelson McGrath in the chapter-opening case or for the Sandy Hook massacre? There is no easy answer to this question. In their search for the causes of mental disorders and for optimal treatments, psychologists—like other scientists—are guided by the scientific method, a set of research principles and methods that helps them to draw valid conclusions about which pieces of the puzzle might be more important for any given mental disorder.

Psychologists test their ideas about the origins and treatment of abnormal behavior by collecting empirical data designed to show whether those ideas are true or false. The process usually starts when the researcher states a hypothesis, a proposition describing how two or more variables are related (e.g., "depression is caused by lack of pleasant social interaction"). Usually, hypotheses are based on whatever model of disorder the researcher finds most convincing—in this example, the psychological model based on learning theory. In any case, as evidence accumulates in support of a hypothesis, the researcher may organize his or her explanations into a theory, a set of propositions used to predict and

scientific method: A systematic process of studying, observing, and recording data to assess the validity of hypotheses.

hypothesis: A theoretical proposition describing how two or more variables are related.

theory: A set of propositions used to predict and explain certain phenomena.

explain certain phenomena. Psychodynamic, behavioral, and cognitive accounts of mental disorders are examples of such theories. But even theories are only tentative explanations, or sets of hypotheses that must be subjected to further scientific evaluation before they can be accepted as valid explanations and guides to future research.

To test a hypothesis empirically, researchers must use methods that allow the hypothesis to be confirmed *or* disconfirmed. Accordingly, the hypothesis must be specific, clear, and stated in terms that have been operationally defined. An **operational definition** is a statement that equates a concept with the exact methods used to represent or measure it. An operational definition of depression, for example, might be a high score on a test that is known to measure depression (e.g., the Beck Depression Inventory-II; Beck, Steer, & Brown, 1996). Two of the most important methods for testing hypotheses are correlational research and experiments.

Correlational Research

A **correlation** is a measure of the degree to which one variable is related to another. When two variables change together in the same direction, they are *positively correlated*. For example, height and weight tend to be positively correlated; taller people usually weigh more than shorter people. When two variables move in opposite directions, they are *negatively correlated*. For example, as more snow falls on a highway, motorists tend to drive slower. If the correlation between two variables is large, knowing about one variable allows for accurate predictions about the second variable.

To test the hypothesis that people feel depressed as a result of having too few pleasant social interactions, a researcher might operationally define "depression" as a score of, say, greater than 28 on the Beck Depression Inventory-II (BDI-II) test and "pleasant social interactions" as the number of conversations during which a person is observed smiling at another person. If these two variables are negatively correlated (the higher the depression score, the fewer smiling conversations), the hypothesis has been supported.

Correlational studies help researchers describe and predict abnormal behavior and evaluate hypotheses about its causes. However, these correlations cannot inform us about *why* two variables are related; that is, they cannot establish that one variable *caused* a change in another. Thus, we do not know whether (1) lack of pleasant social interaction caused depression; (2) depression made people less likely to have pleasant social interactions; or (3) some third factor caused both depression and social withdrawal. For instance, should ice cream be blamed for murders? There is a significant correlation between homicides and ice cream sales—that is, when ice cream sales increase, the rate of homicides also increases (Peters, 2013). Presumably, this does not mean that ice cream is the *cause* of violent behavior (unless you get angry at someone for stealing your cone), but rather that both of these variables are increased by a third variable, such as hot weather.

Experiments

To help them draw cause-effect conclusions about relationships between variables—and thus to choose the most likely explanation for these relationships— researchers conduct experiments. In an **experiment**, the researcher manipulates one variable and measures the effect of this manipulation on a second variable, while holding all other influences constant. The variable that is manipulated by the experimenter is called the **independent variable (IDV)**; the variable that is observed for the effect of the manipulation is called the **dependent variable (DV)**.

In the simplest experiment, the researcher manipulates the independent variable by randomly assigning people to an **experimental group** (which, say, receives treatment for potential cognitive disability, as discussed in this chapter's "Prevention" feature) or to a **control group** (which receives no treatment). The independent variable in this experiment is whether or not the participants receive treatment. The dependent variable here is the degree to which the participants' cognitive abilities improve following treatment or the mere passage of time. In this example, the Abecedarian Project (Campbell et al.,

operational definition: A statement that equates a concept with the exact methods used to represent or measure it.

correlation: A measure of the degree to which one variable is related to another.

experiment: A scientific process of determining cause and effect wherein subjects are randomly assigned to conditions manipulated by a researcher who measures the effect of this manipulation on other variables, while holding all other influences constant.

independent variable (IDV): The variable in an experiment that is manipulated by the experimenter.

dependent variable (DV): The variable in an experiment that is observed to determine the effect of the independent variable.

experimental group: The group that receives an active treatment or manipulation in an experiment.

control group: A group of subjects included in an experiment to control for some variable that could provide an alternative explanation for observed effects on a dependent variable.

2012) showed a wide array of benefits to the treatment group via longitudinal experimental research (i.e., with follow-ups done many years later when the preschool children were 30 years old). **Random assignment** of participants to each condition is vital because it makes it likely that factors such as age, personality characteristics, severity of cognitive disability, and other variables that might affect the dependent variable are distributed randomly, and therefore about equally, between the experimental and control groups. Random assignment, in other words, decreases the chance that variables other than the independent variable will influence the experimenter's results.

Variables that *do* act to confuse or distort results are called **confounding variables**. Their presence makes it harder for researchers to be sure whether the independent variable, the confounding variable, or some combination of the two was responsible for the observed effects on the dependent variable. For example, suppose depressed participants who were randomly assigned to receive a drug treatment improved more than depressed participants in a no-treatment control group. Was the difference due to the drug itself or to the fact that the treated participants had stronger *expectations* for improvement? Perhaps *any* treatment—from drugs to backrubs—that raised their expectations and hope for change would have had the same effect. Even the *experimenter's* expectations about the drug's benefit might have caused her or him to act in a way that gave the treated group greater motivation to improve. Perhaps the parents of the children in the Abecedarian Project had higher hopes for their kids' futures and therefore enrolled them in more enrichment activities throughout their lives.

Improvement stemming solely from expectations or other factors beyond a treatment's active ingredient is known as a **placebo effect**. To assess the role of placebo effects on the dependent variable, researchers often randomly assign some participants to a **placebo control group** that receives an impressive-sounding, but inert or phony, treatment. The progress of the placebo participants is then compared to that of participants in treatment and no-treatment control groups. Of course, if the participants or the therapists know who is receiving real treatment and who is getting placebos, differing expectations for improvement could still bias the results. A **double-blind** study minimizes such bias: Only the director of the experiment knows who is in which group, and everyone else is kept "blind" to the participants' group assignment.

One startling example of the power of placebo occurred in a double-blind study involving patients with osteoarthritis of the knee. One and two years after the surgery, patients in all three groups reported less knee pain and better movement, with no significant differences between the groups (Moseley et al., 2002). This was surprising because two of the groups underwent common surgical procedures—either arthroscopic lavage or arthroscopic débridement of the knee—whereas the third group got only sham surgery (placebo). This placebo group received anesthesia, saw a (fake) video of their surgery, and had skin incisions, but no actual procedure was performed. Yet, they reported similar improvement to the patients who received either of the two actual surgeries.

Regardless of how the initial research is conducted—whether by correlational or experimental research or a hybrid of both—it is essential that the results be subject to **replication**. That is, if the results are duplicated many times with new groups of participants, the researcher can have more confidence that the observed relationship between the independent and dependent variables may be a cause-effect relationship. Accordingly, meta-analyses are becoming more and more important to scientists. These statistical compilations include many different original studies on a given treatment or disorder to yield overall effect sizes or estimates of the overall power of the treatment across multiple replications.

Human Diversity and Research Methods

Replication of research results is important for another reason, as well. Researchers need to know how well their results represent or generalize to people in general, not just their research sample. Do conclusions about social interaction and depression apply to men as well as women? Does the relationship hold among African Americans as well as Asian Americans and Caucasian Americans?

random assignment: A method of assigning members to experimental and control groups such that they have an equal chance of being in either. Random assignment decreases the chance that variables other than the independent variable will influence the result of the experiment.

confounding variable: A variable that confuses or distorts research results, making it difficult to be sure whether the independent variable, confounding variable, or some combination of the two was responsible for observed effects on the dependent variable.

placebo effect: Improvements that result from expectations or other psychological factors rather than from a treatment's active ingredients.

placebo control group: In an experiment, a control group that receives an impressive, but inactive or theoretically inert, treatment.

double-blind study: An experimental design in which only the director of the experiment knows which participants are in the experimental group and which are in the control group.

replication: Repeating a research study with a new group of subjects and/or in a different situation to assess whether prior findings will be found under new circumstances.

To study the effects of human diversity on abnormal behavior, researchers must pay special attention to *sampling*, the methods used for selecting research participants. Ideally, there would be utterly random sampling in which all people on Earth have an equal chance of being included in any given study. In reality, though, it is impossible to draw a truly random sample from the world population, so researchers usually aim for **representative samples** in which participants are selected so as to represent all levels of important participant variables, such as age, gender, and ethnicity. Another option is to focus on a specific participant characteristic and select people as randomly as possible from that group alone. Thus, if researchers are studying whether a treatment that works with adults will also benefit children, they would select their next sample from a diverse population of children. The Abecedarian Project discussed in the "Prevention" feature was based on a sample of 98% African American children in North Carolina. How would these results apply to children of different ethnicities and/or from different regions of the United States or from other countries?

Researchers can also study the impact of human diversity by sampling in such a way that its effects can be analyzed. For example, suppose we are interested in the impact of age or ethnicity on the relationship between social interaction and depression. We can explore these questions by selecting participants in a way that ensures that there are equal numbers of people from each of several age groups and each of several ethnic backgrounds. We can then determine whether the correlation between pleasant social interactions and depression is stronger for people of a particular age or for those in a particular ethnic group.

representative sample: A sample in which participants are selected to represent levels of important subject variables, such as age, gender, and ethnicity; a small group selected from a larger group in such a way that it approximates the characteristics of the larger group.

Understanding Mental Disorders through Scientific Methods

Not surprisingly, the field of abnormal psychology is filled with controversies. Researchers disagree about how best to diagnose mental disorders, what their major causes and consequences are, and how they should be treated. To what extent is schizophrenia inherited? Why are women diagnosed with depression more often than men? Should most children with attention-deficit/hyperactivity disorder be given drugs? Do mental disorders cause people to commit crimes? Can clinicians predict who will be dangerous? Or, as examined in the "Controversy" feature earlier in this chapter, should we study genetic causes of abnormality?

Every chapter of this book includes a special "Controversy" feature that deals with a major dispute about some aspect of abnormal psychology, discusses existing research, and points to gaps in current knowledge. Final answers to controversial questions are difficult to come by, because even though each study provides part of an answer, it also raises new questions that spur researchers to do more research and make new discoveries. Even basic theories about abnormal behavior are constantly being tested, revised, abandoned, and/or refined. Yet, a field without uncertainty and controversy would be a field without progress.

Section Review

The scientific method provides the most vital way for mental health professionals to

- study mental disorders;
- resolve disputes between competing models, theories, or treatment approaches; and
- answer any new questions that arise.

Research can be correlational—examining whether there is a relationship between two variables—or experimental, which involves issues such as sample diversity, random assignment, and control groups to identify causal mechanisms more clearly than other types of research.

Breaking the Cycle of Intergenerational Cognitive Disability

The Head Start program, discussed further in Chapter 3, targets children whose risk for intellectual disability is primarily associated with poverty, not with the intellectual skills of their parent(s). However, parental IQ is a better predictor of the developmental quality of the home environment than family income (Keltner, 1994). For this reason, several programs have targeted infants whose parents have limited intellectual skills (i.e., low IQs). These programs provide a more direct test than Head Start of whether the intergenerational transmission of cultural-familial intellectual delays can be interrupted by early intervention.

One such program was the Abecedarian Project, established in 1972 at the Frank Porter Graham Child Development Center in North Carolina (Ramey & Smith, 1977). The word *abecedarian* refers to one who learns the fundamentals of some area of skill, such as the alphabet. The Abecedarian intervention began in the first 3 months of life and lasted at least until the child's entry into kindergarten. Toddlers participated 6 to 8 hours a day in a nursery school setting, 50 weeks per year. For children 3 and under, the curriculum focused on motor, social, and cognitive skills, often provided in one-to-one instruction. Between ages 3 and 5, small-group instruction was devoted to science, arithmetic,

music, and reading. To test the hypothesis that children in this curriculum would show improved development, selected families were randomly assigned to an intervention or control group. Both groups received free nutritional supplements and health care, but only the intervention group was given the school-based curriculum just described.

Numerous studies have traced the progress of these two groups of children, who are now adults (Ramey & Ramey, 1992; Campbell, Ramey, Pungello, Sparling, & Miller-Johnson, 2002; Campbell et al., 2012). By age 3, the intervention group had IQs that were, on average, 20 points higher than those of children in the control condition. Among control-group mothers with IQs below 70, all but one of their children had IQs in the intellectually disabled or borderline range of intelligence. In contrast, *all* children in the intervention group tested in the normal range of IQ at age 3. The effect of intervention at this age suggested that even children whose intelligence may be influenced partially by heredity are able to benefit from early educational intervention.

Assessments of the Abecedarian children at age 12 showed continuing superiority for the intervention group, although the magnitude of the difference was smaller than it was during the preschool years (Ramey & Ramey,

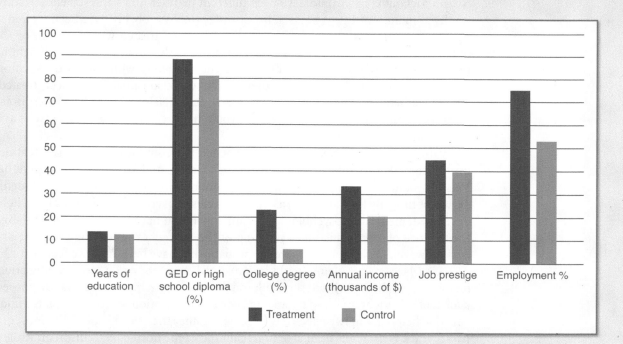

Adult Outcomes for Abecedarian Project Interventions

At age 30, people who had participated in the preschool Abecedarian Project had higher educational attainments and somewhat better financial outcomes than the control group.

Source: Data from Campbell et al. (2012).

Continued

Breaking the Cycle of Intergenerational Cognitive Disability *(Continued)*

1992). The intervention group had IQs that averaged about 5 points higher than the control group. Nearly half of the children in the control group had IQs less than 85, compared with only 13% of the intervention group. And the intervention led to a 50% reduction in the rate of grade failure and to significantly higher reading and mathematical skills. Results showed that intervention group participants earned significantly higher scores on intellectual and academic measures as young adults (age 21), attained significantly more years of total education, were more likely to attend a 4-year college, and showed a reduction in teenage pregnancy compared with preschool controls (Campbell et al., 2002). In other words, the prevention-based treatment was associated with educationally meaningful effect sizes on reading and math skills that persisted into emerging adulthood.

Most impressively, the researchers continued their longitudinal study through the participants' adulthood. Of the original 111 infants enrolled (98% African American), 101 took part in the follow-up when they were 30

years old (Campbell et al., 2012). Overall, the findings provided strong evidence for educational benefits (e.g., 23% of the treatment group had earned a bachelor's degree or higher by age 30 compared with 6% of the control group—see accompanying graph) and mixed evidence for economic benefits (e.g., 75% of the treated group worked full time, whereas 53% of the control group worked full time as adults). However, there was little evidence for treatment-related social adjustment outcomes, such as reduced criminal behavior or higher marital satisfaction as adults (Campbell et al., 2012).

The success of the Abecedarian Project and others like it cast doubt on the idea that ethnic and class differences in intelligence and achievement are immutable facts of life (e.g., Herrnstein & Murray, 1994). We can now be more hopeful that early interventions can prevent intergenerational patterns of cognitive disability (Ramey, 1993). Unfortunately, the positive results of early intervention programs are not typically matched by the public's will to fund them.

Revisiting the Case of Nelson McGrath

Nelson McGrath's fate would have been different in other times and societies. Had Nelson lived in ancient Egypt or Asia, his disorder would probably have been viewed as a sign of demonic possession, and he would have been treated with exorcism or some other religious ritual. In Classical Greece or in the early Roman Empire, he might have received a prescription for moderation in behavior, along with special diets, calming words, and physical therapy. In medieval Europe, Nelson might have been treated as a religious heretic. In the 15th-century Renaissance, Nelson might have been isolated from society in a large asylum, where he would have received little in the way of actual treatment.

By the 18th century, Nelson could have benefitted from the humanitarian treatments introduced by such reformers as Pinel. But as more and larger hospitals were built, Nelson would more than likely have been confined in an institution for an indefinite period of time. By the late 1800s, as the specialties of psychiatry and clinical psychology developed, medical or psychological treatments might have been used with Nelson. In the absence of a scientific understanding of the biology or psychology of most disorders, however, these treatments would probably not have been highly effective for him.

Today, Nelson's problems would be explained as emerging due to a combination of biological, psychological, and sociocultural factors. In fact, his disorder was diagnosed as a form of schizophrenia, and he was treated with medication and behavioral techniques aimed at helping him live effectively in society, rather than in a hospital. For most of the past 5 years, Nelson has been able to remain out of the hospital. His disorder, while not fully understood, is now the subject of research studies around the world. These studies continue to yield important information about the causes and treatment of schizophrenia, to be covered in Chapter 4.

Why was Nelson diagnosed with schizophrenia? How should you interact with someone with schizophrenia? In the previous chapter, we reviewed the processes and criteria by which mental health professionals diagnose and classify abnormal behavior. In the coming chapters, we discuss the various categories of mental disorders in more detail. We describe the major characteristics of each disorder, along with some case examples, and summarize research on causal factors and the most effective methods of treatment. To giv e added perspective to this material, many chapters also include a brief interview with a leading expert on the disorder under discussion, such as our conversation with Dr. Lee Sechrest, an expert on research methods, that concludes this chapter.

As you learn about specific mental disorders in each subsequent chapter of this textbook, we invite you to think critically about all aspects of these disorders: how to prevent, diagnose, and treat them; what causes these disorders and what key questions about them remain unanswered; and, perhaps most important, how to have healthy interactions with all kinds of people with mental disorders without prejudice. For, as Barney (2014) found, your own learning about abnormal psychology can be a vital force for social change, especially for reducing the stigma associated with many mental disorders (discussed in Chapter 1), so that sufferers like Nelson McGrath are treated as fairly as possible by the world around them.

Summary

Making Sense of Abnormality: A Brief History of Early Models of Mental Disorders

We have reviewed the major explanations for abnormal behavior that have prevailed across much of recorded history. From the most ancient civilizations, through the early Greek and Roman periods, and throughout the Middle Ages, supernatural and natural explanations vied for dominance. Depending on which view was most popular, religious rituals or naturalistic therapies were the treatments of choice. Neither proved to be effective. Beginning in the Renaissance and extending through the Enlightenment to the beginning of the 20th century, views of abnormality became more and more naturalistic in orientation, mainly because of the influence of the scientific method. Current models of abnormality combine biological, psychological, and sociocultural explanations, each of which has been supported by results of scientific research.

The Biological Model

Abnormal behavior can be explained in terms of disturbances in the nervous system caused by illness, trauma, or genetic factors. The nervous system has two main parts: the central nervous system (spinal cord and brain) and the peripheral nervous system (composed of the somatic nervous system and the autonomic nervous system). In the autonomic nervous system, the sympathetic division generally increases physiological arousal, preparing the body for action, and the parasympathetic division usually decreases arousal. Malfunctions can occur in any of the main structures of the nervous system, but the forebrain is particularly important because it helps regulate emotion, planning, and thinking and because it is linked to other regulators of the body's functions, such as the glands that make up the endocrine system. Much research has also focused on the role of disturbances in chemical messengers known as neurotransmitters and on the influence of genes. Although genes control the development of every cell and organ of the body, the unique physical and psychological characteristics of each person reflect the interaction between genetic predispositions and the environment. To understand this interaction, behavioral geneticists conduct family, twin, and adoption studies.

Psychological and Sociocultural Models

The first formal psychological theory of abnormal behavior was Sigmund Freud's psychoanalysis. By the middle of the 20th century, several alternative psychological theories had been proposed, including variations on psychoanalysis, as well as behavioral, cognitive, and humanistic theories. Although biological and psychological models of abnormality emphasize internal causes of disorder, sociocultural models point to external factors, such as poverty, stress, and family hardships, as the major causes.

The Diathesis-Stress Model

The diathesis-stress model combines internal factors (the diathesis) with external factors (stressors) to explain abnormal behavior. When a predisposing diathesis is aggravated by a stressor, the risk of developing a disorder increases.

Scientific Methods and Models of Mental Disorders

Scientists collect empirical data to test hypotheses about various models and theories of abnormal behavior. To verify hypotheses, scientists use operational definitions, describing concepts in terms of the operations used to measure them. They then employ correlational and ex-

Lee Sechrest

Source: Reprinted with permission from Dr. Lee Sechrest.

Dr. Lee Sechrest is Professor Emeritus of Psychology at the University of Arizona. He is known widely for his many contributions to research methodology and has been regarded as a leading spokesperson for ensuring that clinical psychology is based on scientific principles and findings.

Abnormal Psychology Research

Q Abnormal psychology texts typically cover biological, psychodynamic, interpersonal, behavioral, cognitive, humanistic, sociocultural, and diathesis-stress explanations of abnormal behavior. Which of these explanations of abnormality do you see as most influential today and why? Which approaches do you see as being most influential in the next century?

A "Most influential" could mean the ideas that are most widely prevalent and that affect the most people; on the other hand, it could mean the ideas that are scientifically most important. In my view, the ideas that have been most influential in determining our views of abnormal behavior are the psychodynamic, biological, and diathesis-stress explanations. That is because the psychodynamic explanation was so widely adopted, but also because it had such substantial correspondence with people's own experiences. Consequently, it became widely influential both among professionals and in the public mind—an influence that was unmerited on the basis of evidence. The biological views of abnormal behavior have existed for centuries, so they have always been influential in determining the views of professionals and the lay public. Finally, diathesis-stress explanations are influential because they square with our everyday experience. It is easy to believe that stress has an important impact on abnormal behavior. In the future, I think a combination of a biological and a sociocultural view of abnormal behavior will be most influential. The biological influence on abnormal behavior cannot be avoided, and I suspect that we will continue to be influenced by the notion that abnormal behaviors are conditioned by social expectations and that a variety of social conditions and pressures come together in some instances to produce phenomena we think of as abnormal behavior.

Q *What do you see as the value and the limitations of scientific methods in making professional decisions about abnormal behavior?*

A The value of scientific methods in making professional decisions about abnormal behavior is that they provide clinicians with relative certainty that their decisions are the best available under the circumstances. Scientific methods also provide uniformity with respect to the treatment of patients or clients. It may be true that some individual clinicians are astonishingly good at what they do, but a great many are not, or would not be if they did not have guidance from the scientific literature. It is still possible for the best clinicians to go beyond what the written prescriptions might be from the literature and to elaborate on them in useful ways and to try new things.

The two greatest limitations of reliance on scientific methods are, first of all, that clinical acts and clinical decisions are made in real time, and science can be slow and plodding; therefore, it takes a long time for science to produce information that is useful. Second, there is often a considerable difference between the nature of scientific studies and the work that clinicians actually have to do. Science cannot guarantee that it will produce findings that are immediately relevant and that will answer questions that clinicians have, such as, "Well, what exactly should I do now?"

Q *Should clinicians be allowed to use only therapy techniques that are empirically validated in controlled experimental research?*

A We have to have better theory so that, if clinicians are using interventions or following plans that are not substantiated by research, they should at least be closely guided by the theory toward which the research is contributing. Whether they should stick to empirically validated methods depends, in my view, on two things: (1) who is paying for their work, and (2) how their work is presented to their clients and the public. If clinicians do not ask the public—either through public legislation or through insurance—to pay for what they do, then I have no objection to anything they do, whether it is empirically validated or not, as long as it is not harmful. I have sometimes referred to this in relation to the FTC regulations regarding toys. Toys must be safe; they need not necessarily be any fun. But clinicians should not be allowed to pretend that what they are doing has been scientifically validated when there is no basis for their clinical work. When clinicians engage in experimental treatments, even within the context of a generally scientific approach, patients or clients should know that the interventions they are receiving are experimental in nature, that they are not validated. Furthermore, if clinicians want to be paid by public funds or through insurance companies, I think that their work should be based directly on what has been evaluated and what has been shown to be effective. They should not simply follow their own theoretical bent or other predilections without regard for whether they have been validated.

Q *Where do you stand on the question of what is abnormal behavior?*

A I have a fairly restricted view of abnormal behavior. I do not believe that all behavior that we call abnormal because it is statistically infrequent or because it bothers us should be regarded as psychopathology. Much of what we see as abnormal behavior and even psychopathology is really a manifestation of the range of human behaviors; that is, that people differ—some people are more intact, some people are more effective, some people are easier to deal with than others. The idea of labeling every human frailty and every human foible and every difficulty that people have as psychopathology and suppose that it could be cured or even substantially altered by psychologically oriented clinicians is simply wrong. We may be able to effect changes in people's behavior over brief periods of time and under special conditions, but we are not changing the people, themselves, fundamentally. We are not capable of taking, let's say, an introverted person who is shy and unresponsive to people and changing that person into a party animal, someone who is outgoing and expansive. People are just different in this way, so I want to confine clinical efforts to what I see as the major forms of psychopathology that most closely resemble what we would think of as diseases.

Q *In historical perspective, from Hippocrates to today, what do you see as the three most important developments in efforts to explain psychopathology?*

A The three most important developments in understanding psychopathology are the discovery of the mind, the discovery of the brain, and the discovery of religion. The discovery of the mind and the idea that behavior is related to people's views of the world and to their perceptions must have been a slow process, but once that process led to the discovery that people had minds, their abnormal behaviors came to be seen in a different kind of way. The discovery of the brain— by that I mean the discovery that what goes on in the brain has implications for behavior—is also a fairly profound discovery because it led to the connection of behavior to what's going on in the body and the notion that we might intervene at the somatic level to produce changes at the behavioral level and maybe vice versa. Finally, one of the critical things that is related to religion is the recognition and the generation of guilt, and I think that was an important element in our views of psychopathology—the notion that people's behavior could be influenced by their morals and that internal states such as guilt resulting from misbehavior and so on could result in psychopathology.

In another way, the three most important developments could be seen as Freud, the DSM (the official classification system of mental disorders in North America), and the explosion of knowledge about the brain. Freud was important because he conditioned the views of psychopathology for nearly a century. His influence was enormous, although I think much of his doctrine was ultimately incorrect. The *DSM* was an important development in framing our approach to psychopathology because it provided a set of diagnostic categories suggesting that disordered behaviors could be classified as diseases. This had great influence on our approaches to explaining and treating psychopathology, and it threatens to continue to distort our views. Finally, brain science has been important because it is increasing our understanding of the workings of the brain and of the relationships between events in the brain and events in the rest of the body and in behavior. I think that it is tremendously important to know that behavior can stem from biological sources.

perimental research methods to test their hypotheses. Correlational studies help describe and predict abnormal behavior, but cannot explain why two variables are related or confirm that a change in one variable actually caused a change in another. To draw causal conclusions, scientists conduct experiments, studies in which one variable—the independent variable—is manipulated, and its effect on a second variable—the dependent variable—is observed. To guard against the distortion of placebo effects and other confounding variables, true experiments include random assignment of participants to experimental and various control groups. Especially in treatment studies, double-blind designs are vital to protect against experimenter bias. Regardless of the designs used, researchers try to study samples of people who represent the full range of human diversity. This effort makes it more likely that research results will be widely applicable.

Key Terms

abnormal behavior, p. 44
acetylcholine, p. 54
adoption study, p. 56
appraisal, p. 65
attribution, p. 66
axon, p. 54
behavior modification, p. 64
behavior therapy, p. 62
behavioral genetics, p. 56
behavioral theory, p. 62
biological model, p. 51
biopsychosocial model, p. 73
cerebral cortex, p. 53
cerebrum, p. 53
classical conditioning, p. 63
clinical psychology, p. 50
cognitive theory, p. 65
cognitive therapy, p. 66
concordance rate, p. 56
confounding variable, p. 77
control group, p. 76
correlation, p. 76
culture-bound syndrome, p. 71
defense mechanism, p. 60
dendrite, p. 54
deoxyribonucleic acid (DNA), p. 55
dependent variable (DV), p. 76
developmental psychopathology, p. 73
diathesis, p. 73
diathesis-stress model, p. 72
dopamine, p. 54
double-blind study, p. 77
ecological model, p. 69
ego, p. 59
ego analyst, p. 60

empathy, p. 68
endocrine system, p. 52
epigenetics, p. 56
etiological factor, p. 51
experiment, p. 76
experimental group, p.76
extinction, p. 62
family study, p. 56
forebrain, p. 51
gamma-aminobutyric acid (GABA),
    p. 54
gene, p. 55
genotype, p. 55
heritability, p. 56
hindbrain, p. 51
hormone, p. 51
humanistic model, p. 67
hypothalamus, p. 51
hypothesis, p. 75
hysteria, p. 50
id, p. 59
independent variable (IDV), p. 76
interpersonal theory, p. 61
learning theory, p. 62
libido, p. 59
medical model, p. 51
midbrain, p. 51
models of abnormality, p. 51
neuron, p. 54
neuroscience, p. 51
neurotransmitter, p. 54
norepinephrine, p. 54
nucleotide, p. 55
object relations theory, p. 60
observational learning, p. 65

operant conditioning, p. 62
operational definition, p. 76
penetrance, p. 55
phenotype, p. 55
pituitary gland, p. 53
placebo control group, p. 77
placebo effect, p. 77
pleasure principle, p. 59
psychiatrist, p. 48
psychoanalysis, p. 59
punishment, p. 62
random assignment, p. 77
rational emotive therapy (RET), p. 66
reality principle, p. 60
reinforcement, p. 62
replication, p. 77
representative sample, p. 78
repression, p. 60
resilience, p. 69
reuptake, p. 54
scientific method, p. 75
self-efficacy, p. 65
serotonin, p. 54
social causation theory, p. 70
social drift hypothesis, p. 70
social learning theory, p. 65
social relativism, p. 71
sociocultural model, p. 69
stressor, p. 73
superego, p. 60
synapse, p. 54
thalamus, p. 51
theory, p. 75
twin study, p. 57

Disorders of Childhood and Adolescence

Source: alphaspirit/Shutterstock.com.

Chapter Outline

A Developmental Perspective

Classification and Diagnosis of Children's Disorders

Neurodevelopmental Disorders

Oppositional Defiant and Conduct Disorders

After reading this chapter, you will be able to answer the following key questions:

- How does child development generally unfold, and at what points might disorders occur?

- What are the key disorders that typically first present in childhood or adolescence, and how are they described in the *DSM-5*?

- What are the possible causes of these disorders?

- What are the best treatments for these disorders?

From the Case of Tom

Tom was 7 when his mother called a child psychiatry clinic asking for an evaluation of attention problems. She told the intake worker that Tom's teacher had complained all year about his "tuning out" in the classroom and not finishing assignments. At home, he never listened to his parents. Tom's mother had read a magazine article about children with attention problems, and according to her, Tom had every single one of the 10 warning signs.

During their first visit to the clinic, Tom and his parents were interviewed by a clinical child psychologist, and many of the mother's concerns were verified. Tom *did* have significant problems getting things done. He was forgetful, and he was always losing his lunch and homework. But this was not the whole story. Tom's problems, the psychologist learned, had begun years before. As a baby, he had been difficult, often fussy, and unusually fearful of new situations. As a preschooler, he was reluctant to join the other kids in play. His family life had not been easy either. When Tom was 10 months old, his mother returned to full-time work, and he was placed in daycare about 40 hours a week. He cried and screamed when his mother left him in the morning, and he was angry and resistant when she came to get him at the end of the day. His parents had experienced considerable marital friction during Tom's early years, including a couple of arguments that got out of hand in front of him. Shortly after the birth of Tom's younger brother, when Tom was 3, his parents separated. Tom's mother was subsequently treated for depression. Tom began to experience stomachaches and to worry about the safety of his parents when he was away from them. He also reported social anxiety in school and challenges in connecting with other kids.

In addition to these anxiety-related symptoms, Tom's inattention was a problem in school. This issue was compounded by what Tom did and thought about when he was not paying attention. Usually, he was thinking about his favorite activity—fishing! When Tom was not doing his work at school, he was drawing pictures of fish, or daydreaming about fishing, or pretending that his pencils were fishing poles and his paper clips were fish. At home, Tom would spend hours playing with his dad's fishing gear, casting his line into an imaginary stream in the backyard. Sometimes, he would refuse to go to school, wanting to stay home and "fish." When he played with other children—which was not too often—he always wanted to talk about fishing, a topic that quickly grew boring to others.

As the initial clinic visit drew to a close, Tom's parents bombarded the psychologist with questions: Did he have an attention disorder? Could their marital conflicts have had anything to do with this? Were Tom's problems the early signs of something really serious or simply a difficult phase that he would grow out of? Was medication the answer?

If Tom's clinic visit had taken place 50 years ago, his parents' questions would have been very difficult for the psychologist to answer. Only within the past few decades has research capable of answering these questions been done. In previous years, clinical research focused far more on *adult* mental disorders than on children's problems. Children were regarded simply as miniature adults, and their problems were viewed as less-intense versions of adult disorders.

Longitudinal studies have allowed investigators to follow the same group of children across time into adolescence, and in some studies, into adulthood. Longitudinal studies have advantages over **retrospective research**, in which adults with a given disorder are asked to recall information about their childhood, resulting in potentially biased accounts of childhood experiences (Sroufe, Egeland, Carlson, & Collins, 2005; Sroufe, 2005). As discussed in Chapter 2, prospective longitudinal methods give researchers the opportunity to examine the many outcomes associated with childhood problems and to analyze the conditions that make positive and negative outcomes likely. Thanks in part to these advances, and to increased attention to various theories of child development, psychologists can now better appreciate the complex interaction of factors that affect disorders of childhood, a field known as **developmental psychopathology** (Rutter & Sroufe, 2000).

In this chapter, we first provide a developmental perspective on childhood and adolescence, followed by a description of the classification of the disorders that typically occur during this period. Then we discuss these *DSM-5 (Diagnostic and Statistical Manual of Mental Disorders)* disorders, which include neurodevelopmental disorders, behavioral disorders involving disruptive, aggressive, and antisocial behavior, and other disorders of childhood in greater detail. Finally, we review what has been learned about the questions Tom's parents asked, discuss how we might explain Tom's problems, and describe the treatments Tom received and how well they worked.

A Developmental Perspective

Developmental perspectives of child development provide a framework for understanding how experiences in infancy and early childhood are linked to disorders appearing during middle childhood, adolescence, and even adulthood. In a classic essay introducing the basic tenets of developmental psychopathology, Alan Sroufe and Michael Rutter (1984) listed important **developmental tasks** that children must accomplish as they grow from infancy to adolescence. These tasks, originally described by well-known developmental

longitudinal study: A study in which an investigator repeatedly assesses the same individuals or variables over a period of time.

retrospective research: Research done by asking respondents about past experiences.

developmental psychopathology: A field of study that focuses on how problems that first appear in childhood or adolescence are linked to disorders occurring later in life.

developmental task: A psychological or cognitive task to be mastered during the course of development from infancy through adolescence; these tasks form a foundation for later learning and adjustment.

TABLE 3.1 Developmental Tasks Crucial to Later Competence

Age (years)	Tasks
0–1	Regulating biological needs such as hunger and thirst; forming effective attachment to parent(s)
1–3	Exploring the environment; experimenting and manipulating objects; using parents as a "secure base" while developing autonomy; responding to external (parental) control of impulses; using language
3–5	Developing self-reliance and flexible self-control of impulses; learning to take initiatives; identifying with same-sex parent to form sense of gender; establishing effective peer contacts; learning to empathize
6–12	Acquiring an understanding of fairness and equity; developing gender constancy; forming same-sex friendships; gaining a sense of "industry" or competence; adjusting to demands of school
13+	Learning to take different perspectives and engage in "as if" thinking; forming loyal friendships; separating from family and developing a unique identity.

Source: Adapted from Sroufe & Rutter (1984).

theorists such as Erik Erickson, Jean Piaget, John Bowlby, and Lawrence Kohlberg, are the foundation on which a child's later adjustment depends. Examples of these tasks include forming an effective *attachment relationship* with a parent during infancy, attaining *empathy* and *self-reliance* during the preschool years, developing *academic competence* during the middle-school years, and developing *autonomy* (or separating from the family) during later adolescence. All are critical in setting the stage for normal social and emotional development (see Table 3.1).

Developmental Tasks and Mental Disorders

A child's quality of adaptation or "fit" with the environment can be expressed in terms of how well and in what manner developmental tasks have been mastered. The major link between developmental tasks and mental disorders is that a *child's failure to effectively handle an early developmental task can impair his or her capacity to handle later tasks successfully*. Early problems in completing a developmental task may increase the likelihood of later maladaptation and the child's need for support from the environment to succeed with later tasks. In the case of Tom from the chapter-opening case, his developmental trajectory through age 7 suggests an increased risk for adolescent difficulties, perhaps in the areas of *separation and individuation* (Meeus, Iedema, Maassen, & Engels, 2005). This parallel process is a critical transition in which adolescents begin to decrease contact with family and to develop their own personal identity. Given Tom's pattern of poor adaptation in early life, when he is a teenager, he might require a parent who can understand and support his pursuit of independence more than teenagers who have less-troubled developmental histories.

Viewing a child's problems in relation to developmental tasks shows more clearly how a child's efforts to adapt to an unfavorable or threatening caregiving environment might lead to deficits later on (Cicchetti & Toth, 2009). For example, some infants learn that it is best to avoid or minimize contact with an abusive parent. Although this might be an adaptive short-term response, in the long term, the lost opportunity to use an adult caregiver as a secure base from which to gather emotional support may cripple that child's ability to be close with others (Sroufe et al., 2005).

"A raise in my allowance is fine, dad. But what I'm really after is power of attorney."

Source: Cartoonresource/Shutterstock.com.

Developmental psychopathologists believe that a child's progress with important developmental tasks is a powerful predictor of later functioning. For this reason, it is important to consider not only the symptoms listed in the *DSM-5* but also a child's patterns of adaptation to these specific developmental tasks (Sroufe & Rutter, 1984).

Analyzing Development: The Example of Attachment

To study the consequences of problems in accomplishing developmental tasks, researchers must first have reliable methods for studying performance on these tasks. One such method is the **Strange Situation**, a 20-minute laboratory assessment of infant-parent attachment developed by psychologist Mary Ainsworth (Ainsworth, Blehar, Waters, & Wall, 1978). The Strange Situation allows an experimenter to observe how an infant responds to separations from a parent, usually the mother. It begins when the parent and infant are brought into a room containing toys. A stranger then enters the room, and after a couple of minutes, the parent is cued to depart, leaving the infant with the stranger. The parent then returns for a reunion with the child. Later, the parent leaves the infant alone in the room again and then returns once more for a final reunion.

Infants respond to this series of separations and reunions in a variety of ways. Most explore the room and the toys at first, but their interest in exploration wanes when the stranger enters. Most infants also protest strongly when the parent first leaves, and they make strong efforts to regain physical contact when the parent returns. Some infants, though, become upset when the parent leaves and cannot be comforted when the parent returns. Others show little emotional distress when the parent leaves and actually *avoid* the parent when he or she returns to the room.

Ainsworth and later researchers used these variations in how infants respond to the Strange Situation to describe several attachment patterns. The most common pattern—in which infants show moderate separation distress, coupled with a strong approach to the parent during reunions—is called **secure attachment**. Researchers have also identified three patterns of **insecure attachment**: (1) minimal separation distress and avoidance of the parent during reunion, (2) excessive and unrelenting separation distress manifested by resistance and anger that is not relieved when the parent returns to the room, and (3) contradictory, undirected, or confused behaviors during reunion (Main & Hesse, 1990; Sroufe et al., 2005).

What do infants' responses to the Strange Situation mean? In longitudinal studies, children who as infants showed secure behavior during the Strange Situation function better later in life than children who showed any of the three insecure attachment patterns (Sroufe et al., 2005). For example, people who were securely attached to their parent as children were more likely to report mutually supportive adult relationships; conversely, those who were insecurely attached endorsed statements more frequently as adults such as "I am uncomfortable being close to others" or "I find that others are reluctant to get as close as I would like" (Hazan & Shaver, 1987). In an interview study of more than 100 adults, 80% of those who had been involved in a romantic relationship for at least 2 years were primarily attached to their partners (Hazan, 1992). However, most of the rest were still primarily attached to a parent, as are many college students (how about you?). Thus, these attachment patterns tend to persist throughout our lives.

Because insecure infants are at greater risk for behavioral problems in childhood and adolescence (Greenberg, Speltz, & De-Klyen, 1993; Sroufe et al., 2005), many clinicians believe that early attachment difficulties play a major role in the development of mental disorders. However, it is important to note that results from longitudinal research on child development indicate that other experiences, such as early peer relationships, also have a

Strange Situation: A laboratory assessment of infant-parent attachment that allows observation of how an infant responds to separations from parents.

secure attachment: A pattern of infant-parent attachment in which infants show moderate separation distress, coupled with a strong approach to the parent during reunions.

insecure attachment: A pattern of infant-parent attachment in which infants show minimal separation distress, coupled with avoidance of the parent during reunions.

Source: Piotr Marcinski/Shuttestock.com.

In the Strange Situation task, the child and parent are first taken to a room where they play with toys. After a stranger enters the room, the parent is asked to leave, and the child's response is noted. The parent returns shortly thereafter. If the child has formed a secure attachment with the parent, he or she will be soothed by the parent's return. If the attachment is insecure (a risk factor for later developmental problems), the child's distress will not be easily calmed by a reunion with the parent.

significant influence on long-term outcomes (Sroufe et al., 2005). In fact, modern developmental psychopathology models suggest that developmental pathways are more complex than originally thought (Rutter & Sroufe, 2000).

Section Review

A developmental perspective on psychopathology requires:

- prospective longitudinal studies of the effects of childhood experiences,
- understanding of how mastery of major developmental tasks provides the building blocks for adolescent and adult competence, and
- tracing the long-term consequences of problems in developmental tasks, such as infant attachment, through research methods such as the Strange Situation.

Classification and Diagnosis of Children's Disorders

Efforts to classify children's disorders follow one of two strategies: a categorical or a dimensional approach. As noted in Chapter 1, the *categorical approach* assumes that mental disorders, like physical disorders, have relatively clear boundaries that distinguish normal behavior from abnormal behavior and one disorder from another. Disorders are like "boxes" into which an individual can be placed, depending on the particular behaviors (or symptoms) shown. In contrast, the *dimensional approach* assumes that most forms of mental disorders are *not* categorically different from normal behavior, so psychopathology is described along one or more continuous dimensions that reflect the degree to which the child shows a maladaptive behavior or emotion.

As discussed in Chapter 1, the *DSM-5* is the most widely used categorical approach for mental disorders in North America. Clinicians using the *DSM-5* begin the diagnostic process with hypotheses about which disorders (or diagnostic categories) are most relevant to the child's main problems. Then they interview the child, the parents, and sometimes, teachers or daycare workers to confirm or rule out the presence of various symptoms. One strategy for improving the reliability of children's diagnostic categories is to use *structured interviews* in which the order and wording of diagnostic questions are standardized. Clinicians might also administer formal psychological tests to the child, as described in Chapter 1.

Clinicians or researchers who employ a dimensional approach favor different methods, however. They usually assess the child's psychopathology by asking parents or teachers to complete behavior checklists that rate the extent to which the child shows specified problem behaviors or social competencies in the home or in the classroom. The resulting data are subjected to statistical procedures to determine which maladaptive behaviors should be grouped together. One widely used and well-researched dimensional method is the Child Behavior Checklist, or CBCL (Achenbach, 1997). Statistical techniques, such as factor analysis, of the CBCL have uncovered two broad dimensions of child behavior problems, called *externalizing* and *internalizing*. **Externalizing problems** represent an excess of undesirable behavior. They are primarily disruptive behaviors that are a nuisance to others, such as aggression, hyperactivity, or impulsivity. **Internalizing problems** refer to maladaptive problems in which there are deficits in desired behaviors, usually accompanied by subjective distress in the child—for example, failing to interact with peers or avoiding school because of anxiety or a depressed mood. Child psychologists commonly use these two dimensions to describe problematic behavior.

externalizing problem:
A disruptive childhood behavior that is a nuisance to others, such as aggression, hyperactivity, impulsivity, or inattention.

internalizing problem:
A deficit in desired child behaviors, usually accompanied by subjective distress in the child.

Section Review

Clinicians can classify children's disorders using:

- a categorical approach such as the *DSM-5* or
- a dimensional approach, using standardized tests such as the Child Behavior Checklist.

The primary dimensions of childhood psychopathology are:

- the externalizing dimension, involving excesses of unwanted or disruptive behaviors, and
- the internalizing dimension, involving deficits in desirable behaviors.

Neurodevelopmental Disorders

neurodevelopmental disorders: In the *DSM-5*, a category of disorders that affect children and adolescents and involve impairment in brain development or functioning. The neurodevelopmental disorders include intellectual disability, autism spectrum disorder, specific learning disorder, and attention-deficit/ hyperactivity disorder.

gross motor skill: The ability to control large muscle movements and body posture.

Several of the psychological disorders that affect children and adolescents are classified in the *DSM-5* as **neurodevelopmental disorders**. All disorders that fall into this category involve impairment in brain development or functioning that affects the child's emotional, cognitive, or psychosocial development. The neurodevelopmental disorders include:

1. Intellectual disability
2. Autism spectrum disorder (ASD)
3. Specific learning disorder
4. Attention-deficit/hyperactivity disorder (ADHD)

To set the stage for the discussion of neurodevelopmental disorders, we begin by providing a brief overview of the different areas or *domains* of growth in a child's developmental progress and the ages at which young children are expected to master certain skills. These expectations illustrate the usual sequence of progressively developing more-advanced skills that build on each other, and they define approximate standards for diagnosing neurodevelopmental disorders. As stated previously, it is important for clinicians to understand the normal course of human development and how disruptions in that course might lead to the disorders discussed in this chapter.

"There's nothing I like more than creating content."

Source: Cartoonresource/Shutterstock.com.

fine motor skill: Involved in smaller movements that occur in the wrists, hands, fingers, feet and toes; fine motor skills coordinate actions such as picking up objects between the thumb and finger, writing carefully, and even blinking.

visual-motor skills: The ability to control eye-hand coordination.

Domains of Development

Research by developmental psychologists has helped establish the ages at which infants and children typically reach important developmental milestones, such as smiling, talking, and walking. However, the rate of development varies considerably, both among children and for the same child across different developmental domains, which are typically divided into four categories: motor skills, language, cognition, and adaptive functioning. Consequently, a sizeable minority of normal children will not achieve a particular milestone at the same age that the "average" child does. Nevertheless, age norms provide a rough gauge as to whether a given child is significantly behind or ahead of schedule.

Table 3.2 outlines the typical course of a child's development in two domains: motor skills and language. Motor skills include **gross motor skills**, which refer to success in controlling large movements involving body posture and moving from one place to another, and **fine motor** and **visual-motor skills**, which include upper extremity and hand and finger movements, as well as eye-hand coordination. Early language development involves progress in both **expressive language**, the use of language to communicate one's thoughts or needs, and **receptive language**, the understanding of language. In most infants, receptive abilities precede expressive skills. The babbling and other vocalizations heard during an infant's first year are forerunners of expressive language. By age 2, typical infants know at least 50 words in their native language.

Skills in another key domain, cognition, are more difficult to assess in infancy and early childhood. **Cognition** refers to a variety of mental processes that determine the individual's capacity to learn, to retain acquired information, and to use such information to solve problems in a flexible and creative way. Before children can speak, assessment of cognitive skills typically revolves around the child's progress in other related areas, such

TABLE 3.2 Developmental Milestones: Motor and Language Skills

Average Age	Language Milestones	Motor Milestones
6 months	Cooing changes to distinct babbling by introduction of consonants	Sits using hands for support; rolls over; unilateral reaching
1 year	Beginning of language understanding; one-word utterances	Pulls to stand; walks holding on to furniture ("cruising") or hand
12–18 months	Says several single words; has repertoire of approximately 30–50 words; points to show what he or she wants	Grasping and release fully developed; walking; creeps downstairs backward; drinks from cup; eats with spoon
18–24 months	Uses two-word phrases; has vocabulary of 50 to several hundred words	Begins to run; walks up stairs with assistance
2 years	Learns new words nearly every day; says two- to four-word sentences; follows simple instructions; points to pictures when named	Jumps with both feet; builds tower of six cubes; climbs without help; throws ball overhead
3 years	Uses full sentences; has few errors; has vocabulary of around 1,000 words; follows multiple-step instructions; carries on conversation using two to three sentences	Runs easily; walks stairs with alternating feet; pedals a tricycle
4 years	Has close to adult speech competence	Jumps over rope; hops on one foot; walks on a line

Source: Adapted from the Centers for Disease Control and Prevention (2014a).

as physical, motor, sensory, or early language abilities. Additionally, a good predictor of later cognitive performance among young children is **habituation speed**, or the amount of time it takes an infant to habituate (or lose interest in) a repetitively presented stimulus. Six-month-old infants with relatively long habituation times are more likely to have low IQs in later childhood than are infants with shorter habituation times (Bornstein & Sigman, 1986; Bornstein et al., 2006).

Psychologists typically assess cognitive ability in post-infancy children, adolescents, and adults with standardized intelligence tests, such as the Stanford-Binet Intelligence Scale and the Weschler Intelligence Scale for Children (WISC-IV; Wechsler, 2003), discussed in Chapter 1. Such tests involve a series of problem-solving tasks ordered by difficulty that assess a variety of domains, including verbal abilities (e.g., identifying the way in which two words are conceptually similar), perceptual reasoning (e.g., putting together a puzzle), working memory, and processing speed. Performance on intelligence tests is usually described in terms of IQ scores. Today, intelligence tests use *deviation IQ scores*; that is, they indicate the child's relative standing in a group of same-aged children. The score distribution has a mean of 100 and a standard deviation of 15. Thus, if a 5-year-old child has a *raw score* (the number of correctly answered test items) that is one standard deviation below the *average* raw score for 5-year-olds, he or she has an IQ score of 85 (100 × 15 = 85).

Intelligence tests are widely used to assess children, and IQ scores figure prominently in definitions of intellectual disability and learning disorders. However, these tests have been criticized for measuring a narrow range of skills. Critics argue that IQ tests fail to capture both what is important for everyday survival and what is truly exceptional achievement (Gardner, 1993). They may also underestimate the cognitive abilities of individuals from cultures that differ substantially from that of the test developers (MacMillan, Gresham, & Siperstein, 1993; Reynolds, 2000). For example, a picture recognition test that assesses a child's ability to name various farm animals would probably be biased against children from an urban background; conversely, a child who grew up in

expressive language: Language that is used to communicate thoughts or needs.

receptive language: The understanding of language.

cognition: Mental processes involved in an individual's capacity to learn, understand, retain, and use information.

habituation speed: The amount of time it takes to habituate, or lose interest in, a repetitively presented stimulus.

MAPS - Prejudicial Pigeonholes

Chapter 3 Disorders of Childhood and Adolescence

a country without mandatory schooling would do poorly on tests designed to measure factual knowledge typically taught in school.

adaptive behavior: Behavior that enables an individual to meet the cultural expectations for independent functioning associated with a particular age.

Adaptive behaviors represent another important developmental domain. They enable an individual to meet the cultural expectations for independent functioning associated with a particular age. At the age of 5, children in the United States, for example, are expected to be toilet trained, to use utensils to feed themselves, and to be emotionally capable of being away from their parents for several hours a day at school. Although adaptive behavior is clearly influenced by other skills (e.g., using money correctly requires the ability to count), it cannot be fully explained by intelligence or other types of skills. For example, most of us know someone who is intellectually skilled but lacks common sense in handling the challenges of everyday life.

Measurement of adaptive behavior usually involves observations by parents or teachers. Tests of adaptive behavior include the Vineland Adaptive Behavior Scales (Sparrow, Balia, & Cicchetti, 1984) and the American Association on Mental Retardation Adaptive Behavior Scale (Nihira, Leland, & Lambert, 1993). Both tests use a structured interview in which detailed questions about an individual's behavior are used to establish the level of adaptive skill. Research with large samples of children, adolescents, and adults has established the ages at which most individuals display specific adaptive skills. The number of items successfully passed on these tests can be converted to a score distribution that, like IQ tests, has a mean of 100 and a standard deviation of 15.

Although standardized tests of adaptive functioning, such as the Vineland, help establish realistic expectations about development, it is essential to remember that different children develop adaptive skills at different rates. Just because a child is slow to acquire a certain skill does not mean that the child will inevitably remain delayed or show deficits in that skill in adulthood. Not every developmental delay is a symptom of a disorder. Many children go through periods when their speech is a bit hard to understand or they reverse letters when spelling certain words. These behaviors are usually a normal part of development, not a sign of disorder. As long as clinicians and parents keep these caveats in mind, the concept of adaptive behavior is a useful supplement to IQ in the definition of intellectual disability.

Section Review

Research by developmental psychologists has helped establish the ages at which infants and children typically reach important developmental milestones across the following four domains:

- motor skills, such as walking;
- language (i.e., talking);
- cognition, such as how they think and solve problems; and
- adaptive functioning, including toilet training and other skills for independence.

Although the rate of development varies considerably, both among children and for the same child across different developmental domains, knowledge of typical developmental patterns can help shed light on abnormal behaviors and potential mental disorders.

Intellectual Disability

intellectual disability: Significantly subaverage intellectual functioning occurring before the age of 18 that is associated with significant limitations in adaptive functioning.

Intellectual disability (formerly *mental retardation*) is diagnosed when an individual has below-average intellectual functioning and impairments in adaptive functioning (i.e., problems with independently meeting the demands of daily living) that occur prior to the age of 18. Although previous versions of the *DSM* required an IQ score of less than 70 (two standard deviations below average) to make a diagnosis of intellectual disability, the *DSM-5* does not indicate that a specific IQ score is *required* to make this diagnosis, although it suggests that a similar cutoff range be employed (i.e., an IQ of 65–75).

A Classification of Intellectual Disability

How many people meet the criteria for intellectual disability? The answer depends on the criteria used to reach a diagnosis, but the worldwide prevalence is between 1 and

3%. People with intellectual disability differ considerably in intellectual impairment and personality characteristics. Researchers have organized this diversity by developing sub-groups of intellectual disability:

- *Mild intellectual disability.* Subtle deficits in adaptive behavior and an IQ of 50–70 characterize mild intellectual disability. About 85% of all persons with intellectual disability fall into this category. Children with mild intellectual disability are delayed in their acquisition of basic language and cognitive abilities. However, their slower-than-average rate of development may not become obvious until middle childhood or adolescence. Before middle childhood, their near-normal social and communication skills allow children with mild intellectual disability to get by and acquire basic academic skills, albeit with intense effort. These children can usually acquire what Americans consider third- to approximately sixth-grade skills. However, in middle childhood (10–12 years), when typical children show more complex cognitive and communication skills (such as advanced problem solving), the limitations of children with mild intellectual disability become more obvious. It is at this point that many show problems in their thinking skills, awkwardness in social relationships, and poor emotional control. As adults, most persons with mild intellectual disability hold semiskilled jobs and get married, although during stressful periods, their parenting skills and ability to take care of themselves may suffer, and they may require some guidance and support.

- *Moderate intellectual disability.* Moderate intellectual disability is associated with an IQ score ranging from 35–49 and limited adaptive behavior. About 10% of individuals with intellectual disability function in this range of impairment. In early childhood, individuals show significant delays in language and cognitive skills and sometimes in motor abilities. Most eventually develop expressive language, although speech errors remain common. Most persons with moderate intellectual disability can learn to read and do simple addition and subtraction problems. In adult life, the majority can perform unskilled jobs in a closely supervised setting; a few are able to work under less-supervised conditions when job tasks are routine and the goal is well specified (e.g., lawn mowing, laundry, assembly-line work). Most adults with moderate intellectual disability live in supervised group homes where assistance with personal finances and health care are provided.

- *Severe intellectual disability.* Severe impairment is indicated by an IQ score of 20–34 and marked adaptive behavior impairments. About 3–4% of persons with intellectual disability fall in this category. In early childhood, their verbal communication is limited. By late middle childhood, the majority can talk, although articulation may be compromised, and the content of speech is simple. Although some people with severe intellectual disability can be taught to recognize survival words on road signs, store signs, and product labels, most do not learn to read. Motor and visual-motor deficits are common and may limit capabilities for self-care and vocational training. Even in the absence of motor problems, however, cognitive limitations usually lead to poor adaptive behaviors, and help with self-care is often required. Vocational opportunities are usually limited to simple assembly work in sheltered workshops.

- *Profound intellectual disability.* About 1–2% of persons with intellectual disability fall within this category, displaying an IQ below 20. Pervasive neurological damage is almost always present, and it has significant adverse effects on all developmental domains. Gross motor deficits usually limit locomotion; many are wheelchair bound. Constant supervision is required, and self-care is nearly impossible without assistance. Individuals with profound intellectual disability do not usually acquire speech, but many develop a repertoire of vocalizations for use in greeting others and signaling basic needs.

Causes of Intellectual Disability

Intellectual disability results from biological factors, psychosocial factors, or a combination of the two. Biological causes include genetic disorders, infectious diseases, and maternal alcohol use during pregnancy. Such factors account for 25–50% of all cases of intellectual disability. The remaining 50–75% of cases result from psychosocial causes, including exposure to impoverished environments lacking in intellectual stimulation.

Down syndrome: A form of intellectual disability caused by a genetic malfunction on chromosome 21.

trisomy 21: Three chromosomes instead of the normal two on pair 21; another name for Down syndrome.

Down Syndrome **Down syndrome** is the most commonly identified cause of intellectual disability. This chromosomal abnormality is characterized by an extra chromosome on the 21st pair of chromosomes. For this reason, Down syndrome is also known as **trisomy 21**. The extra chromosome disrupts cell metabolism, producing a variety of anomalies in physical growth and damage to the central nervous system. The incidence of trisomies increases dramatically with the age of the mother. For example, mothers giving birth before the age of 30 have only about 1 chance in 1,500 of having a child with Down syndrome. If the mother is between 40 and 44 years old, however, the chances increase to 1 in 130 (Smith & Wilson, 1973).

Infants with Down syndrome usually show normal sociability early in life. In fact, Cicchetti and Beeghly (1990) found that 12-month-old infants with Down syndrome are as likely as normal babies to be securely attached to their mothers in the Strange Situation.

Source: Monkey Business Images/Shutterstock.com.

Trisomy 21 accounts for about 10% of all cases of moderate and severe intellectual disability and occurs once in approximately 700 to 800 births. The syndrome is named after the British physician Langdon Down, who first identified this cluster of symptoms in the late 19th century. Down syndrome is the result of an error during the reproductive process, but it is *not* inherited from one generation to another.

The diagnosis of Down syndrome is almost always made shortly after birth on the basis of the newborn's physical features, which tend to include a broad, flat nose, rounded face, and small sloping folds of skin around the corners of the eyes. Individuals with Down syndrome are also likely to be shorter than average and stocky, with small hands and short fingers. Children with Down syndrome have intellectual deficits that are particularly evident in higher-level cognitive skills, such as concept formation and flexible problem solving (Sanchez et al., 2012). Children with Down syndrome usually show expressive language deficits that are disproportionally more severe than their mental age would suggest and more severe than their receptive language problems. They have relatively well-developed rote learning and visual-motor abilities (Pueschel, Gallagher, Zartler, & Pezzullo, 1987) that enable them to acquire many daily living skills with relative ease. Persons with Down syndrome are known for their sociability, relatively stable emotions, and good mental health, at least in comparison with other individuals with intellectual disability. As individuals with Down syndrome reach middle age, they are likely to experience memory loss similar to that seen in the context of dementia.

sex-linked chromosome: Chromosome 23 is known as the sex-linked chromosome because it consists of duplicate chromosomes in the female (designated XX) but not in the male (designated XY).

fragile X syndrome: A heritable genetic aberration involving chromosome 23 that results in moderate intellectual disability and physical anomalies.

Fragile X Intellectual disability can also result from the addition or deletion of genes. For instance, in fragile X syndrome, the aberration involves chromosome 23. This is known as the **sex-linked chromosome** because it consists of duplicate chromosomes in the female (designated XX) but not the male, who normally has an X and a Y chromosome. In **fragile X syndrome**, an excess of genetic material on one tip of the X chromosome makes it appear thin and threadlike—or "fragile." Fragile X syndrome is the result of a genetic error that—unlike Down syndrome—*is* heritable. In fact, it is the most commonly inherited cause of intellectual disability. Fragile X occurs in about 1 in 750–1,000 males, and 1 in 500–750 females (Dykens, Hodapp, & Leckman, 1994). Most males and about one third of females with fragile X experience moderate intellectual disability. Because females have two X chromosomes, they still have an undamaged X when the other is defective, so their intellectual disability tends to be less severe. Certain physical features are associated with the disorder, including a long, thin face with a broad, flat nose and large ears. Affected males also tend to have enlarged testicles.

Although children with fragile X and Down syndrome suffer the same moderate level of intellectual disability, the two syndromes lead to different learning abilities and social behaviors (Hodapp et al., 1992). For example, children with fragile X cannot perform tasks that require them to learn information presented in a sequential order, such as imitating a series of hand movements. Moreover, children with fragile X have difficulties in social relationships. And unlike the typical case of Down syndrome, children with fragile X often develop oppositional and disruptive behavior, sometimes in combination with attention deficits and hyperactivity.

Phenylketonuria (PKU) Mutations in a single gene can also cause intellectual disability. Such errors can be passed on to future generations. An example is a rare condition called **phenylketonuria**, or **PKU**, in which an abnormality in protein metabolism is carried by a recessive gene. If the fetus inherits this gene from both parents, the newborn infant will be literally poisoned by the intake of an amino acid called *phenylalanine*—common in foods such as meat and cow's milk. Normally, phenylalanine is converted to another harmless amino acid, *tyrosine*, but in infants with PKU, the enzyme required for this conversion is missing, and phenylalanine is instead converted to *phenylpyruvic acid*—a substance that is toxic to the central nervous system and that produces moderate-to-severe intellectual disability, marked hyperactivity, and sometimes, extremely fearful or bizarre behavior. Today, newborns are routinely screened for this condition. Identified infants are immediately placed on a diet low in phenylalanine, preventing toxicity and permitting normal development. Untreated children with PKU have average IQs of about 25, whereas children who follow a low-phenylalanine diet from early infancy are likely to have IQs in the 90s (Zigler & Hodapp, 1986).

phenylketonuria (PKU): A genetic cause of intellectual disability that results from an abnormality in protein metabolism.

Environmental Damage to the Central Nervous System Genetic problems represent only one of the organic sources of intellectual disability. Many cases can be traced to the following insults to the central nervous system that occur before, during, or after birth:

- Prenatal hazards include viral and bacterial infections in the mother that cross the placental barrier and harm the fetus, sometimes permanently. One example is German measles—also known as *rubella*. When occurring during the first trimester, rubella can cause intellectual disability, among other physical conditions. Other maternal infections that can result in intellectual disability in the infant include syphilis and genital herpes.

- Another potential prenatal hazard comes from chemical substances that the mother ingests during pregnancy, such as alcohol or other drugs. Substances that cross the placenta and damage the fetus are known as **teratogens**. As few as two alcoholic drinks per day in the midcourse of pregnancy can produce an average drop of 7 IQ points in children (Streissguth, Barr, & Sampson, 1990). Maternal alcohol binges during and just before pregnancy have been associated with mild to severe intellectual disability and a distinctive pattern of abnormal features, including small head circumference, shortened eyelids, flattened jaw line, poorly developed philtrum (cleft palate), and thin upper lip. The term **fetal alcohol syndrome (FAS)** is used to describe these facial abnormalities when they occur in conjunction with retarded physical growth and any of several signs of neurological deficit, including intellectual disability, attentional problems, or learning disabilities.

teratogen: A substance that crosses the placenta and damages the fetus.

- Several factors associated with labor and delivery can result in intellectual disability for infants, such as premature birth and low birth weight, although these are usually temporary delays, rather than permanent deficits (Crnic, Greenberg, Ragozin, Robinson, & Basham, 1983).

- Head injuries, brain tumors, and infectious diseases such as encephalitis are the leading causes of intellectual disability after birth (Rodriguez, 1990).

fetal alcohol syndrome (FAS): A pattern of abnormalities resulting from maternal ingestion of alcohol during pregnancy. FAS is associated with mild to severe intellectual disability, distinctive physical abnormalities, and social and emotional difficulties.

Psychosocial Adversity Adversity in a child's psychosocial environment can also limit intellectual development. The term *cultural-familial* is used to describe mild intellectual disability with no known organic (biological) cause. The term suggests that the intellectual disability is due to psychosocial disadvantage. Not surprisingly, the prevalence of intellectual disability is affected by social and demographic characteristics, such that boys are more often diagnosed than girls, and African-American children receive the diagnosis more often than Caucasians, a difference that probably reflects the influence of socioeconomic class on cognitive attainments.

One view of how adverse psychosocial conditions might lead to intellectual disability focuses on parents with limited intellectual skills or little education. These parents may interact with their children in ways that do not promote cognitive and social development (Keltner, 1994). Parents with limited skills are more likely to be critical of the child's efforts and to be less attentive and responsive to the child during interactions (Barnard & Kelly, 1990). Such parents talk less frequently and elaborately to their children, thus limiting the child's development of verbal abilities (Chaney, 1994; Walker, Greenwood, Hart, & Carta,, 1994). Parents with limited skills are also less able to provide homes with stimulating items, such as educational toys, games, music, or books. These limitations in parent-child interaction and in the quality of the home environment may be regarded as a form of *environmental deprivation.*

In many cases, both organic and psychosocial factors contribute to mild intellectual disability (Baumeister, Kupstas, & Klindworth, 1991). For example, young, poorly educated mothers living in poverty are more vulnerable to illness and disease and are less likely to receive adequate prenatal health care. They are also more likely to use or abuse alcohol or other drugs during their pregnancies. Whatever damage to the infant's central nervous system that results from these organic factors is likely exacerbated by additional limitations in the postnatal caregiving environment.

Detecting and Preventing Intellectual Disability

Efforts at detecting and preventing intellectual disability can take place at each stage in the process of raising a child, beginning with planning for conception and arranging for prenatal health care.

Prenatal Detection and Prevention Prospective parents who want to know their chances of having a child with a genetic disorder can seek this information through genetic counseling. They complete a detailed interview to provide family history and submit a blood sample for analysis of their chromosomes. Similar screening information can be collected early in a pregnancy by obtaining samples of blood or **amniotic fluid** (the fluid surrounding the fetus). The procedure for extracting amniotic fluid, known as **amniocentesis**, does pose a risk to the fetus, however, and it cannot be performed until about the fourth month of pregnancy.

amniotic fluid: The fluid surrounding the fetus.

amniocentesis: The medical procedure of extracting amniotic fluid for the purpose of screening for potential fetal problems.

Some prevention strategies during the prenatal period aim at fostering good physical and psychological health in young mothers. These efforts try to prevent the maternal illness, malnutrition, and prolonged emotional distress that can increase the chances of fetal complications or premature birth, which in turn increase the likelihood of intellectual disability. Another approach attempts to modify the behavior of prospective parents to reduce teratogenic effects. For example, television ads and warnings on bottles and posters have increased awareness of the dangers of maternal alcohol consumption (Baumeister et al., 1991).

Postnatal Detection and Early Childhood Education After a child is born, intellectual disability associated with a genetically determined metabolic deficiency can sometimes be prevented by early detection. In one example described earlier—PKU—intellectual disability can be prevented or lessened if dietary modifications are made early in life (Zigler & Hodapp, 1986).

The infants and young children who are most likely to show mild intellectual disability can be identified on the basis of both familial high-risk characteristics and cognitive tests that were described earlier. Once identified, children at risk for poor intellectual development can be helped through nursery or preschool programs that provide an intellectually enriched environment. The best-known example of this approach in the United States is Project Head Start, a federally funded program begun in the 1960s that is discussed in the "Prevention" feature in Chapter 1. Head Start exemplifies a two-generational intervention that provides services to both children and their parents (Zigler & Styfco, 1993). For example, while the child is trained in early reading skills, the parent is taught how to read effectively to the child, to stimulate the child's interest, and to teach important letter-sound associations. Parent groups that focus on topics ranging from nutrition to behavior management are included in many Head Start programs, both to educate parents and to provide them with much-needed social support. Many Head Start programs also provide medical checkups and dental exams as routine parts of the program. These programs alone have resulted in improvement of about a quarter of a standard deviation across all cognitive and achievement outcomes (Shager et al., 2013). Whereas Head Start assists children mainly based on the socioeconomic level of their parents, though, several other programs have targeted infants whose parents have limited intellectual skills (i.e., low IQs) regardless of their income. One such program was the Abecedarian Project, described in the "Prevention" feature in Chapter 2, in which children of low-IQ parents who were given high-quality educational interventions showed superior achievement (more college degrees and employment) to a control group at age 30 (Campbell et al., 2012).

Treatment of Intellectual Disability

The goals of most interventions are to maximize children's developmental progress and adaptive behavior skills, eliminate or reduce disruptive or self-injurious behavior, and help families adjust to their children's disabilities.

Procedures based on operant learning principles are the most widely used techniques for individuals with intellectual disability. The term **applied behavior analysis** describes an operant teaching process in which complex skills are broken down into a series of smaller units. For example, the process of eating with utensils might be divided into four or five specific steps or *target behaviors*, beginning with picking up a spoon, centering the spoon over a bowl, and so on. Positive consequences are then used as part of a process called **shaping**; that is, rough approximations of the target behavior are first reinforced, and as performance improves, better approximations are required for reinforcement. Reinforcement is eventually given less often or in smaller amounts, and when possible, finally removed altogether, with the expectation that the target behavior will persist (called **maintenance**) and will occur in new situations (called **generalization**). Formal applications of these procedures are called behavior modification programs. Behavior modification programs are used to teach self-care (e.g., toileting, washing, dressing, eating), communication, social, and vocational skills. These programs have consistently succeeded in teaching individuals with severe and profound intellectual disability to acquire many basic, life-enhancing skills.

Institutionalization and Normalization In the United States prior to the 1970s, children with severe to profound intellectual disability were usually placed in an institution for long-term care. Even many children with moderate intellectual disability were sometimes institutionalized from their early years. This practice was supported by the belief that a residential program staffed with professionals could provide better care and education than untrained parents could and that out-of-home placement would protect the family from psychological distress.

In the 1970s, these beliefs were supplanted by the idea that service delivery should be "normalized" as much as possible. The **normalization** movement was based on the idea that persons with intellectual disability should experience the "norms and patterns of the mainstream society" in their everyday lives (Wolfensberger, 1972). Normalization thus involved a retreat from large, centralized institutions and a new emphasis on family care for persons with intellectual disability, on the education of children with disabilities in public school settings, and on providing community-based facilities for residential care.

For people with severe and profound intellectual disability who require nearly continual supervision, the normalization movement led to creative alternatives to institutional

applied behavior analysis: A behavioral modification intervention based on the principles of operant conditioning (i.e., learning theory) that is commonly used to teach new skills and enhance social functioning among children with autism spectrum disorder (ASD) and intellectual disability.

shaping: An operant learning technique in which successive approximations of a target behavior are reinforced until the final target behavior is performed or learned.

maintenance: The persistence of a learned behavior.

generalization: The process by which a learned behavior tends to occur in novel situations.

normalization: A social policy based on the idea that persons with intellectual disabilities should experience mainstream society in their everyday lives; associated with deinstitutionalization and an emphasis on family care, community-based facilities, and public school education of children with disabilities.

Connections

Does the deinstitutionalization of children with intellectual disabilities share similarities with other changes in the treatment of people with serious mental disorders? See Chapter 4.

living. For example, programs that provide supervised apartment dwelling allow persons with intellectual disability to live in their own units (Burchard, Hasazi, Gordon, & Yoe, 1991), and frequent monitoring by trained staff enables them to receive immediate assistance when needed. Other alternatives include family-like group homes in residential neighborhoods and specialized foster homes in which a family is trained to care for one or two individuals with severe mental disabilities.

Special Education and Mainstreaming Normalization and deinstitutionalization put increased responsibility on neighborhood schools to educate all children with disabilities, including those with severe and profound intellectual disability. In the United States, the 1975 Individuals with Disabilities Education Act (IDEA) made special educational services for children with disabilities mandatory, in the least-restrictive environment possible.

In the early years of special education, most children with intellectual disability were placed in self-contained classrooms in regular public schools. IQ testing was emphasized as a means of determining which of these classrooms was most appropriate for a given child (Ysseldyke, Algozzine, & Epps, 1983). More specific assessment data—for example, scores on tests of motor ability, language, social skills, and so on—were also used to determine a child's *individualized education program*, or *IEP*, a formal record of the goals for a child and teaching strategies for reaching those goals.

Opposition to self-contained special education has steadily increased. Many self-contained programs take place in buildings that are removed from regular classrooms, and critics warn that such segregation works against normalization and promotes anti-disability biases in nondisabled students (e.g., Heller, Holtzman, & Messick, 1982). Most school districts have developed alternatives to self-contained programs in which children with disabilities—primarily those with mild or moderate intellectual disability—are partially served in regular classrooms for nondisabled students, a process known as **mainstreaming** (Dunn, 1968). Some schools have eliminated their special education programs altogether, instead serving students of all ability levels in the same general program (Stainback & Stainback, 1992).

mainstreaming: An educational policy in which children with disabilities spend part of their school time in regular classrooms.

Section Review

Intellectual disability refers to:

- significantly below-average intelligence occurring during childhood and
- deficits in adaptive behaviors, such as feeding, dressing, and basic social skills.

Organic causes of intellectual disability:

- account for 25–50% of all intellectual disability cases and
- include genetic disorders, prenatal problems, perinatal and postnatal diseases, and childhood head injuries.

Cultural-familial causes of intellectual disability:

- account for the majority of cases of mild intellectual disability and
- involve parental limitations, family hardships, and other kinds of psychosocial disadvantages.

Services for persons with intellectual disability:

- include attempts at both prevention and treatment, and
- have been guided by the principles of normalization and mainstreaming.

Autism Spectrum Disorder

Kathy Mills sits at her kitchen table, watching her 3-year-old son, Devon, play in the den. For the last hour, Devon has been sitting on the floor peering intently at his right hand, which he holds over his head as he slowly opens and closes his fingers. Devon is looking at changes in the lighting that he makes by waving his fingers in front of the ceiling light.

He has been going through this exercise every day for months, creating his own private kaleidoscope, so fascinated with it that he pays attention to nothing else.

Kathy dreads what she knows is coming next. Devon will stay so absorbed in his finger-and-light ritual that soon he will defecate in his pants. As soon as Kathy tries to pick him up to change his clothes, he will fly into a tantrum, and Kathy might get kicked before she can get Devon changed.

Sometimes, Kathy feels as if she won't be able to cope with Devon's strange behavior another day. Even before Devon was a year old, Kathy had begun to notice all sorts of problems. Devon would never reach out for toys or babble like other babies. He wouldn't even splash around in the water when she gave him a bath. He refused to eat solid food until Kathy devised maneuvers to trick him into eating. Perhaps most upsetting of all, Devon didn't use language and didn't seem to notice other people. If another child walked over to him, Devon would shrink back and begin to cry. If his mother called his name, he usually ignored her. The only words he ever uttered were "hi," "off," and "bye-bye." Sometimes, he used these words correctly, but more often, he merely seemed to be chanting them to himself.

The term *autism* is derived from the Greek word *autos* (self) and literally means a preoccupation with the self. Psychiatrist Leo Kanner first used this term in 1943 to describe a group of infants that he followed in his clinical practice at Harvard. These infants seemed incapable of relating to their parents or to other people; they often engaged in repetitive, purposeless activities called *stereotyped behavior*; and they seemed more interested in objects than in their parents, like Devon's interest in his finger-and-light ritual. At ages 2 and 3, these infants either failed to develop language or made only bizarre speech sounds.

Classification of Autism

In the *DSM-5*, the diagnosis of autism in now included in a very broad diagnostic category referred to as **autism spectrum disorder**, or **ASD**. This term reflects consensus within the psychological community that four previously distinct disorders (*autism, Asperger's disorder, childhood disintegrative disorder*, and *pervasive developmental disorder not otherwise specified or PDD-NOS*) are best conceptualized as a single condition with different levels of severity.

ASD is now characterized by (1) deficits in social communication and interaction, and (2) restrictive, repetitive behaviors, interests, and activities. When making this diagnosis, psychologists rate the severity of the ASD as mild, moderate, or severe (American Psychiatric Association, 2013a). The diagnosis of ASD has been on the rise in recent decades, with current estimates suggesting that 1 in 68 children (or more than 1% of children) in the United States is diagnosed with some form of an ASD (Centers for Disease Control and Prevention, 2014b). ASD is diagnosed four times more often in males than in females (American Psychiatric Association, 2013a). When present in females, it is more likely to co-occur with intellectual disability (American Psychiatric Association, 2013a). Experts believe that the rise in rates of diagnosis of ASD is related to several factors, including increased awareness of the disorder among health-care professionals, improved diagnostic practices, and expansion of the disorder criteria to include less-severe symptoms (Charman, 2011; Kim et al., 2011; Kuehn, 2012). It is too early to determine whether the conceptualization of autism as a spectrum disorder in the *DSM-5* will affect that diagnostic rate going forward. Early field trials revealed that the revised criteria may actually result in 9–12% of those previously diagnosed with Asperger's or PDD-NOS in the *DSM-IV* not meeting the threshold for ASD in the *DSM-5* (Frazier et al., 2012; Huerta, Bishop, Duncan, Hus, & Lord, 2012), although smaller studies have suggested that this number could be as high as 40%, especially for those with PDD-NOS (Frances, 2012b).

Even though symptoms of autism spectrum disorder may be evident during the first year of life, signs of ASD are typically recognized starting during the second year, when

autism spectrum disorder (ASD): A broad category of neurodevelopmental disorders that are characterized by (1) deficits in social communication and interaction, and (2) restrictive, repetitive behaviors, interests, and activities.

TABLE 3.3 The *DSM-5* in Simple Language: Diagnosing Autism Spectrum Disorder

Autism spectrum disorder is diagnosed based on two main symptoms:

1. persistent deficits in social communication/interaction across multiple contexts (e.g., reduced pointing, eye contact, and other nonverbal communication; challenges making friends or engaging in imaginative play); and
2. a narrow range of behavior, interests, or activities (e.g., idiosyncratic movements or speech, rigid rituals, preoccupation with unusual objects or activities).

Source: Adapted from American Psychiatric Association (2013a).

delays in language become more apparent. Early behavioral markers of ASD are exhibited in early childhood, with symptoms such as a lack of interest in or unusual social interaction, strange patterns of play (e.g., repetitive, stereotypical play), and atypical communication styles (e.g., being able to count to 10 but failing to respond to one's name). It is common during this period of time for parents to question whether their child is deaf and for a hearing evaluation to be conducted. Furthermore, during the child's second year of life, repetitive, stereotyped behavior becomes more pronounced, and the failure to engage in age-appropriate play becomes more apparent. Among children with milder forms of ASD, the disorder may not be recognized until the child enters school. The *DSM-5* criteria for ASD are shown in Table 3.3.

Symptoms of Autism Spectrum Disorder

Social Relationship Problems "Gross and sustained" impairment in reciprocal social interaction is one defining feature of ASD. Children with ASD lack many of the *nonverbal* behaviors that regulate social discourse, such as eye contact, "open" facial expression, and the body postures and hand gestures that facilitate interaction. They have trouble using gestures and eye contact to coordinate attention with another person, a process called **joint attention** (Mundy, Sigman, & Kasari, 1994). Many nonverbal cues ordinarily used to share the experience of an interesting object or event with another person—showing, pointing, head nodding, eyebrow raising—are absent or poorly developed in persons with ASD. Children with ASD often seem unaware of others or view them as objects rather than people. One 13-year-old boy diagnosed with ASD, while playing with the fingers of the examining psychologist, began to bend one of them back at an impossible angle—not maliciously, but seemingly unaware that the finger was part of a person, or that such an action would hurt the person. Children with ASD are often said to "look through" rather than "look at" other people, much like the case of Devon described earlier.

joint attention: The process of coordinating attention with another person.

The nature of these social problems changes as the child grows older. Infants with ASD are disinclined to cuddle or smile directly at their parents (Kanner, 1943). Preschool children with ASD seldom show any observable interest in peers, although they may be quite dependent on close contact with their parents. Older children with ASD may begin to show discernible interest in peers, but only in a mechanical, detached style.

Expressive Language Deficits Spoken language is absent or minimal in about half of the individuals with ASD (Volkmar, 1992). In the other half, vocabulary size is close to mental age expectations, but the pragmatic use of language—for communication or self-expression—is

"For Show and Tell I've brought individual credit reports on the entire faculty that I've downloaded from the internet."

Source: Cartoonresource/Shutterstock.com.

extremely limited. Speech may have an unusual tone, rate, or rhythm. Certain words or phrases, sometimes borrowed from television commercials or songs, or formed from idiosyncratic associations that make sense only to those who know the autistic person well, may be stated repeatedly. For example, a teenager with ASD constantly repeated the phrase "antenna head goes down" whenever he saw his father drive up to the family's home. It took his parents several weeks to discover that this phrase stemmed from a song their son heard on the radio ("Antenna Head" by ZZ Top) and his fascination with the retractable radio antenna on his father's car!

Stereotypic Behavior **Stereotypic behavior** often takes the form of inflexible adherence to a specific routine, such as dressing in a particular order that never changes or lining up toys in an exact way at the end of every play period. These routines reflect a pervasive **insistence on sameness** in the physical and psychological environment. Many children with ASD seem to rely on unspoken rules that they regard as unbreakable. Some experts speculate that this insistence on, or efforts to preserve, sameness may be a strategy—*an attempted answer*—that children with ASD use in an effort to make sense of an environment that may be frightening or incomprehensible to them due to their inability to read social cues.

The body movements of children with ASD may also be stereotyped. Odd hand movements (clapping, flapping, finger flicking), whole body activity (rocking or swaying), and abnormal body posture or limb positioning (moving the hands and arms in an unusual way) are common. Stereotyped body movements can also take the form of self-injurious head banging, biting, scratching, and hitting, sometimes leaving permanent scars and injuries.

What about Tom from the chapter-opening case? He showed some symptoms consistent with ASD, such as difficulty in peer relationships and a preoccupation with pretend fishing. How would you decide whether he met full diagnostic criteria for ASD or whether another mental disorder might better explain his behavior?

Distinguishing Autism Spectrum Disorder from Intellectual Disability

Most individuals with ASD have some degree of intellectual disability, and many persons with intellectual disability show limited language development and stereotyped behaviors, such as rocking and self-injurious behavior. Still, clear differences between these two disorders are evident when individuals with ASD and intellectual disability of the same mental age are compared. Children with intellectual disability usually engage others socially and show reciprocal interaction and social skills that are commensurate with their mental age. They also use whatever language they possess to communicate with others.

stereotypic behavior: Behavior commonly seen among children diagnosed with autism spectrum disorder (ASD) and characterized by inflexible adherence to a specific routine, such as dressing in a particular order that never changes or lining up toys in an exact way at the end of every play period.

insistence on sameness: Also referred to as "preservation of sameness," this phenomenon is seen among children diagnosed with autism spectrum disorder (ASD) and involves a persistence that certain aspects of the environment be maintained across time. Since children with ASD often find the social environment to be puzzling, many believe that these "unspoken rules" may be a strategy that children use to make sense of the social world.

Source: wallybird/Shutterstock.com.

Repetitive or stereotyped behavior may also be manifested as an all-encompassing preoccupation with a particular activity, object, or special interest. Some children with ASD maintain an abnormal fascination with mechanical devices or other objects (clocks, vacuum cleaners, stereo equipment). Others are preoccupied with a special topic (e.g., trains, animals, plants, etc.) about which they know a surprising number of specific facts, although the expression of knowledge is usually repetitive and uninformative.

Finally, whereas most children with intellectual disability have uniformly low scores on subtests that tap various abilities measured by an IQ test, children with ASD are likely to show extreme variability in their scores. In particular, children with ASD generally have notable weaknesses in language and abstract reasoning, but some are near average in nonverbal intellectual skills.

Causes of Autism Spectrum Disorder

Experts once believed that ASD was due to inadequate parenting. This view was based on theories that parents of children with ASD were often overly formal in their social interactions (Kanner & Lesser, 1958). It was thought that cold parenting produced the social and emotional deficits seen in ASD. However, subsequent studies showed few differences between the personalities of parents of children with ASD and typically developing children (Cantwell, Baker, & Rutter, 1978; McAdoo & DeMeyer, 1978), and theories that focus on parenting are no longer in favor. Current research points to neurobiological models, which consider the interaction of biological and environmental influences, in explaining the development of ASD.

Biological Causes Whereas the causes of ASD are unknown, there are structural and functional differences in the brains of people diagnosed with ASD. Initially, researchers found that the cerebellum and the frontal lobes were less well developed in some individuals with ASD when compared to typically developing controls (Courchesne, Yeung-Courchesne, Press, Hesselink, & Jernigan, 1988; Gaffney, Kuperman, Tsai, & Minchin 1989). More recently, studies using brain-imaging techniques described in Chapter 1 have revealed abnormalities in frontal lobe regions and in the orbitofrontal cortex and posterior cingulate cortex, part of the limbic system that is involved with emotional and memory processing (Ecker et al., 2013; Uddin et al., 2011). Overall, ASD has been shown to involve deficits in the default mode network of the brain, a set of remote, functionally connected cortical nodes less active during executive tasks than at rest (Washington et al., 2014). The default mode network includes the brain structures just mentioned (prefrontal and posterior cingulate cortex) and is implicated in Theory of Mind (discussed later in the chapter), episodic memory, and other self-reflective processes. Experts have reason to suspect that this abnormal brain development is the result of a combination of factors that include both genetic and environmental influences.

Heritability studies suggest that ASD is more common among identical (monozygotic) twins than fraternal (dizygotic twins) and that having a sibling diagnosed with ASD puts an individual at greater risk for being diagnosed with, or experiencing symptoms of, ASD (Folstein & Piven, 1991). Heritability of ASD was estimated to be approximately 50% in a population-based study of over 2 million people (Sandin et al., 2014), with extreme autism symptom levels showing even higher heritability (Frazier et al., 2014). However, this research conclusively suggests that genetics alone does not cause ASD. As a result, cutting-edge research is currently underway to better understand environmental factors that may contribute to the development of ASD (Newman, 2011; Weintraub, 2011). For instance, there is some evidence linking prenatal risk factors, such as influenza and prolonged fevers in the mother during pregnancy, to increased risk for ASD (Atladottir, Henricksen, Schendel, & Parner, 2012). In a related line of research, there is also evidence to suggest that parental age may be related to increased risk for ASD, but there is controversy about whether maternal or paternal age plays a greater role in this pathway (i.e., Kong et al., 2012; Weintraub, 2011).

Faulty Biological Causes In 1998, Dr. Andrew Wakefield and 11 other co-authors published a study in a top medical journal, *The Lancet*, with the unremarkable title: *Ileal-lymphoid-nodular hyperplasia, nonspecific colitis, and pervasive developmental disorder in children.* Such a title would hardly grab a science journalist's attention, but the small study sparked widespread hysteria about a possible connection between the mumps-measles-rubella (MMR) vaccine and ASD (Novella, 2010).

frontal lobe: The area of the cerebral cortex that controls executive functions, such as planning and carrying out goal-directed activities.

default mode network: A set of remote, functionally connected cortical nodes in the brain that are less active during executive tasks than at rest; this network has functions that involve Theory of Mind, episodic memory, and other self-reflective processes.

Theory of Mind: A cognitive process that allows an individual to infer the mental states of others.

Given real concerns related to the links between environmental toxins and ASD and the fact that symptoms of ASD become apparent around the age of 2 (when vaccines are commonly administered), it is perhaps not surprising that many parents of children with ASD have accepted Wakefield's faulty conclusions and questioned whether vaccinations are to blame. And public opinion was further shaped by celebrities like Jenny McCarthy and Jim Carrey, who jumped aboard the antivaccination campaign.

In 2007, the court case of *Michelle Cedillo v. Secretary of Health and Human Services*, also known as the omnibus autism proceeding, opened in Washington, DC. This was a case involving the family of Michelle Cedillo, a girl with ASD whose parents sued the U.S. government because they believed that her disorder was caused by her receipt of both the MMR vaccine and thimerosal-containing vaccines. On February 12, 2009, the special masters (attorneys appointed by the judge) ruled that the Cedillos were not entitled to compensation as they had failed to demonstrate that thimerosal-containing vaccines in combination with the MMR vaccine could cause ASD. Special master George Hastings stated that "the Cedillos have been misled by physicians who are guilty, in my view, of gross medical misjudgment" (Wikipedia, n.d.).

No credible research to date has found any evidence that childhood vaccines of any kind—with or without preservatives—play a role in the development of ASD (Fombonne, 2008; Weintraub, 2011). In addition, the original Wakefield study stating otherwise was retracted by *The Lancet* in 2010 for methodological errors and possible ethics violations (Novella, 2010). Yet the American public remains unconvinced; once scared, it is difficult to un-scare people. In fact, a recent survey on the issue revealed that 33% of U.S. parents with children under the age of 18 believe that vaccines cause ASD, despite the link being widely discredited by the scientific community (Heasley, 2014). Unfortunately, one possible result of this lack of critical thinking is that vaccination rates have declined in recent years, and diseases that had long been eradicated have been making comebacks, with a recent outbreak of mumps in Ohio (as well as among NHL hockey players) and a rise in measles cases in California and New York (Heasley, 2014).

Psychological Causes Simon Baron-Cohen (1995) theorizes that the social deficits of people with ASD are the result of what he terms mindblindness—their lack of Theory of Mind ability that people without ASD take for granted. This theory, which merges psychological (cognitive) and biological findings (e.g., the brain's default mode network deficits discussed earlier), helps to explain the impairment in the social development, as well as in the communication skills, of people with ASD. Mindblindness can be described as a cognitive disorder in which an individual is unable to attribute mental states to the self and to others. That is, the individual is not capable of attributing beliefs, intentions, and desires to others (Gallagher & Frith, 2003). As a result, it becomes difficult to explain even simple social behavior (e.g., why is that guy yelling?). Without this fundamental understanding of what people are doing and why, the world becomes a potentially threatening place.

However, one of the most important limitations of this original theory is that it is unable to explain the highly repetitive behaviors described earlier that constitute the second main diagnostic feature of ASD. This second cluster of symptoms has been explained instead by the more comprehensive empathizing-systemizing (E-S) theory (Baron-Cohen, 2004). The term *empathizing* extends the idea of Theory of Mind and involves two components: (1) the ability to attribute mental states to oneself and to others and (2) the drive to respond with an appropriate emotion to that mental state (Baron-Cohen, 2004, 2010). A different process—*systemizing*—is conceptualized as the drive to understand and derive rules about a system (Baron-Cohen, 2004). Systemizing allows an individual to predict the behavior of a system and therefore to control it (Baron-Cohen, 2010). A system is defined as anything that takes inputs and delivers outputs, and includes everything from technical systems (e.g., a machine) to natural (e.g., the weather), abstract (e.g., mathematics), social (e.g., a company), collectible (e.g., a library), and motoric (e.g., a tennis top-spin) systems that the brain can analyze or construct (Baron-Cohen, 2004).

thimerosal: An organomercury compound also known as thiomersal, it is a well-established antiseptic and antifungal agent used as a preservative in vaccines, ophthalmic and nasal products, and tattoo inks. Its use as a vaccine preservative was controversial, and it was phased out from routine childhood vaccines in the United States and many other countries in order to assuage popular but unfounded fears.

mindblindness: A cognitive deficit thought to underlie autism spectrum disorder wherein a person is not able to understand other people's behavior in terms of mental states.

empathizing-systemizing (E-S) theory: A theory postulating that the causes of autism spectrum disorder are deficits in empathizing (reading and responding appropriately to other people's emotions) and excesses in systemizing (a drive to understand and apply rules to a system).

Mary Temple Grandin (born August 29, 1947) is an American doctor of animal science, a professor at Colorado State University, a best-selling author, an autistic activist, and a consultant to the livestock industry on animal behavior. She also created the "hug box," a device to calm those with ASD. The subject of the award-winning 2010 biographical film *Temple Grandin*, starring Claire Danes, she also was listed in the *Time* list of the 100 most influential people in the world in the "Heroes" category. Grandin says that "the part of other people that has emotional relationships is not part of me," and she has neither married nor had children. Grandin is a strong advocate for those with ASD and explains how it can benefit society (2008): "What would happen if the autism gene was eliminated from the gene pool? You would have a bunch of people standing around in a cave, chatting and socializing and not getting anything done."

applied behavior analysis: A behavioral modification intervention based on the principles of operant conditioning (i.e., learning theory) that is commonly used to teach new skills and enhance social functioning among children with autism spectrum disorder (ASD) and intellectual disability.

According to the empathizing-systemizing (E-S) theory, ASD is best explained by a deficit in empathy alongside intact or even superior systemizing (Grove, Baillie, Allison, Baron-Cohen, & Hoekstra, 2013). In this way, the social and communication impairments seen in ASD are accounted for by deficits in empathizing, and the pockets of hyperability, repetitive behavior, and restricted interests or obsessions with systems are accounted for by an interest in systemizing (Baron-Cohen, 2004, 2010). There is a large evidence base suggesting that individuals with ASD show impaired performance on measures of empathizing and intact or elevated performance on tests of systemizing ability (e.g., Baron-Cohen & Wheelwright, 2004; Lai et al., 2011; Lawson, Baron-Cohen, & Wheelwright, 2004). For instance, one study found a three- to sevenfold increase for ASD among mathematicians, providing support for the notion that systemizing is an ability associated with the disorder (Baron-Cohen, Wheelwright, Burtenshaw, & Hobson, 2007). Temple Grandin, a renowned professor and leading designer of livestock facilities who has ASD, also shows these superior systematizing abilities.

Treatment of Autism Spectrum Disorder

The most extensive and thoroughly researched treatment program for individuals with ASD is a behavioral modification intervention described by Ivar Lovaas and his colleagues (Lovaas & Smith, 1989) and referred to as **applied behavior analysis**. Based on the principles of operant conditioning, this training program requires intensive training sessions (i.e., daily or near-daily sessions that can continue for a number of years, depending on the severity of the ASD) in the child's home and other environments, and includes the child's parents and peers. The treatment focuses on language development, academic skill development, and cooperative play. Efforts are also made to curtail stereotyped behaviors, tantrums, and aggressive behavior.

In a now-classic study of this intervention, Lovaas (1987) found that children who began treatment prior to age 4 gained an average of 20 IQ points by age 7, and about 50% were able to attend a regular (nonspecial education) first-grade class. Children in an untreated control group did significantly worse; less than 5% were able to attend regular education. A 5-year follow-up of these children indicated that the impressive, early gains seen in the treated children were maintained (McEachin, Smith, & Lovaas, 1993). Subsequent research has replicated the results of this study and provides further evidence that this is an effective method for teaching language, enhancing learning, improving social functioning, and reducing maladaptive behavior (e.g., Eldevik et al., 2009). In terms of timing and duration of treatment, research indicates that the more rigorous the treatment and the earlier it is initiated (ideally before age 5), the more promising the results (Vismara & Rogers, 2010). As such, applied behavior analysis is viewed as the "intervention of choice" for young children with ASD and is the only intervention that meets the criteria to be considered a "well-established" treatment for ASD at this juncture (Rogers & Vismara, 2008).

When Devon was about 4, Kathy and Devon moved, and she found a home-care setting for Devon that he was able to accept. She also enrolled him in an intensive behavior modification program developed by Dr. Lovaas. A team of psychology graduate-student therapists worked with Devon for about 30 hours per week. They used reinforcement techniques to help Devon increase his attention, play, and social skills. Devon also began to learn how to use language to communicate. After 3 months of this program, in conjunction with private speech therapy, Devon learned how to imitate the behavior of an adult, and his ability to understand and use language increased considerably. His mother also reported that Devon began to show a better attention span, to control his bowels, and to comply with instructions more easily.

Psychotropic medications, such as antipsychotic drugs, have been used along with behavior modification and educational programs to treat ASD, usually when there are problems related to disruptive behavior, aggression, or self-injurious behavior (McDougle et al., 2005). In fact, research suggests that antipsychotic drugs (such as risperidone) are more effective when treatment includes parents in the behavioral treatment intervention (Scahill et al., 2012). However, it must be emphasized that medications are not evidence-based treatments for ASD.

MAPS - Medical Myths

In general, the long-term prognosis for ASD varies widely, depending on the symptom profile and severity of symptoms. Traits of ASD commonly persist into adulthood, though a growing group of children with ASD obtain advanced degrees and are able to function independently. As a result of early and intensive behavioral treatment, more and more children with ASD are succeeding academically and going on to college, with an increased need for support programs (Pinder-Amaker, 2014) and campus education regarding the features of the disorder (Tipton & Blacher, 2014). Unfortunately, research suggests that this group of individuals with ASD is the minority (Fein et al., 2013).

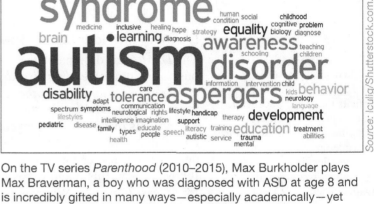

Section Review

Autism spectrum disorder (ASD) is characterized by:

- deficits in social communication and interaction, and
- restricted, repetitive behaviors, interests, and activities.

The severity of ASD is rated as mild, moderate, or severe, making it a spectrum of disorders along one continuum of similar symptoms.

ASD is moderately heritable and may be caused by an interaction of biological factors, such as advanced parental age or illness (e.g., influenza) and psychological factors such as mindblindness, likely resulting from brain deficits to the default mode network. A leading theory to explain ASD is empathizing-systemizing (E-S) theory, which postulates that the causes of ASD are deficits in empathizing (reading and responding appropriately to other people's emotions) and excesses in systemizing (a drive to understand and apply rules to a system).

Treatment of ASD:

- relies on behavior modification procedures to teach communication, academic, and socialization skills and
- is most effective when administered in an intensive format as soon as symptoms become evident.

ASD is not caused by vaccines and is not effectively treated by any medication.

On the TV series *Parenthood* (2010–2015), Max Burkholder plays Max Braverman, a boy who was diagnosed with ASD at age 8 and is incredibly gifted in many ways—especially academically—yet struggles socially. Max is often tormented by his peers in school, due to his poor conversational skills, perseverations, and lack of perspective-taking, as well as reciprocating social cues. At one point during the series, Max worked consistently with a behavioral aide doing applied behavior analysis, which provided a good example of the types of supports and adjustments that may be needed to ensure the academic persistence of children with ASD.

Specific Learning Disorder

It was oral reading time in Carl's fourth-grade classroom. He grew increasingly uncomfortable as the teacher made her way around the room, calling on students to take a turn. It wasn't Carl's lucky day. His name was called. Carl slowly rose to his feet, vaguely aware of laughter coming from the back of the classroom. He began to read, "John . . . cam . . . him from the . . . stair?" The laughter grew a little louder.

"No, Carl, that's 'John came home from the store.' Can you say that?" asked Carl's teacher, glaring in the direction of the laughter.

Carl tried, but he could not improve on his first attempt. The teacher corrected him again, and he tried once more but finally gave up, too frustrated and angry to continue. His teacher was sympathetic. "That's okay, Carl, we'll try again tomorrow," she said, before calling on another student. Carl's reading difficulties were puzzling. He seemed at least average in intelligence, and he came from an educated and apparently well-functioning family. What could account for his inability to read?

To answer this question, Carl was sent to the school psychologist for IQ and achievement testing. The results indicated that Carl had an average overall IQ but that he was reading at only a beginning second-grade level. He was also behind his grade level in spelling but was close to average for his age and grade in math. A multidisciplinary assessment team concluded that Carl had a learning disorder. Consequently, he was placed, for part of each day, in a special education class for individualized reading and spelling instruction, although he still remained with his friends in his regular classroom for most of the school day.

Defining and Identifying Specific Learning Disorder

specific learning disorder: A single overall diagnosis in the *DSM-5* incorporating deficits that impact academic achievement. The criteria describe general shortcomings in academic skills and allow for specifiers in areas such as reading, writing, and mathematics.

The *DSM-5* has designated the term **specific learning disorder** to encompass four previously used terms (*reading disorder*, *mathematics disorder*, *disorder of written expression*, and *learning disorder not otherwise specified*). A specific learning disorder is diagnosed when an individual has learning problems in reading, writing, and/or mathematics. This diagnosis is made when achievement in reading, writing, or mathematics is substantially below that expected for age, schooling, *and* level of intelligence. *Substantially below* is defined as a discrepancy of two or more standard deviations between achievement and IQ. Moreover, this diagnosis is not made unless the learning difficulties have persisted for at least 6 months. Whereas many school districts accept this definition, others define learning disorders as a deviation from grade level without regard to IQ.

The case of Carl illustrates the IQ discrepancy method. All the tests given to Carl were based on an average population score of 100 with a standard deviation of 15. He received an IQ score of 100, and scores of 65 and 89 on tests of reading and mathematics, respectively. Because Carl's reading score was more than two standard deviations below the mean (i.e., 2×15, or 30 points below average), he was diagnosed as having a learning disorder.

Problems with Reading

A specific disability in the domain of reading, previously referred to as *dyslexia*, is the most frequent type of learning problem and affects about 4% of school-aged children. Persistent problems with reading are more commonly seen among boys than girls; however, it is important to note that boys are also more likely to exhibit disruptive behavior and consequently be referred for a psychological assessment in the first place (Rutter et al., 2004).

Contrary to popular belief, children who have reading difficulties do not perceive letters and words as reversed (e.g., mistaking *was* for *saw*) any more often than children without reading problems (Black, 1973; Kaufman & Biren, 1977). They may, however, perceive letters upside down or reversed. For instance, they might confuse the letter *w* for *m* or the letter *b* for *d*. One important difference between those with and without learning disorders in reading is *linguistic*: Those with reading problems tend to read at a slower pace and make more errors when speaking (i.e., distorting, neglecting, or substituting words). People with reading difficulties also have difficulty decoding letters (*phonetic decoding*) and combinations of letters, translating them into sounds, and remembering verbal information (Meyler, Keller, Cherkassky, Gabrieli, & Just, 2008; Vellutino & Scanlon, 1985).

Causes of Reading Problems Many reading specialists regard problems in phonetic decoding as the primary deficit in most cases of reading disorders. Research studies investigating specific learning disorder in the domain of reading have discovered brain abnormalities related to visual and auditory information processing (Golden, 2008; Nicolson & Fawcett, 2008). Moreover, additional research indicates that these brain abnormalities may be the result of genetics (Gabrieli, 2009; Paracchini et al., 2008). For example, research has shown a higher concordance of reading disability in monozygotic twins than in dizygotic twins (DeFries, Fulker, & Labuda, 1987; Olson, Wise, Conners, Rack, & Fulker, 1989).

Problems with Writing

Individuals with a specific learning disorder involving impairments in written expression exhibit problems with spelling, grammar, and/or punctuation in their writing. Difficulties in this domain are also characterized by problems with legibility or fluent handwriting or by problems with constructing clear, organized sentences and paragraphs. Problems with writing typically become evident by the time a child reaches the second grade (approximately age 7), but it is certainly feasible for mild disorders of written expression to go unnoticed until later in a person's education.

Problems with Math

When children are diagnosed with a specific learning disorder with impairment in mathematics, it means that they likely have difficulty with understanding basic math processes, like addition and subtraction, learning and memorizing multiplication tables, or developing math reasoning skills. It may also suggest that they have difficulty performing math calculations. Generally speaking, learning disorders in the math domain become evident around age 6 (i.e., first grade), but they are most commonly diagnosed when a child reaches the age of 8 or 9.

Treatment of Learning Disorders

More is known about the treatment of learning disorders with impairments in reading because these are the most common forms of learning disorders. Speech and language pathologists, along with special educators, often work closely with children diagnosed with specific learning disorder in reading to help them understand phonetics and other aspects of language. Two methods of reading instruction have been emphasized: One is a *whole language* approach that teaches the child to recognize whole words based on the meaning of

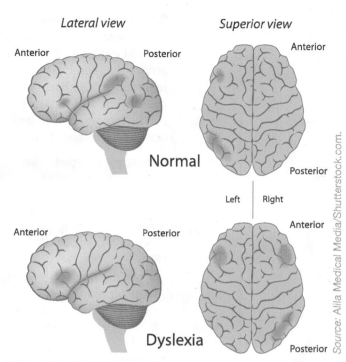

The brains of children with reading disorders ("dyslexia," bottom diagram) tend to show reduced activity in the left occipito-temporal regions (blue and green areas involved in language comprehension, shown in top diagram) during reading, and increased activation instead in those same brain regions in the right hemisphere (Raschle, Chang, & Gaab, 2011; Vlachos, Andreou, & Delliou, 2013). How and why this pattern results in the symptoms of reading disorders is not yet entirely clear.

"Do you believe in life after Math?"

the material being read, and the other is a *sound-based* approach that teaches word recognition in terms of phonetic decoding. Many children learn to read regardless of the teaching method used, and the minority that require special help benefit from an individualized approach that combines phonetic and meaning-based procedures (Lyon, 1985). Many problem readers also benefit from direct instruction in the comprehension of reading passages (Berninger, 1994). Given recent research highlighting links between brain abnormalities (in the realm of visual and auditory information processing) and learning problems in the context of reading, interventions should be tailored to each individual student.

Section Review

Current definitions of learning disorders focus on the discrepancy between the child's academic achievement and IQ or grade level.

A specific learning disorder is diagnosed when an individual has learning problems in reading, writing, and/or mathematics.

Reading problems:

- are the most frequent type of specific learning disorder diagnosed,
- may be due to an impaired ability to decipher and effectively use the smallest sound units of language, called *phonemes*, and
- are linked to brain abnormalities related to visual and auditory information processing.

Treatment of learning disorders often involves special educators and/or speech and language pathologists.

Attention-Deficit/Hyperactivity Disorder (ADHD)

attention-deficit/hyperactivity disorder (ADHD): A childhood mental disorder marked by inattention, impulsivity, and/or high motor activity.

Very few childhood disorders have generated as much interest and controversy as **attention-deficit/hyperactivity disorder (ADHD).** Popular magazines and talk shows periodically list the symptoms of ADHD, and it is not uncommon for a parent coming to a children's mental health clinic to remark that a friend, relative, or teacher "thinks my child has ADHD." TV and comic-strip characters such as Bart Simpson (of *The Simpsons*) and Calvin (of *Calvin & Hobbes*) portray various aspects of ADHD behaviors.

But exactly what is ADHD? The core symptoms entail inattention, hyperactivity, and impulsivity. The symptoms are most readily observed when the child is required to perform structured activities, such as academic tasks. Like Tom in the chapter-opening case,

When so many symptoms are associated with a single disorder and the symptoms are readily observable among typically developing children, diagnoses like ADHD are met with criticism. Many wonder whether the term ADHD is so broad that it could be applied to just about any child with academic and behavior problems. Mike Myers played "Phillip the Hyper-Hypo," a child with ADHD and hypoglycemia, on several *Saturday Night Live* skits in the 1990s. Phillip once said: "I've worn my way through six harnesses. One time, my mom's car ran out of gas so she gave me a Snickers bar and a can of Coke; I towed the car home, 7 miles. When we got home, I was tired." Celebrities with probable ADHD in real life include decorated Olympian Michael Phelps, actor Ryan Gosling, singers/actors Justin Timberlake and Will Smith, and former baseball player Pete Rose ("Famous People with ADHD," 2014).

Source: Suzanne Tucker/Shutterstock.com.

children with ADHD commonly fail to finish school assignments or do them carelessly. It appears as if they are not listening, and they are easily distracted and disorganized. Children with ADHD appear fidgety and restless. They squirm in their seats, fiddle with objects, misplace toys and clothes, climb over furniture, and run through the house. These children have trouble waiting their turn, often blurt out comments, may grab at other people, or interrupt others' activities. Children with ADHD always seem to have their "engines revved up and ready to go" to the point that they may wear their parents and teachers to a frazzle.

So how is it determined if inattention and hyperactivity are simply normal childhood behavior or symptoms of an underlying disorder? First, symptoms must produce problems in at least two settings in which the child functions (e.g., at school *and* at home), and these problems must result in "clinically significant impairment" in the child's day-to-day functioning. Likewise, it is not enough for the child to show inattention, activity, or impulsiveness that are excessive when compared to same-aged peers; such behavior must also be a *primary cause* of functional problems. Thus, a child who is highly active and often impulsive, but who completes school work consistent with his or her ability and has reasonably good peer relations, would not meet ADHD diagnostic criteria (no matter how much the child frustrates or annoys adults). Experts also contend that there is a qualitative difference between the hyperactivity observed among children with ADHD and typical hyperactivity in that developing children typically are able to exert voluntary control over their actions and display goal-directed behavior. Children with ADHD also

Source: Brian L. Burke, Tucson, AZ.

MAPS - Superficial Syndromes
This saguaro has lots of energy and arms in all directions without a clear focus, which is the cactus equivalent of ADHD.

have problems with working memory; that is, they have difficulty holding information in their mind while problem solving (Kasper, Alderson, & Hudec, 2012). This is apparent in children with ADHD when they have difficulty focusing their attention on the task at hand.

Three-subtypes of ADHD have been identified:

1. ADHD primarily marked by *inattention*
2. ADHD primarily characterized by *hyperactivity* or *impulsivity*
3. ADHD combined type (in which both *inattention* and *hyperactivity-impulsivity* are present)

Among children, underachievement in school is exhibited across all subtypes of ADHD (Barkley, DuPaul, & McMurray, 1990), but the underlying reasons for these problems may differ. Research has documented several consistent differences among children diagnosed with the inattentive, hyperactive, and combined subtypes. For one, the hyperactive subtype is four to five times more common than the inattentive subtype. Moreover, children with the hyperactive subtype of ADHD are more likely to exhibit:

- other externalizing behavior problems (i.e., noncompliance, aggression),
- low popularity among peers, and
- comorbid conduct disorder.

On the other hand, children with the inattentive type are more likely to exhibit:

- internalizing behavior problems (i.e., anxiety, depression),
- a slow pace of problem solving, and
- comorbid learning disorders.

Table 3.4 summarizes the *DSM-5* criteria for a diagnosis of ADHD.

Which subtype might Tom (in the chapter-opening case) be diagnosed with? His inattention and off-task behavior at school suggest a diagnosis of *ADHD, inattentive type*.

Chapter 3 Disorders of Childhood and Adolescence   **109**

TABLE 3.4 The *DSM-5* in Simple Language: Diagnosing Attention-Deficit/Hyperactivity Disorder

ADHD is diagnosed based on individuals having six or more out of nine symptoms in either (or both) of two categories—inattention and hyperactivity/impulsivity—before age 12.

Inattention includes the following nine symptoms, where the person often has difficulty with:

1. details of tasks,
2. sustaining attention in tasks or activities,
3. listening to others,
4. finishing tasks,
5. organizing tasks and activities,
6. engaging in tasks that require concentration or other mental effort,
7. keeping track of his or her stuff (e.g., they often lose belongings),
8. not getting distracted, and
9. remembering what to do next.

Hyperactivity/impulsivity includes the following nine symptoms, where the person often:

1. fidgets or squirms,
2. is unable to stay seated,
3. climbs or runs around,
4. cannot play quietly,
5. looks restless,
6. talks too much,
7. answers questions before they are completed,
8. cannot wait his or her turn, and
9. interrupts others

Source: Adapted from American Psychiatric Association (2013a).

Learning disorders are frequently associated with this subtype, and they may contribute to some of Tom's off-task behavior in school.

Prevalence

ADHD occurs in most cultures and affects 7–9% of children in the United States, with over 6 million children between the ages of 4 and 17 diagnosed with ADHD (Schwarz & Cohen, 2013). ADHD is more frequently diagnosed in males than females, and more frequently among Caucasian children than African-American and Hispanic children in the United States (Schneider & Eisenberg, 2006). Females are more likely than males to present primarily with inattentive features.

Changes to the diagnosis of ADHD in the *DSM-5* (e.g., requiring that symptoms be present since age 12 rather than age 7 in the *DSM-IV*) may expand the already-worrying overdiagnosis of ADHD (Paris, 2013), which approaches prevalence rates ranging from 5–15% in several studies worldwide (Faraone, Sergeant, Gillberg, & Biederman, 2003; Polanczyk, de Lima, Horta, Biederman, & Rohde, 2007). This reversal in prevalence—with ASD diagnoses decreasing and ADHD diagnoses increasing in the *DSM-5*—is worth thinking about in greater depth: Why have some diagnostic criteria become more stringent and others less so in the *DSM-5*? Research is one possible answer, although a more realistic reason may lie in considering the strongest interest group in the *DSM-5* and a key sponsor of American Psychiatric Association in general—the pharmaceutical industry (Paris, 2013). In fact, except for ASD, virtually all the *DSM-5* changes loosen diagnosis and threaten to turn the current diagnostic inflation into diagnostic hyperinflation (Frances, 2012a), possibly because most *DSM-5* disorders other than ASD have medications that are commonly used as front-line treatments (Trost, Burke, & Schoenfeld, 2014).

MAPS - Medical Myths

Use and misuse of psychotropic medication is perhaps most relevant for ADHD, where stimulant prescriptions are increasing rapidly (Toh, 2006), despite limited long-term evidence to indicate their effectiveness (Molina et al., 2009), as described further later in the chapter.

Longitudinal Course

The primary symptoms of ADHD are highly persistent over time (Klein & Mannuzza, 1991). About 70% of children who are diagnosed with ADHD in elementary school still meet criteria for this disorder in mid-adolescence (Barkley et al., 1990). Although fewer adults than children and adolescents meet the criteria for ADHD (approximately 4% of adults in the United States), it is clear that symptoms of the disorder persist into adulthood. In fact, the *DSM-5* has elaborated on the criteria for ADHD to ensure that it reflects both child and adult symptomology. Among adults, it is more common to exhibit the inattentive rather than the hyperactive subtype of ADHD.

The diagnosis of ADHD is itself controversial. Some researchers contend, for example, that ADHD is simply a matter of a poor fit between the child's skillset and the environmental demands of 21st-century schooling. In other words, children with ADHD have high energy and the ability to focus especially well when outdoors, so these kids may have been tremendously valuable on the farm, but they are unable to sit and learn in conventional ways in modern (and indoor) schools. An extreme position is taken by Rogers Wright (2010), who contends that ADHD is not a real disorder, but rather a "fad diagnosis." According to Wright, there are a number of complex reasons why a child may show distractibility and/or hyperactivity other than ADHD, such as stress and fatigue as well as neurological and/or emotional problems. Wright (2010) argues that the diagnosis of ADHD can distract mental health professionals from assessing for these other possible causes of distractibility and hyperactivity, leading to misdiagnosis and inappropriate treatments. What do you think?

Causes of ADHD

Current research suggests that the development of ADHD is largely influenced by genetics. The specific genes linked with ADHD are not known. However, it is important to keep in mind that genetics do not operate in isolation. That is, environmental factors that could interact with genetic predispositions must be considered. Accordingly, a diathesis-stress model (as discussed in Chapter 2) may be useful in explaining ADHD: The presence of neurobiological vulnerability aggravated by psychosocial risk factors and/or biological toxins may lead to a significantly increased likelihood of ADHD.

Biological Causes There is a higher risk for ADHD among first-degree relatives, and twin studies indicate that there is a higher rate of ADHD among monozygotic twins than dizygotic twins (Waldman & Gizer, 2006). The heritability of ADHD symptoms was high at 82% for parent ratings, 60% for teacher ratings, and 48% for self-ratings (Merwood et al., 2013). Scholars believe that ADHD is related to deficits in the *frontal lobe* (discussed earlier) of the cerebral cortex (Hynd, Hern, Voeller, & Marshall, 1991; Lou, Henriksen, & Bruhn, 1984). Specifically, brain-imaging studies have identified brain abnormalities and delayed maturation in the frontal lobe among children with ADHD (Hart, Radua, Nakao, Mataix-Cols, & Rubia, 2013; Ivanov et al., 2010; Shaw et al., 2011). This area of the brain controls executive functions, such as planning, self-regulation, and carrying out goal-directed activities, and its impairment could result in deficits in attention and impulse control as seen in ADHD. Further, anatomical asymmetry of the *caudate nucleus* (larger left relative to right volumes) is a marker of ADHD symptoms (Dang et al., 2014); this nucleus is a part of the basal ganglia and has been implicated with voluntary movement, learning, memory, sleep, and social behavior.

Environmental factors such as low birth weight and maternal smoking during pregnancy are often cited as being associated with higher rates of ADHD (Thapar, Cooper, Eyre, & Langley, 2013). However, there is growing evidence from studies using genetically sensitive designs, based on children who remain unrelated to their mothers through assisted conception and siblings where the mother has smoked during one pregnancy and not the other (D'Onofrio et al., 2008; Rice, Harold, Boivin, van den Bree, & Thapar, 2009; Thapar et al., 2009), that associations between maternal smoking, stress during pregnancy, and ADHD (D'Onofrio et al., 2010; Rice et al., 2009) are due, at least in part, to confounding genetic or other household-level factors. Exposures to other toxins in prenatal and/or postnatal life have also been considered as increasing the risk of ADHD. In particular, organic pollutants and lead may damage the neural systems implicated in ADHD (Nigg, 2008), although more research is needed.

Finally, nutrition is a biological factor that has been widely proposed as part of the causal mechanism of ADHD and related symptoms. Several factors have been suggested as causing or aggravating the disorder, including food components such as phosphates, glucose, lactose, preservatives, and dyes (Eigenmann & Haenggeli, 2004). A study in the 1970s led to the introduction of the *Feingold diet*, named after the investigator (Feingold, 1975). Since then, several conflicting findings have been reported (Egger, Stolla, & McEwen, 1992; Pollock & Warner, 1990; Warner, 1993). While there are biologically plausible hypotheses as to why diet might be implicated in the development or maintenance of ADHD symptomatology, especially in some individuals, there is not yet consistent enough evidence from research into diet to wholeheartedly support the notion that such factors play a major role in ADHD (Eigenmann & Haenggeli, 2004; Thapar et al., 2013).

Psychosocial Causes One of the leading psychological (cognitive) models that explains ADHD symptomology is called the **functional working memory model** (Kofler et al., 2014). At the neurobiological level, this model proposes that ADHD results from delayed cortical maturation (Shaw et al., 2007) and associated chronic cortical underarousal (e.g., Dickstein, Bannon, Castellanos, & Milham, 2006), particularly in prefrontal and interconnected regions implicated in working memory processing, storage, and rehearsal. ADHD symptoms are viewed as byproducts of the interaction between environmental demands and the impaired working memory functioning that results from these neurobiological vulnerabilities (Rapport et al., 2008). Working memory is a limited capacity system responsible for the temporary storage, rehearsal, and manipulation of information for use in guiding behavior. The boss of working memory capacity is termed the *central executive* (Baddeley, 2007), a supervisory attentional controller responsible for processing, reordering, and updating information held in short-term memory (Wager & Smith, 2003). Specifically, recent behavioral and neurocognitive research suggests that central executive/working memory deficits may underlie ADHD-related impairments in attentive behavior (Burgess et al., 2010; Kofler, Rapport, Bolden, Sarver, & Raiker, 2010), hyperactivity (Rapport et al., 2009), impulsive responding (Raiker, Rapport, Kofler, & Sarver 2012), and behavioral disinhibition (Alderson, Rapport, Hudec, Sarver, & Kofler 2010; Lee, Riccio, & Hynd, 2004), and strongly predict ADHD-related social problems (Kofler et al., 2011).

What about possible social causes of ADHD? The impact of severe early deprivation on development of ADHD symptoms has been seen in the English and Romanian Adoptees study (O'Connor & Rutter, 2000; Rutter et al., 2007). At present, though, with the exception of rare exposure to extreme forms of early adversity, there is no clear-cut evidence that psychosocial adversity causes ADHD, although such factors may well modify its expression and outcomes (Thapar et al., 2013). Note that, in line with the lack of evidence for the social causes of ADHD, parents of children with this disorder are more likely to stress dispositional or internal causes of ADHD behavior (i.e., neurological and genetic factors) and attribute less responsibility to parenting behavior and the home environment (Dryer, Kiernan, & Tyson, 2006). However, recent research has revealed another potential contribution of the home environment: There is a small but significant relationship between media use and ADHD-related behaviors, such that kids who consume higher levels of media (via TV, movies, or video games) show elevated ADHD symptoms (Nikkelen, Valkenburg, Huizinga, & Bushman, 2014).

Connections

What other disorders involve possible dysfunctions in the brain's basal ganglia? See Chapter 8 for answers.

functional working memory model: A neurocognitive model that proposes that delayed cortical maturation and associated chronic cortical underarousal create working memory deficits that cause the symptoms of attention-deficit/hyperactivity disorder (ADHD).

Treatment of ADHD

Biological Interventions The most frequently employed treatment for ADHD is the use of prescribed medications, such as stimulants. The most common **stimulant** medications are substituted phenethylamines: amphetamine, methylphenidate (sold as Ritalin), dexmethylphenidate (sold as Focalin), dextroamphetamine (sold as Dexedrine), and mixed amphetamine salts (sold as Adderall). Additionally, there is an extended-release version of methylphenidate that is taken once daily (*methylphenidate HCl*, or Concerta), which is also prescribed often. **Ritalin** facilitates the release (and blocks the reuptake) of norepinephrine and dopamine, amplifying the impact of these neurotransmitters in the brain. The result is that children taking Ritalin are better able to focus on relevant stimuli. This change also reduces the core symptoms of ADHD—namely, inattention, hyperactivity, and impulsivity (Chronis, Jones, & Raggi, 2006; van der Oord, Prins, Oosterlaan, & Emmelkamp, 2008). Stimulant medications have been prescribed to children as young as 3–5 years of age.

Critics of Ritalin use to manage symptoms of ADHD cite concerns related to side effects. The short-term side effects of these stimulants can include decreased appetite, insomnia, abdominal pains, headaches, and increased heart rate and blood pressure (Julien, 1992). Further, there is evidence that long-term use of stimulant medications can result in physical growth delays without evidence of growth rebound (Swanson et al., 2007). Use of periodic *drug holidays* (i.e., suspending medication on weekends or during school vacations) helps prevent substantial growth stunting, and reductions in dosage levels can counter (but not eliminate) such common side effects as sleep disturbance and emotional irritability. Additional questions regarding the use of stimulant medications are addressed in the "Controversy" feature.

Beyond the use of stimulants, *atomexetine* (sold as Strattera) is the first nonstimulant medication that has been approved as a viable treatment option for ADHD. Unlike stimulant medication, Strattera is a selective norepinephrine reuptake inhibitor, meaning it makes the neurotransmitter norepinephrine more available in the brain. Because Strattera is a newer medication, there has been far more research supporting the efficacy of Ritalin and related drugs. However, there is research evidence to suggest that Strattera may also be effective for treating the symptoms of ADHD (Newcorn et al., 2008).

Other biological treatments for ADHD include attention to physical staples such as sleep, diet, and exercise (Segal & Smith, 2014). Along with the core symptoms of the disorder, parent-reported sleep problems (see Chapter 12) occur in an estimated 25–50% of children and adolescents with ADHD (Corkum, Tannock, & Moldofsky, 1998). A recent survey of the families of 239 children with ADHD reported that mild to severe sleep problems affected as many as 73.3% of all children participating in the study (Sung, Hiscock, Sciberras, & Efron, 2008). The most common sleep problems reported by children or their parents include difficulties initiating sleep (i.e., delayed sleep onset or bedtime resistance), maintaining sleep (i.e., frequent nocturnal awakenings or restlessness), tiredness on waking, and daytime sleepiness (Sung et al., 2008; Lecendreux & Córtese, 2007; Owens et al., 2009; van der Heijden, Smits, & Gunning, 2005). There is mounting evidence that the treatment of these sleep disorders can ameliorate some symptoms of ADHD (Weiss & Salpekar, 2010). Further investigation of the complex interplay between sleep quality and ADHD symptoms is clearly warranted (Gruber, 2014).

Research has also shown that, like for depression (see Chapter 6), an effective and low-cost treatment for ADHD may be physical exercise (Segal & Smith, 2014). Findings indicate that acute exercise has positive effects on executive functioning in children with ADHD (Chang, Liu, Yu, & Lee, 2012). Furthermore, even single bouts of moderately intense aerobic exercise may serve as a transient nonpharmaceutical treatment option for children with ADHD to improve the cognitive health and academic performance in this population (Pontifex, 2013). Accordingly, some experts have proposed an approach to treating ADHD that employs directed play and physical exercise to promote longer-term brain growth (Halperin & Healey, 2011).

stimulant: A drug that has an excitatory effect on the central nervous system.

Ritalin: A drug that facilitates the release, and blocks the reuptake, of norepinephrine and dopamine, amplifying the impact of these neurotransmitters in the brain; commonly used to treat attention-deficit/hyperactivity disorder.

Weighing the Risks of Ritalin

Prescribing Ritalin for children with ADHD has long been controversial, in large part because of the steady increase in its use during the 1970s and 1980s (Safer & Krager, 1984). In the late 1980s, representatives of the Church of Scientology claimed that Ritalin was a dangerous drug that was being used as a "chemical straitjacket" by unskilled or intolerant adults to control normal, "feisty" children (Barkley, 1990). These accusations led to extreme polarization of the issues; parents were told that Ritalin was either a miracle drug or a virtual poison for their children (Note the similarities here to Prozac, discussed in the "Controversy" feature in Chapter 6).

Today, research has permitted a more clear-headed examination of the issues. There is no longer any doubt that stimulants reduce the core symptoms of ADHD in the majority of children who receive them, at least in the short term, although they have no discernible positive longer-term effects (Molina et al., 2009).

Current concerns focus on the drug's psychological costs to children and on the broader social implications of using medications that can so effectively control children's behavior. First, there is concern that children prescribed psychotropic medication will come to believe that medication, not personal effort, controls their behavior. Critics worry that this attribution could erode a child's self-confidence and motivation to persist at challenging tasks. However, evidence from special ADHD summer camp programs suggests that medicated children experience *enhanced* self-confidence and attribute post-medication improvements to their own efforts (Pelham et al., 1992).

A second concern focuses on the sheer number of children receiving medication for ADHD. Stimulant use quadrupled from 1987 (0.6%) to 1996 (2.4%) among children and adolescents under the age of 18 (Zuvekas, Vitiello, & Norquist, 2006). Data from the Medical Expenditure Panel Survey, a nationally representative annual survey of U.S. households, has revealed a slow but steady increase since then—from 2.4% in 1996 to 3.5% in 2008. The rate grew an average of 3.4% each year, substantially less than the growth rate between 1987 and 1996, which averaged about 17% per year (Zuvekas & Vitiello, 2012). Experts estimate that about 60% of children with ADHD are treated with medication (NIMH, 2011).

A third concern pertains to the possibility that children who take medication for ADHD might be at increased risk for drug abuse later in life. Longitudinal studies of children with ADHD reveal that children with ADHD are at higher risk for developing substance use in adolescence than their age-matched peers (Molina et al., 2009). Importantly, however, multi-site, longitudinal studies found that stimulant treatment was not related to adolescent substance use or substance use disorders (Molina et al., 2009). That is, although children with ADHD are more likely to develop problems related to substance use, this is not likely the result of stimulant use during childhood and adolescence. Further research is needed to explore the possible neurobiological and psychological underpinnings that may lead to both ADHD and subsequent problems with substance use in adolescence and adulthood.

Questioning the psychological cost and social implications of a drug so widely used with children seems a healthy response to lingering questions regarding drug therapy for ADHD and a paucity of good long-term follow-up studies.

Thinking Critically

1. How do you think we as a society should approach the treatment of kids with ADHD?

2. What is your opinion of the rise in stimulant medication and whether it should be routinely prescribed to young children?

Finally, whereas diet is likely not a key part of the causal mechanism for the vast majority of children with ADHD, there is evidence that synthetic food colors or other food sensitivities may play a role for some children (up to 8%) with the disorder, thus meriting treatment with a restriction diet (Nigg, Lewis, Edinger, & Falk, 2012). In addition, several meta-analyses report a small but significant positive effect for supplementation with free fatty acids on ADHD symptomology (Sonuga-Barke et al., 2013; Stevenson et al., 2014).

behavior modification (behavior therapy): Behavioral treatments based on learning theory that are aimed at helping people decrease specific maladaptive behaviors and increase adaptive behaviors.

Psychological Interventions The most promising psychosocial treatment for ADHD is **behavior modification**, based on the principles of operant conditioning and similar to that used for ASD but often targeting different behaviors. In behavioral management programs for ADHD, children are rewarded by parents or teachers for listening to directions carefully, remaining on task, staying in their seats during classroom projects, or performing other behaviors that are incompatible with primary ADHD symptoms. For example, a child might earn extra free time for remaining seated, or peers might be included in *group contingencies*, in which the child with ADHD and classmates earn bonus free time when the child with ADHD remains seated (Speltz, Shimimura, & McReynolds, 1982). With coordinated home-school procedures, parents and teachers use the same behavior program to increase adaptive behavior. In cognitive-behavioral therapy (CBT) interventions, children with ADHD are taught to ask and then answer a series of questions that direct their behavior toward completion of a specific task (e.g., *How do I begin? How am I doing? Who can I ask to check my work?*) and to pause and reflect on their response before acting. Overall, the behavior modification—rather than the cognitive—components have been among the most effective psychosocial treatments for ADHD in kids (Hodgson, Hutchinson, & Denson, 2014). According to a recent meta-analysis, these interventions are generally more effective for girls and least effective for people with the combined ADHD subtype described earlier (Hodgson et al., 2014).

Other psychosocial treatments for ADHD include psychoeducation, family therapy, school-based interventions, social skills training, parent management training (National Collaborating Centre for Mental Health, 2009), and *mindfulness* training for children and their parents (van der Oord, Bögels, & Peijnenburg, 2012). Research on the effectiveness of these approaches has been sparse. However, parent training and education have been found to have positive short-term benefits (Pliszka & AACAP Work Group on Quality Issues, 2007). Moreover, the initial effectiveness of multimodal treatments that include medication and family therapy are largely due to the impact of the stimulant medication, but in the long term, systemic interventions with families, schools, and children play an increasingly important role (Carr, 2009). CBT is the most useful psychological treatment for ADHD symptoms in adults, and it also helps with the commonly comorbid symptoms of anxiety and depression (Huang, Qian, & Wang, 2013).

Finally, a relatively new treatment that integrates biological and psychosocial approaches is *neurofeedback*, which involves rewarding the child for producing certain focused brainwaves (Arns, de Ridder, Strehl, Breteler, & Coenen, 2009). It is a type of biofeedback that uses real-time displays of brain activity—most commonly electroencephalography (EEG)—to teach self-regulation of brain function. Typically, sensors are placed on the scalp to measure activity, with measurements displayed using video displays or sound. A meta-analysis of neurofeedback trials for ADHD found a large positive effect for improving inattention and reducing impulsivity, along with a medium effect on reducing hyperactivity (Arns et al., 2009).

What Works the Best for Treating ADHD? For the last three decades, a multi-site *randomized controlled trial* (RCT) referred to as the **MTA study (Multimodal Treatment Study of ADHD)** attempted to determine what works the best for treating ADHD (MTA Cooperative Group, 2004a). In this large-scale longitudinal study, children diagnosed with ADHD either received (1) medication alone, (2) behavioral modification therapy alone, (3) a combination of medication and behavioral therapy, or (4) routine community care. Results of this study indicate that children receiving either medication alone or the combination of medication plus behavioral therapy had a greater reduction in ADHD symptoms over the short term (14 months) than the groups receiving behavioral therapy alone or community care (MTA Cooperative Group, 1999). Furthermore, although the medication alone and combination treatment groups did not differ significantly in the reduction of ADHD symptoms, researchers found that the combination group had

John finally figured out how to make good use of his son's ADHD energy levels.

Source: Cartoon written by Brian L. Burke; illustrated by Emily Stout.

MTA study (Multimodal Treatment Study of ADHD): A multi-site randomized controlled trial that was conducted over the course of 3 decades among children with ADHD; results indicated that children receiving either medication alone or the combination of medication plus behavioral therapy showed a greater reduction in ADHD symptoms over the first few years—but not after 6–8 years—compared to the groups receiving behavioral therapy alone or community care (which typically included medication).

significantly lower internalizing symptoms, higher social skills (as rated by teachers), better parent-child interactions, and improved reading achievement (MTA Cooperative Group, 1999). The effects of this treatment were maintained for a portion of the original sample over 2 years, although not as strongly as at 14 months (MTA Cooperative Group, 2004a). However, the long-term follow-up over 6–8 years showed that there were no sustained differences between medication and non-medication groups, suggesting that the current first-line treatment for ADHD (Ritalin) did not result in significant benefits for these children as teenagers or emerging adults (Molina et al., 2009). As a group, despite initial symptom improvement during treatment that is largely maintained for a few years, children with combined-type ADHD exhibited significant impairment in adolescence (Molina et al., 2009). Innovative treatment approaches targeting specific areas of adolescent impairment and possibly involving multiple components (diet, sleep, exercise, neurofeedback, behavior modification, and family approaches) are therefore needed.

Section Review

Three subtypes of ADHD have been identified:

1. ADHD primarily marked by *inattention*
2. ADHD primarily characterized by *hyperactivity* or *impulsivity*
3. ADHD combined type in which both *inattention* and *hyperactivity-impulsivity* are present

ADHD occurs in most cultures and affects 7–9% of children in the United States, with symptoms commonly persisting into adulthood.

Current research suggests that the development of ADHD may be associated with both genetic and environmental factors, along with psychological factors, such as working memory deficits, and potential social factors, such as media use and extreme early deprivation.

Brain-imaging studies have identified abnormalities in the frontal lobe, the area responsible for executive functions such as planning and organization, among individuals diagnosed with ADHD, as well as parts of the basal ganglia like the caudate nucleus.

Effective treatment of ADHD generally involves a combination of medication (stimulant) management and behavioral interventions, although few longitudinal studies exist to make a firm recommendation at this time. Other treatment components could include diet, exercise, sleep, family approaches, mindfulness, and neurofeedback.

Oppositional Defiant and Conduct Disorders

comorbidity: When two disorders occur together, or simultaneously.

Connections

Does comorbidity indicate a flaw in the *DSM* system, or does it describe the way disorders occur? For possible explanations of comorbidity, see Chapters 1 and 16.

oppositional defiant disorder (ODD): A childhood mental disorder involving a pattern of negativistic, disobedient, and defiant behavior, usually shown at home and sometimes at school.

The most common reasons for a child's referral to a mental health service are behavioral problems, such as disruptive behavior and deficits in attention. In this section, we discuss two disorders that involve disruptive and antisocial behavior: (1) oppositional defiant disorder (ODD), a pattern of negativistic, disobedient, and defiant behavior usually shown at home and sometimes at school, and (2) conduct disorder (CD), characterized by more serious antisocial behavior at home or in the community, including significant physical aggression, property damage, deceitfulness, or rule violations. ODD, CD, and ADHD are examples of behaviors described by the *externalizing* dimension of the Child Behavior Checklist. These disorders show high levels of co-occurrence, or **comorbidity**, with one another.

The symptoms of ODD usually precede those of CD; in fact, many clinicians view ODD as an early form of conduct disorder. Despite frequent overlap among ODD, CD, and even ADHD, all of these disorders, but especially ADHD, can occur independently.

Oppositional Defiant Disorder (ODD)

Oppositional defiant disorder (ODD) can be diagnosed in a person of any age, but the diagnosis is usually given to children aged 3–7. Typically, these children have poor control of their emotions, are extremely uncooperative and argumentative with parents and teachers, and have repeated conflicts with peers as a result of provocative and hostile interactions (Campbell, 1990). They blame other people for their mistakes and always seem to have a chip on their shoulders. These behaviors seem to reflect a high need for control of social interaction, as if the oppositional child is forever thinking "Everything must go MY WAY, all of the time." Many parents of children with ODD report that being around them requires "walking on eggshells," as any little conflict can escalate into a full-blown tantrum, such as in the case of Nick:

> Nick is a 9-year-old boy brought to a mental health center by his mother because of his increasing disobedience at home and school. Within the last month, Nick has been sent to the principal's office three times for swearing at his teacher in front of other children. At home, Nick can be an affectionate child, but more often, he is argumentative and spiteful. He has to be told again and again to do the smallest of household chores, and even then, he bickers and complains about all the work that is expected of him. Nick has received fairly good grades in school, but his parents report that they have to argue with him about finishing his homework almost every night. His mother says she is fed up with Nick, claiming that "It's just one battle after the next with him; I've had it up to here. It's time for him to grow up."

A major problem in diagnosing ODD is that some of its symptoms occur at a very high base rate in the general population, particularly during the preschool and adolescent years, when concerns over self-assertion come to the forefront (remember the developmental tasks outlined at the onset of this chapter). Many youngsters in the United States argue with their parents at times, do not follow rules, try to avoid their household chores, act angry and spiteful, and could thus be potentially diagnosed with a mental disorder.

Recent versions of the *DSM* have attempted to solve the problem of overdiagnosing ODD by stipulating that, before a youngster can be diagnosed with ODD, the clinician must find evidence that the individual's oppositional behavior—not some other disorder or condition—is producing impairment in social relations, school performance, or other aspects of adaptive functioning expected of someone of the child's age.

Most of us have encountered oppositional toddlers or preschoolers and wondered whether they will ever grow out of it. Longitudinal research suggests that a significant minority of preschoolers continue to engage in troublesome, severe, and age-inappropriate behavior. Susan Campbell (1990) found that about 50% of the preschool children referred to her mental health clinic for externalizing behavior problems continued to have significant difficulties through their early grade-school years. About one third of these children still had significant problems at age 9. Other studies suggest that the majority of grade-schoolers (particularly boys) referred for ODD will show later conduct problems, usually aggression and other antisocial behaviors during adolescence (Verhulst, Eussen, Berden, Sanders-Woudstra, & Van Der Ende, 1993). For a significant subgroup of very young children referred to clinics with ODD, this early pattern will persist and increase over time (Robins, 1991). Beyond this, children diagnosed with ODD are also at higher risk for depression, anxiety, and impulse-control disorders (Nock, Kazdin, Hiripi, & Kessler, 2007).

So how can young children who are likely to have continuing problems be distinguished from those with temporary (and more developmental) problems? Continuing problems are more likely when:

- they are observed in more than one setting (i.e., home and school);
- aggression and hyperactivity co-occur with core ODD features;
- the child engages in covert behaviors, such as lying and stealing, in addition to overt behaviors, such as excessive arguing and aggression; and
- there is a high level of stress in the family.

TABLE 3.5 The *DSM-5* in Simple Language: Diagnosing Conduct Disorder

> Conduct disorder is a disorder in which adolescents violate the rights of others repeatedly and cannot follow social rules or laws, with three or more of the following symptoms (in four categories) in the past year. The four categories are:
>
> 1. violence toward people and/or animals (e.g., physical fights, cruelty, use of weapons),
> 2. property destruction (e.g., setting fires),
> 3. lying or stealing (e.g., breaking and entering), and
> 4. constant rule violations (e.g., missing school, running away from home).

Source: Adapted from American Psychiatric Association (2013a).

Conduct Disorder (CD)

conduct disorder: A childhood mental disorder pattern of antisocial behavior at home or in the community, including significant physical aggression, property damage, deceitfulness, or rule violations.

Compared with ODD, a diagnosis of **conduct disorder (CD)** requires the presence of more-serious antisocial behaviors that substantially infringe on the basic rights of others and that violate community rules. It is not enough to throw tantrums and disobey rules. To be diagnosed with conduct disorder, a child must exhibit behaviors that are potentially harmful to the child, to others, or to property. The *DSM-5* symptoms of CD are shown in Table 3.5. The majority of symptoms pertain to physically aggressive actions; other items describe vandalism, truancy, or taking advantage of people for personal gain. The diagnosis of CD requires a repetitive and persistent pattern consisting of at least three of these symptoms during the previous 12 months and at least one symptom in the previous 6 months.

Conduct disorder is exemplified by a 14-year-old boy ("Eric") recently seen in one of the authors' clinics.

> Eric had a history of unusually violent temper tantrums at age 4, followed by a series of shoplifting incidents at age 8. In the eighth grade, he began to miss school regularly as a result of truancy or being suspended for fights that he usually started. Eric was known as a mean fighter who went out of his way to hurt his adversaries. His parents tried desperately to change his behavior. They paid him to attend classes, took him to a counselor, and hired a tutor to help him with his reading, which had always been poor. None of these strategies worked. Just prior to being brought to the clinic, Eric was discovered in a school bathroom, where he had cut another student's arm with a knife. When questioned about this incident, Eric first blamed the other student, but later admitted to instigating the fight. When asked why he did it, Eric said that the victim—a boy in his shop class—had looked at him "the wrong way." Although the two had never spoken, Eric was convinced that the boy planned to harm him. The only regret Eric expressed about this incident was that he didn't get the chance "to do some real damage."

Children and adolescents with CD vary greatly in social class, age, and characteristic types of antisocial behavior. For example, an adolescent member of an inner-city gang who has stolen, used weapons, seriously injured other teens, and broken into cars with his buddies is very different from the socially isolated, suburban 9-year-old who has set fires, skipped school, and played roughly with the family cat. But both individuals might be diagnosed with CD. As a result, when making this diagnosis, practitioners are asked to specify whether the severity is:

1. *mild* (adolescent has just enough symptoms to make the diagnosis; problems cause minor harm to others, such as lying or staying out after dark without permission),
2. *moderate* (number of conduct problems and effect on others are intermediate, such as stealing without confronting a victim), or
3. *severe* (adolescent exhibits multiple conduct problems that cause harm to others, such as forced sexual activity, physical cruelty, or use of a weapon).

Distinguishing CD from ODD

The typical age of onset of symptoms of ODD is approximately 2–3 years prior to the symptoms of CD (Nock et al., 2007). Given the amount of overlap between symptoms of ODD and CD, many have speculated that ODD may be a precursor to CD. Yet, longitudinal research does not support this theory. In fact, this work indicates that 75% of children with ODD *do not* go on to develop CD. Approximately half maintain their ODD diagnosis, whereas 25% no longer display any ODD symptoms at all (Hinshaw, Lahey, & Hart, 1993). On the other hand, it should be noted that *almost all* cases of CD are preceded by symptoms or a diagnosis of ODD (American Academy of Child and Adolescent Psychiatry, 2007).

Longitudinal Course

In addition to severity, the *DSM-5* also distinguishes between **childhood-onset conduct disorder** and **adolescent-onset conduct disorder**. Several longitudinal studies suggest that youngsters whose symptoms begin prior to age 10 are more likely to be male, demonstrate more aggressive and illegal behavior, experience academic failure, and persist in their antisocial behavior over time. Children whose symptoms begin in childhood, such as Eric, are often called "early starters" (Lahey & Waldman, 2003; Patterson, DeBaryshe, & Ramsey, 1989). Those with adolescent-onset CD do not exhibit the same type of psychopathology evident in childhood-onset CD and are less likely to commit violent offenses or to persist in their antisocial behavior. In fact, the antisocial behavior evident in adolescent-onset cases generally dissipates by the end of the teenage years (Lahey et al., 1999; White, Moffitt, Earls, Robins, & Silva, 1990).

What happens to teenagers such as Eric? About 40% of the children who meet the *DSM-5* criteria for CD before age 15 go on to be diagnosed with antisocial personality disorder as adults (Lahey, Loeber, Burke, & Applegate, 2005). Antisocial personality disorder (discussed in Chapter 16) shares many characteristics of conduct disorder, such as aggressiveness, irresponsibility, deceitfulness, an overt disregard for the feelings and rights of others, and illegal behavior. Adolescents with CD are also at higher risk than typically developing peers for substance abuse and emotional disorders such as depression and anxiety in adulthood (Robins, 1991). Even when CD does not lead to later psychiatric dysfunction, it is associated with major life problems, such as divorce, negative parenting, and higher death rates due to risky or self-destructive behaviors (Rydelius, 1988). Clearly, CD has negative adult consequences that are pervasive and long-standing. It is one of the most valid early-warning signs of serious problems of aggression in adulthood, which is why prevention is so important, as discussed in the "Prevention" feature in this chapter.

Causes of Conduct Disorder

Biological Factors What causes some children to engage in aggressive or antisocial behavior? Adoption and twin studies have shown that about half of the variance in antisocial behavior can be accounted for by genetics (Baker, Jacobson, Raine, Lozano, & Bezdjian 2007), suggesting that both genetic and environmental factors play a role in the development of CD. Several prenatal factors have been linked to CD in children, including malnutrition, lead poisoning, and maternal substance use (Brennan, Grekin, & Mednick, 2003); however, it is important to note that these associations are correlational, and no evidence for a causal mechanism is indicated in this research. Further, neurobiological research tells us that children diagnosed with CD show lower levels of cortical arousal and low autonomic reactivity, particularly in the childhood-onset type of CD. This work suggests that children with a predisposition to CD may have a poor response to punishment and have a tendency to seek out highly stimulating environments (Lorber, 2004; Raine, 2002). One can see how this could potentially lead to the type of uncooperative and impulsive behavior seen in CD, and how similar it is to the biological risk factors for antisocial personality disorder discussed in Chapter 16. In support of this, a prospective study measured physiological arousal in 101 15-year-old boys in England. About 10 years later, these researchers checked court records to determine which boys had been arrested in the interim; 17 of the participants had a criminal record. As shown in Figure 3.1, the

childhood-onset conduct disorder: Children diagnosed with conduct disorder whose symptoms began prior to age 10; these children are more likely to be male, demonstrate more aggressive and illegal behavior, experience academic failure, and persist in their antisocial behavior over time.

adolescent-onset conduct disorder: Children diagnosed with conduct disorder after age 10; these children are less likely to commit violent offenses or to persist in their antisocial behavior into adulthood.

Connections

Is there a genetic basis for criminal behavior? Is just one gene involved? See the discussion of behavioral genetics in Chapter 2.

Derailing Conduct Disorder: The Fast-Track Approach

As noted earlier, children at greatest risk for conduct disorder in adolescence can often be identified early in life, usually by the time they enter grade school. Are such children destined to become "troublemakers" for the rest of their lives, or can something be done to prevent a problematic future?

A number of investigators have developed school-based prevention programs for children believed to be at risk for behavioral and educational problems. An early example of this approach was the Primary Mental Health Project (PMHP; Cowen, Gesten, & Wilson, 1979). The PMHP first identified primary schoolers with potential conduct problems. These at-risk children were then seen in schools by trained, nonprofessional child aides, who taught the children new skills for coping with stressors and controlling impulsive behavior.

Children participating in the PMHP and similar projects experience behavioral and educational gains, but these improvements tend to be modest and often do not generalize well to settings outside of school. Numerous attempts to prevent conduct disorder suggest an important lesson: Preventing or changing major aspects of serious childhood disorders requires lengthy interventions that simultaneously target social, familial, economic, and psychological difficulties.

Some of these requirements were met by a nationwide prevention project called **Fast Track**. Developed by a group of scholars called the Conduct Problems Prevention Research Group (1994) and funded by the National Institute of Mental Health, Fast Track offered a variety of psychological and social services to over 400 families of high-risk children. The program began when children entered the first grade and continued for the following 10 years. It was based on a developmental model hypothesizing that the probability of conduct disorder in a high-risk child could be lowered if:

1. the child's parents are actively involved in the child's school program and develop trust in the school system;

2. the child experiences some measure of academic success, particularly in reading;

3. the child acquires social-cognitive skills that promote the development of friendships and cooperative relationships;

4. the child learns to regulate emotions effectively; and

5. the child develops a mentoring relationship with a same-sex adult.

To accomplish these goals, Fast Track provided services to parents, teachers, and children, and it focused on critical time periods, such as school entry, transition to middle school, and critical high school

years. Fast Track staff members went to the child's school to teach social-cognitive skills such as anger management, to run "friendship groups," and to work with teachers. They also made regular visits to the family's home to help parents acquire child-rearing skills and to become better at managing daily hassles and major stressors ranging from overdue rent to joblessness. The adolescent phase of the program involved curriculum-based parent and youth group meetings to aid in the transition to middle school, as well as individualized prevention planning during high school. Fast Track then measured how much prevention could be achieved when families are given a broad range of intensive treatments in multiple settings and are supported for remaining in the program.

So was Fast Track effective? Results of the 10-year Fast Track intervention on externalizing disorders across childhood suggest that the intervention was successful at preventing the development of ADHD, ODD, and CD, but it is important to note that it was only effective for those participants who were at *highest initial risk* (i.e., those children who were rated by teachers and parents as exhibiting the highest frequency and severity of disruptive behavior; Conduct Problems Prevention Research Group, 2011). In addition to providing evidence to support the efficacy of this prevention program, this study also highlighted the importance of *early screening* of children at risk for antisocial and aggressive behavioral problems.

The "Prevention" feature in Chapter 16 provides yet another excellent example of a multicomponent program designed to prevent early antisocial conduct: The Montreal Longitudinal Experimental Study (Lacourse et al., 2002). In this study, a group of kindergarten boys from inner-city, lower-socioeconomic neighborhoods in Montreal, Quebec, were identified by their teachers as being at risk for later antisocial behavior because of the disruptive behavior they were already showing at school. After the boys received social skills training and their parents got trained in more effective discipline strategies, these boys displayed significantly less delinquent behavior than the control group boys about a decade later.

Hence, prevention involves two steps: (1) early screening and (2) a multicomponent, long-term prevention model that involves the child, parents, and teachers. This exciting and encouraging work has many important implications for educators, clinicians, and public policy makers alike, and gives the broader community hope that children previously viewed as "untreatable" or on a path that was "unchangeable" are capable of making and sustaining positive changes over time (Conduct Problems Prevention Research Group, 2011).

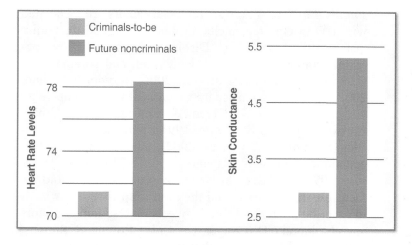

FIGURE 3.1 Adolescent Underarousal and Adult Criminality

A study in England used court records to determine which of the teenagers examined had criminal records 10 years later. Both heart rate and skin conductance (a perspiration index of arousal) were significantly lower for criminals-to-be than for noncriminals when measured at age 15. These results provide evidence that physiological underarousal during childhood is one risk factor for externalizing disorders.

Source: Adapted from Raine, Venebles, & Williams, 1990.

criminals had also had significantly lower heart rates and skin conductance levels than the nonoffenders when they were measured at age 15 (Raine, Venebles, & Williams, 1990).

Psychosocial Factors A substantial body of research supports the link between children's cognitions, or the way that children think about things, and symptoms of CD. Some research suggests that children with CD are more egocentric than their typically developing peers and have problems with taking the perspectives of others (Selman, Beardslee, Schultz, Krupa, & Podorefsky, 1986). Similarly, other research points to deficits in neuropsychological abilities (such as memory, problem solving, language facility) and how these contribute to disruptive behavior. Tests of these abilities in children with disruptive behavior have revealed deficiencies in the ability to comprehend, retain, and utilize language and (just like in ADHD) in **executive functioning**, the ability to attend to relevant information in the environment and to make thoughtful decisions based on that information. Neuropsychologist Terrie Moffit and her colleagues have shown that deficits in these areas are correlated with children's antisocial behaviors, even after controlling for the influence of low socioeconomic status, poor test motivation, or school failure (Lynam, Moffitt, & Stouthamer-Loeber, 1993). Moffit believes that problems in language processing and executive functioning are the primary causal factors in cases where there is early onset of disruptive behavior. However, these factors may be less important in children who first show disruptive behavior in early adolescence, an age when peer group influences (which ultimately are more amenable to change) are more likely to be the determining factor.

Finally, other important research indicates that children with CD have a tendency to interpret neutral events as hostile or threatening, a cognitive distortion known as the **hostile attributional bias** (Crick & Dodge, 1994). That is, they tend to jump to the conclusion that if something negative happens, it is because someone else did it to them on purpose. Ken Dodge and his colleagues have shown that aggressive elementary schoolchildren can be distinguished from nonaggressive peers by the way they handle social information during conflicts (Dodge & Coie, 1987; Lochman & Lenhart, 1993). Aggressive children are less able to remember relevant social cues in many interactions and more likely to perceive hostile intentions in the everyday behaviors of peers. Thus, they may interpret any accidental physical contact by a peer as a deliberate act of aggression. They are also more inclined to believe that aggression on their part will result in positive outcomes (Dodge, Pettit, McClaskey, & Brown, 1986). Some disruptive children are very poor at communicating their sides of an issue in conflict situations. In short, disruptive children may be ill-equipped to handle the *cognitive demands* of interpersonal conflict, making physical aggression the most accessible strategy for them. Dodge and Pettit (2003) have gone on to present a formal *social-cognitive framework* for better understanding aggressive and antisocial behavior in children with CD, which proposes that children with CD view the world in a biased manner (as described earlier), come up with few options for their behavior, have the tendency to generate primarily aggressive responses, and then choose the most aggressive response in many social situations.

Fast Track approach: A nationwide prevention project delivered to over 400 families of children at high risk for disruptive, aggressive, and antisocial behavior; the intervention was successful at preventing the development of ADHD, ODD, and CD for participants who were at highest initial risk (children who were rated by teachers and parents as exhibiting the highest frequency and severity of disruptive behavior). This work also highlighted the importance of early screening of children at risk for aggressive behavioral problems.

executive functioning: The cognitive ability to attend to relevant information, plan or organize activities, and make good judgments about events in the environment.

hostile attributional bias: A cognitive distortion common among children with conduct disorder that results from the tendency to interpret neutral events as hostile or threatening.

"Most of the other parents actually watch the games, mom."

Source: Cartoonresource/Shutterstock.com.

amplifier hypothesis: A theory that explains how family stress may lead to aggressive, antisocial behavior in children and that suggests that stress in the family amplifies negative traits among parents, disturbs family functioning, and limits parents' ability to engage in effective, positive parenting behavior.

coercive cycle: Research suggests that the parent-child interactions in families of boys with aggression are characterized by cycles in which one person's aversive behavior is reinforced by termination of the other's aversive behavior.

transactional process: Children with conduct disorder are thought to both influence and be influenced by their environment; for example, exposure to community violence is associated with conduct disorder, but it is also true that children who are predisposed to violence impact the neighborhood climate.

Family Factors A number of social factors are associated with CD in children, including but not limited to: family instability and stress (e.g., Dishion & Patterson, 2006); parental criminality, maternal depression, and parental substance use (Dishion & Patterson, 2006; Herndon & Iacono, 2005; Lahey, 2008); insecure attachment with parents (e.g., Greenberg, Speltz, DeKlyen, & Endriga, 1991; Urban, Carlson, Egeland, & Sroufe, 1991); parental marital conflict (Cummings & Davies, 2002); adverse family socio-economic status (e.g., Pagani, Boulerice, Vitaro, & Tremblay 1999); and access to weapons in the household. In fact, researchers have used the term **amplifier hypothesis** to describe the relationship between adverse family factors and childhood CD (Conger, Ge, Elder, Lorenz, & Simons, 1994). This theory argues that stress in the family serves to amplify negative traits among parents; in turn, this disturbs family functioning and limits parents' ability to engage in effective, positive parenting behavior and promote a supportive home environment.

In a similar vein, substantial research suggests that negative parenting practices impact the development of CD. According to Gerald Patterson and his colleagues, parent-child interactions in families of aggressive boys are characterized by **coercive cycles**, in which one person's aversive behavior is reinforced by *termination* of the other's aversive behavior (Patterson, Reid, & Dishion, 1992). Here is an example of a coercive cycle from the chapter-opening case of Tom:

Tom whines and becomes verbally abusive when his parents won't turn on the TV. His father yells at him to stop whining and talking back, but Tom continues more intensely. Eventually, the father gets tired of this interchange and allows Tom to turn on the TV. Tom abruptly stops his negative behavior.

In this example, Tom's aversive behavior is reinforced when his father stops yelling and gives in to Tom's request. In turn, the father's giving in is reinforced when Tom stops whining. Because both parties are reinforced for their behavior, this vicious cycle is likely to become well entrenched in the family's interactions during conflicts, leading to parent-child relationships that emphasize the exchange of negative behavior.

Parents of children with disruptive and aggressive behavior are more likely than parents of typically developing children to behave in ways that encourage the development of coercive cycles. For example, they criticize more often, react more strongly to negative child behavior, and issue more frequent commands (Campbell, Ewing, Breaux, & Szumowski, 1986). It is tempting to conclude that such parental behaviors cause child conduct problems, but research suggests that this is a **transactional process**—meaning that both parenting strategies and difficult-to-manage child behaviors play a role in maintaining the cycle (Patterson, et al., 1992).

In summary, multiple biological, psychological (social-cognitive), and social/family factors are associated with aggressiveness, disruptive behavior, and other aspects of conduct disorder. On the whole, evidence suggests that these multiple causes are best conceptualized as risk and protective factors that operate in a transactional manner across time and circumstances.

Treatment of ODD and CD

The most widely used and promising treatment models for ODD and CD involve a combination of approaches applied across multiple settings, including the child's home, school, and community environments (Kazdin, 2007). Moreover, it is important to note that, for treatment to be optimized, family disturbances, such as marital conflict or parental mental health problems, must be addressed simultaneously (McMahon, Wells, & Kotler, 2006). Further, because these problems tend to follow a developmental progression, treatment must change over time to ensure that it is developmentally appropriate and "matches" whether the child is in preschool or elementary, middle, or high school.

Frick (2000) suggests that the treatment of ODD and CD should involve both early *intervention/prevention efforts*, such as those described in the FAST Track model (see the "Prevention" feature in this chapter) as well as *ongoing intervention* to maintain the gains made in the initial treatment and to support adolescents and their parents as they deal with any lingering psychosocial and academic challenges. The following approaches have had some success in reducing the disruptive, aggressive, and antisocial behaviors observed in ODD and CD:

1. **Parent management training.** This method involves teaching parents to change their child's behavior by using *contingency management techniques*. In other words, parents are trained to effectively use positive reinforcement and punishment procedures to modify child behavior. Similarly, tips for reducing negative parent-child interactions are provided. Research supports the effectiveness of this method for reducing aggressive and disruptive behavior by up to one-and-a-half standard deviations, up to a decade later, and with children under the age of 12 (e.g., Eyeberg, Nelson, & Boggs, 2008; Dishion & Patterson, 1992; Hurlburt, Nguyen, Reid, Webster-Stratton, & Zhang, 2013; Lacourse et al., 2002; McMahon et al., 2006).

2. **Problem-solving skills training.** This method targets the social-cognitive deficits exhibited by children with conduct problems. Clinicians provide education and opportunities to role-play, and then deliver targeted feedback to children to help them learn how to deal with problems in their social lives. Research suggests that this method is effective for reducing aggressive, disruptive, and antisocial behavior, particularly among those presenting with less-severe conduct problems (e.g., Kazdin, 2003; Kazdin & Wassell, 2000).

3. **Multisystemic treatment.** As the name implies, this treatment method is an approach that targets a child's maladaptive interactions with his or her family and community. The intervention involves the child, all family members, teachers and other school personnel, friends, and other individuals who interact regularly with the child. Using principles similar to parent management training, problem-solving skills training, and other approaches, multisystemic treatment attempts to modify the interactions between the child and important others in his or her environment. This approach is supported by a great deal of research in both the short and long term, and the positive effects are seen not only in child behaviors but also in child social relationships, general family functioning, and the like (e.g., Henggeler, Sheidow, & Lee, 2007; Henggeler & Lee, 2003).

parent management training: A treatment method used in the context of childhood behavioral disorders that involves teaching parents to change their child's behavior by using contingency management techniques; this strategy is effective for reducing aggressive and disruptive behavior.

problem-solving skills training: A treatment method used in the context of childhood behavioral disorders that targets the social-cognitive deficits exhibited by children with conduct problems and teaches them to solve their problems differently; this method is effective for reducing aggressive, disruptive, and antisocial behavior.

multisystemic treatment: A treatment method used in the context of childhood behavioral disorders that targets the child's maladaptive interactions with his or her family and community; this approach is supported by research, and the positive effects are seen not only in child behaviors but also in child social relationships and overall family functioning.

Section Review

Oppositional defiant disorder (ODD) is characterized by a pattern of negativistic, disobedient, and defiant behavior.

Conduct disorder (CD), on the other hand, involves more serious antisocial behavior, including significant physical aggression, property damage, deceitfulness, or rule violations.

ODD and CD are caused by a combination of etiological factors that are thought to interact and influence one another over time in transactional fashion. These factors may include:

- biological factors,
- psychological (social-cognitive) factors, and
- social/family factors.

Effective treatments include:

- preventative efforts, such as the FAST Track program, and
- developmentally appropriate treatment modalities that are delivered across settings and that change over time, such as parent management training, problem-solving skills training, and multisystemic treatment models.

Revisiting the Case of Tom

What do the theories and research discussed in this chapter tell a psychologist about how to help Tom, the boy described in the chapter-opening case? His inattention and off-task behaviors at school suggest a diagnosis of ADHD, probably the inattentive subtype. His worries about the safety of his parents and frequent stomachaches suggest anxiety as well, although further questioning would be required to confirm the presence of other symptoms of an anxiety disorder. The combination of ADHD/inattentive type and R/O (rule out) for an anxiety disorder is a likely tentative diagnosis of Tom's problems. His social issues likely stem from his ADHD and do not merit a separate diagnosis of autism spectrum disorder (ASD).

What treatment is indicated? To the psychologist at the clinic, Tom's case history suggested some possible goals for treatment, as well as some probable explanations for his difficulties. Tom's fearful behavior during infancy and the preschool years are reminiscent of behavioral inhibition (Kagan, 1989) and suggest a biological diathesis for his anxiety. This vulnerability may have been made worse by Tom's rocky family life, which featured unresponsive parenting, his mother's depression, and his parents' severe marital conflict. These early problems probably led to and were exacerbated by Tom's troubled relationships with his peers. Although none of these factors alone is likely to have caused problems, their cumulative effects are the probable causes of Tom's abnormal behavior.

For 8 months, Tom and his family participated in a multicomponent treatment that involved family therapy and parent training. For example, his parents were taught how to organize their time so they could regularly engage in child-directed play with Tom and his younger brother (see Eyberg, 1988). When it became evident that Tom's parents did not have an effective system for sharing child-care responsibilities, some sessions were devoted to marital communication skills.

In addition, a behavior management program was instituted in which Tom earned points for productive 30-minute work intervals; the points could be exchanged for special privileges, such as going to the movies. This program worked well enough that medication was unnecessary. Because Tom experienced severe social anxiety and had few effective coping strategies, a cognitive-behavioral intervention was undertaken in which the therapist taught Tom how to join a group of children who were playing and to remain calm while doing so.

At the end of about 6 months, Tom showed improvements in some areas but not in others. His off-task behavior at school decreased substantially, and conflict with his mother diminished. However, his peer interactions did not improve, and problems remained in communication between his parents. Nevertheless, the psychologist and the family decided to stop treatment temporarily, mainly because the family had exhausted its insurance benefits for mental health services. At last report, Tom was getting better grades at school, but he was still socially awkward and had no close friends.

Tom is typical of cases seen in child mental health clinics today. He is a boy, he was referred for an externalizing behavior problem and academic failure, and his parents and teacher believed that ADHD was responsible for his difficulties. Tom's problems were complex and reflected a suspected biological predisposition for inhibition, coupled with adverse family conditions and an unstable caregiving environment during critical periods. Unfortunately, Tom is typical of most children referred to clinics in yet another way: Treatment alleviated some difficulties but by no means affected a cure. Only time will tell how well Tom will be able to master the increasingly challenging developmental tasks that lie ahead.

Summary

A Developmental Perspective

The quality of a child's adaptation to the social environment is determined by the manner in which the child approaches and masters certain developmental tasks, such as the formation of secure attachments during infancy and the development of effective peer relationships during the early school years. Difficulties in resolving early tasks may adversely affect the child's accomplishment of later tasks, elevating the probability of psychopathology. Children's disorders rarely emerge in fully developed form but are often preceded by earlier patterns of maladaptation (i.e., oppositional behavior often precedes conduct disorder; social inhibition and fearfulness often lead to anxiety and depression).

Classification and Diagnosis of Children's Disorders

A categorical approach to classifying childhood mental disorders such as the *DSM-5* assumes that mental disorders are discrete entities that can clearly be distinguished from normal behavior and other disorders. By contrast, a dimensional approach to classification organizes children's various problems along a few continuous dimensions that are identified by the statistical procedure of factor analysis. The Child Behavior Checklist, a leading example of this approach, identifies two major dimensions of childhood psychopathology—internalizing and externalizing problems.

Neurodevelopmental Disorders

Domains of Development. Disorders originating in infancy or very early childhood involve a lifelong impairment in mental or physical functioning and substantially limit adaptive functioning. Cases of intellectual disability and autism spectrum disorder meet these criteria. Learning disorders also originate in childhood and can have lifelong effects; however, they have less impact on adaptive behaviors than intellectual disability and autism spectrum disorder do. These disorders are often identified with the help of standardized tests of a child's progress in key domains of development, which include motor skills, language, cognition, and adaptive behavior.

Intellectual Disability. Intellectual disability is characterized by below-average intellectual functioning and impairments in adaptive behavior. The vast majority of persons with intellectual disability fall in the mild range of disability. Organic causes—such as genetic disorders, prenatal problems, perinatal and postnatal diseases, and childhood head injuries—account for 25–50% of all cases of intellectual disability, with most children having IQs below 50. The most common genetic disorder involving intellectual disability is Down syndrome; it results from an error during reproduction that is not passed on to future generations. Fragile X is the most common heritable form of intellectual disability. About 50–75% of cases of intellectual disability are without clear biological cause and are typically in the mild range; they are said to have cultural-familial causes, presumably related to multiple psychosocial disadvantages. Behavior modification programs can be effective in teaching people with intellectual disability a wide range of basic skills. In the United States, normalization and mainstreaming have been promoted for the education of people with intellectual disability.

Autism Spectrum Disorder. Autism is characterized by deficits in social communication and interaction and restrictive, repetitive behaviors, interests, and activities. Some individuals show severe deficits in these areas, whereas others exhibit milder symptoms. As a result, autism is now referred to as autism spectrum disorder (ASD), which represents a cluster of symptoms with varying degrees of severity. A genetic basis for ASD is suggested both by twin studies and an elevated rate of ASD among siblings of children with ASD. Moreover, experts indicate that genetics alone does not explain the development of ASD; rather, the interaction of genetics and the environment is the most likely explanation. Behavior modification programs and educational interventions can enhance the academic and social functioning of children with ASD, and medications have had some success in reducing disruptive or self-injurious behavior. Although some individuals with milder forms of ASD are able to function independently as adults, attend college, and attain advanced degrees and job success, the overall prognosis for people with ASD is guarded at best.

Specific Learning Disorder. Learning disorders are characterized by a discrepancy between a child's academic achievement and IQ or grade level, usually requiring a discrepancy of two or more standard deviation units. Reading deficits are the most common learning disorder. Individuals with reading difficulties have problems in phonetic decoding; that is, the use of phonemes to help them read. Specific learning disorder in reading is linked to brain abnormalities related to visual and auditory information processing.

Susan Campbell

Dr. Susan B. Campbell is professor of psychology at the University of Pittsburgh, where she was formerly director of clinical psychology training and chair of the developmental psychology program. She is a leading expert on the emergence and developmental course of behavior problems in young children, focusing on family and social risks that predict the onset and persistence of childhood disorders.

Q *Treatments for some childhood disorders have shown good short-term effects, but long-term efficacy is generally poor or not established. Will this change? How?*

A We know a good deal about the multiple interacting biological and psychosocial risk factors in the family, peer group, and wider social environment that are associated with more serious childhood disorders. Given the complexity of these disorders, it is hardly surprising that multifaceted treatments will be needed to lead to long-term changes. Change is not easy, and it requires an understanding of the child in context, as well as interventions that may need to support new parenting strategies and rebuild parent-child relationships; often, change is also needed in the family (marital conflict, parental mental health), school, and peer systems in which children are embedded. Although treatments that target specific symptoms or aspects of a problem may show short-term effects, long-term change will require more-complex solutions that engage and motivate parents and provide them with sufficient support to follow through with treatment recommendations. Multimodal treatments are often needed, but empirically supported treatments with adequate follow-up are rarely available in community mental health settings, which lack the resources to translate well-validated treatments from the university to the clinic.

Q *Which treatments do you think are most effective?*

A In line with my prior answer, the most effective treatments are multimodal; that is, treatments containing multiple components that address different aspects of the problem and involve several individuals in the child's environment, such as parents and teachers. For example, some treatment programs include a parent training component, social skills training for the child, and a behavior management program in the classroom. But of course this gets us into political issues regarding the cost. Many people question the worth of this investment. The trend has been to rely on medication as a "quick fix," rather than to address the whole child and the family system.

Q *Do high rates of comorbidity for most children's disorders threaten the validity of the DSM?*

A In general, children showing symptoms of one disorder almost always have symptoms of another disorder. This is evident from numerous epidemiological and clinical studies. For example, most children with ADHD also have ODD or CD, depending on their age. In adolescence, many of these individuals may also be depressed. This is not likely to change with the *DSM-5* because, in some ways, the classification system has become more unwieldy, especially with the modifications to the ADHD criteria, allowing for later age of onset with fewer symptoms. The childhood disorders are still not well defined in terms of developmental course or what the manifestations might be in early versus middle childhood or adolescence. It is difficult to see how the problem of comorbidity will be alleviated by the adoption of the *DSM-5*.

Q *What's the solution?*

A I am very sympathetic to the dimensional approach to assessing children's problems, especially since most dimensional measures include age- and gender-specific norms. It is important to make a distinction between age-related levels of an annoying behavior and clinically significant levels. A dimensional approach to assessment allows the clinician to evaluate the severity of children's problems across different dimensions, to understand where the child falls relative to peers, and to evaluate the association between a child's behavior problems and other characteristics of the child and the child's social context. This can be used along with a structured interview to identify categorical disorders, thereby providing additional information.

Susan Campbell *(Continued)*

Q Do you think there is any reason for concern over the high use of medication for children with ADHD?

A The widespread use of psychotropic drugs to treat children's problems has become a very serious concern. Reports show that even very young children are being prescribed powerful drugs at an alarming rate, and these are almost always "off label." We have no idea how these drugs affect early brain development. Even commonly used medications prescribed for ADHD do not have long-term positive effects. Drugs are used much more widely in the United States than in Canada or Europe. In addition, medication is all too often the only treatment used, and no effort is made to teach the child new skills or to work with the parents to support the child's development. This problem is only going to get worse because the mental health, pediatric, educational, and social service systems work in parallel at best, and there are few integrated services available for children and families dealing with developmental and/or psychiatric problems, which also often co-occur with academic difficulties.

Q What impact, if any, do you think the new diagnostic criteria for autistic spectrum disorder in the DSM-5 will have on rates of diagnosis and treatment?

A It is difficult to know yet whether there will be a further increase in the number of children who are diagnosed with an autism spectrum disorder or whether the combined criteria mean that some of the children at the milder end of the autism spectrum will no longer meet criteria in the *DSM-5*. It is just too soon to tell.

Q Although research consistently fails to find links between autism and childhood vaccinations, there are still many parents who fear that vaccinations cause autism. What does your research on infants and toddlers at high risk for autism suggest?

A It is well known that there is absolutely no link between vaccines and autism, and the research that supposedly supported an association was totally fabricated. Unfortunately, a good deal of money has gone into debunking this, money that could have been better spent on understanding the genetics and neurobiology of autism. My research, part of a larger set of studies, is examining the early development of infants and toddlers with an older sibling with autism because they are at higher-than-average genetic risk for a disorder on the autism spectrum. This is because around 18% of younger siblings are likely to develop autism, and another 20–30% may show subclinical atypical social behavior and/or a language delay. This research is only beginning to identify early behavioral signs that predict a later diagnosis of autism. The goal is to use age-appropriate developmentally informed measures to understand the emergence and developmental progression of early signs of autism. Early identification allows for early interventions, which show promise for long-term outcomes.

Attention-Deficit/Hyperactivity Disorder (ADHD). The development of ADHD may be associated with both genetic and environmental factors, along with psychological factors, such as working memory deficits, and potential social factors, such as media use and extreme early deprivation. ADHD is likely best treated with a combination of stimulant mediation (e.g., Ritalin) and behavioral therapy. However, neither treatment has shown strong evidence of effectiveness in the long run (6–8 years), and a host of other treatment components (diet, exercise, sleep, family approaches, mindfulness, and neurofeedback) may be employed.

Oppositional Defiant and Conduct Disorders

Oppositional defiant disorder (ODD), conduct disorder (CD), and attention-deficit/hyperactivity disorder (ADHD) are examples of behaviors described by the externalizing dimension of the Child Behavior Checklist. Comorbidity is common among these disorders, although each can occur independently. There are multiple causes of ODD and CD, including biological factors, social-cognitive deficits, and a number of family factors (adverse conditions, marital conflict, insecure attachment, presence of negative parenting behavior). Usually, a combination of two or more of these factors is necessary to produce a diagnosable disorder. ODD and CD are treated most effectively with interventions that focus on preventing and treating maladaptive interactions between the child and the systems in which they function (i.e., home, school, community) that may reinforce and maintain the child's disruptive, aggressive, and/or antisocial behavior. Research suggests that prevention efforts are effective for reducing problematic child behavior and maintaining gains over time. The efficacy of intervention methods are also supported by research, with most demonstrating appreciable effectiveness at least in the short term.

Key Terms

adaptive behavior, p. 92

adolescent-onset conduct disorder, p. 119

amniocentesis, p. 96

amniotic fluid, p. 96

amplifier hypothesis, p. 122

applied behavior analysis, p. 97, 104

attention-deficit/hyperactivity disorder (ADHD), p. 108

autism spectrum disorder (ASD), p. 99

behavior modification, p. 114

childhood-onset conduct disorder, p. 119

coercive cycle, p. 122

cognition, p. 90

comorbidity, p. 116

conduct disorder (CD), p. 118

default mode network. p. 102

developmental psychopathology, p. 86

developmental task, p. 86

Down syndrome, p. 94

empathizing-systemizing (E-S) theory, p. 103

executive functioning, p. 121

expressive language, p. 90

externalizing problem, p. 89

Fast Track approach, p. 120

fetal alcohol syndrome (FAS), p. 95

fine motor skill, p. 90

fragile X syndrome, p. 94

frontal lobe, p. 102

functional working memory model, p. 112

generalization, p. 97

gross motor skill, p. 90

habituation speed, p. 91

hostile attributional bias, p. 121

insecure attachment, p. 88

insistence on sameness, p. 101

intellectual disability, p. 92

internalizing problem, p. 89

joint attention, p. 100

longitudinal study, p. 86

mainstreaming, p. 98

maintenance, p. 97

mindblindness, p. 103

MTA study (Multimodal Treatment Study of ADHD), p. 115

multisystemic treatment, p. 123

neurodevelopmental disorders, p. 90

normalization, p. 97

oppositional defiant disorder (ODD), p. 116

parent management training, p. 123

phenylketonuria (PKU), p. 95

problem-solving skills training, p. 123

receptive language, p. 90

retrospective research, p. 86

Ritalin, p. 113

secure attachment, p. 88

sex-linked chromosome, p. 94

shaping, p. 97

specific learning disorder, p. 106

stereotypic behavior, p. 101

stimulant, p. 113

Strange Situation, p. 88

teratogens, p. 95

Theory of Mind, p. 102

thimerosal, p. 103

transactional process, p. 122

trisomy 21, p. 94

visual-motor skill, p. 90

Schizophrenia Spectrum and Other Psychotic Disorders

Chapter Outline

Copyright: karakoysya/Shutterstock.com.

From the Case of Lionel Aldridge

During the 1960s, the Green Bay Packers were the dominant team in professional football. Under the leadership of their legendary coach Vince Lombardi, they won three world championships and the first two Super Bowls. Key to the Packers' success was Lionel Aldridge, a defensive end who was a stalwart of the Packers' defense for almost a decade. Chosen as an All-Pro and elected to the Green Bay Packers' Hall of Fame, Lionel Aldridge was one of the best ever to play his position.

Born in the bayou country of Louisiana on Valentine's Day in 1941, Lionel was raised by his grandparents until he was a teenager. They were poor, but Lionel remembers his childhood as a normal and stable period of life. He ultimately won a football scholarship to Utah State University. After college, Lionel joined the Packers and helped them dominate professional football throughout the 1960s. After retiring from football in 1973, Lionel began to work in broadcasting.

But Lionel Aldridge's life was slowly falling apart. One year after retiring from football, at age 33, he began to hear voices telling him that he was a fraud and a con man and that his past would catch up with him. Lionel heard the voices even while announcing sports on TV. He grew increasingly

After reading this chapter, you will be able to answer the following key questions:

- What is schizophrenia, and how are schizophrenia spectrum and other psychotic disorders categorized in the *Diagnostic and Statistical Manual of Mental Disorders (DSM-5)*?

- How does schizophrenia typically develop and progress?

- What causes schizophrenia?

- What are the main treatments used today to help people with schizophrenia and related disorders?

paranoid that people were out to get him, a fear that was magnified by his nightly appearance on TV, where all his "enemies" could see him. The voices told Lionel that his boss was after him, that his wife was a witch, and that his dog was causing all his problems and had to be killed. Then Lionel began to see things that were not there—the wind chased him, the food on his dinner plate transformed itself into a mass of worms, and his children's balloons became snakes trying to bite him.

There had been few, if any, warning signs of the disorder earlier in his life. In fact, he had enjoyed a life of remarkable success. However, over the next several years, delusions and hallucinations robbed Lionel of his grasp on reality. He was hospitalized more than 20 times during the 1980s with a disorder that left him impoverished and alone. His condition would improve when he took his prescribed medications, but he so hated their side effects (they left him unable to speak for hours at a time) that he often refused to take them. Aldridge lost his job, his family, his financial security, and his home. He began to live on the street, pawning his possessions, as he fought or ran from enemies he was sure were surrounding him.

What could make Lionel Aldridge and millions of other people around the world hear voices, see visions, cower in terror, think that loved ones want to kill them, and retreat into desperate solitude? What causes this devastating and bewildering condition, and how can it be treated? This chapter examines the current knowledge about schizophrenia, a psychosis that can impair almost all aspects of psychological functioning.

Clinicians employ differing definitions of *psychosis*, but in general, the term refers to a serious mental disorder in which individuals lack an accurate perception or understanding of reality and have little insight into how their behavior appears to others. A psychosis typically includes periods of **hallucinations**, sensory experiences that seem real to the person but are not based on any external stimulation of the relevant sensory organ, and **delusions**, false beliefs about reality that are so firmly held that no evidence or argument can convince the person to give them up. Often, psychoses also involve thinking and behavior that are so jumbled and disorganized that onlookers conclude that the person is crazy or insane. Several disorders are accompanied by one or more of these psychotic symptoms; schizophrenia is often marked by the presence of many such symptoms at once.

In this chapter, we examine several disorders for which the presence of psychotic symptoms is a defining feature, but our main focus is on schizophrenia. First, we discuss how schizophrenia has been defined over the past 200 years, how the *DSM-5* describes it today, and how it differs from other psychotic disorders. Then we discuss the lives of people afflicted with schizophrenia—who they are, how they are similar, and how they differ. Next, we turn to an examination of the biological and psychosocial factors that appear to contribute to the development of schizophrenia, followed by descriptions of the treatments that are most effective in controlling the disorder.

The Definition of Schizophrenia Spectrum and Other Psychotic Disorders

Schizophrenia is not, as popular culture sometimes suggests, a split or multiple personality, which, as described in Chapter 10, is called *dissociative identity disorder*. Instead, **schizophrenia** is a psychosis that is marked by a fragmentation of basic psychological functions—attention, perception, thought, emotion, and behavior—that are normally integrated to help us adjust to the demands of reality. People with schizophrenia misperceive what is happening around them, often hearing or seeing things that are not there. They have trouble maintaining attention to the present environment, and their thinking is often so confused and disorganized that they have difficulty communicating with others. Some people with this disorder display a blunting of emotional feelings and a lack of motivation that leaves them immobile and unresponsive. Or their emotions may be highly

hallucination: A sensory experience that seems real but is not based on external stimulation of the relevant sensory organ.

delusion: An extreme, false belief that is so firmly held that no evidence or argument can convince the person to give it up.

schizophrenia: A psychotic mental disorder marked by serious impairments in basic psychological functions—attention, perception, thought, emotion, and behavior.

inappropriate, including uproarious laughter at events that are not funny or uncontrollable crying when nothing sad has taken place. Bizarre behavior is another common symptom, sometimes involving an outlandish or disheveled appearance and odd mannerisms. In other cases, the person avoids social contact as much as possible, withdrawing into private fantasy.

What holds this collection of symptoms together? Not all of them occur in all cases of schizophrenia, and many of them are displayed by people with other disorders. Does it make sense to talk about one disorder called *schizophrenia*? Or is schizophrenia a label that is applied to several different disorders that should be viewed on a continuum? The concept of schizophrenia is anything but simple, as its history shows.

The Evolving Concept of Schizophrenia

The first formal description that unequivocally matches the current conception of schizophrenia is over 200 years old (Gottesman, 1991). In 1809, the classic symptoms of schizophrenia were first documented in descriptions of patients written by John Haslam at London's Bethlehem Hospital and by Philippe Pinel at Paris's Bicetre (Gottesman, 1991). Another 50 years passed before Belgian psychiatrist Benedict Morel grouped a constellation of symptoms into a description of a specific syndrome (Kolb, 1968). Morel described the case of a previously bright 14-year-old boy whose intellectual and emotional abilities gradually deteriorated until he lost all of his prior knowledge and many mental functions. Morel called this condition *demence precoce* (or *dementia praecox*, in Latin), meaning premature loss of rational thought.

By the late 1800s, dementia praecox and several related psychoses had been documented by a number of German psychiatrists. The most influential of this group was Emil Kraepelin, a psychiatrist at Heidelberg Clinic who had examined thousands of mental patients by the 1890s. Through his systematic observations, Kraepelin concluded that three forms of psychosis were all variations or subtypes of a single syndrome that he called dementia praecox. The subtypes were: (1) *hebephrenia*, in which the person behaved in a silly, immature, and disorganized manner; (2) *catatonia*, in which the person held rigid, immobile postures and was mute for long periods; and (3) *paranoia*, in which the person had delusions of grandeur or persecution. Later, Kraepelin added the *simplex* or *simple* subtype, marked by gradual withdrawal and lack of responsiveness to the environment. Kraepelin differentiated these conditions from what he believed was the other major mental disorder—manic depression (known today as bipolar disorder, as discussed in Chapter 5). He thought that dementia praecox was a progressive, deteriorating disease that terminated in "mental weakness" (Gottesman, 1991, p. 7).

By the beginning of the 20th century, however, Swiss psychiatrist Eugen Bleuler espoused different ideas. Bleuler recognized (as Kraepelin ultimately admitted) that dementia praecox did not always begin at an early age; therefore, the term *praecox* was not always appropriate. Furthermore, some people with the disorder got better, so *dementia* was not an appropriate description either. The central problem, said Bleuler, was a loosening or disharmony among various mental processes. There was a split ("schizen") in the mind's ("phren") normally integrated processes of mood and intellect, creating a condition he called *schizophrenia* (Bleuler, 1911/1950).

In his classic 1911 book, *Dementia Praecox: The Group of Schizophrenias*, Bleuler categorized schizophrenia's symptoms as either primary or secondary. According to Bleuler, four primary symptoms are responsible for the split of mental functions:

1. *loosening of associations*, such that thoughts and ideas are not coherently linked;
2. *ambivalence*, wanting two contradictory things at once and being unable to choose between them;
3. *autism*, or total self-centeredness in which reality is replaced by a fantasy life; and
4. *affective disturbance*, in which emotional responses are inconsistent with actions.

MAPS - Attempted Answers

These symptoms—known as Bleuler's four As—force the person with this disorder to try to adapt to a chaotic mental life. According to Bleuler, the adaptations—attempted answers—lead to other common symptoms of schizophrenia: delusions, hallucinations, mutism, and rigid postures.

Bleuler's conception of schizophrenia broadened Kraepelin's original criteria. By Bleuler's definition, a diagnosis of schizophrenia did not require early onset, continuous deterioration, or hallucinations or delusions. Thus, compared with Kraepelin's view of the disorder, many more cases met Bleuler's definition of schizophrenia. For example, Lionel Aldridge in the chapter-opening case would not have satisfied Kraepelin's criteria for schizophrenia, but he did fit Bleuler's more flexible conception of the disorder.

During the first part of the 20th century, Kraepelin's definition of schizophrenia remained dominant among diagnosticians in Europe, while Bleuler's ideas found favor in North America. Over time, the two conceptualizations became increasingly divergent. A landmark study comparing the practices of mental health professionals in New York and London found that people who were diagnosed with schizophrenia according to North American (Bleulerian) criteria were likely to be diagnosed with manic depression (bipolar disorder), major depression with delusions, or neurosis by British clinicians (Cooper et al., 1972). Obviously, such differences in diagnosis hindered communication and reduced the comparability of research by North American and European scientists.

Partly to resolve this discrepancy, American mental health professionals began to search for an approach that would allow an operational definition of schizophrenia. The solution was derived from the work of the German psychiatrist Kurt Schneider (1959), who believed that particular kinds of delusions and hallucinations were the "first rank" or defining features of schizophrenia. Schneider's first-rank symptoms were relatively easy to observe and agree on; however, he ignored the quieter features of schizophrenia that are now known to also be important (Andreasen & Carpenter, 1993). A synthesis of the definitions of Kraepelin, Bleuler, and Schneider was eventually achieved in the *DSM-III* and remains the basis for the *DSM-5* definition. The *DSM-5* eliminated the clinical subtypes (e.g., paranoid) formerly used to organize the vast heterogeneity of the disorder because they were invalid (Tandon et al., 2013). Yet, it still is not understood why schizophrenia presents so differently in so many people and whether it is truly a single disorder (Paris, 2013).

Schizophrenia According to the *DSM-5*

According to the *DSM-5*, the presence of any one symptom of schizophrenia is not enough to diagnose the disorder. Rather, as Table 4.1 shows, there are several characteristic psychotic symptoms, some combination of which must be present for a diagnosis, with at least one of the symptoms being a delusion, hallucination, or disorganized speech. Furthermore, the symptoms must have been active for a minimum of 1 month, along with other signs of disturbance that have lasted for at least 6 months. These symptoms must be

TABLE 4.1 The *DSM-5* in Simple Language: Diagnosing Schizophrenia

Schizophrenia is diagnosed when a person shows at least two of the following five symptoms for over a month, with some symptoms lasting 6 or more months:

1. false beliefs (delusions),
2. false perceptual experiences (hallucinations),
3. hard-to-understand speech (e.g., loss of train of thought, sentences only loosely connected in meaning),
4. unusual behavior (in which the individual acts in any number of ways—from silly and childlike to angry and aggressive—and has inappropriate moods) or catatonic behavior (in which the individual is unresponsive to external stimuli with disturbances in movement from immobility to excessive activity), and
5. negative symptoms (decrease or absence of normal function, such as social withdrawal, sloppiness of dress and hygiene, and loss of emotion, motivation, or judgment).

Source: Adapted from American Psychiatric Association (2013a).

accompanied by marked deterioration in the person's ability to function at work, engage in social relationships, and maintain self-care, and they must not be due to another mental disorder, substance abuse, or a medical condition.

The symptoms of schizophrenia are often classified as either positive or negative. **Positive symptoms** are distortions of normal psychological functions that produce excess behaviors, such as hallucinations, delusions, bizarre behavior, confused thinking, and disorganized speech. (Obviously, the term *positive* in this context does not mean that these behaviors are desirable, but rather that they are present in the lives of those with the disorder and are absent in those without schizophrenia.) **Negative symptoms** involve a diminution, absence, or loss of normal function; examples include apathy, flat emotions, lack of self-help skills, and social withdrawal. Positive symptoms tend to respond to antipsychotic medications better than negative symptoms. As will be noted later in this chapter, there is some evidence that positive and negative symptoms might have different causes.

Positive Symptoms of Schizophrenia

Most people with schizophrenia exhibit both positive and negative symptoms at one time or another. Although a greater number of negative symptoms suggests a worse overall prognosis, positive symptoms are often more bizarre and therefore more immediately noticeable, even frightening, to observers. The two hallmark symptoms of schizophrenia—delusions and hallucinations—are discussed in detail next, along with other positive symptoms of the disorder.

Delusions Delusions are present in about 90% of people with schizophrenia and 66% of people with bipolar disorders during acute episodes (Baethge et al., 2005). Usually, delusions involve misinterpretations of normal perceptual experiences. In other words, a person experiences the world as others do but forms obviously incorrect interpretations of those experiences. For example, if a police officer waves to pedestrians at a busy street corner, delusional individuals might interpret this not as a sign to cross the intersection, but as a signal to a would-be assassin, suggesting a deficit in their ability to infer the actions of others (Ozguven et al., 2010). Explanatory delusions are likely related to the misinterpretation of sensory events, such as a hallucination. In other words, the delusion is an attempted solution—a way for individuals to make sense of their unusual and confusing sensory experiences. Another possibility is that the delusion functions to increase the person's meaning in life; Roberts (1991) found that people with systematized delusions possessed more favorable contents to their beliefs than a comparison group.

The range of beliefs that may constitute a delusion is quite broad. Flagrant, *bizarre delusions* are fairly easy to identify. Truly implausible beliefs—for example, that a person's heart has been removed by aliens or that Brian Williams is spying on a person's home every time he broadcasts the evening news—are easily recognized as delusions. But in other instances, distinguishing a delusion from a mistaken belief can be difficult. A Division II college athlete's belief that he can become a professional athlete runs contrary to much of the evidence, but it is not so extreme that it would be considered delusional. Generally, the clinician tries to determine whether a given belief is odd enough to qualify as a delusion, which usually depends upon how strongly held the belief is, particularly in the face of contradictory evidence.

Religious beliefs that are not endorsed by a clinician's culture or that are not familiar to the clinician may present particular diagnostic problems. Are such beliefs delusional or just rare conclusions accepted as the truth by a group with different cultural beliefs and practices? Most Westerners consider beliefs in the healing powers of witch doctors to be misguided, but many groups endorse such beliefs, and it would typically be improper to label them delusions. Usually, a delusion can be distinguished from a false belief on the basis that the delusion is recognized by almost everyone in a given society as obviously false.

Some delusions are classified by specific content. For example, in *somatic delusions*, people believe that something is wrong with their bodies. They may be convinced that they are infested with parasites or that they are being bombarded with poisonous rays.

MAPS - Attempted Answers

MAPS - Prejudicial Pigeonholes

In other cases, a man may believe he is losing his penis, or a woman may be convinced she is pregnant, despite clear evidence to the contrary.

Delusions of persecution, the most common delusions in schizophrenia (Appelbaum, Robbins, & Roth, 1999), are beliefs that the person is being tormented or harassed by an individual or group such as the FBI, a foreign government, or extraterrestrials. Lionel Aldridge's belief that enemies were tracking him while he was on TV was a persecutory delusion. These delusions lead the person to always be on guard, lest an enemy sneak up undetected. Ambiguous events are usually interpreted in the most threatening terms. For instance, Aldridge's false belief that his wife was a witch may have been strengthened whenever he saw her cooking soup on the stove, as he may have interpreted that as a witch's potion.

Delusions of reference are also relatively common and occur when people misinterpret sounds or other stimuli as having special reference only to them. For example, static from a radio may be interpreted as a sign that someone is trying to communicate with the listener. A newspaper article about a celebrity's troubles may be viewed as an exposé of a personal foible. Delusions of reference may also be triggered by highway billboards, song lyrics, and movies.

Delusions of control involve beliefs that an enemy or foreign entity is controlling a person's thoughts, feelings, or behavior. One individual was convinced that his mind was manipulated by deceased relatives who were living on Jupiter and "controlling earth's equipment as well as its people." Another believed that a dentist had implanted a microchip in his tooth, causing his bowels to lock up (Brown & Lambert, 1995). Related delusions include *thought withdrawal*, the belief that thoughts are being stolen out of a person's brain; *thought insertion*, the belief that bad thoughts are being forced into the delusional person's head; and *thought broadcasting*, the belief that a person's thoughts are being transmitted so that others can hear them.

People displaying *delusions of grandeur* believe that they are famous or important, often someone who can save the world from famine or war. These delusions are also common in bipolar disorders (see Chapter 5's opening case). Religious themes are prominent in many delusions of grandeur. Perhaps the most famous example occurred in the 1960s, when three male patients at different mental hospitals in Michigan all claimed to be Jesus Christ. Ultimately, they were transferred to the same ward of a state hospital in Ypsilanti, Michigan, where they lived together for 2 years. Their encounters are described in Milton Rokeach's classic book *The Three Christs of Ypsilanti* (1964). In the book, the three men are referred to by the fictitious names of Clyde, Joseph, and Leon. They met for the first time on July 1, 1959, in a small room at the Ypsilanti State Hospital. According to Rokeach, the first meeting began with a round of routine introductions. After giving his real name, Joseph was asked if there was anything else he wanted to tell the group. "Yes, I'm God," he replied. Clyde introduced himself next, also giving his straight name first, and then proceeding, "I have six other names, but that's my vital side and I made God five and Jesus six . . . I made God, yes. I made it 70 years old a year ago. Hell! I passed 70 years old." Last came Leon.

"Sir," Leon began, "it so happens that my birth certificate says that I am Dr. Domino Dominorum et Rex Rexarum, Simplis Christianus Pueris Mentalis Doktor. [This is all the Latin Leon knows: Lord of Lords, and King of Kings, Simple Christian Boy Psychiatrist.] It also states on my birth certificate that I am the reincarnation of Jesus Christ of Nazareth, and I also salute, and I want to add this. I do salute the manliness in Jesus Christ also because the vine is Jesus and the rock is Christ, pertaining to the penis and testicles; and it so happens that I was railroaded into this place because of prejudice and jealousy and duping that started before I was born, and that is the main issue why I am here. I want to be myself. I do not consent to their misuse of the frequency

Connections

Are delusions an excuse for criminal behavior? For a discussion of the relationship between legal concepts of responsibility and mental disorders, see Chapter 17.

"It makes you look forty years younger."

There are different types of delusions. In a delusion of grandeur, individuals have a false belief that helps them seem better or more important than they are.

Source: Cartoonresource/Shutterstock.com.

of my life." When asked "Who are 'they' that you are talking about?" Leon responded: "Those unsound individuals who practice the electronic imposition and duping. I am working for my redemption. And I am waiting patiently and peacefully, sir, because what has been promised to me I know is going to come true. I want to be myself; I don't want this electronic imposition and duping to abuse me and misuse me, make a robot out of me. I don't care for it."

As this first session wound down, Clyde and Joseph became very annoyed, each believing the other was an imposter, each shouting divine warnings and orders to the other. Leon, who had sat quietly throughout much of the diatribe, announced that he was not coming back to any more meetings, which he claimed were "mental torture." However, the very next day, when Rokeach told the men it was time to get together again, they all assembled in the same room without the slightest protest. This went on for 2 years, and none of the men relinquished his delusional identity in that time period.

Hallucinations It is important to distinguish hallucinations from illusions, which are more common. **Illusions** occur when an actual sensory experience is misperceived or misinterpreted; the "man in the moon," for example, is an illusion, not a hallucination; likewise, mistaking a cat's meow for a human voice is an illusion. Hallucinations should also be distinguished from a range of unusual experiences that occur among mentally healthy people (Holroyd, Rabins, Finkelstein, and Lavrisha, 1994). After driving for an extended time without sleep, for example, people might begin to see things swimming in front of their eyes, or if they are alone in a strange building, they might easily be convinced that they hear noises that are not there. Unusual sensory experiences such as these are not considered hallucinations unless the person acts as if they are real, is unable to stop them, and reports that they persist no matter what the person does (Bentall, 1990; Heilbrun, 1993).

illusion: The misperception or misinterpretation of actual sensory experiences.

Hallucinations are characteristic of schizophrenia and occur in all modalities (Goghari, Harrow, Grossman, & Rosen, 2013). Hallucinators have difficulty discriminating between real events and their own subvocalizations, thoughts, daydreams, or mental images. They often misattribute these sensations to external sources; therefore, hallucinations give people the "illusion of reality" that seems to exist outside of their control. Baethge and colleagues (2005) examined the past-week prevalence of hallucinations in 4,972 hospitalized psychiatric patients and found that hallucinations were most common in the patients with schizophrenia, compared to those with other mental disorders. Sixty-eight percent of the people with schizophrenia were hallucinating, as compared to 11–23% of the people with bipolar disorders (depending upon the nature of the mood disorder) and 6% of the people with depression. Hallucinations were also more severe and less treatment responsive in the people with schizophrenia. Auditory-verbal hallucinations were the most common, being experienced by 75% of the people with schizophrenia. Prevalence rates vary, however, depending upon the sample (e.g., inpatient versus outpatient and cultural group; Ndetei & Vadher, 1984; Thomas et al., 2007), rating period (e.g., lifetime versus current), and grouping of modalities, with visual hallucinations typically reported to be the second most common in schizophrenia (Langdon, McGuire, Stevenson, & Catts, 2011). Across several studies, auditory hallucinations have been estimated in 47–98%, visual hallucinations in 14–69%, and other modalities (including somatic, olfactory, and gustatory) in 4–25% of people with schizophrenia (Langdon et al., 2011).

Auditory hallucinations, which usually involve hearing hallucinated voices, are the most common and often include content that is negative or abusive (Copolov, Mackinnon, & Trauer, 2004). Typically, the voices accuse the person of wrongdoing, belittle the person, or command the person to perform some act (as they did with Lionel Aldridge in the chapter-opening case). At times, two or more voices may seem to be conversing about the person, as was the case with Mark, a client who reported hearing the voices of a man, a woman, and a child, all telling him that he was Harry Truman and that he was responsible for killing thousands of

"The therapist says I've really made progress now that I've stopped talking to the cat."

Japanese people. They warned him that if he "was ever out of his house after 11 P.M.," he would be set on fire and burned to death. The voices usually taunted him, saying, "go out and burn," "come take your turn" over and over again. Most people with schizophrenia report that their voices are negative in content (53%), with 17% mixed and 27% neutral; no voices are described as having positive content only (Close & Garety, 1998). The type of perceived threat from the voice can vary greatly from one voice hearer to the next, and many people employ a range of "safety-seeking" behaviors designed to mitigate threats from malevolent voices. These safety-seeking behaviors are associated with beliefs about the voice (e.g., whether it is harmful, all-powerful, or all-knowing) and include things like hypervigilance, avoidance, compliance, or prayer (Hacker, Birchwood, Tudway, Meaden, & Amphlett, 2008).

Visual hallucinations are experienced in about one third of cases of schizophrenia. They usually involve visions of people or faces, although less distinct figures, objects, or flashes of light may be experienced as well. One person with schizophrenia reported seeing a computer screen behind her that displayed orders from her "higher in command" to audit the tax forms of her high-school classmates. A common visual hallucination involves the faces of devils and demons, who may also serve as the sources of hallucinated voices (Brewerton, 1994). It was originally thought that visual hallucinations were infrequent for those living with schizophrenia. However, recent evidence suggests that these symptoms are more common than originally believed, particularly in those on the more severe side of the spectrum of schizophrenia (Goghari et al., 2013).

Depending on the study, up to a fourth of people with schizophrenia report *somatic hallucinations*, in which the person feels bizarre sensations within the body—such as electricity shooting through the limbs. The most common forms of somatic hallucinations are tactile—for instance, feeling like bugs or other things are crawling under or on the skin (also known as formication). Actual physical sensations stemming from medical disorders (perhaps not yet diagnosed) and somatic symptom preoccupations with normal physical sensations (see Chapter 11) are not thought of as somatic hallucinations. *Gustatory* (taste) and *olfactory* (smell) *hallucinations* are less common experiences in people with schizophrenia, but they almost always have an unpleasant character. One person reported that he knew his food had been poisoned because he could taste arsenic in it. Others claim that their flesh smells as if it were rotting. Taste and smell hallucinations are more frequently seen in medical diseases, such as epilepsy, migraines, or Parkinson's disease, rather than mental disorders like schizophrenia.

Disordered Thought Processes Whereas delusions are disturbances in the *content* of thoughts, other positive symptoms of schizophrenia involve fundamental disturbances in the *form* of thought—in how thoughts are organized, controlled, reasoned, and processed (So et al., 2012). Almost all experts on schizophrenia agree that this **formal thought disorder** is also a key feature of the disorder. In fact, a meta-analysis comparing the cognitive performance of those with and without schizophrenia across multiple studies found that those with schizophrenia had significantly lower cognitive performance, suggesting that cognitive deficits in general are features of the disorder (Heinrichs, 2005). Because clinicians cannot directly observe how people think, however, they must infer thought processes from how people communicate through speech. Therefore, the *DSM-5* focuses on the presence of disorganized speech as evidence of formal thought disorder.

In thought disorder, which is present in 80–90% of people with schizophrenia during acute phases (Marengo, Harrow, & Edell, 1993), the speaker cannot maintain a specific train of thought. While conversing or answering a question, the person "slips off track," leaving the listener trying to follow a wandering stream of talk. Such speech makes little or no sense and has consequently been called *derailment, cognitive slippage,* or *loosening of associations.* At extreme levels, speech becomes a *word salad*, in which words seem to be mixed, tossed, and flung out at random. The following excerpt from the comments of a person with schizophrenia illustrates some of the common characteristics of this disordered speech:

formal thought disorder: Symptoms involving disturbances in the way thinking is organized.

If things levels in regards and "timed" to everything: I am referring to a previous document when I made some remarks that were also tested and there is another that concerns my daughter has a lobed bottomed right ear, her name being Mary Lou. . . . Much of abstraction has been left unsaid and undone in this product/milk syrup and others, due to economics, differentials, subsidies, bankruptcy, tools, buildings, bonds, national stocks, foundation crap, weather, trades, government in levels of breakages and fuse in electronics too all formerly "stated" not necessarily factuated. (Maher, 1968, p. 395)

Although most of the words in this passage are familiar, their arrangement does not make sense or communicate clear meaning. People with schizophrenia often show little awareness that they cannot be understood when speaking this way. Another sign of disordered thought processes is the creation of words, or *neologisms*, the meaning of which appears to be known only to the speaker. Two neologisms are italicized in the following example:

"...And that, in a nutshell, is my marketing plan. Any questions?"

The players and boundaries have been of different colors in terms of black and white, and I do not intend that the *futuramas* of supersonic fixtures will ever be in my life again because I believe that all known factors that would have its effect on me even the chemical reaction of ameno [sic] acids as they are in the process of *combustronability* are known to me. (Maher, 1968, p. 395)

Disordered thought processes may also be revealed through *perseveration*, in which the person seems to get stuck on a word or concept and repeats it over and over. Another sign of disordered thought is the presence of *clang associations*—words that are spoken apparently only because they sound alike.

Whereas delusions and cognitive deficits are distinct, they influence each other in that inaccurate cognitions increase or strengthen the central beliefs of delusions. In a study of 300 people with at least two psychotic episodes, having a strong conviction related to delusional beliefs, jumping to conclusions, and having less belief flexibility were distinct cognitive constructs (So et al., 2012). Forty-one percent of the sample had 100% conviction in their delusions, and 50% showed a jumping-to-conclusions bias. In addition, 50–75% showed a lack of belief flexibility, which was inversely related to delusional conviction (i.e., less belief flexibility meant stronger endorsement of one's delusions). Whereas cognitive deficits are clearly a part of schizophrenia, cognitive abilities do not appear to deteriorate over time (Heaton et al., 2001), although they also do not improve in response to medication or psychological therapy (So et al., 2012).

Disordered Behavior Another class of symptoms associated with schizophrenia is *disorganized behavior* that makes it impossible for individuals with schizophrenia to get dressed properly, prepare food, or take care of other daily needs. These people may also giggle or sob inappropriately or uncontrollably. Inappropriate sexual behavior, such as masturbating in public, is not uncommon. Some less dramatic behavioral anomalies associated with schizophrenia include facial grimaces, lip smacking, and other stereotyped behavior. One older male client would stuff all his pockets with magazine advertisements of attractive female models, while repeating again and again, "Oh, so that's what I'm doing." By the end of each day, so much ink from the magazines had rubbed off on him that his clothes were filthy.

In addition to strange behavior, people with schizophrenia may also make peculiar movements, hold themselves in contorted postures, walk in a peculiar fashion, and make absurd or obscene gestures. The most dramatic behaviors range across a dimension of **catatonia**. At one end of this dimension, the person becomes virtually immobile, maintaining an awkward body position for hours at a time. At the opposite extreme of catatonia, people may display great excitement, extreme motor activity, repetitive gestures and

catatonia: A dimension of disordered behavior ranging from immobility (where a person may maintain awkward body positions for hours at a time, appearing stuporous) to great excitement, extreme motor activity, repetitive gestures or mannerisms, and undirected violent behaviors.

mannerisms, and undirected violent behaviors (Kleinhaus et al., 2012). In the *DSM-5*, catatonia is a specifier of schizophrenia, meaning that a diagnosis of *schizophrenia with catatonia* is given when this symptom is present; this decision was based on evidence that there are different risk factors for schizophrenia with and without catatonia (Kleinhaus et al., 2012). Over the past few decades, catatonic symptoms have occurred less often with schizophrenia and more often in mood disorders (Stompe, Ortwein-Soboda, Ritter, Schanda, & Friedmann, 2002; Taylor & Fink, 2003). This has lead experts to question whether catatonia is necessarily a core symptom of schizophrenia or rather a behavioral pattern that can occur in the context of several disorders, including neurodevelopmental (see Chapter 3), bipolar (Chapter 5), and depressive disorders, as well as other medical conditions, such as autoimmune or paraneoplastic disorders (American Psychiatric Association, 2013a). Catatonia prevalence rates vary from 1–32%, depending on diagnostic criteria used, but current estimates put the occurrence of catatonic signs in psychiatric patients at about 7–15% (Kendurkar, 2008; Sayegh & Reid, 2010).

Negative Symptoms of Schizophrenia

Negative symptoms of schizophrenia contribute substantially to the morbidity and functional impairment seen in people with the disorder (Fervaha, Foussias, Agid, & Remington, 2014). These symptoms include social withdrawal, **anhedonia** (the inability to enjoy almost anything, as discussed in Chapter 6), flat affect (empty mood), alogia (diminished speech output), and avolition (no motivation). About a fourth to a third of people with schizophrenia present during an acute episode with primary negative symptoms, meaning that the symptoms are due to the disorder itself rather than to some other cause (Chang et al., 2011; Mäkinen, Miettunen, Isohanni, & Koponen, 2008). Even after taking medication, one or more negative symptoms were present in 57.6% of people with schizophrenia, with primary negative symptoms in 12.9% (Bobes, Arango, Garcia-Garcia, & Rejas, 2010). The most frequent negative symptoms were social withdrawal (45.8%), emotional withdrawal (39.1%), poor rapport (35.8%), and flat affect (33.1%; Bobes et al., 2010).

Flat Affect Many people with schizophrenia often stare straight ahead with an empty or glazed look (54% in one study of hospitalized patients; Selten, Wiersma, & van den Bosch, 2000). Even when spoken to, they make no eye contact with the speaker. Their faces are like emotionless masks. Their facial muscles appear slack, and they often speak in a voice so toneless it sounds robotic. Their entire demeanor is drab and listless. This 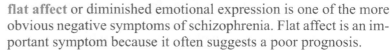 **flat affect** or diminished emotional expression is one of the more obvious negative symptoms of schizophrenia. Flat affect is an important symptom because it often suggests a poor prognosis.

Why does flat affect lead to exacerbation of schizophrenia? Much research over the last decade has investigated this very question. In one study, people with schizophrenia were compared to controls with regard to their emotional processing (Gur et al., 2006). More-prominent flat affect was associated with worse past and current quality of life. Overall, those with schizophrenia were less able to identify happy and sad emotions, and were less able to identify changes in the intensity of these emotions. Flat affect, above and beyond other negative symptoms of schizophrenia, predicted poor performance with emotional processing. Not being able to identify the emotions in others or the intensity of those emotions has critical implications, particularly related to interpersonal interactions and relationships, increasing the morbidity for those living with schizophrenia.

Alogia The failure to say much, if anything, in response to questions or comments is called **alogia**. This negative symptom is present in about half of hospitalized patients with schizophrenia (Selten et al., 2000). People with alogia do not appear especially

anhedonia: Loss of the ability to enjoy activities central to a person's life.

flat affect: Blunted emotionality, often consisting of minimal eye contact, an emotionless face, little or no tone in the voice, and a drab or listless demeanor.

alogia: A negative symptom of schizophrenia involving the failure to say much, if anything, in response to questions or comments.

The negative symptoms of schizophrenia—including social withdrawal, apathy, and dulled emotions—are among its most disabling features. Suicide attempts, although not officially listed as a negative symptom of schizophrenia, are a frequent complication of the disorder. Among people with schizophrenia, suicide is the leading cause of premature death, occurring in approximately 10% of individuals with the disorder (Bromet, Naz, Fochtmann, Carlson, & Tanenberg-Karant, 2005).

Source: dabjola/Shutterstock.com.

negativistic; they just seem to have little to say. Trying to talk with a person who is alogic often leaves a person wondering, "Is that all there is?" In other people, alogia takes the form of slow or delayed responses that become so frustrating that people finally give up trying to sustain the conversation.

Avolition   The behavioral counterpart to alogia is **avolition**. Avolitional people may simply sit for hours on end, making no attempt to do anything. If they do begin some activity, they often wander off in the middle of it, seeming to lose interest or to forget what they were doing.

avolition: A negative symptom of schizophrenia in which patients may sit for hours, making no attempt to do anything.

Avolition is present in over 90% of hospitalized patients with schizophrenia (Selten et al., 2000) and is often accompanied by social withdrawal and anhedonia. People may stare blankly at a television or become agitated by a hallucination, but otherwise, they seem to lack any capacity to be engaged by the environment. Sensitivity to painful stimulation and recognition that another person is experiencing pain is even reduced in some cases. People living with schizophrenia show less of an ability to detect and categorize their own pain or pain in others when presented with a sequence of videos of pain-inducing events (Wojakiewicz et al., 2013). Thus, negative symptoms such as avolition result in severe deficits in fundamental human processes, ranging from engagement in social activity to pain detection.

Distinguishing Schizophrenia From Other Psychotic Disorders

Before diagnosing schizophrenia, a clinician should consider other possible sources of the symptoms observed as part of what is termed a *differential diagnosis* (i.e., a list of disorders that might fit the symptom profile). As noted in Chapters 5 and 6, for example, severe mood disorders can produce some of the symptoms described here. Psychotic symptoms can also be produced by intoxication from alcohol or other drugs and by several medical conditions. For instance, hallucinations and delusions can result from Huntington's disease, multiple sclerosis, central nervous system infections, endocrine disorders such as hypo- or hyperthyroidism, metabolic disorders such as hypoglycemia, and liver or kidney disease (American Psychiatric Association, 2013a). In these cases, the disorder is classified as **psychotic disorder due to another medical condition**.

psychotic disorder due to another medical condition: A mental disorder involving psychotic symptoms caused by a medical illness or condition.

Clinicians also need to consider the symptoms of schizophrenia on a spectrum of number and severity of symptoms. Some disorders are schizophrenia-like, but they do not meet all the diagnostic criteria for schizophrenia, and they tend to be less severe. A common disorder considered on the spectrum of schizophrenia includes schizotypal personality disorder, discussed further in Chapter 16. Spectrum disorders also include several disorders classified by the *DSM-5* as **other psychotic disorders**: delusional disorder, brief psychotic disorder, schizophreniform disorder, and schizoaffective disorder. Most of these disorders are relatively rare, and research on their characteristics and causes is scant. Their symptoms are usually more limited in duration and less intense than those of schizophrenia.

other psychotic disorders: A group of mental disorders whose psychotic symptoms are usually more limited in duration and less intense than those of schizophrenia; includes schizophreniform disorder, schizoaffective disorder, delusional disorder, and brief psychotic disorder.

Delusional Disorder

People who display a rare form of psychosis known as **delusional disorder** show only minimal impairment in their daily life apart from the presence of at least one delusional belief. Usually, the delusion is persistent and causes these individuals to organize much of their life around it. Other than the delusional belief and its consequences, though, these individuals do not display odd or bizarre behavior. Perhaps for this reason, and because these people usually avoid clinicians, this disorder tends to be diagnosed later in life than schizophrenia. Table 4.2 describes the main subtypes of delusional disorder.

delusional disorder: A mental disorder in which the main symptom is the presence of at least one systematic delusional belief.

Brief Psychotic Disorder

"Nervous breakdown" and "falling to pieces" are familiar phrases used to describe people whose psychological functioning has rapidly deteriorated, usually after they have experienced a severe stressor. These cases are best described by what the *DSM-5* classifies as brief psychotic disorder.

TABLE 4.2 Subtypes of Delusional Disorder

Subtype	Description	Typical Behaviors
Erotomanic	Individuals believe that some other person, typically someone of notoriety or higher status, is secretly in love with them.	Stalking the love object, sending annoying texts or gifts, making unwanted phone calls, or taking other steps to contact the loved object (such as the woman who insisted that she was the secret lover of David Letterman)
Jealous	Individuals believe that their romantic partners are being unfaithful, despite very little evidence.	Following the partner or constantly checking on the partner's whereabouts through phone calls or repeated demands for the partner's attention
Grandiose	Individuals believe that they have a special talent, have made an important discovery, know someone of great importance, or have a special relationship with God beyond that associated with established religion.	Trying to convert others into followers or provoking confrontations with authorities (such as David Koresch, leader of the Branch Davidian sect)
Persecutory	Individuals believe that they are being spied on, cheated, followed, or otherwise taken advantage of.	Becoming increasingly isolated and bitter, often trying to bring about opportunities to fight their alleged persecutors or to obtain legal remedies for problems
Somatic	Individuals hold beliefs about their bodies, such as the delusion that a rancid odor is seeping out, that their ears are grossly misshapen, or that they have foreign organisms under the skin.	Becoming preoccupied with hiding the defect or hypersensitive to signs that someone else has noticed it

brief psychotic disorder: The sudden onset of psychotic symptoms marked by intense emotional turmoil and confusion.

Unlike most cases of schizophrenia, **brief psychotic disorder** is characterized by the sudden onset of an episode marked by intense emotional turmoil and confusion and the appearance of positive psychotic symptoms, such as hallucinations, delusions, incoherent speech, and catatonic or disorganized behavior. During this episode, the person is at high risk for attempting suicide. By definition, the episode must last at least 1 day but less than 1 month, after which the individual returns to a normal level of functioning. If the symptoms last longer than 1 month, the diagnosis should be changed to one of the other psychotic disorders.

Often, brief psychotic disorder is a reaction to a severe stressor, such as the death of a loved one, but occasionally, no precipitating stressor can be identified. Whether a stressor precipitated the symptoms is specified when making the diagnosis. Also, when brief psychotic disorder follows childbirth, it is specified as having a **postpartum onset**.

postpartum onset: Beginning of a disorder shortly after giving birth.

Schizophreniform Disorder

schizophreniform disorder: A disorder in which people experience symptoms of schizophrenia for only a few months.

People who experience the symptoms of schizophrenia for only a few months are given the diagnosis of **schizophreniform disorder**. There are two major differences between schizophrenia and schizophreniform disorder. First, impaired social or occupational functioning is not required for a diagnosis of schizophreniform disorder. Second, in schizophreniform disorder, the symptoms are present for at least 1 but not more than 6 months. About one third of people with schizophreniform disorder recover and go on to live without impairment in daily functioning or changes in mood; the other two thirds eventually warrant a diagnosis of schizophrenia or schizoaffective disorder (Bromet et al., 2011).

schizoaffective disorder: A mental disorder in which the person displays symptoms of both schizophrenia and a mood disorder without satisfying the full criteria for either diagnosis.

Schizoaffective Disorder

In **schizoaffective disorder**, people display either hallucinations or delusions that resemble those experienced in schizophrenia, but during the same psychotic episode, the symptoms of a mood disorder are also present. However, to distinguish schizoaffective disorder from depressive or bipolar disorder with psychotic features, the individual must also display delusions or hallucinations for 2 weeks in the absence of a major mood disorder. Whereas interruption in daily functioning may be present, it is not a defining characteristic of the disorder. Therefore, the prognosis for schizoaffective disorder is generally better than for schizophrenia but worse than for mood disorders. Unfortunately, the presence of depressive symptoms increases the risk for suicide (Hor & Taylor, 2010). Schizoaffective disorder is less prevalent than schizophrenia and is more often diagnosed in females than in males (Malhi, Green, Fagiolini, Peselow, & Kumari, 2008).

Substance-Induced Psychotic Disorder

Hallucinations and delusions can result from ingestion of various substances, including drugs of abuse (such as cocaine and cannabis), medications (such as corticosteroids), or toxins (such as organophosphate insecticides). When people begin to experience hallucinations or delusions during or shortly after intoxication, exposure to, or withdrawal from a substance, and the symptoms are not attributable to an episode of delirium (see Chapter 15), they qualify for the diagnosis of substance/medication-induced psychotic disorder. In fact, many substances of abuse, including alcohol, nicotine, cannabis, and cocaine, have been associated with schizophrenia onset—psychotic symptoms that persist for months after the drugs have left the person's system—and may be implicated in the causal mechanisms of the disorder (Frisher, 2010; Jordaan & Emsley, 2014; Lieberman, Kinon, & Loebel, 1990).

substance/medication-induced psychotic disorder: A mental disorder in which a person experiences psychotic symptoms beyond what is expected from intoxication or withdrawal from a substance, and in which the person is not aware that the substance is producing the psychotic symptoms.

Section Review

The current definition of schizophrenia evolved from:

- Morel's original description, in the mid-1800s, of dementia praecox as a syndrome marked by the premature loss of the ability to reason;
- Kraepelin's identification, in the late 1800s, of dementia praecox as a major mental disorder with several subtypes; and
- Bleuler's broader definition of the disorder, which he named *schizophrenia*, because he viewed the splitting of psychological functions as the core of the problem.

Schizophrenia is a heterogeneous disorder in terms of its presentation, and its symptoms can be divided into two main categories:

- positive symptoms, which include delusions, hallucinations, disturbances in the form of thinking, and disorganized and grossly inappropriate behavior; and
- negative symptoms, which include social withdrawal, anhedonia, flat affect, alogia, and avolition.

Disorders associated with schizophrenia can be viewed dimensionally, based on:

- the type of symptoms present and the longevity of those symptoms;
- the presence of severe mood disorders; and
- intoxication from alcohol or other drugs.

Living With Schizophrenia

Schizophrenia comes in many shapes and forms. It can appear suddenly, as it did with Lionel Aldridge in the chapter-opening case, or it can develop slowly over several years. It can affect teenagers, or it can first occur in people who are over 50. In some cases, the most prominent symptoms are hallucinations or delusions; other people suffer primarily from negative symptoms (Paris, 2013). Some people make a complete recovery, others only partial, and roughly a fourth of people with schizophrenia continue to suffer symptoms of the disorder even when they take medications. Some remain hospitalized for years, unimproved by any treatment. In truth, the term *schizophrenia* encompasses several disorders that vary dramatically in onset, number, type, and intensity of symptoms, impairment, and prognosis (Paris, 2013). To highlight these differences, contrast the case of Lionel Aldridge that begins this chapter with that of Louise:

Louise is a pale, stooped woman of 39 years, whose childlike face is surrounded by scraggly blond braids tied with pink ribbons. She was referred for a psychiatric evaluation by her family doctor, who was concerned about her low level of functioning. Her only complaint to him was, "I have a decline in self-care and a low life level." Her mother says that there has indeed been a decline that has occurred over many years. In the last few months, Louise has remained in her room, mute and still.

Twelve years ago, Louise was a supervisor in the occupational therapy department of a hospital, living in her own apartment, and engaged to a young man. After he broke off the engagement, she became increasingly disorganized, wandering aimlessly in the street and wearing mismatched clothing. She was fired from her job, and eventually, the police were called to hospitalize her. They broke into her apartment, which was a shambles, filled with papers, food, and broken objects. This hospitalization lasted 3 months, after which Louise was discharged to her mother's house.

Following discharge, her family hoped that Louise would pull herself together and get back on track, but over the years, she became more withdrawn. She spent most of her time watching TV and cooking with bizarre combinations of ingredients, such as broccoli and cake mix, which she then ate by herself because no one else in the family would. She hoarded stacks of cookbooks and recipes. Often, when her mother entered her room, Louise would grab a magazine and pretend to be reading, when in fact she had just been sitting and staring into space. She stopped bathing and brushing her hair or her teeth. She ate less and less, although she denied losing her appetite, and over a period of several years, she lost 20 pounds. She slept at odd hours.

On admission to the psychiatric hospital, Louise sat with her hands clasped in her lap and avoided looking at the doctor who interviewed her. She answered questions and did not appear suspicious, but her mood was shallow. She denied having depressed mood, delusions, or hallucinations. However, her answers became odder as the interview progressed. In response to a question about her cooking habits, she replied that she did not wish to discuss recent events in Russia. When discussing her decline in functioning, she said, "There's more of a take-off mechanism when you're younger." Asked about ideas of reference, she said, "I doubt it's true, but if one knows the writers involved, it could be an element that would be directed in a comical way." Between answers she repeated the mantra, "I'm safe. I'm safe." (Based on Spitzer, Gibbon, Skodol, Williams, & First, 1994)

Connections

What are the symptoms of autism spectrum disorder? How do its suspected causes differ from those of schizophrenia? See Chapter 3.

premorbid phase: The time period before the prodrome, in which it is possible to identify delays in early neurodevelopment (e.g., not meeting key pediatric milestones) that may suggest an increased risk of developing schizophrenia in the future.

prodromal phase: The usual first phase of schizophrenia in which there is an insidious onset of problems, suggesting psychological deterioration.

The Course of Schizophrenia

Only about 4% of all diagnosed cases of schizophrenia develop before age 15. After that age, the rate of onset increases rapidly, reaching a peak around the age of 25 (great news for most college students!). The average age of people first admitted to a hospital because of schizophrenia is about 30. Contrary to early views, schizophrenia can develop when people are as old as 50–60 years, with about 23% of people living with schizophrenia experiencing their first onset of symptoms after the age of 40 (Howard, Rabins, Seeman, & Jeste, 2000).

Recent conceptualizations of schizophrenia suggest that the disorder constitutes at least three phases (Agius, Goh, Ulhaq, & McGorry, 2010): prodromal phase, active phase (acute psychosis), and residual phase (chronic illness), although at times demarcation between these phases is imprecise (Tandon, Nasrallah, & Keshavan, 2009). Recent biological research supports these phases, suggesting that schizophrenia may be a disorder of both neurodevelopment and neurodegeneration (see the "Controversy" feature). In some classifications, a fourth phase is described, called the **premorbid phase**, a time period before any symptoms are present. Instead, this phase represents the genetic vulnerability coupled with the environmental exposures that together confer risk for the disorder. Although the onset of symptoms of schizophrenia may begin abruptly, most cases start with a **prodromal phase**, in which affected persons show an insidious onset of problems that suggest that something is going wrong with them. They may start to avoid meals with

Schizophrenia: An Appropriate Diagnostic Label or One in Need of Reconceptualization?

A significant amount of evidence supports the *DSM-5* diagnostic category of schizophrenia. The diagnosis does have characteristic symptoms, including positive, negative, motor, mood, and cognitive symptoms that are modestly responsive to antipsychotic medication (Tandon, Keshavan, & Nasrallah, 2008). Also, there is much evidence that schizophrenia is a valid diagnostic entity because the conceptualization of the disorder across cultures is highly similar, and the interrater reliability of the diagnosis is high (Jakobsen, Frederiksen, Parnas, & Werge, 2006), meaning that different clinicians would diagnose schizophrenia after assessing the same person. Tandon and Maj (2008) argue that the diagnosis itself is a seemingly parsimonious construct that carries with it a wealth of information to society, researchers, clients, and clinicians.

However, there is mounting evidence suggesting that the current conceptualization of schizophrenia does not come close to grasping the heterogeneity—vast differences—in symptom presentation and course that is repeatedly seen in research studies (Paris, 2013; Tandon et al., 2009). Although there have been significant developments in determining potential causes of the disorder, as presented later in this chapter, there is yet to be a reliable biological model of schizophrenia that adequately incorporates the different courses of individuals living with it. For example, neurobiological findings that have been discovered in one study with one group of people living with schizophrenia have not always been replicated in other cohorts.

One significant change that was made from the *DSM-IV* to the *DSM-5* suggests that the definition of schizophrenia is changing. In the previous *DSM*, there were a number of subtypes that could be diagnosed for the purpose of attempting to account for the heterogeneity in symptom presentation. These included designations for disorganized cognitions and behaviors, paranoia, and mood disturbances. In a large part because these subtypes were unstable over time (Helmes & Landmark, 2003) and because their designation did not help to differentiate treatment (Regier, 2007), they were abandoned when the diagnosis was reviewed for the current diagnostic manual.

Whereas this represents some progress in redefining this disorder, Tandon and colleagues (2009) suggest that more changes are needed. For example, instead of individuals being categorized by their most prominent symptom, they could be evaluated across the multiple symptom domains that are characteristic of the disorder because these are likely representative of related, yet distinct, entities. Take the diagnosis of schizoaffective disorder. The characteristic features include a mood disturbance along with psychotic symptoms. There is also the possibility that one could have a major depressive disorder along with psychotic features. Instead of considering two separate disorders, a new method of understanding symptoms could include a severity rating on the psychotic symptoms and then the mood symptoms separately over the course of the disorder. This would entail more of a dimensional rather than an entirely categorical approach to diagnosis, as discussed further in Chapter 16.

Tom Insel, a researcher at the National Institute of Mental Health, has proposed that a new conceptualization should involve the view that schizophrenia is a neurodevelopmental disorder (see Chapter 3). He argues that, given all of the evidence highlighting perinatal and adolescent risk for schizophrenia, the beginning of severe symptoms in late adolescence to early adulthood should be seen as the later stage of the disorder, rather than its onset (Insel, 2010). If schizophrenia is viewed from a developmental perspective, with stages of the disorder starting during infancy and early childhood, when particular factors arise that confer risk for the disorder, then treatment efforts can be more targeted. Some researchers believe that it is only within a new conceptualization of schizophrenia that we can move more effectively toward its prevention.

Thinking Critically

1. Does removing the subtypes of schizophrenia (e.g., paranoid schizophrenia) represent progress in understanding the disorder or a step backward in your view?

2. What do you think about the idea—for schizophrenia as well as for other mental disorders—of using a dimensional (rating on each domain) rather than categorical (you have a disorder or you do not) approach to diagnosis?

3. Does it make sense to view schizophrenia as a developmental disorder and look for early signs in children? How could that help people?

their families or stop paying attention to their appearance and hygiene. Often, they start to talk in unusual ways, behave just a little strangely, and seem easily irritated and frustrated, resulting in difficulties at school, work, or socially. As a general rule, the longer this prodromal phase lasts, the poorer the prognosis.

"You know, Mr. Symes, you are not actually a doctor. . . . You're just in the active phase of your schizophrenia right now so you think that you work here."

Source: Cartoonresource.com.

active phase (of schizophrenia): The stage of schizophrenia during which one or more psychotic symptoms, such as delusions or hallucinations, appear.

residual phase (of schizophrenia): A stage of schizophrenia during which most psychotic symptoms have subsided in frequency and intensity; the affected person may still be withdrawn and apathetic, behave strangely at times, and continue to show social and occupational impairments.

Eventually, but usually after some crisis, prodromal symptoms progress to an **active phase**, sometimes called the first-episode phase, in which one or more psychotic symptoms, such as delusions and hallucinations, break into the open. The disorder appears most serious and obvious to other people during this phase, as those living with the disorder lose insight into the problems they are experiencing.

Following the active phase is a **residual phase**, during which the psychotic symptoms subside in frequency and intensity; this is also referred to as the chronic or stable stage of the disorder. This stage may resemble the prodromal phase; individuals may be withdrawn and apathetic, behave strangely at times, and continue to show social and occupational impairments that may result in a lower level of functioning than even during the prodromal phase. There tend to be peaks and valleys to the intensity of the symptoms, depending upon engagement in treatment and psychosocial stressors present in the individual's life.

Whereas it is helpful to think about the progression of schizophrenia in stages for treatment purposes, it is just as important to acknowledge that the course of schizophrenia is highly variable and individualized. Clearly, schizophrenia does not inevitably result in permanent disability, although most people with schizophrenia continue to suffer recurring symptoms. In some cases, the symptoms improve so that people can live almost completely on their own. In other cases, people improve for a while and then suffer a relapse in which the symptoms can be serious enough to require rehospitalization. Remission has a reported rate of 17–78% in first-episode schizophrenia and 16–62% in people with multiple episodes (AlAqeel & Margolese, 2012). The pattern of symptom exacerbation and de-escalation may be repeated several times, but as people age, they are hospitalized less often. The rate of rehospitalization in those over the age of 65 living with schizophrenia is about 19% but exceeds 28% in people ages 45–64 years, with a disproportionate number of rehospitalizations occurring in those with public (rather than private) health insurance (Elixhauser & Steiner, 2013).

An important study completing a 15- to 25-year follow-up of 644 people living with schizophrenia found that over half had favorable outcomes following the initial onset of the disorder, with minimal symptoms, reasonable functioning, and employment (Harrison et al., 2001). A systematic review also supported the notion that outcome from first-episode psychosis may be more favorable than previously reported, with 42% of people experiencing good outcomes across 37 studies and 4,100 participants (Menezes, Arenovich, & Zipursky, 2006). However, reaching functional recovery earlier in the onset of the disorder is less common, with only about 14% of people recovering for more than 2 years in the first 5 years of the disorder (Robinson, Woerner, McMeniman, Mendelowitz, & Bilder, 2004). Overall, a diagnosis of schizophrenia is associated with a poorer outcome than other diagnostic groups, such as mood disorders, and symptom patterns seem to be stable over the course of the disorder (Lang, Kösters, Lang, Becker, & Jäger, 2013). The variables most frequently associated with remission are better premorbid function, milder symptoms at baseline (especially fewer negative symptoms), early response to treatment, and shorter duration of untreated psychosis (AlAqeel & Margolese, 2012). As it is evident that the course of schizophrenia is highly variable, it is essential to consider who is more or less impacted by the disorder.

Who Is Affected by Schizophrenia?

Even though schizophrenia is less common than most other mental disorders in this textbook, it nonetheless has a huge impact in terms of disease burden, hospitalizations, and even homelessness (see Chapter 17; Centers for Disease Control and Prevention, 2014). Worldwide, about 51 million people suffer from schizophrenia, approximately 2.2 million of whom live in the United States (Narrow, Rae, Robins, & Regier, 2002; Torrey, 2001). Annually, new cases arise at a rate of 8 to 40 per 100,000 persons (McGrath et al., 2004), and at any given time, 0.3–1.0% of the population has a diagnosis of schizophrenia (Goldner, Hsu, Waraich, & Somers, 2002), with a 0.7% lifetime risk of developing the disorder (Saha, Chant, Welham, & McGrath, 2005).

Cultural Background

Does culture make a difference in the risk for schizophrenia? Interest in this question dates back to the late 1800s, when Kraepelin himself explored this issue by touring several countries to examine their mental patients. After traveling to Singapore, where he examined patients from Java, China, and Malaya, Kraepelin concluded that their symptoms were remarkably similar to those of his patients in Germany. Such experiences convinced Kraepelin that the disorder was transmitted genetically and was universal.

The strongest support for the universality of schizophrenia comes from a series of studies sponsored by the World Health Organization (WHO) called the "International Pilot Study on Schizophrenia" (IPSS) and the "Determinants of Outcome of Severe Mental Disorders" (DOSMD) (World Health Organization, 1978). Beginning in the 1960s, these studies were conducted in 12 research centers in 10 countries: Denmark, India, Nigeria, Columbia, Russia, China, Czechoslovakia, Japan, the United Kingdom, and the United States. The WHO studies reached several conclusions. First, the descriptions of symptoms for people with schizophrenia in the various countries were similar; in fact, based on symptom patterns alone, it was not possible to identify the country from which people were drawn (Jablensky et al., 1992)—a finding confirmed by subsequent research (Crow, 2008). Second, the **morbidity risk**, defined as the risk that a given person has of developing the disorder over his or her lifetime, averaged 1%. Third, at each site, the prevalence of schizophrenia (whether defined by broad or narrow criteria) was significant. More recent research confirms these findings and even expands them, suggesting that the prevalence rates of schizophrenia are stable across such factors as culture, gender, religion, and geographic region (Jablensky, 1999).

However, other studies have found greater variation in schizophrenia prevalence than those found by the initial WHO studies. For example, a study by Goldner, Hsu, Waraich, and Somers (2002) determined that, particularly in Asian countries (Hong Kong, Taiwan, and Korea), lifetime prevalence rates of schizophrenia are only 0.12 to 0.41 per 100 persons, whereas rates in Finland, the United States, and Puerto Rico are significantly higher (1.0 to 2.6 per 100 persons). Whether geographic and cultural variations play a role in the onset of schizophrenia, culture does seem to matter when it comes to the prognosis for schizophrenia, and it matters in a surprising way (Kalra, Bhugra, & Shah, 2012). People with schizophrenia from so-called developing or Third World countries show *higher* rates of improvement than people from more developed countries (Hopper, Harrison, Janca, & Sartorius, 2007). For example, in a cross-national clinical study of people living with schizophrenia, over a 3-year time period, 84% of those diagnosed with the disorder in East Asia achieved remission, whereas only 60% achieved remission in northern Europe (Haro et al., 2011). Whereas many different biopsychosocial reasons have been offered to explain this puzzling finding (Kalra et al., 2012), two leading factors may be the interrelated arms of treatment and relationships. In many non-Western societies, schizophrenia may be treated with more informal, community-led methods rather than the medications described later in the chapter (Hopper et al., 2007). Researchers hypothesize that the

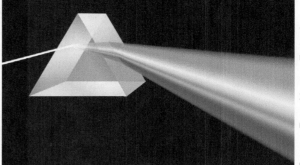

Source: Peter Hermes Furian/Shutterstock.com.

Syd Barrett (1946–2006) was a founding member of the band Pink Floyd, whose classic album *Dark Side of the Moon* had an album cover similar to the image shown here. Barrett was one of the most legendary rock stars to develop schizophrenia, likely triggered by significant drug use, as well as the stress and pressure of his career. Floyd classics such as "Shine on You Crazy Diamond" and "Wish You Were Here" were written as tributes to Barrett, who spent the last 3 decades of his life in a quiet cottage in Cambridge, England. Other famous cases of schizophrenia include Jack Kerouac, an American novelist at the forefront of the Beat Generation in the 1950s and 1960s, and John Forbes Nash, Jr. (1928–), an American mathematician and 1994 Nobel Prize winner. Nash is the subject of the 2001 Hollywood movie *A Beautiful Mind*. The film, loosely based on the biography of the same name, focuses on Nash's mathematical genius and also his battles with schizophrenia.

morbidity risk: The risk of individuals developing a disorder over their lifetime.

better outcomes for those with schizophrenia in developing nations are due to relative levels of social connectedness and acceptance in these cultures (Vedantam, 2005), although further cross-cultural studies are seeking to clarify the findings.

Even if cultural variation in the prevalence of schizophrenia is small, culture might make a difference in other ways. For one thing, it might affect the form of some hallucinations. For example, visual hallucinations have declined since the 19th century, whereas auditory hallucinations have increased. The content of hallucinations also tends to reflect themes that are prominent in a person's culture (Al-Issa, 1977). Among younger people in Western societies, hallucinations often include technological features—neon lights explode, loud noises buzz, and computer screens flash. In contrast, the voices of ghosts, dragons, or animals are likely to appear in the hallucinations of people in cultures with less modern technology. Furthermore, culture may play a role for individuals who immigrate to countries where racism and discrimination are present. In a study of second-generation Afro-Caribbeans living in the United Kingdom, significantly higher incidence rates of schizophrenia were evident, suggesting that the stress related to a potentially hostile social climate may lead to an increase in reported symptoms (Cantor-Graae & Selten, 2005). In the United States, higher rates of schizophrenia are also seen in migrant and ethnic minority groups (Kalra et al., 2012). We return to this issue when we discuss social causes of schizophrenia later in this chapter.

Gender, Morbidity, and Mortality Risk

The morbidity risk for schizophrenia is essentially equal for males and females in Western developed countries (Thara, 2004). However, as Figure 4.1 shows, males tend to be diagnosed with schizophrenia at earlier ages than females (Rajji, Ismail, & Mulsant, 2009), with the typical age of onset for men being 10–25 years (average of 21), but 25–35 years (average of 27) for women. As a result, males account for the majority of cases of schizophrenia with onset before age 30; females predominate among cases with later onset (Hafner et al., 1998). Women also tend to have a bimodal distribution of age at onset, while men display a unimodal distribution, with a peak for men and women from age 18–30 years, but a second peak later in life among women (American Psychological Association, 2013a). The prognosis for men diagnosed with schizophrenia also tends to be worse (Lang et al., 2013). In comparison to men, women tend to have less-severe premorbid symptoms, fewer negative symptoms (which is in itself a positive prognostic factor), and lower cognitive impairment. Women with schizophrenia also have lower rates of suicide than men, even though their reported mood symptoms tend to be worse (Lester, 2006; Grossman, Harrow, Rosen, Faull, & Strauss, 2008; Koster et al., 2008). Finally, women have better treatment outcomes. Interestingly, though, gender differences related to the symptom presentation and age at onset are less evident in people living in non-Western and developing countries (Venkatesh et al., 2008; Thara, 2004).

FIGURE 4.1

Hospitalizations for Schizophrenia in General Hospitals per 100,000 by Age Group, Canada, 1999/2000

As this figure shows, younger males are hospitalized at the greatest rate across the age spectrum of schizophrenia.

Source: Based on data from the Centre for Chronic Disease Prevention and Control, Health Canada.

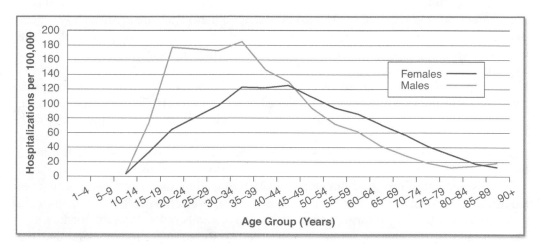

Whereas people living with schizophrenia experience a number of symptoms related to the disorder, they are also at a two-fold greater risk for mortality, compared to same-aged individuals without schizophrenia, with a lifespan shortened by approximately 15–20 years (Parks, Svendsen, Singer, & Foti, 2006; Auquier, Lancon, Rouillon, & Lader, 2007). This abbreviated lifespan is partially attributable to a higher rate of death by suicide and accidents (Pompili, Lester, Innamorati, Tatarelli, & Girardi, 2008). Within the population of individuals with schizophrenia, almost one in three people attempts suicide, and 5–10% die from suicide (Hor & Taylor, 2010; Hunt et al., 2006). In addition, other medical conditions account for greater than half of the risk for increased mortality, due in part to an under-recognition and poor treatment of those medical conditions (Szpakowicz & Herd, 2008). The increased morbidity and mortality associated with schizophrenia substantially increases the disease burden of this mental disorder.

Section Review

Schizophrenia usually follows a course of four stages:

- the premorbid phase,
- the prodromal phase,
- the active phase, and
- the residual phase.

Schizophrenia occurs:

- worldwide at a prevalence rate of about 1%,
- equally in males and females,
- earlier for males than females, and
- usually in the late teens or early 20s, but also as late as the 50s.

Cross-cultural and gender research suggests that:

- the prevalence of schizophrenia is equal across culture, religion, and countries;
- the prognosis is poorer for people living in more developed industrialized nations;
- higher rates of schizophrenia are seen in migrant and ethnic minority groups in those nations;
- women have a better prognosis than men; and
- morbidity and mortality are high and increase the disease burden of schizophrenia.

Biological Causes of Schizophrenia

Schizophrenia has always been considered a complex disorder, and most modern researchers agree that it has no single cause. Researchers are studying many potential biological and environmental determinants of the disorder, and some of the factors examined include heritability, neurodevelopment, fetal and perinatal factors, drug use, trauma, and socioeconomic status (Brown, 2011). The sections that follow review some of the evidence suggesting that risk for schizophrenia stems from a combination of biological and environmental factors.

Genetic Vulnerability

Kraepelin's examination of patients in various countries persuaded him that dementia praecox was not due to differences in childrearing, food, climate, or the environment. Because the disorder occurred in widely varying cultures, Kraepelin argued that it must be a biological disease transmitted genetically. Today, scientists have far better evidence that genetics play an important role in the development of schizophrenia.

The closer a person's biological relationship to someone diagnosed with schizophrenia, the greater that person's risk of developing schizophrenia or one of the schizophrenia spectrum disorders. The evidence for these conclusions comes from three major lines of investigation: family aggregation studies, twin studies, and adoption studies. Collectively, these types of studies have revealed the following:

- Schizophrenia "runs" or aggregates in families.
- This aggregation is found regardless of the type of research methodology (family, adoption, or twin studies) used or the country in which the study is performed.
- In many cases, a vulnerability that predisposes a person to schizophrenia (scientists do not know exactly what) is genetically transmitted.
- Estimates for the heritability of schizophrenia, defined as the observable variance that is attributable to genetic factors, vary from 60–70% (McGue, Gottesman, & Rao, 1983; Rao, Morton, Gottesman, & Lew, 1981).
- Genes alone are not sufficient to account for the development of schizophrenia.

Family Aggregation Studies

Family aggregations of schizophrenia have been examined since the early part of the 20th century. These studies begin with identified people with schizophrenia, called *proband* or *index cases*. The percentage of their family members who are also diagnosed with schizophrenia is then compared with the percentage diagnosed among family members of control cases, matched for age and other relevant variables. Family studies tell researchers the extent to which the disorder runs in families, but not why it does so.

Family studies agree on one fundamental point: The closer an individual's genetic relationship to a person with schizophrenia, the higher the risk of developing schizophrenia. This relationship is dramatically illustrated in Figure 4.2, which shows data compiled in a classic paper by Irving Gottesman, a psychologist at the University of Virginia, from 40 of the most reliable family studies conducted between 1920 and 1987 in Germany, Switzerland, Scandinavia, and the United Kingdom. The progression of increasing risk for schizophrenia with an increasing degree of family relationship is striking. Equally striking, however, is the fact that, even at the highest degree of genetic relationship, the majority of relatives to an index case are *not* diagnosed with schizophrenia.

Given that the majority of relatives of individuals with schizophrenia are not themselves diagnosed with the disorder, how can researchers evaluate other possible contributors to schizophrenia? As they have for other disorders, twin studies provide one way of exploring the roles of genetic and environmental factors.

Twin Studies

Because monozygotic (MZ) identical twins are virtual genetic clones of one another, if one MZ twin has schizophrenia, then the other should as well *if* schizophrenia were due solely to genetic transmission. Similarly, because nonidentical or dizygotic (DZ) twins share only half of their genes, if schizophrenia were due only to genetic factors, and if a DZ twin develops schizophrenia, the co-twin should have a 50% chance of becoming schizophrenic. To the extent that observed rates of *concordance* (sharing the disorder) differ from these anticipated percentages, factors other than genes must contribute to the disorder.

FIGURE 4.2 Family Risks for Developing Schizophrenia

The degree of risk for developing schizophrenia increases with the extent of shared genes with a person who has schizophrenia.

Source: Based on data from Gottesman (1991).

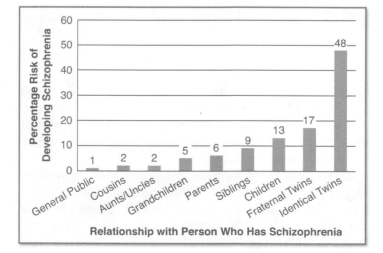

As Figure 4.2 indicates, averaged across several studies, the schizophrenia concordance rate is 48% for MZ twins and 17% for DZ twins (Gottesman, 1991). Another study found that the concordance rate for one twin having schizophrenia if the other twin has the disorder is 25–50%, compared to about 6–15% for nonidentical twins (Cardno et al., 1999). Thus, the difference between MZ and DZ rates supports a role for genetic influence, but the fact that only about half of the identical twins of people with schizophrenia develop the disorder themselves means that genetics alone cannot account for all of the causality.

Adoption Studies

Another method for evaluating the genetic contribution to schizophrenia examines children born to parents with schizophrenia who are then adopted and raised by families without schizophrenia in the home. Such adoption studies have usually been conducted in Europe because of the superior adoption records maintained there. If children born to parents with schizophrenia but then raised by normal adoptive families later develop schizophrenia at a higher rate than do adopted children born to parents without schizophrenia, there is support for a genetic contribution to schizophrenia.

The first published adoption study of schizophrenia examined the adult offspring of 47 female patients at the Oregon State Mental Institution (Heston, 1966). These children had been placed in adoptive families within 3 days of birth. By age 36, 5 of them had been diagnosed with schizophrenia. In contrast, not one member of a comparison group of 50 adopted children born to mothers without schizophrenia had developed schizophrenia by age 36. The most comprehensive adoptive studies of schizophrenia were conducted in Finland and yielded similar results (Tienari, 1991; Tienari et al., 1987, 2004). These studies were able to compare three different groups of children raised by adoptive families: two groups with biological mothers with schizophrenia and the third group with biological mothers without the disorder. Additionally, the researchers rated the level of discord or tension in the adoptive home, and categorized the homes as either healthy or disturbed. Results showed that children of biological mothers with schizophrenia who were raised in an adoptive family with low levels of discord had only a 1.5% lifetime risk of schizophrenia, higher than the general population (<1%) but still fairly low. Conversely, children without maternal history of the disorder but with high levels of adoptive family discord had a 4.8% lifetime risk of developing schizophrenia. But the mean risk for schizophrenia was over 13% in children of mothers with schizophrenia who were reared in dysfunctional (high-conflict) families, indicating how genetic and environmental risks interact to produce the disorder (Tienari et al., 2004).

Thus, whereas genetics play a role in the development of this disorder, it is also quite clear that the environmental factors one is exposed to during childhood are a large part of the picture. In fact, some researchers have concluded that a closer look at the studies used to compile Figure 4.2 might lead psychologists to decide that, in addition to problems in schizophrenia adoption research and the ongoing failure to find postulated "schizophrenia genes," the evidence supporting a genetic basis for schizophrenia is far weaker than is currently believed (Joseph & Leo, 2006).

A Model of Genetic Influence

For decades now, scientists have been trying to pinpoint a gene or pattern of genes that might explain how genetic transmission of schizophrenia occurs. The difficulty in finding the sites of genes influencing schizophrenia is probably due in part to the complexity of genetic influence. The genes that contribute to schizophrenia do not operate as simply as those determining hair color. For example, if you have brown hair, there is a very high probability that at least one of your parents also has brown hair. However, almost 80% of people with schizophrenia do *not* have a parent with schizophrenia, and 60% of people with schizophrenia have a negative family history for the disorder (Gottesman, 2001).

What kind of genetic model can explain such patterns? Today, most investigators believe that the genetic contribution to the majority of cases of schizophrenia is *polygenic*, meaning that a mosaic of different genes act in concert to influence the development, probability, and severity of schizophrenia. No single dominant gene or no two recessive genes determine vulnerability in most cases of schizophrenia, although certain genes probably play a major role in the presence of several smaller genetic influences. Approximately 10 gene variations are linked to schizophrenia, and it is believed that, if a person exhibits any number of these gene variations, then the risk for schizophrenia increases.

Many authorities in the field believe that a **diathesis-stress model** probably best explains most cases of schizophrenia (Zubin & Spring, 1977) and that genes are at least one major source of the diatheses. In other words, schizophrenia may be a disorder that results from the interacting effects of a predisposition or genetic vulnerability for the disorder (the diathesis) and stressors that trigger the diathesis into a full clinical disorder. The diathesis could be a characteristic of the central nervous system resulting from lead exposure during pregnancy, birth complications, high-stress experiences when young, brain-altering drugs that the person uses, or a feature of a person's basic personality that makes up the core of schizophrenia, a kind of fuel that is inert until a match brings about combustion. This model fits with the genetic information available that suggests that schizophrenia is genetically influenced but not genetically determined (Gottesman, 2001). When individuals have a couple of the gene variants that increase risk for schizophrenia but a number of severe and frequent environmental exposures, they may develop schizophrenia. Likewise, other individuals may have a number of gene variants implicating risk for schizophrenia and, even with few environmental stressors present, the threshold for developing schizophrenia is met.

Several research teams have been searching for a behavior that could serve as a *genetic marker* for schizophrenia, thereby allowing identification of people who are at risk for the disorder, with the hopes of targeting primary prevention efforts. Ideally, such a marker would be easily detected and highly correlated with incidence of schizophrenia, but would not actually be a symptom of the disorder itself. In other words, the marker gene may be next to one of the genes implicated in schizophrenia such that they often get inherited together (like books next to each other on the bookshelf ending up near each other in a garage sale). One of the leading behavioral candidates involves the inability to follow or track a stimulus such as a spot of light as it moves across the visual field. This subtle change in the perception of motion occurs in many people with the disorder, as well as their close relatives. In one study, the impaired ability to track moving objects could distinguish those people with schizophrenia from those with depression and healthy controls (Kojima et al., 2001). In another study, a genetic link was discovered for this *smooth-pursuit eye tracking* dysfunction. When individuals have two copies of the dopamine D3 receptor gene (DRD3), they score significantly worse on eye tracking, such that the tracking is interrupted by rapid eye movements (Rybakowski, Borkowska, Czerski, & Hauser, 2001). Whereas the explanation for the link between difficulty tracking and schizophrenia is not simplistic, the behavior may be a promising marker of schizophrenia.

Early Physical Trauma and Stress

Other biological factors apart from genes may also create a predisposition to schizophrenia. Obstetric complications, including prenatal exposure to a viral infection such as influenza, may be one specific risk factor for schizophrenia (Thomas et al., 2001). Indirect support for this contention comes from findings that, compared with controls, a greater proportion of people with schizophrenia are born during the winter or early spring months (e.g., Mortensen et al., 1999). Presumably, during these times of year, pregnant women and their fetuses are more likely to succumb to viral infections. Related research has found that maternal infections such as rubella during the first or early second trimester of pregnancy have been associated with an increased risk for developing schizophrenia (Brown et al., 2001). This **season-of-birth effect** is relatively small (less than a 10% differential in risk; Davies, Welham, Chant, Torrey, & McGrath, 2003), but it is speculated that the maternal immune response to these infections might in fact interfere with proper brain development in the fetus if the infection occurs during specific periods of brain development (Ashdown et al., 2006).

diathesis-stress model: A model that explains how a mental disorder can result from the interaction of a predisposition (diathesis) for a disorder with a trigger (stressor) that converts the predisposition into the actual disorder.

season-of-birth effect: The finding that a greater proportion of people with schizophrenia are born in the winter or early spring months, when, in utero, they would presumably have been more likely to be exposed to viral infections that could affect brain development.

TABLE 4.3 Summary of Relative Environmental and Genetic Risk Factors for Schizophrenia

Risk Factor	Average Approximate Relative Risk of Schizophrenia
Family history of schizophrenia	2–70
Any specific gene variant	1.1–1.5
Urbanicity (living in a crowded city)	2–3
Migration	2–3
First and second trimester infection or malnutrition	2–3
Winter birth	1.1
Obstetric and perinatal complications	2–3
Cannabis or stimulant use	2–3
Paternal age greater than 35 years	1.5–3
Male gender	1.4

Source: Adapted from Tandon et al. (2008).

Other sources of stress and trauma that might affect development and ultimately increase the risk of schizophrenia are complications during pregnancy and birth. Whereas the types of complications are multiple and findings related to risk for schizophrenia remain inconsistent, what appears to mediate the relationship between complications and the disorder is whether or not the fetus experienced hypoxia (lack of oxygen) during this critical time (Byrne, Agerbo, Bennedsen, Eaton, & Mortensen, 2007). Beyond the maternal contribution, paternal age at the time of conception also increases risk for schizophrenia (Wohl & Gorwood, 2007), possibly due to an increase in mutations from impaired spermatogenesis (Cheng, Ko, Chen, & Ng, 2008).

Table 4.3 summarizes the current risk factors for schizophrenia with their relative effects (relative risk means how many times more likely that person is to develop schizophrenia if he or she has that risk factor). How might these traumas—alone or in tandem with genetic predispositions—lead to schizophrenia? All of these traumas are capable of affecting the functioning of critical brain structures, and in recent years, evidence linking schizophrenia with abnormalities in the structure and functioning of the brain has mounted, as discussed in the next section.

Brain Structures and Functions

In the 1800s, Kraepelin speculated about structural abnormalities in the brains of people with schizophrenia (Bruton et al., 1990). In the 1920s, it was reported that some people with schizophrenia have enlarged **ventricles**, the cavities in the center of the brain that are filled with cerebrospinal fluid. But structural problems in the brain could not be documented clearly until recently. Today, methods for studying brain structures include not only postmortem examinations of the brains of deceased people with schizophrenia but also several *neuroimaging* techniques that provide "live," fine-grained pictures of the brain in action. These neuroimaging methods, as discussed in Chapter 1, include computerized tomography (CT) scans, magnetic resonance images (MRIs), positron emission tomography (PET) scans, and the single photon emission computed tomography (SPECT) technique.

Initial neuroimaging studies of brain structure were able to substantiate the much earlier claim that the brains of some people with schizophrenia have enlarged lateral ventricles (Steen, Mull, McClure, Hamer, & Lieberman, 2006). The ventricle enlargement

ventricle: A cavity in the center of the brain that is filled with cerebrospinal fluid.

FIGURE 4.3 Brain Regions Implicated in Schizophrenia

Areas of the brain that control cognitive, behavioral, and emotional functions are important in the development of some cases of schizophrenia. Abnormalities of the frontal lobe, temporal lobe, and the thalamus have been linked to schizophrenia.

Source: Image provided by the Lundbeck Institute at www.cnsforum.com.

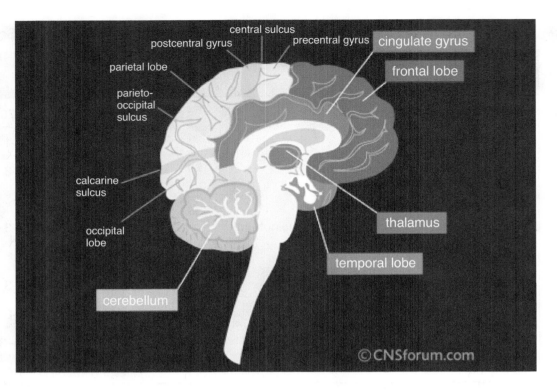

frontal lobe: The area of the cerebral cortex that controls executive functions, such as planning and carrying out goal-directed activities.

thalamus: A key structure in the forebrain that receives, analyzes, and sends on information from all the senses except smell.

hypofrontality: Diminished activity in the frontal lobe of the brain.

Connections

Have abnormalities of the frontal lobes been linked to any other mental disorders? For answers, see Chapters 3, 5, 6, and 16.

suggests that the gray matter and whole brain volume in surrounding areas has been diminished; in other words, ventricle enlargement points to the possibility of either abnormal neurological development or pathological brain deterioration. Ventricle enlargement is not observed in every person with schizophrenia (Andreasen, 1988), nor is it specific to schizophrenia, as ventricular enlargement has also been observed in people with mood disorders, although the effect is smaller (Strasser et al., 2005).

Where do other structural deficits occur, and what are their results? In recent years, researchers have focused on three areas of the brain that most consistently show structural problems in people with schizophrenia: (1) the **frontal lobe**, (2) the temporal lobe and parts of the limbic system that lie beneath the temporal lobe, and (3) the **thalamus** (see Figure 4.3).

Evidence of Hypofrontality

The frontal lobes play a critical role in executive functions, such as planning, decision making, and abstract thinking. Using neuroimaging techniques, scientists have found both decreased frontal lobe volume (e.g., Konick & Friedman, 2001; Baiano et al., 2007) and diminished neuronal and blood flow activity (Carter, MacDonald, Ross, & Stenger, 2001) in some people with schizophrenia. This diminished activity is called **hypofrontality**, and it appears to have important consequences. Hypofrontality has been associated with lowered performance on problem-solving tests and on working memory tasks by people with schizophrenia (Berman & Meyer-Lindenberg, 2004; Hill et al., 2004).

Hypofrontality is more common in men, and it is associated with negative symptoms. In one study with 90 people at high risk for schizophrenia, those with comorbid depression had less activation in the frontal gyrus with functional magnetic resonance imaging (fMRI), compared to those without depression and those who were healthy controls (Whalley et al., 2007). These data suggest that the negative symptoms of schizophrenia (like depression) may reflect diminished activity in the frontal lobe, which is normally heavily involved in problem solving, planning, and thinking. The findings are exciting because they begin to link particular brain regions to specific symptoms of schizophrenia. However, scientists must remain cautious about concluding that hypofrontality is a cause of schizophrenia. First, the extent of hypofrontality among those with schizophrenia tends to be small, compared with controls. Furthermore, not all studies have found that schizophrenia is associated with hypofrontality (Gur & Gur, 1995), perhaps because they have used different scanning techniques and different participant samples. At this point, it is best to consider the hypofrontality hypothesis as having only moderate support.

Temporal Lobe Abnormalities

The second brain area under intense investigation is the temporal lobe and certain structures of the limbic system underneath it. For example, fMRI studies have found that the amount of abnormal activity in parts of the auditory association cortex is associated with the severity of people's auditory hallucinations (Barta, Pearlson, Powers, Richards, & Tune, 1990). A study investigating auditory processing in people with schizophrenia compared to healthy controls revealed that lower-level processing (separating an auditory stream into distinct groups) was performed equally well in both groups (Bourdet, Brochard, Rouillon, & Drake, 2003). However, higher-level processes, including irregularity detection and attentional focus, were performed less efficiently in those with schizophrenia, confirming earlier research that there is abnormal auditory functioning in schizophrenia, with impairment possibly related to more-complex processing in the temporal lobe (Kircher et al., 2004; Wible et al., 2001).

Thalamic Irregularities

Linked to the limbic system is the thalamus, a kind of information relay station in the midline of the brain. An important function of the thalamus is that it filters, sorts, and transmits sensory information to the entire cortex, including the frontal lobes. The thalamus also acts as a regulator of sleep, arousal, and attention. Irregularities in the thalamus have been found in people with schizophrenia (Lisman, 2012). In a study by Guller and colleagues (2012), healthy controls and individuals with schizophrenia received single-pulse transcranial magnetic stimulation (spTMS) to the precentral gyrus, while fMRI was used to measure the response in the thalamus. Individuals with schizophrenia showed reduced thalamic activation in response to pulses delivered to the cortex, indicating abnormal functioning (Guller et al., 2012).

Deficits in the thalamus and its function could help explain many of the symptoms of schizophrenia. For example, if the thalamus does not adequately filter out irrelevant information and sends a scrambled signal to the frontal or temporal lobes, the person could suffer attentional lapses, lose the ability to process information clearly, become overwhelmed by sensory input, and experience hallucinations or delusions. In addition, people with schizophrenia tend to have fewer and smaller sleep spindles, which are waxing and waning oscillations on an electroencephalogram (EEG); these are initiated in the thalamus (Ferrarelli et al., 2010).

Though research has historically focused on dysregulation in specific brain regions, more-recent research suggests that there also exists disturbance in connectivity between different brain regions. The use of fMRI has been able to document disruptions in the interactions between the hippocampus and the prefrontal cortex in those with schizophrenia (Meyer-Lindenberg et al., 2005). As brain-imaging techniques continue to evolve, such as using resting-state connectivity to map the brain, more refined assessments of disturbed network models will hopefully be able to elucidate the unique brain abnormalities implicated in schizophrenia (Ragland, Yoon, Minzenberg, & Carter, 2007).

Hallucinations and the Brain

Neuroimaging studies have also begun to reveal which areas of the brain are involved in hallucinations. The connections can be studied by having people lie in a brain-scanning machine and then asking them to push a button when they experience auditory or visual hallucinations. Pictures taken at the time the button is pushed reveal activation of the brain's surface and certain subcortical areas, where thoughts, emotions, and perceptions are usually integrated. It seems as if activity in these areas—primarily the temporal cortex, the thalamus, and limbic structures such as the amygdala and hippocampus—simulates external sensory input so convincingly that the person believes it is coming from the outside world. When controls hear real noises, the same surface areas of the brain tend to become activated, but fewer subcortical areas are turned on. Other studies have shown that, when people with schizophrenia "hear" hallucinated voices, blood flow in Broca's area, a part of the brain that helps control the production of speech, changes substantially (McGuire, Shah, & Murray, 1993). This implies that the voices are literally coming from these individuals' own head (internal world), rather than from the outside world, but the individuals with schizophrenia are unable to distinguish their own voices from those of others. Finally, research has shown that auditory hallucinations are associated with a number of activations throughout the brain, including the insula, anterior cingulate, temporal cortex, thalamus, and hippocampus, suggesting that hallucinations may be the result of faulty networking between cortical and subcortical areas (Shergill, Brammer, Williams, Murray, & McGuire, 2000).

Some Preliminary Conclusions

As exciting and promising as they are, the results of brain-imaging research remain speculative and must be interpreted with great caution. First, even though various research teams reliably find differences in brain structures and functions, these differences do not appear in all people with schizophrenia; they are not even seen consistently within relatively homogeneous subgroups, such as those who display primarily positive or negative symptoms. Second, the bulk of earlier brain-scanning studies used older people who had taken antipsychotic drugs for many years. These potent drugs may have been responsible for some of the observed brain abnormalities. More-recent studies have tried to correct this flaw by using only people who have not been on antipsychotic medication, studied early in their first episodes of schizophrenia. Third, many of the observed brain deficits are not specific to schizophrenia but occur also in mood disorders and in various medical diseases affecting the brain.

Neurotransmitter Dysregulation

Historically, schizophrenia was viewed as a disorder of dopamine, a neurotransmitter that sends signals from one nerve cell to another in various brain regions, as shown in Figure 4.4. This influential theory holds that positive symptoms of schizophrenia are associated with problems in the dopamine neurotransmitter system. After over 50 years of research related to this neurotransmitter, it is now fairly clear that dopamine systems are implicated in at least some cases of schizophrenia. Several well-established lines of evidence support this conclusion:

1. Early studies found that the tissues and fluids of people with schizophrenia had higher levels of certain dopamine by-products than did those of controls, suggesting that an excess of dopamine was a primary culprit in schizophrenia. This excess has been hypothesized to arise either from an overabundance of dopamine receptors at the synapses or hypersensitivity of these receptors.
2. Drugs that increase dopamine activity in the brain (such as L-dopa and amphetamines) tend to intensify symptoms of schizophrenia and may even induce paranoid, schizophrenic-like positive symptoms in controls (Curran, Byrappa, & McBride, 2004).
3. Drugs that block the action of dopamine in the brain are effective in relieving some positive symptoms of schizophrenia (Syvalahti, 1994).
4. The degree to which these drugs, called *neuroleptics*, block dopamine is correlated with their clinical ability to reduce symptoms of schizophrenia (Seeman, 1987).
5. There may be particular genes that code for the mechanisms involved in dopamine functioning, which also increases the risk for schizophrenia (Arguello & Gogos, 2008).

Although these findings suggest a role for dopamine in schizophrenia, scientists now know that the situation is much more complicated than the initial dopamine-excess hypothesis suggested. First, fewer than 70% of the people taking dopamine-blocking neuroleptics improve, and progress is primarily in the positive symptoms only (Davis, 2010). Furthermore, some brain areas, such as the limbic system, show excess dopamine activity, but other areas, notably the frontal lobes, show *deficiencies* in dopamine. Excessive activ-

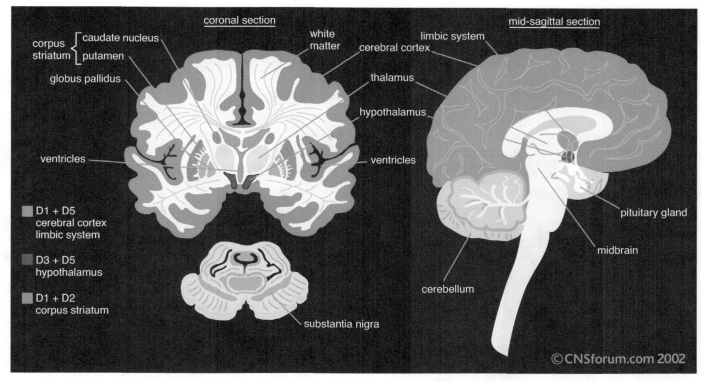

FIGURE 4.4 Range of Dopamine Receptors in the Brain

There are five subtypes of dopamine receptor, and subtypes D1–D5 are widely distributed throughout both the cerebral cortex and the limbic system.

Source: Image provided by the Lundbeck Institute at www.cnsforum.com.

ity may occur largely in schizophrenia with predominantly positive symptoms, whereas deficits in dopamine activity in the frontal lobes may be more typical in people with schizophrenia with more pronounced negative symptoms (Davis, Kahn, Ko, & Davidson, 1991). More-recent research suggests that there is a disruption in the lateralization of the neurochemistry in the brain, such that people with schizophrenia may use more dopamine in one side of their brains versus the other (Hsiao, Lin, Liu, Tzen, & Yen, 2003).

Further exploration of the role of neurotransmitters in schizophrenia has implicated serotonin and glutamate, either on their own or in interaction with dopamine. For example, in postmortem studies of the brains of people who were diagnosed with schizophrenia, the prefrontal cortex and the hippocampus were found to have reduced expression of glutamate receptors (Harrison, Law, & Eastwood, 2003). Simultaneous hyper- and hypoactivation of two different types of serotonin receptors in the hippocampus of people with schizophrenia compared to controls give support for dysregulation of the serotonergic system (Lopez-Figueroa et al., 2004). However, these findings are also true for people with mood disorders (see Chapters 5 and 6) and borderline personality disorder (see Chapter 16), which suggests that serotonin deficiencies are not specific enough to account for the unique symptoms of schizophrenia. As usual, the key may lie in the relative balance of various neurotransmitters in the brain.

Section Review

The diathesis-stress model argues that certain people are predisposed to schizophrenia but that stressors are usually needed to precipitate its development. Genetic factors predispose some people to develop schizophrenia, as indicated by the results of:

- family aggregation studies,
- twin studies, and
- adoption studies.

However, because the majority of people with schizophrenia do not have close family members who also have the disorder, nongenetic factors must also be involved. Biological traumas that might contribute to the development of schizophrenia include:

- prenatal viral infections,
- difficulties during delivery that affect brain structures and functions, and
- abnormalities in neurotransmitter systems.

The brain structures and functions most often implicated in schizophrenia involve:

- the frontal and temporal lobes, and
- subcortical areas, such as the thalamus and other structures such as the hippocampus and amygdala that are part of the limbic system.

Serious mental disorders such as schizophrenia plague many homeless people. The cognitive and behavioral impairments associated with the disorder put these people at increased risk for physical illnesses and victimization by criminals. Homeless people with schizophrenia also are hard to treat because they often refuse to take antipsychotic medication or to participate in psychotherapy.

Psychosocial Causes of Schizophrenia

Like biological factors, environmental and psychosocial stressors have long been suspected of being involved somehow in the causation of schizophrenia (Gottesman, 2001). As difficult as it is to document the role of biological factors that might contribute to schizophrenia, it is even harder to isolate the environmental experiences that might translate a diathesis into the actual disorder.

For one thing, most psychological stressors are not single events that can be easily catalogued; rather, they take the form of a long series of events that accumulate to tax a person's coping resources. In addition, these events are themselves probably affected by genes to some extent. A temperamentally withdrawn and shy child is more likely to seek an isolated social environment than is an extroverted and upbeat child. A child with early brain abnormalities faces increased risks of educational failure and possible social rejection. As people grow older, the distinction between genes and environment becomes less meaningful until a point is reached at which the dichotomy no longer makes much sense.

The Role of Social Class and Urbanicity

Studies spanning 60 years show that, whereas laypeople understand that many factors influence schizophrenia, they place far more emphasis on adverse life events than on biology or genetics (Read, Magliano, & Beavan, 2013). Stroll through the streets of any American city, and you will see shocking examples of how serious mental disorders can ravage people's lives. Whether it is on Broadway, the Sunset Strip, or Michigan Avenue, an astounding number of people with apparent mental disturbances are homeless and wandering the streets (see Chapter 17 for more on homelessness). Do such appearances reflect a reality, or are they just a false stereotype about big-city life? Is there a connection between social conditions and the prevalence of schizophrenia?

In the United States, across over 75 years of research, two enduring facts about the prevalence of schizophrenia reveal that it is highly correlated with (1) living in an urban setting and (2) being a member of a lower social class (Faris & Dunham, 1939; Freeman, 1994; Torrey & Bowler, 1990; Kirkbride et al., 2006). Several hypotheses have been proposed to explain the relationship between urban living, social class, and the prevalence of schizophrenia. The **social drift hypothesis** suggests that, as people develop symptoms of schizophrenia, they cannot maintain adequate occupational functioning and thus gradually slip down the socioeconomic ladder. They migrate to the poorer areas of cities, where lodging is cheaper and where they become more entrenched in lifestyles of marginal subsistence. Social drift links lower socioeconomic class to schizophrenia as one of the ultimate consequences of the disorder itself (Freeman, 1994). Another possible explanation,

social drift hypothesis: Also called the *social selection hypothesis*, it explains higher rates of mental disorders among lower socioeconomic groups as the consequence of disordered people sinking to lower socioeconomic levels because of their disorders.

MAPS - Prejudicial Pigeonholes

sometimes called the **social causation theory**, suggests that the chronic psychological and social stressors, social disorganization, and greater environmental hazards associated with urban living and poverty breed new cases of schizophrenia (Mortensen et al., 1999; Kirkbride et al., 2006). The evidence for this hypothesis comes from the relative-dose response found between level or degree of urbanicity and risk of schizophrenia, strongly supporting the notion that something about the urban environment is causally related to schizophrenia (Pedersen & Mortensen, 2001). Urban culprits that increase risk may include urban versus rural rates of cannabis and other substance use, degree of social stressors such as poverty and violence, environmental toxins, poorer pre- and perinatal health, and migration (Tandon et al., 2008).

Thus far, research has supported both of these hypotheses, suggesting that it may be a combination of lower socioeconomic stressors, along with the depletion of resources that can occur after the onset of the disorder, that explains the link between socioeconomic status and schizophrenia. Relatedly, a number of studies have investigated migration as a risk factor for schizophrenia. In a meta-analysis examining 18 studies, the relative risk for developing schizophrenia was 2.7 for first-generation migrants and rose to 4.5 for second-generation migrants (Cantor-Graae & Selten, 2005). But why does migration impact risk for schizophrenia? Evidence from particular cultural groups who have migrated provides a clue. When individuals migrate from a country that is predominately black to a country where the population is predominately white, or where there are fewer people in a given area from the same ethnic group, there tends to be a higher incidence of psychotic disorders in that migrated group (Veling et al., 2008). This effect might best be explained by migration to a place where stressors related to discrimination and fewer social advantages may contribute to the etiology of this disorder.

However, even if social drift, social causation, and migration influence the epidemiology of schizophrenia, it is still the case that many people with schizophrenia come from families that are socially and economically advantaged. Other forces must therefore be at play in regulating the course of schizophrenia, and family environment turns out to be one of the most important of those additional areas to consider.

The Role of Family Environments

Historically, the psychosocial factor most frequently hypothesized to be related to schizophrenia has been some type of family disturbance. One of the earliest views was that certain kinds of mothers (who came to be known as schizophrenogenic mothers—say that phrase 10 times fast!) were key to the development of schizophrenia, particularly in boys (Fromm-Reichmann, 1948). The **schizophrenogenic mother** was characterized as domineering, overprotective, cold, rigid, and uncomfortable with sex and physical intimacy—all qualities thought to induce schizophrenia in her offspring.

Dad could be over-protective.

Source: Cartoonresource/Shutterstock.com.

Another family theory that was influential in the 1950s and 1960s was the **double-bind hypothesis** of Gregory Bateson and his colleagues (Bateson, Jackson, Haley, & Weakland, 1956). According to this view, schizophrenia sometimes developed when a child was raised by parents who communicated incompatible messages to the child. Typically, the parent was thought to send repeated conflicting messages that a child could not possibly answer in a consistent way, leading to anxiety and confused thinking. For example, a mother might complain to her son that he does not show her enough affection but then stiffen or give him the "cold shoulder" whenever he tries to hug her. Because no one in these families was able to clarify these paradoxical communications, they were thought ultimately to wreak havoc on a child's development.

These theories and others like them never earned much empirical support, and so they are no longer taken seriously by most clinicians. However, family interactions most certainly do play a role in the management of its members who have schizophrenia as elucidated further next.

social causation theory: A theory suggesting that stress, poverty, racism, inferior education, unemployment, and social changes are sociocultural risk factors leading to mental disorders.

schizophrenogenic mother: A formerly popular term for a type of mother thought to cause schizophrenia in her children by her domineering, overprotective, cold, and rigid manner and her discomfort with physical intimacy.

double-bind hypothesis: An early theory suggesting that schizophrenia could arise from the confusion produced when a child was raised by parents who communicated incompatible messages to the child.

The Role of Expressed Emotion

How do you think you would act if you lived with a person who had schizophrenia? Would you feel afraid? Would you be a nag? Would you challenge the person to become more socially involved, or would you feel sorry for the person? Perhaps you would be like the sister of one person with schizophrenia who stated, "I can go from tears to rage in a matter of minutes. He either ignores me or threatens to hit me. Nothing I do ever seems to matter."

Life in all families is stressful at times, but some families are more stressful than others. Members of a family in which one member is disruptive and behaves irrationally are especially likely to react with anger and demands for conformity and accountability. What effects might these reactions have? Years of research on the families of people with schizophrenia show a strong relationship between a certain family climate, called **expressed emotion (EE)**, and the rate at which that person suffers relapses of schizophrenia. EE usually involves high levels of:

- criticism ("You don't do anything but sit in front of the TV"),
- hostility ("I'm sick and tired of your craziness"), and
- overinvolvement ("Don't you realize how hard I try to help you out?").

expressed emotion (EE): A measure of the family environment describing criticism, hostility, and emotional overinvolvement with a person; a risk factor for relapse of mental disorders such as schizophrenia.

Vaughn and Leff (1976) led a pioneering study that illustrated the importance of EE in relation to relapse and the use of antipsychotic drugs. After the people in this study had entered the hospital, social workers interviewed their families and classified them as high or low EE. People who returned to high-EE homes were much more prone to relapse within 9 months of release than those returning to low-EE families. In addition, the amount of contact with members of high-EE families was a critical variable in the relapse rate. If people had more than 35 hours of direct EE family contact per week, then they relapsed twice as often as people with fewer than 35 hours of EE contact. The amount of family contact had no effect on relapse rates among low-EE families. Finally, people's compliance in taking their antipsychotic drugs appeared to protect those in high-EE families against relapse, whereas compliance had little differential effect on relapse rates of people from low-EE families.

In a meta-analysis of 26 studies, when people with schizophrenia were living in a home with high EE, the baseline relapse rate doubled 9–12 months after the index hospitalization (Butzlaff & Hooley, 1998). High EE has been found to have similar effects on the relapse of other mental conditions, such as mood disorders. But how might EE lead to relapse? One possibility is that caring for a person with schizophrenia can lead to a significant amount of burden and depletion of resources for family members, ultimately decreasing their ability to provide emotional support to the person with the disorder (Webb et al., 1998). Additionally, family members who are high in EE tend to be inflexible and less tolerant on personality measures, compared to family members with low EE (Hooley & Hiller, 2000), and tend to have a more internal locus of control (Hooley, 1998) with more self-criticalness (Docherty, Cutting, & Bers, 1998). These findings suggest that family members with high EE may have contributing characteristics that are stable over time, leading to a continued hostile environment when they are under stress (Hooley & Gotlib, 2000).

The research reviewed in this section points to the importance of psychological and environmental factors in the development of schizophrenia. Although several exciting discoveries about the genetic, anatomical, and biochemical irregularities involved in schizophrenia have recently been made, scientists should not ignore the role of psychosocial variables. Indeed, biological and psychological factors work hand in hand in bringing about most cases of schizophrenia, as Figure 4.5 illustrates. Asking whether schizophrenia is caused by biological *or* psychological factors makes no more sense than asking whether a rectangle is formed by its sides or ends. Both dimensions of schizophrenia must be studied carefully if researchers are ever to understand this complex disorder more fully.

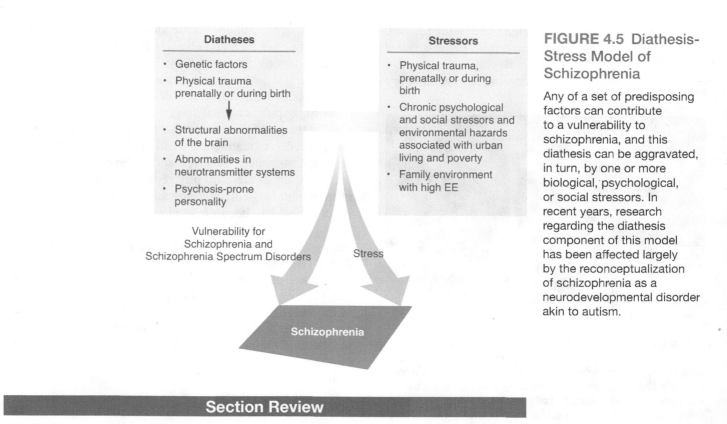

FIGURE 4.5 Diathesis-Stress Model of Schizophrenia

Any of a set of predisposing factors can contribute to a vulnerability to schizophrenia, and this diathesis can be aggravated, in turn, by one or more biological, psychological, or social stressors. In recent years, research regarding the diathesis component of this model has been affected largely by the reconceptualization of schizophrenia as a neurodevelopmental disorder akin to autism.

Section Review

The diathesis-stress model proposes that schizophrenia is caused by an interaction of biological, psychological, and social factors. The two psychosocial factors receiving the most attention in the study of schizophrenia are:

- socioeconomic class and associated stressors, and
- family environments and family communication patterns.

Explanations for the disproportionate rate of schizophrenia among urban and lower socioeconomic groups include:

- the *social drift* hypothesis, which suggests that, as people develop symptoms of schizophrenia, they gradually slide down the socioeconomic ladder, and
- *social causation* theory, which suggests that the social stressors and environmental hazards associated with poverty breed episodes of schizophrenia in vulnerable individuals.

Families high in expressed emotion (EE) are defined by:

- a tendency to make negative comments,
- hostility, and
- emotional overinvolvement regarding the family member with schizophrenia.

High expressed emotion:

- predicts relapse of schizophrenia and
- is probably both a cause and consequence of the person's symptoms.

Treatments for Schizophrenia

Prior to the 1950s, there was little hope for successful treatment of schizophrenia. The typical treatment was to confine people in large public mental hospitals, where hundreds of patients lived for decades in drab, crowded wards. For the most part, all that this hospitalization accomplished was to segregate these people from the rest of society. Some patients received experimental therapies—psychosurgery, electroconvulsive shock, prolonged isolation, and restraint—but most were simply left to languish in the hospital year after year. Their mental abilities, social interests, and self-help skills gradually declined until they became almost totally dependent on the institution. It is difficult to decide which group of patients suffered

phenothiazines: A chemically similar group of neuroleptic drugs that act by blocking specific neurotransmitter receptors.

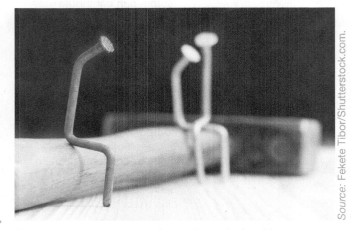

Source: Fekete Tibor/Shutterstock.com.

One of the obstacles to wellness that people with schizophrenia must overcome is *stigma*, the inaccurate views that many people in society hold about them and their disorder. Schizophrenia is significantly associated with the most negative stereotypes of all mental disorders. Although the sufferers are least blamed for their disorder, they are also viewed as least likely to recover, compared to anxiety and depression (Wood, Birtel, Alsawy, Pyle, & Morrison, 2014). Why is the public's view so bleak? Media portrayals of mental disorders most often feature dangerousness or crime (e.g., John Nash threatens to kill his wife in *A Beautiful Mind*), even though research suggests that people with mental disorders are more likely to be victims than perpetrators of violence (Tartakovsky, 2009).

more harm—the recipients of the aggressive treatments or the victims of neglect. In either case, most patients ended up spending much of their adult lives in these institutions.

Beginning in the 1950s, the bleak outlook for patients with schizophrenia began to change. A new category of drugs—the **phenothiazines**—positively impacted the treatment of schizophrenia. As discussed further in Chapter 17, many of the public mental hospitals have been vastly downsized in the past 5 decades so that many people with schizophrenia receive treatment instead in shorter-term inpatient facilities, outpatient facilities, and in the community. Antipsychotic drugs are currently regarded as the cornerstone of treatment for schizophrenia and other psychoses. Their introduction has been credited with a reduction in long-stay, hospital-based care; however, others have pointed out that this reduction began before the drugs were introduced (Ross & Read, 2004). Most often, drug treatment takes place during a 2- to 3-week period of hospitalization that (1) gives the patient a respite from the stressors that often precede a rapid worsening of symptoms, (2) allows clinicians to observe how the patient responds to the medication, and (3) permits intensive treatment with methods other than medication.

In comprehensive treatment programs, drug treatment is combined with various kinds of psychosocial treatment—in particular, training in social and stress-coping skills, family-oriented therapy, and community-based psychosocial treatments. In some instances, the psychosocial component may be limited to the time the person is in the hospital. More commonly, the treatment begins in the hospital and is continued in the community after the person has been discharged. We first consider drug treatments in more detail and then turn our attention to psychological treatments.

Biological Treatments

neuroleptic: A drug that blocks the action of neurotransmitters in the brain, thereby relieving many positive symptoms of schizophrenia.

The drugs most commonly used for schizophrenia are called *antipsychotics* or **neuroleptics**. Within hours of taking neuroleptics, most people are calmed. After a few weeks of drug treatment, most patients who entered the hospital with paranoid delusions or with vivid hallucinations are conversing calmly and much more normally. Within days to weeks, many are relieved of most of the symptoms of thought disorder, as their incoherent speech becomes more logical and organized. However, negative symptoms of schizophrenia, such as withdrawal, muteness, and negativism, are less dramatically affected. The prevalence of negative symptoms in people with schizophrenia spectrum disorders treated with antipsychotics in routine clinical practice not only is still considerably high (57%) but also seems to be related to poorer functioning, unemployment, greater severity, and less-positive symptomatology and higher antipsychotic dose (Bobes et al., 2010). Overall, 60–70% of patients receiving neuroleptic drugs show some improvement, but fewer than 30% respond well enough to live in communities entirely on their own.

The Phenothiazines

extrapyramidal symptoms: A group of side effects that result from neuroleptic drugs, consisting of movement abnormalities, such as tremors, rigidity, spasms, and agitation.

The major neuroleptics, commonly referred to as first-generation antipsychotics (FGA), belong to a general chemical group called the phenothiazines (see Table 4.4). The phenothiazines exert their antipsychotic action primarily by blocking the action of the neurotransmitter dopamine. In particular, they fully or partially block a specific type of dopamine receptor, the D2 receptor in the mesolimbic pathway (Miyamoto, Miyake, Jarskog, Fleischhacker, & Lieberman, 2012).

TABLE 4.4 Sample of Drugs Commonly Used in Treating Schizophrenia and Related Disorders

Class of Drug	Generic Name	Brand Name	Generic Name	Brand Name
Phenothiazines	Chlorpromazine	Thorazine	Fluphenazine	Prolixin
	Thioridazine	Mellaril	Triflupromazine	Vesprin
	Trifluoperazine	Stelazine	Prochlorperazine	Compazine
Butyrophenones	Haloperidol	Haldol	Pimozide	Orap
Thioxanthenes	Thiothixene	Navane		
Atypical antipsychotics	Clozapine	Clozaril	Olanzapine	Zyprexa
	Quetiapine	Seroquel	Paliperidone	Invega
	Aripiprazole	Abilify	Iloperidone	Fanapt
	Ziprasidone	Geodon	Asenapine	Saphris
	Risperidone	Risperdal	Lurasidone	Latuda

The antipsychotic benefits of the phenothiazines do not come without cost, however. These drugs produce a series of side effects that range from controllable nuisances—dry mouth, hypersensitivity to sun, constipation, sleepiness—to incapacitating, irreversible, and even life-threatening complications. One important group of serious side effects involves abnormalities of movement known as **extrapyramidal symptoms**. Among these are symptoms of **Parkinsonism** (motor disturbances that resemble the difficulties caused by Parkinson's disease), which affect about 50% of people treated with phenothiazines; these include fine tremor of the hands, a slow shuffling gait, a blank stare, muscular rigidity, and slowness of movement. **Acute dystonia** is an extrapyramidal side effect involving uncontrollable muscle contractions or spasms of the head, neck, tongue, back, and eyes. **Acute akathesia** is a condition in which people are constantly restless and agitated; they feel they have to keep their limbs moving constantly or they will experience discomfort. Finally, **tardive dyskinesia (TD)** is a serious side effect that affects 20–25% of people who take phenothiazines over long periods of time (Bakker, van Harten, & van Os, 2006). TD symptoms include involuntary and uncontrollable spasmodic jerks, tics, and twitches of the face, tongue, trunk, and limbs. The lips make smacking and sucking sounds, the jaws grind, the limbs may writhe uncontrollably, and speech is progressively impaired. As the disorder progresses, larger portions of the body become involved in these involuntary movements. TD typically begins only after people have been taking phenothiazines for several years, and it usually worsens as long as the drugs continue to be taken.

Neuroleptic malignant syndrome (NMS) is a potentially fatal disorder affecting approximately .01–.02% of people taking neuroleptics (Strawn, Keck, & Caroff, 2007). This disorder occurs within the first few days of taking the drug and involves extremely high fever, muscle rigidity, and irregular heart rate and blood pressure. It is fatal in about 10% of cases (Strawn, Keck, & Caroff, 2007).

Some of the side effects of the phenothiazines can be controlled by taking anti-Parkinsonism medications or by reducing the dose of the phenothiazine. Regardless, taking a person off of the medication and/or switching to an atypical antipsychotic (see the next section) may be the best course of action to treat TD (Sachdev, 2000). However, the side effects of these drugs often prompt many patients to simply stop taking their medication, as Lionel Aldridge in the chapter-opening case did for a time. This problem is widespread among patients once they leave mental hospitals and have less supervision.

Parkinsonism: An extrapyramidal side effect of some neuroleptic drugs, leading to symptoms that mimic Parkinson's disease, such as tremors, shuffling gait, blank facial expression, muscular weakness and rigidity, and slowed movement.

acute dystonia: An extrapyramidal side effect of some neuroleptics, involving tics in the head, neck, and face.

acute akathesia: An extrapyramidal side effect of some neuroleptics, involving uncontrollable restlessness and agitation.

tardive dyskinesia (TD): An extrapyramidal side effect of some neuroleptic drugs, involving spasmodic jerks, tics, and twitches of the face, tongue, trunk, and limbs, as well as speech impairment.

neuroleptic malignant syndrome (NMS): A rare side effect of neuroleptic drugs that is potentially fatal and involves extremely high fever, muscle rigidity, and irregular heart rate and blood pressure.

In fact, the majority of nonhospitalized people with schizophrenia probably experiment with medication-free periods lasting weeks or months at a time. Most neuroleptics work only for as long as the person continues to take them, so these drug "holidays" may lead to relapses of schizophrenia.

Atypical Antipsychotic Drugs

atypical antipsychotics: Drugs that do not have the same biochemical or physiological effects as standard neuroleptics.

Antipsychotics have been characterized as falling into two main groups: "typical" or "first-generation" antipsychotics, developed in the 1950s, and "atypical" or "second-generation" antipsychotics (SGAs), which emerged in the 1990s. Typical antipsychotics include the phenothiazines, as well as thioxanthenes and butyrophenone derivatives like Haldol (see Table 4.4). Newer, second-generation antipsychotic medications initially brought new hope to the treatment of schizophrenia, particularly for those who either do not respond well to standard neuroleptics or who cannot tolerate their side effects. These drugs are called **atypical antipsychotics** because they do not have the same biochemical effects and therefore may produce less extrapyramidal symptoms than do the standard neuroleptics in some individuals (Bruijnzeel, Suryadevara, & Tandon, 2014; Miyamoto et al., 2012). In many instances, these have become the first line of treatment today for people experiencing psychotic symptoms. They are also frequently used with children, adolescents, older adults, and prisoners to treat a range of other mental disorders, ranging from mood to personality disorders (Ross & Read, 2004).

Limitations of Drug Treatments

MAPS - Medical Myths

Second-generation antipsychotics (SGAs) were once thought to be more effective than typical antipsychotics with fewer adverse effects. However, the results of two large effectiveness studies and comprehensive reviews have undermined this distinction (Jones et al., 2006; Leucht et al., 2009; Lieberman et al., 2005; Tyrer and Kendall, 2009), with some calling for it to be abandoned (Kendall, 2011). Most now agree that the perception of SGAs as a major breakthrough in the treatment of schizophrenia was largely a consequence of aggressive marketing by the pharmaceutical industry (Kendall, 2011). Both first-generation and second-generation antipsychotics carry the risk of severe adverse effects. Nearly everyone prescribed antipsychotics has some adverse effects, with almost one in four describing the effects as intolerable and one in three citing them as the most important reason for stopping the medication (Hutton, Weinmann, Bola, & Read, 2013). There is also growing evidence that antipsychotics may be responsible for some of the problems commonly thought to be a sign or symptom of schizophrenia itself. Further, there are many other adverse effects of antipsychotics that, together with the limited efficacy of these drugs, make them less-than-perfect interventions. And the facts about antipsychotic medications appear to be changing. For people with a schizophrenia spectrum diagnosis, evidence is accumulating that the benefits of medication have been overestimated and adverse effects underestimated. The drugs are not successful at treating the negative symptoms, such as anhedonia, and the cognitive deficits, such as lack of mental flexibility, that impede successful engagement or re-engagement that could lead to a higher quality of life (Miyamoto et al., 2012). Moreover, there is a dearth of good-quality evidence that addresses the long-term effects of initial treatment with antipsychotic medication, compared with short-term medication postponement in early-episode schizophrenia research, which casts doubt on the notion that aggressive drug treatment of the first signs of schizophrenia is always the best course of action (Bola, 2006).

Most clinicians now understand that best practices involve an integrated approach to treatment that must include psychosocial interventions (Insel, 2010). For one thing, drugs do not teach people with schizophrenia how to interact more effectively or how to manage stressful situations more successfully. Nor do they help families and friends learn how to cope with the frequent frustrations and conflicts involved in living with a person who has schizophrenia. And even if drugs ameliorate many of the worst symptoms of schizophrenia, they still do not guarantee that people will feel a sense of really belonging or being connected to people around them. Carpenter (2001) succinctly summarized the role of antipsychotic agents: "The benefit of maintenance drug treatment is relapse prevention, not comprehensive treatment of schizophrenia."

Connections
What other treatments are compromised by noncompliance? For examples, see Chapter 5.

Consider the remarks of George Atwood, a clinical psychologist and professor emeritus at Rutgers University, with many years of experience working with people presenting with psychotic symptoms. He describes a case study in which a young woman presented with a central delusion in which she "believed evil 'death rays' were emerging from the eyes of her enemies, and these rays crossed space and impacted against her face," eventually penetrating her brain and calcifying in her very core, stopping her from having thoughts or feelings (Atwood, 2011, p. 12). The course of Dr. Atwood's treatment with this individual spanned decades, and the death rays eventually flowed from his eyes as well. This persecutory delusion persisted until shortly after he expressed a genuine understanding of the symbolism of this delusion to his client as representing the invalidating effect of being labeled, medicated, and objectified. He offered this empathic response to the individual within the context of their relationship:

> My dear, I have something important to say to you, and I want you to listen very closely. I know that I have been hurting you, and it has been very, very bad. I see it clearly, and I did not before. Please know that I never intended to bring you harm; it has just been that I didn't understand. Now I do. I hope and I pray that you and I will find a way to undo the damage that has occurred.

> The rays from my eyes then ceased to flow. . . . I do not want to give the impression that Anna's struggles were over as a result of this little intervention. Her severe difficulties and vulnerabilities continued for a great many years. The delusion of the rays and the solidifications, however, vanished and never returned. She was eventually able to leave the hospital, where she had spent such a long time, and live with her mother and father. (Atwood, 2011, pp. 16–17)

The simple intervention that Dr. Atwood describes illustrates why it is a mistake, in our view, to think about the treatment of schizophrenia in purely biological terms. Drugs can be valuable for controlling the acute-phase symptoms of schizophrenia, but they cannot make a new life for people, validate their experiences as autonomous human beings, or teach them how to cope with the negative consequences of the disorder. These goals are more likely to be accomplished through psychosocial treatments, described next.

Psychosocial Treatments

The first well-documented use of psychosocial treatments for psychosis appeared in the moral era of the 19th century (see Chapter 2), during which several European and American reformers insisted that institutionalized mental patients could be helped—rather than merely hidden—if they were treated with kindness and taught to take more responsibility for their own lives.

In the United States, the use of psychosocial treatments for schizophrenia has a long history. In the 1920s, Harry Stack Sullivan used a form of psychoanalysis, combined with specially organized living arrangements on hospital wards, to work with young people with schizophrenia. His student, Frieda Fromm-Reichmann, continued this tradition, as have other psychoanalytically trained psychiatrists. However, because of a lack of empirical research documenting that psychoanalysis produces significant long-term benefits (Stone, 1986), this is not the treatment of choice for people with schizophrenia.

During the 1960s and 1970s, as new medications and other factors resulted in people with schizophrenia leaving public mental hospitals in droves, two important changes occurred in psychosocial interventions. First, psychologists began to design milieu programs to help hospitalized patients develop the self-help skills that years of living in a mental hospital had eroded. **Milieu programs** were intended to resocialize patients in the hospital so that they could learn to manage their lives and engage in appropriate behavior in the community. These programs attempted to create hospital-ward environments that rewarded patients for resuming independent living.

milieu program: A hospital program that intends to resocialize patients with severe mental disorders so that they can learn how to manage their lives better and engage in appropriate behavior in the community.

token economy: A procedure that uses operant reinforcement principles to alter the behaviors of individuals or groups by giving tokens (such as poker chips) that can be exchanged for other tangible rewards.

Many milieu programs took the form of **token economies**, systems of reinforcing desired behaviors with poker chips or other tokens that could be exchanged for access to television, snacks, or other rewards. In essence, token economies use the principles of operant conditioning to teach patients new skills that ideally will generalize to life in the community (Ayllon & Azrin, 1968). In the 1970s, Gordon Paul and his colleagues at the University of Illinois compared the effects of standard mental hospital care, milieu therapy, and milieu therapy based on token economy principles (Paul & Lentz, 1977). This classic study found that, compared with standard hospital treatment, both forms of milieu therapy produced significantly greater improvements in patients' adjustment skills; and the token economy milieu program produced the highest rate of improvement.

The second important development in psychosocial treatments was a move toward delivering more treatment outside of hospitals, in community settings known as *therapeutic communities* or *group homes*. Whereas these homes and communities have largely been replaced by assertive community treatment (ACT; described later in the chapter), the underlying themes of providing individualized services, offering support beyond psychiatric care, and providing assistance from a skills-based model have persisted.

This facet of psychosocial treatment has not been immune to the sweeping tide of the evidence-based movement. Like other branches of psychological treatment, the likelihood of the adoption of psychosocial treatments for schizophrenia hinges upon the ability of researchers to demonstrate the effectiveness of each approach on an empirical basis. The Schizophrenia Patient Outcomes Research Team (PORT) conducts comprehensive reviews of the current accumulated evidence for different approaches and has made the following recommendations for treatment: skills training programs, cognitive-behavioral therapy, family-based services, assertive community treatment (ACT), token economies, supported employment, and psychosocial interventions for other disorders (substance use or weight management) that the person with schizophrenia may also have (Dixon et al., 2010). Further explanations of skills training programs, cognitive-behavioral therapy, family-based services, and ACT are presented next.

Social Skills Training

Social skills training programs focus on people's social skills across the various domains that individuals might encounter on a routine basis (i.e., social and occupational). Social skills are a component of overall psychosocial functioning, and impairments in social skills can make activities of daily living a struggle for many people with schizophrenia.

The goal of these programs is thus to help people learn the skills needed to assist with day-to-day tasks, such as carrying on conversations, expressing needs clearly, refusing unreasonable demands, and interacting appropriately with friends and relatives. This training can be tedious because the symptoms of schizophrenia interfere with people's ability to learn new skills. Their attention and concentration are often impaired, memory is sometimes disturbed, and motivation is frequently absent. To counteract these obstacles, program staff members often break down social skills into simple steps, such as making eye contact when greeting others, listening carefully to what others say, taking turns during conversations, and talking in a normal tone of voice (Bellack & Mueser, 1993). Social skills training usually takes place in structured groups that rely on modeling, goal setting, role playing, lots of practice, and social reinforcement.

Social skills training programs have demonstrated improvements in the acquisition or reacquisition of interpersonal skills, social and independent living skills, and overall psychosocial functioning, and in the reduction of negative symptoms (Kurtz & Mueser, 2008). However, these improvements can deteriorate after participants leave a skills program. To counteract the drop-off in improvements, clinicians often use booster training to reestablish the initial gains. However, even with booster training, the ability of these programs to prevent relapse is not yet well established (Kurtz & Mueser, 2008).

Cognitive-Behavioral Therapy

Cognitive-behavioral therapy (CBT) for schizophrenia has been gaining in popularity and specificity recently, as a result of the cognitive model of schizophrenia, which provides a new way to think about the core symptoms of hallucinations and delusions (Beck & Rector, 2003). For example, like other psychiatric symptoms, hallucinations commonly occur following acute stressors. One person described the voices he heard as reminding him of all the bad experiences he had experienced in his life (Mayhew & Gilbert, 2008). In other instances, people hear voices that make comments or criticisms that are frequently heard in their own day-to-day situations (Beck & Rector, 2003). A woman with schizophrenia heard the voice of a Chinese warlord stating, "You're useless" or "You're weak," the same critical comments made by her father throughout her childhood. In fact, the voice content in auditory hallucinations is strikingly similar to the automatic or intrusive thoughts that are observed in other mental disorders, such as depression, mania, and obsessive-compulsive disorder (Baker & Morrison, 1998). In other words, negative automatic thoughts and obsessions are powerful and internally driven "voices" that may readily be transformed into hallucinations in susceptible people who fail to recognize internal experiences as belonging to the self (Beck & Rector, 2003; Bentall, 1990).

Regarding delusions, the other key symptom of schizophrenia described earlier, research has yielded strong support for a reasoning bias that is best described as a tendency for people with delusions to gather less evidence than controls so that they jump to conclusions (Garety & Freeman, 1999). Second, there is strong evidence of an attributional bias in people with persecutory delusions, which leads to externalizing blame for negative events; there are early indications that this may result from a particular tendency to personalize—that is, to blame people rather than situations when things go wrong (Garety & Freeman, 1999). An example of how to target these cognitive biases in treatment comes from a case that one of the authors worked on at a college counseling center. The student, a college senior, had a delusional system surrounding his belief that the FBI was after him for petty crimes he had committed while he was a freshman, such as writing graffiti on the dormitory walls. After several sessions of psychotherapy, the counselor pointed out that real events from the student's life were recounted differently from faulty (delusional) events, which were always relayed in the form of a question—for example, "Was that guy following me?" "Did the police officer look at me strangely?" From that point on, the student thus had a new way to do reality testing (cognitive work) on his delusions: Whenever he thought of events in his head as a question, he reminded himself that those events were probably not real.

As a result of accumulating evidence for the cognitive explanation of hallucinations and delusions, the past 2 decades has seen rapid growth in the number of clinical trials aimed at evaluating psychological interventions for schizophrenia, resulting in the recommendation of CBT as a treatment for this disorder in both the United Kingdom and the United States. Therapists are now able to target specific presentations with specialized CBT protocols (Steel, 2013). For the first time, this powerful form of therapy can be tailored to the treatment of discrete symptoms, such as command hallucinations, violent behavior, or comorbid post-traumatic stress disorder (see Chapter 9). In one pilot study, clients reported fewer dysfunctional beliefs about their cognitive abilities, performance, emotional experience, and social exclusion, and this reduction partially mediated the change in negative symptoms (Staring, ter Huurne, & van der Gaag, 2013).

Overall, CBT has been shown to produce significant clinical effects on measures of both positive and negative symptoms of schizophrenia (Rector & Beck, 2012). However, one meta-analysis concludes that these effects are small (Jauhar et al., 2014), and another suggests that CBT may not outperform other forms of supportive therapy in this regard (Newton-Howes & Wood, 2013). Thus, there is promise for the role of CBT in the treatment of schizophrenia, although additional research is required to test its efficacy, long-term durability, and impact on relapse rates and quality of life (Rector & Beck, 2012).

Family Interventions

Therapy for families of people with schizophrenia often focuses on educating them about the nature of schizophrenia and on training family members in effective problem-solving and communication skills (see Table 4.5). This approach is based on a bidirectional view of family environments—that is, that a person's symptoms and erratic behavior

TABLE 4.5 Elements in Effective Psychosocial Family Treatments

Element	Description
Reframe the problem.	Provide family members with alternate ways of conceptualizing the person's disorder so that they do not feel guilty or blamed for it.
Focus on communication.	Enhance family communication to prevent arguments and to ensure that each other's point of view is understood. This activity changes the family atmosphere from high to low expressed emotion (EE).
Focus on present interactions.	Concentrate on current stressors and problems.
Learn behavioral techniques for problem solving.	Break problems down into manageable elements, and train family members in specific problem-solving strategies.
Create structured, stable programs.	Structure all program elements clearly, and make them accessible to all family members.
Provide psychoeducation.	Educate the family about the biological and psychological elements of schizophrenia, what medications may be used in treatment, and how they affect people with the disorder.

Source: Adapted from Lam (1991) and Strachan (1986).

can aggravate family members, whose actions and reactions can, in turn, exacerbate the person's condition (e.g., Bellack & Mueser, 1993). Accordingly, families are trained to increase their awareness of expressed emotion (EE), discussed earlier in the chapter, which includes hostility, criticism, and overinvolved emotional reactions, and to foster positive comments and warmth (Berglund, Vahlne, & Edman, 2003). Whereas there is variability in the contents of various approaches to family interventions (i.e., group versus individual families), these interventions are more effective than many other types of interventions at preventing relapse in the year following intervention and at increasing compliance with medication regimens (Pilling et al., 2002). In fact, multiple controlled studies of family treatment for schizophrenia have shown a significant reduction in relapse and rehospitalization rates (Dixon et al., 2001; Pitschel-Walz, Leucht, Bauml, Kissling, & Engel, 2001). This effect is even greater when the intervention is provided via single-family treatment regimens, rather than in larger groups (Pilling et al., 2002).

Gerard Hogarty and his research team examined the independent and combined effects of client-oriented social skills training and family therapy in preventing relapse (Hogarty et al., 1986). One group received *family treatment* focused on decreasing family guilt and family stressors, increasing understanding of the disorder, decreasing expressed emotion (EE), and increasing social networks for the family. In the *social skills* group, treatment focused on helping people learn how to respond to hostile remarks by family members, to express positive feelings, and to develop more accurate perceptions of others. A third group received *both* family treatment and social skills training. People in a fourth group received only medication from a supportive nurse. One year after being released from the hospital, 41% of the medication-only group had relapsed, compared with only 19% of the family treatment group and 20% of the social skills group. None of the people in the combined family treatment and social skills group relapsed. The positive effects in this study were moderated by EE: In families that changed from high to low EE, no patient relapsed, but among families showing no change in EE status, relapse prevention occurred only if the family received both the family and social skills interventions.

The Recovery Movement and Psychosocial Rehabilitation

The most comprehensive psychological treatments for schizophrenia involve a set of interventions spawned in part by today's **recovery movement**, which promotes the notion

recovery movement: A movement that promotes the idea that individuals recovering from mental disorders should be able to successfully live and work in the community, enjoy active social lives, attend school, and maintain a healthy lifestyle, all while managing their own disorders with the supports that they may need.

Can Schizophrenia Be Prevented or Controlled?

Current research focusing on the prevention of schizophrenia indicates that, whereas genes play an important role in making certain people vulnerable to the development of a serious mental disorder, it is most likely the interaction between genes and environmental factors (i.e., nutrition, psychological trauma, substance abuse) that dictates the full expression of the disorder (Uher, 2014). Although currently there is no specific way to prevent schizophrenia, psychosocial rehabilitation coupled with regular medication comes the closest to constituting a form of *secondary prevention*, which initiates rapid treatment to lessen the lifelong impact of the disorder. For this reason, many programs pay special attention to serving relatively young people with schizophrenia, who are not yet chronically disabled from the disorder. Individuals experiencing first-episode psychosis (FEP) usually receive pharmacological intervention in the form of first- or second-generation antipsychotics in the acute phase, coupled with psychosocial interventions during the stable (residual) phase.

Family therapy, assertive community treatment (ACT), supported employment, psychotherapy, and training in social and self-help skills are all regular components of psychosocial rehabilitation programs, but the most successful programs offer even more services than these. People may be assigned to *case managers*, who serve as advocates and help them to obtain necessary services involving transportation, housing, medical services, and financial aid. In addition, efforts are made to create social support that "wraps around" individuals with schizophrenia and holds them in the community. Peer support groups meet frequently so that people have a place where they can engage in recreation and also learn from and encourage one another. "Safe houses" or temporary, sheltered living arrangements are also offered to people with schizophrenia who are homeless.

Some programs design individualized plans to help clients avoid or manage crises. The plans may include agreements to go to a safe house if family conflict is getting out of hand or to ask a buddy to come stay with the person. In some cases, clients help write what is known as a *proactive crisis plan*, which lists the typical symptoms and warning signs they experience at the beginning of a breakdown. This crisis plan, based on clients' understanding of how their disorder usually progresses, specifies the steps that should be taken to help contain or forestall the crisis.

Vocational rehabilitation has generally yielded positive overall outcomes; however, there has been speculation that this may be due to selection effects (Kilian et al., 2012). That is, less-impaired individuals will find and hold jobs, and those with jobs who experience an exacerbation of their symptoms will leave and not try to find jobs, potentially creating an inaccurate positive representation of studies examining psychiatric outcomes as they relate to having a job. One critical

Source: Alexander Raths/Shutterstock.com.

Learning how to anticipate and manage various crises is crucial to people's ability to avoid schizophrenia relapses. Family therapy, social skills training, and vocationally oriented psychosocial rehabilitation have all shown promise in relapse prevention in young people.

finding in this area is that working more hours results in decreased symptomatology among people with schizophrenia (Kilian et al., 2012).

Beyond even the key steps of managing family tension and life crises, getting housing, and securing a job, some places have attempted to involve the entire community in the treatment and care of people with schizophrenia. Community models go back as far as the Middle Ages (see Chapter 2), when the church was the primary source of treatment for those besieged with various forms of mental disorders. Many sought such assistance by making their way to St. Dymphna Church in Geel, Belgium. As those seeking treatment filled the church and city, there was a lack of housing for the visitors, whereupon church canons instructed townspeople to open their homes to the pilgrims. Thus was planted the seed of what would become an enduring system of foster family care for people with mental disorders. Geel's legendary foster family care system continued to evolve over the centuries and even today, in the 21st century, functions as one part of a modern comprehensive system of mental health services located in Geel and serving the entire region (Goldstein, 2009).

In the United States, as we strive to implement mental health programs that promote community integration, it can be helpful to look for guidance and inspiration to Geel, the oldest continuous community mental health program in the Western world. Geel's history offers a microcosmic view of the challenges that society in general has faced, relative to how the community deals with mental disorders. In the United States, we currently lack convincing evidence that early treatment of psychosis makes a difference in terms of long-range prognosis (Bosanac, Patton, & Castle, 2010). Yet, perhaps the true "preventive medicine" for those with schizophrenia lies not in the specific treatment components—medication, family therapy, or social skills training—but rather in meaningful integration into their communities.

that people with schizophrenia can and do recover to live worthwhile lives. According to Stephen Marder, MD, professor of psychiatry at the University of California, Los Angeles:

> For many years we've underestimated the ability of people with schizophrenia to change and improve their lives, and in fact, clinical care in many settings actually constrains patients and creates lower expectations about what they can achieve. (Friedrich, 2014)

Recently, the recovery movement has not only challenged previously held contentions about the prognosis of schizophrenia but has also highlighted how recovery involves attaining both objective and subjective markers of wellness (Roe, Mashiach-Eisenberg, & Lysaker, 2011). This has led to many calls for a recasting of the kinds of services that should be offered for persons with schizophrenia, renewing debate about the potential role of psychotherapy, including its purposes and nature relevant to schizophrenia (Hamm, Hasson-Ohayon, Kukla, & Lysaker, 2013). Specifically, one consequence of this work has been the proposal that many of the different threads involved in the psychotherapy of schizophrenia could now be integrated under newly developing holistic models of mental health.

Arthur C. Evans Jr., PhD, commissioner of Philadelphia's Department of Behavioral Health and Intellectual Disability Services, is a member of the Recovery Advisory Committee of the American Psychological Association, whose members are striving to ensure that future psychologists learn how to help their clients recover from serious mental disorders and reclaim their lives (Clay, 2014). The team has released a 15-module curriculum for doctoral, internship, and postdoctoral psychology programs that teaches students how to provide recovery-oriented behavioral health care. Says Evans:

> If I break my leg, I not only want it to heal but want to walk again and do all the activities I did before my leg was broken. It's no different with mental illness. People want more than just to not have symptoms; they want to regain their lives to whatever extent they can.

psychosocial rehabilitation: A set of interventions focused on preventing unnecessary hospitalizations, reducing impairments in daily functioning, and strengthening independent living skills by teaching patients with severe mental disorders how to cope with these disorders.

assertive community treatment (ACT): An intensive and highly integrated approach for community mental health service delivery, ACT programs serve outpatients whose mental disorders result in serious functioning difficulties in several major areas of life, often including work, social relationships, residential independence, money management, and physical health and wellness.

The recovery movement has promoted **psychosocial rehabilitation** interventions that try to strengthen people's competencies to maintain health, get a job, live in stable housing, and be able to take care of their personal daily needs (Cook, 1995). A specific approach to this relatively broad concept of psychosocial rehabilitation is the **assertive community treatment (ACT)** approach. ACT programs involve the provision of care through an integrated team that can include psychiatrists, psychologists, nurses, social workers, vocational rehabilitation, and peer support. These services are tailored to the individual, are usually available 24/7, and are delivered in the community. Various ACT programs have been shown to reduce homelessness, hospitalization, and symptomatology, while increasing medication adherence, days in community housing, and the use of outpatient services (Dixon et al., 2010). For example, a 2-year study of an ACT program for individuals with schizophrenia or bipolar I disorder with psychotic features (see Chapter 5) consisted of specialized inpatient and outpatient units, where clients received services at their home or at other places within their community. Nurses, psychiatrists, and psychologists were trained in cognitive, dynamic, and family therapies (Schöttle et al., 2014). Program retention was high, with only a 3.4% dropout rate, along with a decrease in involuntary hospital admissions, a high rate of medication adherence, improved overall functioning, and higher client satisfaction compared to previous treatment (Schöttle et al., 2014). Despite sound evidence for their effectiveness, though, ACT programs are not as widely available in the United States as they perhaps should be, leaving us still with a ways to go to more fully implement the lofty ideals of the recovery movement.

Section Review

Antipsychotics, the primary treatment for schizophrenia:

- are typically classified as either first-generation or second-generation antipsychotics,
- relieve positive symptoms for 60–70% of the people taking them,

- cause several kinds of serious side effects and have limited effects on negative symptoms (low motivation, depression, etc.), and
- lack clear evidence supporting their aggressive and early use for all people with schizophrenia.

Some of the most effective psychosocial treatments for schizophrenia focus on:

- training people in self-help and social skills;
- changing people's faulty cognitions that may lead to hallucinations or delusions;
- family therapy, in which families are taught how to effectively interact with members who have schizophrenia and how to reduce expressed emotion (EE); and
- psychosocial rehabilitation such as assertive community treatment (ACT), which helps people with schizophrenia live in communities by strengthening their independent living skills and creating more supportive environments toward recovery.

Revisiting the Case of Lionel Aldridge

A hundred years ago, Lionel would not have been diagnosed with schizophrenia. Because his condition did not start at an early age and did not progressively deteriorate, he would not have fit Kraepelin's definition of the disorder. However, although Lionel was initially misdiagnosed in the 1970s, clinicians using the *DSM* eventually diagnosed him with the paranoid type of schizophrenia (note that the *DSM-5* does not use these subtypes anymore).

As Lionel Aldridge discovered, medication alone is not a sufficient treatment for most cases of schizophrenia. The support of friends and the opportunity to relearn how to live successfully in the community are crucial. In the late 1980s, using a combination of medication, community support, and his personal resolve to overcome schizophrenia, Lionel began to put his life back together. He learned to cope with the side effects of his medication, and he accepted the fact that he had to take it regularly to function adequately. In cognitive therapy, he found that he could "make friends" with the hallucinated voices he sometimes still heard, so that he was no longer terrified by them. He also learned—from therapists and from friends—how to stop thinking negative and destructive thoughts when bad things happened to him.

Lionel Aldridge spent the last part of his life in Milwaukee, where he was well known not only for past athletic successes but for his ongoing role in educating the public about severe mental disorders. He was an advocate and board member for the mental health association of Milwaukee until his death in 1998. His story illustrates how medication, social support, understanding, and constant effort can help a person overcome even the most severe mental disorders.

Summary

The Definition of Schizophrenia Spectrum and Other Psychotic Disorders

Clinicians have formally recognized the disorder of schizophrenia for fewer than 200 years. Schizophrenia was originally called *dementia praecox* because it was believed to start at a young age and to result in progressive mental deterioration. In the late 1800s, Emil Kraepelin concluded that there were four subtypes of dementia praecox: hebephrenic, catatonic, paranoid, and simple. Eugen Bleuler's ideas eventually led to a broadening of the concept to include conditions that did not always start at an early age or deteriorate progressively. Eventually, *DSM* diagnoses of schizophrenia followed an operational approach to defining the disorder that represented a compromise between the traditions of Kraepelin, Bleuler, and the proposals of German psychiatrist Kurt Schneider.

Schizophrenia is categorized by two major kinds of symptoms: positive symptoms that include delusions, hallucinations, formal thought disorder, and disordered behavior; and negative symptoms that include flattened affect (mood), alogia (poor speech), and avolition (low motivation). Delusions are faulty beliefs that have little or no basis in reality, and hallucinations are faulty perceptual experiences. Schizophrenia is a heterogeneous disorder in

Erin Williams

Erin B. Williams received her PhD in counseling psychology from Indiana State University. Her focus is on community inclusion and psychosocial rehabilitation for persons with severe mental disorders. Dr. Williams is currently a staff psychologist at the Clement J. Zablocki Veterans Affairs Medical Center in Milwaukee, Wisconsin, where she manages Operation HOPE. Operation HOPE is a coalition of psychosocial rehabilitation programs for veterans diagnosed with severe mental disorders (such as schizophrenia) who experience serious and/or persistent functional impairment. These programs are founded on the understanding that people with significant mental health disabilities can, and do, overcome the limitations of their disorders and successfully fill valued roles in their community.

Q *What is your role in treating people living with schizophrenia?*

A I am a psychologist and also the manager of Operation HOPE, a collaborative of local VA programs, established to combat the stigma associated with severe mental illness by helping veterans reclaim their lives and secure meaningful, self-determined roles in their community of choice. We have the privilege of partnering with individuals and their families by utilizing a strength-based, recovery-oriented approach. Studies about recovery from serious mental illness began appearing as early as the 1980s. Since then, researchers have continued to confirm that people who have been diagnosed with schizophrenia desire so much more in their life than simply getting stable on medicine and staying out of the hospital. Psychosocial rehabilitation is the preferred practice, as it is based on the philosophy of healing and human potential. This holistic strategy involves shared responsibility, individualized skill development, and environmental change, resulting in hope becoming a viable outcome.

Q *What treatment model(s) do you use, and what types of symptoms do you see the most improvement in?*

A For persons who experience frequent mental health crises, we provide a community-based program to assist them in better managing the challenges and sequelae of the illness. Focused support includes practical problem solving, crisis resolution, adaptive skill building, transition to self-care and greater independence, and for those interested, competitive employment. Whether individuals are in frequent crisis or not, additional evidence-based programming is available. Social and independent skills training is taught in a supportive setting through small-group interactions using workbook exercises, role playing, and structured problem solving. A transitional learning center is also provided where veterans can access personalized empowerment and recovery planning, mental health advanced directives, peer support services, wellness programming, illness management education, support groups (e.g., Voice Hearers), socialization opportunities, brief psychotherapy, and community inclusion activities that are individualized based on self-identified interests. Family education, support, and therapy are also available. The negative symptoms commonly identified in a diagnosis of schizophrenia are most notably impacted by participation in psychosocial rehabilitation.

Q *Do you see schizophrenia as multiple disorders or as on a spectrum of severity?*

A Schizophrenia is not an illness, but a label that first came into being more than 100 years ago. The criterion of the label has evolved since then, and greater still has been the need for an expanded breath of understanding about the conditions that are included underneath this umbrella term. These conditions do not neatly fit side by side within a spectrum, as they are overlapping, complex, and in some cases, poorly defined. This array of psychotic disorders features contradictory symptoms (e.g., typical date of onset), variable course, and differences in genetic contribution, neuroanatomy, and neurochemistry. Researchers seem to be slowly, but steadily, unraveling these dissimilarities; it is hoped that burgeoning insight will be the catalyst for not only new interventions, but also the impetus to increasingly welcome these people from the shadows of society. This will further shape practice and opinion beyond mere symptom relief to promoting the necessity of an improved quality of life, pursuit of personal satisfaction through meaningful roles, and the realistic quest for these people to reach their dreams and goals "just like everyone else."

that some people have more prominent positive symptoms (hallucinations and delusions), whereas others may have strong negative symptoms (little interest or engagement in life) without a clear delusional system.

In addition to schizophrenia, the *DSM-5* lists several other psychotic disorders that involve hallucinations or delusions. These disorders usually involve fragments of a full schizophrenic syndrome or are reactions to specific events that cause a limited episode of psychosis. They seldom cause the intense symptoms and long-term impairment and suffering found in many cases of schizophrenia.

Living With Schizophrenia

About 1% of the world's population is diagnosed with schizophrenia. Approximately equal proportions of males and females are affected, but the disorder usually begins earlier in males than in females. Initial onset is usually in the teens and 20s, but schizophrenia can develop at any time, even as late as the 50s or 60s. Recovery rates for schizophrenia vary considerably among cultures, with the best outcomes often occurring in developing nations.

Biological Causes of Schizophrenia

It is not possible to pinpoint the causes of any individual case of schizophrenia, but most researchers believe that a diathesis-stress model best explains the disorder's development. Evidence from family aggregation, twin, and adoption studies clearly shows that genes provide one kind of diathesis to schizophrenia. However, in cases in which one identical (MZ) twin has schizophrenia, the co-twin is also diagnosed with schizophrenia only about half the time. Nongenetic factors must therefore be involved as well.

Exactly what is inherited remains unknown. Biological abnormalities, personality patterns, neurological problems involving attentional and cognitive deficits, and structural abnormalities in the brain are all possibilities. Early evidence implicated overactivity of dopamine, but recent studies have cast doubt on this hypothesis as an adequate explanation; other neurotransmitters such as serotonin and glutamate may also be involved. Brain-scanning procedures show that many people with schizophrenia have significant structural brain deficits, particularly in the frontal lobe, thalamus, and certain subcortical structures under the temporal lobe, including parts of the limbic system. The origin of these deficits is currently unknown: They may be inherited, they may be caused by complications during pregnancy or birth, or they may be the result of early viral infections.

Psychosocial Causes of Schizophrenia

In the United States, most people with schizophrenia come from inner cities and from the lower socioeconomic classes. Whether their disorder causes them to drift down to these levels or whether the stressors of urbanicity and poverty breed schizophrenia is still unresolved.

A family climate high in levels of expressed emotion (EE) is a predictor of schizophrenic relapse. However, EE appears to be both a cause and a consequence of the disorder.

Treatments for Schizophrenia

The most common treatments for schizophrenia are antipsychotic drugs, administered initially in the hospital and then continued in the community. The phenothiazines act by blocking dopamine receptors and reduce positive symptoms in about two thirds of patients. These therapeutic effects are offset by potentially serious, sometimes irreversible side effects, such as tardive dyskinesia. As a result, many people stop taking these medications. Atypical (or second-generation) antipsychotic drugs, which have somewhat different neurotransmitter effects than the phenothiazines, are effective for many people who do not respond to traditional neuroleptics or who suffer serious side effects from them. However, second-generation medications also have serious side effects. And, overall, there is little evidence that these medications improve negative symptoms and make a large difference in terms of the person's long-time functioning and quality of life.

Medication alone is thus not a sufficient treatment for most cases of schizophrenia. Psychosocial treatments need to be provided as well. Some of these treatments focus on training people in basic social and survival skills or in changing their faulty thinking about hallucinations and delusions. Others stress family therapy, including educating the family about schizophrenia, enhancing communication among family members, and reducing high levels of expressed emotion in the family. Psychosocial rehabilitation is a broad intervention that teaches people how to cope with the disabilities of schizophrenia and that increases the amount of support available to these people in their home communities as they move toward recovery. All of these psychosocial programs have proved to be important in preventing relapses among people with schizophrenia.

Key Terms

active phase, p. 144

acute akathesis, p. 161

acute dystonia, p. 161

alogia, p. 138

anhedonia, p. 138

assertive community treatment (ACT), p. 168

atypical antipsychotics, p. 162

avolition, p. 139

brief psychotic disorder, p. 140

catatonia, p. 137

delusional disorder, p. 139

delusions, p. 130

diathesis-stress model, p. 150

double-bind hypothesis, p. 157

expressed emotion (EE), p. 158

extrapyramidal symptoms, p. 161

flat affect, p. 138

formal thought disorder, p. 136

frontal lobe, p. 152

hallucinations, p. 130

hypofrontality, p. 152

illusions, p. 135

milieu programs, p. 163

morbidity risk, p. 145

negative symptoms, p. 133

neuroleptic malignant syndrome (NMS), p. 161

neuroleptics, p. 160

other psychotic disorders, p. 139

Parkinsoniam, p. 161

phenothiazines, p. 160

positive symptoms, p. 133

postpartum onset, p. 140

premorbid phase, p. 142

prodromal phase, p. 142

psychosocial rehabilitation, p. 168

psychotic disorder due to another medical condition, p. 139

recovery movement, p. 166

residual phase, p. 144

schizoaffective disorder, p. 140

schizophrenia, p. 130

schizophreniform disorder, p. 140

schizophrenogenic mother, p. 157

season-of-birth effect, p. 150

social causation theory, p. 157

social drift hypothesis, p. 156

substance/medication-induced psychotic disorder, p. 141

tardive dyskinesia (TD), p. 161

thalamus, p. 152

token economies, p. 164

ventricles, p. 151

Bipolar Disorders and Suicide

Chapter Outline

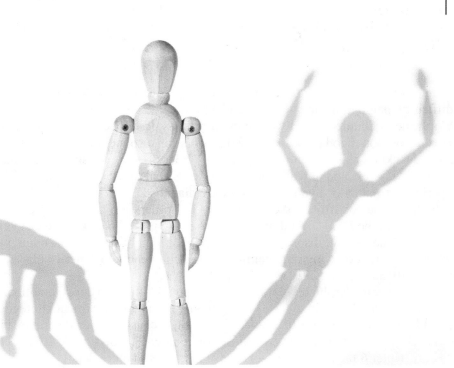

Source: luisrsphoto/Shutterstock.com.

From the Case of John

By the time John was admitted to the hospital, he was talking a mile a minute to anyone who would listen. His wife brought him in after he had been up all night, describing how he needed to be on a plane to Stockholm for the Nobel Prize ceremony, as he claimed he had recently been awarded the world's top prize for physics. John had gone on a spending spree the day before, purchasing a tuxedo and an airline ticket to Sweden.

John is a 37-year-old married man who has been unemployed for several years and who went back to school recently, taking night classes in physics at the local community college. His wife brought him to the hospital following a week in which John had been partying every night and shopping every day. John's troubles had begun 7 years earlier when, while working as an insurance adjuster, he suffered symptoms of depression and anxiety for a few months. He blamed these problems on stress, and within a couple of months and without any formal treatment, the symptoms declined, and John was back to his usual self. A few years later, following thyroid surgery, John experienced some dramatic mood changes. For 2 or 3 weeks, he would feel so full of energy that he was hyperactive and euphoric and barely needed to sleep; these periods were then followed by several days of almost-constant

After reading this chapter, you will be able to answer the following key questions:

- How are bipolar and related disorders described and categorized in the *Diagnostic and Statistical Manual of Mental Disorders (DSM-5)*?

- What causes bipolar disorders?

- What are the main treatments for helping people with bipolar disorders?

- What are the causes of and prevention strategies for suicide?

sleep and feelings of deep depression. This pattern of alternating elation and depression repeated itself continuously over the next several years.

During his energetic periods, John was full of self-confidence, but he became short-tempered easily. He often spent large sums of money on unnecessary purchases, such as high-priced stereo systems, expensive pedigreed dogs, and airline tickets. He also had several impulsive sexual flings. During his depressed periods, he stayed in bed all day, feeling unmotivated and guilty about his irresponsibility and previous excesses. He frequently refused to eat, bathe, or shave during these periods of withdrawal. In fact, during his most recent depressive episode, John had constant thoughts of suicide and even purchased a firearm, which he now keeps under his bed. (Based on Spitzer, Gibbon, Skodol, Williams, & First, 1994)

mood disorders: A group of mental disorders associated with serious and persistent difficulty maintaining an even, productive emotional state.

depression: An extremely low, miserably unhappy mood, along with other physical and cognitive symptoms.

mania: An excited mood in which a person feels excessively and unrealistically positive and energetic.

hypomania: A mild form of mania.

Mood disorders refer to a group of emotional disturbances associated with serious and persistent difficulty maintaining an even keel and a productive emotional state. Whereas **depression** (sad mood coupled with low interest in life, as described in detail in Chapter 6) is the most common mood disorder, these disorders can also include extremely high or agitated moods—known as **mania** (or **hypomania**, a less intense version)—in which the person feels excessively and unrealistically positive or goal directed. Individuals who experience periods of mania or hypomania often are diagnosed with one of the *bipolar disorders*, which are the focus of this chapter. These disorders are separated from the depressive disorders in the *DSM-5*. And in this text, they are placed between the chapters on schizophrenia and depressive disorders in recognition of their bridging these other two diagnostic classes in terms of symptoms, family history, and genetics (American Psychiatric Association, 2013a; Hickie, 2014).

In this chapter, we consider the bipolar disorders in detail—their physical, emotional, and cognitive symptoms; the main theories about their causes; and treatment strategies. The chapter ends with a discussion of suicidal behavior because bipolar disorders and depression, respectively, constitute the two most common causes of suicide (Chehil & Kutcher, 2012). Chapter 6 then examines depressive disorders in more detail.

Bipolar Disorders

bipolar disorders: Mood disorders marked by alternating periods of depression and mania.

People suffering from **bipolar disorders** usually experience periods of depression, as well as periods of either extremely elevated mood known as *mania*, or mixed episodes in which mania and depression alternate so rapidly that both are experienced within the same day. It is unclear whether bipolar disorders are independent of, or a variant of, major depressive disorders (Clayton, 1986). The two classes of disorders obviously overlap, since the depression experienced in each looks the same clinically. However, some features of the two are quite different, and that is why the *DSM-5* now has them in separate categories. For example:

- Major depressive disorders are more common in women, whereas men and women are at about equal risk for bipolar disorders (Hamilton, 1989).
- Bipolar disorders usually start in the late teens to early twenties, earlier than the age at which major depressive disorders usually first appear.
- Bipolar disorders seem to be more frequent among people of higher socioeconomic status (Weissman, Bruce, Leaf, Florio, & Holzer, 1991), which is the opposite pattern of depression.
- Compared with unipolar depression, bipolar disorders are less often triggered or worsened by such psychosocial stressors as the breakup of a relationship.
- Bipolar disorders have a greater genetic basis (higher heritabilities) than major depressive disorder, with familial transmission of manic and major depressive episodes largely independent, despite the high magnitude of comorbidity between these mood states (Merikangas et al., 2014).

(a)   (b)

MAPS - Superficial Syndromes

Manic episodes are common all over the world, including in cacti. The photo in (a) shows a cactus in the Atacama region of Chile in the throes of a high-energy manic episode (as evidenced by the very high arms), whereas the photo in (b) depicts similar symptoms in a saguaro cactus in Tucson, AZ.

Source: Brian L. Burke.

Prevalence and Characteristics of Bipolar Disorders

Lifetime risk for bipolar disorders in the general U.S. population has been estimated at 2–3% (Kessler, Petukhova, Sampson, Zaslavsky, & Wittchen, 2012), with higher risk associated with a family history of bipolar disorders, early onset of major depression, and a history of manic symptoms in response to antidepressant medication (Strober et al., 1988). Twelve-month prevalence is about 1% for bipolar II disorders and slightly less than 1% for bipolar I disorders (bipolar I vs. II is described further in the next section). Bipolar disorders are recurring and chronic disorders. The vast majority (90%) of people with these disorders experience several episodes of depression or mania during their lives (American Psychiatric Association, 2013a), interspersed with periods of relatively normal functioning.

In a combined sample of 61,392 adults from 11 countries, the average lifetime prevalence estimate for bipolar disorders was 2.4% worldwide (Merikangas et al., 2011). The severity of symptoms was greater for depressive than manic episodes. Approximately 74.0% of respondents with depression and 50.9% of respondents with mania reported severe role impairment. Three quarters of those with bipolar disorders worldwide also met criteria for at least one other mental disorder. Anxiety disorders (see Chapter 7), especially panic attacks, were the most common comorbid condition. The surveys found that the treatment needs for people with bipolar disorders are often unmet: Fewer than half of those with lifetime bipolar disorders received mental health treatment, particularly in low-income countries, where only 25.2% reported contact with the mental health system (Merikangas et al., 2011).

In this worldwide study, the United States had the highest lifetime rate of bipolar disorders at 4.4%, and India the lowest, with 0.1% (Merikangas et al., 2011). The United States ranked higher in every category of bipolar disorders, as did, in general, other high-income countries. Two exceptions to this trend were Japan (a wealthy nation), which had a lifetime prevalence of 0.7%, and Colombia, a lower-income nation, with a relatively high prevalence of 2.6%. However, despite cross-site variation in the prevalence rates of bipolar disorders, the severity, impact, and patterns of comorbidity were remarkably similar internationally (Merikangas et al., 2011). As to why the United States may be higher than other nations, researchers can only speculate. One theory is that the type of people who are attracted to the United States to live are entrepreneurs and leaders who took risks to come to America, a self-selected sample of people who may have a higher rate of grandiose and impulsive tendencies that could be precursors for bipolar disorders (Gartner, 2011).

MAPS - Prejudicial Pigeonholes

Bipolar disorders are about equally common in men and women (Kessler et al., 2012). However, in most cases, women with bipolar disorders experience one or more depressive episodes before the first manic phase. Men with bipolar disorders, however, are more

TABLE 5.1 The *DSM-5* in Simple Language: Diagnosing Depression

The person shows at least five of the following nine symptoms most days for two or more weeks:

1. Sad mood
2. Lack of interest or pleasure in activities

Physical changes, like:

3. Low energy
4. Sleeping more or less than usual
5. Eating more or less than usual
6. Moving faster or slower than usual

Changes in thinking, like:

7. Thinking negative thoughts about himself or herself
8. Trouble making decisions
9. Thoughts of suicide

Source: Adapted from the American Psychiatric Association (2013a).

likely to have manic episodes first. Approximately 10–20% of people who have more than one major depressive episode go on to display a bipolar disorder (Post, 1993). This is more likely in individuals with onset of their disorder in adolescence, those with psychotic features, and those with a family history of bipolar disorders (American Psychiatric Association, 2013a). Table 5.1 lists the key criteria in defining depressive episodes in bipolar disorders, which are described in greater detail in Chapter 6.

Unlike typical depressive episodes, manic episodes can develop rapidly—in some cases in a matter of hours, but more typically, over a few days. Table 5.2 lists the key criteria in defining a manic episode. During these episodes, which must last at least 1 week (if untreated) to be officially defined as such, the person displays an abnormally elevated, expansive, or irritable mood, along with unlimited energy and enthusiasm for unrealistic goals. One woman's housecleaning became so extreme that she began cleaning the outside of her house with a toothbrush; one man turned his car headlights on his home so that he could begin painting it at 2 A.M. Manic persons may try to strike up intense conversations with strangers on the street, only to become irritated if they are ignored or rebuffed. Sometimes, in mixed episodes of bipolar disorder, the person feels invincible and omnipotent one minute and in utter despair the next.

It is not unusual for people in a manic episode to go for days with only a few hours of sleep each night. In fact, reduced need for sleep and insomnia/hypersomnia are common symptoms of the manic and depressive phases of bipolar disorders, respectively (Kaplan, Talbot, Gruber, & Harvey, 2012). Furthermore, sleep disturbance persists in the period between episodes and may be a mechanism contributing to relapse, as sleep loss can trigger episodes of mania (Barbini et al., 1998). For example, one study found that 70% of an inter-episode bipolar disorders group had a clinically significant sleep problem, and 55% met diagnostic criteria for insomnia while between mood episodes (Harvey, Schmidt, Scarna, Semler,

Source: Cartoonresource/Shutterstock.com.

"Don't anyone say, 'That's the fax, Jack.'"

Like Jack, people with bipolar disorders often experience irritable rather than elevated moods during their manic or hypomanic episodes.

TABLE 5.2 The *DSM-5* in Simple Language: Diagnosing Mania

The person goes through a period of a significantly elevated or irritable mood, along with high energy and activity as indicated by at least three (or four if the mood is irritable) of the following seven symptoms most days for at least 1 week. The symptoms may involve an increase in:

1. Waking hours (i.e., a reduced need for sleep)
2. Self-esteem
3. Talking
4. Thinking
5. Getting distracted
6. Activity or agitation (i.e., doing more than usual)
7. Dangerous or risky activities (e.g., driving too fast, spending too much)

Source: Adapted from the American Psychiatric Association (2013a).

& Goodwin, 2005). A second study revealed that sleep disturbance is the most common prodrome (a symptom appearing before the full episode) of mania and the sixth most common prodrome of bipolar depression (Jackson, 2003). Furthermore, a prospective study utilizing daily monitoring reported that changes in self-reported sleep duration (change in total sleep time of more than 3 hours) were strongly suggestive of an impending mood episode (Bauer et al., 2006), providing further evidence that sleep may be the most sensitive sign of mania.

In addition, as in the chapter-opening case of John, people with bipolar disorders often show rapid and "pressured" speech; they talk on and on as if they cannot stop, seldom taking into account the remarks or needs of the listener. In addition, like with John, their judgment tends to be poor, leading in some cases to wild spending sprees, questionable business ventures, or sexual promiscuity. Many people experience racing thoughts, and they are so easily distracted that their attention and conversational topics shift rapidly.

"We love the fact you are a doer. We just don't like what you do."

People with bipolar disorders may get a great deal done, but what they are actually doing may, in fact, be risky and not well conceived.

In bipolar disorders, as in major depressive disorders, mood disturbance is only part of the clinical picture. During manic episodes, there is an inflated sense of self-esteem known as *grandiosity*. John's belief that he won the Nobel Prize in physics (when he was, in fact, just a student in physics at a community college) is an example of extreme grandiosity. Individuals may feel they possess special powers or are invulnerable to harm. For example, one man who had few technical or mechanical skills became convinced that he could invent a machine to eradicate the earth's trash disposal problems. Exhausted after working day and night, he became more and more agitated until, wildly out of control, he crashed through a plate-glass window because he was sure that it could do him no harm.

Grandiosity can take on delusional proportions with religious, political, financial, or sexual themes predominating. The person working on the trash disposal machine believed he was receiving instructions from God, and another man who talked incessantly about having special powers to solve all the world's problems became convinced that he had far-reaching political connections. Confusion, memory loss, and fear of death are also frequently seen in manic episodes. The psychotic features typical of some manic episodes may interfere so seriously with an individual's functioning that psychiatric hospitalization is required, as it was for John. If left untreated, manic episodes typically last from a week to about 3 months (Grof, Angst, & Haines, 1974), and for any one person, may occur from two to more than thirty times in a lifetime, with a median of nine episodes (Angst, Felder, & Frey, 1979).

Interestingly, despite being diagnosed with the disorder at about the same rate, men and women tend to show different symptom presentations during manic episodes (Bhattacharya et al., 2011). In men, there is significantly higher motor activity, psychosis, and grandiosity (like John's case), whereas up-and-down mood, depressed mood, guilt, suicide, and anxiety are frequently higher in women in the throes of manic episodes. There are also small gender differences in the course of the episodes. Women experience faster mania improvement and a higher risk of developing a depressive episode during the 12-month follow-up period than do men (Miquel et al., 2011).

Classification of Bipolar Disorders

As with depressive disorders, there are variations in how bipolar disorders manifest themselves. Many people with bipolar disorders experience separate episodes of both depression and mania, others

Kay Redfield Jamison (born June 22, 1946) is an American clinical psychologist, professor of psychiatry at the Johns Hopkins University, and writer whose work has centered on bipolar disorder, which she has suffered since early adulthood. Jamison (1996) describes her disorder as follows: "I have often asked myself whether, given the choice, I would choose to have [bipolar disorder]. If lithium were not available to me, or didn't work for me, the answer would be a simple no . . . and it would be an answer laced with terror. Strangely enough, I think I would choose to have it. I honestly believe that as a result of it I have felt more things, more deeply; had more experiences, more intensely; loved more, and have been more loved; laughed more often for having cried more often; appreciated more the springs, for all the winters. . . . Depressed, I have crawled on my hands and knees in order to get across a room and have done it for month after month. But normal or manic, I have run faster, thought faster, and loved faster than most I know."

have mixed episodes of depression and mania within the same day, and about 10% have only recurring episodes of mania (Clayton, 1986; Keller et al., 1992). Approximately 60% of manic episodes occur immediately before a major depressive episode (American Psychiatric Association, 2013a).

Bipolar I and Bipolar II

For cases in which there are severe, full-blown manic symptoms, usually accompanied by one or more periods of major depression, the *DSM-5* uses the label **bipolar I disorder**. The designation of **bipolar II disorder**, which is slightly more common in the United States (Kessler et al., 2012), refers to cases in which a major depressive episode has occurred in addition to hypomanic (but not manic) episodes. A hypomanic episode involves the exact same clinical symptoms as a manic episode (see Table 5.2), except that the episode is shorter (4 days as opposed to a week or more), less intense, and does not significantly disrupt the person's daily life or require hospitalization, even though the symptoms may be obvious and sometimes irritating to others. Also, by definition, if the episode involves psychotic features (e.g., John believing he won the Noble Prize in physics), then it is termed a manic rather than hypomanic episode (American Psychiatric Association, 2013a).

Although bipolar II disorder can begin in late adolescence and throughout adulthood, the average age of onset is the mid-20s, which is slightly later than for bipolar I disorder (age 18) but earlier than for major depressive disorder (American Psychiatric Association, 2013a). The number of lifetime episodes—both hypomanic and major depressive episodes—tends to be higher for bipolar II disorder than for major depressive disorder or bipolar I disorder. However, people with bipolar I disorder are actually more likely to experience hypomanic symptoms than are people with bipolar II disorder. In addition, if a full-blown manic episode occurs at any time, the person's diagnosis should be changed from bipolar II to bipolar I disorder.

In terms of course and prognosis, the mania or hypomania–depression–euthymia (normal mood) interval course-pattern is most common (34.4%) and is associated with psychotic or manic onset; the depression before mania pattern (25.0%) most often follows anxiety (38.8%), depression (30.8%), or mixed onsets (13.3%; Baldessarini, Tondo, & Visioli, 2014). Both of these patterns were predicted by initial mania–depression sequences, indicating the value of early patterns for prognosis and long-term planning. New evidence suggests that a chronic course and multisystem involvement is the rule in bipolar disorder, rather than the exception, and that together with disturbances of circadian rhythms, mood instability, and cognitive impairment, a high rate of medical burden (comorbid medical diagnoses) is often observed (Soreca, Frank, & Kupfer, 2009). In other words, dysfunction is high in bipolar disorders (El-Mallakh & Hollifield, 2008), which are among the top 10 greatest causes of disability worldwide (Murray & Lopez, 1996). Specifically, it has been repeatedly reported that functional recovery is delayed after symptomatic recovery (Tohen et al., 2000; Tohen et al., 2003). For example, in a study of 162 people with bipolar I disorder followed for 2–4 years after discharge for their first lifetime manic or mixed episode, nearly all (97.6%) had achieved syndromal recovery (no longer meeting criteria for mania) about 14 weeks later, and half recovered in only 5.4 weeks (Tohen et al., 2003). However, at 6 months, only 39.5% had functionally recovered (regaining their pre-disorder occupational or residential status), and after 2 years, the majority were still functionally impaired, with only 43.1% achieving functional recovery (Tohen et al., 2003).

To identify other key variations in how bipolar disorders present, which may affect their treatment and course, clinicians are encouraged to use one of ten different **specifiers**, different subtypes of the disorder based on symptom patterns. The four most important specifiers are:

1. **With mixed features.** This specifier corresponds to the most recent mood episode and is relatively common (20–30%; McIntyre, Tohen, Berk, Zhao, & Weiller, 2013). People with bipolar disorders who have at least three depressive symptoms during a manic episode or at least three manic symptoms during a depressive episode

---

bipolar I disorder: A mood disorder in which severe, full-blown manic symptoms are accompanied by one or more periods of major depression.

bipolar II disorder: A mood disorder in which a major depressive episode has occurred in addition to manic episodes that are mild, or hypomanic.

MAPS - Superficial Syndromes

This saguaro cactus in Tucson, Arizona, appears to be experiencing both episodes of depression (as indicated by the droopy arms on the left) and mania (extremely high arm on the right). Based on these superficial symptoms, the cactus would be diagnosed with bipolar I disorder.

specifier: A descriptor used in the *DSM-5* to indicate the likely course, severity, and specific symptom characteristics of certain mental disorders.

Source: Brian L. Burke.

can be given a "mixed features" specifier for that particular mood episode. Typically, manic episodes with mixed features also entail more anxiety and irritability/agitation compared to "pure" manic episodes (Vieta, Grunze, Azorin, & Fagiolini, 2014). Another study showed that people whose most recent manic episode had definite mixed features were more likely to be young at admission, to be female, to have a family history of mood disorders, and to have a history of suicidality relative to the mania (Shim, Woo, Jun, & Bahk, 2014). Research generally supports the use of the *DSM-5* mixed features specifier and its value in research and clinical practice and treatment (Vieta et al., 2014). For instance, with increasing baseline severity of depressive features during a manic episode, treatment outcome was poorer with olanzapine (Zyprexa, an atypical antipsychotic medication), but remained stable with asenapine, a different atypical antipsychotic medication (McIntyre et al., 2013).

2. **With psychotic features.** This specifier is given if delusions (false beliefs) or hallucinations (faulty perceptual experiences) are present at any time during the mood episode (American Psychiatric Association, 2013a). There is growing evidence that schizophrenia (see Chapter 4) and bipolar disorders overlap significantly in terms of risk factors, neurobiological features, clinical presentations, and outcomes (Yüksel et al., 2012). One such overlap is the presence of psychotic features during many (perhaps nearly 50% of) manic episodes (Kerner, 2014; Özyildirim, Çakir, & Yazici, 2010). The psychotic features can be described further as being either *mood-congruent* or *mood-incongruent*. Mood-congruent psychosis means that the content of all delusions and hallucinations is consistent with the typical manic themes of grandiosity and invulnerability (American Psychiatric Association, 2013a). For example, in the chapter-opening case, John believed that he had won the Nobel Prize (a delusion) during one of his manic episodes; this would be categorized as a mood-congruent psychotic feature because it fits with the inflated self-esteem and unrealistic goals of mania. Conversely, if John believed during a manic phase that the president of his community college was wire-tapping his phones and computer because she (the president) suspected that John was a terrible student who would bring ruin to the college, this would constitute a mood-incongruent (and persecutory) delusion. Interestingly, though, psychotic features may not have predictive value for manic episodes, although they do for depressive episodes (Coryell et al., 2001). In one study, people with psychotic mania at intake did not differ significantly from those with nonpsychotic mania in response to acute lithium treatment, suicidal behavior during follow-up, or risk for mood disorders among first-degree relatives; nor did they have high psychosis ratings during follow-up (Coryell et al., 2001).

3. **With rapid cycling.** This specifier is used when four or more discrete, full-blown mood episodes (depression, mania, and/or hypomania) are experienced within a 1-year period. It is applied to women more frequently than to men. A systematic review of the research literature suggests that rapid cycling affects a significant proportion of people with bipolar disorders (26–43%) and is related to a longer course of illness, an earlier age at onset, more illegal drug and alcohol abuse, and increased suicidality (Carvalho et al., 2014). The etiology remains unclear, although a causal or triggering role for the use of antidepressants and hypothyroidism has been implicated. Also, there is not currently any good evidence that rapid cycling represents a discrete subtype of bipolar disorder, rather than a pattern that can occur at any point during the disorder and that may indicate a worsening outcome.

4. **With seasonal pattern.** Like rapid cycling, this specifier applies not to an individual mood episode, but rather to the broader pattern of mood episodes. The basic feature is a regular seasonal pattern of at least one type of mood episode. Whereas the most common seasonal pattern is that depressive episodes recur at characteristic times of the year (e.g., dark winters in high-latitude climates), it is unclear whether a seasonal pattern is more likely in such depressive episodes that happen during recurrent major depressive disorder (Chapter 6) or as part of bipolar disorders (American Psychiatric Association, 2013a). However, a seasonal pattern is more likely

in bipolar II compared to bipolar I disorder. Further, a study of 314 individuals with bipolar I or bipolar II disorder revealed that both disorders exhibit the lowest frequency of depressive symptoms in summer and the highest around the winter solstice (Akhter et al., 2013). Variation of manic symptoms was more pronounced in bipolar II disorder, with a significant peak in hypomanic symptomatology in the months surrounding the fall equinox. A seasonal pattern is correlated with a lifetime history of rapid cycling, comorbid eating disorders, and total number of depressive episodes (Geoffroy et al., 2013).

Cyclothymic Disorder

In another form of bipolar disorder, known as **cyclothymic disorder**, moods fluctuate over a long period—2 or more years in adults, 1 year or more in children and adolescents—but neither the depressive nor the manic phase is as severe as in bipolar I or II disorders (American Psychiatric Association, 2013a). Cyclothymic disorder, which occurs in 3–4% of young adults (Akiskal, 1992) and about 1% of all adults (American Psychiatric Association, 2013a), is characterized by irritability and oscillations between behavioral extremes, such as pessimism and optimism, low and high self-esteem, and sleeping much more, then much less, than usual (Akiskal, 1992; Depue et al., 1981). Cyclothymic disorder is a parallel term with persistent depressive disorder (discussed in Chapter 6); both suggest less severe but more chronic mood disturbances. In cyclothymic disorder, periods of elevated mood never reach the state of elation commonly associated with mania or hypomania, and low moods neither warrant a diagnosis of major depressive disorder nor interfere significantly with daily functioning.

Over the last three decades, cyclothymic disorder has been positioned in one of two principal ways: (1) formally classified as a mood disorder, and (2) less formally categorized at a "cyclothymic temperament" level, almost like a personality disorder (see Chapter 16; Parker, McCraw, & Fletcher, 2012). Researchers recently recommended that cyclothymia's expression as a mood disorder should be positioned within the bipolar II disorder class—albeit perhaps having briefer mood swings and fewer episodes, more rapid cycling, and greater reactivity to environmental factors than is conceptualized currently for bipolar II disorders (Parker et al., 2012). However, neglect has contributed to confusion about the diagnosis and clinical presentation of cyclothymic disorder. Accordingly, it is rarely diagnosed clinically, in spite of evidence that it may be the most prevalent form of bipolar disorder (Van Meter, Youngstrom, & Findling, 2012).

So what exactly is the relationship between cyclothymic disorder and bipolar I and II disorder? Individuals with cyclothymic disorder are at increased risk for eventually developing bipolar I or II disorder, according to representative prospective studies. Alloy et al. (2012) found that 42.1% of individuals with cyclothymic disorder at baseline met criteria for bipolar II and 10.5% for bipolar I at follow-up, whereas another prospective study found that 63.8% of children and adolescents with a history of major depressive episodes coupled with cyclothymic temperament developed bipolar II disorder during 2–4 years of follow-up (Kochman et al., 2005). Similarly, Birmaher and colleagues (2006, 2009) found that 38% of their child/adolescent patients (ages 7 to 18 at outset) converted to a bipolar I or II diagnosis during four4 years of follow-up (Birmaher et al., 2009). A retrospective study showed that, compared to youth with non-bipolar disorders, youth with cyclothymic disorder had higher irritability, more comorbidity, and greater sleep disturbance, and were more likely to have a family history of bipolar disorders (Van Meter, Youngstrom, Demeter, & Findling, 2013). Thus, cyclothymic disorder appears to have found its home among the bipolar and related disorders.

Bipolar Disorders and Creativity

Bipolar disorders affect people from all socioeconomic classes, ethnic groups, and occupations, but its victims seem to include an unusually large number of well-known creative people. Prominent examples include composers Handel and Tchaikovsky, writers Jack London, Ernest Hemingway, Sylvia Plath, and Virginia Woolf, filmmaker Ingmar Bergman, and possibly, artists Jackson Pollock and Vincent van Gogh. A more recent example is actor Robin Williams, who tragically committed suicide during a depressive episode of bipolar disorder in August 2014. Other celebrities with bipolar disorders include musicians Amy Winehouse and Kurt Cobain, and beloved children's author Robert Munsch, who wrote *Love You Forever* and other children's classics. The incidence of mood disorders among successful artists and writers appears to be higher than among the general population (Goodwin & Jamison, 1990; Jamison, 1989).

Are bipolar disorders and creativity somehow linked? Could creativity lead to an increased risk for bipolar disorders, or could bipolar disorders lead to increased creativity? Perhaps after prolonged creative concentration and introspection on emotional material or after a particularly productive burst of achievement, artists' moods intensify to the point that they are maladaptive. Or perhaps the intense emotions of the bipolar disorder, when they are at manageable levels, lead some artists to creative or dramatic insights or to prolonged periods of absorption in a creative task. The link between bipolar disorders and creativity is often explained through the occurrence of hypomanic episodes (e.g., Furnham, Batey, Anand, & Manfield, 2008; Kyaga et al., 2011, 2013). In support of this idea, during manic or hypomanic episodes, people with bipolar disorders report engaging more in writing, painting, work, or business ideas, as well as in "other" forms of art (McCraw, Parker, Fletcher, & Friend, 2013).

Another possibility is that creativity and mood disorders share common roots. One study of 30 creative writers found that the rate of mood disorders was significantly higher among the writers than among a control group of socioeconomically similar adults, and also that the prevalence of mood disorders among the writers' first-degree relatives was nine times greater than among the relatives of the control group (Andreasen, 1987). People with bipolar disorders are also significantly more likely to report creative personality styles more generally outside of a mood episode (McCraw et al., 2013).

However, the incidence of bipolar disorders among creative artists suffering from mood disorders appears to be much lower than that of depressive disorders (Ludwig, 1995). In Chapter 6, the link between depression and creativity will be revisited. Whereas researchers have not yet solved the puzzle of the apparent relationship between creativity and mood disorders, they have learned a great deal about potential causes of mood disorders themselves, as discussed next.

Vincent van Gogh was hospitalized several times during his life for mental disorders and likely suffered from bipolar disorder, among various other illnesses (Blumer, 2002; Grey, 2011). This cartoon illustrates a self-portrait by Van Gogh that he painted right after cutting off his own ear. Shortly before dying from a self-inflicted gunshot wound (likely during a depressive episode), Van Gogh told his brother why he no longer desired to live: "The sorrow will last forever."

Section Review

Bipolar disorders:

- are mood disorders characterized by periods of depression and mania, often in a recurring, sometimes alternating, period over many years;
- occur about equally in males and females; and
- appear to lie between depressive disorders (Chapter 6) and schizophrenia/ psychotic disorders (Chapter 4) in terms of symptoms, family history, and genetics.

Manic episodes, the hallmark of bipolar disorders, involve:

- a persistently elevated or irritable mood, along with an increase in goal-directed activity;
- high energy and grandiose self-esteem;
- high distractibility with unrealistic goals and risky pursuits; and
- little sleep.

Bipolar disorders can be classified as:

- bipolar I disorder if they include periods of mania;
- bipolar II disorder if they include hypomanic episodes without full-blown mania and if several different subtypes or specifiers can be used to describe the pattern of

mood episodes (rapid cycling, seasonal pattern) and/or the characteristic features of each episode (mixed features, psychotic features); and

■ cyclothymic disorder if they involve numerous periods over 2 years with hypomanic symptoms and depressive symptoms that do not meet criteria for full-blown episodes.

Bipolar disorders (and depression even more so) may be overrepresented among creative people, such as artists and writers.

Biological Causes of Bipolar Disorders

Like most other mental disorders, bipolar disorders result from the complex interplay of biological (including genetic), psychological, environmental, and sociocultural factors.

Most researchers view bipolar disorders as stemming primarily from biological causes. This conclusion is suggested by data from studies of genetic influences on mood disorders, from research on biological processes and symptoms accompanying these disorders, and from the results of drug treatments for bipolar disorders.

Genetic Influences on Bipolar Disorders

In the 1980s, several scientific teams appeared to find clear-cut evidence linking bipolar disorders to a specific genetic culprit. The evidence came from examining the unusually high rates of bipolar disorders in certain families. One team, for example, concentrated on a small set of families in a Pennsylvania Amish community of about 12,000 (Egeland et al., 1987; Kolata, 1987). Because the Amish are a close-knit group who tend to marry only within their group and whose religious values strongly discourage the use of alcohol or other addictive substances (the abuse of which often accompanies mood disorders), they provide an ideal population in which to study genetic transmission of a disorder. The researchers discovered that most of the active cases of bipolar disorders in this particular community involved descendants of just a few couples (Egeland et al., 1987).

linkage analysis: A study of the linked occurrence of a disorder and some genetic marker across several generations.

Hoping to pinpoint a specific gene that would account for this finding, these researchers conducted a linkage analysis; this type of study traces the occurrence of a disorder and some *genetic marker* across several generations. This genetic marker is some characteristic (e.g., color blindness) for which the genetics are well understood. If the marker and the disorder show similar patterns of inheritance, then the genes influencing the disorder are likely to occur at a similar location on the same chromosome as the genes controlling the marker. In this case, the researchers claimed that bipolar disorders were linked to two genetic markers on the tip of the 11th chromosome. However, several other studies since then have consistently failed to find the same pattern or have reported different genetic linkages (Greenwood et al., 2013). As of yet, no specific genetic cause of bipolar disorders (or depression) has been demonstrated.

Other studies, however, do support the idea that, whatever their location, genes play a strong role in creating a predisposition to bipolar disorders. One way to explore the contribution of genetic factors to disorders is to contrast the appearance of a disorder in identical *(monozygotic)* twins who have exactly the same genes versus nonidentical *(dizygotic)* twins who share only about 50% of their genetic endowment. Such studies have generated very high heritability estimates for bipolar disorders—in the range of 70–80% (Edvardsen et al., 2008; McGuffin et al., 2003), perhaps higher than any other disorder in the *DSM-5* and in this textbook.

Recent studies have suggested different genetic pathways for bipolar I versus bipolar II disorders (Lee et al., 2012), with the latter being less heritable (Merikangas et al., 2014). Further, research has shown that there is no significant cross-aggregation between mood disorder subtypes, suggesting that the familial transmission of manic and major depressive episodes is independent, despite the high magnitude of comorbidity between these mood states (Merikangas et al., 2014). Finally, bipolar disorders may be genetically correlated with alcohol use disorder (with which they has 50% comorbidity), nicotine dependence, and anxiety disorders (Carmiol et al., 2014).

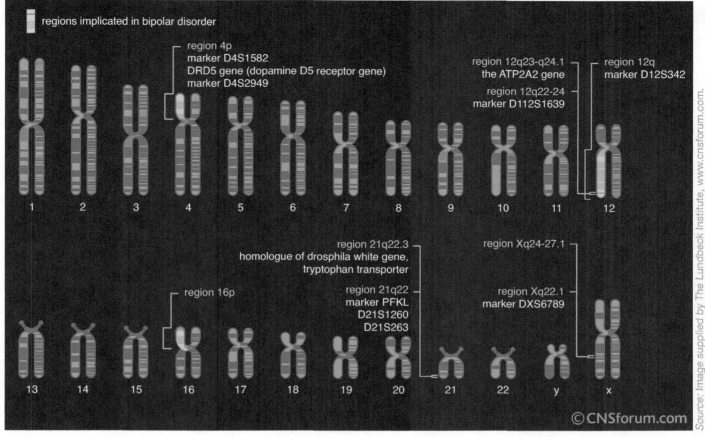

Although no single gene has been identified in the inheritance of bipolar disorders, genetic linkage studies have indicated distinct regions on several chromosomes that may be associated with a family history of the disorder. Among others, regions on chromosomes 4, 12, 16, 21, and X have been implicated, as shown in this image (Craddock & Jones, 2001). However, the precise genes associated with these regions and their functions in the brain have not been identified, and different studies identify entirely different chromosomes as being involved in bipolar disorders.

Neurobiological Influences on Bipolar Disorders

Mood disorders are accompanied by a number of abnormalities in the central nervous system. Whereas imbalances in neurotransmitters have long been postulated to play a central role in depression (see Chapter 6), they have also been associated with bipolar disorders. For instance, lithium, the most effective medication for bipolar I disorder, lowers norepinephrine activity in the brain (Bunney & Garland, 1983). A similar pattern for serotonin can be expected, which may be depleted in depression and therefore should be elevated during manic periods. However, as with unipolar depression, matters are not so simple. The principal metabolite of serotonin—5-HIAA—is sometimes lower in the spinal fluids of people with bipolar disorders than in controls, and lithium increases serotonin levels in many people, leading to the puzzling conclusion that both depression and mania are sometimes accompanied by low levels of serotonin. Recent neuroimaging findings have also indicated a trend toward increased dopamine receptors in both depression and mania, along with a complex pattern of increases in different types of serotonin receptors for depression than for mania (Nikolaus, Hautzel, Heinzel, & Müller, 2012).

So how can all of this confusion be resolved? One possibility is that low levels of serotonin introduce the risk of a mood disorder in general, but that the specific form of the disorder is shaped by either lowered (depression) or heightened (bipolar disorder) activity in other neurotransmitters, such as norepinephrine or dopamine. Another possibility is that mood disorders occur when the neurons themselves, rather than the chemicals they use to communicate, are not working properly. Lithium is chemically similar to sodium, and sodium ions are critical in controlling how neurons fire their messages back and forth across the nervous system. Some researchers suspect that disruptions in sodium ions may

Connections

What other mental disorders may be linked to increased levels of the neurotransmitter dopamine? See Chapter 4 for answers.

make neurons fire irregularly. If they fire too quickly or easily, manic symptoms would result; if they are too sluggish, depressive symptoms would occur. Some early findings supported this hypothesis (e.g., Hirshfield & Goodwin, 1988), but like other biological abnormalities, firm evidence that this factor specifically causes mood disorders is currently lacking.

What about the involvement of specific brain structures in bipolar disorders? Results of newer studies using magnetic resonance imaging (MRI; see Chapter 1) suggest that a reduction in the volume of the orbitofrontal cortex, which plays a role in the automatic regulation of emotions and is a part of the medial prefrontal network, is associated with the heritability of bipolar disorders (Eker et al., 2014). Functional MRI (fMRI) findings suggest that abnormal modulation between ventral prefrontal and limbic regions, especially the **amygdala**, is likely to contribute to poor emotional regulation and mood symptoms (Strakowski et al., 2012). Conversely, increased dorsolateral prefrontal cortex volume may be a neural marker of a resistance factor (i.e., lower likelihood of developing bipolar disorders), as it is part of a network of voluntary emotion regulation that may balance the effects of the disrupted automatic emotion regulation system (Eker et al., 2014).

amygdala: A structure in the forebrain that is part of the limbic system and is linked to emotions.

Evolutionary Influences on Bipolar Disorders

Evolutionary biologists have hypothesized that bipolar disorders could have come from an adaptation to extreme climactic conditions in the northern temperate zone. The evolutionary origin of bipolar disorder (EOBD) hypothesis (Sherman, 2001) states that, during the short summers of extreme climactic zones, hypomania would be adaptive, allowing the completion of many tasks necessary for survival within a short period of time. During long winters, the lethargy, hypersomnia, lack of interest in social activities, and overeating that is symptomatic of depression would be adaptive to group cohesion and survival (Sherman, 2001). Whereas the EOBD hypothesis remains largely unproven, some supporting evidence includes an association between bipolar disorders and a cold-adapted build, a correlation between seasonality and mood changes in those with bipolar disorders, and low rates of bipolar disorders in African Americans (Sherman, 2012).

Section Review

Among the biological factors believed to contribute to bipolar disorders are:

- genetic risks, which are particularly strong for bipolar disorders;
- disturbances in the level, functioning, or regulation of one or more neurotransmitters, such as norepinephrine, serotonin, and dopamine;
- irregularities in the way neurons fire their messages across the nervous system;
- structural brain deficits involving specific regions in the frontal lobes and functional deficits in frontal-limbic circuits involving the amygdala; and
- possible contributions from evolutionary pressures.

Psychological Causes of Bipolar Disorders

Most psychological theories about mood disorders focus on unipolar depression, mainly because—unlike bipolar depression—it has proved treatable via psychological methods.

Because biological causes appear to play a larger role in bipolar disorders than in unipolar depression, psychological and environmental factors have not been heavily emphasized as explanations of bipolar disorders. It must also be acknowledged, though, that bipolar disorders have received substantially less research funding and focus than other serious mental disorders (Clement, Singh, & Burns, 2003), leaving far too many questions unanswered. Further, psychological and biological theories do not necessarily compete with each other as explanations of bipolar disorders. In fact, most current psychological theories view biological factors as one of many risks that predispose some people to develop these disorders.

Psychoanalytic Theories of Bipolar Disorders

One early psychoanalytic theory suggested that bipolar disorders represented a flight from depressed feelings (Freeman, 1971)—an attempted answer to solve the problem of depression. According to this view, manic behavior serves as a kind of defense mechanism that helps a person escape or avoid pain or loss. A small number of studies have investigated this hypothesis in people with bipolar disorders and in normal participants with hypomanic traits (Bentall & Thompson, 1990; French, Richards, & Scholfield, 1996; Thomas & Bentall, 2002). Despite some intriguing findings, the mechanism underlying the idea that mania is in part triggered by efforts to defend against depression is poorly understood and is likely just a small piece of the puzzle (Thomas & Bentall, 2002).

MAPS - Attempted Answers

Cognitive-Behavioral Theories of Bipolar Disorders

More current models explain how key biological and psychological processes might operate in bipolar disorders. Two psychological characteristics that have been theorized to relate to the underlying biological vulnerability to bipolar disorders are: (1) reward sensitivity and (2) emotional reactivity (Johnson, Fulford, & Eisner, 2009). For both characteristics, there is some evidence that (1) these traits differentiate people with bipolar disorders from those without bipolar disorders and (2) these traits predict the course of the disorder.

For instance, one laboratory study examined the behavioral activation system, a motivational system relating to pursuit of incentives (i.e., reward sensitivity), which has been hypothesized to be involved in the genesis of manic symptoms (Johnson, Ruggero, & Carver, 2005). A reward for fast performance was offered partway through a button-pressing task, and participants received both success feedback and a monetary reward. Current manic symptoms significantly predicted higher success expectancy, as well as greater positive mood after reward, suggesting that the increase in goal-directed and risky behavior (such as John, in the chapter-opening case, buying a plane ticket and a tuxedo) during manic episodes may be triggered or facilitated by people's faulty cognitive and affective reactions to rewards (i.e., expecting too much and getting too excited about good things that happen).

Regarding the second psychological vulnerability factor—emotional reactivity—researchers have shown that people with bipolar disorders may be higher in this factor across the board: They have both higher positive *and* negative affect on trait and daily ratings than people without any mood disorders (Lovejoy & Steuerwald, 1995). Whereas negative affect was associated with depression, positive affect and anxiety were associated with both hypomanic and depressive symptoms (Lovejoy & Steuerwald, 1992).

It is worth noting that these are only two of the potential models of psychological vulnerability for bipolar disorders. For example, increasingly robust research documents that other neuropsychological deficits can be found among people with bipolar disorders, even during periods of euthymia (normal mood), as summarized within a recent meta-analysis (Martínez-Arán et al., 2000). Although cognitive dysfunctions in psychosis have classically been associated with schizophrenia (see Chapter 4), there is clinical evidence that some people with bipolar disorders show cognitive disturbances, such as changes in the fluency of thought and speech, learning and memory impairment, and disturbances in associational patterns and attentional processes, either during acute phases or in remission periods. Most of these cognitive deficits seem to remit during periods of euthymia, but some of them may persist in approximately one third of people with bipolar disorders (Martínez-Arán et al., 2000). Finally, in Lam's psychological model of bipolar disorders, the mechanism for the biological-psychological interaction is via cognitive traits such as an extreme drive for achievement and perfectionism (Jones, Sellwood, & McGovern, 2005; Lam & Wong, 1997). This sets the stage for a feed-forward mechanism whereby a biological predisposition to sad moods is amplified into depression, and a biological predisposition to excitement and anxiety is amplified into hypomania or mania.

Bipolar disorders may be influenced by several psychological factors, including:

- manic episodes being an attempted defense against periods of depression,
- reward sensitivity (e.g., being too focused on unrealistic/risky rewards),
- emotional reactivity (as with depressive disorders, except a heightened emotional reaction in terms of both negative and positive affect),
- other widespread cognitive deficits that may persist even between mood episodes, and
- an extreme drive for achievement and perfectionism.

Social Causes of Bipolar Disorders

Social factors have some effect on the *course* of bipolar disorders, although their roles appear less consistent and central than in unipolar depression (Monroe & Depue, 1991). Stressful events, especially those that disrupt social schedules or upset biological rhythms, exert some not yet fully understood influence on the course of bipolar disorders (Johnson & Roberts, 1995). For example, the birth of a child, frequent changes in work schedules, or hectic jet travel have all been suggested as particularly disruptive of the social and biological schedules that are usually affected in bipolar disorders. Stressful events seem to be more important in affecting initial, rather than later, episodes of bipolar disorders (Post, 1992), perhaps because, once the disorder has begun, each repeated episode itself weakens the person and makes later episodes more likely. Post (1992) has argued that repeated or chronic stressors ultimately lead to biological changes that cause neurotransmitter systems to become increasingly sensitive to stressors. As a result of this process, the brain becomes more easily affected by stressors until, eventually, even minor events can trigger the mood swings seen in bipolar disorders.

Overall, there is fairly consistent evidence from prospective studies that recent life events and interpersonal relationships contribute to the likelihood of onsets and recurrences of bipolar mood episodes, as they do for onsets and recurrences of unipolar depression (Geddes & Miklowitz, 2013). There have been repeated findings that 30–50% of adults diagnosed with bipolar disorders report traumatic/abusive experiences in childhood, which are associated, on average, with earlier onset, a higher rate of suicide attempts, and more co-occurring mental disorders such as post-traumatic stress disorder (PTSD) (Brietzke et al., 2012). The total number of reported stressful events in childhood is higher in those with an adult diagnosis of bipolar disorders (compared to those without)—in particular, events stemming from a harsh environment rather than from the child's own behavior (Miklowitz & Chang, 2008). A 2-year prospective study revealed that negative life events were significantly associated with both subsequent severity of manic and depressive symptoms and functional impairment, whereas positive life events only preceded functional impairment due to manic symptoms (Koenders et al., 2014). Finally, life events that result in disruptions in social routines, whether psychologically stressful in the traditional sense or not, have been shown to be significantly associated with the onset of manic episodes in individuals with bipolar disorders (Frank & Swartz, 2004).

Several lines of evidence suggest that **social support** may impact well-being and illness course in bipolar disorders (Eidelman, Gershon, Kaplan, McGlinchey, & Harvey, 2012). For instance, lower levels of perceived social support have been found to predict depressive relapse (Cohen, Hammen, Henry, & Daley, 2004; Johnson, Winett, Meyer, Greenhouse, & Miller, 1999), while higher levels of social support have been theorized to reduce the risk of relapse, possibly by improving medication adherence (Kleindienst, Engel, & Greil, 2005) or yielding more stable sleep (Eidelman et al., 2012). Conversely, **social strain** encompasses adverse social experiences (e.g., being criticized, ignored, overburdened) that cause people to have a negative reaction to or concerns about their relationships (Rook, 1990). A study indicated that people with bipolar I disorder reported

social support: The feeling that you are cared for by others or belong to a valued group.

social strain: Adverse social experiences (e.g., being criticized, ignored, overburdened) that could cause individuals to have a negative reaction to or concerns about their interpersonal relationships.

higher social strain than the control group, which was positively correlated with manic and depressive symptoms (Eidelman et al., 2012).

More specifically, research strongly suggests that the way in which family members relate to one another significantly influences the course of bipolar disorders (Butzlaff & Hooley, 1998). **Expressed emotion (EE)** is a measure of how hostile and critical the attitudes of caregivers/relatives are toward a family member with a mental disorder. There is a clearly documented link between high-EE families and relapse among people with bipolar disorders (e.g., Miklowitz, Goldstein, Nuechterlein, Snyder, & Mintz, 1988). Retrospective and prospective studies have found that risk for relapse and/or hospital admissions among people in high-EE families is from five to nine times greater than the risk among people in low-EE families (Miklowitz et al., 1988). These findings form the basis for one of the top psychosocial treatments for bipolar disorders, discussed later in the chapter.

expressed emotion (EE): A measure of the family environment describing criticism, hostility, and emotional overinvolvement with a person; a risk factor for relapse of mental disorders such as schizophrenia.

Section Review

Bipolar disorders are influenced by social factors, notably stressful life events such as:

- early trauma and abuse;
- conflicts in interpersonal relationships;
- recent negative life events;
- other chronic stressors, such as frequent schedule changes or travel; and
- lack of social support and high social strain, as well as high family expressed emotion.

Treatment of Bipolar Disorders

Bipolar disorders are one of the few categories of disorders, perhaps along with schizophrenia and other psychotic disorders discussed in Chapter 4, for which the optimal frontline treatment is medication, with psychotherapy helping in terms of relapse prevention and family support.

Drug Treatments for Bipolar Disorders

Because an acute manic episode can be so severe, hospitalization and drugs may be required to bring the symptoms under control. Since the 1970s, the primary drug treatment for acute manic episodes has been **lithium carbonate**, commonly known simply as "lithium." The clinical history of lithium began in the mid-19th century, when it was used to treat gout. In 1940, it was used as a substitute for sodium chloride in patients with high blood pressure, but it was later banned due to its major side effects. In 1949, Cade reported that lithium could be used as an effective treatment for bipolar disorders, and subsequent studies confirmed this effect.

lithium carbonate: A drug used to treat mania; commonly known as lithium.

Over the years, different authors have postulated many possible biochemical and biological effects of lithium in the brain. The main proposed mechanisms of lithium action include ion dysregulation, effects on neurotransmitter signaling, the interaction of lithium with the adenylyl cyclase system, inositol phosphate and protein kinase C signaling, and possible effects on arachidonic acid metabolism (Marmol, 2008). However, none of these mechanisms is definitive, and sometimes, results have been contradictory.

Whereas lithium's mechanism of action is not yet precisely known, the drug's effects usually begin 5 to 7 days after treatment commences. During this time, extremely agitated patients are sometimes also given antipsychotic or anticonvulsant drugs for sedation.

People receiving lithium must be monitored closely because lithium can be toxic, particularly to the kidneys and thyroid gland. Lithium blood levels must be watched closely to guard against organ damage. Lithium treatment often requires the person to take maintenance dosages of the drug for years, sometimes for life. However, either as a result of side effects—such as tremors or weight gain—or feelings of invulnerability that occur during manic episodes, many people with bipolar disorders do not comply with long-term lithium therapy regimens (Clayton, 1986).

anticonvulsants: A diverse group of pharmaceuticals used in the treatment of epileptic seizures. Anticonvulsant drugs are also increasingly being used in the treatment of bipolar disorders, since many seem to act as mood stabilizers, and for the treatment of neuropathic pain. Also commonly known as antiepileptic drugs or as antiseizure drugs.

MAPS - Medical Myths

atypical antipsychotics: Drugs that do not have the same biochemical or physiological effects as standard neuroleptics.

Source: Ramon Espelt Photography/ Shutterstock.com.

According to another recent meta-analysis, controlled trials of anti-manic drug treatments for the depressive (not manic) episodes in bipolar I and II disorder remain scarce, although findings with olanzapine, quetiapine, and perhaps carbamazepine and valproate were encouraging; lithium requires adequate testing in this regard (Selle, Schalkwijk, Vázquez, & Baldessarini, 2014). Notably, drugs were superior to placebo in fewer than half of the 24 medication trials in the treatment of depressive episodes. In other words, depressive episodes may be harder to treat than manic ones for people with bipolar disorders.

On the one hand, bipolar disorders are one of the very few categories of mental disorders in the *DSM-5* for which medication represents a viable, bona fide front-line treatment approach. Evidence for the efficacy of lithium in the treatment of acute mania is available and well documented, partly by statistically robust meta-analyses of the initial controlled studies, and partly from lithium versus placebo direct comparisons in modern drug trials (Grandjean & Aubry, 2009). Lithium is also an effective treatment for reducing the risk of suicide (discussed further later in the chapter) in people with mood disorders (Cipriani, Hawton, Stockton, & Geddes, 2013). Lithium may exert its anti-suicidal effects by reducing relapse of mood disorders, but additional mechanisms should also be considered because there is some evidence that lithium decreases aggression and possibly impulsivity, which might be another mechanism mediating the suicidal prevention effect (Cipriani et al., 2013). The majority of experts, and the most recent treatment guidelines, thus still consider lithium as a keystone therapy of bipolar disorders (Grandjean & Aubry, 2009).

On the other hand, though, the overall effectiveness of lithium is a bit unclear. Initial studies suggested that two thirds to three quarters of people receiving lithium improved and that those who took maintenance doses of the drug were much less likely to relapse than people not receiving lithium (Goodwin & Jamison, 1990; Suppes, Baldessarini, Faedda, & Tohen, 1991). Other studies, however, have not been quite as encouraging, suggesting that as many as half of the people taking lithium suffer relapses (Smith & Winokur, 1991). These contradictory findings, coupled with the lack of any definitive meta-analyses supporting lithium and its potentially severe side effect profile (i.e., organ damage), have encouraged researchers to explore alternative medications in the treatment of bipolar disorders.

The past three decades have seen increased use of the **anticonvulsant** (i.e., seizure prevention medication) carbamazepine to treat mania because it has fewer side effects and can be used for long periods with people who respond poorly to lithium (Post, 1990, 1993). Valproate, another anticonvulsant, also acts rapidly to reduce manic symptoms and is effective for some people—especially those with prominent depressive features— who have not been helped by lithium or carbamazepine (Pope, McElroy, Keck, Hudson, 1991). More recently, other medications classified as **atypical antipsychotics** have been used with increasing frequency in the treatment of bipolar disorders (in addition to schizophrenia, where their usage began). Examples of this class of pills include quetiapine (sold as Seroquel), risperidone (sold as Risperdal), and olanzapine (sold as Zyprexa). As explained in Chapter 4, both generations of antipsychotic medication tend to block receptors in the brain's dopamine pathways, although atypicals are less likely than the most widely used typical antipsychotic haloperidol to cause extrapyramidal motor control disabilities in the people taking them (Leucht et al., 2009).

So how have these newer drugs fared in the treatment of bipolar disorders, compared to the gold standard, lithium? A systematic review suggests that carbamazepine might be comparable to lithium in terms of efficacy and safety, and is therefore a valuable option in the treatment of both manic and maintenance phases of bipolar I disorder (Ceron-Litvoc, Soares, Geddes, Litvoc, & de Lima, 2009). Furthermore, the efficacy of both anticonvulsants (carbamazepine and valproate) was found to be equal to lithium in another meta-analysis, with the anticonvulsants showing some evidence of fewer adverse events and better treatment tolerance than lithium (Emilien, Maloteaux, Seghers, & Charles, 1996). Antipsychotic medications are also effective for short-term treatment of bipolar manic episodes and appear to be superior to lithium and anticonvulsants for this purpose (Geddes & Miklowitz, 2013). However, other medications such as lithium are preferred for long-term use (Geddes & Miklowitz, 2013). Olanzapine is effective in preventing relapses, although the evidence is not as solid as it is for lithium (Cipriani, Rendell, & Geddes, 2010).

A meta-analysis examined the effectiveness of continuing to take medication for maintenance when the person is not in an acute manic or depressive episode (Vieta at al., 2011). No single agent was associated with a significantly reduced risk for both manic/mixed and depressive relapse. Of the combination treatments, only quetiapine combined with lithium or valproate was associated with a significantly reduced risk for relapse at both the manic/mixed and depressed poles of bipolar I disorder. The evidence base for switching medications in bipolar disorders (i.e., when the original prescription is not working) is scant though, and little controlled data are available (Grande et al., 2014). However, switches from quetiapine to lithium and from risperidone to olanzapine have proven successful in various studies.

Given a lack of strong evidence for the utility of mood-stabilizing medication (lithium, anticonvulsants, or antipsychotics) in treating the *depressive* episodes associated with bipolar disorders, clinicians often prescribe **antidepressants** (discussed in Chapter 6) to people with bipolar disorders, along with one of the mood stabilizers. Antidepressants are a class of medications that have been shown to reduce symptoms of depression. However, the risk-benefit profile of antidepressant medications in bipolar disorders is controversial. The International Society for Bipolar Disorders recently convened a task force of experts to seek consensus recommendations on the use of antidepressants in bipolar disorders (Pacchiarotti et al., 2013). The task force concluded that there is striking incongruity between the wide use of and the weak evidence base for the efficacy and safety of antidepressant drugs in bipolar disorders. Few well-designed, long-term trials of prophylactic benefits have been conducted, and there is insufficient evidence for treatment benefits with antidepressants combined with mood stabilizers. The task force acknowledged that some individuals with bipolar disorders may benefit from antidepressants but that antidepressants should only be prescribed as an adjunct to mood-stabilizing medications.

Psychotherapy for Bipolar Disorders

Although comprehensive psychotherapy research in bipolar disorders has lagged behind research in other mental disorders, such as anxiety or unipolar depression, a shift in emphasis over the last decade has resulted in psychosocial interventions being viewed as critical to bridging the gap between the theoretical efficacy of drugs and their (often lower) real-world effectiveness. Several important manualized (i.e., treatment done according to specific guidelines), reproducible, adjunctive psychosocial interventions have been developed, including **cognitive-behavioral therapy (CBT), family-focused treatment (FFT), interpersonal and social rhythm psychotherapy (IPSRT),** and **psychoeducation** (Zaretsky, Rizvi, & Parikh, 2007). These focused psychotherapies for bipolar disorders were developed on the basis of previous experience in treating both unipolar depression and schizophrenia and were subsequently evaluated in larger controlled studies (Zaretsky et al., 2007). All of these psychosocial interventions have solid evidence demonstrating their effectiveness when used as an adjunct (companion treatment) to medication for bipolar disorders (Crowe et al., 2010).

In general, psychotherapy of bipolar disorders is aimed at alleviating core symptoms, recognizing episode triggers, reducing negative expressed emotion in relationships, recognizing early (prodromal) symptoms before full-blown recurrence, and practicing the factors that lead to maintenance or remission, such as healthy sleep and activities (Crowe et al., 2010). Psychological therapy specifically designed for bipolar disorders is effective in preventing or delaying relapses, and there is no clear evidence that the number of previous mood episodes moderate this effect (Lam, Burbeck, Wright, & Pilling, 2009). Specific mediating mechanisms include, but are not limited to, increasing medication adherence, teaching self-monitoring and early intervention with emergent episodes, and enhancing interpersonal functioning and family communication (Miklowitz & Scott, 2009). CBT, FFT, and psychoeducation have the most evidence for efficacy in regard to relapse prevention (Zaretsky et al., 2007), whereas CBT, FFT, and IPSRT appear efficacious in treating depressive symptoms and preventing new episodes (Sylvia, Tilley, Lund,

antidepressants: A broad class of medications commonly used in the treatment of depressive and sometimes bipolar disorders; these drugs include monoamine oxidase inhibitors, tricyclics, and selective serotonin reuptake inhibitors (SSRIs), such as Prozac.

MAPS - Medical Myths

cognitive-behavioral therapy (CBT): A psychotherapy that uses learning principles and rational thinking strategies to alter maladaptive thoughts and beliefs that accompany behavior problems.

family-focused treatment (FFT): A psychotherapy that provides families of people (often adolescents) with bipolar disorders with education and skills training relevant to the unique characteristics and developmental problems of teenagers. These problems include rapid onsets and offsets of irritable and/or depressed moods, disturbances in sleep/wake cycles, and high levels of family conflict (expressed emotion).

interpersonal and social rhythm psychotherapy (IPSRT): A psychotherapy designed to help people with bipolar disorders improve their moods by understanding and working with their biological and social rhythms. The treatment emphasizes techniques to improve medication adherence, manage stressful life events, and reduce disruptions in social rhythms that may be involved in mood episodes.

Medication for Children with Bipolar Disorders: Helpful or Dangerous (or Both)?

The onset of bipolar disorders most commonly occurs in adolescence; about 60% of adults with bipolar disorders exhibit their first mood symptoms before 19 years of age (Nandagopal & DelBello, 2010). Children and adolescents with bipolar disorders have high rates of psychosocial morbidity and mortality, and they frequently undergo several unsuccessful medication trials before achieving adequate mood stabilization.

A number of clinical trials have tested the efficacy of medications for children diagnosed with bipolar disorders. Placebo-controlled studies of 3–6 weeks duration have documented the efficacy of several atypical antipsychotics, including risperidone, aripiprazole, quetiapine, and olanzapine, in the acute management of manic and mixed symptoms in children aged 10–17 years (Fraguas et al., 2011). In the United States, these four drugs have been approved by the Food and Drug Administration (FDA) for pediatric use in bipolar mania or mixed states (Vitiello, 2013).

The evidence base for the efficacy of non-antipsychotic mood stabilizers in children is much weaker, however (Vitiello, 2013). Lithium and the anticonvulsants (valproate, carbamazepine, and oxcarbazepine) are used in clinical practice to stabilize severe mood instability, but thus far, no published placebo-controlled trial has demonstrated that this works (Wagner et al., 2009). Nonetheless, lithium has an FDA-approved indication for bipolar disorders in children aged 12 years and older.

Recently, a large, publicly funded clinical trial compared the effectiveness of two non-antipsychotic mood stabilizers and one atypical antipsychotic in pediatric mania (Geller et al., 2012). The treatment of early age mania (TEAM) study randomized 279 children (aged 10–15 years), who were diagnosed with bipolar I disorder in a manic or mixed phase and had not been previously treated with antimanic medications, to receive risperidone, lithium, or valproate for 8 weeks. At the end of week 8, the 68.5% of patients randomized to risperidone were deemed to be much improved on the Clinical Global Impression for Bipolar Illness Improvement-Mania scale, as compared with 35.6% of those on lithium and 24.4% of those on valproate.

However, despite these promising findings for the use of antipsychotics in treating children with bipolar disorders, more information is needed regarding their long-term safety and efficacy in this population (Nandagopal & DelBello, 2010). It is possible that younger children with bipolar disorders may require different treatment approaches than adolescents due to developmental differences, but comparative data on this issue are lacking. Further studies examining the neurobiological effects of psychotropic medications and predictors of response in youth are therefore necessary (Nandagopal & DelBello, 2010).

Until such research is done, should children with bipolar disorders be put on medications with potentially serious side effects for a prolonged period of time? Between 2002 and 2009, pediatric prescriptions for atypical antipsychotics increased by 65%, from 2.9 million to about 4.8 million (Jacobson, 2014). Given the lack of consistent efficacy data, clinical decision making should be based on individual clinical aspects and safety concerns (Díaz-Caneja et al., 2014), rather than using these drugs as the default front-line treatments. Antipsychotics may also be associated with severe side effects, such as diabetes, high cholesterol, and cardiovascular disease, along with a small risk (4%) of tardive dyskinesia—a neurological disorder resulting in compulsive movement (Jacobson, 2014).

Moreover, although most treatment research has examined pharmacotherapy for pediatric bipolar disorders, a growing literature suggests that psychosocial interventions are also important to provide families with an understanding of symptoms, course, and treatment; to teach youth and parents methods for coping with symptoms (e.g., problem solving, communication, emotion regulation, cognitive-behavioral skills); and to prevent relapse (Fristad & MacPherson, 2014). The Task Force on the Promotion and Dissemination of Psychological Procedures guidelines concluded that family psychoeducation plus skill building is probably efficacious and that cognitive-behavioral therapy (CBT) is possibly efficacious in the treatment of pediatric bipolar disorders, although dialectical behavior therapy and interpersonal and social rhythm therapy were deemed experimental in children at this point (Fristad & MacPherson, 2014).

Thinking Critically

1. If you had a child with bipolar disorder, would you want your child treated with medication or psychotherapy or both?

2. What types of research studies are needed in the future to help us make these vital long-range decisions?

& Sachs, 2008). Psychoeducation appears helpful against the recurrence of hypomania or mania, but not depression (Sylvia et al., 2008). Most studies have been based only on bipolar I disorder, however, and psychotherapeutic treatment during the acute phase of a manic episode can be a particular challenge (Zaretsky et al., 2007). In fact, none of the psychosocial interventions claims benefit for the acute treatment of hypomania or mania (Sylvia et al., 2008).

The different psychosocial interventions for bipolar disorders share many common elements, but also some key differences (Miklowitz, Goodwin, Bauer, & Geddes, 2008). With regard to CBT and psychoeducation, both teach people about the disorder, how to recognize prodromes (early symptoms of an acute episode), and what coping mechanisms to use to manage symptoms (Miklowitz et al., 2008). However, CBT adds cognitive and behavioral techniques, such as cognitive restructuring, behavioral activation, and activity scheduling, in a personalized, individual treatment, to be discussed in more detail in Chapter 6. Psychoeducation, in contrast, is typically provided in a standardized group format with a specific focus on education rather than behavior changes (Parikh et al., 2013). Given the similar change in coping styles and mood burden, teaching people with bipolar disorders about how to cope in adaptive ways with the symptoms of mania may be a shared mechanism of change for CBT and psychoeducation (Parikh et al., 2013). A meta-analysis found a low to medium overall effect size of CBT as adjunctive treatment to medication for people diagnosed with bipolar disorders at posttreatment and follow-up, as well as a positive impact of CBT on clinical symptoms, treatment adherence, and quality of life (Szentagotai & David, 2010). However, researchers believe that new CBT strategies are needed to increase and enrich the impact of CBT at posttreatment and to maintain its benefits during follow-up (Szentagotai & David, 2010).

Family-focused treatment (FFT; Miklowitz & Goldstein, 1997) for bipolar disorders typically focuses on adolescents and their families, and has evolved to be delivered in four phases (Miklowitz, 2012). The first phase is an *engagement phase*, in which the objective is to connect with the client and parents (and, where possible, siblings) and relay information about the treatment's structure and expectations. The second phase involves *psychoeducation*, in which therapists lead the family in discussions of the nature, causes, and management of their bipolar disorder and its symptoms. Third, there is *communication enhancement training*, in which clients and family members rehearse more effective speaking and listening skills (e.g., how to give praise and constructive criticism and how to listen more actively). And fourth, the treatment concludes with *problem-solving skills training*, in which clients and family members define, generate, evaluate, and implement solutions to problems in the family's or the client's life. Treatment is usually 21 sessions over the course of 9 months (Miklowitz et al., 2014). When practiced in the community, clinicians and families sometimes opt for shorter versions or longer intervals between sessions (Miklowitz, 2012). A controlled trial of FFT for adolescents showed more-rapid recovery from mood symptoms and lower depression severity scores over 2 years among people who received 21 sessions of FFT, compared with those who received three sessions of family psychoeducation instead (Miklowitz et al., 2008). However, a newer study led by the same researcher found comparable efficacy for both treatment groups (21 sessions of FFT and three sessions of family psychoeducation; Miklowitz et al., 2014), which brings up important questions about the effective components for treating bipolar disorders to be explored in future research (Swartz, 2014).

Interpersonal and social rhythm psychotherapy (IPSRT) was developed by Frank and colleagues (2000, 2004) by integrating standard interpersonal psychotherapy (IPT; see Chapter 6) for major depression with social rhythm therapy—a treatment approach that attempts to stabilize social and circadian rhythms based on the social zeitgeber hypothesis, which posits that unstable or disrupted daily routines lead to circadian instability and mood episodes in vulnerable individuals (Ehlers, Frank, & Kupfer, 1988). According to

psychoeducation: A key component of many psychotherapy treatments for a variety of mental disorders, this involves giving clients information regarding what is known about a specific disorder and how to identify and manage the symptoms.

"My therapist plays with my mind."

Psychotherapy can be challenging with a person who is acutely psychotic, which can happen sometimes with clients who have bipolar I disorder.

the model, major (and minor) life events may act as specific precipitants by inducing the rhythm disruptions that form a direct link to the biomedical features of mood episodes (Frank & Swartz, 2004). Psychosocial stress leads to disrupted sleep and social routines, resulting in the onset and exacerbation of mood episodes in individuals with a diathesis for mood disorder (Wehr & Sack, 1987). IPSRT helps people with bipolar disorders regularize their daily rhythms and facilitates good sleep hygiene to promote mood stability. Additionally, IPSRT builds on the model of interpersonal psychotherapy for depression (Klerman, Weissman, Rounsaville, & Chevron, 1984) that targets the connection between mood symptoms and interpersonal difficulties in one of four interpersonal problem areas (grief, role disputes, role transitions, and interpersonal deficits). Data indicate that IPSRT prevents or delays bipolar disorder episode recurrence and improves acute mood symptoms in adults by helping people stabilize daily social routines and sleep/wake cycles (Frank et al., 2005; Miklowitz et al., 2007) and also has potential to bolster outcomes in adolescents who are at-risk for bipolar disorders (Goldstein et al., 2014). Although IPRST is a model-driven psychotherapy for bipolar disorders, the actual therapy itself contains many different elements in addition to IPT, including CBT, psychoeducation, and self-monitoring of social rhythms (Zaretsky et al., 2007).

Some clinicians also emphasize the need to talk with individuals experiencing mania, to develop a therapeutic alliance in support of recovery (Havens & Ghaemi, 2005). Overall, psychotherapy of any type focusing on a strong therapeutic alliance (i.e., a good relationship between counselor and client) leads to a 17.5-fold decrease in the suicidal rate of people with bipolar disorders (Fountoulakis & Siamouli, 2009), the most potentially dangerous consequence of these disorders that is discussed further in the next section of this chapter.

Section Review

Bipolar disorders are treated with:

- lithium, along with monitoring of blood levels of the drug;
- anticonvulsants (carbamazepine or valproate) or antipsychotics (risperidone, aripiprazole, quetiapine, or olanzapine), in cases in which lithium has not been successful or as a combined treatment; antipsychotics are often used as the front-line treatment of pediatric bipolar disorders in the short term, although the long-term effects of these (and any medications for bipolar disorders) are not yet known;
- antidepressant medications for the depressive episodes in bipolar disorders, though there is a striking incongruity between the widespread use of these drugs and their weak evidence base; and
- psychotherapy, such as cognitive-behavioral therapy (CBT), family-focused treatment (FFT), interpersonal and social rhythm therapy (IPSRT), and psychoeducation, usually as an adjunct to medication; all of these treatments have shown benefit in reducing the harmful effects of bipolar disorders, as well as the associated suicide risk.

Suicide

We discuss suicide at the end of this chapter on bipolar disorders and right before the next chapter on depression because these are the two most common causes of suicide. Mood disorders increase the risk of suicide 20-fold (Chehil & Kutcher, 2012). The lifetime risk of suicide associated with a diagnosis of major depression in the United States is estimated at 3.4%, which averages two highly disparate figures of almost 7% for men and 1% for women (Blair-West & Mellsop, 2001), although suicide *attempts* are more frequent in women (Oquendo, Bongiovi-Garcia, & Galfalvy, 2007). For those with bipolar disorders, lifetime suicide risk may be up to 5% among women and 8% among men (Nordentoft, Mortensen, & Pedersen, 2011). Although previous attempts and poor social support magnify risk, the time spent depressed is likely the major factor that determines a person's overall long-term risk of committing suicide (Holma et al., 2010). Of the primary care patients with depressive disorders, 10% attempted suicide in 5 years (Riihimäki, Vuorile-hto, Melartin, Haukka, & Isometsä, 2014); this number rose to almost 15% for psychiatric patients (Holma et al., 2010). However, risk of suicidal acts for primary care patients was almost exclusively confined to those in the throes of a major depressive episode, with or without concurrent active substance abuse (Riihimäki et al., 2014).

Suicide thus remains one of the most serious problems associated with mood disorders, although it is also linked to a host of other mental disorders, health difficulties, and social problems. Mental disorders are often present at the time of suicide, with estimates ranging as high as 90% or more of the cases (Bertolote, Fleischmann, De Leo, & Wasserman, 2004; Chang, Gitlin, & Patel, 2011). Among all diagnoses, mood disorders accounted for one third to one half of suicides worldwide (Arsenault-Lapierre, Kim, & Turecki, 2004), fol-lowed by substance use disorders (17.6%), schizophrenia (14.1%), and personality disor-ders (13.0%; Bertolote et al., 2004). In the remainder of this chapter, we review the current knowledge about suicide, with special attention to warning signs, causes, and ultimately, prevention.

Who Is Suicidal?

The traditional definition of suicide is the willful taking of one's own life. By this definition, approximately 40,000 suicides occur in the United States each year (about half via firearm), making it one of the nation's "top ten" causes of death (Centers for Disease Control and Prevention, 2011). However, any statistics on suicide may be underestimates for several reasons. First, many deaths that are thought to be accidental (e.g., single car crashes) might actually have been suicides. In addition, high-risk behavior, such as driving at excessive speed or using dangerous drugs, may be a form of suicide, even though the person's inten-tion to end his or her life is not obvious. Finally, social and religious prohibitions still make some relatives, police, and physicians reluctant to identify a death as a suicide.

A Profile of Suicide Attempts

Far more people make suicide attempts than actually kill themselves (American Associ-ation of Suicidology, 2014a). There are an estimated 8 to 25 attempted suicides for every one completion, meaning that there may be over 700,000 suicide attempts every year in the United States. Although a suicide attempt is the best predictor of a subsequent suicide, the profile of suicide attempters is different from that of people who actually kill them-selves. Unlike completed suicides, which are three to four times more common in males, *attempted* suicides are more frequent among females than males by a ratio of about 3 to 1. About 70–90% of attempted suicides involve drug overdoses or self-poisoning (Bongar, 1991); wrist cutting is the next most common method of attempted suicide. In completed suicides, the act usually involves a gunshot, hanging, or carbon monoxide inhalation.

Some people respond to an onslaught of stressors with thoughts of death and self-harming behaviors. Their reactions may include mild drug overdosing, mixing alcohol and other drugs, or minor cutting of the wrists. These actions, called **parasuicidal behaviors**, are especially common among those who have experienced early abuse or trauma or who have borderline personality disorder (see Chapter 16). Although not as risky as more overt suicide attempts, parasuicidal behaviors may eventually lead to more lethal attempts.

parasuicidal behavior: A behavior suggestive of suicide attempts, such as mild drug overdosing, mixing alcohol and other drugs, or minor cutting of the wrists.

Completed Suicide: Who Is at Risk?

As discussed earlier, completed suicide is strongly associated with mental disorder. Stud-ies of the characteristics of individuals at the time of their suicides—known as *psycholog-ical autopsies*—indicate that the vast majority of people who kill themselves displayed ei-ther a mood or alcohol use disorder or both (Cavanagh, Carson, Sharpe, & Lawrie, 2003).

There are substantial differences in completed suicide rates around the world (World Health Organization, 2014). In some northern European countries (such as Latvia, Russia, Ukraine, and Lithuania) and Japan, for example, the suicide rate is estimated to be ap-proximately 20 per 100,000 individuals. In countries with stronger religious prohibitions

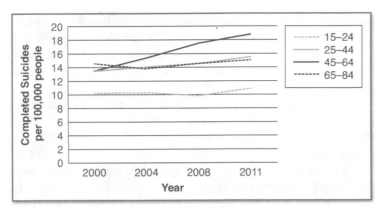

FIGURE 5.1 Suicide Rates by Age

The highest suicide rate is now typically among people ages 45–64, and that rate has continued to rise over the last decade.

Source: Based on data from the American Association of Suicidology (2014b) and the American Foundation for Suicide Prevention (n.d.).

against suicide, such as Greece, Italy, Mexico, and Costa Rica, the rate is more like 5 or 6 per 100,000. In the United States, the estimated suicide rate is somewhere between those two extremes at about 12 per 100,000 people.

Suicide rates among ethnic groups within the United States also vary considerably. For instance, Caucasians (about 14 per 100,000) have higher rates of completed suicides than Asian, Hispanic, or African Americans (each about 5 per 100,000). Native American suicide rates (about 11 per 100,000) are intermediate overall, except among the 15- to 24-year-old group, where rates are considerably elevated (over 20 per 100,000), especially among young males (over 30 per 100,000). In terms of regional variation, five U.S. states, all in the West, had suicide rates in excess of 20 per 100,000 in 2010: Wyoming (23.2), Alaska (23.1), Montana (22.9), Nevada (20.3), and New Mexico (20.1).

The demographics of suicide may be changing. Over the past decade, overall rates of suicide in the United States rose by 15% (Rocket et al., 2012). However, as shown in Figure 5.1, rates of suicide among adults ages 45–64 rose even more sharply (American Association of Suicidology, 2014b). Based on the risk factors discussed here, how high a risk is John, the subject of the chapter-opening case, for committing suicide?

In summary, key risk factors for suicide (Hawton, Comabella, Haw, & Saunders, 2013; Centers for Disease Control & Prevention, 2014) include:

- being a psychiatric patient, particularly with a diagnosis of severe depression, bipolar disorder, alcohol use disorder, or schizophrenia;
- being male, older than 45, and living alone;
- being of Caucasian or Native American background;
- having a history of prior suicide attempts;
- having a family history of a mental disorder;
- experiencing hopelessness;
- misusing alcohol or other drugs;
- having easy access to lethal means (e.g., firearms, pills, etc.); and
- experiencing stressful life events, particularly events involving loss of loved ones and social support.

Adolescent Suicide

Suicide rates among adolescents in the United States between 1960 and 1990 increased dramatically (Garland & Zigler, 1993). In fact, the suicide rate for those youths ages 15–24 has more than doubled since 1950, and suicide is now the second or third leading cause of death in this age group. Recent studies indicate that the incidence of suicide attempts among adolescents may exceed 10% annually (Pompili, Innamorati, Girardi, Tatarelli, & Lester, 2011). Suicide results in almost 5,000 young lives lost each year in the United States, with the top three methods used in suicides of young people including firearm (45%), suffocation (40%), and poisoning (8%; Centers for Disease Control and Prevention, 2014). However, as Figure 5.1 illustrates, prevention programs like the one discussed in the "Prevention" feature in this chapter may be working, as the suicide rate for adolescents has stabilized over the last decade after declining somewhat since its peak in 1994.

The factors associated with adolescent suicide differ in important ways from those seen in adult suicides. Whereas social isolation and hopelessness characterize the older person at risk for suicide, young suicide victims often appear to have responded impulsively to an acute stressor (Shaffer, Garland, Gould, Fisher, & Trautman, 1988). Thus, it is not surprising that adolescents who commit suicide are less likely than adults to leave notes explaining their motives or to give away their belongings as signs of potential suicide risks. The most common scenario involves a youngster who has gotten into trouble or was humiliated in public (Shaffer, 1990). Maybe a young boy was dropped by a girlfriend at a party or lost a fight in front of peers. Bullying, including cyberbullying, can contribute as well (Bauman, Toomey, & Walker, 2013; Dupper, 2013), such as in the case of Tyler Clementi, an 18-year-old student at Rutgers University in New Jersey, who jumped to his death from the George Washington Bridge on September 22, 2010 after his roommate filmed him in a romantic encounter with another man. Research has shown that most adolescent suicides occur after school hours and in the teen's home. Within a typical high school classroom, it is likely that three students (one boy and two girls) have made a suicide attempt in the past year. The typical profile of an adolescent nonfatal suicide attempter is a female who ingests pills, whereas the prototypical suicide completer is a male who dies from a gunshot wound (American Association of Suicidology, 2014b).

Suicide among young people has other unique characteristics, including the so-called contagion effect. Contagion occurs by hearing about another person's suicide. Even the death of another teen reported on the news or talked about at school has been associated with increased suicidal behavior among adolescents (Gould, Jamieson, & Romer, 2003). Clusters of teen suicides have been described, in which the suicide of one adolescent seemed to set off the same behavior in others. Research on the impact of the media's portrayal of suicide also points to a possible contagion effect. Programs aired on TV depicting youth suicide have been associated with an increase in suicides within the viewing area (Gould, 1990). Contrary to popular belief and a few high-profile cases (e.g., Harris and Klebold in the Columbine rampage in 1999), however, suicide pacts are exceedingly rare (fewer than 1% of suicides) and typically occur in elderly (married couples over 50) rather than young populations (Prat, Rérolle, & Saint-Martin, 2013).

Similar to adults, about 80% of adolescents who kill themselves had long-standing mental health problems (Shaffer, 1990). Although depression is associated with suicide in some young people, the majority of boys who kill themselves had externalizing behavioral disorders (see Chapter 3), often accompanied by substance use disorders. Some studies suggest that as many as 50% of all youths who commit suicide had an immediate relative with a history of suicide or suicide attempts.

Causes of Suicide

As is true of the mood disorders often associated with it, suicide can stem from multiple causes. Characteristics of people's social environments and their prevailing belief systems appear to play a central role in suicide, but genetic and biochemical factors cannot be ignored.

Biological Factors in Suicide

Although there are too few twin studies of suicide to provide conclusive findings, the data available indicate greater concordance for suicide among monozygotic than dizygotic twin pairs (Tidemalm et al., 2011). Adoption studies also suggest a higher incidence of suicide among biological relatives in contrast to adopted relatives (Petersen, Sørensen, Andersen, Mortensen, & Hawton, 2014). The results of twin and adoption studies are difficult to interpret, however, because of the overlap of suicide with mental disorders such as depression, bipolar disorders, and schizophrenia. Thus, it is impossible to determine whether the genetic loading is related to the suicidal behavior itself or to the mental

Curbing Adolescent Suicide

Although the overall suicide rate for those ages 15–24 has been relatively steady for the past decade after more than doubling since the 1950s, other disturbing trends have continued. For instance, there is an increase in the rate of suicide among male youth from when they are 11 years old to when they turn 21 (Conner & Goldston, 2007). Further, suicide rates are rising for African American teens (perhaps more in boys), Latino teens (especially Latina girls), Asian American youth, Native American youth, Alaskan Native youth, and Hawaiian American youth (Balis & Postolache, 2008). What explains these troubling trends?

Many clinicians point to increases in substance abuse and major stressors as possible factors. But experts in the area of adolescent suicide suggest that a more significant factor might be that society has inadvertently lowered its taboos about suicide (Shaffer, 1988). Ironically, some of this effect may stem from school-based curricula that attempt to prevent suicide by educating young people on how to detect risk factors for suicide. Some of these programs try to reduce the stigma of suicide by depicting the problem (inaccurately) as a normal response to stress, rather than as a serious difficulty that is usually tied to mental disorders. This normalizing strategy may have backfired because vulnerable youth may be more likely to see suicide as an acceptable solution to life's difficulties. Media often make these messages even worse. For instance, in the wake of the suicide of Robin Williams in 2014, the Academy of Motion Picture Arts and Sciences tweeted, in memory of him and one of his legendary roles in *Aladdin*, "Genie, you're free."

Another critical factor in adolescent suicides may be the growing availability of firearms. Most teen suicide is the result of an impulsive gesture. Access to a deadly weapon allows this impulsive behavior to have deadly consequences, even if the youth may not have been totally resolved to die.

Finally, more and more teens are connecting online instead of in person, which could reduce their social support and also make them more susceptible to bullying in a variety of ways. A recent survey showed that the prevalence of bullying in U.S. high schools was 55%, with 18% of respondents reporting cyberbullying (Gan et al., 2014).

These findings have clear implications for prevention programs. First, family and societal taboos against suicide must be reiterated. Suicide is not an acceptable alternative for a young person faced with stressors, even when the stressors are of overwhelming proportions, and adolescents should not be given any

Because guns are used in the majority of teen suicides, many experts believe that stricter control over the availability of guns would reduce suicide rates.

message, even inadvertently, that suicide is acceptable or "normal."

Second, successful prevention programs should target those specific behaviors or psychological variables that research has shown to be the most significant risk factors for teen suicide. Included among these factors are adolescent mood disorders and alcohol use disorders, all of which have been found to predict adolescents' suicidal behavior (Reifman & Windle, 1995).

Third, access to weapons should be restricted. At the social policy level, stricter gun-control laws may be an effective form of prevention. For example, one study found that the stricter the gun-control laws in a state, the lower the rate of suicides and the smaller the increase in suicides over a 10-year period (Lester & Murrell, 1980). More recently, another study showed that firearm availability at the state level was associated with significantly higher odds of individual suicide in that state compared to other states (Kposowa, 2013). So when mental health professionals determine that a young person is at risk of self-harm, they should work with parents to provide adequate supervision and to remove firearms or other potential means of suicide from the home.

Finally, comprehensive bullying prevention efforts should be extended from middle school students to include high school students, as victimization in person or online increases the risk of suicide in teens (Bauman et al., 2013; Kowalski, Giumetti, Schroeder, & Lattanner, 2014). Because many of the current antibullying programs in use across the United States are not effective (Jeong & Lee, 2013), the future use of these programs should be based on the evidence of which ones are working and why (Strohmeier & Noam, 2012).

Source: Stokkete/Shutterstock.com.

disorder that often accompanies it. And because the risk of suicide is especially common in people with depression who are also impulsive and aggressive, any genetic component of suicide may not even be related to mental disorder per se but to the tendency to engage in violent or impulsive behavior (Kety, 1990).

Similar questions surround the interpretation of biochemical abnormalities found in individuals who attempted or completed suicide. In a meta-analysis, people who had attempted suicide, especially using violent methods, had lower levels of 5-HIAA (the main metabolite of the neurotransmitter serotonin) in their cerebrospinal fluid (CSF) as compared with psychiatric controls; those making subsequent suicidal actions also had lower levels of CSF 5-HIAA (Lester, 1995). However, the serotonin-deficiency hypothesis of human aggression itself lacks empirical corroboration (Duke, Bègue, Bell, & Eisenlohr-Moul, 2013).

Even if abnormalities in neurotransmitter systems are tied to suicide, how they operate to make suicide more likely is unknown. Other biological markers, in addition to serotonin products, that have been implicated in suicide are inflammatory cells (cytokines), which are discussed more in Chapter 6 regarding the causes of depression (Lindqvist et al., 2011). A potential mechanism could be that pro-inflammatory cytokines induce an increased turnover of monoamine neurotransmitters like serotonin, which in the long term results in lower levels of their metabolites (Lindqvist et al., 2011). Unfortunately, no biological test capable of assessing suicide risk exists at this time.

Psychological Factors in Suicide

Psychological ingredients in suicide—such as impulsive personality and mental disorders—are key risk factors, as already mentioned. Psychological theorists generally confine their models to the cause of the mental disorders themselves, although one extra layer has been added to explain suicide. Individuals vary greatly in their psychological vulnerability to stressors, leading some theorists to suggest that extreme vulnerability to stress could predispose a person to suicide. They trace this vulnerability to the quality of a child's early experiences with parents. Various models of abnormality offer different views of how suicide might be linked to these early experiences:

- Traditional psychoanalysts view suicidal thoughts as reflecting intense, unresolved, internalized anger at the primary parent figure. Such thoughts are activated when a person feels unable to maintain a sense of self-worth and self-caring.

- Object-relations and interpersonal theories stress the role of disturbed family relationships in suicide. These theories see family dysfunction early in life as hampering the child's ability to cope with negative affect, develop a positive sense of self, and master the skills necessary to develop and sustain relationships throughout life. Such problems, in turn, may generate interpersonal conflicts, social isolation, and eventually, too little of the support that makes it easier to deal with life's stressors.

- From the cognitive perspective, early negative experiences can increase a person's tendency to feel hopelessness in the face of significant stress. Hopelessness, or a sense of overwhelming pessimism about the future, is one of the best predictors of suicide attempts.

Although cause-effect links have not been established, numerous studies do indicate that early loss of a parent, as well as chaotic, neglectful family life, are associated with suicide in later life (Brent & Silverstein, 2013).

Social Factors in Suicide

Along with psychological risk factors, social and cultural influences appear to be much more strongly related to the prevalence of suicide than are biological factors. In fact, over the years, many cultures have viewed suicide as a respectable response to social disgrace or public failure. In World War II, for example, Japanese *kamikaze* pilots willingly took on the honorable and patriotic duty of crashing their planes directly into American ships,

altruistic suicide: A suicide type proposed by Emile Durkheim, committed by people who choose suicide because they place a social goal or group ahead of personal survival.

anomic suicide: A suicide type proposed by Emile Durkheim, committed by people who feel lost or abandoned by society, often because of social upheaval such as divorce or job loss.

fatalistic suicide: A suicide type proposed by Durkheim, committed by people such as prisoners or slaves who experience severe isolation or rejection and who hold little hope for social integration.

Source: Alan Light.

Beloved actor and comedian Robin Williams was found dead at his home in northern California in August 2014 from an apparent suicide by hanging. Williams, who had a history of bipolar disorder as well as substance use disorders, had reportedly been in a severely depressed state before the suicide attempt, possibly due to recent career failures and/or recent medical news. Other celebrities to die by suicide include author Ernest Hemingway (1961), singer Kurt Cobain (1994), and All-Pro football player Junior Seau (2012). Celebrities who reportedly attempted suicide in their younger years include *The Price is Right* host Drew Carey, singer Eminem, and actress Halle Berry.

even though it meant certain death for the pilot. Even today, individuals set themselves on fire or starve themselves for social or political causes they consider more important than their own lives, such as the 9/11 terrorists who committed suicide flying airplanes into the World Trade Center. The willingness to embrace death for the sake of religious beliefs has been documented throughout history.

Emile Durkheim (1966) was an early proponent of the sociocultural view of suicide. In late 19th-century France, Durkheim proposed distinct types of suicide, ranging from **altruistic** (*kamikaze* pilot) and **anomic** (disenfranchised person) to **fatalistic** (doomed prisoner), each related to people's integration into the social, religious, and political fabric of their cultures. Whereas there is still no definitive taxonomy of suicide, despite researchers' calls for its development (Edlavitch & Byrns, 2014), Durkheim's seminal work illustrated how important the social milieu was to suicide rates (Hassan, 1998).

Studies conducted since Durkheim's time have consistently found that rates of attempted and completed suicide are indeed related to social changes and social mores. Among Native Americans, tribes that are loosely structured and that stress greater individuality tend to see higher rates of youth suicide than do more traditional tribes that emphasize the importance of community over individuals (Earls, Escobar, & Manson, 1990). The rising tide of suicide among young, urban African Americans that has occurred in recent decades (Compton, Thompson, & Kaslow, 2005) appears closely linked to the growing violence and poverty in many cities, along with a decline in social connectedness and support, which is a protective factor (Kuramoto, Wilcox, & Latkin, 2013). The relatively low rate of suicide among Hispanics appears to be due in part to strong family systems and the predominance of Catholicism, which fervently prohibits suicide (Earls et al., 1990).

Social stressors are also highly related to suicide. Suicidal behavior tends to be positively correlated with unemployment, marital instability, legal problems, and limited social support. High unemployment during the Great Depression in the 1930s in the United States was associated with an increased suicide rate. In addition, during more recent periods of increased unemployment (2000s), suicide rates rose markedly in the 45- to 64-year-old group of Americans (see Figure 5.1 earlier). In Australia, longer durations of unemployment were associated with higher male suicide rates (Milner, Page, & LaMontagn, 2013). Another monumental social stressor that appears to increase risk for suicide is war. Beginning in 2008, the rate of suicide among U.S. soldiers exceeded that of the general population for the first time in decades, a trend not observed during prior military conflicts (Nock et al., 2013).

A less obvious but significant source of stress is also the media. For instance, a meta-analysis indicated that there is an average increase in suicide rates (of 0.26 suicides per 100,000 population) in the month after a celebrity suicide (Niederkrotenthaler et al., 2012), such as that of Robin Williams in August 2014. In fact, suicides that tend to be reported in the media are a skewed sample overall and themselves represent a social stressor; the reported suicides tend to be those that may either heighten the risk of lethal imitative behaviors or serve to distort public perceptions about suicide (Machlin, Pirkis, & Spittal, 2013).

Simply put, social support reduces the risk of suicide (Compton, et al., 2005; Denney, 2014), and social isolation or exclusion increases it (Yur'yev et al., 2013). For example, suicide is more common among single, divorced, separated, or widowed people than among married people. Suicide is also less common among people who have children living in their homes (Qin, Agerbo, & Mortensen, 2003). Figure 5.2 summarizes the factors that might lead to suicide. How can knowledge of these factors be used to prevent suicides?

Suicide Prevention

Efforts to prevent suicide involve societal (social) and individual (psychological) components (Mann & Currier, 2011). The societal angle involves changing social factors that increase suicide risks in the general population and increasing public

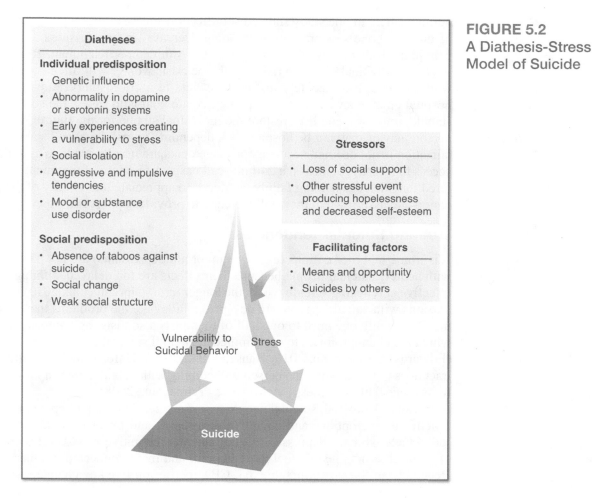

FIGURE 5.2
A Diathesis-Stress Model of Suicide

awareness about suicide, as described in the "Prevention" feature. Note, though, that evidence for many commonly accepted suicide prevention strategies is sometimes sparse or absent (Mann & Currier, 2011). With that in mind, the U.S. Department of Health and Human Services updated its *National Strategy for Suicide Prevention* in 2012 to include 13 goals, among them integrating suicide prevention and clinical training into all health-care reform efforts, promoting research on suicide prevention strategies, and improving the accuracy of news media and entertainment industry portrayals of suicide and mental disorders.

Most individually oriented efforts to prevent suicide have three basic components: (1) assessing the person's risk of suicide using the factors listed earlier, (2) helping the person cope with the immediate crisis, and (3) treating any mental disorders that increase a person's risk for later suicide attempts.

Assessment and Crisis Intervention

Police officers, 911 operators, counselors, and telephone hotline workers use the risk factors listed earlier to respond to suicidal people more effectively. For example, when crisis workers for suicide hotlines take emergency calls, they try to provide support to callers while also determining the degree to which there is an imminent danger of suicide. They ask questions to determine callers' demographic characteristics, whether they are alone, whether they have someone they can contact for support, whether they are being treated for their problems, whether they have a suicide plan or a weapon in hand, and whether they are intoxicated.

Data about the effectiveness of suicide hotline services are difficult to gather, but what information exists is mostly disappointing (Lester, 1993). Studies that have compared the rates of suicide in communities before and after the establishment of suicide hotlines have not found an overall reduction in suicides (e.g., Miller, Combs, Leeper, & Bartan, 1984), although there is some evidence that certain groups of people who call hotlines most frequently (e.g., younger, white females) may benefit more from their availability. Further, hotline callers in one study showed significant decreases in suicidality during the course of the telephone session, with continuing decreases in hopelessness and psychological pain in the following weeks (Gould, Kalafat, Munfakh, & Kleinman, 2007).

If the individual's suicide risk is high, the crisis worker will often summon the police, who will then bring acutely distressed callers to a crisis intervention program or to a hospital emergency room. Here, the immediate goal is to assess the suicide risk, thwart suicidal impulses, and help restore the individual's hope for the future. At this point, the person may or may not be hospitalized, depending on risk level and state laws. If hospitalization is not deemed necessary, arrangements are usually made to give the individual access to a care provider on a 24-hour-call basis. A program of treatment may also be offered that includes helping family or friends to appreciate the severity of the person's situation and assuring that they will be ready to provide support and supervision as needed.

Treating Suicidal Tendencies

It is ironic that medications (e.g., lithium or antidepressants) are not particularly helpful with acutely suicidal people because their effects are too delayed, although they may be effective at reducing suicide risk in the longer term (Cipriani et al., 2013). Psychotherapy sessions with suicidal people are designed to alleviate the problems that prompt suicidal urges. Roughly one third to one half of therapists also insist on a *no-suicide contract*, in which the client promises to seek immediate help if suicidal urges become overwhelming (Edwards & Sachmann, 2010; Hansen et al., 2012). Unfortunately, signing such a contract does not assure that the person will comply with it, and there is a lack of evidence as to its clinical effectiveness (McMyler & Pryjmachuk, 2008).

Because depressed, suicidal people report greater feelings of hopelessness, more dysfunctional assumptions and cognitive distortions, and fewer reasons for living than do individuals who are depressed but not suicidal, cognitive-behavioral therapy (CBT) is often used to help people feel more hopeful and more connected to others (Weishaar & Beck, 1990). As shown in Table 5.3, CBT focuses on five key characteristics of the sui-

TABLE 5.3 Cognitive Techniques for the Treatment of Suicidal Behavior

Cognitive Characteristic	Intervention
Dichotomous (all-or-none) thinking	Help clients build a range of options between their extreme points of view (e.g., between "life is terrible" and "life is perfect").
Problem-solving deficits	Teach problem-solving training, including accepting problems as a normal part of life, precisely defining the problems, generating alternatives, and implementing solutions.
Cognitive rigidity	Employ collaborative empiricism: Teach clients to test their assumptions logically and empirically. Look for evidence of alternative interpretations so that clients can more flexibly see others' points of view.
Hopelessness	Explain to clients that their hopelessness is a symptom, rather than an accurate reflection of their life situation. List all the problems making clients feel hopeless. Use problem-solving training and any skills training as needed to aid implementation of solutions (e.g., assertiveness or social skills training).
View of suicide as desirable	Elicit reasons from clients for dying and reasons for living. Describe advantages and disadvantages of suicide relative to other solutions. Correct cognitive distortions about advantages of dying.

Source: Adapted from Weishaar & Beck, 1990.

cidal person: dichotomous thinking, ineffective problem solving, cognitive rigidity, hopelessness, and viewing suicide as a desirable solution. For example, the therapist helps the client understand that hopelessness stems from negative expectations and interpretations of events, rather than an inevitable reality, and encourages efforts to identify alternative solutions to life's problems. The therapist also aims to reduce clients' tendencies to think in rigid, either/or terms (e.g., "I will *never* succeed at anything") by encouraging them to think more flexibly (e.g., "I am not as good at some things as I am at others"). As problem-solving skills are honed, the individual is less likely to view suicide as a desirable solution. A meta-analysis showed that, overall, there was a strong significant effect for CBT in reducing suicide behavior; however, it was more effective for adult samples (but not adolescent) and when delivered as an individual treatment rather than in a group format (Tarrier, Taylor, & Gooding, 2008). Other evidence-based psychotherapies for suicide prevention include different cognitive-behavioral approaches, such as dialectical behavioral therapy (see Chapter 16) and problem-solving therapy, as well as some non-CBT psychotherapy models like psychodynamic treatments (Winter, Bradshaw, Bunn, & Wellsted, 2013).

Section Review

Suicide:

- is a complex problem most often associated with mental disorders such as bipolar disorders, depression, schizophrenia, and personality disorders;
- is three to four times more common in males, although *attempted* suicides are more frequent among females than males by a ratio of about 3 to 1;
- is typically highest in the 45–64 age range in the United States, with those rates continuing to rise over the past decade;
- is caused by a diathesis-stress model where biological or psychological vulnerabilities are exposed during stressful life events in the absence of adequate social support;
- may be able to be prevented, especially in adolescents; and
- is usually treated with cognitive-behavioral or other psychotherapies, possibly along with medication in the longer term.

Revisiting the Case of John

John from the chapter-opening case was diagnosed with bipolar I disorder because he had experienced several full-fledged manic and depressive episodes. During his manic episodes, John typically went through a period of a significantly elevated or irritable mood, along with high activity. For instance, he felt energized despite sleeping very little, he talked more quickly than usual, and he often spent large sums of money on unnecessary purchases, such as airline tickets to a Nobel Prize ceremony in which he thought he was involved. Conversely, during his depressed periods, John experienced severe sadness and a lack of interest in his usual activities; he stayed in bed all day, feeling unmotivated and guilty about his irresponsibility and previous excesses. In fact, during his most recent depressive episode, John had thoughts of suicide and even purchased a firearm, which he was keeping under his bed.

After his wife brought him to the hospital, John's psychiatrist (Dr. Kate) decided to re-evaluate John's medication. John had been taking lithium for the past 2 years, but he was still having consistent mood episodes, despite good compliance and blood-level monitoring on the lithium. In the past year, John had now had four discrete, full-blown mood episodes, two of depression and two of mania, and he therefore met *DSM-5* criteria for bipolar I disorder with rapid cycling. Dr. Kate prescribed an atypical antipsychotic medication (olanzapine, sold as Zyprexa) for John instead of lithium. John also began a course of CBT with Steve, a counselor in the community.

Throughout the course of 3 months of weekly sessions, Steve helped John to understand the research on bipolar I disorder and the triggers for his mood episodes, and how to cope with his stress in healthier ways. For example, one of John's frequent stressors was his academic work; his most recent episode of mania had occurred shortly before an important exam in one of his physics classes at the community college. Steve and John worked on different ways of thinking about exams, as well as study skills and the value of preparing for the exams early rather than "cramming," which often sent John over the top with stress. Steve and John also worked on medication adherence—that is, why John should keep taking the new pills, despite annoying side effects such as weight gain (he had gained 8 pounds in the first month following hospitalization). Steve had also read the treatment manual for family-focused treatment (FFT) of bipolar disorder, and he implemented aspects of that treatment with John and his wife. Specifically, John's wife attended several of John's therapy sessions. John (with Steve's help) educated his wife about his bipolar I disorder during session 5, and they then worked on communication skills and problem solving in sessions 6 through 10.

Early on in the treatment, Steve did a thorough suicide assessment and determined that John was a moderate risk. Whereas John denied abusing alcohol or drugs, having made any suicide attempts in the past, or having any active suicidal ideations, he did have easy access to lethal means (i.e., a gun under his bed), he had a history of bipolar disorder (the mental disorder associated with the highest risk of completed suicide), and he experienced consistent stress in his daily life. Steve therefore focused some of the CBT sessions directly on the notion of suicide, such as by asking John to make a list of pros and cons of living, and by working on reducing John's cognitive rigidity and all-or-none thinking. By their fifth session, John had agreed to keep his firearm in a locked safe rather than under his bed. John also learned problem solving in his individual sessions with Steve before they opened up the sessions to include John's wife, where they then reviewed problem-solving strategies as a couple.

In the 3 months following his new medication and his work with Steve, John did not have any full-blown mood episodes, although as spring approached, John was beginning to sleep less and less. He was currently sleeping 4–6 hours nightly and did not report feeling tired. This "high-energy" period could be the harbinger of an upcoming manic episode, John and his wife had learned. John's wife therefore scheduled an appointment for him with Dr. Kate (the psychiatrist), along with a booster session with counselor Steve.

Summary

Bipolar Disorders

People diagnosed with bipolar disorders suffer periods of depression as well as episodes of highly elated mood and grandiosity. Manic episodes involve a persistently elevated or irritable mood along with an increase in goal-directed activity that usually comes along with high energy and inflated self-esteem, high distractibility, dangerous activities, and little sleep (without feeling tired). Bipolar I disorder is typified by one or more manic episodes or mixed episodes (in which both depression and mania are experienced nearly every day), usually accompanied by periods of major depression. Bipolar II disorder involves at least one major depressive episode along with at least one hypomanic period (a period of elevated or irritated mood that is not as pronounced as a full-blown manic episode). In another form of bipolar disorder, known as cyclothymic disorder, moods fluctuate over a long period—2 or more years in adults, 1 year or more in children and adolescents—but neither the depressive nor the manic phase is as severe as in bipolar I or II disorder.

Biological Causes of Bipolar Disorders

Mood disorders are caused by an interplay of biological, psychological, and social factors. Genetic factors play an important role in bipolar disorders, perhaps because they are linked to disturbances in the level, functioning, or regulation of various chemical neurotransmitters, such as norepinephrine, serotonin, and dopamine. Bipolar disorders may also be caused by structural brain deficits involving specific regions in the frontal lobes and functional deficits in frontal-limbic circuits involving the amygdala, along with possible contributions from evolutionary pressures.

Colin Smith

Colin Smith is a licensed professional counselor (LPC) who currently works as the training director of the Fort Lewis College Student Counseling Center. For a small liberal arts college, Fort Lewis College maintains a large and vibrant counseling center that sees over 20% of the student body. Colin first got into counseling as a teacher who wanted to teach those most human and avoided of subjects—our life problems—that needed to be discussed in the greatest detail. He has worked at the Fort Lewis College Counseling Center since 1989. Before that, Colin worked as the community counselor and head of psychology/philosophy/religion at Colorado Timberline Academy. Over the years, Colin has also taught many courses at both the undergraduate and graduate levels. Colin has always found that problems properly confronted can provide a path to growth and development.

Q *In your clinical experience, how do bipolar disorders typically manifest in college students and other young adults?*

A Besides the textbook presentation, which really needs to be experienced, bipolar disorders typically show up in a radical change from baseline mood and behavior. There's a current of emotional energy that disrupts sleep, impulse control, and choice. Often, our counseling center gets a call from the hospital or police.

Q *What are some of the challenges for clinicians in accurately diagnosing bipolar disorders?*

A Because baseline is central to diagnosis, I have often known in a few minutes when one of my clients is in a manic episode. We are often called by close acquaintances or faculty, who tell us that the person has not been acting like themselves. However, accurate diagnosis can be difficult, since both the client and others resist the seriousness of the diagnosis and deny that anything is wrong. Knowing the checklist of symptoms is critical. A bipolar depression, if that presents, adds complexity to diagnosis. A good and thorough history on the client is mandatory.

Q *What do you see as the main causes of bipolar disorders?*

A Whereas the cause appears to have definite biological roots, there are many environmental triggers of bipolar disorders. The disorder is also psychologically complex. Many of the clients with bipolar disorders that I have seen in my career are highly creative and bright people. Somehow, though, due to substance use, relationship instability, sleep, or some intellectual or spiritual passion, their minds and mood have caught on fire with an often religious intensity.

Q *What in your view is the optimal treatment for someone with a bipolar disorder?*

A We have a saying when it comes to treatment: stability, stability, stability. Whereas we use medication as the standard of care, a great deal of therapy is needed to accept the diagnosis and comply with medical regimens. Often, there is collateral damage from the episode and even a suicidal impulse to be worked through. As always, personality development matters, and we work to turn adversity into growth.

Q *What is the usual prognosis or course for these treated clients?*

A Prognosis is guarded, since success depends upon so many factors. Many people with bipolar disorders have done exceptionally well, given compliance with medication and therapy. Others, however, have continued to relapse, often with increasing severity.

Psychological Causes of Bipolar Disorders

Several psychological variables have been proposed as causes of bipolar disorders, including manic episodes serving as a defense against periods of depression, heightened reward sensitivity (e.g., being overly focused on unrealistic/risky rewards), and elevated emotional reactivity (as with depressive disorders). People with bipolar disorders also have numerous cognitive deficits that seem to persist even between mood episodes, and some may possess an extreme drive for achievement and perfectionism.

Social Causes of Bipolar Disorders

Environmental and sociocultural factors involving stressful events and the lack of adequate social support have also been implicated in the cause—and, even more so, in the course—of bipolar disorders. Stressful life events, such as early trauma and abuse, chronic schedule changes, and conflicts in interpersonal relationships, have been shown to play a role, along with high social strain and high expressed emotion in people's family life.

Treatment of Bipolar Disorders

Both medication and various kinds of psychotherapy are effective treatments for bipolar disorders. However, this is one mental disorder for which medication is the clearly recommended front-line treatment, with psychotherapy typically employed as an add-on to the pills. Bipolar disorders are treated primarily with lithium, which is holding onto its place as the gold standard. However, other medications, such as anticonvulsants (carbamazepine or valproate) and antipsychotics (risperidone, aripiprazole, quetiapine, or olanzapine) are being used with increasing frequency. These drugs are prescribed in cases in which lithium has not been successful or as part of a combined treatment. Furthermore, antipsychotics are often used as the front-line treatment of pediatric bipolar disorders in the short term, although the long-term effects of these (and any medications for bipolar disorders) are not yet known. Antidepressant medications are commonly used to treat the depressive episodes in bipolar disorders, even though there is presently little evidence for their effectiveness in that capacity. Four different models of psychotherapy have been shown to be effective as an adjunct to medication in the treatment of bipolar disorders: cognitive-behavioral therapy (CBT), family-focused treatment (FFT), interpersonal and social rhythm therapy (IPSRT), and psychoeducation, which is often used along with one of the other three psychotherapy models.

Suicide

Several of the risk factors that predict attempted suicide differ from those predicting completed suicides. The most important risk factors for completed suicides are having attempted suicide previously; being male, older, and unmarried; having access to lethal means; experiencing social stressors; and suffering from mental disorders, such as depression, bipolar disorders, alcohol use disorder, or schizophrenia. Like most mental disorders, suicide has been linked to multiple, interacting causes. Suicide is associated with a moderate genetic vulnerability, possible neurotransmitter abnormalities, social instability and isolation, and a chronic sense of hopelessness and pessimism. Suicide prevention depends on accurately assessing a person's risk for suicidal behavior, helping the person resolve the immediate crisis that surrounds most suicide attempts, and providing additional treatment that addresses the social and psychological problems that often lead to repeated suicide attempts.

Key Terms

altruistic suicide, p. 198

amygdala, p. 184

anomic suicide, p. 198

anticonvulsants, p. 188

antidepressants, p 189

atypical antipsychotics, p. 188

bipolar disorders, p. 174

bipolar I disorder, p. 178

bipolar II disorder, p. 178

cognitive-behavioral therapy (CBT), p. 189

cyclothymic disorder, p. 180

depression, p. 174

expressed emotion (EE), p. 187

family-focused treatment (FFT), p. 189

fatalistic suicide, p. 198

hypomania, p. 174

interpersonal and social rhythm psychotherapy (IPSRT), p. 189

linkage analysis, p. 182

lithium carbonate, p. 187

mania, p. 174

mood disorders, p. 174

parasuicidal behavior, p. 193

psychoeducation, p. 191

social strain, p. 186

social support, p. 186

specifier, p. 178

Depressive Disorders

Source: kwest/Shutterstock.com.

Chapter Outline

Depressive Disorders
Causes of Depressive Disorders
Treatment of Depressive Disorders

From the Case of Margaret

Margaret had been a little scared about leaving home for college. She grew up in a small town, where she had always excelled at everything she attempted. Success was important to Margaret. Her parents expected it, and she believed it was the key to her popularity.

At first, Margaret worried that college might not prove as easy for her as high school, but she made friends quickly and soon began enjoying campus life. She dated several men during her freshman year; then she met Jack early in her sophomore year. After 6 months of being a couple, though, their relationship began to sour. They quarreled often and felt increasingly tense when they were together. Jack suggested that they start dating other people, try to stay friends, and "see what happens." Margaret was upset but also relieved. She had thought about suggesting the same thing but had never had enough courage to do so.

Despite her relief, though, Margaret has not bounced back emotionally. Now a 21-year-old college junior, she has been plagued with frequent headaches and stomach pains for about 3 months. She has no energy, has periods of feeling "down in the dumps," and sometimes feels hopeless and overwhelmed. Typically a competent and motivated student, Margaret's grades

After reading this chapter, you will be able to answer the following key questions:

- How are depressive disorders described and categorized in the *Diagnostic and Statistical Manual of Mental Disorders (DSM-5)*?

- What causes depressive disorders?

- What are the main treatments for helping people with depressive disorders?

during the previous term were lower than usual, and she has fallen further and further behind in her current academic work. She has started to skip classes, especially early in the morning, because she finds it difficult to get out of bed. Much of the time, she feels too tired to study. When she tries, her mind wanders, and she wastes time reading the same pages over and over. Even though she feels exhausted, on some nights she has difficulty falling asleep. Recently, she has begun to avoid her friends because she has to "fake it" to act like her former, happier self.

Most nights, Margaret stays in her room alone. She knows this is abnormal and has at several times resolved to "turn things around," but when the next day comes, Margaret feels even more demoralized and discouraged about her life. As she confided to her roommate, "It's as if I can't move; my body feels pulled down by some extra gravity in the room." She has also stopped calling her parents every week because she feels that they will just nag her to "snap out of it." In fact, she is increasingly annoyed with her parents for pushing her so hard all her life. If they keep it up, she fears that she will end up a moody, bitter woman just as her mother seems to be.

Margaret finally went to the Student Health Center for help because of her physical problems, but a medical examination and initial lab tests failed to find any specific issue. Are Margaret's symptoms a normal response to the end of a relationship, or do they reflect something more serious?

mood disorders: A group of mental disorders associated with serious and persistent difficulty maintaining an even, productive emotional state.

mania: An excited mood in which a person feels excessively and unrealistically positive and energetic.

depression: An extremely low, miserably unhappy mood along with other physical and cognitive symptoms.

depressive disorders: A group of emotional disturbances in which a person experiences a low, unhappy mood and has difficulty maintaining a more neutral or positive emotional state.

We saw in Chapter 5 how **mood disorders** can also include extremely high or agitated moods—known as **mania**—in which the person feels excessively and unrealistically positive. In *bipolar disorders*, individuals experience both episodes of depression and periods of mania. The most common mood disorder in Western cultures, however, involves episodes of **depression**—a low, unhappy mood—without any manic (or hypomanic) periods. The term *unipolar depression* is sometimes used to refer to cases such as Margaret's in which only depressive symptoms are present. **Depressive disorders** refer to a group of emotional disturbances associated with negative moods and serious and persistent difficulty maintaining a comfortable and productive emotional state. However, these disorders usually involve more than just emotional symptoms; they also interfere with an individual's ability to work, to stay involved in relationships, to enjoy family life, and even to maintain good physical health. A depressive disorder can hinder almost all aspects of a person's functioning, and it can come and go many times in a person's life.

In this chapter, we consider the four main depressive disorders in detail—their physical, emotional, and cognitive symptoms; the main theories about their causes; the research data available to support these theories; and efforts at prevention and treatment. We then revisit the case of Margaret to see how she fared and what her experience can tell us about depressive disorders.

Depressive Disorders

Most people have bad moods and even entire days when they feel especially sad or unusually irritable. And most people feel a bit dejected and demoralized when their grades are disappointing or their friends let them down. Usually, these moods do not last long, disappearing once individuals get past a difficult deadline, do something fun with a friend, or just catch up on their sleep (see Chapter 12). A depressive disorder is differentiated from the relatively common bad mood in the following ways:

1. The depressed mood seen in depressive disorders is, like Margaret's, not temporary or easily shaken off. It typically persists for weeks, months, or even years.
2. A depressive disorder is severe enough to impair an individual's ability to work or interact with friends or family.

3. People suffering from depressive disorders show a cluster of other physical and behavioral symptoms, such as reduced appetite, sleep disturbance, or loss of interest in their usual pursuits. One way to think about this is that depression is a full-body disorder.

Major depressive disorder, the most common mood disorder and one of the most frequent mental disorders, is the number one cause of disability and a leading cause of suicide worldwide (Gotlib & Hammen, 2002; Hollon, Thase, & Markowitz, 2002). Over the last few decades, the rate of depression in the general population has increased substantially (Gotlib & Hammen, 2002). In fact, the World Health Organization Global Burden of Disease Study recently ranked it as the single most burdensome disease in the world (World Health Organization [WHO], 2008).

Depression affects approximately 15 million adults in the United States—about 7% of the population—every year (Kessler, Chiu, Demler, & Walters, 2005). It is estimated that one in five adults in the United States will experience at least one episode of significant depression at some time in life, and many of these individuals will have recurrent episodes (Hamilton, 1989). In fact, researchers using prospective rather than retrospective data have found that *up to half of all individuals* in the general population may meet criteria for depression at some point in their life (Moffitt et al., 2010). About one third of U.S. college students had difficulty functioning in the last 12 months due to depression, according to the 2013 National College Health Assessment, which examined data from 125,000 students from more than 150 colleges and universities (Novotney, 2014).

Whereas depression appears relatively evenly across different ethnic groups in the United States, African Americans and Mexican Americans show significantly higher depression chronicity and significantly lower depression care use than Caucasians (González, Tarraf, Whitfield, & Vega, 2010). Females experience 1.5- to 3-fold higher rates of depression than males beginning in early adolescence (American Psychiatric Association, 2013a), a difference to which we will return when we consider the causes of depression and the "A Conversation With" feature later in this chapter. Note, however, that recent research has found that men may experience as much depression as women, but merely in a different form—with higher rates of anger attacks/aggression, substance abuse, and risk taking compared with women (Martin, Neighbors, & Griffith, 2013).

As with other mental disorders, depression is often exacerbated by comorbid problems (Gadermann, Alonso, Vilagut, Zaslavsky, & Kessler, 2012). The highest physical comorbidities with depression include hypertension (high blood pressure), asthma, and anxiety disorders, although 26 other diseases were also disproportionally increased in people with depression, many of them linked to chronic lung diseases and to diabetes (Schoepf, Uppal, Potluri, Chandran, & Heun, 2014).

Depression also often co-occurs with other mental disorders. In fact, over 90% of people with depression also meet criteria for another *Diagnostic and Statistical Manual (DSM)* disorder (and an average of 3.6 other disorders), with the most common being anxiety disorders, substance use disorders, and attention-deficit/hyperactivity disorder (ADHD) (Gadermann et al., 2012; Kessler et al., 2005). For example, many individuals with depression abuse alcohol or other drugs (Grant et al., 2006). Indeed, substance use

Many famous and creative people have suffered from depression, including author J. K. Rowling, who invented the magical world of Harry Potter and platform 9 3/4 in the photo. In an interview with Ann Treneman (2000), Rowling described her depression, which inspired the dementors in her books, this way: "Depression is the most unpleasant thing I have ever experienced. . . . It is that absence of being able to envisage that you will ever be cheerful again. The absence of hope. That very deadened feeling, which is so very different from feeling sad. Sad hurts but it's a healthy feeling. It is a necessary thing to feel. Depression is very different."

MAPS - Attempted Answers

Toby Allen, a prominent artist, completed a project in which he expertly illustrated a variety of mental disorders as anthropomorphized monsters, such as the depression monster shown here.

Depression

The depression monster floats around endlessly, always covering his eyes to hide itself from the outside world. Because of this it always bumps into people or other monsters causing more distress to itself each time.

Its only relief is to wrap its fluid tail around a victim and share its depression with them. The victim is unaware of the monster but will register a heaviness and will develop a state of deep depression. Meanwhile the monster absorbs any positive emotion from its host until it has had its fill and moves onto another host.

zestydoesthings.tumblr.com

Toby Allen 2013

disorders may reflect the efforts of people with depression to relieve their depressive symptoms. Such relief is only temporary, however, and the long-term complications of substance abuse multiply the impairments that mood disorders cause and often lead to legal problems and financial ruin. In other cases, people develop mood disorders as a result of their chronic struggles with substance abuse. In either case, depression makes the substance use disorder worse and more difficult to treat (McKowen, Tompson, Brown, & Asarnow, 2013).

Anxiety and depression often co-occur, and their comorbidity may be even more common in children and adolescents (Cummings, Caporino, & Kendall, 2014). In such cases, individuals feel overwhelmed with negative emotions—despair and guilt over past problems, apprehension and fear about future threats—and they frequently have difficulty sleeping. In fact, the overlap between depression and anxiety is so extensive (over 50%; Hirschfeld, 2001) that some investigators believe they are both parts of a larger emotional state known as **negative affect**, made up of a mixture of anxious and depressive symptoms (Kendall & Watson, 1989). In fact, low positive affect seems to distinguish depression from anxiety, whereas high negative affect is associated with both depression and anxiety (Riskind, Kleiman, & Schafer, 2013).

Depressive disorders tend to fall into two major categories: major depressive disorder and persistent depressive disorder (formerly called dysthymia). The core symptoms associated with these two categories overlap considerably, but they differ in severity and course. Major depressive disorder is typically more severe and episodic, whereas persistent depressive disorder is milder but more chronic.

Major Depressive Disorder

The diagnostic criteria for **major depressive disorder** are described in Table 6.1.

The predominant mood in major depressive disorder is typically a dull despair, a constant sadness that may leave the person thinking that nothing is worthwhile. A passage from Samuel Coleridge's "Dejection: An Ode," which has similarities to J. K. Rowling's description of depression (see earlier photo), captures the oppressive sadness that often engulfs the person with depression:

A grief without a pang, void, dark, and drear,

A stifled, drowsy, unimpassioned grief,

negative affect: An emotional state that is a mixture of anxious and depressive symptoms.

major depressive disorder: One of the most severe forms of depression, characterized by constant sadness or despair, irritability, guilt, physical symptoms, insomnia, and lack of energy.

TABLE 6.1 The *DSM-5* in Simple Language: Diagnosing Depression

The person shows at least five of the following nine symptoms most days for two or more weeks:

1. Sad mood
2. Lack of interest or pleasure in activities

Physical changes, like:

3. Low energy
4. Sleeping more or less than usual
5. Eating more or less than usual
6. Moving faster or slower than usual

Changes in thinking, like:

7. Thinking negative thoughts about himself or herself
8. Trouble making decisions
9. Thoughts of suicide

Source: Adapted from the American Psychiatric Association (2013a).

Which finds no natural outlet, no relief,

In word, sigh, or tear—

Along with this profound sadness, the second most sensitive symptom of depression is **anhedonia**, which means that the person no longer gets joy or pleasure out of things or activities that she or he used to like. Thus, the avid basketball fan loses interest in the game, the involved and active parent finds it difficult to attend to child care, or the once-productive employee becomes disengaged from work.

anhedonia: Loss of the ability to enjoy activities central to a person's life.

In fact, these two features together—sadness (negative affect) and loss of interest or pleasure (lack of positive affect)—can accurately assess depression (Li, Friedman, Conwell, & Fiscella, 2007). For instance, the Patient Health Questionnaire-2 (PHQ-2; Kroenke, Spitzer, & Williams, 2003), which uses these symptoms in a two-item depression screening test in primary care settings, has good sensitivity (83%) and specificity (90%). The sensitivity of a clinical test refers to its ability to correctly identify those people with the disorder, whereas the specificity of a clinical test refers to its ability to correctly identify those people who do not have the disorder (Lalkhen & McCluskey, 2008). In other words, just using these two main symptoms of depression—depressed mood and anhedonia—can allow clinicians to correctly distinguish between those who have and do not have depression over 80% of the time.

As stated earlier, though, depression is a full-body disorder, rather than merely sad mood. Physical symptoms often accompanying major depressive disorder include loss of appetite, persistent fatigue, and complaints about an upset stomach or a variety of aches and pains. As in the chapter-opening case about Margaret, depression may cause the person to feel so drained of energy that body movements are slowed or reduced to the point of near immobility.

About three quarters of people with depression suffer from insomnia (see Chapter 12; Nutt, Wilson, & Paterson, 2008). People with depression may have trouble falling asleep, but their most common sleep disturbances involve waking up during the night—or too early in the morning—and being unable to return to sleep, and they often have disordered REM (rapid eye movement) sleep (Hu, Xie, & Yang, 2010). In fact, insomnia is a significant risk factor for the development of new or recurrent episodes of major depressive disorder in the first place (Perlis et al., 2006).

Although it is not an official criterion of major depressive disorder, people with depression also tend to suffer impairment in immune system functioning, which increases their vulnerability to infections and other illnesses (Tanaka & Kinney, 2011). Such impairment is particularly apparent among older people who are depressed and among people whose depression is severe (German et al., 2006).

Skunky suspected he may be clinically depressed because spraying cocky teenagers with his vile odor did not give him the same sustained pleasure that it once did...

Source: Cartoon written by Brian L. Burke and illustrated by Leslie B. Goldstein.

Cognitive symptoms associated with depression include a sense of guilt and worthlessness and difficulty concentrating on such simple daily activities as reading or watching TV. People who are depressed often postpone decisions for fear of making mistakes. They may feel demoralized and hopeless. They are often self-critical, blaming themselves for their problems and feeling pessimistic about their lives and futures. Their recollection of the past is also grim and unforgiving. This kind of thinking can lead to suicide attempts, as discussed in Chapter 5.

Because of their somatic (body) symptoms and preoccupation with physical well-being, many individuals with depression first seek relief from their physicians, such as Margaret's visit to the Student Health Service of her college. In fact, major depressive disorder is one of the most common problems encountered in family practice and by primary care providers (Katon & Russo, 1989). However, these practitioners must be careful in their diagnoses because the physical symptoms associated with major depressive disorder can also stem from other conditions, including cancer, tumors, infections, hypothyroidism, nutrition deficiencies, and drugs such as steroids and narcotics (Tollefson, 1993).

Course and Recurrence

Depressive disorders can occur across the entire life span (Hamilton, 1989). Although they usually first appear when people are in their late 20s—and are especially common between ages 20 and 45—depressive disorders can also occur in children and adolescents (Klerman, 1988; Ruderman, Stifel, O'Malley, & Jimerson, 2013), and they are a significant problem among older people (e.g., Solhaug, Romuld, Romild, & Stordal, 2012).

Some episodes last only a couple of weeks, whereas others can last for years. The average duration of an untreated episode is between 8 to 10 months (Tollefson, 1993). However, perhaps in as many as two thirds of the cases, episodes of major depressive disorder are recurrent, meaning that a person with depression recovers or improves for a period of time, only to suffer another episode at a later time (Yiend et al., 2009). The long-term course of major depressive disorder typically consists of a dynamic and fluctuating continuum of different levels of depressive symptom severity, mostly below the diagnostic threshold for major depressive disorder (Judd, 2012). People with major depressive disorder spend less than half of their long-term course without any depressive symptoms (asymptomatic); and every increase in the level of depressive symptom severity is associated with a significant stepwise increment in psychosocial disability (Judd, 2012). Longitudinal research over periods as long as 20 years finds that people with depression suffer an average of five to six episodes in their lifetimes (Winokur, 1986; Yiend et al., 2009). As might be expected, recurrent depressive episodes take an ever-growing toll on a person's relationships and productivity.

Being rich or successful does not protect a person from depressive disorders. Results of a worldwide study showed that 15% of the population from high-income countries (compared to 11% from low/middle-income countries) were likely to get depression over their lifetime, with 5.5% having had depression in the last year (Bromet et al., 2011). The United States had one of the highest lifetime rates of depression (19.2%), along with France (21%) and the Netherlands (17.9%; Bromet et al., 2011). Cross-national data also reveal that depression can lead to many other problems, including difficulties in role transitions (e.g., low education, high teen childbearing, marital disruption, unstable employment), reduced role functioning (e.g., low marital quality, low work performance, low earnings), elevated risk of a wide range of other mental disorders, and increased risk of early mortality due to physical disorders and suicide (Kessler & Bromet, 2013).

(a) (b)

MAPS - Superficial Syndromes

These photos depict the superficial view of depression in saguaro cacti near Tucson, Arizona. The photo in *(a)* shows a single episode, whereas the photo in *(b)* illustrates the more common recurrent pattern, with more than one major depressive episode in the cactus's lifespan.

Subgroups of Major Depressive Disorder

Differences in the pattern of depressive episodes and in their predominant symptoms have led diagnosticians to propose subcategories of major depressive disorder. These subtypes, coded as **specifiers** in the *DSM*, may have different causes and prognoses and may respond best to different treatments. Of the nine different specifiers available in the *DSM-5*, clinicians often use one of the following six to describe the current or most recent episode of major depressive disorder:

specifiers: A descriptor used in the *DSM-5* to indicate the likely course, severity, and specific symptom characteristics of certain mental disorders.

1. **With atypical features.** This specifier applies to approximately 15–29% of individuals diagnosed with major depressive disorder or persistent depressive disorder (Thase, 2007). These people show a pattern of symptoms slightly different from those outlined so far: Rather than losing their appetite or having difficulty sleeping, they sleep and eat more than usual, often gaining significant weight (Pae, Tharwani, Marks, Masand, & Patkar, 2009). They may even cheer up briefly following some positive event, such as a phone call from an old friend. In addition to the usual fatigue and psychomotor retardation that can accompany depression, people with atypical features may experience "leaden paralysis," heavy feelings in their arms or legs (like Margaret's description of being weighed down by gravity). Many of these individuals also show such intense sensitivity to rejection that it disrupts their social relationships. This variant on major depressive disorder is more likely to occur among younger people, and it frequently has a more chronic course than typical depression (Stewart, McGrath, Quitkin, & Klein, 2007). In addition, current findings suggest that atypical depression has preferential response to specific types of antidepressant medications (monoamine oxidase inhibitors over tricyclics, as described in more detail later in the chapter; Pae et al., 2009). However, the diagnostic reliability and validity of atypical depression remains elusive and open to further evolution (Pae et al., 2009).

2. **With melancholic features.** This specifier was once termed *endogenous depression*, suggesting that the depression was caused by internal, biological causes. People with melancholic features tend to display severe anhedonia, along with a

Depression with melancholic features, a severe variety of major depressive disorder, occurs frequently in older people. People suffering this disorder are unable to feel pleasure from almost any activity, and their feelings of depression are usually worse in the morning.

lack of reactivity to good events (i.e., no temporary mood brightening), sleep disturbances that involve being unable to get back to sleep after awakening as early as 4 or 5 A.M., changes in bodily activity characterized either by extreme agitation or slowness, and significant weight loss. The depressed mood has a distinct quality (sometimes called "empty mood") and is typically worse in the morning. Melancholic symptoms are more likely to be seen in older people with depression (Mallinckrodt, Watkin, Liu, Wohlreich, & Raskin, 2005). In one study, 36% of people with major depressive disorder met criteria for the melancholic subtype (Melartin et al., 2004). However, the validity of this subtype has been called into question, as there appear to be no major differences in comorbidity or course of depression between melancholic and nonmelancholic subtypes (Melartin et al., 2004).

3. **With catatonia.** This specifier is used for depression marked by extreme psychomotor disturbances; similar problems are also observed in some cases of schizophrenia and bipolar disorders. Individuals may stay immobile for long periods or stay fixed in bizarre postures, sometimes showing a *waxy flexibility* that allows them to be manipulated like a toy action figure. Others may engage in agitated, purposeless behavior; may resist any attempt to move them; or may mimic every movement someone else has made, a condition called *echopraxia*. Some become mute or engage in *echolalia*, a parrotlike repetition of other people's speech (American Psychiatric Association, 2013a). Evidence suggests that catatonia may be best treated by benzodiazepine medication or electroconvulsive therapy (ECT; discussed in more detail later in the chapter; Carroll, 2001).

4. **With psychotic features.** Individuals with severe depression may experience psychotic symptoms, including delusions (e.g., false beliefs about being persecuted) or hallucinations (e.g., seeing or hearing things that are not actually there). Usually, these symptoms are *mood congruent*, meaning that they are consistent with the person's depressed thinking (Winokur, Scharfetter, & Angst, 1985). For example, people with depression who are preoccupied with death and dying might think that others are trying to kill them, or they might hear a voice telling them to kill themselves. *Mood incongruent* psychotic symptoms are less common in depression (more common in schizophrenia) and might involve the delusion that someone is trying to insert thoughts in their minds through electromagnetic airwaves. Individuals with depression and psychotic symptoms present a more severe course of illness, as indicated by longer hospitalizations and lower rates of remission (Buoli, Caldiroli, & Altamura, 2013).

Moreover, a proportion of individuals who initially appear to have major depressive disorder will prove, in time, to instead have a bipolar disorder, discussed in depth in Chapter 5. This change in diagnosis is more likely in those with a family history of bipolar disorders, early onset of depression, or psychotic features (American Psychiatric Association, 2013a). In a prospective longitudinal community study, a total of 3.6% of the initial unipolar major depression cases subsequently developed (hypo)mania, with particularly high rates (9%) in adolescent onset depression before age 17 (Beesdo et al., 2009). However, 13% of people who had major depressive disorder with psychotic features had a manic or hypomanic episode within a 2-year follow-up period, making it especially important to reassess and follow up with people who show this depression subtype (DelBello et al., 2003).

5. **With seasonal pattern.** This specifier, also known as **seasonal affective disorder**, refers to depressive episodes that have a clear seasonal pattern (Flaskerud, 2012). For

seasonal affective disorder: Mood disorders that are linked to a particular season of the year; probably caused by shifts in overall exposure to light.

example, some individuals experience depressive episodes only during the winter months, and then spontaneously recover in the spring. This type of depressive disorder is most commonly seen in locations where winter days are short and exposure to daylight is limited—that is, the rate in low-latitude countries is significantly lower than that in higher-latitude countries in the Northern Hemisphere (Whitehead, 2004). Similar to atypical depression, winter depression often presents with low energy, extreme fatigue, and greater than normal amounts of sleeping, along with increased appetite, often characterized by a craving for carbohydrates. Prevalence estimates of seasonal depression in community-based surveys have ranged from 1.4–9.7% in North America, 1.3–3.0% in Europe, and 0.0–0.9% in Asia (Levitt, Boyle, Joffe, & Baumal, 2000). However, in a study of over 6,500 participants, seasonal differences in severity or type of depressive symptoms were absent or small in effect size (Winthorst, Post, Meesters, Penninx, & Nolen, 2011).

6. **With peripartum onset.** This specifier is used for cases of depressive disorder that begin during pregnancy or within 4 weeks after the birth of a child in 3–6% of women (American Psychiatric Association, 2013a). Young mothers and mothers with a low education level have a heightened risk of developing depression following delivery (Reck et al., 2008). The symptoms are similar to typical depressive disorder, but they tend to fluctuate more often and are frequently accompanied by attacks of severe anxiety and obsessive worries about harm befalling the baby. Women with peripartum episodes often feel guilty because their symptoms are at odds with the joy they were taught to expect following the birth of a baby. This shame often makes these women less willing to talk about their problems, thus making successful treatment less likely (Wisner, Moses-Kolko, & Sit, 2010).

Source: Sarah Fields Photography.

The Guadalupe River in Kerrville, Texas, near the mental hospital where Andrea Yates resides. Yates was a former Houston, Texas, resident who confessed to drowning her five children in their bathtub on June 20, 2001. On July 26, 2006, a Texas jury in her retrial found that Yates was not guilty by reason of insanity because of her mental disorder (which, in *DSM-5*, would be diagnosed as major depressive disorder with peripartum onset and psychotic features). Yates claimed that she killed her children to protect them from Satan. Yates was consequently committed by the court to the North Texas State Hospital and later to a mental hospital in Kerrville, Texas, where she remains today (Hlavaty, 2014).

The existing empirical evidence casts doubt on whether peripartum onset depression actually constitutes a special category of the disorder (Cunningham, Brown, Brooks, & Page, 2013). Other researchers question whether the peripartum period is even associated with any increased rate of depressive disorders (O'Hara, Zekoski, Phillipps, & Wright, 1990). What does seem clear is that, if a mother suffers a depressive disorder shortly after delivering one child, she is at greater risk for depressive disorders following future deliveries (Depression Guideline Panel, 1993). In fact, this recurrence risk is especially high—30–50% with each subsequent delivery—once a woman has had a peripartum episode with psychotic features (American Psychiatric Association, 2013a).

Cultural Factors and Limitations in Diagnosing Major Depressive Disorder

As noted in Chapter 1, it is essential to consider cultural context when diagnosing any mental disorder. For instance, some countries outside the Western world do not use depression as a concept of sadness and suffering; instead, other expressions are used, such as "neurasthenia" and "nerves," which contain symptoms similar to the construct of depression (Lehti, Johansson, Bengs, Danielsson, & Hammarstrom, 2010). This may explain the fairly wide variation of lifetime depression rates worldwide, with the United States topping the list (Bromet et al., 2011). In addition, clinicians need to realize that,

MAPS - Prejudicial Pigeonholes

in many cultures, an individual with depression is more likely to present with somatic symptoms, most commonly low energy/fatigue or insomnia, rather than overt mood or anhedonia symptoms per se (American Psychiatric Association, 2013a).

Furthermore, the link between depression and **bereavement**—grieving the loss of a significant person in one's life—has been muddied by the current diagnostic manuals. It is not by chance that the *DSM-IV*, in its introduction (1994, p. xxi), identified as one of the components of the definition of mental disorder the fact that "the syndrome or pattern must not be merely an expectable and culturally sanctioned response to a particular event, for example, the death of a loved one." In the *DSM-IV*, the bereavement exclusion prevented clinicians from diagnosing a major depressive episode in someone who had recently (within the past 2 months) lost a loved one. The approach of both the *DSM-5* and *ICD-11* has shifted, however, in that it is now possible to diagnose a major depressive disorder in individuals who are actively in mourning (Maj, 2012). The *DSM-5* provides a footnote outlining what it considers key differences between bereavement/grief, which typically involves feelings of emptiness and loss and waves of dysphoria (along with positive emotions) associated with thoughts of the deceased, and depression, which instead entails worthlessness and self-loathing as well as persistent sad mood (American Psychiatric Association, 2013a). The *DSM-5* also lists "persistent complex bereavement disorder" in an appendix of conditions for further study. Formerly called a *pathological grief reaction*, this diagnosis (if it makes it out of the appendix and into future editions of the manual) would be made when individuals are experiencing reactive distress to the death of a loved one at least a year later, as well as social and identity disruptions in their own life.

This grief issue is closely linked to the more general question of what constitutes a mental disorder versus homeostatic reactions to major life events (Maj, 2012). A major depressive disorder is indeed an "expectable response" to the death of a loved one: In the United States, its prevalence among bereaved people ranges from 29–58% 1 year after the loss, and about 50% of all widows and widowers meet criteria for depression at some time during the first year of bereavement (Zisook, Paulus, & Shuchter, 1997). As pointed out in Chapter 1, some scholars now worry that "normal grief will become major depressive disorder, thus medicalizing and trivializing our expectable and necessary emotional reactions to the loss of a loved one and substituting pills and superficial medical rituals for the deep consolations of family, friends, religion, and the resiliency that comes with time and the acceptance of the limitations of life" (Frances, 2012). Parker (2007) further claims that depression was already overdiagnosed even before the slackening of the bereavement exclusion and that depression will remain a nonspecific "catch all" until common sense brings current confusion to order.

Persistent Depressive Disorder

The *DSM-5* conceptualizes chronic forms of depression in a somewhat modified way. What was referred to as dysthymia in the *DSM-IV* now falls under the category of **persistent depressive disorder**, which includes both chronic major depressive disorder and the previous dysthymic disorder. An inability to find scientifically meaningful differences between these two conditions led to their combination (e.g., Blanco et al., 2010; Klein, Shankman, & Rose, 2006), with the same specifiers included as described previously for major depressive disorder in order to identify different presentations and courses.

In adults, the diagnosis of persistent depressive disorder is reserved for individuals who have had difficulties with chronically depressed mood and related symptoms for at least 2 years. In children, the prominent mood is often irritability rather than depression, and the minimum duration of symptoms is 1 year. Table 6.2 lists the key criteria for this diagnosis. Persistent depressive disorder tends to develop more gradually than major depression and typically does not involve an acute disruption of the person's life. It is analogous to a nagging cold that is never severe but, over time, can drag a person down (like the one you get during exam week). People with persistent depressive disorder often feel inadequate and brood about the past. They appear almost accustomed to their demoralized feelings, and,

---

bereavement: Feelings of sadness that follow the death of a loved one and that are best characterized as normal grief reactions to loss.

persistent depressive disorder: A depressive disorder in which depressed feelings and low self-esteem are present for at least 2 years but not as intensely as in major depressive disorder.

TABLE 6.2 The *DSM-5* in Simple Language: Diagnosing Persistent Depression

Consistently depressed (or irritable) mood for at least a year in children or 2 years in adults, which includes two or more of the following symptoms:

Changes in (1) appetite, (2) sleep;

Reduction in (3) energy levels, (4) self-esteem, (5) ability to concentrate, (6) hope.

Source: Adapted from American Psychiatric Association (2013a).

in some cases, will say such things as "I've always felt like this." Persistent depressive disorder is associated with increased risk for major depression (Keller, Baker, & Russell, 1993), which suggests that the two disorders may share a common causal pathway.

Around the world, there is little regional variation in prevalence estimates of dysthymia (one of the former diagnoses combined to generate persistent depressive disorder), with global estimates of 1.5% (Charlson, Ferrari, Flaxman, & Whiteford, 2013). Prevalence of dysthymia peaks at around 50 years, with slightly higher frequency in women than men (Charlson et al., 2013). Lifetime prevalence of persistent depressive disorder in the United States—dysthymia plus chronic depression—is estimated at around 4% (Blanco et al., 2010). Persistent depressive disorder generally lasts far longer than the 2 years required for diagnosis; in one U.S. study, the median time to recovery was well over 4 years (52 months) and was associated with a high risk of relapse (Klein et al., 2006). However, due to its less acute (but more chronic) presentation than major depressive disorder, individuals with this disorder continue to face substantial unmet treatment needs (Blanco et al., 2010).

As many as one quarter of all people with major depressive disorder experience **double depression**, in which a major depressive episode is preceded or followed by persistent depressive disorder (Keller et al., 1992; Wells, Burnam, Rogers, Flays, & Camp, 1992). Research suggests that both persistent depressive disorder and double depression involve a similar course, which is worse than the course of major depression only, with longer duration and more relapses (Rhebergen et al., 2009).

double depression: A condition in which both major depression and dysthymia are experienced.

Despite findings indicating the utility of distinguishing between chronic and non-chronic forms of depression (Klein et al., 2006), other research indicates that persistent depressive disorder is a heterogeneous diagnosis that encompasses many different depressive conditions, as well as anxiety disorders (Chapter 7) and personality disorders (Chapter 16), and without clear evidence of its validity as a separate diagnostic entity (Rhebergen & Graham, 2014). It is feasible, therefore, that the disorder might eventually become a subtype or specifier of major depressive disorder in future *DSM*s.

Premenstrual Dysphoric Disorder

Based on scientific evidence, **premenstrual dysphoric disorder (PMDD)** has been moved from the *DSM-IV* Appendix B, "Criteria Sets and Axes Provided for Further Study," to the main body of the *DSM-5* (American Psychiatric Association, 2013a). Premenstrual disorders, including PMDD and premenstrual syndrome (PMS, which is not a *DSM* disorder), involve significant mood, physical, and behavioral changes occurring during the premenstrual phase of the menstrual cycle (Sigmon, Craner, Yoon, & Thorpe, 2012). Common symptoms include sad mood, anxiety, irritability, social withdrawal, sleep problems, food cravings, and physical symptoms (e.g., breast tenderness, joint or muscle pain, headache; Sigmon et al., 2012). PMS is estimated to occur in 20–40% of menstruating women, whereas PMDD is estimated to affect 2%–9% (Clayton, 2008). Although PMS and PMDD involve similar symptoms, PMDD symptoms are more severe and primarily affective in nature (e.g., depressed mood, anxiety, irritability, loss of interest; Sigmon et al., 2012).

premenstrual dysphoric disorder (PMDD): A mental disorder that involves significant mood swings and irritability that occur during most menstrual cycles and then remit when menstruation occurs.

Although up to 95% of women report noticing premenstrual changes, in PMDD, these changes are severe enough to cause significant distress and impairment (Craner, Sigmon, Martinson, & McGillicuddy, 2014). PMDD is associated with impairment in numerous areas of quality of life and daily functioning, such as dissatisfaction with social relationships, impaired social adjustment, and increased interpersonal difficulties during the premenstrual phase (Di Guilio & Reissing, 2006), and approximately 15% of women with PMDD report at least one suicide attempt (Cunningham, Yonkers, O'Brien, & Eriksson, 2009). Premenstrual disorders are also associated with lower health-related quality of life, greater health-care utilization, reduced occupational productivity, and more frequent absenteeism at work (Borenstein, Dean, Leifke, Korner, & Yonkers, 2007).

Critics cite two concerns with PMDD becoming a full-fledged disorder, rather than an appendix listing in the *DSM-5*: First, the potential stigmatization of women, who are already diagnosed with depression far more frequently than men are; and second, the diagnostic criteria for PMDD are too easily met, which may result in unnecessary treatment of individuals whose symptoms are mild (Paris, 2013).

Disruptive Mood Dysregulation Disorder

disruptive mood dysregulation disorder: A mental disorder in children between 6 and 18 years old that involves persistent irritability and temper outbursts that are grossly out of proportion to the situation or developmental level.

To address concerns about potential overdiagnosis and overtreatment of bipolar disorder in children, another new diagnosis in the depressive disorders category—**disruptive mood dysregulation disorder**—was included in the *DSM-5* for children from age 6 up to age 18 who exhibit chronic, persistent irritability (American Psychiatric Association, 2013a). Alongside this irritability, the child has recurrent temper outbursts that are manifested verbally (e.g., screaming rages) and/or behaviorally (e.g., physical aggression) and that are grossly out of proportion to the situation or provocation or to the child's developmental level.

Irritability is a mood symptom present in the criteria for a large number of mental disorders and refers to easy annoyance and touchiness that can manifest in anger and temper outbursts (Stringaris, 2011). Depending on the stringency of threshold, prevalence rates of irritability range from 3% for severe, chronic irritability strictly (Brotman et al., 2006) to as high as 20% (Pickles et al., 2010). A possible advantage of this new diagnosis is to cement what experienced clinicians already know—that depression frequently does not present with low mood (Miller, 2013). Irritability, anger, anhedonia, or disruptive behavior may be equally defining of a depressive disorder, and difficulty with regulating such emotion may be—at least for some—the primary deficit, more apparent than low mood per se (Miller, 2013). Most findings so far suggest that chronic, severe irritability is not a developmental presentation of mania or a precursor to bipolar disorder, thus justifying this new disorder for use instead of bipolar disorder in children (Mikita & Stringaris, 2013). In fact, children who suffer from disruptive mood dysregulation disorder typically develop major depressive disorders or anxiety disorders as adults, rather than bipolar disorders (Roy et al., 2013). However, offspring of parents with bipolar disorder are more likely to meet criteria for disruptive mood dysregulation disorder than are offspring of community control parents, suggesting that there may be at least some link between those two disorders (Sparks et al., 2014).

Critics contend that there is little research to support this new disorder (Paris, 2013), which is puzzlingly listed in the *DSM-5* under depressive disorders, rather than under disruptive behavioral disorders (see Chapter 3). In any case, because children often have temper tantrums and typically grow out of them, this diagnosis should be used only with extreme caution (Paris, 2013).

Section Review

Depressive disorders are among the most common mental disorders in the world and:

- affect women about twice as often as men;
- can occur at any age, but develop most frequently when people are in their 20s;
- are so often accompanied by anxiety that some experts believe that depression and anxiety are both components of one emotional state called (high) negative affect; and
- also involve a low positive affect, characterized by anhedonia, a loss of interest in previous activities.

The two most common depressive disorders are:

- major depressive disorder, characterized by at least one, but usually several, major depressive episodes throughout one's lifetime;
- persistent depressive disorder, characterized by chronically depressed mood lasting for at least 2 years in adults or 1 year in children;
- often experienced together or in sequence, a condition known as double depression; and
- sometimes separated into subtypes via specifiers based on their different symptom presentations and courses.

The other depressive disorders in the *DSM-5* are both new and include:

- premenstrual dysphoric disorder—disruptive mood swings and irritability that occur during most menstrual cycles; and
- disruptive mood regulation disorder, which can be diagnosed in children who show profound irritability and temper tantrums.

Both of these diagnoses have been subject to criticism about stigmatizing women and children and labelling typical hormonal or developmental trajectories as disordered.

Causes of Depressive Disorders

Now that we have a strong sense of how to detect depressive disorders, we move on to a discussion about causality. How do these disorders develop in the first place? Like most other mental disorders, depressive disorders result from the complex interplay of biological, psychological, and social factors. And, as with most other disorders, the relative contribution of each of these factors is probably slightly different in each person's case.

Surveys of the public in a range of Western countries have shown a predominant belief in social stressors as causes of mental disorders, whereas genetic factors were much less frequently endorsed (Link, Phelan, Bresnahan, Stueve, & Pescosolido, 1999; Nakane et al., 2005). Social factors covered in these surveys included stressful life events, traumatic experiences, family problems, and social disadvantages. One study compared public perceptions of depression in Japan and Australia, again illustrating that the public had a predominant belief in social causes and risk factors. However, there were also some major differences between the countries, such as the belief in weakness of character as a cause of depression, which was stronger in Japan (Nakane at al., 2005).

In the United States, life stress (a social cause) was endorsed by 95% of participants as being the most likely cause of a person's depression, whereas biological causes of a "chemical imbalance in the brain" (73%) and a genetic or inherited problem (53%) were seen as second and third most likely causes, respectively (Link et al., 1999). Public notion of the cause of depression is of particular interest and concern because it may reduce the likelihood of seeking professional help and support from others (e.g., if "weakness of character" is seen as the cause) or result in improper front-line treatment (e.g., if "chemical imbalance" is seen as the cause).

We discuss the biopsychosocial approach to understanding and sorting through the potential causes of depression next.

Source: alphaspirit/Shutterstock.com.

Most researchers believe that depression results from an interaction between biological, psychological, and social factors, as in the diathesis-stress model, a biopsychosocial model of abnormal behavior discussed in Chapter 2.

Biological Causes of Depressive Disorders

Most researchers—like the public—view depressive disorders as stemming at least partly from biological causes, as per the diathesis-stress model discussed in Chapter 2.

The current thinking is that biological mechanisms responsible for early life calibration of stress response systems may generate persistent sensitization to stressors, thereby increasing the risk of depression following exposure to stressful events later in life (Patten, 2013). Biological findings regarding depression and bipolar disorders (see Chapter 5) show some interesting similarities, but also key differences, suggesting that these are distinct underlying constructs (Hickie, 2014).

Genetic Influences on Depressive Disorders

It is estimated that 30–40% of the risk for major depression is heritable (Heim & Binder, 2012), defined as the proportion of observable differences in the disorder between individuals that is due to genetic differences. Gene-environment interactions may explain some of the heterogeneity in the way people respond to stressful life events, as may epigenetic changes occurring during development (Heim & Binder, 2012). Many studies support this idea that genes play a role in creating a predisposition to depressive disorders (Patten, 2013).

Recall from Chapter 2 that one way to explore the contribution of genetic factors to disorders is to contrast the appearance of a disorder in identical (*monozygotic*) twins who have exactly the same genes versus nonidentical (*dizygotic*) twins who share only about 50% of their genetic endowment. If a depressive disorder appears in both members of monozygotic twin pairs more frequently than in dizygotic pairs, there is evidence of a genetic contribution to the disorder. Indeed, major depressive disorder is about four times more likely to occur in both members of identical twins, compared with nonidentical twins (Bowman & Nurnberger, 1993).

Evidence for a genetic component in depressive disorders has also been found in family studies comparing the risk for various relatives of people with such disorders (see Figure 6.1). These studies have consistently shown that close relatives of adults with major depressive disorder are at higher risk for such disorders than are more distant relatives. One study suggested that loss of appetite or weight in parents with a history of recurrent depression may be the strongest marker of risk for depression in their offspring (Mars et al., 2013).

Of course, greater environmental similarities in the lives of close relatives might help account for the results of family studies, so researchers have also used adoption studies to determine the relative contributions of genetic versus environmental factors. If depressive disorders are determined to any significant degree by genetic factors, then depression

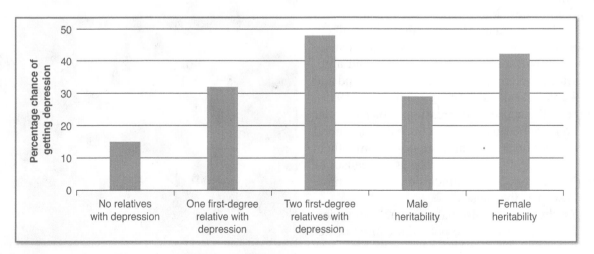

FIGURE 6.1 Depressive Disorders Run in Families

First-degree relatives of people with major depressive disorder have about two or three times the lifetime risk of developing major depression compared to those whose first-degree relatives do not have any major depressive disorders. If that relative has chronic depression, then the person has a 2.5-to-1 chance of also having a chronic form of the disorder. In addition, the heritability of depression is higher in women (approximately 42%) than in men, where it is approximately 29%.

Source: Based on data from Kendler, Gatz, Gardner, & Pedersen (2006); Mondimore et al. (2006); and Wilde et al. (2014).

should be more frequent among the biological relatives of an individual with depression, even if that individual was raised in an adoptive family. However, several studies have shown that children living with parents (especially mothers) who have depression are at higher risk to later develop depression themselves, regardless of whether or not these parents were adoptive or biological, indicating that the risk may be primarily environmental (Marmorstein, Iacono, & McGue, 2012; Tully, Iacono, & McGue, 2008).

Taken together, twin, adoption, and family studies suggest that genetic factors play a weaker role in unipolar depression versus bipolar disorders (see Chapter 5) and that there is a more clearly defined genetic risk for major depressive disorder than for persistent depressive disorder (Newman & Bland, 2009). Clearly, genetics alone do not tell the whole causal story of depressive disorders. For one thing, not everyone who is closely related to a person with depression becomes depressed, and some people with depression are the only people in their families to display the disorder. Furthermore, genetic models do not tell us *how* genetic endowment leads to depression. To understand that link, we must look at how alterations in biological functioning might affect mood.

Neurobiological Influences on Depressive Disorders

Depressive disorders are accompanied by a number of abnormalities in the central nervous system (Pandey & Dwivedi, 2009). These may include abnormalities in the body's regulatory functions—especially in the production and utilization of the chemical messengers in the brain known as *neurotransmitters* and in the production and impact of stress hormones. Much research on the relationship between neurotransmitters and depression has focused on dopamine, serotonin, and the *catecholamines*—norepinephrine and epinephrine. These neurotransmitters are thought to regulate several important behavioral systems relevant to depressive disorders, including motivation, concentration, and interest in others (Rogeness, Javors, & Pliszka, 1992).

Neurotransmitters and Depression Theories about the biological processes underlying depression first appeared in the 1950s, when physicians noted symptoms of depression in patients being treated for high blood pressure with reserpine—a drug that lowers catecholamine levels (France, Lysaker, & Robinson, 2007). Further evidence for this "chemical imbalance" theory came from studies showing that medications that *increased* levels of norepinephrine in the brain could diminish depressive symptoms (France et al., 2007).

However, later research discovered that not all people with depression have low levels of norepinephrine, nor do they all improve after taking drugs that increase norepinephrine levels (France et al., 2007). Since the **catecholamine theory** was first proposed, scientists have discovered that many other neurotransmitters and related chemicals may be involved in depressive disorders. Furthermore, mood-related neural activity may be affected not only by the amount of a neurotransmitter at a synapse but also by a neurotransmitter's effects on other neurotransmitters and on the number and receptivity of receptor sites. Finally, the long-term effects of a change in the amount of a neurotransmitter may differ from its short-term effects, and the amount of chemical available can be affected at several steps in the life cycle of the neurotransmitter. These discoveries help explain why there is no simple, direct correspondence between moods and the amount of any one neurotransmitter in the brain.

catecholamine theory: The idea that low levels of norepinephrine lead to depression and high levels of norepinephrine lead to mania.

The most prominent (though likely incorrect) current theory—the serotonin monoamine theory—holds that low serotonin levels may allow other neurotransmitters such as dopamine and norepinephrine to swing increasingly out of control, leading to extreme moods (Leventhal & Antonuccio, 2009). Some studies, including a meta-analysis, reveal that one or two different polymorphisms (a specific nucleotide sequence in one's genetic code) in the single gene that makes tryptophan hydroxylase-2 (TPH2) may play a role in depression (Gao et al., 2012). TPH2 is an important enzyme (helper protein) in the synthetic pathway for brain serotonin and is considered a key factor for the maintenance of normal serotonin transmission throughout the central nervous system. This line of research provides a vital integration of genetics and neurotransmitters in the possible causes of depressive disorders.

Connections

What other mental disorders are treated with medications that affect neurotransmitters? See Chapters 4, 5, 7, and 8.

Further circumstantial evidence for the role of neurotransmitters in the etiology of depression comes from the fact that medications such as fluoxetine (sold as Prozac), which inhibits the brain's reuptake of serotonin, and bupropion (sold as Wellbutrin), which selectively blocks reuptake of dopamine, have both proved to be somewhat effective antidepressants. These medications do not have the same effect on all individuals, however. In the past decade, scientists have searched for neurotransmitter-related genes that could predict antidepressant response, with some success. For instance, in Caucasians, a polymorphism in the serotonin transporter gene (the widely studied 5-HTTLPR; Karg, Burmeister, Shedden, & Sen, 2011) may be a predictor of antidepressant response and remission, whereas in Asians, it does not appear to play a major role (Porcelli, Fabbri, & Serretti, 2012). Further, stressors in early life may interact with polymorphisms in genes that produce norepinephrine and dopamine to influence response to antidepressant treatment (Xu et al., 2011).

However, the largest and most extensive trial of antidepressants ever conducted cast serious doubt on the idea that different people with depression require different neurotransmitter boosts to get better (Leventhal & Antonuccio, 2009). The STAR*D (Sequenced Treatment Alternatives to Relieve Depression) project used state-of-the-art methods to treat people (over 4,000 of them!) coming to a hospital or psychiatric clinic for relief from depression (Boren, Leventhal, & Pigott, 2009). The main finding was that drugs with different neurochemical actions were equivalent to each other and not much better than placebo, a finding we return to later in the chapter, when we discuss treatment for depression.

Despite the mixed evidence, the lay public in the United States—including 54% of college students—has shown a strong adoption of the chemical imbalance theory of depression as depicted in many drug company advertisements (France et al., 2007). Overall, though, studies have failed to show a consistent and predictable causal link between depression and serotonin or norepinephrine levels (Healy, 2004). A meta-analysis showed that monoamine neurotransmitter (e.g., serotonin, norepinephrine) depletion did not directly or reliably decrease mood (Ruhé, Mason, & Schene, 2007). Thus, after more than 4 decades of research, and contrary to popular belief (and drug company pamphlets), neurotransmitter theories of depression have failed to achieve empirical support (Leventhal & Antonuccio, 2009). Because it is unlikely that depression is related to only one neurotransmitter or another, even in a particular person, interactions among various biochemical, as well as life events, may ultimately prove to be the key causal factors in depressive disorders (e.g., Karg et al., 2011; Sharpley, Palanisamy, & McFarlane, 2013).

In addition, neuroscientists have pointed out that, even when chemical abnormalities have been found in people with depression, they are as likely to be effects of depression as causes. Thus, although it is common for the behaviors associated with depression to be ascribed to biological causes, there is no good answer to the question: Are the behaviors commonly found in people with depression, such as inactivity, absence of appetite, sleep disturbance, excessive alcohol consumption, and so forth, caused by *or the cause of* chemical changes in the brain (Horwitz & Wakefield, 2007)?

Depression and the Endocrine System With this caveat in mind, depression has also been related to the functioning of the endocrine system. This system includes the hypothalamus, which regulates functions such as sleep and appetite; the pituitary gland, which regulates growth; and the adrenal glands. A key part of the endocrine system (described in Chapter 2) is the hypothalamic-pituitary-adrenal (HPA) axis, which plays a critical role in the body's response to stress. In times of stress, the adrenal glands respond to messages from the hypothalamic-pituitary system by increasing their output of cortisol and adrenaline (epinephrine), hormones that help the body cope with stressors via "fight-or-flight" mechanisms.

Certain groups of people with depression show elevated levels of cortisol, abnormal daily variations in cortisol secretion, and increased levels of cortisol metabolites (Nabeta et al., 2014). These data have been used to support the theory that disruptions in the regula-

MAPS - Medical Myths

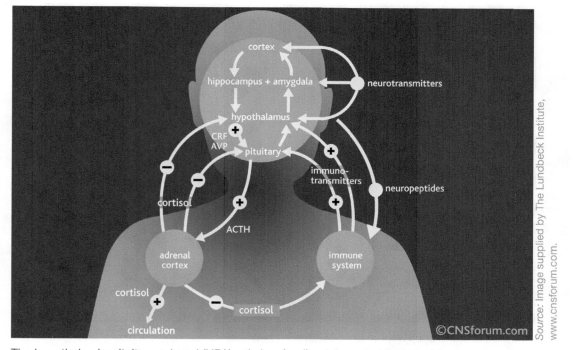

The hypothalamic-pituitary-adrenal (HPA) axis is a feedback loop that includes the hypothalamus, the pituitary, and the adrenal glands. The release of cortisol into the circulation has a number of effects, including elevation of blood glucose for increased metabolic demand. Cortisol also negatively affects the immune system and prevents the release of certain immune cells. Interference from other brain regions (e.g., the hippocampus and amygdala) can modify the HPA axis, as can neurotransmitters (Goodman & Gilman, 2001).

tion of the HPA axis contributes to depression. This theory has also been explored through *biological challenge tests*, which involve giving people with depression **dexamethasone**, a substance that temporarily suppresses the production of cortisol in healthy adults. Initial dexamethasone challenges showed that, when given a nighttime dose of dexamethasone, some people with depression failed to show normal cortisol suppression the next day (e.g., Gibbons, 1969). This outcome was interpreted to mean that people with depression may have an overactive HPA axis. However, further research revealed that similar "non-suppression" effects occur in people without depression, as well as in individuals who had suffered broken bones or other physical trauma (Carroll, 1986; Knorr, Vinberg, Kessing, & Wetterslev, 2010). Therefore, despite its early promise, the *dexamethasone suppression test* is no longer considered a specific or reliable tool for exploring the neuroendocrinological aspects of depression (Knorr et al., 2010).

dexamethasone: A substance that temporarily suppresses the production of cortisol in healthy adults.

Nevertheless, researchers have continued to investigate a possible connection between depression and the HPA axis, which also fits with the catecholamine theory of depression discussed earlier, because the hypothalamus is strongly influenced by catecholamines. One study showed a higher cortisol awakening response among both participants with current and remitted major depressive disorder (Vreeburg et al., 2009). Other research indicates that dysregulation of the HPA axis may be related to poor verbal memory functioning (Hansson, Murison, Lund, & Hammar, 2013) and poor coping strategies in people with depression (Hori et al., 2014).

Other Biological Factors in Depression Researchers are also using sophisticated technology—particularly functional magnetic resonance imaging (fMRI) and positron emission tomography (PET), discussed in Chapter 1—to explore differences in the brain activity of people with and without depressive symptoms. PET studies have found, for example, that people with major depressive disorder have reduced blood flow and metabolism in the prefrontal cortex, particularly when they exhibit psychomotor retardation (Videbech, 2000), and increased activity in the limbic system, which processes emotions

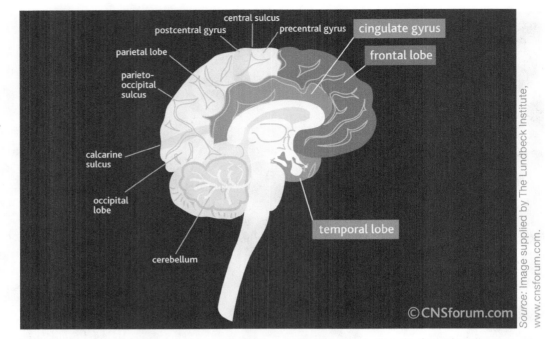

Many areas of the brain appear to be involved in depression, including the frontal and temporal lobes and parts of the limbic system, such as the cingulate gyrus. However, it is not clear if the changes in these areas are the causes of or the result of depression (Gotlib, Joormann, & Foland-Ross, 2014).

(Mayberg et al., 1999), relative to individuals without depression. Accordingly, fMRI studies reveal that people with depression have left amygdala hyperarousal (a part of the limbic system), even when processing stimuli outside conscious awareness and especially for fearful faces, which normalizes with antidepressant treatment (Sheline et al., 2001). The frontal lobe and limbic system contain brain circuits that are involved in attention, alertness, reward, and emotion and are influenced by the neurotransmitters described earlier. Functional and structural anomalies in these brain regions may be stable vulnerability markers for major depressive disorder that precede the onset of symptoms (Gotlib, Joormann, & Foland-Ross, 2014).

Finally, a new theory on biological causes of depression has emerged that contends that inflammation may play a significant role (Dantzer, O'Connor, Freund, Johnson, & Kelley, 2008). This line of research focuses on pro-inflammatory cytokines, proteins produced by our immune systems that elicit systemic inflammation—that is, increased immune cell activities that we notice as heat, redness, pain, or swelling in response to illness. This inflammatory response has been postulated to lead to depression via several mechanisms, including by influencing serotonin (a neurotransmitter) and/or cortisol (a hormone; Dantzer et al., 2008). This cytokine theory of depression is certainly attractive for a field (biological causes of depression) that has been short of real innovations, but it remains far from proven at this point (Dantzer et al., 2008).

Section Review

Among the biological factors believed to contribute to depressive disorders are:

- genetic risks, which are not as strong for major depressive disorder as for bipolar disorder, but stronger than for persistent depressive disorder;
- disturbances in the level, functioning, or regulation of one or more neurotransmitters such as norepinephrine, serotonin, and dopamine;
- abnormalities in the endocrine (hormone) system, particularly the HPA axis, which is a critical system in the body's response to stress; and
- changes in blood flow or inflammation that could interact with the neurotransmitters and/or endocrine system.

Psychological Causes of Depressive Disorders

Psychological and biological theories do not necessarily compete with each other as explanations for depressive disorders. In fact, most current psychological theories view biological factors as one of many risks (diatheses) that predispose some people to develop depressive disorders, as per the diathesis-stress model. But beyond these risks, what factors influence the development of these disorders?

In one way or another, psychological theories assert that depression results from a person's sense of lost control and diminished power (Gilbert, 1992). When people believe they have lost the ability to direct their own lives, they feel hopeless and become demoralized. Eventually, their actual power does diminish, and they give up many of their former productive or enjoyable activities.

Intimate Relationships and Depression

Some psychological theories (see Chapter 2) suggest that problems with intimate relationships can create a predisposition (diathesis) or act as a trigger (stress) for depression.

Psychoanalytic Theories   Psychoanalytic theories of depression are based on a classic paper by Sigmund Freud called *Mourning and Melancholia* (1917/1957). In Freud's model, individuals prone to depression suffered the loss of caregivers or were disappointed by them in some way during their childhood. The diathesis for later depression was their reaction to this early disappointment, which was that they became abnormally dependent on others to make them feel adequate, and were prone to anger when their dependency needs were not met. Freud said that depression results when this anger is eventually turned inward against the self.

Freud's theory was embedded in a particular historical and scientific context and was constrained by the metaphors of his day (Dozois, 2000). In fact, Freud himself raised the issue of limited generalizability and later questioned the complexity of his theory, yet researchers and theorists (e.g., Bradbury, 2001) have continued to overgeneralize from Freud's work on depression (Dozois, 2000). One kernel of wisdom that emerged from Freud's theory, though, is the distinction between mourning and depression—notably, the self-loathing and loss of self-esteem that is more typical of depression than mourning, part of what the *DSM-5* describes in an effort to help users distinguish these two states.

Attachment Theories   Other psychoanalytic theorists, described in Chapter 2, have downplayed the importance of Freud's "anger turned inward" view of depression and emphasized other factors instead (Arieti & Bemporad, 1978). For example, John Bowlby (1980, 1988a, b) proposed a model of psychopathology that draws on biological and social research on animals and humans. Like Freud, Bowlby stressed the importance of early mother-infant attachment. He noted that the nature of this attachment serves as the child's working model of the world and helps the child learn to regulate emotions. As discussed in Chapter 3, disturbance of this attachment can lead to impaired emotional adaptation (Cassidy, 1988; Kobak & Sceery, 1988). Children with secure attachments learn how to recognize their own distress and how to seek support from caregivers. However, children with various kinds of insecure attachments may inhibit their support-seeking when distressed, either because they have learned that support will not be forthcoming or

Because baby rhesus monkeys form close attachments to their mothers, they provide an excellent opportunity for researchers to study the consequences of disrupted attachment. Stephen Suomi (1991) has found, for example, that some baby monkeys suffer an emotional reaction similar to depression after being briefly separated from their mothers.

Source: Im Perfect Lazybones/Shutterstock.com.

Connections

What kinds of family relationships might place children at risk for depression? See Chapter 3 for some answers.

because they are fearful of what form the support might take (Kobak & Sceery, 1988; McCauley, Pavlidis, Kendall, 2001).

Support for Bowlby's view comes from the results of animal research. In a series of studies, Stephen Suomi has demonstrated that separating baby rhesus monkeys from their mothers can produce symptoms of depression and anxiety in the infants that mimic the signs of insecure attachment in children (Suomi, 1991). Bowlby suggested that insecure attachments provide a basis for depression because the individual fails to develop successful methods for dealing with the stressors of life and negative emotions such as anxiety.

Interpersonal Theories Bowlby's ideas, along with earlier contributions by Adolf Meyer and Harry Stack Sullivan, laid the groundwork for current interpersonal theories about the origins of depression. These theories emphasize sociocultural and family causes of psychopathology (Karasu, 1990; Klerman, Weissman, & Rounsaville, 1984) and suggest that unsatisfactory relationships during childhood or adult life place people at increased risk for depression. Intimate interpersonal relationships can protect against depression; however, divorce, loss of friendships, and other deterioration in social support are seen as potential triggers for depression (Karasu, 1990; Monroe & Depue, 1991).

But does loss of social support precede or follow depression? James Coyne's (1976) classic interactional model of depression has emerged as one of the most influential frameworks for studying interpersonal aspects of depression (Starr & Davila, 2008). In this model, people with mild depression attempt to assuage feelings of guilt and low self-worth by seeking reassurance from others. At first, others provide support, but people with depression doubt the authenticity of the support and continue to seek reassurance until others grow annoyed and reject them. The rejection exacerbates the symptoms of people with depression as the cycle continues (Starr & Davila, 2008). In short, people with depression may provoke exactly the interpersonal encounters that are most threatening and aversive, thus assuring that their interpersonal relationships become increasingly unstable and contentious (Coyne & Downey, 1991).

Several experiments have shown that people who interact with a person with depression become more depressed, rejecting, and hostile themselves. Other studies have found that the behavior of people with depression adversely affects the mood and behavior of their family members and friends, thereby decreasing the social support otherwise available to individuals with depression (e.g., Coyne et al., 1987). Further, a meta-analysis supported the significant link between excessive reassurance seeking and depression (Starr & Davila, 2008). Finally, romantic partners' criticism may play a significant role in the maintenance of depressive symptoms (Meuwly, Bodenmann, & Coyne, 2012).

In all likelihood, decreased social support is both a contributor to and a consequence of depression. As people with depression withdraw and shut off contact with existing friends and loved ones (as shown in the chapter-opening case about Margaret), fewer and fewer people are available to provide the support and understanding that could lessen their depressed feelings. At the same time, people with depression may place an undue burden on specific friends and partners, and those people might become frustrated and critical, thus exacerbating the depression.

Learning, Cognition, and Depression

Cognitive and behavioral theories seek to explain depression by focusing on current patterns of thinking and reinforcement, rather than on early childhood events per se. These theories fit with interpersonal models of depression described earlier: People with depression lose their social reinforcement or begin to think about themselves differently as a result of their loss of important relationships, which may have been caused, in part, by their own excessive reassurance seeking in the first place. Some of the cognitive-behavioral theories begin with the idea that past learning experiences, including early experiences of loss, can sensitize a person to later losses, but they place greater emphasis on how such losses influence a person's current cognitive processes. Most prominent among these theories are the hopelessness model (Abramson, Metalsky, & Alloy, 1989),

Beck's (1987) seminal cognitive theory, and Nolen-Hoeksema's (1991) response style theory. We discuss these in the context of other important ideas about the psychological causes of depression.

The Role of Reinforcement Peter Lewinsohn and his colleagues (1974, 1979, 1984) proposed that depression develops when people stop receiving adequate positive reinforcement from their environments, while also having many "punishing" experiences. Lewinsohn suggests three general reasons for the development of such reinforcement patterns:

"I'll only give you the paper if you promise not to let the news upset you."

1. An individual's environment may actually contain few positive elements and many negative ones; for example, living in an isolated area would be a deprivation for someone who craves many friendships.
2. Even more important, the individual may lack the skills necessary to obtain positive results or cope with negative consequences; a person who desires friendships may be too shy or fearful of criticism to talk to strangers.
3. The individual may interpret events in a way that minimizes the positive and accentuates the negative, as when a person who desires friendships avoids new acquaintances because they all seem to be "snobs."

If some combination of these environmental and personality characteristics triggers a decrease in people's efforts to obtain life's rewards, a downward spiral of depressed behavior and reduced reward may appear. As the depressed behavior interferes with reward-seeking efforts, the likelihood of finding positive reinforcement is further reduced, causing depression to deepen and eventually to eliminate efforts to find rewards (Lewinsohn, Youngren, & Grosscup, 1979). See Figure 6.2.

Learned Helplessness, Hopelessness, and Depression The twice-revised **hopelessness** model of depression suggests that if people feel they are unable to control life events—especially stressful events—they learn a sense of hopelessness that will eventually lead to depressive symptoms. This theory grew out of research on the response of animals to uncontrollable stressors, an environment that Lewinsohn (see previous section) would describe as having many more "punishers" than positive reinforcers. In this classic (though no longer ethical) research, dogs were exposed to episodes of electric shock from which they could not escape. When these animals later experienced shocks from which they *could* escape, many did not even try to do so; they just tolerated the shock, looking helpless and miserable (Seligman & Maier, 1967).

Similar results were observed in humans who had been exposed to sessions of inescapable aversive noise (Hiroto & Seligman, 1975). These and other results led Martin Seligman (1975) to hypothesize that this **learned helplessness** (a precursor to hopelessness) in humans (1) interferes with the ability to learn responses that could solve or help them cope with life's problems, (2) causes them to give up even trying to solve such problems, and (3) eventually so impairs motivation, mood, and self-efficacy as to leave them in a state of depression. See Figure 6.2.

More recent versions of this model of depression—now known as the hopelessness model—have stressed the importance of the individual's interpretation of aversive events in determining whether a sense of helplessness occurs (Abramson, Seligman, & Teasdale, 1978). People at risk for depression are thought to have a characteristic way of interpreting things that happen to them, known as a **negative attributional style**, which involves

hopelessness: A chronic tendency to view negative events as inevitable and positive events as unlikely, with no prospect for changing this pattern.

learned helplessness: An explanation of depression suggesting that, if people feel chronically unable to control life events, they learn a sense of helplessness that leads to depressive symptoms.

negative attributional style: A tendency to interpret successes in life as the result of external, temporary, and specific factors beyond a person's control, and to interpret failures in life as the result of internal, stable, and global factors within a person.

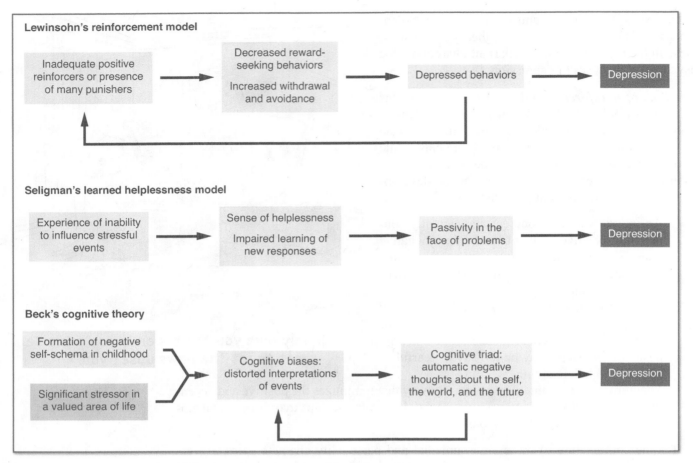

FIGURE 6.2 Psychological Mechanisms Involved in Depression

Peter Lewinsohn, Martin Seligman, and Aaron Beck originally developed important psychological theories describing the development of depression. Each theory has received considerable empirical support, and each has spurred important psychotherapeutic approaches to depression.

three domains: internal, stable, and global (Seligman & Nolen-Hoeksema, 1987). Internal attributions focus on one's own contribution to negative life events ("Getting a bad grade on this test was entirely my fault"). Stable explanations view negative outcomes as enduring and unchangeable ("I will never be able to improve my grade"). Global attributions involve negative inferences about life in general or one's overall self-worth as a result of negative events ("I am a complete idiot, and I will never do well in any college class"). Conversely, people whose thinking is characterized by optimism tend to explain bad events in terms of unstable and specific causes, thereby making hopelessness and depression less likely (e.g., "I will make sure my bad grade won't happen again, plus I'm still doing well in all my other classes"). Hopelessness develops when an individual attributes a negative event to stable and global causes (with the first dimension, internal vs. external causes, significantly less important) and believes that the consequences of the negative event will be dire (Abramson, Metalsky, & Alloy, 1989). Hopelessness theory provides yet another application of a *diathesis-stress model* in which a negative attributional style is the diathesis or predisposition that leads to depression in the face of stressful life events (Metalsky, Joiner, Hardin, & Abramson, 1993).

Beck's Cognitive Triad One of the most influential theories of depression has been and remains Aaron Beck's (1987) *cognitive theory*. According to this theory, vulnerability to depression develops during childhood when basic beliefs about the self are formulated. Beck says that these beliefs—a person's **self-schemas**, such as "I'm likable" or "I'm unlikable"—are determined by the quality of the developing child's interactions with the environment.

self-schemas: Core assumptions and beliefs about the self.

TABLE 6.3 Typical Systematic Errors in the Thinking of People with Depression

Type of Error	Description
Arbitrary inference	Drawing a specific conclusion without solid evidence (e.g., assuming someone does not like you without any proof)
Selective abstraction	Taking a piece of data out of context (e.g., if your boss gives you nine compliments and one constructive criticism, you would come away thinking you are a bad employee)
Overgeneralization	Drawing a general rule or conclusion on the basis of isolated incidents (e.g., thinking the universe is against you because you spilled your coffee and did poorly on a test that same day)
Magnification and minimization	Overfocusing on a perceived failure and ignoring or discounting a perceived success (e.g., thinking that the test you did poorly on will cause you to fail out of school and that the test you aced was easy)
Personalization	Assuming that other people's behavior is about you (e.g., thinking that people are in a bad mood today because of you)
Dichotomous (all-or-none) thinking	Placing all experiences in one of two opposite categories, positive and negative (e.g., thinking that if you do not win "employee of the month" this time, then you are a bad employee)

Source: Adapted from Beck, Rush, Shaw, & Emery, 1979.

Negative self-schemas may have little influence until they are activated by the threat that accompanies significant life stressors. For example, in the chapter-opening case, Margaret placed high value on her popularity and her academic achievement; after the breakup of her relationship, she began to falter in both of these areas. When a person suffers a loss in the arena that he or she values most, negative self-schemas become activated as the person's thinking and interpretation of events become distorted, In fact, Beck, Rush, Shaw, & Emery (1979) identified several cognitive distortions or "thinking errors" that characterize how people with depression process information (see Table 6.3). These irrational thoughts pop up involuntarily ("automatic thoughts") to bias people's view of events. Soon, the person begins to see neutral or even pleasant events in a negative light. For example, Margaret might interpret her professor's compliments as insincere or her friend's cancellation of dinner plans as a sign of rejection and her waning popularity. As a consequence of these cognitive processes, the person begins to experience sadness and other symptoms of depression, including loss of motivation and interest in activities, which could make the cognitions even more negative.

Ultimately, the thinking of people with depression is characterized by a **cognitive triad** of automatic, repetitive, and negative thoughts about the self, the world, and the future (Beck et al., 1979). Individuals with depression see themselves as inadequate and, therefore, worthless; they perceive the world's demands as overwhelming; and they dread that the future will bring nothing but more of the same (similar to the hopelessness model discussed earlier).

cognitive triad: Automatic, repetitive, and negative thoughts about the self, the world, and the future that are characteristic of people with depression.

In general, research supports Beck's ideas that people with depression engage in an excess of negative thinking, are prone to the negative triad of beliefs, and tend to distort even positive feedback as negative (Beck & Alford, 2009). See Figure 6.2. It is less clear whether these dysfunctional cognitions precede or follow the onset of depression (Haaga, Dyck, & Ernst, 1991; Gotlib et al., 2014). In fact, studies have shown that such dysfunctions may be both the cognitive consequences of being depressed *and* the long-term styles of thinking that predispose people to either first or subsequent depressive episodes (Otto et al., 2007). However, negative self-schemas did predict depressive episodes and severity

"He puts a positive spin on everything."

The way people interpret their life events and whether they develop learned helplessness has to do with their attributional style and cognitive schemas.

9 years later (Halvorsen, Wang, Eisemann, & Waterloo, 2010), and children at familial risk for depression who were not (yet) depressed themselves showed depression-prone cognitive styles prior to their depressive symptoms (Gotlib et al., 2014).

Other studies provide support for combined models/theories of depression. For instance, perceived trauma and insecure adult attachment (discussed earlier) predicted cognitive schemas such as irrational beliefs, which in turn predicted depression (Riggs & Han, 2009). Moreover, interpersonal schemas—irrational beliefs about other people—may be particularly important in cognitive vulnerability to depression (Dozois, 2007). Findings from the Cognitive Vulnerability to Depression (CVD) Project, a prospective and collaborative two-site study, provided strong support for both the hopelessness and cognitive models of depression (Alloy, Abramson, Grant, & Liu, 2009), and these two theories also show promise for explaining depression in children and adolescents (Lakdawalla, Hankin, & Mermelstein, 2007). In another study offering support for both of these cognitive theories, hopelessness interacted with stress to predict adolescent depression 1 year later, whereas positive cognitive styles and low stress levels were protective factors for females specifically (Morris, Ciesla, & Garber, 2008).

Response Style, Personality, and Depression

Major life stressors, especially in the form of loss or trauma, appear to be social factors that can trigger depressive reactions, as we discuss further later in the chapter. They do not always do so, however. Why do some people become depressed after a trauma while others do not? According to response styles theory, the way people define and cope with stressors is essential in determining the severity and length of a depressive episode (Nolen-Hoeksema, Morrow, & Fredrickson, 1993).

For example, using *distraction* as a way of coping with stressful events appears to soften the events' impact and help ameliorate depression. Distracting responses, such as doing something fun with a friend, may be beneficial because they allow people to temporarily get their minds off their depression, while also providing an opportunity for positive feedback from others. However, *ruminative* responses tend to amplify and prolong periods of depression, as the individual obsesses about the causes, symptoms, or consequences of depression (Nolen-Hoeksema et al., 1993). Ruminative responses include endlessly thinking, writing, or talking about the depression in an effort to understand it. As suggested by Pyzsczynski and Greenberg's (1987) self-awareness model of depression, excessive ruminative responses may keep the individual so obsessed with depression as to alienate those who might provide social support and, at the same time, may preclude more rewarding social interactions. For instance, Margaret (from the chapter-opening case) made her symptoms worse by withdrawing from her parents, her friends, and her classmates in the wake of her relationship breakup.

Susan Nolen-Hoeksema (1987) has proposed that men and women differ in their characteristic responses to stressors and that these differences may explain why women are more prone to depression. She points out that, in many cultures, socialization throughout childhood teaches boys to emphasize action rather than feelings and teaches girls to be introspective and passive. Consequently, when faced with stressors, men are more likely than women to employ beneficial distracting strategies, whereas women fall into ruminative patterns that accentuate personal responsibility for the problems at hand and therefore facilitate depression. Indeed, research indicates that, in both men and women, learning to decrease ruminative responses and increase distracting strategies leads to improvement in depressed mood (Morrow & Nolen-Hoeksema, 1990; Nolen-Hoeksema et al., 1993).

Several studies have investigated the neural mechanisms—what is happening in the brain—for these three prominent psychological theories of depression: hopelessness, Beck's cognitive model, and response styles theory (Auerbach, Webb, Gardiner, & Pechtel, 2013). This psychobiological research, which centers chiefly on frontal lobe and limbic system structures and functions, has found support for each model (Auerbach et al., 2013). For instance, the amygdala (part of the limbic system) may be critically implicated in the negative self-referential processing that leads to rumination (Auerbach et al., 2013). In addition, high rumination was associated with delayed post-stressor cortisol recovery among adolescents with depression, indicating another possible cognitive-biological connection (Stewart, Mazurka, Bond, Wynne-Edwards, & Harkness, 2013).

Actor Ewan McGregor (famous for his role in *Star Wars*—see photo) has acknowledged bouts of depression, as have a number of other creative people, including talk-show guru Oprah Winfrey, late-night TV host Conan O'Brien, singers Beyoncé Knowles and Gwen Stefani (who claimed depression was the reason she dyed her hair pink in 2000), actors Jim Carey and Angelina Jolie, and baseball players Zach Greinke and Ken Griffey, Jr.

Creativity and Depression

An ongoing line of research may help illuminate the depression-rumination connection. Remember the link between bipolar disorders and creativity discussed in Chapter 5? Studies of creative individuals and historical analyses have shown an even stronger link between creative behavior and depression (Verhaeghen, Joorman, & Khan, 2005). For instance, in his survey of the biographies of 1,004 eminent individuals living in the 20th century, Ludwig (1995) found a lifetime prevalence of depression of 50% for people working in the creative arts, compared with 20% of those in the field of enterprise, 24% of scientists, and 27% of important social figures. A common underlying psychological characteristic—a tendency for self-reflective rumination—may be the source of this correlation; specifically, self-reflection appears to independently increase the risk for depression and also spurs interest in and ability for creative behavior (Verhaeghen et al., 2005).

Other research has shown that there may be two distinct types of rumination: *brooding*, which is characterized by a neurotic tendency to dwell passively on undesirable aspects of the self and the sense that one's feelings are threatening, confusing, and inescapable; and *reflectiveness*, which is characterized by an openness to explore negative feelings, a sense that one's feelings are clear and controllable, and a willingness to contemplate strategies for alleviating unpleasant feelings (Trapnell & Campbell, 1999). How individuals ruminate determines whether they will be more prone to creativity or depression: Reflectiveness has a positive effect on creative behaviors but no effect on low mood, and brooding is linked positively to low mood but has no effect on creativity (Verhaeghen, Joormann, & Aikman, 2014).

The Value of Depression

The psychological models just reviewed suggest that depression is associated with problems in cognitive processing, particularly with distorted, negatively biased thinking. Other research suggests, however, that distortion or bias at certain junctures may be more characteristic of nondepressed people and that depression may actually have several positive aspects to it, in addition to creativity.

Shelley Taylor (1994) and her colleagues (Taylor & Brown, 1988) have found that most nondepressed people have views of themselves, their accomplishments, and their futures that are slightly unrealistic. They also tend to selectively remember the positive aspects of their lives, a style similar to what Seligman called "optimism." This tendency to see themselves and the future in a positive, if slightly illusory, light appears to promote feelings of happiness (Gibbons, 1986; Taylor & Brown, 1988), adaptive social functioning (Diener, 1984), the capacity for productive work (Isen, Daubman, & Nowicki, 1987), and a measure of protection from the stress of life (Taylor & Brown, 1988). Research seems to converge on the adaptive value of positive illusions in the short term, and these may be particularly constructive in instances that would typically incur depression and lack of motivation (Robins & Beer, 2001). One study, for example, showed that adolescents who were below average in their math achievement overestimated their performance, and their positive illusions were negatively related to depressive symptoms (Noble, Heath, & Toste, 2011).

Taylor (1994) believes that depression may result from perceiving life without the protective benefits of rose-colored glasses; as a result, people with depression are often more deliberate, careful, and skeptical—and at times more accurate—in how they process information from their environment (Rottenberg, 2014). Thus, negative cognitive processes of people with depression may simply reflect an unforgivingly accurate pattern of self-judgment. For this reason, some investigators refer to people with depression as "sadder but wiser" (Alloy & Abramson, 1979, 1988).

In fact, research suggests that other aspects of depression—in addition to creativity and accuracy—may also be valuable in certain situations. For instance, the dark pull of depressive disorders may arise from adaptations that evolved to help our ancestors ensure their survival (Rottenberg, 2014). Low mood may operate as a kind of "stop mechanism," activated in situations in which persisting in a goal is likely to be futile or even dangerous (Rottenberg, 2014). Numerous experiments demonstrate that negative affect can improve memory performance, reduce judgmental errors, improve motivation, and result in more effective interpersonal strategies (Forgas, 2013). Further, some researchers suggest that depression—with its links to the immune system and inflammatory response described earlier in the chapter—may even help individuals fight existing infections (Anders, Tanaka, & Kinney, 2013). However, whereas low mood may have worked well for our ancestors, our modern environment—in which daily survival is no longer a sole focus and life stressors take on a more chronic form—makes it all too easy for a sad mood to slide into severe, long-lasting depression (Rottenberg, 2014).

MAPS - Attempted Answers

Section Review

Depressive disorders are influenced by several psychological factors, including:

- early experiences with loss or disappointment that may make a person unusually sensitive to later adversities;
- insecure attachments that leave a child less able to feel worthwhile, regulate emotions, and be satisfied in intimate relationships;
- a relative lack of positive reinforcement and an excess of punishment;
- a perceived lack of control over important events, leading to hopelessness;
- distorted thinking in which a person exaggerates negative aspects about the self, the world, and the future and ignores or minimizes positive information;
- a tendency to perseverate or ruminate about the self, particularly brooding about inescapable faults or failures; and
- the possibility that some aspects of depression (such as low mood) may have been advantageous to our ancestors for a variety of reasons.

Social Causes of Depressive Disorders

One of the key social causes of depression is likely the nature of our modern world. Differences in the prevalence of depression across cultures and generations underscore the potentially important role of the environment. Two well-done, large-scale studies revealed that the lifetime prevalence of depression in young people growing up in the 1990s exceeded by roughly a factor of 10 the prevalence in young people growing up in the 1950s (Seligman, 1990). As Figure 6.3 shows, there is also evidence that the rise in de-

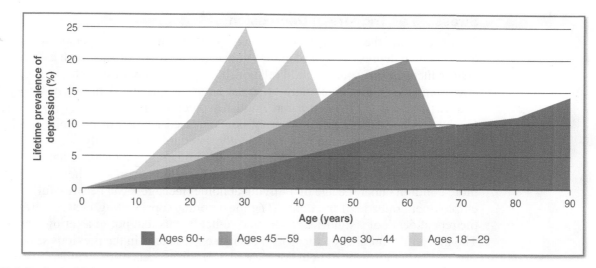

FIGURE 6.3 Age Changes in Depression

According to one large-scale study of over 9,000 Americans, more people are becoming depressed and are experiencing their first major depressive episodes at increasingly earlier ages. The graph shows how the youngest cohort in the study (18–29-year-olds) has already had a higher lifetime prevalence (almost 25% depressed) than any other cohort. Depression expert Constance Hammen discusses the reasons behind these alarming trends in the feature "A Conversation With" that closes this chapter.

Source: Based on data from Kessler et al. (2003).

pression over the second half of the last century has continued into this one: In Denmark, rates of depression more than doubled in the first 6 years of the new millennium (Andersen, Thielen, Bech, Nygaard, & Diderichsen, 2011), whereas chronicity and symptoms in the United States have continued to increase in women (Eaton, Kalaydjian, Scharfstein, Mezuk, & Ding, 2007) and in adolescent populations (Bertha & Balázs, 2013). Martin Seligman (1998), then president of the American Psychological Association, spoke to the National Press Club about an American depression epidemic:

> We discovered two astonishing things about the rate of depression across the century. The first was there is now between 10 and 20 times as much of it as there was 50 years ago. And the second is that it has become a young person's problem. . . .

These changes have occurred over too brief a time span to be explained by genetic factors. Psychologist Stephen Ilardi (2009) began examining the social causes of depressive disorder after being inspired by the extraordinary resilience of aboriginal groups like the Kaluli of Papua New Guinea, who rarely suffer from depression. The Kaluli practice a similar lifestyle to our ancestors, as they hunt, forage, and garden for their food, and live what we might consider very challenging lives, with none of the material comforts or medical advances that we often take for granted. So what is it about the Kaluli lifestyle that makes depression so rare (about 0.05% or 1 in 2,000 people, compared to 20–25% in our culture)?

There may be something about modern industrialized life that creates fertile soil for depression (Seligman, 1990). Rising depression rates are thought to reflect the growing influence of social stressors, such as disintegration of the family, unemployment, increased mobility, violence, and the resulting disillusionment found particularly in urban populations (Gershon, Hamovit, Guroff, & Nurnberger,, 1987). As Ilardi (2013) put it in his excellent TEDx talk at Emory University: "We were never designed for the sedentary, indoor, socially isolated, fast-food-laden, sleep-deprived, frenzied pace of modern life." Seligman (1990) further suggests that the modern Western exaltation of the self, along with the weakening of common institutions (such as religious or cultural organizations), has made it so that when people do not succeed at something, they have few larger beliefs to fall back on for consolation. In his view, hope lies in striking a healthier balance between commitment to the self and dedication to the common good (Seligman, 1990).

Stressors as Triggers of Depression

As noted, many theorists view depression from a diathesis-stress perspective (see Figure 6.4) in which depressive symptoms do not emerge until a diathesis such as genetic risk or disturbances in early parent-child relationships combines with stressful events or harmful environments. In a classic study of social environment and depression, George Brown and Tirril Harris (1978) compared English women being treated in a psychiatric clinic for depression with a control group of nondepressed women from similar backgrounds. They found that depression was more likely if certain vulnerability factors were coupled with specific stressors or "provoking agents." Vulnerability factors (diatheses) included lack of a close confidant or friend; death of their mother in childhood, having four or more children under the age of 14 living at home (teenagers can be stressful!), and lack of employment outside of the home. The most common provoking factors (stressors) were the recent death of a significant person or other events that posed a serious threat of loss. The greater the number of stressors a woman experienced in the previous several months, the greater her chances of being depressed. Certain aspects of the women's current social situations—especially a lack of social support—increased the risk of depression following a loss (Brown & Harris, 1978).

Subsequent research has consistently documented that onset or relapse of depression is more likely following a major loss, either of a significant relationship through death or divorce or loss of self-worth related to unemployment or the like (Brown, Adler, & Bifulco, 1988; Monroe & Depue, 1991). Both acute and chronic stressors have been implicated in depression (Harkness, Theriault, Stewart, & Bagby, 2014). For instance, after the 2010 BP Deepwater Horizon oil spill spewed more than 200 million gallons of oil into the Gulf of Mexico, more than 80% of those who suffered loss of income became de-

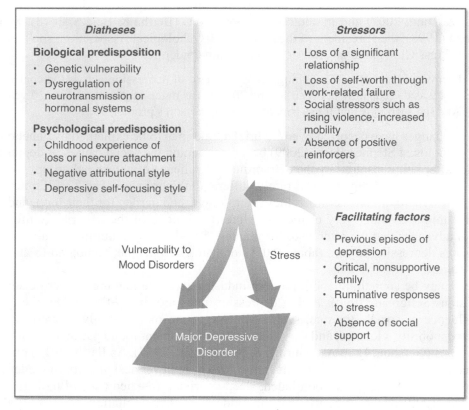

FIGURE 6.4 A Diathesis-Stress Perspective on Major Depressive Disorder

There are a multitude of theories about major depressive disorder and a multitude of biopsychosocial factors that might be involved in its etiology. Perhaps there are also many ways in which the disorder develops. Shown here are the major factors we have discussed that seem to play a role.

pressed in the following year (Morris, Grattan, Mayer, & Blackburn, 2013). Peer stressors through adolescence increase the incidence of depressive disorders, especially in the context of poor relationships with parents during that span (Hazel, Oppenheimer, Technow, Young, & Hankin, 2014). Academic stressors, such as Margaret's falling college grades in the chapter-opening case, can also contribute to or maintain symptoms of depression (O'Reilly, McNeill, Mavor, & Anderson, 2014). Interestingly, adult women were significantly more likely to report a severe life event prior to major depressive disorder onset than were adult men, although this gender difference was not present in adolescent depression (Harkness et al., 2010).

Stressful family environments also influence the course of a depressive disorder (Davila, Hammen, Burge, & Paley, 1995). For example, individuals with depression who live with highly critical, unsupportive families with poor problem-solving skills are more likely to suffer recurrent episodes of depression and be less able to get back to a productive life than those whose families have a more positive emotional climate (Hooley, 1987; Miller et al., 1992). Higher expressed emotion—indicated by family members' making more than a specified threshold number of critical comments or showing any signs of hostility or emotional overinvolvement during the interview—was associated with a greater likelihood of having a future onset of a depressive episode in high-risk and children and adolescents with depression (Silk et al., 2009). Further, continued exposure to maternal criticism appears to be an important risk factor for initial depression in children (Burkhouse, Uhrlass, Stone, Knopik, & Gibb, 2012).

Connections

Does a negative emotional climate in families ("expressed emotion") contribute to relapses of other types of mental disorders? For more on this subject, see Chapter 4.

Section Review

Our modern social environment may be a poor fit for our current bodies and brains, with a lack of outdoor activity, improper nutrition and sleep, and an inappropriate pace of life leading to a rise in depression compared to previous generations.

Depressive disorders are also influenced by other social factors, such as exposure to major stressful events, especially if these events:

- occur to someone lacking in social support or with a critical family, and
- involve some kind of chronic or acute loss.

Treatment of Depressive Disorders

During the last six-plus decades, clinicians have made significant progress in developing and testing both biological and psychological treatments for depressive disorders. Here, we consider the results of some of this work.

Drug Treatments for Depressive Disorders

Drugs have been used to treat depressive disorders for many years, with varying effectiveness. Researchers discovered the first **antidepressants** purely by chance in the 1950s. Seeking a treatment for schizophrenia, scientists at the Munsterlingen asylum in Switzerland found that a drug that tweaked the balance of the brain's neurotransmitters sent patients into bouts of euphoria. On first trying it in 1955, some patients became newly sociable and energetic and called the drug a "miracle cure." The drug, called imipramine and marketed as Tofranil in 1958, was quickly followed by dozens of rivals—known as tricyclics for their three-ring chemical structure—as drug companies rushed to take advantage of a burgeoning market (Fitzpatrick, 2010). Tricyclics have now largely been replaced as the first-line drug treatment of depression by selective serotonin reuptake inhibitors (SSRIs, discussed shortly), and there is also a third (less widely used) class of antidepressant medications called monoamine oxidase inhibitors (Nemeroff & Schatzberg, 2007).

antidepressants: A broad class of medications commonly used in the treatment of depressive and sometimes bipolar disorders; these drugs include monoamine oxidase inhibitors, tricyclics, and selective serotonin reuptake inhibitors (SSRIs), such as Prozac.

The net effect of antidepressant drug action is to alter activity in the brain cells that use norepinephrine, serotonin, and other mood-related neurotransmitters discussed earlier in the chapter. The best-known antidepressants fall into the three categories already mentioned:

monoamine oxidase (MAO) inhibitor: A drug that blocks monoamine oxidase, an enzyme that breaks down neurotransmitters such as serotonin and norepinephrine, resulting in greater availability of these neurotransmitters at neural synapses.

tricyclics: Drugs used primarily to treat depression; they increase levels of neurotransmitters such as norepinephrine and serotonin by blocking their reuptake.

selective serotonin reuptake inhibitors (SSRIs): A type of drug used to treat mental disorders such as depression that works by slowing the reuptake of serotonin in the brain.

- **Monoamine oxidase (MAO) inhibitors**, such as phenelzine (sold as Nardil) and tranylcypromine (sold as Parnate), block monoamine oxidase, an enzyme that breaks down neurotransmitters such as serotonin and norepinephrine, resulting in greater availability of these neurotransmitters at neural synapses.

- **Tricyclics**, such as imipramine (sold as Tofranil), amitriptyline (sold as Elavil), and desipramine (sold as Norpramin), also increase levels of neurotransmitters such as norepinephrine and serotonin, but they do so by blocking the reuptake of these neurotransmitters.

- **Selective serotonin reuptake inhibitors (SSRIs)** include fluoxetine (sold as Prozac), sertraline (sold as Zoloft), citalopram (sold as Celexa), and paroxetine (sold as Paxil). These drugs slow the reabsorption of serotonin by the neurons that secrete it, thus keeping more serotonin in the synapse longer. There are also drugs that act as serotonin-norepinephrine reuptake inhibitors (SNRIs), such as venlafaxine (sold as Effexor) and duloxetine (sold as Cymbalta). Another antidepressant—bupropion (sold as Wellbutrin)—acts by blocking reuptake of dopamine.

Studies suggest that 50–60% of adults with depression are helped by these antidepressant medications, with various therapeutic effects, including brightened mood, improved sleep, and increased energy (Ruhé, Huyser, Swinkels, & Schene, 2006). Antidepressants may work better for persistent depressive disorder than for major depression (von Wolff, Hölzel, Westphal, Härter, & Kriston, 2013).

Although the chemical action of many antidepressants is known, it is still unclear how they actually alter depressive symptoms. For example, antidepressants have an immediate impact on neurotransmitter levels, but depressive symptoms usually are not alleviated until after at least 2 weeks (and sometimes up to 8 weeks) of treatment. However, some studies suggest that antidepressants can work as early as 3 days after treatment and that early response may even predict eventual outcome (Katz, Bowden, Berman, & Frazer, 2006; Posternak & Zimmerman, 2005). In any case, scientists speculate that this delay—ranging from days to weeks—may reflect the time it takes for neuronal receptors to adapt to changes in neurotransmitter levels (Frazer & Benmansour, 2002). In other words, it may be a change in how brain cells use neurotransmitters—and not simply the levels of available neurotransmitters—that is critical to symptom reduction. Still others have postulated that antidepressants do not act as direct mood enhancers but rather change the relative balance of positive to negative emotional processing and actually work in a manner consistent with cognitive theories of depression (Harmer, Goodwin, & Cowen, 2009).

In clinical studies of antidepressants, approximately one third of people with depression achieve a full remission, one third experience a response, and one third are nonresponders (Tranter, O'Donovan, Chandarana, & Kennedy, 2002). Several meta-analyses have even suggested that the differences between drug and placebo are not clinically significant for most people with depression (Kirsch, 2009); in other words, much of the response to antidepressant medications may be due to the placebo effect (see Chapter 2), which results from the person's expectancy and conditioning, rather than any specific chemical action of the drug per se. A few years ago, one meta-analysis (Fournier et al., 2010) rocked the media and the pharmaceutical industry with the following conclusion:

> The magnitude of benefit of antidepressant medication compared with placebo increases with severity of depression symptoms and may be minimal or nonexistent, on average, in patients with mild or moderate symptoms. For patients with very severe depression, the benefit of medications over placebo is substantial.

Interestingly, herbal antidepressants such as hypericum (a medicinal plant known as St. John's wort) have also produced similar effects to prescribed medications in treating depression (Walach & Kirsch, 2003). Whereas hypericum showed only minor effects over placebo (Linde, Berner, Egger, & Mulrow, 2005), it worked as well as SSRIs with significantly fewer withdrawals (i.e., people who stopped taking the pills) due to side

MAPS - Medical Myths

effects (Rahimi, Nikfar, & Abdollahi, 2009). Finally, there is little evidence that either of the common medical practices of augmentation (prescribing more than one antidepressant at a time) or switching (prescribing a different antidepressant if no response is observed to the first medication) are effective treatment options, despite their widespread usage in clinical practice (Bschor & Baethge, 2010; Yury, Fisher, Antonuccio, Valenstein, & Matuszak, 2009).

The STAR*D (Sequenced Treatment Alternatives to Relieve Depression) project has been the largest antidepressant clinical trial in the United States to date conducted without pharmaceutical company support and continues to stimulate debate (Insel & Wang, 2009). Fewer than 30% of participants achieved remission—enough of a reduction in their depressive symptoms that they were no longer diagnosable—at each treatment phase of the trial, and the percentage decreased with each phase a few months apart (Sinyor, Schaffer, & Levitt, 2010). Of the 4,041 people enrolled in STAR*D, all of whom were initially started on citalopram (Celexa, an SSRI), only 1,518 of them (37.6%) obtained remission after up to four medication trials over a year, and only 108 (7.1%) survived continuing care without relapsing and/or dropping out of the study (Pigott, 2011). One researcher (Ghaemi, 2008), reflecting on STAR*D and other outcome studies, concluded: "The widely held clinical view of 'antidepressants' as highly effective and specific for the treatment of all types of depressive disorders is exaggerated."

Despite these significant limitations, in 2011, the Centers for Disease Control and Prevention reported that antidepressant use in the United States had increased nearly 400% in the last 2 decades, making antidepressants the most frequently used class of medications by Americans ages 18–44 (Levine, 2013). By 2008, 23% of women ages 40–59 were taking antidepressants (Levine, 2013). With direct-to-consumer advertising from the pharmaceutical companies legally permitted since 1997, antidepressant use in the United States doubled over the following decade (Olfson & Marcus, 2009). As a result, the world's 11 largest drug companies (6 of which are headquartered in the United States) made a net profit of $711.4 billion from 2003 to 2012, and "Big Pharma" remains the largest political lobbying group worldwide (Drugwatch, n.d.). See the "Controversy" feature for more on this topic.

The major types of antidepressants are all about equally effective, so the choice of which one to prescribe depends on a variety of other considerations (Del Re, Spielmans, Flückiger, & Wampold, 2013). Common side effects include sluggishness, weight gain, sexual dysfunction (especially with SSRIs), suicidal ideation (Smith, 2009), and with tricyclics, possible death from overdose (Palmer, Kleinman, Taylor, & Revicki, 1998). FDA (2007) warning labels on these drugs further state that suicidality, anxiety, agitation, panic attacks, insomnia, irritability, hostility, aggressiveness, impulsivity, akathisia (psychomotor restlessness), hypomania, and mania have been reported in people being treated with antidepressants. The tricyclics also have cardiac side effects and can trigger manic episodes in people prone to bipolar disorder (Geller, Fox, & Fletcher, 1993; Prien & Potter, 1993), and some MAO inhibitors cause high blood pressure if combined with certain foods.

Ideally, drug treatment of depressive disorders begins with the gradual introduction of medication, followed by a period of active treatment lasting for 4 to 6 months after depressive symptoms have been alleviated (Andreasen & Black, 1991). Further to this, antidepressant *prophylaxis*—sustained treatment for a few years or indefinitely—may be beneficial in any person with a history of three or more major depressive episodes, or two or more episodes in the last 5 years (Montgomery, 2006). Some clinical guidelines suggest switching to a different antidepressant at 3 months if remission does not occur (Olgiati, Bajo, Bigelli, Montgomery, & Serretti, 2013). One of the issues with these medications is that they should

"What is the point of filling my prescription? My primary care doctor told me that the medication would only work if I took it while drinking an organic fruit smoothie lying on a tropical beach with waves lapping at the shore and a majestic orange sunset on the horizon after I finished my surfing lesson. . . ."

Prozac: Wonder Drug or Perilous Pill?

Since it was introduced in the late 1980s, Prozac (fluoxetine, an SSRI) has been at the center of a storm of controversy. Heralded by some as a wonder drug and condemned by others as a dangerous substance, Prozac has been prescribed to over 40 million people worldwide. Headlined in major news publications and the topic of countless TV talk shows, the debate over Prozac rages on.

Advocates for Prozac, including Peter Kramer, the psychiatrist whose book *Listening to Prozac* (1993) popularized the drug for millions of readers, claim that it relieves depression and is also safer than other antidepressants. According to case reports, Prozac can even improve basic personality features, helping shy introverts become assertive extroverts or converting pessimists into optimists. No wonder Prozac is known in some circles as the drug that can help people become "better than well." In the book and later feature film *Prozac Nation*, the author laments that the drug did not really work for her but describes it as "a pill that doesn't make you happy but does make you feel not sad" (Wurtzel, 1995, p. 340).

Critics of Prozac blame it for a number of problems, including what they claim is a heightened risk for suicide and violent behavior among people taking the drug. They point to incidents such as on September 14, 1989, when Joseph Wesbecker opened fire on his coworkers in a printing plant in Kentucky with an AK-47 assault rifle. By the end of his rampage, Wesbecker had killed 8 people and wounded 12 more before turning the gun on himself and taking his own life. When it was subsequently discovered that Wesbecker had begun taking Prozac about a month before the shootings, families of the victims filed a lawsuit against Eli Lilly, the manufacturer of Prozac. This lawsuit, the first of hundreds like it across the nation, claimed that Prozac causes previously nondangerous people to turn violent.

Whereas the Westbecker case (resolved in 1994) and many others like it ended with judges or juries deciding that Prozac was not responsible for the violence, a precedent-setting case in Canada in 2011 had a different result. In the 2011 case, Judge Robert Heinrichs listened to expert psychiatric testimony for the defense by Peter Breggin, MD and agreed that Prozac caused a stimulant-like syndrome leading to manic-like behavior, suicidality, and violence in a teenage high school student with no prior history of violence who, while chatting in his home with two friends, abruptly stabbed one of them to death with a single wound to the chest.

Accordingly, the risk of possible dangerous side effects, plus the ethical concerns about a drug that offers the false promise of making over personalities, is the topic of *Talking Back to Prozac* (Breggin & Breggin, 1994), a book intended to refute Kramer's book. The Breggins pick through the studies used to justify Prozac's safety, often uncovering flaws and shoddy science, and detail the FDA approval process, including who on the panel was paid by whom. Other books in the new millennium have attacked the pharmaceutical industry even more directly. *Let Them Eat Prozac: The Unhealthy Relationship Between the Pharmaceutical Industry and Depression* (Healy, 2004) draws on the author's own research and expertise to demonstrate the potential hazards associated with these drugs and Big Pharma's abuses of power (and the author's own bad experiences with the industry). *Medicines Out of Control? Antidepressants and the Conspiracy of Goodwill* (Medawar & Hardon, 2004) is another broad-scale critique of drug companies and their regulation in England and the United States. More recently, *Antidepressants and Advertising: Marketing Happiness* (Hunter, 2007) examines the volatile issue of marketing antidepressants through direct-to-consumer appeals, which is only legal in the United States (since 1997) and New Zealand (since 1981) among Western nations.

So what evidence is there for the pro- and anti-Prozac positions? First, thoughts about suicide and violence do sometimes increase in a small number of people who are treated with antidepressant medication. After individuals take their medicine and begin to feel less depressed, their energy level rises, thereby increasing, at least temporarily, their risk for harming themselves or others. Moreover, the U.S. Food and Drug Administration (FDA; 2004) issued warnings that use of antidepressant medications poses a small but significantly increased risk of suicidal ideation/suicide attempt for children and adolescents. However, subsequent research has shown that antidepressants reduce more suicides in children than they produce (Bridge et al., 2007), and FDA warnings since 2007 point out that scientific data did not show this increased risk in adults older than 24 and that adults ages 65 and older taking antidepressants actually have a decreased risk of suicidality (U.S. Food and Drug Administration, 2007). Further, Prozac is the only selective serotonin reuptake inhibitor (SSRI) currently approved by the FDA to treat moderate to severe depression in children 8 years of age and older (Guirguis-Blake, Wright, & Rich, 2008).

Both sides in this controversy have often relied on dramatic anecdotes and uncontrolled case histories rather than well-designed scientific studies to support their arguments. As a result, both proponents and opponents of Prozac have exaggerated the powers of the drug, and the public has been too influenced by the

Prozac: Wonder Drug or Perilous Pill? *(Continued)*

latest incident reported in the media. The likely truth is that Prozac works for some people in some situations and not others, but that psychotherapy is a better first-line treatment for depression and related issues, as described later in this chapter.

Thinking Critically

1. What other factors besides medication might account for suicides by people with depression?

2. How often does any adverse effect of a medication need to occur before it is considered a serious side effect? Is once enough, or should several examples be required before we decide that the risks of the drug outweigh its benefits?

3. Has the development and widespread marketing of Prozac and other drugs helped or hurt our society?

be gradually reduced if the person wants to discontinue drug treatment, as sudden withdrawal can cause several unpleasant side effects (Prien & Potter, 1993).

Other Biological Treatments for Depressive Disorders

In the 1930s, clinicians noted the remission of psychotic and depressive symptoms in some people who experienced spontaneous seizures (Endler, 1988). On the assumption that the convulsions were responsible for the improvement, **electroconvulsive therapy (ECT)** was developed at a clinic at the University of Rome in Italy—and imported to the United States in the 1940s—to purposely induce brief seizures in individuals with severe mental disorders by passing an electric current through their brains (Endler, 1988).

The early ECT treatments were frightening procedures associated with many negative side effects (Winokur, 1986), including broken bones due to muscle stiffening during the ECT-induced seizures, marked memory loss, periods of disorientation, and even some deaths. Consequently, throughout the 1960s and 1970s, clinicians and hospitals began to limit or abandon the use of ECT.

To minimize problematic side effects, ECT is now administered only on one side of the head (a procedure known as *unilateral ECT*) and is accompanied by medication to control heart rate and relax muscles. Oxygen is also administered because most people stop breathing on their own during the seizure activity (Avery, 1993; Winokur, 1986). These precautions have eliminated ECT's most serious long-term side effects, although temporary memory loss and disorientation are still common, and one third of people treated with ECT still report persistent memory loss (Rose, Wykes, Leese, Bindman, & Fleischmann, 2003).

The use of ECT persists in spite of these difficulties because it is somewhat effective for people whose depression is severe or who do not respond to antidepressant medication (UK ECT Review Group, 2003). Remission rates of just over 50% have been reported for people with depression following treatment with ECT (Berlim, Van den Eynde, & Daskalakis, 2013; Dierckx, Heijnen, van den Broek, & Birkenhäger, 2012). In addition, the efficacy of ECT has been found to be better in people without previous pharmacotherapy failure, as compared with people for whom antidepressants did not work (Heijnen, Birkenhäger, Wierdsma, & van den Broek, 2010).

However, relapse remains a problem. Even with continuation treatment of some sort (e.g., medication), over half of the people who initially respond well to ECT suffer a recurrence of their depressive disorder in the next year (Jelovac, Kolshus, & McLoughlin, 2013). Furthermore, ECT was once thought to be the treatment of choice for people with melancholic depression (discussed earlier in the chapter) but that turns out not to be the case (Rasmussen, 2011). Finally, it is still not clear why ECT works, although it appears that the seizure, not the shock itself, is somehow responsible and that ECT affects the activity of neurotransmitters (Fink, 2013). One research team hypothesizes that ECT affects the brain in a similar manner as severe stress or brain trauma in that it activates the HPA

electroconvulsive therapy (ECT): A treatment for severe depression that induces brief seizures through the use of an electric current.

axis (discussed earlier) and the dopamine system at the same time as it reduces activity in the frontal and temporal lobes (Fosse & Read, 2013). Another theory stipulates that ECT changes the wiring in the hippocampus and amygdala, key components of the brain's limbic system (Tendolkar et al., 2013). Overall, though, the uncertainty surrounding its mechanism of action, its inherently frightening nature, and its negative side effects make ECT one of the most controversial treatments currently in use for depressive disorders.

One proposed therapeutic alternative to ECT has been repetitive transcranial magnetic stimulation (rTMS), a noninvasive technique for modulating cortical and subcortical function through the use of rapidly changing electromagnetic fields generated by a coil placed over the scalp (George & Post, 2011). However, the remission rates with rTMS have been significantly lower (34%) than those with ECT (52%; Berlim, Van den Eynde, & Daskalakis, 2013).

light therapy: Exposing patients to a bright light source during the early morning hours to reduce symptoms of seasonal depression and to correct problems in body temperature or hormone output.

Another biological treatment—one with far fewer risks—being employed for depressive disorders is **light therapy**, especially with depression that has a seasonal pattern (discussed earlier in the chapter). Individuals with these disorders appear to develop a phase delay in their circadian rhythms due to reductions in the amount of early morning light they experience (Avery et al., 1990; Lewy et al., 1987). Light therapy consists of exposure to bright lights during the day as well as "dawn simulation," a bright light source that comes on gradually during the early morning beginning about 2 hours before normal waking (Avery et al., 1994). It has been associated with remission of the symptoms of seasonal pattern depression and also appears to correct phase delays in functions such as body temperature and hormone output (Lewy, 1993; Sack et al., 1990). A meta-analysis suggests that bright light treatment and dawn simulation for seasonal affective disorder, as well as bright light alone for nonseasonal depression, yield a reduction in depression equivalent to those in most antidepressant pharmacotherapy trials (Golden et al., 2005).

However, one of the most promising biological treatments for depression may actually not be medications, electricity, or light, but rather lifestyle in general. For instance, several recent meta-analyses show that physical exercise—whether aerobic or strength training—is as effective in treating depression as medication (Josefsson, Lindwall, & Archer, 2014; Silveira et al., 2013). Another meta-analysis found moderate evidence for the short-term beneficial effects of yoga, compared to usual care in the treatment of depression (Cramer, Lauche, Langhorst, & Dobos, 2013). However, two other meta-analyses suggest that the benefits of exercise may fade over time (Krogh, Nordentoft, Sterne, & Lawlor, 2011) and that it has only a small positive effect on depression in children and adolescents (Brown, Pearson, Braithwaite, Brown, & Biddle, 2013).

In addition to physical exercise and yoga, other lifestyle factors that have been implicated in improving depression include nutrition and sleep. For example, weight loss in obese individuals reduces symptoms of depression (Fabricatore et al., 2011), omega-3 fatty acids have antidepressant properties (Lin, Huang, & Su, 2010), and sleep abnormalities are early markers for later depression (Augustinavicius, Zanjani, Zakzanis, & Shapiro, 2014). Combining all these lifestyle data, psychologist Stephen Ilardi has created a treatment for depression called Therapeutic Lifestyle Change

Source: Brian L. Burke.

Exercise is a biological and behavioral treatment for depression that works as well as antidepressant medication when used as prescribed, especially when combined with nature (e.g., sunlight).

(TLC). TLC encourages people to integrate the following six elements into their lives: (1) an omega-3 rich diet, (2) exercise, (3) plenty of natural sunlight, (4) ample sleep, (5) social connections, and (6) participation in meaningful tasks that leave little time for negative thoughts—all things that our ancestors had in abundance (Ilardi, 2009). Early studies of TLC revealed that, whereas 25–33% of people with depression in community-based treatment (typically medication) improved, the response rate among people receiving TLC was over three times higher (Ilardi, 2009; Karwoski, 2008).

Psychotherapy for Depressive Disorders

Although drugs and other biological elements may be an important aspect of treatment for depressive disorders, especially for severe depression, medication alone does not address the social, emotional, or personality factors that may also underlie people's problems. Therefore, psychotherapy that emphasizes psychodynamic, interpersonal, behavioral, cognitive, or motivational aspects are also commonly used to treat people with depressive disorders. In fact, the psychotherapy approaches described here are as effective as antidepressant medications in the short-term treatment of depression and are likely more effective than medication in the longer-term management of depressive symptoms (Spielmans, Berman, & Usitalo, 2011).

Psychodynamic Approaches

Traditionally, psychodynamic therapies have attempted to alter the individual's personality structure—usually by exposing and working through various unconscious conflicts—rather than to treat a specific problem such as depression. Contemporary versions of psychodynamic treatment seek to address depression specifically and more directly. Examples of these therapies are *time-limited dynamic psychotherapy* (Strupp & Binder, 1984), *short-term dynamic psychotherapy* (Davanloo, 1994), and *supportive-expressive therapy* (Luborsky, 1984). Short-term psychodynamic psychotherapies (defined as 40 or fewer sessions) may also be effective in children and adolescents (Abbass, Rabung, Leichsenring, Refseth, & Midgley, 2013). Overall, though, psychodynamic therapies for depression are the least-examined treatment methods for depression, compared to cognitive-behavioral therapy and interpersonal therapy (discussed in the next sections; Dekker et al., 2014). Accordingly, it is difficult at present to draw firm conclusions about the value of psychodynamic therapies in the treatment of depressive disorders (Jakobsen, Hansen, Simonsen, & Gluud, 2011), although some researchers argue that they are indeed evidence-based treatments (Dekker et al., 2014).

Interpersonal Therapy

Emerging from psychodynamic therapy, the interpersonal approach to treating depressive disorders focuses on the client's current social support system (Klerman et al., 1984). In the case of a depressive disorder, the therapist begins by asking the client to view depression as an illness so as to minimize any sense of guilt over being depressed. Then, attention is directed to one of four interpersonal problems presumed to be central to depression: (1) severe or prolonged grief reactions, (2) role conflicts in interpersonal relationships (as when a woman tries to excel in occupational, marital, and parental roles, all at the same time), (3) role transitions (such as becoming a widow or widower or a college student), and (4) deficits in interpersonal skills (such as extreme shyness or social awkwardness).

The specific treatment strategies depend on which interpersonal problem is most important. For instance, if the core problem is a role transition, attention might center on exploring the losses associated with the change and on preparing for the new role. Overall, the goal is to reduce dependency and increase self-esteem by helping people improve their relationships in family and work environments (Karasu, 1990).

One of the largest comparison studies of different treatments for depression was the National Institute of Mental Health's Treatment of Depression Collaborative Research

Study, which compared the effects of the antidepressant imipramine, placebo medication, cognitive therapy, and interpersonal psychotherapy (Elkin et al., 1989). In this study, conducted at three clinical sites in the United States, 250 adults who had been diagnosed with depression were randomly assigned to one of the four treatments. Among the most important findings was that most people tended to improve, regardless of whether they received the antidepressant drug, cognitive therapy, or interpersonal therapy. In addition, antidepressants were superior to cognitive therapy for patients with severe depression (Elkin, Gibbons, Shea, & Sotsky, 1995). The long-term effectiveness of the treatments was less impressive, but there were tendencies for the psychotherapies to slightly outperform imipramine (a tricyclic antidepressant, the first one on the market). At 18-month follow-ups, only 30% of the original cognitive therapy clients, 26% of the interpersonal therapy clients, 19% of the antidepressant drug clients, and 20% of the placebo clients had recovered and not suffered any relapses. Overall, the value of interpersonal therapy in the treatment of depression is clear but probably small (Jakobsen et al., 2011), yet it deserves its place in treatment guidelines as one of the most evidence-based treatments for depression (Cuijpers et al., 2011).

Behavioral Approaches

As might be expected from the discussion of theories of depression, behavioral therapists seek to reduce clients' depressive symptoms by helping the clients to increase or gain access to positive events in their lives. Sometimes, this means teaching or enhancing the skills (e.g., assertiveness) that clients need in order to experience support and other rewards in social situations. The most prominent current behavioral therapies are social skills training, problem-solving therapy, and behavioral activation. Behavioral activation, which involves increasing people's overt behavior to bring them in contact with reinforcing environmental activities or events (as opposed to the social withdrawal and avoidance that is typical of depression), may be considered a well-established and advantageous alternative to other treatments of depression (Mazzucchelli, Kane, & Rees, 2009).

Furthermore, a series of meta-analyses has shown that behavioral therapies perform as well as—and in some cases better than—other psychotherapies in the treatment of depression (Cuijpers, Andersson, Donker, & van Straten, 2011). Evidence also suggests that starting with a behavioral component in psychotherapy may actually increase client retention over the span of the therapy (Ahmed & Lawn, 2012). However, whereas behavioral activation may outperform cognitive therapy in the short term for people with severe depression (Dimidjian et al., 2006), long-term relapse is reduced when therapists also include a cognitive component to the treatment (Dobson et al., 2008).

Cognitive-Behavioral Therapy

Cognitive-behavioral treatments for depression usually include educational, behavioral, and cognitive techniques and are known overall as CBT. One of the most prominent of these therapies is a short-term (8–16 sessions) intervention based on Beck's (1987) cognitive model of depression discussed earlier in the chapter (and in Chapter 2).

In this cognitive therapy, the client and therapist work together as collaborators to identify and change the client's maladaptive thinking patterns (negative self-schemas). The therapist first introduces the cognitive-behavioral model of depression, explaining that how people interpret events influences how they feel. Next, the therapist helps the client keep track of, or monitor, daily activities and mood to clarify which thoughts and activities are associated with changes in mood. Clients learn, for example, that, even when they are depressed, their moods fluctuate during the course of the day. They may also begin to see links between brighter moods and certain activities, companions, or thoughts. Finally, clients are helped to identify and test the validity of their "automatic thoughts" and often distorted underlying assumptions about the world. Since these thoughts and assumptions guide how clients interpret their experiences, this phase of treatment usually challenges clients' personal belief systems, as illustrated by the ongoing case of Margaret:

Margaret, the 21-year-old woman whose case opens this chapter, has suffered from symptoms of depression since she was a sophomore in college. The youngest of four children in her family, Margaret has always felt as if she has lived in the shadows of her older brothers, each of whom has his own family and has already been successful in the business world. Margaret has always felt pressure to do well academically to impress her parents, who had hoped she would attend medical school after college. Margaret's breakup with Jack, as well as her subsequent academic decline, has left her with many negative self-thoughts. In cognitive therapy, Margaret has begun to learn that her depressive symptoms are worse after events in which she feels like a failure. As an example, the therapist asked Margaret to concentrate on a recent incident in which a friend from her residence hall wordlessly walked by Margaret in the hallway. Because of Margaret's underlying sense of inferiority and current mood, she automatically assumed that her friend was ignoring her, thus adding to her feelings of inferiority and insecurity. However, the therapist asked Margaret to think of alternative explanations for her friend's behavior and asked her to test these explanations by talking to the friend about the event and by watching the interactions of other people in the residence halls. The goal was to help Margaret recognize that the friend could have been preoccupied, might not have seen her, or was perhaps too ill to be sociable. The therapist also helped Margaret realize that, had she automatically assumed one of these other explanations, she would have likely experienced different, nondepressed feelings afterwards.

Mindfulness-based cognitive therapies (MBCT) are a recent development within the cognitive-behavioral tradition and an important element of the third-wave cognitive-behavioral therapy models (Williams et al., 2014). One type of MBCT is a manualized group skills training program (Segal, Williams, & Teasdale, 2002) that integrates psychological educational aspects of CBT for depression with meditation components of mindfulness-based stress reduction developed by Kabat-Zinn (1990). The program teaches skills that enable participants to disengage from their habitual dysfunctional cognitive routines (negative self-schemas) and thus reduce the risk of relapse into depression (Lau, Segal, & Williams, 2004). MBCT has garnered growing empirical support (McCarney, Schulz, & Grey, 2012). In a recent trial, though, whereas MBCT provided significant protection against relapse for participants with increased vulnerability due to history of childhood trauma, it showed no significant advantage in comparison to an active control treatment and usual care over the whole group of people with recurrent depression (Williams et al., 2014).

Overall, research evaluating all types of CBT has found that it is an effective treatment for depression that may also reduce the risk of relapse (Dobson et al., 2008; Hollon, 1993). In addition, CBT may have an advantage over medication in terms of long-term benefits (Antonuccio, Danton, & DeNelsky, 1995). For instance, CBT is equal to SSRIs in initial response and symptom reduction, but superior in terms of relapse prevention (Driessen & Hollon, 2010). Similar to medication and to other psychological treatments, much of the effect of CBT may be due to placebo effects, but there is also a significant specific component of CBT when given for an adequate length (Honyashiki et al., 2014).

CBT is also highly amenable to different delivery formats, ranging from groups to books and electronic media. One meta-analysis showed that group CBT had a moderate effect on the level of people's depression and a small effect on the relapse rate of depression (Feng et al., 2012). CBT can be implemented in a self-guided manner, which typically involves using a book, the Internet, or a phone app with or without the support of a therapist, such as Lewinsohn's *Coping with Depression* course (Lewinsohn & Clarke, 1984), Burns's (1999) *The Feeling Good Handbook*, or apps such as MoodKit (Thriveport, 2011) or the Depression CBT Self-Help Guide (Excel at Life, 2014). CBT self-help treatments for depression have a small but significant effect on depressive symptoms (Cuijpers et al., 2011).

Finally, there are indications that CBT may work through processes specified by Beck's theory to produce changes in cognition that, in turn, mediate subsequent changes in depression, although evidence in that regard is not yet conclusive (Driessen & Hollon, 2010).

Motivational Interviewing

Motivational interviewing (MI; Miller & Rollnick, 2013) is both a treatment philosophy and a set of methods employed to help people increase intrinsic motivation by exploring and resolving ambivalence about behavioral change. It has been described as a therapeutic approach that integrates the relationship-building principles of humanistic therapy (Rogers, 1951) with more active cognitive-behavioral strategies targeted to the client's stage of change (Prochaska, DiClemente, & Norcross, 1992). In the past few decades, MI has become a well-recognized brand that has been used in psychotherapy, medicine, addictions, public health, and beyond (Lundahl & Burke, 2009). Whereas MI has primarily been implemented in the treatment of substance use disorders, as discussed further in Chapter 14 (Lundahl & Burke, 2009), it may also be valuable in treating depression (Arkowitz & Burke, 2008). The specific focus of MI on increasing motivation may be a good fit—either as an adjunct to another type of psychotherapy or as a stand-alone treatment—to the motivational deficit that people with depression show. First, loss of interest and pleasure in most or all usual activities—that is, low motivation—is a core symptom of depression, as described earlier in the chapter (American Psychiatric Association, 2013a). Second, motivation—as measured by willingness to participate actively in treatment, to explore one's problems, and to make changes and sacrifices to improve—significantly predicted improvement in depression treatment (Burns & Nolen-Hoeksema, 1991).

Two recent studies showed early promise for training primary care providers to use MI with their patients who suffer from depression (Keeley et al., 2014; Keeley et al., 2015, in preparation). First, providers were able to effectively learn MI in 8–16 hours of training (Keeley et al., 2014). Further, a single brief session (15 minutes) of MI tripled depressive remission for a group of patients with comorbid diabetes and depression, from 7% (control group) to 23% (MI group) at 8-month follow-ups (Keeley et al., 2015, in preparation).

Comparing and Combining Treatments

Overall, psychotherapy of any type yields a 62% remission rate of depression at follow-up, generally with about 12–18 sessions (Cuijpers et al., 2014). Psychotherapy is not only effective in adults with depression in general, but also in older adults, women with postpartum depression, people with general medical disorders, inpatients, primary care patients, individuals with chronic depression, and individuals with sub-threshold depression (Cuijpers, Andersson, Donker, & van Straten, 2011). Note, however, that psychotherapy is not as effective for people with dysthymia—one component of the new category "persistent depressive disorder"—as it is for people with other depressive disorders; it still has a small but significant positive effect, although SSRIs are significantly more effective (Cuijpers et al., 2010). Further, several meta-analyses have shown that all bona fide psychotherapies for depression are about equally effective, with the exception of supportive psychotherapy (Rogers, 1951), which has a slightly lower effect size than the other treatment models (Braun, Gregor, & Tran, 2013; Cuijpers, van Straten, Andersson, & van Oppen, 2008).

Some researchers suggest that the optimal treatment program for depression may be a combination of antidepressants and either cognitive or interpersonal psychotherapy (Hollon, 1993). The logic of this advice is that drugs can quickly relieve physical symptoms, such as sleep disturbance, while psychotherapies address the cognitive and behavioral patterns that perpetuate depressive symptoms and increase the risk of recurrence. In one meta-analysis, medications and cognitive therapy led to different patterns of response to specific symptoms of depression; medications worked faster than cognitive therapy or placebo on suicidal ideation and other cognitive symptoms, whereas cognitive therapy was superior at treating vegetative (i.e., low energy) symptoms of depression (Fournier et al., 2013). Overall, the combination of psychotherapy and medication had a small yet significant effect over and above the combination of psychotherapy and placebo (Cuijpers, van Straten, Hollon, & Andersson, 2010).

Psychotherapies for children and adolescents with depression are in a more formative stage than the adult counterpart; most of them focus on group interventions. School-based CBT interventions for depression in youth hold considerable promise, although investigation is still needed to identify features that optimize service delivery and outcome (Mychailyszyn, Brodman, Read, & Kendall, 2012). Beneficial treatments have common elements, including activities designed to promote competence, enhance relationship and communication skills, teach systematic problem solving, change unrealistic negative cognitions, and use behavioral activation strategies to increase activity and show its relationship to feelings (McCarty & Weisz, 2007).

Overall, the prognosis for people suffering from depressive disorders is mixed. The good news is that most people recover, even without any treatment, from an episode of depression, in a matter of months. Treatment with psychotherapy and/or medication is relatively effective for the majority of adults. The bad news is that the risk of relapse is high no matter which treatment or combination of treatments is employed. Therefore, many individuals face a life of repeated episodes that result in heavy financial and personal burdens. Even with the plethora of treatment options, it has been estimated that by the year 2020, depression will be the second leading cause of disability throughout the world, trailing only ischemic heart disease (Murray & Lopez, 1996). Whether psychotherapy or medication is the preferred treatment for adult depression remains a hotly debated topic among mental health professionals and often comes down to advertising and accessibility. Drug companies market their medications very heavily, and it is easier to get people access to pills than a trained psychotherapist or counselor, although this may be changing with the current push for more integrated care in the United States. Despite these obstacles, though, the fact that psychotherapy carries fewer side effects and medical risks and achieves slightly superior long-term and relapse prevention effects than medication suggests that it should be the treatment of first choice for depressive disorders—with the possible exception of persistent depressive disorder or very severe depression—whenever feasible.

Section Review

The three main categories of antidepressant medications are:

- monoamine oxidase (MAO) inhibitors,
- the tricyclics, and
- selective serotonin reuptake inhibitors (SSRIs).

These medications:

- are about equally effective, producing improvements in 50–60% of adults;
- are heavily marketed by pharmaceutical companies; and
- have significant side effects that could be distressing to people taking them.

Other biological treatments for depression include electroconvulsive therapy (ECT), light therapy, and lifestyle factors, such as nutrition, sleep, and exercise.

Depression can also be treated effectively with psychotherapy—in particular, interpersonal therapy, behavioral therapy, and cognitive therapy. These therapies:

- achieve improvement rates that do not usually differ from those of medication and
- lead to relapse rates that may actually be lower than with medication and may have fewer adverse side effects.

Even with all of these treatment options, however, depression remains a serious and potentially debilitating disorder that often recurs throughout a person's life.

Constance Hammen

Dr. Constance Hammen is a Distinguished Professor in the Departments of Psychology and Psychiatry and Biobehavioral Sciences at UCLA. She is a leading researcher in the area of mood disorders, particularly the development of depressive disorders.

Q *What do you think underlies the growing rates of depression in our population? Why do we see so much depression, especially in younger people?*

A Rates of depression seem to be increasing worldwide, and in the United States, most studies have shown that younger people were reporting more major depression by their early 20s than did previous generations. Depression rates rise in the late teens and early 20s and throughout young adulthood and then are relatively lower in older age populations. Probably the simplest explanation is that higher rates tend to occur in relation to stressful events and circumstances. Early adulthood is a period of considerable change and challenge for many people, and stressors that overwhelm one's coping skills and resources may trigger depression. It has also been argued that younger people have more exposure to stress now than did previous generations. Their lives are full of family disruption, pressure to succeed and be financially independent, and social mobility. I think they also have many more negative cognitions about themselves and their ability to control circumstances. Certainly, families and social support are very important in helping people deal with stressful circumstances. Young people today may have fewer of those ties, and many do not have resources such as a good education or a good job.

Q *Depression is still more common among women. Any thoughts about why?*

A In my view, four separate factors contribute to the gender differences. One factor has to do with the ex-

pression of the symptomatology itself. We know that women are more willing to admit to emotional difficulties, to express emotions, and to play the role of the weak and needy. So in that sense, they are more likely to admit and feel the symptoms of depression than men are. But there is more to it than that.

A second factor has to do with causal factors that may be more prevalent with women. Women have greater exposure to stress because women experience not only their own stressors but also those of people they are close to. In a sense, women are lightning rods for stressors of other people, as well as feeling their own greater exposure to stress. Women are raised to value close relationships, whereas men are raised to value achievement. Because women tend to value social relationships, they feel stressed when those relationships are threatened.

A third factor would be differences in how people cope with stress. Men and women cope somewhat differently with provoking situations. Men's coping methods may reduce the likelihood of depression. Men, generally speaking, are more active copers. They are more likely to go out and do things to solve the problem, avoid the problem, or distract themselves. Men also may turn to pathological forms of coping, such as drugs and alcohol; nonetheless, they try not to let themselves experience depressive symptoms.

Women, on the other hand, are somewhat less active copers, more likely to use what we call emotion-focused coping; that is, they will think about their problems and symptoms, cry, talk about their problems with other people, and focus on their feelings. Women tend to ruminate about their problems and feelings, and this kind of focus and repetition of negative experiences may consequently exacerbate the symptoms of depression.

Fourth, it has long been suspected that biological differences affecting hormonal balance and interactions among brain circuits, neurotransmitters, and gonadal hormones play a role. However important those factors may be, they are subtle and highly complex to study, and need to be thought of in terms not of levels of female hormones but of interactions among very complicated levels of biological and environmental factors.

Q *What new directions should clinicians and researchers take to better understand and treat depression?*

A One fruitful approach to the origins of depression might be to study how previous stressful experiences may alter the brain or neurochemistry to make people susceptible to depression in response to later stress-

Constance Hammen *(Continued)*

ors. One strong finding in our field is that past depression predicts future depression. Part of the explanation might be that past depression alters the organism in ways that make the person more susceptible to depression. Depression may also alter the brain's processing of information so that it is difficult to inhibit negative cognitions or to shift the focus away from negative content. More knowledge of the specific mechanisms behind becoming depressed and remaining depressed will help to focus on both cognitive-behavioral and pharmacotherapy treatments that are more specific to the underlying deficits.

I think we are also going to see more research on the heterogeneity of depression. It really is a group of different disorders, both mixtures of depression with other disorders and different forms or aspects of depression. The better we can describe the specific clinical and un-

derlying features, the more we might be able to tailor treatment for those specific disorders.

Finally, our treatments just do not cover the need. We must conduct more research on the problem of lower-grade chronic depression. It may be subclinical depression, but if it is enduring, if it persists or recurs, it can still cause a lot of disruption in people's lives and in the lives of those around them. Also, we need better methods of disseminating treatments and making them more accessible to people. Thus, treatments must be better developed to apply to people who might not typically seek out help and should include Internet-based applications (or mobile apps), coordination within the medical primary care system, making interventions appealing and acceptable to all ages and ethnicities, and greatly expanded services for children and adolescents.

Revisiting the Case of Margaret

The primary care doctor at the Student Health Center referred Margaret to the psychologist, Dr. Jane, who interviewed Margaret and asked her to complete an MMPI-2-RF personality test (see Chapter 1). Margaret's MMPI-2-RF restructured clinical (RC) scales showed an elevated RCd (demoralization) and RC2 (low positive emotions), in the context of a low RC9 (hypomanic activation). This is a typical profile for someone suffering from depression, whereas a person with bipolar disorder is more likely to have an elevated RC9 (Watson, Quilty, & Bagby, 2011). Based on the clinical interview and MMPI-2-RF profile, the psychologist diagnosed Margaret with depression. Depression can take many forms, and Margaret had many of the common symptoms. She felt hopeless and overwhelmed; she could not sleep or eat well. She withdrew from her friends and from school. The decades of research reflected in the findings discussed in the chapter proved to be helpful in Margaret's treatment.

The psychologist, Dr. Jane, also assessed Margaret for suicidal ideation by asking her if she thought about killing herself, how or when she might do it, and whether she had access to lethal means. Margaret reported having passive thoughts of "not wanting to be here anymore" but denied any active ideation and said she would never take her own life and had never tried to do so in the past. She was therefore considered low risk for a suicide attempt. Dr. Jane was aware of research suggesting that cognitive or interpersonal psychotherapy is at least as effective as medication in treating moderate depression such as Margaret's. Based on that knowledge, she discussed those treatment options with Margaret, who chose to return to the Student Counseling Center for 8–10 sessions of CBT, to be focused on Margaret's excessively high standards and expectations for herself.

Gradually, Margaret learned to think more flexibly and that she did not have to be perfect to be happy. After eight sessions of therapy, Margaret reported feeling much better. She began going out with her friends again and, by the end of the semester, she had caught up on her academic work. Although her grades were not as good as in the past, Margaret was satisfied with them. Her parents were disappointed, but for once in her life, Margaret decided that she would not apologize to her parents because of their disappointment. Two years after her treatment concluded, Margaret has not suffered a relapse of depression, and she continues to use her "daily thought record" (from her CBT) every once in a while to combat her distorted thoughts when she is in a bad mood.

Summary

Depressive Disorders

The most serious depressive disorder—major depressive disorder—involves prolonged periods of sad moods and demoralized, hopeless feelings; a loss of interest in almost all activities; and disturbances in appetite, sleep, and energy levels. Persistent depressive disorder is a depressive disorder in which depressed feelings and low self-esteem are present for at least 2 years but not as intensely as (though more chronically than) in major depressive disorder. Premenstrual dysphoric disorder involves mood swings and irritability that occur during most menstrual cycles and that remit when menstruation occurs. Disruptive mood dysregulation disorder can be diagnosed (with caution) in children between 6 and 18 years old and involves persistent irritability and temper outbursts that are grossly out of proportion to the situation or developmental level.

Causes of Depressive Disorders

Depressive disorders are caused by a complex interplay of biological, psychological, and social factors. Genetic factors play an important role in depressive disorders, perhaps because they are linked to disturbances in chemical neurotransmitters, such as norepinephrine, serotonin, and dopamine. Depressive disorders have also been related to problems in the endocrine system (hypothalamic-pituitary-adrenal [HPA] axis), as well as possible inflammatory responses of the immune system.

Several psychological variables have been proposed as causes of depressive disorders, including heightened sensitivity to loss or failure, problems in early attachment relationships, interpersonal conflicts, learned helplessness/ hopelessness, deficient reinforcement, cognitive distortions, negative self-schemas, and specific types of rumination. Environmental and sociocultural factors involving our modern world, stressful life events, and a lack of adequate social support have also been implicated.

Treatment of Depressive Disorders

Both medication and various kinds of psychotherapy are somewhat effective treatments for depressive disorders. Antidepressant medications, such as monoamine oxidase (MAO) inhibitors, tricyclics, and selective serotonin reuptake inhibitors (SSRIs), are effective for many adults with major depressive disorder and for persistent depressive disorder, but they are less useful for children and adolescents and may have serious side effects. Some people with severe depression, especially those who do not respond well to medication, may be helped by electroconvulsive therapy (ECT). Other biological treatments include light therapy and lifestyle factors, including exercise, sleep, and nutrition.

Because of its effectiveness in preventing relapse and lack of side effects, psychotherapy is the best treatment in most cases of depression. In many instances, psychotherapy and medications are used in combination to treat depressive disorders. Cognitive-behavioral therapy and interpersonal therapy have been particularly successful in cases of depression, but well-controlled comparison studies have not clearly established any one psychotherapy to be consistently superior to another in the treatment of depression. Even with adequate treatment of any type, the chances of a relapse of depression remain high for many people.

Key Terms

Anxiety Disorders

Chapter Outline

Source: Radharani/Shutterstock.com.

From the Case of Joan

Joan is a 22-year-old Caucasian college senior who presented to the Student Counseling Center in acute distress. Joan reports worrying about "a great many things" in her life since she started college. She says she goes over and over future events in her mind, ranging from exams to school-break plans and from boyfriends to finances. Because of these worries, Joan states that she has difficulty sleeping, typically tossing and turning for hours before finally falling asleep most nights. Studying is challenging for Joan, as she is often unable to concentrate due to future worries that come into her mind involuntarily. She has also had head and neck aches since high school, and reports feeling especially fatigued in the past year.

Joan recently had what she called an "anxiety attack" in her American History class. She felt like her chest was tightening and that she "couldn't breathe" and "might pass out," so she left the class immediately and went to the Campus Health Center, where they thoroughly examined her and then referred her across the hall to the Student Counseling Center for an intake meeting. Joan says she has only had "two or three" of these acute attacks before, all while she was in college and during various classes for her history major. When she has these symptoms, she starts thinking about how she might suffocate or pass out, and it makes her breathing difficulties even worse.

After reading this chapter, you will be able to answer the following key questions:

- What is the difference between anxiety, fear, and panic?
- How are anxiety disorders described and categorized in the *DSM-5*?
- What causes anxiety disorders?
- What are the main treatments used today to help people with anxiety disorders?

FIGURE 7.1 Prevalence of Anxiety Disorders in the United States

This graph shows the lifetime prevalence of anxiety disorders by age and gender in the National Comorbidity Survey Replication (NCS-R) and Adolescent Supplement (NCS-A). Note that prevalence rates of all anxiety disorders are higher for women than for men.

Source: Data from Kessler et al. (2012).

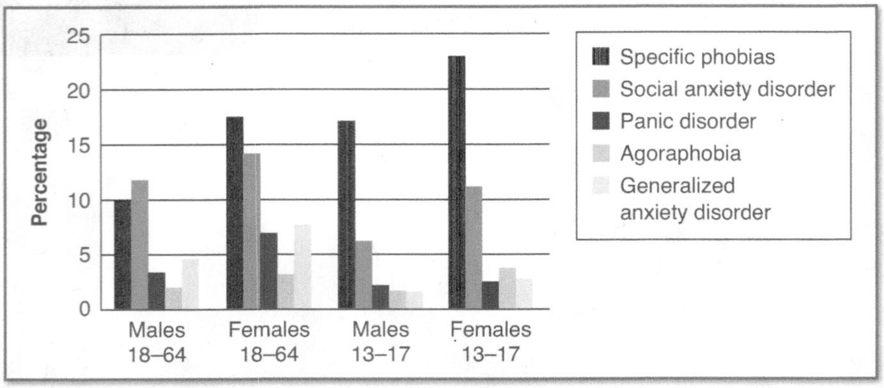

anxiety disorder: A group of mental disorders in which fear or anxiety and associated maladaptive behaviors are the core of the disturbance.

Anxiety disorders like the one(s) Joan is suffering from have consistently been among the most prevalent of all mental disorders in the United States (Kessler et al., 1994; Kessler, Petukhova, Sampson, Zaslavsky, & Wittchen, 2012) and perhaps throughout the world. The global current prevalence of anxiety disorders is about 7% and ranges from 5% in African cultures to 10% in Euro/Anglo cultures (Baxter, Scott, Vos, & Whiteford, 2013). Current epidemiological research shows that about one fourth of American adolescents and adults have experienced one or more of these disorders during their lifetime, and almost 20%—roughly 60 million people—either have had an anxiety disorder within the past year or are currently experiencing one (Kessler et al., 2012). According to the 2013 National College Health Assessment, which examined data from 125,000 students from more than 150 colleges and universities, almost half of the students reported feeling overwhelming anxiety in the last year (Novotney, 2014).

In this chapter, we describe the main anxiety disorders as they are classified in the *Diagnostic and Statistical Manual of Mental Disorders (DSM-5)*: specific phobias, social anxiety disorder, panic disorder, agoraphobia, and generalized anxiety disorder (see Figure 7.1). Two currently separate categories of disorders in the *DSM-5* that are closely related to the anxiety disorders are obsessive-compulsive and related disorders, covered in Chapter 8, and trauma- and stressor-related disorders, described in Chapter 9. Although the rate of comorbidity among anxiety disorders is quite high (Simon, 2009), each disorder has distinct clinical features. Following the clinical description of each disorder, we discuss theories that might explain the disorder's occurrence and the most effective treatments for alleviating it.

Fear and Anxiety Gone Awry

Fear and anxiety lie at the core of all of the anxiety disorders. Both emotions are expressed through three channels:

1. Cognitive distress, distortions, and ruminations
2. Physiological arousal
3. Behavioral disruptions and avoidance

fear: A set of emotional, behavioral, and physical responses to danger.

Although people often talk about fear and anxiety as if they were identical, researchers have found it useful to distinguish between the two emotions. **Fear** refers to a set of responses to a specific perceived danger. It is thought to be a biologically primitive alarm system that sets off a series of cognitive, physiological, and behavioral responses designed to deliver a person from impending harm. A person would likely feel "fear" in a car that is stalled on a railroad track as a train approaches (or at college freshman orientation!). Fear is an abrupt response to real danger that prepares us for immediate action via our "fight-or-flight" response, which is triggered by the hypothalamic-pituitary-adrenal (HPA) axis and neurotransmitters such as norepinephrine (discussed in Chapter 6). **Panic** is closely related to fear; in fact, panic is physiologically identical to fear, except that no real danger or severe threat is actually present.

panic: Fear when no actual danger is present.

These facial expressions show fear in a human being and a monkey, with the wide eyes allowing us to take in more of the fear-provoking situation before deciding whether to freeze, fight, or take flight (run away). Of the 44 muscles in the human face, 40 are devoted to facial expression (the other 4 are devoted to annoying your siblings!). Some facial muscles are activated by positive thoughts, others by negative thoughts, such as those involving fear. The brains of primates are also highly sensitive to faces and their messages. Scientists like Dr. Paul Ekman, on whom the TV series *Lie to Me* (2009–2011) was based, can now read our feelings by measuring changes in our facial expression.

Source: ArtFamily/Shutterstock.com.

Source: Francis Wong Chee Yen/ Shutterstock.com.

Anxiety is related to, but different from, fear; it is a more diffuse or vague sense of apprehension that some aversive event will occur. David Barlow (1988) uses the term *anxious apprehension* to convey the idea that anxiety is a future-oriented concern about events that might happen and over which a person appears to have little or no control. The result is a gnawing sense of foreboding or what we typically call *worry*. For example, people generally feel anxiety after completing an interview for a job they really want, recalling several answers that, in hindsight, seemed incomplete or inaccurate, and then having to wait 2 weeks to find out whether they got the job. Anxiety is longer lasting (more chronic) but less intense than fear, and involves a real or imagined "future" threat.

anxiety: A diffuse or vague sense of apprehension accompanied by fearful behavior and physiological arousal.

The *DSM-5* lists as anxiety disorders specific conditions in which fear or anxiety and their associated avoidance behaviors are clearly experienced as the core of the disturbance. Table 7.1 shows how fear and anxiety interact to yield anxiety disorders (and also obsessive compulsive disorder [Chapter 8] and post-traumatic stress disorder [Chapter 9]).

TABLE 7.1 How Fear and Anxiety Interact to Produce the Anxiety, Obsessive, and Trauma-Related Disorders

1. *Phobias (specific phobia, social anxiety disorder, and agoraphobia)*
   Fear = "Expected" panic ("learned alarm" with fight-or-flight in response to a situation)
   Anxiety = Worry about possible panic and/or being in that feared situation (e.g., elevator, party, crowds)

2. *Panic Disorder*
   Fear = Unexpected panic ("false alarm" with fight-or-flight system being triggered accidentally or unpredictably in different situations)
   Anxiety = Worry about possible future panic attacks or their consequences (e.g., losing control)

3. *Generalized Anxiety Disorder (GAD)*
   Anxiety = Extreme worry producing fatigue, insomnia, and muscle tension

4. *Obsessive-Compulsive Disorder* (Chapter 8)
   Anxiety = Extreme worry with a specific focus (e.g., germs) and a behavioral solution (e.g., cleansing rituals)

5. *Post-Traumatic Stress Disorder* (Chapter 9)
   Fear = "Expected" panic (past "true alarm" when there was a clear danger—for example, an assault)
   Anxiety = Worry about re-experiencing the true alarm (e.g., getting assaulted again)

How are these disorders viewed today? The core emotions—anxiety and fear—can be adaptive when they serve as alarms that enable people to avoid danger or escape harm. In fact, evolutionary theory suggests that natural selection made it advantageous for individuals to be highly fearful of predators and other potentially lethal stimuli because those animals whose fears led to successful escape or avoidance were the most likely to survive (Kendler, Neale, Kessler, Heath, & Eaves, 1992a). When historically useful alarm systems are triggered by stimuli that are not dangerous, however, they become false alarms that may lead to anxiety disorders, as described in Table 7.1.

In this chapter, we describe anxiety disorders as disturbances in biologically based danger response systems that were of importance in helping our ancestors survive the threat of predators or other people. As the coming sections show, though, these anxiety response systems are further shaped into specific patterns by learning and conditioning experiences, by cognitive processes, and by cultural norms and expectations.

Section Review

Fear and anxiety interact to produce all of the disorders in this and the next two chapters. Fear is a quick response to immediate danger that prepares us to fight, flight (run away), or freeze, whereas anxiety—also called worry—is a more chronic and diffuse response to future threats. Panic is fear when no severe danger is actually present.

Specific Phobias and Social Anxiety Disorder

phobia: An irrational, excessive fear that causes intense emotional distress and interferes significantly with everyday life.

The term *phobia* comes from the name of the Greek deity, Phobos, a fearsome creature who was a son of Ares, the god of war. A **phobia** is an irrational, excessive fear that causes intense emotional distress and interferes significantly with everyday life. In the midst of a phobic reaction, a person feels engulfed by a terror that blots out almost all other experience. The fear usually grips an individual with a rush of physiological symptoms of panic, including trembling, a racing heart, sweating, choking, and dizziness or light-headedness. The phobic person may "freeze" or may run from the frightening situation. Phobias are among the most commonly diagnosed mental disorders in the United States (Kessler et al., 2012). In the *DSM-5*, phobias are classified as specific phobias, social phobias (social anxiety disorder), and agoraphobia without history of panic disorder. We discuss agoraphobia—the fear of public places, crowds, or forms of transportation from which escape is difficult—in the section on panic disorder because the two so often occur together (American Psychiatric Association, 2013a).

Specific Phobias

specific phobia: Intense, persistent fear of specific objects or situations that pose little or no actual threat.

Intense, persistent fear of specific objects or situations that objectively pose little actual threat (or a threat far less serious than the person's reaction to it) characterize **specific phobias**. Of course, most people fear and prefer to avoid some situations. It is not unusual for a person to fear swimming in the ocean or flying, for example. For a fear to meet the *DSM-5* diagnostic criteria for a specific phobia, however, it must cause intense distress each time the person is, or anticipates being, exposed to the feared situation. Furthermore, the fear must be intense enough that the resulting cognitive and physiological distress and behavioral avoidance interfere significantly with the person's educational, occupational, or social life.

As many as 14% of adults and 20% of children will develop diagnosable specific phobias in their lifetimes (Kessler et al., 2012), but many more people report specific fears that fall short of the *DSM-5* criteria for phobias. Most types of specific phobias are almost twice as likely in women as in men, except for blood-injection-injury, which some studies report occurring somewhat more equally across genders (American Psychiatric Association, 2013a). In the United States, Asians and Latinos report significantly

The years of Grass Phobia Therapy were starting to pay off for Gunther.

Source: Cartoonresource/Shutterstock.com.

TABLE 7.2 Specific Phobias

Type	Phobia	Type	Phobia
Animals		*Blood, Injury, and Injection*	
Bees	Apiphobia	Blood	Hematophobia
Spiders	Arachnophobia	Needles	Belonephobia
Snakes	Ephidiophobia	Injury	Traumatophobia
Mice	Musophobia	Pain	Algophobia
Animals	Zoophobia	Contamination	Mysophobia
Natural Environment		*Situations*	
Stars	Siderophobia	Enclosed places	Claustrophobia
Wind	Anemophobia	Travel	Hodophobia
Rain	Ombrophobia	Bridges	Gephyrophobia
Thunder	Brontophobia	Empty rooms	Kenophobia
Darkness	Nyctophobia		

lower rates of specific phobias than Caucasians, African Americans, and Native Americans (American Psychiatric Association, 2013a).

Table 7.2 lists some common phobias. Specific phobias are named by placing the Greek word for the feared object or situation before the word *phobia*. Public speaking is sometimes listed ahead of death as one of the top American phobias, prompting comedian Jerry Seinfeld to muse that this means that, when you are attending a funeral, more people there would rather be in the casket than giving the eulogy.

Animal phobias are the most common type of specific phobias, especially in children, and may include (among others) snakes, mice, spiders, cats, or dogs. Animal phobias usually develop in early childhood, with the majority first appearing between the ages of 4 and 10 and only rarely occurring after the early teens (Öst, 1987). In *Harry Potter and the Chamber of Secrets* (Rowling, 2000), Ron Weasley is forced to come face-to-face with his worst fear—spiders—in the Forbidden Forest (except that these giants spiders really are dangerous!). Even if they are not treated, most animal phobias tend to diminish over the years, so that by the time a person reaches the age of 60 or 70, relatively few remain (Grenier et al., 2011).

Because of her snake phobia, Martha had nearly become a prisoner in her own house. She, her husband, and small child had moved to a new home in the country during the winter. One spring day, Martha saw a snake in her yard. After that, she would not allow her child out alone nor would she venture into the yard herself. When she had to leave the house, she would run to the car carrying her child, lock the doors, and speed away before she could see a snake. While in the house, she was constantly vigilant for snakes, and she would not eat vegetables from the garden for fear that snakes might have touched them. (After Kleinknecht, 1991)

Natural environment phobias may be the most common specific phobia type across the lifespan (Burstein et al., 2012; Grenier et al., 2011); they involve exaggerated fears of storms, deep water, heights, or other aspects of the physical world. All infants and many animals, such as dogs, pigs, and cats, have an intense fear of heights. In most cases, this phobia probably involves the fear of falling, rather than of height itself. Fortunately, with maturation and experience, this seemingly innate fear eventually abates. When it does not or if it is reactivated, victims may be unable to walk down flights of stairs, look through high windows, walk across bridges, or visit the majestic Grand Canyon.

At 9 years old, Jessica's fear of heights was so strong she was unable to attend schools with more than one story. She was panic stricken when her class went on field trips where there were steps. She was both frightened and embarrassed in front of her classmates on their trip to a museum. Jessica was able to climb the stairs to the second floor with only a little assistance. However, she had to lie face down and slide on her stomach to get back down.

Another common cluster of phobias involves fears of *blood*, *injections*, and *injury*, the majority of which develop by the early teens. Specific fears within this group include receiving injections, seeing blood or having it drawn, and having stitches to close a wound. This cluster has at least two distinctive features. First, these fears may lead people to delay seeking needed medical attention and thus impair their health (Kleinknecht & Lenz, 1989). Second, approximately 75% of people with blood and injury phobia faint when they are exposed to the critical stimuli, such as a needle (Ducasse et al., 2013). Although as many as 15% of adults have experienced a blood- or injury-related fainting spell (Kleinknecht & Lenz, 1989), they are considered phobic only if their reaction is severe enough to cause significant avoidance, disrupt their daily lives, or impact their health.

Situational phobias are also relatively common—they are the most common subtype in older adults (Grenier et al., 2011)—and include fear of closed places, such as elevators, tunnels, airplanes, and small rooms. Fear of flying (airplanes) is one situational phobia that garnered increased attention in the United States after 9/11. In the year following September 11, 2001, there were an estimated 1,600 more accident-related deaths on American roads than would have been expected statistically, presumably due to fear of flying and increased car traffic (Gaissmaier & Gigerenzer, 2012). In their review of scientific articles in North American and Western European countries, Oakes and Bor (2010) found an estimated prevalence rate ranging from 10–35% for fear of flying. Fear of flying actually appears to be a manifestation of fears of other stimuli (e.g., heights, narrow spaces) embedded in the flying situation but not specific to it (Hawkins-Gilligan, Dygdon, & Conger, 2011).

Claustrophobia—fear of enclosed or narrow spaces—is another common situational phobia. One of the most common manifestations of claustrophobia is refusal to ride in an enclosed elevator. Other common precipitators of claustrophobia include closets, tunnels, airplanes, and certain medical testing machinery and procedures, such as magnetic resonance imaging (MRI), hyperbaric oxygen treatment, and computed tomography (CT) scan (Botella, Villa, Baños, Perpiñá, & García-Palacios, 1999). About 10% of the population has a mild to marked form of claustrophobia, with 2% having severe claustrophobia; in roughly 33% of individuals with claustrophobia, the fear begins in childhood (Wiederhold & Wiederhold, 2005).

Specific phobia of any of the four subtypes shown in Table 7.2 is often the first anxiety disorder to present over the course of development (Beesdo, Knappe, & Pine, 2009). Moreover, prospective community stud-

Source: Black Russian Studio/Shutterstock.com.

The World Trade Center Tribute in Light at night, as seen from Brooklyn across the East River, on September 11, 2012, the 11-year anniversary of the 9/11 airplane attacks. In the year following the tragic event, fear of flying increased, and so did driving, especially in the New York area (Gaissmaier & Gigerenzer, 2012).

ies have demonstrated that this condition is comorbid with other disorders of anxiety and precedes several additional mental disorders, including major depressive disorder and substance use disorders (Lewinsohn, Zinbarg, Seeley, Lewinsohn, & Sack, 1997). Given its early onset and association with later psychopathology, investigators have suggested that the presence of specific phobia in youth may be an initial indication of vulnerability to subsequent impairment. In fact, both the overall number of phobias and certain *DSM-5* subtypes—blood-injection-injury and situational—were uniquely associated with severity and later psychiatric comorbidity in a study of adolescents (Burstein et al., 2012).

Social Anxiety Disorder

Excessive fear of situations in which a person might be evaluated and possibly embarrassed marks **social anxiety disorder (SAD)**, formerly called *social phobia*. People with SAD fear situations in which they believe that they will be exposed to scrutiny by others and in which they might humiliate or embarrass themselves.

> **social anxiety disorder (SAD):** A mental disorder that involves intense fear or anxiety of social situations in which the individual may be scrutinized by others.

Maria was a substitute school teacher who blushed easily when embarrassed. When students or others whom she did not know well asked her a question that she was unable to answer immediately, her face turned bright red, and she felt hot all over. She feared that others would conclude that she was embarrassed because she did not know what she was doing and would evaluate her negatively. As her anxiety grew and she became less able to think and to speak, her fear became a self-fulfilling prophesy. The fear of negative evaluation kept her from accepting jobs that she knew she was competent to perform.

The most common situations that evoke SAD involve speaking or performing in public, meeting strangers (particularly authorities and members of the opposite sex), using public restrooms or dressing rooms, and eating or writing in public. In each case, people with SAD fear that others will find them lacking in some way, that they will be ridiculed, or that they will become the target of public scrutiny. This fear either keeps them from situations that include possible public scrutiny or causes them to live in fear of self-humiliation.

Often, only a single situation, such as public speaking, is the focus of concern. Many people with such specific SAD function adequately by avoiding their phobic situations. For some, however, virtually all public or social situations elicit intense anxiety. This more *generalized* manifestation of SAD affects most aspects of the person's life and may be extremely distressing and disruptive (Burstein et al., 2011).

SAD is about as prevalent as specific phobias but is only slightly more common in women than in men (Kessler et al., 2012). SAD also differs from specific phobias in that it develops a bit later in life, with 75% of cases beginning between 8 and 15 years old, as opposed to 7 to 11 years old for specific phobias (American Psychiatric Association, 2013a). As many as 13% of the population in the United States have had SAD at some period in their lives (9% of adolescents), and about 8% have suffered from SAD in the past year (Kessler et al., 2012). In the United States, being Native American, being young, and having low income increases the risk for developing this disorder, whereas being male; being of Asian, Hispanic, or African American ethnicity; or living in urban or more populated regions reduces this risk (Hofmann, Asnaani, & Hinton, 2010). Worldwide, the epidemiological literature suggests a large range in the lifetime prevalence rates of SAD, with Asian samples (e.g., China, Japan, Korea) having some of the lowest rates (0–2% lifetime prevalence) and Russian samples having some of the highest rates (30+% lifetime prevalence; Hofmann et al., 2010).

SAD appears in all cultures and is thus referred to as *culture-general*. However, because cultural norms and standards shape the expression of fear, the disorder may look different from one culture to another. For example, the culture of Japan, as well as many other Asian countries, tends to emphasize an *interdependent* or *collective* social orientation in which individuals' identities are intimately tied to their families or close friends;

in other words, personal identity is defined largely by others. Many Westerners, on the other hand, have more *independent* identities and are concerned with how others think of them as individuals. *Taijin kyofusho* (TKS) has frequently been discussed as a culture-specific expression of SAD that is particularly prevalent in Japanese and Korean cultures (Hofmann et al., 2010). Similar to individuals suffering from SAD, those with TKS are concerned about being observed and consequently avoid a variety of social situations; they worry that they will emit offensive odors, have a displeasing blemish, or speak in an offensive fashion (Takahashi, 1989). However, the major difference is that a person with TKS is concerned about doing something or presenting an appearance that will offend or embarrass the *other* person. In contrast, SAD is defined as the fear of embarrassing *one-self*. Like SAD in Western cultures, TKS typically begins during the teenage years, but unlike SAD, it is predominantly a male phenomenon (Takahashi, 1989).

Causes of Specific Phobias and Social Anxiety Disorder

The possible causes of specific phobias and social anxiety disorder are examined next, using the biopsychosocial lens.

Biological Theories

If there is a genetic component to phobias, then phobias should appear more often in both members of monozygotic twin pairs than in members of dizygotic twin pairs; in other words, the **concordance rate** should be higher among monozygotic pairs. The concordance rate was higher in monozygotic than in dizygotic pairs for animal phobias, SAD, and agoraphobia (Kendler et al., 1992a). A meta-analysis performed on results from 15 different twin studies indicated that fears and specific phobias were moderately heritable: The highest mean heritability was found for animal (45%) and blood-injection-injury phobias (33%; Van Houtem et al., 2013). Further, SAD appears to be heritable at a similar rate (48%; Stein, Jang, & Livesley, 2002). However, two twin studies found no evidence for heritability of the other two phobia subtypes—natural and situational (Kendler et al., 1992a; Skre, Onstad, Torgersen, Lygren, & Kringlen, 2000).

Although evidence indicates that most phobias have a genetic component, the genetic contribution does not automatically determine the presence of a phobia. The heritability studies just described show that even the most heritable phobias had estimates below 50%; thus, environmental experiences, such as individual traumas, vicarious influences, informational processes, and family history, were primarily responsible for triggering most phobias. This combination of genetic predisposition (a diathesis) and environmental experiences (stressors) illustrates how the diathesis-stress model (described in Chapter 2) applies to phobias.

What neurobiological factors might be associated with a genetic vulnerability to some types of phobias? Most of what is known about fear and anxiety comes from over 3 decades of research using animal models, mainly rats (Winerman, 2005). Research indicates that intense fear appears to originate with signals from the **amygdala** (Carvalho, Santos, Bassi, & Brandão, 2013), a mass of gray matter in the **limbic system**, a complex circuit of brain structures that regulates emotions (see Chapter 2). When activated in mammals, the amygdala can trigger the adrenal gland to produce epinephrine (adrenaline), thereby increasing the physiological arousal related to fear. LeDoux (2003) and others have found that there is a double fear pathway leading to and from the amygdala. One path leads directly from a frightening sensory stimulus—such as the sight of a snake or the sound of a loud crash—to the amygdala in just a few thousandths of a second and produces the biological "fight-or-flight" reaction of fear and panic described earlier. A second, slower pathway travels first to the higher cortex before reaching the amygdala, thereby giving the individual time to appraise the situation and make decisions about how to act; the higher cortex (frontal lobe) is also involved in the "worry" aspect of phobias and SAD.

Whereas the neuroanatomical substrate of phobias has not yet been consolidated (Linares et al., 2012), several possibilities have been proposed that all emphasize the idea that the phobic person is particularly prone to excessive physiological activity in certain

concordance rate: The rate at which a trait or disorder is shared with close relatives, such as a twin.

amygdala: A structure in the forebrain that is part of the limbic system and is linked to emotions.

limbic system: A complex circuit of brain structures (including the thalamus, hippocampus, cingulate gyrus, hypothalamus, amygdala, septum, and parts of the cortex) that helps regulate emotions, memory, and certain aspects of movement.

situations. Two systematic reviews combining studies that used fMRI, PET, SPECT, and structural MRI (neuroimaging techniques discussed in Chapter 1) found that people with various specific phobias and SAD showed greater activation in specific brain regions—including the amygdala, prefrontal cortex, and other limbic system structures—compared to controls (Freitas-Ferrari et al., 2010; Linares et al., 2012). Another possibility is that levels of one or more of the brain's neurotransmitters are disturbed. For example, **gamma aminobutyric acid (GABA)** is a neurotransmitter that inhibits postsynaptic activity. When the level of GABA is low, neurons tend to fire more rapidly, thereby increasing physiological arousal and anxiety. The hypothesis that low levels of GABA might be associated with anxiety is bolstered by the fact that the **benzodiazepines** (drugs that reduce anxiety) increase the activity of GABA (Watanabe, Churchill, & Furukawa, 2007). However, benzodiazepines also have effects that are unrelated to GABA, such as at peripheral receptor sites located outside the central nervous system (Barnard et al., 1998), which may be less plentiful in people with SAD (Johnson et al., 1998). Furthermore, one study showed no difference in GABA levels among people with and without SAD (Laufer et al., 2005).

None of this explains why people develop some types of phobias—animal and social—more often than others. **Preparedness theory** proposes that people are *biologically prepared* to develop fears of certain classes of stimuli, such as snakes and spiders, which were potentially dangerous to our ancestors (Seligman, 1971; Cook & Mineka, 1987). In other words, some stimuli are more easily associated with fears than are others because, in past eras, these stimuli could threaten a person's survival. According to Martin Seligman (1971), who originated this theory, these fears are not inherited directly; rather, it is the capacity to acquire certain fears through traumatic or vicarious conditioning that is inherited. The theory proposes that a single traumatic exposure to a "prepared stimulus," such as snakes or high places, is sufficient for a phobia to develop. It is much more difficult to develop fears of "unprepared stimuli," such as electrical outlets (which some parents want their kids to fear so they can remove those silly plug covers!) or microwave ovens, that have no history of evolutionary threat.

Preparedness theory has focused primarily on phobias of snakes and spiders (Seligman, 1971; Cook & Mineka, 1987) and on SAD involving fear of stares or potentially threatening facial expressions (Öhman, 1985). Experimental research with humans has provided only partial support for preparedness theory (McNally, 1987), but Susan Mineka and Michael Cook have reported some remarkable supportive evidence from studies of vicarious conditioning of fear in young rhesus monkeys (Cook & Mineka, 1987; Mineka & Cook, 1986; Zinbarg & Mineka, 1991). For example, when a monkey, referred to as the "demonstrator," displayed a fear reaction to a snake, a previously fearless "observer" monkey became strongly and persistently fearful of snakes on the basis of seeing this single fear reaction (Mineka, Davison, Cook, & Keir, 1984). However, when a fearless monkey observed a demonstrator monkey displaying fear in the face of a "nonprepared stimulus," such as flowers, no fear reaction developed (Cook & Mineka, 1987). In humans, though, it appears that fear conditioned to social stimuli is less robust than fear conditioned to animal stimuli, as it is susceptible to cognitive influence and may instead reflect on negative stereotypes and social norms (Mallan, Lipp, & Cochrane, 2013).

Psychological Causes

Behavioral, cognitive, and biological theories currently provide the most influential accounts of how phobias develop. However, psychoanalysis has a historically important perspective on phobias, so our discussion of how phobias develop begins with a review of Freud's original ideas on this topic.

Psychoanalytic Formulations Sigmund Freud proposed that phobias, especially animal phobias in young males, were due to an unconscious fear of castration (Freud, 1936/1963). (According to Freud, a snake can be a symbolic reminder to a male that he might lose his penis, or to a female, that she already has. The 2006 film *Snakes on a Plane* takes on a whole new meaning now, does it not?) Freud believed that, when unconscious sexual impulses threaten to emerge in consciousness, the ego transfers the anxiety to another

gamma-aminobutyric acid (GABA): A neurotransmitter that inhibits postsynaptic activity.

benzodiazepines: A class of drugs derived from benzoic acid that are prescribed to alleviate anxiety and panic; includes Valium and Xanax.

preparedness theory: The hypothesis that people are biologically prepared to develop fears of certain classes of stimuli, such as snakes and spiders, that were potentially dangerous to our evolutionary ancestors.

object, such as a snake, that can be rationalized as truly dangerous. Freud's most famous phobia case was Little Hans, the son of one of Freud's medical colleagues (Freud, 1936/1963). Little Hans developed a fear of horses and would not go into the street for fear of being bitten by one. Freud conjectured that Little Hans had incestuous desires for his mother and wished to destroy his father, whom he feared would castrate him if he discovered Little Hans's desire for his mother. Little Hans unconsciously transferred his castration anxiety into a fear of horses, which symbolically represented his father.

According to Freud, SAD also resulted from unconscious impulses stemming from sexual urges. For example, he believed that fear of crowds stemmed from an unconscious fear that one might expose oneself in public (Freud, 1933/1965). Freud's analysis of phobias has not been well supported by empirical research, and psychoanalytic treatment is no longer considered a preferred intervention for phobias.

Behavioral and Cognitive Factors An alternative to the Freudian conception of phobias was proposed early last century by John B. Watson, an American behaviorist. Watson believed that all emotional learning developed from conditioning processes. In his view, a phobia develops because of a direct traumatic experience with a formerly neutral object. For example, suppose a youngster locks a younger sibling in a dark closet and terrifies the trapped child with menacing noises or threats. This experience sets the stage for the traumatized child to avoid closets or other confining places at all costs, thereby reducing feelings of anxiety but also leaving the child convinced that all such situations are dangerous. As a result of this avoidance, the child remains afraid of enclosed spaces and develops into an adult who suffers claustrophobia. Another illustration of Watson's theory is when Ron Weasley told his friends in *Harry Potter and the Chamber of Secrets* (Rowling, 2000) that his arachnophobia stemmed from his childhood, when his mischievous brother Fred turned his teddy bear into a spider.

The most famous early example of this work was Watson & Rayner's (1920) case of "Little Albert," as discussed in Chapter 2. Current psychological detective work suggests that this case study was likely more of an advertisement for Watson's lab than good science and that Albert B. may, in fact, have been a composite of two different baby boys (Beck, 2014). In any event, it is now clear that direct conditioning is an incomplete explanation of phobias (Menzies & Clarke, 1995). For one thing, many phobic persons appear not to have suffered a traumatic conditioning experience that could account for their fears. Second, there are dramatic differences in the ease with which people can be conditioned to fear various stimuli, as suggested by preparedness theory discussed earlier. People develop fears of the dark or of small enclosed spaces far more easily than they do of electric outlets or automobiles, even though they experience many more traumatic events with the latter stimuli.

In light of these potential gaps in the direct conditioning explanation for phobias, what other mechanisms might help account for them? Cognitive processes play an important role in causing some phobias. Remember that neurobiological models of fear describe two pathways—one immediate and centered in the amygdala, and the other slower and involving the prefrontal cortex and other "cognitive" brain regions. Individuals with SAD likely have an overactive amygdala (Freitas-Ferrari et al., 2010), but they may also have flaws in that second, slower system: They experience negative images of themselves performing poorly in social situations, and they also interpret external social information in a less positive way than those without SAD (Hirsch,

Source: Cummings Center for the History of Psychology, the University of Akron.

Watson set out to prove his behavioral theory of fear by conditioning an 11-month-old child, Albert B., affectionately called "Little Albert," to fear a white rat (Watson & Rayner, 1920). Watson and his assistant, Rosalie Rayner, first tested Albert to be sure that he had no fear of white rats or other furry objects. Then, as Albert reached for the rat to play with it, Watson struck a steel bar with a hammer that frightened Albert. After six pairings of the frightening sound with Albert's close proximity to the rat, the rat and any other white or furry objects caused Albert to recoil in fear. From this demonstration, Watson concluded that fears and phobias were conditioned (learned) responses.

Clark, & Mathews, 2006). Another key cognitive factor in the development of SAD is a shift in focus of attention and a particular type of negative self-processing (Clark, 2001). When individuals with SAD believe that they are in danger of negative evaluation by others, they shift their attention to detailed monitoring and observation of *themselves*. They then use the internal information made accessible by self-monitoring to infer how they appear to other people and what other people are thinking about them. In this way, they may become trapped in a closed system in which most of their evidence for their fears is self-generated and any disconfirmatory evidence (such as other people's positive responses to them) becomes inaccessible or is ignored (Clark, 2001).

Also, as described in Chapter 2, learning occurs not only through direct conditioning but also through observation involving the cognitive system—that is, through modeling and vicarious conditioning. For example, some people report that their phobias developed after observing others undergo a trauma (Mineka et al., 1984). In fact, Bandura (1986) argued that modeling processes could explain Little Hans's fear of horses better than Freud's original psychoanalytic account could: Little Hans had witnessed a number of incidents that sensitized him to horses, and he had been repeatedly warned that horses were dangerous and could hurt him. Here is another case of how modeling can lead to a phobia.

Johnny was 10 years old when he and his classmates lined up in the school gym for vaccinations. The boy in front of Johnny screamed and jumped when he got his shot and pulled the syringe off the needle, which remained lodged in his arm. Having observed this traumatic incident, Johnny ran screaming from the gym and avoided needles for 12 years. He missed dental appointments on several occasions. When he finally had to go to the dentist for severe tooth pain, he was clearly phobic and would not allow the dentist to give him an anesthetic injection. (adapted from Kleinknecht, 1991)

Social Causes

Developing a phobia after seeing a fear-provoking situation happening to someone else bridges the cognitive (how one interprets the event) and social causes of these disorders. Similarly, people can also develop phobias by hearing or reading vivid accounts of the dangers associated with certain stimuli. Phobias of air travel are typically acquired in this way. Few people who fear flying have actually experienced a plane crash. They have often, however, seen pictures or heard stories of horrible air disasters, as in the 9/11 examples described earlier. And yet, despite the fact that almost everyone has read or seen the gruesome details of plane crashes like the ones on 9/11, relatively few people become phobic as a result. Other factors—probably involving an inherited biological sensitivity to anxiety and cognitive biases—must be involved as well.

Additional social risk factors for phobias, studied especially in application to SAD, include parenting and family environment, adverse life events, and gender roles (Brook & Schmidt, 2008). The research community has successfully correlated parenting as one small, but integral, part of the mechanism in developing SAD and other anxiety disorders. In particular, parenting attributes such as overcontrol that result in less child autonomy, and to a lesser extent, lack of warmth or rejection resulting in insecure attachment, may lead to SAD in children and adolescents. Researchers are also beginning to realize that parenting is not the exclusive domain of mothers and are now including fathers or partners in their studies (e.g., Greco & Morris, 2002).

A number of different traumatic events may be part of the conditioning response for SAD (Brook & Schmidt, 2008). Events that have been recently studied and thought to contribute to the environmental causes of SAD are losses, such as death or separation, negative family environment or marital discord, family violence, sexual and physical abuse, childhood illness, and bullying. Interestingly, males and females may be triggered by different types of adverse events (Brook & Schmidt, 2008). For instance, boys' (but not girls') risk for SAD increases after changing schools (Tiet et al., 2001). Further, females

FIGURE 7.2
A Diathesis-Stress Model of Phobias

Phobias are most likely to occur when a person who is genetically prone to overreact physiologically to prepared stimuli and/or cognitively prone to self-focus has generally had early adverse experiences and later has a specific frightening experience with one of these prepared stimuli.

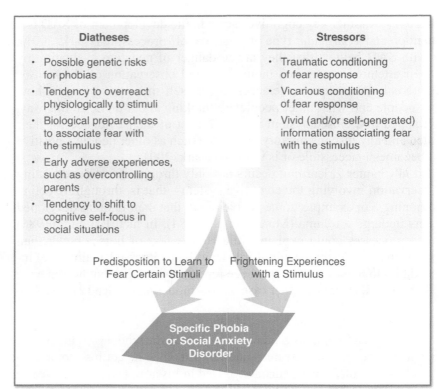

with SAD are more likely to report sexual abuse in their history, whereas males with SAD are more prone to report contact with the juvenile justice system (Chartier, Walker, & Stein, 2001). Not only are reactions to trauma different between genders, but SAD is more common in those who adopt traditional female gender roles (Brook & Schmidt, 2008). Finally, low socioeconomic status (SES) appears to be a stronger risk factor for SAD and other disorders in developing countries, whereas its link to SAD in Western nations has been less clearly delineated to this point (Brook & Schmidt, 2008).

To summarize, a person is mostly likely to develop a phobia when the conditions illustrated in Figure 7.2 are in place. First, certain people have an inborn neurological capacity to physiologically overreact to specific stimuli and therefore feel anxious. If such people directly undergo or vicariously learn about a traumatizing experience with an object or situation, they are at increased risk of becoming phobic of that stimulus. Their chances of becoming phobic are heightened even further if the stimulus has a history of evolutionary importance that "prepares" them for the development of a fear. Finally, people's own cognitive schemas can "create" a traumatizing experience socially where none existed by generating their own negative (and unchecked) assumptions of how other people view them.

Treatment of Specific Phobias and Social Anxiety Disorder

Phobias are the most treatable of the anxiety disorders and perhaps of all mental disorders, especially by psychotherapy; this is the area where psychology has proved its worth most strongly over the past few decades. For instance, over 90% of specific phobias (particularly animal phobias) respond well to treatment (Bandura, Blanchard, & Ritter, 1969). Among the many approaches to treating phobias, those using learning-based procedures have proved most consistently successful (Rachman, 1990). These procedures include systematic desensitization, exposure techniques, and modeling.

Systematic Desensitization

The first treatment that was found to be effective for specific phobias was systematic desensitization, developed by Joseph Wolpe (1958). The procedure begins by teaching the person with the phobia to become proficient at muscle relaxation, which in turn leads to calmness and reduced physiological arousal. The client and therapist then construct an

anxiety hierarchy, a list of fear-provoking stimuli or situations ranked according to how threatening each one is to the client. For example, the following is an anxiety hierarchy for a person with an injection and blood phobia (adapted from Kleinknecht, 1993):

1. Feeling the hypodermic needle in my arm and watching blood pump out when having blood drawn
2. Feeling the needle in my arm for injection
3. Waiting for the injection during "countdown"
4. Seeing the nurse come toward me with the hypodermic needle
5. Feeling the rubber tourniquet on my arm
6. Waiting in a room to get an injection or to have blood drawn
7. Watching someone else get blood drawn
8. Being told I'll need an injection or blood drawn in the future
9. Holding a hypodermic needle
10. Seeing a picture of a hypodermic needle in a magazine

While in a deeply relaxed state, the client is asked to imagine the least frightening item on the anxiety hierarchy (the bottom item on the previous list: seeing a picture of a hypodermic needle). Once able to do so without losing the feelings of relaxation, the client moves up the list, successively imagining each item until he or she is able to imagine the most threatening item (feeling the needle in the arm) while remaining relaxed.

Extensive research has shown that being able to remain relaxed while imagining items in a hierarchy generalizes to live, or *in vivo*, situations (Rachman & Wilson, 1980). If a person with acrophobia can remain calm while visualizing standing at the top of a tall building, chances are good that the person will also be able to climb to the top floor of the building without becoming terrified. Although highly effective, systematic desensitization is time consuming and laborious. Exposure procedures often provide more efficient treatments for clients with phobias.

"Visualize yourself not falling off the wall."

Source: Cartoonresource/Shutterstock.com.

Exposure Procedures

The principle of extinction is the basis for exposure procedures (see Chapter 2). Once a conditioned fear response has been acquired by directly pairing or vicariously associating a fear-provoking stimulus (e.g., a panic attack) with a previously neutral stimulus (e.g., an elevator), the fear response can be extinguished by arranging for multiple exposures to the conditioned stimulus (the elevator) in the absence of the fear-provoking one (i.e., without having a panic attack).

Exposure is usually the opposite of what clients do on their own, which is *avoidance.* This avoidance is actually the main behavior to treat because it is what makes the fear worse; when you avoid a feared situation, you immediately feel relief (less anxiety, a reward), which serves to maintain the problem. (Imagine the relief you would feel if your professor told you that your next abnormal psychology exam was cancelled!) Even people who do not avoid their feared situation entirely often perform various *safety behaviors* (e.g., wearing their lucky scarf or memorizing their entire speech) during the situation that are intended to prevent or minimize the feared catastrophe. If the catastrophe then fails to occur, people ascribe the nonoccurrence to the safety behavior, rather than inferring that the situation is less dangerous than they previously thought (Clark, 2001). Every successful treatment for phobias or SAD must therefore include a component that helps clients reduce their avoidance and safety behaviors in feared situations.

One way to do this is via **graduated exposure**, in which clients are given live, rather than imagined, exposure to items from an anxiety hierarchy similar to those used in systematic desensitization that they must face without their safety behaviors. Using the needle phobia hierarchy, for example, the client would first view a picture of a hypodermic

MAPS - Attempted Answers

syringe, then observe another person holding one, and eventually actually receive an injection and have blood drawn with the guidance of the therapist. People with SAD would be encouraged to face their social fears gradually, starting with minor ones (e.g., ordering food at the university cafeteria to go) and working their way up to higher risk social situations (e.g., attending a college party without any friends there). New technologies, such as virtual reality, are now being used to create vivid, but safe, exposures to feared stimuli such as airplanes so that the therapist can guide the client through a situation without having to actually take a plane trip together. A meta-analysis revealed large declines in anxiety symptoms following virtual reality exposure therapy (Parsons & Rizzo, 2008).

flooding: A treatment technique to extinguish phobias or overcome anxiety by exposing persons to prolonged presentations of the most intense version of the feared stimulus.

A more concentrated exposure procedure called **flooding** involves immediate and prolonged presentation of the most intense version of the feared stimulus. This procedure results in an initial increase in anxiety, followed by relatively rapid fear reduction. Öst (1992, 2012) has shown significant fear reduction in people with specific phobias using this procedure in a single 3-hour session in which clients are exposed to steps of their fear hierarchy using therapist-directed behavioral experiments. This classic single-session approach is also a highly effective intervention for the treatment of specific phobias in children and adolescents (Ollendick & Davis, 2013). A 20-session flooding program, in which clients imagined and then actually faced their most intense social fears, was superior to antianxiety medication and placebo control in the treatment of SAD (Turner, Beidel, & Jacob, 1994).

Modeling Procedures

Just as phobias can be acquired by observing another person undergo a traumatic experience, vicarious learning can be used to reduce fears. Albert Bandura (2012) has extensively studied the effectiveness of modeling treatments in which fearful clients observe a model interacting with the feared stimuli. Someone fearful of heights, for example, would observe another person (perhaps the therapist) gradually ascend a flight of stairs, climb a ladder, or peer out a high window. A person afraid of dogs would observe another person happily playing with a puppy. The repeated observation of others displaying fearlessness communicates to people with phobias that the situation is safe for them.

Source: Brian L. Burke.

Modeling can help someone with a dog phobia try exposure, which is ultimately the key component to any successful phobia treatment.

Participant modeling, a combination of *in vivo* exposure and modeling, is one of the most effective of all treatments for specific phobias. This procedure begins with the therapist demonstrating the feared behavior until the client's fear has diminished somewhat. Next, the therapist

participant modeling: A treatment technique in which a model demonstrates fearless behavior while a client is given increasingly close contact with the feared situation under protected circumstances.

helps the client approach the feared situation step by step, each time arranging the circumstances to maximize the client's success and confidence about further progress. In treating a child for dog phobia, for example, the therapist might hold the child while, together, they pet a friendly, calm dog. The child would gradually be encouraged to pet the dog independently, and the therapist would eventually move away as the child's fear diminishes.

Cognitive-Behavioral Treatments

Whereas the primarily behavioral treatments just discussed are highly effective in treating simple phobia, adding a cognitive component is more common in the treatment for SAD, although it does not necessarily produce better results than exposure alone (Feske & Chambless, 1995; Gil, Carrillo, & Meca, 2001). For example, one of the main cognitive features of phobias and SAD is fear overprediction. The stimulus estimation model asserts that this fear overprediction stems from two factors: (1) overprediction of the dangerous elements of a phobic stimulus and (2) underprediction of existing safety resources or the person's own ability to cope with the threat (Wright, Holborn, & Rezutek, 2002). Individuals with an elevator phobia, for instance, likely overestimate the probability of the elevator falling or getting stuck (which is probably less than 1 in 100,000 rides), whereas they also underestimate the elevator's safety features in the event of a mishap, as well as their own ability to cope with the situation; they think they would "go crazy" in a stuck elevator when, in reality, they would likely experience panic symptoms for 20–30 minutes that would eventually subside. Cognitive therapy helps people with phobias to more rationally and realistically estimate danger and probable coping responses.

Social skills training is another effective component for SAD on its own or as part of a broader cognitive-behavioral treatment (CBT) package (Gil et al., 2001). This involves teaching clients to improve their basic social skills, ranging from making culturally appropriate eye contact, smiling, and speaking up in class to starting and deepening conversations and going on dates (that do not end up like the first date between Adam Sandler and Drew Barrymore's characters in the film *Blended*, which took place at a Hooters restaurant!). As with depression (see Chapter 6), CBT for SAD is also effective in a group format (Wersebe, Sijbrandij, & Cuijpers, 2013). Group CBT for SAD usually includes in-session exposure and social skills training, along with regular homework assignments to gradually face one's social fears and practice emerging social skills outside of the group. Finally, treatment of specific phobias and SAD can also be effective when done in a self-directed manner (without any or much therapist assistance), using widely available books (e.g., Bourne, 2005), apps, or Internet programs (Abramowitz, Moore, Braddock, & Harrington, 2009; Boettcher, Carlbring, Renneberg, & Berger, 2013).

Pharmacotherapy—mainly selective serotonin reuptake inhibitors (SSRIs) like Prozac discussed in Chapter 6—and CBT for SAD are both superior to control conditions in the short term with comparable dropout rates (Canton, Scott, & Glue, 2012). However, CBT is more beneficial for the long-term outcome and is thus considered the treatment of choice (Canton et al., 2012; Gould & Johnson, 2001). For children with SAD, social skills training may be a critical component, and medication alone is not an effective treatment option (Scharfstein, Beidel, Finnell, Distler, & Carter, 2011).

The fact that all of these cognitive-behavioral treatments work well, even though their rationales and details differ considerably, has led to speculation that a common underlying mechanism is responsible for fear reduction in all of them. Albert Bandura believes that the common mechanism is the enhancement of clients' sense of **self-efficacy**, their confidence that they can approach and tolerate their feared objects or situations. Behavioral progress, whether gradual or concentrated (as in flooding), engenders this confidence and change in cognition (Bandura, 1986). Each accomplishment builds clients' self-efficacy so that they can take the next step. Thus, any procedure that enhances self-efficacy should reduce fear behavior.

self-efficacy: A person's belief that he or she can successfully perform a given behavior.

Section Review

Phobias, the most common form of anxiety disorder:

- are irrational, excessive fears of specific objects or situations that cause intense distress and interfere with everyday life;
- include specific phobias that are usually focused on animals, events in the natural environment, blood-injection-injury fears, or other specific situations;
- also include social anxiety disorder, an excessive fear of social encounters involving potential evaluations or public scrutiny;
- are most likely in persons who are predisposed to overreact physiologically to stimuli and who have had or have heard of some frightening experiences with a stimulus; and
- may be effectively treated by procedures that expose the person to the feared stimulus so that he or she gains confidence (self-efficacy) about being able to control or tolerate it rather than avoid it.

Panic Disorder and Agoraphobia

As described in Table 7.1, fear and anxiety combine to produce the different categories of anxiety disorders. In phobias and SAD, the panic—fear out of proportion to the actual danger—typically occurs in specific, predictable situations (e.g., in an elevator, near a dog, before giving a public speech, etc.). These situations then become triggers that generate panic-like symptoms in the future, unless the individual chooses to avoid the situations (an attempted answer that creates the clinical problem). In some cases, however, the panic happens "out of the blue" in a variety of seemingly random situations so that no clear connection can be made between any specific situations and those distressing symptoms. This may result in panic disorder and/or agoraphobia. Because these two disorders are usually considered to be connected (American Psychiatric Association, 2013a; Goisman et al., 1995), they are described together.

Characteristics and Prevalence

The hallmark of **panic disorder** is periodic and unexpected attacks of intense, terrifying fear, called **panic attacks**, that leave victims feeling as if they are going crazy or are about to die. The attacks come on suddenly, reach peak intensity within a few minutes, and may last for minutes or hours (American Psychiatric Association, 2013a; Barlow, 1988). The person then develops persistent anxiety that another attack will occur or that such attacks will be uncontrollable should they recur. The course of untreated panic disorder is variable. An individual may go months or even years without an attack and then suddenly experience an episode. With treatment, prognosis is good: About 70% of people will have a remission of their symptoms in a 3-year span, with 12% relapse, though the relapse rate rises to 21% if the person also has agoraphobia (Nay, Brown, & Roberson-Nay, 2013).

Table 7.3 lists the detailed symptoms of a panic attack, which resemble the fear experienced in phobias, including physical symptoms such as a racing heart, sweating, trembling, choking or smothering sensations, chills, dizziness, nausea, and shortness of breath (Craske, Zarate, Burton, & Barlow, 1993). In panic disorder, however, at least some of the attacks appear to come on suddenly for no apparent reason and with little warning. Other panic attacks seem to be elicited by specific aspects of a situation, but unlike the fear associated with phobias, they occur only intermittently. For example, being in a crowded shopping mall may often, but not always, precipitate a panic attack. Panic attacks are sometimes so strong that they leave people feeling as if the surrounding objects or events are not real (derealization) or as if they have become detached from themselves (deper-

Edvard Munch (1863–1944) was a Norwegian painter whose intensely evocative treatment of psychological themes built on some of the main tenets of late 19th-century Symbolism and greatly influenced German Expressionism in the early 20th century. One of his most well-known works is *The Scream* of 1893, caricaturized here. Munch wrote of how the painting came to be after he had a panic attack (Faerna, 1995, p. 16): "I was walking down the road with two friends when the sun set; suddenly, the sky turned as red as blood. I stopped and leaned against the fence, feeling unspeakably tired. Tongues of fire and blood stretched over the bluish black fjord. My friends went on walking, while I lagged behind, shivering with fear. Then I heard the enormous, infinite scream of nature."

Source: NLshop/Shutterstock.com.

panic disorder: An anxiety disorder marked by panic attacks, coupled with persistent anxiety that another attack will occur.

panic attack: A period of unexpected, intense, terrifying anxiety that leaves victims feeling as if they are going crazy or are about to die.

TABLE 7.3 The *DSM-5* in Simple Language: Diagnosing Panic Disorder

Panic disorder occurs when a person has recurrent panic attacks (described below) and reacts with either worry about having another attack or what the attack means and/or with behavior changes such as avoidance.

A panic attack develops quickly and peaks within minutes; it involves intense fear, along with four or more of the following thirteen symptoms:

Physical symptoms, like		And/or psychological symptoms, like:
1. Racing heart	6. Pain in chest	11. Feeling that things are not real
2. Sweating	7. Pain or nausea in stomach	12. Thinking that you are going crazy
3. Shaking	8. Dizziness	13. Worrying that you are going to die.
4. Difficulty breathing	9. Heat or chills	
5. Choking sensations	10. Numbness	

Source: Adapted from American Psychiatric Association (2013a).

sonalization). Culture-specific symptoms, such as headache, ear ringing, or uncontrollable screaming or crying, may also occur during panic attacks, but they do not count as one of the four required symptoms from the list of thirteen in Table 7.3.

Agoraphobia

In the *DSM-5*, panic disorder and agoraphobia are diagnosed separately, and a person can have one without the other, but they are often comorbid. Indeed, about a third to a half of individuals report panic attacks or panic disorder prior to the onset of agoraphobia and vice versa (American Psychiatric Association, 2013a; Kikuchi et al., 2005).

Agoraphobia means fear of open spaces (*agora* is Greek for *marketplace*). People with agoraphobia, which is the single most common phobia that clinicians treat, typically fear leaving home alone, being in public, and traveling. Their most basic fear, however, is having a panic attack while being away from a place they consider safe. They fear having an attack in a situation in which they will be embarrassed and from which they cannot readily escape (Barlow, 1988; Faravelli, Pallanti, Biondi, & Parerniti, 1992). In other words, their attempted answer—that is, to avoid situations in which they might have a panic attack in public—becomes their clinical problem. The chapter-opening case about Joan, elaborated on further in this section, illustrates comorbid panic disorder and agoraphobia.

Connections

In what other disorders do people experience symptoms of derealization and depersonalization? For the answer, see Chapter 10.

agoraphobia: A fear of open spaces or of being separated from a safe place.

MAPS - Attempted Answers

Joan came to the Counseling Center after having what she called an "anxiety attack" in her American History class. Joan says she has only had "two or three" of these acute attacks before, all while she was in college and during various classes for her history major. When she has these symptoms, she starts thinking about how she might suffocate or pass out, and it makes her breathing difficulties even worse. Recently, Joan had another attack, but this time, it was while she was driving to the grocery store. She felt a wave of terror sweep over her, and she thought she was dying. She had an overwhelming urge to run but did not know why or from what, and besides, she was too weak. She could only pull the car over and shake in terror. After what seemed like hours (actually only 25 minutes), the panic subsided. Now, Joan is reluctant to go out of her residence hall, and when she does, she no longer drives for fear of having another attack. Despite her roommate's urging, she ventures only a couple of blocks from campus to ensure that she can return quickly in case of another attack.

Earl Campbell, a Heisman Trophy winner in college and then a professional football running back, experienced his first panic attack about 5 years after retiring from football while taking a short trip in his car. The attacks continued, and Campbell went to eight different doctors trying to find out what was wrong. After each attack, Campbell grew more worried about what was happening to him. "I'd go to bed at night and just lie there because I knew that if I went to sleep, I'd have an attack. I used to cherish being by myself," he said. "I used to jog, hunt deer, and work out, but I stopped. I'd enjoyed running my own company, but instead, I stayed home." Other celebrities with panic disorder (but without agoraphobia) include actress Scarlett Johansson, who revealed that she often experiences panic attacks before having to get in front of the camera, as well as singer Adele, who once snuck out of a show in Amsterdam through a fire escape to get away from all the pressure.

As in Joan's case, most clients' agoraphobia develops following a series of unpredictable and uncontrollable panic attacks (Barlow, 1988; Faravelli et al., 1992). They begin to avoid places where the attacks occurred, or places like them, until they come to suffer what has been called a "fear of fear" (Arrindell, 1993; Goldstein & Chambless, 1978). Panic attacks can occur in so many places or with such severity in a few places that people with agoraphobia may become totally housebound.

Although clinicians usually assume that most cases of agoraphobia are accompanied by a history of panic attacks (Goisman et al., 1995; Horwath, Johnson, & Hornig, 1993), the presence of agoraphobia without a history of panic disorder may represent roughly half of the cases (American Psychiatric Association, 2013a; Kikuchi et al., 2005). The confusion over the frequency of agoraphobia without panic disorder may be due to differences in the way clinicians and

Source: Brocreative/Shutterstock.com.

epidemiologists have assessed this condition. Obviously, the relationship between agoraphobia and panic disorder requires more research.

Persons displaying panic disorder with agoraphobia are vulnerable to problems that go beyond restricted activities and fear of panic attacks. Their frequent use of alcohol and other drugs as self-prescribed anxiety medications places them at risk for substance abuse (Kushner, Sher, & Beitman, 1990; Pollard, Detrick, Flynn, & Frank, 1990). Self-medication and prescription medications for anxiety are potentially addictive and can add to the individual's misery (Rickels, Schweizer, Weiss, & Zavodnick, 1993). People who suffer from panic disorder with agoraphobia also frequently suffer depression (Weissman et al., 1989) and have a significantly increased risk of premature death from various causes, including suicide (Markowitz et al., 1989; Weissman, Klerman, Markowitz, & Ouellette, 1989).

Source: Brian L. Burke

MAPS - Superficial Syndromes

This cactus from the Atacama region in Chile has agoraphobia and wants to get as far away from the other cacti as possible.

MAPS - Prejudicial Pigeonholes

sleep paralysis: A symptom associated with panic disorder; it occurs when a person is waking up or falling asleep, and involves a brief inability to move.

Prevalence

Most cases of panic disorder have their onset between adolescence and the mid-30s, with a mean age of onset of 20–24 years old (American Psychiatric Association, 2013a). The 12-month prevalence in the United States is about 2–3%, with lifetime prevalence at around 5% (Kessler et al., 2012). In most epidemiological studies, females are found to suffer panic disorder almost twice as often as males (Burnam, Hough, Escobar, & Karno, 1987; Katerndahl & Realini, 1993; Kessler et al., 2012). Estimates of panic disorder in other countries, such as Germany, Switzerland, and Sweden (Amering & Katschnig, 1990; Carlbring, Gustafsson, Ekselius, & Andersson, 2002), yield similar 12-month figures, ranging from 1 to about 2.5%. One exception to this pattern was found in two Asian countries—Taiwan and Hong Kong—both of which have 12-month prevalence estimates of panic disorder at only about a quarter of a percent of the population (Chen et al., 1993; Hwu, Yeh, Chang, & Yeh, 1986).

Prevalence of agoraphobia is similar to that for panic disorder, though perhaps a bit lower at roughly 2.6% lifetime and less than 2% prevalence over 12 months (Kessler et al., 2012). Agoraphobia is found in most parts of the world, but it accompanies panic disorder in the northern latitudes more often than in the southern latitudes (Amering & Katschnig, 1990).

Rates of panic disorder have not been found to differ among ethnic groups in the United States (Burnam et al., 1987; Canino et al., 1987; Horwath et al., 1993; Katerndahl & Realini, 1993); however, agoraphobia appears to occur at a higher rate among African Americans than among Caucasians (Neal & Turner, 1991). African Americans may also experience different symptoms of panic, such as sleep paralysis, a symptom that is uncommon in other ethnic groups. **Sleep paralysis** occurs when a person is waking up or falling asleep, and it involves an inability to move; it is often accompanied by visual hallucinations, hyperventilation, and acute fear. Sleep paralysis is also associated with hypertension (high blood pressure) in African Americans, leading researchers to look for possible causal links between these conditions (Neal & Turner, 1991).

The *DSM-5* lists *ataque de nervios* (ADN; "attack of nerves") as being potentially related to panic disorder. ADNs were first seen in Hispanic culture, although they can occur in anyone: In one study, 32% of Hispanic participants reported at least one lifetime ADN, along with 27% of Caucasian participants and 23% of African American participants (Keough, Timpano, & Schmidt, 2009). ADNs can vary widely but are typically described as an experience of distress characterized by a general sense of being out of control (Keough et al., 2009). The most common symptoms include uncontrollable shouting, attacks of crying, trembling, and heat in the chest rising into the head. Dissociative symptoms, suicidal gestures, and seizure or fainting episodes are observed in some ADNs. Research shows that 36% of ADNs fulfill criteria for panic attacks and between 17% and 33% for panic disorder, depending on the overlap method used (Lewis-Fernández et al., 2002). The main features distinguishing ADNs that fulfill panic criteria from those that do not include whether the episodes were provoked by an upsetting event in the person's life (common for ADNs) and the rapidity of crescendo of the actual attack, with ADNs often reaching a peak more slowly and not necessarily within minutes.

Causes of Panic Disorder and Agoraphobia

As with all mental disorders, there are various biopsychosocial factors that may help explain the cause of panic disorder and agoraphobia.

Biological Factors

Panic disorder and agoraphobia tend to run in families. In one study, Raymond Crowe and his colleagues found that over 17% of the family members of people with panic disorder also had the disorder. The percentage was even greater for female relatives: 46% also had panic disorder, compared with less than 2% of the general population (Crowe, Noyes, Pauls, & Slyman, 1983). Similar findings have been reported for relatives of people with agoraphobia (Noyes et al., 1986). Twin studies of panic disorder typically find greater concordance between monozygotic than between dizygotic twins (Mosing et al., 2009). Thus, researchers today acknowledge a genetic contribution to panic disorder (about 40% heritability; Hettema, Neale, & Kendler, 2001) and agoraphobia (as high as 48% heritability; Mosing et al., 2009), and they have proposed several inherited neurophysiological and biochemical mechanisms that could make a person vulnerable to panic attacks. Moreover, the high genetic correlation ($r = .83$) between panic disorder and agoraphobia and the increased odds ratio for both disorders in siblings of those who have agoraphobia without panic disorder supports the theory of a common genetic etiology (Mosing et al., 2009).

Although the genes involved in the susceptibility and development of panic are still not fully understood, substantial progress has been made in the past 10–15 years (Maron, Hettema, & Shlik, 2010). Despite this progress, only one polymorphism (a different version of a gene called "Val158Met") has been clearly implicated in panic disorder and confirmed via meta-analysis, but it is moderated by gender and ethnicity, and is not exclusive to panic disorder (Maron et al., 2010).

The intense terror of the panic experience must be a basic, primitive alarm mechanism (Barlow, 1988; Gorman et al., 1989). The neurological underpinnings of this alarm system center in a small area of the brain stem called the **locus coeruleus (LC)**. Artificial stimulation of this area in animals results in panic-like behavior (Gorman, Leibowitz, Fryer, & Stein, 1989). Conversely, if the LC is removed, the animal does not show panic. Panic disorder might be caused, in part, by hypersensitivity of this LC-based alarm system. Other areas of the brain, especially the amygdala, hypothalamus, and the frontal and temporal lobes, are also involved in panic and anxiety experiences due to the limbic system's involvement in a circuit with the LC. See Figure 7.3.

locus coeruleus (LC): A small area of the brain stem in which abnormalities are associated with alarm or panic.

So how might LC sensitivity lead to panic disorder? One possibility is that, in people with LC hypersensitivity, certain substances are more likely to trigger panic attacks. There is evidence that many people with panic disorder are particularly sensitive to such substances. For example, *hyperventilation* (rapid breathing) or injection of lactic acid, a natural byproduct of muscle activity during exercise, results in panic attacks in 54–90% of people with panic disorder but only 25% of people without panic disorder (Barlow, 1988). A similar hypersensitivity also occurs to substances such as caffeine, carbon dioxide, sodium lactate (lactic acid), and norepinephrine (Papp et al., 1993).

Hypersensitivity to these substances cannot completely explain panic disorder, however. For one thing, sodium lactate does not cross the blood-brain barrier in lower primates, and thus it might not directly affect the LC as some have theorized (Coplan et al., 1992). Furthermore, if people with panic disorder are led to believe that they can control the amount of carbon dioxide they inhale, they are no more likely to have panic attacks than those not inhaling it (Carter, Hollon, Carson, & Shelton, 1995; Rapee, Brown, Antony, & Barlow, 1992; Sanderson, Rapee, & Barlow, 1989). It has also been demonstrated that, when people with panic disorder are given a placebo they think is sodium lactate, they respond with panic attacks that are virtually identical to those of patients who *are* given

FIGURE 7.3 Brain Structures Involved in Anxiety and Panic

Emotions such as fear, anxiety, and panic are mediated by various brain circuits that involve structures such as the frontal and temporal lobes, the amygdala, the hypothalamus (de Carvalho et al., 2010), and the locus coeruleus (LC), a blue-colored nucleus in the pons (part of the brain stem) that is involved with physiological responses to stress and panic. The LC is also the principal site for brain synthesis of norepinephrine (Goddard & Charney, 1997).

Source: Image supplied by The Lundbeck Institute, www. cnsforum.com.

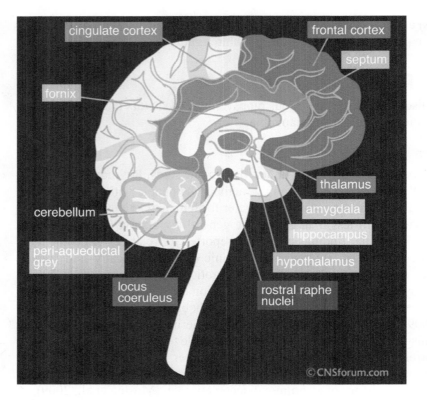

sodium lactate (Goetz et al., 1993). Because a person's perception of control seems to affect responses to these biochemicals, the onset of panic attacks must involve psychological processes as well.

Although neuroscientists are identifying brain areas that are implicated in panic attacks, just how the attacks are triggered in people with panic disorder is not yet established (Goetz et al., 1993). The *suffocation-false alarm theory* (Klein, 1993) postulates the existence of an evolved suffocation alarm system that monitors information about potential suffocation. Panic attacks maladaptively occur when the alarm is erroneously triggered. The expanded theory further hypothesizes that neurotransmitter dysregulation (of opioids such as endorphin) may underlie the respiratory pathophysiology and suffocation sensitivity in panic disorder (Preter & Klein, 2014). This dysregulation increases sensitivity to carbon dioxide as well as to potential psychosocial stressors that involve separation—such as sudden loss, bereavement, and childhood separation anxiety. Tests of the theory have yielded mixed results (McNally, Hornig, & Donnell, 1995). Consistent with Klein's (1993) original theory, suffocation sensations had the largest effect on panic of any physiological symptom (McNally et al., 1995). Yet, as implied by cognitive theories discussed next, catastrophic thoughts best discriminated panic attacks that went away from those that became clinical problems. The precise mechanism of panic attacks is still not understood, and there may even be different types or multiple pathways that produce these distressing symptoms.

Cognitive-Behavioral Models

Cognitive theorists such as Aaron Beck (1976) and David Clark (1986) claim that panic attacks result from misperceptions that benign bodily sensations or harmless external stimuli are actually harbingers of doom. In some clients, these misperceptions can escalate into repetitive thoughts about potentially catastrophic events. The more convinced they become that their normal sensations are really dangerous, the more their anxiety grows. This anxiety then drives the activation of the sympathetic nervous system even higher. Therefore, according to Beck (1976), panic attacks really begin as *false alarms* exacerbated by distorted thinking.

A complementary but even more comprehensive synthesis comes from David Barlow (1988, 2000), who incorporates aspects of biological theories with the cognitive theories

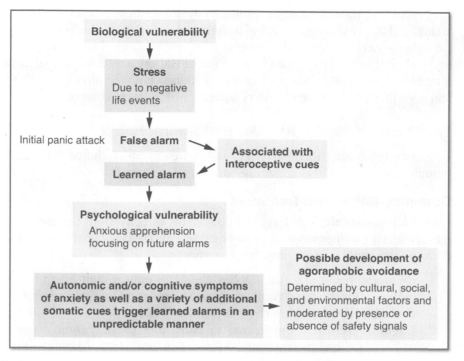

FIGURE 7.4 Barlow's Model of the Causes of Panic Disorder and Agoraphobia

Source: Adapted from Barlow (1988, 2000).

of Beck and Clark to produce a diathesis-stress model of panic disorder (see Figure 7.4). Within Barlow's (2000) triple vulnerabilities model of anxiety disorders, three factors are proposed to yield panic disorder: (1) a genetic contribution to the development of anxiety and negative affect (i.e., a generalized biological vulnerability); (2) a diminished sense of *perceived control* over aversive events and emotional experiences (i.e., a generalized psychological vulnerability common to all anxiety disorders); and (3) elevated levels of *anxiety sensitivity*, a specific psychological vulnerability to developing and maintaining panic disorder that manifests as an anxious focus on the somatic (bodily) cues that signal imminent panic attacks.

Barlow (2000) begins with the assumption that people can have a hereditary predisposition to panic in the form of a highly reactive autonomic nervous system and/or a tendency to be highly sensitive to anxiety symptoms. When biologically vulnerable individuals are exposed to major life stressors, they are prone to experience a panic attack because they interpret the stressor as a signal of mortal danger. The attack is a *false alarm* because there is no immediate danger from which to escape. However, when the cues (e.g., crowded place) and sensations (e.g., rapid heart rate) associated with this first attack occur in the future, they can once again trigger panic. The cues and sensations have become *learned alarms*. As the attacks continue, people may become highly vigilant for early warning signs. The specific psychological vulnerability—*anxiety sensitivity*—leaves the person ready to interpret many different bodily sensations (shortness of breath, rapid heart rate, sweaty palms) as signs of an impending panic attack (Asmundson & Norton, 1993). Further, people with low perceived control over negative events in their lives—a general psychological vulnerability to anxiety disorders—are more likely to view these physical sensations as uncontrollable and develop *anxious apprehension* (persistent worry) regarding future panic attacks. Such anxious apprehension may then produce the avoidance strategies often employed to manage these unpredictable panic attacks, such as agoraphobia or an attempt to avoid the panic-related bodily sensations generated by activities like exercise (White & Barlow, 2002).

Barlow's theory suggests that the triggering role of substances such as lactic acid stems from the fact that these substances create physiological sensations that mimic the early internal cues associated with previous panic attacks. If a person mistakenly believes that these sensations are signs of an impending attack, worry, anxiety, and a full-blown attack may ultimately follow. A similar process may occur when people with panic disorder hyperventilate, misinterpret the resulting physiological sensations as the beginning of an attack, and thereby hasten its actual occurrence (Ley, 1985). Barlow's theory has received strong empirical support and is the prevailing psychological model of panic today (Bentley et al., 2013). One important implication of Barlow's model is that effective treatments for panic disorder and agoraphobia should address both the physiological and psychological contributions to these disorders as described in the next section.

Treatment of Panic Disorder and Agoraphobia

Cognitive-behavioral therapy (CBT) is the treatment of choice for panic disorder, although medication is also commonly used (and overused).

Cognitive-Behavioral Treatments

CBT for panic disorder and agoraphobia stems directly from the view that these problems reflect a misinterpretation of physical sensations as signs of danger. These treatment packages typically contain three basic elements:

1. *Breathing retraining* that teaches clients to reduce their breathing rate, thus promoting relaxation and combating hyperventilation to give them more of a sense of control (self-efficacy) over what their body does.
2. *Cognitive restructuring* geared to correcting clients' chronic misinterpretations of harmless bodily sensations (Gould & Clum, 1995; Margraf, Barlow, Clark, & Telch, 1993; Zinbarg, Barlow, Brown, & Hertz, 1992). Therapists teach these skills to clients using logic and evidence. For instance, clients worried about suffocating during a panic attack would investigate the odds of that happening. Clients learn to effectively challenge their own catastrophic thinking (e.g., "my quick breaths mean I will suffocate") by coming up with viable alternatives and rational responses (e.g., "No, my fast breathing just means that I am experiencing a false alarm when I am not actually in danger"). Once they can do this, they can move on to step 3.
3. *Interoceptive exposure* to somatic cues (such as changes in heart rate or dizziness) that often trigger an attack. This involves actually encouraging clients to have panic-type symptoms during sessions, which can often be brought on by accentuating whatever clients report as their key physical sensation of panic. For instance, if clients' main signal for an impending panic attack is their rapid heart rate, the therapist could have them jog in place during the session to get their heart racing. This graded exposure is intended to reduce clients' anxiety about physical sensations (e.g., by showing them that it is safe for their heart to beat quickly during exercise). As clients experience the panic-type symptoms in session, they are guided through using their cognitive skills (step 2) to challenge their catastrophic misinterpretations of what is happening in their body.

CBT has been reported to eliminate panic attacks in 80–90% of treated clients over follow-up periods as long as 4 years (Chambless & Gillis, 1993; Margraf et al., 1993). These procedures are equally effective whether used in group or individual therapy (Telch et al., 1993). A review of meta-analyses reported large effect sizes for CBT for treating panic disorder with or without agoraphobia (Butler, Chapman, Forman, & Beck, 2006). Other meta-analyses have shown that CBT is significantly better than medications in the treatment of panic disorder (Roshanaei-Moghaddam et al., 2011) and more cost-effective with superior overall health benefits (Heuzenroeder et al., 2004).

A specific cognitive-behavioral intervention known as *panic control treatment* (Craske & Barlow, 1993) has an especially good track record not only in relieving the symptoms of panic disorder, but also in reducing symptoms of other anxiety disorders that are often comorbid with panic disorder (Brown, Antony, & Barlow, 1995). This treatment usually entails a combination of the three components just described—breathing retraining, cognitive restructuring, and interoceptive exposure—after educating clients about how panic arises from their tendency to overreact to and *catastrophize* physical sensations (i.e., false alarms). In one study, clients who completed 12 sessions of panic control treatment experienced a significant decrease in panic-related symptoms, and a majority maintained their improvements over a 2-year follow-up. However, even among clients who improved, many still had setbacks; more than half of them occasionally suffered panic attacks during the 2-year period, and more than one quarter sought additional treatment (Brown & Barlow, 1995). Another study showed that panic control treatment was also effective for adolescents, where their clinical severity of panic continued to improve from post-treatment to 3-month follow-up and then remained stable at 6-month follow-up (Pincus, May, Whitton, Mattis, & Barlow, 2010).

Cognitive-behavioral treatment of agoraphobia is similar to that used for panic attacks, but additional techniques may be necessary to eliminate agoraphobic avoidance behavior, even after panic attacks have diminished. The most effective procedure for treating avoidance involves the same kinds of exposure methods used for specific phobias. People with agoraphobia are encouraged and assisted to confront such feared situations as leaving home, going to department stores or shopping malls, or using public transportation. Exposure can be carried out in graduated fashion or via more intense flooding procedures (Zinbarg et al., 1992).

Drug Treatments

Certain anxiolytics (anti-anxiety drugs) as well as antidepressants have been found useful for treating panic disorder.

The main type of anxiolytic used to treat panic disorder is the class of drugs called *benzodiazepines* (e.g., Valium, Ativan, Xanax), with over half of the people seeking treatment at specialty psychological clinics for panic disorder already taking them as prescribed by their primary care providers (Barlow, 1997). As described earlier, these drugs facilitate the action of inhibitory neurotransmitters such as GABA and thereby reduce anxiety by slowing down the activity of neurons in the brain. Benzodiazepines work rapidly to relieve anxiety, but they also produce undesirable side effects, such as drowsiness and reduced motor coordination. In addition, clients can quickly become dependent on, or even physically addicted to, these drugs. As a result, experts recommend helping clients to discontinue benzodiazepine use (or for doctors not to prescribe them so freely in the first place), as research shows that the pills can make panic disorder relapse after a course of CBT more likely (Barlow, 1997). In a study comparing the effectiveness of alprazolam (sold as Xanax) to CBT in the treatment of panic disorder, 87% of those receiving CBT were panic free, compared with 50% of drug-treated clients after 3 months of treatment (Klosko, Barlow, Tassinari, & Cerny, 1990).

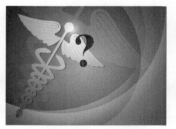

MAPS - Medical Myths

Antidepressants such as selective serotonin reuptake inhibitors (SSRIs; e.g., Prozac) or tricyclics (imipramine) are equally effective as each other and as benzodiazepines in reducing panic symptoms (Offidani, Guidi, Tomba, & Fava, 2013; Otto, Tuby, Gould, McLean, & Pollack, 2001), but they too have troubling side effects, such as dizziness, impotence, and extreme thirst, which often cause people to stop taking them (see Chapter 6). Some clinicians believe that a combination of psychological and pharmacological treatments might be more effective than either one by itself (Marks et al., 1993; Mavissakalian & Michelson, 1986), but research has not found combined treatment to be superior to CBT alone with regard to long-term outcome in people with panic disorder and/or agoraphobia (Gould, Otto, & Pollack, 1995; Pull & Damsa, 2008). Overall, then, the use of medications for panic disorder and/or agoraphobia is generally not necessary, and caution is warranted to limit its increasingly widespread usage (Danton & Antonuccio, 1997).

Section Review

Panic disorder:

- consists of intense, unexpected attacks of panic coupled with the dread of having more attacks;
- is often linked with agoraphobia because many people with panic disorder try to avoid situations in which they might have an attack and might not be able to escape to safety;

- appears in most parts of the world and is more prevalent in females than males;
- may be caused by a biological predisposition to overreact physically to stressors, followed by a tendency to misinterpret bodily sensations as signs of danger, along with low perceived control over negative events, leading to constant apprehension about further attacks; and
- can usually be treated effectively with cognitive-behavioral treatment packages with no strong evidence supporting the highly common use of medication.

Generalized Anxiety Disorder

In contrast to the disorders previously described, anxiety may occur alone in the absence of fear or panic, and it may not be focused on any one particular object, situation, or person. Rather, people with **generalized anxiety disorder (GAD)**, like Joan in the chapter-opening case, are chronic worriers who experience "free-floating anxiety" that is sufficiently pervasive to dominate their lives and interfere with their daily functioning. Note that Joan meets criteria A and B in Table 7.4 and also has at least four of the six symptoms in criteria C (count 'em).

generalized anxiety disorder (GAD): A mental disorder in which anxiety is experienced as "free floating" (not connected to any specific stimulus) and is pervasive enough to interfere with daily functioning.

> Since starting college, Joan has worried about many different areas of her life, especially any important events coming up, ranging from exams to school-break plans and from dates to job interviews. Joan also reports difficulty sleeping and studying, as her worrying often gets in the way of both of these things, and she cannot control it. Physically, Joan states that she has experienced head and neck aches since high school and had felt especially tired for the past year.

GAD is predominantly a cognitive disorder in that its major symptoms involve worry and other negative thought processes. Like Joan, people with GAD worry endlessly over numerous events and are generally overwhelmed by anxious expectations (Barlow, 1988). Although people with GAD worry about the same things as most other adults, such as family, money, work, and illness, their worry is more constant and extreme. For example, one sample of people with GAD reported that, on average, they spent over half of their time in a worried and anxious state (Barlow, 1988). Typically, this worrying is not productive because it interferes with their ability to concentrate and to arrive at optimal solutions for life's problems.

The persistent and uncontrollable worry also produces consequences for the body. As a result, people with GAD report a large number of physical complaints: They are keyed up, irritable, tense, and easily fatigued, and like Joan, they tend to have trouble concentrating and difficulty falling or staying asleep.

The age at onset of GAD differs from that of other anxiety disorders: Prevalence rates are low in adolescents and young adults but increase substantially with age (Wittchen & Hoyer, 2001). GAD is frequently associated with comorbid depression and other anxiety and somatic symptom disorders (see Chapter 11). Like other anxiety disorders, GAD is more prevalent among females; the "Controversy" feature in this chapter discusses

TABLE 7.4 The *DSM-5* in Simple Language: Diagnosing Generalized Anxiety Disorder (GAD)

GAD is a disorder in which individuals worry excessively about various things in their lives most days for 6 or more months and have difficulty controlling (i.e., shutting off) the worry.

The person's anxiety or worry is also associated with three or more of the following six physical symptoms:

1. Sleep problems	3. Trouble concentrating	5. Muscle tension (e.g., headaches)
2. Tiredness	4. Irritable mood	6. Feeling restless or fidgety

Source: Adapted from American Psychiatric Association (2013a).

possible reasons for this gender difference. Current estimates suggest that about 7.7% of females and 4.6% of males in the U.S. adult population will suffer from GAD at some time in their lives, with 2.9% meeting criteria in the past year (Kessler et al., 2012). In the United States, lifetime risk for GAD is higher for Caucasians than for Asian Americans, African Americans, and Latinos (Lewis-Fernández et al., 2010). Individuals of lower socioeconomic status seem to be particularly vulnerable to GAD (Moffitt et al., 2010). Most Western nations have similar 12-month GAD rates to the United States (around 2–3%), but other countries like Mexico, Japan, South Korea, and China have significantly lower rates at around 1% each (Lewis-Fernández et al., 2010). Perhaps there is something about more collectivist cultures' prioritization of groups over individuals that reduces each individual's sense of worry.

Causes of Generalized Anxiety Disorder

Theories about the biopsychosocial causes of GAD are less well developed than those for other anxiety disorders. Indeed, debate continues over whether it is even a discrete disorder at all (Simpson, Neria, Lewis-Fernández, & Schneier, 2010). For example, Massion, Warshaw, & Keller (1993) found that, among a group of 123 clients with GAD, only two did not have either another anxiety disorder or major depression. Some clinicians suggest that GAD is not a separate disorder, but a basic anxiety state from which other disorders develop or another form of major depressive disorder (Massion et al., 1993; Simpson et al., 2010). Others have suggested that, since GAD is so strongly associated with social and economic factors, it should be considered more a response to chronic economic stressors than a true anxiety disorder (Blazer, Hughes, George, Swartz, & Boyer, 1991).

However, a 10-year longitudinal study showed that, whereas GAD predicted that the person would have persistent depression in the future, depression did not predict GAD, and people had significant functional impairment attributable to GAD alone (Kessler et al., 2008). The existence of differences in risk factors for GAD and depression also argues against the view that the two disorders are merely different manifestations of a single underlying internalizing syndrome or that GAD is merely a precursor or severity marker of depression (Kessler et al., 2008). For instance, parental death predicted onset of depression in adolescence (as discussed in Chapter 6) but did not predict the onset of GAD.

Finally, depression and GAD may involve distinct cognitive processes (Yang et al., 2014). Rumination, discussed in Chapter 6, can be defined as the compulsively focused attention on the symptoms of one's distress, and on its possible causes and consequences, as opposed to its solutions (Nolen-Hoeksema, Wisco, & Lyubomirsky, 2008). Rumination is similar to worry except rumination focuses on bad feelings and experiences from the past, whereas worry is concerned with potential negative events in the *future*. Rumination is more commonly associated with depression, and worry is more often linked to GAD (Yang et al., 2014). One possibility to explain the fact that GAD can cause depression but not vice versa is that GAD and worrying about the future may exhaust people so much that they begin to also ruminate about the past and subsequently become depressed.

Biological Causes

Genetic research via family and twin studies shows a GAD heritability of about 32% according to a meta-analysis, which is lower than that for panic disorder (Hettema et al., 2001). A more recent community study concluded that GAD exhibits mild to moderate familial aggregation (Newman & Bland, 2006). Research on the neurobiological basis of GAD has considerably expanded in recent years. A meta-analysis shows that studies have identified abnormal amygdala and prefrontal cortex activation—just like for other anxiety disorders—as well as decreased functional connectivity between these areas in people with GAD (Hilbert, Lueken, & Beesdo-Baum, 2014). Another study showed that anxiety in GAD involves frontal lobe circuits ("worry") more than the amygdala, which contributes in larger portions to fear and panic instead (Blair et al., 2008). Neuroendocrine findings are less consistent, but increased reactivity of the norepinephrine system and in cortisol secretion (a stress hormone implicated in depression) have been reported (Hilbert et al., 2014).

Explaining Gender Differences in Anxiety

Significantly more females than males are diagnosed with anxiety disorders, at a ratio of almost 2 to 1 for every disorder in this chapter except for social anxiety disorder (SAD), where the ratio is only 1.2 to 1 (Kessler et al., 2012). Are females more anxious, more fearful, and more vulnerable to anxiety disorders than males? Or do clinicians diagnose anxiety disorders in females more often because of differences in the way males and females report their fears? Three explanations for the observed differences have been offered: (1) biological differences between the genders, (2) differential socialization and gender-role expectations for males and females, and (3) response-style differences in which males portray themselves in accordance with a typically masculine role, which includes fearlessness and bravery.

It has been suggested that hormonal differences between males and females are one source of differential fearfulness. Isaac Marks (1987) suggested that males' greater exposure to the class of hormones known as *androgens* makes them more aggressive and less reticent in potentially fear-provoking situations—especially after puberty, when much of the gender difference emerges. Another relevant finding is that the onset of several anxiety disorders in females is often associated with hormonal fluctuations. For example, the onset of panic disorder and agoraphobia has been observed to occur during or closely following pregnancy, miscarriage, or hysterectomy (Last, Barlow, & O'Brien, 1984; Neziroglu, Anemone, & Yaryura-Tobias, 1992; Shulman, Cox, Swinson, Kuch, & Reichman, 1994). These correlational data are intriguing, but they offer little direct evidence that hormonal differences explain the gender differences in the prevalence of anxiety disorders.

Some researchers argue that gender differences in the prevalence of anxiety disorders are due to distinctions in the types of behaviors that are expected and encouraged in males and females (McLean & Anderson, 2009). For example, boys are often expected to play rougher than girls, to experience more cuts and bruises, and to play with spiders, snakes, and insects. Repeated exposure to these stimuli might help extinguish fears that boys initially experience. Girls, who are often discouraged from many of these activities, may therefore have fewer opportunities to extinguish early fears. Indeed, some of the largest gender differences in phobia prevalence are related to fears of snakes, spiders, and the like (Bourdon et al., 1988; Marks, 1987). Other theorists have proposed the idea that femininity may lead to fears that are adaptive in certain situations; in other words, the fears and anxiety keep individuals closer to home so that they can contribute to the social functioning of the group (VanderLaan, Gothreau, Bartlett, & Vasey, 2010).

In an entire book devoted to this topic, Michelle Craske (2003) makes the point that women are ultimately more likely to develop anxiety disorders not because of increased levels of fear, but because of their *reactions* to fear. She concludes that, whereas females start off less emotionally reactive than males, they become more inhibited by around 2 years of age. Women's innate tendency to "tend and befriend" in response to threat, as opposed to "fight or flight," is similar to an avoidant style of coping, rendering them less likely than men to develop self-efficacy or to learn effective ways to deal directly with threat in the environment. These tendencies increase socialization but also support a proneness to worry and increase avoidant behavior.

Further evidence for sociocultural factors in gender differences among anxiety disorders comes from examining disorders in which these differences are small or are reversed. For example, in the United States, gender differences in shyness and SAD are typically small or insignificant (Kessler et al., 2012), possibly because gender-role expectations in many social situations are often similar for American males and females. *Taijin kyofusho* (TKS), a cultural variant of SAD in Japan, however, is reported to be more common in males than in females by a 3 to 2 ratio (Takahashi, 1989). Cross-cultural differences in gender ratios are, therefore, more likely a result of differences in social and cultural expectations rather than in biological makeup.

Some psychologists believe that observed gender differences in anxiety disorders do not reflect true differences in fear, but rather, a combination of male reluctance to admit to fear and female willingness to do so. Although there is little direct evidence for this theory, one ingenious study provided some support. Kent Pierce and Dwight Kirkpatrick (1992) administered a questionnaire in which university students rated how much they feared a variety of stimuli, with females reporting more fear than males. But then they had the students retake the questionnaire, this time while attached to a polygraph that, they were told, would be able to tell whether their reports were true. Under the threat of "lie detection," males reported significantly more fear than they had the first time (though still less than the women), whereas females' second fear reports were unchanged. Perhaps some of the differential in reported fears might therefore be due to males' trying to live up to gender-role expectations of fearlessness.

Each of the preceding explanations probably contributes to gender differences in the prevalence of anx-

Explaining Gender Differences in Anxiety (Continued)

iety disorders. Further research is necessary to clarify the psychological and biological mechanisms through which these effects are exerted.

Thinking Critically

1. What role does parenting play in the development of anxiety disorders?

2. Why might certain fears be adaptive or valuable for people?

3. Does the relationship between anxiety disorders and pregnancy indicate that gender differences are created by hormonal differences between the sexes? What factors other than hormones might be involved?

Psychosocial Causes

Most psychological theories of GAD have focused on the role of chronic and excessive worrying because it is this symptom that most clearly distinguishes GAD from other anxiety disorders. In most anxiety disorders, anxiety is focused on specific fear experiences, such as the panic attacks in panic disorder or the obsessive thoughts in obsessive-compulsive disorder (discussed in Chapter 8). But in GAD, the anxiety is spread across many situations. Perhaps the tendency to worry about almost everything is an attempt to maintain tight control over all aspects of life. Chronic worriers believe that, if they stay alert enough to anything that could possibly go wrong, all mistakes or mishaps can be prevented. Of course, this constant "on alert" status carries a heavy price; people with GAD believe that they can never let down their guard or else they will be victimized by a bad event. Consequently, they stay on edge, tense and nervous, always ready to confront the next threat.

Worry may also function as a way to avoid the emotional or physical feelings of anxiety. The *cognitive avoidance theory* of worry (Borkovec, Alcaine, & Behar, 2004) posits that images of negative future events during worry are avoided by engaging in worrisome verbal thoughts instead. Consequently, verbal thought predominates during worry. Consistent with this theory are studies showing that people who worry excessively experience *less* physiological arousal (e.g., increases in heart rate) to a feared stimulus than do nonworriers (Borkovec & Hu, 1990). A person who is always *thinking* about threats may have less opportunity to *feel* upset or to visualize vivid images that are physiologically

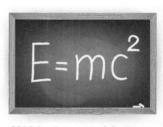

MAPS - Attempted Answers

Toby Allen, a prominent artist, completed a project in which he expertly illustrated a variety of mental disorders as anthropomorphized monsters, such as the Anxiety Monster pictured here.

Anxiety

The anxiety monster is small enough to sit on its victim's shoulder and whisper things in to their unconscious, eliciting fearful thoughts and irrational worries. The anxiety monster is often seen as weak in comparison to others, but it is one of the most common and is very hard to get rid of.

They often carry small objects linked to their victim's anxieties such as clocks which represent a common but irrational fear of things that might never happen. No one has ever seen the face of the anxiety monster for it always wears a skull as a mask.

Toby Allen 2013

zestydoesthings.tumblr.com

Source: "Real Monsters" Illustrations by Toby Allen 2013. Reprinted with permission.

Chapter 7 Anxiety Disorders 273

arousing. Worrying may therefore be a means of avoiding strong feelings of fear by concentrating on more abstract concerns (Hirsch, Hayes, Mathews, Perman, & Borkovec, 2012). College students without GAD report worrying to motivate themselves, prepare for the worst, and avoid negative outcomes. People with GAD report those same three reasons for worrying plus an extra one—to distract themselves from more emotional topics (Borkovec & Roemer, 1995). However, because chronic worriers do not actively confront the situations they find distressing, their high levels of anxiety continue, thus perpetuating the worry cycle (Stokes & Hirsch, 2010).

Treatment of Generalized Anxiety Disorder

Both cognitive-behavioral treatment (CBT) and drug therapy have shown promise in reducing GAD.

Cognitive-Behavioral Treatment

Virtually all data on psychological treatment for GAD come from cognitive-behavioral methods. These methods include *cognitive restructuring*, in which clients are trained to identify and challenge irrational anxiety-generating thoughts and to replace them with more rational beliefs that are then applied in everyday life (Beck & Emery, 1985). Many treatment programs also include relaxation training designed to reduce excessive physiological arousal (Barlow, Rapee, & Brown, 1992; Chambless & Gillis, 1993).

Two different meta-analyses yielded strong evidence that CBT is the treatment of choice for GAD (Cuijpers et al., 2014; Hofmann & Smits, 2008). CBT was also effective at follow-up, resulted in reduction of comorbid depressive symptoms, and was more effective than applied relaxation alone in the longer term (Cuijpers et al., 2014). Further, CBT may work equally well via computer or Internet delivery with minimal therapist assistance (Andrews, Cuijpers, Craske, McEvoy, & Titov, 2010). Overall, CBT for GAD results in better overall health and is more cost effective than medications (Heuzenroeder et al., 2004).

A relatively recent effort to enhance the impact, efficiency, and disseminability of CBT has been the development of transdiagnostic treatments (e.g., Barlow et al., 2011). Transdiagnostic CBT approaches distill and integrate core therapeutic change strategies from existing evidence-based CBT interventions across spectrums of disorders. In other words, because symptom overlap tends to be the norm rather than the exception, and all of the disorders discussed in this chapter (and even the previous and next chapters) have many similarities, transdiagnostic CBT has one general set of procedures to learn that can then be applied to all of these disorders. Results from a meta-analysis indicated that, overall, transdiagnostic group treatments for anxiety disorders are associated with a very large pre- to post-treatment effect size and stable maintenance of gains through follow-up (Norton & Philipp, 2008).

Drug Treatments

Despite the evidence for CBT, drugs are still the most widely used treatment for GAD. Until the new millennium, the most commonly prescribed medications for GAD were the benzodiazepines (Berger et al., 2011), such as Valium (diazepam), Xanax (alprazolam), Ativan (lorazepam), and Klonopin (clonazepam). Initially, these drugs were believed to provide significant relief for this disorder, but recent evidence has called this conclusion into question.

The benzodiazepines begin to relieve symptoms of anxiety in about 20 minutes. This rapid calming effect reduces worry and tension and facilitates sleep in the short run. However, the long-term effects of the benzodiazepines are problematic. First, as previously described, these drugs produce several adverse side effects, such as drowsiness, reduced motor coordination, and physical dependence. Second, the benzodiazepines do not seem to produce lasting reductions in anxiety. In one large-scale study in Scotland, diazepam (Valium) taken alone or in combination with CBT was compared with placebo medication alone and placebo medication combined with CBT (Power, Simpson, Swanson, &

Connections

Are depression and anxiety disorders distinct conditions, or are they different labels for a negative emotion? See Chapter 6.

MAPS - Medical Myths

Wallace, 1990). During 10 weeks of treatment, people with GAD who received CBT—whether alone, with Valium, or with a placebo—showed the greatest anxiety reduction. Conversely, the effects of Valium alone were no greater than the placebo alone.

Benzodiazepines may therefore have robust efficacy in the short-term management of GAD, but they have not been shown to be effective in producing long-term improvement overall (Martin et al., 2007). According to the United Kingdom's National Institute for Health and Care Excellence (NICE; 2011), benzodiazepines should not be given for longer than 2–4 weeks. The only medications NICE recommends for the longer-term management of GAD are antidepressants, and these are now taking over as the most prescribed medication for GAD in the United States as well. One study showed that over half of people treated for GAD received antidepressants (mainly SSRIs), whereas 34% received benzodiazepines (Berger et al., 2011). Perhaps due to the strong overlap between anxiety and depression, antidepressant medications, which include the SSRIs and tricyclics discussed in Chapter 6, have proved somewhat effective in relieving symptoms of GAD (Heuzenroeder et al., 2004). Finally, there is a newer drug called Pregabalin that has a similar molecular structure to the inhibitory neurotransmitter GABA but appears to act on the voltage-dependent calcium channel to decrease the release of neurotransmitters such as glutamate; it is showing initially promising effects in the treatment of GAD (Baldwin, Ajel, Masdrakis, Nowak, & Rafiq, 2013).

Section Review

Generalized anxiety disorder (GAD) is a disorder in which individuals:

- worry excessively about various things in their lives most days for 6 or more months, and
- have difficulty shutting off the worry.

The worry is accompanied by physical symptoms like sleep issues, difficulty concentrating, fatigue, muscle tension, irritable moods, and restlessness.

Because GAD overlaps with other conditions, such as panic disorder and depression, some have questioned whether GAD is a separate disorder at all. Like all of the anxiety disorders discussed in this chapter, GAD is caused by an interaction of biopsychosocial factors, likely involving:

- brain areas such as the frontal lobe (the origins of worrying),
- the limbic system (amygdala) to a lesser extent, and
- worry as cognitive avoidance, whereby people avoid images of negative future events by engaging in worrisome verbal thoughts instead.

The only effective treatments for GAD are antidepressant drugs and cognitive-behavioral therapy. While drugs currently are still the most widely used treatment for GAD, cognitive-behavioral therapy should be the first-line choice due to fewer side effects, higher cost effectiveness, and better overall outcomes.

Revisiting the Case of Joan

In the chapter-opening case, Joan was diagnosed with comorbid GAD and panic disorder. She chose to participate in CBT at her college counseling center, and the treatment consisted of several components over a 16-week period. First, Joan engaged in *worry control*, where she would write down her specific anxious thoughts and learn to challenge them, with the help of her therapist (Dr. Lara) and the handouts that her therapist provided. For example, Joan was worried because she picked the place where she and her friends were staying in early January on school break. She had automatic thoughts like "If they don't like it, it will all be my fault." With the help of Dr. Lara, she generated alternative possibilities, such as "They probably will like it" and "Even if they don't, they all chose to come based on the same information that I had, so it's not my fault."

Another treatment component was *worry exposure*, where Joan was told to set aside time each night before bed to worry (i.e., planned worry to gain more control over it). While she worried, she was asked to identify her worst feared outcome related to the worry (e.g., that the hotel she chose for break would be a dump) and imagine it in vivid detail in her mind for 20–30 minutes. Following this imaginal exposure, she was to use her cognitive techniques (worry control) to challenge the accuracy of the prediction and generate alternative scenarios. Further, after about 6 weeks of treatment, Dr. Lara introduced the technique of *worry behavior prevention*. Joan was asked to identify behaviors that served to maintain or strengthen her worries, such as checking her boyfriend's cell phone when he was asleep so she could make sure he was not cheating on her. Joan was then told to decrease this behavior and see what happened—that is, that reducing her checking behaviors did not increase the odds of an unfaithful boyfriend, and may even have decreased them.

Joan had two more panic attacks in class during the first 8 weeks of treatment, so the second half of the 16-week treatment focused on her panic disorder. Dr. Lara had recommended a yoga class at the college gym, which Joan had started early in therapy. By her 9th visit with Dr. Lara, then, Joan was good at *breathing retraining*, one vital component for combatting panic disorder. She was able to slow and deepen her breathing voluntarily. Joan was also adept at cognitive restructuring, the second component of panic treatment, from the first half of her CBT for her GAD. With repeated and almost daily practice (as part of her counseling homework), Joan was finding it easier to generate alternatives and challenge her distorted and anxiety-producing thoughts.

Finally, Dr. Lara had a session of *psychoeducation* with Joan, in which she explained the nature of panic and that panic attacks were in fact "false alarms" maintained by what Joan told herself when she noticed her chest tightening. Dr. Lara took Joan out for a 10-minute run around campus at the beginning of their 10th session, which used the principle of exposure. When they returned to the counseling center to continue their 50-minute session, Joan was breathing hard and her chest was tightening. Together, they talked through Joan's physical symptoms and generated alternative explanations (e.g., "your chest is tightening because you exercised, not because you are going to pass out.") The third time they did this activity together, Joan's fear of her bodily sensations of chest tightening decreased. After her 4 months of treatment (which ended in March of her senior year of college), Joan was doing much better. She was panic-free and no longer dreaded going to class, and she was sleeping and studying more effectively. However, Joan was still a "worrier" and thought a great deal about her impending graduation, how her divorced parents would get along that weekend, and what she wanted to do after college.

Summary

Fear and Anxiety Gone Awry

Fear and anxiety are the emotions at the core of all of the anxiety disorders. Fear refers to a set of physical, behavioral, and emotional responses to a specific danger. It is an adaptive emotion when it signals an organism to avoid or escape danger. Panic is fear without actual danger present. Anxiety is a diffuse and chronic sense of apprehension about some aversive event in the future that people fear they cannot control. Fear and anxiety interact to produce all the anxiety disorders in this chapter, as well as in Chapters 8 and 9.

Specific Phobias and Social Anxiety Disorder

Phobias of circumscribed objects or situations are classified as specific phobias. Social anxiety disorder (SAD), formerly called social phobia, involves intense fear regarding social situations in which people fear that they will embarrass themselves or attract negative attention from others. Phobias are the most common anxiety disorders. They can be acquired by direct or vicarious conditioning and through information about the alleged danger of an object or situation. Preparedness theory postulates that people are biologically predisposed to become afraid of objects or situations that were dangerous to our evolutionary ancestors and therefore had significance for survival.

Effective treatment of phobias and social anxiety disorder requires a component called exposure, in which avoidance behavior is discontinued and people gradually (or all at once) face the feared situation, possibly in their imagination first (systematic desensitization). The key to successful treatment of phobias appears to be increasing the client's sense of self-efficacy about coping with the feared stimulus.

Panic Disorder and Agoraphobia

Panic disorder consists of intense attacks of panic that are unexpected and not necessarily triggered by specific phobic stimuli. Repeated attacks, and the dread of having more attacks, lead many people with panic disorder to avoid situations in which they have previously had an attack or in which they believe they might have one. This avoidance constitutes agoraphobia. Panic and agoraphobia often, but do not always, co-occur.

Panic disorder appears in some form in most parts of the world. It is more prevalent among females. Biologically based theories suggest a genetic contribution to panic disorder. It is becoming more clear that specific areas of the brain, such as the locus coeruleus, may be involved in panic attacks, but just how these attacks are triggered is still unclear. Cognitive-behavioral theorists propose that misinterpretation of bodily sensations as signs of danger escalate into panic attacks. Antidepressant and anti-anxiety drugs decrease panic attacks, but the results of cognitive-behavioral treatment programs are better and longer-lasting.

Generalized Anxiety Disorder

Chronic worriers whose anxiety is free floating and persistent but without a strong fear-based component may be diagnosed with generalized anxiety disorder (GAD). Since GAD overlaps with other conditions such as panic disorder and depression, some have questioned whether GAD is a separate disorder. However, other evidence indicates that people with GAD do not experience the same type of physiological arousal seen in other anxiety disorders; in fact, people with GAD use worrying to distract from and protect themselves against images of negative future events. Like all of the anxiety disorders discussed in this chapter, GAD is caused by an interaction of biopsychosocial factors, likely involving brain areas such as the frontal lobe and the limbic system (amygdala), though the latter plays a larger role in phobias and panic. The only effective treatments for GAD are antidepressant drugs and cognitive-behavioral therapy, which should be the first-line choice due to fewer side effects, higher cost effectiveness, and better overall outcomes.

Key Terms

agoraphobia, p. 263

amygdala, p. 254

anxiety, p. 249

anxiety disorder, p. 248

anxiety hierarchy, p. 259

benzodiazepines, p. 255

concordance rate, p. 254

fear, p. 248

flooding, p. 260

gamma aminobutyric acid (GABA), p. 255

generalized anxiety disorder (GAD), p. 270

graduated exposure, p. 259

limbic system, p. 254

locus coeruleus (LC), p. 265

panic, p. 248

panic attacks, p. 262

panic disorder, p. 262

participant modeling, p. 260

phobia, p. 250

preparedness theory, p. 255

self-efficacy, p. 261

sleep paralysis, p. 264

social anxiety disorder (SAD), p. 253

specific phobia, p. 250

Tiffany O'Meara

Dr. Tiffany O'Meara has spent the majority of her career working as a counseling psychologist in university counseling centers. She has worked at UCLA and USC, and has spent the past 13 years at UC–San Diego. There, she runs two highly popular therapy groups: "Building Social Confidence" and "Advanced Building Social Confidence." The Building Social Confidence group is a cognitive-behavioral group treatment for social anxiety disorder. Dr. O'Meara is also the creator and coordinator of the Wellness Peer Educator program. The Wellness Peer Educators are a group of students who educate fellow students about topics of mental health and well-being, work to reduce the stigma of seeking mental health assistance, and provide information about counseling services on campus.

Q *In your years working in university counseling centers, what have you noticed in terms of student trends? Have any DSM diagnoses become more or less common over the past decade?*

A I have noticed a big shift in the number of students utilizing our services. We are much busier now than when I started working over 15 years ago. We currently see about 11% of the total university population. About 8 years ago, it used to be that adjustment disorders [see Chapter 9] and relationship problems were the top two diagnoses seen at our counseling center. Now, anxiety is the most common mental health problem seen at our center, with depression as the second most common diagnosis.

Q *How do you diagnose social anxiety disorder (SAD)?*

A I diagnose social anxiety disorder through a clinical interview, using the *DSM-5* criteria, which describes SAD as "a persistent fear of one or more social or performance situations in which the person is exposed to unfamiliar people or to possible scrutiny by others" in which the individual fears acting in a way (or showing anxiety symptoms) that will be embarrassing and humiliating.

SAD is more than just being shy. Although there are similar qualities to shyness, social anxiety is more severe. It can cause overwhelming anxiety and impair school, work, and/or social functioning. Individuals with social anxiety are often afraid of not knowing what to say in a conversation and typically worry a great deal about what others are thinking about them. These fears keep them from interacting socially. Avoidance is very common in social anxiety, and it can seriously interfere with their life. For example, some students I have seen with SAD have difficulty making friends and dating, interacting in groups, participating in class (or even attending class), presenting in front of a class, talking to a professor during office hours, or applying for jobs and internships because they are afraid of going on an interview. I always tell my students that there is nothing wrong with shyness in itself, but if their anxiety is keeping them from doing things they want to do and reaching their goals, then it may be a disorder.

Q *What, in your experience, are the best treatments for SAD?*

A I have worked with students in both individual and group counseling, and whereas I think that both treatment modalities are effective, I find cognitive-behavioral group therapy to be the most effective treatment for SAD. One of the most helpful things about the group therapy that a student cannot get from individual counseling is the opportunity to meet others with similar symptoms and similar experiences. This is immediately validating and normalizing. Often, after the first group, students will say something such as, "Now I don't feel like such a freak," or "It's been so helpful just to hear that I'm not alone, that others have these same fears." Social anxiety is maintained through a pattern of negative thinking patterns and avoidance behaviors. So cognitive-behavioral treatment helps students challenge those thought patterns to create more realistic thinking and to start facing their fears through setting specific behavioral change goals.

Q *Can you explain a bit about your Building Social Confidence group, such as how you run it and what treatment components it involves?*

A The Building Social Confidence group is a cognitive-behavioral treatment with three main components. The group is part *didactic*, with me (and my co-leader) explaining social anxiety concepts and the rationale be-

Dr. Tiffany O'Meara *(Continued)*

hind cognitive-behavioral treatment, and also teaching specific conversational and social skills. Another part of the group is *experiential*, with group members practicing conversations in pairs and with the larger group (8–10 members). A third and final component is *supportive group therapy*, in which the members share personal experiences and provide each other with all-important social support. As mentioned earlier, a key feature of treating social anxiety is challenging negative thought patterns and creating behavioral change goals. Doing this in a group setting allows students to observe each other in terms of how many of their behavioral goals end up turning out successful and how they cope when things do not go exactly as planned.

A pattern of social avoidance is successful in reducing short-term anxiety, but it also reinforces the anxiety in that individuals never learn whether their fears are as bad as they think they are. When students stop avoiding and start to face their fears, they quickly learn that either their fear is not as bad as they thought it was, or they are better able to cope than they had imagined. These successful experiences start to change negative thinking patterns and can help build confidence (self-efficacy), which then makes it easier to approach the next social situation.

Q Can you tell us about a success story or two that you have had in working with people with SAD?

A Over the years, I feel fortunate to have witnessed many success stories. Much of the progress made by students involves small but meaningful changes: a student who is able to participate more in class, a student who is able to approach a professor to ask for a letter of recommendation, or a student who is able to start sending out resumes for an internship. But there are also students who have made quantum changes: One student, who had never been involved in any clubs or activities, got involved in his first club and the next year was elected president of that club. Another student who was very anxious about talking in front of others ended up performing karaoke in front of hundreds of

people. The first client I ever saw with SAD was upset because he had never had a girlfriend. Over the course of the school year, he took risks to talk with women and was entering his first romantic relationship by the end of that year.

Each week, students assign themselves a homework goal. Those students who are willing to face their fears, step out of their comfort zone, and make small changes end up making the best progress. It's not that one small change changes their life, but rather that small changes over time make a big difference.

One of my favorite success stories was of a graduate student, "Jacob," who came to see me because at the end of the school year he would need to defend his dissertation in front of a large group of people. He was extremely anxious about the idea of speaking in public. I explained to him the rationale behind cognitive-behavioral treatment and how we were going to start small and work our way up to his greatest fear. Jacob started by making a hierarchical list of social situations that would cause him anxiety and ranked them from lowest anxiety to highest anxiety. The top (scariest) item was defending his dissertation. The first (least-scary) item on the list was to speak to a server in a restaurant. Jacob started at the bottom of his list by talking to the server. The first time, he simply ordered food. The next time, he set a goal to ask a more personal question, such as, "How are you doing?" Every week, he set a new goal and moved up his list. His progress was slow but steady. Sometimes, he had great success, whereas other times, his homework goals would not go so well. But he learned how to cope with rejection and failure, and continued to focus on the actions he was taking, rather than on a specific outcome that he was hoping for. We also worked on challenging his patterns of negative thinking and on providing him with some tools to reduce his physiological anxiety and to improve his social skills. He took a class on public speaking, interviewed and got a job off campus, and started to provide tours as part of that job. By the end of the academic year, he was able to successfully defend his dissertation!

Obsessive-Compulsive and Related Disorders

Source: maryp/Shutterstock.com.

Chapter Outline

Obsessive-Compulsive Disorder

Hoarding Disorder

Body Dysmorphic Disorder

Hair-Pulling and Skin-Picking Disorders

Causes of Obsessive-Compulsive and Related Disorders

Treatment of Obsessive-Compulsive and Related Disorders

After reading this chapter, you will be able to answer the following key questions:

- How are obsessive-compulsive and related disorders described and categorized in the *Diagnostic and Statistical Manual of Mental Disorders (DSM-5)*?

- What causes obsessive-compulsive and related disorders?

- What are the main treatments used today to help people with obsessive-compulsive and related disorders?

From the Case of Jim

Jim is a 31-year-old Manhattan lawyer who recently went through a messy divorce with his wife of 7 years. Jim has always been considered a somewhat anxious and "high-strung" person, but lately, his anxiety has manifested itself in new ways. For example, Jim has been late to work—and even to court— several times in the past month because he has had to return home 10–15 times each morning to make sure he did not leave the stove on or the door to his apartment unlocked. When his boss, one of the partners at the law firm, asked Jim why he kept returning to his house, Jim was hard-pressed to give a good answer:

> I know it is unreasonable and downright silly. It's just that I have this recurrent thought about how I forgot to do something important . . . and how the entire building could explode because of my failure to turn off my stove after cooking my breakfast in the morning. I have to go back until it feels right.

Jim described his childhood as "normal," although he portrayed his parents as very strict and as demanding that Jim do things perfectly, like clean his room or organize his clothes and schoolbag. Jim remembers meticulously arranging his baseball cards as a kid and getting upset if someone (like his annoying older sister) would mess them up. Jim also recalls having tics as a child, mainly having to do with a stereotypical way of clearing his throat and blinking his eyes frequently. Jim is currently at his wit's end and worried that, if he cannot stop himself from returning to his apartment multiple times each day, he will lose his prestigious and hard-earned job at the law firm.

Obsessive-compulsive and related disorders in the *DSM-5* reflect the increasing evidence of these disorders' relatedness to one another in terms of diagnostic features, as well as the clinical utility of grouping these disorders in the same chapter (American Psychiatric Association, 2013a). Like the anxiety disorders covered in Chapter 7, obsessive-compulsive and related disorders all involve significant anxiety. However, the hallmarks of these disorders are specific preoccupations (e.g., order, parting with possessions, body appearance), along with the performance of repetitive behaviors or mental acts in response to those preoccupations. Some of these disorders—hair pulling and skin picking—involve recurrent body-focused repetitive behaviors and repeated attempts to stop these compulsive actions.

Obsessive-Compulsive Disorder

Obsessive-compulsive disorder (OCD) involves recurrent obsessions or compulsions that are serious enough to adversely affect a person's life (see Table 8.1 for the criteria for this diagnosis). **Obsessions** are unwanted, disturbing, often irrational thoughts, feelings, or images that people cannot get out of their minds. When clinicians use the term *obsession*, they are not referring to the preoccupation a person might feel about a romantic partner or the daydreams a person has about an upcoming weekend. Such repeated thoughts are usually experienced with some pleasure. Most people occasionally experience intrusive thoughts such as these, and such thoughts are perfectly normal. Clinical obsessions, however, seem to force their way into the mind and stay there for long periods of time. They usually involve frightening images or aggressive urges, and bring with them significant anxiety.

Most people have experienced a minor, temporary obsession in the form of a tune or advertising jingle that they cannot get out of their minds. Others may frequently worry when they are away from home that they have forgotten to lock a door or turn off an appliance. In OCD, however, the obsessions are much more distressing. The main diagnostic *specifier* for OCD concerns the level of insight involved. About two thirds of individuals with OCD, including Jim in the chapter-opening case, recognize that their obsessive beliefs are definitely or probably not true and are diagnosed with *OCD, with good or fair insight* (American Psychiatric Association, 2013a; Brakoulias, 2013). Some think that their beliefs are probably true (*OCD, with poor insight*), whereas a small subset of people are completely convinced that their obsessive beliefs are true (*OCD, with absent insight/delusional beliefs*). Surprising to some clinicians is that the nature or theme of the obsessions themselves is not currently

obsessive-compulsive disorder (OCD): An anxiety disorder that involves recurrent obsessions or compulsions that are serious enough to adversely affect a person's life.

obsession: An unwanted, disturbing, often irrational thought, feeling, or image that people cannot get out of their minds.

Source: Alan Light.

Fictional character Monica E. Geller, played by actress Courteney Cox (shown here), was known for her obsessive-compulsive features in the American sitcom *Friends* (1994–2004). Examples of Monica's obsessive-compulsive cleanliness included labelling cups, sorting towels into 11 different categories (four of which were "everyday use," "fancy," "guest," and "fancy guest"), and describing her new workplace as being "not just Health Department clean, but Monica clean." She was also extremely territorial when it came to cleaning, as shown when her husband Chandler announced that he had hired a maid, and Monica snapped that she hoped he meant "mistress."

TABLE 8.1 The *DSM-5* in Simple Language: Diagnosing Obsessive-Compulsive Disorder

> ■ *Obsessive-compulsive disorder (OCD)* is diagnosed when individuals have *obsessions* or *compulsions* or both that take lots of time and impair their functioning.
>
> ■ *Obsessions* are upsetting thoughts, impulses, or images that pop into a person's head and will not simply go away, despite the person's attempts to ignore or stop them or to satisfy them by performing a compulsion.
>
> ■ *Compulsions* are repetitive behaviors (e.g., washing hands, ordering, checking) or mental acts (e.g., praying, counting) that individuals believe they must do to neutralize their obsession or prevent some dreaded event, even though these compulsive acts are excessive or ineffective.

Source: Adapted from American Psychiatric Association (2013a).

a specifier in the *DSM-5*, despite mounting evidence supporting the role of these themes in explaining the heterogeneity of the disorder (Brakoulias, 2013).

Factor analysis of symptom data from thousands of people with OCD has consistently yielded four different dimensions (e.g., Bloch, Landeros-Weisenberger, Rosario, Pittenger, & Leckman, 2008; Leckman, Grice, Boardman, & Zhang, 1997). The first dimension (accounting for about 30% of the variance in individual symptoms of those with OCD in Leckman et al., 1997) includes obsessions associated with *aggressive*, *sexual*, and/or *religious forbidden thoughts* (e.g., taboo thoughts such as "I have an urge to harm someone" or fears of committing a crime or shouting obscenities). The second dimension accounts for 13.8% of the variance and includes OCD symptoms concerning *symmetry/ordering* (e.g., "Things must be in their proper place"). The third dimension accounts for 10.2% of the variance and is composed of *contamination* obsessions (e.g., "I will get germs" or other fears of harm). Other contamination-related obsessions include disgust over body secretions or, as evident in the chapter-opening case, Jim's worry that he did not turn off the stove or lock the door to his apartment. The fourth dimension includes *hoarding* obsessions (not throwing things away), which accounts for 8.5% of the variance and is now considered a separate disorder in the *DSM-5*, discussed in more detail later in the chapter.

MAPS - Superficial Syndromes
This cactus is obsessed with symmetry and organization, always maintaining even numbers of projections.

Source: Brian L. Burke.

People with OCD find their obsessions so uncomfortable that they feel compelled to take some action to suppress them or to ease the anxiety and guilt caused by them. Research reveals that all individuals with OCD experience both obsessions and compulsions (Leonard & Riemann, 2012), with about 95% self-reporting both symptoms and the other 5% of people found to have both kinds of symptoms upon further examination of their medical records. **Compulsions** are repetitive, nearly irresistible acts that temporarily relieve the anxiety derived from the obsessions. Common compulsive rituals are connected to the specific obsessions and include:

compulsion: A repetitive, nearly irresistible act that a person performs, often in response to some obsessive thought.

- checking doors or windows, water or gas taps for safety (like Jim checking the stove and locks) or checking that you did not actually harm someone in obsessions with *aggressive/sexual/religious* content;

- counting objects a precise number of times or repeating certain actions (such as going through a doorway) a set number of times or constantly organizing objects for *symmetry/ordering* obsessions; and

- repetitively washing the hands or other objects or not touching people/things that may be a source of germs or dirt in *contamination* obsessions.

Sometimes, compulsions take the form of performing some small act in exactly the same manner, over and over, so that the individual labors through each day at an extremely slow pace. Putting dishes and silverware away in a precisely aligned pattern, hanging clothes in a closet so that exactly the same gap is maintained between hangers, sorting food on shelves according to their caloric content, or insisting that books be always maintained in alphabetical order on shelves are typical compulsive routines. Although people with OCD try to resist performing these rituals and understand them to be unreasonable and excessive, the impulse to use them to reduce mounting tension eventually wins out. As discussed in Chapter 7, avoidance behaviors for anxiety disorders become stronger because they are rewarded by anxiety reduction—that is, not going into the elevator or refusing to give a public speech leaves the individual feeling relieved. Similarly, the compulsion in OCD brings about immediate—albeit very short-lived—relief from the nagging anxiety brought on by the obsessions, which by definition are recurrent and unyielding.

In fact, one study showed that it is the nature of the attempted solution—what individuals do in response to their anxiety—that determines which *DSM-5* disorder they may develop (Ladouceur et al. 2000). Ladouceur and associates found that people without any mental disorders also had unwanted thoughts but that their most common reactions were to use distraction or self-talk (convince themselves that they were all right), seek reassurance, or do nothing. Conversely, those with anxiety disorders were more likely to

MAPS - Attempted Answers

Everyone waited as Allen figured out how much the meal had cost per bite.

try different cognitive strategies to combat the intrusive thoughts, such as thought-stopping (e.g., consciously saying "Stop!" whenever they experienced these thoughts) or self-questioning (e.g., asking themselves whether that thought was really true). Finally, people with OCD were most likely to engage in an overt compulsion or mental checking that was specifically linked to the unwanted thoughts. This behavioral solution typically becomes the clinical problem for those with OCD, as the compulsions cause the bulk of the dysfunction and distress, like making Jim from the chapter-opening case late for work and at risk of losing his job.

Characteristics and Prevalence

The tyrant in your head will second-guess you no matter what you do. That voice of dread is terrified, terrifying, loud, and repetitively destructive. Demote it by making it your pesky backseat driver. You can steer without it.

—*Becky Wolsk, OCD sufferer (n.d.)*

How does the compulsive behavior performed in response to obsessional thoughts compare to behavior involved in other conditions, such as overeating, gambling, and substance use disorders? In all of these compulsive disorders (including OCD), people, at least in the short run, derive pleasure (or anxiety reduction and relief) from performing the behavior. In addition, just like with these other addictions, OCD rituals can be highly debilitating in the longer term. For example, people with contamination obsessions and its accompanying washing compulsions might wash their hands for several hours each day, leaving little time for other activities. Hand washers have been known to continue their compulsion even after they have rubbed off several layers of skin. However, one key difference between OCD and the other compulsive disorders is that people in the latter case often seek the opportunity to engage in the desired behaviors (i.e., actively seeking buffets, casinos, or substances of choice), whereas people with OCD are typically not looking for opportunities to perform their compulsive acts. Rather, the obsessive thoughts fueling their compulsions are intrusive and unwanted.

Howard Hughes, the famous industrialist, aviator, and movie producer, suffered from OCD related to his dread of contamination. His obsessive behavior led to virtual isolation from the world. Anything that came into his penthouse apartment had to be wrapped in special paper. His attempts at cleanliness became so involved that he was unable to continue them, and eventually, he abandoned all efforts to cleanse himself (CIBA-GIEGY, 1991). Dr. Samuel Johnson, the 18th-century English lexicographer, essayist, and biographer, apparently had a version of OCD. One of his contemporaries described Johnson's behavior as he approached a door: "Johnson would take a prescribed number of steps from a certain point in the room, and just before crossing the threshold, he would twist, turn, and make strange gesticulations. Finally, he would leap over the threshold. . . ." (Rapoport, 1989). Other famous people who have reportedly battled with OCD include Leonardo DiCaprio, who ironically played Howard Hughes in the 2004 film *The Aviator* (New Health Guide, 2014). DiCaprio has revealed that he has to force himself not to step on chewing gum stains when walking and has the urge to walk through doorways multiple times. Jessica Alba, an American model and actress who starred in *Fantastic Four* (2005), disclosed that she has OCD that causes her anxiety if she does not repeat activities such as combing her hair or washing her hands. Soccer player David Beckham is one of the most high-profile athletes to reveal his OCD symptoms; he said that odd numbers and objects that are misaligned can aggravate his symptoms. Finally, actress Cameron Diaz mentioned in a 1997 article that she has a germ phobia and described herself as a "frequent hand washer." She is afraid of touching doorknobs and will often use her elbows to open doors instead.

Similarity to Tourette's Disorder

Clinical researchers have noted similarities between OCD and tic-related conditions like the one Jim from the chapter-opening case reported as a child. For example, a condition known as **Tourette's disorder**, originally noted by Gilles de la Tourette in the 19th century, is characterized by both repetitive vocal tics or vocalizations (teeth clicking, coughing, grunting) *and* motor acts and tics, such as rapid eye blinking, retracing footsteps or twirling around, and facial grimaces. Because Tourette's disorder usually begins in childhood or early adolescence, the *DSM-5* classifies it as a neurodevelopmental disorder (see Chapter 3 for more disorders in this category). In addition to motor tics, which many children have at some point in their development but then outgrow, about one third of children with Tourette's disorder also display **coprolalia**, the involuntary shouting or repeating of obscene words. They also tend to have problems involving impulsive behavior and socially annoying actions.

Gilles de la Tourette himself noted a possible association between Tourette's disorder and obsessive-compulsive behavior, and many contemporary clinicians have observed increased rates of OCD among people with Tourette's disorder, as well as among their relatives (George, Trimble, Ring, Sallee, & Robertson, 1993; Leckman & Cohen, 1994; Pauls, Raymond, & Robertson, 1991). Based on these findings and the fact that the motor rituals of Tourette's often appear similar to OCD, several researchers currently believe that people with Tourette's and OCD share a genetic vulnerability. Up to 30% of individuals with OCD have a lifetime tic disorder, and they are diagnosed with a special subtype of OCD called *tic-related*, which is more common in males who have OCD onset in childhood (American Psychiatric Association, 2013a).

Prevalence of Obsessive-Compulsive Disorder

OCD appears worldwide and affects 1–3% of the general population around the globe, with little variation among countries studied in terms of lifetime prevalence (Leckman et al., 2010; Ruscio, Stein, Chiu, & Kessler, 2010) or even symptom structure involving taboo thoughts, symmetry, cleaning, or fear of harm (American Psychiatric Association, 2013a). Interestingly, one study directly comparing OCD in people from the United States and Costa Rica found that, though the core symptoms were the same in both countries, severity and comorbidity were both higher for U.S. participants (Chavira et al., 2008). Therefore, some features of OCD, such as impairment, may be culturally influenced.

Between 2–3% of U.S. adults and 1% of children and adolescents suffer OCD at some time in their lives (Kessler, Petukhova, Sampson, Zaslavsky, & Wittchen, 2012; Robins & Regier, 1991). Up to half of the cases begin in childhood or adolescence, with some compulsive behaviors starting as young as 3 years of age (Rapoport, 1989). In their extensive studies of children with OCD, Judith Rapoport and her colleagues (1981, 1989) found that gender distribution varies by age. In particular:

- those with onset in early childhood are predominantly male;
- the gender distribution is fairly even among people who develop OCD during adolescence; and
- adult-onset cases are predominantly female.

Males and females are equally represented among those whose compulsions involve counting and checking, but the majority of "washers" are female (Minichiello, Baer, Jenike, & Holland, 1990; Rachman & Hodgson, 1980). Paul Emmelkamp (1982), a psychologist from the Netherlands, has proposed that this phenomenon reflects an extension of traditional gender-role differences in which women are typically cast as cleaners. Overall, among all adults with OCD, there is a 2:1 ratio of females to males in terms of lifetime prevalence (Kessler et al., 2012).

Section Review

Individuals who suffer from obsessive-compulsive disorder:

- experience recurring intrusive thoughts (obsessions) or repetitive behaviors (compulsions) that are time consuming and disruptive to normal life (usually, both symptoms are present);

OCD Onscreen: Has OCD Been Portrayed Accurately on TV and in Movies?

America's fascination with mental disorders—and perhaps especially OCD—has resulted in various films and TV shows featuring main characters with OCD symptoms. But how accurate and realistic have these portrayals been? Here, we discuss three examples: one TV drama series, one popular film, and one TV "reality" show.

Monk (2002–2009) was an American comedy-drama detective mystery television series created by Andy Breckman and starring Tony Shalhoub as the eponymous character Adrian Monk. Monk was a brilliant detective for the San Francisco Police Department until his wife, Trudy, was killed by a car bomb in a parking garage. Trudy's death led Monk to suffer a mental breakdown. He was then discharged from the force and became a recluse, refusing to leave his house for 3-1/2 years. Monk eventually began to work as a private detective and as a consultant for the homicide unit, despite limitations rooted in his OCD, which had grown significantly worse after the tragedy, along with several other phobias.

Monk's compulsive habits were numerous, and a number of phobias, such as his fear of germs, compounded his situation. Monk had 312 fears, some of which were milk, ladybugs, harmonicas, heights, imperfection, claustrophobia, driving, food touching on his plates, messes, and risk. At various points in the series, Monk tried to conquer his fears by doing various exposure (cognitive-behavioral therapy) activities. For example, he tried drinking milk, climbing a ladder, and putting a ladybug on his hand, but when things were scattered unorganized across a table, he could not resist the compulsion to arrange them neatly. The OCD and plethora of phobias inevitably led to awkward situations that caused problems for Monk and anyone around him as he investigated cases. At the same time, however, some of his OCD-related skills, such as his obsessive focus and sharp attention to detail, aided him in solving cases.

As Good As It Gets was a 1997 American romantic comedy film directed by James L. Brooks and starring Jack Nicholson as misanthropic novelist Melvin Udall and Helen Hunt as a single mother with an asthmatic son, both of whom won the Academy Award for Best Actor/Actress for their work. In the film, Melvin Udall suffered from OCD, which, paired with his grumpiness, alienated nearly everyone with whom he interacted. Melvin's most prominent obsession was a strong fear of contamination, which he managed by overwashing himself in scalding hot water, wearing gloves and not touching people, and using disposable plastic utensils in restaurants. Another of Melvin's

Jack Nicholson won an Oscar for his role as an author with OCD in *As Good As It Gets* in 1997.
Source: Alan Light.

obsessions was about organization and control. For example, he had jars in his apartment filled with hundreds of candies that were separated by their color. Melvin's days had to be standardized and routine. He went to the same restaurant every day for breakfast, stepping over sidewalk cracks on his way there, and always had the same waitress, which in turn gave him a sense of control. When the waitress was not there to serve him one day, he became extremely anxious. One last obsession Melvin showed was that of safety/doubt. He had a compulsion of locking the door to his apartment several times, just to make sure it was locked.

Both of these projects (*Monk* and *As Good As It Gets*) did a reasonable job of illustrating the main symptom clusters of OCD, as well as the debilitating distress and dysfunction that OCD can cause, not just for the sufferers but also for those around them. However, the purpose of each of these shows was obviously entertainment, and so audiences were encouraged to laugh at the disorder without truly understanding the terror, shame, and self-loathing that many OCD sufferers endure (Wortmann, 2013). Another shortcoming of these portrayals was the perpetuation of the medical myth—that is, that pills are the only answer. In the episode "Mr. Monk Takes His Medicine," Monk's psychologist convinces him to try medication for his OCD, which works magically to cure his symptoms but also takes away his crime-fighting superpowers. In *As Good As It Gets*, Udall states that he is feeling much better because he has started taking his pills (presumably selective serotonin reuptake inhibitors [SSRIs]), with no mention of cognitive-behavioral therapy (CBT), which should be the treatment of choice.

These inaccuracies have been largely remedied by the more recent "reality" show *Obsessed*, an American documentary series that began airing on the A&E network on May 29, 2009. The series depicts the real-life struggles and treatment of people with OCD and anxiety disorders. For example, the episode that aired on June 8, 2009 featured Nidia, a mysophobe (afraid of germs) who washed her hands several times a day. She had a fear of bowel movements and felt compelled to take long showers and to use enemas and

OCD Onscreen: Has OCD Been Portrayed Accurately on TV and in Movies? *(Continued)*

toothbrushes to clean her rectum. She had been hospitalized twice due to internal bleeding as a result of her cleaning rituals. Her marriage to her husband was rocky due to her OCD. The same episode also featured Rick, who was afraid of growing old and ritually visited several gyms before and after work for short workouts. He had anxiety if he did not get to do a certain number of workouts per day. He also had anxiety about turning his body counterclockwise and had a tendency to add up the numbers on car license plates while driving.

Nidia was helped through CBT (exposure and response prevention, discussed later in the chapter). For example, Dr. Shana Doronn requested that Nidia have an outdoor picnic with her husband. The picnic consisted of high-fiber foods to help Nidia face her fear of having a bowel movement. Dr. Doronn also instructed Nidia to gradually reduce the length of her showers.

Rick, on the other hand, made only minimal progress through therapy. Dr. John Tsilimparis described

Rick as "just visiting," rather than as being committed to therapy to stop his ritual behavior, which highlights the importance of a motivational phase to the treatment.

Robert Sharenow of A&E has said about the show: "The series sheds a light on the vast world of anxiety disorders, while offering those who suffer from these debilitating afflictions a path to recovery. . . ." (The Futon Critic, 2009).

Thinking Critically

1. What other films or TV shows have you seen that feature people with OCD or other mental disorders? How accurate were these depictions?

2. What impact do you think it has on public opinion and pharmaceutical sales when popular shows portray disorders like OCD as being treatable only via psychotropic medication?

- have common obsessions of taboo thoughts/impulses, cleanliness/contamination, or order/symmetry; and
- have compulsions that fit with these obsessions—for example, cleaning rituals in someone with a contamination obsession or ordering rituals in someone with an order/symmetry obsession.

Hoarding Disorder

Hoarding disorder was formerly considered a subtype of OCD, as described earlier, but as of the *DSM-5* (American Psychiatric Association, 2013a), it is now a separate category. The change was due to research that has demonstrated that a large percentage of individuals who hoard display no other OCD symptoms (Pertusa et al., 2010; Samuels et al., 2008). In addition, hoarding is more commonly correlated with symptoms of depression rather than OCD (Wu & Watson, 2005).

Hoarding, as Table 8.2 shows, is defined as the acquisition of and inability to discard large quantities of possessions that appear to be of limited value, to the extent that one's living spaces are significantly cluttered (Frost & Hartl, 1996). The core symptom of the disorder—a reluctance to throw stuff out—is in itself very common; in fact, the prevalence of difficulty discarding worn-out/worthless items in the general population is over 20% (Rodriguez, Simpson, Liu, Levinson, & Blanco, 2013). However, in hoarding disorder, the inability to discard useless items is persistent and leads to severe blockage of individuals' living spaces. For instance, individuals may not be able to cook in the kitchen, sleep in their bed, or sit on their couch due to the accumulation of objects of little or no actual value. Of course, many people without any disorders have collections of various objects, from stamps to baseball cards. However, whereas collectors usually proudly display their collections and keep them well organized, people who hoard seldom seek to display their possessions, which are usually kept in disarray (International OCD Foundation, 2014).

hoarding disorder: A mental disorder in which individuals have persistent difficulties discarding or parting with possessions, regardless of their actual value, leading to the severe cluttering of their personal living spaces.

"You may want to send a search party into Konklin's cubicle. No one has heard from him in three days."

Source: Cartoonresource/Shutterstock.com.

TABLE 8.2 The *DSM-5* in Simple Language: Diagnosing Hoarding Disorder

Hoarding disorder is diagnosed when individuals have persistent difficulty getting rid of material possessions because doing so would be upsetting and/or they believe that they need to save the items. As a result, their active living areas become clogged and even unusable.

Source: Adapted from American Psychiatric Association (2013a).

Hoarding is associated with high levels of disability and impairment (Tolin, Frost, Steketee, Gray, & Fitch, 2008). This impairment includes but is not limited to illnesses due to unsanitary conditions, social isolation, work disability, and even death (Frost, Steketee, & Williams, 2000; Frost, Steketee, Williams, & Warren, 2000; Kim, Steketee, & Frost, 2001). One study found that hoarding participants were significantly more likely to report a broad range of chronic and severe medical concerns and had a five-fold higher rate of mental health service utilization compared to controls; several had been threatened with eviction due to hoarding, and some even had a child or elder removed from their home by the authorities (Tolin et al., 2008). These results suggest that compulsive hoarding represents a profound public health burden in terms of occupational impairment, poor physical health, and social service involvement.

Characteristics and Prevalence

Because hoarding disorder is a new disorder in the *DSM-5*, nationally representative prevalence studies are not yet available. Community surveys in the United States and Europe, however, estimate the point prevalence of clinically significant hoarding to be 1.5–6% (American Psychiatric Association, 2013a; Nordsletten et al., 2013; Samuels et al., 2008). In one study in the United Kingdom (Nordsletten et al., 2013), those with hoarding disorder were older and more often unmarried (67%) compared to people without the disorder. Members of this group were also more likely to be impaired by a current physical health condition (52.6%) or comorbid mental disorder (58%) and to claim benefits as a result of these issues (47.4%). Further, individuals with hoarding disorder were more likely to report lifetime use of mental health services, although access in the past year was less frequent. A community-based study found that alcohol use, personality disorder traits,

Source: Songquan Deng/Shutterstock.com.

In the New York based TV show *Friends*, it was Monica Geller who kept a secret closet filled with junk and had OCD tendencies, as described earlier. However, in real life, Lisa Kudrow, who played quirky character Phoebe Buffay on the show, has publicly acknowledged her hoarding tendencies. Kudrow has reported that she keeps old documents, faxes, and day planners from the 1980s. Hoarding of objects is one of the common compulsive rituals seen in hoarding disorder, which previously was considered a type of OCD. Frequently hoarded items include paper (e.g., mail, newspapers), books, clothing, and containers (International OCD Foundation, 2014). How would you determine whether Lisa Kudrow has hoarding disorder?

and specific childhood adversities may be associated with hoarding, which was greater in men than in women and inversely related to household income (Samuels et al., 2008).

Another study surveyed over 750 adults online to delineate the typical onset and course of hoarding behavior (Tolin, Meunier, Frost, & Steketee, 2010). Median age of onset for hoarding disorder was 11–15 years, with most respondents reporting symptom onset before age 20. Late-onset hoarding (e.g., after age 40) was rare. Most respondents described a chronic course of illness, with a significant minority describing an increasing or relapsing/remitting course. Stressful and traumatic events were common in this sample; changes in relationships and interpersonal violence were disproportionately associated with periods of symptom onset or exacerbation.

"Oo, I see we have two more strays to add to the database."
Leroy was not only a cattle herder—he was also a cattle *hoarder*.

Animal hoarding, defined as the accumulation of a large number of animals (pets), along with a failure to provide minimal standards of nutrition and care, may be a special type of hoarding disorder (American Psychiatric Association, 2013a; Frost, Patronek, & Rosenfield, 2011). Like object hoarders, people who hoard animals have great difficulty relinquishing them to others who can more adequately care for them, and they form intense attachments (urges to save) that result in significant impairment.

Several other similarities between animal and object hoarding are noteworthy (Frost et al., 2011). Both appear to follow a chronic course and are characterized by an exaggerated sense of responsibility, need for control over objects/animals, and intense emotional attachments to objects/animals. Both show impaired insight into the nature of the problem. However, there are significant differences as well. The vast majority of animal hoarding cases are characterized by very poor living conditions, whereas only a small number of object hoarding cases involve such living conditions (Frost et al., 2011). One exception to the animal squalor trend is celebrity Paris Hilton, who claims that she has 35 pets (Lambe, 2013), although she would not be diagnosed with animal hoarding because her pets have high-quality living conditions (e.g., a two-story dog mansion for her seven dogs!).

The American documentary series *Hoarders* on A&E (2009–2013) depicted the real-life struggles and treatment of people who suffer from hoarding.

Section Review

Individuals with hoarding disorder:

- experience persistent difficulties discarding or parting with possessions, regardless of their actual value, leading to the severe cluttering of their personal living spaces;
- can have significant disability and impairment as a result of their hoarding; and
- may also hoard animals, who usually reside in poor living conditions.

Body Dysmorphic Disorder

Body dysmorphic disorder (BDD) was first documented in 1886 by Enrico Morselli, an Italian psychiatrist who referred to it as "dysmorphophobia," meaning fear of having a deformity (Hunt, Thienhaus, & Ellwood, 2008). Morselli noted the obsessive thoughts and compulsive behaviors that characterize the disorder, which he believed to be similar to the symptoms of OCD (Wolrich, 2011). Most people have something they do not like about their appearance—a crooked nose, an uneven smile, or eyes that are too large or too small. And though they may fret about their imperfections, the imperfections do not interfere with their daily lives. People with BDD, however, think about their real or perceived flaws for hours each day. They cannot control their negative thoughts and do not believe people who tell them that they look fine. Their thoughts may cause severe emotional distress and interfere with their daily functioning. They may miss work or school, avoid

body dysmorphic disorder (BDD): A mental disorder in which individuals are preoccupied with one or more perceived defects in their physical appearance and perform repetitive behaviors or mental acts in response to these appearance-related concerns.

BDD is sometimes called "imagined ugliness" because people think that there is something wrong with some aspect of their appearance, such as their skin (e.g., perceived acne or scars), hair (e.g., excessive body hair), or nose (e.g., size or shape).

Like OCD, many celebrities have acknowledged suffering from BDD (Health Research Funding, 2014), including two very famous people who are now deceased. Michael Jackson, shown here, popularly known as one of the best musical performers of all time, likely had BDD, as he underwent many different types of surgical operations and treatments to change his nose (several times) and even lighten the color of his skin. Marilyn Monroe was thought to be suffering from BDD to the extent that she frequently changed her face and appearance whenever she appeared on TV.

social situations, and isolate themselves, even from family and friends, because they fear that others will notice their bodily flaws.

Like people with OCD, individuals with BDD have obsessions—preoccupations that are intrusive, unwanted, and time consuming, occurring 3–8 hours daily on average (American Psychiatric Association, 2013a)—as well as compulsions. The obsessions typically involve the belief that they are unattractive or deformed, despite the fact that others do not observe this abnormality. According to data collected from over 500 study participants, individuals with BDD most often focus on their skin (73%), hair (56%), nose (37%), stomach (22%), weight (22%), breasts/chest (21%), eyes (20%), thighs (20%), and teeth (20%; Butler Hospital, 2008). However, preoccupation with any body part or area of the body is possible, and it can shift from one body part to another over time (Phillips, 2005).

Just like with OCD, the compulsions are individuals' drive to perform repetitive behaviors or mental acts, which may increase their anxiety in the long run. Nearly all individuals diagnosed with BDD engage in time-consuming, compulsive behaviors, which typically include efforts to hide, check, and improve perceived appearance flaws. The most common of such BDD behaviors typically include: (1) camouflaging the body part (with body position/posture, clothing, accessories, makeup, or one's hair) (91%); (2) comparing the body part with that of others or scrutinizing the appearance of others (88%); (3) checking one's appearance in mirrors or reflective surfaces (87%); (4) undergoing plastic surgery and seeking dermatological, dental, or other medical treatments, often repeatedly, to eliminate or repair the defect (72%); and (5) seeking reassurance or attempting to convince others that the perceived defect is real and unattractive (54%; Phillips, 2005). Furthermore, 46–59% of people with BDD perform compulsive grooming rituals (e.g., brushing hair, applying makeup, removing hair) and excessive clothing changes or purchasing of beauty products; 38% engage in skin picking or self-mutilation (to alter, reduce, or remove the defect); 24% avoid mirrors altogether, sometimes for days at a time; and 18–39% engage in excessive dieting, tanning, exercising, or weight-lifting (Butler Hospital, 2008). BDD is relatively frequent (6–15%) among plastic surgery and dermatology patients, who undergo unnecessary surgeries to correct perceived imperfections, rarely finding satisfaction with the results (Kisely, Morkell, Allbrook, Briggs, & Jovanovic, 2002; Pavan et al., 2006). The "Prevention" feature discusses this process in more depth.

Characteristics and Prevalence

One specifier (subtype) of BDD—muscle dysmorphia—occurs almost exclusively in males. Muscle dysmorphia consists of preoccupation with the idea that one's body is insufficiently muscular or lean, or is "too small" (Pope, Gruber, Choi, Olivardia, & Phillips, 1997). In reality, these men look normal or may even be very muscular. Many men with muscle dysmorphia attend to a meticulous diet and time-consuming workout schedule, which can cause bodily damage, and use anabolic-androgenic steroids and other substances in an attempt to get bigger (Pope, Phillips, & Olivardia, 2000). One study compared men with muscle dysmorphia (86% of whom had additional appearance concerns) to men with BDD without muscle dysmorphia, finding similarities in demographic features, BDD severity, and number of overall body areas of concern (Pope et al., 2005). However, people with the muscle dysphoria subtype of BDD were more likely to lift weights excessively (71% versus 12%), diet (71% versus 27%), and exercise excessively (64% versus 10%), and generally had poorer quality of life than other people with BDD (Phillips et al., 2010). Some researchers have suggested that muscle dysmorphia is more closely related to eating disorders (see Chapter 12) than to BDD (Murray, Rieger, Touyz, & De la Garza García, 2010).

Although there are limited data on the prevalence of BDD, it may be far more common than generally recognized (Wolrich, 2011). From 0.7–2.4% of the general population

Can/Should Some Plastic Surgeries Be Prevented?

People with body dysmorphic disorder (BDD) suffer from a severe preoccupation with an imagined or grossly exaggerated perception of a bodily defect. Accordingly, people with BDD often attempt to rectify their perceived defect by seeking cosmetic surgery, but they are typically unhappy with the results of their procedures. After surgery, patients commonly experience an exacerbation of symptoms, as their original preoccupation intensifies or is transferred to another part of the body (Steiner, 2002). These patients often undergo numerous surgeries in futile attempts to rectify their original procedure. Further, the plastic surgeon is usually blamed for the perceived outcome, sometimes leading to lawsuits or, in one case, homicide of the doctor (Steiner, 2002). Thus, the costs of simply allowing people with BDD to have plastic surgeries are high; many potentially negative outcomes could be avoided if these cosmetic surgeries were preempted in the first place.

Two pathways for preventing excessive plastic surgeries in those with BDD are to educate the two key parties involved in these procedures: (1) the patients themselves and (2) their plastic surgeons. In one study, data were collected from 449 patients aged 18–70 undergoing elective cosmetic surgery in Australia (Jackson, Dowling, Honigman, Francis, & Kalus, 2012). Just under half of the sample indicated that they had been teased or bullied about their appearance. Teased patients showed significantly higher levels of anxiety, depression, and dysmorphic concern about their bodies; lower levels of physical attractiveness and appearance satisfaction; and lower levels of satisfaction with discrete aspects of their appearance than patients who were not teased. Teasing also contributed to longer periods of considering surgery as an answer to body dissatisfaction concerns, even when controlling for age (Jackson et al., 2012). Therefore, one front-line pathway to prevention would be to provide educational initiatives on appearance-related teasing to adolescent students. This could both reduce victimization and teasing in the first place (thereby lowering the incidence of both BDD and eating disorders, as discussed in Chapter 12), and possibly help victims generate alternatives to surgery before their body image concerns become too entrenched.

However, the next line of defense for the prevention of unnecessary surgeries must target the plastic surgeons themselves. As detrimental consequences for both patient and doctor may result after these cosmetic procedures, plastic surgeons should be familiar with the signs and symptoms of BDD so that they can identify prospective patients who have it (Steiner, 2002). However, this is typically not the case at all. One survey showed that 82% of plastic surgeons were unfamiliar with the *DSM* diagnostic criteria for BDD, whereas 28% were unaware of even the main clinical feature of the disorder (Steiner, 2002). Clearly, more doctors need to become familiar with the signs and symptoms of BDD and should be educated about the typical outcome of plastic surgery for those suffering from BDD. This would help to minimize detrimental consequences for both the patients and the plastic surgeons.

Dr. Isaac Schweitzer (1989), a psychiatrist from the University of Melbourne, Australia Department of Psychiatry, believes that, "for effective preoperative collaboration, the psychiatrist must develop specific skills and recognize particular problems that are unique to these patients. Successfully establishing liaison with the surgeon will result in a fascinating mix of body image problems challenging the psychiatrist." Schweitzer went on to develop four aspects of preoperative assessment that he recommends be used before all cosmetic surgeries:

1. *Motivation:* What are the patient's motivations for surgery? Does the motivation arise from the patient or someone else? A personal—and rational rather than distorted—wish for change is essential to prevent later resentment.

2. *Expectations:* What are the patient's expectations of surgery? Are these realistic, or does the patient believe that surgery will improve his or her life situation radically and globally?

3. *Risk:* Does the patient understand the risks and implications of surgery? Is the patient sufficiently well informed to make a reasonable decision about surgery?

4. *Anxiety:* How anxious is the patient? A patient who shows little or no anxiety demonstrates denial and possibly a failure to fully appreciate the implications of surgery.

Such psychiatric screening of patients considering cosmetic plastic surgery may be helpful to the plastic surgeon in optimizing patient satisfaction and outcome. Plastic surgeons can incorporate the psychiatric referral into the broad, comprehensive, presurgical work-up. For example, the surgeon may tell a prospective patient: "As part of my evaluation, I often find it helpful to have a patient meet with a psychiatrist to help sort out the complex issues motivating possible surgery" (Ericksen & Billick, 2012).

These two complementary pathways—educating patients and their plastic surgeons—may help reduce the number of ill-advised cosmetic surgeries that take place regularly in the United States and throughout the Western world. Decide for yourself: Should some of these surgeries be prevented?

worldwide may suffer from BDD, including over 5 million individuals in the United States alone (Hunt et al., 2008), with more similarities than differences across cultures and nations (American Psychiatric Association, 2013a). These results indicate that BDD may be as common as many other better-known mental disorders, such as schizophrenia, bipolar disorder, and eating disorders. BDD is chronic (especially without appropriate treatment), with an average duration of 16 years, and onset is typically during adolescence (Phillips, 2005). It appears to be equally prevalent in adult men and women; however, some research supports a different rate for adolescents and young adults, and in particular, females. For instance, one study found that adolescent girls experience BDD symptoms more intensely than adolescent boys (Mayville, Katz, Gipson, & Cabral, 1999). In addition, studies using college student samples have found even higher rates of BDD on college campuses than in the general population, ranging from 5–13% worldwide, as well as a higher prevalence among female college students (Bartsch, 2007; Bohne, Keuthen, Wilhelm, Deckersback, & Jenike, 2002; Cansever, Uzun, Doenmez, & Ozsahin, 2003).

Section Review

People with body dysmorphic disorder:

- have a preoccupation with one or more perceived physical defects that are not observable to others (obsessions);
- at some point have performed repetitive behaviors (compulsions) that are time consuming and disruptive to their life, such as checking mirrors or seeking reassurance about their perceived flaws; and
- may also experience muscle dysmorphia, which is the preoccupation with the idea that one's body build is too small or not muscular enough, a condition found more commonly in men.

trichotillomania (TTM; hair-pulling disorder): A mental disorder that involves recurrent pulling out of one's hair, resulting in distress and hair loss, along with repeated attempts to decrease or stop the pulling.

excoriation (skin-picking) disorder: A mental disorder that involves recurrent skin picking, resulting in distress and skin lesions, with repeated attempts to decrease or stop the picking.

Hair-Pulling and Skin-Picking Disorders

Trichotillomania (TTM; also known as **hair-pulling disorder)** is characterized by the repetitive pulling out of one's hair, despite repeated attempts to stop, resulting in noticeable hair loss and significant distress or impairment. Although no longer part of the formal *DSM-5* diagnostic criteria, many pullers (especially adults) report a sense of tension before, or when resisting, pulling, as well as pleasure, gratification, or relief during/after pulling (Himle, Hayes, Mouton-Odum, & Golomb, 2014). TTM is listed in the category of "OCD and related disorders" in the *DSM-5* because of its compulsive underpinnings—a body-checking behavior that is involuntary and hard to stop. TTM is a heterogeneous disorder in regard to manifestation, severity, and impairment.

For more than a century, researchers and clinicians have recognized people who repeatedly pick at their skin without an underlying dermatological problem. Prior to the *DSM-5*, an American Psychiatric Association working group recommended that **excoriation (skin-picking) disorder (SPD)** be included as a separate diagnosis in the *DSM-5* and proposed a set of diagnostic criteria (Snorrason, Stein, & Woods, 2013). The criteria define SPD as recurrent skin picking that results in skin lesions, clinically significant distress or functional impairment, along with repeated attempts to stop or decrease the picking behavior. SPD shares similarities with TTM in phenomenology (e.g., high incidence in women) and clinical symptoms (e.g., repetitive and compulsive grooming behaviors; Bohne, Keuthen, & Wilhelm, 2005). However, some important differences exist between the two diagnoses. The onset of TTM is typically in adolescence during or after puberty, whereas SPD has a bimodal onset, peaking both right after puberty (often with the development of acne) and then again in the early 20s (American Psychiatric Association, 2013a;

There is a common expression about anxiety that it can make you want to "tear your hair out." People with trichotillomania (hair-pulling disorder) literally do this.

Source: Aaron Amat/Shutterstock.com.

Odlaug & Grant, 2008a). Comorbidity of bipolar disorder and borderline personality disorder has also been found to be more common in individuals who have SPD than in individuals with TTM (Odlaug & Grant, 2008b).

Characteristics and Prevalence

Hair-pulling and skin-picking disorders (TTM and SPD) are thought to be related to OCD because both involve compulsive, body-focused behaviors, and both have been listed in the OCD category starting with the *DSM-5* (American Psychiatric Association, 2013a). Accordingly, both of these disorders are more common in people with OCD. In one study, 5% of people with OCD also met criteria for TTM, and over 16% met criteria for SPD. Individuals who met criteria for both OCD and either TTM or SPD tended to be younger women with a higher level of education and with comorbid BDD (Lovato et al., 2012).

Excoriation (skin-picking) disorder often begins in adolescence after puberty or in one's early 20s and may coincide with a dermatological condition such as acne (pimples).

The ways individuals pull hair in TTM can vary (McDonald, 2012). The most common pulling sites are the scalp, eyelashes, and eyebrows, although pulling may occur anywhere on the body, including the pubic region (Duke, Keeley, Geffken, & Storch, 2010). There is a difference in pull sites among ethnic lines: Caucasians have reported pulling from lashes and eyebrows more often than have racial/ethnic minorities (Neal-Barnett et al., 2010). The number of places that people with TTM pull from increases with age (Flessner, Woods, Franklin, Keuthen, & Piacentini, 2008). Approximately one third of individuals pull from multiple sites (Himle et al., 2014). Hair may be pulled one strand at a time (most common) or in clumps (Duke et al., 2010) and is most often pulled with fingers, tweezers, combs, or brushes (Walther, Ricketts, Conelea, & Woods, 2010).

Researchers have identified three subsets of hair pulling: early onset, automatic, and focused. Early-onset TTM occurs in children 8 years or younger and is generally self-correcting without therapeutic intervention (Duke et al., 2010). Automatic hair pulling is unconscious and happens while the individual is focused on something else (e.g., watching television or reading), whereas individuals with focused hair pulling are aware of the pulling. This type of pulling has been described as goal-directed, usually to reduce tension or to regulate a negative emotional state (Himle et al., 2014). Focused hair pulling is characterized by urges and tension often associated with OCD (Duke et al., 2010). These three subsets of TTM are not mutually exclusive; an individual may have co-occurring hair-pulling types (Duke et al., 2010). Only 25% of individuals report primarily focused pulling, with the majority reporting automatic or mixed pulling (Himle et al., 2014).

SPD is characterized by excessive scratching, picking, gouging, lancing, digging, rubbing or squeezing of skin with no or only minor surface irregularities (Arnold, Auchenbach, & McElroy, 2001). Skin lesions such as acne, scabs, scars, and insect bites are sometimes excoriation sites. Excoriation may also occur in response to itching or other skin sensations, such as burning, tingling, dryness, and pain (Arnold et al., 1998). Most people with SPD excoriate skin with their fingernails and fingers, but the teeth and instruments (e.g., tweezers, nail files, pins, or knives) are also sometimes used. Excoriations are usually found in areas that are easily reachable (e.g., the face), and most people excoriate multiple sites. Similar to TTM, one fifth to one quarter of those with SPD endorsed tension or nervousness before picking, tension or nervousness when attempting to resist picking, and pleasure or relief during or after picking (Keuthen, Koran, Aboujaoude, Large, & Serpe, 2010). Direct associations were found between skin picking and depressive, anxiety, and obsessive-compulsive symptoms, which may indicate that people with SPD are engaging in the behavior for emotional relief (Hayes, Storch, & Berlanga, 2009). Furthermore, one study showed that people with SPD were more likely to be female, to report higher rates of co-occurring compulsive nail-biting, and to have a first-degree relative with a grooming disorder compared to people with OCD, who spent significantly more time on their thoughts and behaviors and were more likely to have co-occurring BDD (Grant, Odlaug, & Won Kim, 2010).

Current prevalence estimates for TTM are largely established through college student surveys and vary from 1–13.3% (Duke et al., 2010); the prevalence of SPD is likely 1.4–5.4% (Hayes et al., 2009; Keuthen et al., 2010). Both of these disorders are much more common in women than in men, by a 10 to 1 ratio in TTM and a 3 or 4 to 1 ratio in SPD (American Psychiatric Association, 2013a).

Section Review

People with hair-pulling (trichotillomania [TTM]) or skin-picking disorders (SPD):

- engage in recurrent pulling out of their hair or picking at their skin to the point that they create bald spots and/or skin sores or infections;
- are focused abnormally on their body (hair or skin) as a target of their compulsive behavior; and
- usually develop these disorders during or after puberty.

Causes of Obsessive-Compulsive and Related Disorders

The biopsychosocial approach is helpful for exploring the causes of OCD and related disorders. As for most anxiety disorders (Chapter 7), biological and cognitive-behavioral theories are currently the leading explanations for how OCD develops.

The Role of Genetics

In addition to the genetic clues derived from OCD's association with Tourette's disorder, genetic contributions to OCD have been examined in both family studies and twin studies. Family studies indicate that OCD has a significant hereditable component, with relatives of OCD patients four times more likely to develop the disorder than the general population (Bloch & Pittenger, 2010). Twin and family studies support a significant genetic contribution to related disorders as well, such as chronic tic disorders, TTM, SPD, BDD, and hoarding disorder (Browne, Gair, Scharf, & Grice, 2014). Researchers have unpacked OCD's heritability by symptom factor, finding that heritability estimates (the proportion of observed differences in OCD symptoms that are due to genetic differences) range from about 32% for contamination/cleaning to 58% for taboo sexual/religious/aggressive thoughts (Katerberg et al., 2010). Findings for related disorders have been similar: Twin studies have shown a 50% heritability for hoarding disorder (Iervolino et al., 2009) and a 44% heritability for BDD (Monzani et al., 2012).

There are disorder-specific genetic factors unique to OCD, BDD, and hoarding disorder, whereas TTM and SPD are largely influenced by the same latent genetic factor (Monzani, Rijsdijk, Harris, & Mataix-Cols, 2014). Candidate gene studies in OCD have thus far focused on genes involved in the neurotransmitter pathways of serotonin, dopamine, and glutamate (discussed in the next section). These studies have been, for the most part, inconclusive; the only genetic association replicated by multiple groups has been with a glutamate transporter gene (SLC1A1; Bloch & Pittenger, 2010). Other research suggests that people with OCD are at increased genetic risk for any anxiety disorder (see Chapter 7), as more OCD family members compared with controls (30% versus 17.1%) had one or more anxiety disorders (Black et al., 1992). This research suggests that there may be an inherited general diathesis for OCD and for anxiety, rather than genetic transmittal of specific symptoms (Black, Noyes, Goldstein, & Blum, 1992).

Neurobiological Factors

glutamate: The body's most prominent neurotransmitter, the brain's main excitatory neurotransmitter, and also the precursor for GABA, the brain's main inhibitory neurotransmitter.

In additional to genetic research, other neurobiological research on OCD also implicates **glutamate**, which is the brain's main excitatory neurotransmitter and also the precursor for gamma-aminobutyric acid (GABA; see Chapter 7), the brain's main inhibitory neurotransmitter. For example, brain-imaging studies (e.g., MRI; see Chapter 1) have revealed altered glutamate concentrations in the basal ganglia and anterior cingulate cortex of people with OCD (Wu, Hanna, Rosenberg, & Arnold, 2012). This glutamate hypothesis of OCD, if it turns out be correct, may generate novel treatment approaches for OCD and related disorders (Wu et al., 2012).

The **serotonin** hypothesis of OCD has had a similar trajectory to that of depressive disorders (see Chapter 6)—first thought to be a major breakthrough, now cooled off somewhat, though several researchers refuse to abandon the hypothesis (Stengler-Wenzke, Müller, Angermeyer, Sabri, & Hesse, 2004), despite mixed evidence (Bloch & Pittenger, 2010). Part of the reason that the hypothesis persists is that, as for depression, **selective serotonin reuptake inhibitors (SSRIs)** have played a role in the treatment of OCD and related disorders, as described further later in the chapter. A separate line of research regarding serotonin involves OCD-type symptoms in dogs. Many of the compulsive behaviors observed in people with OCD involve excessive grooming, washing, and cleaning rituals. As veterinarians and many dog owners can testify, a common behavioral disorder seen in several larger breeds of dogs, especially Labrador retrievers, is incessant licking of the paws and sides, officially known as *canine acral lick dermatitis*. Although researchers obviously cannot know for sure how biologically or psychologically similar canine acral lick dermatitis is to OCD, its behavioral similarity makes it an excellent model for exploring the causes of OCD. In one study (Rapoport, Ryland, & Kriete, 1992), 42 dogs who had suffered canine acral lick dermatitis for at least 6 months were treated with one of several drugs. Based on owners' ratings, only the drugs that inhibited serotonin reuptake (SSRIs) significantly decreased the dogs' licking behaviors.

Checkers the dog lives for playing ball, even when the ball is thrown into the water; his obsession with balls has a compulsive quality to it. Other dogs show compulsive licking and checking behaviors similar to OCD in humans.

serotonin: A neurotransmitter that influences emotion, sleep, and behavioral control.

selective serotonin reuptake inhibitor (SSRI): A type of drug used to treat mental disorders such as depression and that works by slowing the reuptake of serotonin.

Structural and functional neuroimaging studies point to the involvement of pathways leading from the cortex through the basal ganglia to the thalamus (Leckman, 2002). The **basal ganglia** are situated at the base of the forebrain and are associated with a variety of functions, including control of voluntary motor movements, procedural learning, routine behaviors or "habits," cognition, and emotion. The basal ganglia use both GABA and glutamate to facilitate the ability to effectively switch between motor and mental behaviors, which is required for producing new behavior. Failures to do so may result in the repetitive production of stereotyped movements, thoughts, or behaviors that is common in OCD and related disorders (tics, BDD, SPD, and TTM).

basal ganglia: Clusters of brain cells (nuclei) that are situated at the base of the forebrain and that are associated with a variety of functions, including control of voluntary motor movements, procedural learning, routine behaviors or "habits," cognition, and emotion.

Although the evidence is far from conclusive, researchers believe that several interconnected brain areas are implicated in OCD and related symptoms. In addition to the basal ganglia, these include the *orbitofrontal cortex* (a portion of the **frontal lobes** just above the eyes) and the *cingulate gyrus* (a region of the cortex just overlaying the caudate nucleus of the basal ganglia). These areas are thought to form a circuit that, when overactivated, results in the repetitive symptoms seen in OCD (Insel, 1992; Rapoport, 1989). Similar brain structures have been implicated in BDD (Rivera & Borda, 2001). In particular, it appears that the circuit from the basal ganglia to the frontal cortex is involved in a variety of control mechanisms, ranging from impulsive to compulsive disorders (Grant, Stein, Woods, & Keuthen, 2012).

frontal lobe: The area of the cerebral cortex that controls executive functions, such as planning and carrying out goal-directed activities.

Brain-imaging studies have shown these areas to have higher-than-normal metabolism in people with OCD before treatment and more normal activity following successful behavior therapy or drug therapy (Baxter et al., 1992; Swedo et al., 1992). Additional support for neurological contributions to OCD comes from studies showing that a large proportion of people with head injuries and neurological diseases such as Huntington's, Sydenham's chorea, and Tourette's disorder also have obsessive or compulsive symptoms (Insel, 1992; Rapoport, 1989). Finally, circumstantial evidence about an intriguing correlation between streptococcal infections and tic disorders and OCD is also accumulating—possibly via an autoimmune process whereby the person's immune system attacks its

Chapter 8 Obsessive-Compulsive and Related Disorders **295**

The Basal Nuclei

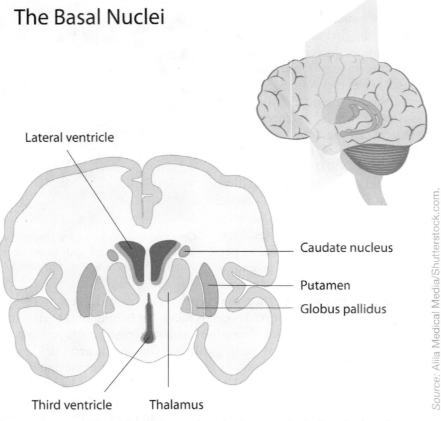

Lateral ventricle

Caudate nucleus

Putamen

Globus pallidus

Third ventricle   Thalamus

Source: Alila Medical Media/Shutterstock.com.

Researchers have postulated that various brain areas, including the basal ganglia (clusters of brain cells [nuclei] that are situated at the base of the forebrain, as shown here), are implicated in OCD and related symptoms.

own basal ganglia—that may account for a small percentage of cases of pediatric OCD (Hoekstra & Minderaa, 2005).

Cognitive-Behavioral Factors

Cognitive behaviorists believe that OCD involves a vicious cycle in which (1) physiological reactivity and obsessive thinking increase during times of heightened stress; (2) the obsessive thoughts are experienced as "bad" or "unacceptable" and thus are anxiety-provoking; (3) ritualistic behaviors or thoughts are used to neutralize the anxiety; and (4) these compulsive responses are then reinforced and become persistent because of their anxiety-reducing ability.

This model begins with a component that is also implicated in the cause of all the anxiety disorders discussed in Chapter 7—physiological overreactivity to certain events. This high reactivity is likely caused by individuals' *anxiety sensitivity*, which refers to their fear of behaviors or sensations associated with the experience of anxiety. Higher levels of anxiety sensitivity are thought to amplify anxious reactions and fear-related responding, which subsequently leads to greater levels of avoidance for people with phobias or panic disorder (Taylor, Koch, & McNally, 1992).

However, unlike people with phobias who avoid specific objects or situations or people with panic disorder who become distressed over increased physical sensations, people with OCD become particularly upset about their own intrusive thoughts. Why do certain people feel intense anxiety about their own thoughts? The answer might be found in early experiences that teach people that some thoughts are so dangerous that they must be avoided at all costs. It is almost as if the person with OCD believes that thinking aggressive or destructive thoughts is as bad as performing the acts themselves. Therefore, people prone to OCD constantly strive to undo such thoughts as soon as they occur, typically

MAPS - Attempted Answers

through compulsive behavior, which then becomes the problem—much like avoidance behavior does for those with anxiety disorders.

When these cognitive factors are combined with what is known about the neurobiological underpinnings of anxiety, the following integrative explanation for OCD emerges. Certain individuals are prone to overreact physiologically to many events and to experience anxiety as a result. Furthermore, although people are generally prone to think a bit more obsessively after stressful events, those who are more physiologically reactive to stress are more likely to experience obsessions than are less-reactive people (Barlow, 1988; Rachman & Hodgson, 1980). Even though many people experience obsessions from time to time, people with OCD are further predisposed to become extremely distressed by their obsessions. These predispositions, acquired through early learning experiences that established specific thoughts or ideas as taboo, convince the person that certain thoughts are dangerous, immoral, or threatening (Rachman, 1993; Rachman & Hodgson, 1980). When these distressing thoughts occur, they cause great anxiety, which the person feels must be nullified by compulsive rituals.

Frost and Hartl (1996) were the first to propose a cognitive-behavioral model of hoarding. Within this framework, compulsive hoarding is viewed as a multifaceted problem resulting from information-processing deficits, extreme emotional attachments to possessions, erroneous beliefs about the nature of possessions, and behavioral avoidance. Numerous studies have demonstrated that individuals who hoard experience cognitive-processing problems in the areas of decision making, categorization, and attention (Grisham, Norberg, Williams, Certoma, & Kadib, 2010; Hartl, Duffany, Allen, Steketee, & Frost, 2005; Wincze, Steketee, & Frost, 2007). These difficulties are posited to directly contribute to the organizational problems and extreme clutter associated with hoarding.

Just like the inaccurate beliefs that people with OCD may have about their obsessions, faulty beliefs about the nature of one's possessions are associated with hoarding behaviors. For example, many people who hoard have mistaken beliefs regarding the future utility of their possessions, leading them to save worthless or worn-out objects "just in case" they are needed in the future (Frost, Hartl, Christian, & Williams, 1995). In addition to these beliefs, individuals who hoard also experience extreme emotional attachments to their possessions (Frost & Gross, 1993). Beliefs such as "throwing this item away means losing a part of my life" or "without this possession, I will be vulnerable" undoubtedly lead to saving behaviors (Medley, Capron, Korte, & Schmidt, 2013). Instead of the performance of a compulsive behavior to ward off the anxiety brought on by these cognitive distortions (as in OCD), hoarding involves behavioral avoidance, which occurs via the act of saving possessions to postpone making decisions (Frost & Hartl, 1996). Specifically, it has been suggested that the act of saving is an avoidance behavior aimed at reducing the distress associated with potentially making a wrong decision regarding a cherished possession (Coles, Frost, Heimberg, & Steketee, 2003). As with compulsions in OCD, the avoidance transiently reduces the person's anxiety and so becomes a hard habit to break.

Specific psychological models for the etiology of the other OCD-related disorders (BDD, TTM, and SPD) have been less well developed. A preliminary, hypothetical model for BDD involves a complex interplay in which genetic and biological susceptibilities interact with environmental events, such as teasing or abuse (Feusner, Neziroglu, Wilhelm, Mancusi, & Bohon, 2010). The subsequent development of distorted cognitions and reinforcing repetitive and avoidance behaviors may then serve to maintain the symptoms of the disorder.

Research has also supported the negative reinforcement (i.e., when a behavior is strengthened by removing a negative outcome or aversive stimulus such as anxiety) model of TTM (McDonald, 2012). Specifically, an increase in negative emotions (e.g., tension, anxiety, boredom, and sadness) often occurs before pulling, pleasurable emotions occur during pulling, and there is again an increase in negative emotions (e.g., guilt, anger, and sadness) after pulling (Diefenbach, Mouton-Odum, & Stanley, 2002; Diefenbach, Tolin, Meunier, & Worhunsky, 2008; Shusterman, Feld, Baer, & Keuthen, 2009). In other words, the emotional experience of hair pulling is a cyclical process that may set the stage for future hair pulling, just like obsessions and compulsions become coupled in people with OCD. Pulling hair may therefore be a strategy for managing undesirable emotions (Diefenbach et al., 2002), similar to hoarding behaviors, compulsions, or body-checking behaviors.

Social Factors

As with the anxiety disorders discussed in Chapter 7 and post-traumatic stress disorder (PTSD) discussed in Chapter 9, both parenting and adverse life events play a role in the etiology of OCD and related disorders. For instance, authoritarian parenting is a risk factor for OCD; this parenting style is low on warmth/nurturance and very high on behavioral control, and represents parenting that is rigid and values strong adherence to rules with relatively less affection and nurturing (Timpano, Keough, Mahaffey, Schmidt, & Abramowitz, 2010). Jim in the chapter-opening case described his parents as being very strict. In addition, compared with controls, people with OCD perceived higher levels of rejection from their fathers (Alonso et al., 2004). There is also evidence that the specific form of obsessions and compulsions is influenced by early family experiences that dictate which thoughts and behaviors are particularly unacceptable. For example, Gail Steketee and her colleagues found that parents of "checkers" are more meticulous and stricter than parents of "washers," who tend to stress cleanliness (Steketee & White, 1990). In general, the parents of adults with OCD appear to have held rigid expectations for proper conduct and to have placed tight controls on their children's behavior, like Jim's parents did. Hoarding can also be partially predicted by parental traits, specifically low parental emotional warmth (Alonso et al., 2004).

Research has documented a relationship between childhood trauma and OCD; however, this relationship is not direct in nature but is influenced by peoples' past experiences with significant others and associated difficulties in emotional processing (Carpenter & Chung, 2011). One study indicated that hoarding severity was positively associated with the number of traumatic events that occurred prior to symptom onset, supporting the notion of cumulative trauma in hoarding (Przeworski, Cain, & Dunbeck, 2014). Those with hoarding symptoms alone also had higher rates of physical assault and transportation accidents prior to symptom onset than those with OCD symptoms alone. Finally, those with hoarding and OCD symptoms reported higher rates of sexual assault prior to symptom onset than those with OCD alone.

Adverse life events also play a role in BDD, such as the impact of childhood teasing about one's body or appearance (Feusner et al., 2010). Furthermore, people with BDD reported more retrospective experiences of sexual and physical abuse in childhood or adolescence than did controls (Buhlmann, Marques, & Wilhelm, 2012), although there was no significant group difference in reports of emotional abuse in early life. Not much is known about the social causes of habit disorders such as TTM or SPD, except that mother-child relations were once postulated to play a role (Asam & Trager, 1973), but that has not been confirmed by modern research. Diefenbach, Reitman, and Williamson (2000) proposed that TTM may be modeled and learned from peers and family members. In addition, people with TTM have an elevated frequency of trauma in their past, compared to people without any disorders, and researchers have speculated that hair pulling may represent their attempts to self-soothe or self-harm in the wake of such trauma (Gershuny et al., 2006).

Section Review

Biopsychosocial causes of obsessive-compulsive and related disorders include:

- genetic contributions;
- brain studies that suggest involvement of the frontal lobes and basal ganglia, and the possible implication of the neurotransmitters glutamate and serotonin (again);
- cognitive and behavioral loops whereby people develop faulty thinking around the meaning/danger of obsessions, their material possessions, and/or their body image (as in BDD), along with compulsive, avoidance (hoarding), or body-checking/

- pulling/picking behaviors that get stronger because they temporarily reduce anxiety; and
- social factors, such as overly harsh parenting styles and/or adverse life events such as trauma, which may activate or exacerbate symptoms.

Treatment of Obsessive-Compulsive and Related Disorders

OCD is not an easy disorder to treat. In fact, some people become so desperate to rid themselves of OCD symptoms that they undergo a special form of psychosurgery known as a *cingulotomy*, in which a small amount of tissue in the cingulum is destroyed. Unfortunately, this extreme form of treatment is successful in only a minority of patients (Cosgrove et al., 1995; Jenike et al., 1991; Sachdev, Hay, & Cumming, 1992). The newest biological treatment for OCD that has shown promise is repetitive transcranial magnetic stimulation (rTMS), which uses a magnet instead of an electrical current (as in electroconvulsive therapy [ECT]) to activate the brain (Berlim, Neufeld, & Van den Eynde, 2013), and is also discussed in Chapter 6 as a potential treatment for depression. However, to date, only two approaches have shown consistent success as treatments of OCD and related disorders: a specific class of drugs that affect the neurotransmitter serotonin and a form of cognitive-behavioral therapy (CBT; Olatunji, Davis, Powers, & Smits, 2013; Watson & Rees, 2008). However, like for depression, OCD symptoms usually persist at moderate levels even following adequate treatment (Eddy, Dutra, Bradley, & Westen, 2004).

Drug Therapy

Clomipramine (sold as Anafranil), a drug that inhibits the reuptake of serotonin, was the first effective pharmacological treatment for OCD (Lickey & Gordon, 1991). Indeed, only drugs that inhibit serotonin reuptake (SSRIs such as Prozac, Zoloft, and Anafranil, discussed in detail in Chapter 6) seem to reduce OCD symptoms (Leonard et al., 1989; Lickey & Gordon, 1991). Enthusiasm for these drugs must be tempered, however, because—much like for depressive disorders—they produce clear improvement in only about half of people with OCD (Saxena, Brody, Maidment, & Baxter, 2007), symptoms return quickly after discontinuation of the drugs (Pigott et al., 1990), and the medications produce notable side effects, such as nausea, fatigue, and loss of sexual desire.

MAPS - Medical Myths

Whereas some researchers have suggested that these drugs do not work for people with hoarding disorder (Cullen et al., 2007), others disagree (Saxena, 2011). In one study, a similar proportion of hoarders and nonhoarding people with OCD were significantly (28% versus 32%) or partially (22% versus 15%) helped by the medication, yielding almost identical response rates to SSRIs (Saxena et al., 2007). Now that hoarding disorder is its own separate disorder in the *DSM-5*, more research will surely follow to determine whether medications have a role to play in its treatment.

Cognitive-Behavioral Therapy (CBT)

Behavioral treatments for OCD are the only psychological treatments that have consistently been shown to reduce OCD symptoms (Olatunji et al., 2013). These procedures, sometimes combined with drug treatments, are based on the principle of extinction (described for treating phobias in Chapter 7). Two treatment components are usually combined: **exposure** to the stimulus that elicits obsessive rumination and anxiety, and **response prevention**, in which the person is kept from performing the anxiety-reducing ritual (Steketee & White, 1990).

For example, if a client compulsively washes as a way of allaying fear of contracting the AIDS virus, the therapist might arrange for the client to go to a local health department or hospital where HIV testing is done. The client would likely fear that the AIDS virus is lurking on door knobs or tabletops, so exposure might require having the client touch or

exposure and response prevention (ERP): A behavioral treatment for obsessive-compulsive and related disorders that involves having individuals face (rather than avoid) their anxiety-provoking obsessions, material possessions, or body concerns without engaging in their usual compulsive or avoidant behavioral rituals.

OH MY GOD, I MAY HAVE TO WALK ON THE FLOOR!

even rub these surfaces. This exposure would generate anxiety and set up a strong urge to wash the contamination away. However, the therapist would help the client resist washing at this point. In some cases, the therapist can prevent the compulsion by simply being present and reminding the client not to give in to the urge to wash. In more severe cases, the client might need to be locked out of all areas where water is available. In either case, the client's anxiety will rise and might remain high for 30–60 minutes, after which it will begin to decline, along with the urge to wash. Repeated exposure and response prevention trials at different locations and for different stimuli eventually help the client learn that the obsessions are exaggerated concerns and that the rituals related to them are not necessary. Exposure and response prevention (ERP) can be an effective treatment whether administered to individuals or via a group (Jónsson & Hougaard, 2009). When direct exposure is impossible, *imaginal exposure* can be substituted. For example, a client's fear of making an error at work can lead to anxiety-provoking obsessions about being fired and anxiety-reducing compulsions to check all work repeatedly. Here, the client could be asked to imagine making errors while resisting the urge to perform compulsive checking (Steketee & White, 1990). In some cases, clients can carry out effective ERP programs on their own.

Just like for depression and anxiety, cognitive-behavioral therapy (CBT) is the front-line treatment of choice for OCD, as it outperforms medication and does as well as combined treatment (CBT plus medication) in meta-analyses of randomized controlled trials (Huang, Li, Han, Xiong, & Ma, 2013). For pediatric OCD, CBT and pharmacotherapy were also the only treatments effective beyond control in alleviating OCD symptoms but, once again, CBT showed a greater effect size than medication at follow-up, even more pronounced than for adults (Abramowitz, Whiteside, & Deacon, 2005; Watson & Rees, 2008). More specifically, exposure and response prevention was the best type of cognitive-behavioral therapy for OCD, therapist-guided exposure was better than therapist-assisted self-exposure, and exposure in vivo (real life) combined with exposure in imagination was better than exposure in vivo alone (Rosa-Alcázar, Sánchez-Meca, Gómez-Conesa, & Marín-Martínez, 2008). Moreover, family-based treatments offer the potential of increasing the effectiveness of existing interventions for OCD by broadening the context of treatment and providing family members with important information and skills to support the recovery of affected individuals (Thompson-Hollands, Edson, Tompson, & Comer, 2014).

In studies of OCD, however, the presence of hoarding symptoms has often been associated with poorer response to exposure and response prevention, compared to people who did not display hoarding behaviors (Muroff, Bratiotis, & Steketee, 2011). These findings confirm the clinical impressions of experienced OCD researchers that hoarding is more difficult to treat than other subtypes of OCD, such as contamination/washing and harming/checking symptoms, and imply that alternative interventions may be needed for hoarding problems. Over the past decade or so, an increasing number of studies have tested the efficacy of CBT interventions that have been tailored specifically for hoarding rather than OCD per se. The gold-standard treatment manual for hoarding now has sections on organizing and problem-solving skills training, exposure and practice methods to reduce acquiring and remove clutter, cognitive strategies to facilitate this work, and motivational interviewing methods to address ambivalence whenever it occurs during treatment (Steketee & Frost, 2007). Of considerable interest is the potential for delivering treatment using newer technologies over the Internet and via webcam that can provide direct services in locations where hoarding occurs (Muroff et al., 2011).

The best treatment for BDD is also a version of cognitive-behavioral therapy (Prazeres, Nascimento, & Fontenelle, 2013), which yields even better results than SSRI medication

(Williams, Hadjistavropoulos, & Sharpe, 2006). This treatment includes the behavioral components of exposure and response prevention, just like for OCD (Wilhelm, Phillips, & Steketee, 2013). For instance, individuals with BDD who think that their skin looks funny might be asked to go out to brightly lit public places where attention could be called to their skin (exposure); they would then be taught how to reduce their usual body-checking behaviors, such as by not looking in a mirror/reflection or not repeatedly inspecting other people's skin or not asking others if their own skin looks all right (response prevention). The cognitive component of the treatment for BDD includes evaluating and combating self-defeating thoughts (as for depression), such as "I always need to look my best," or "My skin needs to look amazing at all times."

Whereas individuals with BDD will be helped to cut down on their mirror use in the short term, *perceptual retraining* for mirror checking is an additional technique for developing a healthier relationship with mirrors in the long run (Wilhelm et al., 2013). The rationale for perceptual retraining is that people with BDD usually zoom in on their disliked body areas in excruciating detail. People are taught instead to describe their entire body, going from head to toe, nonjudgmentally while viewing it from 3–4 feet away, thereby interrupting their typical overfocusing and selective attention.

Few randomized controlled trials have examined the effects of CBT or SSRIs for the treatment of trichotillomania (TTM). As for all OCD-related disorders, though, the studies that exist converge on the finding that CBT is the treatment of choice, with SSRIs also showing moderate effectiveness (McGuire et al., 2014). Bloch et al. (2007) found that a type of CBT called **habit reversal training** is currently considered the most effective intervention for TTM. Grounded by a landmark 1973 study by Azrin and Nunn, habit reversal training consists of three main elements: awareness training, competing response training, and social support. Awareness training is simply empowering clients to be cognizant of their hair pulling, as well as the thoughts and emotions that precede the pulling. Competing response training is the act of doing something that makes pulling impossible (e.g., balling up the hand into a fist for 60 seconds instead of pulling hair). Social support is brought in so that clients have someone who can help them to identify their hair pulling and who can remind them to participate in the competing response training.

Habit reversal has also been used effectively to treat skin-picking disorder (SPD; Rosenbaum & Ayllon, 1981). Other CBT approaches for SPD have included combinations of differential reinforcement (e.g., rewarding nonpicking behaviors), providing distracting activities (e.g., toys), wearing protective clothing (e.g., helmets or gloves), response interruption and redirection, punishment, and extinction (Lang et al., 2010). SSRIs have also shown some success in a small number of clinical trials for SPD (Arnold et al., 2001).

habit reversal training: A cognitive-behavioral treatment used for hair pulling, skin picking, tics, or other problem habits and that involves awareness training, competing response training, and social support.

Section Review

Treatment of obsessive-compulsive and related disorders usually involves cognitive-behavioral therapy (CBT) or drugs that inhibit the reuptake of serotonin (SSRIs). CBT:

- typically takes the form of exposure and response prevention, which includes exposure to the anxiety-provoking obsessions or impulses and then a reduction in the person's usual behavioral responses (compulsions, hoarding, body checking);
- in the case of hair pulling or skin picking, involves a similar technique called habit reversal, whereby individuals learn to become more aware of the impulse and practice an incompatible response, such as tucking their hands inside their pockets, whenever the urge arises; and
- is the treatment of choice because it does as well as or better than medication (especially for children with OCD), has fewer side effects, and can be delivered in a variety of formats, ranging from individual to family to group settings, or even using newer technologies like websites and apps.

Revisiting the Case of Jim

Jim from the chapter-opening case was diagnosed with obsessive-compulsive disorder with good or fair insight, tic-related (due to his past history of motor tics and vocalizations). He did not have symptoms of any other OCD-related disorders, such as hoarding, BDD, or body-focused repetitive behaviors (hair pulling or skin picking). Jim's treatment consisted mainly of exposure and response prevention (ERP), a version of cognitive-behavioral therapy that is considered the front-line treatment of choice for people with OCD.

The first session after the intake/diagnosis was spent on psychoeducation. Jim's doctor—Dr. Joe—explained that OCD was like a false alarm. When Jim's anxiety would "go off" like an alarm system, it communicated information that Jim was in danger. Unfortunately, with OCD, Jim's brain tells him that he is in danger a lot, even in situations where Jim "knows" that the likelihood that something bad might happen (like leaving the stove on or the door unlocked) is very small. Dr. Joe explained that this is one of the cruelest parts of the disorder. He told Jim that his compulsive behaviors are his attempts to keep himself safe when that alarm goes off. Dr. Joe also said that when Jim engaged in those compulsive behaviors, he was reinforcing the brain's idea that he must be in danger. In other words, Jim's compulsive behavior (the checking) fueled that part of his brain that sounded the many false alarm signals. Dr. Joe explained that, to reduce Jim's anxiety and obsessions, Jim would have to decide to stop the compulsive behaviors.

Dr. Joe also explained that the "exposure" in ERP refers to Jim exposing himself to the thoughts, images, objects, and situations that make him anxious and/or start his obsessions, while the "response prevention" part refers to making a choice not to do a compulsive behavior once the anxiety or obsessions have been "triggered." Dr. Joe told Jim that all of this would be done under Dr. Joe's guidance at the beginning, but that, eventually, Jim would learn how to do his own ERP exercises to help manage his symptoms.

Jim was anxious about starting ERP treatment, so he and Dr. Joe agreed to spend the next visit discussing the pros and cons of the therapy versus other possible treatments (e.g., SSRI medication). During this second visit, Dr. Joe employed motivational interviewing. Instead of telling Jim what to do, Dr. Joe asked him exploratory questions and listened actively and reflectively to Jim's responses. At the end of the session, Jim decided that he did not want to take medication but that he would be willing to give ERP a try.

Currently, Jim is about halfway through (eight sessions into) his treatment with Dr. Joe, and the ERP is working fairly well, though not completely. Jim has cut down his checking so that he typically only returns to his house 3–4 times (instead of 10–15), and he has been on time for work more often in the past month. He is still bothered by his obsessions, but they do not seem as fierce and all-consuming as they once were.

Summary

Obsessive-Compulsive Disorder

The *DSM-5* includes five main disorders in the obsessive-compulsive and related disorders category: (1) obsessive-compulsive disorder (OCD), (2) hoarding disorder, (3) body dysmorphic disorder (BDD), (4) trichotillo-mania (TTM, hair-pulling disorder), and (5) excoriation (skin-picking) disorder (SPD). Individuals who suffer from OCD experience recurring intrusive thoughts (obsessions) and/or repetitive behaviors (compulsions) that are time consuming and disruptive to their normal life. In 80% of cases, both obsessions and compulsions are pres-

ent. The most common obsessions involve taboo thoughts/impulses, order/symmetry, and cleanliness/contamination, and the compulsions that individuals develop typically match their obsessions. For instance, someone with a contamination obsession may use cleaning rituals, whereas someone with an order/symmetry obsession may develop counting or neatening compulsions instead.

Hoarding Disorder

Hoarding disorder used to be considered a subtype of OCD but is now diagnosed as a separate disorder. People with hoarding disorder experience persistent difficulties

Hal Arkowitz

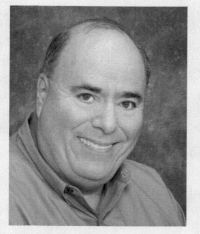

Hal Arkowitz, PhD, is emeritus associate professor of psychology at the University of Arizona. He has been a scientist-practitioner for his entire career, meaning that he values how science (research) can inform practice and how practice can inform science. In terms of research, Dr. Arkowitz has contributed to the study of psychotherapy integration—how different models of therapy can be used together—as well as to how people change. He is past editor of the Journal of Psychotherapy Integration. *More recently, he has done research and given workshops on motivational interviewing, co-edited a book entitled* Motivational Interviewing in the Treatment of Psychological Disorders *(now in its second edition), and is a co-columnist, with Scott O. Lilienfeld, for* Scientific American Mind *on a series that addresses common myths and misconceptions about various topics in clinical psychology and corrects them with findings from psychological science. Dr. Arkowitz also practices psychotherapy as he has throughout his career.*

Q *How do you diagnose OCD and how commonly do you see it in clinical practice?*

A I diagnose OCD according to the criteria in the DSM-5, precisely as you have outlined in this chapter. On average, I see about two clients a week with OCD in my clinical practice as a psychotherapist.

Q *What have you observed about the triggers for OCD in your clients?*

A When people have OCD, it is always with them to one degree or another, in part because of the genetic contribution to it. High stress makes it more severe, and low stress makes it less severe.

Q *What treatments do you use for your clients with OCD?*

A The best treatment for OCD consists of a psychotherapy method called exposure and response prevention (ERP), a type of cognitive-behavioral therapy. In ERP, clients are first exposed to what they fear—for instance, dirt and contamination. They are then encouraged not to engage in the compulsion (e.g., hand washing) for as long as possible. The goal is to extinguish the anxiety associated with the obsessions so that these obsessions and their associated compulsions will be reduced in power.

I also include treatment methods to help clients reduce stress—which is a trigger for OCD as I mentioned earlier—such as relaxation training. This can also help clients endure the anxiety-provoking nature of the ERP treatment that I described.

Further, many clients respond best to a combination of medication and psychotherapy. I often refer people to a psychiatrist for an evaluation, as certain antidepressants may be helpful, especially SSRIs.

Q *How well do these treatments work, and how hard is it for your clients to follow through?*

A In my experience, people with mild or moderate cases without any other diagnoses (comorbidity) can be helped significantly by treatment, but most will still have some residual symptoms. When the OCD is severe and comorbidity (i.e., another mental disorder) is present, the prognosis is much poorer.

It is extremely difficult to have people follow through since it means that they have to repeatedly experience anxiety. As such, one of the approaches that I have used, along with CBT, is motivational interviewing [MI, also discussed in Chapters 6 and 14] to boost the client's motivation and tolerance for the anxiety-provoking ERP treatment. One of my research studies in 2009 showed that adding MI pretreatment to CBT was specifically and substantively beneficial for individuals with generalized anxiety disorder [GAD, discussed in Chapter 7] who had high worry severity at baseline. It remains to be seen whether MI will turn out to be helpful for people with OCD as well.

discarding or parting with possessions, regardless of their actual value, leading to the severe cluttering of their personal living spaces. Individuals can have significant disability and impairment as a result of their hoarding, including illness due to unsanitary conditions, social isolation, work disability, and even death. Some people hoard animals rather than objects. The most prominent difference between animal and object hoarding is the extent of unsanitary living conditions, which is typically worse for animal hoarders.

Body Dysmorphic Disorder

In body dysmorphic disorder (BDD), people develop a preoccupation with one or more perceived physical defects that are not observable to others (obsessions) and then perform repetitive behaviors (compulsions) that are time consuming and disruptive to their lives to try to neutralize their bodily concerns. For example, people may wear loose clothing, check mirrors, or seek reassurance about their perceived flaws. Some people (more commonly men) experience muscle dysmorphia, a subtype of BDD in which there is a preoccupation with the idea that one's body build is too small or not muscular enough.

Hair-Pulling and Skin-Picking Disorders

People may also develop body-focused repetitive behaviors such as hair-pulling (trichotillomania [TTM]) or skin-picking disorder (SPD). Individuals with these disorders engage in recurrent pulling out of their hair or picking at their skin to the point that they create bald spots and/or skin sores or infections. They focus abnormally on their body (hair or skin) as a target of their compulsive behavior. These disorders usually manifest themselves during or after puberty.

Causes of Obsessive-Compulsive and Related Disorders

Biopsychosocial causes of obsessive-compulsive and related disorders include genetic contributions, brain stud-ies that suggest involvement of the frontal lobes and basal ganglia, and the possible implication of the neurotransmitters glutamate and serotonin. Cognitive-behavioral explanations involve cognitive and behavioral loops whereby people develop faulty thinking around the meaning/danger of obsessions, their material possessions, and/or their body image (as in BDD), along with compulsive, avoidance (hoarding), or body-checking/pulling/picking behaviors that get stronger because they temporarily reduce anxiety. These disorders may also be activated or exacerbated by social factors, such as overly autocratic parenting styles and/or early adverse life events, such as trauma.

Treatment of Obsessive-Compulsive and Related Disorders

Treatment of obsessive-compulsive and related disorders usually involves cognitive-behavioral therapy (CBT) or drugs that inhibit the reuptake of serotonin (SSRIs). CBT is the treatment of choice across the board because it does as well as or better than medication (especially for children with OCD), has fewer side effects, and can be delivered in a variety of formats, ranging from individual to family to group settings, or even using newer technologies like websites and apps. CBT typically takes the form of exposure and response prevention, which includes exposure to the anxiety-provoking obsessions or impulses and then a reduction in the person's usual behavioral responses (compulsions, hoarding, body checking). In hair-pulling or skin-picking disorders, CBT involves a similar technique called habit reversal, whereby individuals learn to become more aware of the impulse to pull or pick and practice an incompatible response, such as tucking their hands inside their pockets or making a tight fist, whenever the urge to pull or pick arises.

Key Terms

Trauma- and Stressor-Related Disorders

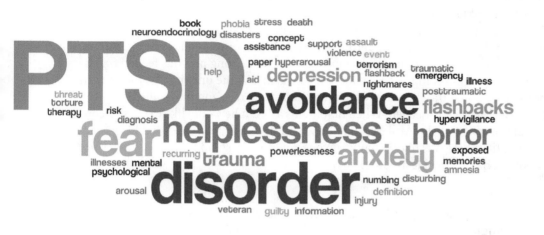

CHAPTER 9

Source: lculig/Shutterstock.com.

Chapter Outline

The Nature of Stress

Physical Reactions to Stress

Psychological Reactions to Stress

Mental Disorders after Stress and Trauma

From the Case of Arul

It was an ordinary fall day on campus for Arul. He was sitting outside one of the more modern buildings on the campus while enjoying his coffee before heading into the auditorium for his last class of the day. It was a large lecture taught by a graduate student he had come to really like. As he was walking to the class and the door was closing behind him, he noticed a group of students running and looking panicked, but he was not able to process what this might mean in that particular moment. He set his backpack down and took his seat in the back of the big lecture hall. Class began at that same moment.

"Good aftern …" his instructor started before he was interrupted with what sounded like fireworks or a loud popping sound outside. Just then, another student kicked the door open, and he was covered in more blood than Arul had ever seen in his life. He and the rest of the students in the room were silent for what felt like an eternity. As the blood-covered individual collapsed in front of them, pandemonium set in, and students started running in every direction. Screams drowned out the sound of gunfire for a moment, and Arul was frozen with panic. He was momentarily unable to move and began to feel like he was out of his body, despite having a strong impulse to help the student who had collapsed.

After reading this chapter, you will be able to answer the following key questions:

- What is stress?
- How does the body respond to stress?
- How does the mind respond to stress?
- What are the symptoms of mental disorders that occur after stress and trauma?
- How can post-traumatic stress disorder (PTSD) be prevented?

He ran toward the front of the auditorium and through a door he had never noticed before. The door led to a small room with extra desks, podiums, and other materials for the lecture hall. Once inside, he noticed several other students taking cover behind some of the objects in the room. He thought about how the other students looked terrified and pathetic hiding behind things that would never stop a bullet. However, Arul realized that he was trapped in there and would have to do the very same thing. He remained in this room until the mass shooting was over.

By the time Arul left the room, the incident had exploded on media, and his parents were already on campus to take him home. He was overcome with emotion and relief when he saw his parents. Paramedics, police, firemen, media vans, and others lined the streets and filled the campus. When his parents asked him what had happened and if he was OK, Arul said that he did not want to talk about it, and they did not push the issue. He said that he wanted to leave the campus right this instant, and on the way home, he stated in no uncertain terms that he would never return.

The next couple of nights for Arul were filled with restless sleep and steady, intrusive memories of the student standing in the doorway. When his parents would stir in another room, he would jump up and feel overcome with a strong nervous feeling that he had a hard time controlling. He was not able to watch TV; the one time he did, he saw a reporter discussing the shooting, which made his heart race and his hands sweat, and made him feel very light-headed. When his parents asked if he would like to see someone who might be able to help, Arul said that he would. However, he stated that he was not "crazy" and that there was likely no way anyone could understand him, given that, since the shooting, he sees people as not to be trusted.

Severe trauma, such as the incident described in the chapter-opening vignette, usually leaves psychological marks on its victims, and Arul was no exception. His sleep problems, fear, and personal insecurities were all signs of stress. What precisely is stress, and how does it affect people? Are some stressors more disruptive than others? What is the difference between trauma and stress? What are the best ways to cope with stress? What emotions do people feel when experiencing stress? Which specific mental disorders are caused by overwhelming stress?

The Nature of Stress

stress: An ongoing process that occurs when environmental or social threats place demands on individuals.

Stress occurs when environmental or social threats (called *stressors*) place demands on individuals. Stress is an ongoing process that involves interactions between environments and people. The way in which an individual experiences stress depends on (1) the nature and timing of the stressors, (2) the person's psychological characteristics and social situation, and (3) biochemical variables that influence stress responses. Figure 9.1 presents a summary of this process.

Types of Stressors

Predictable stressors arise from life's milestones, such as getting married, having children, starting college, or beginning a new job. Other common stressful events include academic setbacks, financial losses, occupational failures, relationship difficulties, unemployment, and the illness or death of loved ones. These events happen regularly as people live their lives. Even relatively minor events, such as car trouble, getting stuck in a traffic jam, or losing your lecture notes the night before an exam, can be significant stressors. The effect is worse when several of these daily hassles pile up in a short period of time.

Many stressors are linked to occupational demands. For example, air-traffic controllers are under constant pressure to make quick, life-and-death decisions; servers in restaurants are urged by customers to hurry; and underground miners live with the constant danger of cave-ins. Jobs that do not offer a balance of positive job characteristics (i.e., control,

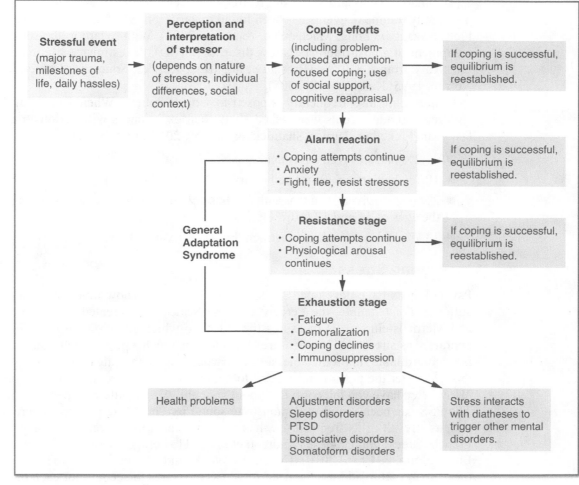

FIGURE 9.1 The Process of Stress

social support) to counteract the negative characteristics and demands of the job (i.e., interpersonal conflict, job insecurity) generate the greatest amount of stress (Demerouti, Bakker, Nachreiner, & Schaufeli, 2001).

Beyond everyday life stress, stress can come in the form of unpredictable traumas, such as single incidents like experiencing an earthquake or flood, motor vehicle crash, or a violent mass casualty event, such as the one involving Arul in the chapter-opening vignette. Traumas can also be repetitive in nature, such as childhood sexual abuse over a long period of time or combat exposure in the military. Whereas resilience after a potentially traumatic event is the norm (deRoon-Cassini, Mancini, Rusch, & Bonanno, 2010), a significant minority of people go on to develop lasting psychological distress following trauma. Even if such events happen only once in a person's lifetime, these events are often so powerful that they can leave significant impairment. Attempts to prevent such traumas from happening in the first place, called primary prevention, are the best intervention strategies. However, after a trauma has occurred, secondary prevention efforts to prevent the development of psychological distress are often employed, as described in detail later in this chapter.

In stressful situations, time distortion is a common reaction. A faster-than-normal rate of psychological processing following a rapid stressor conveys an impression that more time has elapsed; a decreased rate of psychological activity during an extended stressor suggests that less time has passed. Both kinds of distortions may facilitate coping. With quick stressors, like a motor vehicle crash, a sense of slowed time may suggest that evasive action is possible, despite the speed of the threat. With prolonged stressors, a feeling of shortened time may suggest to victims that they can "hold out" a little longer.

Traumatic events are surprisingly frequent. The lifetime prevalence of exposure to potentially traumatic events has been found to vary from 51–89.6% (Breslau et al., 1998; Flett, Kazantzis, Long, MacDonald, & Millar, 2002). With regard to the subsequent development of a post-traumatic stress disorder (PTSD), the estimated lifetime prevalence rates vary from 6.8–9.2% (Breslau et al., 1998; Kessler, Sonnega, Bromet, Hughes, & Nelson, 1995; Kessler et al., 2005).

Children are also frequently exposed to violent trauma. When a national sample of children and adolescents were asked about their experiences with serious trauma in the last year (Finkelhor, Turner, Shattuck, & Hamby, 2013), reports indicated that:

- 41.2% had survived a physical assault;
- 10.1% had an assault-related injury;
- 2% had survived sexual assault or abuse, with a higher rate among girls between the ages of 14 and 17 (10.7%); and
- 13.7% had survived maltreatment by a caregiver.

Measuring Stress

Psychologists have developed several scales to measure how much stress a person has suffered. For example, the Perceived Stress Scale (PSS) created by Cohen, Kamarck, and Mermelstein (1983) measures the extent to which situations in a person's life are appraised as stressful. This measure taps into how much a person feels that his or her life is uncontrollable, unpredictable, and overwhelming. The scale asks about feelings and thoughts over the past month related to a general state of stress, with questions such as "How often have you felt confident about your ability to handle your personal problems?" The PSS has been found to demonstrate sound psychometric properties across cultures and, as a result of its frequent use, has been translated into several languages, including French, Greek, and Chinese (Andreou et al., 2011; Lesage, Berjot, & Deschamps, 2012; Leung, Lam, & Chan, 2010). Cohen, Kamarck, and Mermelstein (1983) developed this measure in part to address the need for stress measures to account for each person's subjective experience or appraisal of a stressor.

Another common stress measure, the Schedule of Recent Experience (SRE), assesses the occurrence of specific stressful situations from a list of 42 events involving health, work, family, and social and financial difficulties (Amundson, Hart, & Holmes, 1986). Examples include:

- major changes in eating or sleeping habits,
- being fired from work,
- death of a relative or close friend,
- a violation of the law, and
- a major business readjustment.

Respondents check the events they have experienced during the previous 6, 12, 24, and 36 months. Each event is then given a predetermined weight based on prior research in which subjects rated the amount of adjustment that was needed to cope with it (ranging from 1 = very little adjustment to 100 = maximal adjustment). These weights are added to give a total *Life Change Units* score, which provides an overall index of how much stress the person has experienced in a given time period. In the 57-item Life Experiences Survey (LES), the respondents themselves rate the positive or negative impact of an event (Sarason, Johnson, & Siegel, 1978). Allowing individualized ratings of events should make instruments such as the LES more sensitive to individual and cultural influences. Addition-

"I've been feeling a lot of work-related stress."

Source: Cartoonresource/Shutterstock.com.

ally, the LES allows for the measure of positive change after stress, rather than assuming that stress leads solely to negative emotional outcomes.

Effects of Stressors

Although stressors differ in many ways, they produce an amazingly similar pattern of closely entwined physiological and psychological reactions. Some of these reactions occur so quickly and automatically that we are unaware of them. Others extend over longer periods of time. The physiological reactions to stress include hundreds of biochemical changes, but a clear pattern underlies them all. This pattern is *adaptive*; it helps people adjust to stressors. Hans Selye (1936) first described this system of reactions as the **general adaptation syndrome (GAS)**. He identified three stages of response to stressors:

1. The first stage is the *alarm reaction*, which Selye (1982) said is a "general call to arms of the body's defensive forces." This stage, also discussed in Chapters 2 and 7, is sometimes called the **fight-or-flight response** because the autonomic nervous system is jolted into activity either to fight or to escape the stressor.
2. If a stressor lasts only a short time, the alarm reaction and its aftereffects are little more than an unpleasant reminder of how close disaster came. But if the stressor persists, or if new stressors are piled on top of old ones, alarm is followed by a **stage of resistance**, in which coping mechanisms are used to defend against the continuing effects of stress.
3. Eventually, if stressors continue for long enough, the **stage of exhaustion** begins as a result of the long-term effects of resistance. Physical signs of exhaustion include indigestion, loss of weight, insomnia, and fatigue. When a person's energy is finally depleted, the ability to cope with stressors is lost, and the person suffers a "breakdown." In extreme situations, the stage of exhaustion can end in death.

general adaptation syndrome (GAS): A three-stage physiological reaction to a stressor, consisting of alarm, resistance, and exhaustion.

fight-or-flight response: The immediate response to a stressor in which the individual's autonomic nervous system is activated to fight or to flee from the stressor.

stage of resistance: The second stage of the general adaptation syndrome, in which various coping mechanisms are used to defend against a stressor.

stage of exhaustion: The third stage of the general adaptation syndrome, in which organ systems break down.

Section Review

Individuals undergo stress when they are exposed to environmental or social threats called *stressors*. Stressors can involve:

- severe traumatic events,
- milestones of development,
- occupational demands, and
- daily hassles.

Psychologists have developed several scales to measure how much stress a person has suffered, such as:

- the Perceived Stress Scale (PSS), which measures the extent to which situations in a person's life are appraised as stressful; and
- the Schedule of Recent Experience (SRE), which assesses the occurrence of specific stressful situations from a list of 42 events.

Selye's general adaptation syndrome (GAS):

- is a description of the sequence of physiological changes occurring in response to a stressor; and
- consists of alarm, resistance, and exhaustion stages.

Physical Reactions to Stress

Selye's description of the GAS was an attempt to organize the physiological changes underlying stressful experiences. It is a rough approximation of these changes, not a precise schedule. Selye did not focus on the psychological or behavioral changes that take place during stress, but since the GAS was first described, other research has shed more light on these aspects of stress reactions. Table 9.1 summarizes key physical, emotional, behavioral, and cognitive reactions that typically occur during the stages of the GAS sequence. In this section, we look at these reactions in more detail.

TABLE 9.1 Typical Reactions to Stress

Stage	Physiological Reactions	Emotional Reactions	Cognitive and Behavioral Reactions
Alarm	• HPA axis is activated; hypothalamus releases CRH • Sympathetic nervous system aroused • Epinephrine and norepinephrine activate organs throughout the body	• Fear • Excitement • Panic • Anger	• Mental activity increases, particularly attention and concentration • Fight or flee stressors
Resistance	• Body expends its energy supplies, but more slowly to resist stressors • Immune system weakens	• Tension • Anxiety • Defense mechanisms • Insomnia	• Cognitive appraisal of stressor • Organize efforts at coping • Emotion-focused coping • Problem-focused coping • Elicit social support
Exhaustion	• Immunosuppression • Physical energies depleted • Weight loss • Organ damage • Death	• Hopelessness • Desperation • Insomnia • Helplessness	• Disorganized thinking • Impaired attention and concentration • Weakened coping efforts

Physiological Reactions

The autonomic nervous system (ANS) regulates both the emotions and the body's responses to stressors. The ANS is divided into two branches—the sympathetic and parasympathetic nervous systems—that stimulate the endocrine glands, the heart, and many other organs. The two branches of the ANS usually work to balance each other; what one system speeds up, the other slows down. As Figure 9.2 shows, the sympathetic nervous system helps mobilize the body for fighting or fleeing stressors by releasing *epinephrine* (adrenaline), quickening the heartbeat, dilating the pupils of the eyes, sending more blood to the muscles, and inhibiting digestion. The parasympathetic branch conserves the body's supplies by constricting the pupils, slowing the heart, and stimulating digestion. It may also be activated during stress, but it generally does not help in coping with immediate stressors.

The Alarm Reaction

The alarm stage of the GAS is really a two-alarm alert, involving separate but integrated systems (Chrousos & Gold, 1992). In response to a sudden stressor, a chemical relay system, known as the **hypothalamic-pituitary-adrenal (HPA) axis**, a major part of the neuroendocrine system, swings into action. The hypothalamus first secretes a substance known as **corticotropin-releasing hormone (CRH)**. CRH, in turn, jump-starts a chain of coordinated physiological and biochemical defenses against the stressor. CRH signals the pituitary to secrete **adrenocorticotrophic hormone (ACTH)**, which, in turn, directs the cortical (outer) portion of the adrenal glands to release **adrenal corticosteroids**, such as cortisol and other glucocorticoids (discussed in Chapter 6). These chemical messengers, sometimes referred to as **stress hormones**, intensify the alarm and prepare the body to cope with the stressor. Activity in the parasympathetic division of the autonomic nervous system temporarily shuts down, directing energy away from the digestive and reproductive systems in favor of more immediately vital functions. Heart rate increases, as does blood pressure, respiration, and production of glucose. Pupils dilate, and muscles tense. At the same time, immune responses are slowed down in order to conserve energy for answering the immediate threat. The corticosteroids also direct the hypothalamus to inhibit further production of CRH, thereby completing a *negative feedback loop* in the HPA axis.

hypothalamic-pituitary-adrenal (HPA) axis: The feedback loop that plays a critical role in the body's response to stress. In times of stress, the adrenal glands respond to messages from the hypothalamic-pituitary system by increasing their output of cortisol and adrenaline (epinephrine), hormones that help the body cope with stressors via "fight-or-flight" mechanisms.

corticotropin-releasing hormone (CRH): A hormone that starts a chain of coordinated physiological and biochemical defenses against a stressor, and signals the pituitary gland to secrete adrenocorticotrophic hormone (ACTH).

adrenocorticotrophic hormone (ACTH): A hormone that, in response to a stressor, directs the adrenal glands to release adrenal corticosteroids.

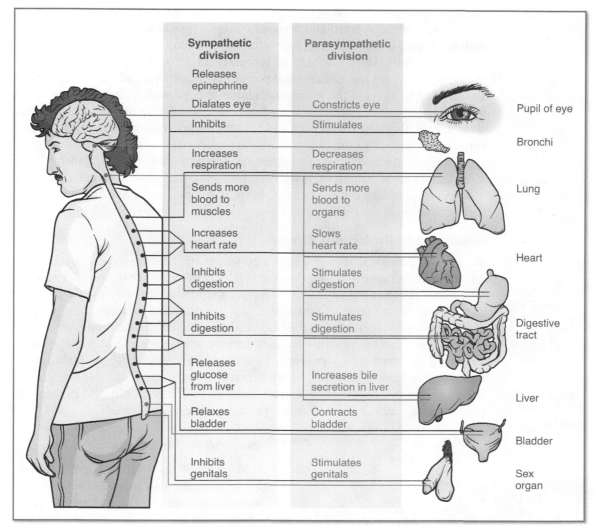

Sympathetic division	Parasympathetic division	
Releases epinephrine		
Dialates eye	Constricts eye	Pupil of eye
Inhibits	Stimulates	Bronchi
Increases respiration	Decreases respiration	Lung
Sends more blood to muscles	Sends more blood to organs	
Increases heart rate	Slows heart rate	Heart
Inhibits digestion	Stimulates digestion	
Inhibits digestion	Stimulates digestion	Digestive tract
Releases glucose from liver	Increases bile secretion in liver	Liver
Relaxes bladder	Contracts bladder	Bladder
Inhibits genitals	Stimulates genitals	Sex organ

FIGURE 9.2 Activation of the Autonomic Nervous System

These are some of the changes involved when the sympathetic and parasympathetic divisions of the autonomic nervous system are activated.

The second initial alarm originates in the hypothalamus, which influences the brain stem and spinal cord to stimulate the adrenal medulla (inner part of the adrenal glands) to release the *catecholamines*, epinephrine and norepinephrine. The catecholamines stimulate heart rate and raise blood pressure; at the same time, they stimulate the central nervous system, increasing attention and concentration. These changes make the alarmed person more vigilant to danger, but feelings of heightened anxiety, or even panic, may accompany these changes.

The two stress alarms interact to produce other biological changes. For example, they activate the production and release of *endogenous opioids*, opiates that exist naturally in the body. **Endorphins** are a special type of endogenous opioid that help regulate cardiovascular activity, reduce the perception of pain, increase feelings of euphoria that can facilitate psychological coping with stress, and enhance the immune system response (McCubbin, 1993). The body "prescribes" endogenous opioids following a stressor to help people cope with intense threat. The stress-coping benefits of physical exercise may be linked to the fact that exercise helps release extra endorphins, which is why exercise can feel really good (especially when you stop!).

adrenal corticosteroid: A chemical messenger, also known as a stress hormone, that intensifies alarm and prepares the body to cope with a stressor.

stress hormone: A chemical messenger, also known as an adrenal corticosteroid, that intensifies alarm and prepares the body to cope with a stressor.

endorphin: An endogenous opioid that helps regulate cardiovascular activity, relieve pain, and facilitate psychological coping.

Experiencing the Alarm Reaction

It is not uncommon to feel these short-term adjustments to a stressor after a near-accident in an automobile. Arms and legs shake, the heart thumps against the chest, and breaths come in gasps. Dizziness or light-headedness is common. All of these sensations are by-products of the sympathetic nervous system's rush to protect against threat. Likewise, if sickness and a knotted-up stomach follow, it is partly because of rapid changes in the digestive system, which has become less relevant during the emergency.

During the alarm reaction, several perceptual, cognitive, and behavioral adjustments—all intended to increase the immediate ability to cope with a stressor—are quickly made. First, as noted earlier, attention is riveted on the stressor so that it can be perceived more clearly. This heightened vigilance and concentration can take extreme forms. Survivors of automobile accidents commonly recall the experience as unfolding in slow motion; individuals who have been shot may remember seeing the bullet coming toward them. At the same time, focused attention is a distraction from many other stimuli. Shooting victims often report that they did not hear the blast of the gun, and assault victims may not recall suffering some of their injuries.

Reactions to Prolonged Stress

If a stressor persists long enough for a person to enter the resistance phase, the biological reactions can become harmful. Prolonged release of stress hormones can cause chronically high blood pressure, damage muscle tissue, and inhibit the body's ability to heal after injury. Sustained secretion of corticosteroids also produces wear and tear on various parts of the nervous system, such as the hippocampus, and because it suppresses the body's immune system, prolonged stress reduces the immune system's strength (Herbert & Cohen, 1993a). If the immune system remains suppressed for too long, the body becomes more vulnerable to various diseases. Many experts believe that this **immunosuppression** is the basis for the association between stress and increased risks of physical illness, such as cancer and certain autoimmune diseases (Kiecolt-Glaser, McGuire, Robles, & Glaser, 2002).

immunosupression: A decrease in immune system effectiveness that sometimes follows sustained stress.

"Do the workers feel we are milking them for too many hours a week?"

Source: Cartoonresource/Shutterstock.com.

Stress and the Immune System

Over 40 years of research has demonstrated that exposure to stressors can interfere with certain aspects of the immune response (Segerstrom & Miller, 2004). This research initially relied on demonstrations with animals in which loud noises, electric shocks, cold temperatures, separation of newborns from mothers, and crowding suppressed aspects of the animals' immune systems. More recent research with human beings has found compromised immunity resulting from sleep deprivation, final examinations, divorce, loss of a loved one, and caring for chronically ill relatives (Herbert & Cohen, 1993a; Kiecolt-Glaser & Glaser, 1992). In addition, as discussed in Chapter 6, depressed or angry mood and negative thinking have also been linked to altered immunity (Glaser, Robles, Malarkey, Sheridan, & Kiecolt-Glaser, 2003).

The Relationship between Stress Responses and Immune Functioning

How does the immune system respond to stressors? The nervous system and the immune system have two lines of connection. First, the autonomic nervous system innervates (is connected to) major immune system organs, such as the spleen, bone marrow, and lymph nodes. Sympathetic nervous system neurons release the catecholamines, which are then received by receptors on immune cells. The second line involves the hypothalamic-pituitary-adrenal (HPA) axis described earlier. The HPA axis is activated by stressors in a chemical chain reaction that results in the cortical part of the adrenal glands secreting **glucocorticoids** such as cortisol, the steroid hormones that the body uses to fight stress. Immune cells have receptors for the glucocorticoids, thereby creating a specific mechanism by which stress can exert an influence on immune functioning.

glucocorticoid: A steroidal hormone the body uses to fight stress.

The relationship between a stressor and changes in the immune system is delicate and selective. Identical stressors may affect people in different ways (Krantz & Manuck, 1984). For example, a socially isolated person often suffers a substantially greater amount of immunosuppression than does someone who can turn to close friends for aid (Pressman et al., 2005). The nature of the stressor can also make a difference. Brief stressors, such as the kind studied in most research laboratories, often increase immune cells (Edwards et al., 2006), but exposure to long-term naturalistic stressors usually results in a decline in immunological strength (Segerstrom & Miller, 2004). Recent research on **adverse childhood experiences (ACEs)** shows a clear positive relationship between the number of types of ACEs exposed to during childhood and risk for disease in adulthood, including autoimmune disease (Dube et al., 2009). Finally, the same stressor may affect only selected aspects of immunity (e.g., the number of specific immune cells), leaving other aspects (e.g., the amount of antibody released) untouched.

The biochemical foundations of stress responses and immune defenses help explain how stressors suppress immune functioning, in turn increasing the risk for illness. Both stress responses and immune system defenses require large amounts of energy. The fight-or-flight nature of the alarm reaction calls for energy to be transferred to the muscles and brain immediately. The immune defenses, on the other hand, require that energy be directed almost entirely to other systems, such as white blood cell production and temperature increases that are involved in inflammation at the site of an injury or infection. Faced with both the immediate threat of a stressor and the more leisurely progress of a pathogen, the body responds to the imminent danger first, thus depriving the immune system. Stress-induced immunosuppression is usually adaptive in the short run, but when stress responses are maintained for too long, the costs of continued immunosuppression appear in the form of greater susceptibility to disease and slowed recovery from illness.

adverse childhood experiences: Stressful or traumatic experiences, including abuse, neglect, and a range of household dysfunction, such as witnessing domestic violence or growing up with substance abuse, mental disorders, parental discord, or crime in the home.

Section Review

Physical responses to a stressor differ in the various stages of Selye's general adaptation syndrome (GAS). In the alarm stage of the GAS, the person is jolted into action, and the body prepares to fight or flee the stressor. The initial physiological responses to a stressor consist of two chemical alarms:

- the HPA axis and the corticosteroids and
- the sympathetic nervous system and the catecholamines.

In the resistance stage, the person attempts to cope with the stressor. In the final exhaustion stage, the person's capacity to resist breaks down, and the ability to cope with stressors is ultimately lost.

If a stressor persists long enough for a person to enter the resistance phase, the biological reactions can become harmful. Whereas acute stressors boost immune function, prolonged or chronic stressors lead to suppression of the immune system, which, in turn, results in greater susceptibility to illness.

Psychological Reactions to Stress

Individuals cope with stress in many ways (Lazarus, 1993). **Coping** refers to people's efforts to modify or tolerate stressors (Folkman & Lazarus, 1980). Richard Lazarus and Susan Folkman developed the *transactional model of stress* to highlight that stress is the result of transactions between individuals and the environment. How successfully a person copes with a stressor depends on the individual, the stressor itself, and the context in which the stressor is experienced. Therefore, according to the transactional model, stress is not the direct response to an event but results when individuals perceive the demands of the event to exceed their ability to cope. When individuals are faced with a stressor, they make a **primary appraisal**, which is a cognitive evaluation of whether the stressor is manageable or uncontrollable. Next, they evaluate coping resources and, consequently, what can be done about a situation. Finally, they respond to these appraisals by enacting coping strategies.

coping: A person's efforts to modify, manage, or tolerate stressors.

primary appraisal: The evaluation of the significance of a stressor or threatening event.

People often change their coping strategies from one situation to another. They may even select different coping strategies as a single, stressful event unfolds.

Types of Coping

problem-focused coping: An attempt to reduce stress by directly changing the stressor itself.

People who try to reduce stress by directly solving a problem are using **problem-focused coping**. Problem-focused coping is aimed at changing the stressor itself. For example, if daily arguments between you and your roommate are a major source of stress, you might try to change the stressor by moving out, by asking your roommate to move out, by trying to resolve the disagreements (usually about the dirty dishes!), or by trying new activities together that would help you and your roommate to become better friends.

People also attempt to change the way they think about a stressor so that, even if they cannot eliminate it, they can at least make it less upsetting. This strategy is known as **cognitive reappraisal**, and it is often a powerful tool for reducing stress responses.

cognitive reappraisal: An attempt to reduce stress by thinking about a stressor in ways that make it less upsetting.

Another form of coping is the use of defense mechanisms, which can be thought of as any mental process that helps protect a person from psychological or emotional distress. Although to the layperson there is an implicit negative connotation when describing a person as defensive, psychoanalytic literature describes defense mechanisms as being potentially adaptive and healthy (McWilliams, 1994). Defense mechanisms are similar to cognitive reappraisal in that they can happen automatically (outside of conscious awareness). Moreover, defense mechanisms can alter reality to make a person feel better. However, a defense might be considered pathogenic or maladaptive when an overreliance on a particular defense seems harmful to the individual. Examples of this are evident in people with post-traumatic stress disorder, where there might be an overreliance on *withdrawal* and/or *dissociation*, in which individuals might be reluctant or terrified to engage behaviorally (isolating themselves from friends or family) or to engage with the thoughts or emotions associated with the traumatic memory during therapy.

emotion-focused coping: Attempts to reduce stress by changing a person's emotional responses to a stressor.

People who try to reduce stress by managing the emotional effects of the stressor are using **emotion-focused coping**. Their efforts are not aimed at eliminating the stressor itself but at changing their emotional responses to it. If you responded to your roommate conflicts by talking to a friend about how angry you are, or by trying to cheer yourself up by concentrating on your roommate's good qualities, or by practicing meditation to reduce feelings of tension, you would be using an emotion-focused strategy.

social support: The feeling that you are cared for by others or belong to a valued group.

Another way of coping with stressors is to seek or use **social support**. Social support requires more than just the presence of other people; it involves feeling that the social support provided is helpful. Therefore, more important than the sheer number of social contacts is the belief that you are cared for and valued. Social support can take the form of advice, guidance, feedback, and direct help. A friend can provide social support by offering advice, by listening to vented feelings, or by taking the person under stress out for the evening to get a break from the stressor. In a sense, social support is divided among two dimensions: (1) a structural dimension, which involves the size and frequency of social interaction, and (2) a functional dimension, which encompasses emotional (such as receiving empathy and love) and instrumental (practical help, such as financial help or getting a ride to a doctor's appointment) components (Charney, 2004). Although both components of social support are important, most research has found that the quality of the support, or the functional dimension, is a better stress buffer than the actual amount of social support (Southwick, Vythilingam, & Charney, 2005). Experiencing social support helps people feel esteemed, loved, and part of a community of people who care for one another.

"I think it's important to note that we really did try hard."

Source: Cartoonresource/Shutterstock.com.

Effects of Coping Strategies

Are certain stressors managed better with one type of coping than another? In general, most people are flexible in how they cope; therefore, it is difficult to identify the "best" coping style (Gil & Caspi, 2006). Regardless of type of coping, what is important is how effective individuals feel their coping is in response to the stressful event, referred to as *coping self-efficacy* (Benight & Bandura, 2004).

People tend to cope best with the adversities of a protracted stressor (e.g., a painful, chronic illness such as arthritis) by seeking information about the stressor so they can anticipate and control it better (Revenson & Felton, 1989) or at least convince themselves that they can control it. Information gathering is a part of problem-focused coping. On the other hand, given a truly uncontrollable condition, emotion-focused coping might be the most effective strategy (Meyerowitz, Heinrich, & Schag, 1983).

Several studies suggest that stressors are less likely to have harmful effects on people who enjoy high levels of social support (Wang, Wu, & Liu, 2003). One study of over 400 college students revealed that the number of Facebook friends someone had was associated with stronger perceptions of social support, which in turn were associated with reduced stress, less physical illness, and greater well-being (Nabi, Prestin, & So, 2013). In another study with over 300 rural pregnant women, satisfaction with social support during pregnancy contributed to a reduction in depression following childbirth (Jesse, Kim, & Herndon, 2014). Specifically, satisfactory social support during a stressor predicts better psychosocial adjustment, quality of life, well-being, and engagement in health promotion behavior. Why is this so?

One possibility is that social support acts as a *buffer* against the harmful effects of stressors. By serving as an additional resource in a person's attempts to manage stressors, social support bolsters coping efforts. New research suggests that effective social support may lead to better health by reducing chronic activation of the HPA axis (Charney, 2004). An increase in support can decrease stress, which in turn decreases the body's activation of the stress response, potentially making the person less susceptible to immunosuppression, thereby resulting in better health. Conversely, social isolation has been linked to morbidity and mortality in a host of medical illnesses. People without adequate social support are 2 to 3 times more likely to die from heart disease, cancer, and additional chronic conditions compared to those who have adequate support (Berkman, 1995). Support may also deter a person from responding to stressors with harmful behaviors, such as excessive drinking. Several studies have shown that married men suffer fewer psychological difficulties after a traumatic event than do their widowed counterparts (e.g., Siegel & Kuykendall, 1990), and a few investigations suggest that married women live somewhat longer than unmarried women do (Hibbard & Pope, 1993).

A second explanation for the beneficial effects of social support is that it exerts *direct effects*. In this view, social support is seen as helpful, regardless of the stressors a person experiences, because there are general benefits to being embedded, and feeling that you belong, in supportive relationships (Baumeister & Leary, 1995).

A third possible answer is that higher levels of social support and lower levels of stress reflect the influence of a common underlying characteristic such as *social competence*. Socially competent persons are more likely to have friends, to manage their lives effectively, and to encounter fewer major adversities (Adler & Matthews, 1994). Social competence may be a general characteristic of some individuals that accounts for both supportive relationships and good adjustment.

Of course, a combination of all three explanations may be at work. In reality, it is difficult to separate the effects of personal competence, social support, and exposure to fewer (or buffered) stressors. Each of these qualities makes the others more likely. What does seem clear is that a lack of social support generally puts people at higher risk for both physical and psychological disorders and even mortality (Ozbay et al., 2007).

Social support does not always produce positive results, however. It can create guilt and discomfort if recipients feel overly burdensome or dependent because the support is one-sided. In other instances, well-intentioned helpers may give too much help or behave in other ways that lead recipients to see themselves as weak or incompetent (Wortman & Lehman, 1985). When assistance starts to feel like supervision, it may no longer be helpful.

Connections

Can social support help protect people against other mental disorders, such as schizophrenia, when they are under stress? For a discussion of this possibility, see Chapter 4.

One of the most serious stressors a person can face is the death of a loved one. Funerals facilitate the coping process by serving as a ritual that mobilizes both social support and emotion-focused coping.

Therefore, social support can buffer against stress only when the person receiving the support views it as effective.

Individual Differences and Potential Stressors

Stress is the result of interacting biological, psychological, and sociocultural forces. People differ in the ways they respond to a stressful event, depending, in part, on the meaning they give to the event. These meanings are shaped by their personal histories and past experiences, which include numerous social and cultural forces.

Exposure to Stressors: Individual and Cultural Differences

Certain people seem more likely than others to repeatedly experience stressful events. What accounts for their greater risk of adversity? First, some people, as a result of poor social skills or long-term psychological handicaps, unintentionally bring about more stressful events in their lives. Another possibility is that repeated financial or interpersonal setbacks have a cumulative effect so that one bad event (e.g., getting fired) leads to more problems (e.g., divorce) later on. Finally, severe stressors such as violence might even cause changes in brain chemistry that could contribute to future problems. Experiments in which young hamsters were repeatedly attacked by older animals have shown that the stress actually changed the brains of the youngsters (Melloni, Delville, & Ferris, 1995). Depending on the environments they encountered as adults, these traumatized hamsters tended to be either overly aggressive or timid, bringing more stress into their lives in either case. In another study, where young mice were exposed to social aggression, the mice as adults became socially isolated and exhibited anxious and helplessness behaviors (Kovalenko et al., 2014). Obviously, all of these factors might also interact, resulting in a series of life problems that are the result of biological processes, personal limitations, and previous adversities.

Ethnic differences, gender, and age can affect the frequency and types of stressors people encounter. African Americans, for example, must confront a host of cultural and social stressors more frequently than Caucasian Americans (Anderson, 1989). In general, members of minority groups are more likely than Caucasian Americans to face poverty, discrimination in housing and jobs, difficulties in single parenting, and pressure to conform to the norms of the majority culture. Similarly, women are much more likely than men to suffer sexual assaults, a major source of trauma related to psychological problems in the United States. Women are also more likely to be single, custodial parents, a status accompanied by numerous major stressors. Older persons may be particularly likely to face the stressors of economic setbacks, deaths of loved ones, chronic illnesses, and gradual loss of physical abilities. Given the premium that American society places on physical beauty and a youthful countenance, older people also often face the stress of discrimination against their changing appearance. Aging women are especially apt to encounter this stressor.

Reactions to Stressors: Individual and Cultural Differences

Research has demonstrated how different coping styles can be embedded in ethnic identity and/or culture as well, explaining some of the variability seen among cultures with regard to rates of different physical illnesses and mental health disorders (Mezuk et al., 2010). The harmful impact (and even the definition) of stressors seems to exist largely in the minds of those who experience them. The amount of *subjectively perceived* stress is more strongly correlated with later adjustment problems than is the sheer frequency of negative life events (Coyne & Downey, 1991). Not getting an "A" grade in an abnormal psychology course may be demoralizing to one student, whereas being turned down for a

Connections

What role do stressors play in depression and suicide? See Chapter 6.

date may be much more upsetting to another. Unexpected stressors take more of a toll on a person than stressors that are expected and prepared for. Accordingly, many researchers who study stress ask individuals to describe their subjective feelings in order to learn as much as possible about how each person perceives upsetting life experiences.

A host of factors determine how a person reacts to and copes with potential stressors. In addition to the stronger impact of unexpected events, several other characteristics tend to amplify the impact of stressors. For example, people usually feel more harmed by stressors when:

- they have to cope alone rather than with the aid of social support,
- they feel helpless or unable to control what is happening to them, and
- they believe that their stress was caused by the intentional or careless behavior of another.

In addition, people who are generally more optimistic and have greater self-esteem tend to be less threatened by stressors. A confident person may view many stressors as challenges or opportunities for growth. By contrast, an introverted or shy person or one who lacks self-assurance may be traumatized by the same stressors. The point is that identical events affect individuals in different ways. Not all stressors are created equal, and neither are people's capacities for coping with them.

Resilience and Stress

As stated earlier in the chapter, most people are exposed to significant stressors in their lives, and although a minority of those exposed to a traumatic event will develop post-traumatic stress disorder (PTSD; Kessler et al., 2005), most do not. Whereas much of psychology has focused on this minority who do get diagnosed with PTSD, a reorientation toward a nonpathologizing approach to adult trauma focusing on psychological well-being has emerged in the trauma literature (Bonanno, 2008); this reflects the larger overall shift in recent psychological research toward positive psychology, discussed in Chapter 2 (Huppert, 2010). Researchers have utilized a variety of methodological techniques to identify aspects of *resilience* in adults who have experienced a traumatic event, although there has been little consistency in the definitions and constructs measured (i.e., personality, coping, ego defense, access to resources, etc.; Agaibi & Wilson, 2005).

Bonanno, Westfall, and Mancini (2011) described four symptom trajectories (paths of functioning across time after a stressor) that emerge in studies that take into account the heterogeneity of responses to potentially traumatic events: (1) a resilient trajectory, which is the most common; (2) a recovery trajectory, whereby symptoms are elevated initially and then decrease over time, returning to baseline levels of functioning; (3) a chronic trajectory, with high symptom levels soon after a stressor that remain high; and (4) a delayed trajectory, with worsening symptoms over time (Bonanno et al., 2011).

Research that takes into account protective factors can potentially aid in identifying those who present with normative distress following a trauma but who may be on a recovering or resilient trajectory. Although some protective factors may intuitively be the inverse of some risk factors (i.e., social support; Bonanno, 2008), research and theory in this area have been explicit that resilience is not simply the absence of disorder (Almedom & Glandon, 2007). Therefore, additional research designed to measure protective factors might eventually contribute to more robust measures and a clearer understanding of post-traumatic resilience.

In their review of the literature, Bonanno and Diminich (2013) identified several key factors that increase people's ability to bounce back in the face of stressors, such as having a resilient personality, being the right age (not too young or too old), having experienced less past and current stress, being able to cognitively appraise difficult events as challenges rather than threats, and having *coping flexibility*, which means using a number of the different coping strategies as needed to get through the trauma.

Research also is beginning to reveal that a relatively common response to trauma is not a mental disorder but rather post-traumatic growth (PTG; Helgeson, Reynolds, & Tomich, 2006). Whereas resilience is the maintenance of well-being and few symptoms after a traumatic event, post-traumatic growth is when individuals surpass their pre-trauma well-being, usually after a period of post-trauma distress. PTG may include any number of affirming life changes—including a greater sense of personal strength, deepening of relationships with others, heightened appreciation for life, an increase in spirituality, and greater acknowledgment of new possibilities—all due to the trauma experienced as a result of the struggle with highly challenging circumstances (Tedeschi & Calhoun, 1996). PTG is correlated with positive affect (mood) and inversely related to depression, and these relationships are stronger when examining only traumatic events that are central to a person's identity (Boals, Steward, & Schuettler, 2010).

A meta-analysis clearly supported the hypothesis that optimism, social support, spirituality, acceptance coping, reappraisal coping, religious coping, and seeking support coping are all associated with PTG (Prati & Pietrantoni, 2009). Results from 70 studies revealed a small to moderate gender difference, with women reporting more PTG than men (Vishnevsky, Cann, Calhoun, Tedeschi, & Demakis, 2010). Finally, active intervention via psychotherapy augments PTG and can thus help people make the most of adversity (Roepke, 2014).

Section Review

When continued over long periods of time, stress can lead to:

- immunosuppression, a weakening of the immune system;
- extreme emotional and behavioral changes; and
- certain mental disorders.

People undergoing stress can cope with it through various strategies, including:

- cognitive reappraisal and defense mechanisms;
- problem-focused and emotion-focused coping; and
- eliciting social support.

The normative psychological response to stress is resilience, which is currently being studied throughout the life span to identify who is able to endure trauma and emerge without mental disorders and perhaps even with post-traumatic growth.

Mental Disorders after Stress and Trauma

MAPS - Attempted Answers

Just as physical reactions to stressors are adaptive in the short run but harmful if they become chronic, some psychological reactions can become maladaptive if they continue for too long. Heightened attentiveness and concentration can become obsessiveness and restlessness. Concern about a stressor may intensify into constant anxiety, depression, or feelings of helplessness. Preparation and planning can become so preoccupying that a person is unable to sleep. Memories of the details of a traumatic incident may turn into terrifying flashbacks or nightmares. Indeed, anxiety, helplessness, frustration, hostility, sleeplessness, and demoralization are the most common psychological effects of stress. Severe and traumatic stress also contributes to several specific mental disorders, the first two of which are discussed further in this chapter:

1. *Adjustment disorders*—Maladaptive behavioral and psychological reactions to a stressor occurring within 3 months of a stressor.
2. *Post-traumatic stress disorder (PTSD)*—A stressor-related disorder triggered by an unusually severe and traumatic event. PTSD involves several distinct symptoms of disturbance that last for at least 1 month and has a shorter version called *acute stress disorder*.
3. *Sleep-wake disorders*—Disturbances in latency, amount, or quality of sleep that are serious enough to cause social or occupational impairments (see Chapter 12).

4. *Dissociative and somatic symptom and related disorders*—Disorders that are often preceded by intense stressors or emotional conflict but involve symptoms that mask or substitute for feelings of anxiety (see Chapters 10 and 11).

5. *The onset or recurrence of other psychological disorders*—The role of stress in obsessive-compulsive disorders (Chapter 7), depression (Chapter 6), bipolar disorder (Chapter 5), and schizophrenia (Chapter 4) has received special research attention. Stressful events have been implicated as triggers for the onset of these disorders and for repeated episodes of them.

Adjustment Disorders

A person with an **adjustment disorder** suffers significant behavioral or psychological symptoms in response to a stressor. To be classified as an adjustment disorder according to the *Diagnostic and Statistical Manual of Mental Disorders (DSM-5)*, these symptoms must occur within 3 months after the stressor's appearance and last no longer than 6 months after the stressor or its consequences have ended—see Table 9.2. With chronic stressors or those that have enduring consequences (e.g., the financial setbacks associated with divorce), the symptoms may last longer than 6 months. The symptoms must also exceed what would normally be expected from exposure to the stressor or be serious enough to impair the person's occupational, social, or academic functioning. On the other hand, the symptoms should not be so severe as to constitute one of the other mental disorders in the *DSM-5* (e.g., depression, anxiety, or PTSD). If, as is sometimes the case, the symptoms last more than 6 months after the stressor or its consequences end, the diagnosis is changed, usually to a mood disorder or anxiety disorder.

adjustment disorder: Maladaptive behavioral and psychological reactions to a stressor occurring within 3 months of the stressor.

All stressors cause some disruption, so it is often difficult to distinguish between reactions that are normal consequences of a stressor (such as grief over the death of a loved one) and those causing enough impairment to constitute an adjustment disorder. Generally, if individuals believe that they are handling the stressor adequately, no diagnosis is made. If, however, individuals experience enough distress that it impairs their ability to function on a daily basis, an adjustment disorder will probably be diagnosed.

Usually, an adjustment disorder appears as a milder version of some other mental disorder. Depending on the nature of the symptoms, five subtypes of adjustment disorders can be specified: adjustment disorder (1) with anxiety, (2) with depressed mood, (3) with disturbance of conduct, (4) with mixed disturbance of emotions and conduct, and (5) with mixed anxiety and depressed mood. (A sixth, unspecified, subtype is used for cases that do not fit any of the five main subtypes.) For example, if the primary symptoms are nervousness and tension, adjustment disorder with anxiety would be diagnosed. If symptoms involve both emotional upset and behavioral difficulties (such as not meeting financial responsibilities, missing work frequently, or illegal activities), adjustment disorder with mixed disturbance of emotions and conduct would be the diagnosis. The mixed emotions/conduct subtype is most common among adolescents, whereas the depressed subtype is most common among adults. Research shows that adjustment disorder with depressed mood and adjustment disorder with mixed anxiety and depressed mood together account for 80% of adults diagnosed with this disorder, and that there really is no clinically

TABLE 9.2 The *DSM-5* in Simple Language: Diagnosing Adjustment Disorders

An adjustment disorder may be diagnosed when individuals have difficulty adjusting to a specific stressful event in their lives within 3 months of the event.
"Difficulty adjusting" is defined as experiencing emotions (anxiety or depressed mood) or behaviors that are either out of proportion to the severity of the stressor and/or that significantly impair individuals' daily functioning.
Two qualifiers are that the distressing emotions or behaviors are not a part of normal grief and that the symptoms do not continue for more than 6 months after the stressful event ends.

Source: Adapted from American Psychiatric Association (2013a).

meaningful distinction between these two very similar subtypes (Zimmerman, Martinez, Dalrymple, Chelminski, & Young, 2013).

Adjustment disorders, post-traumatic stress disorder (PTSD), and acute stress disorder are all linked to a precipitating stressful event, but adjustment disorders differ from the others in two important respects. First, adjustment disorders can arise in response to stressors of any magnitude, while PTSD and acute stress disorder are diagnosed only in response to unusually severe stressors, typically traumatic in nature. In contrast to PTSD, index events of adjustment disorders are single or ongoing severe life events (e.g., divorce, illness, job loss, conflicts at work) or other stressors (ongoing psychosocial difficulty or a combination of stressful life conditions, such as family conflicts, moving from one place to another, or particular refugee conditions; Maercker et al., 2012). Second, PTSD and acute stress disorder involve a specific set of symptoms, including heightened anxiety and disruptions in behavior, as well as disruptions in the autonomic nervous system. The symptoms of adjustment disorders range widely in form, but are typically more diffuse, milder, and of limited duration.

Adjustment disorders are diagnosed frequently. Although only 1–3% of the general population meet criteria for an adjustment disorder at any given time (Casey, 2009), 5–20% of clients in outpatient mental health clinics and 50% of hospital psychiatric patients receive this diagnosis (American Psychiatric Association, 2013a). Comorbidity with other mental disorders is high, reaching almost 50% (Maercker et al., 2008), and adjustment disorders are diagnosed about equally in males and females (Zaiontz, Arduini, Buren, & Fungi, 2012). Clinicians often use this diagnosis to indicate that a person's symptoms are mild, are unlikely to last a long time, and are not the result of a more serious condition. Therefore, the adjustment disorder label carries few of the negative stereotypes often associated with other mental disorders. Adjustment disorder shows a distinct profile as an intermediate category between no mental disorder and affective disorders such as depression and anxiety disorders (Fernández et al., 2012). Unfortunately, adjustment disorder diagnoses tend to be unreliable, probably because the diagnosis is often made to avoid using a more severe diagnosis. Adjustment disorder is also something of a "wastebasket" category, which is used when symptoms do not fit well elsewhere in the *DSM-5*. Thus, clinicians may not be as rigorous in assessing individual criteria for adjustment disorder as they should be. In primary care settings, this diagnosis often goes unrecognized: One study showed that only 2 of the 110 cases of adjustment disorders were accurately detected by general medical practitioners (Fernández et al., 2012).

Triggers for Adjustment Disorders

The stressors that give rise to adjustment disorders may be one-time events, such as divorce, or multiple setbacks, such as repeated occupational failures. They may last a short time (e.g., an earthquake) or stretch on for what seems like forever (e.g., the chronic illness of a loved one). Most adjustment disorders develop following marital, academic, or occupational problems, but people differ so much in their responses to stressors that it is impossible to predict how a particular individual will react to a given stressor. Likewise, even though the *DSM-5* indicates that adjustment disorders occur within 3 months of a triggering stressor and improve within 6 months after the stressor is over, clinicians treat many cases that do not follow this neat temporal pattern.

Adjustment Disorders and Natural Disasters

Manuel Diaz was driving to his home in Oakland, California, around 5 P.M. on October 17, 1989, when his car was suddenly swept off the road and thrown into a road sign. Dazed, but not seriously injured, Manuel sat gripping the steering wheel in terror, while his car bounced wildly from side to side for 2 seemingly endless minutes. Manuel had just lived through the worst earthquake to strike the United States in decades, resulting in 60 deaths and property damage exceeding $5 billion. Manuel's home was spared any structural damage, and his family escaped serious injury. But over the next several weeks, he just did not feel like himself. He was reluctant to leave home for fear that something would happen while he was gone. At work, he was seized by the idea that something horrible had happened to one of his children. He was forgetful about little tasks, and he often found himself bickering with coworkers with whom he had never before had problems. Manuel began waking up at 3 A.M. and could not get back to sleep; often, it seemed as if he had been awakened by a nightmare. He began to make plans to move someplace where he would feel safer.

Manuel's distress was shared by thousands of victims of the 1989 earthquake, as well as victims of more recent earthquakes in Haiti and Chile in 2010 and Napa in 2014, and of the Indonesian tsunami of 2004, Hurricane Katrina (2005), and the Japanese nuclear disaster (2011). His reactions are an example of an adjustment disorder with mixed anxiety and depressed mood, and they illustrate a common type of adjustment disorder following a natural (or human-made) disaster.

The question of how common one of Manuel's symptoms—nightmares—might be was investigated in a study in which undergraduate students from the San Francisco Bay area (San Jose State and Stanford Universities) were asked to write a description of their nightmares every morning for 3 weeks after the earthquake. Undergraduates from another area not affected by the earthquake (University of Arizona, the alma mater of two of your textbook authors) served as a control group. Students from the three universities did not differ in the frequency of nightmares they experienced during the year before the earthquake. However, after the earthquake, the San Jose State students experienced about twice as many nightmares and the Stanford students about 1.5 times as many nightmares as the Arizona students (Wood, Bootzin, Rosenhan, Nolen-Hoeksema, & Jourden, 1992). The content of the students' nightmares was also affected. More than 25% of the nightmares reported by students from the Bay area were about earthquakes, compared with only 3% of the nightmares for the Arizona students. These nightmares did not differ, however, in their overall intensity.

In general, adjustment disorders following disasters typically involve a combination of symptoms that are post-traumatic (e.g., nightmares, avoidance), depressive (e.g., hopelessness), and anxious (e.g., worries about safety). One study based on retrospective reports from 43 children exposed to Hurricane Katrina in Louisiana in 2005 found that the prevalence of children's mental health symptoms was 44–104% higher in the 2 years after Hurricane Katrina compared to pre-Katrina (Roberts, Mitchell, Witman, & Taffaro, 2010). The majority of such symptoms reported had an onset after the hurricane; for example, 79% of the children reported new onset of mental health symptoms in the year after Katrina. The vast majority of these children (56%) continued to experience mental health difficulties 2 years after the disaster.

Heavily damaged homes in the Ninth Ward of New Orleans. One block behind these homes is the industrial canal that collapsed during the storm surge of Hurricane Katrina in 2005.

Source: Brian Nolan/Shutterstock.com.

Adjustment Disorders and Interpersonal Stressors

Margerie Herning discovered that Bob, her husband of more than 10 years, was having an affair with a female coworker. Bob confessed that this relationship had been going on for 4 months and that, although he still cared for Margerie and their two daughters, he needed "more space" and wanted to move out and live on his own. Although Bob promised that he would end his affair, Margerie discovered that he was soon living with his new lover.

Margerie felt that her world had been shattered. She had trusted her husband completely. She had never been romantically involved with anyone except Bob from the time they had begun dating in high school; now she felt alone. She was too embarrassed to tell her friends or parents about Bob's affair, so she stayed at home as much as possible. Margerie found that her girls were getting on her nerves constantly, acting as if it were her fault that their father had left the family. Margerie lost 15 pounds in 5 weeks, feeling sick to her stomach all the time. Her future seemed totally empty. She could not concentrate at work. Two weeks after Bob left, Margerie was driving too fast, lost control of her car, and smashed into a parked pickup truck. She told herself that the wreck was "just an accident," but she realized that she was endangering herself, and shortly afterward, she called a psychologist for help.

Why do interpersonal stressors, such as Margerie's marital difficulties, so often lead to psychological and physical problems? One reason is that interpersonal problems are often chronic, and they can have a substantial impact on all family members (Coyne & Downey, 1991). Children raised in adverse family environments run higher-than-normal risks of suffering even more stressors in the future. Indeed, the correlation between marital stressors and subsequent maladjustment may actually reflect a long series of interpersonal stressors. Furthermore, people who experience a series of stressors often become more difficult to get along with, thus actually creating additional stressors. Finally, interpersonal stressors, such as a troubled marriage, usually have a double impact: They are direct stressors, plus they involve a loss of the partner's social support. In addition, in Margerie's case, shame over her problems also prevented her from using her social support network, which caused her to even further isolate herself.

Adjustment Disorders and Culture

MAPS - Prejudicial Pigeonholes

The diagnosis of adjustment disorders must take into account the personal circumstances of the individual and the expression of symptoms within the person's culture (Casey, 2009). For example, the loss of a job might be acceptable for one person, whereas for another it could heap poverty on their family. Cultural differences in the expression of emotion also need to be considered, since some individuals are more expressive than others. A knowledge of "normal" coping with illness and other stressful events is essential, and the diagnostic process will be guided by the extent to which an individual's symptoms are in excess of this, both in terms of severity and duration. For instance, failure to appreciate that some cultures grant compassionate leave from work following bereavement might lead to a grieving person being identified as disordered in another culture. Further, members of certain subcultures—such as LGBT youth (Volpp, 2012) and immigrant populations (Zaiontz et al., 2012)—are at higher risk for the development of adjustment disorders in the first place.

Treatment of Adjustment Disorders

Although definitive data on the course of adjustment problems is lacking, most mild adjustment disorders probably resolve themselves in a few months without formal treatment. Many persons with adjustment disorders turn to friends or family for support, or they just "wait it out," assuming that once the stressor is over, they will feel better and function normally again. In many cases, this assumption proves correct, and the person regains a satisfactory level of adjustment. Although some sadness or uneasiness may linger long after the stressor is gone, it usually does not significantly impair the person's functioning. More serious adjustment disorders may progress into another mental disorder, usually an anxiety disorder or mood disorder. Still, even serious adjustment disorders have a generally favorable prognosis.

Among those with adjustment disorders in primary care settings, 37% receive at least one medication prescription (Fernández et al., 2012). However, the use of psychotropic drugs such as antidepressants in treating adjustment disorders is not properly supported and should be avoided, whereas the usefulness of psychotherapies is more solidly supported by clinical evidence (Carta, Balestrieri, Murru, & Hardoy, 2009; Casey, 2009). Short-term psychodynamic therapy has shown effectiveness with adjustment disorders, with 12 sessions working just as well as a full year of treatment (Ben-Itzhak et al., 2012). However, cognitive-behavioral therapy (CBT) is likely the frontline treatment of choice (Casey, 2009; van der Heiden & Melchior, 2012). CBT was

helpful when administered to those with adjustment disorder who experienced work-related stress in reducing long-term absenteeism (van der Klink, Blonk, Schene, & van Dijk, 2003), and it is the recommended treatment strategy for these disorders in deployed military personnel (Fielden, 2012). Regardless of the specific psychotherapy model employed, the treatment of adjustment disorder usually focuses on intervening to enhance factors that reduce stress. This type of therapy tends to be solution-focused to enhance a person's coping resources. Ultimately, a person's psychological resilience will be bolstered to better manage current and future stressful situations.

His entire life was about balance.

Source: Cartoonresource/Shutterstock.com.

Enhancing Problem-Focused Coping Strengthening a person's ability to solve problems is an effective strategy for preventing or lessening adjustment disorders. This goal can be attained through family or friends, or through formal counseling in which a client learns effective problem solving (D'Zurilla & Goldfried, 1971).

Problem-solving therapy, often embedded in CBT, has been used with many types of clients and has generally proved successful in helping people cope with a wide range of life difficulties, including divorce, occupational stressors, interpersonal problems, and financial setbacks (Spiegler & Guevremont, 1993). It has had particular success in boosting the coping skills of children and adolescents who face many serious challenges (Kazdin, 1994a).

Effective problem-solving therapy programs follow seven basic steps:

1. Define the problem clearly. This step usually requires the person to identify the major goals that need to be achieved and the obstacles or conflicts blocking the path to these goals.
2. Identify alternative strategies for solving the problem. The goal of this brainstorming is to discover as many general solutions as possible.
3. Evaluate the short-term and long-term consequences of the alternative strategies, and select a general strategy for attempting to solve the problem.
4. List several specific alternative tactics for implementing the general strategy that has been chosen.
5. Choose a tactic that appears to have the best chance of resolving the problem.
6. Act on the decisions reached in the previous steps.
7. Assess the effectiveness of these actions. If the problem is resolved, the problem-solving sequence has been successful. If the problem remains, the person must return to one of the earlier stages and go through the sequence again, selecting different strategies or tactics to solve the problem.

Enhancing Emotion-Focused Coping People often cope more effectively with a stressful event if they have the opportunity to express their feelings about the event and gain a better understanding of it (Greenberg, Elliott, & Lietaer, 1994). Expressing feelings about a stressor is helpful—first, because it unburdens people of the negative thoughts and emotions they have kept bottled up, and second, because it allows them to think about the stressor in new and more effective ways. Emotional expression is one of the key pillars of most psychodynamic therapies, which focus explicitly on bringing emotion into the session so that it can be discussed and processed directly (Maroda, 2010).

Seminal research by James Pennebaker and his associates (Pennebaker & Beall, 1986; Pennebaker, Kiecolt-Glaser, & Glaser, 1988; Petrie, Booth, Pennebaker, & Davison, 1995) has examined the effects of one specific and common type of emotional expression: writing about one's thoughts and feelings after a stressful experience. Writing provides the opportunity to vent negative feelings, clarify and explore them more fully, and consider various methods for coping with them.

In one study (Pennebaker et al., 1988), 25 undergraduate students wrote in a journal for 20 minutes on 4 consecutive days about traumatic events in their lives. Another 25 students wrote for the same amount of time about more trivial events, such as a recent social activity. Before and after completing their daily writing assignments, the students rated their moods and reported any symptoms of physical illness. The researchers also measured the students' immune system functioning and the number of visits they made to the student health center during the study. Students who wrote about personal traumas showed better immune system functioning, made fewer visits to the health center, and reported less emotional distress than did students who wrote about trivial matters. In another study, college students who either wrote about traumatic events or spoke into a tape recorder about them for 20 minutes a week showed better immune system control over latent Epstein-Barr antibodies than did students who wrote about trivial topics instead (Esterling, Antoni, Fletcher, Margulies, & Schneiderman, 1994).

Even though writing or talking about a negative event may cause a short-term surge in negative emotions (Donnelly & Murray, 1991), the long-term effects of emotion-focused coping appear to be largely positive. Writing or talking about a stressful event, even years after it happened, can improve a person's psychological and physical functioning (Pennebaker, Barger, & Tiebout, 1989). For example, survivors of the Nazi Holocaust during World War II who disclosed strong negative feelings in an interview 40 years after their trauma demonstrated greater improvements in health than those who expressed milder feelings. Many studies have now shown that disclosing stressful or traumatic events via journaling or speaking (even into a private tape recorder) promotes physical health, psychological functioning, and subjective well-being (Berry & Pennebaker, 1993; Frattaroli, 2006).

Emotional disclosures seem to give people an opportunity to rid themselves of negative feelings, while simultaneously increasing confidence that they can cope with future stressors. As this confidence grows, individuals may gradually replace a general pessimism about themselves and the future with a more optimistic, upbeat style of thinking. A tendency to take an optimistic perspective on most events has been linked to better physical health and improved psychological adjustment during stress (e.g., Stoeber & Janssen, 2011). A stable optimistic outlook in which a person believes that good things will generally or eventually happen in the future has been termed *dispositional optimism* (Scheier & Carver, 1985). This trait may be genetically influenced to some extent, but it is also likely that a person's unique interpersonal experiences and real-life accomplishments can increase its strength, along with opportunities and outlets for genuine emotional expression.

Enhancing Social Support Therapists typically enhance social support for clients in two ways: directly, by actively listening to their clients and being empathic to their plights, and indirectly, by trying to help their clients become more receptive to social support opportunities in their lives. Some clients place a premium on keeping up an image of sturdy independence and regard turning to others as a sign of weakness that will cause others to lose respect for them. Therapists may challenge this attitude by asking clients how they feel when others solicit help from them. Generally, clients will admit that they feel closer to people who occasionally look to them for assistance. Therapists then ask clients to consider whether the same positive feelings might not come to those whose support they accept (Nietzel, Guthrie, & Susman, 1991). Helping clients increase the social support in their lives may be one of the common beneficial effects of most forms of psychotherapy, as social support is a protective factor for a wide variety of mental disorders.

Post-traumatic Stress Disorder

Fear of dying, which Arul in the chapter-opening vignette experienced during the shooting at his school, is probably the most primitive emotion that human beings experience. This fear is a normal, inborn response to the perception of threat. People who suddenly perceive threats are energized by rushes of chemicals that increase their energy, endurance, and strength, and help them escape or fight off attackers. This alarm system, so crucial in saving people from danger, can also be triggered as a false alarm, however; sometimes, as in Arul's case, the responses can persist long after the danger has passed. Previously neutral stimuli, like being in a classroom, become conditioned to feeling the instant surge of fear. In Arul, that fear became generalized to the point that he could not be in places with many people around without having autonomic nervous system arousal.

Individuals who have experienced a severe trauma and continue to experience intense, fear-related reactions weeks or months later when reminded of the trauma may be experiencing **post-traumatic stress disorder (PTSD)**. Usually, the trauma threatened the victim, or someone close to the victim, with mortal danger or serious bodily harm. In Arul's case, his experience of the shooting at school precipitated his PTSD.

According to the *DSM-5* (American Psychiatric Association, 2013a), features of PTSD fall into four broad classes of symptoms that occur following a severe trauma:

MAPS - Superficial Syndromes
Note the traumatic injuries in this saguaro cactus that eventually resulted in a chronically hypervigilant and anxious state akin to PTSD.

1. Frequent reexperiencing of the event through intrusive thoughts, flashbacks, and repeated nightmares and dreams;
2. Avoidance of stimuli associated with the trauma and a general numbing or deadening of emotions (feeling detached or estranged from others);
3. Negative changes in thinking and mood associated with the trauma, such as a persistent guilt or shame; and
4. Increased physiological arousal resulting in exaggerated startle responses or difficulty sleeping.

post-traumatic stress disorder (PTSD): An anxiety disorder in which a person experiences a pattern of intense, fear-related reactions after being exposed to a highly stressful event.

According to the *DSM-5*, these symptoms must last longer than 1 month to qualify as PTSD. Trauma-related symptoms beginning within 1 month after the trauma and lasting more than 2 days but less than 1 month are diagnosed instead as **acute stress disorder** (American Psychiatric Association, 2013a). However, in some cases of PTSD, trauma-related symptoms may not emerge for months or even years following the actual event.

Table 9.3 lists the full range of symptoms diagnostic of PTSD. A review of Arul's case description reveals that he experienced each of these diagnostic criteria: He was fearful for his life and witnessed injury to others (Criterion A); guns and related stimuli

acute stress disorder: A mental disorder in which a person who has undergone a traumatic event experiences trauma-related symptoms similar to PTSD that begin within 1 month of the trauma and last less than 1 month.

TABLE 9.3 The *DSM-5* in Simple Language: Diagnosing Post-traumatic Stress Disorder

Post-traumatic stress disorder can be diagnosed only if a person has been exposed to a traumatic event and either experienced the event directly or vicariously (e.g., found out that it happened to a loved one) or experienced repeated exposure to negative aspects of the event. After the event, the person then experiences symptoms in each of the following four areas for at least 1 month:

1. intrusions, like flashbacks and nightmares of the event;
2. avoidance, like refusing to go to certain places that may serve as a reminder of the event;
3. arousal, like being hypervigilant or startling more easily as a result of the event; and
4. changes in thinking and mood, like negative beliefs about how dangerous the world is or how the person might have caused or contributed to the event.

Source: Adapted from American Psychiatric Association (2013a).

triggered a reexperiencing of the trauma (Criterion B); he avoided stimuli associated with the trauma (Criterion C); he had thoughts about people's lack of trustworthiness and the danger of the world (Criterion D); and he was hyperaroused and reactive (Criterion E).

Traumatic events known to precipitate PTSD include war, natural disasters (such as tornados, earthquakes, hurricanes, and floods), serious accidents, torture, and various forms of abuse, including physical and sexual assault. All of these situations directly threaten a person's bodily integrity or life. They would cause distress in almost anyone who experienced them. Recent estimates of PTSD prevalence reveal that up to 12% of women and 4% of men will suffer from PTSD in their lifetimes, with the 12-month prevalence at about 4% for both genders combined (Kessler, Petukhova, Sampson, Zaslavsky, & Wittchen, 2012). In people exposed to traumas such as war or sexual assault, the prevalence of PTSD rises. For instance, U.S. war veterans of Iraq and Afghanistan had PTSD rates of 21% for women and 33% for men (Haskell et al., 2010). For comparison, the prevalence of PTSD among women with no history of sexual assault, those victimized for the first time before the age of 18, and those assaulted for the first time at 18 or older were 8.1%, 35.3%, and 30.2%, respectively (Masho & Ahmed, 2007). One way to look at these findings is that fewer than a third of the people exposed to horrible trauma such as combat or sexual assault will experience PTSD symptoms. Why might this be? Why do some people undergo horrible trauma and remain relatively free of symptoms, whereas others who are exposed to similar or less severe stressors develop PTSD? Research on the causes of PTSD may provide some possible answers.

Do Gender and Ethnicity Constitute Vulnerability for Developing PTSD?

When researchers have attempted to identify who is at risk for developing PTSD, female gender and ethnic minority status have been shown to be relatively moderate risk factors across multiple studies. More women than men are consistently diagnosed with PTSD by a factor of close to 3 (Holbrook, Hoyt, Stein, & Sieber, 2002; Kessler et al., 2012). However, female gender is not always found to be a risk factor in the development of PTSD, with significant variations from one study to another (Brewin, Andrews, & Valentine, 2000).

So why do some studies find evidence for gender as a risk factor for PTSD, whereas others do not? One explanation is the occurrence of proxy risk factors—that is, risk factors that are correlated with other risk factors (Kraemer, Stice, Kazdin, Offord, & Kupfer, 2001). For example, in a large retrospective study that assessed risk factors in a community sample, female gender did not remain a significant risk factor when other variables, like type of traumatic event, were included in the model being analyzed (Hapke, Schumann, Rumpf, John, & Meyer, 2006). This was likely due to the fact that women are more frequently the victims of assaultive traumas, such as sexual assault or physical attack, than are men.

Surveys of current rates of PTSD have been conducted in groups exposed to mass trauma (genocide and war) in different countries, including refugees. The range of PTSD in these groups has been wide: 1.7% of a community sample in post-conflict East Timor, 10% of inhabitants in a Senegalese refugee camp, 20% of tortured and imprisoned Tibetan refugees, 59.7% of torture survivors in rural Nepal, and 62% of community-based Cambodian refugees in the United States met criteria for PTSD (Hinton & Lewis-Fernández, 2011). The difference in rates highlights differential cultural responses to stress, as discussed earlier, which is supported by studies that examine rates of PTSD in members of

MAPS - Prejudicial Pigeonholes

different ethnic groups within a single country after a mass trauma such as a natural disaster or a terrorist attack. For example, New Yorkers of Latino origin had significantly higher rates of PTSD 6 months and 2 years after the 9/11 disaster than non-Latino whites (Adams & Boscarino, 2006). Another study, conducted 6 months after Hurricane Andrew (1992 in the United States), showed much higher rates of PTSD among Latinos (38%) and African Americans (23%) as compared to Caucasians (15%; Perilla, Norris, & Lavizzo, 2002).

What is the explanation for these cultural variations? Some of the variability in PTSD rates can be explained by differential trauma exposure. For example, African Americans in New Orleans tended to have fewer evacuation routes/options and more poorly constructed houses that were vulnerable to destruction during Hurricane Katrina (Chan &

Rhodes, 2014). Minority groups are thus more likely to bear the full brunt of the trauma, and there is a significant correlation between exposure severity and post-traumatic stress (Chan & Rhodes, 2014). For example, being African American was shown to be a risk factor for PTSD in the earlier literature for Vietnam veterans. However, further studies found that it was not their ethnicity but the fact that African American men were more likely to have been exposed to more severe direct combat during service, which predicted their PTSD severity. Moreover, there is evidence to suggest that immigrants and minority groups are often worse off not merely during but also in the *aftermath* of natural disasters, due to their lack of economic resources compared to their counterparts in majority groups (Chan & Rhodes, 2014). Other explanations for culture differences in PTSD include the effect of racism and discrimination, predisposing vulnerability factors (e.g., unemployment), less effective coping styles, and

Moorice was causing vicarious PTSD in the Reece Dairy cows by regaling them with tall tales from the Texas slaughterhouse where he came from.

differential symptom expression (e.g., members of some African cultures do not show avoidance/numbing symptoms, whereas members of Native American cultures may be more likely to have nightmares; Hinton & Lewis-Fernández, 2011).

Multiple surveys have shown that PTSD is diagnosable in diverse cultures around the world (Hinton & Lewis-Fernández, 2011). But the precise rates vary: 12-month community prevalence ranges from 0% in the Yoruba-speaking areas of Nigeria to around 4% in the United States, even when using the same diagnostic instrument (the Composite International Diagnostic Interview, discussed in Chapter 1). Other rates are 0.2% in metropolitan China (Beijing and Shanghai), 0.4% in Japan, 0.6% in Mexico, 0.6% in South Africa, 0.7% in South Korea, 0.9% in Europe, and 1.3% in Australia. Thus, most 12-month rates of PTSD worldwide cluster around 0.5–1.0%. It is unclear why the U.S. prevalence is considerably (4 times) higher than other countries, although one factor may be that PTSD is higher in U.S. military veterans (20–30%; Haskell et al., 2010) than in military personnel of other countries such as the United Kingdom (around 3%; Mulligan et al., 2012), perhaps because conversations about PTSD have become the primary way in which U.S. troops express trauma and other forms of suffering (Hautzinger & Scandlyn, 2013).

Causes of PTSD

PTSD is one of the only mental disorders that requires a specific causal agent—trauma. Although trauma is a necessary cause of PTSD, its occurrence does not tell the whole causal story. In other words, trauma is a necessary—but not sufficient—condition in the causal chain of PTSD. And, while traumatic events differ, there is clear evidence that people who go on to develop PTSD after a traumatic event share common vulnerabilities that may increase their risk for distress (Vogt, King, & King, 2007). The biopsychosocial model discussed in Chapter 2 (and in just about every chapter since) contributes interacting causal factors in the usual three categories.

Biological Causes of PTSD Are some people biologically predisposed to develop PTSD? William True and his colleagues (1993) studied reports of 4,042 twin pairs, in which both members had seen military service during the Vietnam era. Concordance rates for PTSD symptoms between twins led to the conclusion that a genetic predisposition contributes substantially to nearly all symptoms of PTSD. Twin research to date suggests that: (1) exposure to assaultive trauma is moderately heritable, whereas exposure to nonassaultive trauma is not, (2) PTSD symptoms are moderately heritable, and (3) comorbidity of PTSD with other disorders may be partly due to shared genetic and environmental influences (Afifi, Asmundson, Taylor, & Jang, 2010). Overall, PTSD is approximately 30% heritable, indicating that genetic factors are important in the disorder's etiology (Koenen, 2007).

Other biological research has pointed out that PTSD reactions appear to originate from excessive surges of neurotransmitters such as norepinephrine or from hypersensitivity in the same brain structures (e.g., the locus coeruleus) that are involved in panic attacks (Southwick, Yehuda, & Morgan, 1995). Numerous studies have provided compelling evidence that an excessively strong adrenergic (epinephrine) response to the traumatic event may mediate the formation of the durable traumatic memories that in part characterize the disorder (Pitman, 1989). One of the earliest and most replicated PTSD findings is that of heightened autonomic reactivity (such as heart rate and skin conductance) and facial EMG (muscle) reactivity to external, trauma-related stimuli, such as combat sounds and film clips (Keane et al., 1998), as well as to internal, mental imagery of the traumatic event (Pitman, Orr, Forgue, de Jong, & Claiborn, 1987). Thus, people who develop PTSD appear to be biologically primed or sensitive to fear and trauma in the first place.

Newer studies using both structural and functional neuroimaging (MRI and fMRI, discussed in Chapter 1) show that the usual suspects—limbic system brain structures such as the amygdala and the hippocampus—are involved in PTSD, as they are in anxiety disorders discussed in Chapter 7 (Pitman et al., 2012). The amygdala is an almond-shaped structure located at the base of the seahorse-shaped hippocampus that recognizes both conditioned and unconditioned stimuli signaling danger, and also initiates the fear response. Amygdala reactivity is exaggerated in individuals with PTSD and is positively correlated with symptom severity. Other brain parts, such as the ventromedial prefrontal cortex, reduce the amygdala's expression of the fear response and show diminished activity in people with PTSD; ventromedial prefrontal cortex activity is also negatively correlated with symptom severity. Functional neuroimaging findings in the hippocampus, which is involved in memory formation and in recognizing both safe and dangerous contexts, have been mixed in PTSD, with both hypo- and hyper-reactivity observed (Pitman et al., 2012).

Psychological Causes of PTSD The functioning of the hippocampus has served as a sort of bridge between biological and psychological research on PTSD. When stress is high enough to impair the operation of the hippocampus, the resulting memories are different from those formed under more ordinary circumstances (Nadel & Jacobs, 1998). Empirical data suggest that memories of trauma may be available as isolated fragments rather than as coherently bound episodes (Nadel & Jacobs, 1998). Another unusual feature of memories formed under stress is that there is amnesia for the autobiographical context of stressful events, but stronger than normal recall for the emotional memories produced by them. These findings may explain why people with PTSD have strong emotional responses to objects and situations that remind them of the trauma without a solid sense of where and who they are, or even the fact that they are in the present rather than in the past.

Particular aspects of an individual's personality, such as higher levels of hostility and lower levels of self-efficacy, agreeableness, and conscientiousness, have also been found to be associated with PTSD among professionals exposed to traumatic events (Heinrichs et al., 2005; Hodgins, Creamer, & Bell, 2001). Furthermore, researchers have found that higher neuroticism scores and lower extraversion were associated with greater risk for PTSD in burn survivors (Fauerbach, Lawrence, Schmidt, Munster, & Costa, 2000). Finally, two different studies of motor vehicle crash survivors have found evidence that having a personality disorder diagnosis (see Chapter 16) predicted higher scores on measures of PTSD 1 year following the accident (Blanchard et al., 1995; Malta, Blanchard, Taylor, Hickling, & Freidenberg, 2002).

Behavioral and Cognitive Factors in PTSD Behavioral and cognitive theorists have proposed a couple of mechanisms by which PTSD symptoms might develop. Behavioral theories focus on a **two-factor conditioning** model originated by Hobart Mowrer (1939) that involves both classical and operant conditioning (discussed in Chapter 2). According to this explanation, during a trauma such as sexual assault, previously neutral stimuli become conditioned emotional stimuli through their association with fear and pain (which are unconditioned stimuli). Later, the conditioned stimulus, such as the sight of a hunting

two-factor conditioning: A model that combines classical conditioning and operant conditioning to explain disorders such as PTSD and phobias.

knife, can elicit terror as memories of being assaulted at knifepoint come flooding back. Through stimulus generalization, other related stimuli, such as a table knife, may also come to elicit anxiety (Keane, Fairbank, Caddell, & Zimering, 1989). Even the time of day or type of weather associated with the trauma may, through classical conditioning and stimulus generalization, come to elicit PTSD symptoms.

Once a person's emotional responses (fear and panic) become conditioned to an array of stimuli, the victim tries to avoid these stimuli. Unlike with phobias (discussed in Chapter 7), where the person strives to avoid the objects or situations associated with false alarms (i.e., panic when no actual danger exists), individuals with PTSD avoid things that might remind them of their past true alarm (i.e., a terrible event that really did happen to them). As with phobias, though, these avoidance behaviors are further strengthened by operant conditioning—that is, the behaviors are reinforced by their ability to reduce anxiety. Research merging biological and behavioral perspectives shows that people with PTSD are more easily conditioned by fearful experiences and display slower extinction learning in which they might learn that the past alarm is unlikely to recur in the future (Pitman et al., 2012).

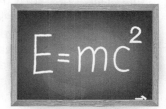

MAPS - Attempted Answers

As noted earlier, this two-factor conditioning theory is similar to behavioral explanations of phobias (Chapter 7), and in some ways, PTSD is like an intense, pervasive phobia. However, several elements of PTSD differ from phobias and are not readily explained by conditioning theory. For example, Edna Foa points out that, unlike anxiety disorders, PTSD involves two paradoxical extremes of consciousness: (1) reliving the traumatic event in nightmares, flashbacks, and intrusive thoughts, and (2) experiencing a numbing of emotional response and denial of the trauma. According to Foa and others, these features of PTSD are better accounted for by cognitive-behavioral theory, discussed later in the chapter; (Foa, Zinbarg, & Olasov-Rothbaum, 1992; Creamer, Burgess, & Pattison, 1992).

fear network: A memory network that connects fear stimuli and fearful responses.

Foa and her colleagues have drawn on network theories of cognition and emotion to posit a theory of **fear networks** for PTSD (Foa & Kozak, 1986; Foa, Steketee, & Olasov-Rothbaum, 1989; Foa et al., 1992; Lang, 1985; Litz & Keane, 1989). They propose that, following a traumatic event, a memory network is automatically set up in the person that interconnects all the fear stimuli and response elements associated with the trauma. The network contains information about trauma-related *stimuli* and *responses* (including verbal, physiological, and behavioral activity), along with information about the *meaning* of the event to the person. These fear networks also include escape and avoidance programs designed to protect the person from harm in situations similar to those in which he or she experienced the life-threatening trauma. When any part of the fear network is accessed and activated, escape and avoidance programs are set in motion to remove the person from danger. Activation of these responses constitutes the PTSD symptoms. For example, flashbacks, in which the victim mentally re-experiences the trauma, can be explained as activation of the whole fear network, including its stimulus and response elements. The network model has considerable appeal because of its implications for treatment and prevention, as noted in this chapter's "Prevention" feature. As you will see later in the chapter, the leading treatment for PTSD is based on both the two-factor and fear networks theories of PTSD.

Another cognitive contribution is that PTSD symptoms are more likely to occur if the victim comes to believe that

Source: albund/Shutterstock.com.

Famous American author J. D. Salinger experienced several traumatic experiences after he was drafted into the Army in 1942, and he certainly displayed some of the classic symptoms of PTSD (Shields & Salerno, 2013). The author of *The Catcher in the Rye* (1951/1985), one of the most influential novels of 20th-century American literature, became an almost total recluse, who struggled to maintain any kind of long-term relationships with women. Salinger was so reclusive that he even built a tall wooden stockade fence around his house in New Hampshire to keep admirers away. The novel's symbolism has much to do with protecting youth, Salinger's innocence before witnessing the ravages of war:

Among other things, you'll find that you're not the first person who was ever confused and frightened and even sickened by human behavior. You're by no means alone on that score, you'll be excited and stimulated to know. Many, many men have been just as troubled morally and spiritually as you are right now. Happily, some of them kept records of their troubles. You'll learn from them—if you want to. Just as someday, if you have something to offer, someone will learn something from you. . . . (p. 197)

Can PTSD Be Prevented?

Natural disasters and other traumas are unfortunate facts of life, but there is reason to believe that PTSD, in some trauma victims at least, can be prevented. Preventing the occurrence of a negative outcome following the potentially traumatic event is called *secondary prevention*, a level of preventive care that focuses on early diagnosis, use of referral services, and rapid initiation of treatment to stop the progress of a mental disorder. For one thing, although many people who experience severe trauma may develop acute stress disorder, most do not go on to develop PTSD. One reason may be that those experiencing trauma, but not PTSD, tend to receive high levels of social support from family, friends, or counselors immediately following the event (e.g., Perry, Difede, Musngi, Frances, & Jacobsberg, 1992; Sutker, Davis, Uddo, & Ditta, 1995). Thus, providing immediate social support for trauma victims may prevent their experiences from triggering an acute stress disorder or progressing into full-blown PTSD symptoms 30 days after the trauma.

Other than social support, two additional characteristics tend to distinguish people who develop PTSD from those who do not. Individuals who suffer chronic PTSD often perceive the world as a dangerous place from which they must retreat, and they usually come to view themselves as incompetent and helpless to deal with stressors. If these two misconceptions could be eliminated after a trauma, more severe cases of PTSD might be prevented in many victims. Edna Foa and her colleagues developed a four-session prevention course designed to attack these two misconceptions in women who have been sexually assaulted (Foa, Hearst-Ikeda, & Perry, 1995). Based on her fear network model of PTSD, Foa included the following elements in her prevention course:

1. education about the common psychological reactions to assault in order to help victims realize that their responses are normal,

2. training in skills such as relaxation so that the women are better prepared to cope with stress,

3. emotionally reliving the trauma through imaginal exposure methods to allow victims to defuse their lingering fears of the trauma, and

4. cognitive restructuring to help the women replace negative beliefs about their competence and adequacy with more realistic appraisals.

Ten women who had recently been sexually assaulted completed Foa's four-week course. Their PTSD symptoms were then compared with 10 other women who had also been sexually assaulted but who did not

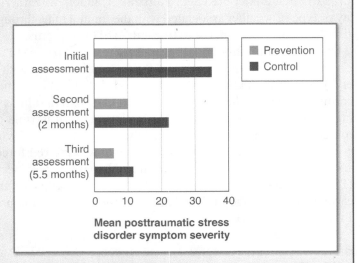

Mean posttraumatic stress disorder symptom severity

Prevention of PTSD in Rape and Assault Victims

Compared with controls, women participating in a PTSD prevention course experienced fewer symptoms of the disorder at assessments conducted at 2 and 5.5 months after their sexual assaults.

Source: Foa et al. in *Journal of Consulting Psychology*, Vol. 64, 1995, p. 952. Reprinted with permission

take part in the prevention course. As the accompanying bar graph shows, at 2-month and 5.5-month post-assault assessment, victims who completed the prevention course had fewer PTSD symptoms than did the no-treatment controls. Two months after their trauma, 70% of the untreated women, but only 10% of the treated women, met the *DSM* criteria for PTSD (Foa et al., 1995). These results suggest that a brief program that facilitates emotionally reexperiencing trauma *and* correcting beliefs about personal inadequacy can reduce the incidence of PTSD.

These secondary prevention efforts can be highly valuable because research suggests that PTSD becomes more difficult to treat the longer a person has had the symptoms (Rauch & Foa, 2003). A meta-analysis suggests that the case for secondary prevention efforts to prevent PTSD has been mounting (Roberts, Kitchiner, Kenardy, & Bisson, 2009), with over 20 early-intervention studies of cognitive-behavioral therapy showing effectiveness for preventing or reducing symptoms of PTSD. For instance, brief exposure-based interventions that are applied in the hospital emergency room in the hours immediately following trauma may have a more significant impact in reducing the prevalence of chronic PTSD, compared to other interventions that have been tested weeks after the initial trauma exposure (Kearns, Ressler, Zatzick, & Rothbaum, 2012). The key is being able to identify those participants who are most at risk so that targeted prevention efforts can be offered.

Can PTSD Be Prevented? *(Continued)*

Note that the often-used Critical Incident Stress Debriefing (CISD), which involves scores of mental health professionals descending upon a town after a trauma and forcing everyone to talk about what happened immediately, has not received much empirical support and may even be a rare psychological intervention that can actually make things worse (Wei, Szumilas, & Kutcher, 2010). Thus, the type of early intervention matters.

Finally, there is new evidence that biological treatments might also be valuable in the prevention of PTSD. For example, a high dose of cortisol given shortly after the traumatic event reduced the probability of developing PTSD in one study (Zohar et al., 2011). Other studies have shown that giving victims the beta-blocking (epinephrine-reducing) drug propranolol within hours of a trauma could reduce PTSD symptoms (Brunet et al., 2008; Brunet et al., 2011). One explanation is that propranolol blocks the reconsolidation of the traumatic memory. However, insufficient human studies exist to date to conclude that this intervention is effective in preventing PTSD (Pitman et al., 2012). Finally, researchers are currently studying the possible role of the protein kinase M-zeta (PKMzeta) in memory persistence (Furini, Myskiw, Benetti, & Izquierdo, 2013), with the possibility that drugs that block PKMzeta could actually erase traumatic memories from the brain (sounds like science fiction, doesn't it?). Renowned memory researcher Elizabeth Loftus (2011) posed a challenging question: *If a pill could remove your worst memory so that you would never know it happened, would you choose to take it?*

the world is a dangerous place and then generalizes danger signs from one traumatic incident to all situations (Kushner, Riggs, Foa, & Miller, 1992). Such overgeneralization may be particularly problematic for people who believe that there is no one to whom they can turn for help or no one with whom they can discuss their fears and coping strategies, which leads into the discussion of social contributions to PTSD's development.

Psychosocial Causes of PTSD Among other factors that contribute to symptom development of PTSD are social factors present prior to the trauma, characteristics of the trauma itself, and what happens to the victim after the trauma.

Pre-trauma Experiences Pre-trauma risk factors, or factors that are present prior to the traumatic event, have been found to increase vulnerability to PTSD after trauma. Younger age in a study of disaster rescue workers substantially increased the odds of developing distress (PTSD or acute stress disorder) after an airplane crash (Fullerton, Ursano, & Wang, 2004). Research has suggested that it may not be younger age itself that predicts PTSD, but rather factors associated with younger age, such as socioeconomic status and engagement in more risk-taking behavior, that make the younger person more vulnerable (Holbrook, Hoyt, Stein, & Sieber, 2002). Other pre-trauma factors that have been shown to protect against the development of PTSD include higher education (Koenen et al., 2002), being in a committed relationship (Fullerton et al., 2004), and having stable employment (Joy, Probert, Bisson, & Shepherd, 2000). Finally, two clear factors that suggest strongest risk for PTSD are past trauma history and previous psychiatric history for self and/or family members (Ozer, Best, Lipsey, & Weiss, 2003; Kleim, Ehlers, & Glucksman, 2007).

Peri-trauma Experiences Factors associated with the trauma itself and the thoughts and emotions during the traumatic event have been shown to increase risk for PTSD. Resnick et al. (1993) found that 26% of women whose trauma was crime-related developed PTSD, whereas only 9% of noncriminal trauma victims developed PTSD symptoms (see Figure 9.3). The extent of injury during motor vehicle trauma also predicted subsequent PTSD symptom development (Blanchard et al., 1995), as did greater emotional distress and physical pain at the time of injury (Zatzick et al., 2007). Moreover, heart rate recorded during emergency medical transport was significantly correlated with PTSD symptoms at 6 weeks and at 6 months for child victims of trauma (Nugent, Christopher, & Delahanty, 2006), indicating that early physiological arousal may be a risk factor. In addition to their biology, victims' psychological perceptions of trauma at the time are also important in

FIGURE 9.3 PTSD in Women Following Crimes and Other Traumas

As the top part of this figure shows, women who experienced crime-related trauma are nearly 3 times more likely to suffer PTSD than are women who suffered noncrime trauma. In addition, among the women who were crime victims, those who believed that their lives were in danger were more likely to develop symptoms than those who did not. Furthermore, those who received an injury *and* perceived their lives to be threatened were significantly more likely to develop PTSD.

Source: Adapted from Resnick, Kilpatrick, Dansky, Saunders, & Best (1993).

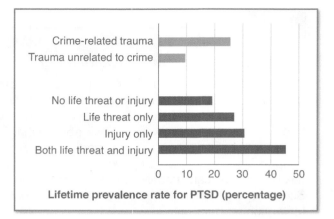

determining the likelihood of PTSD. The belief that the victim's life is in danger and that he or she has no control over the trauma appears to contribute to PTSD symptoms (Green, Grace, Lindy, Gleser, & Leonard, 1990; Kushner et al., 1992).

Post-trauma Events Several studies have shown that the risk of developing PTSD is inversely related to the amount of social support that trauma victims have (Brewin et al., 2000; Ozer et al., 2003). The more embedded in helpful relationships a person feels and the larger the network of friends or relatives the person can call on in time of need, the better the person's ability to cope with severe stressors (Cohen & Wills, 1985). One study found that the male Vietnam veterans most likely to suffer PTSD were those who, upon returning from the war, experienced significant reductions in the size of their social network and the quality of social support they received (Keane, Zimering, & Caddell, 1985). Indeed, the social rejection that was experienced by many returning Vietnam veterans may be one reason why rates of PTSD following combat in Vietnam were so high compared to veterans of earlier wars; in general, there is a 1.5–3.5-fold increase in PTSD risk with deployment, which is highest for Vietnam veterans (Magruder & Yeager, 2009). In addition to a lack of social support, continued life stressors after a trauma tend to increase PTSD risk. This stress may be related to resources; the fewer resources individuals have prior to a trauma, the fewer resources are available to buffer them against stress. In a study with injured trauma survivors, for instance, those without health insurance were twice as likely to be diagnosed with PTSD 1 year after their injury (Zatzick et al., 2007).

Treatments for PTSD

The best treatments for PTSD have come from cognitive-behavioral therapy (CBT) approaches. There have also been advances in psychopharmacologic treatments for PTSD, but the Institute of Medicine (2014) is clear that the first line of treatment for PTSD should be exposure-based (CBT) interventions.

Over the years, PTSD has gone by many names, each one usually linked to the specific trauma giving rise to symptoms. In war, it was called "shell shock" or "war neurosis." In sexual assault, it was called "rape trauma syndrome." Indeed, two major phenomena brought PTSD to the attention of mental health professionals: frequent psychological complications for veterans of the Vietnam War and recognition of the deep trauma experienced by victims of sexual assault. Extreme and unexpected personal tragedies are also leading causes of PTSD.

Source: John Gomez/Shutterstock.com.

Cognitive-Behavioral Therapy Three different yet similar types of CBT packages have been developed for the treatment of PTSD. Direct exposure treatment, called **prolonged exposure therapy**, follows from the idea that the PTSD symptoms are a series of conditioned responses that were acquired at the time of the trauma and have generalized to related stimuli; thus, as in phobia cases, exposure to feared stimuli can be accomplished either imaginally (using imagery) or in vivo (real life). Following their cognitive view of PTSD described earlier in the chapter, Foa and her colleagues suggested that treatment of PTSD should involve prolonged exposure that can both (1) activate the fear memory net-

prolonged exposure therapy: A cognitive-behavioral treatment for PTSD that involves repeatedly exposing individuals to stimuli that remind them of their past trauma in order to alter their fear networks.

work and (2) provide experiences that are incompatible with the information stored in the memory network (Foa et al., 1991). Foa believes that repeatedly exposing PTSD victims to feared stimuli in the absence of negative consequences challenges the fear of danger and allows new, more rational information to become part of the brain's network. Exposure treatments often include other components, such as relaxation training, which can help the client develop new coping skills while extinguishing emotional reactions to the fear-provoking stimuli. Over the past 20 years, there have been more than 40 controlled clinical trials investigating the efficacy of prolonged exposure therapy. A meta-analysis revealed that the average person treated with prolonged exposure fared better than 86% of patients in control conditions at post-treatment on PTSD measures (Powers, Halpern, Ferenschak, Gillihan, & Foa, 2010). Prolonged exposure is thus considered a highly effective treatment for PTSD, resulting in substantial treatment gains that are maintained over time (Powers et al., 2010).

A variant of this treatment, called **cognitive processing therapy** (CPT), has been proposed and tested by Patricia Resick and Monica Schnicke (1993). They extended Foa's methods to include homework, such as writing about the meaning of the event and identifying and challenging beliefs that might maintain the symptoms. CPT still includes the exposure component, but then incorporates specific ways to address secondary emotions, including anger and blame. This treatment has been shown to be effective in a variety of populations, including sexual assault survivors, veterans, and refugees (Resick, Nishith, Weaver, Astin, & Feuer, 2002; Chard, Schumm, Owens, & Cottingham, 2010; Schulz, Resick, Huber, & Griffin, 2006).

Another potentially effective, albeit controversial, cognitive-behavioral treatment for PTSD is **eye movement desensitization and reprocessing** (EMDR; Shapiro, 1995). The goal of EMDR therapy is to process clients' distressing memories, thereby reducing their lingering effects and allowing clients to develop more adaptive coping mechanisms. This is done in an 8-step protocol that includes having clients recall distressing images while receiving one of several types of bilateral sensory input, including side-to-side eye movements. Whereas there is mounting evidence for its overall effectiveness (e.g., Davidson & Parker, 2001), the evidence supporting the use of EMDR to treat combat veterans afflicted with PTSD does not (yet) rise to the threshold of an empirically supported treatment (Albright & Thyer, 2010). Importantly, no incremental effect of eye movements was noted when EMDR was compared with the same procedure without them, meaning that the eye movements themselves may actually be unnecessary (Davidson & Parker, 2001). The efficacy of CPT and EMDR have both shown similar results to prolonged exposure therapy, likely because the central component of each of these three treatments is the same—habituating the individual with PTSD to the fearful stimuli through exposure (Powers et al., 2010).

Other PTSD treatment programs incorporate several procedures that target different aspects of the symptoms. These procedures include cognitive restructuring to improve the client's efforts to manage symptoms of cognitive intrusion, systematic desensitization to decrease physiological arousal, and training in specific coping strategies to deal with daily stressors (Zinbarg, Barlow, Brown, & Hertz, 1992). While these nonexposure-based treatments appear to be better than no-treatment control groups, the three exposure-based interventions already discussed (prolonged exposure, CPT, and EMDR) are the overwhelming favorites in the treatment of PTSD.

Drug Treatments At present, the National Center for PTSD, an organization that leads research and education regarding PTSD, suggests that medication should be viewed as a second-line treatment for PTSD, to be considered only if the exposure-based therapies do not alleviate symptoms. Selective serotonin reuptake inhibitors (SSRIs), a class of medications discussed in Chapter 6 that allow for brain serotonin to be available longer for neurons to absorb it, is a recommended medication to alleviate PTSD symptoms. However, 30–50% of PTSD patients do not respond well to sertraline (Zoloft) and paroxetine (Paxil), the only medications (both SSRIs) currently approved by the Food and Drug Administration (FDA) to treat PTSD (Marshall, Beebe, Oldham, & Zaninelli, 2001;

cognitive processing therapy: A cognitive-behavioral treatment for PTSD that involves repeatedly exposing individuals to stimuli that remind them of their past trauma, in addition to having them process the meaning of their trauma through written exercises.

eye movement desensitization and reprocessing: A cognitive-behavioral treatment for PTSD that involves repeatedly exposing individuals to stimuli that remind them of their past trauma, while they engage in eye or other bilateral movements postulated to facilitate emotional processing.

MAPS - Medical Myths

Marshall & Pierce, 2000), and no single drug has been discovered that will reduce all the symptoms found in PTSD. Additional medications may be used to target specific symptoms, such as sleep disturbance and negative alterations in mood. Many of the medications prescribed for PTSD directly affect the HPA axis mentioned previously, intending to reduce symptoms and alleviate negative mood (Pariante, 2003).

Section Review

Adjustment disorders are a relatively common diagnosis and are:

- in response to traumatic and life-altering stressors,
- commonly diagnosed, and
- treated with problem-focused therapy to reduce the impact of the stressor.

Even though most people are exposed to a traumatic event in their lifetime, a small percentage will develop post-traumatic stress disorder (PTSD) or its shorter version, acute stress disorder. These disorders:

- are theorized to develop due to classical conditioning and to be maintained by operant conditioning, with the emergence of fear networks in the brain; and
- develop based on specific pre-, peri-, and post-trauma risk factors

The most effective treatment for PTSD is cognitive-behavioral therapy (CBT) that has exposure components, such as prolonged exposure or cognitive processing therapy.

Revisiting the Case of Arul

Upon meeting with a psychologist, Arul described his symptoms and explained how they had all started following the mass shooting on his college campus. His psychologist described the possible symptoms of post-traumatic psychological distress following a traumatic event, and she stated that Arul might meet the criteria for post-traumatic stress disorder (PTSD). While Arul did not like the notion of having a "disorder," for the first time he realized that what he was experiencing was not totally unusual, considering what he had been through. Reluctantly, he agreed to begin discussing the shooting, along with his associated thoughts and feelings, with the psychologist. Surprisingly to Arul, this process revealed feelings of anger not only at the shooter, but also at himself for not thinking twice about the students he saw running, and for freezing when he had the impulse to help the student who had been shot. It was only a beginning, but he was willing to work on the confusing thoughts and feelings that seemed to be generated in an instant on what was supposed to be an ordinary day.

Once Arul attended therapy, he learned about the fear conditioning that took place for him during his trauma. Through CBT, Arul learned to overcome the fear that he associated with almost every place or situation that closely resembled his scenario during the shooting. A big part of overcoming that fear involved exposure: revisiting what he was thinking and feeling during the moments of the shooting, which allowed him to process the emotions tied to that day. He never forgot the shooting, but he was able to stop avoiding others, start going out with friends, and engage in life again without constantly being fearful that he was in harm's way. Eventually, for Arul, the nightmares stopped, and he was able to return to school and finish his degree.

Ann Marie Warren

Dr. Warren is a board-certified rehabilitation psychologist, Associate Investigator of Trauma Research at Baylor University Medical Center, Division of Trauma, and Clinical Assistant Professor at Texas A&M Health Sciences Center–Department of Surgery. She is an expert in early assessment and treatment of people who have been traumatically injured.

Q *What kind of patients do you work with, and what role do you have?*

A Currently, I see patients exclusively who are admitted to our Level I trauma service at Baylor University Medical Center following an injury severe enough to require hospitalization. These patients sustain injury from a variety of causes, including motor vehicle collisions, falls, and violence (particularly, penetrating injuries such as gunshot or stabbing injuries), as well as sports-related injuries. In addition, I work with the patients' families, as family members often experience a level of psychological distress that may be above what is experienced by the patient, especially while the patient is in the ICU. My consults come directly from the trauma surgeons, and I begin working with patients and families once admitted to the ICU and/or the trauma surgery floor and follow with them during their acute admission. In addition to direct consults, I work with the multidisciplinary team to provide psychological and behavioral information about the patient that may impact care, as well as contribute to recommendations regarding discharge and referral.

Q *How do you identify who might be at risk for developing PTSD or other psychological distress after trauma?*

A Screening for acute stress disorder/PTSD symptoms is part of the evaluation process whenever I am consulted on a patient. Research shows that certain factors after injury, such as age, history of pre-injury psychiatric disorders, and type of injury (i.e., gunshot wound or other penetrating injury) may be more predictive of later PTSD. However, patients who do not have those types of risk factors should not be excluded from screening for post-traumatic psychological distress.

Q *What types of interventions do you do with trauma survivors?*

A There is very little evidence-based research to suggest what interventions may be most beneficial in the first few hours or days following injury. However, we do know that forms of cognitive-behavioral therapy, particularly prolonged exposure and cognitive processing therapy, have evidence to suggest their usefulness for PTSD in general. In the hospital, providing psychoeducation regarding both normal and abnormal responses to trauma is a general approach to help normalize the experience for people after injury. Brief cognitive-behavioral therapy is also used to help specific symptoms, such as insomnia or nightmares. Helping patients understand the need for follow-up with a mental health care provider in the community if symptoms persist is another form of intervention and secondary prevention.

Q *How do you choose which interventions to use?*

A Keeping up with the literature in this area is important, especially as new information regarding early interventions to reduce later PTSD after injury is continually evolving. There are also some great resources available, such as the National Center for PTSD, which provides information regarding interventions and education for both providers and the public. Additionally, talking with psychologist colleagues in similar settings also helps determine what is considered best practice.

Q *What types of research are you doing related to secondary prevention?*

A The Baylor Trauma Outcome Project (BTOP) is an ongoing, longitudinal prospective study examining the impact of injury on patients admitted to a Level I trauma center. Specifically, we are looking at a variety of outcomes, including psychological outcomes, at the time of hospitalization and then 1, 3, 6, and 12 months post-injury. Using this research, we hope to better identify who may be at risk for the development of later PTSD; ultimately, this research will be used to develop the pilot work needed for interventional studies to help psychologists provide evidenced-based interventions in the acute stage of any injury.

Summary

The Nature of Stress

Stress is a process that results when environmental or social threats place demands on a person. Stressors come in many forms, including predictable challenges and sudden, unpredictable crises. Stress reactions occur in a three-stage pattern of physiological, behavioral, and psychological changes that Selye termed the *general adaptation syndrome (GAS)*.

Physical Reactions to Stress

In the alarm stage of the GAS, the person is jolted into action, and the body prepares to fight or flee the stressor. In the resistance stage, the person attempts to cope with the stressor. In the final exhaustion stage, the person's capacity to resist breaks down and the ability to cope with stressors is ultimately lost.

Physical and psychological reactions to stressors are usually adaptive in the short run because they are aimed at coping with stressors in some way. However, if these defenses must be employed for too long, people begin to experience harmful physical and psychological effects. Prolonged stressors lead to suppression of the immune system, which in turn results in greater susceptibility to illness.

Psychological Reactions to Stress

People use a variety of strategies to cope with stressful events in their lives. Problem-focused coping is aimed at modifying stressors themselves. Cognitive reappraisals involve thinking about stressors in less upsetting ways. Emotion-focused coping attempts to manage the feelings individuals have about a stressful event. Enlisting social support is a fourth general strategy that people use to cope with stress. Depending on the nature and context of a stressful event, any or all coping strategies can be successful. In general, people who are flexible in the strategies they use are most effective at coping with stress.

Mental Disorders after Stress and Trauma

If coping efforts fail and stressors continue, the possible consequences include adjustment disorders, post-traumatic stress disorder, sleep-wake disorders, dissociative and somatic symptom and related disorders, and the onset or recurrence of other psychological disorders.

Adjustment disorders are a common diagnosis for the temporary problems that people suffer following a stressor. Often, the symptoms of an adjustment disorder resemble a milder version of other mental disorders, particularly mood disorders and anxiety disorders. Adjustment disorders are commonly diagnosed following natural disasters and because of chronic problems in relationships or work. Rather than medication, interventions that bolster individuals' resilience through increasing their perceived social support or strengthening their problem-focused and/or emotion-focused coping strategies usually help resolve an adjustment disorder.

Some people exposed to intense, life-threatening traumas develop post-traumatic stress disorder (PTSD), in which they periodically reexperience the trauma, feel the pull to avoid situations and places that are reminders of the trauma, have negative changes in thought patterns and mood, and are easily startled and physiologically reactive. Natural disasters, war, mass shootings, and physical and sexual assault are the major traumas that precipitate PTSD. Although some people may be genetically vulnerable to PTSD, the disorder cannot be fully explained without considering the cognitive and learning processes that exacerbate and perpetuate PTSD symptoms. Cognitive-behavioral treatments (CBT) for PTSD, which involve exposing clients to triggering stimuli and helping them change the way they think about those stimuli, is the first-line treatment, rather than other types of psychotherapy or medications.

Key Terms

acute stress disorder, p. 325

adjustment disorder, p. 319

adrenal corticosteroid, p. 310

adrenocorticotrophic hormone (ACTH), p. 310

adverse childhood experiences (ACEs), p. 313

cognitive processing therapy, p. 333

cognitive reappraisal, p. 314

coping, p. 313

corticotropin-releasing hormone (CRH), p. 310

emotion-focused coping, p. 314

endorphin, p. 311

eye movement desensitization and reprocessing, p. 333

fear network, p. 329

fight-or-flight response, p. 309

general adaptation syndrome (GAS), p. 309

glucocorticoid, p. 312

hypothalamic-pituitary-adrenal (HPA) axis, p. 310

immunosuppression, p. 312

post-traumatic stress disorder (PTSD), p. 325

primary appraisal, p. 313

problem-focused coping, p. 314

prolonged exposure therapy, p. 332

social support, p. 314

stage of exhaustion, p. 309

stage of resistance, p. 309

stress, p. 306

stress hormone, p. 310

two-factor conditioning, p. 328

Dissociative Disorders

Source: i4lcocl2/Shutterstock.com.

From the Case of Louise

Louise is a 30-year-old account representative for an up-and-coming technology company. Her job involves a fair amount of travel, and she works mostly on her own, checking into the office only once or twice a week. Although she is successful in her work, she has only a few close friends and has been estranged from her family since she left home after high school. As soon as a romantic relationship becomes at all serious, Louise feels panicky and cuts it off. She has struggled with depression and terrible headaches for years, and has consulted many doctors, with no real relief. She finally decided to seek psychotherapy because her difficulties have begun to interfere with her work productivity.

In therapy, Louise tried to provide a complete history of her past but could recall only a few memories from her childhood. She remembered not getting along with her stepfather, which led to friction with her mother. When she left home for college, everyone seemed relieved. Her memory problems extended into her adult life. She described having to post lists and written reminders to keep her on target at work. She admitted that she sometimes lost track of time and could not remember what she had done or where she had been. She complained of finding things in her apartment that she could not remember buying.

After reading this chapter, you will be able to answer the following key questions:

- What are the components of dissociation?

- What are the defining features of dissociative identity disorder in the *Diagnostic and Statistical Manual of Mental Disorders (DSM-5)*, and is it a valid diagnosis?

- What other dissociative disorders are described in the *DSM-5*?

- What causes dissociative disorders?

- How are dissociative disorders treated?

The first 6 months of therapy focused on reducing Louise's somatic complaints and feelings of depression and anxiety. As Louise began to feel more relaxed and trusting in the therapeutic relationship, the therapist noticed some striking changes. Typically, Louise had come to sessions in simple, casual dress, but now she began to appear in flamboyant outfits. Moreover, her behavior seemed to change with her dress. Within the same therapy session, Louise would switch from talking and acting like a mature, outspoken adult to behaving like a little girl with a child's voice and demeanor. These changes occurred as Louise started to talk about childhood memories that she had not shared with anyone. Many of these memories involved frightening interactions with her stepfather, such as when he punished her by locking her in a closet.

dissociative disorder: A mental disorder that involves disruptions in a person's normally integrated sense of memory, consciousness, or identity.

In this chapter, we explore dissociative disorders, which often feature dramatic, unexpected, and involuntary reactions to trauma and other emotionally charged situations. **Dissociative disorders** involve disruptions in a person's memory, consciousness, or identity. As a result, these disorders, along with somatic symptom disorders (see Chapter 11), were initially classified as *neuroses* in the *DSM-II*. Historically, a neurosis was defined as a psychological disorder brought about largely by unconscious emotional conflicts and expressed mainly through anxiety-related symptoms. In the case of dissociative problems, various defense mechanisms were seen as converting anxiety into disturbances in memory or identity (dissociative disorders). In the *DSM-III*, the somatic and dissociative disorders were separated into distinct categories, where they currently remain through the *DSM-5*.

In the *DSM-5*, dissociative disorders are purposely placed after trauma- and stressor-related disorders because dissociative disorders are often found in the aftermath of trauma, and post-traumatic stress disorder (PTSD) even has dissociative symptoms as part of the diagnostic criteria. Further, dissociative disorders were placed right before somatic symptom and related disorders (see Chapter 11) to highlight the similarity between those two categories—that both may involve an expression of distress through atypical means, whether via consciousness changes (dissociation) in dissociative disorders or physical symptoms (somatoform dissociation) in somatic disorders. In the sections that follow, we examine the characteristics, causes, and treatments for dissociative disorders.

The Nature of Dissociation

dissociation: The process by which the normally integrated elements of consciousness, memory, and personal identity become splintered.

Dissociation is a process by which the normally integrated elements of consciousness, memory, and personal identity become splintered. In some cases, dissociation takes the form of not being able to remember important personal experiences. In other cases, individuals become confused about their identity or act as if they have a new identity. During some dissociated experiences, people describe feeling as if they, or objects around them, are not real. They feel emotionally detached from ongoing events, like an outsider watching a movie, rather than a person actively participating in real life.

Dissociative experiences are not necessarily pathological. In fact, mild forms of dissociation are common and perfectly normal. For example, people dissociate when they focus their attention on one aspect of experience and ignore another. When students daydream during a boring class (not this one!) or fantasize about being a movie star or a Nobel laureate, they are engaging in mild dissociation. At times, people can become so absorbed in these fantasies that they lose track of events around them until something snaps them back to awareness, such as a professor repeating their name louder and louder in class. Similarly, while driving for several hours at a stretch, some people briefly lose awareness that they have been steering their vehicles.

Children engage in dissociation even more often than adults. They invent imaginary playmates and temporarily assume new identities during play. One of your textbook authors had an invented "friend" named Guy, who used to do mischievous things around the house; one time, Guy even broke a TV. When frightened by an event, some children report "pretending it was happening to someone else" as a way of coping when no other form of help is available.

Most examples of dissociation are passing experiences that offer brief, even pleasurable, respites in the day and do not interfere with work or relationships. But in other instances, dissociation involves complex and disturbing processes in which people temporarily forget where or who they are or what they have been doing. In extreme cases, people behave as if they possess more than one identity, and these identities appear to have unique memories and personal histories.

Cultural Perspectives on Dissociation

Examples of dissociation have been described throughout history and across many cultures. Ancient Greek and Roman mythology is replete with stories of humans assuming different personalities to act out the will of the gods or to make up for past wrongs (Ross, 1989). Early Christianity emphasized the belief that a person's soul could be possessed by evil spirits. Beliefs in Satanic possession have been popular at other points in history; for example, the witch hunts conducted by 16th-century settlers in colonial America were driven by the conviction that some women's personalities had been taken over by demons.

MAPS - Prejudicial Pigeonholes

In many contemporary cultures, dissociative experiences such as trance states, "speaking in tongues," or spirit possession are accepted, even valued, ways of coping with stress or expressing strong emotions. For instance, in a common form of spirit possession in parts of India, another self temporarily "takes over" a person's body and leaves the person with no memory of what transpired (Spanos, 1994). An epidemiological study conducted in Mozambique found that one in five people reported experiencing spirit possession (Igreja et al., 2010). *Ataques de nervios*, another culturally defined form of dissociation discussed in Chapters 7 and 11, is commonly seen as a response to stress in Latin American cultures. It involves uncontrollable shouting or crying, displays of seizurelike behavior, and failure to recall the episode afterward. When such episodes are brief and leave no residual problems, they are considered a form of normal distress. More extreme attacks, though, may be considered a symptom of a mental disorder.

Other forms of dissociation occur as part of religious ceremonies or medical rituals and are therefore viewed as desirable achievements. For instance, high levels of non-pathological dissociation are found in very religious communities in Northern Ireland (Binks & Ferguson, 2013). In many cultures, native healers, or *shamans*, induce trance states to allow communication with spirits or to bring about a hypnotic anesthesia against the pain of branding the skin. In these instances, dissociation is considered normative and nondistressing and is therefore not symptomatic of a dissociative disorder (Spiegel et al., 2013). In other words, culturally accepted dissociative experiences often occur, do not lead to impairment, and may be perceived as beneficial within the culture and by the individual (Binks & Ferguson, 2013; Castillo, 2003; Dorahy et al. 2014).

In many religions, achieving a trancelike state is welcomed because it indicates that an important religious experience has been attained. It is only when these trances are involuntary and lead to emotional distress and impairment that they are considered mental disorders.

Symptoms and Types of Dissociative Disorders

Fantasizing, daydreaming, and culturally bound rituals form the normal end of a continuum of dissociative experiences; dissociative disorders represent the dysfunctional end of the spectrum. Some of the most common symptoms are:

Amnesia: The loss of a person's autobiographical memory, including memory of identity or of periods of the person's past. Dissociative amnesia does not include simple

amnesia: Loss or impairment of memory.

depersonalization: A feeling that individuals have become detached from their real self, as if they are observing themselves from outside the body.

derealization: A feeling that objects or events are strange or unreal, or have suddenly changed shape, size, or location.

identity confusion: Individuals' uncertainty about the nature of their own identity, of who they are.

identity alteration: Behavioral patterns suggesting that individuals have assumed a new identity.

Connections

How do some of these symptoms (e.g., depersonalization, derealization) differ from hallucinations seen in schizophrenia? For examples of some differences, see Chapter 4.

dissociative identity disorder (DID): A mental disorder in which individuals experience a shattering of a unified identity into at least two separate but coexisting personalities with different memories, behavior patterns, and emotions; formerly called *multiple personality disorder*.

forgetfulness of isolated facts (e.g., the capitol of North Dakota) or loss of memory caused by an organic injury or illness (see Chapter 15).

Depersonalization: Detachment from the body, in that individuals feel as if they are observing themselves from outside their body. During such experiences, individuals lose a sense of being real and may feel as if someone else is in control of their body or voice.

Derealization: Detachment from the environment, such as a sense that objects in the external world are strange or unreal or have suddenly changed shape, size, or location. Individuals may feel that their home is unfamiliar or that the trees in the yard have become smaller or look farther away than usual.

Identity confusion: Uncertainty about the nature of individuals' personal identity, of who they are.

Identity alteration: Behavior patterns suggesting that individuals have assumed a new identity.

These dissociative symptoms may develop rapidly or gradually, and may be present only during certain periods, or they may be chronic. Depending on the combination of symptoms, the *DSM-5* classifies three main dissociative disorders: (1) dissociative identity disorder, (2) dissociative amnesia, and (3) depersonalization/derealization disorder. Most dissociative disorders are exceedingly rare; when they do occur, they often disappear in a matter of hours or days. As a result, clinicians do not have many opportunities to study these conditions. The two most common dissociative disorders appear to be dissociative amnesia and depersonalization/derealization disorder, but the one that attracts the most attention is dissociative identity disorder.

Section Review

Dissociation is a process in which:

- periods of divided attention and concentration, amnesia, uncertain or confused identity, and feelings of unreality may occur, and
- cultural factors often play an important role.

The dissociative disorders include:

- periods during which two or more identities appear to take control of an individual's personality,
- episodes of amnesia that are not caused by medical conditions, and
- recurring feelings of being unreal or being detached from the body and of feeling that the outside world is unreal.

Dissociative Identity Disorder

Dissociative identity disorder (DID), formerly known as multiple personality disorder, is one of the most perplexing of all mental disorders. In 1791, German physician Eberhardt Gmelin reported the first detailed case history of a person experiencing multiple identities after being hypnotized (North, Ryall, Ricci, & Wetzsel, 1993). Sporadic reports of cases of what was then called "dual personality" occurred throughout the 1800s, a period that also saw a marked increase in spiritualism in Europe and the United States. French psychologist Pierre Janet wrote about *desaggregation mentale* as a failure to integrate mental components in the usual way in which they worked together. The spiritualism of that era included beliefs in communing with the dead, spirit possession, and the power of devices such as the Ouija board and divining rod (North et al., 1993). Reports of multiple personalities became less frequent in the early 1900s, as spiritualism declined among the general population and naturalistic explanations of unusual behavior gained popularity.

A resurgence of interest in multiple personalities occurred gradually over the middle of the 20th century, likely stimulated by the dramatic cases described in books and movies, such as *Three Faces of Eve* (Thigpen & Cleckley, 1957), *Sybil* (Schreiber, 1973), and *The Minds of Billy Milligan* (Keyes, 1981). *Sybil* was about a young woman who allegedly had 16 different personalities, with a significant history of child abuse at the hands of her mother. In each of these accounts, stories of childhood trauma—often in the form of horrific child abuse—played a central role in the author's explanation of why multiple personalities subsequently emerged.

"I am worried that you will charge me double for this session, Doc, if I tell you that I really have DID and let Alan come out to meet you."

However, this diagnosis remains controversial today. Although some mental health experts strongly believe that DID is a *bona fide* clinical condition, others either question its status as a real clinical phenomenon or doubt that it belongs in a unique diagnostic category. Research suggests that the majority of psychologists believe DID to be a valid clinical diagnosis but perceive it to be rare (Cormier, 1997). In addition, respondents cite extreme child abuse as the foremost cause, although there is some disagreement about other causes (e.g., hypnosis). Approximately half of all psychologists believe that they have encountered someone with DID, but almost a third believe that they have encountered someone who feigned the disorder (Cormier, 1997). Psychiatrists are more skeptical about the reality of DID than psychologists: Close to half of the psychiatrists sampled believe that DID is a legitimate clinical phenomenon, whereas psychologists' general level of skepticism for the existence of DID is low (Dorahy & Lewis, 2002). Others point out that DID follows the classic trajectory of a medical fad (like gluten intolerance) in that it was once considered rare but then was frequently diagnosed during the 1980s and 1990s, after which interest declined (Paris, 2012).

Is it actually possible for a person's sense of identity to disintegrate into several pieces? Could this transformation really take place without the person being aware of it? One of the world's foremost memory experts, Elizabeth Loftus, weighs in on that debate in the "A Conversation With . . ." feature at the end of this chapter.

Symptoms of Dissociative Identity Disorder

In dissociative identity disorder, an individual's personality appears as separate identities or parts, rather than being integrated into a cohesive whole. All of us have multifaceted personalities, and as we go through life, we express these differing parts of ourselves in various situations. Sometimes, we feel ambitious, other times lazy; sometimes outgoing, sometimes shy. Just think about how you might act differently in class, with your roommate, with your family, or at a party. We also struggle to balance the many roles we are asked to play—spouse, parent, student, child, employee. On occasion, we may feel confused about who we really are, but we remain conscious of this confusion and retain a cohesive set of memories and behavior patterns. In short, our identity stays unified. Individuals with DID, however, experience a shattering of their unified identity into at least two separate, but coexisting, personalities with different memories, behavior patterns, and emotions.

As Table 10.1 indicates, the presence of different personalities or experience of **pathological possession** (alternate identity attributed to possession by an external spirit,

pathological possession: The sense that another spirit or being has taken over one's behavior or mental processes.

TABLE 10.1 The *DSM-5* in Simple Language: Diagnosing Dissociative Identity Disorder

Dissociative identity disorder is diagnosed when a person's functioning is guided by two or more distinct identities or personality states, each with its own relatively enduring pattern of perceiving, relating to, and thinking about the environment and self. Further, the person does not remember at least some autobiographical information (e.g., key or traumatic events). The identity alterations are not attributable to accepted religious or cultural practice nor to a substance or medical condition.

Source: Adapted from American Psychiatric Association (2013a).

alter personality (alter): In dissociative identity disorder, one of the different "personalities" that seems to assume control over the individual's functioning in different situations.

power, deity, or other person) is the core symptom of DID. These different personalities, sometimes referred to as **alter personalities**, or **alters**, are internal and appear to assume control over the individual's functioning in different situations. Some alters seem not to know about the existence of other alters and do not usually remember what the others have done. As with Louise in the chapter-opening case, people with DID report finding objects in their homes that they do not remember buying. Sometimes, these people turn up in places with no memory of how they got there or why.

In the late 1800s, most cases of DID described in France and the United States involved only two personalities. However, the average number of alters has increased over the past few decades (Lynn et al., 2012). Currently, the typical case averages over 10 alters (Gillig, 2009). Alters often differ widely among themselves in how they dress, move, talk, and interact with the world. One alter may be prim and proper, another flamboyant and promiscuous. Many times, both male and female alters appear in the same individual. As illustrated in the chapter-opening case of Louise, one alter is usually a child who may report a series of early traumas or upsetting memories not reported or recognized by other alters. Other typical alters include a personality that acts out impulses and forbidden behaviors, such as promiscuous sexual activity or substance abuse, and an alter who engages in suicidal or self-mutilative behavior. Often, one of the alters is a powerful, dominant figure who seems to serve as a protector for the host.

host personality: In dissociative identity disorder, the primary identity that is in charge of the person's functioning most of the time.

Most identities are of ordinary people, though fictional, mythical, celebrity, and animal alters have also been reported. The primary identity, which often has the person's given name, is the **host personality** and is in charge most of the time. The host typically is the personality who seeks psychological treatment, tends to be passive and dependent (with other personalities or alters being more active, aggressive, or hostile), and often has more complete memories (Lynn et al., 2012). The host often reports low self-esteem, depression, and recurrent nightmares. Suicidal or self-mutilative thoughts are also common, as are headaches and other physical concerns.

The symptoms of DID are not simply those of "multiple personalities"—rather, they cause significant disruption in a person's single coherent identity. This includes alterations in sense of self, such as the sense that one is observing oneself (Dell, 2006), or feeling like one has no control over one's own actions. The symptoms can involve changes in mood, actions, continuity of consciousness, memory, perception, thoughts, and even sensory-motor functioning. Part of the criteria for DID includes evidence for amnesia. The type of forgetting usually takes three forms: (1) loss of memory for important life events, (2) loss of memory for everyday activities, and (3) realization that activities have happened without recollection of engaging in those activities (Dell, 2006; Spiegel et al., 2013).

The *DSM-5* has added the culturally sensitive notion that, in some cases of DID, the person describes the dissociation as an experience of possession, as though another being has taken control over the person. For example, the person's actions may represent a ghost of someone who has recently died. The reason for the inclusion of this type of DID presentation in the *DSM-5* is to account for the diverse presentations of the disorder seen in other cultures and countries, such as Africa and Asia, and in immigrants living in Western cultures (Spiegel et al., 2013). Marked impairment in everyday life due to the symptoms is key when considering possession-form DID to clarify that the experiences are not a part of accepted cultural beliefs or practices.

Source: Eugene Onischenko/Shutterstock.com.

Many people think they know the legendary Herschel Walker: 1982 Heisman Trophy winner, pro football star considered one of the greatest running backs ever, and 2008 Olympic torchbearer. But not only does the public not know the real Herschel Walker, the athlete himself says he does not either. In his 2008 book *Breaking Free*, Walker revealed that he suffers from dissociative identity disorder. Asked how many different personality facets, or alters, he had, Walker replied: "To be honest, I have no idea" (Falco, 2008). But in the book, Walker talks about a dozen, each described by their roles or function: the Hero, the Coach, the Enforcer, the Consoler, the Daredevil, and the Warrior, to name a few.

(a) *Source: Brian L. Burke.* (b) *Source: Brian L. Burke.*

MAPS - Superficial Syndromes

Notice the early and later stages of dissociative identity disorder in these cacti. In (a), the cactus shows only mild disruptions in identity, whereas in (b) the cactus depicts several distinct personality states taking hold of the individual.

Switching, the process of changing from one personality to another, is thought to be stimulated by stress (Lynn et al., 2012). Some switches are triggered by flashback memories of prior trauma. Others are linked to stressful events, such as a reprimand by a boss or a request for increased sexual intimacy by a partner. Therapists sometimes witness switching when clients begin to discuss childhood traumas. People with DID generally do not exert voluntary control over the switching of alters. They may be aware of periods of lost time but not of the alter's appearance or actions. Observers may recognize a switch because of changes in the individual's facial expression, body language, or manner of speaking. At times, the changes can be dramatic. The person might suddenly switch from being quiet and depressed to aggressive and angry or might adopt markedly diverse ways of dressing and grooming to suit the alter in control.

switching: In dissociative identity disorder, the process of changing from one personality to another; thought to be stimulated by anxiety.

Prevalence of Dissociative Identity Disorder

At one time, dissociative identity disorder (DID) was thought to be extremely uncommon. In fact, before the 1970s, there were only 80 reported cases of DID worldwide, though by 1998, there were over 40,000 cases (Lilienfeld & Lynn, 2003). Today, the actual numbers are hard to ascertain, but epidemiological studies conducted in communities have found prevalence rates of 1.1% to 1.5% among U.S. adults (Dorahy et al., 2014; Johnson, Cohen, Kasen, & Brook, 2006). The rates of DID rise to as much as 10% for psychiatric patients (Ross, Duffy, & Ellason, 2002), with women more likely to be diagnosed with DID than men. Women also tend to present with more dissociative type symptoms (Ross & Ness, 2010), such as amnesia, whereas men tend to present with more violent behavior (Lewis et al., 1997). Additionally, a large proportion of people with DID have been previously diagnosed with mood disorders, somatic symptom disorders, or personality disorders, with an average of

Source: Complot/Shutterstock.com.

The most famous literary case of a dual personality is undoubtedly Robert Louis Stevenson's 1886 depiction of Dr. Jekyll and Mr. Hyde. Henry Jekyll described his dual nature this way:

(M)an is not truly one, but truly two. I say two, because the state of my own knowledge does not pass beyond that point. . . . I learned to recognize the thorough and primitive duality of man; I saw that, of the two natures that contended in my field of consciousness, even if I could rightly be said to be either, it was only because I was radically both; and from an early date . . . I had learned to dwell with pleasure, as a beloved daydream, on the thought of the separation of these elements. If each, I told myself, could but be housed in separate identities, life would be relieved of all that was unbearable. (Chapter 10) five comorbid diagnoses (Rodewald, Wilhelm-Gobling, Emrich, Reddemann, & Gast, 2011). Cases of pathological possession have been reported in countries such as China, India, Turkey, and the United States, with anywhere from 60–100% of people seeking treatment for DID reporting feeling possessed (Ross, 2011).

Furthermore, the symptoms of DID include a vast array of features that overlap with other disorders, such as depression, borderline personality disorder, somatic disorders, and post-traumatic stress disorder. Because of this overlap, some clinicians have speculated that DID represents a severe variant or complication of one of these disorders, rather than a discrete diagnostic entity (Dorahy et al., 2014; Gleaves, May, & Cardeña, 2001).

Section Review

Dissociative identity disorder involves:

- alterations in one's identity or evidence of pathological possession, along with
- evidence of dissociative amnesia (forgetting key life events).

Individuals with DID do not really have "multiple personalities." Rather, they experience a shattering of their unified identity into at least two separate, but coexisting, personalities with different memories, behavior patterns, and emotions. These alter personalities, often as many as 10, typically differ widely among themselves in how they dress, move, talk, and interact with the world. One may be an aggressive protector of the host, and another may be childlike and immature.

Furthermore, the symptoms of DID include a vast array of features that overlap with other disorders, such as depression, borderline personality disorder, somatization disorders, and post-traumatic stress disorder. Typically, a person with DID has five other comorbid *DSM* diagnoses.

Other Dissociative Disorders

We next discuss two dissociative disorders—dissociative amnesia and depersonalization/derealization disorder—in which personality is intact, but memory and self-awareness may not be.

Dissociative Amnesia

dissociative amnesia: Sudden loss of memory for personally important information that is not caused by a medical condition or other mental disorder, usually following a stressful event:

The key symptom of **dissociative amnesia** is the sudden loss of memory for personally important information that is not caused by a medical condition or another mental disorder. This information should have been stored successfully in memory and otherwise would have been remembered. The memory loss usually follows a stressful event, such as a suicide attempt or violent assault, as in the case of John, which follows.

John was a college-aged man who showed up in a New York City hospital emergency room at 11 P.M. on a Saturday night. His clothes were torn, and he had fresh cuts and bruises on his face and arms. He was able to tell the physician his name and that he came to New York City with a group of college friends for the weekend, but he could not recall anything about where he had been for the past several hours, what had happened to his friends, how he was injured, or how he got to the hospital. Medical tests ruled out most of the possible physical explanations for his condition. John was admitted for further observation and fell asleep for the rest of the night. The next morning, John still felt "fuzzy" about many details. He remembered being separated from his friends somewhere outside a bar in Greenwich Village. He also recalled looking for them near a subway station, at which point he vaguely remembered being accosted at gunpoint by a group of teenagers. He thought that he must have been robbed and beaten, but he really did not know for sure. He knew only that he started the evening with $100 in his wallet, but he had no money when he entered the hospital. When John's friends were eventually contacted, they confirmed that they had been separated from John the night before. When John finally left the hospital, he still could not remember anything more about his assault.

The memory loss in dissociative amnesia can take several forms. **Localized amnesia** refers to loss of memory for a distinct period of time, usually the few hours immediately after a specific trauma. This is the most common type of amnesia. With **selective amnesia**, a person can remember only some of the events surrounding a trauma; the remainder are forgotten. Less common forms of dissociative memory loss include generalized, continuous, and systematized amnesia. **Generalized amnesia** involves total loss of memory for a person's entire life or identity, which may occur among those exposed to extreme stress, such as combat veterans and sexual assault victims (Witztum, Margalit, & van der Hart, 2002). **Continuous amnesia** refers to the loss of memory for events from a particular time or trauma up to the present, and **systematized amnesia** describes the loss of memory for certain classes of information, such as all memories of a person's father or of life in the military. When the amnesia occurs with **dissociative fugue**, a person suddenly leaves home or work and travels to a new location with loss of memory for the reason for travel or even identity. In these cases, the *DSM-5* specifier *with dissociative fugue* is added to the diagnosis.

During World War II, dissociative amnesia or other dissociative episodes accounted for 5–14% of all psychiatric casualties (Ross, 1989), and 35% of soldiers exposed to heavy combat in World War II could not recall major aspects of these experiences (Davis, 1993). Many veterans of the Vietnam war also reported amnesia for battleground experiences, but they were usually diagnosed with post-traumatic stress disorder (PTSD) instead, which shows again how the sociocultural climate can impact diagnosis.

Dissociative amnesia is most common in young adult males and in middle-aged adult females. In a U.S. community study of middle-aged adults, the 12-month prevalence rate for dissociative amnesia was 1% for men and 2.6% for women (Johnson et al., 2006). The relatively high prevalence among young adult males may simply reflect the fact that they are most likely to have faced violent stressors, such as combat. Most reported cases of dissociative amnesia are of the retrograde type, meaning that individuals forget things that happened to them before their symptoms developed; rare cases have been described, though, in which the amnesia is anterograde, so that individuals have difficulty forming new memories (Lips, Mascayano, & Lanfranco, 2014).

Over the past few decades, and peaking in the 1990s, the United States saw an increasing incidence of reported cases of dissociative amnesia, often in the form of lost and then recovered memories of childhood trauma. These claims remain highly controversial among clinicians. Some therapists believe that greater awareness of child abuse has sensitized clinicians to identify more cases of trauma-related dissociation, whereas others believe that dissociative problems are being overdiagnosed or even suggested by overzealous clinicians. For instance, some researchers suggest that the absence of cases before 1800 indicates that dissociative amnesia is not a natural neuropsychological phenomenon, but instead, a culture-bound syndrome, dating from the 19th century (Pope, Poliakoff, Parker, Boynes, & Hudson, 2007).

localized amnesia: Loss of memory for a distinct period of time, usually the few hours immediately after a specific trauma.

selective amnesia: Ability to remember only some of the events surrounding a trauma; the remainder are forgotten.

generalized amnesia: Loss of memory of a person's entire life.

continuous amnesia: The loss of memory for events from a particular time or trauma up to the present.

systematized amnesia: Loss of memory for certain classes of information.

dissociative fugue: A dissociative state in which individuals travel to a new location without remembering their pre-fugue life, often also becoming confused about their identity.

Source: Fer Gregory/Shutterstock.com.

Dead Again was a 1991 psychological thriller/neo-noir starring Kenneth Branagh and his then-wife Emma Thompson, in which the main character appeared to suffer from dissociative amnesia with fugue. *The Bourne Identity*, a 1980 spy fiction thriller by Robert Ludlum made into a film starring Matt Damon in 2002, was the story of a man with remarkable survival abilities who suffered from amnesia (which type do you think it was?) and who sought to discover his true identity and why others wanted to kill him. Real cases of this disorder appear every now and then in the media, such as that of Jeff Ingram, 40, an amnesia sufferer found wandering around the streets of Denver, Colorado, in 2006 (Associated Press, 2006). He had been searching for his identity for more than a month before being reunited in Washington State with his fiancee, who saw his picture on the news, but Ingram still did not remember his past life or what happened. He had reportedly had similar bouts of amnesia in the past, likely triggered by stress, once disappearing for 9 months.

Dr. Elizabeth Loftus (see the "A Conversation With . . ." feature at the end of the chapter) has testified in many cases of recovering memory legal proceedings over the past 2 decades. The case that arguably had the biggest negative impact on Loftus was that of "Jane Doe" (Nicole Taus). In 1997, David Corwin and his colleague Erna Olafson published a study of an apparently bona fide case of an accurate, recovered memory of childhood sexual abuse (Corwin & Olafson, 1997). Skeptical, Loftus and her colleague Melvin Guyer decided to investigate further. Using public records and interviewing people connected to Taus, they uncovered information that Corwin had not included in his original article—information that they thought strongly suggested that Taus's memory of abuse was false (Abramsky, 2004).

Evaluation of people with amnesia should always include a careful assessment to rule out medical conditions that might explain the memory loss, such as neurological illnesses, brain trauma, and substance abuse (Staniloiu, Markowitsch, & Brand, 2010). The person's medical history, a neurological examination, and neuropsychological testing can help clinicians determine the possible causes of memory loss.

Depersonalization/Derealization Disorder

depersonalization/derealization disorder: A disorder in which individuals experience both depersonalization (detachment from others or themselves) and derealization (feeling that the world is not real) in the absence of other physical and mental disorders.

Episodes of depersonalization, derealization, or both are the essential features of depersonalization/derealization disorder. Depersonalization involves detachment from oneself, and derealization involves feeling detached from one's environment. Individuals may feel like a robot or like an actor in a dream or movie; others report feeling as if they have left their bodies and are hovering above them. Sometimes, individuals feel so detached that movement or speech seem to be outside of their personal control. Objects in the external world may seem unreal or bizarre. Both depersonalization and derealization often accompany a number of other physical and mental disorders, so depersonalization/derealization disorder is diagnosed only when there is no evidence of another medical or mental disorder. Brain tumors and some forms of epilepsy can produce depersonalization symptoms, as can drugs such as *Cannabis* (Hürlimann, Kupferschmid, & Simon, 2012).

Two factor analyses of data from large samples of people with **depersonalization/derealization disorder** indicate that it has four clusters of symptoms: (1) anomalous (strange) body experiences, (2) emotional numbing, (3) anomalous subjective recall, and (4) alienation from surroundings (Sierra, 2009).

Depersonalization/derealization disorder usually first occurs in adolescence or young adulthood (average age of onset is 16) and affects women and men about equally (Simeon, Knutelska, Nelson, & Guralnik, 2003). Interestingly, about half of U.S. adults have experienced at least one episode of this depersonalization/derealization, although meeting full *DSM-5* criteria for the disorder is significantly less common, with lifetime prevalence ranging from 0.8–2.0% (Hunter, Sierra, & David, 2004). These isolated depersonalization/derealization experiences are often in the form of fleeting reactions to a severe stressor and do not impair the person in the longer term. Although its prevalence is comparable to that of schizophrenia and bipolar disorder, depersonalization/derealization disorder may be underdiagnosed; the average person with this disorder spends 12 years in the mental health system before receiving the correct diagnosis (Sierra, 2009).

Many studies have found a significant association between low levels of depersonalization/derealization disorder and anxiety (Sierra, Medford, Wyatt, & David, 2012). The fact that high-intensity depersonalization was not correlated with anxiety, however, adds further evidence in favor of depersonalization/derealization disorder being an

Source: dwphotos/Shutterstock.com.

Adam Duritz, front man for the rock music group Counting Crows, whose hits include *Mr. Jones* and *Round Here*, has described his battle with depersonalization/derealization disorder (Singh, 2014): "The dissociative disorder is scary. Being crazy is scary. I would love to not have to deal with that," he said. Duritz first revealed his diagnosis publicly in 2008 and had said previously that his mental health issues hampered his ability to write new songs and release new music with Counting Crows.

independent condition (Sierra et al., 2012). Furthermore, people with depersonalization/derealization disorder have significantly higher self-esteem and are more harm avoidant than people with borderline personality disorder (Hedrick & Berlin, 2012). Thus, although depersonalization/derealization disorder and borderline personality disorder (discussed in Chapter 16) commonly overlap in terms of dissociative symptoms and emotional irregularities, the differences in self-esteem, behavior, and temperament may help identify where they differ (Hedrick & Berlin, 2012). Finally, a high prevalence of depersonalization symptoms is found in people with panic disorder, supporting a link between those two sets of symptoms (Mendoza et al., 2011). The most common immediate precipitants of depersonalization/derealization disorder are severe stress, depression, panic, marijuana ingestion, and hallucinogen ingestion, but none of these predict symptom severity (Simeon, Knutelska et al., 2003).

Section Review

Individuals with dissociative amnesia can present with:

- short-term, long-term, event-specific, or complete amnesia, or
- dissociative fugue, whereby individuals travel, with loss of memory for who or where they are.

Depersonalization/derealization disorder involves individuals experiencing detachment from themselves, their environment, or both, which causes significant distress or dysfunction in their life.

Both disorders require medical exams to rule out possible biological causes of the symptoms (e.g., tumors), and both overlap with many other mental disorders, such as anxiety and borderline personality.

Causes of Dissociative Disorders

There is considerable debate about the model of risk for developing a dissociative disorder. Expert consensus is that people with a history of childhood trauma are at a greater risk for dissociation (Dalenberg et al., 2012). However, beyond this consensus, there are widely divergent views regarding how and why dissociation develops and even how strong this relationship is in the first place. Is dissociation a coping response, or does it develop partly as a result of suggestion?

Two major theories on the etiology of DID have been proposed to date. According to one theory, called the **post-traumatic model (PTM)** of dissociation, DID originates from severe trauma during childhood that produces a splitting of personalities as a defense against the traumatic events. The second theory, called the **sociocognitive model**, suggests that people diagnosed with DID are unduly influenced by social and cultural factors that create or maintain the disorder.

Post-traumatic Model

Childhood trauma was considered a possible contributor to dissociative states as early as the 1920s, but its role started to receive far more emphasis in the 1970s, when therapists began to link severe childhood abuse to DID. Researchers such as Frank Putnam (1995) suggest that DID almost always begins with severe childhood trauma (see Figure 10.1). Sexual abuse, particularly incest, was the most common type of abuse reported in Putnam's studies, followed by a combination of sexual and physical abuse. The participants frequently described ritualistic abuse that was repetitive, lurid, and sadistic. In some cases, people had not endured direct abuse but had witnessed terrifying scenes, such as the murder of a family member.

Putnam argues that exposure to such unrelenting and cruel trauma forced these children to rely on one of the few coping processes at their disposal: psychological escape, usually by imagining themselves to be someone else,

post-traumatic model (PTM): The claim that dissociative identity disorder is caused by childhood trauma, with which the person tries to cope by creating alternate personalities.

sociocognitive model: The claim that dissociative identity disorder is a diagnosis given to people who have learned to enact a role that emphasizes multiple personalities, often in response to suggestions from therapists, media portrayals, or cultural influences; has been extended as the fantasy model.

"OK, Horace, your DID time as Little William is over now. It's time for the conference call with China."

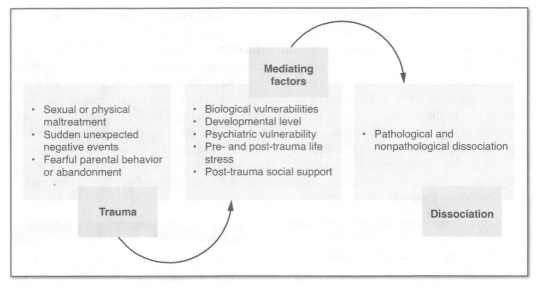

FIGURE 10.1 Post-traumatic Model of Dissociative Identity Disorder

According to the PTM, a major risk factor for dissociative identity disorder is severe trauma in early childhood, which some children deal with through dissociative forms of coping. These dissociative experiences form the beginning of one or more new identities, which may reappear as personality alters when individuals are subjected to severe stressors in adulthood.

often someone strong or smart enough to defeat the abuser or outsmart the assailant. Many children have an excellent ability to engage in spontaneous dissociation, such as fantasy games played with imaginary friends. If repeatedly traumatized, these children become adroit at mental escape through dissociation as a way to protect themselves by believing it is happening to someone else (Ross, 1997).

Dissociation allows children to escape the constraints of reality, to keep traumatic memories and emotions outside of conscious awareness, to feel detached from the traumas (i.e., "It happened to someone else"), and even to avoid feeling the actual physical pain of the abuse. Every time children enter a dissociative state, they accrue memories, feelings, and behaviors that are unique to that state. These episodes form the beginnings of an alternate personality or personality fragment, leading to structural dissociation, or different parts of the personality to handle different stressors in everyday life (Steele, van der Hart, & Nijenhuis, 2009). As these children enter adulthood and are faced with everyday life stressors, they may be unable to self-regulate, since their way of managing emotions previously was through dissociation, promoting a fragmentation of the self that is a core feature of DID (Carlson, Yates, & Sroufe, 2009).

Evaluating the Post-traumatic Model

There is certainly a significant relationship between trauma history and severity of dissociative symptoms, with the probability of high dissociability four times greater in trauma-exposed versus non-trauma-exposed samples (Briere, 2006). However, the exceedingly high numbers (90%) of people with DID who reported trauma histories in some early studies have not been replicated. A more recent meta-analysis of 38 studies found that the strength relationship between trauma and dissociation was $r = .32$ (Dalenberg et al., 2012), which is a medium effect size (correlation coefficient) that indicates a link but not the necessity of DID being triggered by traumatic events; the average in reviewed studies was about 60% (not 90%) of people with DID reporting significant past abuse.

Furthermore, the precise cause-effect relationship between child trauma and DID is still not empirically sound. For instance, not all individuals with documented histories of abuse go on to develop DID. And the validity of the occurrence of abuse is difficult to prove because it is documented only by adults' retrospective recall of childhood events, which may be inaccurate. It also cannot be ignored that many of the research studies investigating the link between trauma and dissociation are cross-sectional in nature, not allowing for causal inferences to be drawn (Merckelbach & Muris, 2001). In one prospective study (meaning that people were not simply asked to report on what had already happened to them), Ogawa and colleagues (1997) followed high-risk children from impoverished backgrounds for 19 years. Although they documented modest positive correlations between childhood trauma and dissociation *during childhood*, they noted that the childhood trauma (sexual abuse) did not significantly predict later dissociation for the children when they were 19 years old.

Even strong proponents of DID's validity acknowledge that therapists can exacerbate a client's symptoms by inappropriately using hypnosis or becoming naively fascinated with the client's presentation (Kluft, 1995). However, they also point to several physiological or behavioral differences that would be difficult (although not impossible) for clients to fake or simulate. For example, alter personalities within the same person have been shown to differ in:

- handedness (some alters are left-handed, whereas others are right-handed),

- visual acuity (some alters need glasses, but others do not),

- allergic reactions (some alters are allergic to pollen, whereas others are allergic to cat hair),

- brain-wave activity (the EEGs of the alters are often different), and

- physical limitations (one alter may be color-blind, whereas others can accurately perceive colors).

Many of these claims remain controversial, however. In some cases, independent observers have not confirmed the alleged differences between alters. Yet, some interesting neuroimaging research suggests unique functioning in the brain for those with DID, compared to healthy controls. For example, in one research program (Reinders et al., 2003, 2006), when an individual with DID was in an emotional alter (one that was associated with trauma memories), compared to an alter that was numb and depersonalized from trauma memories, there was evidence for increased cerebral blood flow in the amygdala, frontal cortex, and other emotion-related brain areas. These findings could not be replicated in healthy controls who were asked to simulate or "fake" two identity states (Reinders, Willemsen, Vos, den Boer, & Nijenhuis, 2012).

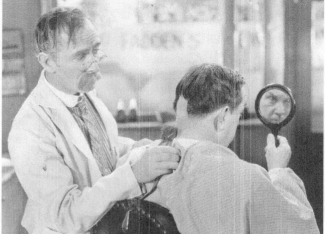

Source: Everett Collection/Shutterstock.com.

Many mistakes have been made in the media portrayals of people with DID. For example, *Me, Myself & Irene* (2000) was an American comedy film starring Jim Carrey and Renée Zellweger. Carrey played a Rhode Island state trooper named Charlie who, after years of continuously suppressing his rage, suffered a breakdown that resulted in a second personality, super-aggressive cop Hank. The film made a number of serious errors in characterizing DID, including calling Charlie a "schizo" (remember from Chapter 4 that schizophrenia has nothing to do with alter personalities), treating his DID with pills, and assuming that the disorder was caused by his wife leaving him several years earlier (there is no evidence that DID is caused by adult traumas). Even in *Sybil*, long considered the classic case study of DID as a 1973 book and 1976 movie, questions regarding the story's accuracy, billed as a true account, have surfaced. In a 2011 book, *Sybil Exposed*, author Debbie Nathan argues that most of the story is based on a lie.

Sociocognitive Model

Nicholas Spanos (1994) offers a sociocultural explanation for why and how people might learn to present multiple selves. He notes that the *enactment* of multiple identities usually serves specific personal goals. In some cultures, acting as if one is possessed by spirits is one of the few acceptable ways of expressing distress or disagreement. In these cultures, brief epidemics of spirit possession occur in times of stress or upheaval. For instance, spirit "possessions" increased dramatically among female factory workers in Malaysia following a tightening of policies that made their tedious and low-paying jobs even more difficult (Spanos, 1994). Spanos (1994, p. 143) argues that, in the United States, DID has become a socially acceptable way to "express failures and frustrations as well as a covert tactic by which to manipulate others and attain succor and other rewards."

Validity of the DID Diagnosis: The Case of the Hillside Strangler

Many people find dissociative disorders difficult to understand and wonder whether people are faking their symptoms and merely pretending to be disturbed. This suspicion is particularly pronounced in the cases of those charged with serious crimes who then plead not guilty by reason of insanity (NGRI). Kenneth Bianchi, the "Hillside Strangler," provides an example of a case in which experts differed publicly in their opinions about DID.

In 1979, Kenneth Bianchi was arrested for the murder of two female college students in Bellingham, Washington. The evidence supporting the arrest was conclusive, but Bianchi insisted that he was innocent and had no memory for the nights the murders took place. Bianchi presented himself as a polite young man, and despite subsequently discovered evidence that he had a long record of antisocial conduct (including faking a college transcript and posing as a psychologist), he steadfastly denied previous criminal or violent behavior.

Nationally known experts representing the defense and the prosecution, as well as evaluators appointed by the judge, evaluated Bianchi's mental health. The defense called John G. Watkins (1984), a psychologist with expertise in hypnosis and DID, to evaluate Bianchi and help him recall the nights when the murders occurred. In a videotaped hypnotic session, Dr. Watkins gave Bianchi the following instructions:

> I've talked quite a bit to Ken but I think that perhaps there might be another part of Ken that I haven't talked to. And I would like to communicate with that part. And I would like that other part to come and talk to me. . . . And when you are here, lift the left hand off the chair to signal me that you are here. . . . Part, would you please come and lift Ken's hand to indicate to me that you are here? (Spanos, 1994, p. 153)

In the course of being hypnotized by Watkins, Bianchi revealed a second identity named "Steve," whose demeanor was strikingly different from Ken's. He was strident and angry, whereas Ken was quiet and cooperative. Steve described taking part in a number of killings in the Los Angeles area. The details corresponded with 10 then-unsolved murders of young women in the late 1970s in the hills surrounding Los Angeles. Steve implicated Kenneth Bianchi, as well as his cousin, Angelo Buono, as being responsible for what had become known as the "Hillside Strangler Murders."

Is it possible that Dr. Watkins's use of hypnosis helped Bianchi to create an excuse in the form of DID? Some mental health and law enforcement experts be-

Source: Carolyn Franks/Shutterstock.com.

Primal Fear was a 1996 American neo-noir crime-thriller film starring Richard Gere, Laura Linney, and Edward Norton in his film debut. Norton played altar boy Aaron Stampler, who after being confronted by his lawyer (Gere), transformed into a new persona—a violent psychopath who called himself "Roy" and confessed to the murder of an archbishop. Molly Arrington, the psychiatrist examining Aaron, was convinced that he suffered from DID caused by years of abuse at the hands of his father. You will have to see the movie for yourself to determine if Dr. Arrington was right.

lieved that Dr. Watkins had created the other personality through hypnotic suggestion; others argued that Bianchi was simply a clever criminal who manipulated the system to avoid punishment. Bianchi pleaded not guilty to the crimes by reason of insanity (NGRI, as described further in Chapter 17), citing multiple personalities (now called DID) as the basis for his claim. Three of the seven mental health experts involved in the case argued vehemently that Bianchi had antisocial personality disorder; the other four concluded he was insane and suffering from some sort of dissociative disorder.

Could alternate personalities appear as a result of a hypnotist's suggestions? Could Bianchi fool so many professionals? A legendary ingenious experiment by Nicholas Spanos and colleagues (Spanos, Weekes, & Bertrand, 1985) investigated whether hypnotic techniques such as those used with Bianchi could provide enough information to enable a group of naive college students to make up convincing multiple personalities. The students were asked to pretend that they were an accused murderer and to role-play how they thought such a defendant would respond in a hypnosis session. They were given no information regarding DID. One group of students then participated in a hypnotic interview that mimicked the one used with Bianchi, including the interviewer specifically asking for "parts" to come forward. Other control groups were also hypnotized but given less-explicit suggestions about different personality "parts."

Validity of the DID Diagnosis: The Case of the Hillside Strangler *(Continued)*

The vast majority of students in the Bianchi hypnosis condition responded by describing alternate personalities, including using a different name, referring to their primary identities in the third person, and claiming amnesia for their alter personalities after the hypnotic session ended. The students given the less-directive interviews provided little or no evidence of alter personalities in their role plays. In a second session, the students who had previously introduced personality alters during hypnosis did so again and exhibited large differences between their various personalities on several psychological tests. In other studies, Spanos asked people who were role-playing DID to describe the kinds of childhoods they would have had. They described childhoods that closely resembled the backgrounds reported by people with DID—a negative and abusive childhood in which the alter personalities emerged early in life as a way of dealing with stressful situations and strong emotions (Spanos, Weekes, Menary, & Bertrand, 1986).

In Bianchi's case, clever investigative work revealed that his multiple personality defense was a fraud. The prosecution hired a noted expert on hypnotism, Martin Orne, to test Bianchi's claims. Orne proceeded to hypnotize Bianchi, but only after telling him that most people with true DID revealed three, rather than two, alters.

As if on cue, after Orne hypnotized Bianchi, a third alter named Billy suddenly emerged. The ruse had fooled Bianchi into confirming Orne's incorrect statement. Furthermore, although Bianchi claimed to know nothing about DID, a search of his room uncovered numerous textbooks on hypnosis and abnormal psychology, from which he presumably learned much about the disorder.

Kenneth Bianchi eventually withdrew his insanity defense and pleaded guilty to murder. The prosecutor dropped his request for the death penalty in exchange for Bianchi's agreement to testify against his cousin Angelo. Bianchi is currently serving a life sentence in a Washington State prison, whereas Angelo Buono died of a heart attack in prison in California in 2002 at the age of 67.

Thinking Critically

1. Research suggests that people can role-play symptoms of DID fairly well. What might this mean about the validity of the disorder and its diagnosis?

2. Some studies show greater discrepancy in physiological measures between the alter personalities of people with DID versus people asked to role-play this disorder. What might explain these larger discrepancies?

As the case of serial killer Kenneth Bianchi in the "Controversy" feature in this chapter highlights, features of DID can be created through suggestions from overzealous therapists or mass media coverage in a culture that has become fascinated with the disorder. Some researchers argue that increases in the appearance of DID may be a result of such fascination; high-profile cases may encourage both vulnerable and suggestible people, as well as some clinicians, to explain certain psychological symptoms as manifestations of multiple identities.

Proponents of the sociocognitive model (Lilienfeld & Lynn, 2003; Lynn & Pintar, 1997; Lynn et al., 2014) point out that therapist influence may account for two well-established facts regarding DID: (1) most clients who are diagnosed with DID, such as Louise in the chapter-opening case, did not begin therapy complaining about multiple personalities; and (2) some therapists diagnose the condition frequently, whereas others report never having seen a single case.

But how, then, does this sociocognitive model account for the well-established link between trauma and dissociation described earlier? If individuals have been abused as children, the chances that they will be given information about enacting multiple personalities increase (Lilienfeld & Lynn, 2003). Because many therapists are convinced that a history of childhood abuse is the primary cause of dissociative disorders, they are likely to ask questions and convey ideas about DID to their clients who were abused, thus becoming a key source of information about enactment of multiple identities. Therapists who are committed to the diagnosis of DID typically use highly leading interviewing techniques to encourage clients to report a disorder that might not otherwise have appeared. Finally, as the Bianchi case in the "Controversy" feature reveals, through the use of hypnotic procedures, therapists can encourage alter personalities to emerge in therapy. The widespread use of hypnosis to elicit recall by people suspected of having DID may be a source of therapist contamination in that memories recalled under hypnosis are particularly subject to distortions and inaccuracies (Loftus, 2000). In response to these suggestive techniques, clients may therefore enact alters and ultimately become convinced that they suffer from DID.

Evaluating the Sociocognitive Model

Researchers suggest that both reported cases of DID and the number of alters per person with DID have increased dramatically over the past few decades, as more attention is paid to the disorder (Lynn et al., 2012). Also, mainstream treatment techniques are purported to reinforce disclosure of alters through suggestive questioning, such as "Is there another part of you with whom I have not spoken?" This is further supported by evidence that most people do not report alters until after attending therapy, and the number of alters tends to increase through the course of treatment. Additionally, therapists using hypnosis tend to have a greater number of people with DID in their caseload than those not using hypnosis (Powell & Gee, 1999). Taking this evidence together, sociocultural theorists suggest that both iatrogenic (therapist-induced) and sociocultural influences play a significant role in the development of DID, but also contend that those who are experiencing pre-existing psychopathology are likely to be vulnerable to these other factors. As the next section highlights, there may be specific factors that lead to this vulnerability.

Fantasy Model

fantasy model (FM): The claim that dissociation makes individuals prone to fantasy, thereby engendering confabulated memories of trauma commonly seen in people with dissociative identity disorders.

The **fantasy model (FM)** extends the sociocognitive model. Proponents of the FM have marshaled evidence that fantasy overlaps with dissociation and that specific fantasy-related traits render some individuals vulnerable to the suggestive influences emphasized by the sociocognitive model (Merckelbach, Horselenberg, & Schmidt, 2002). FM researchers point out that suggestibility and fantasy proneness are related to both inaccurate or exaggerated self-reports of trauma, as well as to dissociative experiences (Lynn et al., 2014). Figure 10.2 displays this model, which identifies fantasy-related factors as mediators between cultural and environmental experiences and retrospective self-reports of trauma, vulnerability to suggestion, and dissociative experiences.

absorption: A dimension of personality that describes a person's tendency to become caught up in private reveries, imaginings, or a current task, to the exclusion of surrounding stimuli; also known as fantasy proneness or imaginative involvement.

Absorption (also called *imaginative involvement* or *fantasy proneness*) is the ability to become absorbed in private reveries or imaginings and varies across individuals (Levin, Sirof, Simeon, & Guralnik, 2004). For example, daydreaming does not come easily to everyone, and not everyone can become equally absorbed in a novel or movie (or even this textbook!). Some people find it easy to get completely caught up in what they are doing, and they lose track of time and of what is going on around them. They can become so immersed in fantasies that they occasionally have trouble distinguishing imagined events from real ones. Others, even when trying hard to attend fully to a TV show, for instance,

FIGURE 10.2 The Fantasy Model of DID Development

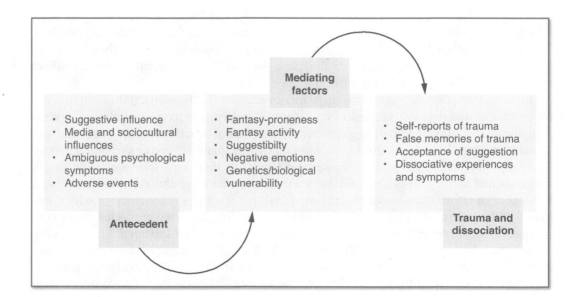

TABLE 10.2 Fantasy Absorption and Dissociative Experiences

Fantasy Absorption Items	Dissociative Experience Items
The sound of a voice can be so fascinating to me that I can just go on listening to it.	I sometimes have the experience of finding myself dressed in clothes that I do not remember putting on.
I can sometimes recollect certain past experiences in my life with such clarity and vividness that it is like living them again, or almost so.	I sometimes find that when I am alone, I talk out loud to myself.
If I wish, I can imagine (or daydream) some things so vividly that they hold my attention in the way a good movie or story does.	I sometimes remember a past event so vividly that I feel as if I were reliving the event.
I am sometimes able to forget about my present self and get absorbed in a fantasy that I am someone else.	I sometimes find myself in a familiar place but find it strange and unfamiliar.
	I sometimes look in a mirror and do not recognize myself.

remain fully aware of their surroundings and are easily distracted. In short, people differ along a dimension of fantasy proneness.

In an important series of studies, Steven Lynn and his colleagues (2014) investigated whether people who score higher on measures of fantasy proneness are also more likely to experience dissociative symptoms. Table 10.2 compares items that are drawn from two different questionnaires used in this research—one that measures fantasy proneness and one that measures dissociative events. In one study, college students who scored in the upper 4% on the measure of fantasy proneness were compared with students scoring in the average range on this measure (Rauschenberger & Lynn, 1995). Two thirds of the high fantasy-prone students met the criteria for a past or present mental disorder, compared with only 31% of the medium fantasy-prone students. High fantasizers also reported three to four times as many dissociative symptoms as medium fantasizers, although no student in either group qualified for a diagnosis of a *DSM* dissociative disorder.

Clearly, fantasy proneness is related to general psychopathology, but the exact nature of the relationship is not clear. Perhaps a tendency to fantasize increases recollection of past negative experiences or a tendency to exaggerate the potential negative aspects of future events. These characteristics could, in turn, lead to demoralization and greater vulnerability to stressors. Another possibility is that high fantasizers are more prone to report symptoms of mental disorders, whether they actually occurred or were merely imagined.

Integrative View of DID

Like so many questions in the field of abnormal psychology, the dispute about whether DID is a valid diagnosis cannot be answered with a simple "yes" or "no." The disruptive effects of severe trauma—a key causal factor cited by proponents of the diagnosis—should not be underestimated. Some traumas are probably severe enough to lead to dissociation. As proponents of the PTM put it (Dalenberg et al., 2014, p. 917): "Dissociation is a response to the reality of trauma, and the connection between the two is no fantasy."

Furthermore, psychologically important ideas and emotions can exist without a person's always being fully conscious of them. The splintering of consciousness and loss of autobiographical memories reported in DID are clearly possible, just like the physical dissociation described in Chapter 11. By the same token, current data do not necessitate the conclusion that all—or even most—claims of DID are caused by severe trauma. Many cases might involve a small degree of genuine dissociation, which individuals then exaggerate either to confirm a therapist's expectations or to provide an explanation for their

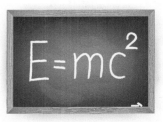

MAPS - Attempted Answers

psychological problems as an "attempted solution" that is operative for so many mental disorders. The fact that dissociative experiences are so often linked in the dominant Euro-American context to situations in which individuals lack control—that is, traumatic and stressful experiences that are themselves defined in part by the way they violate expectations of autonomy and feelings of control—is not coincidental (Seligman & Kirmayer, 2008). Although trauma is not a necessary precursor for dissociation, it can provoke and intensify this process, leading individuals to experience dissociation more frequently or persistently (Seligman & Kirmayer, 2008).

Overall, a variety of pieces of evidence, including commonly prescribed treatment practices of DID proponents, the clinical features of people with DID before and after psychotherapy, the distribution of cases of DID across psychotherapists, data from role-playing studies, and the extremely low prevalence of childhood DID outside of treatment, call into question a "strong" form of the PTM—that is, that all cases of DID are caused by early trauma (Lilienfeld & Lynn, 2015). These data, however, may be consistent with a "weak" form of the PTM that accords a predisposing role to childhood trauma but also grants a substantial causal role to sociocultural influences, including iatrogenesis (Lilienfeld & Lynn, 2015).

Biological Causes of Dissociative Disorders

One question that has received research attention in the last 20 years is whether there are biological factors that increase risk for developing a dissociative disorder. Between 48 and 59% of the variance accounted for in dissociation is attributable to genetics, with the remaining variance related to nonshared environmental influences (Jang, Paris, Zweig-Frank, & Livesley, 1998; Becker-Blease et al., 2004). The neurobiological basis of dissociative disorders is gaining evidence, with reduced serotonin (Simeon, 2004) and an increase in cannabinoids as potential mediators of dissociation (Simeon, Guralnik, Knutelska, Yehuda, & Schmeidler, 2003). Functional magnetic resonance imaging (fMRI) studies have also found abnormalities of the sensory cortex—areas responsible for visual, auditory, and somatosensory processing (Simeon et al., 2000)—that may be involved in the vulnerability to having dissociative experiences.

Trauma-dissociation theorists defend their emphasis on the role of early trauma by pointing to the fact that MRI studies have found reductions in the size of the hippocampus in adults who had been severely abused during childhood and who show current evidence of post-traumatic stress disorder and dissociative symptoms (Vermetten, Schmahl, Lindner, Loewenstein, & Bremner, 2006). The hippocampus is the part of the brain responsible for transferring information between short- and long-term memory; therefore, hippocampal changes may constitute a biological consequence of physical abuse that also influences memory disturbance. Further research is necessary to explore this possibility, however, because it has not been established that abuse is the cause of the brain changes.

Biological Overlap Between Dissociative Disorders and Post-Traumatic Stress Disorder (PTSD)

As discussed in Chapter 9, there is a separate category of trauma- and stressor-related disorders in the *DSM-5* that includes the diagnosis of *post-traumatic stress disorder (PTSD)*. A dissociative subtype specifier for PTSD is applied if there is evidence of persistent depersonalization or derealization following the traumatic event (Friedman, Resick, Bryant, & Brewin, 2011). There is also empirical support that dissociation may play a role in the frequent co-occurrence of PTSD and borderline personality disorder among women (Wolf et al., 2012).

People with PTSD and depersonalization show an increase in activity in the cingulate cortex and medial prefrontal cortex, areas of the brain responsible for modulating arousal and regulating emotion (Hopper, Frewen, Sack, Lanius, & Van der Kolk, 2007; Lanius et al., 2010), as well as evidence for limbic inhibition (Lanius, Brand, Vermetten, Frewen, & Spiegel, 2012). This pattern of prefrontal activation and limbic inhibition has also been seen in people with DID (Simeon, Guralnik et al., 2003) and with depersonalization/

derealization disorder (Spiegel et al., 2013). Moreover, the volume of the hippocampus and amygdala in individuals with either DID (Vermetten et al., 2006) or PTSD (Irle, Lange, Sachsse, & Weniger, 2009) is significantly reduced, suggesting similar neural mechanisms for both disorders. As a result, some researchers question whether PTSD and DID should be in the same diagnostic category and conceived as minor and major forms of personality dissociation (Nijenhuis, 2014). Early trauma (e.g., before age 9) may make an individual more vulnerable to DID, whereas later trauma (e.g., war) may increase risk for PTSD, rather than DID (Barlow & Durand, 2004).

What specifically might be happening biologically during depersonalization/ derealization experiences? There is neurobiological evidence for a "cortico-limbic" model of depersonalization/derealization disorder in which inhibitory activity in the prefrontal cortex disrupts the "emotional tagging" of events by the amygdala and related limbic structures, which results in suppressed autonomic arousal and a sense of disconnection from reality (Seligman & Kirmayer, 2008). For example, the intensity of emotional experiences is specifically attenuated in people with depersonalization/ derealization disorder; in other words, they are under-responsive to emotionally charged stimuli (Sierra, Senior, Dalton, McDonough, & Bond, 2002; Sierra & David, 2011). Emotional intensity depends largely on interoceptive awareness—that is, sensitivity to stimuli originating inside of one's body (Fustos, Gramann, Herbert, & Pollatos, 2013; Herbert & Pollatos, 2012). Stunted emotions may reflect the difficulties that people with this disorder have in integrating their actual visceral and bodily perceptions into a sense of themselves (Michal et al., 2014). In other words, they experience their body but cannot somehow reconcile it with how they feel and/or their overall sense of self in a coherent manner. Another dissociative disorder—dissociative amnesia—is also associated with an altered pattern of cortico-limbic neural activity, one in which the prefrontal cortex has an important role in inhibiting the activity of the hippocampus in memory formation (Kikuchi et al., 2010).

Connections

What other mental disorders might be related to the functioning of the frontal lobes and limbic systems? See most chapters of this book!

Psychological Causes of Other Dissociative Disorders

We have already discussed various psychosocial models of DID, particularly the warring theories of post-traumatic and sociocognitive/fantasy models. What about psychological factors in other dissociative disorders, such as depersonalization/derealization disorder? A cognitive-behavioral model suggests that attributions and appraisals, along with increased attention to symptoms, play important roles in the development and maintenance of this disorder. One study found that people with depersonalization/derealization disorder made less normalizing attributions for physical symptoms, along with more catastrophic appraisals (i.e., assuming the worst) than those in a control group, showing similar patterns to people with panic disorder and obsessive-compulsive disorder (see Chapters 7 and 8; Hunter, Salkovskis, & David, 2014).

With respect to dissociative amnesia, cognitive elements of memory formation likely play a role, though the precise mechanism is yet to be elucidated (Giesbrecht, Lynn, Lilienfeld, & Merckelbach, 2008). For example, DePrince and Freyd (2004) indicated that high dissociators recalled fewer trauma words (i.e., superior forgetting), whereas Devilly and colleagues (2007) found increased memory fallibility in high dissociators, as demonstrated by lower general recall and, in one study, a heightened tendency to produce commission errors (i.e., remembering words that were never shown). Much work remains to be done in this realm before any definite answers are forthcoming.

Section Review

Sudden trauma or strong emotional conflicts can trigger dissociative disorders in individuals who are vulnerable as a result of:

- a tendency to be highly absorbed in imaginative activity,
- a tendency to be suggestible and easily hypnotized, and
- a childhood history of trauma or physical abuse.

Two very different theories have been proposed to explain dissociative identity disorder, emphasizing either:

- a history of early childhood trauma that causes certain people to fall into a repetitive pattern of dissociated identities as a form of defensive coping, or
- a pattern of enacting multiple identities as a result of expectations and suggestions from clinicians and cultural support from modern Western society.

Post-traumatic stress disorder and dissociative disorders have overlapping symptomology and neurobiological findings. Cognitive explanations for the other dissociative disorders (depersonalization/derealization disorder and amnesia) have been put forth, but research remains limited.

Treatment of Dissociative Disorders

Treatment of Dissociative Identity Disorder

The long-term prognosis for dissociative identity disorder (DID) is not favorable, even with treatment. Most people experience chronic impairments from the condition, which, unlike other dissociative disorders, seldom improves spontaneously. Like Louise in the chapter-opening case, individuals with DID have difficulty with interpersonal trust and concerns about rejection (Gillig, 2009), making the idea of therapy difficult to accept. Further, with treatment, many people with DID achieve some fusions—alters merging into their host personality—yet they rarely become fully unified (Brand et al., 2012).

Systematic research on treatment outcomes for people with DID is in its infancy (Brand et al., 2012). The sparse literature on the efficacy of treatment for DID is a reflection of the difficulty identifying people with the disorder, the variability in treatments offered to this population, and the high therapy dropout rates (Gantt & Tinnin, 2007). In some studies, increases in suicide attempts, hallucinations, severe dysphoria, and chronic stress have been reported following termination of treatment (Piper & Merskey, 2004). However, in a more recent study of over 200 people and their therapists from 19 countries over a 30-month period, there was statistically significant evidence for reduction in dissociation, PTSD symptoms, general distress, depression, suicide attempts, and engagement in self-injurious behaviors (Brand et al., 2013).

Although strong research evidence is limited, many therapists are convinced that the person's "real" personality will emerge only after the alters have been *fused* or integrated in therapy, while still retaining the various experiences of the alters. More recently, specific phasic treatment approaches have been developed to reach this goal. These treatments focus on helping clients clarify the alter system, explore emotionally upsetting material, and work through the consequences of childhood trauma.

Whereas some clinicians use medications such as stimulants, antidepressants, and anticonvulsants to treat some of the symptoms of DID (Nemzer, 1996), there is no solid evidence that drugs are helpful in the long-term prognosis (e.g., Loewenstein, 1991). The expert consensus thus far for treating DID includes psychotherapy with three general steps or phases (Dorahy et al., 2014). Phase one of the treatment is centered around establishing safety and stability in the therapeutic relationship so that clients feel comfortable and trust their therapist. Phase two includes exploring trauma narratives and resolving trauma-related emotions, thoughts, and behaviors. This is generally done via a cognitive-behavioral approach and includes exposure to the trauma (see Chapter 9) when individuals are ready (Brand et al., 2012). In phase three, the treatment focuses on integrating identities and reducing reliance on dissociation as a way to cope with stress. When international experts who treat people with DID were surveyed, the follow-

I don't want to wade into that psyche, thought Dr. Frank.

Source: Cartoonresource/Shutterstock.com.

Connections

Why is a trusting relationship so important to the success of most forms of psychotherapy? For a discussion of some reasons, see Chapter 2 (humanistic model).

MAPS - Medical Myths

ing specific components were highly endorsed throughout the treatment: fostering the therapeutic relationship, providing psychoeducation (i.e., information on DID), increasing emotional intelligence, reducing impulsivity, establishing grounding techniques to reduce dissociation, and developing coping strategies to manage stress without the need for alters (Brand et al., 2012).

A current area of debate among DID experts is the extent to which the dissociated self states need to be targeted directly in therapy (Brand et al., 2012). The clinical literature on DID encourages therapists to work with self states, as well as to talk openly to increase internal awareness and cooperation among them. However, some clinicians support a more indirect approach and rarely, if ever, attempt to work with self states other than those spontaneously presenting in therapy sessions. Furthermore, some contend that treatments with a sole or major focus on trauma provide a cautionary example of how not to treat patients with DID and recommend instead treating the emotional dysregulation and manifold symptoms that accompany the typical presentation of the disorder (Lynn, Condon, & Colletti, 2013).

Treatment of Other Dissociative Disorders

Unfortunately, there is limited available research and therefore few treatment guidelines for the treatment of other dissociative disorders. To date, no controlled studies addressing the treatment of dissociative amnesia have been reported. All the information available reflects the experience and case reports of clinicians and treatment centers (Maldonado, Butler, & Spiegel, 2002). Fortunately, though, most individuals who suffer dissociative amnesia or depersonalization/derealization disorder improve without any formal treatment once the triggering stressor is removed or resolved. In cases that require psychotherapy, the goal is to help individuals cope better with the trauma that led to the amnesia or fugue. Attention is also devoted to helping clients deal with their loss of memory and sense of identity and to teaching them new skills for coping with stress. Individuals are sometimes hypnotized to promote the retrieval of memory (MacHovek, 1981). As noted earlier, however, this approach risks the implantation of false memories (Loftus, 2000), which is why many experts recommend that treatment focuses instead on enhancement of functioning, rather than on uncovering buried memories (Loftus, 1994). In most cases, brief interventions that are supportive and/or cognitive-behavioral can be effective. Clients usually regain their memories and return to their prior levels of functioning.

Specific treatments for depersonalization and derealization have received little attention. One study by Hunter and colleagues (2005) examined the benefits of a specific cognitive-behavioral therapy that focused on teaching people to interpret their symptoms in a nonthreatening way, as well as on reducing avoidance and safety behaviors and symptom monitoring. There were significant initial and longer-term improvements for individuals in this sample, with almost a third no longer meeting criteria for the diagnosis at the end of treatment. However, this study lacked the rigorous design (i.e., comparison to a control group whose members did not receive the treatment) to be able to draw clear treatment guidelines from the outcomes. There is also some evidence for dysregulation of endogenous opioid systems in depersonalization/derealization disorder, and a few uncontrolled studies have suggested that opioid antagonists such as naltrexone may help in the treatment of these symptoms (Simeon & Knutelska, 2005).

Source: Image Point Fr/Shutterstock.com.

Note that expert consensus did not include using hypnosis in the treatment of DID (Dorahy et al., 2014); such use is controversial because, as discussed earlier, it can increase false memories (Loftus, 2000). However, one clinician claims that hypnosis played a crucial role in the first successful psychotherapy of DID and continues to be a valuable asset to the contemporary psychotherapist working with these conditions to access alters, gather information, and promote symptom relief (Kluft, 2012). Modern hypnosis differs from what you might imagine, with the use of therapeutic suggestions rather than having people cluck like a chicken, and has been used in the treatment of disorders ranging from chronic pain and depression to anxiety and weight loss (Wark, 2008).

Connections

What other disorders typically involve temporary or even permanent memory loss? See Chapter 15 for details.

Adverse Childhood Experiences: Reducing the Risks for Dissociative Disorders

As the number of reported cases of dissociative identity disorder has increased, so too have concerns about how the disorder can be prevented. There is consensus that sexual and physical abuse of young children contributes to the disorder (though to what extent is under debate); thus, a reduction of child abuse and treatment of abusers are obvious prevention strategies. Several risk factors have been isolated for child abuse (Rodriquez & Richardson, 2007). As examples, abusive parents tend to:

- hold unrealistic expectations for their children, such as the age by which they should be toilet trained,
- become easily annoyed when they are under stress,
- have an external locus of control,
- choose aggressive means of resolving conflicts,
- have low levels of empathy,
- have limited access to social support and help with child care, and
- disagree with each other about child rearing and discipline standards.

Parents who are poor, were abused themselves as children, give birth to children with congenital defects, have children while they are still teenagers, or are embroiled in their own marital conflicts are also at greater risk to be abusers (Milaniak & Widom, 2014). Can these risks be reduced or overcome? (This is our third "Prevention" feature in this textbook that mentions parenting training; can you recall the other two? Obviously, learning how to parent effectively is super important.)

Several studies have shown that parents can learn more-effective child management skills and that abusive interactions with children can also be reduced. For example, Matthew Sanders and several colleagues created the Triple P-Positive Parenting Program, which is a five-level evidence-based intervention designed to strengthen parenting (Sanders, Cann, & Markie-Dadds, 2003). The first level is a widespread community campaign informing parents about parenting issues and informing them of parenting programs. The second level focuses on just one topic, such as toilet training, and the parents either talk on the phone or work in person with a therapist to strategize around that topic. In the third step, parents are involved in multiple sessions that address how to manage behavioral or developmental issues with their children. In the fourth and fifth steps, parents who have children with severe behavioral problems (see Chapter 3) receive 10–12 sessions of intervention that is focused on developing parenting skills specific to the disordered conduct and another 10–12

sessions targeting the parents' unique needs as individuals. After one large-scale study utilized this approach in a community of 100,000 people, there were 340 fewer cases of maltreatment, 240 fewer children being removed from their homes, and 60 fewer maltreatment injuries to children that required medical attention (Prinz, Sanders, Shapiro, Whitaker, & Lutzker, 2009).

In other words, abusive parents can be taught to change their behavior if they learn the necessary skills for managing their children. However, child abuse is not caused solely by the problems of individual parents; they need help from the people around them as well. For example, social support significantly reduces the relationship between mothers' distress and their likelihood of abusing their children (Rodriquez & Tucker, 2014). Community daycare centers that occasionally relieve parents of childcare demands and crisis intervention that helps parents cope with personal stress are two examples of much-needed social services in this realm.

Sociocognitive theorists do not deny the horrors of child abuse, and they do not oppose efforts to prevent it. However, because they argue that DID is also an *iatrogenic* condition (one that is inadvertently caused by treatment), they believe it is essential that therapists avoid implanting ideas of abuse and multiple identities in suggestible clients. Psychologist Elizabeth Loftus (1994, 2000) and sociologist Richard Ofshe have studied claims of repressed memories and the techniques used to retrieve them. They have used laboratory research and real-life cases to document how memories—sometimes for incredibly brutal acts—can be built from the suggestions of others.

Ofshe's involvement in the case of Paul Ingram provides a chilling example. Ingram, a sheriff's deputy in Olympia, Washington, was arrested for child abuse in 1988. He steadfastly denied the allegations, but the police continued to question and pressure him over the next 5 months, even though there was very little evidence to support the allegations that Ingram's children had lodged against him. To help Ingram's memory, a psychologist or a detective would repeatedly describe an act of abuse, such as Ingram and a bunch of other men raping his daughter. Ingram would at first have no memory for such incidents, but after concerted effort, including praying and being hypnotized to help his memory, he started to "recall" some details. Ultimately, Paul Ingram confessed to not just the charges of incest but to rapes, assaults, sexual abuse, and participation in a Satanic cult that was believed to have killed 25 babies.

Adverse Childhood Experiences: Reducing the Risks for Dissociative Disorders *(Continued)*

To check the accuracy of Ingram's memory, Ofshe, who the prosecutor had hired as a consultant, asked Ingram to recall an event that Ofshe had totally fabricated—that Ingram had forced his son and daughter to have sex in front of him. Just as with the police interrogation, Ingram could not remember anything at first, but after thinking and praying about it, he gradually formed images of the event, and within a matter of hours, endorsed a three-page confession to the scene Ofshe had made up. Ofshe concluded that, rather than being a sex offender or a Satanic cult member, Paul Ingram was a vulnerable man with a strong need to please authorities, a highly suggestible nature, and the ability to fall easily into a trance.

Ultimately, Paul Ingram decided to plead guilty to six counts of third-degree rape. He was sent to prison and now insists that he never abused his children. Ingram was released in 2003 after serving his sentence. Ingram's story became the basis of the book *Remembering Satan* by Lawrence Wright (1994). Was Paul Ingram duped into confessing on the basis of false memories, or was he a guilt-ridden abuser who finally admitted his crime? Questions such as these are at the heart of the controversy over whether therapists should aggressively try to help clients recover memories of abuse that may have been repressed. Moreover, the existence of repressed memory itself has been called into question (McNally, 2012).

Section Review

Most treatments for dissociative identity disorder:

- begin with the establishment of a safe and trusting therapeutic environment,
- focus on helping individuals come to terms with past traumas,
- teach information about the disorder, as well as coping skills,
- may or may not help individuals to integrate their various alters into one personality, and
- have not been evaluated in controlled studies, so their overall effectiveness is unknown.

Treatment for other dissociative disorders focuses on helping individuals to cope with any triggering traumas (if present) and is limited to case reports or uncontrolled studies of cognitive-behavioral therapy and opioid medication.

Revisiting the Case of Louise

Louise continued weekly psychotherapy for 2 more years. Her therapist, Dr. Joan, told her about the diagnosis of dissociative identity disorder and what clinicians believe can cause or contribute to it. Thereafter, Louise began to talk more about her childhood and the abuse she suffered, which she said she had always remembered but never wanted to admit to or talk about before. Her dreams and memories of the past also became more intense. Two alters appeared in therapy: One was a child who acted panicky and emerged only when Louise was involved in an angry conflict in which she felt she was "in trouble." The other was a teenage girl who dressed and acted provocatively and seemed to take pride in breaking as many rules or expectations as she could.

As Louise revealed more about her memories of childhood, she reported more about how her drunken stepfather often verbally abused her, sometimes beat her, and would lock her in a closet for several hours at a time. Since her mother was usually at work during these episodes, she never stood up for Louise and even blamed Louise for the arguments with her stepfather.

As a result of therapy, Louise attempted to talk with her mother about the past, but her mother refused to do so, saying, "You didn't have it any worse than most kids. We tried our best." However, Louise was able to talk to her younger brother about their childhood,

Elizabeth Loftus

Elizabeth Loftus, PhD, is a distinguished professor at the University of California, Irvine. She holds positions in the Department of Psychology and Social Behavior and the Department of Criminology, Law and Society. She is also professor of law. Dr. Loftus is one of the world's leading experts on memory and has written and lectured widely on issues relating to sexual abuse charges stemming from claims of repressed and recovered memories.

Q There has been considerable controversy in the United States about "repressed" memories of childhood sexual abuse. Do you think delayed recall of childhood trauma occurs?

A It depends on what you mean by "delayed recall." Can people remember things that they have not thought about for a long time? Can they be reminded of experiences that they once had, but have not recalled in many years? Of course! Go to a high school reunion, and you can experience that. But do people take massive traumas and routinely banish them and reliably recover them later? There is no good scientific proof for that.

Q From your perspective as a cognitive psychologist, how do you view dissociative identity disorder?

A There is no question that something is going on with individuals diagnosed with dissociative identity disorder. But it may be too simplistic to ask, is it real? The question is whether these symptoms are caused by a history of violent, prolonged, early-childhood trauma, or by something else, such as suggestion from a therapist or the culture. Whereas I have become convinced that in some of these cases the effects are caused by suggestion, I cannot say whether there are other cases that are actually caused by a long history of violent abuse.

Q Is there basic research that might be relevant to the hypothesis that traumatized children build separate banks of memories?

A One line of research in cognitive psychology is work on implicit versus explicit memory. Explicit memory is involved when I ask you to remember a specific episode from your life (e.g., your high school prom). Implicit memory is a residual of a prior experience that occurs in the absence of conscious awareness that you even had the prior experience (e.g., learning how to tie your shoe). There is proof that we show a residual from past experiences when we are not even aware we had those experiences. It is possible that a child could be exposed to something traumatic, store a residual of the experience, and express that without explicitly remembering the incident. But it is a stretch to see how it would lead to alters and multiple personalities, although it does not mean that it could never happen.

There is a research literature that demonstrates that you can create amnesias and then restore memories with hypnosis. It is possible that genuine trauma could operate this way and create some amnesias that could be restored. But you really have to stretch to make these things fit with existing theory.

Q Does your work tell about how or whether a therapist or evaluator can determine whether a memory is real?

A Yes, the work tells us that, without independent corroboration, there is no way to know whether a memory is real or whether it is a product of imagination, suggestion, or some other mental process.

Q Do you think social or historical factors have contributed to increases in recalled memories of abuse?

A In our culture, we have a history in which reports of abuse coming primarily from women and children were ignored or not believed. There has been a very useful social movement to bring recognition of and belief in these reports. But in the interest of advancing belief in and respect for victims, the pendulum has swung too far. Now, we tend to believe every single story, no matter how dubious.

Q Where is research on "repressed memory" going?

A My collaborators and I are trying to test the limits of memory creation and the power of suggestion to create false memories. We have shown that you can make people believe they had childhood experiences that they never actually had. For example, by suggesting events to them, we can make them believe that they were lost in a shopping mall, that they were crying and

and she felt some relief from these talks, as her younger brother had similar memories of their abusive stepdad.

After over 2 years of working with Dr. Joan, Louise was transferred to a new job in a different city and discontinued therapy. At that point, she was no longer plagued by separate alters during her daily life and had learned better ways to manage her stress. She was still hesitant about romantic relationships, but she had begun making some female friends, although she had trouble trusting them. She maintained only a superficial relationship with her mother, mostly through phone calls or visits at holidays, although she no longer had frequent nightmares involving her stepfather's abuse. Louise continued to struggle with bouts of depression in her new city, but she did not contact a therapist after she moved.

Summary

The Nature of Dissociation

Abrupt disruptions in the normally integrated processes of memory, consciousness, and awareness are typical of the dissociative disorders. Dissociative symptoms must be understood within a cultural context. In some cultures, amnesia and trance (possession) states are an accepted form of religious experience, and at other times, they may be useful ways to express discontent or emotional distress.

Dissociative Identity Disorder

The most extreme and puzzling of the dissociative disorders is dissociative identity disorder (DID), in which a person's identity appears to fragment into alternate personalities ("alters") that exert control over the person's behavior at different times and without full awareness of the others. In the late 1800s, most cases of dissociative identity disorder involved only two personalities. However, the average number of alters—as well as the prevalence of the disorder itself—has increased over the past few decades.

Other Dissociative Disorders

Dissociative amnesia involves the sudden loss of memory without a clear organic (biological) cause. When it involves travel to another place, the specifier "with dissociative fugue" is utilized. Individuals' recurrent feelings of being detached from themselves or that the outside world is unreal are characteristic of depersonalization/derealization disorder.

Causes of Dissociative Disorders

Dissociative amnesia and depersonalization/derealization disorder are thought to be triggered by sudden severe trauma or strong emotional conflicts occurring in individuals who are prone to dissociation due to suggestibility, fantasy absorption, and biology.

Clinicians disagree on the extent to which dissociative identity disorder is a genuine, distinct disorder arising out of early trauma during childhood or a condition at least partially and unintentionally created by therapists' suggestions, media portrayals, and cultural norms.

The post-traumatic model of dissociative identity disorder suggests that DID originates from early severe childhood abuse that produces a splitting of personalities as a defense against or psychological escape from the traumatic events. Another theory, the sociocognitive or fantasy model, proposes that DID is diagnosed in clients who are prone to dissociative-like experiences and who learn to enact multiple identities from the leading and suggestive techniques used by psychotherapists and from modern cultural expectations.

Treatment of Dissociative Disorders

Psychotherapy for dissociative identity disorder usually aims at helping clients feel safe, come to terms with past trauma, and cope more effectively with life stress; it may sometimes result in the integration or fusion of alters into a unified identity. However, the efficacy of these treatments has not been carefully evaluated. Many people with other dissociative disorders improve without formal treatment, once the triggering stressor has been resolved.

Key Terms

absorption, p. 352

alter personality (alter), p. 342

amnesia, p. 339

continuous amnesia, p. 345

depersonalization, p. 340

depersonalization/derealization disorder, p. 346

derealization, p. 340

dissociation, p. 338

dissociative amnesia, p. 344

dissociative disorder, p. 338

dissociative fugue, p. 345

dissociative identity disorder (DID), p. 340

fantasy model (FM), p. 352

generalized amnesia, p. 345

host personality, p. 342

identity alteration, p. 340

identity confusion, p. 340

localized amnesia, p. 345

pathological possession, p. 341

post-traumatic model (PTM), p. 347

selective amnesia, p. 345

sociocognitive model, p. 347

switching, p. 343

systematized amnesia, p. 345

Somatic Symptom and Related Disorders

Source: Ron and Joe/Shutterstock.com.

Chapter Outline

Somatic Symptom and Related Disorders

Causes of Somatic Symptom and Related Disorders

Treatment of Somatic Symptom and Related Disorders

From the Case of Samantha

Samantha's family doctor referred her to a pediatric neurologist after Samantha experienced a brief period of unconsciousness, followed by an inability to move her legs. She was a pleasant 10-year-old girl with no history of medical or behavioral problems or mental health concerns. Her family was close-knit and active in their church. They lived in a rural setting, where Samantha was admired as a good student and a "model child." She and three younger siblings attended a very small school, where she was making excellent academic progress. Samantha was carefully evaluated, and despite her inability to move her legs, no physical or medical explanations were identified. Her thinking and memory were clear, and she cooperated with the physician. She seemed a bit withdrawn, but she could not identify any psychological stressors in her life.

Samantha's parents were adamant that Samantha had to be suffering a physical, not a mental, problem. They believed that feelings were private and that emotional distress was best resolved through prayer and hard work. Nevertheless, they agreed to let Samantha enter a child psychiatry hospital unit.

During her time on the unit, Samantha continued her schooling, received physical therapy to help her regain muscle strength and walk again,

After reading this chapter, you will be able to answer the following key questions:

■ How are somatic symptom and related disorders described and categorized in the *Diagnostic and Statistical Manual of Mental Disorders (DSM-5)*?

■ What causes somatic symptom and related disorders?

■ How do psychological factors give rise to physical symptoms without an identifiable organic cause?

■ How are somatic symptom and related disorders treated?

■ What is the role of integrated care in the detection and treatment of somatic symptom and related disorders?

and participated in group therapy that focused on education about feelings, coping with stress, problem solving, and interpersonal skills. She began to share some of her fears, such as concerns about going to the "big city" middle school the following year.

Samantha was diagnosed with a conversion disorder (functional neurological symptom disorder), which is one of the **somatic symptom and related disorders** in the *DSM-5* (American Psychiatric Association, 2013a). Could Samantha's inability to move her legs (a physical problem) have been triggered by her psychological distress—that is, unexpressed fears about changing schools and moving into a larger community? Somatic (formerly called **somatoform**) disorders involve physical complaints or disabilities that suggest a medical problem but that typically have no known biological cause and are not voluntarily produced by individuals. The disabilities associated with most of these disorders are assumed to arise from **somatization**—a process by which emotional distress is converted into (or expressed as) physical symptoms. Not all somatic disorders involve the expression of disguised emotions, however. Some disorders are grouped in this category simply because it provides a convenient label for several types of individuals who consult physicians about physical complaints that may not be due to an identifiable medical illness.

Somatic Symptom and Related Disorders

The category of *somatic symptom and related disorders* consists of a grouping of mental disorders all sharing one common feature: the prominence of somatic (physical) symptoms associated with significant distress and impairment. Individuals either experience these physical symptoms without any identifiable organic cause, experience heightened health-related anxiety despite the absence of significant physical symptoms, falsify physical or psychological symptoms in the absence of external rewards, or experience psychological factors that negatively impact a medical condition. In most of these disorders, the physical symptoms that individuals report are truly experienced subjectively, and the inability to find the symptoms' biological cause makes these disorders difficult and often frustrating for health-care professionals to treat. Because most individuals who experience somatic symptoms visit their primary care medical provider first, it is important for physicians to have a basic understanding of somatic symptom and related disorders to make an appropriate diagnosis and refer individuals to mental health care when indicated.

Medically unexplained physical symptoms (MUPS) is an umbrella term that medical providers use to characterize symptoms without corresponding objective (lab, test, or physical exam) findings that could explain the symptoms. MUPS are common and problematic in medical settings, with prevalence estimates ranging from 15–30% in primary care settings (Kirmayer, Groleau, Looper, & Dao, 2004) to as high as 66% in specialty clinics (Nimnuan, Hotopf, & Wessely, 2001). One use of the term *MUPS* is in reference to the overlapping symptoms present in a variety of conditions—in addition to somatic disorders—such as chronic fatigue syndrome, fibromyalgia, multiple chemical sensitivity, and Gulf War illness, which also share a significant overlap in treatment (Burton, 2003). However, just because a person experiences MUPS does not mean that a medical explanation does not exist. It could be that medical providers have yet to identify one or that they have exhausted all currently available medical testing. The term *MUPS* is commonly used synonymously with and to indicate the presence of somatic symptoms, but the *DSM-5* states that a somatic disorder can exist whether or not the symptoms can be medically explained (American Psychiatric Association, 2013a).

In many cases, clinicians assume that the symptoms are an expression of underlying emotional tension or stress, or that they are intensified by such

"This 'dark area' on the x-ray looks suspiciously like chocolate."

Modern medicine does not know everything.

Source: Cartoonresource/Shutterstock.com.

TABLE 11.1 Somatic Disorders From the *DSM-III* (1980) Through the *DSM-5* (2014)

DSM-III	DSM-III-R	DSM-IV	DSM-5
Somatization disorder	Somatization disorder	Somatization disorder	Somatic symptom disorder
Hypochondriasis	Hypochondriasis	Hypochondriasis	Illness anxiety disorder
Psychogenic pain disorder	Somatoform pain disorder	Pain disorder	
	Undifferentiated somatoform disorder	Undifferentiated somatoform disorder	
Conversion disorder	Conversion disorder	Conversion disorder	Conversion disorder (functional neurological symptom disorder)
Atypical somatoform disorder	Body dysmorphic disorder	Body dysmorphic disorder	Same diagnosis (body dysmorphic disorder) but moved to obsessive-compulsive and related disorders (Chapter 8)
	Somatoform disorder NOS (not otherwise specified)	Somatoform disorder NOS (not otherwise specified)	Other specified somatic symptom and related disorder Unspecified somatic symptom and related disorder
Factitious disorder	Factitious disorder	Factitious disorder	Factitious disorder
		Psychological factors affecting other medical conditions (in the section entitled "Other Conditions That May Be a Focus of Clinical Attention")	Psychological factors affecting other medical conditions (in the main manual)

stressors. The symptoms may mimic actual medical disorders, and affected individuals are often convinced that an illness is primarily responsible. Some individuals undergo expensive and invasive medical procedures or visit one physician after another in an attempt to relieve their symptoms. Fortunately, for Samantha in the chapter-opening case, she and her parents followed their doctor's recommendation to seek psychological treatment aimed at alleviating the emotional distress believed to be maintaining her physical inability to move her legs.

Because the *DSM-5* is so new to the fields of behavioral sciences and treatment of mental disorders, much of what is known about somatic symptom and related disorders stems from decades of research on disorders from previous editions of the *DSM*. Table 11.1 outlines the somatic disorders included in previous editions of the *DSM* going back several decades.

Somatic Symptom Disorder

In 1859, French physician Pierre Briquet provided the first formal description of individuals who consulted him about a seemingly endless list of physical complaints that he could not explain medically. These individuals kept coming back for one type of treatment after another, even though none of the treatments was successful. The condition was known as **Briquet's syndrome** until 1980, when the *DSM* relabeled it *somatization*

Briquet's syndrome: First described in 1859 by Paul Briquet, this disorder involves patients who feel they have been sickly most of their lives and who complain of multiple symptoms related to numerous organ systems; the conviction of illness continues, despite negative medical testing, and patients continue to seek medical treatment and undergo procedures.

TABLE 11.2 The *DSM-5* in Simple Language: Diagnosing Somatic Symptom Disorder

> ■ For a diagnosis of somatic symptom disorder, individuals must be experiencing at least one somatic symptom (including pain) that causes significant distress or impairment in daily functioning for at least 6 months.
>
> ■ Individuals must also be spending a great deal of time and effort thinking or worrying about the somatic symptoms or feared health outcome as a result of the symptoms.

Source: Adapted from American Psychiatric Association (2013a).

somatic symptom disorder (SSD): A *DSM-5* disorder describing one or more somatic (physical) symptoms that are distressing or that disrupt a person's life, with a large amount of time spent thinking about or feeling anxiety about personal physical health or symptoms.

"Ooo, I just felt the good cholesterol kick the bad cholesterol."

Mind and body may not be as separate as you think.

Source: Cartoonresource/Shutterstock.com.

MAPS - Attempted Answers

body dysmorphic disorder (BDD): A mental disorder in which individuals are preoccupied with one or more perceived defects in their physical appearance and perform repetitive behaviors or mental acts in response to these appearance-related concerns.

disorder (American Psychiatric Association, 1980), currently defined by the *DSM-5* as **somatic symptom disorder (SSD)**. This new diagnosis captures several other disorders from the *DSM-IV*, as shown in Table 11.1, including hypochondriasis, somatization disorder, and pain disorder.

The cardinal feature of SSD, as described in Table 11.2, is the presence of one or more physical symptoms that cause significant distress or impairment and excessive thoughts, feelings, or behaviors related to those symptoms, such as anxiety about one's physical health. Symptoms must be persistent and last for more than 6 months. Individuals whose somatic symptoms predominately involve pain, labeled *pain disorder* in the *DSM-IV* (American Psychiatric Association, 1994), are now included in this category. For example, if a woman receives medical attention for a miscarriage and then, several weeks later, begins experiencing severe pelvic pain, despite no identifiable medical explanations of the pain, this would now be diagnosed as SSD.

The physical problems in SSD are thought to be generated by somatization, which, as noted earlier, is a tendency to experience psychological distress in the form of bodily symptoms. It is important to note that somatization is a widespread and not necessarily pathological condition. Physical symptoms often serve as a barometer of emotional well-being. Some people get stomach cramps or diarrhea when pressures increase at work; others complain of tension headaches or migraines when they are emotionally upset. Instances of somatization fall along a continuum from ordinary muscle tension after a difficult day to persistent physical symptoms that interfere with a happy and productive life. What this suggests is that mind and body are not distinct, separate entities, but that psychological state can and does exert significant influence over physical well-being, and vice versa, a point that has been made more subtly in most other chapters of this textbook.

A prominent focus on physical concerns is a core feature of SSD. This is another case in which *attempted answers*—individuals' efforts to deal with their symptoms—actually create the clinical disorder. Individuals spend a great deal of time worrying about their physical symptoms and/or engaging in problematic behaviors to find explanations for their problems or to "figure out" solutions to make their physical symptoms go away. Time spent focusing on alleviating symptoms and searching for answers takes them away from important areas of their life, which in effect causes even more distress and impairment in psychosocial functioning (Schoepf, Heun, Weiffenbach, Herrmann, & Maier, 2003).

It may be difficult to distinguish SSD from other mental disorders. For example, the diagnosis of **body dysmorphic disorder (BDD)** was conceptualized as a somatoform disorder in the *DSM-IV*, but is now grouped with *obsessive-compulsive and related disorders* (see Chapter 8) in the *DSM-5*. Some people might confuse BDD and somatic symptom disorder on the basis that they share a preoccupation with a physical concern. BDD is the preoccupation with an imagined or exaggerated *defect* in physical appearance, rather than pain or somatic symptoms that are feared to be related to an underlying illness. Also, approximately 75% of individuals who would have met criteria for **hypochondriasis**, or the excessive preoccupation or fear about having a serious illness based on a misinterpretation of bodily symptoms, in the *DSM-IV* would now receive a diagnosis of SSD if somatic symptoms were present (Sirri & Fava, 2013).

Because SSD is a new diagnostic category, prevalence rates are estimated from somatoform disorders in previous *DSM* editions and studies included in the field trials of the *DSM-5*. It is presumed that approximately 5–7% of the population meets criteria for SSD, with disproportionately higher rates in females, older adults, individuals with fewer years of education, and those who experience significant stressful life events (American Psychiatric Association, 2013a; Dimsdale et al., 2013). Estimates from two recent studies show prevalence rates of SSD ranging from 7.3% in a medically ill sample to 0.6% in a group of healthy individuals (Creed et al., 2012, 2013).

Illness Anxiety Disorder

Illness anxiety disorder (IAD) (see Table 11.3) is new to the *DSM-5* and is defined by persistent concerns about having or acquiring a serious illness without the presence of strong somatic symptoms (American Psychiatric Association, 2013a). IAD would subsume the other 25% of people formerly diagnosed with hypochondriasis in previous *DSMs* (Sirri & Fava, 2013). The key symptom of this disorder is a high level of health-related anxiety and a heightened sensitivity to personal health status. In a manner similar to somatic symptom disorder (SSD), individuals engage in excessive thoughts, feelings, or behaviors, but these actions are directly related to their health-related concern, not to a specific somatic symptom. In other words, people with IAD are not bothered by significant physical symptoms per se or trying to make the symptom go away (as people with SSD are), but rather, they are consumed with worry about the possibility that they have or will get a disease. Clinical examples of IAD include individuals so concerned that their slight headache is a sign of a brain tumor or that their fast heartbeat is a sign of an impending heart attack that they cannot work effectively or manage their interpersonal relationships.

In IAD, the specific illness that is feared may not always stay the same and can change over time (American Psychiatric Association, 2013a). In some cases, these unwarranted fears are limited to a certain organ or disease; in others, several illnesses are feared simultaneously. IAD fears never quite reach delusional proportions, which would be the case if individuals could never entertain the possibility that the feared illness was not present. Some people with IAD even realize their fears are exaggerated, but they still cannot control them. Others become frustrated with doctors and family members who do not take their complaints as seriously as they would like to have them taken.

IAD is now used instead of hypochondriasis because it is less pejorative and provides a category for individuals who experience significant health-related anxiety without the presence of significant somatic symptoms. Many clinicians believe that this change represents a welcome attempt to improve the diagnostic conceptualization of a disorder that has outgrown its ancient origins in the "hypochondrium," the upper part of the abdomen

hypochondriasis: A significant concern about personal health, especially when accompanied by delusions of physical disease.

illness anxiety disorder (IAD): A *DSM-5* disorder defined by persistent concerns about having or acquiring a serious illness without the presence of strong somatic symptoms.

MAPS - Prejudicial Pigeonholes

TABLE 11.3 The *DSM-5* in Simple Language: Diagnosing Illness Anxiety Disorder

Illness anxiety disorder is diagnosed when, for at least 6 months, individuals are preoccupied with having or getting a serious illness and experience both of the following:

- significant anxiety about their health, but without the presence of strongly distressing somatic symptoms, and
- repeated health-related behaviors (e.g., self-examinations, scheduling doctor visits, or avoiding doctors) aimed at relieving or decreasing their health-related anxiety.

Source: Adapted from American Psychiatric Association (2013a).

Somatic Disorders and Recent Diagnostic Controversies

Somatic disorders are at the heart of the diagnostic controversy of the recently published *DSM-5*. Many mental health experts have voiced concerns regarding the newly created diagnosis somatic symptom disorder (SSD) and its addition to the revamped category of somatic disorders. SSD was created, in part, for pragmatic reasons, rather than being informed by scientific research (Frances, 2013a). The *DSM* task force felt that it was practical to replace several rarely utilized somatization disorders with a broader singular disorder. In effect, SSD may function as a "catch-all" label, given to patients whose medical providers struggle to find an appropriate medical explanation for their physical complaints, including people with chronic fatigue syndrome and fibromyalgia.

Allen Frances, former chair of the *DSM-IV* task force and professor emeritus at Duke University School of Medicine, expressed his trepidation about how the broadly defined SSD "would mislabel millions of people as mentally ill when they are really just medically ill" (Frances, 2012). Dr. Frances also noted that, during the *DSM-5* field trials, one in six cancer and coronary heart disease patients also met criteria for SSD, and he fears that patients already struggling with serious primary medical conditions will be burdened by unnecessary psychiatric diagnoses. From a utilitarian perspective, it would be sensible to diagnose medical patients with SSD if and only if it would positively impact treatment and improve health outcomes. However, little is known about the cost-benefit comparison of diagnosing SSD versus other mental disorders, such as adjustment disorder (see Chapter 9), which could be less stigmatizing (Frances, 2013b).

What stigma is there in being diagnosed with SSD, and how might this impact the care that people receive from their medical providers? Will patients be prescribed unnecessary psychotropic medications? In fact, medications for somatic disorders have been shown to be only minimally effective—in part because

research is limited by a lack of conceptual clarity, diagnostic overlap with other disorders and conditions, and the absence of a theoretical or etiological basis for the disorders (Somashekar, Jainer, & Wuntakal, 2013).

Lastly, little is known about how this newly created disorder will impact primary care providers who are already burdened with managing psychological complaints. The limited availability of treatment outcome research for somatic disorders implicates multimodal treatment as being most effective, which requires a wealth of resources that might include evidence-based cognitive-behavioral therapy (CBT), medication, and case management, all integrated and delivered in the primary care setting. Will primary care providers be onboard? Some might contend that the aforementioned diagnostic and treatment obstacles existed prior to the updated version of the *DSM* and thus that the *DSM-5* task force is not imposing new risks or challenges, but Dr. Frances and others note that the *DSM-5* task force failed in its duty and responsibility to make decisions based on available scientific research and instead may have acted for the wrong reasons.

Thinking Critically

The *DSM-5* has sparked controversy regarding the changes it made to somatic disorders. Somatic symptom disorder in particular is a new disorder that is characteristically nonspecific and that risks overdiagnosing individuals with a mental disorder. Some important questions remain, such as:

1. What other factors should the *DSM* task force consider before changing diagnostic criteria?

2. What do you think of the new somatic disorders in the *DSM-5*? Given the nonspecificity of SSD and IAD, are these newly created disorders necessary, or can they be better explained by other mental disorders?

interior to the lowest ribs (Brakoulias, 2014). Use of the term *hypochondriasis* for a state of disease without a known biological cause reflects the ancient belief that the viscera of the hypochondria were the seat of melancholy and sources of the vapor that caused such morbid feelings. Some experts have praised the *DSM-5* because they believe that these new diagnoses (SSD and IAD) are likely to promote collaboration with other medical colleagues. According to these individuals, the descriptive nature of the diagnostic terms acknowledges that not all people react to somatic symptoms or to illness in the same way, and addressing psychological, social, and cultural influences is likely to improve outcomes (Brakoulias, 2014). As the "Controversy" feature describes, however, not all experts agree.

Behaviorally, individuals with IAD often engage in attempted answers, such as performing medical self-examinations, gathering information from various sources to self-diagnose (which is easy in today's information age), or seeking reassurance of good health. As in SSD, however, these individuals are not easily reassured. In light of negative diagnostic testing and ample reassurance from a doctor, individuals might continue to experience ongoing concerns about their health and continue searching for solutions that resolve their anxiety (much like people with compulsions in obsessive-compulsive disorder). Individuals suffering from IAD might also engage in actions that seem counterintuitive to dealing with their concerns, such as **behavioral avoidance** (e.g., missing doctor appointments, avoiding hospitals for fear of getting sicker, avoiding exercise)— activities that could increase the probability of good health but that are avoided because they elicit more anxiety or fear. Behavioral avoidance is characteristic of many anxiety disorders (discussed in Chapter 7) because it is a short-term solution, albeit a maladaptive one, for decreasing anxiety. Over time, the consequences of excessive worry and avoidant behavior actually serve to maintain the disorder, increase levels of health anxiety, and cause significant disruption in social relationships, occupational performance, and overall quality of life (Olatunji, Etzel, Tomarken, Ciesielski, & Deacon, 2011).

Prevalence estimates are based on rates of hypochondriasis as defined by previous editions of the *DSM* and suggest a range of 1–3% in community samples (American Psychiatric Association, 1994). Males and females show equal rates of clinical health concerns, and about one third to one half of individuals with IAD have a fleeting form, or less-severe illness anxiety disorder (American Psychiatric Association, 2013a). From its earlier conceptualization as hypochondriasis, IAD continues to be controversial, in that researchers question whether the disorder is truly unique or if it is simply a variation of another anxiety disorder (Olatunji, Deacon, Abramowitz, 2009). In fact, research has identified shared genetic profiles between anxiety and somatic syndromes (Gillespie, Zhu, Heath, Hickie, & Martin, 2000; Hickie, Kirk, & Martin, 1999; Kato, Sullivan, Evengård, & Pedersen, 2009), and some even consider hypochondriasis (now SSD or IAD) a personality disorder (Tyrer, Fowler-Dixon, Ferguson, & Kelemen, 1990), given its chronic and persistent course. Figure 11.1 illustrates

MAPS - Attempted Answers

behavioral avoidance: A pervasive pattern of avoiding or withdrawing from social interactions; a defense mechanism by which individuals remove themselves from unpleasant situations.

"I'm happy to see you, too."

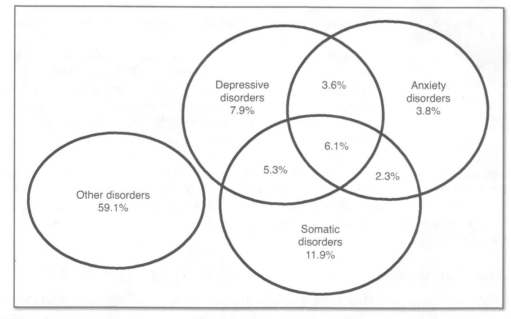

FIGURE 11.1 Percentages of Diagnoses and Mental Comorbidity of Somatic, Depressive, and Anxiety Disorders (Including OCD) in Primary Care

Prevalence rates of somatic, depressive, and anxiety disorders (including OCD) from a sample of 394 people across 18 primary care clinics in Germany. The comorbidity rate of depressive, anxiety (including OCD), and somatic disorders was 17.3%, whereas 13.7% of people who met a diagnosis for a somatic disorder also met a diagnosis for a depressive or anxiety disorder (including OCD) or both (Mergl et al., 2007).

TABLE 11.4 Examples of Dysfunctional Core Beliefs, Cognitions, and Behaviors Among Individuals With Anxiety

Mental Disorder	Beliefs	Cognitions	Behaviors
Obsessive-Compulsive Disorder	"If I have the thought, then it must be true."	"My hands are contaminated."	Wash hands repeatedly.
Panic Disorder	"My body is in danger."	"My heart is going too fast."	Take antianxiety medication.
Social Anxiety Disorder	"People think I'm stupid."	"I am sweating so much that people notice it."	Avoid raising hand in class.
Illness Anxiety Disorder	"Good health means being symptom-free."	"The pain in my neck is something very serious."	Plead with physician to take an MRI.

the rates of overlap among somatic disorders, anxiety disorders (including obsessive-compulsive disorder [OCD]), and depressive disorders. People are often diagnosed with two or more of these disorders, due to diagnostic and symptom overlap.

More recently, a cognitive-behavioral model has been used to better understand the relationships between IAD, OCD, and anxiety disorders. For example, IAD and OCD can both involve a pervasive and repetitive preoccupation with health and disease (Fallon, Qureshi, Laje, & Klein, 2000), and IAD and panic disorder both involve hypervigilance to bodily sensations. Furthermore, as shown in Table 11.4, dysfunctional beliefs precipitate disordered behaviors in many of these disorders. Similar to OCD, a fear of contracting an illness or disease in IAD is associated with increased anxiety and distress, followed by efforts to compulsively check or seek assurance about symptoms with the intention of reducing anxiety (Olatunji et al., 2009). Similarly, people suffering from social anxiety disorder overestimate the probability of being negatively evaluated. This then leads to increased anxiety and distress that is reduced by engaging in behavioral avoidance (Moitra, Herbert, & Forman, 2008). Many maladaptive behaviors associated with anxiety disorders, OCD, and somatic disorders function to alleviate or avoid aversive emotions or anxiety brought on by faulty beliefs or cognitions.

Despite these cognitive and behavioral similarities, however, IAD remains grouped with somatic symptom and related disorders. According to some researchers, the *DSM's* reliance on superficial similarities (e.g., concerns related to physical symptoms or health) to group IAD with the somatic symptom and related disorders obscures the important functional and causal mechanisms that IAD shares with anxiety disorders and OCD (Olatunji et al., 2009).

Source: Brian L. Burke.

MAPS - Superficial Syndromes

Even if this cactus were highly anxious (as indicated by the raised arms) about its physical symptoms, it would be classified as having a somatic symptom disorder, rather than an anxiety disorder. If the physical symptoms were significant, then SSD would be the diagnosis; otherwise, the cactus would be labelled with IAD.

Conversion Disorder (Functional Neurological Symptom Disorder)

conversion disorder: A *DSM-5* psychiatric disorder in which individuals experience problems with motor or sensory abilities that suggest a neurological impairment, but no recognized neurological condition exists to explain the symptoms; also called functional neurological symptom disorder.

In **conversion disorder** (see Table 11.5), individuals experience problems with motor or sensory abilities that suggest a neurological impairment, but no recognized neurological or organic condition exists to explain the symptoms (American Psychiatric Association, 2013a). As illustrated by Samantha in the chapter-opening case, these pseudoneurological symptoms usually develop suddenly after some stressful event or emotional episode, although this connection is generally not apparent to the person in distress. Three types of symptoms are common, and there may be more than one presenting symptom at a time:

TABLE 11.5 The *DSM-5* in Simple Language: Diagnosing Conversion Disorder

For a diagnosis of conversion disorder,

- individuals must have at least one altered voluntary motor or sensory function that causes them significant distress or dysfunction, and
- the altered function must be incompatible with a medical explanation for the symptoms.

Source: Adapted from American Psychiatric Association (2013a).

- *motor deficits*, such as difficulties swallowing, poor balance or coordination, paralysis or weakness of the arms or legs (as in Samantha's case), loss of the voice, or urinary retention;

- *sensory deficits*, such as the loss of sensation to touch or pain, double vision, blindness, or deafness; and/or

- *seizurelike* symptoms.

Although the symptoms of conversion disorder can be temporarily disabling, they differ from disabilities caused by actual neurological disorders. For example, in conversion disorder, the symptoms may come and go, depending on the activity the person is performing. A person might inadvertently use a "paralyzed" arm to get dressed or to scratch an itch ("Conversion Disorder," n.d.). Moreover, visual material influences the behavior of people with conversion blindness, even though they deny ever having seen that material (Bryant & McConkey, 1999).

Furthermore, many conversion symptoms make no anatomical sense because the complaint does not correspond to the body's sensory systems. An example of this is **glove anesthesia**, in which individuals experience a loss of sensation and sometimes paralysis only in their hand, despite the fact that the "wiring" of nerves in the area dictates that the paralysis should run the entire length of the arm and hand. It does not make anatomical sense for the numbness to stop at the wrist.

About one third of people displaying conversion disorders appear strangely indifferent to their symptoms, a nonchalant attitude known as *la belle indifference* (French for "beautiful indifference"). They may chat away about the problem without showing any serious concern over its potential adverse consequences or any viable signs of emotional distress. Freud suggested that such individuals are "unaware" of their anxiety because they suppress the aversive emotional energy that eventually manifests through physical pathways (Stone, 2006). Although there is little direct scientific support for Freud's explanation of the causes of conversion disorder, many believe that the disconnection between the temporary disability and the emotional response is a target for treatment. In contrast, people who malinger (see the next section) or who exaggerate symptoms to achieve secondary gain (external rewards) can be apprehensive about discussing their "symptoms" and remain on guard against being tripped up by an interviewer and having their ruse discovered. *La belle indifference* is not an official symptom of conversion disorder, but it is a common feature in presenting cases. However, most people with conversion disorder, like Samantha in the chapter-opening case, are in fact distressed by their symptoms (Stone, 2002).

The prevalence of conversion disorder in the U.S. general population is about 0.5%, but conversion disorder may

glove anesthesia: Loss of sensation in an area that would be covered by a glove (e.g., one's entire hand up to the wrist).

la belle indifference: A naive, inappropriate lack of emotion or concern for others' perceptions of one's disability; seen in people with conversion disorder.

A comedic illustration of the notion that individuals with conversion disorder do not have an organic neurological impairment but merely believe that they do is shown in the film *Talladega Nights: The Ballad of Ricky Bobby* (2006), starring Will Ferrell. After thinking he is paralyzed, despite no evidence of physical injury, race-car driver Ricky Bobby stabs himself in the leg to show his friends that he is not faking, and promptly begins walking (and jumping up and down while screaming very loudly!), shouting "I can walk" after the pain subsides.

Source: Franck Boston/Shutterstock.com.

account for up to 5% of referrals to neurology clinics (American Psychiatric Association, 2013a). Still, the incidence of this disorder has been declining over the past 100 years, a trend thought to be due to increased education and medical sophistication in the population. Conversion disorder symptoms often reflect how much the person knows about the human body. For instance, in the chapter-opening case, it was Samantha's sudden inability to walk in the absence of any evidence of spinal cord damage that suggested a conversion disorder. An older, more medically sophisticated person might experience just localized weakness, making it more difficult to rule out illnesses such as multiple sclerosis. Conversion disorder is observed more often among women, in rural populations, and in lower socioeconomic groups; and it is the somatic disorder most likely to affect children (American Psychiatric Association, 2013a; Tomasson, Kent, & Coryell, 1991).

With regard to the frequency of different types of conversion symptoms across cultures, relatively few variations are apparent (Brown & Lewis-Fernández, 2011). Loss of consciousness and/or psychogenic nonepileptic seizures (PNES) have been identified as the most frequent pseudoneurological problems in studies of conversion disorder from Turkey, India, and the Sultanate of Oman. In contrast, PNES were relatively rare in a small retrospective study of childhood conversion disorder from Japan; in this study, visual disturbance was the most frequent symptom, followed by motor paralysis. Motor disturbances, particularly paralyses and coordination disorders, were the most common conversion symptoms in the majority of other studies. Pure sensory disturbances, such as glove anesthesia, were relatively less common and broadly comparable across cultures.

The origins of these cross-cultural differences in symptom frequency are unclear at present (Brown & Lewis-Fernández, 2011). A number of possibilities might be considered, including the effects of different diagnostic practices, cultural variations in health service provision and consulting behavior, and/or local concerns about health and illness.

The course of conversion symptoms is typically short-lived. Most symptoms disappear, although in up to a quarter of cases, they recur. A recent longitudinal study documented better long-term adjustment among people who initially displayed conversion symptoms, compared to people with other somatic disorders. Those with conversion disorder reported a lower rate of divorce, fewer psychiatric symptoms, and better adjustment in terms of physical and mental health, and in carrying out their normal social roles (Kent, Tomasson, & Coryell, 1995).

MAPS - Prejudicial Pigeonholes

Factitious Disorder

factitious disorder: Pretending to have a physical illness or mental disorder, despite no obvious external rewards for having the disease.

feigning: To represent fictitiously; to put on an appearance of or to pretend.

malingering: The purposeful production of false or grossly exaggerated complaints with the goal of receiving a benefit that may include money, an insurance settlement, drugs, or the avoidance of punishment, work, jury duty, the military, or some other kind of service or attention.

Factitious disorder is defined by the intentional production or **feigning** of physical or psychological signs or symptoms in oneself or in other people. Factitious disorder is different from **malingering**, for which there is no formal *DSM-5* diagnosis, even though the two produce similar behaviors (faking sickness). Malingering is defined as the intentional production of false or grossly exaggerated physical or psychological symptoms, but the motivation for the behavior involves clearly identifiable external incentives. Examples of such incentives include attracting attention or sympathy, obtaining economic gain, or avoiding legal responsibility (as in the Bianchi case—see the "Controversy" feature in Chapter 10). In contrast, factitious disorder involves the absence of identifiable external reward; individuals fake illness for the sole purpose of assuming the "sick role" and cannot even articulate why they are doing it.

In factitious disorder (see Table 11.6), individuals may engage in pathological lying and provide medical staff with different versions of their chief complaint across visits. Although they may appear to hold a deep knowledge of their symptoms and medical history, the lack of positive results through medical testing and inconsistencies in their reporting across medical visits may make it clear that their presentation is psychologically based. When confronted with this explanation of their symptoms, individuals often refuse to accept this as a valid diagnosis and seek medical attention elsewhere (Krahn, Li, & O'Connor, 2003).

Factitious disorder imposed on another is a variation of the disorder in which individuals act as if someone in their care has a physical or psychological illness, even though that

TABLE 11.6 The *DSM-5* in Simple Language: Diagnosing Factitious Disorder

When imposed on oneself, factitious disorder involves:

- intentional production or feigning of physical or psychological symptoms in the absence of external rewards, and
- when symptoms are not better explained by a medical condition or another mental disorder.

When imposed on another, factitious disorder involves:

- intentional production or feigning of physical or psychological symptoms *in another person*, in the absence of external rewards,
- when symptoms are not better explained by a medical condition or another mental disorder, and
- when the person who evidences the symptoms does not receive the diagnosis.

Source: Adapted from American Psychiatric Association (2013a).

TABLE 11.7 Warning Signs of Factitious Disorder Imposed on Another (Munchausen's Syndrome by Proxy)

- The person is often a parent, usually a mother (although the proxy can be any adult).
- The parent welcomes medical tests of the child, even if the tests are very painful.
- The parent attempts to convince the staff that the patient is sicker than what is apparent.
- There are repeat hospitalizations and medical evaluations without a definite diagnosis.
- The worsening of symptoms is generally reported by the parent but is not evident in the child.
- The child's symptoms disappear when the child is away from the parent.
- The "illness" is prioritized above other things in the child's life, such as school and social relationships.

person is not actually sick. They engage in fabrication and lies so that the victim (often a child) is seen as being ill (Dye, Rondeau, Guido, Mason, & O'Brien, 2013). The diagnosis in these cases is given to the perpetrator rather than the victim, although victims often undergo needless medical testing and are easily manipulated by the person with the disorder (Cordess, 2001). Factitious disorder imposed on another is recognized in the popular media as **Munchausen's syndrome by proxy**, with warning signs listed in Table 11.7. The case of JC depicts a severe and unfortunate instance of this disorder (adapted from Boros & Brubaker, 1992):

Munchausen's syndrome by proxy (MSP): A type of factitious disorder in which people act as if an individual under their care has a physical or mental illness when the individual is not really sick; considered a form of abuse.

JC was a 3-year-old boy who suffered from asthma, severe pneumonia, mysterious infections, and sudden fevers. He was hospitalized 20 times during an 18-month period. Doctors were even concerned that he might have AIDS. However, they soon began to suspect that JC's mother might have caused the child's problems. When the boy complained to his mother's friend that his thigh was sore because "Mommy gave me shots," the authorities were called. Upon searching the residence, investigators seized medical charts and information and hypodermic needles.

JC's mother was a 24-year-old part-time fast-food restaurant worker. When she was 7 years old, her older sister had died of a brain tumor at a children's hospital. During her sister's prolonged illness, JC's mother, by necessity, had spent long periods of time at the hospital. Although this occurred long ago, JC's mother remembered the experience vividly.

During JC's many hospitalizations, his mother seemed almost obsessively involved in medical matters and hospital routines. She spent hours in the hospital library, reading medical texts. She had few friends outside the hospital. JC's father was a 24-year-old church janitor, afflicted with many health problems, the most notable being severe insulin-dependent diabetes. During JC's many hospitalizations, his father appeared distant and only marginally involved. JC's 7-year-old sister was in good health and was named after her mother's deceased sister. JC was removed from his home, assault charges were filed, and the case was taken to court.

Factitious disorder is categorized with somatic symptom and related disorders because most cases are seen in medical settings and because this disorder shows how psychological factors can influence physical symptoms. The deliberate feigning of symptoms may show dramatic improvement if a legal case is favorably settled. However, if attention is what is unknowingly sought, showing attention may solidify the symptoms, making them even stronger by rewarding them. Although epidemiological data on factitious disorder is limited, prevalence rates range from 0.03–9.3% (Kocalevent et al., 2005). A recent survey of outpatient physicians and consulting specialty physicians (e.g., neurologists, surgeons, internal medicine doctors) found that 1.3% of patients may suffer from factitious disorder (Fliege et al., 2007).

Psychological Factors Affecting Other Medical Conditions

Psychological factors affecting other medical conditions (see Table 11.8) is another newly created disorder that was formerly included in the *DSM-IV* section called "Other Conditions That May Be a Focus of Clinical Attention." This disorder was defined to identify individuals who show a clinically significant effect of psychological factors on a medical condition or conditions. To meet criteria for this disorder, a medical symptom or condition must be present. Also, psychological factors must negatively impact the medical problem in one or more of the following ways: through a temporal relationship, where psychological distress precedes the worsening of the medical illness; by interfering with treatment of the medical condition (e.g., the person does not take prescribed pills); and/or by having a clear negative effect on the underlying causes of the medical condition or substantially increasing the person's health risks (American Psychiatric Association, 2013a).

What distinguishes psychological factors affecting other medical conditions from other disorders, such as SSD, is that the problem behavior is not directly related to having somatic symptoms. For example, psychological factors affecting other medical conditions would be an appropriate diagnosis for cardiac patients who are overwhelmed with work stress and experience frequent heart palpitations and elevated blood pressure as a result, placing them at greater risk of experiencing another cardiac event. Conversely, a diagnosis of SSD would be more appropriate for cardiac patients who are highly anx-

"The hospital computer system has a virus. Ironic, isn't it?"

Source: Cartoonresource/Shutterstock.com.

TABLE 11.8 The *DSM-5* in Simple Language: Diagnosing Psychological Factors Affecting Other Medical Conditions

- Psychological factors, such as thoughts, emotions, or behaviors, significantly and negatively influence a concurrent medical or physical condition, or the treatment of that condition.
- Emphasis is on the medical condition, rather than on the psychological factors.

Source: Adapted from American Psychiatric Association (2013a).

ious and fear having another heart attack, and thus engage in excessive worry and blood pressure monitoring in response to their fears.

Section Review

Somatic symptom and related disorders share one major common feature: the prominence of somatic (physical) symptoms associated with significant distress and impairment. The category of disorders includes:

- somatic symptom disorder, in which one or more somatic symptoms cause distress or dysfunction;
- illness anxiety disorder, in which individuals are preoccupied with having or acquiring a serious illness, even though they do not have significant somatic complaints;
- conversion disorder (also called functional neurological symptom disorder), in which individuals suffer from neurological impairment (e.g., paralysis, blindness) without any associated medical findings to explain the deficits;
- factitious disorder, in which individuals feign illness in themselves or in someone for whom they are caretaker for no obvious external gains; and
- psychological factors affecting other medical conditions, in which psychological or behavioral dysfunction significantly affects the course of a medical disease.

Causes of Somatic Symptom and Related Disorders

Diathesis-Stress Model of Somatic Disorders

Although different causal factors have been emphasized for specific somatic disorders, once again, a **diathesis-stress model** provides the most useful framework for organizing these factors into a general explanation of somatic disorders. This model, shown in Figure 11.2, contains the following three elements:

- A predisposition to somatic disorders is conveyed by a combination of biological and psychological vulnerabilities, including genetic and neurological abnormalities, personality dispositions, hypersensitivity to physical sensations, and higher levels of negative emotions.

- One or more of the predisposing factors interact with long-term stressors or a severe trauma to increase the probability that individuals will experience physical symptoms associated with emotional arousal.

- The physical symptoms are likely to be interpreted and experienced as signs of an illness, rather than of a mental disorder, if sociocultural conditions support such interpretations, if the affected individuals lack sufficient medical knowledge, or if the environment provides reinforcement for this interpretation.

diathesis-stress model: A model that explains how a mental disorder can result from the interaction of a predisposition (diathesis) for a disorder with a trigger (stressor) that converts the predisposition into the actual disorder.

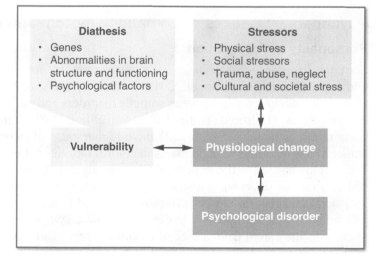

FIGURE 11.2
Diathesis-Stress Model of Somatic Disorders

We now consider the evidence pertaining to each biopsychosocial element of this diathesis-stress model.

Charles Darwin (1809–1882), the British naturalist and scientist most famous for his theory of evolution, likely suffered from what today would be called a somatic symptom disorder. Darwin experienced a great amount of stress and complained of somatic symptoms, including stomach problems, headaches, vomiting, and heart symptoms. He also took to his bed after his wife gave birth to his children. Other famous people who have suffered from somatic symptom disorders include fairy-tale author Hans Christian Andersen, who wrote the stories upon which *Frozen* and *The Little Mermaid* are based; artist Andy Warhol, who died because his fear of hospitals prevented him from seeking medical attention for his gallbladder problems until it was too late; and dictator Adolf Hitler, who was prescribed various medicines for all kinds of ailments, both real and imagined (Forde, 2011).

Biological Causes of Somatic Symptom and Related Disorders

Twin and family studies are used to estimate heritability of genetic factors, and findings suggest that somatic symptom and related disorders run in families (Gillespie et al., 2000). For example, 10–20% of first-degree female relatives of individuals with SSD also have the disorder (Guze, 1993). A recent study estimates the heritability of dimensions of health anxiety at 10–35% (Taylor, Thordarson, Jang, & Asmundson, 2006). These low heritability rates suggest the dominant role that environmental factors play in such anxiety.

The fact that conversion disorders cluster within families might be due to neurological abnormalities that constitute a vulnerability to these disorders. Several studies have demonstrated patterns of brain activity suggesting that conversion involves a cortical inhibitory mechanism that disrupts conscious awareness (Harvey, Stanton, & David, 2006; Sierra & Berrios, 2000). The brain-imaging evidence has been interpreted to mean that somatosensory information continues to be processed at lower levels in such cases, but that inhibition by parietal and prefrontal structures disrupts the link between mechanisms that generate the intent for movement and those responsible for its execution (Athwal, Halligan, Fink, Marshall, & Frackowiak, 2001). In other words, individuals with conversion disorder may be able to produce motor or sensory changes that "bypass" conscious awareness.

Neuroimaging studies of people experiencing somatic distress in general suggest differences in regional and localized brain functioning during emotional tasks, compared to controls, and specifically diminished modulation of activity in the bilateral parahippocampal gyrus and left amygdala, among other areas (de Greck et al., 2012). Furthermore, functional magnetic resonance imaging (fMRI) and positron emission topography (PET) have implicated differences in prefrontal and right parietal region activity in the genesis of somatic symptoms (Hakala, Vahlberg, Niemi, & Karlsson, 2006). Brain research on somatic disorders is in its infancy, though, and future research will likely uncover more specific areas of the brain associated with these disorders.

Psychosocial Causes of Somatic Symptom and Related Disorders

Personality and Cognition

Somatic disorders have been linked to neurocircuitry involved in emotional awareness and expression (de Greck et al., 2012; Wood, Williams, & Kalyani, 2009). Studies have also shown a relationship between somatic disorders and personality disorders (Bornstein & Gold, 2008; Hollifield, Tuttle, Paine, & Kellner, 1999; Starcević, 1990). For instance, male relatives of people with SSD have higher rates of personality disorders and substance abuse disorders than do males in control families (Massachusetts General Hospital, 2008). This has led to the hypothesis that people diagnosed with SSD or personality disorders share an underlying disturbance. For example, impulsivity may lead to recurrent antisocial and risk-taking behaviors in some individuals, resulting in elevated negative emotionality and a propensity to develop somatic symptoms (Lilienfeld, 1992). Somatic symptoms may stem from a lack of emotional processing in those with avoidant personality disorder, primitive defenses for childhood abuse in those with borderline personality disorder, and attention seeking in those with histrionic personality disorder (Bornstein & Gold, 2008).

A personality trait known as **negative affectivity** might also be implicated. People high in negative affectivity tend to worry, be pessimistic, fear uncertainty, feel guilty, tire easily, have poor self-esteem, and be shy and depressed (Gray, 1981). When combined with physiological sensitivity, negative affectivity may enhance the likelihood that people will make unduly negative attributions about benign (harmless) bodily sensations on which they are constantly focused; in a sense, their worries may be "specialized" to the area of health (Lecci, Karoly, Ruehlman, & Lanyon, 1996). Greater negative affectivity, as well as impulsivity or "novelty seeking," predicts increased severity of somatization (Russo, Katon, Sullivan, Clark, & Buchwald, 1994). Thus, when people who are high on negative affectivity become overly concerned about bodily sensations, they may find it difficult to restrain repeated urges to seek medical care—which makes their symptoms worse—if they are also relatively impulsive and seek excitement.

Furthermore, those with somatic disorders are hypersensitive to physical sensations, meaning that they perceive normal bodily sensations as more intense and disturbing than others do. People with SSD, for instance, have a lower threshold for physical discomfort, compared to controls (Barsky, 1989). What accounts for this pain amplification is still unknown. One possibility is that there is an interplay between biological (pain reception), psychological (e.g., depression, anxiety, attention to threat bias), and social (e.g., life stressors, interpersonal relationships) factors.

The psychological contribution to pain amplification may stem from a greater sensitivity to and fear of one's anxious symptoms, similar to panic disorder. Anxiety sensitivity (AS), discussed in Chapter 7, is the fear of anxiety sensations and their believed negative consequences. Cognitive theories suggest that AS might pertain to not just fears of anxiety, but may extend to a broader catastrophic style concerning bodily symptoms and may be a common factor in somatization (Tsao et al., 2009). Such **catastrophizing** may influence physiological reactivity and produce higher levels of physical discomfort, as people distort real or even imagined disasters out of proportion (Knaus, 2008). For example, if a professor asks to speak to several students after class, students who are catastrophizers might spend the entire class thinking they have done something wrong or that they are failing the class. Similarly, individuals with a pain condition might report that their pain is always 10/10 on a severity rating scale, even though physical presentation and behavior are not consistent with that intensity. Put differently, things hurt more when you worry about the worst-case scenario all the time.

The Role of Stress and Trauma

Historically, psychoanalytic theorists have viewed somatization as a way of deflecting strong emotions. Because conversion disorder, in particular, has long been viewed as a way to express repressed conflicts, many clinicians have speculated that this condition and other somatic disorders are triggered by a personal conflict or stressor. In other words, a person's psychological distress might be expressed instead in the form of bodily impairment. For instance, in the chapter-opening case, Samantha's unexpressed anxiety about switching to a new, bigger middle school may have been what fueled her leg paralysis. In the late 1800s, when Freud used the term *conversion* to refer to the substitution of physical symptoms for repressed negative emotions, he became one of the first clinicians to link physical symptoms with a history of trauma or conflict (Tomasson et al., 1991). In fact, one of Freud's earliest recorded cases, Anna O., suffered from conversion disorder (then called *hysteria*), which was reportedly treated successfully via psychotherapy. Modern research supports the notion that people who have difficulty processing their emotions or representing them mentally are more vulnerable to such disorders, as Freud first surmised (Stonnington, Locke, Hsu, Ritenbaugh, & Lane, 2013).

Associated with the view of somatization as deflected emotions is the hypothesis that adults who experience clinically elevated somatic symptoms are more likely to have been

Connections
What other elements of personality disorders might make people who have them more susceptible to somatic disorders? See Chapter 16.

negative affectivity: The experience of negative emotions and poor self-concept; includes a variety of negative emotions, such as anger, disgust, guilt, fear, and anxiety.

catastrophizing: An exaggerated and irrational style of thought in which individuals assume the worst and may blow situations out of proportion.

One of Freud's earliest cases in 1895 (more recently published as Freud & Breuer, 2004) was a 21-year-old he called Anna O.:

Her illness lasted for over 2 years, and in the course of it she developed a series of physical and psychological disturbances which decidedly deserved to be taken seriously. She suffered from a rigid paralysis, accompanied by loss of sensation, of both extremities on the right side of her body. Her eye movements were disturbed and her power of vision was subject to numerous restrictions. . . . In regard to the patient's disturbances of vision, they were traced back to occasions such as one on which, when she was sitting by her father's bedside with tears in her eyes, he suddenly asked her what time it was. She could not see clearly; she made a great effort, and brought her watch near to her eyes. She tried hard to suppress her tears so that the sick man should not see them. Another time, Anna was sitting at the bedside with her right arm over the back of her chair. She fell into a waking dream and saw a black snake coming towards the sick man from the wall to bite him. She tried to keep the snake off, but it was as though she was paralyzed. Her right arm, over the back of the chair, had gone to sleep. When Anna O. had recollected this scene in hypnosis, the rigid paralysis of her arm disappeared, and the treatment was brought to an end.

abused as children. Because preschoolers typically lack the verbal and cognitive abilities necessary to understand and express their emotions, physical symptoms might be one vehicle available to them for conveying their emotional distress. As noted in Chapter 10, another vehicle might be the dissociation from their own identity or consciousness that could lead to a dissociative disorder. Early instances of trauma-triggered somatization might make it more likely that individuals will display emotional upsets via physical symptoms later in life. In fact, physical symptoms are highly common during stressful events, such as people "freezing" and being unable to act (see Chapter 9's chapter-opening case) or going numb during trauma. This has been termed *somatoform dissociation* and is a manifestation of inborn psychobiological animal defensive reactions to protect us from or blunt the harm (Nijenhuis, 2009).

But is there evidence to support an association between somatization and childhood abuse? In one study, the early sexual experiences of 60 women diagnosed with SSD were compared with 31 women diagnosed with a mood disorder (Morrison, 1989). The two groups did not differ in terms of early voluntary sexual experiences, but the women with SSD were more than three times as likely to report having been sexually molested; the average age at the time of this abuse was 10 years. Another study found that individuals with exposure to medically ill parents (a trauma for young children) during childhood were more likely to experience somatization and somatic symptom behaviors in adulthood (Craig, Cox, & Klein, 2002). Moreover, nearly 70% of people who were receiving treatment for chronic oral-facial pain reported that they had suffered sexual or physical abuse (Curran et al., 1995). A large review of the scientific literature on the relationship between childhood abuse and health problems concluded that adult survivors of such abuse experience more health problems and more painful symptoms than those with no abuse history (Sachs-Ericsson, Cromer, Hernandez, & Kendall-Tackett, 2009). As you are beginning to see, abuse makes almost every disorder in this textbook more likely.

In addition to childhood trauma, other stressful life events often immediately precipitate the experience of somatic symptoms, including the onset of clinically elevated symptoms. The nature of the relationship between stressful life events and mental disorders has been well documented for depression (Kendler, Karkowski, & Prescott, 1999; You & Conner, 2009) and anxiety disorders (Rueter, Scaramella, Wallace, & Conger, 1999). Research examining the causal relationships between stressful life events and specific somatic disorders is limited. However, conversion disorder has been associated with a complex array of early and later negative life events (Roelofs, Spinhoven, Sandijck, Moene, & Hoogduin, 2005).

The Role of Culture

That the prevalence of somatic disorders varies considerably among different cultures points to the importance of sociocultural factors (Canino, Bird, Rubio-Stipec, & Bravo, 1997; Noyes, Stuart, Watson, & Langbehn, 2006). In general, somatic disorders are more prevalent in cultures that discourage open discussion of psychological problems and that stigmatize mental disorders (Kirmayer & Young, 1998). Not surprisingly, physical symptoms might take on special significance in these cultures because they provide an acceptable way for individuals to communicate their unhappiness or distress. Furthermore, somatization is influenced by demographic variables, such as low education and economic level, rural residence, and minority ethnicity (Kirmayer & Young, 1998; Noyes et al., 2006). Numerous studies have also shown that immigrants experience more stressful life events and somatic distress than members of native populations, due to the challenges associated with cross-cultural transitions (Ritsner, Ponizovsky, Kurs, & Modai, 2000).

The similarity between conversion disorder and some specific cultural syndromes is also noteworthy. For example, symptoms such as unexplained amnesia, blindness, fainting, paralysis, convulsions, loss of consciousness, weakness, and dizziness characterize some *ataques de nervios* (e.g., Laria & Lewis-Fernández, 2001), which were first seen in Hispanic culture, although they can occur in anyone. In general, some researchers consider that the high number of somatic complaints found in Hispanics, as reported in cross-cultural studies, may be a function of client-physician language barriers, financially limited access to health care, and medically unidentified cultural syndromes (Bravo & Roca, 2013). Thus, reliable, well-validated, and carefully translated measures should be used and administered by culturally sensitive clinicians, who are mindful about idioms of distress, culture-bound syndromes, and cultural differences (Bravo & Roca, 2013).

Connections

What other mental disorders are related to *ataques de nervios*? See Chapters 7 and 10.

Another cultural consideration regarding somatic disorders involves groups of people with specialized knowledge, such as medical students or people studying abnormal psychology (like you!). Medical students who study frightening diseases for the first time routinely develop vivid delusions of having the "disease of the week"—whatever they are currently studying. This temporary kind of somatic disorder is so common that it has acquired the name *medical student syndrome* (Baars, 2001). What about the analog for psychology students? No evidence has been obtained to support *psychology student syndrome* overall; however, a positive correlation was found between neuroticism and psychological health anxiety. In other words, readers of this textbook who are high in neuroticism may be at a higher risk for diagnosing themselves with psychological problems (Deo & Lymburner, 2011). Furthermore, students planning to major in psychology report more worry about their psychological health than those planning to major in some other field (Hardy & Calhoun, 1997). Although the process of learning about various psychological disorders decreases students' anxiety about their own mental health, it increases their anxiety about the mental health of family members. On a brighter note, after completing coursework in abnormal psychology, students are more willing to seek help from campus mental health services for their personal psychological distress (Hardy & Calhoun, 1997).

Maintenance of Somatic Symptoms

Once somatic symptoms are present, they are likely to be maintained or strengthened if they are reinforced by social or cultural factors in the environment. Individuals experiencing clinically significant somatic symptoms may learn from their families that illness is a legitimate way to garner attention, to avoid stressful responsibilities, or to express otherwise unacceptable negative feelings (Fordyce, 1976). These consequences are sometimes referred to as **secondary gain**. So, for example, pain behavior can be learned as a result of inadvertent reinforcement by health-care providers who attempt repeated medical interventions and by family members and friends who offer sympathy and assistance (Romano et al., 1992). A behavioral model of reinforcement has been influential in understanding how the social environment maintains somatic symptoms and complaints (Patterson, 2005).

secondary gain: External rewards, including interpersonal or social advantages, gained indirectly from an illness.

For children, parents are the ones who have the most influence on the consequences of somatic complaints. For example, they can give their children extra treats or relieve them of chores—responses referred to as *parental solicitousness* (Peterson & Palermo, 2004). Although the notion that reinforcement enhances somatic symptoms makes conceptual sense, several studies have found no evidence that parental solicitousness causes an increase in children's and adolescents' somatic complaints (Jellesma, Rieffe, Terwogt, & Westenberg, 2008). However, parental solicitousness is associated with parents' *perceptions* of their children's somatic complaints (Peterson & Palermo, 2004). And there are other processes within the family that might influence children's reports of somatic complaints, such as modeling and overprotection (Garralda, 1996).

The diathesis-stress model can be used as a framework to understand the role of bio-psychosocial factors in the development and course of somatic disorders. Interacting components of the model include biological (genes), psychological (personality disorders, negative affect, difficulty expressing emotion), and social (abuse or life stress) factors that contribute to the development and maintenance of disorder.

Data are limited on the relative contributions of genetic and biological factors in somatic disorders; however, available research findings suggest that:

- somatic disorders run in families; however, it is unclear if the disorders are inherited through genetic or learned pathways; and
- somatic disorders are associated with specific differences in regional brain activity.

In terms of psychosocial causes of somatic disorders, research shows that:

- individuals diagnosed with somatic disorders are more likely to have personality disorders and negative affectivity;
- people with somatic disorders may experience physiological symptoms differently and show a greater sensitivity to both somatic and anxiety symptoms;
- childhood abuse and stress have been linked with somatic disorders, as has greater sensitivity to somatic symptoms such as pain; and
- somatic symptoms and related behavior can be maintained by environmental and cultural factors that reinforce (or reward) specific behaviors or symptoms.

Treatment of Somatic Symptom and Related Disorders

Psychosocial Interventions

The most highly researched, effective, and commonly used therapy for somatic symptom and related disorders is cognitive-behavioral therapy (CBT; Kroenke, 2007; Tazaki & Landlaw, 2006). The goals of CBT for somatic symptom and related disorders include: (1) developing a collaborative and supportive therapeutic relationship, (2) identifying maladaptive thoughts or cognitive errors associated with individuals' somatic symptoms, and (3) modifying unhealthy behaviors that function to maintain the disorder, which may include learning new coping strategies to respond in a more healthy manner to somatic cues and/or stress, as well as using biofeedback therapy aimed at teaching individuals how to voluntarily control some of their physiological processes (e.g., heart rate).

For instance, CBT for somatic symptom disorder (SSD) or illness anxiety disorder (IAD) is designed to help individuals develop and evaluate an alternative understanding of their problems. This understanding focuses on how misinterpretations of health-related information (mainly bodily variations and medical information) lead to a pattern of responses, including anxiety, distorted patterns of attention, safety-seeking behaviors, and physiological arousal. These responses, in turn, account for individuals' patterns of symptoms and functional impairment.

CBT is accomplished through two avenues: (1) cognitive, which has the purpose of making sense of individuals' experiences but ultimately getting them to correct the misperception of their physical symptoms as catastrophic (signs of illness); and (2) behavioral, including active evaluation of the mechanisms involved through collaboratively designed behavioral experiments. Specifically, the behavioral component of CBT for SSD or IAD could include exposure and response prevention (Visser & Bouman, 2001), just as treatment for obsessive-compulsive disorder (OCD) does. For example, individuals with IAD and concerns about contracting HIV due to public toilet seats could begin to use public restrooms more frequently and, after doing so, reduce their previous safety behaviors of taking a 30-minute extremely hot shower. Over repeated trials, individuals' anxiety will lessen, and they will reduce their life-interfering attempted answers/compulsions of taking scalding hot showers after every trip to a public restroom.

Overall findings from a meta-analysis suggest that psychotherapy is effective in treating somatic disorders—more effective than usual treatment for physical symptoms and functional impairment, but not necessarily (or only slightly) for psychological symptoms (Koelen et al., 2014). More recently, "third-wave" behavioral therapies, which emphasize the use of acceptance and mindfulness-based strategies over symptom-control–based strategies, have gained attention as viable treatments for somatic disorders (Eilenberg, Kronstrand, Fink, & Frostholm, 2013; Fjorback et al., 2013). Mindfulness-based stress reduction is effective at reducing chronic pain (Sturgeon, 2014), for example, although it may be differentially effective across populations. A recent longitudinal study noted greater improvements in pain, health-related quality of life, and psychological well-being for back or neck pain than in fibromyalgia, chronic migraine, or headache (Rosenzweig et al., 2010). For conversion disorder, hypnosis, mindfulness, and behavioral interventions are often combined with supportive psychotherapy to help patients overcome physical symptoms and cope with triggering stressors (Allin, Streeruwitz, & Curtis, 2005).

Other forms of psychotherapy that have been used to treat somatic disorders include psychodynamic therapies, humanistic therapies, and integrative therapies. In a meta-analysis of psychodynamic therapies only, treatment yielded significant or possible effects on physical symptoms (91.3% of the studies), psychological symptoms (91.6%), social-occupational function (76.2%), and health-care utilization (77.8%; Abbass, Kisely, & Kroenke, 2009). Another recent meta-analysis reviewed treatment outcome studies for medically unexplained physical symptoms (MUPS) and somatic disorders and found that only CBT had been adequately studied and outperformed treatment as usual (van Dessel et al., 2014). Compared with usual care or waiting list conditions, CBT reduced somatic symptoms, with a small effect lasting up to a year and substantial differences in effects among CBT studies (van Dessel et al., 2014).

Pharmacological Treatments

According to a meta-analytic review, researchers have tried many classes of psychotropic drugs—ranging from antidepressants and herbal medications (St. John's wort) to antipsychotics and anticonvulsants—to find an effective treatment for somatic disorders, resulting in lack of specificity (Somashekar et al., 2013). The selection of a drug or a particular class of drugs in trials has not been based on clear rationales, which does little to guide clinicians in selecting the right drug for a given person (Somashekar et al., 2013).

The use of antidepressants is the most common and effective medical approach to treating somatic disorders and MUPS (Somashekar et al., 2013). This type of medication includes several classes, including tricyclic antidepressants and selective serotonin reuptake inhibitors (SSRIs), described in detail in Chapter 6. Preliminary evidence suggests that, for various somatic disorders, antidepressants may be beneficial through the reduction of comorbid symptoms, including depressive and anxious symptoms, but not through direct reductions in somatic symptoms (Kroenke, 2007). For hypochondriasis (now called SSD or IAD), paroxetine (Paxil, an SSRI) performed as well as CBT, with both interventions effective through 18 months of follow-up (Greeven et al., 2009).

Treatments for somatic disorders with predominant pain usually take place in a medical setting and combine behavioral interventions, other psychotherapy, and pharmacotherapy. The drugs used most often in those cases are antidepressants (again), as well as nonsteroidal anti-inflammatory drugs (NSAIDs), such as aspirin. From a therapeutic class perspective, fibromyalgia patients received antidepressants (46%), anticonvulsants (35%), pain therapies such as NSAIDs (25%), muscle relaxants (8%), and sleep agents (2%; Dussias, Kalali, & Staud, 2010). Unfortunately, none of these medications works well for more chronic or long-term pain (Turk, 2002).

Primary Care Behavioral Health: Integrated Care

Since most people seek help and medical explanations for somatic complaints from their primary care medical provider, many experts believe that the best strategy is to prepare

Connections

How do antidepressant drugs actually work? See Chapter 6.

MAPS - Medical Myths

physicians and psychologists to work with these patients within the general medical care system (Katon, 1993; Samuels, 1995). To reduce "doctor shopping" and constant help seeking, a **behavioral health consultant (BHC)**—a mental health provider trained to work in an integrated care medical setting—may be designated to facilitate the patient's care. In this way, the patient can receive care from a specialist in mental health who works closely with the medical team. Each visit might include a brief physical exam, but tests and medications should be ordered only if necessary. The BHC might also teach the patient alternative ways of communicating emotional needs and coping with stress, while simultaneously providing support and encouragement.

It is important to note that a medical model still predominates in the current understanding of somatic disorders. The *DSM-5* has continued to use the disease perspective in its attempt to explain somatic symptoms, through creating categories of disorders, despite limited theoretical or empirical justification. The medical model works quite well for many biological illnesses that have well-defined characteristics, but it is problematic for psychological conditions. For example, "strep throat" or streptococcal infection is a common illness brought on by a bacterial infection, and a simple swab of the infected area allows physicians to identify it. However, as Paris (2013) put it, advances in neuroscience have not succeeded in explaining *any* mental disorder.

Thus, clinical observation and consensus from experts, rather than hard facts, are still the guiding forces behind the *DSM*. These problems are even more apparent when it comes to somatic disorders, where the current *DSM-5* taxonomy poses inherent problems for the psychosomatic clinician, due to its lack of diagnostic validity and reliability in identifying these disorders (Fink, Rosendal, & Olesen, 2005). Therefore, not only is there an urgent need for an empirically derived classification system of disorders that incorporates psychological, social, and cultural factors, but there is also a need for the integration of properly trained psychologists and psychiatrists who can support medical providers through application of their knowledge and expertise in diagnosing and treating somatic disorders (Fink et al., 2005). Therein lies the bourgeoning movement termed *integrated care*, which has already taken root at many Veteran's Administration (VA) hospitals and other facilities around the United States, as well as worldwide, as discussed in the "Prevention" feature.

Section Review

Various psychological and pharmacological treatments are used to treat somatic symptom and related disorders, with small, though significant, effectiveness. To date, a review of available literature suggests that:

- cognitive-behavioral therapy is the treatment of choice for most cases of somatic symptom disorders,
- antidepressant medications help to decrease the symptoms of anxiety and depression that often co-occur with somatic disorders, and
- primary care behavioral health (and integrated care) is the optimal model of treatment that appears to be most efficient and helpful for people with somatic disorders.

Primary Care Behavioral Health

Generalized somatic complaints comprise a large percentage of primary care visits, and a significant subset of these complaints is related to behavioral health issues (Katon, Ries, & Kleinman, 1984). Typical somatic complaints include various types of pain (back, head, abdominal), functional deficits (insomnia, fatigue, sexual function issues, appetite issues), or abnormal symptoms (tingling or numbness, weakness in a limb, breathing difficulties; Kroenke, 1992). Patients present to primary care physicians first for these symptoms, often because of their interpretation of the symptoms as primarily medically related and/or because obtaining an appointment with their primary care provider, who is often a known and trusted entity, is easier and necessitates less effort than making an appointment with a specialty mental health provider.

Because somatic complaints can legitimately arise from a variety of medical and psychological conditions, a primary care provider is likely to do a thorough medical evaluation, possibly including laboratory tests, a physical exam, screening instruments (e.g., a patient health questionnaire for depression), and an interview. If medically related conditions are ruled out, the primary care provider considers behavioral or mental health factors as either causes of the somatic complaints or mitigating factors. For example, a person presenting with headaches may be encountering work stress or depression, and could benefit from relaxation or problem-solving strategies. Some somatic complaints may not be caused by mental health concerns but may be impacted by the person's behaviors nonetheless. For example, another patient with headaches may have a legitimate migraine disorder, but triggers such as stress and diet can impact outcomes; therefore, addressing these behavioral issues is an important part of the medical treatment (Serrano, 2013).

There are no known published guidelines at this time for the prevention of somatic symptom or related disorders or medically unexplained symptoms (MUPS) that cause significant psychological distress. However, the key to prevention is identifying people who might be prone to somatic disorders within primary care settings. A recent 5-year randomized controlled trial tested the effectiveness of a prevention program for somatic disorders delivered in several primary care health centers in Spain (García-Campayo, Arevalo, Claraco, Alda, & Lopez del Hoyo, 2010). The researchers delivered a

Neftali Serrano, PsyD., is chief behavioral health officer at Access Community Health Centers in Madison, Wisconsin, as well as associate clinical professor in the Department of Family Medicine at the University of Wisconsin–Madison. He is on the cusp of the movement toward integrated care.

manualized intervention program based on psychoeducational and cognitive-behavioral techniques. The intervention consisted of five 120-minute group sessions led by a primary care physician and mental health provider. Group sessions educated patients on the differences between physical symptoms and diseases, patient and family doctor roles, and the use of a self-help book based on cognitive and behavioral strategies to deal with somatic disorders. The intervention was successful, but in surprising ways. The researchers found that their intervention decreased symptoms of somatic symptom disorder and illness anxiety disorder even 5 years later, yet prevalence rates of the diagnoses did not change. Despite this fact, the patients reported decreases in depression and anxiety, and improvements in overall general health.

Because somatic concerns and general mental health issues present with such great frequency in primary care, integrated care—that is, the integration of mental health professionals (or behavior health consultants [BHCs]) in primary care—is an emerging model used to augment and support the work of primary care providers (Serrano, 2013). BHCs work with patients in the same exam room where they are seen by the primary care provider, helping patients to develop strategies for improving their health, while also providing support for primary care providers (Hunter, Goodie, Oordt, & Dobmeyer, 2009).

James Pennebaker

Dr. James Pennebaker is Regents Centennial Professor, Department of Psychology, University of Texas at Austin. His work has focused on how people can effectively cope with the emotional consequences of trauma and on the benefits of writing about trauma, or as he calls it, "putting our feelings into words." A pioneer of writing therapy, he has researched the link between language and recovering from trauma and has been recognized by the American Psychological Association as one of the top researchers on trauma, disclosure, and health. In particular, Pennebaker finds that a person's use of "low-level words," such as pronouns and articles, is predictive of recovery as well as indicative of sex, age, and personality traits: "Virtually no one in psychology has realized that low-level words can give clues to large-scale behaviors." His research has clearly shown the connection between mind (psychological distress) and body (physical health behaviors), which is of great relevance to the somatic disorders discussed in this chapter.

Q *Is Selye's general adaptation syndrome (GAS; Chapter 9) an accurate description of stress reactions?*

A Selye's GAS is still a very useful description of the stress process. However, I think Selye, and many stress researchers since, neglected one important aspect of stress and that is what happens when a stressor stops. Too little attention has been paid to "stressor offset." I have noticed in my research that, very often, people do not break down or become sick until after the stressor ends. For example, remember the American hostages who had been held in Iran for over a year? When they were released, most of them were in reasonably good physical health, but when they returned home, a lot of them got sick. The same pattern holds for college students. They make it through final exam week without

becoming ill, but as soon as vacation starts, they come down with something. Is there a physical and psychological letdown after the stressor is over that leaves people more susceptible to sickness? Or do people become so used to the stressor that, when it is finally over, the change feels like a new stressor?

Q *What is the key to effectively coping with a stressor?*

A I think the key is for persons to put their emotional life into words somehow so that they both acknowledge the emotions they are feeling and begin to coherently understand these emotions. Denial works sometimes, especially in the short run, as a coping strategy, but with major stressors, the person who focuses on his or her deepest thoughts and feelings and consequently understands them better will cope more effectively.

Q *Is writing about feelings more effective than talking to someone about them?*

A Either method can be effective as long as the person actually does it. One advantage that writing has over talking is that writing does not require an audience. When we talk to someone about our troubles, we usually notice that person's reactions, and if we are socially sensitive at all, we may begin to alter what we say so as not to upset or bore the listener. As a result, talking may not allow as deep a processing of our feelings as writing, unless we are lucky enough to have someone to talk to who is a very good listener.

Q *Do certain kinds of people benefit more than others from writing about their traumas?*

A My research suggests that about 60% of all people who write about a personally meaningful trauma derive physical and psychological benefits from it. People who are highly repressed and therefore think it is silly to write about personal feelings do not usually benefit. Those who tend to be helped the most by writing about their feelings are those for whom the trauma is still psychologically active; that is, they are still living with the emotions about the stressor.

Q *What are some of the health effects of using disclosure to cope with stress or trauma?*

A When people are asked to write about an emotional upheaval in their lives for as little as 15–20 minutes for 3–4 consecutive days, a number of health changes have been reported by labs all over the world. This expressive writing exercise has been found to reduce the rate of physician visits for colds and flu for up to

James Pennebaker (Continued)

3 months. Other projects with people suffering from chronic disease find improvements in immune function, blood pressure, white blood cell count among people with AIDS, increased range of movement for people with arthritis, faster wound healing following surgery, and many other positive health effects. Health improvements have been found among people of all ages and across cultures and languages. In other words, as you have stated in this chapter, mind and body are intimately connected—that is, psychological processing is beneficial for physical health and symptoms.

Q What are the most important questions that stress researchers should address in the future?

A I can think of at least four areas that will be exciting to study. First, we need to study the nature of language itself so that we can learn what it is about writing or speaking that can be therapeutic for people. Second, we are witnessing an explosion in biotechnology. We need to harness this technology to learn how the different systems in the body change in real-life situations. Third, most major stressors are interpersonal in nature; they involve arguments between friends, breakups in relationships, or deaths of loved ones. As a result, we need to understand the social dynamics of stressors much better than we currently do. Finally, we need to broaden our research perspectives by focusing on cultural shifts and differences as influences on stress. Early childhood experiences clearly influence people's needs, emotions, and thoughts. I suspect that the cultures in which these experiences are embedded are far more important than we currently give them credit for being.

Revisiting the Case of Samantha

Samantha from the chapter-opening case is an example of someone with conversion disorder who initially sought help from her medical provider, which is commonplace for individuals with somatic disorders. Samantha's symptoms included the inability to move her legs, although many different motor and sensory symptoms may be salient in the presentation of conversion disorder. Samantha's problem received immediate attention from her family and comprehensive care from her medical team.

Samantha's primary care physician ran diagnostic tests to rule out medical or neurological deficits. Fortunately, her doctor had a sufficient understanding of somatic disorders to correctly diagnose Samantha with conversion disorder and refer her for psychological treatment. Samantha participated in a multimodal treatment package, consisting of physical rehabilitation and group psychotherapy, where she was able to gradually express and cope with her negative emotions that she had not shared with her family. She admitted being intensely afraid of leaving her small school to attend the regional middle school—a move that she was scheduled to make at the end of her summer break. At first, Samantha was afraid to try walking, but she was soon doing better each day. By the time she was discharged from the hospital, Samantha was completely mobile and expressed a more positive outlook toward her new school. Further, her family now had a more complete understanding of what gave rise to Samantha's symptoms.

Samantha's case illustrates the importance of having an integrated medical team with an understanding of and appreciation for the relationship between psychological factors and physical health. Without this, Samantha might have continued to go through needless and potentially painful medical testing without finding any symptom relief.

Summary

Somatic Symptom and Related Disorders

Somatic symptom and related disorders involve medically unexplained somatic symptoms or health-related anxiety. Mental health professionals are challenged to estimate the relative contributions of psychological causes to somatic symptoms and the contributions of other causal factors, such as medical illnesses or other mental disorders. Illness anxiety disorder is distinguishable from somatic symptom disorder by the presence of health-related anxiety in the absence of strong somatic symptoms. Conversion disorder involves problems with motor or sensory abilities that suggest a neurological impairment, but clinical data suggest that no recognized neurological or organic condition exists to explain the symptoms. Factitious disorder refers to the feigning of physical or psychological symptoms without obvious external reward. Psychological factors affecting other medical conditions can be diagnosed when a medical condition is negatively impacted by psychological symptoms.

Causes of Somatic Symptom and Related Disorders

Applied to somatic disorders, the diathesis-stress model shows that physical or psychological vulnerabilities interact with various kinds of stressors to produce an increase in and preoccupation with physical symptoms. Genetics may predispose an individual to these biological and psychological vulnerabilities, which may interact with environmental factors that give rise to and maintain somatic disorders. Psychological predispositions can include personality traits (e.g., negative affectivity) or disorders, along with a heightened sensitivity to personal anxiety or physical symptoms.

Moreover, evidence suggests that stressful triggering events, such as abuse, might play a role in the onset of somatic disorders, although the precise link between stress and somatic disorder has yet to be explained. Culture may also play an important part, as somatic disorder patterns differ among people from different cultures. Environmental and cultural factors may actually help maintain disordered behaviors through the availability and delivery of secondary gains (external rewards).

Treatment of Somatic Symptom and Related Disorders

Available interventions for somatic disorders include pharmacological and psychosocial treatments. Antidepressants and NSAIDs are among the most frequently used pharmacological treatments. Cognitive-behavioral therapy is the most effective treatment overall, although outcomes sometimes show only small improvements. Because most people with somatic complaints present to primary care settings first, integrated primary care behavioral health is an important delivery model to optimize treatment for people with somatic disorders.

Key Terms

behavioral avoidance, p. 369

behavioral health consultant (BHC), p. 382

body dysmorphic disorder (BDD), p. 366

Briquet's syndrome, p. 365

catastrophizing, p. 377

conversion disorder, p. 370

diathesis-stress model, p. 375

factitious disorder, p. 372

feigning, p. 372

glove anesthesia, p. 371

hypochondriasis, p. 367

illness anxiety disorder (IAD), p. 367

la belle indifference, p. 371

malingering, p. 372

medically unexplained physical symptoms (MUPS), p. 364

Munchausen's syndrome by proxy (MSP), p. 373

negative affectivity, p. 377

secondary gain, p. 379

somatic symptom and related disorders, p. 364

somatic symptom disorder (SSD), p. 366

somatization, p. 364

somatoform disorders, p. 364

Eating, Feeding, and Sleep-Wake Disorders

Source: Aakov Filimonov/Shutterstock.com.

Chapter Outline

Eating Disorders

Sleep-Wake Disorders

From the Case of Emily

Emily, a 17-year-old who was recently treated in one of the authors' clinics, frequently complained of "looking dumpy" and "feeling fat," despite being well below the average weight for her age and height. Before developing an eating disorder, Emily recalled that normal satiety cues (feeling full just after eating) led to extremely self-deprecating thoughts, such as "I'm fat and ugly," along with feelings of guilt. "Eating made me feel like a bad person, as if I had done something wrong," she said. Emily also shared that her swim coach at school would often make comments to other girls on the team about their weight and clearly favored the thinner girls. Consequently, Emily began to refuse all foods except rice cakes and pickles. She also began to exercise at least 90 minutes per day in addition to swim practice, often doing sit-ups compulsively in her bedroom at night. Shortly before her parents brought her to the clinic, this 5'3" tall young woman weighed only about 80 pounds. Although Emily said she felt healthy at this weight, she still believed that her legs and ankles were "too thick," and she attributed her "fatness" to a lack of self-control. "I still thought I could stand to lose a few pounds; I just needed to try harder," Emily confessed. Emily also said that she constantly thought about food.

After reading this chapter, you will be able to answer the following key questions:

■ What are the characteristics of anorexia nervosa, bulimia nervosa, and binge-eating disorder?

■ What are the potential causes of eating disorders?

■ How are eating disorders treated?

■ What are the characteristics of other eating and feeding disorders, such as pica and avoidant/restrictive food intake disorder?

■ What are the main types of sleep-wake disorders?

Emily began avoiding friends and social gatherings, worried that food would be offered. "At first, I would tell my friends or family that I had already eaten, or that I wasn't feeling well, to avoid having to eat anything," Emily said. After a while, however, Emily said it became increasingly difficult for her to get out of eating without people becoming suspicious, so she began avoiding the situations altogether.

Not only was Emily obsessed with thoughts surrounding food, she was consumed by weighing herself multiple times a day:

> Every morning, the first thing I would do was step on the scale. If I had lost any weight from the day before, I felt happy, like I had accomplished something great. But that just drove me to want to eat even less to keep up the weight loss. If I had gained any weight, even a half-pound, I felt horrible about myself and was convinced that the weight gain was obvious on my body.

Emily also stopped getting her monthly period, which she took as a sign that she was finally getting close to her ideal weight. She entered treatment with little insight into the severity of her condition and expressed minimal interest in changing her eating habits.

To be at your best, your basic human needs must be adequately met. Perhaps you have taken an exam when hungry or given a presentation when sleep deprived. Such tasks become harder and your performance usually suffers when you are not well rested. Being preoccupied with food and feeling tired can affect your mood, concentration, memory, family and social interactions, ability to cope with stress, and physiological health, among other important areas of functioning.

The disorders in this chapter involve dysfunctions in the basic human processes of eating and sleep. We first address the characteristics, causes, and treatment of the three most prevalent eating disorders: anorexia nervosa, bulimia nervosa, and binge-eating disorder. We also describe pica and avoidant/restrictive food intake disorder, two other eating and feeding disorders that clinicians encounter, especially when working with children. We conclude by discussing the process of sleep and how the sleep-wake cycle can become disordered.

Eating Disorders

Anorexia Nervosa

Clinical Description

anorexia nervosa: A disorder whose main characteristics are an unreasonable fear of gaining weight, disturbances in the perception of one's body shape or size, and the relentless pursuit of thinness, leading to significantly low body weight.

Unreasonable fear of gaining weight, disturbances in the perception of one's body shape or size, and the relentless pursuit of thinness, no matter what the consequences, are the main characteristics of **anorexia nervosa**. Affected individuals insist on keeping their weight below a normal level. Some are obsessed with food, despite their reluctance to eat it, devoting enormous amounts of time to reading about food or cooking large amounts of it for others. Anorexia is a serious disorder that sometimes requires hospitalization. Severe malnutrition, skin disease, and even death are some of its possible consequences. In fact, anorexia has the highest mortality rate of any psychiatric illness (Arcelus, Mitchell, Wales, & Nielsen, 2011) and a mortality rate six times higher than that of the general population (Papadopoulos, Ekbom, Brandt, & Ekselius, 2009).

body mass index (BMI): A measure that uses weight and height to identify individuals who may be at risk for weight-related health problems.

Individuals with anorexia nervosa have a significantly low body weight, defined as a weight that is less than minimally normal or less than minimally expected (American Psychiatric Association, 2013a). Clinicians rely on a calculation of **body mass index (BMI)** to determine weight minimums (see Figure 12.1). Individuals are deemed below minimal weight expectations when their BMI is 18.5 or less. For example, a 5-foot, 4-inch-tall woman who is below 108 pounds would not meet the minimum weight expectation for her height. Over the course of their illness, most individuals with anorexia will lose 25–30% of their body weight (Hsu, 1990). Children and adolescents with anorexia may not

Body Mass Index

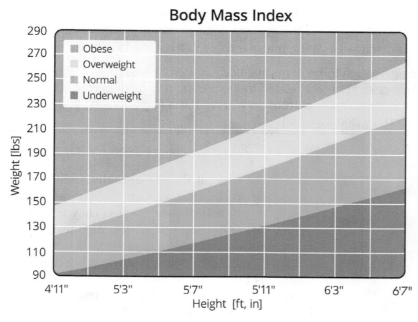

FIGURE 12.1 Body Mass Index (BMI)

A BMI in the lower right area of the diagram may suggest a diagnosis of anorexia.

Source: Zerbor/Shutterstock.com.

lose weight but, rather, fail to make expected weight gains while still growing in height. A loss of appetite for individuals with anorexia is rare.

Some individuals with anorexia try to reduce their weight by extreme dieting, fasting, excessive exercise, or a combination of all three strategies. This subtype of anorexia nervosa is called the **restricting type**. Individuals with this subtype of anorexia often begin by excluding high-calorie foods and progress to an extremely limited diet. Some individuals with this subtype spend hours a day exercising, even when ill or injured (Peñas-Lledó, Vaz Leal, & Waller, 2002).

In the **binge-eating/purging type** of anorexia, binge eating may be followed by purging, which involves self-induced vomiting or misuse of laxatives, diuretics, or enemas in an effort to prevent ingested food from adding to body weight. Sometimes, even small amounts of food are purged (Stoving et al., 2012). Note that this is diagnosed as anorexia, rather than bulimia (discussed later in the chapter), even if purging is occurring, as long as the person is below the minimally expected body weight. It is not uncommon for individuals to show crossover between the two anorexia subtypes over the course of the disorder, as well as to experience episodes of both anorexia and bulimia throughout their lifespan (American Psychiatric Association, 2013a).

Individuals with anorexia also have an intense fear of gaining weight or becoming fat, or they may take measures to prevent weight gain, even though they are already underweight. They may have a fear of losing control over their eating and view weight gain as an unacceptable loss of self-control (Svenaeus, 2013). Ironically, fear of weight gain often increases as a person loses more weight (Zanetti, Santonastaso, Sgaravatti, Degortes, & Favaro, 2013).

Typically, those with anorexia have extremely distorted images of their bodies, or they deny the seriousness of their low body weight. The chapter-opening case about Emily illustrates this point. Emily believed she could never be quite thin enough. Even though other people might perceive them

anorexia nervosa, restricting type: A subtype of anorexia in which an individual tries to reduce weight by extreme dieting, fasting, and/or excessive exercise.

anorexia nervosa, binge-eating/purging type: A subtype of anorexia in which an individual vomits or misuses laxatives, diuretics, or enemas after eating.

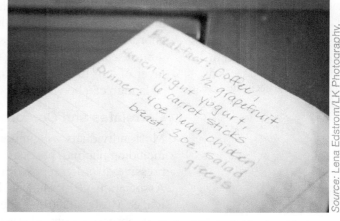

Daily food intake is severely limited for individuals with the restricting type of anorexia nervosa.

Source: Lena Edstrom/LK Photography.

TABLE 12.1 The *DSM-5* in Simple Language: Diagnosing Anorexia Nervosa

Anorexia is a disorder of eating that involves EACH of the following three criteria:

1. Not eating enough to be of normal body weight for your age, height, and sex
2. Persistent anxiety or fear related to the prospect of gaining weight
3. Misperceptions of your current body shape/size (e.g., thinking you are "fat" even though you are underweight)

Source: Adapted from American Psychiatric Association (2013a).

Source: Brian L. Burke.

MAPS - Superficial Syndromes
Saguaro cacti could be "diagnosed" with anorexia, based on superficially observable characteristics of low body weight and malnutrition.

as looking emaciated and unhealthy, individuals with anorexia are preoccupied with any sign of fat, no matter how small, on any part of their bodies. They may weigh themselves frequently throughout the day, use tape measures to gauge the size of various parts of their body, or spend a great deal of time in front of a mirror checking for "problem areas," as Emily did.

While anorexia is diagnosed in females 10 times more often than in males (Button, Aldridge, & Palmer, 2008), men can also struggle with this disorder. Some researchers have argued that the current diagnostic criteria do not capture the kinds of body image concerns that are often found among men with disordered eating (Jones & Morgan, 2010). For example, some men may experience great body dissatisfaction while striving for low body fat or specific musculature, strength, and exercise goals. Such men would not be diagnosed with anorexia because their body weight is not low enough to meet the current diagnostic criteria.

Anorexia should not be confused with the tendency to be extremely weight conscious or overly concerned about caloric intake and exercise. Thinness alone, or wanting to be thin, is insufficient to diagnose anorexia. All the symptoms in Table 12.1 must be observed. With that in mind, people who experience significant distress or impairment stemming from symptoms of an eating disorder—even if they do not meet all diagnostic criteria—may still benefit from treatment.

Medical Complications

Without essential nutrition, the body's ability to function is severely compromised. Cardiovascular complications as a result of starvation can lead to sudden death (Jauregui-Garrido & Jauregui-Lobera, 2012). Kidney failure can result from severe dehydration. Many women with anorexia will experience **amenorrhea**, the absence of menstruation due to their low body weight. This can lead to increased susceptibility to osteoporosis, a disease marked by dry, brittle bones that can easily break. Other medical complications of anorexia include muscle loss and weakness, fatigue, sensitivity to cold temperatures, acne, gum disease, and dry hair, skin, and nails. Some individuals develop **lanugo**, a downy layer of hair that grows all over the body, including the neck and face. The development of lanugo can be viewed as the body's way to stay warm when body fat is depleted.

amenorrhea: The absence of menstruation.

lanugo: A downy layer of hair that grows on the body, including the neck and face.

Correlates and Comorbidity

Most individuals with anorexia nervosa also meet criteria for other psychiatric disorders, including phobias, obsessive-compulsive disorder, posttraumatic stress disorder, major depressive disorder, bipolar disorder, and/or substance use disorders (American Psychiatric Association, 2013; Hudson, Hiripi, Pope, & Kessler, 2007; Kaye, Bulik, Thornton, Barbarich, & Masters, 2004). Other research has shown higher rates of anorexia among women with obsessive-compulsive personality disorder, a disorder marked by perfectionism, control, and rigid adherence to rules (Reas, Ro, Karterud, Hummelen, & Pedersen, 2013). As noted, individuals with anorexia also may have a history of bulimia, an eating disorder described in the next section. Suicide is not uncommon among individuals with anorexia. A recent study showed an eightfold increase in risk for suicide among patients being treated for anorexia compared to those without the disorder (Suokas et al., 2014). In many cases, the onset of eating problems is preceded by a stressful event, such as the birth of a sibling, peer teasing about body weight, or separation from or loss of a parent (Pike et al., 2008).

Some researchers have tried to identify subtypes of anorexia based on personality features. Lavender and colleagues (2013) provide support for three subtypes: underregulated, overregulated, and low psychopathology. The underregulated subtype characterizes individuals with anorexia who are more prone to self-harm, negative affect, risk taking, and impulsivity, while the overregulated subtype describes individuals who display more perfectionism and compulsivity. Those with low psychopathology show less comorbidity with other psychiatric disorders and do not have the personality features of the other two subtypes. Looking for personality distinctions among clients with anorexia may inform our understanding of how this eating disorder is best treated, as described later in the chapter.

An intriguing study conducted in Germany (Brockmeyer et al., 2012) suggests that starvation with low body weight helps to regulate negative emotions among individuals with anorexia. In other words, individuals may starve themselves as a way to manage difficult feelings. Such findings highlight the importance of teaching healthy coping strategies to individuals with anorexia and anyone who may be at risk for the disorder.

MAPS - Attempted Answers

Bulimia Nervosa

When I was in middle school, I liked my body. But when I was 15, I started to get some curves. I remember I gained 8 pounds from the year before. I guess you could tell on my frame because a boy in my class told me that everyone was talking about how I was getting fat. I decided to go on a diet. I kept track of my calories and tried to eat less than 900 each day. It was so hard. I had heard about people who ate whatever they wanted and then threw it up. I was determined to try, and I found that purging wasn't hard to do. Before long, I was bingeing and purging most days a week. I used to binge when I was sure my parents had gone to sleep. I'd eat whatever soft and sweet foods I could find, usually ice cream or pastries. I got very good at quickly making cookie dough, and I'd eat it raw. Sometimes, I ate food I didn't really like that much, like stale bread with cheese. I'd quietly take any empty food boxes or wrappers and put them in the garbage cans in the garage, where I knew my parents wouldn't find them. I'd get so full my stomach would hurt, and I'd feel hot and sick. Then I'd throw it all up while I flushed the toilet and turned the water on in the sink to hide any noise. I'd feel relief that the food was out of me but horribly ashamed because I knew I had a problem.

—*Brittany, age 17*

Clinical Description

The eating disorder known as **bulimia nervosa** is characterized by recurrent binge eating, in which large quantities of food are consumed in one sitting, followed by compensatory behaviors to prevent weight gain. Compensatory behaviors include vomiting, fasting, excessive exercise, and use of laxatives, diuretics, or other medications after binge eating. Unlike anorexics, individuals with bulimia tend to be of normal weight or even somewhat overweight.

People with bulimia nervosa—primarily young women—believe that they cannot control their eating. Their anxiety and remorse after binge eating are relieved somewhat by purging. Unfortunately, purging usually brings about even stronger feelings of shame and disgust, and the individual with bulimia is caught in a downward spiral of emotional distress. Often, binge eating occurs in an attempt to cope with the emotional aftermath

bulimia nervosa: An eating disorder characterized by recurrent binge eating in which large quantities of food are consumed in one sitting, followed by purging or other efforts to prevent weight gain.

TABLE 12.2 The *DSM-5* in Simple Language: Diagnosing Bulimia

Bulimia is a disorder of eating in which a person is overconcerned about her or his body shape/size, along with the following two other symptoms occurring weekly or more for 3+ months:

1. Episodes of binge eating, which means eating more than usual in a short period of time without having control over your eating
2. Compensatory behaviors to prevent weight gain (e.g., self-induced vomiting; misuse of laxatives, diuretics, or other medications; not eating; or exercising too much)

Source: Adapted from American Psychiatric Association (2013a).

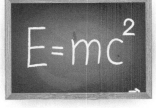

MAPS - Attempted Answers

of purging, but it leads only to more purging. This pattern can accelerate to the point that bulimic individuals may spend the majority of their days locked in binge-purge cycles.

The reduction of anxiety brought about by purging may help maintain the act of purging through negative reinforcement. In other words, when purging helps individuals feel immediately better (albeit briefly), they are more likely to continue the behavior, despite the eventual negative consequences.

The *DSM-5* criteria for the diagnosis of bulimia are listed in Table 12.2. Within an hour or two, individuals with bulimia eat an amount of food that most people would not consume in similar circumstances. Usually, they choose foods they would otherwise avoid: fast food, cake, cookies, ice cream, doughnuts, pudding, and breads, for example. During the binge, they feel like their eating is uncontrollable, with some individuals describing the experience as a "feeding frenzy." Usually, the binge occurs in secret, and individuals attempt to hide what they have consumed by disposing of wrappers or other evidence of the binge. However, there are anecdotal reports of college women engaging in group binges, followed by inappropriate compensatory behaviors.

After bingeing, many individuals report feeling an overwhelming sense of shame, guilt, and embarrassment, as well as worry about weight gain from the binge. They often feel painfully full. The majority of individuals with bulimia purge what they have consumed by vomiting. Vomiting in and of itself is an inefficient way to eliminate calories, reducing just one-third to one-half of calories consumed. Diuretics and laxatives also do not undo the caloric consequences of bingeing (Mehler, 2011; Roerig, Steffen, Mitchell, & Zunker, 2010). Men are more likely to purge via excessive exercise (Weltzin et al., 2005). While bingeing and purging must occur about once a week over the course of 3 months for bulimia to be diagnosed, some individuals may binge and purge multiple times per day.

As is seen in anorexia, body shape or weight is inextricably tied to self-esteem among individuals with bulimia. They may vow to diet after a binge-purge cycle, restrict their food intake, and avoid "fattening foods," only to succumb to an episode of binge eating. Purging follows, and the vicious cycle repeats itself.

Medical Complications

Recurrent binges and compensatory behaviors can cause a host of medical problems, including disruptions of the body's ability to detect fullness and satiety. While the weight loss associated with anorexia can be readily noticed by friends and family, many individuals with bulimia can hide their disorder. As a consequence,

Source: Zoran Karapancev/Shutterstock.com.

Lady Gaga (see mannequin photo), Kerry Washington, Paula Abdul, and Katie Couric have all spoken publicly about their struggles with bulimia to draw awareness to this serious disorder.

they may have the disorder for a longer period of time before starting treatment, and the medical complications associated with bulimia have a longer time to take their toll.

In fact, individuals with bulimia may not seek treatment for their eating disorder, but rather seek care from health professionals for a specific medical complication stemming from bulimia (Mond, Myers, Crosby, Hay, & Mitchell, 2010). Salivary glands can become enlarged from recurrent vomiting, which can give the face a puffy appearance. Gastrointestinal problems and fatigue are commonly reported (Mond et al., 2010). Electrolyte imbalances caused by vomiting can lead to serious complications, including kidney failure and heart irregularities (Brown & Mehler, 2013). Dentists may be in a unique position to identify individuals with bulimia, as the stomach acid released during vomiting can cause serious problems to the teeth and gums, including tooth decay, erosion to tooth enamel, and gum disease (Mehler, 2011; Romanos, Javed, Romanos, & Williams, 2012).

Correlates and Comorbidity

As with anorexia nervosa, individuals with bulimia often experience other psychiatric disorders, including bipolar and depressive disorders (American Psychiatric Association, 2013a). Hudson and colleagues (2007) found that nearly 95% of individuals meeting criteria for bulimia also had another mental disorder: Phobias, posttraumatic stress disorder, major depressive disorder, and substance use disorders co-occurred with bulimia most frequently. Women with borderline personality disorder may have an increased risk for bulimia nervosa (Reas et al., 2013). Impulsiveness and hyperarousal also have been linked to individuals with bulimia (Merlotti et al., 2013), as has a greater reactivity to stress (Peterson et al., 2010). Suokas and colleagues (2014) found that the suicide risk for patients being treated for bulimia was five times higher compared to those without the disorder. As with anorexia, bulimia is often preceded by stressful life events.

Binge-Eating Disorder

Clinical Description

In May 2013, the American Psychiatric Association included **binge-eating disorder (BED)** in its update to the *DSM*. This disorder is marked by recurrent binge eating, but in contrast to bulimia, a person with BED does not use inappropriate strategies such as vomiting, excessive exercise, diuretics, or laxatives to compensate for binge eating. The majority of individuals who seek treatment for BED are overweight or obese (American Psychiatric Association, 2013a).

binge-eating disorder (BED): An eating disorder characterized by recurrent episodes of eating unusually large quantities of food.

However, just because someone is overweight or obese does not mean they have binge-eating disorder. A multitude of factors, including genes and family history, health conditions, medications, work schedules, and lack of access to healthy foods, contribute to being overweight.

Some researchers have questioned BED for the same reason that they question many other new disorders in the *DSM-5*—the criteria describe symptoms that are fairly common and should be classified as a disorder only with caution (Paris, 2013). As with bulimia, individuals with BED engage in a binge and experience a loss of control over what and how much they are eating. They may binge when they are not hungry or until they are painfully full. They may eat more rapidly than usual when bingeing. As with bulimia, individuals with BED usually try to hide their binges. They may dine alone and dispose of food packaging that would suggest a binge. Their behavior causes them a great deal of distress.

MAPS - Prejudicial Pigeonholes

I used to visit the drive-thrus at Taco Bell and McDonald's before pulling into a parking spot and eating by myself in the car. I sensed the people who parked next to me were making fun of me. I felt ashamed and embarrassed, but I still did this four or five times per week.

—*Mark, age 36*

We live in a culture obsessed with food.

People would not be diagnosed with BED if they binge-eat as part of a culturally sanctioned event, like this pie-eating contest in Durango, Colorado.

Medical Complications

The weight gain that often accompanies BED can lead to a variety of long-term health consequences. Being overweight can tax most of our major organs and increase risk for heart disease, diabetes, high blood pressure and cholesterol, stroke, liver and gall bladder disease, and some forms of cancer (National Eating Disorders Association, n.d., "Health Consequences of Eating Disorders;" Office of the Surgeon General, 2001). BED may cause or exacerbate any of these conditions, and it is associated with increased usage of health care (Wonderlich, Gordon, Mitchell, Crosby, & Engel, 2009).

Correlates and Comorbidity

Research studies on BED are still in their infancy, but the field is learning more about this disorder with each passing year. Grilo and colleagues (2009) found that nearly 75% of their sample of individuals with BED experienced another psychiatric disorder at some point in their lives, including substance use, mood, and anxiety disorders. This finding is mirrored by that of Hudson and colleagues (2007), who found almost 80% of their sample to have another psychiatric diagnosis. A study by Grucza, Przybeck, & Cloninger (2007) found that individuals with BED showed higher rates of panic attacks, generalized anxiety disorder, prior suicide attempts, and depression; conversely, individuals who were obese but did not display BED did not report these concerns as often. Davis and colleagues (2008) found that individuals with BED showed more emotionally driven eating and more eating in response to environmental cues compared to those without BED. In terms of personality variables, individuals with BED may be more harm-avoidant and cautious than those without BED (Peterson et al., 2010).

Section Review

The three most common eating disorders are:

- anorexia nervosa, characterized by an unreasonable fear of gaining weight, disturbances in the perception of one's body shape or size, and the relentless pursuit of thinness leading to significantly low body weight (whether by restricting or purging or both);
- bulimia nervosa, characterized by recurrent binge eating of large quantities of food, followed by purging or other efforts to prevent weight gain; and
- binge-eating disorder (BED), which involves recurrent episodes of eating unusually large quantities of food.

Eating Disorder Statistics

The lifetime prevalence of anorexia nervosa among women living in the United States is estimated to be just under 1.0%; for men, the estimate is 0.3% (Hudson et al., 2007); see the "Controversy" feature "Are Eating Disorders Underreported in Men?". Whereas most studies show that rates of anorexia are lower among women from minority subgroups, a 2011 study suggests that rates of anorexia are similar among non-Latino white, African-American, Latina, and Asian women (Marques et al., 2011). Anorexia is more common in wealthier, industrialized countries (e.g., the United States, many European countries, New Zealand, and Japan; American Psychiatric Association, 2013a). Yet, while the prevalence of anorexia is lower in non-Western countries, it appears to be increasing (Makino, Tsuboi, & Dennerstein, 2004). Most cases of anorexia begin during adolescence and young adulthood (American Psychiatric Association, 2013a). A large-scale survey of eating disorders among the U.S. population found the average (median) age of onset for anorexia is about age 18 (Hudson et al., 2007), although symptoms may appear much earlier.

Are Eating Disorders Underreported in Men?

Men have eating disorders, too, and they have throughout history. In fact, one of the first clinical descriptions of a male with anorexia was written by 17th-century physician Richard Morton. Many researchers argue that males with eating disorders are underdiagnosed and undertreated (Strother, Lemberg, Stanford, & Turberville, 2014).

Eating disorders among men have been overlooked for a variety of reasons, including a historical belief tying eating disorders to postpartum concerns, psychoanalytic theorizing that eating disorders are caused by repression of female sexuality (e.g., anorexia as a fear of "oral impregnation"), and the former usage of amenorrhea (the absence of menstruation) as a diagnostic criterion for the disorder (Anderson, 2014). A preponderance of research studies that include only female participants has helped to maintain the lack of focus on males with eating disorders. One man trying to change this is comedian and actor Russell Brand, who has spoken openly about his struggle with eating disorders during his teenage years.

Whereas there is a great deal of overlap across genders in terms of the causes, course, and outcomes associated with eating disorders, important differences remain. Many men with eating disorders desire thinness but also value other body types, including the lean, muscular, celebrity-airbrushed standard, especially in the upper body (Anderson, 2014). Gueguen et al. (2012) have found that men (compared to women) with anorexia are older when they seek treatment, are less likely to have attempted suicide, and are more likely to have been overweight prior to their eating disorder. There is evidence that homosexual men have increased rates of eating disorders compared to heterosexual men (Russell & Keel, 2002).

In one of the only studies of its kind, Weltzin and colleagues (2014) studied 111 men in a male-only residential treatment program for eating disorders. The majority of men reported a history of excessive exercise. Eighty percent of the sample had another psychiatric disorder, most often a depressive disorder. Anxiety disorders and substance use disorders were also reported. Over the course of treatment, the men's weight was restored, and eating disordered behaviors, as well as depression and anxiety symptoms, decreased. The study's authors note that group psychotherapy that includes only men is critically important to the treatment process, as men are allowed to express emotions without judgment and discuss their disorder without experiencing additional shame that they have a "female problem." Weltzin's findings thus suggest that men benefit from all-male treatment centers, where the stigma surrounding their disorder is minimized.

Thinking Critically

As noted in Chapter 2, the scientific method has an important role to play in resolving controversies about abnormal behavior. It provides public, agreed-upon procedures for engaging in *critical thinking* about a dispute. You can use the seven steps to critical thinking discussed in Chapter 1 to examine the issue and ask yourself the following questions:

1. How do sociocultural factors play a role in the development and diagnosis of eating disorders in men?

2. Which sports and activities do you think might contribute to the development of eating disorders in men?

3. Why is it important for researchers to make sure to include different demographics in their study samples (e.g., participants of different genders, ethnicities, and ages)?

The lifetime prevalence of bulimia nervosa is higher than that of anorexia. Estimates suggest that 1.5% of women and 0.5% of men living in the United States will experience bulimia at some point in their lives (Hudson et al., 2007). Marques and colleagues (2011) found rates of bulimia in the United States to be higher among African Americans and Latinos, compared to non-Latino whites and Asians. They also found lifetime rates of bulimia among Latino men to be significantly higher than non-Latino white men. Most cases of bulimia begin during adolescence and young adulthood (American Psychiatric Association, 2013a), with the average age of onset also being about 18 years old (Hudson et al., 2007).

The gender gap narrows in BED, with 3.5% of women and 2.0% of men experiencing this disorder at some point in their lives (Hudson et al., 2007). Rates of BED appear similar across non-Latino whites, Latinos, Asians, and African Americans, although little cross-cultural data on BED is currently available. As with anorexia and bulimia, BED is believed to typically begin in adolescence and young adulthood, but it can also occur in later adulthood (American Psychiatric Association, 2013a).

Causes of Eating Disorders

While a variety of causal factors for eating disorders have been proposed, most researchers agree that there is no single pathway. Rather, there are multiple risk factors. In many cases, the more risk factors individuals have, the greater the likelihood that they will develop an eating disorder. As discussed in Chapter 2, psychological vulnerabilities, biological factors, and sociocultural factors are often identified as playing causal roles in the development of eating disorders.

Psychological Factors

For years, many theorists held a psychoanalytic interpretation of anorexia as a "flight from adult sexuality," in which the individual equates food and eating with "forbidden sexual objects and activities" (Wilson, 1988). Today, a more psychodynamic conceptualization focuses on the role of attachment in the etiology of eating disorders. For example, a child with an insecure attachment to his or her caregivers would have difficulty forming attachments later in life and might be at risk for psychological problems (see Chapter 3), including eating disorders. A recent study examined the efficacy of psychodynamic group therapy for women with binge-eating disorder (Maxwell, Tasca, Ritchie, Balfour, & Bissada, 2014). Conceptualizing binge eating as a form of maladaptive coping that stems from unmet attachment needs and interpersonal conflict, the therapy group focused on teaching clients healthier ways to relate to others. Clients sought to alter long-standing relational patterns and to find adaptive ways to get their attachment needs met. Twelve months after completing the group, the participants reported less anxiety and less avoidance regarding attachments, fewer interpersonal problems, and fewer depressive symptoms. However, no changes in binge eating were noted at the time of follow-up.

Specific personality variables may put one at risk for eating disorders. For many years, researchers have observed a link between perfectionistic personalities and eating disorders (Garner, Olmstead, & Polivy, 1983). For those with perfectionistic qualities, normal shortcomings in life may be experienced as more traumatic. In the same way, a "normal-sized" body is seen as a sign of imperfection. A longitudinal study by Vohs and colleagues (1999) showed that women with perfectionistic attitudes, low self-esteem, and the belief that they were overweight were more likely to engage in bulimic symptoms 9 months later.

Vohs's research is in line with findings suggesting that low self-esteem places one at increased risk for eating disorders (Polivy & Herman, 2002). Add to this the fact that dieting, which is highly prone to disruptions that result in overeating, often produces a downward spiraling of self-esteem that contributes more specifically to eating disorders. Indeed, dieting tends to precede the development of eating disorders in a great majority of cases (Stice, Marti, & Durant, 2011). Fad diets are particularly dangerous in terms of producing eating disorders, as these are typically extraordinarily challenging to follow and implement effectively.

Other researchers have identified eating disorders as a way to regulate overwhelming negative emotion caused by trauma (Rorty & Yager, 1996). Indeed, Lejonclou, Nilsson, & Holmqvist (2013) found that women with a history of repeated trauma were more likely to have an eating disorder. In this way, eating disorders can be viewed as a coping mechanism favored by individuals who may not have more constructive ways of dealing with personal distress (Troop, Holbrey, & Treasure, 1998). The person with anorexia achieves at least partial emotional gratification by avoiding food and achieving slimness (albeit never enough). The person with bulimia or binge-eating disorder gains (temporary) emotional relief by bingeing (and then by purging, for those with bulimia). Striegel-Moore and colleagues (2002) found that African-American and Caucasian women with binge-eating disorder reported higher rates of sexual abuse, physical abuse, and bullying by peers.

Biological Factors

The search for biological causes of eating disorders is especially challenging because eating disorders lead to a host of biological disruptions in the body. Thus, while one

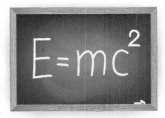

MAPS - Attempted Answers

might observe differences in neurotransmitters, or hormone levels, or even brain activity in those with eating disorders, it is challenging to know whether such differences are the cause or consequence of the eating disorder. Nonetheless, some individuals may have a biological vulnerability that puts them at risk for the development of eating disorders.

Evidence for the role of biology in the development of eating disorders comes in part from **family heritability studies**. Relatives of people with eating disorders are more likely to have an eating disorder themselves (Strober & Bulik, 2002). Twin studies show that anorexia is much more common among identical twins compared to fraternal twins, suggesting that shared genes contribute to the development of the disorder (Strober & Bulik, 2002). However, as discussed in Chapter 2, it is difficult to disentangle a shared family environment (e.g., focus on thinness, attitudes about food, preoccupation with appearance) from shared genetics.

Biological explanations for anorexia have also centered on the role of the *hypothalamus*, discussed in Chapter 2, which controls feeding, drinking, and sexual drive and plays a role in regulating the menstrual cycle. Hypothalamic dysfunction is suspected because some women with anorexia show evidence of amenorrhea (absence of menstruation) *prior* to weight loss, suggesting that menstrual cycle suppression may result from something other than weight loss (Hsii & Golden, 2013; Katz, Boyar, Roffwarg, Hellman, & Weiner, 1978). However, other factors can also cause amenorrhea, including emotional distress. Furthermore, hypothalamic dysfunction seen in individuals with eating disorders may be a consequence, rather than a cause, of disordered eating.

Some researchers have speculated that eating disorders result from an inability to identify internal states: physiological states such as hunger and fullness, as well as emotional states. There may be a biological vulnerability that makes paying attention to internal states more challenging for some individuals. For example, a person may interpret the experience of negative emotions as hunger and thus respond by bingeing. This lack of awareness could be seen as a biological cause of eating disorders, although Bruch (1973) suggested that certain family environments may foster confusion between physiological and emotional states. When caregivers use food to assuage a child's expression of distress, a child's trust in his or her body (i.e., whether one is hungry or not) is eroded. This may set the stage for using food as a means to express one's emotions.

family heritability studies: Studies that examine the degree of risk for relatives to develop mental disorders experienced by other family members.

Sociocultural Factors

The sociocultural view, which may be the most powerful explanatory lens for eating disorders, has focused on societal factors in North America and Europe that influence perceptions of ideal appearance and body weight. According to this perspective, television commercials, magazines, diet ads, and a culture of celebrity encourage an almost obsessive pursuit of slimness, a trend that has become prominent since the middle part of the 20th century and has been documented in films such as the *Killing Us Softly* series. In a classic analysis, *Playboy* centerfolds and Miss America Pageant contestants showed decreasing average body weight from 1959 to 1978, with Miss America Pageant winners having body weights that were about 82% of average, lower than the weight criterion for anorexia at the time (Garner, Garfinkel, Schwartz, & Thompson, 1980).

This constant publicity about thinness as a standard of beauty has not changed and may lead many people to hold unreasonable expectations about how thin they should be to be attractive. Across ethnic groups, there is a correlation between the prevalence of eating disorders and the cultural pressure to be thin (Hsu, 1990). It is interesting that eating disorders occur primarily in cultures in which food is abundant; in cultures in which food is scarce, a rounder physique is considered more desirable (Polivy & Herman, 2002).

This thin ideal begins in childhood, with the ever-popular Barbie doll. As Kate Meehan put it (1998):

> Statistically, Barbie's proportions made life-size are ridiculous. Not only would she be 7 feet, 2 inches tall, but she'd boast an impressive 40-inch bust line, a tiny 22-inch waist, and 36-inch hips. Now is this really a good toy to allow our children to play with?

Due to this and other similarly unrealistic media messages around thinness, people in Western cultures tend to have distorted views of their own body size and attractiveness. In a classic study, Fallon and Rozin (1985) found that men and women differ when choosing the figure drawings that most resemble (a) their own current figures, (b) their ideal figures, and (c) the figure thought most attractive to the opposite sex. For men, the current, ideal, and most attractive figures were almost identical. For women, the current figure was heavier than the most attractive figure, which was even heavier than the ideal figure. In a replication of that experiment, women with high Eating Attitude Test (EAT) scores, indicating abnormal eating patterns, also chose an ideal figure that was significantly thinner than what they thought was attractive to the opposite sex (Zellner, Harner, & Adler, 1989). These two studies suggest that, whereas men are generally satisfied with their figures, women desire to be thinner than they think they are, and women with abnormal eating behaviors desire to be even thinner than what they think other people find attractive.

Not surprisingly, eating disorders are more common among young women who report greater exposure to popular media (Smolak & Chun-Kennedy, 2013), endorse more gender-role stereotypes (Hepp, Spindler, & Milos, 2005), and internalize societal standards about appearance (Fernandez & Pritchard, 2012). Stice and colleagues (2001) randomly assigned adolescent girls to a 15-month fashion subscription. They found that girls who demonstrated initial elevations in perceived pressure to be thin, body dissatisfaction, and deficits in social support were adversely affected by exposure to these images over the long term. Such results suggest that exposure to thin-ideal images may have lasting negative consequences for vulnerable girls.

Eating disorders are also more common among subgroups in which certain physiques are prized; for example, many models, actors, and athletes have reported struggles with eating disorders. Dancers, gymnasts, wrestlers, triathletes, cyclists, and boxers report particularly high rates of eating disorders. Sundgot-Borgen & Torstveit (2004) found that 8% of their sample of elite male athletes met criteria for an eating disorder.

In addition, the current prejudice against overweight people in our society may fuel fear and preoccupation with body shape and size. Self-reports of being teased about one's appearance are associated with symptoms of eating disorders (Lunner et al., 2000). Indeed, body dissatisfaction is a well-known precursor as well as a maintaining factor in eating disorders (Polivy & Herman, 2002).

In addition to looking at the media, performance sports, and teasing as factors that contribute to eating disorders, other sociocultural theorists have looked at family characteristics. Men with eating disorders have reported growing up in families with a distant climate: less physical affection, poorer parental relationships, and family taboos regarding nudity (Mangweth-Matzek et al., 2010). Families having an adolescent with anorexia have been found to be less skilled at conflict resolution and communication, more traditional, rigid, and likely to shift blame from one family member to another and to establish covert alliances (Eisler, 2009; Palazzoli, 1985). For example, in Emily's family from the chapter-opening case, a strong but unacknowledged alliance existed between Emily's mother and her younger sister. This alliance excluded Emily as well as her father, who had recently become increasingly removed from the family. Emily's father even had an extramarital affair that, although supposedly a secret, was known to the whole family. Many clinicians believe that this type of family situation provides fertile ground for the development of eating disorders in already vulnerable adolescents (Cunha, Relvas, & Soares, 2009; Minuchin, Rosman, & Baker, 1978).

In these cases, anorexia may divert attention from trouble spots, such as an unhappy marriage, thereby maintaining the family's equi-

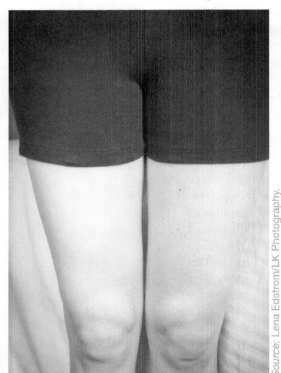

Source: Lena Edstrom/LK Photography.

Social media has increased discussion of the "thigh gap," the space between the inner thighs when standing with knees together. Whether or not one has a thigh gap is largely based on body type, tendon length, and pelvis shape, yet many teens strive for a thigh gap and may do so by adopting unhealthy diet and exercise patterns. What does it say about our society when the thigh gap becomes a status symbol?

librium. Emily's anorexia functioned to unite her parents, as they struggled together to help their daughter. It is not yet clear, however, to what extent these family patterns are causes of anorexia or part of the family's reaction to a child's eating disorder. Thus, it is important to emphasize that, although family factors may have contributed to Emily's eating disorder, they almost certainly were not its sole cause.

Treatment of Eating Disorders

The initial treatment objective in cases of anorexia nervosa is to increase body weight and treat medical complications (American Psychiatric Association, 2006); for bulimia nervosa and binge-eating disorder, the initial treatment objective is to decrease binge-eating episodes. Recovery rates for anorexia are estimated to be as high as 70%, while recovery rates for bulimia are placed at around 55% (Smink, van Hoeken, & Hoek, 2013). Among studies examining BED treatment, recovery rates range between 19% and 65% (Smink, van Hoeken, & Hoek, 2013). The sooner a person seeks treatment, the more likely he or she is to recover from an eating disorder.

Severe anorexia requires treatment in a hospital setting to carefully address the life-threatening consequences of the disorder, including severe malnutrition, electrolyte imbalances, and cardiac problems. The primary and most immediate goal is to increase body weight. This may be done with a nasogastric feeding tube in some cases, in which a tube carries food to the stomach via the nose.

Some individuals with eating disorders seek longer-term treatment, usually for several months, in an inpatient setting. During such residential treatment, clients' health and weight are monitored, food intake is recorded and observed, and schedules are set to include group and individual psychotherapy. Treatment is guided by a multidisciplinary team that includes psychiatrists and other physicians, psychologists, nurses, nutritionists, dieticians, and psychotherapists. In a long-term follow-up study of individuals with anorexia and bulimia who had spent 30 days or more in a residential program, the majority sustained their treatment gains, maintaining a healthy weight and showing improvement in depressive symptoms (Brewerton & Costin, 2011).

Other therapeutic options include day treatment, where a client attends treatment each day but does not stay overnight; intensive outpatient treatment, where a client meets with the treatment team several times per week; and outpatient therapy, where a client meets for group, individual, or family therapy as needed.

Psychological treatments for eating disorders generally include cognitive-behavioral therapy (CBT) and interpersonal psychotherapy (IPT). Cognitive-behavioral approaches teach clients to eat small amounts of food at regularly scheduled times, to quantify and record their eating to gain a sense of control over it, to identify the antecedents/triggers of disordered eating, to identify factors that maintain the vicious cycle, and to use specific statements to themselves or other strategies to counter the irrational thinking that precedes abnormal eating. IPT examines relationships in clients' lives and how attachment needs are (or are not) being met. Clients address the interpersonal context surrounding the development of eating disorders and, importantly, how relationship problems may serve to maintain disordered eating.

For anorexia, clinical trials have not shown one kind of psychotherapy to be more effective than another (Watson & Bulik, 2013). In contrast, CBT has had considerable success in the treatment of bulimia and is considered a first-line treatment approach (Fairburn, Jones, Peveler, Hope, & O'Connor, 1993; Glasofer & Devlin, 2013). IPT also has research support for its utility in treating bulimia and binge eating (American Psychiatric Association, 2006; Wilfley et al., 1993).

A meta-analysis of studies addressing the treatment of BED showed the benefits of CBT in reducing binge eating, as well as in lowering overconcern about shape, weight, and eating (Vocks et al., 2010). CBT did not appear to lower weight in these studies. IPT has also received empirical support, especially for those BED clients with low self-esteem and more severely disordered eating (Iacovino, Gredysa, Altman, & Wilfley, 2012). For

meta-analysis: A statistical technique that combines the results of several studies into an overall average or estimate.

individuals with BED and obesity, a weight-loss component may be necessary, but to date, there is limited research on the efficacy of combined psychological and weight-loss treatments.

A different meta-analysis addressed the effectiveness of dialectical behavior therapy (DBT) among clients with eating disorders (Lenz, Taylor, Fleming, & Serman, 2014). DBT is a psychotherapy that was originally developed to treat individuals with borderline personality disorder (Linehan, Armstrong, Suarez, Allmon, & Heard, 1991; discussed further in Chapter 16). Through a manualized protocol, DBT teaches clients concrete skills to tolerate distress, regulate emotions, and be more effective in interpersonal situations. It also includes a mindfulness component to help individuals become more aware of what they are thinking and feeling. In short, DBT helps clients accept their current difficulties and work toward change through use of new skills. The meta-analysis showed that DBT appeared to decrease the number of eating-disorder episodes among individuals with anorexia, bulimia, and BED. Furthermore, DBT appeared to decrease depressive symptoms among women diagnosed with an eating disorder. Future research may continue to show DBT to be a useful approach to the treatment of eating disorders.

To date, only two prevention programs have significantly reduced risk for future onset of eating disorders in trials (Stice, Becker, & Yokum, 2013). Both of these successful treatments seek to address one of the key components that may fuel maladaptive eating behaviors in the first place—the cultural ideal of unrealistic thinness promulgated by the Western media. One way of combating this ideal is to teach people how to consume their media more critically. For instance, Stice and his team in Texas had female adolescent research participants voluntarily engage in what they termed "a dissonance (body project) intervention"—verbal, written, and behavioral exercises in which they critiqued the thin ideal, such as by writing an essay about the costs associated with the pursuit of this ideal (Stice, Marti, Spoor, Presnell, & Shaw, 2008). Dissonance participants showed a 60% reduction in risk for eating pathology onset relative to assessment-only controls through 3-year follow-up (Stice et al., 2008), and this treatment was effective for participants of different ethnicities (Stice, Marti, & Cheng, 2014). Stice has since replicated these results in real-world settings, including a high school (Stice, Rohde, Shaw, & Gau, 2011) and a college (Stice, Butryn, Rohde, Shaw, & Marti, 2013).

The second effective strategy for combating the thin ideal and preventing eating disorders is to teach people how to make gradual healthy and lasting changes to their diet and physical activity, to balance their energy needs with their energy intake and thereby achieve a healthier weight and body satisfaction (Stice, Rohde, Shaw, & Marti, 2013). In one such study, participants receiving this "healthy weight intervention" showed a 61% reduction in risk for eating pathology onset and a 55% reduction in risk for obesity onset relative to assessment-only controls through 3-year follow-up (Stice et al., 2008). Note the difference between this treatment—learning balanced lifestyle strategies for being fit and healthy—versus the notion discussed earlier in this chapter that fad diets and glorification of thinness (rather than fitness) actually increase eating-disorder symptoms.

MAPS - Medical Myths

What about medication as a component of treatment? For anorexia, a variety of drugs with appetite-enhancing characteristics—including *cyproheptadine* and *THC* (the active ingredient in marijuana)—have been tried, but with little success. Several studies have examined the effectiveness of *olanzapine*, an antipsychotic medication that has a side effect of weight gain. Conclusions are mixed: Most studies show no change in psychological well-being, whereas some studies show a small but statistically significant effect for weight gain (Watson & Bulik, 2013). Other medications, including antidepressants such as *selective serotonin reuptake inhibitors (SSRIs)*, also have limited support for the treatment of anorexia, and the American Psychiatric Association (2006) recommends that medications should not be used as the primary or sole treatment for anorexia. Watson and Bulik (2013) note that the neurochemical imbalances that generally accompany anorexia may render certain medications less effective.

For individuals with bulimia, medications have shown more promise. The SSRI *fluoxetine (Prozac)* is viewed as the "gold standard" of pharmacological treatment for bulimia and is approved by the Food and Drug Administration (FDA) for its treatment (Broft, Berner, & Walsh, 2010). In multiple studies, fluoxetine is associated with a reduction in binge-and-purge episodes and improvements in anxiety and depression (Broft, Berner, & Walsh, 2010).

Individuals with BED may benefit from medications aimed at reducing bingeing and concurrent depressive symptoms. However, research on the efficacy of drugs in the treatment of BED is limited, with medications showing only moderately positive effects (Vocks et al., 2010).

Family therapy is sometimes used in conjunction with individual treatments, and there is growing support for its efficacy, especially among youth with anorexia (Watson & Bulik, 2013). In therapy based on the pioneering work of Salvador Minuchin (Minuchin et al., 1978), anorexic adolescents and their families attend sessions (sometimes while eating lunch) during which discussion and role playing are aimed at (1) clarifying relationships, (2) developing distinct boundaries between and among relationships to give the adolescent breathing room from an overprotective parent, and (3) improving communication among family members. Improved communication is thought to minimize disordered eating behaviors. For example, adolescents might be taught in family treatment to express anger directly to a rejecting or overprotective parent, rather than doing so by refusing food.

The vast majority of treatments for eating disorders have been developed and studied with women as the primary research participants. Whereas it is presumed that these psychological treatments will be helpful for men with eating disorders, it is possible that gender may affect treatment outcomes, as discussed in the earlier "Controversy" feature. Some clinicians have argued that treatments should be tailored to men, incorporating an analysis of how masculinity influences disordered eating patterns (Greenberg & Schoen, 2008). Men may be more concerned with body shape and muscular definition rather than thinness (Nunez-Navarro et al., 2012).

Section Review

Eating disorders:

- are more commonly diagnosed in women, but men also experience these disorders;
- are usually diagnosed in adolescence/young adulthood;
- are caused by a combination of psychological, biological, and sociocultural factors; and
- can be successfully treated, usually by psychotherapy rather than medication, especially if a person seeks treatment sooner rather than later.

Other Eating and Feeding Disorders

In addition to anorexia, bulimia, and BED, other eating and feeding disorders are seen in clinical practice. Two such disorders are pica and avoidant/restrictive food intake disorder, which both typically first occur during childhood.

Pica

Pica is the ongoing consumption of nonnutritive, nonfood items that are inappropriate for an individual's developmental level. For example, a diagnosis of pica might be considered for a 15-year-old who eats sand, but not for a 1-year old who often eats sand when playing in a sandbox. Individuals with pica have reportedly consumed a wide variety of items, ranging from acorns and chalk to nails and lead paint chips. Some individuals consume one or two "preferred" substances, while others ingest many different substances indiscriminately (Stiegler, 2005). One of your textbook authors worked with a client who consumed three boxes of baking powder per day. Pica occurs most often in individuals with developmental disabilities (see Chapter 3); prevalence rates for pica in this population range from 9–25% (Ali, 2001).

pica: The ongoing consumption of nonnutritive, nonfood items that are inappropriate for an individual's developmental level.

TABLE 12.3 The *DSM-5* in Simple Language: Diagnosing Pica

Pica is a disorder of eating that involves one main symptom and two qualifiers:

1. Main symptom: Consistent eating of things that are not food over 1+ months.

Qualifiers:
    a. The main symptom does not fit with the developmental level of the individual (e.g., it is normal for 6-month-olds to put anything in their mouths but not for 6-year-olds).
    b. The main symptom is not part of a specific cultural practice (e.g., eating a certain nonfood substance for spiritual reasons).

Source: Adapted from American Psychiatric Association (2013a).

Soil is sometimes consumed by individuals with pica.

Source: Sinisa Botas/Shutterstock.com.

There is no one clear etiology for pica. It is often suggested that iron and/or zinc deficiencies play a causal role, but these conditions could also be the result of pica (Stiegler, 2005). Others suggest that pica behaviors may be an attempt at self-soothing by those with developmental disabilities or part of a larger impulse-control disorder (Stroman, Young, Rubano, & Pinkhasov, 2011). Behaviors similar to pica are also part of certain cultural traditions, and it is important to note that they are not inherently pathological. For example, some East African women consume soil as part of fertility rituals (Stiegler, 2005), but this does not constitute a disorder unless it causes distress and dysfunction.

Pica can have serious medical consequences, including choking, poisoning, and intestinal obstruction (Williams & McAdam, 2012). Mortality rates for pica are especially high in the elderly with developmental disabilities (Dumaguing, Singh, Sethi, & Devanand, 2003). Corbett and colleagues (2003) did not find pica to independently cause pregnancy complications, although other studies have found pregnant women of immigrant and low socioeconomic status who engage in pica behaviors to be at elevated risk for lead poisoning and associated prenatal complications (e.g., Thihalolipavan, Candalla, & Ehrlich, 2013).

Many treatments exist for pica. Most are behavioral in orientation, and contemporary approaches typically incorporate reinforcement and other strategies that gradually reduce the amount of nonfood consumption (Hagopian, Rooker, & Rolider, 2011). Applied behavior analysis, which utilizes principles of classical and operant conditioning discussed in Chapter 2, is the treatment of choice for individuals with both pica and developmental disabilities (Matson, Hattier, Belva, & Matson, 2013). Treatments that involve the introduction of aversive stimuli or physical restraints are discouraged except in cases where individuals' behaviors are placing them in immediate danger (Williams & McAdam, 2012). Lastly, preliminary research has shown SSRIs (e.g., Prozac) to be effective in reducing pica symptoms in some patients, although the drug class has not yet been approved for this purpose. Pharmacological treatment for pica warrants further research (Herguner, Ozyildirim, & Tanidir, 2008). The *DSM-5* diagnostic criteria for pica are shown in Table 12.3.

Avoidant/Restrictive Food Intake Disorder

Jack is an 8-year-old boy whose mother took him to a pediatrician due to concerns that he is not eating a balanced diet and has not gained any weight for the past 6 months. Jack refuses to eat all fruits, vegetables, and dairy, and he frequently skips meals if he does not like any of the food items offered. At 4 feet tall, Jack is roughly average height for his age, but at 50 pounds, he weighs about 10 pounds less than the national average. The doctor's assessment found no underlying medical conditions. At first glance, Jack's refusal to eat a complete, balanced diet and failure to achieve expected weight gain may appear to indicate anorexia nervosa. However, after careful consideration Jack was diagnosed with avoidant/restrictive food intake disorder (ARFID).

Avoidant/restrictive food intake disorder (ARFID) is a new diagnosis in the *DSM-5*. ARFID was chosen to replace the former *DSM-IV-TR* disorder "feeding disorder of infancy or early childhood" and to improve the ability to identify disordered eating across the lifespan (Fisher et al., 2014).

The crucial distinction between ARFID and anorexia is the lack of disturbance in body image. Individuals with ARFID do not avoid or restrict food intake because they think that they are overweight or unattractive (Bryant-Waugh, 2013). Instead, multiple other reasons contribute to not eating, including a lack of interest in eating or food, sensory-based avoidance of food (e.g., not liking the texture, taste, or smell of food), and avoidance related to fears about eating other than weight gain (e.g., food poisoning or vomiting). Research by Fisher and colleagues (2014) has validated ARFID as a diagnosis distinct from anorexia or bulimia nervosa. Individuals with ARFID have a younger average age of onset than individuals with anorexia or bulimia. They are also more likely to suffer from a related medical condition or anxiety disorder but less likely to have a comorbid mood disorder diagnosis.

The current body of literature for ARFID is very limited, and this disorder does not yet have any evidence-based treatments. Bryant-Waugh (2013) suggests a model similar to treatment for anorexia that incorporates nutritional education, medical monitoring, and CBT. Future research will investigate the effectiveness of this and other approaches to treating ARFID.

The *DSM-5* diagnostic criteria for ARFID are shown in Table 12.4.

avoidant/restrictive food intake disorder (ARFID): A problem with eating/feeding, not due to body image concerns, that results in inadequate nutrition or calorie consumption.

"In what aisle are the 'won't immediately kill you' foods?"

Source: Cartoonresource/Shutterstock.com.

Section Review

Eating disorders that are usually first diagnosed in childhood include:

- pica, the recurrent consumption of nonnutritive, nonfood items, and
- avoidant/restrictive food intake disorder (ARFID), characterized by a lack of interest in eating or food, sensory-based avoidance of certain foods, avoidance related to fears about eating, or other problems with eating/feeding that do not include body image concerns.

TABLE 12.4 The *DSM-5* in Simple Language: Diagnosing Avoidant/Restrictive Food Intake Disorder

Avoidant/restrictive food intake disorder is a disorder of eating with one main symptom and two qualifiers:

1. Main symptom: The person is not getting enough nutrients from food. As a result, the person is either losing weight, nutritionally depleted, or taking supplements.

Qualifiers:

   a. The reasoning for the main symptom has nothing to do with body image concerns (e.g., as in anorexia). Instead, the person shows an apparent lack of interest in eating or food, avoidance based on the sensory characteristics of food, or concern about potentially unpleasant aspects of eating.

   b. The main symptom is not part of a specific cultural practice (e.g., not eating for spiritual or political reasons).

Source: Adapted from American Psychiatric Association (2013a).

Revisiting the Case of Emily

As you may have guessed, Emily from our chapter-opening case was diagnosed with anorexia nervosa, restricting type, due to her low body weight, fear of gaining weight, severe body image distortion, and attempts to lose weight via overexercising and very limited eating. Emily's first stage of recovery from anorexia was 2 weeks of inpatient treatment at a psychiatric hospital. There, she was assigned an integrative treatment team that included a psychiatrist, a pediatrician, a dietician, and a counselor. Emily was also placed on a feeding tube to begin weight restoration and given a meal plan outlining three meals and three snacks per day. Once determined to be medically stable, Emily was transferred to a residential treatment program. She no longer received nutrients from a feeding tube, and her meal plan was adjusted to continue weight restoration. All of her meals and snacks were closely monitored by program staff to ensure that she was compliant with her meal plan and not hiding any food. Emily's dietician educated her about normal eating behaviors and portion sizes, and her counselor helped her challenge her distorted body image and beliefs about food and weight. Emily was discharged from the residential program after 2 months, and she now continues seeing an outpatient psychiatrist, counselor, and dietician. Family therapy was also recommended, and Emily's parents both voiced their willingness to participate.

Over the course of inpatient and residential treatment, Emily gained 21 pounds. This now gives her a BMI of 17.9, which is significantly healthier than her pretreatment BMI of 14.2 but still meets the criteria for mild anorexia. Continued recovery and eventual remission of Emily's eating disorder is possible, especially if she keeps up with her outpatient providers and her parents remain vigilant and supportive. However, relapse is an unfortunate reality for many people with eating disorders, and it is possible that Emily will relapse at least once and may even need to re-enter inpatient or residential treatment. Her prognosis is helped by the fact that her eating disorder was discovered and treated early and that she has no history of self-harm, substance abuse, or trauma. Recovery will not be easy for Emily, but she certainly has the potential to lead a fulfilling adult life.

Sleep-Wake Disorders

Hannah, a 32-year-old woman, frequently complains of feeling tired throughout the day. When asked about her sleeping habits, Hannah shared that for the past 6 months, she has had difficulty falling asleep. Once she eventually falls asleep, she often wakes up during the night and has trouble getting back to sleep. She said she usually feels a sense of dread at bedtime, worried that she will have another tough night of sleep. Some nights, she lies in bed awake more than she sleeps. When she wakes up during the night, she sometimes looks at the clock and calculates how much sleep she can still get if she is lucky enough to fall back asleep. Her daytime tiredness has begun to take a toll on her work performance: "I can't concentrate on the tasks at hand," she said. "I'm constantly yawning, zoning out, and half-awake during the day. Even though I'm exhausted all the time, I still can't sleep at night." Hannah also said she has been feeling increasingly irritable and anxious as a result of not sleeping: "My friends don't seem to want to be around me much anymore, and I can't really blame them," Hannah shared. "I seem to snap at anything and everything nowadays." Hannah said her sleep difficulties occur three to four times a week. Hannah is not taking any medications, nor does she use any recreational drugs.

One of the most frequent complaints reported to physicians and mental health professionals is disturbed sleep. This is not surprising, given that people spend about one third of

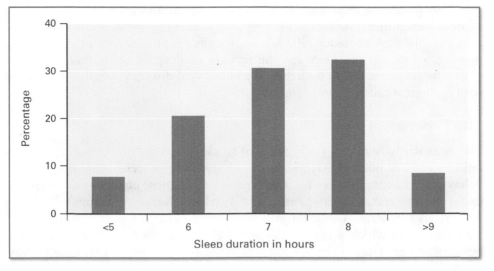

FIGURE 12.2 How Much Do People Sleep?

Most adults report sleeping between 6 and 8 hours a night.

Source: Adapted from Krueger & Friedman (2009).

their lives asleep. Infants sleep about 16 hours a day, school-aged children and adolescents sleep about 10 hours a day, and healthy adults sleep 7–8 hours per day (see Figure 12.2; National Heart, Lung, and Blood Institute, 2011). College students, though, typically sleep less than 7 hours per day, going to bed, on average, after midnight (Galambos, Vargas Lascano, Howard, & Maggs, 2013). Living on campus is associated with later bedtimes and rise times; alcohol use is higher and GPA is lower when bedtimes are later (Galambos et al., 2013). As well, total sleep time is a significant predictor of college academic performance (Taylor, Vatthauer, Bramoweth, Ruggero, & Roane, 2013). However, this pattern of poor sleep predates college, with over two thirds of U.S. high school students reporting insufficient nightly sleep (Eaton et al., 2010).

Any activity that commands that much time is certain to be subject to problems, and almost everyone knows how a sleepless night feels. Most of us have had trouble sleeping on occasion. Lying in bed and not being able to sleep can be extremely frustrating, and usually, the harder a person tries to fall asleep, the less likely sleep becomes. The day after a sleepless night can be miserable, and after a sleepless night, most people go to bed earlier than usual the next night to catch up on the missed sleep. For millions of people, however, it is not that easy. They may struggle with disturbed or inadequate sleep night after night, for years on end, becoming desperately preoccupied with the one thing they cannot achieve—a good night's sleep. The chronic misery of the poor sleeper was described by English novelist Iris Murdoch, who said, "There is a gulf fixed between those who sleep and those who cannot. It is one of the greatest divisions of the human race."

Troubled sleep may stem from several causes. When the disturbance lasts for a few nights or as long as a couple of weeks, the most likely explanation is that an individual is going through a stressful period in his or her life. About 75% of people with insomnia report that their first attack occurred when facing major stressors (Dunkell, 1994; Ellis, Gehrman, Espie, Riemann, & Perlis, 2012). The connection between stress and sleep problems is one that most people experience at some time in their lives. People have trouble falling or staying asleep the night before a big trip, an important test, a major speech, or an important game. Worry about finances, children, or relationships often leads to disrupted and restless sleep.

Sleep disturbance is often tied to other mental disorders, as well as to physical health concerns, such as chronic pain, arthritis, heart disease, and diabetes. In one study, people with insomnia were three times more likely to have another *DSM* mental disorder than were those without sleep complaints (Ford & Kamerow, 1989). Although sleep disturbances can be produced by physical

Not surprisingly, worrying about sleep problems can make sleep problems worse (O'Kearney & Pech, 2014).

or mental disorders, sleep problems can also place an individual at risk for the development of these other disorders in the first place, including substance use concerns (American Psychiatric Association, 2013a). As more is discovered about the biological underpinnings of mental disorders and the process of sleep, it is becoming clear that sleep problems are connected to both mental and physical disorders because they share a common biological cause.

The Process of Sleep

The poet Percy Shelley (1813) referred to sleep as the "brother of death," but sleep, unlike death, is not a passive state; it is a dynamic process made up of physical and behavioral changes. Much of our understanding of these changes comes from research using the **electroencephalogram (EEG)**, which measures changes in the electrical activity of the brain. The EEG is one measure used in a **polysomnographic (PSG) assessment**, in which a person sleeps for a night or two in a sleep laboratory while being observed. During sleep, several biological measures—EEG, muscle movements, heart activity, and eye movements—are monitored. Based on these measures, researchers have identified five distinctive stages of sleep, each with different behavioral and biological qualities.

Stages of Sleep

When people fall asleep, their muscles relax, their body temperature begins to drop, and they drift into a light sleep from which they can be easily awakened. This *stage 1* sleep lasts from 30 seconds to 10 minutes. In *stage 2* sleep, the EEG shows some distinctive changes in brain activity as sleep deepens. A single phase of stage 2 sleep lasts, on average, 30 to 45 minutes; on most nights, half of the total sleep time is spent in stage 2. *Stage 3* and *Stage 4* sleep are sometimes called deep or **delta sleep** because of a predominance of delta brain waves, a slower wave pattern recorded during these stages. These two stages account for 10–20% of total sleep time, and they are the most restorative and revitalizing periods of our sleep. The immune system is thought to replenish itself during deep sleep. It is relatively difficult to wake someone in stage 4 sleep. One complete cycle through these first four stages of sleep takes about 90 minutes.

After 30 to 40 minutes in stage 4, the sleeper ascends into a special phase of lighter sleep in which the eyes dart back and forth quickly under closed lids. This stage, called **rapid eye movement (REM) sleep**, is differentiated from stages 1 to 4, which are called **non-REM (NREM) sleep**. Physiologically, REM sleep looks similar to stage 1 sleep; heart rate, breathing, and brain waves all increase. Paradoxically, however, the muscles become so relaxed during REM sleep that a person is essentially paralyzed, with the exception that penile erections are most likely to occur during REM sleep. On about 85% of awakenings during REM sleep, people report that they had been dreaming, although this percentage can be as high as 94% under controlled laboratory conditions (Yu, 2014). Most of our dreams appear to take place during REM sleep. In fact, the eye movements of this stage may be coordinated with the actions taking place in dreams (Leclair-Visonneau, Oudiette, Gaymard, Leu-Semenescu, & Arnulf, 2010). However, dreams can also occur in other sleep stages; NREM sleep reports are generally more thought-like, less elaborate, and less bizarre than REM sleep reports (Lusignan et al., 2010).

When people are deprived of REM sleep for a few nights, they compensate by entering REM more quickly and remaining in it about twice as long on subsequent nights. This rebound phenomenon suggests that REM sleep serves vital biological functions. First, the *locus coeruleus*, which releases norepinephrine during the waking state, is almost totally inactive during REM sleep. The nervous system becomes less sensitive to norepinephrine if it is released steadily for too long; therefore, one function of REM sleep may be to shut down production of norepinephrine long enough to allow the brain to reset its receptiveness to this neurotransmitter (Mallick & Singh, 2011). Further, people who are deprived of REM sleep have poorer retention of material learned the day before than do people

electroencephalogram (EEG): A measure of changes in the electrical activity of the brain.

polysomnographic (PSG) assessment: A measurement process in which a person sleeps in a laboratory while sleep variables are observed and monitored.

delta sleep: The most restorative period of sleep, in which slower brain waves called delta waves are predominant; it accounts for 10–20% of total sleep time.

rapid eye movement (REM) sleep: A phase of sleep in which the eyes dart back and forth quickly under closed lids; often associated with dreaming.

non-REM (NREM) sleep: Sleep stages 1 to 4, in which REM sleep is not experienced.

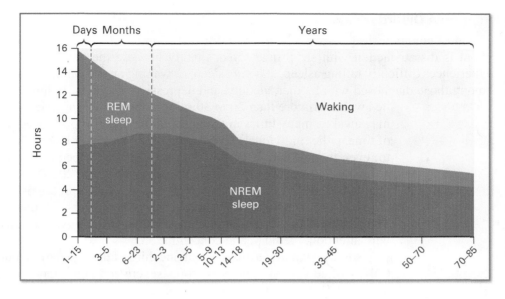

FIGURE 12.3 Sleep Changes with Age

As people age, the amounts of REM (rapid eye movement) and NREM (non-REM) sleep change. REM sleep declines sharply in the first 10 years of life and continues to drop off more slowly after that. The amount of NREM sleep changes less dramatically, falling from about 8 hours during infancy to 5 hours in old age.

Source: Adapted from Roffwarg, Muzio, & Dement (1996).

who are allowed to sleep normally. Therefore, REM sleep may also help individuals consolidate and fortify important learning experiences, as well as process the emotional contents of memory (Groch, Wilhelm, Diekelmann, & Born, 2013).

During a night's sleep, most people pass through the full sleep cycle four to six times. Most deep sleep (stages 3 and 4) occurs in the first 3 to 5 hours of sleep. As a night's sleep continues, more and more time is spent in the shallower stage 2 and REM sleep. Total sleep declines with age—particularly REM sleep, which, as Figure 12.3 shows, declines by about 50% between infancy and old age.

Biological Regulation of Sleep

Sleep, like many other biological functions, takes place on a rhythmic schedule that repeats roughly every 24 hours. These **circadian rhythms** (from the Latin *circa dies*, meaning "about a day") are partially linked to external cues, such as light, but they are maintained even when people are isolated from external cues. Apparently, the body is equipped with a biological clock that maintains circadian rhythms even when external cues are missing. This clock appears to be in the **suprachiasmatic nucleus (SCN)** of the hypothalamus. The eyes send signals to the SCN to link it to external cues of the light/dark cycle. In addition, when the eyes sense darkness, the pineal gland soon begins to produce **melatonin**, a hormone that also informs the hypothalamus of darkness. The SCN then sends signals to areas of the hindbrain (see Chapter 2), such as the locus coeruleus, that activate either wakefulness or sleep.

circadian rhythm: An internally cued rhythmic schedule of biological activity that repeats roughly every 24 hours.

suprachiasmatic nucleus (SCN): A brain structure found in the hypothalamus that maintains the body's circadian rhythms.

melatonin: A hormone that affects the hypothalamus and helps prepare the body for sleep.

Section Review

The normal process of sleep involves:

- repeating stages of progressively deeper NREM sleep and one stage of REM sleep during which dreams occur;
- a circadian rhythm that is regulated by an internal clock in the brain; and
- major decreases in the amount of REM sleep as people age.

Types of Sleep-Wake Disorders

The *DSM-5* classifies a number of sleep-wake disorders that (1) describe problems with the amount, quality, or timing of a person's sleep or (2) involve unusual behaviors or abnormal physiological events during sleep. All of these problems result in daytime distress and impairment among individuals who experience sleep-wake disorders (American Psychiatric Association, 2013a).

Insomnia Disorder

insomnia disorder: A condition in which a person experiences difficulty falling asleep, staying asleep, or waking up too early.

The most common sleep disorder is **insomnia disorder**, in which the predominant complaint is dissatisfaction with sleep quantity or quality because the person consistently experiences difficulty falling asleep, staying asleep, or waking up too early. It is common among those diagnosed with bipolar, anxiety, and depressive disorders. Individuals may lie awake for more than 20 to 30 minutes before falling asleep, or they may awaken many times in the night, sometimes for prolonged periods of time. Other individuals wake up at least a half hour before they want to, even though they have not slept a full night's sleep (i.e., meaning at least 6.5 hours; American Psychiatric Association, 2013a). The poor quality or limited quantity of sleep causes significant problems the next day, in work, school, social, or other important areas of functioning. Many individuals report fatigue, moodiness, irritability, and difficulty with attention, memory, and concentration.

Insomnia symptoms affect about one third of the population, but only 6–10% of adults will have symptoms severe and consistent enough to meet full *DSM-5* criteria for insomnia disorder (American Psychiatric Association, 2013a). Women are affected more than men (Attarian, 2013), a finding that may be due in part to hormonal shifts that occur during and after pregnancy and during menopause. Most often, insomnia first occurs in young adulthood, and it usually involves problems falling asleep. However, insomnia is most prevalent among middle-aged and older adults, who report more difficulties staying asleep (American Psychiatric Association, 2013).

Source: Cartoonresource/Shutterstock.com.

"Your lectures cured my sleep disorder."

Insomnia disorder can be caused by several factors, including irregularities in the timing of the internal biological clock and chronic stress. It can also be caused by poor sleep habits, such as consuming alcohol or caffeine before bedtime, going to bed or getting up at irregular times, trying to go to sleep without first winding down or relaxing, and using the bedroom for studying, problem solving, watching TV, or other nonsleep-related activities. When these activities begin to affect sleep, a person starts to worry that it will be hard to fall asleep. Once this pattern of worry sets in, the person approaches going to bed with apprehension, thereby making sleep more difficult.

Connections

Why is insomnia such a common symptom of depression? For some possible answers, see Chapter 6.

Many people with insomnia engage in more active thinking at night; in particular, they report more negative thoughts, perhaps in anticipation of another night of troubled sleep. This can create a vicious cycle in which worry, concern, and frustration over another poor night's sleep actually contribute to the problem.

Individuals with insomnia often "try harder" to fall asleep but to no avail. A study by Shoham and colleagues (1996) found that insomnia patients who were instructed to stay awake actually fell asleep faster than their counterparts on a wait-list control group.

MAPS - Attempted Answers

MAPS - Medical Myths

sleep hygiene: A psychoeducational approach to sleep in which the person is taught how to develop and maintain effective sleep habits.

The most common treatment for insomnia is medication, particularly prescription drugs such as *Lunesta, Rozerem, Halcion, Sonata, Restoril,* and *Ambien.* However, despite their frequent use, these medications have several notable disadvantages. They produce unwanted side effects, such as sleepiness during the daytime; they often induce dependence; and when they are discontinued, insomnia often becomes worse than before the medication was used.

Several psychological treatments have been employed for insomnia, with much greater success than medication over the long term (Kierlin, 2008). The specific method depends on the nature of the individual's problem. Relaxation techniques can be used to counter physical tension; cognitive therapies can help people reduce tendencies to ruminate and worry, especially about being able to fall asleep. Multicomponent treatments, such as **sleep hygiene** counseling, are among the most effective psychological approaches. Sleep hygiene aims to "clean up" a person's sleep environment to maximize the chances of a good night's sleep. The person is taught to develop good sleep habits, such as not using

Sleep Hygiene

If you are the typical college student, work and study schedules, athletics, social activities, internships, and demanding professors may cause you to sleep a lot less than you might like. You probably can take a nap at the drop of the hat, and the library may be your favorite spot to curl up with a good textbook and snooze. As you know, college will not last forever, and most of you will find jobs that necessitate consistent work schedules, perhaps even an 8 A.M. start time! Knowledge of good sleep habits can help you to avoid sleep problems. If you do not use these strategies now, stash them away so they can be helpful to you in the years to come.

Sleep Hygiene Strategies:

1. *Keep a consistent sleep-wake schedule, even on weekends.* Go to bed at the same time each night, and get up at the same time each morning.

2. *Exercise, but not too late.* Exercise is good for sleep and helps increase the amount of time you spend in stages 3 and 4. But exercising late at night can make it very hard to fall asleep. Try to exercise during the day or at least a couple hours before you intend to go to sleep.

3. *Avoid nicotine and caffeine*, especially in the evening. These substances are stimulants, which can make it difficult for your body to fall asleep and stay asleep.

4. *Be mindful of medications that can disrupt sleep.* Know the side effects of any medications you take. For example, an allergy medication that contains pseudoephedrine can cause wakefulness.

5. *Avoid alcohol before bed.* While alcohol can make you fall asleep faster, your sleep will be less deep, and you will experience more frequent awakenings, thus compromising the quality of your sleep.

6. *Limit food and beverages before bed.* Eating before bed can cause indigestion, and drinking too much can disrupt your sleep by necessitating frequent trips to the bathroom.

7. *Time your naps carefully.* Taking a nap in the late afternoon can make it difficult, if not impossible, to go to bed at a reasonable hour. Do not get stuck in the cycle of (1) late night (because you are not tired), (2) early morning (due to work or school demands), (3) afternoon nap (because you are exhausted)! If you are going to nap, do so in the early afternoon, and limit your naps to less than an hour.

8. *Relax before bedtime.* Listen to soothing music, turn off electronics, take a warm bath, and read a good book. A consistent, pleasant bedtime ritual can set the stage for sleep.

9. *Adjust your sleep environment.* A dark, cool, quiet room can enhance your ability to get a good night's sleep. This may be hard to find in a college dormitory room!

10. *Think about light.* Allow yourself daytime light exposure. Get outside, even on a cloudy day. Limit your light exposure at bedtime, which includes the light emitted from computers, phones, and other electronics.

11. *Do not lie in bed awake.* If you cannot fall asleep after 20 minutes, get out of bed, go to a different room, and engage in a quiet activity until you feel sleepy. Lying in bed awake can make sleep problems worse. Only return to bed when you feel sleepy.

12. After using these strategies, *consult your counselor or doctor if you have trouble sleeping.* He or she may have other ideas to help you get the rest you need.

Source: National Heart, Lung, and Blood Institute (2011).

caffeine or alcohol before bedtime, going to bed at the same time every night, rising at the same hour in the morning, and restricting activities in the bedroom to sleep and sex, rather than work and TV viewing (see the "Prevention" feature on sleep hygiene). This last component (instruction #11 in the "Prevention" feature) is called **stimulus control**, and it is based on the classical conditioning principle (Chapter 2) of strengthening the association of bed with sleep, rather than with anxiety or activity (Kierlin, 2008). In stimulus control, individuals are instructed to get out of bed anytime (at the beginning, middle, or end of the night) that they are lying in bed for a span of time without sleeping, so that they only use their bed for sleep. Although stimulus control instructions appear simple and straightforward, compliance is better if the instructions are discussed individually and a rationale is provided for each instruction (Bootzin, 2013).

stimulus control: A treatment for insomnia in which individuals are instructed to get out of bed anytime they are not sleepy so that the association between bed and sleep is strengthened; this can be used on its own or in conjunction with a broader sleep hygiene approach.

Other Sleep-Wake Disorders

Other prominent sleep-wake disorders include:

1. **Hypersomnolence disorder.** In this disorder, a person complains of excessive sleepiness and engages in prolonged episodes of sleep on an almost daily basis. Individuals with this disorder can have an extremely hard time waking up, despite setting multiple alarms, having friends try to awaken them, or sleeping on a couch or chair instead of a bed. It feels like they can never get enough sleep, even though they get a normal amount of sleep each night (i.e., 6–9 hours). Daytime naps do not help them feel more refreshed or alert. They can very easily fall asleep during activities that are relaxing or unstimulating (e.g., watching movies, reading, sitting in an abnormal psychology class). Many individuals with this disorder show symptoms of depression (American Psychiatric Association, 2013a). Of individuals who seek treatment in sleep disorder clinics, 5–10% will be diagnosed with hypersomnolence disorder; it is diagnosed equally among men and women (American Psychiatric Association, 2013). Stimulant medications are often prescribed to treat this disorder.

2. **Narcolepsy.** This disorder describes a person who experiences excessive daytime sleepiness and suffers sudden attacks of REM sleep. Such sleep attacks can occur multiple times per day, regardless of the amount of nighttime sleep. Moving so quickly in and out of REM sleep can lead to sleep paralysis and hallucinations, both when a person falls asleep and when he or she wakes up. For many individuals, narcolepsy is accompanied by **cataplexy**, a loss of muscle tone that can cause a person to collapse and be immobile for several seconds to a few minutes. Cataplexy is usually preceded by the experience of strong emotions, such as laughter and joking. Narcolepsy is rare, affecting less than 0.05% of the population, with men slightly more likely to have this disorder than women (American Psychiatric Association, 2013a). Stimulant medications are often prescribed for individuals with narcolepsy to help them stay awake during the day. Antidepressant medications can help reduce episodes of cataplexy, sleep paralysis, and hallucinations (Akintomide & Rickards, 2011).

3. **Obstructive sleep apnea hypopnea.** Sleep apnea involves cessation of breathing during sleep. A large tongue, tonsils, or neck, or structural abnormalities that narrow or partially block the airway can cause temporary pauses in breathing. The hallmark of obstructive sleep apnea is snoring—loud, stentorian, rattle-the-house snoring (like your roommate?). The loud snoring is interrupted by silence when breathing stops, followed by a loud snort as the person gasps for air. This pattern occurs throughout the night, at least a handful of times per hour. Multiple brief awakenings during the night generally leave a person feeling exhausted the next day. The person does not fully awaken during these pauses of breathing, so usually it is a spouse or partner who notices the gasps for air. Obstructive sleep apnea is a common disorder, affecting 3–7% of adults worldwide (Punjabi, 2008). It is most often diagnosed in overweight individuals between 40 and 60 years of age, and in men more than women (American Psychiatric Association, 2013a). Individuals with sleep apnea have higher rates of heart disease and heart failure, high blood pressure, stroke, diabetes, and depression (American Psychiatric Association, 2013a). Treatment involves keeping the airway open during sleep. Not sleeping on one's back, avoiding alcohol before bed, and losing weight can help in many cases. Other individuals find relief using a continuous positive airway pressure (CPAP) machine at bedtime, which helps them breathe better during sleep via a mask that is worn over the nose. The machine provides a steady stream of pressurized air that keeps the airways open. While the CPAP machine is effective for most people with sleep apnea, it must be worn for it to work. Some individuals report embarrassment over having to wear a mask at bedtime, others will unknowingly remove the mask during sleep, and still others report that the mask is uncomfortable.

4. **Circadian rhythm sleep disorder.** This disorder involves a pattern of sleep disturbance caused by a mismatch between a person's natural circadian sleep/wake

cycle and the demands of the environment. The most common causes of this disorder are changing shifts at work and air travel across time zones. In such cases, individuals feel ready for sleep at the wrong time or try to sleep when their bodies are not ready. Adolescents are more likely than other age groups to experience a *delayed sleep phase*, such that they are not ready to sleep until late at night. This can make early school start times (or early college classes) especially problematic. The hormonal changes of puberty may exacerbate this problem (American Psychiatric Association, 2013a). Individuals in late adulthood are more likely than other age groups to experience an *advanced sleep phase*, such that they go to sleep more than 2 hours earlier (and thus awaken earlier) than desired (American Psychiatric Association, 2013a). Other individuals have an *irregular sleep phase*, such that they do not have a major sleep session at all and instead take several naps (usually during the day). Treatments for circadian rhythm sleep disorder can involve chronotherapy, where sleep time is gradually shifted to approach the desired sleep schedule; light therapy, which uses bright lights to trigger wakefulness at desired times; and sleep hygiene strategies (see the earlier "Prevention" feature) to facilitate an appropriate sleep schedule.

LONDON BANGKO

MOSCO\

SYDNEY ROME

Source: gualtiero boffi/Shutterstock.com.

The well-known phenomenon of "jet lag" is particularly difficult following travel eastward, when time "is lost." For example, the records of professional sports teams are worse for games played immediately after eastward travel than for games played the day after traveling westward.

5. **Parasomnias.** Parasomnias are a group of sleep-wake disorders that involve unusual behaviors or abnormal physiological events during sleep. The most common parasomnias are nightmare disorder and NREM sleep arousal disorders.

Nightmare disorder involves repeated frightening dreams that interrupt sleep during REM sleep. Often, the nightmares involve a sense of danger and pertain to the themes of survival, security, or safety. The nightmares are easily remembered, and details can be easily described. Usually, a person is highly alert upon awakening from the nightmare, which can make returning to sleep difficult. In occasional cases, multiple nightmares occur in the same night, sometimes revolving around a common theme. Disturbing nightmares can occur in children younger than 5; 1–4% of parents report that their young children have nightmares "often" or "always" (American Psychiatric Association, 2013a, p. 405).

In **NREM sleep arousal disorders**, a person experiences incomplete awakening from sleep, with either sleepwalking or sleep terrors. *Sleepwalking* involves the person leaving the bed and moving about; simply sitting up in bed, talking, or gesturing may also occur. During the episode, the person is unresponsive and can be awakened only with great difficulty. After the episode, the person has no memory of what transpired. Sleepwalking is not uncommon: 10–30% of children have had an episode of sleepwalking (American Psychiatric Association, 2013a).

During *sleep terrors*, the person awakens with a terrified scream or panicky cry. It may be difficult to comfort or reassure the person, who often remains upset for several minutes. The next morning, the person has no memory of the terror. Sleep terrors do not involve story-length nightmares, but they may include frightening images. As many as 37% of 18-month-olds and nearly 20% of 30-month-olds experience sleep terrors, compared to 2% of the adult population (American Psychiatric Association, 2013a). Most childhood cases spontaneously disappear in adolescence.

It is important to note that all individuals experience nightmares from time to time, and sleepwalking and sleep terrors are not unusual, especially among children. Only when nightmares, sleepwalking, and sleep terrors recur and cause clinically significant distress or impairment do clinicians consider diagnosing a parasomnia.

parasomnias: Sleep disturbances involving unusual behaviors or abnormal physiological events during sleep.

nightmare disorder: A parasomnia that involves repeated frightening dreams that interrupt sleep, usually during REM stages.

NREM sleep arousal disorders: Parasomnias in which a person experiences incomplete awakening from sleep, with either sleepwalking or sleep terrors.

Chapter 12 Eating, Feeding, and Sleep-Wake Disorders   411

6. Some sleep-wake disorders can be caused by substances. **Substance/medication-induced sleep disorder** refers to problems of sleep that are the direct physiological result of ingestion of a medication or a drug of abuse. Usually, the substance causes insomnia, hypersomnolence, or a parasomnia. The substance most often associated with sleep disorders is alcohol, but amphetamines, caffeine, cannabis, cocaine, and opioids are other frequent culprits. Sleep disorders can occur either during the intoxication phase or the withdrawal phase of drug use. The use of several medications prescribed for anxiety and sleep problems can ultimately contribute to sleep disorders. For example, although sedatives and tranquilizers produce the desired increase in sleepiness when they are first taken, when used repeatedly, they lead to tolerance, meaning that more and more of the drug must be taken to achieve the desired result. If a person discontinues the drug, a sleep disorder may appear rapidly.

Section Review

The *DSM-5* describes a number of sleep-wake disorders, including:

- those that involve disturbances in the duration, timing, or quality of sleep, including insomnia disorder, hypersomnolence disorder, narcolepsy, obstructive sleep apnea hypopnea, and circadian rhythm sleep disorder.
- parasomnias, which involve abnormal behavioral or physiological events taking place during sleep, including nightmare disorder and NREM sleep arousal disorders (involving sleepwalking or night terrors).
- sleep problems that are the direct result of a medication or a drug of abuse, in which case substance/medication-induced sleep disorder would be diagnosed.

Sleep problems are best treated with psychotherapy, such as sleep hygiene and stimulus control, rather than medication.

Summary

Eating Disorders

Anorexia nervosa is characterized by an unreasonable fear of gaining weight and the relentless pursuit of thinness, even at the cost of serious malnutrition. Individuals with anorexia try to reduce their weight by engaging in extreme diet restrictions and/or excessive exercise. Bulimia nervosa is a pattern of excessive binge eating followed by purging (e.g., self-induced vomiting) or other inappropriate strategies intended to prevent weight gain. Binge-eating disorder is marked by recurrent binge eating, but in contrast to bulimia, a person with binge-eating disorder does not use inappropriate strategies such as vomiting, excessive exercise, diuretics, or laxatives to compensate for binge eating.

Most researchers agree that there is no single pathway to the development of an eating disorder and that multiple risk factors combine to increase the likelihood that a person will develop an eating disorder. Psychological vulnerabilities, biological factors, and sociocultural factors are all identified as playing causal roles in the development of eating disorders.

A variety of psychological treatments for eating disorders have been studied, and several have shown promise.

Cognitive-behavioral therapy (CBT) and interpersonal psychotherapy (IPT) are the most widely studied psychological treatments for eating disorders. For anorexia, no psychological treatment has yet emerged as clearly superior to another, but for bulimia, CBT has had considerable success and is considered a first-line treatment approach. IPT also has research support for its utility in treating bulimia and binge eating. Family therapy and also dialectical behavior therapy (DBT) have shown promise in the treatment of eating disorders. Medications have limited support for the treatment of anorexia, but fluoxetine (Prozac) is widely used to reduce binge-and-purge episodes among individuals with bulimia. More research is needed to understand the role of medications in the treatment of binge-eating disorder.

Pica and avoidant/restrictive food intake disorder are other eating and feeding disorders seen in clinical practice, especially when working with children. Pica involves the recurrent consumption of nonnutritive, nonfood items (e.g., acorns, ash, chalk, charcoal, clay, gum, paint chips, paper, soil) that are inappropriate for an individual's developmental level. Avoidant/restrictive food intake disorder describes a problem with eating/feeding that is not due

Ted Weltzin

Dr. Theodore Weltzin, MD, is Medical Director of Eating-Disorder Services at Rogers Memorial Hospital. He is a leading expert in the treatment and research of eating disorders, and he has spearheaded training and program development at one of the largest eating-disorder treatment centers in the country. Dr. Weltzin is a Fellow of the American Psychiatric Association.

Q *What changes have you observed over the years in the clinical presentation of eating disorders?*

A In general, the clinical presentation has been that there are more co-occurring problems, such as alcohol and drug abuse, depression, and OCD [obsessive-compulsive disorder]. The reasons for this are not clear, but these additional clinical conditions make eating disorders more difficult to treat, as they reduce recovery rates and increase cost and duration of treatment.

Q *What differences exist in the presentation of men and women with eating disorders?*

A Men are more likely to have been overweight and teased about their weight, as well as more likely to focus on muscularity rather than thinness. Also, we do see increased rates of eating disorders with excessive exercise as the primary symptom in men.

Q *How do you see the changes in the DSM-5 impacting the diagnosis and treatment of eating disorders?*

A The biggest impact will be the addition of binge-eating disorder (BED) as a specific diagnosis. Data support that binge eating is very likely more prevalent than anorexia and bulimia, and with a specific diagnostic category, this will increase treatment options for people with BED. Also, as up to 40% of individuals with BED are males, this will further awareness of eating disorders and eating-disorder treatment as not just for women.

Q *Given that many individuals with binge-eating disorder are overweight, is weight loss a treatment goal?*

A The initial focus on binge eating needs to be on normalizing eating, developing a more normal relationship with food, and decreasing emotional eating. Weight loss needs to focus on improved fitness and healthier coping skills and occur ideally under the guidance of a dietician with eating-disorder expertise.

---

to body image concerns and that results in inadequate nutrition or calorie consumption. A person may have a lack of interest in eating or food; avoid certain foods because of their taste, texture, or smell; or avoid food because of fears about eating, such as choking or food poisoning.

Sleep-Wake Disorders

Sleep-wake disorders involve (1) disturbances in the duration, timing, or quality of sleep or (2) parasomnias, which involve abnormal behavioral or physiological events taking place during sleep.

Sleep-wake disorders that involve disturbances in the duration, timing, or quality of sleep include:

- insomnia disorder, in which a person has a hard time falling asleep, staying asleep, or waking up too early;

- hypersomnolence disorder, in which a person sleeps too much;

- narcolepsy, a disorder marked by sleep attacks and sometimes cataplexy;

- obstructive sleep apnea hypopnea, in which a person stops breathing many times during sleep; and

- circadian rhythm sleep disorder, which describes problems with the sleep-wake cycle.

Parasomnias include nightmare disorder and NREM sleep arousal disorders (involving either sleepwalking or night terrors). Front-line treatment for sleep disorders include psychotherapy (sleep hygiene and stimulus control) rather than medication.

Key Terms

Sexual Dysfunctions and Gender Dysphoria

Source: Syda Productions/Shutterstock.com.

Chapter Outline

Overview of Sexual Dysfunctions

Types and Causes of Sexual Dysfunctions

Treatment of Sexual Dysfunctions

Gender Dysphoria

From the Case of Alexandra

Alexandra is a 21-year-old female who was raised in a conservative, religious household. She has long considered herself a role model for her three younger siblings. In high school, she excelled academically, showed respect for her parents and their rules, and never got into any kind of trouble. Alexandra's parents always stressed the importance of Alexandra waiting to have sex until marriage. Even though she dated a couple of boys during high school, she never engaged in sexual contact beyond kissing.

When Alexandra was 18 years old, she started college to become a teacher. A couple of weeks into her first semester, she went to her friend David's place, where his roommates were having a party. David offered Alexandra a beer, which she refused at first. However, she gave in after David started to tease her for not wanting to drink with him and his roommates. After drinking far more than she intended, Alexandra ended up sleeping with David that night.

Confused about her feelings for David, Alexandra called him several times in the following days. He never responded. The next time they happened to run into each other, David told her to leave him alone and that sleeping with each other did not mean he liked her. After this event, Alexandra did not seek out any romantic relationships for several years.

After reading this chapter, you will be able to answer the following key questions:

- What is the sexual response cycle?
- What factors affect sexual responsiveness?
- How has understanding of sexual dysfunctions changed over time?
- What are the characteristics of the sexual dysfunctions described in the *Diagnostic and Statistical Manual of Mental Disorders (DSM-5)*?
- How are sexual dysfunctions treated?
- What is gender dysphoria, and how is it treated?

Now 21, Alexandra spends most of her time studying for her classes and relaxing with her friends. She has grown close to a new guy, Michael, with whom she has been going out for about 6 months. Even though Alexandra likes Michael a lot, she feels uncomfortable kissing Michael and does not usually initiate it. When Michael touches her and tries to be physically close to her, she feels indifferent and tends to pull away from him. Not recognizing Alexandra's mixed signals, Michael coaxed her to sleep with him a couple of days ago. Alexandra agreed because she feared Michael would break up with her. During their sexual encounter, Alexandra did not feel aroused, even though Michael was gentle, caring, and giving. She wants to be in a romantic relationship but feels anxious and tense when thinking about her lack of sexual interest and desire.

Concerns about sexual functioning and gender can be very challenging, impacting relationships, self-concept, and self-esteem. The disorders described in this chapter address problems affecting sexual physiology as well as one's self-concept of gender. We first provide background information regarding sexual dysfunctions before addressing their core characteristics and treatment. We conclude by addressing gender dysphoria, including its prevalence, causes, and treatment.

Overview of Sexual Dysfunctions

sexual dysfunctions: A category of disorders involving problems with sexual response or sexual pleasure.

The category of disorders known as **sexual dysfunctions** involves a variety of difficulties in a person's ability to respond sexually or to experience sexual pleasure. Laboratory research on the biopsychosocial aspects of sexual activity has helped clinicians understand the nature, causes, and treatment of these dysfunctions. We begin by providing an overview of the research on typical sexual responses.

The Sexual Response Cycle

sexual response cycle: A sequence of psychological changes and physiological reactions, consisting of desire, excitement, orgasm, and resolution.

Sexual responsiveness is conceptualized as a sequence of psychological changes and physiological reactions known as the **sexual response cycle**. The original sexual response cycle was conceived by pioneering sex researchers William Masters and Virginia Johnson (1966). At Washington University in St. Louis, they conducted detailed studies of the physiological changes that occurred as paid volunteers engaged in various sex acts in their laboratory. The couple divorced in 1991 after two decades of marriage (hopefully not due to a poor sex life!); Masters died in 2001, and Johnson died in 2013.

vasocongestion: An excessive accumulation of blood in tissue.

According to Masters and Johnson, the first phase of sexual response is *excitement*, characterized by several physiological changes in the sexual organs, skin, and throughout the body. These changes include increased heart rate and respiration; **vasocongestion** (swelling) of the penis or clitoris; lubrication of the vagina; flushing of the abdomen, chest, and face; breast enlargement; and erection of the nipples. A period of high arousal potentially sets the stage for the *orgasmic phase*, when sexual pleasure peaks with involuntary rhythmic contractions of the body and a release of sexual tension. For males, **orgasm** involves ejaculation of semen; for females, orgasm consists of contractions of the labia minora, vagina, and uterus.

orgasm: The phase of sexual response when sexual pleasure peaks with involuntary rhythmic muscle contractions and a release of sexual tension; in males, this typically involves ejaculation, whereas in females, this involves contractions of the labia minora, vagina, and uterus.

During the *resolution phase*, the blood that has collected in the sexual organs disperses. If orgasm has occurred, resolution happens quickly and is experienced as a sense of well-being. Without orgasm, resolution can take up to 6 hours. During and after resolution in men, there is a *refractory period* during which they cannot be stimulated to orgasm. Because women do not enter such a phase, some can experience multiple and successive orgasms (Sadock, 1995).

Since the inception of Masters and Johnson's (1966) sexual response cycle nearly 50 years ago, a number of criticisms have been leveled against the classic theory (Levin, 2008). For example, Tiefer (1991) argued that Masters and Johnson's sexual response cycle depicts a biological parallelism between male and female sexual responses that is largely inaccurate. In particular, Masters and Johnson's model may minimize the intricacies of female sexual response (Tiefer, 1991). In addition, Masters and Johnson's research methods have been criticized. Their sexual response model is based on a small sample of participants who were highly orgasmic and sexually open individuals, willing to participate in what was (and likely still would be) highly controversial research (Tiefer, 1991). The generalizability of findings with such a sample is questionable. Masters and Johnson's model also has been criticized for failing to account for the impact of psychological influences on sexual response. Kaplan (1974) therefore added the stage of *desire*, which is thought to occur prior to the excitement phase. Thus, the sexual response cycle begins with a person's psychosocial desire to have sex, often triggered by thoughts and fantasies about a sexual activity or a sexual partner. As these fantasies continue, the person starts anticipating emotional and physical reactions that occurred in past sexual encounters, which intensifies the level of desire.

Changing Views of Sexual Dysfunctions

Psychoanalytic theories about sexual dysfunction were dominant in the late 19th and early 20th centuries. They held that problems with sexual function reflected unresolved conflicts from early childhood. Treatment relied on long-term individual therapy aimed at resolving these conflicts, but the outcomes of these treatments were generally poor, and mental health professionals then concluded that sexual dysfunctions were difficult to treat (Levine, 1995; Sadock, 1995).

Sex is a natural part of life for all living beings, yet it makes many people uncomfortable. Did you have "the talk" with your parents? How did it go?

The theory and treatment of sexual dysfunctions changed dramatically in the 1960s and 1970s, largely because of the research of Masters and Johnson (1966, 1970). In addition to the sexual response cycle, they also studied individuals with a wide variety of sexual dysfunctions. Their observations contradicted prevailing psychoanalytic wisdom. For example, psychoanalysts had argued historically that orgasm arising from vaginal stimulation was more psychosexually mature than orgasm from clitoral stimulation. Masters and Johnson confirmed the importance of clitoral stimulation, direct or indirect, in all female orgasms and showed that, contrary to popular belief, the physiological responses were the same, regardless of the focus of stimulation (Levine, 1995).

Research by Masters and Johnson also led to a more detailed classification of sexual dysfunctions. They were the first to distinguish between lifelong and acquired sexual disorders and to expand clinicians' understanding of how psychological factors affect sexual dysfunctions. Prior to publication of Master and Johnson's work, the only two sexual dysfunctions described in males were *impotence* (now viewed as a pejorative term describing the inability to attain or maintain an erection) and *premature ejaculation*. Similarly, *frigidity*, or lack of sexual interest and responsivity, was the label used for sexual dysfunctions that women experienced (Levine, 1995). Masters and Johnson identified additional sexual dysfunctions—as did other sex researchers such as Helen Singer Kaplan (1977, 1979)—and described these problems in relation to the different phases of the sexual response cycle.

Traditionally, people have been reluctant to talk about their sexual dysfunctions, and even today, many individuals and couples find it difficult to seek help when these problems occur (Chang, Klein, & Gorzalka, 2013; Heiman, 1993). This reticence is unfortunate because treatment is often easier and more successful than once believed. Sexual dysfunctions are also more common than many people think. In Western cultures, most people experience brief periods of sexual dysfunction at some point in their lives (Heiman, 1993). For example, periods of stress or sorrow are often accompanied by temporary disinterest in sex or lessened sexual responsiveness.

Chapter 13 Sexual Dysfunctions and Gender Dysphoria

Factors Affecting Sexual Responsiveness

Sexual responsiveness depends on the interplay of several physiological and psychological factors (Heiman, 1993; Sewell, 2005).

Neurological, Vascular, and Hormonal Factors

Any factor that has a negative impact on *neurological*, *vascular*, or *hormonal* functioning can interfere with sexual response. These include, for example, chronic medical conditions such as diabetes mellitus, psychological disorders such as major depressive disorder, the use of certain medications, and aging. Thus, although healthy men experience sexual pleasure and satisfaction across the lifespan, there may be age-related decrements in sexual desire, arousal, and activity (Schiavi, Schreiner-Engel, Mandeli, Schanzer, & Cohen, 1990; Strassberg, Perelman, & Watter, 2014). Women, too, report decreased frequency of intercourse and orgasm as they grow older (Katz-Bearnot, 2010). These changes are linked to the decline in estrogen production that comes with menopause. As estrogen levels drop, vaginal lubrication decreases, and blood flow to the pelvic area lessens during intercourse (Clayton, 2012). These changes can make sexual intercourse uncomfortable and even painful, but many age-related changes can be addressed with current treatments.

Attitudes and Beliefs

Sexual response is also influenced by *attitudes* and *beliefs* about sex that have been shaped by cultural and religious heritage, family traditions, and sexual experiences. In North America, various cultural and religious groups endorse different attitudes toward sexual behavior. Thus, a person with a strong religious background might view extramarital sex as strictly forbidden, which is what Alexandra's parents in the chapter-opening case taught her. Someone raised in a predominantly Hispanic community might value *traditional machismo* sexual behavior for men but maintain more conservative ideas about sexual freedoms for women. They might also value *caballerismo*, or the importance of emotional connectedness, honor, and nurturance within close relationships (Arciniega, Anderson, Tovar-Blank, & Tracey, 2008). Family-based learning also influences beliefs about sexuality. When parents punish a young child for masturbating or encourage an adolescent to carry condoms when dating a steady partner, they are passing on to their children certain attitudes about sex. Parents also model sex-related attitudes when they display comfort with physical contact by giving hugs and kisses or when they avoid showing affection for each other in front of their children.

Finally, a person's sexual history can influence comfort with sexual activity. Episodes of criticism, abuse, or coerced sexual activity may inhibit sexual interest or response, as it did for Alexandra. Sexual abuse during childhood can have a profound effect on sexual functioning in adulthood (Aaron, 2012; Wyatt, Guthrie, & Notgrass, 1991). Some individuals who have suffered abuse become sexually inhibited and fearful, whereas others may become sexually promiscuous.

Interpersonal Factors

The relationship between sexual partners also affects sexual behavior. Emotional closeness normally enhances sexual desire, while emotional distance often dampens it. If one partner has a much stronger need for sexual contact than the other, this "desire discrepancy" can cause distress, especially if the desires of one partner are experienced as coercive (Rosen & Leiblum, 1995; Strassberg et al., 2014). The history of the relationship is also important. Many couples become less sexually active as they age and as they deal with careers, child rearing, emotional conflicts, and other stressors. Still, among all sexually active adults in the United States, people in committed partnerships report the highest level of pleasure from their sexual relationships (Michael, Gagnon, Laumann, & Kolata, 1994; Waite & Joyner, 2001).

In summary, clinicians attempting to treat sexual dysfunctions must first carefully assess each client or couple to understand the role of biological factors, attitudes and beliefs, and relationship factors in the problems reported.

Connections

What other mental disorders have been linked to a history of childhood sexual abuse? See Chapters 9 through 12.

The sexual response cycle:

- was studied carefully by the pioneering sex researchers Masters and Johnson,
- describes a sequence of psychological changes and physiological reactions that occurs during sexual activity, and
- now includes the phases of desire, excitement, orgasm, and resolution.

Sexual dysfunctions:

- are no longer viewed through a psychoanalytic lens,
- include a variety of sexual concerns experienced by both men and women, and
- are common and treatable.

Factors that affect sexual responsiveness include:

- neurological, vascular, and hormonal factors;
- attitudes and beliefs that come from one's culture, religion, family of origin, and sexual history; and
- the relationship between sexual partners.

Types and Causes of Sexual Dysfunctions

The *DSM-5* describes a variety of sexual dysfunctions that affect various stages of the sexual response cycle. And like many classes of disorders, the conceptualization and understanding of sexual dysfunctions have evolved over the years.

To more precisely define sexual dysfunction, the *DSM-5* specifies a duration and frequency for a given sexual problem (see Table 13.1). Thus, for a diagnosis of a sexual dysfunction to be given, individuals must have experienced the problem for a period of at least 6 months and in 75% or more of the instances in which they attempted sexual activity. The idea here is that it is normal to experience sexual difficulties every now and then, for any number of reasons, and calling something pathological, when it is actually just a temporary problem, is avoided. Along those same lines, the *DSM-5* acknowledges that even long-standing behavior may be normal *given the circumstances*. If a woman is experiencing significant strain in her relationship—or perhaps physical, sexual, or emotional violence—then it would be normal for her to have difficulty with sexual functioning. In such cases, a diagnosis of sexual dysfunction is not warranted.

The *DSM-5* uses four modifiers to better describe each sexual dysfunction. Specifically, clinicians note whether the problem is **lifelong** or **acquired** to distinguish an individual who has had a sexual dysfunction since becoming sexually active ("lifelong") from one whose sexual dysfunction only develops following a chronic medical condition or a specific sexual trauma. They also note whether the sexual dysfunction is **generalized** or **situational**, meaning whether it is problematic in every situation or only problematic in certain situations or with certain partners. The specific sexual dysfunctions listed in the *DSM-5* are discussed next, beginning with those that are most common in females.

lifelong: A modifier used to describe a sexual dysfunction that has always occurred since one's first sexual experiences.

acquired: A modifier used to describe a sexual dysfunction that develops after a period of normal sexual functioning.

generalized: A modifier used to describe a sexual dysfunction that occurs in most or all sexual situations.

situational: A modifier used to describe a sexual dysfunction that occurs only in certain sexual situations.

TABLE 13.1 The *DSM-5* in Simple Language: Diagnosing Sexual Dysfunction

To diagnose someone with any sexual dysfunction, the following three items must be true:

1. The sexual problem must have lasted at least 6 months and occurred in 75–100% of sexual experiences.
2. The sexual dysfunction must not be primarily due to severe relationship problems or other severe stressors; a substance, medication, or medical condition; or another mental disorder.
3. The symptoms must cause significant distress.

Source: Adapted from American Psychiatric Association (2013a).

In the 19th century, it was a common medical belief that women did not experience sexual desire. As a result of this myth, women often suppressed their sexual urges for fear of being chastised by parents, peers, and potential suitors. Whereas it was considered normal for men to have a healthy sexual appetite, those women who dared to enjoy a more open and adventurous sexual lifestyle were thought to have a mental disorder termed *nymphomania* (uncontrollable sexual desire). Women labeled as nymphomaniacs were told to abstain from substances believed to increase sexual appetite (like red meat and alcohol), to sleep on a horse-hair mattress instead of a more comfortable one, and to clean their vagina with borax, a strong soap. In some cases, such women were even institutionalized (Groneman, 1994; Pouba & Tianen, 2006).

Source: Creativemarc/Shutterstock.com.

Female Sexual Interest/Arousal Disorder

female sexual interest/arousal disorder (FSI/AD): A sexual dysfunction in women marked by low or no sexual interest or arousal.

Female sexual interest/arousal disorder (FSI/AD) is one of three sexual disorders specific to women. It is characterized by an absence of or reduced frequency or intensity of three or more of the following: (1) sexual interest, (2) sexual arousal, (3) sexual thoughts or fantasies, (4) initiation of sexual activity, (5) the experience of sexual excitement or pleasure, and/or (6) physical sensations during sexual activity (American Psychiatric Association, 2013a). FSI/AD represents a merging of two disorders that existed in the previous version of the *DSM*: female hypoactive desire disorder and female arousal disorder. Because researchers found that these two disorders were often comorbid (occurring at the same time) and difficult (and perhaps unnecessary) to tease apart, it was determined that one disorder capturing difficulty with both interest and arousal was more appropriate. Alexandra in the chapter-opening case has symptoms of FSI/AD, as does Kathy in the description that follows:

Kathy and Will had a very active sex life for the first 8 years of their marriage. They both enjoyed sexual intimacy and had sex three or four nights a week, on average. Kathy rarely had trouble in feeling desire to have sex with Will or in becoming aroused. Then, their relationship hit a rough patch. Kathy became frustrated and dissatisfied with the state of their marriage. She felt that she was always taking care of household responsibilities and that Will was not "pulling his weight." What had once been an active sex life was gradually becoming nonexistent, and Will's attempts to have sex with Kathy were now almost always met with disinterest. Will tried using different forms of stimulation, such as erotic stories and videos, to pique his wife's interest, but they had no impact on Kathy's desire to be intimate with her husband.

When they started seeing a marriage counselor, Kathy disclosed feeling emotionally distant from Will. Over the years, they had stopped engaging in many leisure activities together, like going to the movies or out to dinner. As part of treatment, Kathy and Will made a concerted effort to start spending positive time together again. Kathy also learned how to more effectively communicate with Will about helping out around the house, and Will made a corresponding effort to assist more with household chores. They were also given intimacy exercises, gradually incorporating sex back into their lives. For the first time in years, Kathy began to feel a desire to be sexual again. Better communication strategies and a renewed emotional closeness to Will helped Kathy to be more receptive to Will's advances and to actually initiate sex at times.

Identifying when a woman has significantly low sexual interest or desire can be difficult because there is no fixed standard of normalcy. How does one decide when interest in sex becomes abnormally low? Measuring the frequency of sexual fantasies may provide a better way of estimating a woman's sexual interest; fantasy frequency has historically been lower in those with low desire than in sexually functional adults (Wincze & Carey, 2001). It should be noted that some women self-identify as asexual, having experienced low desire throughout their lives without concern. Such a scenario would not warrant a diagnosis (American Psychiatric Association, 2013a).

In practice, problems with interest and desire often occur alongside difficulty with orgasmic ability, sexual pain, relationship problems, and mood disturbance. Age of onset can vary; sexual inhibitions learned during childhood or adolescence often carry over into adulthood (Yates, 1993). However, women typically are not aware of a problem until they begin to have active sexual lives, and still other women may experience no difficulty at first but start to develop problems with changing life circumstances.

Whereas the sexual response cycle was once conceptualized as a linear progression (desire leading to excitement, orgasm, and resolution), it is now understood differently. There is acknowledgment that desire does not always precede arousal, and in fact, women may have any number of reasons for initiating sexual activity outside of feeling sexual desire. For instance, a woman may want to feel emotionally close to her partner or may want to bring pleasure to him or her. In the process, a woman may experience arousal, which then triggers her desire to continue sexual activity and perhaps, though not necessarily, reach orgasm (Basson, 2005).

Prevalence

The prevalence of FSI/AD is unknown, as it is a new disorder. However, it is known that problems with both interest and arousal are quite common. In fact, Shifren and colleagues (2008) found that low desire was the most common self-reported sexual difficulty among women in the United States, endorsed by approximately 39% of a large national sample, followed by low arousal (26%). More desire and arousal problems were reported by: women ages 35–64 (versus women over 64 or under 35); married versus single women; women with co-occurring medical and mental conditions, such as thyroid problems, depression, and anxiety; and women without a current sexual partner (Shifren, Monz, Russo, Segreti, & Johannes, 2008). A review of the literature showed that women who reported low desire also tended to report poor self-image, mood instability, and anxiety (Hartmann, Heiser, Rüffer-Hesse, & Kloth, 2002).

Causal Factors

Like most aspects of sexual behavior, sexual desire is shaped by biological, cognitive, and emotional factors (Levine, 1995). People usually feel desire when a biological drive for sex, determined by neuroendocrine mechanisms and manifested in genital arousal, is joined with positive expectations about sexual behavior and being in the "right mood" to engage in sex with a specific person. In some cases, the biological basis of sexual desire may be impaired, sometimes as a result of natural aging.

The gonadal hormones, especially androgens, help maintain sexual desire. Both men and women have testosterone and estrogen receptors in the brain, concentrated in areas such as the hypothalamus that control emotional and sexual feelings (McEwen, 1991). Although the role of testosterone is not as consistent in women as it is in men, some research has found that testosterone replacement resulted in more sexual activity and sexual pleasure in menopausal women (Shifren et al., 2000). Estrogen in women is important for maintaining vaginal response and comfort during sexual stimulation, but may not affect sexual desire or arousal on its own. In studies of postmenopausal women with low sexual desire, those who were placed on

"Well, maybe I would want to have sexual relations with you more often if you weren't always such a beast."

a combination of estrogen and testosterone supplements had significant improvement in levels of interest and desire, compared to women who just received estrogen treatment alone (Lobo, Rosen, Yang, Block, & Van Der Hoop, 2003; Sherwin, Gelfand, & Brender, 1985).

In many cases of sexual dysfunction, including FSI/AD, a clear-cut biological cause cannot be identified. For some women, problems with interest and desire may be attributed more to psychosocial factors. Consider a woman who grew up in a family or culture where sex was always described in negative terms, as something "bad" that only "dirty" women do, like Alexandra in the chapter-opening case. Such societal messages can have a major impact on how a woman views herself as a sexual being and on her sexual experiences. Contrast this with a woman who grew up in an environment where sex was considered a healthy part of adult and relationship functioning. It is much more likely that this second woman would go on to have positive sexual experiences and normal sexual functioning.

As with all sexual dysfunctions, a history of negative sexual experiences and negative outcome expectations can inhibit sexual arousal (Graham, Sanders, Milhausen, & McBride, 2004), as was the case for Alexandra and her bad experience with David in college. Further, victims of childhood sexual abuse often experience adult sexual difficulties that are closely tied to the form of the abuse. For example, women who were sexually fondled as children may fail to become aroused when engaging in foreplay that resembles the abuse pattern. Given a safe and loving relationship, however, these same women may become aroused during other sexual activities (Becker, Skinner, Abel, & Cichon, 1986; Wincze & Carey, 2001).

Problems with interest and arousal can also be caused by a number of cognitive and interpersonal problems. Anxiety about sex can be one of the major threats to adequate arousal. Any time sexual partners worry about whether they are "doing sex the right way" or whether they will satisfy their partners, they may become distracted from the physical sensations of sexual activity that are naturally arousing. Hostility or mistrust between partners can also chill sexual arousal. For females in particular, feeling emotionally distant from a partner often interferes with sexual arousal. Finally, interest/arousal difficulties occur in some couples because of a long-term pattern of inadequate or inept sexual foreplay. If one partner is uninterested or uninformed about how to give the other partner sexual pleasure, there may simply be too little stimulation to result in arousal.

Female Orgasmic Disorder

female orgasmic disorder: A sexual dysfunction in which a woman cannot experience orgasm, takes an inordinately long time to reach orgasm, or experiences diminished intensity of orgasm.

Women who cannot experience an orgasm, who take an inordinately long time to reach orgasm, or who experience diminished intensity of orgasm may be diagnosed with **female orgasmic disorder**. Here is an illustrative case:

Lola, a 25-year-old laboratory technician, has been happily married to a 32-year-old cab driver for 5 years and has a 2-year-old son. Her only complaint is a lifelong inability to experience orgasm, even though she receives what she considers to be sufficient stimulation during sexual activity. She has tried to masturbate, and on many occasions, her husband has manually stimulated her for long periods. Whereas these methods have not resulted in orgasm, Lola is strongly attached to her husband, feels erotic pleasure during lovemaking, and lubricates copiously. Her husband reports no sexual difficulty. Clinical interviews reveal that, as she nears orgasm, Lola experiences a sense of dread about some undefined disaster. She fears losing control over her emotions, which she normally keeps closely in check. (Based on Spitzer, Gibbon, Skodol, Williams, & First, 1994)

Prevalence

Difficulty with orgasm is a common sexual complaint, with a 20% prevalence in a large national sample of women in the United States (Shifren et al., 2008), and it is the second most common sexual dysfunction in women behind FSI/AD (Lewis et al., 2010). In an online survey of 1,200 U.S. women, 70% reported experiencing a sexual health problem but fewer than 20% had actually consulted a professional about it (Association of Reproductive Health Professionals, 2009). It appears that women want to get help and are willing to talk about their sexual problems when asked, but they prefer that their providers initiate those conversations (Berman et al., 2003). Unfortunately, health professionals are often hesitant to ask about sexual dysfunction for a variety of reasons, including concerns of embarrassing their patients, uncertainty about appropriate treatment, or assumptions that their patients (e.g., elderly people) are not sexually active (Gianotten, Bender, Post, & Hoing, 2006; Solursh et al., 2003). On the other hand, just because women experience a sexual problem does not necessarily mean that they are distressed by it. Women who cannot or who infrequently experience orgasm may still have high levels of sexual satisfaction. In fact, only about half of women reporting difficulty with orgasm endorse feeling distressed about it (Hayes, Dennerstein, Bennett, & Fairley, 2008). This is an important element, since the *DSM-5* requires significant distress to meet criteria for a diagnosis.

Causal Factors

As with other sexual dysfunctions, there may be multiple causes of female orgasmic disorder. Sometimes, the culprit is lack of adequate stimulation, a factor that needs to be ruled out prior to diagnosis. Many women do not experience orgasm with vaginal penetration alone and need added clitoral stimulation to reach orgasm during intercourse.

There is a long list of risk factors for female orgasmic disorder, many of which overlap with other sexual dysfunctions. Some of these include low education level, higher age, anxiety, depression (Shifren et al., 2008), poor communication with a sexual partner (Kelly, Strassberg, & Turner, 2006), and history of abuse (Rellini & Meston, 2007). Having a chronic medical condition, especially neurological conditions such as multiple sclerosis and spinal cord injury that involve nerve damage, can also interfere with orgasmic ability (Basson, Rees, Wang, Montejo, & Incrocci, 2010). Further, taking certain types of medications, such as antidepressants (see Chapter 6), can influence orgasmic function. One study showed that among people taking selective serotonin reuptake inhibitors (SSRIs), 73% experienced sexual problems, two thirds of whom reported orgasmic dysfunction (Bossini, Fagiolini, Valdagno, Polizzotto, & Castrogiovanni, 2007). Finally, sex hormones also contribute to sexual function and dysfunction. For instance, women given testosterone treatment reported improvements in sexual functioning, including more intense orgasms (Shifren et al., 2000).

Other important factors affecting orgasmic difficulty may include the pubococcygeus muscle, alcohol use, and psychosocial factors. The *pubococcygeus* (or PC) *muscle* is located on the pelvic floor and supports the bowel and bladder. The PC muscle can be weakened over time by a number of factors, including pregnancy and childbirth, and pelvic floor weakness can lead to orgasmic difficulties, incontinence, and sexual dissatisfaction (Rosenbaum, 2007). Although research is limited, pelvic floor rehabilitation—such as via the Kegel exercises described in the "Prevention" feature later in this chapter—has been shown to improve sexual functioning, including orgasmic abilities (Beji, Yalçjn, & Erkan, 2002).

Excessive alcohol and drug use impairs sexual functioning, including a woman's ability to reach orgasm. In a review of the literature, Peugh & Belenko (2001) found that higher blood alcohol levels may hinder sexual response, including orgasmic ability. Higher blood alcohol levels have been associated with longer times to orgasm and subjective reports of diminished orgasmic intensity (Wincze & Carey, 2001). Interestingly, many women may cope with sexual dysfunction with problematic alcohol use, compounding their sexual difficulties and potentially creating a vicious cycle (Peugh & Belenko, 2001). Although the literature is mixed with regard to the effects of other drugs on sexual functioning, chronic use of cocaine, amphetamines, opiates, and other drugs tends to impair functioning, including ability to reach orgasm (Peugh & Belenko, 2001).

Madonna was one of many celebrities who changed the direction of sex in world media, starting in the 1980s. Her coffee-table book, Sex (1992), featured photographs that shocked many of her fans, including pictures of people engaging in paraphilic acts like sadomasochism (see Chapter 17). Believe it or not, in your grandparents' era, you could not just pick up a book like that at a neighborhood bookstore or view racy shows like *Sex in the City* on TV.

genito-pelvic pain/penetration disorder (GPPD): A sexual dysfunction in women that describes tension or pain during intercourse or penetration, or fear of pain or penetration.

It may turn out that female orgasmic disorder may be best explained by factors that contribute to diminished desire and arousal (FSI/AD). For many women, problems with sexual desire, arousal, and orgasm occur simultaneously and reflect cultural, religious, and social attitudes and beliefs about how women should express their sexuality. Over the past century, attitudes about women's sexuality have changed dramatically in many parts of the world. Once expected to be passive recipients of sexual activity, women are now far freer to express and act on their sexual interests and needs. However, they continue to receive mixed messages about their sexuality.

Genito-Pelvic Pain/Penetration Disorder

Another new *DSM-5* disorder, **genito-pelvic pain/penetration disorder (GPPD)**, includes four symptom dimensions: (1) difficulty having intercourse, (2) pain during intercourse or penetration, (3) fear of pain or penetration, and (4) pelvic floor muscle tension (American Psychiatric Association, 2013a). A woman need experience only one of these dimensions to meet diagnostic criteria. Although some men may also experience pelvic pain, it is less well understood at this point, and GPPD is currently diagnosed only in women.

In previous versions of the *DSM*, sexual pain disorders included *dyspareunia* (recurring problems with pain before, during, or after sexual intercourse) and *vaginismus* (involuntary spasm of the musculature in the vagina that precludes penile penetration). Given the high degree of comorbidity and frequent difficulty distinguishing these two disorders in clinical settings, they were merged in the *DSM-5* to form GPPD.

Prevalence

Rates of pelvic pain in community samples have been documented as 12–21% (Arnold, Bachmann, Kelly, Rosen, & Rhoads, 2006); however, prevalence of GPPD is unknown since it is new.

Causal Factors

Dysfunction of the pelvic floor muscles has been shown to be a significant contributor to pelvic pain. Specifically, research has shown that abnormal muscle activity (i.e., spasms) when at rest is most important in predicting pain (Bergeron, Rosen, & Morin, 2011; Reissing, Binik, Khalifé, Cohen, & Amsel, 2004). Electromyographic activity (EMG) can be measured using a small dilator that is inserted into the woman's vagina. Of course, even this step can be quite difficult for some women, who may have developed an automatic defensive reaction to attempted penetration.

Biological factors often play a significant role in sexual pain. The most common organic causes include infections of the urinary tract, vagina, cervix, or fallopian tubes; scarring following surgery related to childbirth; ovarian cysts or tumors; and *endometriosis* (a painful condition in which the growth of endometrial tissue occurs in the pelvic cavity outside the uterus). The decline in estrogen associated with menopause can lead to a thinning of vaginal tissue, lack of lubrication, and consequent pain during intercourse. This specific problem can be readily treated with estrogen replacement therapy or by the topical use of estrogen cream or lubricants.

Pelvic pain can also be viewed from a psychosocial perspective, involving cognitive, emotional, and behavioral factors leading to the pain experience. For example, women with higher levels of anxiety and those who were previously abused are more likely to report genital pain later in life (Landry & Bergeron, 2011). Other factors shown to be relevant in the onset and maintenance of pelvic pain include partner responses to the pain (Rosen, Bergeron, Leclerc, Lambert, & Steben, 2010) and hypervigilance/fear of pain (Desrochers, Bergeron, Khalifé, Dupuis, & Jodoin, 2009). Of course, perhaps *all* of these factors—biological, cognitive, emotional, and behavioral—play important roles in the development and maintenance of genital/pelvic pain (Bergeron et al., 2011).

Classical conditioning theory suggests that genito-pelvic pain might develop in women whose initial experience with intercourse was painful and aversive. Such an experience could lead to avoidance of further sexual contact or to tensing/tightening upon penetration, due to expectations of pain. Repeated episodes of tensing the pelvic floor can then result in worsened sexual functioning. Additionally, avoidance may serve to maintain fear and anxiety about sex because, by avoiding sex, individuals are also avoiding opportunities for positive sexual experiences that could challenge existing negative beliefs.

Next, we discuss the sexual dysfunctions that apply to men.

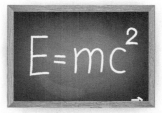

MAPS - Attempted Answers

Male Hypoactive Sexual Desire Disorder

The primary symptoms of **male hypoactive sexual desire disorder (MHSDD)** are deficient or absent (1) sexual or erotic thoughts or fantasies and (2) desire for sexual activity. As noted earlier in the discussion of FSI/AD, hypoactive sexual desire can be difficult to determine because there is no set standard of normal sexual desire. Clinicians are advised to take into account a man's age, current stressors, and other cultural and contextual factors when judging whether or not sexual interest is deficient.

male hypoactive sexual desire disorder (MHSDD): A sexual disorder characterized by a man's lack of sexual thoughts and desire for sexual activity.

Prevalence

The *DSM-5* reports that fewer than 2% of men ages 16–44 struggle with MHSDD (American Psychiatric Association, 2013a). It also notes that as many as 41% of older men (ages 66–74) will experience low sexual desire, although the percentage meeting full diagnostic criteria is unclear. Taken together, studies suggest prevalence rates of 15–25% (Rowland, 2012). As with the other sexual dysfunctions, this disorder can be lifelong or acquired. Men of East Asian ethnicity are reported to have higher rates of low desire (American Psychiatric Association, 2013a).

Causal Factors

Biopsychosocial factors are important to consider when understanding sexual desire. For this and other sexual dysfunctions, the *DSM-5* suggests that clinicians explore medical factors, individual vulnerabilities (e.g., a history of sexual abuse or poor body image), cultural/religious factors (e.g., beliefs about sexuality), as well as relationship and partner factors (e.g., conflicting attitudes about sex, partner is depressed) that may help to better understand the causes and subsequent treatment of this and other sexual disorders (American Psychiatric Association, 2013a).

In some cases of MHSDD, there may be a biological contribution to the impairment of sexual desire. The hypothalamic-pituitary-gonadal (HPG) axis is the way in which the male brain communicates via hormones with the testes. For men in particular, adequate levels of testosterone appear necessary for normal sexual desire (Schiavi, Schreiner-Engel, White, & Mandeli, 1988). Diseases that disrupt the HPG axis, such as Parkinson's disease, may interfere with sexual desire (Rowland, 2012). More generally, any illness that leads to pain or discomfort can lead to diminished desire (Wincze & Carey, 2001).

In many cases of MHSDD, however, biological causes do not appear to contribute to the problem. In these cases, the dysfunction may stem from one or more of the psychosocial factors listed in Figure 13.1. For example, having another mental disorder contributes to loss of sexual desire. Rowland (2012) noted that couples who report low sexual desire have higher rates of past or current depression. In an intriguing study of people with hypoactive sexual desire disorder, 73% of the men and 71% of the women reported a history of depression, compared with 32% of male controls and 27% of female controls (Schreiner-Engel & Schiavi, 1986). For many of these people, sexual desire waned with their first depressive episodes and never fully returned, even if they experienced no further episodes. Schizophrenia also is associated with low sexual desire (Rowland, 2012), as are anxiety disorders and post-traumatic stress disorder (Letourneau, Resnick, Kilpatrick, Saunders, & Best, 1996).

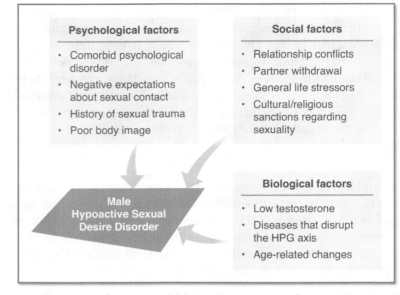

FIGURE 13.1 Possible Causes of Male Hypoactive Sexual Desire Disorder

Interactions of biological, psychological, and social factors can lead to male hypoactive sexual desire disorder.

Sexual inhibitions learned during childhood or adolescence often carry over into adulthood (Yates, 1993). Negative messages about sex learned from parents, or cultural or religious prohibitions about sex can be a source of hypoactive sexual desire (Wincze & Carey, 2001). In addition, a history of childhood sexual abuse or other sexual trauma is associated with impaired desire (Loeb et al., 2002; Wincze & Carey, 2001). Low self-esteem resulting from body image concerns has also been seen among individuals with low sexual desire (Wincze & Carey, 2001).

Distress in a romantic relationship is also associated with hypoactive sexual desire (Becker et al., 1986; Rowland, 2012; Rosen & Leiblum, 1995; Verhulst & Heiman, 1988). For example, lack of attraction to one's partner and poor relationship quality have been linked to low desire (Rowland, 2012; Wincze & Carey, 2001). Accordingly, clinicians are sensitive to the possibility that MHSDD can be a symptom of a more general problem in the partners' relationship. In such cases, couples therapy is recommended first, before addressing the couple's specific sexual issues (Rowland, 2012).

Erectile Disorder

erectile disorder: A sexual dysfunction characterized by a recurrent failure to obtain or maintain an erection adequate for sexual activity.

Erectile disorder occurs when there is a recurrent failure to obtain or maintain an erection adequate for sexual activity. For a diagnosis of **erectile disorder**, these difficulties must occur during all or almost all sexual activities with a partner. A full erection may be possible during masturbation or during REM sleep. Due perhaps to a culture's phallocentric emphasis (i.e., the importance of an erect penis for sex), many men with erectile disorder experience low self-esteem and low self-confidence (American Psychiatric Association, 2013a). Depression and post-traumatic stress disorder often co-occur with erectile problems, along with male hypoactive sexual desire disorder and premature ejaculation (American Psychiatric Association, 2013a).

Prevalence

Erectile difficulties are very common. Estimates from a cross-sectional analysis suggest that 18 million men in the United States experience erectile disorder (Selvin, Burnett, & Platz, 2007). The *DSM-5* notes that 40–50% of men older than 60–70 years can have "significant problems with erections" (American Psychiatric Association, 2013a, p. 427). In a worldwide survey of people from 27 countries about their sex life, the effects of erectile function on aspects of the sexual experience emerged as the most pressing concerns among male participants (Mulhall, King, Glina, & Hvidsten, 2008). Nearly half (48%) of men surveyed reported some degree of erectile dysfunction. A significant proportion of men (65%) were not very satisfied with their erection hardness, and 7% of men reported using a prescription medication for erectile disorders.

Although erectile problems increase with age, the vast majority of physically healthy men can still perform sexual intercourse even after the age of 80 (Bretschneider & McCoy, 1988). Among a large sample of European men, a quarter of those in their 70s and 80s had sex more than weekly (Nicolosi et al., 2006).

In diagnosing erectile disorder, doctors must be aware of the "Viagra effect" (Frances, 2013). Due to the hype surrounding Viagra and other drugs for erectile dysfunction, people may have unrealistic expectations about how strong and long lasting erections should be.

Causal Factors

Clinicians generally recognize that erectile disorder is caused by an interplay of biological, psychological, and social factors.

Biological Factors Because endocrine, vascular, and neurological systems all contribute to erections, problems in any of these areas can lead to malfunction. For example, spontaneous erections diminish in frequency and amplitude with the decreases in testosterone that come with aging. Heart disease and vascular problems, such as arteriosclerosis, can impair erections because a typical erection depends on a threefold increase in blood flow to the penis (Wincze & Carey, 2001). Chronic obstructive pulmonary disease (COPD) may lead to breathlessness during sexual activity, which then leads to worry and indirectly contributes to erectile dysfunction (Wincze & Carey, 2001). Diabetes mellitus is the medical condition most likely to cause erectile problems; over one third of diabetic men are affected (Ackerman & Carey, 1995). More and more cases of erectile problems are now being attributed to a medical condition. In such cases, no *DSM* diagnosis is made.

Erectile impairment is also a side effect of medications (e.g., blood pressure lowering drugs) for some individuals. Finally, smoking and alcohol use are associated with an increased risk of erectile dysfunction. In these cases, the proper *DSM* diagnosis is *substance/medication-induced sexual dysfunction.*

Psychological and Social Factors Even for men whose erectile problems are organically based, cognitive, emotional, and relationship factors are usually operating as well. Performance anxiety, cognitive distractions, stress, and relationship problems are among the psychosocial factors that contribute to erectile disorder. For many years, the leading theory—popularized by Masters and Johnson—was that men who were anxious about their sexual performance and who worried about how their partners would evaluate them were at greatest risk for erectile problems. Preoccupation with sexual performance turned many men into *spectators* who were so worried about the adequacy of their sexual functioning that they were unable to experience arousal themselves. Psychotherapist Albert Ellis's pithy summary was that, in most cases of erectile dysfunction, the man was "scared unstiff."

Anxiety does indeed play a major role in erectile dysfunction, but research has revealed that this role is more complicated than first described. For example, David Barlow and his colleagues have shown that it is not anxiety *per se* that interferes with erections as much as factors that cause a man to become *distracted* and therefore miss out on cues that would sexually arouse him. In a classic study (Barlow, Sakheim, & Beck, 1983), young males were first given a painful electric shock to their forearms and then watched an erotic film under one of three different conditions: One group was assured that they would not be shocked again, a second group was told that they might be shocked while they watched the film, and a third group was told they would probably be shocked during the film *if* they did not attain adequate erections (as measured by a penile strain gauge, a device that measures changes in penile circumference). If theories about the debilitating role of performance anxiety were correct, this third condition—intended to mimic the situation in which a man worries about attaining or maintaining an erection during sex—should have

"I'm afraid you will have to sign a non-disclosure agreement."

led to the weakest erections. However, men in both of the shock conditions had *stronger* erections than those in the no-shock condition. In fact, the "get-an-erection-or-else" instructions led to the strongest erections of all! The researchers speculated that the men's careful monitoring of their own arousal (in anticipation of possible shock) may have actually been helpful in the maintenance of their erections as they watched the erotic film.

So although anxiety *may* impair erections in some cases, it does not always do so when it serves to focus the participants, rather than to distract them. Indeed, it may be that *any* psychological variable that serves as a distractor from sexual sensations may interfere with the natural process of attaining and maintaining an erection. In one experiment, for example, men who were required to concentrate on a nonerotic narrative while watching an erotic film developed inferior erections, compared with men who were allowed to concentrate on the erotic film (Abrahamson, Barlow, Beck, Sakheim, & Kelly, 1985). Other research reveals that men with erectile disorder are more easily distracted by nonsexual stimuli and less aroused by erotic stimuli (Rowland, Cooper, & Slob, 1996). They also tend to underestimate the fullness of their erections (Barlow, 1986). Psychological contributions to erectile disorder are highlighted by research suggesting that a self-critical attribution style (i.e., attributing poor sexual performance to one's personality characteristics) leads to erectile problems (Weisberg, Brown, Wincze, & Barlow, 2001).

Not surprisingly, stressors and significant relationship difficulties affect male sexual arousal and contribute to erectile disorder too (Wincze & Carey, 2001). One of the more destructive myths about male sexuality is that men are always ready to engage in sex, regardless of their psychological or emotional state.

In summary, it appears that men with erectile disorder may approach sexual encounters with anxiety and negative expectations as a result of biological, psychological, and/or social factors. Once in a sexual situation, they can be easily distracted from sexual cues so that they underestimate how aroused they might be. Dismayed and embarrassed about what they believe is inadequate arousal that, they fear, is obvious to their partners, they engage in more and more negative thinking about themselves and their sexual ability. These negative thoughts further block sexual cues and increase negative emotions that make sexual arousal all but impossible.

Delayed Ejaculation

delayed ejaculation: A sexual dysfunction in which a man is unable to ejaculate or experiences an inordinately long delay before ejaculating during sexual activity.

Men with **delayed ejaculation** experience an inability to ejaculate or an inordinately long delay before ejaculation during sexual activity. This difficulty occurs even though the man wants to ejaculate and has adequate sexual stimulation. Most of these men still experience ejaculation when they masturbate or, on occasion, while dreaming. Some men report that their penises feel numb after erection and when intercourse begins (Apfelbaum, 2000). More commonly, they feel sexually excited at the beginning of intercourse, but as it continues, their desire wanes, and the sexual encounter becomes a chore. The distress associated with this disorder is compounded by cultural expectations that men should achieve ejaculation (and orgasm) 100% of the time when engaging in sexual activity (Wincze & Carey, 2001).

Prevalence and Causal Factors

The prevalence of delayed ejaculation is unclear, and the *DSM* notes that it is the least common male sexual dysfunction. Prevalence rates are estimated at less than 1%, and the disorder appears to be more common among men over the age of 50 (American Psychiatric Association, 2013a).

Little research has been done on the causes of this disorder, and the research that exists is largely limited to case studies (Wincze & Carey, 2001). Currently, the best explanation is that some of the physical and psychological factors that lead to erectile problems

Source: Cartoonresource/Shutterstock.com.

also play a role in inhibiting ejaculation for men. In some cases, men become frustrated with the delay or absence of ejaculation and, as a result, find the act of intercourse to be unpleasant.

Some sex therapists believe that this pattern suggests an underlying problem with lack of arousal or with conflict with the partner (Heiman, 1993; Apfelbaum, 2000). The role of performance anxiety has been underscored (McCarthy, 1988), whereas other researchers have suggested that a focus on the partner's pleasure distances the man from his own sexual sensations (Apfelbaum, 2000). Guilt stemming from religious proscriptions against sexual activity may contribute to delayed ejaculation (Perelman, 2009). Behavioral explanations note that many men with delayed ejaculation are able to ejaculate during masturbation. The speed, intensity, and length of time necessary to achieve ejaculation during masturbation—along with accompanying fantasies—are different from those experienced with a partner and may contribute to delayed ejaculation during intercourse (Perelman, 2009). Clinicians must remember to rule out *substance/medication-induced sexual dysfunction* because alcohol, antidepressants, and drugs for high blood pressure can cause ejaculatory problems (Frances, 2013). Spinal cord injury, multiple sclerosis, and diabetes can also cause problems with ejaculation (Perelman, 2009).

Premature (Early) Ejaculation

A much more common sexual dysfunction in men is **premature (early) ejaculation**, in which a man ejaculates after very little sexual stimulation, usually before or almost immediately after he has achieved penetration with a partner. Of course, the "ideal" timing of ejaculation varies, depending on the people involved. What is early ejaculation for one couple may be totally satisfactory for another (McCarthy, 1988). Accordingly, assessment and diagnosis of premature ejaculation must take into account the needs, perceptions, and circumstances of each individual or couple. Still, most men do not want to ejaculate before, or just after, penetrating their partner because it makes satisfactory sexual intercourse nearly impossible. The *DSM-5* therefore defines ejaculation as "premature" if it occurs within 1 minute after penetration. For other sexual activities, time criteria have not been established. In such circumstances, clinicians will consider a diagnosis if ejaculation occurs before the person wants it to and if this pattern causes marked distress or interpersonal problems. Many men with premature ejaculation report feeling a lack of control over ejaculation and worry about their performance in future sexual experiences (American Psychiatric Association, 2013a).

> **premature (early) ejaculation:**
> A sexual dysfunction in which a man ejaculates after very little sexual stimulation, usually before or almost immediately after penetrating a partner.

Prevalence

During their lifetime, 20–30% of men of all sexual orientations experience premature ejaculation (Rowland, 2011). However, the *DSM* estimates that only 1–3% of men would meet the current diagnostic criteria for premature (early) ejaculation (American Psychiatric Association, 2013a).

Causal Factors

What factors might lead to premature ejaculation? Biological factors associated with premature ejaculation include thyroid disease, prostate conditions, and drug withdrawal (American Psychiatric Association, 2013a). In addition, some men simply may be more prone to a rapid ejaculatory response. This biological predisposition may interact with psychological and relationship factors to lead to premature ejaculation (Rowland, 2012).

Although it has a complex relationship with erections, as noted earlier, anxiety is one psychological factor that has been clearly and repeatedly linked to premature ejaculation (Corona et al., 2004; Rowland, 2012). Other psychological factors related to premature ejaculation include negative mood in the presence of erotic stimuli (Rowland, Tai, & Slob, 2003) and, interestingly, alexithymia (Michetti et al., 2007). *Alexithymia* is a clinical term used to describe individuals who have a hard time reading emotional cues in themselves and others. A man with alexithymia may be less able to identify his own sensual cues and thus may be less able to control his own ejaculatory responses.

Relationship factors are also important to consider, as this disorder occurs in the context of partnered sexual activities. Rowland (2012) notes that rapid ejaculation may be more likely to occur when a partner has sexual aversion, avoidance, or pain. More generally, a man and his partner's worry and frustration stemming from episodes of premature ejaculation may exacerbate and perpetuate the problem (Buvat, 2011).

Section Review

The *DSM-5* describes multiple sexual dysfunctions affecting men and women:

- Female sexual interest/arousal disorder (FSI/AD) involves an absence or decrease in sexual interest and/or arousal in women, whereas male hypoactive sexual desire disorder (MHSDD) involves deficient or absent desire for sexual activity in men.
- Female orgasmic disorder pertains to problems with orgasm, such as when a woman cannot experience an orgasm, takes a very long time to reach orgasm, or finds that her orgasms are diminished in intensity.
- Genito-pelvic pain/penetration disorder (GPPD) involves tension, pain, or fear of pain for women during intercourse or penetration.
- Erectile disorder describes problems with erection, such as when a man cannot obtain or maintain an erection adequate for sexual activity.
- Delayed ejaculation describes when a man cannot ejaculate or takes a very long time to ejaculate during sexual activity.
- Premature (early) ejaculation describes when a man ejaculates after very little sexual stimulation.

All sexual dysfunctions must last for at least 6 months, occur in most sexual situations, and cause significant distress.

Sexual dysfunctions are common and may be due to a variety of causes, including hormonal influences, medical conditions, negative beliefs about sex, negative expectations about sexual activity, other mental disorders, sexual trauma, communication difficulties within a romantic relationship, and other biopsychosocial factors.

Treatment of Sexual Dysfunctions

With Masters and Johnson's research in the 1960s and 1970s, treatment for sexual dysfunction was radically transformed. Rather than viewing sexual dysfunction as a symptom of unresolved conflicts, Masters and Johnson argued that inadequate knowledge about sexual functioning, coupled with performance anxiety, was at the root of most sexual problems.

Their treatment model involved working with a couple daily for a 2-week period. First, a male and female co-therapist team conducted an exhaustive history of a couple's sexual functioning and overall relationship. Next, the therapists attempted to dispel various myths about sex and provided the couple with specific information about satisfying sexual functioning. Third, the co-therapists offered the couple an explanation of their sexual problems that stressed how faulty sexual habits can be learned, how successful treatment could eliminate these habits, and how more beneficial habits could be developed. They also coached the couple on how to communicate more clearly about sex and about other topics of importance to their relationship. Couples were then taught—and urged to practice in private—**sensate focus**, the core therapeutic technique of the Masters and Johnson program that is still widely used today.

During sensate focus sessions, the partners take turns providing physical pleasure to each other via kissing, massage, or touch without attempting any direct genital stimulation. In fact, to reduce performance anxiety and excessive demands for coitus, the couple is told not to have intercourse. Masters and Johnson (1970) saw sensate focus as the first opportunity many couples ever had to "think and feel sensuously and at leisure" without worrying about achieving the goal of sexual satisfaction. After a few days, the couple is given permission to add genital stimulation to their sensate focus sessions, but the ban on intercourse is retained. Finally, the couple is told to attempt brief penetration, but to keep

sensate focus: A method of increasing sensuality and the ability to experience physical pleasure by focusing on kissing, massage, or touch without attempting direct genital stimulation of a partner.

their attention mainly on sensate focus. Masters and Johnson anticipated that, as couples were swept up in their passion, they would break the rules and engage in intercourse.

This approach proved highly effective. Masters and Johnson reported that over 90% of men complaining of premature ejaculation improved, and the majority of couples with more complicated problems, such as erectile or orgasmic difficulties, also benefitted. However, few clients or therapists have the luxury of devoting the intensive 2-week period to treatment that this approach required. Consequently, Masters and Johnson's methods have been modified for modern use. Co-therapist teams are now seldom used, and most treatment programs meet with couples once or twice a week rather than every day (McConaghy, 1996), which allows time for couples to complete homework assigned by the therapist (Wincze & Carey, 2001). Evaluations of these streamlined procedures indicate that they, too, are effective, though they seldom achieve recovery rates as high as Masters and Johnson originally reported, and relapse is not uncommon. Today's sex therapists often use modified forms of sensate focus or combine it with techniques adopted from traditional individual and couples therapy. Other cognitive-behavioral techniques have been introduced, and medical interventions are increasingly being applied to sexual problems (Ackerman & Carey, 1995; LoPiccolo, 1994; McCabe, 2001; McConaghy, 1996; Wincze & Carey, 2001). In the next sections, we consider how some of these treatments are applied to specific sexual dysfunctions.

Treating Female Sexual Interest/Arousal Disorder and Male Hypoactive Sexual Desire Disorder

As described earlier in the chapter, there can be many biological and psychosocial factors that contribute to a lack of sexual interest. For example, if a person has negative attitudes about sex, exploring the origins of such attitudes may facilitate treatment. Cognitive-behavioral techniques can be used to challenge and restructure such faulty attitudes. In addition, positive experiences with sex are needed to increase desire (Rowland, 2012). Such experiences can be facilitated through sensate focus and careful use of erotica. Masturbation training may also be helpful in identifying the factors that contribute to a positive sexual experience (Rowland, 2012). Overall, however, there are relatively few empirical studies showing the effectiveness of treatments addressing female sexual interest/arousal disorder and male hypoactive sexual desire disorder specifically (Althof et al., 2005; Heiman, 2002).

That said, a handful of studies have demonstrated the usefulness of cognitive-behavioral therapy in treating low desire. For example, Trudel and colleagues (2001) provided cognitive-behavioral group therapy to women with low sexual desire and their partners. Twelve weekly sessions addressed causes of low desire, communication skills, cognitive restructuring of dysfunctional thoughts related to sex, sexual intimacy exercises, and sensate focus. Remarkably, 64% of the women demonstrated sustained improvement in their low desire symptoms at a 1-year follow-up.

Pharmacological treatments have also been used to treat low desire. For example, testosterone patches and gels and the antidepressant buproprion (Wellbutrin) have all shown promise for increasing sexual interest and satisfaction (Davis et al., 2006; Rowland, 2012; Segraves, Clayton, Croft, Wolf, & Warnock, 2004).

Source: SARYMSAKOV ANDREY/Shutterstock.com.

What do asparagus, caviar, ginseng, okra, oysters, and dried beetle dung have in common? They all have been touted as aphrodisiacs. Although there is no convincing empirical support that these substances stimulate sexual desire, perhaps the belief that they work is all it takes to get people in the mood. But you may still want to skip the beetle poop. . . .

Treating Erectile Disorder

With the advent of pharmacological treatments for erectile disorder, there has been less of a push to distinguish between biologically or psychologically caused erectile dysfunction.

MAPS - Superficial Syndromes
Medications have become very popular in treating erectile disorder. This saguaro cactus in Tucson, Arizona, demonstrates what may happen after swallowing those infamous pills.

Source: Brian L. Burke.

MAPS - Medical Myths

Oral medications, such as sildenafil (Viagra), tadalafil (Cialis), and vardenafil (Levitra), work by increasing blood flow to the penis, causing erection when the penis is stimulated. These medications are effective no matter the origin of the problem, and erectile disorder is now one of the most treatable of all the sexual dysfunctions (Rowland, 2012). Thus, a man can take one of these medications when he anticipates sexual activity; they all work within about a half hour of ingestion.

However, the news regarding sexuopharmaceuticals like Viagra, Cialis, and Levitra is not uniformly positive. First, you have probably heard the long list of side effects while watching television commercials: headaches, nausea, diarrhea, stomach pain, dizziness, hearing loss, vision loss, or an erection that lasts more than 4 hours (which, thankfully, is quite rare!). Second, discourse related to male sexuality and aging has changed significantly over the past few years in response to the increasing biomedicalization of sexuality and the medical restoration of "failing erections." These pills have led to the emergence of a new *antidecline narrative*, which is associated with a new obligation to remain forever functional (i.e., to be capable of sex for life; Marshall & Katz, 2002). Conventional Viagra success stories affiliated with the antidecline narrative and its privileging of frequent coital sex are prolific on the Internet, and in drug company promotions, popular media, and the medical literature. But research indicates that alternative success stories—accounts of changes in erections and sexual practices that are sometimes even welcomed by men and their partners (albeit in retrospect)—are in circulation as well (Potts, Grace, Vares, & Gavey, 2006). Some men adapt to, enjoy, and even prefer sexual experiences and practices that are quite different from their preferences when they were younger and/or when they were able to readily experience erections (Potts et al., 2006). Such accounts disrupt the arguably common-sense notion that a healthy sex life for men (and their partners) requires the maintenance of "rock-hard" erections and frequent penetrative sex.

If erections are still the focus, though, special devices can be used to produce erections in addition to the popular blood flow increasing medications. One of these includes a plastic tube that is placed over the penis and a hand or battery-powered pump that is used to create a vacuum, thus drawing blood into the penis and causing an erection. The erection is maintained by placing a ring at the base of the penis to hold the blood in place. Surgery is usually reserved as a last treatment option (Rowland, 2012). Penile prosthesis surgery dates back to the 1930s and involves implanting a rigid or inflatable rod in the penis. The devices last on average for 10–15 years.

Psychosocial treatments can also be helpful for erectile disorder. Aubin and colleagues (2009) compared medication alone (Viagra) to medication plus couple sex therapy among a sample of 44 men with erectile dysfunction. Couple sex therapy entailed eight sessions that addressed communication and emotional skills training, sexual fantasy training, cognitive restructuring, and sensate focus. Therapeutic exercises were assigned for the couples to try at home. Couples who received medication plus couple sex therapy reported greater improvement or maintenance of sexual function and sexual cognitions (e.g., fewer doubts about self or partner, fewer sexual "shoulds," fewer negative thoughts about sex) compared to those receiving Viagra only.

Treating Female Orgasmic Disorder

Treatment of female orgasmic disorder often involves a combination of approaches, including dealing with relationship problems, using cognitive techniques to lessen performance anxiety during sexual encounters, and encouraging sensate focus. In many cases, however, direct training in masturbation is the primary intervention. It is designed to educate the woman about her sexual responses, encourage her sexual fantasies, reduce any inhibitions about enjoying sex, and teach her how to experience an orgasm. Indeed, this technique helps up to 80% of formerly nonorgasmic women to become orgasmic (Heiman, 2007; LoPiccolo & Stock, 1986). Further coaching about sexual stimulation and fantasy helps transfer this private orgasmic ability to situations in which there is a sexual partner. For many women, simply reading about sexual responsiveness and masturbation allows them to learn to become orgasmic, and sex therapists still highly recommend the classic text *Becoming Orgasmic* (Heiman & LoPiccolo, 1988).

Treating Genito-Pelvic Pain/Penetration Disorder

Treatments for genito-pelvic pain/penetration disorder draw on a combination of psychological techniques. After negative attitudes about sex and physical problems such as lack of lubrication have been addressed, cognitive-behavioral therapy (CBT) is employed to teach the woman how to relax, first as she imagines sexual involvement and then as she attempts sexual intercourse. Sensate focus and pleasuring exercises are also included, as are efforts to improve communication and reduce conflicts with her partner.

For some women, *vaginal insertion* exercises are recommended. After practicing how to maintain vaginal relaxation while imagining sexual intercourse, the woman uses a dilator or her finger to practice penetration and relaxation. The size of the dilator can gradually be increased as the woman begins to feel more comfortable. Eventually, a partner may help insert the dilator or finger and, for heterosexual couples, they will eventually move on to penile penetration (at first, with partial penetration and withdrawal). In this treatment, the woman has complete control over what steps are taken, how fast, and for how long.

According to a review of the research, about three fourths of women have improved sexual functioning and reduced pain after receiving CBT treatment, with about one fifth able to achieve intercourse (LoFrisco, 2011). Initially, bibliotherapy appeared to be more effective, but group and individual CBT are more effective in the long term. Although other treatment types, such as surgery and medication, are found to be more effective, CBT may be preferable due to its noninvasive nature. In addition, there may be other psychosocial treatment types that are equally effective as CBT, such as biofeedback or supportive psychotherapy.

Treating Delayed Ejaculation

Research on treatment for delayed ejaculation is limited (Hartmann & Waldinger, 2007). However, most sex therapists advise masturbation retraining and other self-stimulation techniques to bring about a greater degree of psychosexual arousal (Rowland, 2012). Sexual fantasies can be helpful to block distracting thoughts that lower arousal (e.g., "This is taking too long!"). Relaxation, effective communication, and cognitive reframing that reduce performance anxiety are also advised (Rowland, 2012). It is helpful for a man's partner to be involved in treatment to learn ways to enhance arousal during sex.

Treating Premature (Early) Ejaculation

One of the most notable methods pioneered by Masters and Johnson (1970) for the treatment of premature (early) ejaculation is called the **squeeze technique**. To use this method, the man or his partner firmly squeezes the head of his penis as sexual excitement begins to peak but before the point of ejaculatory inevitability. This maneuver reduces the man's arousal and prolongs his ability to postpone orgasm. Many sex therapists have replaced the squeeze technique with the **stop-start technique**. In this approach, the man is taught to recognize the sensations leading up to ejaculatory inevitability and to control sexual arousal by simply stopping stimulation and relaxing for a few moments. After mastering this technique during masturbation, the man can use it with a partner to delay his orgasm. Initial reports about the squeeze and stop-start techniques were favorable, but more recent studies suggest that improvements gained from these methods alone may fade over a period

squeeze technique: A method of treating premature (early) ejaculation by firmly squeezing the head of the penis as sexual excitement begins to peak but before the point of ejaculatory inevitability, thus prolonging the time to ejaculation.

stop-start technique: A method of treating premature (early) ejaculation by stopping sexual stimulation before ejaculatory inevitability and relaxing, thus prolonging the time to ejaculation.

Kegel Exercises: Not Just for Women?

The Mayo Clinic notes that men with certain health conditions, such as having had their prostate removed, or having an overactive bladder, or being diagnosed with diabetes, may experience weakening of the *pubococcygeus* (or PC) *muscle*. Kegel exercises may help prevent or improve the incontinence men may experi-

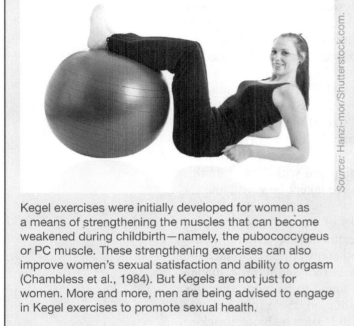

Source: Hanzi-mor/Shutterstock.com.

Kegel exercises were initially developed for women as a means of strengthening the muscles that can become weakened during childbirth—namely, the pubococcygeus or PC muscle. These strengthening exercises can also improve women's sexual satisfaction and ability to orgasm (Chambless et al., 1984). But Kegels are not just for women. More and more, men are being advised to engage in Kegel exercises to promote sexual health.

ence as a result of medical conditions. There may also be the added benefit of increased sexual pleasure and ejaculatory control, although more research is needed in this area.

According to the Mayo Clinic, men should follow these steps to perform Kegel exercises:

1. *Locate your PC muscle*—Your PC muscle is the one that helps you stop urine midstream and is also used to prevent you from passing gas.

2. *Practice*—Now that you know where your PC muscle is, try a little exercise. After emptying your bladder, lie flat on your back with your knees bent and separated. Squeeze your PC muscle for 3 seconds, then relax for 3 seconds. After some time and practice, you will be able to do Kegel exercises while sitting or standing as well.

3. *Focus*—Be sure not to use other muscles, like those in your stomach. It is best to focus on the PC muscle and let it do the work. You should also breathe normally while doing Kegels, just as you would with any other exercise.

4. *Repeat*—You should try to reach three sets of 10 repetitions each and every day for the greatest benefit.

Source: Adapted from the Mayo Clinic (2012).

---

of years. Accordingly, the techniques are now used in the context of more comprehensive CBT, which seeks to resolve faulty beliefs and anxieties about sex (McCarthy, 1988). Couples counseling also is recommended to frame the issue as a "couple-level problem," facilitating communication and changes in the couple's sexual patterns. For example, altering sexual positions or slowing down during intercourse may provide more control over ejaculation (Rowland, 2012). Kegel exercises (see the "Prevention" feature) may strengthen pelvic muscles and thereby also provide more control over ejaculation (Rowland, 2012).

Medications offer some promise, albeit with side effects, for premature (early) ejaculation. For example, clomipramine, a tricyclic antidepressant, can increase ejaculatory latency and improve subjective sexual satisfaction (Rowland, 2012). Delayed ejaculation is also one of the side effects of selective serotonin reuptake inhibitors (SSRIs) such as paroxetine (Paxil), fluoxetine (Prozac), and sertraline (Zoloft). These SSRIs can be taken daily, but they also appear to be effective when taken as needed, 4–6 hours before intercourse (Rowland et al., 2010). Tramadol, an opioid analgesic (pain pill), may also be effective when taken as needed in the short term, although daily paroxetine (Paxil) was more effective over 3 months of follow-up at increasing time to ejaculation (Alghobary, El-Bayoumy, Mostafa, Mahmoud, & Amr, 2010). Another treatment option includes topical ointments and creams; these can be applied to the penis to lower sensory stimulation and prolong arousal (Rowland, 2012).

The Value of Psychoeducation

Another important line of treatment for almost all sexual dysfunctions includes psychoeducation, or obtaining accurate information about sex as you have done via this chapter.

Low knowledge and high acceptance of myths about sex are risk factors for most of the disorders discussed. For example, women with sexual dysfunctions presented with significantly more age-related (e.g., "After menopause, women lose their sexual desire") and body image myths (e.g., "Women who are not physically attractive cannot be sexually satisfied"), whereas men with sexual dysfunctions had higher scores on "macho" myths (e.g., "A real man has sexual intercourse very often") and myths related to women's satisfaction (e.g., "The quality of the erection is what most satisfies women"; Nobre & Pinto-Gouveia, 2006).

Most Americans receive part of this psychoeducation via the ubiquitous "sex-ed" classes featured in one form or another in almost every high school curriculum. But how accurate is the information presented in these classes? What do you remember from yours? It turns out that the precise content of the sexual education class matters in terms of future sexual health. More specifically, abstinence-only sex education does not appear to have positive effects on long-term sexual health (McCave, 2007) or even on whether people practice abstinence (Huberman & Berne, 1995). In one study, Bearman and Bruckner (2001) found that teenagers who pledged abstinence did delay sexual intercourse for approximately 18 months. However, once sexually active, youths who made virginity pledges were 33% less likely to use contraceptives than youths who did not pledge to remain virgins. Further, those who pledged virginity were more likely than their peers to engage in high-risk sexual behaviors, including anal and oral sex. Research suggests that receipt of formal sex education before first sex, particularly including instruction about birth control methods, yields a range of healthier outcomes among adolescents and young adults (Doskoch, 2012).

"Here's a news flash: you don't use your Guardian Angel to provide condoms."

Source: Cartoonresource/Shutterstock.com.

Note that treatment of sexual dysfunctions varies greatly worldwide, based on cultural views of sexuality. For instance, although there is a need for sex therapy in countries like Korea, there are several challenges to overcome before it can be widely accepted by the general public (Youn, 2013). Korean people do not consider it appropriate to discuss sexual problems with anyone, let alone a stranger. The right to women's sexual pleasure is still unrecognized in Korean culture. Sexual medicine is thus at present geared primarily toward the resolution of male sexual dysfunction in male-dominated societies such as Korea (Youn, 2013), as well as other countries like Saudi Arabia with similar gender inequality (Chaleby, Jabbar, & Al-Sawaf, 1996).

Section Review

Treatment of sexual dysfunctions, which always has to take the individual's culture into account, depends on the type of dysfunction and may include:

- behavioral and/or cognitive techniques designed to help a person learn to be less anxious or distracted during sexual activity and to develop a greater awareness of sexual arousal;
- specific strategies, such as the squeeze or stop-start technique;
- couple-focused interventions, such as sensate focus or couples counseling;
- medications; and
- psychoeducation (i.e., accurate sex education).

Revisiting the Case of Alexandra

Recognizing her own discomfort with sexual activity, Alexandra asked Michael if they could slow down their sexual relationship. Although confused by Alexandra's request, Michael agreed and promised not to pressure Alexandra into any activity that she was not comfortable with. Alexandra decided she needed to figure out why she felt so negatively about physical intimacy. She sought out the help of her college's counseling center. The counselor referred her to a therapist in the local community with experience treating sexual dysfunctions.

Alexandra was immediately comfortable with the therapist. They explored the origins of her negative attitudes about sex, and Alexandra began to identify, challenge, and restructure some of her beliefs. For example, Alexandra recognized that part of her believed she was a bad person for having had sex outside of marriage. With the help of her therapist, Alexandra recognized that, while she regretted having sex with David and Michael, the sexual acts did not define her nor make her a bad person. Over the course of therapy, Alexandra clarified her desire to wait to have sex until she found a committed partner. She came to understand that having sexual feelings is not wrong and is, in fact, natural and normal. She accepted that exploring her own body was not shameful, and she engaged in at-home exercises to learn more about her body and what felt good to her. Although her therapist told her about pharmacological interventions that could be helpful in increasing her desire, Alexandra decided she did not need them.

While Alexandra and Michael eventually broke up, Alexandra no longer feels scared and anxious when thinking about sexual activity, and she is looking forward to exploring her sexuality with a life partner when the time is right.

Gender Dysphoria

"Ex-GI becomes blond bombshell." This intentionally provocative headline graced the December 1, 1952 edition of the *New York Post*. It referred to the return to the United States of Christine, formerly George William Jorgensen, Jr., an ex-soldier who had travelled to Copenhagen, Denmark, for one of the world's first "sex change" operations. For a brief time, Ms. Jorgenson was one of the most famous people in the world. To what did she owe her tremendous notoriety? Part of the answer lies in the particular social juncture in which she transitioned from male to female. The postwar period has been identified as one in which gender roles became increasingly defined and polarized. As an ex-GI, the former George Jorgensen embodied a quintessential masculine role. As a woman, Christine Jorgensen embodied the image of feminine grace that was culturally constructed in Western countries at the time. Jorgenson reportedly received thousands of letters, often from gender-variant people who saw her as a positive role model who helped them understand their own lives and conditions. Christine wrote an autobiography and played herself in a movie, *The Christine Jorgensen Story*. She married several times before dying of stomach cancer in 1989 at the age of 62.

Gender Nonconformity

The first question inevitably asked after the birth (or even during an ultrasound examination) of a baby is whether the child is a boy or a girl. As infants, girls and boys are treated differently; to take but one example, fathers often engage in more rough-and-tumble play with their sons than with their daughters. Parents often spend more time discussing emotions with daughters than with sons, except for the emotion of anger. As a result of these and many other influences, the sense of being "male" or "female" is, from the beginning, a deeply felt part of a person's identity. Most toddlers think of themselves as male or female and consistently imitate the same-gender models they see at home and school, and on television. By the age of 3, children have a clearly established gender identity, even if they think they could temporarily "be" the opposite gender by letting their hair grow or by wearing different clothing.

natal sex assignment: One's sex assigned at birth based on physical genitalia.

Natal sex assignment is one's sex assigned at birth based on physical genitalia. In many cultures, this assignment carries with it certain prescribed gender-role behaviors, expectations, and presentation. For example, since women are able to bear children, they are often seen as more capable than males of caring for and nurturing children. Conversely, because males often possess greater physical size and strength than females, men are seen as the protectors and providers in the family. These gender expectations are socially constructed and can be powerful prescriptions for "normative" gender behavior. However, some individuals are uncomfortable with these social constructs or do not fit within them.

Some people experience incongruity between their internal sense of **gender identity** and their natal (biological) sex assignment. Others wish to abandon the gender binary completely and identify as neither gender, or as being "gender-less" or "gender free." The variety of terms and definitions that people have about their gender identity is indicative of the inadequacies of a bi-gender system to describe complex and varying shades of gender identity. Note also that *sex* and *gender* are, in fact, distinct terms: **Sex** refers to the physiological markers that indicate maleness or femaleness, whereas *gender identity* describes the psychological sense of being male or female.

A gender identity continuum is often a difficult concept to embrace because of the heavy reliance in mainstream U.S. society on the gender binary, or the notion that there are two distinct poles of gender: male and female, only one of which can be occupied by an individual at any given time. This belief is evident in the current use of the term **transgender** as a marker for people who view their natal sex assignment as being different from their personal or internal gender identification. Often, people who identify as transgender seek to migrate or "transition" from one gender pole to another. It is during this process of migration and "transition" that problems may arise regarding social acceptance and validation of the person who is between gender poles. Some have described this polar migration, or "crossing," as being "caught in the crossfire," as the following testimonial illustrates:

gender identity: Individuals' subjective sense of their own gender, often (but not always) male or female.

sex: Physiological markers that indicate maleness or femaleness.

transgender: People whose gender identity, gender expression, or behavior is different from what is typically associated with their natal sex.

> I was 3 or perhaps 4 years old when I realized that I had been born into the wrong body and should really be a girl. . . . What triggered so bizarre a thought I have long forgotten, but the conviction was unfaltering from the start. On the face of things, it was pure nonsense . . . by every standard of logic, I was patently a boy. I was James Humphry Morris, male child. I had a boy's body. I wore a boy's clothes. It is true that my mother had wished me to be a daughter, but I was never treated as one. It is true that gushing visitors sometimes assembled me into their fox furs and lavender sachets to murmur that, with curly hair like mine, I should have been born a girl. As the youngest of three brothers, in a family very soon to be fatherless, I was doubtless indulged. I was not, however, generally thought effeminate. As I grew older, my conflict became more explicit to me, and I began to feel that I was living a falsehood. I was in masquerade, my female reality, which I had no words to define, clothed in male pretense. (Jan Morris [1974], author of the book *Conundrum*)

Many transgender researchers and theorists believe that one of the key problems gender-nonconforming people face in society today is not the problem of gender variation, but rather the problem of trying to fit into the relatively confining definitions and practices of dichotomous gendered behavior presentation and expectations. Notions of what is currently called "transgender" in the United States vary considerably from culture to culture. Moreover, these notions often change over time *within* cultures. For example, it was once common in the United States to refer to transgender people as suffering from being "born in the wrong body," a notion that reflects, in part, the Western dichotomy of mind and body.

"Can I be a boy today?"

Aspects of male and female gender identity can exist in one person.

Preventing Miscommunication and Promoting Respect

Using proper terms and language shows respect for people's personal definitions of self. Controversy has surrounded which terms to use, with evolving terms illustrating the fluidity of human gender expression and identity in the modern world. The National Center for Transgender Equality (2014) defines the following terms in an effort to promote understanding and sensitivity:

Transgender: People whose gender identity, gender expression, or behavior is different from what is typically associated with their natal sex.

Transsexual: An older term for people whose gender identity is different from their natal sex and who seek to transition from male to female or female to male.

Transition: The time when individuals begin to live as the gender with which they identify rather than their natal sex assignment. This time period often includes changing one's first name and dressing and grooming differently. Sometimes, transitioning involves medical interventions, such as taking hormones or having surgery, or legal action, such as changing identity documents, to reflect one's gender identity.

Cross-dresser: A term for a person who dresses in clothing traditionally worn by the other gender, but who generally has no desire to live full-time as the other gender (see Chapter 17). *Transvestite* is an older term that has negative connotations and is no longer used.

Genderqueer: A term used by some people who identify as neither entirely male nor female.

Gender nonconforming: A term for people whose gender expression is different from sociocultural expectations related to gender.

FTM: A person whose natal sex assignment was female, but who identifies and lives as a male, and is also known as a "transgender man."

MTF: A person whose natal sex assignment was male, but who identifies and lives as a female, and is also known as a "transgender woman."

Drag queen: A male performer who dresses as a woman for the purpose of entertaining others. This term is sometimes derogatorily used to refer to transgender women. Most drag queens do not identify as transgender but rather as gay men.

Drag king: A female performer who dresses as a man for the purpose of entertaining others. Most drag kings do not identify as transgender but rather as lesbians.
Source: National Center for Transgender Equality, 2014.

Thinking Critically

1. Why do you think people may be uncomfortable with something that makes gender categories more complex?

2. How do the names and terms we use affect people?

3. What other changes have you noticed where you live regarding attitudes toward people with gender nonconformity?

Cross-Cultural Views of Gender Nonconformity

Other world cultures have historically had mixed views on gender nonconformity. For instance, the *hijras* of India are people who are assigned as males at birth but who through social, spiritual, and surgical processes (special ceremonies and the removal of the penis and testicles) have cast off their male identities. Although their physical presentation resembles that of Indian women, they consider themselves to be a "third gender," or as a leading authority on the subject termed it, "neither man nor woman" (Nanda, 1990). Hijras have been long marginalized in Indian society, relegated to roles as entertainers and prostitutes. In recent years, they have acquired limited legal status and a measure of protection, but they continue to suffer from prejudice and violence.

Third-gender people also exist in many Native American cultures. Often called "two-spirit" people (meaning a blending of male and female), these individuals are highly valued in Native American societies. Mexico also has indigenous third-gender people called the *muxes*, a Zapotec word derived from the Spanish word for woman, *mujer*. Like the hijras, they dress and comport themselves in ways similar to women but view themselves, and are viewed by other members of their culture, as a third gender. But, unlike the hijras, they are viewed positively in Zapotec culture, enjoying a similar status to the Native American two-spirit people.

Gender Nonconformity and the *DSM*

As discussed in Chapter 1, the historical and social context changes how a mental health disorder is viewed, as well as what is included in the *DSM* and what treatments are considered effective and ethical. The concept of context surrounding mental health is clearly illustrated in the history of homosexuality in the *DSM*, which was considered a mental disorder until 1973. The famous joke in psychological circles is that with the removal of homosexuality from the *DSM*, thousands of gay men, lesbians, and bisexual individuals were "cured" overnight of their mental disorder. The change in status of homosexuality in 1973 was the direct result of empirical research on adaptive and healthy psychological functioning of gay men, the gay rights movement, and general advocacy and growing familiarity with homosexuality in U.S. society at that time. This change illustrates the relativism inherent in operational definitions of mental health and psychological disorders. Behavior that was once considered "pathological" may come to be considered "normal" merely as a result of changing times and social values.

MAPS - Prejudicial Pigeonholes

In that vein, *gender identity disorder (GID)* existed in the *DSM* from 1980 until the publication of the *DSM-5* in 2013. GID was defined as a "strong and persistent cross-gender identification" and "persistent discomfort" with one's assigned sex (American Psychiatric Association, 2000, p. 581). The *DSM-5* replaced GID with **gender dysphoria**, which is defined as "a marked incongruence between one's experienced/expressed gender and assigned gender" (American Psychiatric Association, 2013a, p. 452). The difference between the two diagnoses lies in the recognition that gender nonconformity and "transgender" are not identity disorders, as was implied in the definition and diagnosis of GID. Instead, gender dysphoria focuses on the psychological distress (dysphoria) that may arise over the mismatch between one's natally assigned sex and one's authentic gender identity. In this way, gender dysphoria is seen by some as a more specific diagnosis than gender identity disorder (Haraldsen, Ehrbar, Gorton, & Menvielle, 2010). The *DSM-5* reports prevalence rates ranging from .005–.014% for natal adult males and .002–.003% for natal adult females (American Psychiatric Association, 2013a), but notes that such rates are likely underestimations.

gender dysphoria: A mental disorder that describes strong incongruence between one's assigned gender and one's experienced or expressed gender.

Though the diagnosis of gender dysphoria in the *DSM-5* does not presume a pathology related to variant gender identity, discussion continues about the presence of *any* gender-related diagnosis in the *DSM*. Some believe that access to insurance coverage for treatment of gender nonconformity and dysphoria is the reason that gender is included in the *DSM-5*. Some propose that the diagnosis and treatment of gender dysphoria should be placed in the medical community instead, rather than within a mental health manual (Allison, 2010; Barron, 2013). This could allow a medical diagnosis of "transgender," for example, to be sufficient for gaining access to cosmetic surgeries, insurance-covered hormone therapy, genital surgery, and other procedures without the resulting mental health stigma.

A male cross-dresser. As noted in the *DSM-5*, gender dysphoria should not be confused with transvestic disorder (see Chapter 17) or with body dysmorphic disorder (see Chapter 8).

Source: Paul Vasarhelyi/Shutterstock.com.

Numerous research studies investigating the comorbidity of mental disorders in transgender adults have reported generally healthy psychological functioning among these individuals (Cohen-Kettenis & Pfäfflin, 2009), which means that they would not meet criteria for gender dysphoria, which requires significant distress or dysfunction (as do all *DSM* diagnoses). As one transgender woman remarked, "I have been fortunate to have the support of my family and friends throughout my gender-affirmation process. . . . I was able to transition on the job. I'm not saying there weren't bumps in the road, but I would say my journey has been one of gender '*euphoria*,' rather than '*dysphoria*'" (Hetzel & Mann, 2014).

Causes of Gender Dysphoria

Research has revealed no single etiological factor underlying variations in gender identity development. To date, investigative inquiries from the psychosocial perspective have failed to produce any evidence that family climate and/or parental behaviors contribute significantly to gender nonconformity. Twin studies indicate that gender dysphoria is 62% heritable, evidencing the genetic influence in its development (Coolidge, Thede, & Young, 2002). In addition, the volume of the central subdivision of the bed nucleus of the stria terminalis (BSTc), a brain area that is essential for sexual behavior, is typically larger in men than in women; a small study found that male-to-female transsexuals had a female-sized BSTc (Zhou, Hofman, Gooren, & Swaab, 1995). However, despite laypeople endorsing biomedical causes and treatments of gender dysphoria most strongly (Furnham & Sen, 2013), research has not yet definitively revealed critical hormonal or neurobiological differences that account for the condition (de Vries & Cohen- Kettenis, 2012; Fraser, Karasic, Meyer, & Wylie, 2010; Steensma, Kreukels, de Vries, & Cohen-Kettenis, 2013).

Gender Nonconformity and Gender Dysphoria in Children

Although gender questioning is relatively rare among elementary schoolchildren, many children occasionally display some type of gender-nonconforming behavior, such as playing with toys usually associated with a different gender (Sandberg, Meyer-Bahlburg, Ehrhardt, & Yager, 1993). The diagnostic criteria in the *DSM-5* for gender dysphoria in children consist of more-concrete behavioral displays of cross-gender activities and preferences than the diagnostic criteria for adolescents and adults (American Psychiatric Association, 2013a).

The World Professional Association for Transgender Health (WPATH) recommended to the *DSM-5* committee that the manual make it clear that the distress in functioning is not due solely to external prejudice, stigma, and negative treatment by others, but rather to the child's internal distress over gender dysphoric feelings (DeCuypere, Knudson, & Bockting, 2011; Fraser et al., 2010). Otherwise, the individual may suffer the label of a disorder because of the intolerance of society (Barron, 2013). The *DSM-5* failed to make this distinction, however.

Prevalence in Childhood

Many children expressing gender variation and nonconformity begin to show a preference for cross-gender toys and activities as early as age 2 or 3. Toy preferences are usually followed by fantasy play in which the child assumes a cross-gender role. For example, by the age of 3, a boy may ask for dolls and stuffed animals as gifts, use towels to simulate long hair or a skirt, and try on female clothes and shoes. Some boys may position their penis between their legs when dressing up or express hope that their penis will go away when they grow up. Girls may demonstrate gender-nonconforming behavior by wanting to wear male clothing, asking for short haircuts, or wishing to participate in traditionally male groups (e.g., scouting organizations). Girls may also use a male name when introducing themselves to strangers. Gender dysphoria is more common in male versus female children, perhaps because such behavior in natal females is less likely to be condemned by parents, teachers, and peers, and is therefore less likely to be brought to the attention of mental health professionals.

Comorbidity

Children referred for treatment for gender dysphoria often show higher-than-average levels of behavioral and emotional concerns, including anxiety, disruptive behavior and impulse control problems, and depressive symptoms. There is also a higher prevalence of autism spectrum disorder and attention-deficit/hyperactivity disorder (ADHD) among children referred to gender clinics (Drescher & Byne, 2012; Strang et al., 2014). Gender-nonconforming children may also show social avoidance, separation anxiety, and even suicidal impulses that may be related to peer, family, and social criticism (Zucker & Bradley, 1995).

Treatment for Children

Debate continues over the treatment of gender dysphoria in children. Some clinicians believe that modifying children's gender-nonconforming behavior to something closer to their natal sex may serve to alleviate their gender dysphoria and assuage the stress, social isolation, and/or maladjustment that may result from general unrest in the family and from difficulty forming and navigating peer relationships (Zucker & Bradley, 1995; Zucker, 2004).

Others believe that such attempts at gender-conforming or "normalizing" behaviors may negatively affect the child's self-esteem and general life satisfaction. Such arguments seem to parallel those pertaining to reparative or conversion therapy, in which the therapeutic goal is to "repair" or "undo" one's homosexual orientation and to "convert" the person to heterosexual orientation. Critics charge that treating gender dysphoria in this way reinforces narrow definitions of gender, and although it may serve to remove the discomfort felt by family and peers, it does not address the child's authentic gender identity. Some children may become anxious, depressed, and even suicidal if not allowed to live in their preferred gender. In these cases, the goal of therapy should be to provide the necessary support and advocacy for children, their families, and the community to make the gender-affirmation experience positive and avowing, rather than distressful and invalidating.

Gender Nonconformity in Adolescence and Adulthood

In many cases, childhood gender nonconformity or gender variation does not persist into adolescence or adulthood, although current estimates of persistence are higher than they have been in the past (Byne et al., 2012). The *DSM-5* reports prevalence rates of gender dysphoria persisting from childhood into adulthood that range from 2.2–30% in natal males, and from 12–50% in natal females. Interestingly, of the cases followed, 63–100% of natal males who had gender dysphoria in childhood that did not persist into adulthood identified as sexually attracted to males. Of natal females whose gender dysphoria did not persist into adulthood, many (32–50%) later identified as lesbian (American Psychiatric Association, 2013a, p. 455). It is therefore important to explore both sexual orientation and gender identity in older children and adolescents, since having a homosexual orientation may in some cases account for gender-nonconforming behavior.

The diagnosis of gender dysphoria in adolescents and adults uses the same basic criteria that exist for children—that is, a persistent and strong incongruence between experienced and assigned gender. As noted in Table 13.2, individuals may wish to be rid of their natal sex characteristics, and they may want the physical characteristics of the other gender. For natal males who seek medical treatment, this may include removal of the Adam's apple and/or testicles, as well as undergoing breast implantation and vaginal reconstruction;

TABLE 13.2 The *DSM-5* in Simple Language: Diagnosing Gender Dysphoria

Gender dysphoria is diagnosed when there is a mismatch between one's assigned gender and one's experienced gender, lasting at least 6 months, and including at least two of the following:

- a belief that one's internal gender does not fit with one's physical sex characteristics or that one is another gender,
- a desire to be rid of one's physical sex characteristics,
- a desire to have the sex characteristics of the other gender,
- a desire to be the other gender, and/or
- a desire to be treated as the other gender.

Source: Adapted from American Psychiatric Association (2013a).

for natal females, this may include having a mastectomy (removal of breasts) and reconstruction of the chest wall, having a hysterectomy (removal of uterus), and participating in testosterone treatments to stimulate facial and other hair growth.

Adolescents and the Gender Identity Clinic

Much of the research that has been conducted on gender nonconformity in adolescence comes from clinical studies conducted at the Gender Identity Clinic at the Vrije University Medical Center (VUMC) in Amsterdam, The Netherlands. Although the legal age of consent for gender-affirmation surgery is 18 in most Western countries, hormonal treatment (pubertal suppression) can be undertaken a couple of years earlier, following therapeutic and medical evaluation (Drescher & Byne, 2012) and after the adolescent has lived for a significant period of time in the preferred gender (Coleman et al., 2011). Such pubertal suppression has been associated with lower rates of comorbidity with mental disorders such as anxiety, mood disorders, and disruptive behavior disorders (de Vries, Steensma, Doreleijers, & Cohen-Kettenis, 2011). In a follow-up study with 70 adolescents who had received pubertal suppression around age 16 at the Gender Identity Clinic at VUMC, it was reported that all 70 case participants underwent gender-affirmation surgery and continued hormonal treatments after the age of 18 (de Vries, Steensma, Doreleijers, & Cohen-Kettenis, 2011). In fact, clinicians at the Gender Identity Clinic concluded that, once proper therapeutic assessment is completed, withholding hormonal and surgical treatments can result in long-term psychological damage to the individual (de Vries & Cohen-Kettenis, 2012). Unlike children who may not experience the persistence of gender nonconformity in adolescence or adulthood, adolescents have a high rate of such persistence.

Ongoing Advocacy for Gender-Nonconforming Individuals

The World Professional Association for Transgender Health (WPATH) developed the Standards of Care (SOC) for the Health of Transsexual, Transgender, and Gender Nonconforming People. The SOC are designed to be used by health care providers, both medical and psychological, to explore treatment options, services, and therapeutic outcomes for transgender and gender-nonconforming people. Services for this population of individuals may include psychotherapy, reproductive care, primary medical care, and hormonal treatments, as well as access to educational information regarding nonsurgical body modification, including breast binding or breast padding, genital tucking, electrolysis, and information pertaining to gender marker changes in legal documentation (e.g., birth certificate, driver's license, Social Security card).

There is no clinical evidence that one type of psychotherapy is more effective than another in treating gender dysphoria. However, WPATH affirms that one of the main goals of psychotherapy is to facilitate better life adjustments and satisfactory functioning within the construct of gender nonconformity. This may include:

- providing support for family and social adjustments (i.e., providing family therapy when a marital partner and/or children are involved; supporting people who transition in the workplace or at school);
- addressing psychological issues, including abuse, anxiety, or depression surrounding gender dysphoria; and
- exploring gender identity and gender-role expressions (Coleman et al., 2011).

Specific issues to cover in psychotherapy with a gender-nonconforming person may include: exploring strategies for living full time in a preferred gender, which may or may not include some form of genital surgery; exploring the possibility that the person is not gender nonconforming but has a homosexual orientation and possesses cross-gender attributes and interests; and exploring possible comorbidity with a mental disorder, such as body dysmorphic disorder, borderline personality disorder, or a psychotic disorder (Byne et al., 2012). WPATH does not endorse psychotherapy that strives to alter one's gender nonconformity.

Outcome Research on Gender-Affirmation Surgery

During the past 3 decades, there have been high rates of self-reported satisfaction among individuals who have undergone gender-affirmation surgery, along with a marked decline in postsurgery regrets (Byne et al., 2012). Much of the research has focused on natal males who have undergone gender-affirmation surgery. Those who transition early in life tend to report having pretransition homosexual orientations, as well as few regrets with surgeries and their transition to preferred gender identity status. Those who transition later in life still report mostly high satisfaction rates with surgery. However, this group often reports having mostly heterosexual orientations (pretransition), which may include being or having been married and having biological children (Byne et al., 2012).

Fewer studies have been conducted on gender-affirmation surgery among natal females. Perhaps this is because fewer natal females undergo such surgical procedures because of high costs and lower satisfaction rates with results. For instance, phalloplasty that achieves functional urine elimination and is sensitive to sexual/erotic stimulation is both difficult to achieve and extremely costly ($60,000) compared to vaginoplasty ($20,000).

Closing Thoughts

The framework for understanding mental disorders and normalcy comes from constructions of standards that are embedded in historical and cultural contexts. In these early decades of the 21st century, the ever-increasing presence of gender-nonconforming individuals and of transgender people in society may serve to expand constructions and acceptance of human variations, while stretching society's comfort level with those who fall outside of common practices and typical behaviors. Perhaps these individuals will help people to see beyond the ordinary and to understand the spectrum of human experience and expression. It will be interesting to see how gender-nonconforming behavior is addressed in the next edition of this text.

Section Review

Gender dysphoria is:

- a *DSM-5* disorder that describes a persistent and strong incongruence between one's assigned gender and one's experienced or expressed gender;
- diagnosed in children, adolescents, and adults; and
- a controversial diagnosis, as some transgender advocates believe that the distress associated with gender dysphoria stems more from societal intolerance than from individual disturbance.

Treatment of gender dysphoria involves:

- helping individuals accept their internal sense of gender;
- helping individuals make adjustments to align their internal sense of gender with their external gender presentation; and
- in some cases, may include referrals for medical interventions to facilitate adjustment to the nonnatal gender.

Summary

Overview of Sexual Dysfunctions

Normal human sexual responsiveness involves a sequence of psychological changes and physiological reactions known as the sexual response cycle. The sexual response cycle involves the phases of desire, excitement, orgasm, and resolution and was studied carefully by the pioneering team of sex researchers, Masters and Johnson. Sexual dysfunctions involve disruptions at various (and sometimes multiple) points in the sexual response cycle. Whereas they were once viewed as problems of unresolved childhood conflicts, sexual dysfunctions are now understood to involve a variety of biopsychosocial causes. For example, medical conditions and psychological disorders, medications, age, attitudes and beliefs, sexual history, and relationship quality can all affect sexual functioning.

Meredith Leischer

Meredith Leischer is a retired psychotherapist with a specialization in gender dysphoria. She provided diagnosis and treatment for depression, anxiety, relationship concerns, and life transitions, and followed the Harry Benjamin Standard of Care guidelines for the treatment of gender change issues. For over 20 years, she has facilitated the Gemini Gender Group, a transgender support group in Milwaukee, Wisconsin. Ms. Leischer is a transgender woman. She has been married for 35 years and has a 28-year-old daughter.

Q *What are your thoughts about the diagnostic change in the DSM-5 from gender identity disorder to gender dysphoria? Do you see this as accomplishing the American Psychiatric Association's stated intent of removing the stigma of pathology surrounding gender identity?*

A As a transgender individual myself and former therapist who worked almost exclusively with individuals exploring gender change or who were in the process of gender change, I see the proposed language in diagnosis as a welcome change. However, other than therapists who have worked with transgender individuals and who are truly nonjudgmental, I suspect that the public at large will keep the stigma alive—especially when reinforced with negative stereotypes presented by the media.

Q *Do you think that the presence of gender dysphoria in the DSM-5 is necessary for receiving mental health care and insurance coverage for diagnosis and treatment?*

A I believe that the diagnosis of a distress-causing condition is a necessary evil at this time as a way to encourage insurance companies to pay for various physical procedures and psychological counseling. At this time, though, few insurance companies will cover psychotherapy if the diagnosis is gender dysphoria. But because the majority of transgender clients can be diagnosed with depression and/or anxiety without the comorbid diagnosis of gender dysphoria, insurance companies have been paying for the counseling services that transgender clients might need.

However, until more studies like those conducted by the Netherlands Institute for Brain Research (e.g., Swaab, Gooren, & Hofman, 1995) indicate that the condition of being transgender is an actual biological condition, as opposed to some sort of psychological disturbance that insurance companies can ignore, little is likely to change. There must also be more widespread acceptance of the condition of transgender within the medical profession.

Q *What do you think the practical implications would be with regard to stigma, access to diagnosis and treatment, and insurance coverage if gender dysphoria was removed from future editions of the DSM?*

A As we all know, insurance companies will resist paying for any type of treatment, medical or psychological, that they consider unnecessary or cosmetic. Therefore, I believe it is necessary for the *DSM* to continue to have a category for the treatment of this condition, even though most insurance companies currently will not pay for services when the diagnosis is gender dysphoria.

Q *Do you see parallels between the diagnosis of gender dysphoria in the current DSM, and the diagnosis of ego-dystonic homosexuality in the DSM in the 1980s?*

A In both cases, individuals self-identify (or diagnose) themselves with their respective condition and quickly understand the familial and social implications of revealing their thoughts or behaviors to family or friends. At this point, a "cognitive dissonance" about their behavior or thoughts is likely to set in, which slowly builds until individuals accept that their thoughts or behaviors are not going to change. At that time, they may seek relief in the form of psychological counseling to affect acceptance or to work on behavioral changes.

Types and Causes of Sexual Dysfunctions

The *DSM-5* describes a number of sexual dysfunctions specific to women and men. These include female sexual interest/arousal disorder (FSI/AD), female orgasmic disorder, genito-pelvic pain/penetration disorder (GPPD), male hypoactive sexual desire disorder (MHSDD), erectile disorder, delayed ejaculation, and premature (early) ejaculation. All sexual dysfunctions must last at least 6 months, occur in most sexual situations, and cause significant distress.

Treatment of Sexual Dysfunctions

A wide variety of treatments exist for sexual dysfunctions, with most tailored to the specific dysfunction. Behavioral and/or cognitive techniques are designed to help a person learn to be less anxious or distracted during sexual activity and to develop a greater awareness of sexual arousal. For example, self-stimulation techniques and masturbation training, the stop-start or squeeze technique, or cognitive restructuring of negative beliefs about sex may be part of a cognitive-behavioral approach, depending on the dysfunction. Couple-level interventions may include sensate focus, communication training, or couples counseling to address relationship concerns that get in the way of sexual functioning. A variety of pharmacological treatments exist for sexual dysfunctions, including medications, testosterone gels or patches, and in some cases, even surgery.

Gender Dysphoria

The main feature of gender dysphoria is a persistent and strong incongruence between one's assigned gender and one's experienced or expressed gender. Gender dysphoria is seen in children, adolescents, and adults. The main treatment is psychotherapy to affirm one's internal sense of gender. Medical interventions are often used to more closely align one's internal sense of gender with one's external gender presentation. This controversial disorder may reflect society's discomfort with gender nonconformity.

Key Terms

acquired, p. 419

delayed ejaculation, p. 428

erectile disorder, p. 426

female orgasmic disorder, p. 422

female sexual interest/arousal disorder (FSI/AD), p. 420

gender dysphoria, p. 439

gender identity, p. 437

generalized, p. 419

genito-pelvic pain/penetration disorder (GPPD), p. 424

lifelong, p. 419

male hypoactive sexual desire disorder (MHSDD), p. 425

natal sex assignment, p. 436

orgasm, p. 416

premature (early) ejaculation, p. 429

sensate focus, p. 430

sex, p. 437

sexual dysfunctions, p. 416

sexual response cycle, p. 416

situational, p. 419

squeeze technique, p. 433

stop-start technique, p. 433

transgender, p. 437

vasocongestion, p. 416

Substance-Related and Addictive Disorders

Source: Joshua Resnick/Shutterstock.com.

After reading this chapter, you will be able to answer the following key questions:

- How does the *Diagnostic and Statistical Manual of Mental Disorders (DSM-5)* classify substance-related and addictive disorders?

- What classes/types of substances are included in the *DSM-5*?

- What causes substance-related and addictive disorders?

- How are substance-related and addictive disorders treated?

From the Case of Jerry

It was a typical night at the Blue Ox Bar & Grill. The place was crowded and smoky, and every conversation had to be shouted over the pounding bass of the band. Jerry, a college junior, was there for the fourth time this week. He had finished only half of the assigned reading for his midterm exam the next morning, but he had already shared four pitchers of beer with his buddy, Ben. It crossed his mind that, at this time last year, drinking two pitchers would have put him under the table, but now that much beer seemed to have much less effect on him.

As Jerry wandered home from the bar, he was troubled. Did he have a drinking problem? Jerry decided that this was a rather remote possibility. After all, most of his friends drank heavily, and so did his father; they could not *all* be "alcoholics." Besides, people with alcohol-related problems were the old guys who drank hard liquor straight out of the bottle and begged money from you on street corners. And Jerry seemed to remember reading somewhere that problem users were unable to stop drinking until they passed out. He was not like that. He drank only beer, and he could stop when he had to.

Or could he? His girlfriend, Alison, had urged him not to drink so much, but as hard as he had tried, Jerry had not been able to cut down on alcohol, and eventually, Alison had broken up with him. Although Jerry did not drink every day, he almost always got drunk whenever alcohol was around, often consuming as many as 12 bottles of beer in an evening. Jerry also drank at the worst possible times: when exams were coming up or just before a date. On nights before exams or paper deadlines, he tried to sober up for studying or writing by snorting the stimulant *methamphetamine*, and then smoking marijuana to "round off the edges" of his post-amphetamine crash. Once a high school senior who had hated the taste of alcohol and who had tried marijuana only a few times, Jerry had rather quickly developed an entrenched pattern in which his use of these and other drugs put him at risk for failing out of college.

Is Jerry correct in assuming that he does not have a problem with alcohol because he does not drink hard liquor, drinks no more than many of his friends, and does not ever pass out? What accounts for his heavy drinking and his use of other drugs? Is he just fitting into the college scene, or is Jerry especially vulnerable to alcohol? Does his use of alcohol and other drugs reflect learning, peer pressure, and/or a mental disorder, and will his current use of these substances lead to even more severe problems in the future? Finally, if he wants to lower the risk for such problems, should Jerry give up drinking and taking drugs altogether, or should he just try to do it less often and in smaller quantities?

These are just a few of the questions we discuss in this chapter about disorders associated with alcohol, marijuana, nicotine, and even a substance that most people in the United States use every day—caffeine. These substances are called **psychoactive drugs** because they affect users' thinking, emotions, and behavior. They include drugs that

psychoactive drugs: Drugs that alter cognitive, emotional, and behavioral processes.

- are widely available and used by many people (such as alcohol, nicotine, and caffeine),
- are legally available only through prescription (such as benzodiazepines and some opioids), or
- are illegal (such as cocaine, methamphetamine, LSD, heroin, and marijuana) in most U.S. states.

In most cases, our discussion of these substances will include a description of their physiological and behavioral effects, typical patterns of use and abuse (including *DSM-5* criteria for diagnosing substance-related disorders), and methods for changing and preventing these patterns.

No mental disorders create more personal and social disruption than those related to psychoactive substances. In 2013, an estimated 24.6 million Americans (almost 10% of the population) age 12 or older were illicit drug users, meaning they had used an illicit drug during the month prior to the survey interview; this was up from about 8% in 2002 through 2008 (Substance Abuse and Mental Health Services Administration, 2014). In 2013, marijuana was the most commonly used illicit drug (80%), with 19.8 million users. Figure 14.1 shows illicit drug use by race/ethnicity over the past decade. Meta-analysis of published results has revealed that substance use—of tobacco, alcohol, and illicit drugs, in that order—is prominently featured on the list of the top modifiable behavioral risk factors contributing to mortality in the United States, along with diet, exercise, accidents, toxic agents, and risky sexual behavior (Mokdad, Marks, Stroup, & Gerberding, 2004).

DSM-5 Diagnosis of Substance-Related Disorders

substance intoxication: A temporary condition in which, as a direct result of ingesting too much of a substance, individuals experience impaired judgment, altered thinking, pronounced mood changes, disturbed perception, or impaired motor behavior.

In the *DSM-5*, *substance-related disorders* include substance-induced disorders and substance use disorders. An individual can be diagnosed as displaying either or both. *Substance-induced disorders* involve impaired functioning as a direct result of the physiological effects of the ingested psychoactive substance. **Substance intoxication** refers to a temporary condition in which, as a direct result of ingesting too much of a substance, individuals experience impaired judgment, disturbed perception, pronounced mood changes,

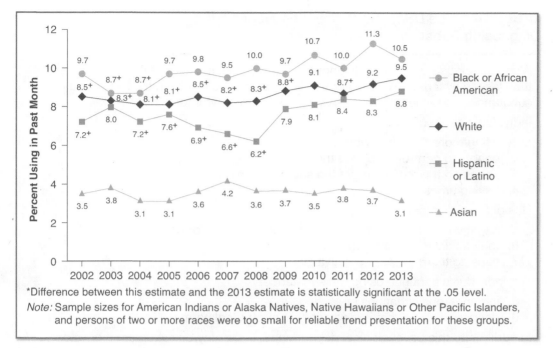

*Difference between this estimate and the 2013 estimate is statistically significant at the .05 level.

Note: Sample sizes for American Indians or Alaska Natives, Native Hawaiians or Other Pacific Islanders, and persons of two or more races were too small for reliable trend presentation for these groups.

FIGURE 14.1 Illicit Drug Use Rising in the United States

In 2013, among persons age 12 or older, the rate of current illicit drug use was 3.1% among Asians, 8.8% among Hispanics, 9.5% among Whites, 10.5% among African Americans, 12.3% among American Indians or Alaska Natives, 14.0% among Native Hawaiians or Other Pacific Islanders, and 17.4% among persons reporting two or more races. The graph shows a slight but significant increase in drug use over the past decade by about a percentage point for every group except Asians.

Source: Substance Abuse and Mental Health Services Administration, U.S. Department of Health and Human Services, http://www.samhsa.gov/data/sites/default/files/NSDUHresultsPDFWHTML2013/Web/NSDUHresults2013.pdf, p. 27.

altered thinking, or impaired motor behavior. Suppose, for example, that a 15-year-old is brought to an emergency room because she displays slurred speech, loss of coordination, and an unsteady gait after drinking beer for the first time. In *DSM-5* terms, she is suffering an *alcohol-induced* disorder—in this case, specifically, from *alcohol intoxication*.

Substance use disorders involve repeated, frequent use of substances, resulting in problematic behaviors or impairments in personal, social, and occupational functioning. Previous *DSMs* distinguished between substance use disorders involving abuse versus those involving dependence. **Substance abuse** was marked by a maladaptive pattern of substance use that results in repeated and significant adverse consequences and maladaptive behaviors. Conversely, **substance dependence** was considered the more serious diagnosis and was indicated by a set of behavioral, physiological, and cognitive symptoms and impairments caused by continued use of a substance, notably **physiological dependence** (**tolerance** and **withdrawal**) and **psychological dependence**. However, in a controversial move, substance abuse and substance dependence were combined into **substance use disorder** in the *DSM-5*. The diagnostic criteria are shown in Table 14.1. Note that the word *addiction* is not applied as a diagnostic term in this classification, although it is in common usage in many countries to describe severe problems related to compulsive and habitual use of substances (American Psychiatric Association, 2013a).

The change in the *DSM-5* relating to substance use disorders was rooted in a growing body of psychometrics literature that shows empirically how faint the distinction is between abuse and dependence (e.g., Saha, Chou, & Grant, 2006). However, some experts argue that combining abuse and dependence means that much valuable distinguishing information will be lost in the amalgam (Frances, 2010a). On the other hand, diagnosing individuals with a substance use disorder even in the absence of physiological dependence (tolerance and withdrawal) could serve as a valuable warning sign for them (Frances, 2010a).

substance abuse: A maladaptive pattern of substance use resulting in repeated and significant adverse consequences and maladaptive behaviors.

substance dependence: A condition indicated by a set of behavioral, physiological, and cognitive symptoms and impairments caused by continued or excessive use of a substance.

physiological dependence: Excessive or frequent consumption of a drug, resulting in drug tolerance or withdrawal.

tolerance: A condition in which increasingly larger doses of a drug are required to achieve the same physical effect or subjective state.

withdrawal: A pattern of physical symptoms that results from discontinuing drug use once individuals have become physically dependent on it.

psychological dependence: Intense desire for a drug and preoccupation with obtaining it.

substance use disorder: A new diagnosis in the *DSM-5* that combines substance abuse and substance dependence into one disorder; involves a problematic pattern of use of one of 10 categories of substances, leading to impairment or distress.

TABLE 14.1 The *DSM-5* in Simple Language:
Diagnosing Substance Use Disorders

A substance use disorder is diagnosed (with specific mention of the substance and the class to which it belongs) when individuals have difficulty in their lives due to the substance, with at least two of the following eleven symptoms over 1 year.

Individuals are frequently:

1. using more than they want to,
2. unable to control or reduce their use, and/or
3. spending time trying to get the substance, along with
4. having urges to use (cravings).

Use of the substance is:

5. negatively impacting individuals' academic, work, or personal goals;
6. their social relationships; and/or
7. causing them to give up activities.

Yet, individuals continue using the substance:

8. in dangerous situations or
9. despite realizing that it is causing them physical harm.

In addition to this psychological dependence, there may be evidence of physical dependence:

10. tolerance and/or
11. withdrawal effects.

Source: Adapted from American Psychiatric Association (2013a).

What these changes will do to the prevalence of substance use disorders going forward remains unclear. Two studies found that alcohol use disorders would likely increase considerably—from 11–60%—under the *DSM-5* (Agrawal, Heath, & Lynskey, 2011; Mewton, Slade, McBride, Grove, & Teesson, 2011), but another found no significant increases in prevalence of alcohol-related disorders in the *DSM-5* as a result of the new criteria (Edwards, Gillespie, Aggen, & Kendler, 2013). Further, research suggests that two fifths of those with *DSM-IV* cannabis abuse could fall *below* the threshold for *DSM-5* cannabis use disorder, resulting in a reduction of those diagnoses (Mewton, Slade, & Teesson, 2013).

The section on substance-related disorders in the *DSM-5* includes those associated with 10 classes of substances: (1) alcohol, (2) caffeine, (3) cannabis (marijuana), (4) hallucinogens (e.g., LSD, phencyclidine/PCP), (5) inhalants (such as glue or spray paint), (6) opioids (e.g., heroin), (7) sedatives (including hypnotics and anxiolytics, which are drugs that reduce anxiety), (8) stimulants (e.g., methamphetamine, cocaine), (9) tobacco (nicotine), and (10) other/unknown substances. All drugs that are taken in excess have in common direct activation of the brain reward system (related to dopamine), which is involved in the reinforcement of behaviors and the production of memories (American Psychiatric Association, 2013a). We emphasize alcohol use disorders in this chapter because they are so common and because much is known about their causes and consequences. We also emphasize treatment of alcohol use disorders because these interventions have been used as models for helping users of other drugs.

Section Review

Substance use disorder is a new diagnosis in the *DSM-5* that combines substance abuse and substance dependence into one disorder; it involves a problematic pattern of use of one of 10 categories of substances that leads to impairment or distress. Abuse refers to a pattern in which individuals spend a great deal of time using or trying to get the substance, despite clear negative consequences, whereas dependence refers to the development of physical addiction to the substance, including tolerance (needing more of the substance to produce the same effect) and withdrawal (having symptoms when substance use is discontinued).

Alcohol

Alcohol consumption is extremely common in the United States, as well as in many other countries. As shown by the most recent World Health Organization (2014a) data, globally, individuals above 15 years of age drink, on average, 6.2 liters of pure alcohol per year, which translates into 13.5 grams of pure alcohol per day. However, total alcohol consumption varies widely around the world. The highest consumption levels continue to be found in the developed countries—in particular, in Europe and the Americas—whereas the lowest consumption levels are found in Southeast Asia. Harmful use of alcohol causes approximately 3.3 million deaths every year (or 5.9% of all deaths), and 5.1% of the global burden of disease is attributable to alcohol consumption.

Alcohol use is fostered by cultural traditions and social conventions and reinforced by intense advertising. Indeed, television and print ads do everything possible to portray the drinking of alcohol in its many forms—beer, wine, or liquor—as a normal part of life and to associate its use with attractive people and happy social situations. Alcohol's popularity stems in part from its perceived ability to lower social inhibitions, facilitate social interaction, and create pleasant feelings. To many people, alcohol is a magic elixir that can increase social competence, sexual prowess, personal confidence, and power.

But alcohol is also a dangerous drug (Centers for Disease Control and Prevention, 2014a) and a poison to the human body. Excessive alcohol use led to approximately 88,000 deaths and 2.5 million years of potential life lost each year in the United States from 2006 through 2010, shortening the lives of those who died by an average of 30 years (Stahre, Roeber, Kanny, Brewer, & Zhang, 2014). The economic costs to society of excessive alcohol consumption in 2006 were estimated at $223.5 billion, or $1.90 a drink and $746 per person in the United States: 72.2% from lost productivity, 11.0% from health-care costs, 9.4% from criminal justice costs, and 7.5% from other effects (Bouchery, Harwood, Sacks, Simon, & Brewer, 2006). Short-term health risks related to excessive alcohol use include injuries, violence, alcohol poisoning, risky sexual behaviors, and miscarriage, whereas longer-term consequences include poor academic or work performance, legal troubles, cancer, mental disorders, and relationship strife (Centers for Disease Control and Prevention, 2014a).

Binge drinking is the most common pattern of excessive alcohol use in the United States (Centers for Disease Control and Prevention, 2014b). The National Institute on Alcohol Abuse and Alcoholism defines binge drinking as a pattern of drinking that brings a person's blood alcohol concentration (BAC; defined in the next section) to 0.08 grams percent or above. This typically happens when men consume five or more drinks, and when women consume four or more drinks, in about 2 hours. According to national surveys:

- One in six U.S. adults binge drinks about four times a month, consuming about eight drinks per binge (Centers for Disease Control and Prevention, 2012).
- Approximately 92% of U.S. adults who drink excessively report binge drinking in the past 30 days (Town, Naimi, Mokdad, & Brewer, 2006).
- About half of all college students report binge drinking each year (Chauvin, 2012).
- The prevalence of binge drinking among men is twice the prevalence among women (Centers for Disease Control and Prevention, 2012).
- Binge drinkers are 14 times more likely to engage in alcohol-impaired driving than nonbinge drinkers (Naimi et al., 2003).
- About 90% of the alcohol consumed by youth under the age of 21 in the United States is in the form of binge drinks (Office of Juvenile Justice and Delinquency Prevention, 2005).

So, given the plethora of pleasant and harmful consequences and the billions of dollars spent on advertising, consuming, and treating disorders related to alcohol, how does the drug actually work?

Alcohol in the Body

When alcohol enters the stomach, a small amount of *ethanol*—the form of alcohol contained in typical alcoholic beverages—is almost immediately absorbed through the stomach wall and into the bloodstream. The rest passes from the stomach to the small intestine, where most of it is absorbed and carried in the blood to various organs of the body, including the brain, heart, and liver.

When alcohol reaches the liver, it undergoes **oxidation**, through which it is converted to *acetaldehyde* by the enzyme *alcohol dehydrogenase*. Acetaldehyde is further *metabolized*, or chemically decomposed, into other products. The liver can metabolize about a half ounce to an ounce of alcohol in an hour. Physiological *tolerance* for alcohol results, in part, from the body's capacity to metabolize alcohol more efficiently after repeated exposure to it. When the amount of alcohol consumed exceeds the liver's capacity to oxidize it, ethanol and acetaldehyde begin to accumulate in body cells, disrupting cell structure and functions, and producing several problems, such as faulty metabolism of vitamins.

The unmetabolized ethanol absorbed into the blood from the small intestine and stomach can be measured as **blood alcohol concentration**, or **BAC**. Alcohol is absorbed more slowly from drinks with lower alcohol content (such as beer) than from those with higher alcohol content (e.g., whiskey). (A *drink* is defined as 1 ounce of 100-proof alcohol, a 12-ounce beer, or a 4-ounce glass of wine.) In an average-sized person, 1–2 drinks yield a BAC of 0.02–0.05%; 3–5 drinks produce a BAC of 0.06–0.10%; and 10–13 drinks create BACs of 0.2–0.25%. When consumed with food, ethanol remains in the stomach longer, resulting in slower absorption into the bloodstream, lower BAC, and less intoxication than when ingested on its own. In the United States, the legal definition of drunken driving (driving under the influence, or *DUI*) is set in terms of some minimum BAC level, currently 0.08%. For those under 21, there is a zero tolerance limit—any amount of alcohol is grounds for a DUI arrest.

Unmetabolized alcohol can have devastating effects on body organs, particularly the liver, the pancreas, and the heart. Chronic alcohol abuse is the single most frequent cause of liver diseases in the United States. The most serious of these is **alcoholic cirrhosis**, characterized by damaged liver cells, development of scar tissue, and the eventual inability of the liver to filter toxins from the blood (Grant, DeBakey, & Zobeck, 1991). Whereas nondrinkers have a slightly higher risk of cardiovascular disease than light or moderate drinkers (Boffetta & Garfinkel, 1990), heavy drinking is a risk factor for several coronary diseases, including high blood pressure, weakening of the heart muscle, arrhythmias, and strokes. Heavy drinking commonly results in **pancreatitis**, a condition in which cells in the pancreas are killed. Chronic alcohol abuse can suppress the body's immune system, leaving individuals vulnerable to infectious diseases, including tuberculosis, pneumonia, and other respiratory illnesses, along with cancer of the mouth, pharynx, larynx, esophagus, breast, and liver (Longnecker, 1994).

So alcohol has a host of deleterious effects on the body, but what about your brain?

Effects of Alcohol on the Brain and Behavior

When blood-borne alcohol reaches the brain, it interacts with neurotransmitters that provide the chemical basis for communication among brain cells.

Depressant Effects in the Brain

The two neurotransmitters particularly affected by alcohol are glutamate and gamma-aminobutyric acid (GABA). **Glutamate** is a major *excitatory* neurotransmitter in the brain; it stimulates activity in the neurons it reaches. *GABA*, the brain's major *inhibitory* neu-

oxidation: The process by which alcohol is converted to acetylaldehyde and metabolized.

blood alcohol concentration (BAC): The amount of unmetabolized ethanol absorbed into the blood.

alcoholic cirrhosis: A disease characterized by damaged liver cells, development of scar tissue, and the eventual inability of the liver to filter toxins from the blood.

pancreatitis: A condition in which cells in the pancreas are killed; commonly caused by heavy drinking.

Connections

How does maternal alcohol consumption affect fetal development? For descriptions of *fetal alcohol syndrome*, see Chapter 3.

glutamate: The body's most prominent neurotransmitter; the brain's main excitatory neurotransmitter, and also the precursor for GABA, the brain's main inhibitory neurotransmitter.

rotransmitter, has the opposite effect—it reduces the activity of the brain cells it reaches. Numerous animal studies show that alcohol reduces the excitatory action of glutamate and increases the inhibitory action of GABA. The net effect is the suppression of brain cell activity, which is why alcohol is considered a central nervous system *depressant*.

Alcohol affects other neurotransmitters as well. Its effects on **dopamine**, for example, may explain the short-term "rewarding" experience that accompanies alcohol consumption. Neuroscientists believe that certain regions of the brain—such as the *nucleus accumbens*—mediate the experience of pleasure. Research has shown that animals will work hard to maintain electrical stimulation of these "reward centers" (Olds & Milner, 1954). Dopamine is a prominent neurotransmitter in these areas, and alcohol increases the level of dopamine in the nucleus accumbens and other reward centers (e.g., Wozniak, Pert, & Linnoila, 1990).

Alcohol's "rewarding" effects may also relate to its ability to increase the level of the neurotransmitter **serotonin** in certain brain regions. When animals are given drugs that increase or mimic the activity of serotonin, they reduce their alcohol intake. Alcohol also increases the release of **endogenous opiates**, also called *endorphins*. These naturally occurring substances are chemically similar to opioid drugs, such as morphine and heroin, which produce a state of euphoria and reduce the experience of pain.

Effects on Behavior

The behavioral consequences of alcohol intoxication are well known. After a drink or two, most people feel less inhibited, more talkative, and more relaxed. As Figure 14.2 shows, however, as the BAC rises, judgment becomes impaired, self-awareness is reduced, and clear thinking becomes more difficult. With a BAC in the range of 0.05–0.07%, slurred speech and mild motor coordination problems are apparent. When the BAC climbs past the 0.08% range, motor coordination problems, such as unsteady gait, drowsiness, and impaired perception, become noticeable enough to mark this level of impairment as "intoxicated" in legal terms. Other typical signs of intoxication include unpredictable mood changes, poor attention and memory, and a lack of inhibition that impairs normal

Connections
Which other mental disorders may involve the neurotransmitters glutamate and GABA? See Chapters 7 and 8.

dopamine: A neurotransmitter that is prominent in several areas of the brain and is linked with several types of mental disorders.

serotonin: A neurotransmitter that influences emotion, sleep, and behavioral control.

endogenous opiate: A naturally occurring chemical, similar to an opioid drug, that produces a state of euphoria and reduces the experience of pain.

Drinks	Body Weight in Pounds																	
	Female									Male								
	90	100	120	140	160	180	200	220	240	100	120	140	160	180	200	220	240	
	.00	.00	.00	.00	.00	.00	.00	.00	.00	.00	.00	.00	.00	.00	.00	.00	.00	
1	.05	.05	.04	.03	.03	.03	.02	.02	.02	.04	.03	.02	.02	.02	.02	.02	.02	Impairment begins
2	.10	.09	.08	.07	.06	.05	.05	.04	.04	.08	.06	.05	.05	.04	.04	.03	.03	
3	.15	.14	.11	.10	.09	.08	.07	.06	.06	.11	.09	.08	.07	.06	.06	.05	.05	Driving skills significantly affected; possible criminal penalties
4	.20	.18	.15	.13	.11	.10	.09	.08	.08	.15	.12	.11	.09	.08	.08	.07	.06	
5	.25	.23	.19	.16	.14	.13	.11	.10	.09	.19	.16	.13	.12	.11	.09	.09	.08	
6	.30	.27	.23	.19	.17	.15	.14	.12	.11	.23	.19	.16	.14	.13	.11	.10	.09	
7	.35	.32	.27	.23	.20	.18	.16	.14	.13	.26	.22	.19	.16	.15	.13	.12	.11	Legally intoxicated; criminal penalties
8	.40	.36	.30	.26	.23	.20	.18	.17	.15	.30	.25	.21	.19	.17	.15	.14	.13	
9	.45	.41	.34	.29	.26	.23	.20	.19	.17	.34	.28	.24	.21	.19	.17	.15	.14	
10	.51	.45	.38	.32	.28	.25	.23	.21	.19	.38	.31	.27	.23	.21	.19	.17	.16	

FIGURE 14.2 Blood Alcohol Concentrations and Behavioral Effects

The concentration of alcohol in a person's blood is directly correlated with increased behavioral impairment. The United States uses a BAC of 0.08% as the legal definition of intoxication. The effects of different BAC levels also depend on such factors as the drinker's weight, how quickly the alcohol was consumed, and whether food was eaten along with the alcohol.

Source: West Virginia Alcohol Beverage Control Administration (2014), http://www.abca.wv.gov/enforcement/Documents/BAC%20Chart.pdf.

social functioning. Some intoxicated individuals become verbally or physically aggressive (Ito, Miller, & Pollock, 1996) or make uncharacteristic and inappropriate sexual advances. At BAC levels over 0.25%, a drinker may lose consciousness and suffer severe respiratory problems that can lead to death. Note that high tolerance does not affect individuals' BAC; it just makes it so that individuals may not feel or notice that their BAC is high. Thus, their bodies are being damaged without their awareness.

The behavioral effects of alcohol are determined partly by its physiological impact on the brain, but they are also strongly influenced by factors such as the situations in which people drink, their prior drinking experiences, and their expectancies about the effects of alcohol. All of these factors can play a role in shaping the behavior that follows alcohol use.

Even though it is a depressant, alcohol can have both sedating and agitating effects on behavior. By depressing inhibitory centers in the brain, alcohol produces some activating effects like those associated with stimulant drugs. The sedating effects of alcohol wear off before the agitating effects do, so heavy drinkers often experience nervousness and tension several hours after a bout of drinking. This rebound effect sets up a vicious cycle of attempted solutions in which the individuals may resume drinking to reduce the agitation that remains from previous drinking. At some point, though, chronic alcohol users find that no amount of additional drinking will completely eliminate their tension and agitation.

As individuals develop a tolerance for alcohol, the normal signs of intoxication become less pronounced, appearing in full force only when unusually large amounts are consumed. Other behavioral effects or personality changes worsen with continued alcohol abuse, however. For example, in some individuals, the aggressiveness characteristic of acute intoxication develops into a brooding, ongoing hostility, often directed at spouses or other family members (Leonard, 1990). Individuals who chronically abuse alcohol tend to show a gradual deterioration in problem-solving skills, especially in concentration and flexibility in finding solutions. As their cognitive abilities become impaired, they may find it even more difficult to communicate effectively with friends and relatives. The resulting deterioration in social relationships and social support exacerbates their problems (Steinglass, Bennett, Wolin, & Reiss, 1987).

Prevalence of Alcohol Use Disorders

Estimates of the prevalence of alcohol use disorders (AUDs) vary, depending on where the line is drawn between normal and pathological use (Tarter & Vanyukov, 1994). All of the surveys point to high levels of maladaptive drinking in the United States, and the same story emerges from studies in the United Kingdom, Australia, Ireland, Korea, and many other countries. Worldwide estimates of AUDs range from near zero in Iran, Iraq, and Yemen to over 15% in males in the Russian Federation or Hungary, with the U.S. rates being somewhere in the middle (World Health Organization, 2014b). Eighteen percent of U.S. college students (24% of men, 13% of women) have suffered from clinically significant alcohol-related problems in the past year, compared with 15% of their non–college-attending peers (22% of men, 9% of women; Slutske, 2005). Approximately 7.2% or 17 million adults in the United States age 18 and older had an AUD in 2012 (National Institute on Alcohol Abuse and Alcoholism, 2014).

In terms of racial/ethnic differences within the United States, as shown in Figure 14.3, the prevalence of what was formerly called alcohol abuse was greater among Caucasians/Whites than among African Americans, Asians, and Hispanics (Grant & Dawson, 2005). The prevalence of alcohol dependence was higher among Caucasians/Whites, Native Americans, and Hispanics than among Asians. These data underscore the need to design culturally sensitive prevention and intervention programs (Grant & Dawson, 2005). Furthermore, recent studies suggest that variations in two of the genes that break down alcohol in the body (linked to the enzyme *alcohol dehydrogenase* described earlier) may influence drinking behavior and the risk for AUDs across different racial/ethnic groups (Ehlers, Liang, & Gizer, 2012). For instance, Asians are more likely to become sick from alcohol consumption due to two different protective alleles (gene variants) in the enzyme

MAPS - Attempted Answers

MAPS - Prejudicial Pigeonholes

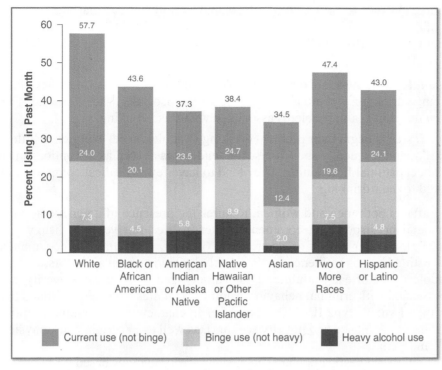

FIGURE 14.3 Alcohol Use by Race/Ethnicity in the United States, 2013

The graph shows that, whereas Causasians/Whites report the highest current usage of alcohol overall, people from other racial/ethnic groups may have higher "binge" or "heavy" use.

Source: Substance Abuse and Mental Health Services Administration, U.S. Department of Health and Human Services, http://www.samhsa.gov/data/sites/default/files/NSDUHresultsPDFWHTML2013/Web/NSDUHresults2013.pdf, p. 39.

gene (Luczak, Glatt, & Wall, 2006), partly explaining their typically low rates of AUDs, whereas Native Americans lack such protective genetic variants (Ehlers et al., 2012). However, the complete explanation for AUD patterns among different cultural groups will most likely be explained by theories that include both genetic and environmental determinants (Ehlers et al., 2012).

Course of Alcohol Use Disorders

The term **alcoholism**—which does not appear in the *DSM-5*—has traditionally referred to a pattern of heavy drinking that steadily worsens until individuals are thought to have lost control over drinking and become so dependent on alcohol that physical and mental health are jeopardized and social and occupational functioning are impaired. This iconic image of the alcoholic stems partly from an influential survey conducted in the 1940s on a small group of men in Alcoholics Anonymous (AA) (Jellinek, 1946). Based on these men's reported drinking histories, Jellinek proposed a four-stage model of how alcohol dependence progresses. In the first phase, the *prealcoholic*, individuals drink only occasionally, mostly in social situations and to relieve tension. In the second, or *prodromal* phase, drinking is heavier, sometimes in secret, but with few signs of gross intoxication. In the third, or *crucial*, phase, individuals lose control over their drinking. Even one drink inevitably seems to lead to binge drinking until blackouts result; health is affected, and social lives begin to deteriorate. The final, *chronic*, phase involves daily drinking, often accompanied by malnutrition, physical tolerance, and—when alcohol is unavailable—withdrawal symptoms.

Researchers have found partial support for Jellinek's progression (Venner & Feldstein, 2006). However, studies from other cultures suggest that adherence to that progression decreases as the studied sample deviates culturally from Jellinek's sample of U.S. White men, which calls into question the cross-cultural applicability of this popular model of

alcoholism: A pattern of heavy drinking in which individuals lose control over drinking and become so dependent on alcohol that physical and mental health are jeopardized and social and occupational functioning are impaired.

AUD course (Venner & Miller, 2001). Researchers now believe that there are different patterns of drinking and impairment that occur for those with AUDs (Venner & Feldstein, 2006). For example, Robert Cloninger and colleagues (1996) distinguished between two types of AUD courses:

■ *Type I AUDs* show a late onset of problem drinking, are prone to anxiety, engage in binge drinking, and are unlikely to behave antisocially when drinking. They often develop health problems associated with their drinking.

■ *Type II AUDs* begin their problem drinking in adolescence, experience little anxiety, and frequently show antisocial tendencies as well as disruptions in social and occupational functioning. They tend to have fewer medical complications linked to their drinking.

Type I affects both men and women, requires the presence of a genetic as well as an environmental predisposition, commences later in life after years of heavy drinking, and can take on either a mild or severe form. Type II, in contrast, affects mainly sons of males with AUDs, is influenced only weakly by environmental factors, often begins during adolescence or early adulthood, is characterized by moderate severity, and usually is associated with criminal behavior. Additional studies have demonstrated that people with type I versus type II AUDs also differ in characteristic personality traits (e.g., harm avoidance and novelty seeking), as well as in certain neurophysiological markers.

Other investigators have created similar typologies based on factors such as age of onset, motivation to drink, and the social/psychological consequences of drinking (Babor et al., 1992; Hill, 1992). Robert Zucker (1987), for example, includes a subtype of a person with an AUD who is not antisocial but who still starts drinking heavily in adolescence, often after being separated from family members, such as in going off to college. Schuckit and colleagues (2002) have argued for a unitary course of AUDs across genders, severity of dependence, care, and comorbidity. What is your drinking pattern, and how would you know if you had a problem with alcohol? Check out Table 14.2.

Other Mental Disorders Associated With Alcohol Use

The *DSM-5* lists 11 alcohol-related disorders: (1) alcohol intoxication, (2) alcohol withdrawal, (3) alcohol intoxication delirium, (4) alcohol withdrawal delirium, (5) alcohol-induced psychotic disorder, (6) alcohol-induced bipolar disorder, (7) alcohol-induced depressive disorder, (8) alcohol-induced anxiety disorder, (9) alcohol-induced sleep disorder, (10) alcohol-induced sexual dysfunction, and (11) alcohol-induced mild or major neurocognitive disorder.

The phrase *alcohol-induced* presupposes that alcohol use precedes and causes other comorbid disorders. Is this assumption warranted? As Figure 14.4 shows, there are four possible explanations for comorbidity between alcohol-related disorders and other mental disorders: (1) the mental disorder precedes and causes the alcohol disorder; (2) the alcohol disorder precedes and causes the mental disorder; (3) a common factor precipitates both disorders; or (4) both disorders—regardless of which came first—exacerbate each other.

As described in Chapter 15, *delirium* refers to a disturbance of consciousness in which there is profound confusion, agitation, and an inability to attend to the environment. Perceptual or cognitive distortions, such as hallucinations or delusions, may also be present. Alcohol-induced delirium occurs primarily during periods of extreme intoxication or withdrawal following prolonged, heavy drinking. It can be accompanied by muscle tremors, hallucinations, and profuse sweating. The phrase **delirium tremens** (or **DTs**) is commonly used to identify this particular set of symptoms, as seen in the following case of *alcohol withdrawal delirium*.

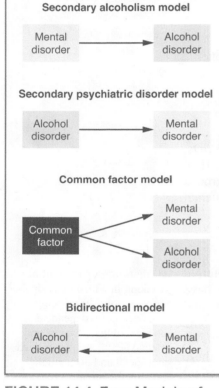

FIGURE 14.4 Four Models of How Alcohol Use Disorders and Other Mental Disorders May Be Related

delirium tremens (DTs): A set of symptoms, including muscle tremors, hallucinations, and profuse sweating, that result from withdrawal from heavy alcohol use.

TABLE 14.2 Take the AUDIT Test

The Alcohol Use Disorders Identification Test (AUDIT) is a simple 10-question test developed by the World Health Organization to determine if a person's alcohol consumption may be harmful. The test was designed to be used internationally and was validated in a study using people from six countries. Questions 1–3 deal with alcohol consumption, 4–6 relate to alcohol dependence, and 7–10 consider alcohol-related problems. A score of 8 or more in men (7 in women) indicates a strong likelihood of hazardous or harmful alcohol consumption. A score of 20 or more is suggestive of an AUD, although some authors quote scores of more than 13 in women and 15 in men as indicating likely dependence. Brief counseling is recommended at a score of 16, with more intensive treatment recommended at scores above 19. Points associated with each answer are listed in parentheses. Keep track of your points as you take this assessment.

1. How often do you have a drink containing alcohol?
   (0) Never (skip to questions 9–10)
   (1) Monthly or less
   (2) 2–4 times a month
   (3) 2–3 times a week
   (4) 4 or more times a week

2. How many drinks containing alcohol do you have on a typical day when you are drinking?
   (0) 1 or 2
   (1) 3 or 4
   (2) 5 or 6
   (3) 7, 8, or 9
   (4) 10 or more

3. How often do you have six or more drinks on one occasion?
   (0) Never
   (1) Less than monthly
   (2) Monthly
   (3) Weekly
   (4) Daily or almost daily

4. How often during the last year have you found that you were not able to stop drinking once you had started?
   (0) Never
   (1) Less than monthly
   (2) Monthly
   (3) Weekly
   (4) Daily or almost daily

5. How often during the last year have you failed to do what was normally expected from you because of drinking?
   (0) Never
   (1) Less than monthly
   (2) Monthly
   (3) Weekly
   (4) Daily or almost daily

6. How often during the last year have you been unable to remember what happened the night before because you had been drinking?
   (0) Never
   (1) Less than monthly
   (2) Monthly
   (3) Weekly
   (4) Daily or almost daily

7. How often during the last year have you needed an alcoholic drink first thing in the morning to get yourself going after a night of heavy drinking?
   (0) Never
   (1) Less than monthly
   (2) Monthly
   (3) Weekly
   (4) Daily or almost daily

8. How often during the last year have you had a feeling of guilt or remorse after drinking?
   (0) Never
   (1) Less than monthly
   (2) Monthly
   (3) Weekly
   (4) Daily or almost daily

9. Have you or someone else been injured as a result of your drinking?
   (0) No
   (2) Yes, but not in the last year
   (4) Yes, during the last year

10. Has a relative, friend, doctor, or another health professional expressed concern about your drinking or suggested you cut down?
    (0) No
    (2) Yes, but not in the last year
    (4) Yes, during the last year

Source: Reproduced, with the permission of the publisher, from *The Alcohol Use Disorders Identification Test: Guidelines for Use in Primary Care, AUDIT*, 2nd edition. Geneva, World Health Organization, 2000 (The AUDIT test: Self-Report Version page 31, http://whqlibdoc.who.int/hq/2001/WHO_MSD_MSB_01.6a.pdf, accessed January 12, 2015).

Joe is a 43-year-old carpenter who, for 5 years, drank more than a fifth of wine daily. He often blacked out during his drinking, ate only one meal a day, and was fired from many jobs because of absenteeism. Recently, Joe ran out of money, and after 3 days with no alcohol, his hands began to shake so severely that he was unable to light a cigarette. He could not sleep and was plagued by panic. Neighbors were concerned because of his rambling, incoherent speech. When taken to the hospital, Joe thought the doctor was his brother; he did not know where he was, and he picked at imaginary insects on his bedsheet. The sound of carts rolling in the hallway provoked intense visual and auditory impressions of "fiery car crashes." (From Spitzer, Gibbon, Skodol, Williams, & First, 1994)

benzodiazepines: A class of drugs derived from benzoic acid that are prescribed to alleviate anxiety and panic; includes Valium and Xanax.

Alcohol withdrawal syndrome can be explained by an imbalance between inhibitory and excitatory neurotransmitters, especially a reduced neurotransmission in GABA and an enhanced neurotransmission in glutamatergic pathways, as well as an enhanced dopamine release (Glue & Nutt, 1990). In one study (Palmstierna, 2001), 6.9% of people with AUDs developed alcohol withdrawal delirium after hospital admission, despite treatment with **benzodiazepines**, which mimic GABA transmission (see Chapter 7). Five risk factors were significantly correlated with the development of alcohol withdrawal delirium: current infectious disease, tachycardia (rapid heart rate), signs of alcohol withdrawal accompanied by an alcohol concentration of more than 1 gram per liter of body fluid, a history of epileptic seizures, and a history of delirious episodes (Palmstierna, 2001).

A more severe form of alcohol-induced delirium is *alcohol-induced psychotic disorder*, which resembles delirium but is less episodic and more likely to include well-developed delusions and hallucinations. The psychotic individual generally does not recognize these delusions and hallucinations as being induced by alcohol. For example, one person with this disorder believed that TV newscasters were sending him instructions in a "secret language," but he vehemently denied any connection between this belief and his drinking. Alcohol-induced psychotic disorder is associated with high comorbidity with other mental disorders, high rehospitalization and mortality rates, and suicidal behavior (Jordaan & Emsley, 2014).

Neurocognitive disorder (see Chapter 15) is a more persistent and pervasive condition, characterized by significant deterioration in memory, language, motor coordination, or executive functions, such as planning, organizing, and attending to specific tasks. Afflicted individuals are often unable to recognize familiar persons or understand where they are or how they got there. It is a more persistent condition than delirium, lasting long after the alcohol intoxication and withdrawal are over. Mild or major neurocognitive disorder can be caused by adverse effects of alcohol consumption on brain functioning (Martin, 2007). Some alcohol-associated neurocognitive deficits may recover with abstinence, whereas others seem to persist for months or years beyond cessation of drinking (Martin, 2007).

Wernicke-Korsakoff syndrome: A rare, alcohol-induced memory disorder in which affected individuals become confused and unable to coordinate voluntary muscle movements, and then lose memory for personal experiences.

A well-known, but rare, alcohol-induced memory disorder, called **Wernicke-Korsakoff syndrome**, is partly caused by a deficiency in vitamin B_{15} or *thiamine* (Osiezagha et al., 2013). Thiamine deficiency is related both to the malnourishment commonly seen among people with chronic AUDs and to the fact that alcohol interferes with vitamin metabolism. Current hypotheses suggest that the syndrome occurs as a result of a disconnection between diencephalic and medial temporal lobe structures, the latter known to play a prominent role in the capacity to learn new information (Nahum et al., 2014). Wernicke-Korsakoff syndrome occurs in two phases. In the first, Wernicke's phase, the individual is suddenly confused and unable to coordinate voluntary muscle movements. In the second, more chronic Korsakoff phase, the individual's memory for personal experiences, even recent ones, is lost, while other types of memory remain intact (Isenberg-Grzeda, Kutner, & Nicolson, 2012). Clinicians miss most cases of Wernicke-Korsakoff syndrome, likely because patients do not present with the classic signs associated with the condition (Isenberg-Grzeda et al., 2012).

Causes of Alcohol Use Disorders

Why do some people develop significant and diagnosable problems with their alcohol use, whereas others appear to be able to use the drug more moderately and without serious consequences? Some theorists argue that problem drinking stems from alcohol's ability to stimulate dopamine receptors in the brain's reward centers, a feature that is common to all substance use disorders (American Psychiatric Association, 2013a). An early classic study showed that rats will seek stimulation of certain dopamine-releasing brain areas over and over, even in the absence of food (Olds & Milner, 1954), which has an analog in the fact that humans will do much the same thing, often persisting in severe and dangerous patterns of substance use, despite clear negative consequences.

But this explanation does not account for why roughly one third of the American population are nondrinkers and one third drink only in moderation. Is there a genetic characteristic that makes certain individuals particularly susceptible to the rewarding effects of alcohol? Or is alcohol abuse shaped by personality, family dynamics, or group norms? No one knows for sure, but biological, psychological, and social factors have all been implicated—singly or in combination—as causes of AUDs.

MAPS - Superficial Syndromes
Observe what the effects of chronic excessive alcohol use have done to this saguaro cactus in Tucson, Arizona.

Genetic Factors

Problem drinking runs in families. The risk of alcohol abuse is seven times greater among the first-degree relatives of people with AUDs than among first-degree relatives of non-problem drinkers (Merikangas, 1990). Evidence that genetic factors contribute to this risk comes from both twin and adoption studies, with overall heritability estimates ranging from 50% (Munn-Chernoff et al., 2013) to over 60% (Wetherill et al., 2014).

Most twin studies have found a higher concordance rate among identical twins than among nonidentical twins for level of alcohol consumption, as well as for susceptibility to the effects of alcohol (Cadoret, 1990). Concordance rates are generally in the 25–75% range, but the rates are affected by the type of AUD and by factors such as gender. Usually, higher concordance rates appear in males, in people who display severe alcohol abuse, and in those—such as Cloninger's Type II AUDs—whose problem drinking began early in life (McGue, Pickens, & Svikis, 1992). Adoption studies provide the strongest support for the role of genetic influence on alcohol-related disorders. Reports of research conducted in the United States, Sweden, and Denmark indicate that adopted children born to parents with AUDs are more likely to develop problem drinking as adults than adopted children born to parents without AUDs (Cloninger, Bohman, & Sigvardsson, 1981; Schukit, Goodwin, & Winokur, 1972).

What exactly is it that people with AUDs inherit? Scientists are hard at work looking for various candidate genes. Earlier, we discussed the possible role of the genes involved in *alcohol dehydrogenase* as conferring protection from AUDs (Ehlers, Liang, & Gizer, 2012). Findings from an extensive meta-analysis also identified five GABA-type A receptor genes that may be involved in the pathogenesis of AUDs (Li et al., 2014). Other genes that might be implicated include the D2 dopamine receptor gene (DRD2; Conner et al., 2005), as well as genetic loci Kcnj9 and Mpdz (Buck, Milner, Denmark, Grant, & Kozell, 2012), DPYSL2 (Taylor & Wang, 2014), and PKNOX2 (Wang et al., 2011).

Neurobiological Influences

What biological mechanisms might link genetic processes with drinking behavior? Potential answers come from research to identify *biological markers* of vulnerability to alcohol. Progress has been made in finding markers that predict people's genetic predisposition to AUDs, such as genetic differences in several neurotransmitters, including GABA, dopamine, serotonin, and beta-endorphin (Peterson, 2004).

Another possible marker may lie in people's brainwaves, the patterns of electrical activity measured by an electroencephalograph (EEG). Some studies have found that the sons of fathers who had AUDs have higher-than-normal rates of a fast-paced brainwave called the *beta wave* (Gabrielli et al., 1982) and show less EEG *change* after alcohol consumption than sons of nonproblem drinkers (Ehlers & Schuckit, 1990).

Differences also occur in **event-related potentials (ERPs)**, which are measured brain responses that occur as the direct result of a specific sensory, cognitive, or motor event (Luck, 2005). One such change—called the *P300* because it occurs about 300 milliseconds after the presentation of a stimulus—is believed to indicate an individual's attentional skills. Meta-analysis evaluated P300 findings from the sons of people with AUDs compared to unaffected male controls (Polich, Pollock, & Bloom, 1994). Analysis of the then 30 available studies indicated that 40% of the reports found statistically reliable P300 amplitude effects, such that low-risk participants exhibited significantly larger components than high-risk participants (i.e., offspring of parents with AUDs). But these effects are moderated by a number of factors, including smoking, gender, age, and comorbidity (Polich & Ochoa, 2004). Researchers today therefore still do not know whether or how the brain's neuroelectrical activity increases vulnerability to alcohol abuse (Cuzen, Andrew, Thomas, Stein, & Fein, 2013).

Another potential biochemical marker for alcohol disorders may lie in the functioning of enzymes and neurotransmitters. One target of research is the enzyme *monoamine oxidase* (MAO), which is involved in the metabolism of the neurotransmitters dopamine and norepinephrine. Recall that dopamine is a suspected mediator of alcohol's effect on reward centers in the brain. Early studies revealed that people with AUDs had less MAO activity than controls, and the effect was more prominent for Type II AUDs (Tabakoff, Whelan, & Hoffman, 1990). However, the role of MAO activity is controversial and complex. First, MAO levels are themselves affected by alcohol consumption and by a variety of other psychiatric conditions. Second, platelet MAO-B activity has in several studies been reported to be low in males with AUDs, but this has not been the case with regard to females with AUDs (Nilsson, Wargelius, Sjöberg, Leppert, & Oreland, 2008). Third, recent research has found that MAO-A levels may be elevated in the brains of people with AUDs (Matthews et al., 2014).

Researchers are also focusing on the neurotransmitter *serotonin* as a possible marker for AUD risk. Abnormally low levels of serotonin have been linked to aggression, impulsivity, and antisocial behavior (see Chapters 5 and 6), all of which are associated with Cloninger's Type II AUDs. Serotonin levels have been found to be related to alcohol craving in both animals and humans. For example, an imaging study provided the first evidence that AUDs in humans, like in rodent models, are associated with increased levels of ventral striatal serotonin 1-B receptors (Hu et al., 2010).

One other potential marker is heart rate change in response to alcohol consumption. The degree to which a substance accelerates the heart rate may reflect an individual's sensitivity to the stimulating properties of that substance, thus providing an index of the reward value of that substance to the user (Wise & Bozarth, 1987). Indeed, men with relatives with AUDs show larger increases in heart rate (reflecting sympathetic nervous system activity) after drinking than do men from families without AUDs (Finn, Zeitouni, & Pihl, 1990), and those men who show relatively large heart rate increases after using alcohol are more likely to drink regularly (Pihl & Peterson, 1991). Perhaps the sons of people with AUDs are more susceptible to the stimulating properties of alcohol—and hence more strongly reinforced by its biochemical effects. In addition, heart rate variability (HRV)—a measure of beat-to-beat changes in heart rate that is a sign of a healthy parasympathetic nervous system, which counteracts the sympathetic nervous system to calm us down—predicted craving in people with AUDs. Those with lower HRV had reduced capacity for self-regulation and lower ability to inhibit their craving (Quintana, Guastella, McGregor, Hickie, & Kemp, 2013). These studies provide evidence for a broader role of the autonomic (sympathetic and parasympathetic) nervous system in the maintenance of dependence disorders.

To summarize, although people with AUDs differ from controls in neuroelectrical activity, the functioning of enzymes and neurotransmitters, and heart rate changes, many of these effects are complicated and difficult to replicate. Furthermore, none of these markers has yet proved to be a consistently reliable indicator of alcohol vulnerability, nor has any of them been conclusively shown to cause AUDs. Still, the fact that there are biological differences in the way that people respond to alcohol implicates a potentially heritable vulnerability. But having this vulnerability does not mean that a person will inevitably develop an AUD. Psychological and social factors undoubtedly interact with biological variables to elevate the risk of problem drinking.

Psychological Factors

Emotional states, expectancies, and personality characteristics can affect an individual's motivation to drink. For example, the **tension reduction hypothesis**—a mainstay of psychological literature on alcoholism for over 60 years (Conger, 1956)—suggests that drinking alcohol is reinforced by its ability to reduce tension, anxiety, anger, depression, and other unpleasant emotions. Therefore, people who have experienced such reinforcement—either firsthand or by seeing others use alcohol to reduce stress—should increase their drinking in stressful situations.

Many laboratory studies have tested this hypothesis by placing animals and humans in various kinds of stressful conflicts and giving them free access to alcohol. Other studies have correlated the amount of alcohol consumption with the number and intensity of stressors that people report in daily life (e.g., family conflict, job change, death of a loved one). The laboratory studies have generally supported the tension reduction hypothesis, but studies of the results of self-reported, real-life stressors have not been as positive (Cappell & Greeley, 1987). The lack of consistent support from studies of naturally occurring stressors appears to be because (1) drinking can be motivated by many factors besides a desire to reduce tension; (2) alcohol has variable effects on tension, depending on how much is consumed; and (3) only certain individuals experience stress reduction after ingesting alcohol.

For example, several studies have found an association between alcohol use and stress only among individuals who have limited skills for coping with stress and who believe that alcohol will relieve their stress (Cooper, Russell, Skinner, Frone, & Mudar, 1992; Shariat, 2003). Trait anxiety (how anxious a person feels most of the time) has not been related to alcohol consumption, but students with a positive family history of AUDs have stronger expectancies of tension reduction from alcohol use (Shariat, 2003). This research attests to the power of expectancies in determining the effects of substances on users.

Alcohol expectancy involves individuals' beliefs about the physical and psychological effects of alcohol—for example, that it can enhance sexual performance, reduce tension, restore confidence, or increase social competence (Marlatt, 1987). According to alcohol expectancy theory, drinking behavior is determined largely by the reinforcement that individuals *expect* to receive from it (Goldman, Brown, & Christiansen, 1987; Thombs, 1994). From this perspective, the physiological effects of alcohol are relatively unimportant in accounting for problem drinking; the fact that high doses of alcohol increase anxiety will probably have little effect on drinkers who are convinced that *any* amount of alcohol will promote relaxation.

How well is this theory supported by research? In a classic study, the late Alan Marlatt (see the "A Conversation With . . ." feature at the end of this chapter) and his colleagues (Marlatt, Demming, & Reid, 1973) compared the drinking behavior of males in the laboratory assigned to one of four groups. Group 1 members were told, correctly, that they were being served vodka and tonic. Group 2 members were told that they were being served vodka and tonic, but they received only tonic. Group 3 members were told that they were being served tonic alone, but they were actually given vodka and tonic. Group 4 members were told, correctly, that they were being served only tonic. The results of this study supported alcohol expectancy theory: Both problem and nonproblem drinkers drank significantly more when told their drinks contained alcohol (Groups 1 and 2), *regardless of the beverage's actual alcohol content*. This finding is significant because it challenges models of AUDs that hold that problem drinking is controlled only by biological

tension reduction hypothesis: The idea that drinking alcohol is reinforced by its ability to reduce tension, anxiety, anger, depression, and other unpleasant emotions.

alcohol expectancy: An individual's belief about the physical and psychological effects of alcohol.

"Tough week or tough life?"

Source: Cartoonresource/Shutterstock.com.

mechanisms triggered directly by alcohol's physiological effects on the body. Instead, how much people drink may be at least partly determined by their cognitive states—that is, expectations about what they are drinking and how it might make them feel (Thombs, 1994).

A related line of research relies on measures such as the Alcohol Expectancy Questionnaire (AEQ) to compare the alcohol-related beliefs of people who differ in their use of alcohol. The AEQ assesses expectancies about alcohol's ability to enhance sexual, physical, and social pleasure; to increase social assertiveness and power; to reduce tension; and to promote other positive changes (Brown, Christiansen, & Goldman, 1987). In Western culture, likely a result of media campaigns and the ubiquitous association between alcohol use and social circumstances (e.g., college parties), people expect social enhancement from drinking, and such expectancies predict use (Smith, Goldman, Greenbaum, & Christiansen, 1995). Other studies have supported a role for post-trauma symptom-specific alcohol expectancies as a potential link between sexual assault and alcohol consumption; in other words, sexual assault survivors may drink because they think it will numb their intrusive symptoms (Vik, Islam-Zwart, & Ruge, 2008). Religiousness and spirituality's protective influence on underage drinking is partly due to their influence on lowering expectations about alcohol's positive effects (Sauer-Zavala, Burris, & Carlson, 2014). Overall, then, people with AUDs are more likely than nonproblem drinkers to believe that positive outcomes will follow alcohol use, as shown in Figure 14.5.

Another psychological mechanism thought to contribute to problem drinking is the inability to discern the internal cues that signal intoxication. For many drinkers, these cues—such as dizziness, lightheadedness, nausea, and the like—act as warning signs that blood alcohol concentrations are high and serve as a "shut-off valve" that inhibits further drinking. Several studies have shown that people with AUDs are not very good at detecting these internal cues, tending to estimate their BAC almost exclusively on the basis of such *external* cues as the number of drinks consumed (Brick, 1990). Conversely, nonproblem drinkers use both internal and external cues (Huber, Karlin, & Nathan, 1976). For example, in one study, people with a positive family history of AUDs made judgmental errors and underestimated their drunkenness relative to individuals without such a family history; and the more they tended to underestimate their drunkenness, the more likely they were to binge drink and drive after drinking (Turrisi & Wiersma, 1999). Further, training people to more accurately estimate their own BAC has been used as an intervention in drunk driving prevention programs because it imparts an ability to

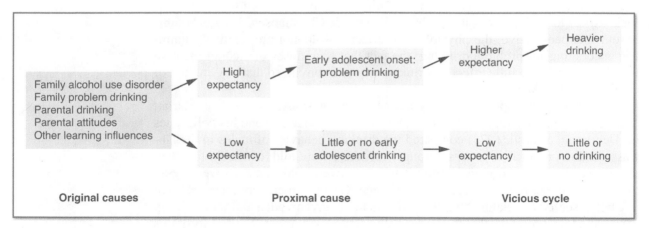

FIGURE 14.5 An Expectancy Model of Alcoholism

In Greg Smith's (1995) expectancy model of AUDs, learning experiences transmitted in families influence the expectancies that young children hold about drinking alcohol. High positive expectancies lead children to experiment with drinking at early ages, and early drinking tends, in turn, to further increase positive expectancies about drinking.

perceive individualized impairment that may be present below the legal limit for driving (Aston & Liguori, 2013).

One final psychological factor to consider is personality. Freud contended that AUDs reflected frustrated oral needs and regression to the oral stage of psychosexual development (see Chapter 2). Whereas that view has not received much empirical support, more-recent studies suggest that a particular type of person may be prone to drinking disorders (Sher, Walitzer, Wood, & Brent, 1991). In adults, this personality pattern has been variously called "antisocial," "sensation-seeking," "novelty-seeking," and "impulsive." In children, it has been called *externalizing*. All of these terms refer to a pattern of risky, impulsive, and sometimes aggressive behavior. Externalizing behavior influences drinking problems in two ways: (1) by directly leading to more exposure to and use of alcohol, and (2) by promoting more positive alcohol expectancies (Sher et al., 1991).

Connections

What other behaviors are typical of childhood externalizing disorders? See Chapter 3.

More-recent work has unpacked the role of impulsivity in AUDs by examining specific facets of the trait, such as negative urgency (the tendency to behave impulsively in the face of strong negative emotions) and sensation seeking (the tendency to pursue stimulation through impulsive behaviors; Karyadi, Coskunpinar, Dir, & Cyders, 2013). In a recent study, among college students high (versus low) in sensation seeking, strong beliefs about alcohol's role in college life were related to significantly greater drinking; among students high (versus low) in negative urgency, endorsing strong beliefs about alcohol's role in college life was related to greater levels of alcohol-related negative consequences (LaBrie, Kenney, Napper, & Miller, 2014). It turns out that these two distinct impulsivity traits—sensation seeking and urgency—may play different roles in escalation of alcohol use and development of AUDs during emerging adulthood (Shin, Hong, & Jeon, 2012).

Sociocultural Factors

Cultural traditions and interpersonal processes, such as family interactions, parenting practices, and peer pressure, also influence alcohol use disorders. For example, patterns of problem drinking differ from country to country. In England and North America, AUDs often involve periods of extremely heavy drinking and a loss of control over consumption. In wine-drinking countries such as France, however, people with AUDs are usually inveterate or steady drinkers who never show a loss of control. In Muslim countries, which discourage alcohol use on religious grounds, the incidence of any kind of AUDs is very low.

Social processes in the home may be partly responsible for the tendency of alcohol problems to run in families. Parenting styles and the quality of parent-child relationships, for example, tend to influence the probability of problem drinking during adolescence. Parents who are nurturing but still use firm discipline (called *authoritative* parenting) are less likely than nonsupportive, authoritarian, or inconsistent parents to have adolescents who drink (Čablová, Pazderková, & Miovský, 2014). Conversely, in one study, parental overprotection in early adolescence had the strongest relationship to regular alcohol use in these children as they grew older (Visser, de Winter, Vollebergh, Verhulst, & Reijneveld, 2013). Preliminary evidence also suggests that risks for adult AUDs are lower when a person's family of origin emphasized family "rituals," such as a family dinner hour, vacations, and holiday celebrations. Because these rituals provide opportunities for family communication and shared experiences, they are ideal for fostering the feelings of support and commitment that are linked to a lower probability of problem drinking (Bennett & Wolin, 1990). Adolescents' drinking tends to mirror that of their parents, suggesting that children imitate the patterns of alcohol use and abuse that they see at home. So if parents use alcohol to deal with stress-induced emotions, adolescents are more likely to believe that alcohol will reduce their own tensions. In general, the more that parents drink, the earlier their children begin to drink (Kandel, Kessler, & Marguiles, 1978).

Peer-group influence is another important social factor in shaping drinking, at least among young people (Visser, de Winter, Veenstra, Verhulst, & Reijneveld, 2013). The socializing effects of friends' drinking on adolescent drinking behavior have been firmly established in previous literature (Deutsch, Steinley, & Slutske, 2014). Indeed, many

Alcohol Abuse: Sin, Disease, or Habit?

The history of alcohol research and treatment and, to a major extent, approaches to other substances of abuse have been shaped by three broad viewpoints (Thombs, 1994). Advocates of each of these viewpoints have often regarded one another's ideas with suspicion, resulting in heated, sometimes hostile, disagreements about the best way to explain and treat substance abuse.

The *moral* perspective regards excessive alcohol use as a sin or weakness of character. Punishment or repentance is often the treatment of choice, and many advocates of this perspective endorse legal sanctions as the primary strategy for reducing problem drinking. Although the oldest view of alcohol use disorders, this perspective—that alcoholism is a matter of choice—is very much alive today. U.S. civil and criminal courts continue to show a reluctance to hold defendants blameless for actions committed under the influence (e.g., toughening laws on impaired driving). The U.S. Supreme Court has ruled that alcoholism can be regarded and treated as "willful misconduct" (Connors & Rychtarik, 1989). And an assumption of freedom of moral choice lies behind all "Just say no" campaigns (Miller & Kurtz, 1999).

MAPS - Prejudicial Pigeonholes

A second perspective, the *disease model*, sees alcohol use disorder as a symptom of an underlying illness. Within U.S. society, this view emerged in the 1930s and 1940s, growing rapidly in popularity after World War II (Johnson, 1973). According to the disease model, certain individuals have physiological vulnerabilities—of genetic or other biological origin—that render them unable to control their consumption of alcohol. In this view, alcoholics (as they are termed) bear no responsibility for the development of their problems. They are, in fact, viewed as incapable of making rational decisions, warranting social intervention to coerce them into treatment (Miller & Kurtz, 1999). The therapy of choice consists of detoxification, education about the disease, admonition to abstain from all psychoactive substances, and medical procedures to alleviate related physical problems, such as nutritional deficits (Milam & Ketcham, 1983). Because the disease model emphasizes individuals' inability to control their drinking, complete abstinence is usually the treatment goal.

A third viewpoint—the psychological or *learning perspective*—contrasts sharply with both previous views in suggesting that alcohol use disorders are acquired patterns of maladaptive behavior, harmful habits that anyone can learn if exposed to environmental conditions that support excessive drinking (like college). According to this view, operant learning, classical conditioning, and cognitive expectations lead to and maintain excessive alcohol use. For example, according to recent dual-process theories, alcohol (mis)use is determined by interplay or imbalance between two systems: faster, automatic, implicit, and impulsive cognitive processes, on the one hand, and slower, more conscious, explicit, and reflective processes on the other hand (Deutsch & Strack, 2006). Studies have shown that both explicit and implicit cognitions are associated with alcohol consumption in adolescents (Thush & Wiers, 2007), undergraduates (Houben & Wiers, 2007), and adults (Reich, Below, & Goldman, 2010). Clinicians adopting a psychological perspective are more likely than others to consider alternatives to complete abstinence (such as controlled drinking, described later in this chapter) as a treatment goal.

Currently, problematic alcohol use is usually publicly portrayed as a disease in U.S. society. Government agencies such as the National Institute on Alcohol Abuse and Alcoholism generally support the recovery movement and, as a corollary, the disease model. Accordingly, this model is frequently advocated by physicians, whose training emphasizes biological causality. It is also endorsed by substance use counselors who follow the 12-step program of Alcoholics Anonymous (AA) and the philosophy that people with drinking problems lack control over their use and must therefore abstain from drinking forever. The popularity of the disease model does have certain advantages. Calling alcoholism a disease makes it less stigmatizing than labeling it a moral problem. Thus, the disease model may reduce guilt, allowing recovering individuals to focus on how to maintain an alcohol-free life (Thombs, 1994).

However, many academic psychologists and some physicians criticize the disease model, contending that empirical data do not support it. They point, for example, to several studies showing that alcohol-dependent drinkers can choose not to

MAPS - Medical Myths

drink under laboratory conditions that provide strong reinforcement for abstinence (Fingarette, 1988). Furthermore, and in contradiction to the loss-of-control

Alcohol Abuse: Sin, Disease, or Habit? *(Continued)*

hypothesis, some people with alcohol use disorders can ingest alcohol and then limit their subsequent intake. So, although the disease model may be comforting and easier to understand, scientific data suggest that this view is by no means the only viable one. Based on this research, modern theories about alcohol use disorders seek to integrate aspects of all three models, bringing the field closer to accepting a diathesis-stress model (e.g., Goldstein, Abela, Buchanan, & Seligman, 2000; Klanecky & McChargue, 2013).

Thinking Critically

1. What is the climate regarding use of alcohol and other drugs on your college campus, and which model do you think best explains it?

2. Which model do you believe holds the most promise for understanding and treating alcohol (or other substance) use disorders? Why?

3. Do you think that scientific data or people's prior beliefs will be more influential in resolving the controversy over the nature of alcohol use disorders?

programs aimed at preventing drinking by young people are based on the assumption that social acceptance is an important reinforcer of drinking, especially during adolescence. However, surprisingly little is known about how peer groups operate in this regard. For instance, peer influence was not reduced by parents' perception of peers or by the person's own self-control (Visser et al., 2013), although its effects were reduced by good, authoritative parenting (Hoffmann & Bahr, 2014). One study showed that, as closeness to male friends decreased, the influence of their drinking behavior on the person actually increased, perhaps indicating that drinking together was being used as a bonding strategy to get closer (Deutsch et al., 2014).

Another sociocultural theory of AUDs and substance use disorders more generally is the *dislocation theory of addiction* (Alexander, 2012). Dislocation denotes a lack of psychosocial integration into a society, and some argue that our modern free-market society mass-produces dislocation as part of its normal functioning, even at the best of times. In other words, people around the world, rich and poor alike, are being torn from the close ties to family, culture, and traditional spirituality that constituted the normal fabric of life in pre-modern times. This kind of global society subjects people to unrelenting pressures toward individualism and competition, displacing them from social life. People adapt to this dislocation by concocting the best substitutes that they can, and addiction provides this substitute—a rite of passage in a sense—for many people (Colin Smith, personal communication, September 2013). History shows that addiction can be rare in a society for many centuries but can become nearly universal when circumstances change—for example, when a cohesive tribal culture is crushed or an advanced civilization collapses (Alexander, 2010). Of course, this historical perspective does not deny that differences in vulnerability are built into each individual's genes, experience, and personal character, but it removes individual differences from the foreground or sole focus of attention. In Alexander's (2010, 2012) view, addiction is much more of a social problem than an individual disorder.

Connections

What other mental disorders are proposed to stem partly from the downfall of society and the pitfalls of modern life? See Chapter 6.

A Multifactor Model

As noted in earlier chapters, in relation to most forms of mental disorder, debates about which causal factor is most important eventually give way to models that recognize the combined and interacting roles of several different factors. As the "Controversy" feature suggests, the field of alcohol abuse was relatively slow to develop this multifactorial perspective, largely because of long-standing, intensely held, and deeply conflicting views about whether alcoholism is a moral failing, a disease, or a learned habit (Thombs, 1994).

Many scientists now argue that AUDs stem from an interplay of several biopsychosocial factors, all of which must be taken into account to fully explain these disorders (Devor, 1994; Epstein & McCrady, 1994). One such multifactor theory has been proposed by Ralph Tarter and Michael Vanyukov (1994), who claim that certain genetically determined *temperaments* interact with various *facilitating environments* to produce a heightened risk for alcohol use problems. Different combinations of high-risk temperaments and environmental liabilities create various *pathways* to an alcohol problem. For example, the combination of *high activity level* (impulsivity) and *ineffective parental discipline* constitutes a pathway that is different from *low sociability* and exposure to a *deviant peer group*. In other words, people may be predisposed toward—and may learn to follow—any of several pathways to problem drinking. Think about your current relationship with alcohol or other substances and whether any of the risk factors discussed in this section might apply to you.

Treatment and Prevention of Alcohol Use Disorders

Given the many patterns of AUDs and the multiple factors and pathways that lead to these problems, it should not be surprising to learn that no single treatment is effective in changing the behavior of all, or even most, problem drinkers. But are some treatments more effective than others? Do some treatments work better for certain types of people with AUDs?

For many years, the most common treatment of AUDs in the United States was based on the *Minnesota model*, in which alcoholism is viewed as a disease. Named for its place of origin, the Minnesota model typically requires patients to be hospitalized for 4–6 weeks, although treatment in outpatient clinics is becoming more popular. For those who show signs of alcohol intoxication or withdrawal, the treatment begins with hospital-based **detoxification**, a supervised period of "drying out," often aided by drugs or other interventions to ease withdrawal symptoms and remedy nutritional deficits. For all patients, the main focus of treatment is on education about the consequences of alcohol use and abuse, individual counseling for psychological problems, group therapy to enhance interpersonal skills, and—at the end of the hospital or clinic program—continued participation in group meetings of Alcoholics Anonymous (AA). Total abstinence from alcohol is nearly always the goal of the Minnesota treatment model, and to emphasize the dangers of relapse, model proponents refer to people who successfully complete treatment as "in remission" or "recovering." The model is still in widespread use today (e.g., Klein & Ross, 2014), although other similar models have been developed, all of which share the fundamental notion of abstinence and strong reliance on the peer-group process in treatment (Borkman, Kaskutas, & Owen, 2007).

detoxification: A supervised period of "drying out" from an abused substance, often aided by drugs or other interventions to ease withdrawal symptoms and remedy nutritional deficits.

Alcoholics Anonymous

People with AUDs need not complete the Minnesota model (or any other) treatments to get help from Alcoholics Anonymous (AA). Indeed, AA works with more people with AUDs than any other treatment organization. First organized in 1935 in Akron, Ohio, by two people with AUDs (Dr. Bob Smith, a physician, and Bill Wilson, a stockbroker), it is a volunteer-supported organization and is thus free of charge. AA is based on the 12 steps to recovery summarized in Figure 14.6. Today, thousands of AA groups can be found in countries all around the world (Sharma & Branscum, 2010).

The AA treatment philosophy is based on the idea that alcoholism (as they call it) is a disease that can be controlled only if a person strives for complete abstinence. AA members are encouraged to attend self-help meetings whenever they wish, and many do so several times a week. At first, they are urged merely to accept that they are alcoholics (called "first stepping"), but they are gradually indoctrinated into all aspects of AA's spiritual approach to staying sober. Members who have maintained sobriety for a time serve as sponsors for newcomers. These sponsors answer questions, offer tips on how to stay sober, and maintain frequent personal contact to help the recovery process.

The effectiveness of the AA approach is difficult to assess scientifically because AA group membership is anonymous, and AA has traditionally not been interested in helping researchers conduct outcome studies. Reviews (e.g., Emrick, Tonigan, Montgomery, &

FIGURE 14.6 The Twelve Steps of Alcoholics Anonymous

Alcoholics Anonymous is a free, nonprofessional, peer-directed counseling program that adheres to a spiritual philosophy defined by 12 steps, summarized as follows:

Step1.	Acknowledging that we cannot control our drinking.
Steps 2 and 3.	Giving ourselves over to a higher power.
Steps 4 and 5.	Taking stock of ourselves and admitting our misguided behavior.
Steps 6 and 7.	Asking God to remove our character flaws.
Steps 8 and 9.	Listing people who were harmed by our misbehavior and making amends when possible.
Step 10.	Continuing to right our past wrongs.
Steps 11 and 12.	Seeking a relationship with God and carrying this message to other alcoholics.

Source: Adapted from Alcoholics Anonymous, www.aa.org.

Little, 1993) do suggest that members who regularly attend AA meetings have a better chance of maintaining sobriety than those who do not. However, it also appears that many people who start AA—perhaps more than half—discontinue participation in the first year. A meta-analysis revealed that attending conventional AA meetings was worse than no treatment or alternative treatment for those coerced into attending meetings, and residential AA-modeled treatments performed no better or worse than alternatives. However, several components of AA were supported—such as using people recovering from their AUD as therapists, having peer-led self-help therapy groups, teaching the 12-step process, and encouraging individuals to conduct an honest inventory of themselves (step 4 in Figure 14.6; Kownacki & Shadish, 1999). Another systematic review of randomized controlled trials evaluating the effectiveness of AA and other 12-step programs did not demonstrate their effectiveness in reducing alcohol use and achieving abstinence, compared with other treatments (Ferri, Amato, & Davoli, 2006).

So the overall efficacy of AA is still unknown. Its advocates believe it is the best AUD intervention available, whereas its detractors argue that other types of treatment are necessary, especially for the many people who avoid or drop out of AA. Taken as a whole, the data suggest that AA may be helpful, especially in conjunction with professional treatment, for many people who are addicted to alcohol. We do not know, however, whether AA might occasionally be harmful. When a group is highly confrontational, for example, people with AUDs may become resistant to change. Nevertheless, in light of the evidence supporting the program, the wide availability of meetings, and the lack of expense, AA is worth considering for many problem drinkers (Lilienfeld & Arkowitz, 2011).

As you can see in Figure 14.6, AA's 12 steps are embedded in a religious (theistic) worldview, which could be a turn-off to some people with AUDs. Thanks to AA, though, there are now many types and styles of addiction recovery groups, all voluntary associations of people who share a common desire to overcome alcohol or drug problems. Different groups use different methods, ranging from completely secular to explicitly spiritual (like AA). A survey of members found that active involvement in *any* addiction recovery group correlates with higher chances of maintaining sobriety and that nonreligious respondents are significantly less likely to participate in 12-step groups (Atkins & Hawdon, 2007).

One alternative to AA is called SMART Recovery (Self-Management and Recovery Training), an international nonprofit organization that provides assistance to individuals seeking help with addictive behaviors. The approach is secular and scientifically based, using nonconfrontational motivational, behavioral, and cognitive methods (Horvath & Yeterian, 2012). SMART Recovery offers a substantially different approach to recovery and a different meeting format than that of the 12-step spiritual fellowship, which is still the dominant addiction mutual-aid group approach in the United States. Founded in 1994, SMART Recovery now appears likely to endure and to be of interest to individuals specifically seeking an evidence-based, self-empowering, and self-reliant approach to addiction recovery. This approach significantly differs from the powerlessness approach of the 12-step spiritual fellowships because it promotes tools for recovery that aim to increase participants' capacity to maintain motivation, identify and cope with cravings, identify and modify irrational thinking and beliefs, and live with greater balance and attention to long-term goals in addition to short-term ones (Horvath & Yeterian, 2012).

Marital and Family Therapy

Alcohol and other problematic substance use patterns are inextricably linked to the close social relationships of the user. In many cases, a spouse, parent, or close friend can inadvertently support someone with an AUD by the way he or she responds to it. Sometimes, the user becomes a preoccupation of another family member, whose "job" becomes protecting, monitoring, or censuring the user, a role perhaps learned in family relationships during childhood (Koffinke, 1991). Such people, described as **codependent**, can become so enmeshed in another person's drinking problems that they actually prevent changes in the use pattern.

codependent: A person who protects, monitors, or censures a person with a substance use disorder, becoming enmeshed in the user's problems and preventing change in the substance use pattern.

Even if there is no codependency, marital and family relationships can contribute to abuse, as when marital conflict stimulates bouts of heavy drinking. One pattern that often appears in such couples is termed nag-withdraw, wherein the person without the AUD nags the person with the AUD (e.g., "Why are you drinking so much lately? You really need to stop."); the other person responds by withdrawing from the critic, often going away to drink more (Rohrbaugh & Shoham, 2002).

Given their potential impact on drinking behavior, it is not surprising that AUD treatment programs can be made more effective by involving the person's spouse and other family members (Bowers & Al-Redha, 1990; Powers, Vedel, & Emmelkamp, 2008). In some programs, the spouse may be present as a spectator, participate in alcohol-focused counseling sessions, or take part in marital therapy aimed at teaching communication skills, conflict resolution techniques, and examining the family's role in supporting problem drinking. In one study, people with AUDs who received marital therapy were found to drink less, report greater marital satisfaction, and experience fewer marital separations 18 months later than did those whose spouses participated only in the person's alcohol-focused (not couple-focused) counseling sessions (McCrady, Stout, Noel, Abrams, & Nelson, 1991).

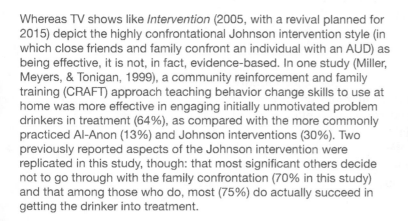

Whereas TV shows like *Intervention* (2005, with a revival planned for 2015) depict the highly confrontational Johnson intervention style (in which close friends and family confront an individual with an AUD) as being effective, it is not, in fact, evidence-based. In one study (Miller, Meyers, & Tonigan, 1999), a community reinforcement and family training (CRAFT) approach teaching behavior change skills to use at home was more effective in engaging initially unmotivated problem drinkers in treatment (64%), as compared with the more commonly practiced Al-Anon (13%) and Johnson interventions (30%). Two previously reported aspects of the Johnson intervention were replicated in this study, though: that most significant others decide not to go through with the family confrontation (70% in this study) and that among those who do, most (75%) do actually succeed in getting the drinker into treatment.

Source: Iakov Filimonov/Shutterstock.com.

Behavioral Treatments

Alcohol can be thought of as an unconditioned stimulus that elicits unconditioned responses in the form of pleasant physical reactions. Behavioral therapists have developed learning-based procedures designed to help people with AUDs associate alcohol with *unpleasant* stimuli, and thus make drinking less likely. For example, in aversion therapy, the sight, smell, and taste of alcohol are repeatedly presented while the person with the AUD is nauseated or vomiting as a result of taking an emetic drug. After repeated trials, these alcohol-related sensory cues should begin to elicit nausea or other unpleasant reactions (see Chapter 2 for a review of classical conditioning principles). By itself, aversion therapy has had limited success in treating AUDs (Costello, 1975; Nietzel, Winett, Macdonald, & Davidson, 1977), but it can enhance the effects of other treatments (e.g., Smith, Frawley, & Polissar, 1991).

Behavioral treatments based on operant conditioning (see Chapter 1) attempt to change drinking by manipulating reinforcement contingencies for alcohol use. Nathan Azrin's **community reinforcement** model (Azrin, McMahon, Donohue, Besalel, & Lapinski, 1994) has proved to be one of the most effective of these operant approaches. Originally tested in the early 1970s, it has repeatedly proven to be successful over the years with larger, diverse populations (Smith, Meyers, & Miller, 2001). In this intervention, several social and environmental influences are used to help people with AUDs maintain sobriety. For instance, they are taught to recognize the circumstances in which drinking is most likely (e.g., college frat parties, weekends), as well as the social reinforcers that help support this drinking (e.g., awkward social situations with many strangers present). They then learn how to arrange reinforcement contingencies to reward sobriety and to avoid situations that encourage drinking.

community reinforcement: A treatment for substance use disorders in which social and environmental influences are used to help maintain sobriety.

Controlled Drinking Treatments

Some people with AUDs avoid AA and other treatment programs because the prospect of living without alcohol is too threatening. Is it possible for them to learn to drink in moderation? This question was raised as a scientific issue more than 40 years ago, and it has generated some of the most intense controversy ever seen in the field of alcohol studies. The controlled drinking debate was sparked by a study by Mark and Linda Sobell, two psychology graduate students, in which they compared a program for teaching people with AUDs to drink in moderation with an abstinence-oriented program similar to AA (Sobell & Sobell, 1973, 1976). Their results showed that people could indeed engage in controlled drinking and that, overall, the moderation group had somewhat better outcomes than the abstinence group. At about the same time, a study by the RAND Corporation (Armor, Polich, & Stambul, 1976) suggested that not all people with AUDs who resumed drinking after treatment inevitably relapsed into problem drinking. In other studies, people with AUDs were helped to moderate their drinking by becoming more sensitive to bodily cues associated with rising blood alcohol levels and by honing better self-control skills (Lovibond & Caddy, 1970; Miller & Munoz, 1982).

These results were decried by advocates of the total abstinence camp, and the Sobells were charged with scientific misconduct and ethical violations when follow-up assessments revealed that only one of the twenty people in the controlled drinking group had been able to maintain his controlled drinking and that four had died from alcohol-induced problems (Pendery, Maltzman, & West, 1982). An independent investigative committee later refuted these charges, and objective reviews of the Sobell's research showed that deaths from alcohol-related problems were about as frequent in the abstinence group.

The emotional fallout from these bitter disputes has led to continuing mistrust between proponents and opponents of controlled drinking goals. The ferocity of the controversy also led to the virtual disappearance of studies designed to compare the value of treatments aimed at controlled drinking versus total abstinence. Several studies have found that people who initially state a preference for abstinence as a goal have a better treatment outcome than those stating a preference for controlled drinking (Adamson, Heather, Morton, & Raistrick, 2010; Meyer, Wapp, Strik, & Moggi, 2014). Higher levels of functioning, lower levels of consequences, no prior involvement in treatment and AA, and a more drinking-saturated social environment were associated with the choice of a nonabstinence goal (DeMartini et al., 2014). However, a research review provides some empirical support for the following statements: (1) reduced-risk drinking is a viable option for at least some problem and dependent drinkers; (2) abstinence- and nonabstinence-based treatments appear to be equally effective; and (3) allowing people to choose their treatment goal increases the treatment success rate (van Amsterdam & van den Brink, 2013).

Motivational Interviewing

Motivational interviewing (MI; Miller & Rollnick, 2013), which first started as a treatment for alcohol-related disorders, is both a treatment philosophy and a set of methods employed to help people increase intrinsic motivation by resolving their ambivalence about behavior change. MI is now a well-recognized model that has been used in psychotherapy, medicine, addictions, public health, and beyond. Because of its emerging importance as a component of treatments for substance use disorders, we describe its theory and evidence base here.

Many professionals interested in helping people make behavioral changes—such as reducing or quitting their alcohol intake—assume that supplying knowledge is sufficient. Well-intended practitioners advise high-risk drinkers to cut down. Individuals addicted to alcohol or other drugs are told to avoid situations that will trigger cravings. However, seasoned practitioners realize that even very good advice often fails to generate behavioral change. After all, too many of us continue to engage in unhealthy behaviors despite *clearly knowing* what we should do and even *how* to change. What is lacking is the motivation to *apply* that knowledge (the *why* of change).

Motivation is essential to the change process. Research has shown that a client's motivation to change is significantly influenced by the therapist's relational style (Norcross, 2002); in one study, the more the therapist confronted (e.g., "you're an alcoholic"), the more the client drank 1 year later (Miller, Benefield, & Tonigan, 2001). MI posits that a good working relationship in which clients are viewed as the expert on their own life and can choose their own drinking goals serves to minimize resistance to change and thereby enhances motivation. MI therapists, in the style of humanist Carl Rogers (Chapter 2), strive to promote a collaborative relationship with their clients based on empathy, which is part of what makes the treatment work (Miller & Rose, 2009). Note how different this approach is from the more traditional approaches for AUDs (Minnesota model or AA) that require breaking through individuals' defenses and getting them to accept a label of "alcoholic."

In addition to this supportive relationship, MI adds a directive component in which the therapist works toward specific goals of directly increasing individuals' motivation to change their drinking. To do so, MI attempts to foster dissonance between clients' unhealthy status quo behaviors (e.g., binge drinking) and their own healthy goals (e.g., live a long life, responsible living, be a good partner or student) in the hope that focusing on the discrepancy will motivate clients to change. Similarly, MI encourages client speech that favors change—what is termed *change talk* (Amrhein, Miller, Yahne, Palmer, & Fulcher, 2003)—which has emerged as a significant predictor of outcome (Magill et al., 2014). In other words, if you can get individuals with an AUD to discuss why and how they might like to change their drinking, rather than nagging or telling them to do so, the probability of them changing is enhanced.

A large and expanding number of controlled research studies of MI have demonstrated that, despite its typically brief duration (one or two sessions), it is significantly (10–20%) more effective than no treatment and at least as effective as other viable treatments for a wide variety of problems, ranging from substance use to reducing risky behaviors and increasing client engagement in treatment (Lundahl, Kunz, Brownell, Tollefson, & Burke, 2010). There is a dose effect, such that more sessions tend to produce more behavioral change, and yet, MI typically operates as a brief treatment, with higher cost effectiveness than the alternatives. MI has proved effective in a variety of formats, although it may work best as a prelude to other treatments, as it was initially designed—for instance, having a session of MI before beginning an inpatient treatment program for an AUD (Lundahl et al., 2010). MI also works for clients regardless of problem severity, age, gender, or race/ethnicity. Finally, MI is equally learnable by practitioners of diverse professions, optimally via a 2-day interactive workshop, followed by ongoing supervision and coaching (Lundahl & Burke, 2009).

Relapse Prevention

With treatment options such as those just discussed, abstinence or controlled drinking rates in the year following treatment range from about 20% to as high as 75%, depending on the length and extent of the people's AUDs. But over longer periods of time, the percentage of successful outcomes tends to decline, as most people with AUDs who are treated—even in abstinence-oriented programs—eventually begin to use alcohol again, a process known as **relapse**.

According to the disease model and to proponents of AA, if a person with an AUD resumes drinking after treatment (or at any other time), out-of-control use will inevitably follow. However, leading people to expect that "one drink leads to twenty" may actually create a self-fulfilling prophecy, increasing the likelihood of continued drinking once any drinking occurs. A different approach aims at teaching problem drinkers specific relapse-prevention skills in an effort to prevent isolated drinking episodes from being repeated and eventually escalating into an AUD. The relapse-prevention approach encourages people with AUDs to believe that a lapse in abstinence can be a valuable learning experience that can potentially strengthen previous treatment gains (Lewis, Dana, & Blevins, 1988).

The late Alan Marlatt (see the "A Conversation With . . ." feature at the end of the chapter) was a pioneer in the field of relapse prevention (Marlatt & Gordon, 1985). Marlatt believed that relapse was most likely when individuals recovering from an AUD engaged in self-defeating thoughts that brought about "inadvertent" exposures to circumstances that increased their risk of drinking. The case of Jim provides an example.

relapse: The return or worsening of a disorder after recovery.

> After 2 or 3 months of abstinence following his diagnosis of an AUD, Jim began purchasing cigarettes and groceries at a store next to a bar frequented by his former drinking buddies. Initially, Jim told himself that he went to this store only because it offered easy parking, but this was a dangerous deception because it soon led Jim to stop by the bar to chat with his old friends. After a couple of visits, Jim started to drink again, "just to be friendly." One night, however, he stayed for 3 hours, drank heavily, and was arrested for drunken driving on his way home.

Marlatt and his colleague Judith Gordon (1985) contended that such cases of self-deception result from *apparently irrelevant decisions* that, if unchecked, accumulate and eventually lead to drinking. Cognitions such as "I owe myself a drink" or any number of positive expectancies about the consequences of "one small drink" may set off a chain of faulty decisions. Once there is a lapse, many people experience intense guilt and shame that generate a cascade of increasingly pejorative self-evaluations ("I've let my family down" or "I'm a complete failure"). These cognitions then increase the probability of continued drinking, an outcome known as the **abstinence violation effect** (Marlatt & Gordon, 1985).

Relapse prevention techniques are cognitive-behavioral, as they teach individuals to monitor self-defeating cognitions and to replace them with different thinking strategies. The ultimate goal is to provide the skills to prevent a complete relapse, regardless of the situation or impending risk factors (Marlatt & Witkiewitz, 2005). For example, Jim learned that it was better for him to shop at a different store, where he did not have to overcome so many temptations to drink. Jogging became a daily ritual, a kind of "positive

abstinence violation effect: A situation in which expectancies about using a drug may set off a chain of faulty decisions for an abuser that then increase the probability of resumed abuse.

addiction" that replaced drinking. Finally, Jim learned that he could lessen his urge to drink if, instead of thinking about how good it felt to drink, he focused on how miserable he felt as he sat in jail after his drunken driving arrest. A meta-analysis found relapse prevention to be useful for a variety of substance use problems, including AUDs (Irvin, Bowers, Dunn, & Wang, 1999).

Other Brief Psychosocial Interventions

Because of how common and costly AUDs are in a variety of settings, the last several decades have seen an explosion in the development of brief treatments that can be delivered in a medical, work, or college environment. Some brief-intervention programs teach controlled drinking skills, such as goal setting ("no more than two drinks a day"), self-monitoring (counting the number of drinks and slowing the rate of consumption), and self-reinforcement ("I'll buy new songs for my iPod whenever I go a week with fewer than 10 drinks;" Harris & Miller, 1990). Other brief interventions include health education seminars, alcohol screening interviews by primary care physicians or nurses, and brief marital counseling. Motivational interviewing (MI), as discussed in detail earlier, is also considered a brief intervention and may be the most effective of all such time-sensitive approaches (Carey, Scott-Sheldon, Carey, & DeMartini, 2007; Hennessy & Tanner-Smith, 2014).

There is current agreement that, after years of limited and halting progress, alcohol brief interventions have finally come of age, certainly from a scientific perspective, if not so much from the perspective of practical implementation (Heather, 2010). From the research viewpoint, the effectiveness of screening and brief intervention in primary health care is well established (Sullivan, Tetrault, Braithwaite, Turner, & Fiellin, 2011), and its evidence in other medical settings is emerging (e.g., Kuokkanen & Heljala, 2005). The more intense versions of these brief interventions (such as those teaching controlled drinking skills) are usually more effective than less intense interventions (e.g., 10-minute screening and feedback by a physician), especially for individuals whose drinking is more severe (Poikolainen, 1999). Note that, with the current move toward integrated care in the United States and beyond, more and more medical professionals are being trained in brief interventions such as MI (Lundahl et al., 2013).

Along with health-care settings, one of the most common places for use of brief intervention has become college campuses. Related to his pioneering work on relapse prevention described earlier, Alan Marlatt ushered in a new era of **harm reduction**, which remains the best practice for addressing college student drinking to this day (Blume, 2012). Harm reduction acknowledges the plain fact that many college students will choose to drink alcohol but strives to reduce the negative consequences and risky behaviors often associated with such use.

Dan Kivlahan, Alan Marlatt, and their colleagues used harm reduction principles when they developed a six-session, cognitive-behavioral group program for light-drinking college students, called the Alcohol Skills Training Program (ASTP; Kivlahan, Marlatt, Fromme, Coppel, & Williams, 1990). ASTP is designed to meet the special needs of college-age drinkers by deemphasizing (1) the goal of abstinence, (2) the long-term health risks of drinking, and (3) authoritative messages. Instead, the emphasis is on promoting (1) controlled drinking through relapse prevention skills and BAC estimation, (2) avoidance of hangovers and other immediate negative consequences of drinking, and (3) nonconfrontational group discussions about the effects of drinking on behavior (Fromme, Marlatt, Baer, & Kivlahan, 1994). One brilliant harm reduction strategy first employed in the ASTP involved research concerning the biphasic effects of alcohol use (Blume, 2012). There is a generally agreed-upon point of diminishing returns when the pleasurable effects of consuming a substance begin to be outweighed by potential negative effects; an increase in BAC levels beyond the point of diminishing returns contributes to worsening effects. College students enrolled in ASTP were instructed in using personalized BAC charts (see Figure 14.2) to determine how to plan and pace their drinking to remain below the point of diminishing returns. In other words, the goal was to drink only to the point

harm reduction: A range of public health policies designed to reduce the harmful consequences associated with various human behaviors, both legal and illegal. Harm reduction policies for alcohol use, for example, encourage drinking responsibly and try to reduce the harmful consequences often associated with excessive consumption.

where they could enjoy the pleasant effects of alcohol without vomiting, blacking out, or putting themselves in danger. The ASTP group interventions set the stage for developing a one-on-one harm reduction intervention referred to as the Brief Alcohol Screening and Intervention for College Students (BASICS) program (Dimeff, Baer, Kivlahan, & Marlatt, 1999), which is in wide use in over 1,800 colleges today.

Whereas individually delivered brief interventions are effective, there is not yet evidence that group-delivered brief interventions are associated with reductions in alcohol use in adolescent populations (Hennessy & Tanner-Smith, 2014), and campus-wide interventions for college students have not been systematically examined (Scott-Sheldon, Demartini, Carey, & Carey, 2009). However, findings indicate that electronically delivered interventions (such as the eCheckup, which can be implemented on a large scale but is individually completed) may be a promising campus-wide prevention approach to address the problem of college student alcohol consumption, especially for campuses that have limited resources (Hustad, Barnett, Borsari, & Jackson, 2010).

Qualitative reviews of the literature support the efficacy of some individual-level college drinking interventions (e.g., brief motivational interventions) but not others (e.g., education-only programs; Larimer & Cronce, 2007; Lewis & Neighbors, 2006; Walters & Neighbors, 2005). A meta-analytic review of 62 randomized controlled trials evaluating individual-level alcohol interventions for college students found a significant reduction in the quantity of alcohol consumed, compared with controls, that lasted up to 6 months after the intervention (Carey et al., 2007). Moreover, interventions targeting personal motives for change and/or changing exaggerated normative perceptions (i.e., "everyone here drinks more than I do") predicted greater reductions in alcohol-related problems. Normative feedback was especially important for students who drank for social reasons (Walters & Neighbors, 2005).

Many brief-intervention programs are offered not as treatment but as *prevention* for problem drinkers who have not yet developed AUDs. Some programs are aimed at secondary prevention in college students who consume an average of four or five drinks per day but who (so far) experience few adverse social consequences. Other programs aim at primary prevention in helping adolescents or children delay drinking, as the "Prevention" feature in this chapter discusses. Finally, brief interventions are not sufficient for everyone. Jerry in our chapter-opening case responded to a campus newspaper notice about a program much like the ASTP. However, an initial evaluation found that his alcohol and drug problems were too severe for this type of program; with his consent, he was referred to an off-campus facility that catered to younger drinkers so that he could receive more intensive one-on-one treatment than the brief intervention could provide.

Medication

Prescription drugs have been used both to treat alcohol withdrawal and to curb drinking behavior. Withdrawal effects can be minimized by a variety of drugs—most with serious side effects or addictive properties themselves—that mimic the neurochemical effects of alcohol. Strong evidence from controlled studies shows that benzodiazepines, carbamazepine (an anticonvulsant), beta blockers (usually used for cardiac arrhythmias), and calcium channel blockers and clonidine (both typically used to treat high blood pressure) reduce unspecific withdrawal symptoms more effectively than placebo does (Franck, 2003). Only benzodiazepines have a documented effect as preventive treatment against withdrawal seizures or delirium tremens, and benzodiazepines are better and safer than GHB and clomethiazole, two sedative/hypnotic drugs also used in the hospital to treat alcohol withdrawal (Ungur, Neuner, John, Wernecke, & Spies, 2013). Unfortunately, benzodiazepines have undesirable side effects, and some researchers question their use on the grounds that they are addictive and that most people with

"The problem is that you're overmedicated. Luckily there are drugs that can help with that."

Delaying and Deterring Drinking by Adolescents

The most severe alcohol use disorders in adults often begin with drinking during adolescence, so many prevention programs are specifically aimed at discouraging teenage drinking. Traditionally, such programs consisted of stricter enforcement of underage drinking laws, along with warnings about the negative consequences of alcohol and drugs. In the 1980s, for example, young people were told to "just say no" to alcohol and other drugs. Today, prevention programs are becoming more sophisticated. Most are school-based and comprehensive enough to target marijuana, tobacco, and other substances that tend to be associated with the use of alcohol.

These prevention programs employ one or more of four components. The first, *affective education*, attempts to enhance adolescents' self-esteem and clarify their personal values about substance use. The second, called *life skills training*, improves skill at interpersonal communication, conflict resolution, and assertiveness. The third component, *resistance training*, is similar to life skills training but focuses specifically on teaching youngsters how to resist pressure from peers to use alcohol and other drugs. Finally, *normative education* promotes peer group norms against alcohol and drug use, corrects false impressions about the prevalence of substance use among peers (e.g., challenging the idea that "everyone is doing it"), and encourages youngsters to make public commitments to remain free of alcohol and other drugs. Most programs also provide education about the negative consequences of drug and alcohol use, with an emphasis on important short-term consequences, such as how drinking leads to elevated risk of pregnancy or sexually transmitted diseases stemming from alcohol-induced sexual behavior. More recently, preventive programs have also included parents; in one program, parents attended a 1-hour instructional presentation that provided information on why adolescents use drugs and alcohol, helpful tips for communicating with adolescents, how to spot drug and alcohol use, and what to do when they find it (Goldberg, 2011).

Many well-designed studies suggest that these programs can result in a certain amount of change in adolescents' drinking attitudes and behavior (Mrazek & Haggerty, 1994). Overall, affective education tends to be the least effective approach, whereas normative education tends to be the most effective (Bledsoe, 2003; Hansen, 1994; Hansen & Graham, 1991). The U.S. Life Skills Training Program can also be effective in reducing drunkenness and binge drinking (Lipp, 2011). Some studies suggest that multicomponent interventions that combine school-based programs with parental involvement and media coverage may be particularly promising. The most effective parenting programs are those that share an emphasis on active parental involvement and on developing skills in social competence, self-regulation, and parenting (Petrie, Bunn, & Byrne, 2007). However, the effects of these programs may differ for people of different racial/ethnic groups. For example, African-American participants benefit from the inclusion of the components of spirituality, violence, and stress (Bledsoe, 2003). Refusal skills (resistance) training is especially effective for Hispanic populations (Bledsoe, 2003).

Finally, preventive programs to reduce high-risk drinking are becoming more common on college campuses throughout the United States. A meta-analysis found that behavioral interventions for freshman college students significantly reduce alcohol consumption and alcohol-related problems (Scott-Sheldon, Carey, Elliott, Garey, & Carey, 2014). The most effective strategies include personalized feedback (getting information on how much you drink and how it compares to others), moderation strategies, expectancy challenge (determining if what you think alcohol will do is actually accurate), identification of risky situations, and goal setting (Scott-Sheldon et al., 2014). What prevention strategies to reduce high-risk drinking exist on your college campus?

AUDs do not experience withdrawal symptoms severe enough to warrant this intervention (Wartenberg et al., 1990).

Medications have been used in two ways to discourage drinking. In the first, people with AUDs are given drugs such as *disulfiram* (sold as Antabuse) that create increased heart rate, nausea, vomiting, and other unpleasant effects if people consume alcohol. Controlled studies show that a dose of disulfiram taken in the morning, for example, is effective in discouraging drinking throughout the day (Fuller et al., 1986), but it has little effect in the long run, simply because most people stop using it whenever they want to drink. Disulfiram also has negative side effects (e.g., it can intensify depression), and if individuals take too much, it can create physically dangerous reactions to alcohol. It is not uncommon for suicidal people to drink heavily after taking an overdose of disulfiram. A meta-analysis showed that supervised treatment with disulfiram has some effect on short-term abstinence and days until relapse, as well as number of drinking days, when compared with placebo, none, or other treatments, although its long-term effect on abstinence has not yet been evaluated (Jørgensen, Pedersen, & Tønnesen, 2011). Another meta-analysis concluded that, based on results with open-label studies (where the participants knew whether they were taking disulfiram or not), disulfiram is a safe and effective treatment, compared to other abstinence supportive pharmacological treatments or to no treatment (Skinner, Lahmek, Pham, & Aubin, 2014). However, blinded studies were incapable of distinguishing a difference between treatment groups, presumably because expectancy is the mechanism of action by which disulfiram works—that is, people expect to feel sick if they drink, and that expectation is what prevents them from drinking (Skinner et al., 2014).

The second way drugs are used to promote sobriety involves the administration of **antagonists**, which block the effects of other drugs. These anticraving drugs target the neurotransmitters—such as dopamine, serotonin, and the endogenous opiates—that mediate alcohol's effects on the brain and create the sensation of craving. The most promising of these anticraving drugs are *naltrexone* (sold as Revia), which interferes with the production of endogenous opiates, and *acamprosate* (sold as Campral), which stimulates GABA transmission and blocks glutamate. Both of these medications are associated with a reduction in return to drinking and are equal to one another when compared directly (Jonas et al., 2014). For some unexplained reason, however, the effects of these drugs in clinical trials are decreasing over the years, with more recent studies showing weaker effects than older studies (Del Re, Maisel, Blodgett, & Finney, 2013).

antagonist: A drug that blocks the effects of neurotransmitters or other drugs.

Long-term effects of these medications depend on how compliant individuals are in taking the medication (Swift, Oslin, Alexander, & Forman, 2011) and whether the anticraving effects of these medications can outweigh the positive alcohol expectancies, the tension reduction effects, the influence of codependents, and the other psychological factors that support alcohol abuse. Clinicians therefore recommend using various strategies (such as motivational interviewing) to monitor or improve medication adherence. Also, through improved adherence, once-monthly injectable extended-release naltrexone (sold as Vivitrol) may provide an advantage over other oral agents approved for AUD treatment (Hartung et al., 2014).

Treatment Stages and Matching

One critical factor related to the likelihood of treatment success is individuals' readiness to change. According to a classic model developed by James Prochaska, Carlo DiClemente, and John Norcross (1992), the process of changing drinking patterns (or any other health-threatening behaviors) occurs in five stages, whether professional treatment is involved or not. These stages of change include:

1. *precontemplation*, in which the person is aware of a problem but has no intention to change;
2. *contemplation*, in which the person is aware of a problem and has begun to think about making changes but has not yet made a commitment to change;
3. *preparation*, in which the person is making small changes in behavior and intends to make more meaningful ones in the future;
4. *action*, in which the person has made substantial efforts to overcome the problem and has already reached a criterion for success in changing the targeted behavior; and
5. *maintenance*, in which the person works to prevent relapse so that positive changes become a new way of life.

People often pass through the early stages several times before they are able to make permanent changes in a problem behavior. What implications does this readiness-for-change model have for finding the right treatment option for people with AUDs? It suggests that action-oriented programs such as those used by behavioral therapists may not be helpful to individuals who are still at the precontemplation or contemplation stages. On the other hand, brief interventions such as motivational interviewing aimed at boosting motivation to change and exploring the disadvantages of drinking might be ideal for people at the first two stages of change.

However, the intuitive idea of matching different treatment choices to different types of drinkers has not been supported by most data. Results from an 8-year research program involving over 1,700 participants—Project MATCH—found that matching clients to treatments designed to address specific needs did not lead to better results. Whether they received cognitive-behavioral therapy, brief motivational treatment (MI), or a program aimed at helping them get involved in AA (called 12-step facilitation), people with AUDs did about equally well in terms of drinking and other related outcomes (Project MATCH Research Group, 1997). In fact, regardless of the "type" of AUD they had, brief and relatively inexpensive treatment was just as effective as more complex treatment. Nine of ten carefully selected primary matching variables failed to exert any significant effect on outcome at 1 year. High-anger clients did better in MI, and those with greater levels of alcohol dependence did somewhat better in 12-step models (Project MATCH Research Group, 1998). The good news is that, consistent with positive outcomes reported in prior national studies, the Project MATCH (1997, 1998) data suggest that substantial improvement occurs during treatment for alcohol problems and that it is largely maintained over time.

Another very large and expensive study for alcohol treatments (the COMBINE study; Anton et al., 2006) assigned almost 1,400 people to nine different combinations of pharmacological and psychological interventions. The psychological intervention combined cognitive-behavioral therapy, 12-step facilitation, and motivational interviewing (the same three approaches shown to work separately in Project MATCH). Results showed that this combined therapy performed as well as naltrexone, but there was no evidence of efficacy for acamprosate and also no evidence of incremental efficacy for combinations of naltrexone, acamprosate, and psychotherapy (Anton et al., 2006). According to some researchers, however, the COMBINE study cannot be regarded as providing strong empirical support for the use of either naltrexone or acamprosate, as the analysis also shows that there is no difference between the treatment groups that received placebo and those given the specific pharmacological interventions (Bergmark, 2008). Due to the paucity of differential and new results obtained in both Project MATCH and COMBINE, others have called for the end to these types of "large-scale black box randomized controlled trials" (Bühringer & Pfeiffer-Gerschel, 2008).

Section Review

Alcohol use disorders:

- are experienced by over 17 million Americans;
- cost society billions of dollars in crime, illness, absenteeism, and serious accidents; and
- are often comorbid with other mental disorders.

Several factors are involved in causing alcohol use disorders, including:

- genetic risk, with several specific variants being identified;
- biological irregularities that increase certain individuals' vulnerability to the rewarding effects of alcohol;
- the reinforcing properties of alcohol, along with the expectancies that individuals hold about alcohol; and
- family, peer-group, and social factors that promote drinking.

Treatments for alcohol use disorders:

- include detoxification and inpatient programs, Alcoholics Anonymous, behavioral treatments (including relapse control), family/couples' therapy, medication, brief interventions such as motivational interviewing, harm reduction approaches, and prevention efforts;

- differ in whether their goal is to promote abstinence or controlled drinking; and
- have, in an attempt to boost their effectiveness, been matched to individual variables. such as type of alcohol use disorder, severity and duration of alcohol dependence, and readiness for change, but this research has been largely disappointing to date.

Other Sedatives

Sedatives are a group of drugs—including alcohol—that enhance the activity of GABA, which, as noted earlier, is the brain's major inhibitory neurotransmitter. The ability of sedatives to reduce neural activity leads to several effects, including sedation, enhanced sleep (a *hypnotic* effect), and reduced anxiety (an *anxiolytic* effect). Most of the more than two dozen drugs in this category fall into one of two major types: barbiturates and benzodiazepines.

Barbiturates

Odorless, white, crystalline derivatives of the chemical compound *barbituric acid* make up the class of drugs known as the **barbiturates**. Drug users tend to prefer short-acting and intermediate-acting barbiturates (Coupey, 1997). Often called "downers," barbiturates are prescribed in tablet form as sedatives or hypnotics for persons suffering from insomnia. Although barbiturates induce sleep in most individuals, they also have certain drawbacks, including reduction of rapid eye movement (REM) sleep. Furthermore, sleep disruptions are common when people stop taking these drugs.

barbiturates: A class of drugs that are addictive and produce relaxation and mild euphoria at low levels and have an effect similar to alcohol intoxication at higher levels.

At low doses, barbiturates typically produce relaxation and mild euphoria, but at higher doses, they bring about a state similar to alcohol intoxication, including impaired motor coordination and poor judgment and concentration. High doses of barbiturates can also depress respiratory functions and lower blood pressure and body temperature to the point of coma and death, especially if taken with another depressant, such as alcohol. Sadly, the ease with which this combination induces loss of consciousness catches many users by surprise. Accordingly, accidental death is a major risk of barbiturate use. Because of this, barbiturates are rarely prescribed anymore, and the number of people who kill themselves by knowingly combining barbiturates with alcohol is declining (Carlsten, Allebeck, & Brandt, 1996).

Benzodiazepines

Drugs derived from *benzoic acid* are called benzodiazepines. Commonly prescribed benzodiazepines include Valium, Librium, and Xanax. Like barbiturates, they bring about feelings of relaxation and mild euphoria but are less likely to produce significant toxicity. For this reason, benzodiazepines are regarded by many family doctors as having a low risk for accidental death and suicide (Dupont & Saylor, 1992).

However, physicians are becoming more aware about the controversy that surrounds the wide use of benzodiazepines in many mental disorders (Dell'osso & Lader, 2013). Toxicity and overdoses do occur when benzodiazepines are taken with other depressants, a common pattern among substance users, and dependency can also occur (Choy, 2007). Many Americans have received prescriptions for benzodiazepines at some point in their lives, typically for sleep disorders (Chapter 12), anxiety disorders such as panic disorder (Chapter 7), or post-traumatic stress disorder (PTSD; Chapter 9). In 2012, prescribers wrote 37.6 benzodiazepine prescriptions per 100 persons in the United States (Paulozzi, Mack, & Hockenberry, 2014). Despite Veterans Affairs clinical guidelines recommending against routine use of benzodiazepines for PTSD, the prevalence of long-term use increased in the veteran population with PTSD, rising from 15.4–16.4% in men and 18.0–22.7% in women, respectively, from 2003 to 2010 (Hawkins, Malte, Imel, Saxon, & Kivlahan, 2012).

The use and abuse patterns associated with benzodiazepines vary substantially (Busto et al., 1986; O'Brien, 2005). One pattern is shown by adolescents and young adults who

MAPS - Medical Myths

engage in "recreational" use of sedatives, hypnotics, or anxiolytics. These people take the equivalent of two or three therapeutic doses to produce a pleasurable high or reduce social anxiety. Recreational users are typically introduced to these drugs by friends who obtain the drugs illegally. Polydrug use is common in these circumstances; downers are often mixed with alcohol and marijuana. For some recreational users, social use escalates to weekly then daily use and leads to high levels of tolerance. Some heavy users may take 10–20 times the therapeutic dose of a benzodiazepine daily.

Another pattern of abuse is observed in middle-class adults who initially take prescribed depressants for anxiety, insomnia, or pain. These people then become dependent on the drug and begin to take more than the amount prescribed, as illustrated by the case of Betty that follows. One study showed that people with benzodiazepine use disorder differed significantly from the control group in particular psychological dimensions, such as higher neuroticism and introversion, adverse life events previous to the disorder, and the prevalence of emotional rather than problem-based coping mechanisms (Konopka, Pełka-Wysiecka, Grzywacz, & Samochowiec, 2013).

Betty was a well-known attorney in her community, though she was highly anxious and preferred to be by herself. After she suffered a pulled muscle in her leg from a minor skiing accident, Betty's physician prescribed 5 mg of Valium daily to help ease the pain. But Betty gradually became "hooked" on the Valium. Unbeknownst to her family and friends, she steadily increased her use of the drug. Over a 2-year period, she visited 17 doctors and 20 pharmacies to maintain what had grown to a daily intake of 70 mg of Valium. Eventually, she spent more and more time going to doctors and driving to out-of-town pharmacies. By this time, her drug habit seriously interfered with the responsibilities of her work.

Even modest therapeutic doses of sedative drugs can lead to withdrawal. Withdrawal from Valium, for example, has been observed in individuals taking as little as 15 mg daily for 6 to 8 months, an amount and duration well within the range that physicians prescribe for several disorders. Following a course of dosages of this amount or somewhat higher, withdrawal symptoms are relatively mild, including anxiety, agitation, tremulousness, and insomnia. Discontinuing daily doses of about 40 mg of Valium can lead to more serious withdrawal symptoms, including increases in coronary activity, sweating, elevated body temperature, nausea, and vomiting. Delirium and seizures like those seen in alcohol withdrawal are likely if the daily dose was 100 mg. The severity of withdrawal symptoms is determined by the length of drug use, dosage, and type of depressant (Cambor & Millman, 1991). Short-acting drugs whose effects last 10 hours or less (e.g., the benzodiazepine *Ativan*) provoke withdrawal within hours after drug use is stopped, and these symptoms usually ease within a few days. Longer-acting drugs such as Valium lead to withdrawal symptoms that may not develop for more than a week after discontinuing the drug and may take a month or more to disappear.

Treatment of Sedative Use Disorders

There are almost no alternatives to abstinence-oriented treatment strategies in the scientific literature for sedative use disorders (Liebrenz, Boesch, Stohler, & Caflisch, 2010). Along with this gradual tapering toward abstinence, many clinicians prescribe non-benzodiazepine anxiolytic drugs or adjunctive medications, such as antidepressants or anticonvulsants, which mimic some of benzodiazepines' effects (Liebrenz et al., 2010). However, evidence for the use of substitutive pharmacotherapy in the management of benzodiazepine dependence remains relatively weak (Parr, Kavanagh, Cahill, Mitchell, & Young, 2009). Brief advice, such as a clinician recommending gradually reducing benzodiazepine dosage for every patient who has been prescribed benzodiazepines for longer than 3 months, yields better cessation rates when compared with continuation of routine care (Oude Voshaar, Couveé, Van Balkom, Mulder, & Zitman, 2006; Parr et al., 2009).

The optimal treatment involves linking people with psychological assistance to further increase the chances of ceasing use successfully (Parr et al., 2009). After detoxification, many individuals experience a mild *abstinence syndrome* in which they suffer insomnia, head and body aches, anxiety, and depression (Cambor & Millman, 1991). These symptoms may last for months, making the recovering user extremely vulnerable to relapse. Many of the same psychological and educational procedures used to treat alcohol use disorders are also used to rehabilitate people who have abused other sedative drugs. These treatments include individual and group therapy (e.g., cognitive-behavioral therapy, motivational interviewing), drug-specific education, and peer support groups such as AA (Halikas, 1993).

Section Review

Sedatives such as barbiturates and, more common today, benzodiazepines:

- reduce neuronal activity, leading to sedating, hypnotic, or anxiolytic effects;
- are often prescribed for a variety of medical and mental disorders, but their prolonged use can escalate into a sedative use disorder;
- can produce strong withdrawal symptoms and dependence; and
- are usually treated with techniques derived from the alcohol field, such as AA-type peer support groups, individual or group cognitive-behavioral therapy, motivational interviewing, and drug-specific education.

Stimulants

Drugs that have an excitatory effect on the central nervous system are called **stimulants**. Some stimulants, primarily *amphetamines*, are called "uppers" or "speed." Other stimulants include cocaine, methylphenidate (sold as Ritalin, a commonly prescribed drug for attention-deficit/hyperactivity disorder), caffeine, nicotine, and over-the-counter diet pills. Most stimulants create their effects by producing temporary elevations in the neurotransmitter dopamine, especially in the *nucleus accumbens*, the major reward center in the brain, discussed earlier as a common end mechanism for all addictive behaviors.

stimulant: A drug that has an excitatory effect on the central nervous system.

Amphetamines

First used medically to control asthma and nasal congestion, **amphetamines** stimulate the sympathetic branch of the autonomic nervous system, increasing heart rate and blood pressure, constricting blood vessels, and shrinking mucous membranes. Increased

amphetamines: A class of drugs that stimulate the sympathetic nervous system, increasing alertness and reducing appetite.

(a)   *Source: Eugene Sergeev/Shutterstock*   (b)   *Source: Brian L. Burke.*

MAPS - Superficial Syndromes

"This Is Your Brain on Drugs" was a large-scale U.S. antinarcotics campaign by Partnership for a Drug-Free America launched in 1987. A simple advertisement showed an egg in a frying pan, similar to (a), suggesting that the effect of drugs on a brain was like a hot pan on an egg. The cactus version of stimulant use disorder is shown in (b).

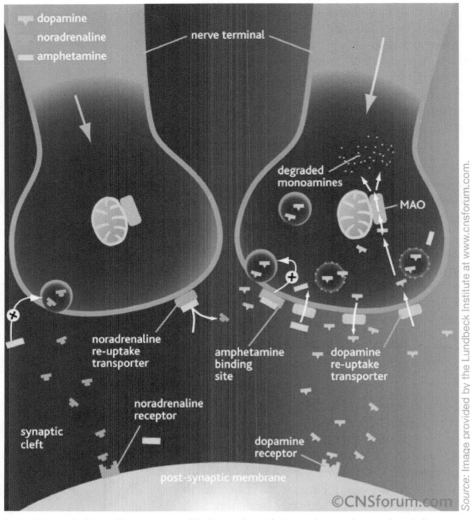

Low-dose amphetamines can modify the action of dopamine and norepinephrine in the brain (Calipari & Ferris, 2013). Amphetamines increase the concentration of dopamine in the synaptic cleft in three ways: (1) They can bind to the presynaptic membrane of dopaminergic neurons and induce the release of dopamine from the nerve terminal; (2) they can interact with dopamine-containing synaptic vesicles, releasing free dopamine into the nerve terminal; and (3) they can bind to the dopamine reuptake transporter, causing it to act in reverse and transport free dopamine out of the nerve terminal. Amphetamines can also cause an increased release of norepinephrine into the synaptic cleft.

sympathetic nervous system arousal also increases alertness and reduces appetite. For this reason, amphetamines have sometimes been used to treat sleep disorders, obesity, and attention-deficit disorders.

In addition to simple amphetamines, many users favor amphetamine variants, such as *methamphetamine*, a particularly pure form of amphetamine known as "crystal," "meth," or "ice." Meth has become more popular over the last decade, as featured on TV shows such as *Breaking Bad* (2008–2013). Methamphetamine is often used recreationally for its effects as a potent euphoriant and stimulant, as well as for its aphrodisiac qualities. Methamphetamine use disorder is now recognized as a global phenomenon responsible for considerable social and financial burdens (Miles et al., 2013).

Amphetamines produce a wide range of behavioral effects, depending on dosage, method of ingestion, frequency of use, and psychological characteristics of the user (Cambor & Millman, 1991). At low doses, amphetamines produce alertness and focused attention that can enhance performance on cognitive tasks such as reading. At higher doses, they lead to feelings of exhilaration and vigor, accompanied by increased talkativeness. Generally, amphetamines do not produce the marked euphoria associated with cocaine. At even higher doses, alertness may give way to hypervigilance and restlessness, whereas talkativeness turns into grandiosity and aggressiveness. When high doses are repeatedly taken for a long time, delirium or paranoia may develop, even in previously stable individuals.

Jabbar is a college student who, over a 2-year period, developed a twice-weekly habit of snorting crystal methamphetamine. At first, he enjoyed the rush of energy he got from the drug, bragging to his friends, "I got ice in my veins." Eventually, however, his behavior took an ominous turn. He began to accuse his roommates of trying to disrupt his studying by leaving "Satanic messages" on his answering machine. He was arrested a couple of times for disorderly conduct, once after he ran through the library and ripped up several books because "they had the wrong pages in them." These symptoms stopped immediately after he quit using methamphetamine.

Amphetamine intoxication also brings potentially dangerous physical changes, including an irregular heartbeat, dilation of the pupils, perspiration or chills, nausea, and muscular weakness. Often, there is a postintoxication period of marked fatigue, irritability, and dysphoria known as *crashing*. Significant physical and psychological harms have been associated with amphetamine use, especially with an increasing frequency of use (Darke, Kaye, McKetin, & Duflou, 2008). These harms include anxiety, suicide, depression, violent behavior, psychosis, cardiovascular complications, and physical dependence (Butler, Wheeler, & Sheridan, 2010).

Three groups of individuals are especially vulnerable to developing amphetamine use disorders: (1) those who initially obtain an amphetamine prescription for a different medical or mental disorder; (2) those who obtain the drug, usually through illegal channels, to stay alert while studying or on the job; and (3) recreational users who obtain amphetamines illegally to enjoy a high. Recreational users are typically young people from high-risk backgrounds (living in poverty in an inner city, with high levels of family adversity), who usually smoke amphetamine or inject it intravenously. Intravenous users, who typically inject high doses every few days, are at high risk for HIV infection because of needle sharing and sexual risk taking (Darke, Ross, Cohen, Hando, & Hall, 1995). Individuals in the other two groups are likely to be older, more stable, and to ingest the drug nasally or orally.

Cocaine

An *alkaloid*, or plant-derived, drug, **cocaine** comes from *erythroxylon coca*, a hearty bush indigenous to mountainous areas of South America. Cocaine's active ingredient is found in the leaves of this coca plant and, for centuries, the native peoples of the region, including the Incas as early as the 1500s, chewed these leaves to obtain a stimulating effect (Cambor & Millman, 1991). In the 1800s, cocaine became a popular treatment for various ailments throughout Europe and the United States, partly because of Sigmund Freud's claim that it cured hysteria. In fact, cocaine was regarded as a harmless substance with invigorating properties; as its name implies, Coca Cola contained cocaine until about 1900, after which caffeine was used instead. It was not until 1914, after cocaine's addictive potential was recognized, that the Harrison Narcotics Act limited the availability of cocaine (and opiates) in the United States.

cocaine: A psychoactive, pain-reducing, stimulant drug.

Cocaine was virtually unknown as an illegal recreational drug in the United States until the drug-permissive era of the 1960s and early 1970s, but even then, it was not as popular as marijuana or LSD. Later in the 1970s, however, there was a surge in the popularity of cocaine use, especially among middle- and upper-income groups. By the mid-1980s, its expense—and the brevity of its effects—made cocaine a "fashionable" drug for the wealthy. One survey in 1988 indicated that 2.3 million Americans had used cocaine within the previous 30 days (National Institute on Drug Abuse, 1991). The majority of affluent social users snorted cocaine in powder form. Many heavier users either mixed cocaine powder with water and injected it intravenously or experimented with *free-basing*, in which a potent form of cocaine is extracted by heating cocaine powder with a volatile substance, such as ether or ammonia. The resulting vapor is then inhaled, producing a rapid and intense infusion of cocaine. As all too many users discovered, this method is especially dangerous because the heated mixture can ignite without warning. In the late 1980s, a form of cocaine known as *crack* became popular, especially among less affluent users. Crack is produced by combining cocaine powder with

Marshall loved his 8-year-old son Cleatus, but he did not like it when Cleatus played with his ready-to-ship merchandise.

Source: Caricatures4you.com/Shutterstock.com.

Source: Photo by Alan Light.

On doing cocaine with her boyfriend in the 1970s while working as an anchorwoman in Nashville, Oprah Winfrey (shown here at her 2004 birthday party) said on her show in 1995: "I did your drug. This is probably one of the hardest things I have ever said. . . . I had a perfect, round, little Afro, I went to church on Sunday, and I went to Wednesday prayer meetings when I could . . . and I did drugs." Many other celebrities have used (and glorified use of) various drugs, such as Angelina Jolie, Megan Fox, George Clooney, Drew Barrymore, Elton John, Nicolas Cage, and Johnny Depp (Jacobs, 2013). Famous people to die from drug-related causes include Philip Seymour Hoffman, Cory Monteith (from *Glee*), Whitney Houston, Amy Winehouse, Michael Jackson, Heath Ledger (who played the Joker), Chris Farley (from *SNL*), Kurt Cobain (lead singer of *Nirvana*), Marilyn Monroe, writer Jack Kerouac, and John Belushi (who ironically was the iconic college partier in *Animal House*). The complete list is far too long to include here.

baking soda and then heating the mixture until brownish crystals settle to the bottom; these are left to harden into "rocks" that can be smoked in a pipe. The term *crack* refers to the noise the rocks make when lit.

Cocaine's physiological and behavioral effects are similar to those of other stimulants. The cardiovascular effects are complicated, but they appear to include rapidly increased blood pressure and irregularities in heart rhythms (Herning, Glover, Koeppl, Phillips, & London, 1994). Cocaine intoxication can cause sudden death due to respiratory arrest or heart failure. However, the effects of cocaine are different in two important ways from those of the amphetamines. First, cocaine produces a more euphoric experience than most amphetamines do, as it results in more serotonin release from the prefrontal cortex (Pum, Carey, Huston, & Müller, 2007), causing a euphoria in which there are instant feelings of well-being and confidence. Second, cocaine produces faster, but less long-lasting, effects than amphetamines. Smoking a single piece of crack, for example, can cause a rush that is immediate but that lasts for less than 5 minutes. Cocaine users must therefore repeat their doses frequently to maintain a cocaine high and forestall the postintoxication crash.

Although both cocaine and methamphetamine increase the levels of dopamine in the brain, animal studies have shown that the levels of dopamine are higher when methamphetamine is administered because of the drug's effect on different mechanisms occurring within nerve cells ("Methamphetamine and Cocaine," n.d.). For example, cocaine blocks dopamine reuptake, prolonging dopamine activity in the brain, whereas methamphetamine not only blocks dopamine reuptake, it also increases the release of dopamine. This, in turn, causes high dopamine concentrations in the synapse and thus longer-lasting effects. In general, methamphetamine causes three times more release of dopamine than cocaine and has a half-life of 12 hours, compared to cocaine's 1 hour. If administered via smoking, methamphetamine produces a high for 8–24 hours, whereas cocaine produces a high for 20–30 minutes (Centers for Disease Control and Prevention, 2007).

Cocaine's highly pleasurable but short-lived effects can lead to extreme psychological dependence in a remarkably short time. Many stable and financially secure individuals have become destitute as a result of their efforts to maintain a cocaine habit that can cost several hundred dollars a week. People with cocaine use disorders from low-income or impoverished circumstances often turn to theft or prostitution to buy crack. Cocaine has thus contributed to a host of medical and social problems, including sexually transmitted diseases (resulting from both sexual contact and needle exchange), as well as violence among adolescents who are recruited to distribute crack.

Caffeine

Caffeine is the most widely used psychoactive drug in the world. In the United States, more than 85% of adults and children regularly consume caffeine (Frary, Johnson, & Wang, 2005). As shown in Figure 14.7, caffeine is a stimulant found in many foodstuffs, including coffee, tea, some carbonated sodas, most energy drinks, and chocolate. Mean daily caffeine consumption among adult caffeine consumers in the United States has been estimated to be 280 mg/day, the equivalent of about two cups of coffee, or seven 12-ounce cans of caffeinated soft drinks (Barone & Roberts, 1996).

Caffeine decreases blood flow to the brain by constricting blood vessels, so it has been used to treat migraine headaches. It also shrinks mucous membranes and widens bronchial airways and is therefore an ingredient in some cold medications and treatments for asthma. Like amphetamines, it is contained in many over-the-counter diet pills. Overall, caffeine is less harmful than other stimulant drugs. At low doses (75–100 mg), caffeine produces mild stimulation that can improve attention, problem-solving skills, and some aspects of memory, and that can induce positive mood (Warburton, 1995). At moderately high doses (100–200 mg, the amount in one small coffee), most people experience nervousness, insomnia, and gastrointestinal discomfort. At very high doses (more than 1,000 mg a day, the amount in 10 ounces of energy shots), caffeine can induce muscle tremor, agitation, excessive talkativeness, disorganized thinking, and rapid or irregular heart rate.

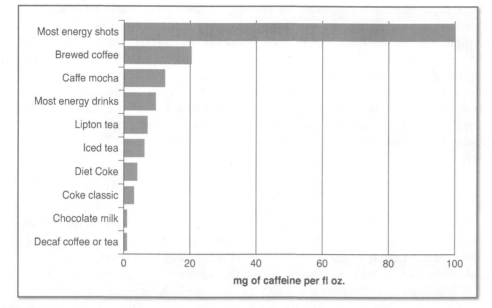

FIGURE 14.7 Average Caffeine Content of Popular Beverages

Source: Based on data from Caffeine Informer (2014).

The connection between caffeine and its potentially detrimental effects on blood markers of cardiovascular disease is controversial (Bennett, Rodrigues, & Klein, 2013). A large prospective study found that, after adjustment for tobacco-smoking status and other potential confounders, there was a small but significant *inverse* association between coffee consumption and mortality (Freedman, Park, Abnet, Hollenbeck, & Sinha, 2012). This means that coffee actually reduced death overall in that population. However, the relationship between caffeine consumption and acute elevations in blood pressure (BP) has been well established, along with vascular mechanisms for this effect (e.g., Hartley, Lovallo, Whitsett, Sung, & Wilson, 2001). One study showed that BP increased more after a stressor if caffeine was also consumed (Bennett et al., 2013). Thus, regular caffeine use by those with predispositions to hypertension (high BP) is probably a bad idea, especially if these people also smoke cigarettes.

Other risks associated with heavy caffeine use include sleeping problems and anxiety. Research has shown that 200 mg of caffeine (a 10-ounce cup of coffee) consumed in the morning can disrupt REM sleep and total sleep time that night (Landolt, Werth, Borb'ely, & Dijk, 1995). Caffeine can also induce panic attacks in persons susceptible to anxiety and can increase symptoms of general anxiety and insomnia. Complete abstinence from coffee by heavy coffee drinkers produces some withdrawal effects, such as headaches and lethargy (Mitchell, deWit, & Zancy, 1995), although it is not clear whether caffeine leads to true dependence.

Caffeine is generally considered to be safe when consumed at normal dietary doses; however, it is not completely innocuous. Heavy caffeine use (greater than 400 mg per day) is associated with increased risk for health problems and pregnancy complications (Nawrot et al., 2003). The *DSM-5* describes several caffeine-related disorders, including *caffeine intoxication, caffeine withdrawal, caffeine-induced anxiety disorder*, and *caffeine-induced sleep disorder*. These diagnoses are made when caffeine's effects cause significant distress or interfere with social or occupational functioning. However, unlike for the other substances mentioned in this chapter, there is no *DSM-5* diagnosis of a caffeine use disorder (much to Starbucks' dismay!). In other words, the *DSM-5* states that you can suffer adverse effects, such as nervousness,

insomnia, rapid heart rate, and rambling speech, from excessive caffeine intake (caffeine intoxication), as well as from its withdrawal (e.g., headache, drowsiness, depression, flu-like symptoms), but not from dependence. However, some researchers disagree with the *DSM-5* approach (Juliano, Evatt, Richards, & Griffiths, 2012). In one study of people seeking treatment for problematic caffeine usage, the most commonly endorsed *DSM-5* substance use disorder criteria were withdrawal (96%), persistent desire or unsuccessful efforts to control use (89%), and use despite knowledge of physical or psychological problems caused by caffeine (87%; Juliano et al., 2012). Whereas the *DSM-5* does not recognize a diagnosis of caffeine use disorder, the *International Classification of Diseases (ICD–10)* does.

Nicotine

nicotine: A stimulant drug found in the leaves of the tobacco plant and usually ingested by smoking.

Found in the leaves of the tobacco plant, *nicotiana tabacum*, **nicotine** is named after the French ambassador to Portugal, Jean Nicot, who began exporting tobacco to Paris in the late 16th century. Like the coca plant, tobacco is indigenous to South America. It was first smoked by the ancient Mayans, who passed on the custom to North American native tribes. In the 15th century, the first Europeans to visit America took up smoking, and by the 17th century, European demand for tobacco exports from the Americas was high, and the tobacco industry was on its way. Today, tobacco is one of the largest cash crops in the United States, and American cigarette manufacturers export their product to most of the world.

In pure form, nicotine is a deadly poison; a few drops on the tongue can cause respiratory failure, paralysis, and death. However, very small amounts of nicotine enter the bloodstream when tobacco leaves are smoked, so the effects of smoking are not immediately lethal. The real danger from nicotine lies in its long-term effects, including its role in making the smoking habit so difficult to break. Many experts consider tobacco smoking to be the number one public-health problem in the United States, where tobacco-related cancer, heart disease, respiratory illness, and other chronic conditions kill half a million people each year (U.S. Department of Health and Human Services, 2014). Cigarette smoking is responsible for about one in five deaths annually in the United States, or 1,300 deaths every day (U.S. Department of Health and Human Services, 2014). Worldwide, tobacco use causes more than 5 million deaths per year, and current trends suggest that tobacco use will cause more than 8 million deaths annually by 2030 (World Health Organization, 2011). On average, smokers die 10 years earlier than nonsmokers (Jha et al., 2013). Most of these health problems are not caused by nicotine, but by the carbon monoxide and cancer-causing chemicals found in tobacco smoke.

The health risks of environmental tobacco smoke (ETS, also called "secondhand smoke") exposure from cigarettes have been extensively studied and, at times, heatedly debated (Rostron, 2013). Several research groups have attempted to quantify the magnitude of mortality attributable to ETS exposure in the United States. Max, Sung, and Shi (2012) estimated that 41,000 deaths among adults in the United States are attributable to ETS each year and that 34,000 of these deaths are due to ischemic heart disease. As an example, a meta-analysis showed that pregnant women who are exposed to secondhand smoke are 23% more likely to experience stillbirth and 13% more likely give birth to a child with a congenital malformation (Leonardi-Bee, Britton, & Venn, 2011). Thanks to public health campaigns, new laws banning indoor smoking in most (80% of) states, and an increasing number of college campuses going entirely smoke-free, ETS exposure has declined dramatically among nonsmokers in the United States in recent years (Rostron, 2013).

In 2013, an estimated 66.9 million Americans age 12 or older were current users of a tobacco product. This represents 25.5% of the population in that age range (Substance Abuse and Mental Health Services Administration, 2014), with a breakdown as follows: 55.8 million (21.3% of the population) were cigarette smokers, 12.4 million (4.7%) smoked cigars, 8.8 million (3.4%) used smokeless tobacco, and 2.3 million (0.9%) smoked tobacco in pipes. In addition, electronic cigarettes have been increasing in popularity since they were introduced into the U.S. market in 2007 (Breland, Spindle, Weaver, & Eissenberg, 2014). Also referred to as electronic nicotine delivery systems or "e-cigarettes," these generally consist of a power source (usually a battery) and heating element (commonly referred to as an atomizer) that vaporizes a solution (e-liquid). The user inhales the resulting vapor. Many questions remain about these products, and limited research has been conducted (Breland et al., 2014), although some researchers contend that allowing e-cigarettes to compete with cigarettes in the marketplace might decrease smoking-related morbidity and mortality (Hajek, Etter, Benowitz, Eissenberg, & McRobbie, 2014).

Nicotine dependence develops quickly, partly because of nicotine's ability to stimulate the release of dopamine in the nucleus accumbens and its effects on the neurotransmitter *acetylcholine* (ACH); "hooked" smokers must then smoke to prevent or postpone the effects of withdrawal. However, other neurochemical systems also participate in the addictive effects of nicotine, including glutamate, cannabinoids, GABA, and opioids (Berrendero, Robledo, Trigo, Martín-García, & Maldonado, 2010). Heavy nicotine use is facilitated by the fact that it is nearly impossible to become intoxicated from the nicotine doses contained in cigarettes. Smokers can thus smoke almost continuously with little or no behavioral impairment. Before the advent of smoking restrictions in the workplace and other public settings, heavy smokers could smoke almost anywhere, all day long. Even with such restrictions in place, avid smokers consume 30 or more cigarettes each day for most of their lives. Experienced smokers need a cigarette to start their day; they often smoke more cigarettes than they anticipate, run out sooner, and anxiously look for a place to buy more. They become upset when they encounter smoking restrictions, and many smokers alter their social or recreational plans to accommodate their need to smoke. Virtually all smokers continue to smoke despite knowing that their health is being compromised. All of this adds up to a tobacco use disorder as defined by the *DSM-5*.

Nicotine produces a clear-cut withdrawal syndrome. The most common symptoms are irritability, depressed mood, lowered heart rate, and weight gain. The average person gains 7–10 pounds after quitting smoking, most of it in the first 6 months after cessation (Perkins, 1993). However, weight gain is not inevitable if the quitter follows a healthy diet and a program of regular exercise (Farley, Hajek, Lycett, & Aveyard, 2012), which can also help reduce tobacco withdrawal and cravings (Ussher, Taylor, & Faulkner, 2012). Withdrawal symptoms usually begin within hours of quitting, peak in a few days, and last for about a month. Certain individuals appear particularly sensitive to the physiological effects of nicotine; as a result, they become dependent on it more easily, develop nicotine tolerance more quickly, and suffer stronger withdrawal symptoms (Pomerleau, Collins, Shiffman, & Sanderson, 1993).

Why do people smoke? Ritualistic use of psychoactive substances has been, and remains, prevalent in virtually all cultures from time immemorial. Children everywhere enjoy spinning around and rolling down hills to make themselves dizzy, suggesting that humans have an innate fondness for alterations of consciousness. People use drugs for many reasons: to feel good, amplify sensory and sensual experiences, alleviate pain, boost energy, increase feelings of power and self-worth, stimulate creativity, enhance social and spiritual connections (as the dislocation theory discussed earlier in the chapter states), and even to manage the anxiety of their own mortality, as counterintuitive as this may sound (Solomon, Greenberg, & Pyszczynski, 2015). A central theory in social psychology, terror management theory (TMT) postulates that investment in cultural worldviews (e.g., one's nation, religion, or sports teams) serves to buffer our potential for death anxiety (Burke, Martens, & Faucher, 2010). Although each psychoactive substance has its own unique biochemical effects, they all can serve to manage terror by reducing the capacity to experience anxiety, dimming self-awareness, distorting perceptions, or altering one's sense of the flow of time (Solomon et al., 2015).

To demonstrate that addictive behaviors are magnified in reaction to reminders of death, Jamie Arndt and his colleagues (2013) had cigarette smokers come into the lab for a study examining "basic personality and smoking behaviors." As part of the experiment, participants pondered either their own mortality or the prospect of failing an upcoming exam. Then everyone got one of their favorite cigarettes and took five puffs while hooked up to a gadget that measured how much they inhaled, how long each puff lasted, and how fast they inhaled. The findings were striking: After thinking about death (but not after thinking about an exam), the highly addicted smokers puffed harder, longer, and faster to jack up the amount of nicotine they inhaled. In other words, smoking is not just serving a physiological function, but rather it may also be serving a deeply rooted psychological function for those most addicted to it.

Treatment of Stimulant Use Disorders

The epidemic of cocaine abuse during the 1980s created an enormous number of cocaine-dependent persons who needed treatment, but the specialized services needed were virtually nonexistent at the time. As a result, these people were initially treated in inpatient or outpatient programs modeled on traditional treatments for alcohol use disorders (AUDs). These programs tried to produce total abstinence through group therapy, individual counseling, and training in relapse prevention skills (McLellan et al., 1994). Cocaine Anonymous, a 12-step program similar to Alcoholics Anonymous, was used to provide follow-up support.

contingency management: Deliberately presenting or withdrawing reinforcers or aversive stimuli following change-worthy behaviors.

The treatment of stimulant use disorders became more sophisticated in the 1990s, thanks to a version of cognitive-behavioral therapy (CBT) called **contingency management**. Two of the most effective contingency management interventions for the treatment of substance use disorders have been abstinence reinforcement and the community reinforcement approach (Stitzer, Jones, Tuten, & Wong, 2011). The primary goals of both treatments are to initiate and sustain drug abstinence and to modify drug-seeking behavior by increasing the number and potency of alternative reinforcers that are incompatible with the drug-using lifestyle. The major premise of both treatments is that if sufficient numbers of alternative reinforcers can be made available, they might effectively compete with the pharmacological reinforcing effects of drugs and with nondrug reinforcers that have become associated with the drug-using lifestyle.

The *abstinence reinforcement* procedures utilize tangible vouchers or prizes to reinforce drug abstinence directly. For instance, people with cocaine use disorders are rewarded with money and social outings with their families or friends if urine tests confirm that they are abstinent from cocaine. The *community reinforcement approach*, discussed earlier as a treatment for AUDs, achieves the same goal by increasing the number of alternative nondrug reinforcers in the natural environment or community of the drug user. The goal is to rearrange multiple aspects of an individual's "community" so that a clean and sober lifestyle is more rewarding than one dominated by alcohol and/or drugs (Hunt & Azrin, 1973). Meta-analytic findings suggest that these CBT approaches are among the most effective for promoting abstinence during the treatment of substance use disorders (Schumacher et al., 2007), although they may work better for cocaine or opiate use disorders than for tobacco or polydrug use disorders (Prendergast, Podus, Finney, Greenwell, & Roll, 2006).

As with AUDs, stimulant use disorders may also be treated with family/couples' therapy, brief interventions such as motivational interviewing (MI), harm reduction approaches, and prevention efforts. Even though these evidence-based treatments produce a moderate effect size, dropout rates in most substance use disorder studies hover in the 30% range (Dutra et al., 2008).

Finally, medication strategies have been used as adjuncts to psychological treatment for stimulant use disorders. As with AUDs described earlier, these approaches have typically lacked precision and effectiveness. The medical field has been trying to come up with a satisfactory treatment for cocaine addiction for almost as long as the drug has been available in Europe and the United States (Kleber, 2003). More than 40 medications have been investigated over the past several decades as treatments for cocaine use disorder, but none has shown adequate effectiveness (Kleber, 2003), and the number of medication trials for substance use disorders with negative findings is striking (Brensilver & Shoptaw, 2013).

One approach has been to prescribe drugs such as antidepressants to offset the protracted dysphoria during withdrawal that contributes to relapse. A second strategy (called

MAPS - Medical Myths

substitution or agonist treatment) aims to reduce drug craving by giving medications such as *bromocriptine* that mimic the dopamine-enhancing effects of stimulants. However, studies comparing antidepressants or bromocriptine with placebos have failed to find that these medications improve outcomes (e.g., Campbell, Thomas, Gabrielli, Liskow, & Powell, 1994; Eiler, Schaefer, Salstrom, & Lowery, 1995). Three separate meta-analyses have yielded little evidence for the benefit of central nervous system stimulants (Castells et al., 2007), anticonvulsants (Álvarez, Farré, Fonseca, & Torrens, 2010), or antipsychotics (Álvarez, Pérez-Mañá, Torrens, & Farré, 2013) in the treatment of cocaine use disorder, as none of those drugs significantly reduces cocaine use or improves retention in treatment compared to placebo, with dropout rates typically in the 50% range.

The third and most recent approach to developing medications that might help treat cocaine and other stimulant use disorders is called **pharmacogenetics**. This approach uses genetic variation to predict individual differences in response to specific medications and can aid in personalizing prescriptions (de Leon, 2009). Although the concept is relatively new, studies of several genes have yielded significant findings suggesting that pharmacogenetic research may lead to the selection of individual-appropriate medication for the treatment of substance use disorders in the future and to increased cessation rates (Sturgess, George, Kennedy, Heinz, & Müller, 2011). For example, one study showed that disulfiram and methylphenidate pharmacotherapies for cocaine use disorder are optimized by considering polymorphisms affecting genes for two dopamine-related enzymes (Haile, Kosten, & Kosten, 2009).

> **pharmacogenetics:** The study of inherited genetic differences in drug metabolic pathways that can affect individual responses to drugs, both in terms of therapeutic effects as well as adverse effects.

Overall, in addition to the high dropout rates already mentioned, the treatment of stimulant users is complicated by several factors. First, these people are especially prone to polydrug use as they attempt to "take the edge off" the crash that follows stimulant intoxication. A study of cocaine users found more than half to be dependent on alcohol (Higgins, Budney, Bickel, Foerg, & Badger, 1994), whereas a study of amphetamine users showed that more than half had abused benzodiazepines (Darke, Ross, & Cohen, 1994). Second, these polydrug users are more prone to having comorbid mental disorders and poor health than are people who abuse a single drug (Darke et al., 1994). Whether such comorbidity is a cause or effect of polydrug use is uncertain. Third, in treating polydrug users, deciding whether to focus on all the drugs involved, or on only one of them (and if so, which one?) is often difficult.

Treatment and Prevention of Tobacco Use Disorders

Programs that educate the public about nicotine risks, alter smoking attitudes, and restrict smoking in offices and public places have been successful in reducing tobacco smoking in the United States. In the 1970s, more than half of the American population smoked, but today, only about 25% do (Substance Abuse and Mental Health Services Administration, 2014). Psychology has helped spur the dramatic reduction in the prevalence of tobacco use since its peak in the 1960s (Abrams, 2014). In fact, cancer death rates are declining for the first time in a century, driven largely by the dramatic reduction in smoking rates, from 54% in 1965 to less than 20% today. Within 40 years, more than 45 million Americans have quit smoking. This has arguably been one of the most successful public health behavior change interventions of all time, and psychology is playing a central role in this success story (Abrams, 2014). Psychological research has spawned a range of programs that include self-help, online and telephone "quit" lines and text messages, brief treatments in primary care, intensive inpatient programs for severely addicted smokers, and treatments of smokers with other medical, behavioral, health, and substance use problems. Other successful programs include youth smoking prevention campaigns and efforts to bring antismoking messages and programs to low-income and underserved populations.

But smoking is still the leading preventable cause of death and disease in the United States. And unfortunately, cigarette smoking has increased in many other countries around the world. Even in the United States, smoking continues to be popular among the young. In 2013, young adults ages 18–25 had the highest rate of current use of a tobacco product (37%) in the United States (Substance Abuse and Mental Health Services Administration,

2014). As smokers grow older and begin to take the health risks of their habit seriously, many try to quit. Quitting smoking is often conceptualized as a series of stages (see the "stages of change" model described earlier in the section "Treatment Stages and Matching;" Prochaska et al., 1992), but chiefly requires two steps: first, making a quit attempt, and then second, succeeding in that attempt. Most, but not all, evidence suggests that different factors influence each of these two steps of the quitting process (Vangeli, Stapleton, Smit, Borland, & West, 2011). For example, smoking duration and number of previous quit attempts (Hyland et al., 2006), along with motivation to quit (Hyland et al., 2006; Zhou et al., 2009), have been more strongly associated with quit attempts than with cessation. In contrast, a review of the literature suggests that nicotine dependence is the single most consistent predictor not of whether a person may try to quit but rather of success following a quit attempt (Vangeli et al., 2011). Most smokers who try to quit, either on their own or with help from cessation programs, fail in their attempt. Fewer than 5% of smokers stop each year, even in countries where the most effective cessation interventions are available (Giovino, 2002; Messer et al., 2007), and it takes multiple quit attempts (between 3 and 10, depending on the survey) to become a nonsmoker.

In recent years, attention has turned to the possibility of encouraging those who are unable or unwilling to quit to reduce their cigarette consumption as an outcome goal (Yong, Borland, Hyland, & Siahpush, 2008). A review of intervention trial studies by Hughes and Carpenter (2005) drew the conclusion that many smokers are able to reduce their smoking spontaneously and maintain significant reductions for long periods. The same review also concluded that adult smokers who try to quit and fail tend to return to a lower level of smoking, but this reduction tends to dissipate over time. So how can smokers get help with one of the most difficult habits to change?

Most of the dozens of formal smoking-cessation treatments available use a variant of cognitive-behavioral therapy (self-monitoring, goal setting, and reinforcement) and have been shown to be effective across age groups (Suls et al., 2012; U.S. Department of Health and Human Services, 2008). Some treatments involve abrupt, "cold turkey" cessation, whereas others seek gradual reduction in smoking. Meta-analyses show that motivational interviewing, described earlier, is also useful for helping people quit (Heckman, Egleston, & Hofmann, 2010), as are interventions that focus on enhancing a smoker's partner's supportive behaviors, while minimizing behaviors critical of smoking (Park, Tudiver, Schultz, & Campbell, 2004). Smoking cessation programs in the workplace are becoming increasingly common, but they are only likely to be effective if participants have moved beyond the contemplation stage so that stopping smoking is a personal priority (Fishwick et al., 2013). Even in the most effective quit programs, though, abstinence rates after a year rarely exceed 50% and average only about 33% (Shiffman, 1993).

Finally, a meta-analytic review provided strong evidence that the three main medications prescribed to smokers—nicotine replacement therapy, bupropion, and varenicline— can all help people quit (Cahill, Stevens, Perera, & Lancaster, 2013). Bupropion (sold as Wellbutrin or Zyban) is an antidepressant drug whose mechanism of action is only partly understood; it has been widely described as a weak norepinephrine-dopamine reuptake inhibitor and an antagonist at acetylcholine receptors (Dwoskin, Rauhut, King-Pospisil, & Bardo, 2006). Varenicline (sold as Chantix) is a nicotinic receptor partial agonist, which stimulates nicotine receptors more weakly than nicotine itself does. Further research into the safety of varenicline is warranted, however, as its side effects include nausea and, in some cases, depression and suicidal thoughts (Cahill et al., 2013). Nicotine replacement is typically accomplished through nicotine gum or patches, which aid in cessation efforts by providing enough replacement nicotine to reduce craving and other withdrawal symptoms. Research on the effects of these nicotine replacement treatments indicates that they can

He had tried many ways to quit smoking but only one worked.

indeed reduce the severity of withdrawal symptoms, including depression and sleep disturbance (Cahill et al., 2013). Because nicotine gum and patches are now available over the counter, and because they can improve abstinence rates—particularly when used in combination with cognitive-behavioral therapy (Stead & Lancaster, 2012)—they are likely to play a continuing role in formal and informal smoking cessation efforts.

Section Review

Stimulants:

- include amphetamines, cocaine, caffeine, and nicotine;
- have excitatory effects on the central nervous system;
- can produce psychological and physiological dependence and are often abused in conjunction with other drugs; and
- can cause several dangerous physical changes in the brain and cardiovascular system.

Treatments for stimulant use disorders:

- include cognitive-behavioral therapy called contingency management (abstinence reinforcement and community reinforcement), family/couples' therapy, brief interventions such as motivational interviewing, harm reduction approaches, and prevention efforts; and
- are complicated by high drop-out rates and other factors.

Treatments for tobacco use disorders:

- include public education, smoking restrictions, behavior modification programs, motivational interviewing, and nicotine replacement strategies (as well as other medications); and
- may be more successful when they take into account that most smokers attempt to quit several times before doing so successfully.

Opioids

An **opioid** is an alkaloid containing opium or one of its derivatives, such as morphine, heroin, codeine, or methadone. Opium comes from the seed pods of the poppy plant, which is indigenous to Asia and the Middle East. Opioids, also known as *narcotics*, were used by the ancient Greeks and Romans to relieve pain and induce sleep. During the American Civil War, morphine was used as a surgical anesthetic. Like cocaine, opioids were regarded as relatively harmless until their addictive potential became known, partly as a result of experiences with opioid-dependent Civil War veterans. As noted earlier, opioids were outlawed (along with cocaine) by the Harrison Act of 1914. Today, opioids are prescribed for pain relief, as antidiarrheals and cough suppressants, and even as antidepressants in rare, intractable cases of depression (Bodkin, Zornberg, Lukas, & Cole, 1995).

> **opioid:** An alkaloid containing opium or one of its derivatives, such as morphine, heroin, codeine, or methadone.

Opioid drugs exert their influence by interacting with the receptor sites used by the body's endogenous (naturally occurring) opiates, including the *endorphins* and *enkephalins*. These receptor sites are located throughout the body—in the brain, spinal cord, and even the bloodstream—and have ties to the immune system (Makman, 1994). The endogenous opiates influence pain and appetite, and they can produce positive moods. However, chronic use of morphine, heroin, or other exogenous opiates may alter the production of endogenous opiates. When individuals stop using exogenous opiates, the production of endogenous opiates is temporarily deficient (Cambor & Millman, 1991). This deficiency may explain why the opioid withdrawal syndrome can include negative mood and increased pain sensitivity.

Opioid Use Disorders

Heroin, a white, odorless powder derived from morphine, is the most commonly abused opioid. In 2013, about 681,000 Americans reported using heroin in the past year, a number

> **heroin:** A white, odorless powder derived from morphine; it is one of the most addictive and commonly abused opioids.

FIGURE 14.8 Rating of Harm Levels of Recreationally Used Substances

Researchers in the United Kingdom developed and explored the feasibility of using a nine-category matrix of harm, with an expert rating procedure, to assess the harms of a range of various recreational drugs in an evidence-based fashion. Ratings were based on two dimensions—potential for dependence (addiction) and physical harm. The results, shown here, were controversial, as the ranking of drugs produced by their assessment of harm differed from those used by current regulatory systems (i.e., governments). Heroin was tops in both dimensions of harm, with cocaine close behind, and alcohol and tobacco (two widely used substances) in the upper range of dependence potential. Critics contend that the scale is skewed by usage frequency and that "if Ecstasy, GHB, or solvents were as widely used as alcohol or nicotine, the extent of drug-related harm would be far greater" (Parrott, 2007, p. 425).

Source: Based on Nutt, King, Saulsbury, & Blakemore (2007).

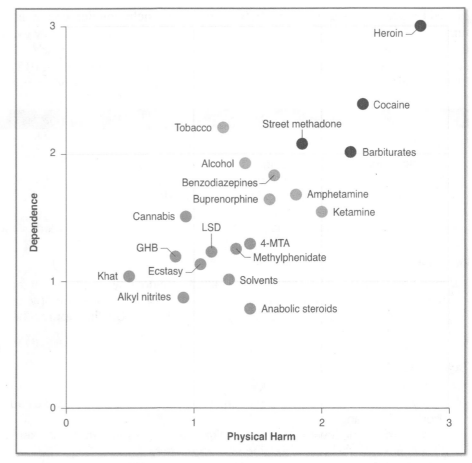

that has been on the rise since there were 373,000 users in 2007 (Substance Abuse and Mental Health Services Administration, 2014). This trend appears to be driven largely by young adults ages 18–25, among whom there have been the greatest increases. Heroin was first derived from opium in the late 19th century by German physicians who wanted to create a stronger, but less addictive, analgesic for use as a substitute for morphine. Heroin was chosen as the trade name for this drug because of its potentially "heroic" effects in the battle against pain. Unfortunately, its creators misjudged heroin's addictive potential: It is one of the most addictive opioids and, according to a recent expert survey shown in Figure 14.8, the most harmful drug of all (Nutt, King, Saulsbury, & Blakemore, 2007).

Heroin use in the United States has historically been most frequent among lower socioeconomic classes, ethnic minority groups, and people living in inner-city areas (Hartnoll, 1994). The same social problems linked to the sale and use of crack cocaine are associated with heroin injection. Although sexual activity has recently overtaken injection drug use as the top HIV risk factor, sharing of contaminated needles remains a serious danger (Keen, Khan, Clifford, Harrell, & Latimer, 2014). Since the 1990s, the demographics of heroin use have begun to shift; its use has increased dramatically among young, relatively affluent individuals, and it is even considered to be chic in some circles. One study revealed that young African-Americans' rates of injection for heroin are declining, whereas rates for young Whites are rising (Broz & Ouellet, 2008).

In pure form, heroin can be smoked or snorted, but the preferred form of ingestion by most heavy users is intravenous injection ("mainlining"), which produces an almost immediate, intense rush. After the rush, heroin produces a sedated, dreamlike euphoria in which the senses are dulled, attention to the environment is reduced, and the desire for food is decreased. This condition differs from the euphoria produced by cocaine, which is characterized by high energy and enhanced attention. People experiencing opioid intoxication appear "spacey," drunk, drowsy, and disconnected from their surroundings. Their speech is often slurred, and their pupils are frequently constricted. Following heroin use, the intense euphoria lasts from 45 seconds to several minutes, peak effects last 1–2 hours, and the overall effects wear off in 3–5 hours, depending on the dose ("How Does Heroin Work?" 2012).

OxyContin, an extended-release version of the opioid oxycodone, is another popular opioid drug, especially on college campuses. In 2013, the number of new nonmedical users of OxyContin age 12 or older was 436,000, which was similar to the estimates for prior years from 2004 through 2012 (Substance Abuse and Mental Health Services Administration, 2014). The number of users of pain relievers in general without a prescription has been near the 2 million mark for the past couple of years (Substance Abuse and Mental Health Services Administration, 2014). The average age at first use of Oxy-Contin among past-year initiates was about 23. It is available by prescription only and is used to treat moderate to severe pain when around-the-clock pain relief is needed for an extended period of time. As with all opioids, OxyContin works by changing the way the brain and nervous system respond to pain.

At high doses, any opioid user can become comatose and suffer respiratory failure. An estimated 1% of all heroin addicts die from overdose each year (Thombs, 1994). However, what constitutes an opioid overdose varies from one user to another and, within the same user, from one occasion to another. Heroin addicts sometimes die from a dose that was no stronger than that which they had tolerated in the past. Why? This question was partially answered several decades ago by an experimental psychologist named Shepard Siegel. He found that tolerance to a given dose of heroin in rats was partially conditioned to the *physical environment* in which the drug was typically received. Being in a familiar environment appeared to produce learned physiological responses that helped prepare the rat's body for

the drug's effects. If an addicted rat received its normal dose of heroin in an unfamiliar cage, death from overdose was very likely (Siegel, 1982). An implication of this *environmental-dependent* opioid tolerance (Bespalov, Zvartau, & Beardsley, 2001) is that a heroin overdose depends not only on how much of the drug is taken, but also on the tolerance level of the drug user and *where* the drug has typically been taken. Finally, a unique analysis of heroin users' behaviors in the 12 hours prior to the overdose event, compared with the same time period preceding the most recent episode of nonoverdose-related heroin use, revealed that using larger quantities of heroin increased the odds for an overdose by a factor of 12, and benzodiazepine use increased that risk 28 times, substantially more so than the other risk factors analyzed (Dietze, Jolley, Fry, & Bammer, 2005).

Opioids produce an intense withdrawal syndrome, with symptoms that are almost the opposite of the drug's intoxicating effects. Thus, instead of euphoria, there is dysphoria, and the senses are heightened rather than dulled, leading to anxiety and increased sensitivity to pain. Excessive body secretions (runny nose, watery eyes), pupil dilation, and diarrhea are common, as are fever, insomnia, and "goose bumps." Some of these effects develop within 8 hours after the last opioid dose and gradually decline after about a week. However, symptoms such as craving, anxiety, depression, insomnia, and sexual dysfunction may continue for several months following last use (Liu, Wang, Hao, & Zeng, 2000).

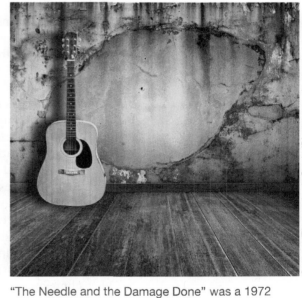

"The Needle and the Damage Done" was a 1972 song by Canadian musician Neil Young that described the descent into heroin addiction by his Crazy Horse guitarist Danny Whitten, who died from a drug overdose at age 29. Many other famous musicians have struggled with heroin addiction, including Eric Clapton and Jimi Hendrix. Both Janis Joplin and Jim Morrison (frontman of the Doors) died from a heroin overdose at the age of 27.

Treatment of Opioid Use Disorders

Medications play a central role in the treatment of opioid users. Opioid antagonists such as *naltrexone* are used during initial stages of detoxification to quell withdrawal symptoms (Legarda & Gossop, 1994), and other drugs are used to reduce opioid craving after withdrawal is over. By far the most common—and most controversial—pharmacological approach to treating heroin addiction is the prescription of the synthetic opioid *methadone*. Methadone is a longer-acting drug than heroin and is more active when taken orally. It produces good pain-reducing effects at relatively low doses, even when taken infrequently, thus limiting its addictive potential. However, as with any opioid, higher doses of methadone produce euphoric effects. And although it can also induce tolerance and withdrawal, the methadone withdrawal syndrome is safer and less painful than withdrawal from heroin. Methadone was first used in the 1960s as a substitute for heroin as addicts went through withdrawal. The next step was to gradually decrease the methadone dose until individuals achieved complete opioid independence, but this goal proved difficult to achieve. Most addicts simply returned to heroin when their methadone treatment ended. To forestall such relapses, many heroin addicts were eventually placed on **methadone maintenance therapy**, in which they continued to receive methadone for as long as they needed it.

methadone maintenance therapy: A treatment designed to help opioid-dependent persons avoid relapses by giving them methadone until they can achieve complete opioid independence.

The results of the methadone maintenance approach are mixed. A meta-analysis concluded that methadone is an effective maintenance therapy intervention for the treatment of heroin dependence as it retains people in treatment and decreases heroin use better than treatments that do not utilize opioid replacement therapy (Mattick, Breen, Kimber, & Davoli, 2009). However, methadone does not show a statistically significant superior effect on criminal activity or mortality. Further, as many as 20% of heroin addicts remain dependent on methadone for 10 years or more (Bertschy, 1995). More worrisome is the fact that reductions in heroin use are often offset by increases in other nonopioid drug abuse, particularly cocaine (Magura et al., 1994). Some programs have combatted drug use by making participants' daily methadone dose contingent on providing clean, drug-free urine tests.

In short, most experts agree that methadone maintenance is preferable to heroin dependence, but few are satisfied with its results. Efforts to provide better treatments have taken several directions. One approach has been to develop methadone substitutes, such as *buprenorphine*, that have fewer reinforcing and addictive properties. Compared to detoxification or no treatment, buprenorphine also significantly reduces drug use and extends treatment retention (Mattick, Breen, Kimber, & Davoli, 2014). Methadone is typically preferred because it is less expensive and more effective (Mattick et al., 2014), but buprenorphine has a slightly different pharmacological action. Making both available may attract greater numbers of people to treatment and improve the matching of patients to appropriate treatments (World Health Organization, 2013).

An alternative to maintenance is to help patients completely withdraw from opioids, a process also referred to as opioid detoxification. Methadone and buprenorphine can be used in reducing doses; alpha-2 adrenergic agonists such as *clonidine* can also be used to ameliorate withdrawal symptoms. Following detoxification, the long-acting opioid antagonist *naltrexone* can be used to help prevent relapse. Naltrexone produces no opioid effects itself and blocks the effects of opioids for 24–48 hours. Compared to maintenance treatment, though, opioid withdrawal actually may result in poorer outcomes in the long term (World Health Organization, 2013).

Other clinicians have focused on combining psychological treatment with methadone maintenance. Psychosocial interventions, including cognitive and behavioral approaches and contingency management techniques, have been used as adjunctive treatments only—that is, combined with agonist maintenance treatment or medications for assisting opioid withdrawal. Present evidence suggests, though, that these psychotherapeutic strategies may not help to enhance the effectiveness of medical treatment (Amato, Minozzi, Davoli, & Vecchi, 2011). Treatment guidelines nevertheless recommend that psychosocial services should be made available to all people, although those who do not take up the offer should not be denied effective pharmacological treatments (World Health Organization, 2013).

Section Review

Opioids, also known as narcotics:

- contain opium or one of its derivatives, such as morphine, heroin, codeine, oxycodone, or methadone;

- usually produce a pleasurable rush, followed by a dreamy euphoria;
- create strong physical dependence, produce intense withdrawal symptoms, and are linked with lifestyles devoted to drug use; and
- are associated with use disorders that are treated by methadone or buprenorphine maintenance, adrenergic agonists to ameliorate withdrawal symptoms, and opioid antagonists to help prevent relapse, often along with adjunctive psychotherapy.

Cannabis

The psychoactive drug derived from the hemp plant *cannabis sativa* is **cannabis**. Originally from Asia, hemp flourishes today in many parts of the world. *Marijuana* (also known as "pot," "weed," "grass," or "boo") is the dried, chopped leaves, tops, and stems of the hemp plant. Typically smoked in cigarette form (called a "joint"), marijuana can also be taken orally by mixing it with food or brewing it as a tea. *Hashish*, which is almost always smoked, is the dried resin from the tops and leaves of the female hemp plant. The psychoactive ingredients of cannabis are called **cannabinoids**, the most important of which is *delta-9-tetrahydrocannabinol*, or *THC*. The concentration of THC in marijuana and hashish varies greatly, depending on the genetic history of the plant and the conditions under which it is grown. Today's marijuana contains nearly five times the THC contained in plants cultivated during the 1960s or 1970s.

In the United States, marijuana is the most commonly used illicit drug, as shown in Figure 14.9. In 2013, 5.7 million Americans age 12 or older used marijuana on a daily or almost daily basis in the past 12 months (i.e., on 300 or more days in that period), which was an increase from the 3.1 million daily or almost daily users in 2006 (Substance Abuse and Mental Health Services Administration, 2014); see Figure 14.10. Its popularity has waxed and waned with changing legal regulations, political attitudes, and moral and social values. In the first part of the 20th century, cannabis could be bought and sold without penalty, and was used primarily by jazz and blues musicians and artists. Social concern over the drug materialized in the 1930s, and it was soon outlawed. In the 1950s, marijuana was thought to cause "reefer madness," but by the late 1960s, it had become such an accepted middle-class recreational drug that some states relaxed criminal codes relating to marijuana, and there were proposals to legalize its use. Use of marijuana among high school and college students has worried many experts because a young person's use of cannabis

cannabis: A psychoactive drug derived from the hemp plant that causes a variety of intoxicating and hallucinatory effects.

cannabinoids: Psychoactive ingredients of cannabis, the most important of which is delta-9-tetrahydrocannabinol, or THC.

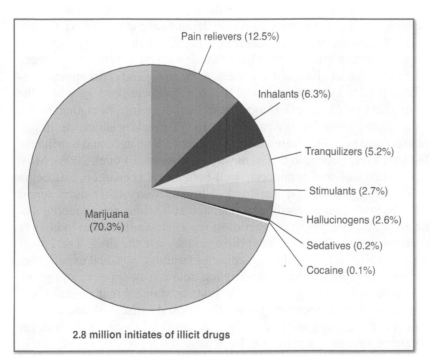

2.8 million initiates of illicit drugs

Pain relievers (12.5%)
Inhalants (6.3%)
Tranquilizers (5.2%)
Stimulants (2.7%)
Hallucinogens (2.6%)
Sedatives (0.2%)
Cocaine (0.1%)
Marijuana (70.3%)

FIGURE 14.9 Gateway to Illicit Drug Use in the United States

In 2013, the specific illicit drug category with the largest number of recent initiates (new users) among persons age 12 or older was marijuana (2.4 million), followed by nonmedical use of pain relievers (1.5 million), followed by nonmedical use of tranquilizers (1.2 million), followed by Ecstasy (0.8 million), followed by stimulants, cocaine, and inhalants (0.6 million each). Among past-year initiates ages 12–49 in 2013, the average age at first use was 17.1 years for PCP, 18.0 years for marijuana, 19.2 years for inhalants, 19.7 years for LSD, 20.4 years for cocaine, 20.5 years for Ecstasy, 21.6 years for stimulants, 21.7 years for pain relievers, 24.5 years for heroin, 25.0 years for sedatives, and 25.4 years for tranquilizers.

Source: Substance Abuse and Mental Health Services Administration, U.S. Department of Health and Human Services, http://www.samhsa.gov/data/sites/default/files/NSDUHresultsPDFWHTML2013/Web/NSDUHresults2013.pdf, p. 59.

FIGURE 14.10 Marijuana Use Rising in the United States

In 2013, 5.7 million persons age 12 or older used marijuana on a daily or almost daily basis in the past 12 months (i.e., on 300 or more days in that period), which was an increase from the 3.1 million daily or almost daily users in 2006. The number of daily or almost daily users of marijuana in 2013 represented 17.4% of past year users. In 2013, 8.1 million persons age 12 or older used marijuana on 20 or more days in the past month, which was an increase from the 5.1 million daily or almost daily past month users in 2005 to 2007. The number of daily or almost daily users in 2013 represented 41.1% of past month marijuana users.

Source: Substance Abuse and Mental Health Services Administration, U.S. Department of Health and Human Services, http://www.samhsa.gov/data/sites/default/files/NSDUHresultsPDFWHTML2013/Web/NSDUHresults2013.pdf, p. 30.

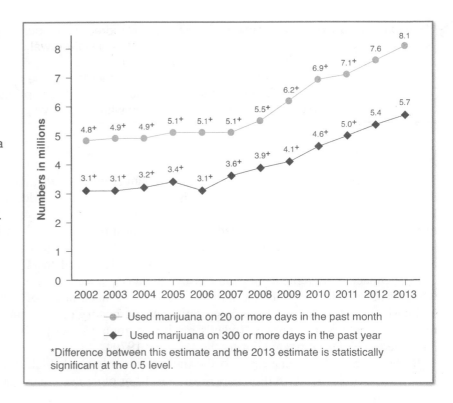

is believed to be a gateway that increases the chances of trying other, more addictive drugs. Indeed, a 25-year longitudinal study offered strong support for the gateway hypothesis; regular or heavy cannabis use was associated with an increased future risk of using other illicit drugs, abusing or becoming dependent upon other illicit drugs, and using a wider variety of other illicit drugs overall (Fergusson, Boden, & Horwood, 2006).

The acute physical effects of cannabis include dilation of the blood vessels in the eye, dry mouth, increased appetite (known as the "munchies"), and rapid heartbeat. Cannabis increases cerebral blood flow, especially in the frontal regions of the brain, and it has primarily sedating effects on the central nervous system (Mackie & Hille, 1992). The neurochemical processes by which THC interacts with the brain and other organs are not fully understood, but research in the last few decades has begun to piece together a probable scenario. Specific cannabinoid receptors have been identified in the brain (especially the cerebellum and hippocampus), spleen, tonsils, and white blood cells (Bouaboula et al., 1993). Cannabinoids seem to mimic endogenous (naturally occurring) substances in the body, including the endogenous opiates, suggesting one way by which cannabis exerts its rewarding effects. THC has several medicinal purposes (Kumar, Chambers, & Pertwee, 2001): Its appetite-enhancing effects have been used to treat anorexia, and because it reduces pressure within the eye, marijuana is also used to treat glaucoma. Cancer patients undergoing chemotherapy are sometimes given marijuana to reduce the nausea and vomiting caused by anticancer drugs.

What is evident is that there is no such thing as a typical marijuana user, and marijuana, like other drugs, affects different people in different ways (Osborne & Fogel, 2008). Most cannabis users report feelings of mild euphoria, well-being, and relaxation that begin within minutes after the drug is used and last for 2–3 hours. Many other users report mildly stimulating effects, such as increased heart rate, and still others report feelings of anxiety or even panic on occasion. Emotional reactions to marijuana often seem to involve intensification of whatever mood people are in at the time they use the drug. The effects of cannabis intoxication usually include enhancement of pleasurable physical experiences and mild perceptual distortions: Music may sound better, colors may appear more vivid, and time may seem to pass more slowly. One research study showed that typical marijuana users differed in terms of their frequency of use, the amount consumed, and the type of recreational activities that they engaged in while under the influence, as well as the manner in which they perceived these activities to be enhanced (Osborne & Fogel, 2008).

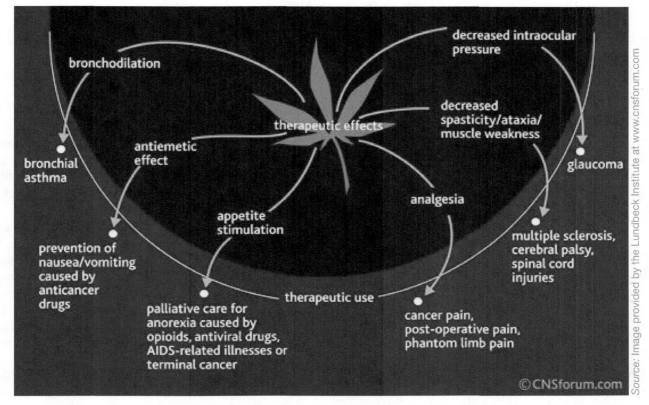

Perhaps the best-known use of cannabis in a therapeutic setting is as an analgesic in the management of cancer pain, postoperative pain, and phantom limb pain. Cannabinoids have also been used in the prevention of nausea and vomiting caused by anticancer drugs and to stimulate appetite in palliative care for anorexia caused by opioids, antiviral drugs, AIDS-related illnesses, or terminal cancer. Other effects include a bronchodilator effect on the small airways of the lungs and an ability to decrease intraocular pressure (Kumar, Chambers, & Pertwee, 2001). It is paradoxical that cannabinoids have been reported to be of therapeutic value in neurological disorders associated with spasticity, ataxia, and muscle weakness because similar symptoms can be caused by cannabis itself. Due to these medicinal properties, about half of U.S. states have passed laws allowing some degree of medical use of marijuana, whereas a third of states have taken steps to decriminalize it to some degree.

The only significant commonalities that these marijuana users shared were their middle-class status and their disassociation with organized religion (Osborne & Fogel, 2008).

The short-term effects of cannabis intoxication are relatively mild, compared with those of other drugs discussed in this chapter. But does regular or high-dose use of cannabis produce significant long-term risks to physical health? During high-dose, acute cannabis intoxication, users may experience hallucinations and other psychotic-like symptoms. Motor performance—especially on fine motor tasks—is usually impaired by cannabis, as are short-term memory, reaction times, and the ability to sustain attention (Riedel & Davies, 2005; Wilson, Ellinwood, Mathew, & Johnson, 1994). These effects may be responsible for the fact that cannabis intoxication is frequently implicated in automobile and motorcycle accidents. At one trauma center, nearly one third of all injured motorcyclists tested positive for cannabis in urine samples (Soderstrom, Dischinger, Kerns, & Trifillis, 1995).

For years, the conventional wisdom held that cannabis was not truly addictive, but this view has been altered due to a number of relatively recent discoveries (Nordstrom & Levin, 2007). Marijuana withdrawal, which typically affects only heavy smokers, has not been well characterized by the research community. Until recently, there was scant evidence in animal models for marijuana tolerance and withdrawal, the classic determinants of addiction (Hanson, 2009). Now, however, several researchers have identified the existence of symptoms brought on by the abrupt discontinuation of regular marijuana use, and a growing body of evidence supports the existence of a clinically significant marijuana withdrawal syndrome in a subset of marijuana smokers (Hanson, 2009). The *DSM-5*, unlike its predecessors, lists criteria for *cannabis withdrawal disorder*. The syndrome is marked by irritability, restlessness, generalized anxiety, hostility, depression, difficulty sleeping, excessive sweating, loose stools, loss of appetite, a general "blah" feeling, and a mental state that has been described as "inner unrest" (Hanson, 2009). Psychological dependence on cannabis also occurs, which is characterized by preoccupation with and compulsive use of the drug, risk taking (e.g., driving while "stoned"), interpersonal conflicts, and legal problems; the *DSM-5* therefore lists *cannabis use disorder* as well.

A great deal of research with animals and humans has so far produced mixed evidence of harmful long-term effects, but several worrisome possibilities are still being investigated. For example, because marijuana smoke contains 50–100 times the carcinogens found in tobacco smoke, chronic marijuana smokers face an increased risk of lung cancer. Pot smokers do suffer deterioration in the linings of the trachea and bronchial tubes; this damage is greatest in people who smoke both marijuana and tobacco. Exposure to marijuana has various biologically based physical, mental, behavioral, and social health consequences and is associated with diseases of the liver (particularly with co-existing hepatitis C), lungs, heart, and vasculature (Gordon, Conley, & Gordon, 2013). The scientific evidence for substantial cannabis-related adverse effects appears strong enough that individuals who use or who are considering using cannabis should be made aware of these potential negative outcomes (Budney, Moore, & Vandrey, 2004). Overall, though, such outcomes appear less severe than those associated with alcohol, tobacco, heroin, or cocaine abuse (Budney et al., 2004).Whereas some have claimed that chronic use of cannabis causes **amotivational syndrome**—a pattern of apathy and inability to meet personal or career goals (Wenk, 2014)—in some users, empirical studies suggest that there is no such thing ("Debunking the Amotivational Syndrome," 2006). However, cross-sectional and longitudinal research indicates that young people who use cannabis are at increased risk of poor school performance and reduced educational attainment (Lynskey & Hall, 2000). There is also longitudinal evidence that early cannabis use independently increases the risks of early school leaving (Lynskey & Hall, 2000).

Public policy surrounding marijuana has shifted significantly in recent years. There are, of course, both pros and cons regarding marijuana legalization, but the debate is often political or emotional rather than rational, with strong views held by both proponents and opponents (van Ours, 2012). Those in favor of legalization tend to ignore the negative health effects of cannabis use, whereas those against legalization tend to ignore the fact that legal substances such as alcohol and tobacco also have adverse effects on health. Evidence is mixed as to the overall effects of marijuana legalization: Whereas residents of states with medical marijuana laws have higher odds of marijuana use than residents of other states (Cerdá, Wall, Keyes, Galea, & Hasin, 2012), there is no evidence of increased marijuana use in adolescents after state policy changes (Choo et al., 2014). Nationally, the University of Michigan's "Monitoring the Future" study, which tracks trends in substance use among students in middle and high schools, found that after 5 years of spikes among teens, marijuana use declined in 2014 (Marcus, 2014). Interestingly, though, some economists have predicted that the legalization of recreational marijuana in Colorado and Washington will lead to increased marijuana consumption in those states, coupled with decreased alcohol consumption, and that, as a consequence, these states will experience a reduction in the social harms resulting from alcohol use (Anderson & Rees, 2014).

Treatment of Cannabis Use Disorders

Often, cannabis use disorder is part of a polydrug problem, and it is usually the other drugs (e.g., alcohol, cocaine, opioids) that pose a more immediate risk and hence become the focus of treatment. Still, some 12-step–type support groups have been adapted specifically for people with cannabis use disorders (e.g., Miller, Gold, & Pottash, 1989), along with cognitive-behavioral therapy (including relapse prevention, behavioral coping skills training, contingency management/vouchers), motivational interviewing, and family therapy approaches (Nordstrom & Levin, 2007). Three main findings arise from considering the studies of psychotherapy for cannabis dependence (Nordstrom & Levin, 2007):

amotivational syndrome: A pattern of apathy and inability to meet personal or career goals that is linked to cannabis-induced alteration of brain functioning.

1. A number of psychotherapies have been shown to be helpful in the treatment of this disorder.
2. Adding vouchers to behavioral coping skills training appears to be the most effective treatment (with over a third abstinent at follow-up), and all other forms of psychotherapy perform about equally to one another.
3. Longer psychotherapies (e.g., 14 sessions of relapse prevention) do not appear to be more advantageous than shorter therapies (e.g., 2 sessions of motivational interviewing).

Despite attempts at using anticonvulsants such as divalproex sodium and antidepressants such as bupropion and nefazodone, no effective pharmacologic treatments for cannabis use disorders yet exist (Nordstrom & Levin, 2007).

Section Review

Cannabis, a psychoactive drug derived from the hemp plant:

- is the main ingredient in marijuana and hashish;
- is the most commonly used illegal drug in the United States;
- usually produces mild euphoria, sedation, and some perceptual distortions;
- produces withdrawal and psychological dependence, along with a mounting list of harmful effects in the long term;
- is at the center of changing public policies in the United States, ranging from legalization for medicinal uses only in some states to outright legalization in a few states;
- is often accompanied by other drug use or abuse that is the primary target of treatment;
- can be treated by a variety of psychotherapies, with behavioral coping skills training plus vouchers likely being the most effective; and
- cannot be treated effectively via any psychotropic medications.

Hallucinogens

Cannabis and hallucinogenic drugs are not members of the same drug category, but some of their effects are similar, as use produces a range of distorted perceptions—usually mild in the case of cannabis, stronger with hallucinogens. Hallucinogenic drugs are also less physiologically addictive than most of the drugs discussed so far, but they can cause psychological dependence.

The drugs already discussed in the chapter have been named after their neurochemical effects (sedatives and stimulants) or the plant from which they are derived (opioids and cannabis). **Hallucinogens**, though, are named for the unusual perceptual experiences they produce. Also sometimes called *psychedelics*, these diverse drugs are best known for creating visual effects in which objects appear to shimmer or waver, colorful "halos" appear, or objects emit visual "trails." Users may also experience visual hallucinations of nonexistent objects or people; less often, the hallucinations may be auditory or tactile (Nelson, 2014). Hallucinogens may produce distortions in body image, as when users feel as though their arms are several feet long. In another common perceptual anomaly known as **synesthesia**, information from different senses is blended so that users claim they can "see" sounds or "feel" colors. In most cases, users understand that these perceptual distortions are drug induced. Tragically, however, there have been cases when people have thought they could fly and then jumped off a roof to try to prove it.

Hallucinogens may also lead to depersonalization, paranoid thinking, and extremely variable moods, in which users go from the heights of euphoria to the depths of depression, or from feelings of security to feelings of anxiety and terror. Hallucinogens' effects usually begin within an hour after ingestion and last from several hours to a day, depending on the type and dose of drug and method of administration (Nelson, 2014).

hallucinogen: A drug that produces unusual perceptual experiences.

synesthesia: A drug-induced perceptual anomaly in which information from different senses is blended so that users "see" sounds or "feel" colors.

Lysergic Acid Diethylamide (LSD)

The best-known hallucinogen is **lysergic acid diethylamide (LSD)**, which first became popular in the 1960s. Also known as "acid," LSD was discovered in 1943 by Swiss chemist Albert Hofmann, who accidentally ingested a small piece of mold growing on rye grain and then recorded his strange experiences. LSD can be synthesized or derived from *ergot*, a fungus that affects cereal plants such as wheat and rye.

The hallucinogenic experiences during an LSD "trip" are the product of central nervous system excitation. LSD also arouses the sympathetic nervous system, causing dilated pupils, increased heart rate, elevated blood pressure, and increased alertness. LSD mimics the neurotransmitter *serotonin* by interacting with serotonin receptors in the cerebral cortex and brain stem. Because of the similarity between the hallucinogenic effects of LSD and the symptoms of schizophrenia, some researchers have used the effects of LSD as a model from which to develop hypotheses about the causes of schizophrenia, discussed in Chapter 4 (Marona-Lewicka, Nichols, & Nichols, 2011).

Source: Brian L. Burke.

MAPS - Superficial Syndromes
The cactus in this photo appears to be suffering from a florid visual hallucination.

lysergic acid diethylamide (LSD): A hallucinogenic drug that excites the central nervous system.

LSD can be taken in tablet form or by eating sugar cubes or paper on which a drop of the drug has been placed. Even heavy users usually take LSD only periodically, allowing several days or weeks to pass between episodes. In one study, 81% of users reported having had a "spiritual experience" on a hallucinogenic drug, and over 90% considered "access to the unconscious mind" to be a specific property of the classic hallucinogens. They also reported relatively less harm associated with the classic hallucinogens (LSD and psilocybin) than other drugs in the questionnaire (MDMA [Ecstasy], cannabis, ketamine, and alcohol; Carhart-Harris & Nutt, 2010). With repeated use, some tolerance develops to LSD's hallucinogenic effects, but tolerance to its effects on the nervous system is rare. However, there are also reports of acute and prolonged adverse responses to these drugs (Carhart-Harris & Nutt, 2010). For instance, LSD-induced behavioral and emotional changes can threaten both physical and psychological well-being. Chief among these problems are panic attacks. When panic occurs, the drug user can usually be "talked down" by a supportive person, although sometimes a sedative must also be given.

Long after LSD's initial effects end, some users report having *flashbacks*—brief recurrences of the perceptual distortions experienced during the LSD "trip." Flashbacks may be triggered by thoughts, by use of other drugs, or by being in an environment with ambiguous or unusual stimuli (e.g., entering a dark room). Some people have reported flashbacks occurring as long as 5 years after their last use of LSD. The *DSM-5* lists a diagnosis called *hallucinogen persisting perception disorder* to describe the condition in which flashbacks of one or more of the perceptual symptoms that were experienced while intoxicated cause clinically significant distress or interfere with day-to-day functioning.

In the United States during the 1960s and 1970s, LSD was primarily used by middle-class White American adolescents and young adults. After the passing of this "hippie" era, the popularity of LSD use declined in favor of such drugs as cocaine and methamphetamine. The number and percentage of persons age 12 or older who are current users of hallucinogens (1.3 million or 0.5% in 2013) have remained fairly stable for the past decade (Substance Abuse and Mental Health Services Administration, 2014).

Other Hallucinogens

mescaline: A hallucinogenic drug derived from the peyote cactus that causes effects similar to LSD.

Mescaline and psilocybin are alkaloids with hallucinogenic effects similar to those of LSD. **Mescaline** is derived from the *peyote* cactus plant; the crown of the cactus (called the peyote button) is chewed or swallowed with water or food. For centuries, peyote has been used in religious services by Native Americans in South and Central America and in the southwestern United States, and the practice continues to this day in the Native American church. **Psilocybin** alkaloids are found in several species of Mexican mushrooms, pieces of which are chewed or swallowed with water. Both mescaline and psilocybin produce visual illusions, distorted body image, and depersonalization. One study showed that psilocybin produced a range of acute perceptual changes, subjective experiences, and labile moods including anxiety, but that it also increased measures of mystical experience (Griffiths, Richards, McCann, & Jesse, 2007). New research is exploring the beneficial effects of psilocybin on a range of issues, from terminal cancer to anxiety and depression, and even smoking cessation (Pollan, 2015). However, "bad trips" can often occur because the amount of active hallucinogen varies widely from one peyote button or mushroom to another, so users can never be certain about the exact dosage unless they are taking the drug as part of a controlled and guided research study.

Methylenedioxy-methamphetamine (MDMA), also called *Ecstasy* (shortened to "E," "X," or "XTC"), is designated as a hallucinogen, even though it is actually a derivative of methamphetamine intentionally designed by unscrupulous chemists. It acts as a serotonin-dopamine-norepinephrine releasing agent and reuptake inhibitor (Schifano, 2004). MDMA is reputed to make users more open and empathic. MDMA is often considered the drug of choice within the rave culture and is also used at clubs, festivals, and house parties (Carvalho et al., 2012). The psychedelic amphetamine quality of MDMA offers multiple reasons for its appeal to users in the "rave" setting (Reynolds, 1999). Some users enjoy the feeling of mass communion from the inhibition-depressing effects of the drug, whereas others use it as party fuel because of the drug's stimulatory effects. Contrary to popular belief, though, MDMA is *not* a safe drug. MDMA induces hyperthermia that can occasionally be fatal (Schifano, 2004). It appears that certain conditions common to such gatherings—overcrowding, extended physical activity, and dehydration—intensify the drug's hyperthermic effects, leading to sudden death (Green, Cross, & Goodwin, 1995). With frequent use, MDMA can also damage serotonin-sensitive receptors in the brain (Green et al., 1995).

Phencyclidine (PCP), also known as *angel dust*, differs in several ways from other hallucinogens. Originally developed as a medical anesthetic, PCP produces analgesia, respiratory suppression, and seizures when swallowed, smoked, or injected. At high doses, coma results. Unlike LSD, mescaline, and psilocybin, PCP overdoses can be fatal. Its hallucinogenic effects are also different. Perhaps because of PCP's analgesic effects, users report a feeling of superhuman power and invulnerability, sometimes to the point of being delusional. Because of these altered perceptions, PCP users may become so aggressive and violent as to injure themselves or others. The effects of PCP develop quickly, but because it is eliminated from the body slowly, frequent PCP use can lead to confusion and personality changes that last for months. Whereas *People* magazine and Mike Wallace of *60 Minutes* called PCP the country's "number one" drug problem in 1978, its use has been on the decline in the United States since that peak (Harrison, 2011). However, PCP is also a frequent component of embalming fluid, which is an occasional drug of use in inner cities (Singer, Mirhej, Shaw, Saleheen, & Vivian, 2005).

Treatment of Hallucinogen Use Disorders

Few treatment programs have specifically targeted users of hallucinogens, since hallucinogens are typically used in conjunction with other, more dangerous drugs. Treatment of LSD intoxication may require a brief period of hospitalization, but because the drug is not physiologically addictive, most therapies focus on helping users curb their psychological dependence on it. Hallucinogen persisting perception disorder may be effectively treated with benzodiazepines (Lerner et al., 2003), although agents such as naltrexone (an opioid receptor antagonist), risperidone (an antipsychotic), and antidepressants have also been employed.

Section Review

Hallucinogens are psychoactive drugs that:

- produce perceptual distortions and other unusual sensory experiences;
- include LSD, mescaline, psilocybin, MDMA, and PCP; and

- are not physically addictive but, like all drugs, can lead to psychological dependence.

Treatments for hallucinogen use disorders involve the usual remedies (cognitive-behavioral therapy, motivational interviewing, etc.), along with medications such as benzodiazepines to treat hallucinogen persisting perception disorder if it arises.

Gambling

gambling disorder: A new disorder in the *DSM-5* that involves persistent and recurrent problematic gambling behavior that leads to clinically significant impairment or distress.

Gambling disorder is a new diagnosis in the *DSM-5* that introduces the notion that people can be addicted in a problematic way to things other than drugs and alcohol. Symptoms are similar to those for the substance use disorders described throughout this chapter, including the need to gamble increasingly high amounts, difficulty cutting back, preoccupation with gambling, lying or damaging personal relationships as a result of gambling, and often gambling when feeling distressed (American Psychiatric Association, 2013a). Disordered gambling occurs at higher rates among certain subgroups in the community, such as individuals with substance use disorders (14%; Cowlishaw, Merkouris, Chapman, & Radermacher, 2014) or other mental disorders, among medical populations, and among adolescents (Morasco, 2013). Gambling problems are associated with an increased 3-year incidence of nicotine dependence in women and alcohol dependence in men (Pilver, Libby, Hoff, & Potenza, 2013). Studies suggest that motivational interviewing and cognitive-behavioral therapy approaches are effective in reducing the frequency and severity of gambling, although additional research is needed to evaluate whether these approaches are appropriate for the majority of potential clients, or if specific interventions need to be developed for certain high-risk or difficult-to-treat groups (Morasco, 2013). A meta-analysis provided little support for the use of any pharmacological agent in the treatment of gambling disorder (Bartley & Bloch, 2013).

The rationale for placing gambling disorder into the substance-related and addictive disorders category in the *DSM-5* is that compulsive behaviors follow the same clinical pattern and may even derive from the same neural network as compulsive substance use (Frances, 2010b). For example, there is a moderate overlap in the genetic risk for alcohol use disorder and gambling disorder (Slutske, Ellingson, Richmond-Rakerd, Zhu, & Martin, 2013). Similarly, the *DSM-5* criteria for hypersexual disorder use the same items that define substance use and gambling disorders, and hypersexual disorder would seem to fit nicely as a behavioral addiction, although it has been placed instead in the Appendix, with other diagnoses requiring more research. Critics contend that opening the door for behavioral addictions in the *DSM-5* may have unintended consequences because repetitive (even if costly) pleasure seeking is a ubiquitous part of human nature (Frances, 2010b). These behavioral addictions could quickly expand from their narrowly intended, appropriate usage to become a popular and much misused label for anything that people do for fun but causes them trouble, ranging from sugar and chocolate to video games, the Internet, smartphones, and pornography. In other words, we can be addicted to a great many things. Think about your own life: What substances or foodstuffs or behaviors do you engage in that you might change if you could?

"Hey, the little guy's kind of cute."

Source: Cartoonresource/Shutterstock.com.

Section Review

Gambling is a new disorder in the *DSM-5* that describes a pattern of ongoing and problematic gambling behavior, leading to clinically significant impairment or distress, as indicated by symptoms like:

- a preoccupation with gambling,
- the tendency to gamble when feeling upset,

- lying or hurting people due to gambling, and
- trying to reduce personal gambling behavior without success.

Some experts believe that including a behavioral addiction in this *DSM-5* category puts us on a slippery slope to other behavioral addictions, which are ubiquitous in modern society.

Revisiting the Case of Jerry

Just how severe was Jerry's polydrug problem? Did he have a substance use disorder? With respect to alcohol use, Jerry fit the *DSM-5* criteria for an alcohol use disorder (AUD). He had developed tolerance to alcohol (he could "handle" two pitchers now, but not a year ago), often drank more than he wanted to, and had unsuccessfully tried to cut down. Further, he kept drinking, despite his emerging relationship problems and at the expense of his academic success. His AUDIT score was 29 (see Table 14.2), and the presence of five *DSM-5* symptoms put him in the "moderate" range of severity for his AUD. In short, Jerry was incorrect in assuming that he did not have an AUD because he drank only beer and could stop drinking before passing out. Drinking and drug use significantly affected his life; nearly all his friends were heavy drinkers.

The best way to describe Jerry's use of marijuana is that he did not yet meet criteria for a cannabis use disorder because it was not interfering with his life or relationships, and he did not show signs of marijuana tolerance or withdrawal. His marijuana use may have been adversely affecting his schoolwork, as he used it to "sober up" before studying, but Jerry did not meet any other *DSM-5* criteria for that substance use disorder. The same is true of Jerry's weekly amphetamine use, which was confined to episodes related to studying. He did not show signs of amphetamine tolerance or withdrawal, nor was he preoccupied with using or obtaining the drug.

There appear to be multiple causes of Jerry's AUD. Jerry's father had an AUD, suggesting that a combination of genetic predisposition, parental modeling, and an adverse family environment contributed to his problems. Jerry also drank heavily prior to exams and before going out on a date. These are situations that cause many people to feel anxious, and it could be that Jerry experienced a stress-dampening effect from alcohol, or at least expected the substance to produce such an effect. Jerry would appear to fall into Cloninger's Type I class of people with AUDs who tend to be anxiety prone and who have a relatively late onset of drinking.

Jerry's family history and college-age polydrug pattern placed him at high risk for continuing—and intensifying—his pattern of drug use. Indeed, for a while it appeared that his frequent visits to the Blue Ox tavern would hurt his grades so much that he would have to leave college, and academic failure might well have worsened his AUD. But Jerry's story has a relatively happy ending. Although his problems were too severe for the university prevention program, Jerry was referred to an off-campus outpatient treatment program, and his university health insurance covered the costs. This program combined training in relapse prevention skills with a peer support group, and his initial intake interview was conducted using motivational interviewing. Jerry came to realize that he did want to change, and he became highly involved in this program. He particularly liked the support group, where he discovered that other students had similar problems, and he appreciated the relapse prevention approach, where it was possible to "mess up" but still follow a plan for getting his life back together. Although he had several lapses, Jerry eventually graduated from college and, at last report, was working full-time and was not using cannabis, amphetamines, or other drugs, except for an occasional "social" drink. He admitted that alcohol was still—and would probably always be—something he had to be "very careful about."

Alan Marlatt (1941–2011), *in Memoriam*

Dr. Alan Marlatt was a professor of psychology at the University of Washington in Seattle. He was one of the world's leading experts on substance use disorders and pioneered the relapse prevention approach to treatment, challenging a once widely held belief that substance addiction was incurable and could only be controlled by abstinence. For 30 years, Dr. Marlatt was director of the Addictive Behaviors Research Center, an arm of the University of Washington in Seattle that nurtured a movement among therapists holding that addiction treatment should take a more moderated approach than is common in traditional 12-step programs calling for complete abstinence, like that of Alcoholics Anonymous. Dr. Marlatt was a leading proponent of the approach called "harm reduction." His data demonstrated that reducing a person's level of alcohol use could lead directly to reduced troubles at home and at work. He maintained that, whereas those with substance use disorders may not be able to stop using a substance immediately, individualized counseling—a "meet them where they are" approach—could bring about changes in their "life conditions" and eventually lead to abstinence. Through his research, much of it involving students on college campuses, Dr. Marlatt also identified factors that could predict a relapse, among them negative emotions, conflicts with others, and recurring thoughts that the substance will make the person feel better.

Substance Abuse

Q *In your view, do mood disorders usually lead to problem drinking, or are mood disorders more often a consequence of heavy drinking?*

A I have found examples of both in my clinical work. Many problem drinkers drink to "self-medicate" their depression or anxiety, although drinking only exacerbates a mood problem. The other direction of causality, in which heavy drinking leads to depression, is less likely.

Q *What were your original goals for relapse prevention as a treatment for alcohol use disorders?*

A Relapse prevention was never designed to be a treatment in and of itself, but rather a supplement to help maintain the impact of other treatments. We developed this approach with two goals in mind. The first was to avoid relapses if possible. An equally important second goal was to *manage* a relapse if and when it occurs. Several recent studies have shown that relapse prevention can, in fact, help contain relapses. Among the people with alcohol use disorders who relapsed in these studies, those taught cognitive-behavioral skills drank less alcohol overall and had fewer "intoxication days" than those without this training.

Q *Is there a risk that you are increasing the chances of relapse by preparing people with alcohol use disorders for its occurrence?*

A The probability of a relapse—with or without relapse prevention training—is extraordinarily high; the vast majority of heavy drinkers eventually experience a return to drinking. The chances of a prolonged relapse are increased by *not* teaching relapse skills. Relapse prevention training is like participating in a fire drill—it's better to know it and need it than to need it and not know it.

Q *What's your view of the Prochaska, DiClemente, and Norcross "stages of change" model?*

A The model has a lot of intuitive appeal, especially the idea that different approaches may be needed, depending on a person's readiness to change. But there have been difficulties in reliably measuring a person's specific stage of change. For example, classifying someone as "precontemplative" or "contemplative" is not easy to do. Another problem is that the process of change that forms the basis of the model has yet to be studied adequately. To really understand how people change, you need to study them *prospectively* over time, but the stages of change model was not developed in this way.

Q *Biologically oriented researchers have been searching for the ideal anticraving medication. Will a drug cure ever be found for alcohol use disorders?*

A I very much doubt that medication alone will ever "cure" alcohol use disorders. Naltrexone, for example, certainly does what it is supposed to do: It effectively blocks the action of opioid receptors that probably account for some of alcohol's rewarding effects on the brain. But naltrexone does not make the person *feel* any better, as alcohol can, at least at lower blood levels. As a result, people with alcohol use disorders on the verge of a relapse may stop taking their naltrexone, so they can maximize the reinforcement they get from alcohol.

Q *What about the combined effects of naltrexone and relapse prevention?*

A In theory, relapse prevention should help people with alcohol use disorders remain on their medication longer by getting them to challenge the seemingly irrelevant cognitions that precede their decision to stop the medication—for example, telling themselves "I don't need meds anymore to not drink." Programs that combine behavior therapy with pharmacotherapy have particular promise, as shown in recent studies for cocaine, nicotine, and opioid use disorders.

Q Are most college students who drink heavily likely to develop an alcohol use disorder in later years?

A It depends on family history. College life promotes high rates of alcohol consumption in many students. If the person comes from a family with a history of alcohol dependence, he or she is more likely to continue the heavy drinking in later years.

Summary

DSM-5 Diagnosis of Substance-Related Disorders

Drug abuse involves patterns of use that are hazardous to a person's health, produce personal distress, or lead to occupational, social, or legal difficulties. Prolonged abuse often causes psychological dependence (marked by craving for the drug and a preoccupation with obtaining it) and physiological dependence or addiction. Addiction to a substance is indicated by two physical effects: withdrawal (experiencing symptoms when one stops using the substance) and tolerance (requiring more and more of the substance to produce the same effect). When a person's judgment, thinking, mood, perception, or motor behavior is impaired directly as a result of using a substance, substance intoxication has occurred.

According to the *DSM-5*, substance-related disorders involve either problems associated with the direct effects of substances on an individual (substance-induced disorders) or problems associated with patterns of heavy substance use (substance use disorders). The main substances of abuse are alcohol and other sedatives (including hypnotics and anxiolytics), stimulants (amphetamines, cocaine, caffeine, and nicotine), opioids, cannabis, and hallucinogens.

Alcohol

Alcohol can damage cells, interfere with metabolism, depress brain cell activity, harm the liver and other organs, and suppress the immune system. The initial effects of alcohol consumption on the brain and behavior are sedating, but as blood alcohol concentrations increase, perception, thinking, and behavior become impaired. Binge drinking and excessive alcohol use are common patterns worldwide, including on college campuses. A substantial percentage of persons with alcohol-related disorders suffer other mental disorders that may cause, follow, or accompany alcohol problems.

Biological, psychological, and social factors help explain who develops an alcohol use disorder (AUD), and different causal patterns may be involved, depending on the type of AUD being explained. Genetics play a role in predisposing some people to AUDs, particularly men who start to drink heavily early in life. Several biological vulnerabilities might underlie alcohol use disorders, including abnormal brain cell activity, low neurotransmitter levels, and heightened physical sensitivity to the effects of alcohol. The psychological variables most likely to be causally related to AUDs are tension reduction, positive expectancies about the effects of alcohol, and a set of antisocial, externalizing, and impulsive personality traits. Cultural traditions, family relationships, parental modeling, and peer associations also influence AUDs.

The options for treating alcohol use disorders reflect differing philosophies about whether alcohol is a disease, a moral problem, or a learned habit. Some success has been achieved through inpatient treatment and detoxification, Alcoholics Anonymous (AA), training in moderate or controlled drinking, relapse prevention, marital and family therapy, aversion therapy, community reinforcement methods, brief interventions such as motivational interviewing, and medications that minimize alcohol withdrawal symptoms, block alcohol's effects, or cause unpleasant reactions to drinking. Some school- or college-based prevention programs have also achieved positive results.

Other Sedatives

Sedatives (also called depressants) inhibit neurotransmitter activity in the brain and lead to sedation, sleepiness, and reduced anxiety. In addition to alcohol, the major sedatives of abuse are the barbiturates and, more common today, the benzodiazepines. Both categories of drugs can cause dependence and withdrawal, with the barbiturates posing the more serious risk. Detoxification, personal therapy (via motivational interviewing and/or cognitive-behavioral therapy), peer support groups such as AA, and educationally oriented programs are the primary treatments for sedative abuse.

Stimulants

Stimulants have an excitatory effect on the central nervous system, increasing the availability of dopamine at synapses. These drugs include amphetamines, cocaine, methylphenidate (Ritalin), caffeine, and nicotine. Many stimulant users are prone to polydrug abuse, and they often drop out of treatment. The recommended front-line treatment for cocaine addiction is contingency management. Cognitive-behavioral therapy, nicotine replacement strategies, and a combination of both approaches have had some success in bringing about abstinence or harm reduction from cigarettes, and prevention programs have had significant impact.

Opioids

Also known as *narcotics*, the opioids include morphine, heroin, codeine, oxycodone, and methadone. Opioids relieve pain and produce dreamlike states of euphoria. They tend to be highly addictive, can lead to an intense withdrawal syndrome, and are often associated with criminal lifestyles. Treatments for opioid use disorders include antagonist drugs, methadone maintenance (the front-line approach), and adjunctive psychotherapy.

Cannabis

Cannabis and hallucinogens produce some similar effects. Derived from hemp plants, cannabis is a psychoactive drug usually used in the form of marijuana or hashish. Cannabis is the most commonly used illegal drug in the United States. It has both sedating and mildly stimulating effects on users, and it produces mild perceptual distor-tions. Cannabis use can lead to withdrawal and psychological dependence and is often accompanied or followed by abuse of other drugs (the gateway hypothesis).

Hallucinogens

Hallucinogens produce unusual perceptual experiences, visual distortions, and highly variable moods in which users swing from euphoria to depression, sometimes in just a few moments. Paranoia, synesthesia, panic attacks, and flashbacks are other effects. The best-known hallucinogen is LSD; others include mescaline, psilocybin, MDMA, and PCP.

Gambling

Gambling is a new disorder in the *DSM-5* that describes a pattern of persistent and recurrent problematic gambling behavior, leading to clinically significant impairment or distress, as indicated by symptoms such as preoccupation with gambling, gambling when upset, lying or hurting people due to gambling, and unsuccessfully trying to reduce personal gambling behavior. Some experts believe that including a behavioral addiction in this *DSM-5* category will open the door to other behavioral addictions, which are quite common in our society.

Key Terms

Neurocognitive Disorders

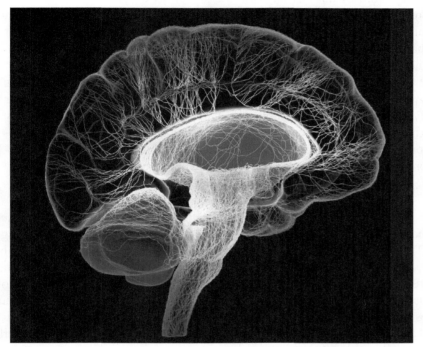

Source: Johan Swanepoel/Shutterstock.com.

After reading this chapter, you will be able to answer the following key questions:

- What are the different functions subsumed under the broad umbrella of cognition?

- What is delirium?

- How are neurocognitive disorders classified in the *Diagnostic and Statistical Manual of Mental Disorders (DSM-5)*?

- What causes neurocognitive disorders?

- How are neurocognitive disorders treated?

From the Case of Dorothy

Dorothy is a 78-year-old retired laboratory technician. She was almost incoherent when the police picked her up in response to a call about an elderly woman walking in the street in a nightgown and slippers. In her brief moments of clear speech, she repeatedly insisted that she needed to "get to the lab." By the time the squad car reached the hospital, half a mile away, Dorothy was unconscious. A wrist bracelet identified her as a diabetic and gave the name and telephone number of a neighbor. After an intravenous tube was started, Dorothy was admitted to the hospital, and her neighbor was notified. The neighbor confirmed that these nocturnal episodes had happened before.

By morning, Dorothy was alert and chatting with the staff. She indicated that she was employed in the chemistry department of a local college and needed to return to the lab as soon as possible. Several times she told her nurses about the research project in which she was involved. A call to the college revealed that Dorothy had been involved in such a project 15 years earlier but that she had retired 13 years ago. A CT scan revealed some atrophy of Dorothy's frontal and parietal lobes, but there was no sign of medical problems other than the diabetes and mild osteoporosis. A structured interview revealed that Dorothy was able to correctly state the day's date and the location of the hospital, but she could not recall the names of three objects she had identified minutes earlier, and she had great difficulty counting backward from 100 by 7s. During evening visiting hours, Dorothy mistook her roommate's husband for a "spy" from another college; she confided to the nursing assistant that he had been "after her for years" because he wanted to prevent her from completing her research project. Several hours later, the nurses found Dorothy pulling at her intravenous tubing and her bedclothes. After receiving a mild sedative, Dorothy slept through the night. The next morning, she was alert, but she showed no memory for the events of the previous day or evening.

Late in the day, Dorothy was discharged to the care of her daughter, who had driven several hundred miles to stay with her mother. The daughter admitted that she had been worried about her mother's lapses of attention and memory over the past year, but that her mother had refused all offers of help. In fact, she and Dorothy had bickered more with each other in the past few months than at any previous time. The daughter also reported that there was almost no food in her mother's house, there were greasy stains on the living room carpet, and the sink was piled with dirty dishes. This was unlike her usually fastidious mother. During the discharge interview, the doctors informed Dorothy and her daughter of their *DSM* diagnosis: delirium, along with a possible major neurocognitive disorder due to Alzheimer's disease, which was upgraded to probable after conducting a more thorough neuropsychological assessment of Dorothy a few weeks later.

neurocognitive disorder (NCD): A mental disorder involving a loss of cognitive function in one or more key domains.

In this chapter, we consider the **neurocognitive disorders (NCDs)**, a group of mental disorders that, as in Dorothy's case, (1) are directly caused by biological changes in the brain, (2) involve impairments in cognition, and (3) can appear at any age but are especially common in older people, in part because many diseases that cause brain deterioration are more likely to affect the elderly. Injuries to the brain, tumors, infectious diseases, gradual degeneration, poisoning, and substance-induced changes are the most common causes of these conditions. When brain damage underlies these disorders, it is often described as being either focal or diffuse. *Focal damage* involves lesions in specific areas of the brain; closed-head injuries and brain tumors are common causes of focal damage. *Diffuse damage* refers to lesions in brain tissue that are spread across the brain or at least to several areas of it; poisoning and infectious diseases such as AIDS can lead to diffuse damage. Psychological and sociocultural factors also influence the severity and course of the disorders reviewed in this chapter, but by themselves, they do not cause cognitive disorders.

Research on the functioning of the brain has demonstrated that several mental functions are localized in specific areas. For example, the left hemisphere controls speech and other language functions for most people, and the right hemisphere specializes in the processing of emotional material. Four different regions, or *lobes*, of the cerebral cortex (discussed in Chapter 2) also have special responsibilities. The **frontal lobes** control motor movements and higher-order thinking and planning. The temporal lobes specialize in the processing of language, perception, and memory; beneath the temporal lobes, other structures, such as the hippocampus and amygdala, are heavily involved in memory and emotions and form part of the **limbic system**. The parietal lobes process sensory information about pain, body temperature, and touch. Toward the back of the head, the occipital lobes specialize in vision. Figure 15.1 shows a few of the brain regions that, if damaged, often lead to specific cognitive impairments related to their key functions.

frontal lobe: The area of the cerebral cortex that controls executive functions, such as planning and carrying out goal-directed activities.

limbic system: A complex circuit of brain structures (including the thalamus, hippocampus, cingulate gyrus, hypothalamus, amygdala, septum, and parts of the cortex) that help regulate emotions, memory, and certain aspects of movement.

Although the brain is divided into many different components, it must also still function as an integrated system. Most complex mental functions, such as perceiving external stimuli, using and understanding language, remembering events, and learning new information, require that many brain areas cooperate and communicate with each other. Thus, a breakdown in an area that controls the perception of sounds can also impair language comprehension, learning, memory, and speech. Further complications arise because many

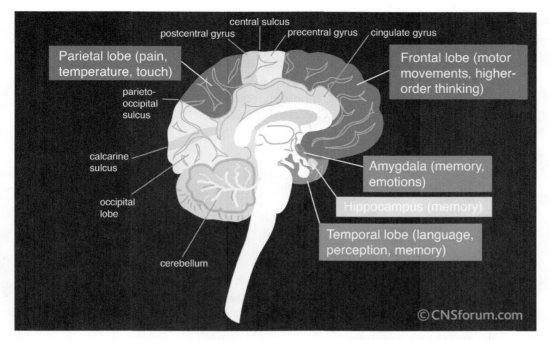

FIGURE 15.1 Brain-Behavior Relationships: Major Structures in the Brain and the Key Functions Associated with Each

The organization of the brain is more complicated than figures such as this suggest. Many parts of the brain are involved in controlling language, thinking, behavior, and emotions, so that it is not always possible to predict how a lesion in a specific part of the brain will affect an individual's overall functioning. The thalamus, hypothalamus, amygdala, and hippocampus collectively make up what is called the limbic system.

Source: Image provided by the Lundbeck Institute at www.cnsforum.com.

forms of brain damage are not limited to a single area or structure. Being struck on one side of the head can cause severe bruising on the opposite side of the brain when it strikes the skull, referred to as a *coup contrecoup injury*. Conditions such as Alzheimer's disease also produce degeneration across many areas of the brain, yielding a mosaic of cognitive problems.

Domains of Cognition

The symptoms of NCDs can take the following forms:

- An inability to remember events that happened only minutes earlier
- Loss of the ability to understand written language while still comprehending speech
- Failure to recognize familiar people or objects
- Loss of the ability to plan simple sequences of behavior
- A clouding of consciousness that leaves the person with incomplete awareness of what is taking place in the environment
- Profound confusion and disorientation, sometimes to the point of delusional beliefs
- Loss of judgment about the appropriateness of behavior
- Difficulties in accurately perceiving spatial arrangements or in coordinating motor behaviors

Which of these impairments did Dorothy in the chapter-opening case display?

The *DSM-5* groups these symptoms into six key domains that form the basis for NCDs. Each domain also has subdomains of cognitive abilities. Table 15.1 lists these domains and the accompanying primary brain regions responsible for the associated cognitive

TABLE 15.1 Brain Regions Involved by Domains of Cognition

Neurocognitive Domain	Subdomains	Brain Regions Implicated
Complex attention	Sustained attention Divided attention Selective attention Processing speed	Intraparietal cortex, superior frontal cortex, temporoparietal cortex, and inferior frontal cortex (Corbetta & Shulman, 2002)
Executive function	Planning Decision making Working memory Responding to feedback Flexibility	Frontal lobes, prefrontal cortex (Miyake et al., 2000)
Learning and memory	Free recall Cued recall Recognition memory Semantic and autobiographical long-term memory Implicit learning	Medial temporal lobe (hippocampus, parahippocampal cortex, entorhinal cortex), striatum, neocortex, amygdala (Squire, 2004)
Language	Object naming Word finding Fluency Grammar and syntax Receptive language	Broca's area, Wernicke's area, middle temporal gyrus, inferior parietal and angular gyrus (Friederici, 2011)
Perceptual-motor abilities	Visual perception Visual reasoning Perceptual-motor coordination	Premotor cortex, motor cortex, cerebellum, occipital lobe (Rosenbaum, Carlson, & Gilmore, 2001)
Social cognition	Recognition of emotions Theory of mind Insight	Temporoparietal junction, medial prefrontal cortex (Van Overwalle, 2009)

Source: Based on American Psychiatric Association (2013a).

ability. Deficits in these domains are the basis for determining diagnosis and etiology of all NCDs.

Each of these areas of cognition allows people to function on a daily basis. Impairments in any of these areas are assessed carefully via neuropsychological testing (see Chapter 1) to establish the etiology and severity of the NCD. Examples of the clinical presentations of people with deficits in each of these six domains of cognition follow. Deficits in one area of cognition often are accompanied by deficits in other areas and are therefore not mutually exclusive.

Complex attention: Jack is a 45-year-old male whose co-workers have recently expressed concern about his ability to perform his job. He is a construction foreman, and his position is at the management level. He has difficulty staying on task at the construction site, often losing his train of thought when talking with his subordinates if there are others things going on around him. When his employees report to him, they provide an update on progress of the day; then, a minute or two later, Jack asks questions that make it seem like he had not been listening before. Also, when people ask questions of him, he takes a long time to respond, almost as if he forgot the question.

Executive function: Maria is an 89-year-old woman whose daughters live out of state. When they came to visit her for her birthday, they entered her home where she lives by herself and could not believe what they encountered. What must have been months of mail was unopened and piled all over the house. They quickly learned that Maria had not been paying her bills. She was not doing laundry either, and dirty clothes were strewn all over the house. After spending several days with her, they realized that she had not been seeing her friends or attending social activities, such as the bridge club that she had previously attended weekly for years.

Learning and memory: Jim is a 76-year-old retired pilot. His wife recently reported to his primary care physician that Jim is often forgetful, which is a big change for him. For example, Jim goes to the store to get groceries and returns with items that were not needed and does not remember the items that were. He also has conversations with his wife or others in which he repeats the stories that he is telling, and it is clear that he is not aware that he is repeating himself.

Language: John is a 34-year-old male who enjoys working hard and playing many different types of sports. In fact, he is involved in a sports league of some sort almost every night of the week. On Wednesday nights, he plays rugby for a local league. During the last game, he took a hard hit and, for a few minutes, felt confused and disori-

"When I asked how much memory you had left I was asking about your computer, not you."

ented. He got up, shook it off for about 10 minutes, and then returned to play. The next day at work, John had difficulty concentrating and had a hard time finding the words he needed to express himself. John went to a work meeting a week later and ran into a colleague he had not seen in a while, but he could not recall the colleague's name, which was something that had never happened to John before.

Perceptual-motor abilities: Alice is an 89-year-old woman who has been single and independently living in her home since her husband died over 20 years ago. Until recently, she had been able to do her own grocery shopping, run errands, and drive to visit her friends. However, in the past 2 months, Alice has been unable to recall how to get to her friend's house, even though she has been there numerous times for their weekly get-together. The other day, when driving to her son's house, Alice realized that she had forgotten how to get there, and she had to call him to get directions. When she goes to her local mall, she finds that she is less comfortable there and is feeling confused, so she has been going only when a friend can go with her.

Social cognition: Alex is a 57-year-old husband and father of two. He and his wife are avid socialites. They are involved with many charity organizations, which often requires participating in events such as dinners and fundraisers, as well as active networking to raise awareness of the causes for which they are raising money. In the past 6 months, Alex's wife Heather has become concerned about attending functions because Alex has started to act "differently" when he is around others. He has been excessively talking politics lately, offering his strong opinion, unaware that others are put off, even though they make attempts to change the conversation. He has even made comments to their adult children that have caused them to ask Heather what is wrong with Alex. His previous ease in social settings has appeared to dissipate, and Heather no longer enjoys these events but instead is anxious and fearful that Alex may say something embarrassing.

Neuropsychological testing can determine the specific areas of cognition that are impaired. Results of an individual's testing are compared to a large sample of others of the same age and education level to determine if there are specific areas of deficit. This type of assessment is very helpful in determining areas of impaired cognition and in documenting change over time in abilities.

NCDs can be caused by numerous diseases and medical conditions that are acquired, rather than developmental. These mental disorders are unique in that the etiology of the cognitive impairment is typically known and determines the specificity of the diagnosis. In the sections that follow, we concentrate on the most common and widely studied medical illnesses involved in NCDs.

<hr>

Section Review

- Domains of cognition include complex attention, executive function, learning and memory, language, perceptual-motor abilities, and social cognition;
- Particular regions of the brain are implicated in specific cognitive abilities.
- When an individual presents with cognitive changes, neuropsychological testing can determine which domains of functioning are impaired, compared to same-aged norms.

<hr>

Delirium

delirium: A disturbance in consciousness involving impairments in attention, disorientation, memory and language problems, and hallucinations.

Delirium, the mildest and most transient NCD, is a clinical syndrome (a set of symptoms) that results from an underlying disease. It is a unique condition in that the cause is attributed to the direct effects of a general medical condition or the persisting effects of a substance (alcohol or other drug of abuse, medication, or a toxin). The essential features, shown in Table 15.2, include a disturbance in attention or awareness that is a clear change in baseline cognition and that is not the result of another NCD. Like Dorothy in the chapter-opening case, people with delirium may be disoriented to time and place, with an altered or clouded sense of the environment; the deficits may develop in a few hours or less and then fluctuate over the day (Choi et al., 2012). As the following case illustrates, people with delirium also experience changes in cognition, such as memory deficits, perceptual or language disturbances, or disorientation.

Leonard, a 67-year-old retired toolmaker, had surgery to correct circulatory problems with his feet, caused by his chronic diabetes. After awakening in the recovery room, Leonard was agitated and drifted in and out of consciousness. At first, his wife thought her husband was experiencing normal postanesthetic confusion, but when Leonard was still confused after several hours, she asked their family doctor to come to the hospital.

Leonard did not appear to recognize his family and repeatedly yelled at his wife, "Who is this woman in my room? Get her out of here!" He insisted on leaving his hospital room as quickly as possible because "they're trying to get my guns out of the basement, and someone has to stop them." Leonard became hostile and threatening to the nurses, and when a physician asked Leonard if he knew where he was, he responded, "I'm in jail on my way to the morgue."

These episodes lasted for several hours, after which Leonard began to settle down and finally fell asleep. His physicians diagnosed his problems as an anesthesia-induced delirium.

As Leonard's case highlights, delirium constitutes reduced orientation to significant others and even oneself (Choi et al., 2012). There is a reduced ability to direct attention, focus, and even shift and sustain attention. When people with delirium are asked questions, their concentration wanders, and they often engage in **perseveration**, meaning that they give the same answer over and over to entirely different questions. At other times, they jump from topic to topic and are easily distracted by external stimuli. An individual with delirium may also switch between a significant increase and decrease in activ-

perseveration: Repeating the same answer over and over to different questions.

TABLE 15.2 The *DSM-5* in Simple Language: Diagnosing Delirium

Delirium is diagnosed when (1) attention (focus) and (2) awareness (orientation to the environment) are disturbed, along with at least one other cognitive deficit (e.g., memory or language). The deficits develop quickly, with an obvious change from previous functioning that fluctuates in severity throughout the day, and there is evidence that the deficits are due to the physiological consequence of a medical condition, substance intoxication or withdrawal, or exposure to a toxin.

Source: Adapted from American Psychiatric Association (2013a).

ity, although the hyperactive state is more easily recognized (Camus, Gonthier, Dubos, Schwed, & Simeone, 2000). The etiology or cause of the delirium (i.e., due to substance intoxication or withdrawal, medication, another medical condition, or multiple etiologies) should be specified when making the diagnosis:

Course, Characteristics, and Prevalence of Delirium

In children, onset of delirium is typically rapid, often coinciding with a high fever. In the elderly, it may develop rapidly (over hours) or slowly (over days). A common pattern among older patients is for problems of awareness to fluctuate during the day and then worsen at night.

Delirium often begins with warning signs similar to those that precede migraine headaches. Some people become especially sensitive to smells or sounds; others report mild perceptual distortions and changes in mood. In some cases, the person begins to lose the ability to judge the passage of time or to maintain concentration. In addition, signs of autonomic nervous system arousal, such as a racing heart, increased blood pressure, sweating, flushed face, and dilated pupils are common. The normal sleep-wake cycle is often reversed; the person suffers agitation and insomnia at night but is drowsy during the day, with significant difficulty falling asleep. Sleep-wake cycle disturbances are so commonly associated with delirium that they have been proposed as a core symptom (Jabbar et al., 2011). Restoration of a more normal sleep-wake cycle is a good sign that the delirium is improving.

As the inner world of people with delirium becomes increasingly disturbed, the individuals often experience emotional changes, including depression, apathy, euphoria, anxiety, or irritability. They may swing rapidly from one emotional extreme to another. Visual hallucinations and paranoid delusions are common. Delusions involving misidentification also are common. For example, as Leonard's case illustrates, **Capgras syndrome**, the delusion that impostors are posing as friends or relatives, is encountered in some cases of delirium (Munro, 2000). This problem is an especially cruel and devastating development for a devoted spouse or friend, and it can complicate the caregiver-patient relationship after discharge from the hospital. However, Capgras delusions associated with a medical etiology usually remit when the medical condition is resolved (Joshi et al., 2010).

During delirium, a person's memory is usually impaired for events that have just occurred, but memory for events that happened long ago remains intact. In most cases of uncomplicated delirium, cognitive losses develop and resolve rapidly, corresponding with the onset and elimination of the medical condition that caused it. Complete recovery from delirium is common, once its underlying cause is treated, usually within a few weeks, although recovery tends to be slower in the elderly than in the young. Unfortunately, delirium increases the risk of death at all ages, especially in the elderly. This is because delirium often occurs when the illness that produced it is severe and because the delirium itself may complicate medical care. The emotional states, delusions, and hallucinations that often accompany delirium can cause people to refuse treatment. In some cases, fear leads to serious injuries as people in the throes of delirium rip out monitors, catheters, and intravenous tubing or fall during an attempt to escape.

Because many cases of delirium develop and resolve so rapidly, it is difficult to estimate the prevalence of the disorder. Mild to moderate cases, in particular, are likely to be missed. Overall, delirium prevalence in the community is low, at about 1–2% (Inouye,

Capgras syndrome: The delusion that impostors are posing as friends or relatives.

2006). Yet setting and age are important factors when considering the prevalence of this condition. As age increases, so does the prevalence of delirium, up to 14% in individuals over 85 years of age. For people admitted to the hospital, prevalence goes as high as 24% (Agostini & Inouye, 2003; Inouye, 1998). Delirium is especially common in older adults after surgery (15–53%; Agostini & Inouye, 2003) and in 70–87% of those receiving intensive care (Pisani et al., 2003). Finally, for those receiving end-of-life care or postacute care and for those living in nursing homes, delirium occurs in 60–83% of cases (Boorsma et al., 2012; Casarett, 2003).

As was the case for Dorothy in the chapter-opening case, the impaired brain function of individuals with a mild or major NCD increases susceptibility to delirium (Cole, McCusker, Dendukuri, & Han, 2002; Inouye, 2006). The cognitive changes in neurocognitive disorders, however, unlike those of delirium, usually develop more slowly and are often irreversible. Also, whereas altered consciousness is the essential symptom for delirium, a mild or major neurocognitive disorder that is unaccompanied by delirium usually causes no major change of consciousness or awareness.

Assessment of Delirium

To identify and treat the underlying cause of delirium, clinicians must obtain an accurate assessment of the person's medical condition and medical history. This assessment can be difficult because, even with mild delirium, the person's reports will often be unreliable. Relatives, friends, or neighbors are often asked to provide collateral information and are heavily relied upon regarding the onset and progression of symptoms (Lindesay, Macdonald, & Starke, 1990).

If reliable informants are not available, a brief examination of the person's home may provide the necessary information. For example, if the home is clean and tidy, the person's cognitive decline is probably the result of uncomplicated delirium. However, the presence of spoiled food in the refrigerator, trash strewn around the home, and stacks of dirty dishes (as in Dorothy's chapter-opening case) may indicate more long-standing problems, such as depression or major NCD. (Note: If your roommates never do the dishes, it does not mean that they have an NCD; they could just be lazy.) Sudden bladder or bowel incontinence also points to delirium, especially in older adults.

Assessing cognitive function in delirium is difficult, and formal neuropsychological assessment is often impossible. However, a structured interview—the *mini-mental state examination* (MMSE; Folstein, Folstein, & McHugh, 1975)—is a type of **mental status examination (MSE;** discussed in Chapter 1) that is widely used to assess delirium. The MMSE is easy to administer in 5–10 minutes and provides a rating of individuals' mental state based on brief assessments of attention, memory, language, concentration, figure copying, and orientation to place and time. It involves questions such as having individuals repeat the three objects that were named for them earlier, count backward by 7s from 100, write a sentence, read short instructions, and copy a small picture. Notice how these items use many of the six key domains of cognition described earlier in the chapter. Another simple bedside method for tracking the progression or remission of delirium is the "draw a clock test," in which individuals are asked to draw a nondigital clock, put in all the numbers, and set the hands at ten past eleven. Though the clock drawing test does offer specific clues about the area of change or damage, it can provide huge amounts of information about general cognitive and adaptive functioning, such as memory, how people are able to process information, and vision. A normal clock drawing almost always predicts that a person's cognitive abilities are within normal limits (Kennard, 2014).

Brain activity is disturbed during attacks of delirium. For example, electroencephalogram (EEG) recordings from the brains of people with delirium typically show widespread slow waves, somewhat like those observed during certain stages of sleep. But EEG recordings alone are not necessarily good indicators of delirium because the EEG also slows with normal aging and especially with other NCDs. Furthermore, delirium induced by drugs or drug withdrawal (e.g., *delirium tremens* during alcohol withdrawal) can be indicated by bursts of fast EEG activity rather than EEG slowing.

mental status examination (MSE): A brief, specialized, and focused interview designed to assess a person's memory, mood, orientation, thinking, and concentration.

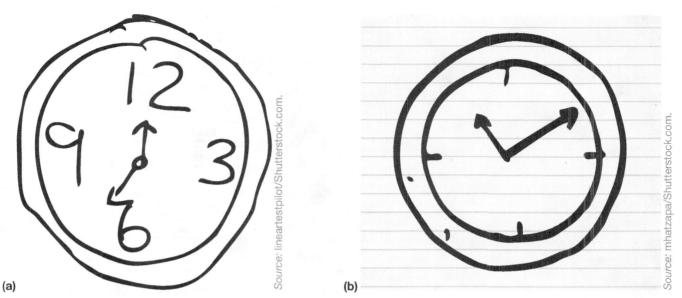

Two examples of the clock drawing test. Maximum potential score is five points. (a) This example would earn two points (one point for the round clock and one for the two hands), whereas (b), which lacks numbers but shows the correct time (11:10), would earn three points on the test.

Causes and Outcome of Delirium

Delirium has many physical causes, but the most common causes are head trauma, postoperative states, the effects of using (or withdrawing from) drugs, exposure to toxins, epilepsy, metabolic disturbances, dehydration, and infections. In many cases, delirium is caused by more than one factor. A common combination of causes among the elderly is an infectious disease, along with medication-induced side effects. Stressful life events can also increase the risk of delirium; bereavement or sudden relocation due to hospitalization can add to the confusion and disorientation felt by people with delirium.

Neuroimaging studies have contributed to understanding the impacted brain regions in people with delirium. Cortical atrophy in the prefrontal and temporoparietal cortex, fusiform and lingual gyri, and deep structures, including the thalamus and basal ganglia, has been seen in elderly people with delirium (Burns, Gallagley, & Byrne, 2004). What is not clear is whether the atrophy is a risk factor for developing delirium or a result of the delirious state and medical comorbidities.

Whereas there are multiple etiologies of delirium, there are also multiple outcomes. Figure 15.2 gives an idea of the various paths following the diagnosis of delirium. Unfortunately, poor outcomes are a possibility, including further medical complications, such as pressure ulcers and decreased ingestion of food, both of which have been shown to be associated with worse prognosis (Inouye & Marcantonio, 2007). Following a delirious state, some people may still report subjective memory ability changes, and neuropsychological testing has revealed significantly reduced performance on executive functioning, attention, and processing speed, with continued impaired performance on the mini-mental state examination (Fann, Alfano, Roth-Roemer, Katon, & Syrjala, 2007; Katz et al., 2001; McCusker, Cole, Dendukuri, Belzile, & Primeau, 2001). Because delirium can result in such negative outcomes, it is important to discuss the treatment of this condition and the impact it can have on an individual's quality of life.

Treatment of Delirium

The most important goal of treatment is to identify and correct the underlying causes of the delirium. It is also critical that treatment be delivered in a supportive environment because delirium can be frightening for both its victims and their loved ones.

Nonpharmacologic strategies are the first-line treatment for anyone with delirium. Psychosocial interventions that include reorientation and behavioral intervention, while

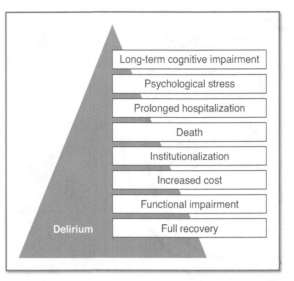

FIGURE 15.2 Possible Outcomes Following an Episode of Delirium

using family members or friends to reassure and reorient the person, are usually helpful. This requires educating all caregivers about delirium, especially delirium that is accompanied by another NCD. If education is not provided, the startling symptoms of delirium, combined with the cognitive deficits of the NCD, may lead caregivers to institutionalize individuals prematurely.

Physical restraint of someone with delirium should be avoided if possible to prevent reinforcement of hallucinations and paranoid delusions that can complicate later treatment. For the same reason, patients should be moved out of "high-tech" environments, such as surgical intensive care units, as soon as it is safe to do so. Bringing a large clock, calendar, or some familiar items from home into the hospital room can help to comfort and reorient the patients. Those who used eyeglasses or hearing aids prior to the disorder should have them returned as soon as it is feasible to do so, and their rooms should always be well lighted to reduce perceptual disturbances. In one study, a nonpharmacological behavioral sleep protocol that incorporated warm milk or tea, relaxation strategies, and massage prior to bed was feasible and effective in hospital environments (McDowell, Mion, Lydon, & Inouye, 1998). If medication is used to treat delirium, it is usually only when individuals' symptoms are severe enough to compromise their safety. However, few high-quality controlled trials have been performed to provide adequate guidance on whether medication should be used with this population at all (Bourne, Tahir, Borthwick, & Sampson, 2008).

Finally, and perhaps most importantly, the dignity of individuals with delirium must be appreciated and protected. Hospitalization can be demeaning, especially to those who are mentally impaired and incapable of understanding what is happening. Insensitivity by caregivers in this setting can threaten individuals' identity and self-esteem, leading to further agitation and frustration for them and their loved ones.

"Mother has settled in."

Source: Cartoonresource/Shutterstock.com.

Section Review

In delirium, the primary cognitive impairments:

- consist of disturbances in consciousness, awareness of the environment, attention, and other cognitive functions;
- develop over a short period of time (hours to days) and fluctuate throughout the day;
- are often accompanied by pronounced swings in emotion, sleep disruption, and agitated behavior; and

- can be caused by drug use or withdrawal, metabolic disturbances, infectious diseases, brain injuries, epilepsy, poisoning, and postoperative states.

Treatment of delirium:

- requires identifying and treating the underlying medical cause; and
- is aided by supportive caretakers who provide repeated reassurance, reorientation, and respect for the individuals experiencing delirium.

Major and Mild Neurocognitive Disorders

As already mentioned at the beginning of the chapter, *neurocognitive disorders (NCDs)* involve an overall (and, unlike delirium, generally permanent) loss of cognitive function in domains that include complex attention, executive function, learning and memory, language, perceptual-motor, and social cognition. The *DSM-5* changes in the diagnostic terminology for NCDs are important to note. The current terminology for *major NCDs* corresponds largely to the previously utilized term *dementia*, which is found in the vast majority of research to date regarding these disorders. However, memory impairment is no longer a necessary criterion for diagnosis of all etiologies of NCD, as was the case for a diagnosis of dementia (Foley & Heck, 2014).

Mild NCD, which was introduced in the *DSM-IV-TR* (American Psychiatric Association, 2000) as an area for further study, now represents its own diagnosis in the *DSM-5* and replaces the previous diagnosis of *cognitive disorder not otherwise specified* (Foley & Heck, 2014). Research is underway to determine the degree to which mild NCD also corresponds to the widely studied and diagnosed concept of *mild cognitive impairment* (Petersen et al., 2014; Sachs-Ericsson & Blazer, 2015). Consistent with previous conceptualizations of mild cognitive impairment, mild NCD is believed to be an early stage along a spectrum of cognitive impairment that is associated with increased risk of further progression to major NCD.

Diagnostic Criteria

NCD diagnosis is made based on four components: First, it is important to discuss differentiation between major and mild NCD. Second, the etiological subtype used to specify the hypothesized cause of the cognitive dysfunction must be identified. The third and fourth components of NCD diagnosis include specifiers regarding behavioral disturbance and disorder severity.

Differentiating Major and Mild NCD

Major and mild NCD are differentiated by two specific factors, as shown in Table 15.3: (1) the degree of cognitive impairment and (2) the extent to which impairment interferes with daily functioning. Whenever possible, standardized neuropsychological testing is conducted to determine whether the degree of cognitive impairment that an individual is exhibiting is best classified as substantial or modest impairment. These classifications are made by comparing an individual's scores to a normative group matched on demographic variables, such as age, level of education, and racial/ethnic group. Scores falling more than two standard deviations below the average of the normative group (less than 3rd percentile) are considered substantially impaired and are consistent with a diagnosis of major NCD. Scores falling between one and two standard deviations below the normative average (3rd–16th percentile) are considered modestly impaired and are consistent with a diagnosis of mild NCD. This objective measure of cognitive decline must also be accompanied by a subject complaint about the individual's cognitive abilities, which can be expressed by the individual, a close friend or family member, or a clinician.

Independence, or lack thereof, in completing **activities of daily living (ADLs)** represents the other critical component differentiating mild and major NCD. In mild NCD, people can complete most ADLs without help. ADLs are commonly broken into two categories: *basic* (e.g., dressing, eating, bathing, toileting) and *instrumental* (e.g., using

activities of daily living (ADLs): A term used in health care to refer to daily self-care activities; health professionals routinely refer to the ability or inability to perform ADLs as a measurement of the functional status of a person, particularly in regard to people with disabilities and the elderly.

TABLE 15.3 The *DSM-5* in Simple Language: Diagnosing Major and Mild Neurocognitive Disorder

Diagnostic Criteria for Major Neurocognitive Disorder	Diagnostic Criteria for Mild Neurocognitive Disorder
Significant cognitive decline from a previous level of performance in one or more cognitive domains based on:	Modest cognitive decline from a previous level of performance in one or more cognitive domain based on:
Concern of the individual or others that there has been a significant cognitive decline AND	Concern of the individual or others that there has been a significant cognitive decline AND
■ Cognitive performance *is substantially impaired*. ■ Cognitive deficit *interferes with independence in daily life*. ■ Delirium and other potential etiologies have been ruled out.	■ Cognitive performance *is modestly impaired*. ■ Cognitive deficit *does not interfere with independence in daily life*. ■ Delirium and other potential etiologies have been ruled out.

Source: Adapted from American Psychiatric Association (2013a).

the phone, managing finances, housekeeping, taking medications). Findings from a longitudinal, population-based study indicated that onset of disability in completing ADLs is associated with accelerated rates of cognitive decline (Rajan et al., 2012). Cognitive functioning declined by over 100% after the onset of any ADL impairments, and numerous studies have shown that such declines in ADL performance predict future NCDs (Fauth et al., 2013; Pérès et al., 2008; Sikkes et al., 2011).

Etiological Subtypes

NCD is not a single mental disorder. It is a syndrome that may accompany a variety of diseases or physical conditions affecting the central nervous system. In addition to determining whether the presentation is reflective of major or mild NCD, clinicians must also specify the cause of the NCD as part of the diagnostic process. Potential etiological subtypes are listed in the *DSM-5*, with the most common ones described briefly as follows (Alzheimer's Society, n.d.):

NCD Due to Alzheimer's Disease

Cognitive impairment: Deficits in memory, learning, and at least one other cognitive domain

Onset: Insidious with gradual decline

Frontotemporal NCD

Two possible variants of cognitive impairment: Behavioral and language

Behavioral variant: Symptoms of behavioral disinhibition, apathy, loss of sympathy/empathy, perseverative behavior, hyperorality (putting inappropriate things into one's mouth)

Language variant: Decline in language abilities, including speech production, object naming, grammar, or comprehension

Learning, memory abilities, and perceptual-motor functioning are relatively spared.

Onset: Insidious with gradual decline

Vascular NCD

Cognitive impairment: Deficits in attention, processing speed, and executive functioning

Onset: Acute, related to cardiovascular conditions such as strokes or arterial diseases that interrupt oxygen supply to the brain, or gradual, with slow progression, such as with small vessel disease

NCD Due to Traumatic Brain Injury

Cognitive impairment: Loss of consciousness, posttraumatic amnesia, disorientation, and confusion

Onset: Occurring immediately following traumatic injury to the brain

Substance/Medication-Induced NCD

Cognitive impairment: Varied, depending upon the substance or drug

Onset: Ingestion of a substance or medication capable of producing the impairment in cognition just prior to the appearance of symptoms

NCD Due to HIV Infection

Cognitive impairment: Problems with short-term memory, language, and thinking; difficulties with concentration and decision making; unsteadiness; mood changes; hallucinations; possible problems with sense of smell

Clinical findings: Diagnosis of human immunodeficiency virus (HIV)

NCD with Lewy Bodies

Cognitive impairment: Cognitive functioning, particularly attention and orientation, fluctuates

Additional symptoms: Recurrent visual hallucinations, spontaneous motor abnormalities (e.g., muscle rigidity, slow movement)

Clinical findings: Abnormal protein deposits, called *Lewy bodies*, which lead to degeneration of the neurons of the cortex and brain stem

Onset: Insidious with gradual decline

NCD Due to Parkinson's Disease

Cognitive impairment: Memory loss, and loss of the ability to think quickly and to carry out everyday tasks; person may become obsessive, with a loss of emotional control and sudden outbursts of anger or distress

Clinical findings: Diagnosis of **Parkinson's disease**, characterized by progressive neurodegeneration and symptoms such as tremor, unsteady or stiff gait, and slowed motor movements; microscopic deposits known as *Lewy bodies* (see previous section) occur in brain-stem nerve cells in people with Parkinson's disease

Onset: Insidious with gradual decline

Parkinson's disease: A degenerative dementia characterized by tremor, difficulty in movement, and reduced production of dopamine.

NCD Due to Huntington's Disease

Cognitive impairment: Early cognitive changes in executive functioning, which may precede the motor abnormalities commonly associated with the onset of **Huntington's disease**

Clinical findings: Diagnosis of Huntington's disease or risk for Huntington's disease based on family history or genetic testing

Onset: Insidious onset with gradual decline

Huntington's disease: A dementia involving progressive subcortical degeneration that leads to motor disturbances, changes in personality, and cognitive difficulties.

Additional Diagnostic Specifiers

Two additional specifiers must be considered with a diagnosis of NCD. For both major and mild NCD, a specifier of "with" or "without behavioral disturbance" should be provided. Examples of behavioral disturbance include psychotic symptoms, mood disturbances, agitation, and apathy. For major NCD only, current severity of symptoms is also specified (i.e., mild, moderate, or severe). A "mild" specifier indicates difficulty completing only *instrumental* activities of daily living independently (e.g., more-complicated tasks like finances), whereas a "moderate" specifier indicates difficulty completing *basic* activities of daily living independently (e.g., laundry, cleaning). A "severe" specifier indicates that the individual is fully dependent on the help of others to complete everyday activities.

Differential Diagnosis

A diagnosis of NCD is always characterized by decline in at least one domain of cognitive functioning, regardless of which etiological subtype characterizes the diagnosis. However, clinicians must be able to tease apart the more-subtle variations in presentation based on these etiologies to determine the appropriate differential diagnosis. That is to say, how do clinicians decide on one cause over another?

Neuropsychological tests and magnetic resonance imaging (MRI) are the most informative diagnostic techniques at present, with 84% and 82% correct classifications in one study of Alzheimer's disease (Schmand, Eikelenboom, & van Gool, 2011). Neuropsychologists, who comprise a subspecialty of psychology interested in brain-behavior relationships, often must act as "brain detectives." Differentiating between etiological subtypes of NCD involves close attention to such factors as time course of symptom onset and progression, the specific cognitive domains impacted, and additional associated symptoms and clinical findings. For example, acute onset of cognitive decline is more likely in NCD due to traumatic brain injury or vascular disease when a particular event such as a head injury or stroke occurred, whereas symptom onset is typically more insidious and gradually progressive in the context of neurodegenerative etiologies, such as Alzheimer's disease or frontotemporal brain degeneration. Deficits in particular cognitive domains also greatly inform the etiological determination. For instance, NCD due to Alzheimer's disease is commonly associated with deficits in learning and memory; however, this cognitive domain is relatively spared in frontotemporal NCD (Braaten, Parsons, McCue, Sellers, & Burns, 2006). Whereas NCD with memory loss has the highest likelihood of being associated with Alzheimer's disease pathology, early **aphasia**, progressive visuospatial deficits, and changes in personality also can be associated with Alzheimer's disease (Weintraub, Wicklund, & Salmon, 2012).

aphasia: A loss or impairment in language.

Finally, MRI can be used to help determine the cause of an NCD. For example, atrophy in the hippocampus or entorhinal cortex could be used to support a diagnosis of NCD due to Alzheimer's disease, whereas evidence of subcortical infarcts or white matter lesions would be more indicative of vascular NCD (O'Brien, 2007). Conversely, NCD due to Lewy bodies, but not Alzheimer's disease, is associated with reduced amygdala volume on MRI (Burton et al., 2012).

Prevalence and Demographic Considerations

Current estimates of NCD prevalence are based on previously reported dementia prevalence. The global prevalence of dementia is estimated to be approximately 4.7% (Prince et al., 2013). Of the geographical regions examined, NCD prevalence was third highest in North America at 6.9%, with western Europe and southern Latin America having the highest prevalence rates at 7.2% and 7.0%, respectively.

NCD prevalence varies greatly across etiologies. Alzheimer's disease accounts for 60–80% of all NCD cases, whereas vascular NCD and frontotemporal NCD account for 10% and 5% of dementia cases, respectively (Prince et al., 2013). There is a large variability in estimates for NCD with Lewy bodies, with this type of NCD accounting for 2–31% of dementia cases, depending on the study.

Demographic factors such as age and gender are also related to prevalence of NCD. For many NCDs, such as those due to Alzheimer's and vascular disease, a steep increase in prevalence is associated with advanced age, particularly between the ages of 65 and 85 (Jellinger & Attems, 2010). Frontotemporal NCD tends to be associated with earlier onset of cognitive impairment, with only 20–25% of cases occurring in individuals over the age of 65. Prevalence of NCD due to Parkinson's disease also increases with age in accordance with the onset of Parkinson's disease itself. NCD due to Huntington's disease is associated with age to a lesser degree, given that Huntington's disease onset is typically around the age of 40.

Gender differences exist within multiple NCD categories. As described previously, frontotemporal NCD is subdivided into two variants—behavioral and language—the former of which is more common in males and the latter of which is more common in females (American Psychiatric Association, 2013a). Prevalence of NCD due to traumatic brain injury is also greater among males, given that males account for the majority (59%) of such brain injuries in the United States (American Psychiatric Association, 2013a).

Cultural Considerations in Assessing for NCD

As described previously, neuropsychological testing is commonly used to determine domains of cognitive impairment and whether the degree of impairment warrants diagnosis of an NCD. This determination is made by comparing an individual's testing scores to normative data collected from a large reference group. Importantly, the effectiveness of this approach requires that individuals are similar to their reference group on demographic variables such as age or level of education. For example, a 95-year-old would be expected to perform more poorly than a 25-year-old on a test of memory. Thus, to determine how well these individuals are performing for their age, it is important that the 95-year-old is compared with other older adults and the 25-year-old is compared with other younger adults. Likewise, it is standard for individuals to be compared to a reference group with a similar level of educational attainment, given that more education is associated with better performance on many of the tests.

Research examining the impact of race/ethnicity on cognitive performance has highlighted differences across racial/ethnic groups on a wide variety of cognitive tests, including those assessing visual and verbal memory, executive functioning, and object naming (Boone, Victor, Wen, Razani, & Pontón, 2007). These findings suggest that racial/ethnic group status should also be considered when determining an appropriate normative reference group. However, this has been a significant challenge for neuropsychologists, who frequently use tests that have only been validated among non-Hispanic, English-speaking whites (Manly & Echemendia, 2007). Whereas there has been some progress in recent years toward developing normative data for additional racial/ethnic groups, such as African Americans and Hispanics, many groups continue to be underrepresented in the normative data for neuropsychological tests, and questions remain about which reference group is best to use when an individual does not fall neatly into one of the options (e.g., when someone is biracial). Examining potential advantages and disadvantages of using race-specific normative data has become the focus of substantial research inquiry (Manly, 2005).

MAPS - Prejudicial Pigeonholes

Differences in language can pose another obstacle when using neuropsychological testing to determine the presence or absence of an NCD. The vast majority of neuropsychological assessments conducted in the United States are done in English, which can result in poorer performance and the perception of greater cognitive impairment among non-native English speakers, though these deficits may be better attributed to language barriers in testing. Translators or translated test materials are frequently used when testing an individual in English is deemed inappropriate. However, questions have been raised regarding the accuracy of these translations and other potential ethical issues in cross-cultural neuropsychology (Artiola i Fortuny et al., 2005; Brickman, Cabo, & Manly, 2006).

Section Review

Neurocognitive disorder (NCD):

- refers to an overall degradation of cognitive function;
- involves impairments in one or more cognitive domains, including complex attention, executive function, learning and memory, language, perceptual-motor abilities, and social cognition; and
- is largely consistent with the term *dementia*, which appeared previously in the *DSM-IV*.

Diagnosis of NCD:

- is specified as either major or mild,
- involves the identification of a specific etiological (causal) subtype, and
- includes specifiers for the presence or absence of behavioral disturbance, as well as for severity (for major NCD only).

Causes of NCD include:

■ neurodegeneration, strokes, and arterial diseases; and
■ Lewy bodies, Alzheimer's disease, Parkinson's disease, Huntington's disease, HIV infection, head trauma, and other medical conditions.

Demographic variables such as age, gender, and racial/ethnic status:

■ are related to the prevalence of various NCDs and
■ play a role in the interpretation of neuropsychological testing data, which are commonly used in the determination of an NCD diagnosis.

Neurocognitive Disorder Due to Alzheimer's Disease

Alzheimer's disease: The most frequent cause of dementia, characterized by memory loss, apathy, cognitive difficulties, language problems, and personality changes.

Because of its increasing frequency, we now discuss NCD due to Alzheimer's disease in more detail, followed by an examination of NCD due to traumatic brain injury as a contrast. The irreversible gradual deterioration of the brain's cerebral cortex called **Alzheimer's disease** is by far the most common cause of NCD; it currently affects more than 5 million Americans (Alzheimer's Association, 2013), and that number is expected to grow rapidly as the population ages. Over 7 million people over the age of 65 are expected to have major NCD due to Alzheimer's disease by 2025, with that number increasing to 13.8 million by 2040. The incidence of NCD due to Alzheimer's disease doubles with every 5 years of increased age between 65 and 85, making advanced age the greatest risk factor. Because the number of older persons in almost all countries will increase dramatically in the next 50 years, the magnitude of NCD due to Alzheimer's disease as a health problem is almost certain to reach crisis proportions. A substantial increase in the prevalence of NCD due to Alzheimer's disease is expected in Africa, Asia, Europe, Latin American and the Caribbean, and North America between now and 2050 (Brookmeyer, Johnson, Ziegler-Graham, & Arrighi, 2007). When onset of NCD due to Alzheimer's disease occurs before age 65, it is diagnosed as *early onset*; when onset occurs after age 65, which is much more common, it is diagnosed as *late onset*.

Several studies have found women to be at higher risk for NCD due to Alzheimer's disease than men (Azad, Al Bugami, & Loy-English, 2007; Kalaria et al., 2008). Women account for approximately two thirds of all Americans with NCD due to Alzheimer's disease, which is predominantly explained by the fact that women live longer than men (Alzheimer's Association, 2013); however, increased rates of hypertension, hyperlipidemia, and diabetes in elderly woman, compared to elderly men, may also play a role (Azad et al., 2007). There are also racial/ethnic differences in NCD due to Alzheimer's disease. Increased rates of NCD due to Alzheimer's disease have been found in African Americans and Hispanics, compared to non-Hispanic whites (Demirovic et al., 2003; Tang et al., 2001). These observed differences in prevalence are likely attributable in large part to variation in the prevalence of risk factors, such as cardiovascular disease (Chin, Negash, Hamilton, 2011; Tang et al., 2001). Other cultural factors that could play a role include perceptions of normal versus abnormal aging, willingness to seek treatment, and access to health care.

Stages of NCD Due to Alzheimer's Disease

The course of NCD due to Alzheimer's disease has recently been divided into three stages: preclinical, mild cognitive impairment, and Alzheimer's disease dementia (Sperling et al., 2011). The two later stages now correspond to mild and major NCD due to Alzheimer's disease, respectively. Inherent in the conceptualization of the preclinical stage of Alzheimer's disease is the idea that pathophysiological changes associated with this disease occur years, possibly even decades, before the emergence of clinical symptoms. This preclinical stage of Alzheimer's disease has been newly acknowledged, based on increased attention to early biomarkers of the disease that may confer increased risk for disease development. In the early stages of cognitive impairment, the primary symptoms are usually increased forgetfulness, especially for emotionally neutral events, and a loss in ability to cope with changes in the environment or in routines.

Later stages of the disease are associated with increasing problems in multiple domains of cognition, such as more extensive memory impairment, coupled with executive functioning deficits. At this point, people with Alzheimer's disease have great difficulty learning new information, as well as recalling and recognizing that information if it is presented again at a later time. They often ask the same questions and tell the same stories repeatedly. Ultimately, people struggle to find their way even in familiar places and fail to recognize familiar people. One of the authors had a father who died of Alzheimer's disease in 2014; when he would visit his father in the long-term care facility, all they could talk about was his father's childhood because his father had virtually no memories of their 4 decades of shared life together; yet, his father remembered his own childhood from 65 years ago. Because of these profound memory lapses, people with Alzheimer's attempt answers—and so they may fill in the gaps in their lives with made-up stories or even act aggressively toward caretakers without recognizing the true extent of their own impairment.

MAPS - Attempted Answers

Whereas subtle cognitive impairments are evident at the point of mild NCD due to Alzheimer's disease, individuals at this stage of disease progression retain the ability to complete activities of daily living. However, even routine tasks, such as dressing, eating, and using the bathroom, become impossible in the later stages of major NCD due to Alzheimer's disease. Eventually, people deteriorate to the point where they are unable to care for themselves. The rate of deterioration varies dramatically from person to person; individuals aged 65 years and older typically survive an average of 4–8 years after being diagnosed with Alzheimer's disease, although the duration of illness from diagnosis to death can be as high as 20 years (Alzheimer's Association, 2013).

Disentangling Normal Aging and NCD Due to Alzheimer's Disease

People commonly notice subtle declines in their cognitive abilities over the course of normal aging. Over the life span, decreased accuracy and slowed reaction times may become evident in the completion of activities that call upon a wide array of cognitive abilities (Ghosh, Agarwal, & Haggerty 2011). Hedden and Gabrieli (2004) highlighted three patterns of age-related change in cognition: (1) lifelong decline, in which abilities consistently decline over the life span, (2) decline late in life, in which abilities are relatively stable throughout most of life but decline in late adulthood, and (3) stability across the life span, in which abilities show overall resilience to decline. Lifelong declines are apparent in cognitive abilities, including processing speed, working memory, encoding of new information, long-term memory, reasoning, and executive functioning. Late-life declines are evident in abilities such as short-term memory, execution of well-practiced tasks (i.e., procedural memory), and execution of knowledge-based tasks. Stability across the life span is noted in domains such as verbal knowledge, emotional processing, automatic memory processing, and autobiographical memory (i.e., remembering your own life).

Whereas age-related changes in cognitive functioning are seen in both healthy older adults and those with NCD due to Alzheimer's disease (they are aging too, after all), researchers have identified distinct patterns of neural pathology that are associated with Alzheimer's disease and that suggest that Alzheimer's disease represents more than simply an exaggerated aging process (Ghosh, Agarwal, & Haggerty, 2011; Ohnishi, Matsuda, Tabira, Asada, & Uno, 2001).

Neuropathology of NCD Due to Alzheimer's Disease

The brains of patients with NCD due to Alzheimer's disease usually show atrophy—in the form of neuron and synapse loss—in several areas. Particularly hard hit are areas that mediate memory, including the medial temporal lobe, hippocampus, entorhinal cortex, and parahippocampal gyrus. Primary sensory and motor cortices are largely spared. Whether these changes are a more-or-less expected consequence of aging for many individuals or a unique kind of brain pathology is a topic of much debate. Atrophy of the hippocampus specifically, however, is more pronounced in patients with Alzheimer's disease. Estimates of hippocampal atrophy range from 0.2–3.8% per year as a result of normal aging, versus 4.9–8.2% in people with Alzheimer's disease (Ghosh et al. 2011).

Alzheimer's disease was first identified by German neurologist Alois Alzheimer in 1907. During an autopsy of a 51-year-old woman who had suffered serious cognitive deterioration, he discovered two features of her brain that are now recognized as the most distinctive signs of the disease: tangles and plaques. **Neurofibrillary tangles** are twisted clumps of protein fibers found in dying cells (see Figure 15.3). **Neuritic plaques** are composed of the residue of dead neurons and cellular garbage. These plaques and tangles are characteristic of Alzheimer's disease.

The *DSM-5* criteria for NCD due to Alzheimer's disease only describes diagnoses of *probable* and *possible* NCD, which is why Dorothy and her family in the chapter-opening case could not be told definitively that she had Alzheimer's disease. Evidence of particular patterns of cognitive decline, in conjunction with genetic risk factors, increases the likelihood of an Alzheimer's disease etiology. As dementia progresses from early to late stages, however, symptom domain boundaries become blurred, and distinctive profiles are difficult to discern (Weintraub et al., 2012). Thus, currently, a definite diagnosis of Alzheimer's disease can only be made based on a postmortem autopsy during which tangles and plaques are found in the person's brain.

neurofibrillary tangles: Twisted clumps of protein fibers found in dying brain cells.

neuritic plaque: The residue of dead neurons and cellular debris; found in patients diagnosed with Alzheimer's disease.

FIGURE 15.3 Brain Regions Affected by Alzheimer's Disease

In Alzheimer's disease, cortical neurons develop neurofibrillary tangles, consisting of hyperphosphorylated tau. The neurons eventually die. Many of these are from the temporal lobe and associated limbic system, as shown here, and play a role in memory formation (van de Nes, Nafe, & Schlote, 2008).

Source: joshya/Shutterstock.com.

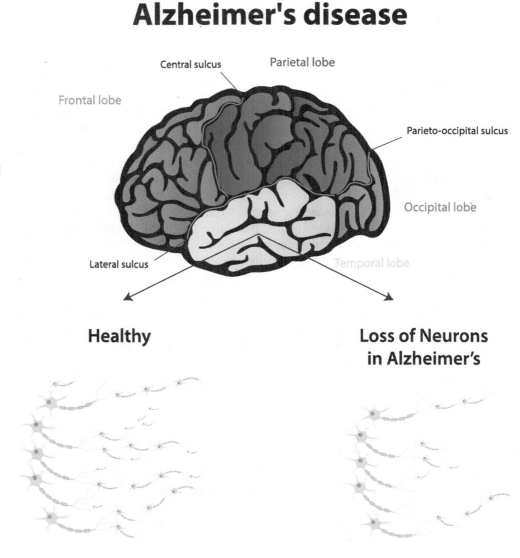

Alzheimer's disease

Central sulcus

Parietal lobe

Frontal lobe

Parieto-occipital sulcus

Occipital lobe

Lateral sulcus

Temporal lobe

Healthy

Loss of Neurons in Alzheimer's

Genetic Factors and NCD Due to Alzheimer's Disease

Extensive research over the last several decades has led to the establishment of the well-known amyloid hypothesis of Alzheimer's disease (Hardy & Selkoe, 2002). Early research leading to this hypothesis stems from individuals with Down syndrome, who carry three copies of chromosome 21 and are extremely likely to develop Alzheimer's disease by age 40. Their brains develop large numbers of **amyloid (senile) plaques**. The form of the amyloid protein, **beta-amyloid-4**, found in these plaques is an abnormal derivative of **amyloid precursor protein (APP)**, which is produced by a gene on chromosome 21. Individuals with one type of early-onset Alzheimer's disease also develop large numbers of these amyloid plaques, presumably caused by a mutation of the same APP-producing gene on chromosome 21 that people with Down syndrome have. Advances in research are increasing abilities to visualize these amyloid plaques in-vivo through the use of imaging with positron emission tomography, which could someday make a diagnosis of Alzheimer's disease possible while the person is still alive (Klunk et al., 2004; Small et al., 2012).

A gene on chromosome 19 has been linked to the much more common late-onset variety of Alzheimer's disease. This gene is known to produce **apolipoprotein E (ApoE)**, a protein that transports cholesterol in the blood. There are three variants of the ApoE gene, but only ApoE-ε4 increases the risk of Alzheimer's disease, whereas ApoE-ε2 may actually protect against the disease. Being an ApoE-ε4 carrier does not guarantee the development of Alzheimer's disease; however, it is estimated that 40–65% of individuals with Alzheimer's disease carry either one or two ApoE-ε4 alleles (Alzheimer's Association, 2013; Twamley, Ropacki, & Bondi, 2006). Family history of Alzheimer's disease is another prominent risk factor for disease development that is not completely accounted for by the genetic risk associated with ApoE-ε4. Having a first-degree relative with Alzheimer's disease is associated with greater risk, and that risk grows with increasing numbers of afflicted first-degree relatives.

Other Risk Factors for NCD Due to Alzheimer's Disease

Discoveries of possible genetic factors linked to Alzheimer's disease have added to understanding of this illness and may eventually lead to its prevention. But the exact cause of Alzheimer's disease is not yet known, so scientists continue to pursue leads based on other risk factors. In addition to increased age as a primary risk factor for NCD due to Alzheimer's disease and the genetic risk factors described previously, the Alzheimer's Association (2013) identified the following risk factors: history of mild NCD, increased risk of cardiovascular disease, low educational attainment, minimal social and cognitive engagement, and traumatic brain injury.

Whereas mild cognitive impairment is associated with increased risk of developing major NCD due to Alzheimer's disease, the relationship between these disease stages is complicated. This is largely due to the fact that minor NCD does not always progress to major NCD due to Alzheimer's disease, and it is difficult to discern what causes one person with mild NCD to further decline, whereas another person with mild NCD may remain cognitively stable or even improve. In recent years, the clinical conceptualization of mild NCD has evolved to differentiate between those characterized by either a presence or lack of memory impairment (**amnestic** versus nonamnestic) and deficits in one or more cognitive domains (single- or multiple-domain). Some research suggests that amnestic NCD, coupled with deficits in additional domains, such as psychomotor speed and executive functioning, is most predictive of progression to major NCD due to Alzheimer's disease (Tabert et al., 2006). Consideration of additional factors, such as atrophy in brain regions associated with memory impairment and Alzheimer's disease (i.e., the hippocampus), has been shown to improve the prediction of who will likely convert to the more severe stage of major NCD due to Alzheimer's disease (Devanand et al., 2007).

Source: Brian L. Burke.

MAPS - Superficial Syndromes
A saguaro cactus showing the amyloid (senile) plaques associated with Alzheimer's disease in Tucson, Arizona.

amyloid (senile) plaque: A deposit found in large numbers in the brains of people who are likely to develop Alzheimer's disease.

beta-amyloid-4: An abnormal form of a common protein that is essential for life.

amyloid precursor protein (APP): A form of protein produced by a gene on chromosome 21; thought to mutate in people with Alzheimer's disease.

apolipoprotein E (ApoE): A protein that transports cholesterol in the blood.

amnestic disorder: A disorder that involves primarily memory loss.

How Cognitive Ability and Physical Activity Impact NCD Due to Alzheimer's Disease

The prevalence of NCD due to Alzheimer's disease is on the rise as the percentage of the population over the age of 65 continues to increase. As such, the identification of risk factors for NCD due to Alzheimer's disease and potential mechanisms for preventing this disease have become the focus of substantial research. For example, reducing head injuries, preventing cardiovascular disease, and controlling blood pressure and stress should reduce the risk for Alzheimer's. Research has also been pivotal for understanding the role of education and cognitive ability as well as physical activity in protecting against the development of Alzheimer's disease.

The Role of Cognitive Resilience

One of the more surprising discoveries about the risks for developing NCDs is that non-biological factors in early life, such as education and certain cognitive abilities, may be related to the functioning and even the survival in old age. A particularly intriguing demonstration of this possibility is known as the "Nun Study," a longitudinal study of aging and Alzheimer's disease in 678 Roman Catholic nuns who were first evaluated between 1991 and 1993. What makes this study especially interesting is that, because they lived together for over 60 years in the same environment, the nuns did not differ in income, diet, access to health care, use of drugs or alcohol, or exposure to toxins. That is an ideal situation for an experiment.

Researchers found that sisters who had at least a bachelor's degree lived 89.4 years on average and were less likely to require nursing care, whereas those without a college education lived an average of about 82 years and showed a decline in self-care in their later years (Snowdon, Ostwald, & Kane, 1989). What could account for education's relationship to longer life and better mental functioning? One possibility is that advanced education is a form of mental exercise that somehow strengthens brains, much as vigorous physical exercise builds muscles. As a result, individuals who use their minds actively throughout their lives may have more mental capacity in reserve and are relatively better protected against cognitive impairments in old age—in a sense, developing cognitive resilience.

Findings from the Nun Study also revealed a negative correlation between NCD and the frequency of complex ideas in autobiographical essays written by the nuns in their 20s, just before they took their vows (Snowdon et al., 1996). A rater analyzed the *idea density* of these essays without knowing the current status of the nuns who wrote them. Essays judged high in idea density contained a greater number of ideas per words than essays judged to have low idea density. For example, the nun with the lowest idea-density essay wrote, "I was born in Eau Claire, Wisconsin, on May 24, 1913 and was baptized in St. James Church." The nun with the highest idea-density essay wrote, "The happiest day of my life so far was my First Communion Day, which was in June nineteen hundred and twenty when I was but eight years of age, and four years later in the same month I was confirmed by Bishop D. D. McGavick." Idea density in these essays significantly predicted cognitive functioning and presence of Alzheimer's disease 58 years later! All of the nuns who had died of Alzheimer's disease had written low idea-density essays; none of the sisters who had died from other causes had written low idea-density essays. This pattern was the same, regardless of how much education the nuns had received.

Whereas results based on the Nun Study were first published over 20 years ago, novel publications continue to emerge as new data from this study are examined. In addition to participating in annual cognitive and physical exams, the nuns who participated in this study also agreed to brain donation upon death. Recent work regarding the Nun Study has focused heavily on evaluating neuropathology in the brains of deceased participants and its relationship to their previously assessed cognitive abilities. Through this research, lower idea-density scores based on early-life autobiographical essays have been linked to greater severity of Alzheimer's disease pathology in the brain (e.g., amount of neurofibrillary tangles; Snowdon, Greiner, & Markesbery, 2000). As the Nun Study participants continue to age, additional work related to the associations between early-life cognitive ability and late-life neuropathology is likely to emerge.

The Role of Physical Activity

Exercise has long been emphasized as important for the maintenance of good physical health. Indeed, engagement in physical activity can prevent chronic diseases, such as cardiovascular disease, hypertension, diabetes, and some cancers (Hamer & Chida, 2009). However, less attention has historically been paid to the impact of physical activity on cognitive functioning, a trend that has been changing substantially in recent years.

At what point in our lives should we start worrying about exercise and really put those New Year's resolutions into practice? Research suggests that the answer is now! Middleton and colleagues (2010) conducted a study of 9,344 women aged 65 and older, asking them to report how frequently they engaged in low-,

How Cognitive Ability and Physical Activity Impact NCD Due to Alzheimer's Disease *(Continued)*

moderate-, and high-intensity physical activities during their teenage years, at age 30, at age 50, and currently. When all four time points were included in the same statistical model, physical activity during the teenage years was most significantly related to decreased odds of cognitive impairment later in life. However, women who were inactive as teenagers recouped some cognitive benefits of physical activity if they became active at age 30 and 50, compared to those who remained inactive.

In addition to identifying *what* impact physical activity has on cognitive processes, researchers are also trying to understand the *underlying mechanisms* by which this impact occurs. This has sparked research related to the structure and function of the brain as it relates to engagement in physical activity. Dr. Carson Smith (see "A Conversation with Carson Smith" at the end of this chapter) is one researcher conducting work on this topic. In several studies of older adults with varying degrees of genetic risk of Alzheimer's disease (i.e., the presence or absence of the ApoE-ε4 allele), Smith and colleagues (2011, 2014) found that physical activity had protective effects on atrophy of the hippocampus and boosted performance on a semantic memory task among ApoE-ε4 carriers, but not among participants without this heightened risk. These results speak to the importance of specifically targeting individuals at increased risk of developing Alzheimer's disease, as physical activity interventions may be particularly beneficial for these individuals.

A number of risk factors for cardiovascular disease are also associated with increased risk of Alzheimer's disease (Stampfer, 2006). One study found that diabetes and smoking conferred the greatest risk of Alzheimer's disease, although hypertension and heart disease were associated with increased risk as well (Luchsinger et al., 2005). A critical element of these risk factors is that, unlike genetic factors, they are typically modifiable through changes in behavior, such as increased physical activity or dietary changes. Such behavioral changes could have substantial preventive benefits in reducing the risk of various diseases, including Alzheimer's, as the "Prevention" feature in this chapter illustrates.

Low levels of education are also linked with Alzheimer's disease. Having more than 15 years of education is associated with decreased risk of the disease, compared to having fewer than 12 years of education (Kukull et al., 2002). Moreover, one study found a 17% decrease in risk for Alzheimer's disease with each additional year of formal education (Evans et al., 1997), so you are doing yourself a big favor by taking this course and being in school! Why should education matter? One possibility is that individuals with higher levels of education often enjoy higher levels of health care and are better able to avoid other risk factors associated with the disease, such as head trauma and heart disease. Another factor may be that better-educated individuals maintain higher levels of mental activity early in their lives, which can protect against developing Alzheimer's disease. The role of education and premorbid cognitive ability are described further in the "Prevention" feature.

Numerous studies have found that continued engagement in social and cognitively stimulating activities decreases the risk of NCD due to Alzheimer's disease. For example, Saczynski et al. (2006) found that older adults who were not socially active had a greater risk of developing Alzheimer's disease than those who were more socially engaged. Additionally, a decrease in the level of social engagement from midlife to late life was associated with greater risk of disease onset. The role of social engagement in risk for Alzheimer's disease has been linked to the concept of cognitive reserve, which is founded on the idea that certain characteristics or life experiences may increase the brain's resistance to damage that commonly occurs with increased age and the onset of neuropathology.

Finally, traumatic brain injury (TBI) also increases the risk of NCD to Alzheimer's disease. A study of World War II navy and marine veterans found that the risk of Alzheimer's disease was twice as great among veterans who had suffered a moderate TBI and 4.5 times as great among veterans who had suffered a severe TBI (Alzheimer's Association, 2013; Plassman et al., 2000). *Dementia pugilistica*, a form of dementia seen in boxers who have suffered repeated heavy blows to the head, has been recognized for a

Pat Summitt, who coached the University of Tennessee women's basketball team to eight national championships and paved the way for female coaches, was diagnosed with early-onset Alzheimer's in 2011 at the age of 58. Other celebrities diagnosed with the disease have included former President Ronald Reagan, actor Charlton Heston, and artist Norman Rockwell.

tacrine: A drug treatment approved for Alzheimer's disease, it slows the breakdown of acetylcholine.

MAPS - Medical Myths

long time as a contributor to the disease. Sports-related head trauma has become a hot topic in relation to football, where players commonly incur numerous TBIs over the course of their career. A recent study of 3,439 retired National Football League (NFL) players found that mortality due to Alzheimer's disease was four times greater in this sample than the general population (Lehman, Hein, Baron, & Gersic, 2012).

Pharmacological Treatment of NCD Due to Alzheimer's Disease

Alzheimer's disease is a chronic condition that may involve a long period during which symptoms are not yet obvious or are manageable. Interventions during this period may delay the onset of Alzheimer's disease or may slow its progress. Most attempts to treat Alzheimer's disease have been disappointing to date, though, because relatively little is known about the specific causes of the disease or its underlying biological mechanisms, making it difficult to develop effective interventions. However, knowledge in this area has grown substantially in recent years, and several large-scale clinical trials of possible treatments are now being conducted that suggest benefits from a number of strategies. In 2012, the Obama administration launched a National Alzheimer's Plan that takes a two-pronged approach: focusing on future treatments plus help for families suffering today. It includes funding for a prevention study in high-risk patients and tests on an insulin nasal spray that has shown promise in earlier studies. The plan was created to meet the requirements of the National Alzheimer's Project Act, signed into law in 2011, intended to find a cure or means of prevention by 2025 (Loeffler, 2012).

Five drugs are currently approved for the treatment of Alzheimer's disease. Four of these medications—specifically, donepezil (Aricept), rivastigmine (Exelon), galantamine (Reminyl), and **tacrine** (Cognex)—fall into the category of acetylcholinesterase inhibitors, which are believed to improve the decreased cholinergic transmission that occurs as a result of early loss of neurons in Alzheimer's disease (Mangialasche, Solomon, Winblad, Mecocci, & Kivipelto, 2010). Figure 15.4 demonstrates how these inhibitors work at the cellular level. The fifth drug, memantine (Namenda), is an N-methyl-D-aspartate (NMDA) receptor antagonist that protects neurons from toxicity that results from an increase in extracellular glutamate associated with neurodegeneration in Alzheimer's disease (Scarpini, Scheltens, & Feldman, 2003). However, although these medications provide a much-sought-after treatment option, they have generally been associated with only modest benefits and tend to simply slow the progression of symptoms, rather than actually changing the underlying mechanisms of the disease (Relkin, 2007).

Though still in the development stage, new drugs are being examined that may better target the specific neuropathology of Alzheimer's disease. For example, building on what is known about the amyloid hypothesis, drugs to reduce beta-amyloid-4 production, prevent its aggregation, and promote its clearance are currently being studied (Mangialasche et al., 2010).

The sad news is that none of the pharmacological treatments available today are effective for stopping the neuronal death and malfunction that leads to Alzheimer's disease and eventual mortality (Alzheimer's Association, 2013). However, active management of the disease can improve the quality of life for both individuals with Alzheimer's and their caregivers, which is accomplished by:

1. appropriate use of all available treatment options;
2. effective management of coexisting medical or mental conditions (e.g., depression);

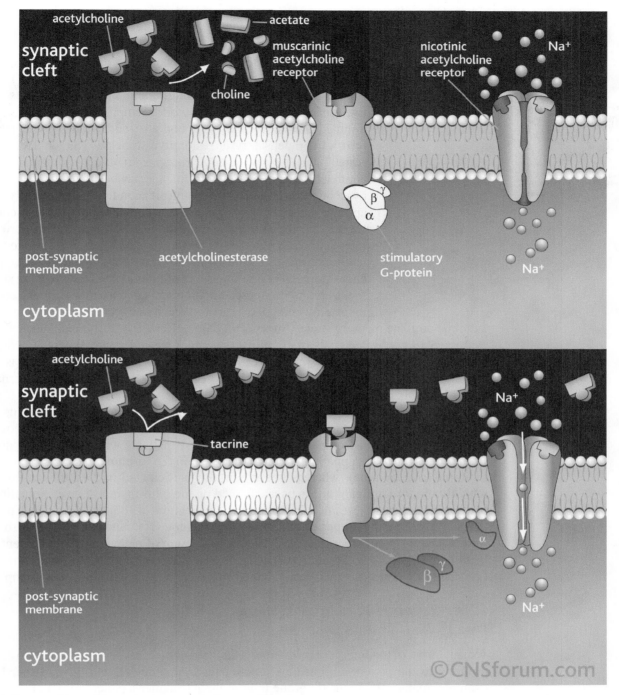

FIGURE 15.4 How Most Alzheimer's Drugs Work

Acetylcholinesterase inhibitors like tacrine are either short-acting, medium-duration, or irreversible inhibitors, which differ in their interactions with the active site of acetylcholinesterase.

Source: Image provided by the Lundbeck Institute at www.cnsforum.com.

3. coordination of care among physicians, other health care professionals, and lay caregivers;
4. encouraging individuals with Alzheimer's to participate in activities and/or adult daycare programs; and
5. encouraging individuals with Alzheimer's and/or their caregivers to take part in support groups and related services.

Source: Cartoonresource/Shutterstock.com.

Cognitive Training as a Treatment for NCD Due to Alzheimer's Disease

Another approach to treating the cognitive impairment in NCD due to Alzheimer's disease is nonpharmacological in nature. Through engagement in cognitive training, commonly referred to as cognitive rehabilitation, people can work to improve their cognitive functioning. One meta-analysis found that such training can take the form of compensatory or restorative strategies (Sitzer, Twamley, & Jeste, 2006). *Compensatory strategies* involve learning new ways to approach tasks in which performance has been negatively impacted by a cognitive deficit. For example, if an individual frequently misses appointments due to poor memory, a compensatory strategy could be writing the appointment time in a notebook or calendar to provide a memory aid. *Restorative strategies*, on the other hand, aim to specifically improve functioning in the cognitive domain that is impaired and restore it to a previous level of functioning. A restorative strategy for dealing with missed appointments due to poor memory could be repeatedly cuing the patient to recall and recite the appointment date and time until the memory sticks (Sitzer et al., 2006). Results of this meta-analysis, which examined 19 controlled trials of cognitive training, revealed improvements in cognitive and functional abilities, with small effect sizes seen for cognitive domains such as visual learning and motor speed and large effect sizes seen for executive functioning, verbal and visual learning, and activities of daily living.

Cognitive rehabilitation has been combined with pharmacological treatments in an attempt to maximize improvement. Bottino et al. (2005) examined the effects of these treatment options in a comparison of two groups of patients with Alzheimer's disease. Both groups received a pharmacological treatment in the form of an acetylcholinesterase inhibitor (rivastigmine), whereas one group also participated in 2 months of cognitive rehabilitation. Significant differences emerged on the mini-mental state examination and backward digit span test after the cognitive intervention, with those who participated in the cognitive training outperforming those who did not. Giordano et al. (2010) also found improvements in cognition lasting 2 months in a group of patients who underwent treatment with cognitive rehabilitation in addition to a different acetylcholinesterase inhibitor (donepezil), whereas no significant change was seen in the medication-only group.

Other Psychosocial Interventions for NCD Due to Alzheimer's Disease

A main thrust of treatment for Alzheimer's disease involves training caregivers to respond properly to the patient's immediate emotional, psychological, and physical needs. For example, many caregivers are prone to urge the Alzheimer's patient to practice intellectual or social skills so as to hold on to these skills as long as possible. Once the disease has taken hold, however, these drills accomplish little, other than frustrating the patient and the caregiver. However, caregivers can take numerous small steps to ease daily problems, such as the following:

- Offering gentle reminders and making lists can prop up the memories of the person with Alzheimer's disease.
- Sewing labels on clothing and placing reminders in strategic locations (e.g., "Turn off the stove") can help the person with Alzheimer's disease to navigate through confusing environments and to maintain some independence.
- Maintaining familiar schedules, keeping personal possessions in the same locations, and adhering to daily routines may reduce stress and help the person with Alzheimer's disease to cope with daily demands.

- Providing comfortable, loose-fitting clothing with few buttons, snaps, or zippers is advisable.
- Maintaining a well-lit environment, with nightlights and a comfortable auditory environment (e.g., a radio tuned to a station with familiar, favorite music) to reduce troubling behavior, such as the tendency for people with advanced Alzheimer's disease to wander aimlessly or become agitated at night.

Even with these strategies, however, taking care of a person with Alzheimer's disease—which often results in losing your life partner before your very eyes—can be highly frustrating and challenging. Research indicates that male caregivers mainly adopt task-focused strategies (see Chapter 9), whereas female caregivers mainly adopt emotion-focused strategies, which result in more distress (Iavarone, Ziello, Pastore, Fasanaro, & Poderico, 2014). The patient factors associated with increased caregiver burden are severity of symptoms and functional status, whereas among caregivers, being the sole caregiver, poor mental health, and living with the patient result in higher psychological burdens (Conde-Sala et al., 2014).

Section Review

Alzheimer's disease accounts for 60–80% of the cases of major NCD. The exact cause of the disorder is not yet fully understood, but:

- the presence of amyloid plaques, which result from an abnormal derivative of amyloid precursor protein (APP) on chromosome 21, and the ε4 allele of apolipoprotein E (ApoE), produced by a gene on chromosome 19, have been linked to increased risk of Alzheimer's disease; and
- family history of Alzheimer's disease, a history of mild cognitive impairment, increased risk of cardiovascular disease, low levels of education, decreased social and cognitive engagement, and traumatic brain injury are other possible risk factors.

Alzheimer's disease cannot yet be cured or prevented, but:

- new medications that can temporarily reduce some of its symptoms are being developed,
- cognitive rehabilitation yields significant improvements in cognitive and functional abilities lasting for a number of months, and
- psychosocial interventions can help people with Alzheimer's disease and their caregivers cope better with many of the disease's inevitable impairments.

Major or Mild Neurocognitive Disorder Due to Traumatic Brain Injury

Significant attention has been directed toward the impact that traumatic brain injuries (TBIs) have on a person's life, particularly in cognitive functioning. Not only can such injuries increase risk for later NCDs, such as Alzheimer's disease, but they can also cause NCDs more immediately and directly. Major or mild NCD due to a TBI is the result of an impact to the head or displacement of the brain within the skull, as in blast injuries, sports injuries, or rapid momentum changes that occur in car crashes (Ropper & Gorson, 2007). In addition to evidence of a mechanism of injury, the presence of loss of consciousness, post-traumatic **amnesia** (loss of memory immediately following the event), reported disorientation and confusion, and neurologic evidence of an injury, such as positive findings on a neuroimaging exam, are common symptoms (American Psychiatric Association, 2013a). Interestingly, not all TBIs are evidenced on a neuroimaging exam, and therefore, a negative finding does not rule out the diagnosis. The severity of the brain injury can vary and is based on the length of the loss of consciousness, the length of the post-traumatic amnesia, and the level of disorientation and confusion, often rated using the Glascow Coma Scale (GCS) score (Teasdale & Jennett, 1974) by the medical provider

amnesia: Loss or impairment of memory.

TABLE 15.4 Scoring of the Glasgow Coma Scale to Rate Potential TBIs

	1	2	3	4	5	6
Eye	Does not open	Opens in response to pain	Opens in response to sound	Opens spontaneously		
Verbal	No verbalization	Incomprehensible sounds	Utters words	Confused, disoriented	Talks normally	
Motor	No movements	Extension to pain	Flexion to pain	Flexion/ withdrawal to pain	Localizes painful stimuli	Obeys physical commands

Note: A higher score indicates better orientation and therefore less impairment, with scores ranging from 3–15.
Source: Adapted from Teasdale & Jennett (1974).

administering care in the acute phase of the injury (see Table 15.4). Providers can then use the GCS at multiple time points after injury to track change in orientation over time.

The diagnosis of a TBI and the diagnosis of an NCD due to a TBI are not the same. A diagnosis of an NCD due to a TBI requires that the person also has to present with additional symptoms that meet the criteria for a mild or moderate NCD, with the etiology being the brain injury. The cognitive impairment has to present immediately following the TBI and persist past the acute postinjury period (American Psychiatric Association, 2013a). TBIs also increase the risk for later NCDs due to Alzheimer's or Parkinson's disease, which do not occur immediately following the injury but rather as a result of long-term brain changes.

Prevalence and Risk Factors for NCD Due to TBI

concussion: From the Latin *concutere* ("to shake violently"), concussion is the most common type of traumatic brain injury.

TBIs, which are also often referred to as **concussions**, are a major public health problem. Approximately 1.7 million TBIs are reported per year, which result in more than 1 million emergency room visits, 275,000 hospitalizations, and over 50,000 deaths (American Psychiatric Association, 2013a). The highest rate of TBI is in children younger than 4 years of age, older adolescents, and individuals over age 65. The cause of TBIs varies, with falls the most significant mechanism of injury, followed by motor vehicle crashes. Sports-related concussions are the most significant contributor in the younger population.

Whereas most people recover from a TBI, about 2% develop immediate NCDs. Repeated blows to the head, through contact sports or exposure to multiple blast injuries, may reduce the likelihood that the symptoms will subside, suggesting the potential for a cumulative effect with persistent NCD from multiple brain injuries (McAllister et al., 2012) that can result in neuropathological encephalopathy (abnormal brain function; Baugh et al., 2012) or other long-term NCDs.

Course of TBI

The most significant neurobehavioral symptoms typically are found immediately following a mild TBI, with gradual improvement in associated symptoms to complete resolution in 3 months (Rohling et al., 2011). Co-occurring symptoms include dizziness and even double vision. In moderate to severe injuries, there may be more persistent neurocognitive deficits that never resolve back to baseline, with associated mood, behavioral, and neurophysiological changes (Institute of Medicine, 2008). The course of the TBI also relates to the type of injury and whether it is localized, like in cases related to a penetrating injury. For example, a bullet wound to the brain may cause injury to a specific area of the brain where the bullet passed through. There are also more diffuse brain injuries, typically referred to as closed head injuries, where multiple areas of the brain are impacted due to

TABLE 15.5 Criteria for Severity Rating of TBI

Symptoms	Mild	Moderate	Severe
Loss of consciousness	< 30 minutes	Minutes to 24 hours	> 24 hours
Post-traumatic amnesia	< 24 hours	1–7 days	> 7 days
Glascow Coma Scale score (range from 0–15, with 15 = no disorientation or confusion)	13–15	9–12	3–8

Source: Based on American Psychiatric Association (2013a).

the crashing of the brain against the skull. Regardless, the sequence of recovery afterward is similar, from regaining of consciousness (particularly in the more severe cases) to an acute phase of disorientation and confusion (Goldstein, 2012). Table 15.5 lists the criteria for mild, moderate, and severe TBI.

Factors that can affect the course of an NCD due to TBI include older age, history of prior TBI, lower Glasgow Coma Scale (GCS) score, worse motor function, and significant anatomical injury as evidenced by computed tomography (Rohling et al., 2011). Also, as discussed in this chapter's "Controversy" feature, some people experience psychological symptoms after a TBI that result in depression (Kim et al., 2007) or post-traumatic stress disorder (PTSD; Bryant, 2011), which can help to maintain and may overlap with the symptoms of the NCD.

Postconcussion syndrome, which is a complex of symptoms that continue for weeks to up to a year, occurs in approximately 15% of those who experience a mild TBI (Mittenberg & Strauman, 2000). Although postconcussion syndrome is not represented in the *DSM-5*, it is a diagnosis in the worldwide *International Classification of Diseases (ICD-11)* system discussed in Chapter 1. This diagnosis may be made when symptoms resulting from the concussion last longer than 3 months. These symptoms vary and can include headaches, difficulty concentrating, dizziness, sleep problems, irritability, and lowered tolerance for noise and light (Bigler, 2008). When these symptoms include modest cognitive (in addition to physical) deficits, mild NCD can be diagnosed in the *DSM-5*. Otherwise, many clinicians diagnose "Unspecified Neurocognitive Disorder" in the *DSM-5* in these cases (Marisa Menchola, personal communication, December 2014), which applies to presentations in which there are symptoms characteristic of an NCD that cause clinically significant distress or impairment but do not meet the full criteria for any of the disorders in the NCD diagnostic class (American Psychiatric Association, 2013a). It is unclear why some people's symptoms resolve by 3 months after a mild TBI and why other people go on to develop postconcussion syndrome (King, 2003). However, research has found that pre-TBI medical or mental diagnoses, expectations of disability, being older, and being female increase the chances of developing postconcussion syndrome (Ryan & Warden, 2003). Although some experts believe that this syndrome is the result of structural changes in the brain from the injury, others believe that it is due to psychological distress, such as depression, anxiety, and PTSD (Bigler, 2008).

postconcussion syndrome: A set of symptoms that may continue for weeks, months, or a year or more after a concussion, a minor form of traumatic brain injury; also known as postconcussive syndrome or PCS.

Concussions and Sports

Particular attention is being paid to concussions in adolescent athletes, as their brains are still developing and are therefore vulnerable to persistent effects of any brain injuries. A large-scale epidemiological study examined the rates and patterns of concussions in high school athletes across 20 different sports (Marar, McIlvain, Fields, & Comstock, 2012), finding an overall injury rate of 2.5 per 10,000 athlete exposure events, with a higher rate during competition versus practice. The majority of concussions resulted from participation in football (47.1%), followed by girls' soccer (8.2%), boys' wrestling (5.8%),

Are Traumatic Brain Injury Symptoms and Psychological Distress Related?

Consider this scenario: An individual is brought to the hospital emergency department following a motor vehicle crash in which he sustained a traumatic brain injury (TBI). As the doctors are assessing the patient's physical injuries, they notice that he seems to be experiencing memory deficits and having difficulty paying attention to what is going on around him. The patient undergoes brain imaging to assess potential damage to his brain, and there are no abnormal findings. A few weeks after the incident, though, the patient is referred for neuropsychological testing because he is continuing to experience cognitive deficits. Test results indicate subtle deficits in several areas of cognitive functioning, including processing speed and attention. The patient also reports that he has been feeling extremely depressed since the car crash.

Is the patient's depression related to the TBI specifically? That is, is he experiencing depression *because* the crash disrupted the functioning of his brain? Or is the depression a co-occurring issue related to the fact that the patient experienced a trauma? Whether psychological distress is indicative of co-occurring symptoms or a syndromal sequela of TBI is debatable (Arciniegas & Wortzel, 2014; van Reekum, Cohen, & Wong, 2000), and clinicians are seeking to understand the relationship between TBIs and the psychological distress that often follows.

Major depressive disorder (see Chapter 6) and post-traumatic stress disorder (PTSD; see Chapter 9) are two mental disorders that commonly occur following an incident that also resulted in a TBI. In a study of 599 individuals who were hospitalized due to a TBI, Bombardier and colleagues (2010) found that 53.1% experienced major depressive disorder in the first year following their TBI. Another study found that 17% of participants exhibited moderate to severe depression 3–5 years after their TBI (Dikmen, Bombardier, Machamer, Fann, & Temkin, 2004), and psychological symptoms have been shown to persist up to 30 years post-injury (Koponen et al., 2002). Hoge and colleagues (2008) assessed rates of PTSD among veterans who incurred a TBI in combat. Among those who reported a loss of consciousness in the course of their TBI, 43.9% met criteria for PTSD. Moreover, after accounting for PTSD and depression, the other symptoms of the TBI (e.g., loss of consciousness) did not significantly predict most of the long-term health outcomes. These findings suggest that psychosocial functioning plays a substantial—perhaps even the key—role in recovery following a TBI.

The potential influence of premorbid psychological symptoms is often considered when attempting to better understand the relationship between TBI and post-trauma psychological distress. The presence of mental disorders prior to injury has consistently been associated with increased risk of psychological distress following a TBI (Dikmen et al., 2004; Whelan-Goodinson, Ponsford, Johnston, & Grant, 2009). However, such distress is not uncommon even among those with no previous history of psychological problems. Bombardier et al. (2010) found that rates of post-TBI major depressive disorder were higher among individuals with a previous history of depression; however, 41% of individuals with no history of depression also experienced major depressive disorder following their injury. Whelan-Goodinson et al. (2009) found that 72% of participants who developed depression following a TBI had no prior history of depression. Taken together, it appears that novel psychological symptoms are common following a TBI, and previous psychological symptoms may be exacerbated.

So why is it important whether or not psychological distress is distinct from TBI symptoms? Two primary reasons include: (1) it can impact the treatment plan for patients who have experienced a TBI, and (2) it can impact the approach to research regarding TBI. With regard to treatment, a great deal of focus is often placed on the person's medical recovery following a TBI, with the assumption that this alone will lead to amelioration of psychological symptoms. On the other hand, if psychological distress is considered distinct from the physical injury to the brain, psychological interventions are more likely to be employed, which could include treatment of both premorbid and post-injury psychological distress.

The second reason why this controversy is important regards how it informs research. With the large number of veterans returning from combat in Iraq and Afghanistan, much research is being conducted on the topic of TBI in this population, based on findings that one in four of these veterans has incurred head or neck injuries, including brain trauma (Hoge et al., 2008). Another burgeoning area of research is repetitive TBI, which commonly occurs in football players. Whereas many of the research studies focus specifically on psychological symptoms in the context of TBI, other research studies—in an effort to minimize potentially confounding effects—exclude individuals from study participation due to the presence of psychopathology. Although this may serve to simplify the interpretation

Are Traumatic Brain Injury Symptoms and Psychological Distress Related? *(Continued)*

of some findings, it may also limit the types of individuals who are included in the research and jeopardize the degree to which findings can be generalized to the larger population, in which comorbid psychological distress is the rule rather than the exception.

Thinking Critically

Consider the following questions regarding the relationship between TBIs and psychological distress:

1. What other information might help resolve this controversy? How would you design a research study related to TBIs to obtain this information?

2. Should researchers include or exclude participants with a significant psychiatric history as they continue to conduct research to identify markers of recovery and outcome following a TBI?

3. Should treatment recommendations following a TBI vary, based on whether or not the patient has a previous history of psychological distress, or should a psychological follow-up be recommended for all TBI patients?

and girls' basketball (5.5%). Football had the highest concussion rate per event (6.4), followed by boys' ice hockey (5.4) and boys' lacrosse (4.0). When sports that both boys and girls play were compared, girls had a higher concussion rate than boys, with the most common mechanism of injury being player-to-player contact. In a study of high school and NFL football players, neuropsychological testing showed a slower back-to-baseline recovery in the high school athletes compared to the NFL players, with the majority of NFL players showing complete recovery in 2 days (Pellman, Lovell, Viano, & Casson, 2006).

However, of particular concern in NFL athletes are the repeated concussions experienced and the cumulative neurologic impact of those injuries. The concern reached the level of the U.S. federal government when the House Judiciary Committee convened a session in 2010 regarding the evidence of permanent brain damage caused by repeated concussions and the impact this has on retired players. Research over the past decade has certainly brought about concentrated attention on the topic of brain injury in football players, which has led to more cautious monitoring and more time off prior to return to play.

Whereas athletes who play in contact sports like hockey and football are at an increased for a TBI, even noncontact sports like soccer and basketball pose a risk for brain injury, suggesting that safety precautions should be taken in all sports to protect developing brains. Four leading physicians with ties to the NFL (National Football League) recently requested improvement in how the league's concussion protocol is followed (Marvez, 2014). Jim McMahon, who led the Bears to the 1986 Super Bowl title, is among the retired players suing the NFL for damages resulting from concussion-related brain trauma.

TBI and the Military

In 2008, a groundbreaking study examined the occurrence and predictors of TBIs in army infantry soldiers returning from the war in Iraq (Hoge et al., 2008), as concerns about the long-term effects of blast-related TBIs were emerging (Warden, 2006). Of 2,525 soldiers studied, 124 (4.9%) reported TBIs with loss of consciousness, and 260 (10.3%) reported TBIs with altered mental status during their deployment. Of those reporting loss of consciousness, 43.9% met criteria for PTSD, as compared with 27.3% of those reporting altered mental status, 16.2% with other injuries, and 9.1% with no injury. Soldiers with a TBI reported significantly worse general health outcomes, more missed work, an increase in medical visits, and more somatic and postconcussion symptoms than soldiers with other injuries. However, when controlling for the effects of PTSD and depression on the health outcomes of these soldiers, the relationship between a TBI and physical health was no longer significant, suggesting that the effects' impairments were due to psychological distress, rather than to the TBI directly.

Prevention and Treatment

Unlike most neurological disorders and NCDs, head injuries are preventable. The Centers for Disease Control and Prevention (n.d.) has issued a safety statement regarding behaviors that can help to reduce the occurrence of a head injury for people of all ages. These behaviors include:

1. wearing a seatbelt;
2. properly restraining children in car seats;
3. wearing a helmet when riding a bike or horse, when skating, snowboarding, or skiing, when playing baseball or softball, and when playing contact sports;
4. keeping firearms and bullets properly stored and locked; and
5. avoiding falls by using step stools when reaching for items that are high up, installing and using handrails on stairways, installing window guards to prevent children from falling out of open windows, and using safety gates on stairs.

After a TBI has occurred, emergent medical attention is needed to stabilize an individual to prevent further injury. Depending upon the severity of the brain injury/damage, restoring oxygen supply to the brain, maintaining blood flow, and controlling blood pressure are the primary foci. For milder brain injuries, such as concussions that occur due to sports, players are taken out of play, evaluated by medical personnel, and not allowed to return to play until resolution of symptoms (e.g., as per the NFL's concussion protocol).

After the acute phase of a TBI, rehabilitation is an important part of the recovery process. Following proper acute medical care, and depending upon the severity of the injury, people may receive rehabilitation that incorporates physical therapy, occupational therapy, speech and language therapy, physical medicine, psychology/psychiatry, and social support. A neuropsychologist may perform repeated tests to assess functioning in the cognitive domains throughout treatment to document improvements and areas still in need of focused therapy. Many high school and collegiate programs are now requiring baseline neuropsychological testing prior to engagement in varsity sports, with assessment of athletes shortly after any concussions and then again weeks or months after the injury to document symptom course (Schatz, 2011). Time will tell whether the emerging emphasis on brain safety will reduce future NCDs, both those directly and indirectly related to TBIs.

Section Review

Neurocognitive disorders (NCDs) due to a traumatic brain injury (TBI):

- are the result of mechanisms of injury, such as falls, motor vehicle crashes, blasts due to explosions, and sports, and
- present with the most severe symptoms in the acute phase but with gradual improvement over time.

TBIs are a unique neurocognitive condition where prevention can make a considerable impact.

Treatment for an NCD due to a TBI:

- should incorporate a multidisciplinary approach to rehabilitation that is individualized, depending upon the symptom presentation and course, and
- involves repeating neuropsychological tests to monitor recovery.

Revisiting the Case of Dorothy

After Dorothy's initial bout of delirium, she was more formally assessed back at the hospital a few weeks later, where she was given neuropsychological testing, including a Wechsler Memory Scale–Revised, a verbal learning test, the *mini-mental state examination*, clock drawing tests, and a clinical dementia rating scale. The profile of Dorothy's results on these tests closely matched those of a typical patient with Alzheimer's disease, so she was given a diagnosis of probable NCD due to Alzheimer's disease. This news devastated Dorothy's daughter, confirming her worst fears, and made her feel extremely guilty for what she now felt was her mistreatment of her mother in the previous few months. The neuropsychologist who was part of the team evaluating Dorothy encouraged Dorothy's daughter to contact the local chapter of the Alzheimer's Association for information about the disease and about caregiver support groups.

After returning home from the hospital, Dorothy insisted that she was well enough to live on her own. She refused her daughter's offers to stay with her or to move to her daughter's home. Over the next 18 months, she was hospitalized three times; on one occasion, she sustained second-degree burns after leaning against her stove and catching her blouse on fire. After this incident, Dorothy's daughter insisted that she sell her house and come live with her.

At first, the arrangement worked reasonably well. Dorothy had her own apartment in the basement, so she was able to keep many of her personal possessions, and because one of her three teenaged grandchildren was usually home, she was seldom alone. She had begun taking tacrine (Cognex), which seemed to restore some of her memory and ability to concentrate, and she was able to help out around the house. Although she missed seeing some of her old friends, she was reasonably content. After about 2 years, however, things took a turn for the worse. Soon, she was more confused and forgetful than ever. She was shaky on her feet and increasingly irritable. Her grandchildren were less and less interested in staying home with her; in fact, Dorothy once overheard them tell their mother they "were sick and tired of having to look after Grandma all the time; besides, she just sits there and acts like she doesn't even know us."

Soon, Dorothy had to be lifted out of her bed or onto the toilet, and she spent more and more time just lying in bed. After Dorothy scalded her leg by absentmindedly pouring boiling water on herself, her daughter knew something had to be done. She felt guilty about the thought of moving her mother into an institution, but a couple of sessions with an Alzheimer's support group helped her make that decision. Luckily, the family could afford to keep Dorothy in a full-time nursing home. They had watched many other families spend all of their savings and even sell their homes to cover the nursing and housing costs required to support their sick, elderly parents.

Once in the nursing home, Dorothy seemed to deteriorate even more quickly. She lost her appetite and became incontinent; ultimately, she was unable to speak. During her final months, Dorothy did not appear to recognize any of her beloved family members. Her daughter continued to visit her each day, often leaving the nursing home in tears, heartbroken at how ill her mother had become. Dorothy finally died of pneumonia, 15 months after entering the nursing home.

Summary

Domains of Cognition

There are six domains of cognition that are the basis for neurocognitive disorders (NCDs). Complex attention, executive function, learning and memory, language, perceptual-motor, and social cognition deficits are the primary presenting problems of individuals diagnosed with NCDs. The presenting cognitive complaints of NCDs vary, depending on the etiology of the disorder and the severity of the condition.

Delirium

The primary feature of delirium is a disturbance in consciousness that often develops quickly and fluctuates throughout the day. People with delirium have trouble maintaining and shifting their attention, and they often also suffer perceptual distortions, memory problems, and disorientation. Delirium is most common in young and old people because both groups are more susceptible to the various illnesses, injuries, and physical conditions that are

A CONVERSATION WITH

Carson Smith

Carson Smith, PhD, is an associate professor in the Department of Kinesiology at the University of Maryland. His research is focused on understanding how exercise and physical activity affect human brain function and mental health. Dr. Smith investigates the effects of acute and chronic exercise on brain function, as measured using multimodal magnetic resonance imaging (MRI) and electroencephalography (EEG). Dr. Smith and his team are interested in the potential efficacy for exercise to affect brain function and memory in healthy older adults at genetic risk for Alzheimer's disease, people diagnosed with mild neurocognitive disorder, and those who are at increased risk for neurocognitive disorders due to metabolic disease and stroke.

Q *Could you describe your overall research agenda?*

A My overall research agenda is to describe how exercise and physical activity works within a person, its impacts on both brain structure and brain function. I am interested in brain function related to cognition and aging and the prevention of Alzheimer's disease. So I am interested in documenting how exercise not only effects cognitive outcomes that we would detect on a neuropsychological test, but how exercise is effecting brain systems and brain networks that are related to broader memory and cognitive functions. I am also interested in brain function related to emotion and how exercise may be protective against anxiety and depressive disorders.

Q *Are there certain types of physical activity that are better than others in terms of the impact on cognitive functioning?*

A I think that is an unanswered question. Certainly, there is some evidence that a combination of exercises is more effective than just one on its own. When you combine aerobic exercise with strength training, we tend to see larger effects. But those are only a few studies and mostly in healthy older adults, so we do not really know if the combination is better in all types of people. But it seems from animal research that you need to have cardiovascular benefit to stimulate neurogenic effects [i.e., brain cell growth] in the hippocampi.

Q *Is there any consensus on how much exercise is needed to see positive effects on cognition?*

A More than zero! Being physically active and doing something is better than nothing. We see this for many different types of clinical disorders. For instance, you are less likely to be depressed or anxious or have cognitive decline if you are engaging in minimal amounts of physical activity. It seems that exercise has a protective effect on a wide variety of mental disorders.

Q *Is there a particular age group that exercise seems to be most important for? Is there a particular time that you should jump into starting to do exercise, or is it something to be worried about your whole life?*

A That is a delicate question because we want people to be physically active through their whole life, and there are probably many benefits that accumulate over time. But we do know that even if you start being physically active when you are older, there are still many benefits that you can have from starting an exercise program. However, generating those habits is probably better done when you are younger; from a behavioral prospective, we want to see people adopting a lifestyle with physical activity earlier in their lives. We do not really know if exercise would be more protective, for example, for ApoE-ε4 carriers if they were to start exercising earlier in life versus later in life. But the research literature to date suggests that the effects of exercise on cognitive outcomes are greater in the age group of 60–75 years old. A single session of exercise, though, will affect all different age groups. So you could actually document some effects of a single session of exercise in younger adults. It is just that the training effects are not as easy to detect in these younger people because they have higher cognitive functioning overall.

Q *Where do you think that physical activity rates among all potential interventions for cognitive decline, such as medication and cognitive rehabilitation?*

A At the top, of course! It by far exceeds what medication or cognitive training can do. Cognitive training is specific, so you can train cognitively on a working

Carson Smith (Continued)

memory task, and you can be really good working memory tasks, but it does not transfer necessarily to other types of cognitive tests or domains, whereas exercise has much more generalizable benefits on cog-

nitive function. Beneficial effects do occur when you are learning a new language or learning something with doing a puzzle, for example, but physical exercise may be even more potent and generalized.

the most frequent causes of the disorder. In many cases, appropriate treatment of the underlying condition causing the delirium will bring about a complete recovery.

Major and Mild Neurocognitive Disorders

Major and mild NCDs refer to a loss of functioning in one or more of the cognitive domains, compared to a previous higher level of performance. The level of impairment determines the mild or major designation, with the degree interference in daily living being a large contributing factor. Many NCDs are progressive disorders for which no effective treatment or prevention is available.

There are multiple possible etiologies for NCDs. The most significant cause of cognitive decline is Alzheimer's disease. Additional causes include traumatic brain injury, substances/medications, HIV infection, vascular disease, Parkinson's disease, Huntington's disease, Lewy bodies, and frontotemporal dysregulation.

Neurocognitive Disorder Due to Alzheimer's Disease

The most frequent cause of NCDs, accounting for 60–80% of the cases, is Alzheimer's disease, a progressive disease of the brain. The specific cause of Alzheimer's disease is not yet known, but various genetic abnormalities appear to be involved (e.g., in chromosomes 19 and 21). Other factors that may contribute to the risk of developing Alz-

heimer's disease are a history of mild cognitive impairment, increased risk of cardiovascular disease, low levels of education, decreased social and cognitive engagement, and traumatic brain injury. Currently, there is no cure for Alzheimer's disease, although new medications and various psychosocial interventions, including exercise, can be useful in managing some of its symptoms and slowing the progression of the disease.

Major or Mild Neurocognitive Disorder Due to Traumatic Brain Injury

Concussion or traumatic brain injury (TBI) can lead to an NCD, particularly if an individual experiences repeated brain injuries, resulting in more-permanent impairment. TBIs occur most often due to falls, and then motor vehicle crashes, although sports- and military-related injuries have received more attention of late. Because TBIs are an external and modifiable event, there is much focus on primary prevention. The expected course of recovery is a gradual improvement in symptoms, although that can be complicated by psychological distress, possibly leading to postconcussion syndrome. Treatment for TBIs involves coordinated multidisciplinary efforts that include different medical specialties that focus on the individual symptom presentations.

Key Terms

Personality Disorders

Chapter Outline

Source: KenDrysdale/Shutterstock.com.

From the Case of Ted Bundy

Theodore Robert Bundy seemed destined to live a charmed life. He was intelligent, attractive, and polished. He had been a Boy Scout in his youth and later an honor student in psychology (yes!) at the University of Washington. He also served as a work-study student in a Seattle crisis clinic. One of Bundy's psychology professors wrote of him: "He conducts himself more like a young professional than a student. I would place him in the top 1% of the undergraduates with whom I have interacted" (Leyton, 1986).

Of course, this rosy biography omits the fact that Ted Bundy hunted down, raped, and killed young women for the sheer thrill of possessing and controlling them. It was early in January 1974 when Ted Bundy attacked his first victim: a young woman who Bundy maimed while she was asleep, leaving her with permanent brain damage. From 1974 through 1978, Bundy stalked, sexually assaulted, and killed 30 or more victims in Washington, Oregon, Utah, Colorado, and Florida. He used his good looks and charm as lures to trap his victims. Looking helpless and harmless—he would walk on crutches or wear a fake cast on his arm—Bundy would enlist the aid of a young woman, and after securing her trust, would choke her to death and mutilate and

After reading this chapter, you will be able to answer the following key questions:

- How do personality disorders differ from other mental disorders?
- What are the defining characteristics of the 10 personality disorders described in the *Diagnostic and Statistical Manual of Mental Disorders (DSM-5)*?
- What are the potential causes of personality disorders?
- How can personality disorders be treated?

Ted Bundy, one of the most notorious U.S. serial killers, was an extreme example of someone with an antisocial personality disorder. Some clinicians use the terms *psychopath* or *sociopath* to describe such people.

sexually abuse her body before disposing of it in a remote area. No one knows for sure how many women he killed because he never gave a complete confession.

Who was the real Ted Bundy? Were there early signs that he was capable of such carnage? Did Bundy have a mental disorder, and if so, what diagnosis should he have received? Beneath the superficial charm of Bundy's overt behavior lurked a far different person, one who was driven by a lust to dominate people and who was incapable of feeling guilt. In Bundy's own words, he was the "most cold-hearted son of a bitch you'll ever meet" who did not "feel guilt for anything" and felt "sorry for people who feel guilt" (Jeffers, 1991).

Bundy's quest for domination may have begun with his shame for having been the son of his 22-year-old mother and a sailor with whom she had had a brief sexual encounter. Bundy was born in 1946 in the Elizabeth Lund Home for Unwed Mothers in Burlington, Vermont. From an early age, he was embarrassed by his illegitimacy and his family's poverty. He told people how humiliated he was to be seen riding in his stepfather's run-down car. As a juvenile, he constantly sought to create an impression of being a sophisticated and successful member of the upper class who deserved admiration. He went to great lengths to further this impression, even wearing fake mustaches and makeup to change his appearance. He stole cars in high school to maintain his image and occasionally affected an English accent. He sought out women whose physical appearance satisfied his craving for escaping what he called his "common" origins. He was never interested in an emotionally close relationship with these women; his main desire was to be seen with them and to have other people admire him for being with an attractive woman.

Despite the time he spent creating the right impression, Bundy was not popular in high school, and he knew it. He told interviewers, "In junior high, everything was fine, but I got to high school and I didn't make any progress. I felt alienated from my old friends. They just seemed to move on and I didn't. . . . I wasn't sure what was wrong and what was right. All I knew was that I felt a bit different" (Leyton, 1986). As time passed, Bundy's snobbery and social pretensions grew insatiable. He wanted to possess certain women to gratify his need for power and control. His preferred victims were upper-class sorority women who became, in their final hours, Bundy's ultimate possessions, mere objects with whom he could do whatever he wished.

After two escapes and a third capture, Bundy was tried for the murder of two sorority sisters at the University of Florida. Apparently convinced of his brilliance and legal acumen obtained while attending two different law schools, Bundy served as his own attorney in the trial. Like many people with antisocial personalities, Bundy overestimated his skills; he was convicted of the sorority sisters' murders and the kidnapping, murder, and mutilation of a 12-year-old Florida girl. Ted Bundy died in the electric chair at Raiford Prison in Starke, Florida, on January 24, 1989.

personality: The unique pattern of consistency in behavior that distinguishes each person from every other person.

If we were proposing a moral taxonomy of behavior, we would no doubt reserve a particularly ignominious corner for Ted Bundy. But in a formal classification of mental disorders, where should he be placed? Bundy did not hear voices or see visions, he was not out of touch with reality, he did not experience any pronounced physical problems, and he did not suffer attacks of anxiety or bouts of depression. Instead, Ted Bundy's problems seemed to be part and parcel of his **personality**, that unique pattern of consistency in behavior that distinguishes each person from every other. The way we interact with friends and family, the attitudes we hold toward work and school, and the approach we use to solve life's problems all reveal our unique constellation of traits that we call our personalities. Bundy represented an extreme example of what is called *antisocial personality disorder*, one of ten patterns that the *DSM-5* identifies as personality disorders.

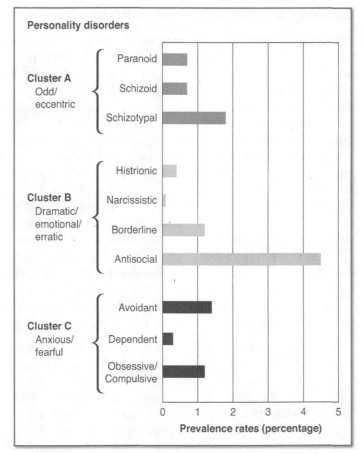

Personality disorders

Cluster A
Odd/
eccentric
- Paranoid
- Schizoid
- Schizotypal

Cluster B
Dramatic/
emotional/
erratic
- Histrionic
- Narcissistic
- Borderline
- Antisocial

Cluster C
Anxious/
fearful
- Avoidant
- Dependent
- Obsessive/
Compulsive

0 1 2 3 4 5
Prevalence rates (percentage)

FIGURE 16.1
Overview of Personality Disorders and Their Prevalence

The *DSM-5* describes 10 main personality disorders, organized into three clusters. Because of the nature of personality disorders, it is difficult to determine their prevalence accurately. Shown here are conservative estimates of personality disorders in a large community sample in the United States.
Source: Based on Samuels et al. (2002).

A **personality disorder** is an enduring pattern of inner experience and behavior that is extremely inflexible, pervasive across contexts, and stable across time; deviates markedly from the expectations of a person's culture; and causes significant distress or impairment in work, social, or other important areas. These problematic patterns can be traced back at least to adolescence or early adulthood, and in some cases, even to childhood. People diagnosed with personality disorders have some consistently distorted ways of thinking, expressing emotions, controlling behavior, or interacting with others that impair their adjustment to everyday demands and often lead to misery for others and/or themselves. People who have antisocial personalities such as Bundy's can maintain a facade of coolness and charm, but behind it lies a long-standing core of aggressiveness and deceit with no regard or empathy for the rights of others.

In this chapter, we describe the clinical characteristics of each of the 10 personality disorders included in the *DSM-5*. As shown in Figure 16.1, the *DSM-5* groups the 10 personality disorders into three clusters, based on similarities of their characteristics: (1) odd/eccentric, (2) dramatic/emotional/erratic, and (3) anxious/fearful. We also examine what is known about the causes of personality disorders and their treatments. First, though, we take a closer look at the concept of personality disorder and why these disorders may be particularly difficult to diagnose and treat.

personality disorder: An enduring pattern of inner experience and behavior that is inflexible, pervasive, and stable; deviates markedly from the expectations of a person's culture; and causes significant distress or impairment.

Fateful Patterns: An Overview of Personality Disorders

French novelist Andre Malreaux's observation that "character is fate" provides a superb shorthand description of personality disorders. A personality disorder comes to define a person's fate; it is a streak of vulnerability that affects almost all of a person's endeavors. People with personality disorders appear "stuck" in their problems; their behavior is so inflexible and persistent that they never seem able to change to a new approach, even when it is obvious that their old strategies are not working.

Defining Characteristics and Prevalence of Personality Disorders

Personality disorders differ in several important ways from other psychological problems. Everyone knows someone whose personality seems odd, but personality disorders involve more than eccentricity. For a personality disorder to be diagnosed, an individual's personality traits must be maladaptive. A **personality trait** is a psychological attribute that is relatively stable over time and across different situations. Personality traits distinguish one person's typical behavior from that of others. For example, people who show a high degree of the trait of extroversion tend to be outgoing, energetic individuals who feel comfortable in many different social situations and seem to make friends easily. Almost any trait, when it becomes too rigid and extreme, can cause problems for an individual and for society. For example, extroverted people can be too extroverted, becoming annoying pests who talk too much or fail to respect other people's privacy (like your college roommate). Accordingly, the *DSM-5* defines a personality disorder in terms of personality traits that are "inflexible and maladaptive and [that] cause significant functional impairment or subjective distress" (American Psychiatric Association, 2013a, p. 647). These disorders are characterized by the three Ps: they are persistent (long lasting), pervasive (present in multiple areas of one's life), *and* pathological (dysfunctional or maladaptive).

The long-term, ingrained patterns of behavior seen in personality disorders are related to four other important features of these disorders:

personality trait: A psychological attribute that is relatively stable for an individual over time and across different situations.

1. People with personality disorders often do not see themselves as troubled, let alone as suffering from a mental disorder. Thus, personality disorders are sometimes said to be **ego-syntonic**, meaning that those who display them tend to experience them not as aberrations but as natural parts of themselves. The extreme traits associated with the disorder just feel like part of the person's basic personality structure. Indeed, many people with personality disorders think that their only problem is that other people mistreat or misunderstand them. However, not all personality disorders are ego-syntonic; in some cases, individuals are aware that extreme traits are causing them trouble and feel a desperate need to gain better control of their behavior.

ego-syntonic: Experiences that seem to be a natural part of the self.

2. Personality disorders may be difficult to treat. Part of this difficulty stems from the fact that clients who believe that their problems are due to the actions of others are usually reluctant to seek or cooperate in treatment in the first place.

3. Personality disorders are often more distressing for others than for the person displaying them. Many mental disorders tax the resources and patience of friends and relatives, but personality disorders can be particularly troubling to others. As the case of Ted Bundy illustrates, a severe personality disorder can leave a trail of disaster in its wake.

4. Personality disorders often appear in combination with other mental disorders, particularly anxiety disorders, depressive and bipolar disorders, substance use disorders, and other personality disorders. This is especially true for individuals diagnosed with Cluster B personality disorders. For example, Lenzenweger and colleagues (2007) found that 70% of individuals diagnosed with antisocial personality disorder also experienced another mental disorder. For those diagnosed with borderline personality disorder, nearly 85% met diagnostic criteria for at least one other mental disorder. Because of this comorbidity, it is often difficult to determine whether a client truly suffers two or more distinct disorders, or whether the problems attributed to a mental disorder such as depression or a substance use disorder are actually the result of a pervasive personality disorder.

The definition of a personality disorder also implies several things about its course. Just as personality traits begin to stabilize by young adulthood, personality disorders are also usually apparent by that time. By definition, then, the onset of personality disorders occurs no later than young adulthood. However, these disorders often do not come to a clinician's attention until years later, after a series of difficulties have forced clients into treatment or after they have become motivated to change a life of constant emotional turmoil. Also, by definition, personality disorders are relatively stable through the years, although certain disorders tend to diminish in severity after the age of 40.

The prevalence of personality disorders in the United States is difficult to estimate, in part because many people with these disorders refuse to acknowledge their problems and avoid contact with clinicians. Nonetheless, a large-scale epidemiological survey suggests that approximately 9% of the U.S. population meet criteria for a personality disorder, with personality disorders in Clusters A and C more commonly diagnosed (Lenzenweger et al., 2007). These disorders are even more common in psychiatric clinics, accounting for almost a third of all cases (Zimmerman, Rothschild, & Chelminski, 2005).

The picture regarding gender differences is complicated. Most of the personality disorders—paranoid, narcissistic, and antisocial personality disorders being the most obvious examples—are diagnosed more often in men than in women. Conversely, border-line personality disorder is the prime example of a personality disorder that is diagnosed about three times more often in women than in men. A few disorders, such as avoidant personality disorder and dependent personality disorder, seem to affect men and women about equally.

Scientists still know very little about cultural differences in the prevalence of personality disorders. The approximate 3–4% rate of antisocial personality disorder holds true for Canada and New Zealand, but in Taiwan, the prevalence is believed to be less than 0.5%. Western European countries report a prevalence rate for all personality disorders combined that is similar to that of the United States. However, the picture is much less clear in non-European nations, where until recently, clinicians have been less likely than their Western colleagues to diagnose certain types of personality disorders.

Diagnosing Personality Disorders

Table 16.1 lists the criteria for diagnosing a personality disorder. Reliable diagnosis of these disorders is complicated by several factors, including their comorbidity with other mental disorders.

Personality Disorders and Comorbidity with Other Mental Disorders

Comorbidity between personality disorders and other mental disorders can be understood in several ways. First, a personality disorder and another mental disorder may simply coexist at the same time. When they do, one disorder is likely to aggravate the other. For example, the general suspiciousness of paranoid personality disorder may cause people to mistrust and shun treatment that is necessary for managing their accompanying bipolar disorder. A depressive disorder may lead people with dependent personality disorder to feel even more desperate for someone else's guidance.

It is also possible that one of the disorders predisposes a person to develop the other. For example, the emotional instability that is a hallmark of borderline personality disorder may cause people to react more intensely to life stressors, ultimately leading to a major depressive disorder. In other cases, another mental disorder may lead to a personality disorder. A childhood depressive disorder may undermine a child's confidence about

TABLE 16.1 The *DSM-5* in Simple Language: Defining a Personality Disorder

A persistent, pervasive, and pathological pattern that reveals itself in at least two of the following areas:

1. Thinking (e.g., the way you perceive yourself or others)
2. Emotions (e.g., the way you react to others)
3. Behavior:
   a. The way you treat others
   b. Your ability to control your impulses around others

Source: Adapted from American Psychiatric Association (2013a).

making new friends or mastering new challenges. As a result, the child may avoid social situations, thereby setting the stage for an avoidant personality disorder.

Yet another interpretation of comorbidity is that it is an artifact of the criteria used for various diagnoses. Because the diagnostic criteria for several mental disorders overlap, two diagnoses may be given when only one disorder is present. For example:

- Comorbidity may simply be the result of definitional similarity. Borderline personality disorder shares criteria with depressive and bipolar disorders; the symptoms of antisocial personality disorder and substance use disorders are similar; and avoidant personality disorder and social anxiety disorder have similar definitions. It is therefore not surprising to find these pairs of disorders often diagnosed together.

- A personality disorder and another mental disorder may represent different levels of severity along the same basic dimensions of disturbance. For example, some clinicians believe that schizotypal personality disorder may be a mild form of schizophrenia and that borderline personality disorder is an early or alternative manifestation of bipolar or cyclothymic disorder. The *DSM-5* acknowledges these issues by occasionally listing personality disorders in two places. Schizotypal personality disorder is listed in both the *Personality Disorders* and *Schizophrenia Spectrum and Other Psychotic Disorders* chapters, and antisocial personality disorder is listed in both the *Personality Disorders* and the *Disruptive, Impulse-Control, and Conduct Disorders* chapters in the *DSM*.

Connections

Is comorbidity also high for any other mental disorders? Consider comorbidity for depressive disorders in Chapter 6 and anxiety disorders in Chapter 7.

Other Diagnostic Difficulties

At least three other problems make reliable diagnosis of personality disorders difficult. First, the criteria used to define different personality disorders often overlap considerably. As a result, the same behavioral characteristics may be associated with several personality disorders. For example, impulsive behavior is symptomatic of both borderline personality disorder and antisocial personality disorder. Distress or impairment due to a lack of close friends and confidants is associated with schizoid, schizotypal, and avoidant personality disorders. This overlap of symptoms may account for high rates of comorbidity among personality disorders themselves. Torgersen and colleagues (2001) found that among individuals with personality disorders, 29% met criteria for two or more personality disorders. As an example, despotic former world leaders Adolph Hitler, Saddam Hussein, and Kim Jong-il all met criteria for at least three personality disorders—paranoid, antisocial, and narcissistic—along with schizoid in Jong-il's case (Coolidge & Segal, 2007).

A second obstacle to reliable diagnosis of personality disorders is that, by definition, they refer to long-standing behavior patterns, rather than acute or current symptoms. This definition requires that the clinician assess a person's adolescence or childhood to determine whether the individual has been, for example, chronically mistrustful of people (in the case of paranoid personality disorder) or always aloof and emotionally cold (in the case of schizoid personality disorder). Yet, an accurate social history of a person's styles of interaction as a child or adolescent may be difficult to obtain. Memory of distant events can be faulty and are sometimes distorted by clients who put their own "spin" on the past. Such distortions might be particularly likely in the case of personality disorders because of their long-standing nature and their tendency to affect many aspects of behavior, emotion, and thinking simultaneously.

Finally, the problems associated with the *DSM-5*'s categorical approach to classification are particularly obvious in the case of personality disorders. As noted in Chapter 1, the *DSM-5* directs the clinician to assign a diagnosis if a client meets a particular number out of a fixed set of criteria. For example, if five out of the nine criteria for narcissistic personality disorder are met, the diagnosis is made. But there is little or no evidence to support a particular cutoff (such as five of nine instead of six of nine criteria) as being the "true" boundary between normal and abnormal personality (Samuel & Widiger, 2006; Widiger & Trull, 1991). Furthermore, if the rule requires that five of nine criteria be met, two peo-

"He is the world's foremost expert on himself."

Source: Cartoonresource/Shutterstock.com.

ple could be diagnosed as displaying narcissistic personality disorder even though they share only one defining feature. Other people who share four defining features might not be diagnosed because they do not display a fifth criterion.

Future Directions: The *DSM-5*'s Alternative Model for Diagnosing Personality Disorders

For decades, the difficulties in diagnosing personality disorders have encouraged the development of alternative dimensional approaches (Cloninger, 1987; Costa & Widiger, 1994; Watson, Clark, & Harkness, 1994; Widiger & Costa, 1994; Widiger, Livesley, & Clark, 2009; Widiger & Trull, 2007; Wiggins & Pincus, 1989). Recall from Chapter 1 that a *dimensional* approach involves describing individuals along various dimensions or traits of personality. Despite a strong push for a dimensional understanding of personality disorders, the categorical approach to diagnosis remains unchanged in the *DSM-5*. However, in the appendix of the *DSM-5*, the American Psychiatric Association introduces an alternative model that "aims to address numerous shortcomings of the current approach to personality disorders" (American Psychiatric Association, 2013a, p. 761). Future research using the new model will determine whether the categorical approach will be replaced in upcoming editions of the *DSM*.

The new model is presented as a hybrid dimensional-categorical model. Individuals are first assessed on their level of impairment in personality functioning in two realms—self (identity and self-direction) and interpersonal (capacity for empathy and intimacy)—with a range from 0 (little to no impairment) to 4 (extreme impairment). Individuals who score 2 or higher (i.e., at least a moderate level of impairment) in two or more of these four areas of personality functioning would subsequently be assessed for a diagnosis of a personality disorder. The clinician then identifies the presence of core, pathological personality traits that further differentiate the personality disorders. These traits include the five broad trait domains of negative affectivity, detachment, antagonism, disinhibition, and psychoticism. Within these five broad traits, twenty-five trait facets or subtraits are identified to show the nuances among the personality disorders. Are you following? Early concerns are that the new model is too complex for use in clinical practice (American Psychiatric Association, 2013b).

Section Review

Unlike most mental disorders, personality disorders:

- do not involve discrete periods of specific clinical symptoms,
- do not come and go or vary widely in intensity,
- are often ego-syntonic (feel normal and natural to the person), and
- are often more distressing for others than for the person displaying them.

Because they involve stable, long-lasting patterns of maladaptive behavior, personality disorders:

- are often diagnosed along with other mental disorders and
- are in many cases difficult to treat.

Concerns about the reliable diagnosis of personality disorders include:

- high rates of comorbidity among the personality disorders,
- the need to establish a long-standing pattern of dysfunction, and
- use of a categorical instead of a more dimensional assessment approach.

Types of Personality Disorders

While the American Psychiatric Association's hybrid dimensional-categorical model is being studied, clinicians will continue to use categorical diagnoses to identify individuals with personality disorders. Consequently, in this text, the descriptions of personality disorders are organized around the current *DSM-5* categories. However, even this organization implies something of a dimensional approach because the disorders are clustered to emphasize particular personality attributes: odd/eccentric, dramatic/emotional/erratic, and anxious/fearful. Further, it is likely that many of the following diagnoses will only be of historical significance in the future, as borderline and antisocial personality disorders are the only two with strong empirical foundations (Paris, 2013).

We all know people who have unusual or even "difficult" personalities. Having such a personality does not mean that one has a personality disorder. As with other disorders, a person must experience significant distress or impairment in functioning to fulfill the diagnostic criteria. As the proverb says, "It takes all kinds to make the world go round." With that in mind, though, it may be helpful to think about someone you know who meets at least some of the criteria for each specific personality disorder discussed in the next sections, as it will help you to learn and remember the clinical descriptions better.

MAPS - Prejudicial Pigeonholes

Cluster A: Odd/Eccentric Personality Disorders

In the *DSM-5*, Cluster A describes personality disorders marked by *oddness or eccentricity*. These include paranoid, schizoid, and schizotypal personality disorders. Table 16.2 describes the primary characteristics of these disorders.

Paranoid Personality Disorder

paranoid personality disorder: A personality disorder characterized by habitual suspicion, mistrust, irritability, and hostility.

People with **paranoid personality disorder** are habitually suspicious, constantly on guard, and mistrustful. They assume that others will take advantage of or harm them unless carefully watched and prevented from doing so. They are prone to anger and intense jealousy, and they tend to misinterpret innocent actions or remarks as threats or insults directed at them. Often, these attitudes are accompanied by an air of moral superiority and condescension based on a strong belief that other people are usually corrupt or conniving.

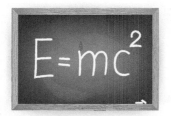

MAPS - Attempted Answers

As a result of their chronic irritability and thinly disguised hostility, individuals with paranoid personality disorder succeed at creating exactly the kind of social interactions that confirm their most dire predictions about others. They are drawn toward litigation and other official proceedings as a way of settling their grievances and evening the score over perceived slights. People with paranoid personality disorder tend to burn their bridges before they get to them. They appear to dislike other people and seem incapable of intimacy. People with paranoid personalities have loner tendencies, coupled with their chip-on-the-shoulder attitudes, which lead others to avoid them, a response that only heightens their paranoid suspicions.

The features of paranoid personality disorder are illustrated by Bill A., a 45-year-old auto mechanic who worked in a large car dealership:

> For the first 2 years on the job, Bill performed well, according to his supervisor. But in the next few months, his work and his relationships with coworkers deteriorated. These problems started when Bill accused a fellow mechanic of sabotaging his work by putting grease on his tools. Bill insisted that the coworker was jealous because Bill was a better mechanic. Bill believes that the other mechanic, whom he calls a "management mole," has turned everyone in the agency against him, and he has asked the police to investigate the telephoned death threats he claims to have received, as well as the flat tires that he is convinced have been caused by nails that coworkers have put under his car.

TABLE 16.2 Cluster A: The Odd/Eccentric Personality Disorders in the *DSM-5*

Primary characteristics:

- Paranoid: Suspicious, chronically hostile, envious, or tense
- Schizoid: Isolated from others, with a lack of emotional expression
- Schizotypal: Odd mannerisms, appearances, and experiences; pervasively detached from others

Because of the secretiveness and isolation of persons with paranoid personality disorder, accurate assessment of its prevalence is difficult, but this disorder is estimated to occur in 1–4% of the general U.S. population (American Psychiatric Association, 2013a; Samuels et al., 2002). Its effects are most often observed in occupational settings, where, as with Bill A., it leads to frequent conflicts with superiors and coworkers. This disorder is diagnosed more often in men than in women, and there is some evidence of increased prevalence of paranoid personality disorder among individuals who have relatives diagnosed with schizophrenia (American Psychiatric Association, 2013a).

Schizoid Personality Disorder

The hallmarks of **schizoid personality disorder** are an indifference to social relationships and a pervasive emotional blandness. People with this disorder usually lack close friends, and they appear to take no pleasure from positive events and to feel no unhappiness after setbacks. It is as though emotional color has been bleached from their lives. As a result, they lack social skills and seem to be lethargic and aloof.

Individuals with schizoid personality disorder prefer solitary activities and occupations. The work of nighttime security guard or lighthouse keeper would be ideally suited to them, although their interpersonal apathy and lack of initiative make it less likely that they would succeed at any job. They prefer mechanical or abstract activities, such as computer or mathematical games, over those that involve working with other people. Although they may passively accept sexual attention from others, they are typically indifferent to potential romances or friendships. They are unlikely to date and often do not marry.

Diagnosed slightly more often among males, the overall prevalence of schizoid personality disorder is estimated to be 1–5% (American Psychiatric Association, 2013a; Samuels et al., 2002). It is rarely seen in formal clinical treatment settings. Like paranoid personality disorder, schizoid personality disorder may also be more prevalent among relatives of people with schizophrenia or schizotypal personality disorder.

schizoid personality disorder: A personality disorder characterized by extreme indifference to social relationships and a pervasive emotional blandness.

Schizotypal Personality Disorder

People with **schizotypal personality disorder** are like those with schizoid personality disorder in that they, too, are socially isolated and tend to shun close relationships. However, people with schizotypal personalities are more noticeable because they tend to act, dress, and/or talk in odd ways. In addition, unlike those with schizoid personality disorder, people with schizotypal personality disorder are usually socially anxious and apprehensive. This anxiety appears to be tied to general self-consciousness and discomfort with others that does not diminish with further acquaintance. The person with schizotypal personality disorder often appears quirky and reacts stiffly in social situations. People with this disorder seldom have close friends outside their own families, and other people tend to see them as silly and absurd. Such social isolation may explain why 30–50% of individuals with schizotypal personality disorder seen in clinical settings also have a diagnosis of major depressive disorder (American Psychiatric Association, 2013a).

The odd thinking and speech associated with schizotypal personality disorder is not so eccentric as to qualify as psychotic, but it is certainly unusual enough to draw attention and sometimes frighten other people. Individuals with schizotypal personality disorder frequently express superstitions and beliefs in telepathy or clairvoyance. *Ideas of reference*, which involve the belief that one is being monitored or talked about by others, are prominent, as are associated feelings of paranoia and suspiciousness. People with this disorder also often report bizarre perceptual experiences, such as holding conversations with dead relatives or believing that spirits or nonexistent people are inhabiting a room. They may sometimes talk to themselves or others in vague, confusing, or tangential ways, but their speech is seldom incoherent, as is often the case with schizophrenia.

The prevalence of schizotypal personality disorder ranges from 2–5% and may be slightly more common among males (American Psychiatric Association, 2013a; Samuels et al., 2002). Reliable diagnosis of this personality disorder has proved challenging, in part because of its substantial overlap in symptoms with schizoid, paranoid, avoidant,

schizotypal personality disorder: A personality disorder characterized by odd ways of talking, thinking, acting, and dressing, as well as social isolation and a lack of close relationships.

Connections

How much evidence is there for a genetic basis for schizophrenia and the conditions that are part of the schizophrenia spectrum? For answers, see Chapter 4.

An example of someone who may meet criteria for schizotypal personality disorder is the quirky and odd character of Cosmo Kramer, played by Michael Richards (shown here) on the well-known TV sitcom *Seinfeld* (1989–1998). Another is beloved character Luna Lovegood from the *Harry Potter* series: "The girl gave off an aura of distinct dottiness. Perhaps it was the fact that she had stuck her wand behind her left ear for safekeeping, or that she had chosen to wear a necklace of Butterbeer caps, or that she was reading a magazine upside down" (from *Harry Potter and the Order of the Phoenix* by J. K. Rowling, 2004).

histrionic personality disorder: A personality disorder characterized by extreme attention-seeking behaviors, flamboyance, and suggestibility.

and borderline personality disorders. As noted earlier in the chapter, schizotypal personality disorder is also listed in the *Schizophrenia Spectrum and Other Psychotic Disorders* chapter of the *DSM-5*. This personality disorder has often been viewed as a mild form of schizophrenia or as part of the schizophrenia spectrum. It is more common among first-degree relatives of individuals with schizophrenia.

Cluster B: Dramatic/Emotional/Erratic Personality Disorders

The *dramatic/emotional/erratic* personality disorders include histrionic, narcissistic, borderline, and antisocial personality disorders. Table 16.3 summarizes the clinical descriptions of these disorders, which tend to be typified by active, sometimes uncontrolled, behaviors. This cluster contains the two personality disorders that have received the most attention from researchers and are the most useful in clinical practice: antisocial and borderline personality disorders.

Histrionic Personality Disorder

The major features of **histrionic personality disorder** are a set of attention-seeking behaviors that include seductiveness, exaggerated displays of emotions, and demands for reassurance and praise. Individuals with this disorder love to be the center of attention and frequently use physical attractiveness or flamboyant emotionality to get there. They describe events with hyperbolic speech that sounds empty in spite of its hyperbole; phrases such as "unbelievably unique," "incredibly beautiful," and "horribly awful" characterize their speech. All of their actions, even their manner of dress, are designed to make others notice them.

These strategies may at first strike others as creative, entertaining, or even charming, but tend, in most cultures, to wear thin over time, revealing shallow exhibitions driven by self-centered needs. As the charm wears off and people grow weary of paying constant attention and tribute, histrionic individuals must seek new audiences. When their social charm or physical attractiveness fails to gain the stimulation that these people crave, they may develop attention-getting physical complaints.

The interpersonal style of those with histrionic personality disorder has been described as actively dependent: "Their clever and often artful social behaviors give the appearance of an inner confidence and independent self-assurance; beneath this guise, however, lies a fear of genuine autonomy and a need for repeated signs of acceptance and approval" (Millon, 1990, p. 121). People with histrionic personality disorder are easily bored and susceptible to group pressures and to joining in fads (Atkins diet, anyone?). They are also suggestible and therefore drawn to strong authority figures whose admiration they especially desire.

Histrionic personality disorder is estimated to occur in 0.6–1.8% of the U.S. population (American Psychiatric Association, 2013a; Samuels et al., 2002), and it has been diagnosed more often in females than in males. The reasons for this gender difference remain unclear. It may reflect: (1) general trends of women coming into contact with mental health professionals more frequently than men; (2) cultural influences that lead females,

TABLE 16.3 Cluster B: The Dramatic/Emotional/Erratic Personality Disorders in the *DSM-5*

> Primary characteristics:
> - Histrionic: Shallow; always seeking attention; exaggerated emotions; seductive
> - Narcissistic: Inflated self-esteem; low empathy for others; feels entitled to special privileges
> - Borderline: Unstable moods; impulsive behaviors; angry; lack of a coherent sense of self; interpersonal turmoil
> - Antisocial: Constantly violating rights of others; callous, manipulative, dishonest; does not feel guilt

especially, to believe that attention for physical beauty is important; or (3) diagnostic biases described in Chapter 1. In a study by Maureen Ford and Tom Widiger (1989), clinicians were asked to diagnose fictitious cases. One case involved a typical description of antisocial personality disorder for which the person was said to be either a man or a woman; the other described a histrionic personality disorder, again presented as either a man or woman. The results showed that clinicians were more likely to diagnose a female with histrionic personality disorder even when she met the criteria for antisocial personality disorder. Likewise, histrionic behavior attributed to a female increased clinicians' use of the histrionic diagnosis.

MAPS - Prejudicial Pigeonholes

Researchers' interest in histrionic personality disorder appears to have declined; it may be diagnosed less frequently in the future, since it overlaps considerably with other personality disorders in the dramatic/emotional/erratic cluster. Due to a lack of empirical evidence, some researchers have argued that histrionic personality disorder should be removed from the *DSM* altogether (Paris, 2013; Skodol et al., 2011). It is notable that histrionic personality disorder is not featured in the appendix of the *DSM-5* during the presentation of the hybrid dimensional-categorical model, suggesting that this disorder may not appear in future *DSM*s.

Narcissistic Personality Disorder

Christina Aguilera addresses the concept of narcissism in her 2010 song, *Vanity*: "Every day I see myself, I love me even more." The term *narcissism* derives from the Greek myth of Narcissus, who was so enthralled with his reflection in a pool that he died of protracted longing after his own beauty. The main feature of **narcissistic personality disorder** is an overinflated sense of importance and worth, leading to a sense of entitlement to special privileges and to exemptions from the rules that apply to others. Individuals with this disorder entertain grandiose ideas about their abilities and importance, and they are prone to feelings of rage or humiliation if others overlook or criticize them. Indeed, they sometimes behave irresponsibly because they do not feel that normal social constraints should apply to them; at such times, their behavior may turn antisocial. Jack Nicholson's character in the 1997 film *As Good As It Gets*—misanthropic writer Melvin Udall—displayed many aspects of narcissistic personality disorder.

narcissistic personality disorder: A personality disorder characterized by an overinflated sense of self-importance and worth that leads to a sense of entitlement to special privileges and exemptions from the rules that apply to others.

As in histrionic personality disorder, those diagnosed with narcissistic personality disorder crave attention and feature themselves as stars in fantasies of success and power. Preoccupied with their own status, they lack empathy for others and exploit social relationships for their own gain. They are frequently envious or believe that others envy them. If criticized or reprimanded, their arrogance often turns to hostility and even abuse. Unable to admit weaknesses or to appreciate the effect their behavior has on others, people with narcissistic personality disorder are often poor candidates for psychotherapy.

MAPS - Superficial Syndromes
(a) Individuals with narcissistic personality disorder are sometimes preoccupied with fantasies of brilliance, power, or beauty and require excessive admiration from others (and themselves). (b) This saguaro cactus is also narcissistically admiring its own reflection.

(a)

(b)

Is our society becoming more narcissistic? Do Facebook and Twitter engender an excessive focus on the self? What does it mean that the word *selfie* is now in our popular lexicon?

borderline personality disorder: A personality disorder characterized by impulsivity and instability in several areas of functioning, including mood, behavior, self-image, and interpersonal relationships.

The prevalence of narcissistic personality disorder is not clearly established, but estimates range from 0.1–6.2% of community samples (American Psychiatric Association, 2013a; Samuels et al., 2002). This disorder appears to have grown more common over the past decade or so. It is unclear whether the increased incidence represents a genuine upswing in new cases or simply greater clinical interest in and attention to the disorder. Males are diagnosed with narcissistic personality disorder slightly more often than females.

Borderline Personality Disorder

Because it is a disorder that involves potentially destructive behavior, clinicians and researchers have studied borderline personality disorder extensively. In fact, it is the most commonly researched and treated personality disorder.

The clinical term *borderline* has carried different meanings over the years. Historically, some clinicians used the term to capture the similarity between borderline personality disorder and brief or mild schizophrenic symptoms, thus describing a person who is in "a borderline area between neurosis and psychosis" (Kernberg, 1967, p. 641). In the *DSM-5*, the essential qualities of **borderline personality disorder** are impulsivity and instability in several areas of functioning, including mood, behavior, self-image, and interpersonal relationships. In fact, individuals with borderline personality disorder are sometimes described as being predictable only in their unpredictability. During periods of increased stress, they may display psychotic-like symptoms for a brief time. Nancy, a 23-year-old veterinary assistant, exemplifies many features of borderline personality disorder:

Three months before Nancy's admission to a hospital, she learned that her mother had become pregnant. She began drinking heavily, ostensibly to sleep nights. While drinking, she became involved in a series of "one-night stands." Two weeks before admission, she began feeling panicky and having experiences in which she felt as if she were removed from her body and in a trance. During one of these episodes, she was stopped by the police while wandering on a bridge late at night. The next day, in response to hearing a voice repeatedly telling her to jump off a bridge, Nancy ran to her work supervisor and asked for help. Her supervisor, seeing her distress and also noting scars from a recent wrist-cutting incident, referred her to a psychologist, who then arranged for her immediate hospitalization.

In the hospital, Nancy acknowledged that she had had feelings of loneliness and inadequacy and brief periods of depressed mood and anxiety since adolescence. Recently, she had been having fantasies that she was stabbing herself or a little baby with a knife. She complained that she was "just an empty shell that is transparent to everyone."

Nancy's parents divorced when she was 3, and for the next 5 years, she lived with her maternal grandmother and her mother, who had a severe drinking problem. She had night terrors during which she would frequently end up sleeping with her mother. When Nancy was 8, her maternal grandmother died, and she recalls trying to conceal her grief about this from her mother. She spent most of the next 2 years living with various relatives, including a period with her father, whom she had not seen since the divorce. When she was 9, her mother was hospitalized with schizophrenia. From age 10 through college, Nancy lived with an aunt and uncle, but had ongoing and frequent contacts with her mother. Her school record was consistently good.

Since adolescence, Nancy had dated regularly, having an active, but rarely pleasurable, sex life. Her relationships with men usually ended abruptly after she became angry with them when they disappointed her in some apparently minor way. She then concluded that they were "no good to begin with." She had several roommates but had trouble establishing a stable living situation because of her jealousy about sharing her roommates with others and because of her manipulative efforts to keep them from seeing other people. Since college, she has worked steadily, and at the time of admission, was working a night shift in a veterinary hospital and living alone. (Based on Spitzer, Gibbon, Skodol, Williams, & First, 1994.)

TABLE 16.4 The *DSM-5* in Simple Language: Diagnosing Borderline Personality Disorder

Since adolescence, there has been a persistent, pervasive, and pathological pattern of relationship issues, instability, and a hard time regulating mood, including five or more of the following nine features:

Relationship issues, such as:

1. Sensitivity to someone possibly leaving or letting the person down
2. Chaotic relationships with others
3. Unstable identity

Instability in other areas, such as:

4. Risky or impulsive behavior (e.g., substance abuse, sex)
5. Suicidal or self-mutilating behavior

Mood problems, such as:

6. Unpredictable moodiness
7. Anger
8. Feeling empty
9. Dissociative symptoms (like feeling detached or out of body)

Source: Adapted from American Psychiatric Association (2013).

One way to remember the main symptoms of borderline personality disorder delineated in Table 16.4 is via the acronym RIM: relationships, instability, and mood. As Nancy's case illustrates, the interpersonal relationships of individuals with borderline personality disorder are especially turbulent. They can quickly develop strong, impassioned romances in which they idealize the partner as being almost perfect. However, when negative experiences occur, as they do in any relationship, people with borderline personality disorder overreact with extreme mood swings. They are especially frightened by signs of abandonment or rejection, and will alternate between rage and desperate pleas for the other person to stay with and care for them. They can be very sensitive to other people's behavior, such that they tend to overinterpret its meaning, often in a quasi-paranoid way. Thus, if someone is especially helpful at work, it might be viewed as a sexual overture. Conversely, if someone forgets to say "hello" or says it too matter-of-factly, this might be seen as a put-down that has to be confronted.

The core deficit in borderline personality disorder appears to be **emotional dysregulation** (Linehan, 1993), a term used in the mental health community to refer to the inability of individuals to control or regulate their emotional responses to provocative stimuli. In borderline personality disorder, this can express itself either as emotional instability and/or in terms of poor emotional awareness—that is, emotional numbing. Whereas the first dimension is closely related to symptoms such as impulsivity, suicidal behaviors, or inappropriate anger, the latter can be associated with dissociative experiences and chronic feeling of emptiness (Speranza, 2013). People with borderline personality disorder typically have trouble regulating their moods and are particularly unable to tolerate negative emotions. When something bad happens to them, they appear to be unable to say, "I'll get over it." Consequently, one negative emotion leads to another. For example, feeling slighted leads to depression, which leads to rage, which generates some extreme behavior, which ultimately produces guilt.

emotional dysregulation: A mental health term that refers to the inability of a person to control or regulate his or her emotional responses to provocative stimuli.

Source: MitarArt/Shutterstock.com.

In *Girl, Interrupted*, Winona Ryder portrayed Susanna Kaysen, a young woman diagnosed with borderline personality disorder. In the film, which is based on a true story, Susanna recounts 2 years spent in a psychiatric hospital for teenage girls. If you have seen the film (or read the book), do you think borderline personality disorder is an accurate diagnosis for Susanna, or were her symptoms merely signs of a troubled adolescence?

Chapter 16 Personality Disorders   **551**

Connections

What other disorders are associated with disturbances in identity or memory? See Chapter 10.

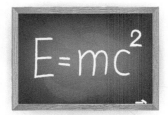

MAPS - Attempted Answers

antisocial personality disorder: A personality disorder characterized by repeated rule breaking, chronic manipulativeness, a callous outlook toward the rights of others and society, and tendencies to behave impulsively, dishonestly, irresponsibly, and without remorse.

Toby Allen, a prominent artist, completed a project in which he expertly illustrated a variety of mental disorders as anthropomorphized monsters, such as the Borderline Personality Disorder Monster pictured here.

Through such repeated emotional cycles, those with borderline personality disorder create most of their own life crises.

In addition to the aforementioned mood swings, people with borderline personality disorder also tend to display uncertainty about their self-image and identity. Under extreme stress, they can temporarily lose control of or "forget" their personal identities.

The instability seen in borderline personality disorder is also reflected in impulsive, sometimes dangerous, behavior. People often lose control of their tempers and are prone to getting into physical fights. They may go on sprees of spending, eating, drinking, or sex, usually to ward off the feelings of emptiness or loneliness to which they are prone. Suicidal behavior, gestures, or threats, or self-mutilating behavior are hallmarks of borderline personality disorder. Up to 80% of individuals with this disorder have suicidal behaviors (Linehan et al., 2006), and completed suicide occurs in 8–10% of individuals with borderline personality disorder (American Psychiatric Association, 2013a). Self-harm—including cutting, burning, hitting, hair pulling, or head banging—can be viewed as a means to regulate emotions, punish oneself, or express pain (Kleindienst et al., 2008).

The reasons for cutting and other forms of self-harm are often hard for outside observers to understand. Individuals with borderline personality disorder may engage in self-harm in an attempt to manage their distressing emotions. As one client put it, "I'd rather feel physical pain than emotional pain. Feeling the physical pain grounds me and somehow soothes me." Treatment for borderline personality disorder, described later in the chapter, teaches healthy coping strategies so that individuals can manage distress without harming themselves.

Borderline personality disorder is considered one of the most severe personality disorders because of the intensity, range, and unpredictability of its symptoms. These manifestations tend to be most severe for people in their 20s but ease somewhat as they reach their 30s and 40s. The overall prevalence of borderline personality disorder is estimated at 1–2% among the general population and at approximately 20% among psychiatric inpatients (American Psychiatric Association, 2013a; Samuels et al., 2002). Females are diagnosed with the disorder about three times more often than males (American Psychiatric Association, 2013a).

Antisocial Personality Disorder

Antisocial personality disorder describes people who are chronically callous and manipulative; who trample on the rights of others; who ignore social rules and laws; who behave

impulsively, dishonestly, and irresponsibly; who fail to learn from punishment; and who lack remorse or guilt over crimes and other misdeeds. In decades past, this pattern has been called moral insanity, psychopathy, and sociopathy. Notorious exemplars of this disorder include Ted Bundy (from the chapter-opening case), David Berkowitz, John Wayne Gacey, Charles Manson, Aileen Wuornos, and Jeffrey Dahmer, along with fictional characters Sideshow Bob (of *Simpsons* fame) and Hannibal Lecter (created by Thomas Harris in *Red Dragon*, 1981, and *The Silence of the Lambs*, 1988). Other, less violent criminals reveal antisocial features through their exploitation of others for personal gain.

Over 2 decades ago, psychiatrist Hervey Cleckley (1976) offered an influential description of individuals then called "psychopathic personalities." According to Cleckley, psychopathic personalities possess superficial charm and intelligence and do not show signs of delusions, irrational thinking, or anxiety about matters that might upset most people. What the psychopath does display is unreliability, insincerity, a disregard for the truth, a lack of remorse over misdeeds, a failure to learn from experience, and an incapacity to feel normal emotional reactions, including a genuine love for anyone. In addition, according to Cleckley, psychopaths are manipulative, impulsive, and fail to follow through on any kind of overall life plan. They often have superficial, promiscuous sex lives and are prone to suicide threats that they seldom carry out.

Some psychopaths are sufficiently sophisticated in their manipulations, clever enough in their exploitations, and smooth enough in their mistreatment of others to escape legal sanctions. In fact, some are so successful as to be envied for the power, prestige, and wealth they amass. Society seems to have no shortage of "successful psychopaths," who somehow manage to escape paying for their lives of irresponsibility and deceitfulness (Ronson, 2011). Some experts argue that features of psychopathy are compatible with the skills and temperament required of many high-powered CEOs (Ronson, 2011).

Robert Hare's (2003) Psychopathy Checklist—Revised (PCL-R) provides a highly regarded description of the psychopath (see Table 16.5). Similar to Cleckley's model,

TABLE 16.5 The Psychopathy Checklist–Revised

Each of the 20 items in the PCL-R is scored on a three-point scale (0 = not at all; 1= somewhat; 2 = definitely) according to specific criteria obtained through file information and a semistructured interview. The resulting total score is between 0 and 40, with most studies using either 25 or 30 as the cutoff score above which the person is considered to be a psychopath (Guy & Douglas, 2006). This assessment is often used in forensic settings to predict the future dangerousness of the individual and to make decisions about parole.

Items on the checklist include *personality traits*, such as:

- being charming, impulsive, and irresponsible;
- having an inflated self-esteem;
- needing constant stimulation;
- experiencing shallow moods;
- lacking empathy or guilt; and
- not accepting blame for one's actions.

Behaviors are also included on the checklist, including:

- engaging in consistent lying and manipulative behavior,
- living at the expense of others (e.g., living rent-free in someone else's house),
- being unable to control one's behavior,
- having frequent sexual and short-term relationships,
- having few feasible long-range plans,
- showing a history of behavioral problems and juvenile delinquency,
- violating one's probation or parole, and
- displaying criminal versatility (i.e., committing lots of different types of crimes).

Source: Adapted from Hare (2003).

There was a certain "Dark Wizard" who made things very difficult for the kids on the train to Hogwarts School. Which characteristics of psychopathy from the PCL-R are displayed by Lord V . . ./He-Who-Must-Not-Be-Named from the Harry Potter series?

Hare emphasizes two defining characteristics: emotional-cognitive instability and behavioral deviance (Hare, Hart, & Harpur, 1991). A meta-analysis showed that the PCL-R, while commonly used in criminal justice settings, has only medium predictive accuracy and that the core personality features of psychopathy (charm, narcissistic self-worth, no guilt/empathy, shallow mood, etc.) have no significant link to violence (Yang, Wong, & Coid, 2010). In fact, it appears to be the behavioral aspects entirely—that is, previous criminal history and antisocial actions—that account for the validity of the PCL-R (Yang et al., 2010).

Although many clinicians use these terms interchangeably, *psychopathy* and *antisocial personality disorder* are actually not synonymous. The *DSM-5*'s definition of antisocial personality disorder, as shown in Table 16.6, stresses repeated violations of the rights of others and overt criminal behavior more than devious traits and interpersonal tendencies. As currently construed in the *DSM-5*, the diagnosis of antisocial personality disorder grossly overidentifies people with offence histories as meeting the criteria for the diagnosis (Ogloff, 2006). For example, research shows that 50–80% of prisoners meet the criteria for a diagnosis of antisocial personality disorder, yet only approximately 15% of prisoners are psychopathic, as assessed by the PCL-R (Ogloff, 2006). As such, the characteristics and research findings drawn from psychopathy research may not be entirely relevant for those with antisocial personality disorder.

Figure 16.2 outlines the sequence of problems that typically precedes antisocial personality disorder. The disorder begins prior to the age of 15 as symptoms of conduct disorder (see Chapter 3), in which a youngster is repeatedly involved in lying, stealing, vandalism, aggressiveness, and even physical cruelty. Ted Bundy, for example, stole cars to impress people, while "Son of Sam" serial killer David Berkowitz poisoned his mother's pet parakeet. By age 18, when the diagnosis of antisocial personality disorder can officially be made, the antisocial conduct typically includes both crimes against property and assaults against persons. The severity of antisocial personality disorder, like most other personality disorders, tends to diminish after age 40.

The overall prevalence of antisocial personality disorder is 1–5% (American Psychiatric Association, 2013a; Samuels et al., 2002), with men diagnosed much more frequently than women. Many individuals with antisocial personality disorder have a concurrent substance use disorder (Grant et al., 2004). Not surprisingly, the prevalence rate is much higher (greater than 70%) in substance abuse clinics, prisons, or other forensic settings (American Psychiatric Association, 2013a).

TABLE 16.6 The *DSM-5* in Simple Language: Diagnosing Antisocial Personality Disorder

Since adolescence, there has been a persistent, pervasive, and pathological pattern of trampling on the rights of others, including three or more of the following seven features:
1. Legal trouble   5. Doing dangerous things 2. Lying to and manipulating people   6. Being irresponsible 3. Inability to be planful   7. Not feeling guilty about any 4. Verbal or physical fighting   harmful actions

Source: Adapted from American Psychiatric Association (2013).

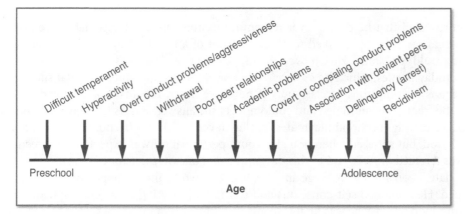

FIGURE 16.2 Precursors of Antisocial Personality Disorder

Signs of antisocial personality disorder are often evident in early childhood. Aggressive children tend to grow up to be aggressive adults, and the precursors of chronic antisocial conduct can frequently be seen in temperamental, interpersonal, and academic problems that show up in the elementary school years.

Source: Based on Loeber (1990).

Cluster C: Anxious/Fearful Personality Disorders

The *anxious/fearful* personality disorders include avoidant, dependent, and obsessive-compulsive personality disorders. Table 16.7 summarizes characteristics of these disorders.

Avoidant Personality Disorder

The main characteristics of **avoidant personality disorder** are constant feelings of inadequacy and ineptitude, especially in social situations. Persons with this disorder are afraid of being embarrassed, criticized, or ridiculed by others, and consequently, they avoid social situations whenever possible. If forced into a social encounter, they are usually very inhibited, afraid at every step of making a mistake that will bring the rejection they are sure is forthcoming. They seek constant reassurance that others will like them and tend to avoid occupations requiring social interaction. However, unlike persons with schizoid personality disorder, who appear indifferent to social interaction, those with avoidant personality disorder long for affection and social acceptance and are distressed by its absence. People with avoidant personality disorder are overly cautious. Afraid that new situations will "throw them a curve" for which they are not prepared, people with avoidant personalities tend to follow a set routine and try to stay out of situations in which they would be called on to act spontaneously. They are unusually timid, and as adolescents, they may have experienced less involvement in extracurricular activities and less popularity compared to others (Rettew et al., 2003). As substitutes for the real interpersonal contacts they desire but avoid, they may often fantasize about "perfect" relationships that await them in the future. Leon, who came to a clinic complaining of feeling "down" and lonely, is an example of a person with avoidant personality disorder:

avoidant personality disorder: A personality disorder characterized by constant feelings of inadequacy, especially in social situations.

TABLE 16.7 Cluster C: The Anxious/Fearful Personality Disorders in the *DSM-5*

Primary characteristics:

- Avoidant: Feels inadequate, needs constant reassurance; timid and cautious
- Dependent: Requires excessive advice and guidance; very submissive; low self-esteem
- Obsessive-compulsive: Overly conscientious, inhibited, and perfectionistic; preoccupied with staying controlled

Leon revealed that he cannot ever remember feeling comfortable socially. Even before kindergarten, if he were asked to speak in front of a group of his parents' friends, his mind would "go blank." He felt overwhelming anxiety at children's social functions, such as birthday parties, which he either avoided or, if he went, attended in total silence. He could answer questions in class only if he wrote down the answers in advance. Even then, he frequently mumbled and could not get the answer out. As he grew up, Leon had a couple of neighborhood playmates, but he never had a best friend. His school grades were good, but suffered when oral classroom participation was expected. As a teenager, he was terrified of girls, and to this day has never gone on a date or even asked a woman for a date. Leon attended college and did well for a while, then dropped out as his grades slipped. He remained self-conscious and terrified of meeting strangers. He had trouble finding a job because he was unable to answer questions in interviews. He has no friends as an adult and avoids all invitations to socialize with coworkers. (Based on Spitzer et al., 1994, pp. 124–125)

dependent personality disorder: A personality disorder characterized by excessive self-sacrifice, an inability to make decisions without exorbitant help, and a dread of being alone.

obsessive-compulsive personality disorder: A personality disorder characterized by a preoccupation with rules, details, and organization in many aspects of life, so much so that the person is stubbornly perfectionistic.

The prevalence of avoidant personality disorder is placed at 1.5–2.5%, and it is seen equally in males and females (American Psychiatric Association, 2013a; Samuels et al., 2002). It is often difficult (and perhaps not even clinically vital, as the treatment is similar) to distinguish between avoidant personality disorder and social anxiety disorder, a common anxiety disorder discussed in Chapter 7 (Chambless, Fydrich, & Rodebaugh, 2008; Herbert, Hope, & Bellack, 1992).

Dependent Personality Disorder

People with **dependent personality disorder** are unable to make decisions without exorbitant amounts of advice and reassurance. Rather than shunning social contact, as is the case with avoidant personality disorder, they cling to others and make excessive self-sacrifices to win the smallest signs of appreciation. Typically, they prefer to have others make decisions for them about where to live, what job to seek, and how to dress and act. People with dependent personalities typically behave in a submissive, ingratiating manner to win affection. They dread being alone, and although their interpersonal strategies may win some temporary friendships, their excessive dependency eventually becomes annoying and ends up driving people away.

People with dependent personality disorder have little self-confidence, and their constant need to lean on others only confirms their sense of being incapable of functioning successfully on their own. Although precise prevalence figures are unknown, estimates hover at only 0.3–0.6% of the population (American Psychiatric Association, 2013a; Samuels et al., 2002). Dependent personality disorder has been diagnosed slightly more often in women, which may be due to the fact that women are treated more often in formal clinical settings.

Obsessive-Compulsive Personality Disorder

People with **obsessive-compulsive personality disorder** are preoccupied with rules, details, and organization in many aspects of life. They tenaciously manage their lives by always trying to make them predictable and safe. Rigidly committed to the minutiae of life, individuals with obsessive-compulsive personalities tend to lack a larger perspective on most activities; they lose sight of the forest because they are so focused on the individual trees. They may hoard worthless possessions, apparently out of a conviction that "someday I might need them." This pack-rat mentality may also be reflected in stinginess with money. People tend to refer disdainfully to these individuals as "bean counters," "nitpickers," or "worrywarts."

Source: Brian L. Burke.

MAPS - Superficial Syndromes
This cactus is reluctant to venture far from its partner.

Indeed, many individuals with obsessive-compulsive personality disorder are so stubbornly perfectionistic about every task that they may make little or no progress on them, or they take so long at them that they miss important deadlines. At the same time, they are unwilling to delegate tasks to others for fear that the work will not be done in accordance with their standards. In such individuals, conscientiousness becomes so extreme as to be a liability. For all their concern about doing things perfectly, most people with obsessive-compulsive personalities are ineffective and indecisive, often worrying themselves into mediocre performance.

Individuals with obsessive-compulsive personality disorder also tend to be inflexible about moral and ethical matters, and in personal and romantic relationships, to be controlling and aloof, as if emotional spontaneity were too threatening to tolerate. Consequently, they sometimes appear cold and insensitive. Describing a character who displayed an obsessive-compulsive personality in *The Man in the Case*, playwright Anton Chekov (1898/2000) wrote that the man "displayed a constant and insurmountable impulse to wrap himself in a covering, to make himself, so to speak, a case which would isolate and protect himself from external influences."

Estimates of the overall prevalence of obsessive-compulsive personality disorder range from 1–8% (American Psychiatric Association, 2013a; Samuels et al., 2002). It is diagnosed about twice as often in men as in women. Obsessive-compulsive personality disorder should be distinguished from *obsessive-compulsive disorder*, discussed in Chapter 8. Obsessive-compulsive personality disorder is a chronic lifestyle governed by perfectionism, obstinacy, and rigid habits. However, it lacks the specific obsessions and compulsive rituals that are hallmarks of obsessive-compulsive disorder (OCD).

Sheldon Cooper of TV's *The Big Bang Theory* endears himself to us with his rigid adherence to rules and routine, all characteristics of obsessive-compulsive personality disorder. The studio set of his faculty office is shown here.

Source: Carlos Duarte do Nascimento (@chesterbr).

Avoidant = "No way am I going; it makes me too nervous."

Schizoid = "I wasn't invited."

Narcissistic = "I bet I was the first one Lola invited!"

Dependent = "I'll only go if you're going too."

Histrionic = "This is a disaster; I don't even have anything to wear..."

Borderline = "I know Lola used to be my best friend, but now I hate her guts."

Happy Birthday Lola!

Antisocial = "How can I use this party to my advantage?"

Schizotypal = "Even though it's not a theme party, I think I'll wear a costume."

OCD = "The party is called for 7 PM, so I better leave my house at 6:48 PM because Google maps says it will take precisely 12 minutes to get there from my house..."

Paranoid = "I'm sure that Lola made the party on that date because she knew I had other plans that day!"

Source: Cartoon written by Brian L. Burke and illustrated by Leslie B. Goldstein.

How someone with each of the 10 *DSM-5* personality disorders might react to finding out that Lola's birthday party was coming up.

As diagnosed in the *DSM-5*, the 10 basic personality disorders are classified under three general clusters:

- Cluster A: Paranoid, schizoid, and schizotypal personality disorders involve behavior patterns that appear odd or eccentric.
- Cluster B: Histrionic, narcissistic, borderline, and antisocial personality disorders involve behavior that is dramatic, emotionally unstable, or erratic.
- Cluster C: Avoidant, dependent, and obsessive-compulsive personality disorders involve behavior that is anxious and fearful.

Causes of Personality Disorders

We first consider what theories of personality reveal about personality disorders in general, given that extreme, rigid personality traits are the central characteristics of these disorders. Then we examine specific theories about the causes of the two most studied disorders: borderline and antisocial personality disorders.

Theoretical Perspectives on Personality Disorders

People develop their unique combinations of personality traits through the interaction of inherited tendencies with the experiences they have while adapting to the environmental demands of a particular culture. Although personality never becomes fixed at any particular age, most people's main traits develop during childhood. In adulthood, individual qualities become more consistent and may not change much across many years (McCrae & Costa, 1994), although variation exists among individuals in terms of how stable their personalities are (Allemand, Steiger, & Hill, 2013).

No one type of personality is best or healthiest. The important questions are how well an individual's style fits with environments in which that person most often functions, and how adaptive and flexible the person is in dealing with changing environmental demands. Theories about the causes of personality disorders attempt to explain how people develop styles that do not fit their environment and why those styles are rigidly maintained in spite of the problems they cause. Any general theory of personality could be extended to become a theory of personality disorders, but a few theoretical perspectives dominate the field. Here, we examine the biopsychosocial aspects—ranging from genetics to a variety of psychological theories—regarding the causes of personality disorders.

Genetics and Personality Disorders

Can genetic factors account for personality disorders? Are some people genetically predisposed to develop personality disorders associated with extreme versions of certain traits? Are any particular traits more heavily influenced by genetics than others? For most personality disorders, these questions are difficult to answer because few family, twin, or adoption studies have shed light on a possible genetic basis for a given disorder (Dahl, 1993; Torgersen et al., 2000). The odd/eccentric cluster of personality disorders provides evidence that the rates of both paranoid and schizoid personality disorders are slightly higher among relatives of individuals diagnosed with schizophrenia than they are among normal controls (American Psychiatric Association, 2013a), but no direct evidence of a genetic risk for either of these two disorders has yet been clearly established. The data suggesting a genetic contribution to schizotypal personality disorder are stronger (Bollini & Walker, 2007). As noted earlier, studies indicate that schizotypal personality disorder is more common among first-degree biological relatives of individuals diagnosed with schizophrenia than among the population in general (American Psychiatric Association, 2013a; Dahl, 1993). Also, individuals with schizotypal personality disorder often show deficits in attention and short-term memory, as do individuals with schizophrenia, further suggesting a genetic link between the two disorders (Bollini & Walker, 2007). The fact that schizotypal personality disorder is dually listed in the *DSM-5* (in both the *Person-*

ality Disorders and *Schizophrenia Spectrum and Other Psychotic Disorders* chapters) suggests that the field is moving toward viewing this disorder as part of the schizophrenia spectrum.

For the cluster of dramatic/emotional/erratic personality disorders, numerous studies support the role of genetics in antisocial personality disorder (Waldman & Rhee, 2006), and there is a growing body of literature supporting a genetic role in the development of borderline personality disorder. For example, close relatives of individuals with borderline personality disorder are much more likely than the general population to also have borderline personality disorder (American Psychiatric Association, 2013a; Torgersen et al., 2000), although it is difficult to tease apart the role of shared family environment. There is little research to suggest a genetic role in the development of narcissistic or histrionic personality disorder.

Very little research has been conducted on the anxious/fearful cluster of personality disorders. With that in mind, though, a study of over 1,300 adult twin pairs in Norway concluded that Cluster C personality disorders are moderately heritable overall (Reichborn-Kjennerud et al., 2007).

Psychodynamic Theories of Personality Disorders

Even if genetics is assumed to play a role in governing personality traits, the extreme and rigid forms that these traits assume in personality disorders must be shaped by other substantial developmental influences. Freud proposed that problems of personality—his term was "character"—arose from fixations during specific points of development. As an example, according to traditional Freudian theory, fixation during the anal stage of development was thought to occur when parents were overly strict or unusually permissive in toilet training a child. As adults, some anal characters become overly controlled, highly organized, stingy, and obstinate. These behaviors are similar to the perfectionistic and inflexible patterns of obsessive-compulsive personality disorder. But this intriguing account of personality disorders has received little research support, so relatively few clinicians see traditional psychoanalysis as a viable explanation of personality disorders.

More-recent psychodynamic formulations, particularly those arising from object relations theories, have received better empirical support (Eagle, 1984; Fonagy, Target, & Gergely, 2000; Ribeiro et al., 2010). Object relations theorists believe that the nature and quality of early attachments between infants and their caregivers largely determine children's expectations about how other people will respond to them. These expectations, in turn, color all other close relationships and help determine a person's strongest needs and vulnerabilities. These needs and vulnerabilities often form the core of personality disorders. Because these expectations are established so early, often before a child has learned to speak, they are resistant to change, especially through verbal means such as psychotherapy. According to object relations theory, when these expectations become rigid and extreme, the person becomes locked into the troubling behavior patterns known as personality disorders.

Interpersonal Learning Theories

If genetics and early relationships cannot by themselves explain personality differences, though, what other factors might be involved? According to interpersonal theorists, most personality traits involve interpersonal themes, such as how outgoing people are, how trusting or dependent they tend to be, how comfortable they feel with different types of people, and how much empathy or warmth they show to others. Differences in these traits may have a genetic basis, and they may also be associated with varying amounts of security in a child's early object relations. But once traits are established, they are solidified into enduring personality patterns as a result of interpersonal learning experiences.

As described in Chapter 2, Harry Stack Sullivan's interpersonal theory of personality (1953) suggests that people desire to be with others who reinforce their typical ways of behaving. According to this view, personalities are shaped by the interpersonal experiences that people prefer and seek out. Personality disorders result when an individual

MAPS - Attempted Answers

relies too heavily on extreme and maladaptive behaviors toward others. For example, the submissive behavior found in dependent personality disorder tends to invite or "pull for" dominant behavior from another (and vice versa). The aggressive behavior seen in paranoid personality disorder often engenders hostility from others (and vice versa). For people who tend toward personality disorders, the effect of their attempted solutions is to entrench themselves even further in their problematic styles. Their rigid behavior tends to perpetuate itself by evoking behaviors from others that are reinforcing and that validate their initial dysfunctional personality styles.

Evolution-Based Personality Theory

Renowned psychologist Theodore Millon (1990) proposed a theory that views personality differences in terms of their evolutionary significance. According to Millon, three fundamental *polarities* underlie the biological structures and psychological processes that constitute human personality. The first of these polarities involves the *minimization of pain* and *the maximization of pleasure*. This polarity involves two basic aims of life: to enhance life through the pursuit of pleasurable activities and to preserve life by protecting against danger. The degrees to which a person pursues pleasure and avoids pain are separate bipolar dimensions; a person can be high or low on either or both. Thus, a person who acts to maximize pleasure may or may not also seek to minimize pain.

The second fundamental polarity is adapting to environmental demands through *passive accommodation* or *active modification*. Passive accommodation requires little initiative; one can "fit in" by quietly accepting and adjusting to environmental changes. Active modification demands more direct, proactive attempts to make the environment fit an individual's needs. These two poles are mutually exclusive; the more people tend to use one strategy, the less they use the other one.

The third polarity involves the degree to which a person is oriented toward *advancing the self* and/or *caring for others*. As in the first polarity, a person can be high or low on either or both. One can maximize self-interests, displaying egotism and little consideration for others. One can also focus on others by seeking relationships that are caring or intimate.

But how do these polarities relate to personality disorders? Millon believed that, as a result of genetic influences, psychodynamics, and learning histories, some people develop deficiencies, imbalances, or conflicts in one or more of the three polarities. When this happens, troubled personalities result, several of which resemble the *DSM-5* personality disorders. For example, persons displaying schizoid personality disorder are deficient in their capacity to feel either pleasure or pain, and they maintain a passively detached style toward most events. People with dependent personalities, by contrast, are oriented almost exclusively toward others as a means of producing pleasure and avoiding pain. They passively wait for others to take care of them and believe that the best way to secure this guidance is to always assume a submissive role with others. At the other end of these polarities are the people with antisocial personalities who actively pursue independence (advancing the self) throughout life. They crave autonomy and power for themselves, often at others' expense.

Each of the previous theories is concerned with explaining the ways in which personality traits, in general, may become fixed and maladaptive. But these viewpoints do not focus on particular disorders per se. In the next two sections, we examine theories and research concerned with specific causes of the two most-studied personality disorders—borderline personality disorder and antisocial personality disorder.

Causes of Borderline Personality Disorder

Theories about the causes of borderline personality disorder have emphasized biological contributions, psychodynamic factors, and social factors, such as early childhood trauma. These influences may operate as separate pathways leading to borderline personality disorder, or more likely, they may interact to produce the condition.

Biological Contributions

There seems to be a plausible sequence leading from neurological impairments to borderline personality disorder. Children with neurological impairments often show hyperactivity, poor attention, unstable moods, fussiness, and impulsivity that can translate into interpersonal problems, academic difficulties, and troubles with parents. These problems, in turn, may ultimately lead to the poorly regulated emotions, impulsive behavior, and identity confusion that typify borderline personality disorder.

But what type of biological vulnerability sets the stage for borderline personality disorder? A few empirical studies have found an association between early organic brain dysfunction and adult borderline personality disorder (Andrulonis et al., 1981; van Reekum, Conway, Gansler, White, & Bachman, 1993). Current research has focused on the use of functional neuroimaging that links emotional dysregulation, a hallmark symptom of borderline personality disorder, to increased activity in the *amygdala*, part of the limbic system (Bradley, Conklin, & Westen, 2007). Other lines of research have examined the role of the neurotransmitter serotonin, with lower levels linked to a higher frequency of self-harm and suicidal behavior (Audenaert et al., 2001). However, a recent meta-analysis found no evidence that serotonin-related genes are implicated in borderline personality disorder (Calati, Gressier, Balestri, & Serretti, 2013).

Another clue to a biological influence on borderline personality disorder is the discovery of a high prevalence of depressive and bipolar disorders among relatives of individuals diagnosed with borderline personality disorder (American Psychiatric Association, 2013a; Dahl, 1993). Some clinicians believe that this increased prevalence indicates a basic similarity between borderline personality disorder and disturbances that affect mood, along with a possible shared genetic diathesis for these disorders. Of course, the mere fact that two disorders tend to co-occur does not necessarily mean that they are genetically related.

Psychodynamic Factors

Various psychodynamic theorists suggest another possible progression from early childhood problems to borderline personality disorder. They argue that the seeds of the disorder are sown in the first 2 years of life, when excessively aggressive impulses in the child or inadequacies in parenting impair the child's ability to form a stable self-identity. More particularly, many object-relations-oriented theorists believe that borderline personality disorder results from a lack of bonding between infants and primary caregivers. The result is that neither a secure sense of self nor an abiding trust in others ever develops. Without a stable self or a belief that relationships can be trusted to last, people are always on the lookout for any sign of rejection or criticism. As a result, they typically feel disillusioned and desperate.

Although this theory may be intuitively attractive, most empirical research on child development does not support the idea that early parent-child conflicts over dependence and independence lead to adult borderline pathology (Crowell, Waters, Kring, & Riso, 1993). However, research does suggest a relationship between borderline personality disorder and an unstable family environment (Bradley et al., 2007), which includes the occurrence of trauma in the first several years of a child's life.

Early Childhood Trauma

Many researchers have focused on childhood loss and abuse as causes of borderline personality disorder. For example, a meta-analysis found that 20–40% of individuals with borderline personality disorder experienced a traumatic separation from a parent (Gunderson & Sabo, 1993). Special attention has focused on the link between early abuse and borderline personality disorder, and several studies have found that as many as 80% of individuals diagnosed with this disorder suffered an early history of physical or sexual abuse (Crowell et al., 1993; Herman, Perry, & Van der Kolk, 1989). Other research has found that people who have experienced childhood sexual abuse are almost four times more likely to exhibit borderline behaviors, compared to those with no such history (Zelkowitz, Paris, Guzder, & Feldman, 2001). Witnessing violence is also believed to be a risk factor (Zelkowitz et al., 2001). Most researchers agree that childhood trauma is an important developmental characteristic of many—but not all—individuals who develop borderline personality disorder (Bradley et al., 2007).

Putting the biopsychosocial causes together, results from a meta-analysis suggest that hippocampal volumes are reduced in people with borderline personality disorder, relative to healthy controls, but particularly in cases in which people have been diagnosed with comorbid post-traumatic stress disorder (PTSD; see Chapter 9) as a reaction to a severe trauma (Rodrigues et al., 2011). Thus, trauma may affect brain regions in the limbic system, such as the hippocampus and the amygdala, which then results in specific constellations of symptoms that meet criteria for borderline personality disorder.

Causes of Antisocial Personality Disorder

The causes of antisocial personality disorder and repeated criminal conduct have been researched extensively. As a result, clinicians now know quite a bit about the precursors of the disorder. For example, men who engage in repeated antisocial behavior tended in early childhood to be more hyperactive, physically awkward, and impulsive, and to have more trouble regulating their emotions than did their prosocial peers. They also had more learning disabilities and speech problems and were prone to break rules frequently both at home and at school. It is easy to see how this cluster of problems soon leads to conflicts with parents, peers, and teachers (Moffitt, 1993). Academic failures and early school dropout often follow as well. Some of these difficulties probably originate from physiological disturbances in the child's nervous system, and this biological diathesis appears to set the stage for a long chain of behavioral and social adversities that ultimately leads to chronic antisocial behavior.

Biological or Psychological Predispositions

Evidence from twin and adoption studies confirms that genetic factors contribute to the risk of antisocial personality disorder (Black & Blum, 2014; Dahl, 1993; Nigg & Goldsmith, 1994; Waldman & Rhee, 2006). Exactly how a genetic risk translates into actual antisocial conduct remains unknown, though many clues are emerging.

A variety of biological markers have been observed among individuals who engage in antisocial behavior. For example, electroencephalographic (EEG) measures of central nervous system activity indicate that psychopaths have a higher rate of EEG abnormalities compared with normal controls (Reyes & Amador, 2009). An intriguing study by Kiehl and colleagues (2001) showed that criminal psychopaths are more likely to show functional abnormalities in their frontal cortex and limbic systems when processing emotional material, compared to criminal nonpsychopaths. Morgan and Lilienfeld (2000) reviewed evidence showing that adults with antisocial behavior exhibit deficits in frontal lobe tasks of executive functioning, which include key cognitive tasks like planning, judgment, and decision making.

Further, skin conductance arousal is lower among adolescents who exhibit delinquent behavior and have tendencies toward sensation seeking (Gatzke-Kopp, Raine, Loeber, Stouthamer-Loeber, & Steinhauer, 2002). Individuals with antisocial personality disorder also show lower resting heart rates (Raine, 2002), as well as lower levels of the neurotransmitter serotonin (Patrick, 2007). Taken together, research suggests that individuals with antisocial personality disorder have deficits in emotional and/or cognitive processing that may be biologically based: difficulty feeling anxiety or processing emotion, combined with risk seeking and poor judgment and decision-making skills (Patrick, 2007).

Conceptually, how are these biological markers of antisocial personality disorder understood? Psychopathy expert Robert Hare (Hare & McPherson, 1984) has suggested that psychopaths suffer from an "immature cortex" that makes it difficult for them to inhibit behavior. One possibility is that cortical defects impair the ability of people with antisocial personalities to plan and regulate behavior carefully. A related and influential

Connections

Has childhood abuse been linked with other disorders? See Chapter 10 for answers.

idea is Herbert Quay's theory that people with antisocial personalities suffer chronically low levels of cortical arousal, and they therefore are constantly trying to find ways to "bump up" their excitement. According to Quay's (1965) *stimulation-seeking* theory, the thrill-seeking and disruptive behavior of the psychopath serves to increase sensory input and arousal to a desired level.

The tendency to be underaroused may help to explain why individuals with antisocial personality disorder are less strongly affected by aversive stimuli, such as social rejection or electric shocks (Lykken, 1957). They are also less able to detect punishment and are less responsive to environmental threats (Herba et al., 2007). As a result, people with antisocial personalities appear to have difficulty learning to inhibit their behavior in response to cues that signal punishment or that cause others to feel anxious. Underarousal in both central nervous system and autonomic nervous system functioning has been related to several early precursors of antisocial personality disorder, such as difficult temperament and moodiness, attention deficits and hyperactivity, and oppositional defiant and conduct disorders. Individuals with antisocial personality disorder also tend to score higher on measures of trait impulsivity (Swann, Lijffijt, Lane, Steinberg, & Moeller, 2009), with impulsive or sensation-seeking behavior possibly serving to increase their levels of arousal. These findings paint a picture of the person with antisocial personality disorder as someone who is impulsive, while being adroit at wriggling out of whatever trouble the disinhibited behavior causes. Add to these factors an enhanced attraction to rewards and excitement, and there exist the underpinnings of several well-known features of this disorder, including impulsivity, callousness, and exploitiveness.

Imagine that a young boy is planning to steal food from a grocery store. If this boy has been caught and punished for similar transgressions in the past, his contemplated theft should lead to fear (signaled by physiological reactions, such as sweaty palms or a racing heart) that he will be punished for this act as well. The emotion of fear should cause the boy to inhibit the theft on his own. Once he decides not to steal, the boy will be reinforced by the reduction in fear that follows, and gradually he will learn that stealing is not worth the fear it engenders. But what if that lesson is not learned, either because his parents have not monitored his behavior closely enough or because, even when he is punished, he has a biological tendency to not experience strong fear? Under these circumstances, the boy will not learn the lessons that fear imparts. Without such restraints, the boy will feel no particular need to engage in self-control or to inhibit antisocial behavior; instead, he will charge ahead with whatever behavior happens to please him at the moment, without considering whether it is appropriate or whether it might hurt someone else.

Family and Parenting Practices

Historically, families have been the major social institution for teaching conventional moral standards of conduct. Thus, it is not surprising that family factors have been emphasized in several theoretical accounts of antisocial personality disorder. An early example was provided by Arnold Buss (1966); he claimed that parents who are cold and detached or who are inconsistent and lax in their discipline foster antisocial behavior in their children. These children, said Buss, fail to learn to control their impulsive behavior, and this early deficit in impulse control eventually results in more serious behavioral, academic, and social problems as the child grows older. Marlene Moretti (2013), a Canadian expert on youth violence, further states that she has seen only one or two true child psychopaths in her career; the rest, in her view, have all been victims of dysfunctional family and peer situations.

Several specific family and social variables have been consistently associated with antisocial behavior, including:

1. A history of family criminality (Farrington, 2006; Farrington, Jolliffe, Loeber, Stouthamer-Loeber, & Kalb, 2001; Loeber & Dishion, 1983). Not only does family criminality, especially by fathers, provide a role model for youthful antisocial conduct, but it is also likely to disrupt family stability and limit family resources like finances and quality time spent together.

FIGURE 16.3
Biological/
Psychological
and Family/Social
Contributions to
Early Precursors of
Antisocial Personality
Disorder

Biological, psychological, family, and social factors often interact to produce a set of childhood problems involving a difficult temperament, aggressive behavior, and childhood behavior disorders. These early precursors can set the stage for antisocial personality disorder.

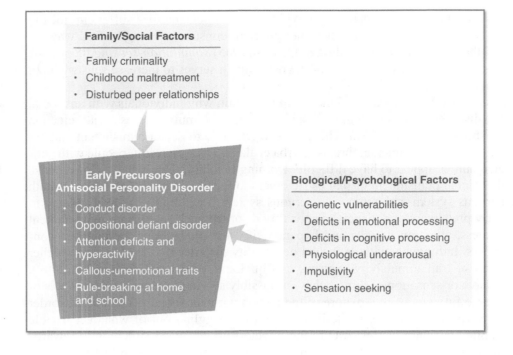

2. Childhood maltreatment, including chronic parental uninvolvement, erratic discipline, neglect, physical or sexual abuse, and poor supervision of children (Graham, Kimonis, Wasserman, & Kline, 2012; Lang, af Klinteberg, & Alm, 2002; Patterson, 1986; Weiler & Widom, 1996). Any of these factors make it more difficult for a child to learn the basic rules of society and to feel committed to obeying these rules. In addition, abusive relationships serve to teach the child that violence and boundary violations are acceptable means of influencing others.

3. Disturbed peer relationships (Black, 2013; Elliott, Huizinga, & Menard, 1989). Children who become habitually antisocial often learn some of this conduct from peer groups who model antisocial behavior and reinforce it by granting highest status to the most antisocial members of the group (e.g., gangs).

As summarized in Figure 16.3, when these family and social influences are combined with the biological/psychological predispositions previously described, they substantially increase the risk of a young person developing the early precursors of antisocial personality disorder (Nietzel, Hasemann, & Lynam, 1999). Once the early precursors are in place, a child is at risk for gradually developing a chronically antisocial pattern of life.

Section Review

The major theoretical explanations of extreme, rigid personality traits that make up personality disorders are that:

- genetic factors influence major personality traits, suggesting a genetic vulnerability for personality disorders;
- early developmental disturbances in attachment relationships determine adult personality patterns;
- repeated interpersonal learning experiences solidify personality traits into enduring personality patterns; and
- deficiencies or conflicts in the pursuit of pleasure and avoidance of pain, active or passive adaptation to the environment, and advancing the self or others produce disordered personalities.

Theories about the causes of borderline personality disorder have focused on:

- possible organic brain dysfunction,
- genetic links to depressive and bipolar disorders,

- conflicts in early infant-caregiver relationships involving themes of independence and dependence, and
- early childhood trauma, especially in the form of loss or physical/sexual abuse.

Theories about the causes of antisocial personality disorder have focused on interactions between:

- biological/psychological factors, including genetic vulnerabilities, deficits in emotional and cognitive processing, physiological underarousal, impulsivity, and sensation seeking; and
- family/social factors, including higher rates of family criminality, childhood maltreatment, and disturbed peer relationships.

Treatment of Personality Disorders

As already mentioned, personality disorders are challenging mental disorders to treat because of their association with other disorders and, especially, because of their status as a long-standing lifestyle rather than an acute episode. People often become comfortable with their personality disorders, just as many of us become comfortable with an old pair of jeans that may not look attractive to others (and may even have holes in them!). And just as we are unwilling to part with those jeans, many people with personality disorders are not motivated to seek treatment. Often, they must be coerced into it by friends or relatives, or even through legal means. For this reason, motivational interviewing (Miller & Rollnick, 2013), also discussed in Chapters 6 and 14, could be of great value in the pretreatment phase or first part of treatment (Verheul & Herbrink, 2007). Problems in treating personality disorders have increased interest in preventive efforts, such as in the case of antisocial personality disorder, as discussed in the "Prevention" feature in this chapter.

In general, psychotherapy is the treatment of first choice for personality disorders (Verheul & Herbrink, 2007). When the course of treatment is obstructed by severe symptoms or in cases of severe comorbidity, psychotherapeutic treatment can be supported by symptom-oriented pharmacological therapy. Nonetheless, given the state of the art in psychiatric research, one should be reserved in prescribing additional medication to people for their personality pathology (Verheul & Herbrink, 2007). Evidence suggests that medical interventions in general add limited value to psychotherapy for personality disorders (Teusch, Bohme, Finke, & Gastpar, 2001) and that the routine prescription of drugs for people with personality disorders is simply not warranted (Paris, 2011).

MAPS - Medical Myths

Ironically, though, most of the traditional forms of psychotherapy into which people with personality disorders may be pushed may not be well suited to their specific problems. Therapists have thus responded to the challenge of treating personality disorders by creating new variations on the standard approaches and by proposing specific treatment goals that are matched to specific personality disorders. For example, Heinz Kohut pioneered a therapeutic approach known as *self psychology* (Kohut, 1977) for treating narcissistic personality disorder. The task for the therapist, says Kohut, is to provide the client with a relationship in which needs that were unmet during infancy can be recognized and even gratified; then the person can enjoy a more realistic and healthy sense of self-worth. To date, Kohut's psychoanalytic treatment approach has received little empirical support (Paris, 2014). In fact, some theorists have proposed that psychotherapy could even backfire for people with narcissistic personality disorder because it promotes the same sort of cultural narcissism about the centrality of the self, driven by recent social changes associated with modernity and technology, that has led to an increase in this disorder in the first place (Paris, 2014).

Tailored strategies have been proposed for other personality disorders as well. Specific cognitive-behavioral and psychodynamic therapies are effective interventions for reducing symptoms and personality pathology and for improving social functioning among people suffering from borderline, dependent, and avoidant personality disorders, with less evidence for effectiveness with other personality disorders (Verheul & Herbrink, 2007).

Can Personality Disorders Be Prevented? The Case of Antisocial Behavior

Personality disorders are difficult to treat, but can they be prevented? Considering the case of antisocial personality disorder, for which much research is available, current knowledge of predisposing risks suggests several prevention goals. First, because some biological vulnerabilities to antisocial personality disorder can be caused by prenatal exposure to drugs or alcohol and by inadequate nutrition for infants, public health programs that improve the health of women during pregnancy are essential. Second, programs such as school-based mindfulness or martial arts training that help children learn how to control impulsive behavior are critical. Third, parenting programs have had significant impacts on reducing children's antisocial behavior later in life (Moretti, 2013). For example, *The Incredible Years* is a series of interlocking, evidence-based programs for parents, children, and teachers, supported by over 30 years of research. The goal is to prevent and treat young children's behavior problems and promote their social, emotional, and academic competence. These programs are used worldwide in schools and mental health centers, and have been shown to work across cultures and socioeconomic groups to reduce future antisocial behavior (Menting, de Castro, & Matthys, 2013). Fourth, keeping children engaged in school and improving their ability to achieve academically are particularly important in the late elementary and middle-school years.

Because conduct disorder is a known precursor of antisocial personality disorder, special attention has been given to developing interventions that reduce this problem. An excellent example of a multicomponent program designed to prevent early antisocial conduct is the Montreal Longitudinal Experimental Study (Lacourse et al., 2002; Tremblay et al., 1992; Tremblay, Pagani-Kurtz, Masse, Vitaro, & Pihl, 1995). In this study, a group of kindergarten boys from inner-city, lower socioeconomic neighborhoods in Montreal, Quebec, were identified by their teachers as being at risk for later antisocial behavior because of the disruptive behavior they were already showing at school. These boys were then randomly assigned to a preventive intervention or a control group. Boys in the control group were repeatedly observed at school, and their parents filled out questionnaires on their behavior over the years, but they received no systematic treatment. Boys in the prevention program received two types of interventions: (1) They were taught new social skills to use at school so they could improve their ability to make friends and solve different kinds of social conflicts, and (2) their parents were trained in more-effective child discipline and behavior management practices. Parenting training programs emphasized close supervision of children's behavior, positive reinforcement of prosocial behavior, consistent, nonabusive discipline strategies, and management of family crises. The preventive intervention lasted for 2 years, when the boys were 7–9 years old.

The long-term impact of the intervention was measured in terms of the boys' adjustment up to age 17. Compared with control-group boys, a significantly greater percentage of boys in the prevention program were in an age-appropriate classroom up to the end of elementary school. However, this difference disappeared once the boys entered high school. By age 15, only 40% of all the boys in the study were in their age-appropriate grade at school. Overall, though, the boys receiving the intervention reported significantly less delinquent behavior than the control-group boys, and their rates of delinquent behavior did not differ from that of a large sample of boys selected at random from other elementary schools in Quebec. Thus, it appears that prevention programs targeted on both child and parental skill building can prevent some cases of antisocial behavior.

For instance, specialized cognitive-behavioral therapy for people with avoidant personality disorders emphasizes reducing avoidance of social encounters through techniques also used to treat social anxiety disorder, including systematic desensitization, gradual exposure to socially threatening situations, improvements in social skills, and challenges to dysfunctional assumptions (Alden, 1989; Emmelkamp et al., 2006; Rees & Pritchard, 2013).

Treatment of Borderline Personality Disorder

Borderline personality disorder presents a particularly difficult therapeutic challenge, partly because the clients' interpersonal problems intrude on the very process of therapy. Clients with this disorder often idealize their therapists, only to become angry at them later because of some disappointment for which the therapists are held responsible (e.g., going on vacation). As a result, these clients often vacillate between loving and hating their therapists. They may also cross boundaries that most other clients honor, such as intruding into therapists' personal lives or engaging in dramatic, even dangerous, behavior in an effort to gain extra attention. For instance, they may call therapists in the middle of the night, complaining that they are too upset to sleep. Sometimes, in a crisis, they will show up at their therapist's office and demand to be seen immediately. It is no wonder that some therapists refuse to treat people with borderline personality disorder or limit the number they will see at any one time.

Because symptoms of borderline personality disorder often include disturbances in mood, individuals can be misdiagnosed, usually with depression or bipolar disorder. This can lead clients to receive treatments that do not work. Research shows that treating depression alone is not effective for individuals with personality disorders (Newton-Howes, Tyrer, & Johnson, 2006). Specialized psychotherapy approaches for people with borderline personalities have been developed by interpersonal (Benjamin, 1993), analytic (Marziali & Munroe-Blum, 1987), and cognitive-behavioral therapists (Beck et al., 1990; Linehan, 1993). Medication is commonly used as an adjunctive treatment, as the current evidence suggests that drug treatment, especially with mood stabilizers (see Chapter 5) and second-generation antipsychotics (see Chapter 4), may be effective for treating a number of core symptoms and associated psychopathology; however, the evidence does not currently support drug effectiveness for reducing the overall severity of borderline personality disorder (Lieb, Vollm, Rucker, Timmer, & Stoffers, 2010).

Psychodynamic therapy based on an object relations model has been a particularly prominent form of treatment for people with borderline personality disorder. Perhaps the most influential version of this approach is the **transference-focused psychotherapy** of Otto Kernberg (1984; Kernberg, Selzer, Koenigsberg, Carr, & Appelbaum, 1989). Kernberg concentrates on analyzing the *transference* that develops in therapy—the process through which a client transfers to the therapist strong feelings and attitudes that are tied to a significant person from the client's past. Rather than seeking to uncover childhood conflicts that shape the transference as Freud did, Kernberg focuses on how the client with borderline personality disorder distorts the relationship in the present. A prominent example of this distortion is what Kernberg calls *splitting*, in which clients so exaggerate the negative and positive qualities of their therapist that they are unable to see that the qualities are actually just different aspects of the same person. Instead, they oscillate between seeing their therapist as either all good or all bad. Kernberg also structures treatment sessions and clients' day-to-day environment to help people with borderline personality disorder maintain firmer controls over their erratic, and sometimes aggressive, behavior. Transference-focused psychotherapy is receiving mounting empirical support and appears to be an effective treatment for borderline personality disorder (Levy, Meehan, & Yeomans, 2012).

Another effective psychotherapy for borderline personality disorder is a form of cognitive-behavioral therapy, first pioneered by Marsha Linehan (who has acknowledged being a sufferer of this same disorder herself in the past), known as **dialectical behavior therapy** or **DBT** (Linehan, 1993; Linehan & Kehrer, 1993). DBT is a comprehensive approach to helping clients with borderline personality disorder gain better control of what Linehan believes is their core problem—namely, difficulty in regulating their emotions and the consequent development of an incoherent self-image. Applying a diathesis-stress model, Linehan sees borderline personality disorder as arising when children with emotionally unstable temperaments are raised in *invalidating environments* in which almost all emotions are tightly controlled, ignored, punished, or trivialized. The result is that the children never learn to cope with any of their intense emotions.

Given that the causes of borderline personality disorders are multifaceted, Linehan's DBT focuses on several goals. Initially, DBT helps clients to develop basic skills in containing problematic behaviors. Clients are taught how to reduce their suicidal preoccupations and gestures, substance abuse, and other high-risk behaviors as they gradually develop a greater tolerance for painful emotions. In a group format to supplement their individual sessions, clients are taught concrete skills to tolerate distress, regulate emotions, be more effective in interpersonal situations, and increase mindfulness skills that

transference-focused psychotherapy: A treatment for borderline and other severe personality disorders that is based on psychoanalytic concepts and techniques that work with clients' early relationship templates to help clients construct a more stable adult identity.

dialectical behavior therapy (DBT): A comprehensive form of cognitive-behavioral therapy designed specifically for the treatment of borderline personality disorder. It focuses on increasing skills that allow individuals to accept current difficulties and work toward change.

will enable them to approach life in a less reactive manner. Skills are practiced during and between group sessions, and also addressed during individual therapy. In addition, therapists help individual clients to confront any traumatic experiences (such as physical or sexual abuse) that took place in their invalidating environment in childhood or later. This phase of treatment concentrates on recalling memories of past traumas, eliminating self-blame associated with these traumas, reducing post-traumatic stress symptoms, and resolving questions of whom to blame for the traumas (Linehan & Kehrer, 1993).

By consistently helping clients with borderline personality disorder to see that almost all events can be viewed from different perspectives, DBT therapists encourage clients to see the world in a more integrated or balanced way. A dialectical attitude by therapists also balances the goals of accepting clients as they currently are, while seeking to promote change in their behavior and thinking.

In comparison with other treatment approaches, DBT is associated with better overall adjustment up to 1 year after treatment (Linehan Armstrong, Suarez, Allmon, & Heard, 1991; Linehan et al., 2006; Linehan, Tutek, & Heard, 1992). Nonetheless, the treatment is intense, it may take years, and it is not effective for all clients (Linehan & Kehrer, 1993). Furthermore, DBT is effective at stabilizing and controlling self-destructive behavior and improving clients' compliance with treatment, but it may not be significantly better than treatment-as-usual at reducing symptoms of depression (Panos, Jackson, Hasan, & Panos, 2014).

Overall, rates of improvement for treatment of personality disorders such as avoidant, dependent, and borderline have approached 50% (Verheul & Herbrink, 2007), similar to that for other mental disorders like depression (see Chapter 6). The 10-year course of borderline personality disorder is characterized by high rates of remission (85% of clients have remission in a 10-year period), low rates of relapse (only 12%), but severe and persistent impairment in social functioning (Gunderson et al., 2011).

Treatment of Antisocial Personality Disorder

Clinicians have suggested several guidelines for treating people with antisocial personalities: (1) Treatment should be in a controlled environment, preferably a residential center; (2) treatment staff must maintain strict limits on clients' antisocial behavior; and (3) people with antisocial personalities must be taught to substitute less deviant means of gaining stimulation and to value cooperation as a basic moral principle (Meyer, 1993). However, even as clinicians suggest these strategies, they also recognize that there are virtually no data supporting the long-term effectiveness of psychological interventions for antisocial personality disorder (Wilson, 2014).

In fact, antisocial personality disorder is so difficult to alter that most clinicians regard it as essentially untreatable. Adults displaying antisocial personality disorder are seldom motivated to change (they are typically in treatment only through legal coercion), and they find it difficult to trust or have genuine rapport with a therapist unless it is part of a manipulation for personal gain (such as release from prison). Indeed, no form of psychotherapy has proved useful in treating antisocial personality disorder, nor have drugs or other biological treatments fared any better. It may be that the deficits in emotional and cognitive processing seen among individuals with antisocial personality disorder limit the effectiveness of therapy or other treatments (Patrick, 2007).

Fortunately, the severity of antisocial personality disorder tends to decline somewhat after about age 40, even without treatment. Why this phenomenon, termed *burnout*, occurs is not yet known. The other good news is twofold: There is emerging evidence that prevention efforts can be helpful in antisocial personality disorder (see this chapter's "Prevention" feature) and that adolescents at high risk for antisocial personality disorder (those with high scores on the PCL-R youth version) can be successfully treated via intensive psychotherapy, which cuts their likelihood of committing a future crime in half (Caldwell, Skeem, Salekin, & Van Rybroek, 2006).

- The long-standing patterns seen in personality disorders are challenging to treat, in part because clients may not be motivated to seek treatment.
- Medication is not typically effective in the treatment of any of the personality disorders.
- Tailored psychotherapy treatment approaches have shown success, particularly for individuals with borderline personality disorder, for whom dialectical behavior therapy (DBT) is recommended, as well as for dependent and avoidant personality disorders.
- There is no established treatment for antisocial personality disorder in adults, which suggests that early prevention (which can be successful) may be society's best option for addressing this disorder.

Revisiting the Case of Ted Bundy

In an interview shortly before he was executed on January 24, 1989, Ted Bundy expressed remorse for his crimes and blamed them on his addiction to violent pornography. However, most mental health professionals saw Bundy's statements as just one more example of the self-serving justifications that individuals with antisocial personality disorder are so adept at creating, in this case, to buy time and perhaps avoid the death penalty.

Fortunately, not all people with antisocial personality disorder are as dangerous as Ted Bundy, but they almost always victimize someone, whether by creating conflict in their families, taking credit for others' achievements, swindling people out of their money, or engaging in other forms of violent or nonviolent crime. Because these violations are chronic and there is no known effective treatment for antisocial personality disorder at this time, incarceration remains the dominant strategy for constraining repeated adult antisocial conduct (although treatment and prevention strategies work if the interventions occur before the person becomes an adult).

However, incarceration seems to be no more successful than treatment. One follow-up study of 231 Canadian male criminals released from prison revealed that almost two thirds of those identified as psychopaths had violated the conditions of their release or had committed a new crime within 1 year. Three years after getting out of prison, 80% of the psychopathic criminals had their releases revoked (Hart, Kropp, & Hare, 1988). Psychopathy also predicted violent reoffenses among Swedish criminals (Grann, Långström, Tengström, & Kullgren, 1999). In short, data such as these suggest that imprisoning psychopaths is unlikely to rehabilitate them; however, it does punish them and offers society a period of protection from their crimes.

For other personality disorders, the prognosis is not quite so dim. Special forms of psychotherapy for avoidant personality disorder and borderline personality disorder have been developed, and research suggests that these cognitive-behavioral therapies can lead to improvements and that the long-term prognosis is good.

Summary

Fateful Patterns: An Overview of Personality Disorders

According to the *DSM-5*, a personality disorder is an enduring pattern of inner experience and behavior that deviates markedly from the expectations of a person's culture, is pervasive and inflexible, begins in childhood or adolescence, lasts a long time, and results in distress or impairment. Ten personality disorders are described in the *DSM*, and they are often comorbid with one another or with other mental disorders. The chronic, long-lasting qualities of personality disorders set them apart from most other mental disorders, which are often more episodic in nature.

Mark Lenzenweger

Mark F. Lenzenweger, PhD, is a distinguished professor of psychology in clinical science, cognitive neuroscience, and behavioral neuroscience at the State University of New York at Binghamton, adjunct professor of psychology in psychiatry at the Weill Cornell Medical College, and senior research fellow at the Personality Disorders Institute of the New York Presbyterian Hospital. He directs the Laboratory of Experimental Psychopathology at SUNY-Binghamton, where he conducts research in several areas: schizotypy and schizophrenia, neurocognition in borderline personality disorder, and longitudinal research in personality disorders. Dr. Lenzenweger is internationally renowned for his research in schizotypy and has long advocated the view that schizotypic psychopathology is a variant of schizophrenia liability. This perspective has shaped the current diagnostic status of schizotypal pathology in the DSM-5. Dr. Lenzenweger directs the landmark NIMH-funded Longitudinal Study of Personality Disorders, which was the first prospective multiwave study of personality disorders, personality, and temperament. He is the author of over 110 peer-reviewed scientific articles, as well as six edited volumes and one monograph in psychopathology and clinical science. A fellow in both the Association for Psychological Science and the American Psychopathological Association, as well as a NARSAD distinguished investigator, he is also a licensed clinical psychologist who continues to work with clients in psychotherapy.

Q *What progress are we making in the treatment of personality disorders?*

A The treatment of personality disorders has made great gains in the past 10 years. In the past, psychologists and psychiatrists lacked any specialized treatment approaches to the personality disorders. In fact, many engaged in what is referred to as "treatment as usual," and this implied a relatively unfocused, somewhat haphazard, approach to the treatment of these debilitating conditions. The treatment-as-usual approach, which could involve both drug treatments and psychological treatments, often did not help individuals with personality disorders improve and some people actually became more impaired. However, the treatment scene for personality disorders is much different today. We now have several empirically supported treatments (treatments with a solid scientific basis) that are known to be quite useful in the treatment of personality disorders. Leading new specialized treatments for the personality disorders (particularly borderline personality) are Kernberg's transference-focused psychotherapy and Linehan's dialectical behavior therapy.

Q *Are there neurobiological markers that can help identify individuals at risk for certain personality disorders?*

A At this time, there are no highly predictive neurobiological markers for personality disorders. There are some effective screening tools that have been used to tap into likely risk for personality disorders. One particularly effective screening tool is the *International Personality Disorder Examination Screen (IPDE-S)*, which was developed as a supplemental tool for use in larger-scale epidemiological studies. The *IPDE-S* has shown remarkable ability to detect risk or the likelihood of a personality disorder. We are making headway, however, with respect to a better understanding of underlying neural systems and how they are related to both what we might call "normal" personality, as well as personality disorder. Along with my colleague Dr. Richard Depue at Cornell University, I have proposed a neurobehavioral model of personality and personality disorders. This model links important underlying brain circuits, along with their primary neurotransmitters (such as dopamine, norepinephrine, serotonin) as well as other agents (e.g., endogenous opiates), to major personality systems. We have proposed that when these underlying brain systems, in interaction with the environment, come together in certain combinations, the groundwork for a personality disorder is laid. This is a new and exciting perspective that links modern personality neuroscience with clinical science, especially personality disorders research.

Q *Why do personality disorders tend to show such high levels of overlap or comorbidity with one another?*

A The issue of overlap or what some might call "comorbidity" is a challenging issue, and it has to do primarily with the crude classification system we use for

Mark Lenzenweger, PhD (Continued)

personality disorders. The classification system that has received the most attention in psychology and psychiatry has been the one proposed originally in the *DSM-III* in 1980, and it has remained largely the same over the years. The original system really represented a descriptive approach to personality disorders, and the tendency was to include more disorders, rather than fewer. This means that the original classification scheme was not based in a solid body of empirical research findings, which could have led to excessive overlap. Moreover, some of the personality disorders in the *DSM* share conceptual similarities, and in some cases, the same diagnostic criteria are represented in different disorders. Thus, the system was constructed in a way that implicitly built in overlap. To make matters worse, the *DSM* approach to diagnosis has explicitly encouraged the assignment of multiple diagnoses to the same patient. The end result is what appears to be elevated covariation or comorbidity across the different personality disorders. The question remains: Is this true comorbidity, or is this an artifact of the diagnostic classification system and recommended diagnostic practice? It may be that fewer personality disorders should be designated in the diagnostic system, but only further empirical research will settle this issue. The alternative system for personality disorders description and diagnosis in the *DSM-5* is an important effort to try to address this problem of excessive overlap in this area.

Q In what ways are schizotypal personality disorder, schizoid personality disorder, and schizophrenia related?

A This is an issue that has long been of interest to both researchers and clinicians working with individuals affected with schizophrenia and related conditions. Early observers of schizophrenia speculated that the illness often expresses itself in dilute forms, and in fact, it was thought that these diluted forms might be the most common expressions of schizophrenia liability. Today, we know, as a result of research done in my laboratory and that done by others, that schizotypal personality pathology is strongly related to schizophrenia. Schizotypal persons display many of the same neurocognitive, perceptual, and language-related deficits as those seen in patients with actual schizophrenia. In fact, we now think of schizotypal personality as a variant or alternative manifestation of the liability for schizophrenia. This view has now been included in the *DSM-5*. Schizoid personality disorder, which is relatively rare, is also thought to share a connection with schizophrenia but has not been studied nearly as much as schizotypal pathology. However, available evidence from the study of biological relatives of persons affected with schizophrenia supports a connection between schizoid personality disorder and schizophrenia, albeit of lesser strength.

Types of Personality Disorders

DSM-5 groups the 10 personality disorders into three clusters, based on the similarity of their major symptoms: Cluster A, the odd/eccentric group (paranoid, schizoid, and schizotypal personality disorders); Cluster B, the dramatic/emotional/erratic group (antisocial, borderline, histrionic, and narcissistic personality disorders); and Cluster C, the anxious/fearful group (avoidant, dependent, and obsessive-compulsive personality disorders).

Causes of Personality Disorders

Theories of personality disorders tend to emphasize genetic predispositions, early childhood conflicts, the learning of stable interpersonal patterns of behavior, and interactions among these variables that produce rigid, dysfunctional personality patterns. The suspected causes of borderline personality disorder include brain dysfunctions, genetic ties to depressive and bipolar disorders, infant-caregiver conflicts, and early childhood trauma. The suspected causes of antisocial personality disorder include genetic vulnerabilities, deficits in emotional and/or cognitive pro-

cessing, physiological underarousal, impulsivity, sensation seeking, and a combination of family and social factors that undermine the ability of parents to control early manifestations of aggressive and rule-breaking behavior.

Treatment of Personality Disorders

Treatment or prevention of personality disorders is challenging because of their long-standing nature and their complicated causation. Medication is not very effective for personality disorders. No single treatment or preventive strategy will be effective for all, or even most, disorders, suggesting that each disorder requires interventions that are guided by knowledge of specific risk factors. Special forms of psychotherapy have been developed for borderline personality disorder and avoidant personality disorder, and research results suggest that they can bring about positive changes. There is no effective treatment for antisocial personality disorder at this time. Because personality disorders begin to emerge in adolescence, prevention is not likely to be effective unless it targets childhood antecedents to the disorders.

Key Terms

Paraphilic Disorders and Legal Issues

CHAPTER 17

Source: Lena Edstrom/LK Photography.

Chapter Outline

From the Case of Justin

Justin is 23 years old and has his first "real" job at an elementary school. He loves his job as a third-grade teacher, mostly because of how young students react to new and exciting discoveries. Justin enjoys incorporating fun and interactive play into his daily lessons about science. He often fondly recalls his own memories of elementary school and distinctly remembers experiences he had with his own fourth-grade teacher, Mr. Wallace.

Justin recalls that Mr. Wallace took him under his wing and provided him with a lot of personal attention, far more than the other students in the class. Justin never knew his father, and he liked having an older man to look up to. Mr. Wallace often offered Justin rides home from school. Justin's mother worked long hours at the diner to support her son, and she greatly appreciated Mr. Wallace's generosity in looking after Justin. It was during these car rides home when Mr. Wallace would tell Justin how special a boy he was. On about a dozen occasions over the course of that year, Justin remembers how Mr. Wallace would stop off at an old, deserted factory on the way home and have Justin remove his pants; then Mr. Wallace would perform oral sex on him. Justin remembers Mr. Wallace telling him that this was how people showed that they loved one another.

After reading this chapter, you will be able to answer the following key questions:

- What is the difference between a paraphilia and a paraphilic disorder?
- What are the key characteristics of the eight paraphilic disorders described in the *Diagnostic and Statistical Manual of Mental Disorders (DSM-5)*?
- What are the possible causes of paraphilic disorders?
- What treatments exist for paraphilic disorders?
- What are the legal and ethical issues that relate to mental disorders and mental health professionals?

Justin vividly recalls that this is what he thought to be true from then on, throughout the rest of his childhood and teenage years. Justin has struggled with intimacy as an adult and has never really had any serious girlfriends. Though his experiences with Mr. Wallace were troubling, he still recollects all of the positives that came from the relationship and strongly associates Mr. Wallace with happy, yet confusing, memories. Now a teacher himself, Justin feels a strong bond with the boys in his third-grade classroom. He notices that he gets sexually aroused when they hug him. Justin is disturbed by this but also enjoys it. He tells himself that this is a natural part of caring for others, and he hopes that he can provide the type of love and support that he received from his past teachers, especially Mr. Wallace.

Does Justin have a mental disorder, or does his case represent an extreme variation on the almost endless variability of normal human sexual expression? Is Justin's sexual attraction to young boys caused by a biological abnormality, or is it the result of the experiences he had as a young child? Can he learn to stop being attracted to young boys, or is this the way he will always be? We consider such questions in this chapter as we address paraphilic disorders, disorders involving sexual arousal that is repeatedly elicited by unusual or inappropriate stimuli or situations. Later in the chapter, we also consider legal and ethical issues that could arise in diagnosing or treating people with paraphilic or a host of other mental disorders.

Paraphilia Versus Paraphilic Disorder

Everyone has sexual fantasies and preferences for certain kinds of sexual partners, activities, or stimuli, and finding a partner who is willing to share or fulfill such fantasies and preferences adds interest to a person's sex life. Some people have atypical sexual interests, either involving unusual erotic activities or uncommon erotic targets. But just because a person has an unusual sexual interest does not necessarily mean that he or she has a mental disorder.

According to the *DSM-5*, people can have anomalous sexual practices without having a disorder, and the terms *paraphilia* and *paraphilic disorder* define the distinction. The main feature of a **paraphilia** is an intense and persistent sexual interest in fantasies or actions involving atypical stimuli. Some paraphilias are harmless, as when a man becomes sexually aroused only if his partner wears black leather or when a woman cannot be orgasmic unless her partner wears cowboy boots. Other behaviors are far more problematic because they involve engaging in illegal behaviors, such as exposing one's genitals in public or secretly watching others' sexual activities. Such actions often lead to relationship problems, unemployment, or even arrest. In these cases, a **paraphilic disorder** would be diagnosed because the paraphilia causes negative consequences, either for the individual or for others. Such negative consequences include clinically significant distress, impairment in functioning, or risk of harm to self or others. A paraphilic disorder is diagnosed when the paraphilic behavior, urges, or fantasies are persistent, defined as lasting for at least 6 months.

Delineating what is normal versus deviant or disordered sexuality is one of the biggest challenges when using the term *paraphilia* (McManus, Hargreaves, Rainbow, & Alison, 2013). The definitions under *paraphilia* within the *DSM* have been highly debated and controversial (Wakefield, 2011). The malleability of sexual pleasure across time and cultures creates problems for those defining and diagnosing paraphilia. Furthermore, for some people with the disorder, paraphilic stimuli are always necessary for arousal, whereas for others, they become important only during periods of stress. Thus, individuals with paraphilic preferences may routinely engage in sex with a regular adult partner, but periodically seek sexual satisfaction by molesting children, exposing themselves in public, or cross-dressing. The specific paraphilic disorders diagnosed depend on the object of inappropriate sexual arousal, as described in the next section.

paraphilia: An intense and persistent sexual interest in fantasies or actions involving anomalous stimuli.

paraphilic disorder: A disorder in which a paraphilia causes (1) distress or impairment in social, occupational, or other important areas of functioning or (2) harm or risk of harm to others.

MAPS - Prejudicial Pigeonholes

The *DSM-5* distinguishes between having atypical sexual interests and having a mental disorder due to one's sexual interests:

- A paraphilia is not a mental disorder and refers to an intense and persistent sexual interest in fantasies or actions involving anomalous stimuli.
- A paraphilic disorder describes when a paraphilia causes (1) distress or impairment in social, occupational, or other important areas of functioning or (2) harm or risk of harm to others.

The *Fifty Shades of Grey* trilogy has sold over 100 million copies worldwide. If you have read this erotic thriller, would you consider Christian Grey to have a paraphilia or a paraphilic disorder? Why?

Source: Veronica Louro/Shutterstock.com.

Types of Paraphilic Disorders

The *DSM-5* identifies eight specific paraphilic disorders, all of which are seen much more often in men. These include voyeuristic disorder, exhibitionistic disorder, frotteuristic disorder, fetishistic disorder, transvestic disorder, sexual sadism disorder, sexual masochism disorder, and pedophilic disorder.

Voyeuristic Disorder

The hallmark of **voyeuristic disorder** is that individuals achieve intense sexual arousal through repeated, clandestine observation of others naked, disrobing, or engaging in sexual activity. These "peeping Toms" typically seek no sexual contact with the people they watch; the thrill seems to come from attempting and getting away with behavior that is taboo and risky. Individuals with voyeuristic disorder often masturbate, either while watching others or later, as they relive what they saw (Becker, Johnson, & Perkins, 2014). Some may also expose themselves to their victims after watching them for a while. Note that the individuals they watch are not consenting to be observed. Individuals can also be diagnosed with voyeuristic disorder if they are distressed or impaired by urges or fantasies of watching unsuspecting others, even if they do not attempt to create the fantasy or act upon the urge. Since many adolescents are sexually curious, and thus may temporarily engage in voyeuristic behavior as they explore their sexual identities, only adults (18 years or older) can be diagnosed with voyeuristic disorder. However, voyeuristic behavior typically begins in adolescence and can continue into adulthood (American Psychiatric Association, 2013a).

Lifetime prevalence rates for voyeuristic disorder are pegged at 12% in males and 4% in females (American Psychiatric Association, 2013a). Exhibitionistic disorder (described in the next section) appears to co-occur in some individuals with voyeuristic disorder.

voyeuristic disorder: A paraphilic disorder in which individuals achieve sexual arousal through the clandestine observation of others who are naked, disrobing, or engaging in sexual activity.

Exhibitionistic Disorder

In **exhibitionistic disorder**, the recurrent act of exposing one's genitals to an unwilling observer brings intense sexual arousal. Many exhibitionists follow a consistent pattern, exposing themselves in the same setting or to similar kinds of people, but most attempt no other contact with the observer. They may masturbate during the exposure, and their sexual arousal seems to be stimulated by the surprise or shock that their act causes (Becker et al., 2014). Most exhibitionists are not physically aggressive. Individuals can also be diagnosed with exhibitionistic disorder without exposing themselves to others: As for voyeuristic disorder, having exhibitionistic fantasies or urges that are distressing or cause impairment is enough to warrant a diagnosis.

Prevalence rates are unclear, but the American Psychiatric Association estimates that 2–4% of males meet criteria for exhibitionistic disorder; prevalence rates in females are less certain and are believed to be much lower (American Psychiatric Association, 2013a). This disorder appears to remit with age. Children, adolescents, and women are the primary targets of individuals with exhibitionistic disorder (Murphy & Page, 2008).

exhibitionistic disorder: A paraphilic disorder in which individuals gain sexual arousal by exposing their genitals to an unwilling observer.

Frotteuristic Disorder

frotteuristic disorder: A paraphilic disorder involving recurrent touching or rubbing against a nonconsenting person to become sexually aroused.

Frotteuristic disorder involves recurrent touching or rubbing against a nonconsenting person to become sexually aroused. A common pattern is for a man to approach a female victim in a crowded public place, such as a subway train, bus, or shopping mall. He then moves next to the woman and, while fully clothed, begins to push or brush his penis against her buttocks or legs as he fantasizes about having intercourse with her. Individuals with frotteuristic disorder are seldom apprehended, in part because their victims are slow to realize what is taking place or are too embarrassed to call attention to it. As with the other paraphilic disorders mentioned thus far, a person need not engage in frotteurism to be diagnosed with this disorder; being distressed or impaired by fantasies or urges to touch a nonconsenting person would merit a diagnosis of frotteuristic disorder.

Approximately 10–14% of adult men seen in clinical settings for paraphilic disorders and hypersexuality meet criteria for frotteuristic disorder (American Psychiatric Association, 2013a). Rates among women are unknown, but they are believed to be substantially lower than rates for males. This disorder appears to remit with age. Exhibitionistic disorder and voyeuristic disorder have been known to co-occur with frotteuristic disorder (American Psychiatric Association, 2013a).

Fetishistic Disorder

fetishistic disorder: A paraphilic disorder in which individuals focus sexual interest on a nonliving object or specific nongenital body part to become aroused.

In **fetishistic disorder**, the person recurrently experiences intense sexual arousal from an inanimate object or a specific nongenital body part. In addition, the fantasies, urges, or behaviors involving the inanimate object or body part cause distress or impairment in functioning. Common fetishes include shoes, leather garments, underwear, rubber items, feet, toes, and hair (American Psychiatric Association, 2013a). In many cases, individuals masturbate while gazing at, holding, tasting, rubbing, or smelling the fetish. Others coax their partner to wear the fetishistic item during sex because, without the fetish, they may experience sexual dysfunction (see Chapter 13). Almost any object can serve as a fetish, whether or not it is normally associated with sex. One 33-year-old man developed a fetish for baby carriages; he hoarded pictures of them and masturbated while looking at them (Raymond, 1956).

The American Psychiatric Association (2013a) reports that fetishistic disorder is found almost exclusively in men and that the fetish can develop prior to adolescence. Darcangelo (2008) reviewed studies that show fetishistic disorder to be rare, even among forensic populations.

Transvestic Disorder

transvestic disorder: A paraphilic disorder in which individuals cross-dress to become sexually aroused and experience distress or impairment as a result.

The diagnosis of **transvestic disorder** is made if a person experiences distress or impairment as a result of arousal from cross-dressing fantasies, urges, or behavior. Sexual arousal may occur from the fabrics or the garments themselves, or from thoughts or images of being the opposite sex. Individuals with this disorder may wear only one or two articles of clothing (e.g., women's underwear) or fully dress as the opposite sex (including wigs and/or makeup). They may masturbate or engage in sexual activity while cross-dressed. Others become so aroused by cross-dressing that they ejaculate spontaneously. Individuals cross-dress to become aroused, but over time, the sexual excitement may give way to a sense of comfort. (One highway tollbooth attendant we know of, for example, relaxed after work each evening by lounging around in nightgowns.) The partners of individuals with transvestic desires frequently know about these people's preferences, and those preferences can disrupt their sexual relations and lead to relationship problems.

Without distress or impairment, transvestic disorder is not an appropriate diagnosis for someone who cross-dresses for sexual arousal. Distress may be suggested by a pattern of "purging and acquisition" (American Psychiatric Association, 2013a, p. 703). In this pattern, individuals get rid of all of their articles of clothing (which they may have purchased at great expense) in an effort to stop cross-dressing. Before long, unable to resist the desire to cross-dress, they acquire a brand-new wardrobe. This pattern may repeat itself many times.

Unfortunately, some individuals may confuse transvestic disorder with the term *transgender*, which describes when one's biological sex does not match one's gender identity. Thus, a biological male may dress in female-typical clothing because such clothing is a truer expression of her gender identity. Her clothing choice is a function of her gender identity and is not motivated by sexual arousal. Gender dysphoria is discussed in Chapter 13.

Whereas the prevalence of transvestic disorder is unknown, it is believed to be rare. It occurs almost exclusively in men, the majority of whom are heterosexual (American Psychiatric Association, 2013a). Transvestic disorder may begin in childhood or adulthood, and it may be temporary or long-lasting (Becker et al., 2014).

Sexual Sadism Disorder and Sexual Masochism Disorder

Obtaining sexual excitement or gratification by inflicting physical pain or humiliation on a sexual partner is the chief feature of *sexual sadism*. *Sexual masochism* describes when sexual arousal depends on receiving painful stimulation or being humiliated. It is important to recognize that sexual fantasies or enactments involving bondage, blindfolds, or minor discomfort do not necessarily constitute paraphilic disorders. It is not uncommon, for example, for individuals to fantasize about a sexual partner overpowering them, and many couples act out shared fantasies in which they bind each other to the bed with a necktie or piece of lingerie. Individuals who rely exclusively on sexual masochism or sadism for sexual release are not diagnosed with a paraphilic disorder unless they experience distress as a result of their behavior (i.e., shame, guilt, anxiety) or if their behavior impairs important areas of functioning (i.e., relationships, work, school). It is only when sexual gratification depends on pain or humiliation—and when these activities lead to harm or distress when forced on or coerced from a partner—that **sexual sadism disorder** or **sexual masochism disorder** is diagnosed—see Tables 17.1 and 17.2.

Individuals with sexual masochism disorder may act out their urges through masturbatory fantasies or sexual contacts in which they are bound, whipped, cut, electrically shocked, stuck with pins, forced to crawl or imitate animals, or are urinated and defecated on. Sometimes, police find the bodies of men who died accidentally while trying to heighten their arousal during masturbation by self-strangulation (described as *sexual masochism disorder with asphyxiophilia*).

Individuals with sexual sadism derive pleasure from inflicting pain on others, and although some of these people find willing partners, mainly masochists, others become a public menace because they attain fullest arousal with victims they do not know and

sexual sadism disorder: A paraphilic disorder describing when sexual arousal depends on the physical or psychological suffering of another person.

sexual masochism disorder: A paraphilic disorder describing when sexual arousal depends on being humiliated or made to suffer.

TABLE 17.1 The *DSM-5* in Simple Language: Diagnosing Sexual Sadism Disorder

> The person has experienced consistent sexual arousal, over a period of at least 6 months, from someone else's suffering (physical or psychological) and has either acted on these urges with a nonconsenting person or the urges have caused significant distress or dysfunction to the person.

Source: Adapted from American Psychiatric Association (2013a).

TABLE 17.2 The *DSM-5* in Simple Language: Diagnosing Sexual Masochism Disorder

> The person has experienced consistent sexual arousal, over a period of at least 6 months, from his or her own suffering (physical or psychological), and the urges have caused significant distress or dysfunction.

Source: Adapted from American Psychiatric Association (2013a).

whom they can terrify. Indeed, many serial killers would be described as having sexual sadism disorder, as the act of controlling and hurting victims is intensely pleasurable to them. This kind of sadist often chooses victims who are easy targets, such as adolescent runaways or prostitutes. Sexually sadistic fantasies are usually present by early adulthood but may have even begun in childhood (Becker et al., 2014).

In some cases, sadistic or masochistic acts remain consistent over time, but in others, the desired intensity of pain inflicted or endured gradually increases, placing these people at a growing risk for arrest, injury, or death. The frequent use of pornography involving sadism and masochism is sometimes reported among people with these paraphilic disorders. Precise prevalence data are unknown. The American Psychiatric Association (2013a) reports that fewer than 10% of civilly committed sexual offenders in the United States have sexual sadism. Among individuals who have committed sexually motivated homicides, rates range from 37–75%. As with other paraphilic disorders, sexual sadism and masochism disorders appear to remit with age.

Another Paraphilic Disorder: Lust Murder

A lust murder is a homicide in which the offender searches for erotic satisfaction by killing someone. Lust murder is synonymous with the paraphilic term *erotophonophilia*, an extreme form of sadism that involves sexual arousal or gratification contingent on the death of a human being (Purcell, 2001). Commonly, this type of crime is manifested either by murder during sexual intercourse and/or by mutilating the sexual organs or areas of the victim's body. The mutilation of the victim may include evisceration and/or displacement of the genitalia (Aggrawal, 2009), which usually takes place postmortem (Hickey, 2010). It sometimes includes such activities as removing clothing from the body, posing and propping up of the body in different positions (generally sexual ones), insertion of objects into bodily orifices, anthropophagy (the consumption of human blood and/or flesh), and necrophilia, the performing of sex acts on a human corpse, as in the case of Jeffrey Dahmer (Purcell, 2001).

Most cases of lust murder involve male perpetrators; however, accounts of female lust murderers do exist (Ramsland, 2007). In general, lust murder is a phenomenon most common among serial killers. These offenders have made a connection between murder and sexual gratification. When they choose a victim, there must be something about that victim that they find sexually attractive. Once they have found a victim who is ideal, they might engage in stalking or other predatory behaviors before acting out their fantasy on the victim.

Fantasies are a key component in lust murders and can never be completely fulfilled. Lust killers typically have a fantasy that continues to evolve over time and becomes increasingly violent as they struggle to fulfill it (Holmes & Holmes, 2010). Examples of lust murderers who killed multiple victims include Jeffrey Dahmer, Ted Bundy (discussed in Chapter 16), and historically famous cases such as the Boston Strangler and Jack the Ripper. Whereas these cases clearly represent only a small portion of those with paraphilic disorders, research indicates that paraphilic behavior is a common denominator in sexual crimes (Purcell, 2001). Lust murders are an extreme example of how a series of paraphilic disorders (i.e., sexually deviant behaviors), coupled with other deficits (e.g., antisocial personality disorder), can give rise to violent conduct (Arrigo & Purcell, 2001).

King Joffrey of *Game of Thrones* displays characteristics of sexual sadism disorder, along with antisocial personality disorder (see Chapter 16).

The *DSM-5* allows the diagnosis of other paraphilic disorders that cause significant distress or impairment with the category *Other Specified Paraphilic Disorder*. An example is necrophilia, or sexual arousal involving corpses. Serial killer Jeffrey Dahmer was a notorious example of someone who engaged in *necrophilia*. In general, crime scene behaviors often reflect paraphilic disturbances in those who commit serial sexual homicides (Myers et al., 2008).

Sadism and Rape

Are individuals with sexual sadism disorder responsible for the hundreds of thousands of rapes that occur each year around the world? No. Although an unknown percentage of rapes are committed by true sexual sadists, rape is a crime that is often fueled by motives such as power, hatred, or aggression, and may thus have little or no relationship to sexual arousal or satisfaction. Rape is viewed as a crime of violence, not sex (Brownmiller, 1975), and it is not considered a paraphilic disorder. Proposals to include rape as a mental disorder under the label *coercive paraphilic disorder* have been rejected by the creators of the *DSM-5* (Paris, 2013).

According to various researchers, including Allen Frances (2011), who was the chair of the *DSM-IV* task force, this sends an important message to everyone involved in approving psychiatric commitment under sexually violent predator statutes that the act of being a rapist almost always is an indication of criminality, not of mental disorder. Four *DSM*s have unanimously rejected the concept that rape is a mental disorder. As Frances (2011) put it:

> Rapists need to receive longer prison sentences, not psychiatric hospitalizations that are constitutionally quite questionable. This *DSM-5* rejection has huge consequences both for forensic psychiatry and for the legal system. If "coercive paraphilia" had been included as a mental disorder in the *DSM-5*, rapists would be routinely subject to involuntary psychiatric commitment once their prison sentence had been completed. Whereas such continued psychiatric incarceration makes sense from a public safety standpoint, misusing psychiatric diagnosis has grave risks that greatly outweigh the gain. . . .

Pedophilic Disorder

According to the *DSM-5*, **pedophilic disorder** involves recurrent and intense sexually arousing fantasies, urges, or behaviors involving sexual activity with a prepubescent child (usually defined as younger than 13) by a person who is at least 16 years of age and is at least 5 years older than the child. Some people with pedophilic disorder are attracted only to children; others are aroused by adults as well.

Individuals with pedophilic disorder typically develop extensive justifications for their behavior, claiming that the child "enjoys it" or that it "teaches the child valuable lessons about love." With the exception of sexual sadists, child molesters are not usually overtly aggressive toward their victims. Typically, they take advantage of the child's trust, or they convince the child that there is nothing wrong with sexual contact, like in the chapter-opening case about Justin. When the victims are family members, the relative often bribes or intimidates the child to keep her or him from reporting the abuse. Many of those with pedophilic disorder create and take advantage of special opportunities to gain easy access to children, as the following case illustrates:

> Dr. Crone, a 35-year-old unmarried child psychiatrist, was prominent in his community and came from a stable family. He had chosen a profession devoted to caring for children, and for many years, had been a Cub Scout leader and a member of the local Big Brothers organization. Thus, it was a shock to all who knew him when he was arrested, and later convicted, of fondling several young neighborhood boys. In a psychiatric interview following his arrest, Dr. Crone reported that, at the age of 6, a 15-year-old male camp counselor performed fellatio on him several times over the course of the summer. In later years, as his male friends began expressing sexual attraction toward girls, his secret was that he was attracted to boys. Whenever he masturbated, he fantasized about a young boy, and on a couple of occasions, he felt himself to be in love with such a youngster. He felt little, if any, sexual attraction toward females of any age or toward adult men. Dr. Crone knew that others would disapprove of his sexual involvement with boys, and he kept promising himself that he would stop, but temptation always got the better of him. (Based on Spitzer, Gibbon, Skodol, Williams, & First, 1994)

pedophilic disorder: A paraphilic disorder involving sexual activity with a prepubescent child by a person who is at least 16 years of age and at least 5 years older than the child.

The American Psychiatric Association (2013a) places prevalence rates of pedophilic disorder in males as high as 3–5%. Women with pedophilic disorder are believed to be but a fraction of that found in men, but they do exist (Grayson & De Luca, 1999). This disorder is lifelong, although the frequency of sexual behavior with children appears to decrease with age. Use of child pornography is suggestive of pedophilic disorder (Seto, Cantor, & Blanchard, 2006).

Whereas pedophilia may be limited to fantasies and impulses, pedophilic behaviors are the primary concern of both the mental health and criminal justice systems because of the potential for serious harm to children and adolescents. Remote risk factors for development of pedophilia include the individual having been sexually abused as a child (Fagan, Wise, Schmidt, & Berlin, 2002). Proximate risk factors for its behavioral expression are the prevalence of comorbid mental disorders (Fagan et al., 2002). For instance, antisocial personality disorder appears to be a risk factor for pedophilic disorder in men with pedophilia (American Psychiatric Association, 2013a); the lack of empathy and remorse in those with antisocial personality disorder makes these individuals more likely to act on their fantasies of having sexual contact with minors. Treatment goals, discussed further later in the chapter, focus on stopping the behavior and achieving long-term behavioral control in the community.

Connections

What symptoms and behaviors are typical of antisocial personality disorder? Are these individuals always physically dangerous? See Chapter 16.

Prevalence of Paraphilic Disorders

It is difficult to estimate the prevalence of paraphilic disorders in the general population because most people whose sex lives are dominated by these preferences are not willing to admit to them. A rough estimation of the problem can be made from the fact that over 70,000 arrests occur in the United States each year for sexually related crimes not including rape (Federal Bureau of Investigation, 2010). Yet, even this estimate is skewed, as not every sexual offender's behavior is driven by a paraphilic disorder (First, 2014), some individuals with paraphilic disorders never commit a sex crime (Becker et al., 2014), and many individuals with paraphilic disorders who are public offenders are never caught.

In one of the only studies of its kind, Abel and colleagues (1988) interviewed 561 men seeking evaluation and/or treatment for a possible paraphilic disorder. The researchers obtained a special federal Certificate of Confidentiality that guaranteed the anonymity of the participants. The certificate enabled researchers to circumvent mandatory reporting laws, so that participants could disclose sexual offenses without fear of legal prosecution. Nearly 40% of the men had engaged in 5–10 different forms of paraphilic behavior, either concurrently or in sequence, with the overall pattern of results suggesting that individuals with only one paraphilic disorder are rare (Abel, Becker, Cunningham-Rather, Mittelman, & Rouleau, 1988). For example, among individuals with exhibitionistic disorder, 46% reported behavior consistent with pedophilic disorder, 28% reported behavior consistent with voyeuristic disorder, and 16% reported behavior consistent with frotteuristic disorder (Abel et al., 1988). The researchers also found that individuals with pedophilic disorder were very likely to have offended several times against both family and nonfamily.

A more recent study from Germany revealed that paraphilic arousal patterns are quite common in the community as well (Ahlers et al., 2011). The percentage of men reporting at least one paraphilia-associated sexual arousal pattern (PASAP) was 62.4%. In 1.7% of cases, PASAPs were reported to have caused distress. The presence of a PASAP was associated with a higher likelihood of being single, masturbating at least once per week, or having a low general subjective health score. Pedophilic PASAP in sexual fantasies and in real-life sociosexual behavior was reported by 9.5% and 3.8% of participants, respectively. These findings suggest that paraphilia-related experiences cannot be regarded as unusual from a normative perspective. At the same time, many men experience a PASAP without accompanying problem awareness or distress, even when PASAP contents are associated with potentially causing harm to others.

Another study showed that paraphilic disorders may be more common than previously thought among psychiatric inpatients (Marsh et al., 2010). In the sample, 13.4% of men reported symptoms consistent with at least one lifetime *DSM* paraphilic disorder.

Is Sex Addiction a Mental Disorder?

Sex addiction, otherwise known as hypersexual disorder, is not a mental disorder according to the *DSM-5*. In fact, despite being initially proposed as a new diagnosis for possible inclusion in the *DSM-5*, it is now not even listed in the appendix of the *DSM-5* as a condition for further study. Why not?

Hypersexual disorder is defined as recurrent and intense sexual fantasies, urges, and behaviors that last at least 6 months (Reid et al., 2012). In turn, the fantasies, urges, and behaviors lead to significant distress or impairment. In a field trial, the diagnostic criteria for hypersexual disorder showed good validity with theoretically related measures of hypersexuality, impulsivity, emotional dysregulation, and stress proneness, as well as good internal consistency (Reid et al., 2012).

Many clinicians work with individuals whose lives have been turned upside down by out-of-control sexual activity. Individuals (including prominent politicians) have been divorced for extramarital affairs, fired for viewing pornography at work, and shamed in the court of public opinion for "sexting." Some therapists argue that inclusion of hypersexual disorder in the *DSM-5* would encourage empirical studies about appropriate treatments for sex addiction. Others note that a psychiatric diagnosis would facilitate reimbursement for clinical services. Still others believe that conceptualizing hypersexuality as "addiction" would allow greater compassion for individuals who struggle with a behavior that threatens to destroy their personal and sometimes professional lives.

Conversely, other experts believe that including so-called "behavioral addictions" sets up a slippery slope such that any behavior that is outside the norm could be pathologized. What about shopping addiction or exercise addiction? What about spending hours on Facebook at the expense of doing one's job or schoolwork? How do we decide what is a mental disorder and what is a problem of daily living?

Hypersexual disorder was not included in the *DSM-5*, presumably because of insufficient research establishing it as a reliable and valid diagnosis (see Chapter 14 for a discussion of behavioral addictions). Yet, there may have been other unstated reasons as well. It is interesting, for example, that "excessive sexual drive" is included in the *International Classification of Diseases (ICD)*, a diagnostic tool maintained by the World Health Organization and used by clinicians around the world (discussed in Chapter 1). But the *DSM-5* decided not to go down what could have been quite a slippery slope.

Thinking Critically

1. Do you think there is a difference between the various behavioral addictions (shopping, Facebook, sex, chocolate, etc.)? How would the treatment be similar?

2. Do you think hypersexual disorder should be included in the *DSM-6*? Why or why not?

The most common paraphilic disorders were voyeurism (8.0%), exhibitionism (5.4%), and sexual masochism (2.7%). Patients who screened positive for a paraphilic disorder had significantly more psychiatric hospitalizations and were significantly more likely to report having been sexually abused than patients without a paraphilia.

Most paraphilic disorders begin in adolescence or early adulthood, peak during adulthood, and gradually become less intense as the person ages (Meyer, 1995). Individuals with paraphilic disorders generally are male (Becker et al., 2014). According to Abel and colleagues (1988), among individuals with multiple paraphilic disorders, one will typically dominate for months or years before another paraphilic disorder takes precedence over the first. The first paraphilic disorder will then lessen in intensity. Substance use disorders, mood disorders, and personality disorders are often comorbid with paraphilic disorders (Becker et al., 2014).

In Western societies, a wide range of sexual behaviors are described in a number of surveys and studies. However, not only are such data often not available from other societies, the accuracy of the data that do exist is often questionable. Even so, not all cultures appear to manifest fetishes or certain paraphilic practices, or to view them as an issue (Bhugra, Popelyuk, & McMullen, 2010). That in itself may be a reflection of first, whether the culture sees itself as sex-positive or sex-negative, and second, whether the function of sexual intercourse is seen as pleasure or procreation. Furthermore, other characteristics of the society may play important roles; for example, paraphilic disorders may be more common in egocentric and sex-positive cultures, where sexual intercourse is predominantly practiced for pleasure and where arousal becomes a predominant theme. In contrast, sociocentric, kinship-based, preindustrialized societies that emphasize sex for reproduction may well have rates of paraphilic disorders that are different from those reported in the West (Bhugra et al., 2010).

Section Review

The eight paraphilic disorders described in the *DSM-5* are:

- voyeuristic disorder, in which individuals achieve sexual arousal through the clandestine observation of others who are naked, disrobing, or engaging in sexual activity;
- exhibitionistic disorder, in which individuals gain sexual arousal by exposing their genitals to an unwilling observer;
- frotteuristic disorder, which involves recurrent touching or rubbing against a non-consenting person to become sexually aroused;
- fetishistic disorder, in which individuals focus sexual interest on a nonliving object or specific nongenital body part to become aroused;
- transvestic disorder, in which individuals cross-dress to experience sexual arousal;
- sexual sadism disorder, which describes when sexual arousal depends on the physical or psychological suffering of another person;
- sexual masochism disorder, which describes when sexual arousal depends on being humiliated or made to suffer; and
- pedophilic disorder, when individuals who are at least 16 years of age engage in sexual activity with a child who is at least 5 years younger.

Whereas their exact prevalence is difficult to estimate, paraphilic disorders may be more common than previously thought. In one sample of psychiatric inpatients, 13.4% of men reported symptoms consistent with at least one lifetime *DSM* paraphilic disorder. The most common paraphilic disorders were voyeurism (8.0%), exhibitionism (5.4%), and sexual masochism (2.7%). Even in the community, the majority of men report at least one paraphilia-associated sexual arousal pattern, with almost 2% indicating significant distress as a result.

Causes of Paraphilias and Paraphilic Disorders

Determining the causes of paraphilias and paraphilic disorders is as difficult as estimating their prevalence. First, many in the academic community are unable to agree on operational definitions for paraphilic behaviors, stemming in part from the ongoing debate regarding whether or not paraphilic preferences should be considered mental disorders rather than simply exotic forms of sexual interest. In addition, designating a behavior as a paraphilia is often largely motivated by cultural norms, and there is a great deal of variance from one culture to the next in what is considered a socially acceptable activity (Thibaut, De LaBarra, Gordon, Cosyns, & Bradford, 2010). Without consistent definitions, research on paraphilic behaviors has been all the more challenging.

In short, clinicians know less than they need to know about why paraphilias and paraphilic disorders develop. A few cases may have an organic basis, and some can probably be traced to extreme childhood trauma, but the vast majority of paraphilias and paraphilic disorders appear to be caused by multiple and interacting biopsychosocial factors that are still not well understood.

Biological Factors

Multiple lines of evidence suggest that biological factors may play a role in the etiology of some paraphilic behavior. Several studies show a higher-than-expected incidence of temporal and parietal lobe abnormalities in some men who engage in pedophilia, fetishism, and sadism (Cantor & Blanchard, 2012; Cantor et al., 2008; Langevin, 1993; Meyer,

1995; Wright, Nobrega, Langevin, & Wortzman, 1990). Case reports describe the onset of paraphilic behavior among individuals with Parkinson's disease with the start of medications that increase dopamine levels (Shapiro, Chang, Munson, Okun, & Fernandez, 2006). Head injury is also associated with paraphilic behavior (Chughtai et al., 2009). Other studies have linked abnormal androgen levels to paraphilic arousal, but the findings are dated, inconsistent, and limited to violent sexual offenders (Bradford & McLean, 1984).

One study used functional magnetic resonance imaging (fMRI, discussed in Chapters 1 and 2) to compare the brains of pedophilic and nonpedophilic men while viewing their preferred sexual stimuli (Polisois-Keating & Joyal, 2013). All activated brain regions associated with sexual arousal in the nonpedophilic group were also found in the pedophilic group, such as the fusiform gyrus, the occipital (visual) cortex, the cerebellum, the anterior cingulate cortex, the amygdala, and the substantia nigra. However, the number of significant brain areas activated during sexual arousal was higher in the pedophilic group, perhaps indicating that people with pedophilia show a stronger response to sexual stimuli overall.

At this point, not enough is known about these biological influences, yet it is unlikely that they can completely account for paraphilias and paraphilic disorders.

Psychological Factors

Most psychological explanations of paraphilias and paraphilic disorders suggest that they appear in people whose early experiences (1) undermined their ability to be aroused by consensual sexual activity with another adult, (2) increased their susceptibility to sexual arousal through atypical stimuli, and (3) lowered their ability to empathize with victims and appreciate the harmfulness of their actions.

In the early 20th century, it was believed that sexual deviation stemmed from developmental disruptions in the sexual maturation process (Thibaut et al., 2010). For example, object relations theorists argue that paraphilic interests begin early in life when a child fails to establish a secure bond with the mother or other primary caregiver. Failure at this early developmental task may not only lead to separation anxiety when the child enters preschool or elementary school, but may also interfere with the ability to form intimate relationships later in life. If the father was also absent or uncaring, the child (usually a boy) may begin using paraphilic objects such as the mother's shoes or underwear to be comforted or sexually aroused.

John Money's model of paraphilic development emphasizes the importance of sexual stressors during childhood that shape future patterns of sexual arousal and sexual behavior (Money & Pranzarone, 1993). Money suggested that children engage in a series of behaviors that serve as "practice" for sexual arousal and sexual activity in adulthood. These behaviors include learning how to approach and initiate social interactions with people who attract them. In early childhood, boys learn to chase or tease girls on the playground, and in middle school, boys and girls may start learning how to flirt with each other. Various stressors can interrupt or distort these early sexual learning experiences. For example, children may be punished or humiliated for engaging in normal sexual play or rehearsal, thus making them less likely to continue the normal course of sexual practice that would eventually have led to typical sexual attractions and skills.

A more extreme situation arises for those who are coerced into inappropriate sexual play or otherwise victimized by a pedophile, such as Justin in the chapter-opening case. Money says that these sexually stressed children find themselves in a bind: They feel "in trouble" for engaging in sexual behavior, but they worry about causing even more trouble by reporting it. He believes that these children often resolve their dilemma by continuing to endure the sexual stressor. As the inappropriate sexual behavior is repeated, it may gradually seem less unusual or improper, thus helping the children to neutralize or master the strong emotions that initially accompanied the behavior. Money's theory has been invoked to explain why pedophiles, particularly those who abuse boys, are more likely to have been abused as children than are men who engage in other types of abuse (Jespersen, Lalumiere, & Seto, 2009; Worling, 1995).

The most widely accepted psychological explanations of paraphilias and paraphilic disorders today are based on the principles of learning, especially on the roles of classical and operant conditioning in transforming normal sexual arousal into fetishes or other paraphilic preferences. Learning theorists suggest, for example, that a youngster may become sexually aroused by inappropriate stimuli as the result of a chance association between those stimuli and sexual arousal. Thus, if a young child is sexually aroused while seeing or touching a certain piece of clothing, that stimulus may become associated with sex. This initial association may be magnified if the child begins to include the stimulus in masturbatory fantasies. After being repeatedly associated with sexual arousal, this originally nonsexual stimulus may acquire the power to elicit that arousal, much like a stimulus can acquire fear-related properties, as discussed in Chapter 7. Eventually, the stimulus becomes a fetish that allows the person to reliably produce sexual arousal. If there are no negative consequences resulting from the paraphilic behavior and the behavior continues to be reinforced through masturbation (strong positive reinforcement!) and fantasy, the behavior is likely to continue (Becker et al., 2014).

One experimental study illustrated how a fetish might be learned. The experimenters showed men pictures of boots, along with arousal-eliciting pictures of nude women (Rachman & Hodgson, 1968). After many pairings, the boots themselves elicited sexual arousal. In this laboratory situation, when the boot pictures were no longer paired with the nude photos, they lost their erotic allure for most of the men. However, if the men had repeatedly masturbated while fantasizing about boots, and if they had had few other sexual outlets, an enduring boot fetish might have developed (though the study authors would then have had trouble getting any future research past an Institutional Review Board!).

In addition to the learning model just described, paraphilic behavior often is maintained due to individuals' attempts to solve an actual problem in their lives. The problem could be related to their lack of social skills and/or their sexual dysfunctions (see Chapter 13), both of which are common among sex offenders (Emmers-Sommer et al., 2004; Raymond, Coleman, Ohlerking, Christenson, & Miner, 1999). Relying on one object or activity for their sexual arousal may therefore be a way of navigating a challenging sex life. People displaying paraphilic behavior often develop highly ritualized sexual encounters that must be acted out according to a fixed script to achieve satisfaction. These scripts are the focus of masturbatory fantasies and tend to have two other effects as well: (1) they substitute for real people, thereby compensating for shyness, sexual inhibitions, and a lack of social skills, and (2) they tend to reduce attention to the effects that sexual behavior has on real people, thereby minimizing empathy for victims.

MAPS - Attempted Answers

I'm sorry darling, but it's "that time of the month" again.

Hooray, that means we can talk.

Source: Vhrsti/Shutterstock.com.

Social Factors

Finally, the social roles expected for men and women, the ways in which sex and aggression are linked in popular media, and social values regarding sex are all factors that might contribute to the unusual sexual arousal seen in paraphilias and paraphilic disorders. Consider as one example the differences in how society views masturbation. The fact that masturbation is condoned or accepted more for men than for women results in men more frequently using masturbation to reinforce sexual fantasies. This is just one example explaining why men constitute the vast majority of individuals with paraphilias and paraphilic disorders.

Baldwin and Baldwin (1997) proposed a hypothesis to explain this well-known gender difference by arguing that biological and social factors operate together. Males are often more interested in physical sexuality than females for biological reasons (Greer & Buss, 1994). Men think about sex more frequently (Peplau, 2003) and emphasize the physical pleasure of sex (Frazier & Esterly, 1990), whereas women are less likely to engage in sexual intercourse without an emotional attachment (Carroll, Volk, & Hyde, 1985). Furthermore, from a developmental perspective, the male child develops differently from the female child. Boys learn genital pleasure more readily and perhaps earlier (Galenson & Roiphe, 1974), and parents often apply double standards in encouraging boys toward sexuality while proscribing it for girls. Noncoital learning through peers and other sources influence male attitudes toward sex, sexuality, masturbation, and erections. Pubertal girls, on the other hand, often learn about genitalia and sex in an embarrassing way. These roles related to sex, gender, sexual activity, and masturbation are strongly influenced by cultural values, as are the perceived purpose and inherent pleasure related to sexual intercourse (Bhugra et al., 2010). The bottom line is that men's overfocus on sexual gratification may set the stage for the emergence and development of paraphilic behaviors.

Section Review

While the causes of paraphilias and paraphilic disorders are unclear, they are likely due to a combination of biopsychosocial factors. Possibilities include:

- temporal and parietal lobe abnormalities, elevated dopamine, abnormal androgen levels, and head trauma;
- childhood experiences that (1) undermine the ability to be aroused by consensual sexual activity with another adult, (2) increase susceptibility to sexual arousal through atypical stimuli, and (3) lower the ability to empathize with victims and appreciate the harmfulness of actions; and
- social factors that permit and encourage male (rather than female) sexual expression.

Treatment of Paraphilic Disorders

Because those who have a paraphilic disorder are seldom motivated to enter or actively participate in programs designed to alter their patterns of sexual arousal and behavior, the successful treatment of paraphilic disorders is not easy. Once in treatment, individuals with a paraphilic disorder may be only minimally motivated to cooperate because they may not be distressed by their behavior and may not want to change (Guay, 2009; Meyer, 1995). Indeed, many of these individuals, especially those with pedophilic disorders, engage in extensive justification for and rationalization of their sexual behavior (Abel & Rouleau, 1995). Consequently, many clinicians, and most members of the public, are convinced that paraphilic disorders are nearly untreatable, though this is not necessarily true. These beliefs, however, along with concerns about the sexual victimization of children, have led to social policies aimed at preventing sexual offenses. Two such policies—civil commitment and public notification—are discussed in this chapter's "Prevention" feature.

Behavioral Methods

Given the apparent learned aspects of many paraphilic disorders, it is not surprising that behavioral therapy forms the crux of the treatment. The earliest forms of behavior therapy for sex offenders consisted mainly of aversive conditioning techniques—**aversion therapy**—designed to reduce arousal to problematic stimuli (Nietzel, 1979). For example, those with a sexual fetish were given an electrical shock as they fondled a leather handbag, those experiencing exhibitionistic disorder were given drugs that made them nauseous while they thought about exposing themselves, and those with frotteuristic disorder were instructed to imagine rubbing against a woman in the subway and having horrible consequences befall them. **Covert sensitization** is an aversive conditioning technique in which clients imagine a paraphilic stimulus or behavior. Then, just as they begin to become aroused by these images, the therapist adds images of the clients suddenly developing open sores, of rats crawling all over their body, or of other disgusting stimuli. In a variation of this method called *olfactory aversion therapy*, aversive images are accompanied by the presence of a foul odor (Maletsky, 1973). Whereas this treatment is not widely used, Marshall (2006) notes in a case study of pedophilic disorder that

aversion therapy: A behavioral treatment in which clients pair aversive events (e.g., foul smells or imagining friends watching them commit their paraphilic sex acts) with their preferred paraphilic stimuli in an attempt to reduce the sexual arousal conditioning to those stimuli.

covert sensitization: A behavioral treatment in which clients imagine their preferred paraphilic stimuli and then substitute unpleasant, aversive images in an attempt to reduce the sexual arousal conditioning to their paraphilic stimuli.

Civil Commitment and Public Notification

As fears about sex offenders continue to grow in the United States, social policies have emerged in an effort to curb repeated sex offenses.

Twenty states have laws that allow *civil commitment* of sex offenders, such that convicted sex offenders who are deemed most likely to repeat their offenses are committed to secure treatment facilities even after their prison terms expire. This preventive detention can continue as long as authorities judge an offender to be dangerous, and in theory, it can last for life.

Proponents of civil commitment for sex offenders note that the law is targeted at a small subgroup of individuals who are deemed most likely to reoffend. They argue that civil commitment is an important safeguard that keeps the most high-risk sex offenders away from communities. In addition, civil commitment provides treatment that may not have been available in prison.

Yet, some legal experts argue that civil commitment is a form of *double jeopardy*, which means multiple punishments for the same offense. Others note that the "secure treatment facilities" for civilly committed sex offenders are largely unable to provide successful treatment. Still others point out that determining who is likely to recommit a sexual crime is an impossible task and that civil commitment laws are a threat to American liberties (Yung, 2011). Despite arguments against civil commitment laws, the U.S. Supreme Court has upheld challenges to the constitutionality of these laws three times.

A second legislative approach to prevention is embodied in *registration and notification* laws that require convicted sex offenders to register with the state immediately after their release from prison. The goal is to inform the public about where these offenders are living so that police (and neighbors) can maintain close surveillance of them. The first notification law was passed in New Jersey following the rape and murder of Megan Kanka by a neighbor who had spent 6 years in prison for attempting to murder another little girl. In 1996, President Clinton signed federal legislation known as "Megan's Law" that requires law enforcement authorities in all states to notify communities when convicted sex offenders move into their neighborhoods. Megan's Law has since been supplemented with new registration requirements and a low-, medium-, and high-risk classification of sex offenders.

It is unclear whether such laws, in fact, protect the public by making repeat offenses less likely. Some have argued that the registry is an invasion of privacy, leading to "vigilante justice," with sex offenders becoming targets for crime. Conversely, others believe that individuals and families have the right to know if they are living among people with a history of sexual crimes. You can search for registered sex offenders in your own area by visiting the U.S. Department of Justice National Sex Offender Public Website: http://www.nsopw.gov/

What do you think? Does knowing the addresses of registered sex offenders keep our communities safer?

---

olfactory aversion therapy was successful in reducing deviant sexual interests, effects that reportedly endured over time. In *shame aversion therapy*, clients imagine friends or relatives watching them commit paraphilic acts and expressing their disgust and disapproval. Although such methods have been studied for decades, aversive conditioning techniques have been largely unsuccessful in permanently changing sexual preferences (Camilleri & Quinsey, 2008).

A final behavioral approach to treating paraphilic disorders is **masturbatory reconditioning**, which involves having clients use masturbation to modify their sexual preferences. For instance, clients might be directed to masturbate using their preferred paraphilic stimuli as usual, but then to alternate more appropriate sexual stimuli (e.g., consenting adults) at the last minute while continuing to masturbate (Laws & Marshall, 1991). Although large-scale and long-term research is lacking, behavioral and cognitive-behavioral methods (described in the next section) remain the standards according to which all other treatments for paraphilic disorders should be judged (Maletzky, 2002).

masturbatory reconditioning: A behavioral treatment for paraphilic disorders that involves having clients use masturbation to modify their sexual preferences.

Other Psychological Treatment Methods

Cognitive-behavioral therapy (CBT) has been used in the treatment of paraphilic disorders, most notably pedophilic disorder. CBT focuses on attitudes and thinking errors that maintain paraphilic behavior, and involves cognitive restructuring to challenge and change a person's beliefs that lead to paraphilic acts. For example, individuals with pedophilic disorder who think that their sexual interactions with children are harmless would be challenged with evidence showing lasting psychological harm to victims. The development of *empathy for victims* is often included in treatment, as well as *social skills training* (Becker et al., 2014). Specifically, clients are trained in the social skills that can help them establish more-appropriate sexual contacts. They may also be helped to overcome depression and problems in existing relationships, including a component on how to be close to others, termed *intimacy training* (Marshall & Fernandez, 1998). Whereas some research shows minimal long-term treatment gains for CBT among sex offenders (Marques, Wiederanders, Day, Nelson, & van Ommeren, 2005), other research suggests that CBT is the most helpful form of psychological treatment for this population (Losel & Schmucker, 2005).

CBT is often used to target **relapse prevention**, discussed in Chapter 14, which focuses on identifying high-risk situations, stimuli, or stressors that lead to paraphilic arousal and teaching individuals to avoid these triggers whenever possible. Thus, individuals with pedophilic disorder are asked to have no contact with children, even if this means temporarily leaving home; those suffering from frotteuristic disorder are required to stay away from crowds; and individuals with voyeuristic disorder are told to avoid places where they have "peeped" before. In addition, clients learn to spot those seemingly irrelevant decisions that, on closer scrutiny, increase the risk of offensive sexual behavior. Those suffering from voyeuristic disorder who know that they are more likely to "peep" when drunk are taught to recognize the significance of agreeing to meet a friend for a drink after work. Similarly, individuals with pedophilic disorder must understand that deciding to go home by a different route is not a random decision if the new route happens to take them past a schoolyard. Relapse prevention includes paying attention to and avoiding these so-called casual decisions, as well as developing ways to delay gratification when old arousal patterns are triggered. Many sex offenders have a history of giving in to their urges almost immediately, then viewing their transgression as an excuse to give up all efforts to change. In relapse prevention, clients are helped to recognize this phenomenon, known as the *abstinence violation effect*, and to learn that isolated slips need not indicate total failure.

Biological Methods

Modern records show that biological treatment for paraphilic preferences was first documented in the late 1800s with the use of surgical castration (Thibaut et al., 2010). This irreversible technique involves removal of the testes (where testosterone is largely produced) as a means of reducing sexual interest, drive, and the ability to maintain an erection (Weinberger, Sreenivasan, Garrick, & Osran, 2005). Surgical castration has been widely used in Europe among incarcerated sex offenders. In the United States, it is used in several states as a means of obtaining a reduced criminal sentence (Scott & Holmberg, 2003). Weinberger et al. (2005) note that surgical castration, though not a mainstream treatment for sexual predators, is used in cases when other treatment has not been effective. Evidence shows that surgical castration reduces the instance of sexual criminal **recidivism**, or repeat offenses, and is often voluntarily selected by offenders, since it potentially may be their only option of ever living in the community again (Weinberger et al., 2005).

Medication that reduces sexual libido (sometimes referred to as **chemical castration**) has also been used as a treatment, especially for sexual offenders who are deemed to be high risk to reoffend (Becker et al., 2014). In fact, in California, chemical castration is mandatory for repeat child sexual offenders (Thibaut et al., 2010). These medications, such as cyproterone acetate and medroxyprogesterone acetate, are commonly prescribed but can have serious side effects (Briken, Hill, & Berner, 2003); they work by lowering testosterone (sex hormone) levels. Some research shows that luteinizing hormone-releasing hormone agonists may offer a new treatment option for treatment of people with paraphilic disorders (Briken et al., 2003). Selective serotonin reuptake inhibitors (SSRIs) are also sometimes prescribed because a reduction in sexual arousal is a side effect of these antidepressant drugs. However, Becker and colleagues (2014) note that much of the current understanding of using SSRIs—and any of the medications just described—to

relapse prevention: Part of the cognitive-behavioral treatment for many mental disorders, it focuses on identifying high-risk situations, stimuli, or stressors that lead to the unwanted behavior (drugs, alcohol, eating, paraphilias) and then teaching the client to avoid these triggers whenever possible.

Connections

How is relapse prevention used in the treatment of other disorders? Is it effective? See Chapter 14.

recidivism: Repeating an undesirable or illegal act that the person has been punished for in the past.

chemical castration: The use of medication to suppress the male sex hormones such as androgen; sometimes used as treatment for sex offenders and people with paraphilic disorders.

MAPS - Medical Myths

treat paraphilic disorders is based on case reports, rather than controlled clinical trials. Thus, although SSRIs and hormonal treatments are used in practice to treat paraphilic disorders among sex offenders, the U.S. Food and Drug Administration (FDA) has not approved these medications for this usage.

Conclusions About Treating Paraphilias

Overall, the results of treatments for paraphilic disorders are mixed. Some studies indicate that specialized treatment programs can reduce the likelihood of recidivism (Weinberger et al., 2005; Marshall & Eccles, 1996), whereas others suggest that treatment has no significant effect (Marques et al., 2005; Furby, Weinrott, & Blackshaw, 1989; Hanson, Steffy, & Gauthier, 1993). There is also a growing body of evidence for the effectiveness of sex offender treatment for child molesters and exhibitionists (Beech & Harkins, 2012). These conflicting conclusions may reflect differences in client characteristics. In one study of treated sex offenders, those most likely to be treatment failures had engaged in a higher number of previous sex offenses, had victimized boys more often than girls, and had never been married (Hanson et al., 1993). Further, some researchers recommend combined treatment for severe paraphilias in adult males—that is, antiandrogen medical treatment combined with CBT (Assumpção, Garcia, Garcia, Bradford, & Thibaut, 2014).

Clearly, treatment modalities of paraphilias are insufficiently explored and evaluated. Specific clinical recommendations on what and when to treat, how long to treat, with what to treat, and how to possibly prevent paraphilias and especially their consequences also are lacking (Balon, 2013).

Section Review

Whereas the efficacy of treatments for paraphilic disorders is unclear, a variety of treatments have been used, including:

- behavioral methods, typically involving aversive conditioning techniques;
- cognitive-behavioral therapy, which is often combined with relapse prevention; and
- biological methods, including surgical castration and antilibido medications.

Legal and Ethical Issues Involving People With Mental Disorders

At age 22, Wilson was diagnosed with schizophrenia. For the next 10 years, he was in and out of public mental hospitals, where his treatment consisted mainly of various kinds of psychoactive drugs. Starting at the age of 32, Wilson spent 15 months living with his girlfriend, after which time he went home to live with his parents. Last month, Wilson stopped taking his medication and stopped seeing his case worker at the local community mental health center. In a matter of days, Wilson's behavior began to deteriorate. He heard voices telling him that his mother was having sex with his former doctors and was stealing his social security check. When he heard voices from the trash cans accusing him of stealing, Wilson would retaliate by setting the cans afire, then urinating on them. His neighbors grew so afraid of him that they would hide indoors if they saw him nearby. They begged Wilson's parents to do something "before it was too late." One evening, as his father was cooking dinner, Wilson picked up a chair and threw it at him to, as he later told police, "stop the SOB and his whore-wife from poisoning my food." His mother called 911, and when the police arrived minutes later, they found Wilson huddled in a corner of the kitchen, hallucinating and terrified. When they told him they were going to take him to the state hospital, Wilson did not resist. A hospital psychiatrist concluded that Wilson was dangerous and ordered him committed to the hospital on an emergency basis for a 72-hour observation period.

We discussed the notion of civil commitment regarding sex offenders earlier in the chapter, but people with a wide variety of mental disorders—not just paraphilic disorders—come into contact with the legal system. Whereas the vast majority of people with schizophrenia and other mental disorders are not dangerous, some (like Wilson in the previous case) could be. So does that mean he needs to be treated, even if he does not consent? Throughout this text, we have pointed out that all mental disorders occur in a social and cultural context, but now we focus more directly on that context by considering some of the ways in which mental disorders can affect society at large, not just the diagnosed clients and the mental health professionals who work with them.

There is worldwide concern about finding the most socially beneficial way of dealing with people who have mental disorders. In the United States, for example, elaborate policies and procedures are designed to ensure that the constitutional rights of people with mental disorders are protected, which has not always been the case throughout history (see Chapter 2). Leaders and policy makers in government, business and industry, law, and the mental health professions play a central role in deciding these issues, and their choices reveal society's values regarding people with mental disorders. At issue is the need to balance the rights of individuals with mental disorders against the rights of other citizens to be protected from potentially dangerous people. To what extent, if any, should the right of all people to feel safe be constrained to preserve freedoms for those who display mental disorders?

If this man is about to jump to his death (see Chapter 5 for more on suicide), how much power should the state have to hospitalize him against his will? Under current laws, people with mental disorders cannot be involuntarily committed to a hospital just because they suffer a mental disorder that could be helped by treatment or because others see them as a nuisance. In most states, however, they can be hospitalized if they are a danger to themselves (or others).

The Rights of Individuals Versus the Rights of Society

The past 50 years have seen especially intense debate in the United States over how to balance the rights of people with mental disorders against society's concern for the safety and protection of all citizens. The debate tends to focus on two areas: (1) Should the state hospitalize people against their will, and (2) should people with mental disorders be allowed to refuse treatment ordered by mental health professionals?

Civil Commitment

In the United States in the 1950s and 1960s, it was relatively easy for people displaying serious mental disorders to be committed to a psychiatric hospital against their will through a legal order known as **civil commitment**. Such orders were issued whenever the state believed that individuals required psychiatric treatment, and the length of hospital confinement—which in many cases extended for decades—was determined by the hospital's staff; patients were released only when their doctors thought the time was right. This approach to civil commitment began around the time of the Civil War (1860s), when the United States first started to construct large public mental hospitals. It was based on two interrelated principles: (1) *parens patriae* ("the country as parent"), which holds that certain types of impairment can render people incapable of deciding what is best for them so the state, like the parent of a young child, has the duty to make decisions for them; and (2) *police power*, which dictates that the state has a duty to consider the welfare of all people living within its boundaries, along with the right to write statutes for the benefit of society at large, even when this may come at the cost of restricting the liberties of certain individuals (Testa & West, 2010).

In the late 1960s, though, many states began to reform their rules for involuntary commitment to expand the rights of people with mental disorders. The new rules allowed people to resist psychiatric hospitalization and to be protected against indefinite periods of commitment. These reforms were part of the social upheaval that occurred in the

civil commitment: The legal order by which an individual can be involuntarily committed to a psychiatric hospital.

The Kings Park Psychiatric Center, known by Kings Park locals simply as "The Psych Center," was a former state-run psychiatric hospital located in Kings Park, New York. It operated from 1885 until 1996, when New York State closed the facility, releasing its few remaining patients or transferring them to the still-operational Pilgrim Psychiatric Center.

Source: littleny/Shutterstock.com.

United States during a period of intense debate about the wisdom of virtually all government policies. Civil liberties activists were concerned about abuses of *parens patriae* and police power—for example, that people with mental disorders were being deprived of legal due process during commitment proceedings. A strong bias against psychiatry also developed during this period, and critics argued that psychiatrists' lack of success in treating severe mental disorders made involuntary hospitalization little more than imprisonment without trial (Appelbaum, 1994).

Along with the civil rights movement came a shift in the legal standard for civil commitment away from a need-for-treatment model to the **dangerousness model** that exists today (Testa & West, 2010). In 1964, Washington, DC, instituted a standard for civil commitment that established that individuals must be determined to have a mental disorder before they could be hospitalized against their will. Second, the individuals had to pose an imminent threat to the safety of themselves or others or be "gravely disabled," meaning that they could not provide for the necessities for basic survival (Anfag & Appelbaum, 2009). It is commonly

dangerousness model: A model of civil commitment in which people with mental disorders can only be hospitalized against their will if they are an imminent danger to themselves or others.

interpreted that dangerousness refers to physical harm to self (suicide) or physical harm to others (homicide), and that the requirement for imminence means that the threat must be likely to occur in the near future (Testa & West, 2010). California adopted a similar statute 5 years later (Anfag & Appelbaum, 2009). One by one, other states followed suit until the prevailing standard for civil commitment in the United States required the presence of dangerousness as a result of mental disorder(s). Currently, there are only a few states that do not follow the trend. Delaware requires only proof that individuals are not able to make "responsible choices" about hospitalization or treatment for them to be committed, whereas Iowa's statute mandates only proof that individuals are likely to cause "severe emotional injury" to people who are unable to avoid contact with them, such as family members (Testa & West, 2010).

Public Mental Hospitals and Deinstitutionalization

Therefore, by the end of the 1970s, virtually every state had passed laws that allowed involuntary hospitalization of people with mental disorders *only* if some version of the previous conditions (i.e., a mental disorder involving imminent danger to self or others) was met. These new rules, combined with new psychoactive medications capable of controlling psychotic behavior, led to the release of large numbers of people from mental hospitals. The number of patients in state and county mental hospitals peaked at around 550,000 in the mid-1950s. By 1970, this number had fallen below 400,000; by 1979, fewer than 150,000 psychiatric inpatients were in state hospitals; and by the late 1980s, the number was around 100,000 (Manderscheid, Atay, & Crider, 2009).

"Bad news, Stevens. Legal has decided it's not a good idea to let you go home at the end of the day."

Source: Cartoonresource/Shutterstock.com.

The decline in mental hospital populations that occurred in the past 5 decades has generally been described as a shift from inpatient to outpatient treatment of mental disorders in the United States. This shift, known as *deinstitutionalization*, was an important goal of the community mental health movement. As promising as deinstitutionalization appeared on paper, however, its implementation has turned out to be a combination of myth and missed opportunity (Kiesler, 1991; Kiesler & Simpkins, 1991).

The myth stems from the fact that the decreased numbers of patients in state mental hospitals or Veterans Administration

(VA) hospitals does not mean that inpatient care is a thing of the past. Statistics on treatment provided in *all* of these inpatient facilities (including private for-profit institutions) contradicts the notion of widespread deinstitutionalization: The total number of inpatient cases has actually increased somewhat, with most of the increase appearing in general medical and private psychiatric hospitals. In fact, inpatient days in short-term facilities rose for people with mental disorders between 1996 and 2007, most dramatically for youth, although they decreased among elderly individuals (Blader, 2011). In other words, mental health care in the United States has not been deinstitutionalized to the extent that is often claimed (Kiesler & Simpkins, 1991).

The missed opportunity piece comes from the difference between just being deinstitutionalized and receiving adequate treatment in the community. One of the reasons for optimism surrounding deinstitutionalization several decades ago was the advent of newer medications for serious mental disorders (see Chapters 4 and 5). However, the pattern with most psychotropic drugs has been one of initial excitement followed by ultimate disappointment that these are not quite the "miracle cures" that the pharmaceutical companies marketed.

MAPS - Medical Myths

Furthermore, the United States now leads the world—by far—in terms of the prison population per capita; whereas the United States has about 5% of the world's population, it houses around 25% of its prisoners (Holland, 2013). This disturbing trend may be perpetuated by inadequate treatment of people with mental disorders (Baillargeon, Binswanger, Penn, Williams, & Murray, 2009). At least 15% of the prison population likely requires mental health treatment (Magaletta, Diamond, Faust, Daggett, & Camp, 2009), and there is a significantly higher risk of recidivism—that is, probability of individuals returning to prison after they are released—among inmates with mental disorders (Baillargeon et al., 2009). The overall failure of the deinstitutionalization movement is suggested by the large percentage of people with mental disorders who, during the past few decades, have either drifted into homelessness or become wards of the criminal justice system. In fact, reduced hospital capacity causes an increase in crime and arrest rates in part through its increase of homelessness (Markowitz, 2006).

Mental Disorders and the Homeless As many as 3.5 million people experience homelessness in a given year in the United States (1% of the entire U.S. population or 10% of its poor), or about 842,000 people in any given week (National Law Center on Homelessness and Poverty, 2011). About a third to half of the permanently homeless have alcohol or other substance use disorders (Dennis, Bray, Iachan, & Thornberry, 1999; Paquette, 2011), and a quarter to a third of them suffer from severe mental disorders, such as schizophrenia or bipolar disorders (Paquette, 2011; Tessler & Dennis, 1989). In other words, homelessness has become an enormous public health problem in the United States, and it is strongly related to mental disorders.

The policy of confining people in state mental hospitals in the 1950s and 1960s may not have been the ideal answer, but at least it usually assured them a minimum level of safety and shelter. Today, with public mental hospitals a less-ready refuge, there is a continuing struggle to provide the broad range of services these individuals need.

Accordingly, over 2 decades ago, the National Institutes of Mental Health Task Force on Homelessness and Severe Mental Illness ("Outcasts on Main Street," 1992) proposed the creation of an integrated system of care with three main components (see Figure 17.1). The first major component of this system is to provide adequate housing, ranging from temporary *safe havens* to more-permanent living options. Modern efforts to reduce homelessness include "housing-first models," where individuals and families are placed in permanent homes with optional wrap-around services (Lee & Tyler, 2010). Furthermore, this effort is less expensive than the cost of institutions that serve tangled needs of the homeless, such as emergency shelters, mental hospitals, and jails. Overall, this alternative approach has shown positive outcomes. For example, one study reports an 88% housing retention rate for those in Housing First, compared to 47% using traditional programs (Raphael & Stoll, 2013).

FIGURE 17.1 An Integrated System of Care for People With Mental Disorders Who Are Homeless

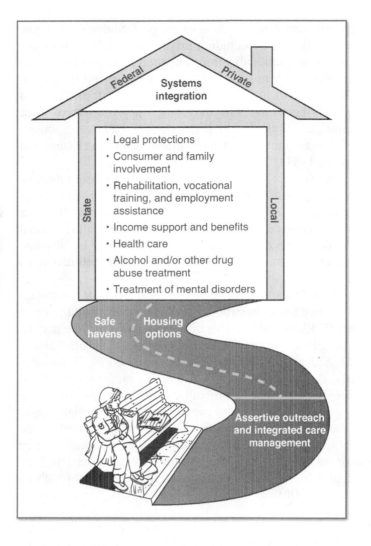

The second component of the integrated system to help reduce homelessness is *assertive outreach orientation*, meaning that service providers would seek out and bring treatment to homeless people with mental disorders on the streets and in shelters, rather than waiting for these clients to ask for help. Service providers would also offer *integrated case management*, helping clients obtain necessary health and welfare benefits, arranging appointments with health care providers, and making sure that clients are receiving appropriate services. The third and final component in this integrated system of care consists of a collection of income support, health-care, psychosocial rehabilitation, mental health and substance abuse treatment, education, and vocational services.

Although it took 2 decades after the task force recommendations, the Obama administration launched *Opening Doors*, the nation's first comprehensive strategy to prevent and end homelessness (U.S. Interagency Council on Homelessness, 2010). In addition to the integrated care model just outlined, the government's plan also includes an overarching goal to "transform homeless services to crisis response systems that prevent homelessness and rapidly return people who experience homelessness to stable housing." The U.S. Department of Housing and Urban Development's 2014 Annual Homeless Assessment Report to Congress detailed a 25% drop in the unsheltered population since 2010, the year that *Opening Doors* was implemented.

People With Mental Disorders in the Criminal Justice System The process of deinstitutionalization has placed ever-greater responsibility for supervising people with severe mental disorders on police and the criminal justice system. Police officers have wide discretion in their response to disruptive people who may also have mental disorders. They can arrest them or force them into a hospital. They can attempt on-the-spot counseling, refer them to a mental health agency, or return them to the care of friends or relatives. Consider the classic research of Linda Teplin (1984), a sociologist at Northwestern University, who trained a team of psychology graduate students to observe police-citizen interactions over a 14-month period in two Chicago precincts. In 800 police-citizen encounters, over 500 citizens were considered suspects eligible for arrest, but only 29.4% of them were actually arrested. However, of the 30 suspects rated by the observers as having an overt mental disorder, 46.7% were arrested, a significantly higher rate than for suspects who did not appear to display a mental disorder. Similar results have been reported in other cities.

In other words, when something must be done about a disruptive person with a mental disorder, police officers may prefer arrest over hospitalization. Thus, homeless people with mental disorders are being "criminalized" to a certain extent because society does not know what else to do with them. They are often treated like petty criminals, and for many, local jails have become their major source of shelter, food, medical treatment, detoxification, remedial education, and other services. Commenting on this situation as it affects African-American youngsters, the Reverend Jesse Jackson discussed why jail might be a palatable option for them:

MAPS - Prejudicial Pigeonholes

> Once in jail, they are no longer homeless. They have doctors in jail. They have libraries in jail. They have organized recreation in jail. They have everything in jail they should have had out here! (Rodricks, 1992)

One approach that has helped alter police response in these situations is the implementation of crisis intervention teams (CIT). The CIT program trains officers in crisis intervention skills to adequately handle interactions with individuals with mental disorders (Broussard, McGriff, Neubert, D'Orio, & Compton, 2010). Furthermore, in addition to the training, the program was developed in an effort to promote partnerships among law enforcement, mental health professionals, and advocates. The training component of CIT provides police officers with 40 hours of lectures and role-playing activities based on the Memphis Model of CIT (Bower & Pettit, 2001). The CIT model is being implemented widely, with over 400 programs currently operating (Watson, Morabito, Draine, & Ottati, 2008). The limited evidence on CIT effectiveness is promising (Watson et al., 2008). CIT-trained officers have consistently better scores on knowledge about mental disorders and their treatments, self-efficacy for interacting with someone with psychosis or suicidality, de-escalation skills, and referral decisions (Compton et al., 2014a). CIT training appears to increase the likelihood of referral or transport to mental health services and to decrease the likelihood of arrest during encounters with individuals thought to have a behavioral disorder (Compton et al., 2014b).

So Has Deinstitutionalization Worked? Deinstitutionalization was pronounced unsuccessful over 20 years ago, and little has changed since then (Paulson, 2012). However, deinstitutionalization could have been, and still could be, successful if policy makers would support evidence-based, cost-effective community alternatives (Searight, 2013). For example, there is no evidence that inpatient treatment (of any length) for substance use disorders (see Chapter 14) is more effective than outpatient treatment, but inpatient treatment can cost 10 times as much (Kiesler, 1993). The majority of people with schizophrenia (see Chapter 4) showed enhancements in social functioning after being released from hospitals into the community, which indicates that even long-stay patients could achieve better functioning by deinstitutionalization (Kunitoh, 2013). In addition, deinstitutionalization appears to have had positive effects for people with intellectual disability (see Chapter 3), where living outside the hospital resulted in gains in 75% of the adaptive

Partly as a result of laws that make it harder to hospitalize people with mental disorders against their will, increasing numbers of individuals with mental disorders are being detained in local jails, where they can be observed for a day or two to determine whether a hospital commitment is justified. One jailer, commenting on individuals who are repeatedly arrested for this reason, said, "It is as if they are serving a life sentence a few days at a time."

behavior domains assessed (Hamelin, Frijters, Griffiths, Condillac, & Owen, 2011). Several decades of research have repeatedly demonstrated that the assertive community treatment model (recommended by the task force on homelessness discussed earlier) reduces hospital admissions and improves quality of life for people with severe mental disorders (Phillips et al., 2001). Thus, although deinstitutionalization has not been a panacea, the idea of treating people with mental disorders primarily outside of psychiatric hospitals remains viable today if ample resources (i.e., money) could be allocated to grant access to outpatient treatments to those who need them.

The Right to Refuse Treatment

Aside from the complex results of deinstitutionalization, fundamental questions about patients' rights are raised when a person in a psychiatric hospital does not want to take medication that a physician believes would be beneficial. Should society "help" people with mental disorders by giving them treatment against their will?

Since the mid-19th century, the treatment of medical patients has been governed by rules that require patients to give informed consent before receiving medication, surgery, or other procedures. The rules of **informed consent** presume that medical patients are competent to decide whether they want to receive a treatment after being told about its potential benefits and risks and the alternative treatments available (see Figure 17.2). For many decades, however, informed consent rules were not usually applied in the treatment of people with serious mental disorders because it was assumed that their disorders made them incompetent to render such decisions.

In the past few decades, though, several landmark legal proceedings have helped shaped U.S. national policy on refusing treatment. By the late 1970s, for instance, courts in Massachusetts *(Rogers* v. *Okin,* 1979) and New Jersey *(Rennie* v. *Klein,* 1978), among others, had decided that committed mental patients should not be automatically presumed incompetent and that they therefore retained the right to refuse medication, even if it was likely to be beneficial. Still, the right to refuse treatment is not recognized in all states; some state courts have decided that committed patients can be ordered to comply with treatment that a mental health professional has deemed necessary.

Even in states that recognize a patient's right to refuse treatment, this right is not absolute. A patient's refusal can be overridden if the patient is behaving dangerously and medication is likely to lessen the emergency, or if the patient is judged to be incompetent to make a decision about treatment. In the latter instance, a judge or a panel of clinicians and citizens can give "substituted" consent on the patient's behalf if they conclude that the patient would have consented to treatment had he or she been mentally competent to do so.

Formal refusals of treatment are surprisingly infrequent. On average, in jurisdictions recognizing the right to refuse treatment, only about 10% of patients actually do so (Appelbaum, 1994). Even fewer refuse medication for very long, and those who do almost always have their refusal overridden eventually by a judge or review panel (Appelbaum & Hoge, 1986). Finally, data on whether compulsory treatment works are lacking. For instance, compulsory refeeding in people with anorexia (see Chapter 12) appears to be beneficial, but the longer-term effects remain uncertain (Elzakkers, Danner, Hoek, Schmidt, & Elburg, 2014). In addition, another review found little evidence to indicate that compulsory community treatment was effective for people with severe mental disorders, such as schizophrenia or bipolar disorders (Kisely, Campbell, & Preston, 2005). These underwhelming results may be because treatments of all kinds—ranging from psychotherapy to medication—work better in the context of a therapeutic relationship based on mutual trust and empowerment of the treated individual (Bassman, 2005; Onken, Dumont, Ridgeway, Dornan, & Ralph, 2002).

Other Legal Rights of People With Mental Disorders

In addition to rules and regulations covering involuntary hospitalization and refusal of treatment, state and federal courts have decided a number of cases that give people with mental disorders other basic rights.

informed consent: Obtaining agreement from individuals to participate in research or receive treatment after they have been informed of the procedure's potential benefits and risks and the alternatives that are available.

CONSENT TO TREATMENT AND RELEASE OF INFORMATION

Consent to Treatment: I/we voluntarily authorize the rendering of such care, including diagnostic procedures and medical treatment, by authorized agents and employees of the University _____ Hospital (hereafter referred to as the Hospital), and _____ and the medical staff, or their designees, as may in their professional judgment be deemed necessary or beneficial, and may include testing for HIV (the virus that causes AIDS) and other blood borne diseases. I/we acknowledge that no guarantees have been made as to the effect of such examination or treatment on my condition or the condition of the person for whom I am duly authorized to sign. I/we understand that I/we have the right to make decisions concerning my health care or the health care of the person for whom I am duly authorized to make such decisions, including the right to refuse medial and surgical procedures.

❏ I have formulated Advance Directives (living will, health care surrogate declaration, durable power of attorney) and request that these directives govern my course of care, in as much as is possible under state or federal law. I understand that it is my responsibility to provide the Hospital with a copy of my Advance Directives and that those directives will not govern my course of care until they have been filed in my medical record.

   ❏ Advance Directives attached   ❏ Advance Directives not attached

❏ I have not formulated Advance Directives (living will, health care surrogate declaration, durable power of attorney), but I understand that it is my right to make decisions regarding my course of treatment, including the executing of advance directives.

Release of Information: I authorize the release from my medical records or the records of the person for whom I am duly authorized to do so, of such medical and/or psychiatric information as may be required by:
1. Any health, sickness and accident insurance carrier, workman's compensation, or agency (social welfare, governmental) which is legally responsible, or which the Hospital has good cause to believe is legally responsible for all or any part of the Medical Center's charges and/or professional fees.
2. Physicians or health care facilities rendering professional care to the patient.
3. The Peer Review Organization responsible for reviewing medical care under Public Law 92-603.

Procurement of Information: I/we authorize the release of any medical records from other physicians, hospitals or health care facilities that the Hospital needs for my present medical care or the present medical care of the person for whom I am duly authorized to sign.

*This consent may be revoked at any time, except to the extent that action has already been taken, by the patient/duly authorized agent and will expire automatically one year from the date below.

_____   _____   _____

Signature of Patient or Next of Kin, Legal   Signature of Witness   Date
Agent/Guardian and Relationship to Patient

FIGURE 17.2 Informed Consent

Under normal conditions, patients are treated only after they have been made familiar with the potential risks and benefits of a medical or psychological procedure and have explicitly agreed to it. In cases of individuals with severe mental disorders, the capacity to give informed consent may be impaired, requiring special procedures designed to protect their rights.

The Right to Treatment In addition to the right to *refuse* treatment, several courts have held that people committed to mental hospitals have the right to be *treated*, not merely confined. In the landmark 1966 case of *Rouse* v. *Cameron*, Charlie Rouse had been confined to a hospital for 4 years after being found not guilty by reason of insanity on a weapons charge. Rouse petitioned the court for his release, claiming that he had been confined without receiving treatment for longer than the 1-year maximum prison sentence he could have received, had he been found guilty. The court of appeals agreed and ruled that involuntary commitment required hospitals to make at least a reasonable effort to treat committed patients.

Rights of Nondangerous Patients In 1975, the U.S. Supreme Court considered the case of *O'Connor* v. *Donaldson*. Kenneth Donaldson was a 49-year-old man who had been diagnosed with schizophrenia and confined in the Florida State Hospital at Chattahoochee for about 15 years. His father had had him committed because Donaldson was supposedly delusional and dangerous, but the evidence for his alleged dangerousness at the time of commitment was questionable. Indeed, hospital staff notes and testimony later revealed that he was never dangerous to himself or anyone else. Donaldson repeatedly asked to be released from the hospital on the grounds that he was not receiving treatment, that he was not a threat to anyone, and that he could live independently outside the hospital. A jury agreed with Donaldson that he had been improperly confined and awarded him $38,500 in damages.

The state of Florida appealed the jury's verdict to the U.S. Supreme Court. *O'Connor* was a landmark case because it marked the first time that the Supreme Court agreed to hear arguments about the constitutional rights of a civilly committed mental patient, and it required the Court to evaluate the state's justifications for involuntarily committing people with mental disorders to a hospital. Its ruling seriously undercut the *parens patriae* rationale for involuntary commitment described earlier. Writing for the Court, Justice Potter Stewart ruled that a "state cannot constitutionally confine . . . a nondangerous individual who is capable of surviving safely in freedom by himself or with the help of willing and responsible family and friends." In other words, the Supreme Court decided that having a mental disorder and the need for treatment alone were not enough to justify involuntary commitment. The effect of this decision and others since then (e.g., *Foucha* v. *Louisiana*, 1992) was to limit states' powers so that they cannot force hospitalization of persons who, even though they may have a mental disorder, are not dangerous and can live outside the hospital on their own or with the support of others.

Rights of Criminal Defendants With Mental Disorders The Supreme Court has also recognized the need for extra protection of people with mental disorders who are accused of crimes. In 1986, for example, the U.S. Supreme Court ruled that the Eighth Amendment of the Constitution forbids the execution of any inmate who is mentally incompetent at the time of execution. Definitions of mental incompetence for execution vary, but in most states, condemned prisoners are considered incompetent if they are judged to be insane or if, as the result of a mental disorder, they are unaware of the nature of the death penalty and the reasons it is being imposed.

This ruling came in *Ford* v. *Wainwright*, a 1974 Florida case in which Alvin Bernard Ford had been sentenced to death for killing a police officer during an attempted robbery. After 8 years on death row, Bernard began to manifest symptoms of a mental disorder. In letters to various people, he claimed to be the target of a complex conspiracy involving the Klan and others that would ultimately force him to kill himself. He believed that his prison guards, whom he saw as part of this conspiracy, were killing people and burying their bodies in concrete. He thought that female members of his family were being tortured and sexually abused in the prison and that up to 135 of his relatives had been taken hostage. Ford's mental condition eventually deteriorated to the point that he spoke mostly in a private code, saying things such as "Hands one, face one. Mafia one. God one, father one, Pope one. Pope one. Leader one" (Perlin, 2013, p. 209).

Ford's lawyers asked for an evaluation of Ford's mental competence. Two psychiatrists, one of whom had been seeing Ford in prison, stated that Ford suffered from schizophrenia and was not capable of appreciating what was happening to him. However, the governor of Florida appointed three other psychiatrists to evaluate Ford's competence, and after a single 30-minute meeting with Ford, they unanimously pronounced him competent for execution. The governor signed Ford's death warrant, but Ford's lawyers appealed to the Supreme Court, which ruled that it is unconstitutional to execute insane people and that the state of Florida had not given Ford sufficient due process in assessing his mental condition. Alvin Ford ultimately died in prison of natural causes, but other inmates have been executed despite indications that they might have been suffering from serious mental disorders at the time. Mental health clinicians continue to debate whether it is ethical for them to participate in competence-to-be-executed proceedings (Appelbaum, 1986; Heilbrun, 1987), once again highlighting the delicate balance between individual rights and public safety for those with mental disorders.

Source: Keith McIntyre/Shutterstock.com.

Varnall Weeks, described by prosecution and defense experts alike as having a serious mental disorder, was executed in Alabama's electric chair on May 13, 1995. Even though Weeks was apparently racked by delusions (e.g., he believed that after his death, he would take the form of a godlike turtle and rule all of humankind), the courts held that Weeks was competent for execution because he was capable of understanding that he was being executed for his crime of murder. More recently, Robert Ladd was executed in Texas in 2015, despite having an IQ of 67, which indicates intellectual disability (Chapter 3).

Section Review

The conflict between autonomy rights of individuals with mental disorders and society's rights to be protected is revealed most clearly:

- in the changing principles and procedures for involuntarily hospitalizing people with severe mental disorders and
- in the debate over whether patients have a right to refuse treatment.

Commitment of people with mental disorders in virtually every state in the United States is now possible only if the individuals have a mental disorder and pose an imminent danger to themselves or others. Because of reductions in involuntary commitments, there are fewer people in public mental hospitals today (deinstitutionalization), along with more people in private hospitals and other inpatient facilities, prisons, and on the streets (i.e., homeless) than there were in the United States several decades ago.

Other legal rights of people with mental disorders concern:

- the right to effective treatment with informed consent and
- special rights for criminal defendants with mental disorders.

Mental Health Professionals in the Legal System

As explained in Chapter 1, the *DSM-5* opens with a cautionary statement about its use in forensic (legal) settings:

> Although the *DSM-5* diagnostic criteria and text are primarily designed to assist clinicians in conducting clinical assessment, case formulation, and treatment planning, the *DSM-5* is also used as a reference for the courts and attorneys in assessing the forensic consequences of mental disorders. As a result, it is important to note that the definition of mental disorder included in the *DSM-5* was developed to meet the needs of clinicians, public health professionals, and research investigators, rather than all the technical needs of the courts and legal professionals. (American Psychiatric Association, 2013a, p. 25)

In other words, the *DSM-5* is not intended to be a legal manual but a psychological one. However, mental health professionals often interface with the legal system, and in so doing, they necessarily or inadvertently bring *DSM-5* concepts and categories into the legal area. Mental health professionals generally provide the legal system with one or more of four main services (Wrightsman, Nietzel, & Fortune, 1994):

1. As *basic scientists*, they study a phenomenon to learn as much as they can about it, with no regard for whether their work has relevance to the legal system. For example, a psychologist studying the development of cognitive ability tests might examine whether the predictive validity of the test is affected by the ethnicity or gender of the people being tested. This research might subsequently play a role in litigation about the legally acceptable use of the test in hiring decisions (Gottfredson, 1994).

2. As *trial consultants* to attorneys, mental health professionals participate, for example, in jury selection or trial preparation to help one side win the trial (Costanzo & Krauss, 2010).

3. As *policy evaluators or researchers*, they study the effects of changes in correctional programs, legislation, or social services.

4. As *expert witnesses*, they testify on a wide variety of subjects in civil and criminal trials, including issues related to criminal responsibility.

From the public's point of view, the mental health professional's role as expert witness is surely the most controversial. Psychologists and psychiatrists have testified in some of the most notorious trials in recent American history, including those of Jeffrey Dahmer, James Holmes, Andrea Yates, and John Hinckley. One commentator summed up the skepticism of many Americans when he referred to trial testimony by mental health experts as the time to "send in the clowns." Of course, as you likely now realize after reading this entire textbook (right?), mental health professionals may have much to contribute to legal proceedings due to their fundamental knowledge about abnormal behavior and its causes. Next, we discuss special considerations regarding the interface between mental health professionals and the legal system, an area known as **forensic psychology**.

Confidentiality

The laws of most states recognize several types of **privilege**, which protects certain people from public disclosure in court of what they have said in confidence to certain other people. Privilege exists, for example, between a minister and parishioner, a husband and wife, a lawyer and client, and a doctor and patient. Most states have laws that also establish privileged communications between a psychotherapist and client. These communications are considered privileged because society believes that the relationships in which they occur could not survive without the assurance of nondisclosure, even if it means that the whole truth about some matters may never be revealed.

Privilege is similar, but not identical, to *confidentiality*. **Confidentiality** is not a legal requirement but an *ethical* obligation that therapists owe their clients. Indeed, most therapists believe that confidential communication is absolutely essential to effective therapy because, without it, clients might be unwilling to talk about the embarrassing, terrifying, or socially inappropriate things that may hold the key to understanding and addressing their problems. As desirable as it may be, though, a client's right to privileged or confidential communication—like the right to refuse treatment—is not absolute. A therapist may be forced to breach confidentiality in the following situations:

1. If the therapist believes that the client needs to be involuntarily committed to a hospital (e.g., the client is a danger to self or others)
2. If the client raises the issue of his or her mental condition in a trial and the therapist is called on to testify on the client's behalf
3. If the client has undergone a court-ordered psychological evaluation
4. If the therapist learns from the client that the client is abusing other people
5. If the client tells the therapist of an intent to harm another specific person

The *Tarasoff* Decision

The fifth exception to maintaining confidentiality in the preceding list creates a particularly thorny problem: Should a therapist be required to break confidentiality whenever a client threatens to harm another person? Since the famous case of *Tarasoff* v. *Regents of the University of California*, the answer, in most states, is yes.

Prosenjit Poddar was a client of psychologist Lawrence Moore when he confided to Moore that he intended to kill Tatiana Tarasoff because she had rebuffed his romantic interest in her. Moore told his supervisor, Dr. Harvey Powelson, of this threat and then called and wrote the campus police, requesting that they detain Poddar. They did so, but then released him because they were convinced that he was rational and would keep his promise to stay away from Tatiana (who was out of the country at the time). Poddar did not

forensic psychology: The use of psychological knowledge or research methods to advise, evaluate, or reform the legal system.

privilege: The protection from being made to publicly disclose in court what individuals have said in confidence to certain other people (e.g., between a lawyer and client or doctor and patient).

confidentiality: The ethical obligation of a therapist to keep in confidence the information that is discussed with a client.

keep his promise. About 2 months after terminating therapy with Dr. Moore, Poddar went to Tatiana's home and stabbed her to death. He was subsequently convicted of murder.

Because no one had directly warned Tatiana or her parents of Poddar's threats, her parents sued the university, psychotherapists employed by the university, and the campus police to recover damages for the murder of their daughter. The Supreme Court of California found for the plaintiffs (*Tarasoff* v. *Regents of the University of California*, 2008). The Court tipped the scales in society's favor because it viewed psychologist Moore's situation as being like that of a physician who would be held liable for failing to warn people about a contagious disease carried by one of the physician's patients: "Protective privilege ends where the public peril begins," concluded Judge Tobriner (Simone & Fulero, 2005). As a result, therapists in California are required to take steps to protect victims from clients who the therapists believe are dangerous.

In the American Psychological Association's (2010) Ethical Principles of Psychologists and Code of Conduct, the therapist's **duty to warn** is implicitly contained within the guidelines for disclosure of confidential information without the consent of the client:

> Psychologists disclose confidential information without the consent of the individual only as mandated by law, or where permitted by law for a valid purpose such as to (1) provide needed professional services; (2) obtain appropriate professional consultations; (3) protect the client/patient, psychologist, or others from harm.

duty to warn: An ethical and often legal obligation that requires a clinician who has reasonable grounds to believe that a client may be in imminent danger of harming himself or herself or others to warn the possible victims.

In situations when there is cause for serious concern about a client harming someone, the clinician must therefore breach confidentiality to warn the identified victim/third party about imminent danger (Corey, Corey, & Callahan, 2010). This is not just an ethical but a legal duty in all but a few states, such as Nevada and North Dakota, which do not have a duty to warn. Currently, clinicians in 33 jurisdictions are compelled to follow *Tarasoff* and in 7 others to decide whether to take action (Bersoff, 2014).

The Impact of *Tarasoff*

Now that 40 years have passed since the *Tarasoff* case, it is possible to assess its effects on clinical practice. First, *Tarasoff* made therapists more alert to the potential for dangerous behavior by their clients. Survey after survey has indicated that, since *Tarasoff*, therapists are more aware of potential complications involving client dangerousness, are more concerned about their legal liability in such situations, and have changed the way they practice to reduce their legal risks (Shapiro, 1984; Wise, 1978). Along with this heightened awareness, clinicians have worried that, as a result of *Tarasoff* and other more-recent court decisions continuing the erosion of psychotherapist-client privilege, a greater possibility exists that more persons will be hospitalized, perhaps inappropriately, and that therapists will be forced to testify against their clients in later criminal proceedings (Yufik, 2005).

However, there is considerable evidence that *Tarasoff* has not had the adverse impact that many clinicians initially predicted (Buckner & Firestone, 2000). Researchers have found little evidence that *Tarasoff* has deterred many clinicians from treating potentially dangerous clients or has caused such clients to avoid therapy (Givelber, Bowers, & Blitch, 1984). There has been no evidence that clients have been unnecessarily hospitalized (Appelbaum, 1988). Even more surprisingly, even when a therapist breaks confidentiality by warning a potential victim or the police, this act typically does *not* have a negative effect on the client, particularly if the therapist first

Confidentiality laws may be even stricter in other countries. For instance, patient privacy is sacrosanct in Germany, where Andreas Lubitz is suspected of deliberately flying a Germanwings jet into a French mountainside, killing himself and 149 others in March 2015. Lubitz reportedly suffered from suicidal ideation before becoming a pilot, along with a more recent medical issue. How much should his doctors have shared with the airline without Lubitz's consent?

discusses with the client the need to give the warning (Binder & McNiel, 1996). In fact, under these conditions, warning a third party sometimes has a positive effect on the client. Perhaps the warning helps establish for the client clear limits on what behavior is acceptable or not acceptable, stimulates the client's involvement in self-control, or demonstrates the therapist's willingness to take decisive action that could ultimately benefit the client.

Criminal Competence and Responsibility

Beyond confidentiality issues, another area of law that illustrates the controversies surrounding mental health professionals is expert testimony about a defendant's mental condition. In most societies, it is seen as immoral to punish people who, as a result of a mental disorder, either do not know that their actions are wrong or are unable to control their conduct. Societies see punishment as fully deserved only by those who can comprehend the nature and wrongness of their criminal behavior.

Criminal Competence

competency to stand trial: A legal decision that an individual is mentally able to understand the nature of trial proceedings, participate meaningfully in the trial, and consult with an attorney at the time of the trial.

Indeed, in the United States, it is not even permissible to continue criminal proceedings against a defendant who is unable to understand the nature and purpose of those proceedings. Thus, before a court ever considers whether a defendant was sane or insane during the commission of a crime, it must first decide about the defendant's **competency to stand trial**, which is the ability to participate adequately in criminal proceedings and to aid in one's own defense (Costanzo & Krauss, 2010). Note that competence refers to the defendant's mental condition *at the time of the trial*, whereas insanity, described next, refers to the defendant's mental condition *at the time of an alleged offense* (Costanzo & Krauss, 2010).

The question of criminal competence can be raised at any point in the criminal process by the prosecutor, the defense attorney, or the presiding judge. In practice, this question is usually raised by defense attorneys who have reason to believe that their client may be suffering from a mental disorder. Typically, when the judge orders a competency assessment, the defendant is taken to a special forensic hospital for observation and examination. In fact, the majority of offenders with mental disorders who have been committed to hospitals are there either because they are awaiting a competency evaluation or they have been found incompetent and are receiving treatment to restore their competence. In most states, psychiatrists, psychologists, and social workers are authorized to perform competency evaluations, and they often use special structured interviews to do so (see Chapter 1).

Being found competent to stand trial does not certify robust mental health or normal mental functioning. Even people suffering from severe mental disorders, psychosis, or intellectual disabilities are often judged competent. In fact, a study of over 8,000 competency evaluations in Virginia found that over two thirds of individuals suffering from these severe disorders were still found competent to stand trial (Warren et al., 2006). Defendants found to be not competent may be committed to a hospital for medication and other treatment. In most states, this mandatory treatment can last up to 6 months, after which time, if a person is still judged incompetent, a different form of hospitalization might be arranged, or the person might be released (Costanzo & Krauss, 2010).

The Insanity Defense

insanity: A legal term that describes a state of mind and implies that a defendant cannot be held responsible for his or her illegal conduct.

In all states, defendants are initially presumed to be mentally responsible for the crimes with which they are charged. Therefore, if defendants plead not guilty by reason of **insanity**, they must present evidence to show that they lacked a state of mind necessary to be held responsible for their crimes. Because *insanity* is a legal term, not a psychological concept, it is defined in the United States by legal standards that have evolved over time and vary from state to state.

These standards had their origins in 1843, when Englishman Daniel McNaughton tried to assassinate then British Prime Minister Robert Peel. McNaughton suffered the paranoid delusion that Peel was conspiring against him, so he waited outside the prime minister's house at Number 10 Downing Street, and he shot and killed Peel's secretary, whom he mistook for the prime minister. McNaughton was charged with murder but pleaded not guilty by reason of insanity (NGRI), essentially claiming that he did not know the difference between right and wrong. Nine medical experts testified that McNaughton was insane, and after hearing instructions from the judge, the jury did not even leave the courtroom before deciding that McNaughton was not guilty by reason of insanity. Even though

McNaughton spent the rest of his life in Broadmoor insane asylum, this verdict infuriated the British public (Costanzo & Krauss, 2010). Queen Victoria, particularly upset because she herself had been the target of several assassination attempts, demanded that Britain toughen its definition of insanity.

After extended debate in the House of Lords and among the nation's highest judges, a definition of insanity known as the McNaughton rule (sometimes spelled M'Naghten) was enacted, stating that,

> . . . to establish a defense on the grounds of insanity it must be clearly proved that, at the time of committing the act, the accused was laboring under such a defect of reason, from disease of the mind, as not to know the nature and quality of the act he was doing or, if he did know it, that he did not know what he was doing [was] wrong. (quoted in Post, 1963, p. 113)

McNaughton became the rule in Great Britain, and it remains the standard for insanity in about 20 states in the United States to this day. Under this law, defendants have to prove that they suffered from a mental illness that affected their ability to understand what they were doing and/or their ability to understand that what they were doing was wrong (Costanzo & Krauss, 2010). However, the McNaughton rule has been severely criticized over the years because it focuses only on cognition—knowing right from wrong—and ignores how mental disorders might affect motivation and control.

An alternative to McNaughton is the ALI rule, which was developed in the 1970s by the American Law Institute (ALI) in an appellate case in which the defendant, Archie Brawner, Jr., had been convicted of the murder of Billy Ford. This rule holds that a defendant is not responsible for criminal conduct if "at the time of such conduct as a result of mental disease or defect [the defendant] lack[s] substantial capacity either to appreciate the criminality [wrongfulness] of his conduct or to conform his conduct to the requirements of the law." The ALI standard has enjoyed great success, being eventually adopted by 26 U.S. states, with the federal courts adopting a somewhat modified version (Costanzo & Krauss, 2010). The ALI rule differs from McNaughton in three main ways:

1. By using the term *appreciate* instead of *know*, the ALI rule acknowledges that emotional factors as well as cognitive ones can influence criminal conduct.
2. The ALI rule does not require that offenders have a total lack of appreciation for the wrongfulness of their conduct—only that they lack "substantial capacity."
3. The ALI rule defines insanity in both cognitive and volitional terms. Under this rule, defendants can be considered insane even if they appreciated that certain conduct was wrong, as long as a mental disorder rendered them unable to control their conduct at the time of the offense.

The Insanity Defense Under Fire

After John Hinckley was found not guilty by reason of insanity for shooting President Ronald Reagan, Press Secretary James Brady, and three other people in 1982, an ABC News poll showed that 67% of Americans believed that justice had not been served in the case. Highly publicized cases such as Hinckley's (and McNaughton's) tend to be followed by widespread public dissatisfaction and cynicism about the insanity defense. Among the greatest concerns are that a large number of defendants successfully use the insanity defense, that defendants found NGRI are quickly released from the hospital after their trials, and that insane criminals are more dangerous than other criminals. How realistic are these concerns?

Prevalence and Success of the Insanity Defense The insanity defense is employed much less frequently than most people assume and with far less success than defendants would wish. One study in Wyoming found that the public assumed that the insanity defense was used in about half of all criminal cases and was successful about 20% of the time. In fact, the insanity defense was used by only 102 of 22,102 felony defendants studied (less than 0.005%) and was successful only once (Pasewark & Pantle, 1981). Across the United

McNaughton rule: A legal definition of insanity requiring that, at the time the wrongful act was committed, the person accused was, as a result of a mental disorder, unable to know the nature and quality of the act or to know that the act was wrong.

ALI rule: A legal rule that holds that a defendant is not responsible for criminal conduct if he or she lacks substantial capacity to either appreciate the wrongfulness of the act or to control his or her conduct as required by law. ALI stands for American Law Institute.

John Hinckley, Jr., was a loner who dropped out of Texas Tech in 1976 and set out for Hollywood in the hopes of making it big in the music industry. During his time in California, he became obsessed with the film *Taxi Driver* (1976) and one of the movie's stars, Jodie Foster. He traveled to Yale University, where Ms. Foster was a student. In a delusional attempt to reenact a scene from *Taxi Driver* and win the love of Ms. Foster, Hinckley attempted to assassinate then President Ronald Reagan, whose sculpture (shown here) sits in President's Park, Black Hills, South Dakota. Hinckley was found not guilty by reason of insanity. The Hinckley case set off a public furor regarding the insanity defense, even though Hinckley remains confined today at St. Elizabeths Hospital in Washington, DC.

James Eagan Holmes (born December 13, 1987) is the accused perpetrator of a mass shooting that killed 12 people at a Century movie theater in Aurora, a suburb of Denver, Colorado, on July 20, 2012 during a midnight screening of the film *The Dark Knight Rises*. Holmes was hospitalized after attempting suicide several times while in jail in November 2012. He is currently held without bail and pleaded not guilty by reason of insanity on June 4, 2013. Holmes's trial is scheduled for 2015 (Johnson, 2014). Another famous insanity case in this millennium was discussed in Chapter 6: Andrea Yates, who confessed to drowning her five children in their bathtub on June 20, 2001 and was found not guilty by reason of insanity in 2006 because of her mental disorder (Hlavaty, 2014).

States, experts estimate that fewer than 1% of all criminal cases result in a finding of NGRI (Costanzo & Krauss, 2010). Of those cases that were successful, 90% of the defendants had been previously diagnosed with a mental disorder, typically involving psychosis (Schmalleger, 2001). In general, the more often the insanity defense is used, the lower its rate of success (Appelbaum, 1994). Simply put, juries are reluctant to find violent offenders NGRI, mainly out of fear that these offenders will be prematurely released and will repeat their violence.

The Likelihood of Early Release NGRI defendants seldom "go free," however. One study found that NGRI defendants in New York were hospitalized for an average of 3.5 years (Steadman & Braff, 1983). The same study showed that defendants who had committed more-serious offenses tended to be confined longer. In many states, the norm is to keep NGRI defendants in mental institutions until a judge is convinced that it is safe to release them. In an effort to err on the side of caution, judges often use criteria for releasing NGRI defendants that are stricter than those set for noncriminal involuntary commitments. This results in people found NGRI potentially spending as much or even *more* time confined to a mental hospital than they would have had they been found guilty of their crime and sent to prison (Melton et al., 2007; Silver, 1995). For people charged with offenses less serious than homicide or attempted homicide, for instance, insanity acquittees stay locked up significantly longer than do their convicted counterparts (Harris, Rice, & Cormier, 1991).

Do hospital confinement and treatment have any clear benefits for defendants found NGRI? No one knows for sure. Some studies show that individuals who complete their hospital treatment do better than those who run away from the institution (Nicholson, Norwood, & Enyart, 1991), but another study found no difference in the posthospitalization behavior among NGRI defendants who were officially discharged and those who escaped (Pasewark, Bieber, Bosten, Kiser, & Steadman, 1982). Robert Nicholson and his colleagues (1991) collected data on all NGRI defendants in Oklahoma who had been treated in the state forensic hospital over a 5-year period. Within 2-1/2 years of their release, half of these patients had been rearrested or rehospitalized, a rate that is about the same as for criminals in general. These data confirm the results of earlier studies (Melton et al., 1987).

Dangerousness of Insane Defendants The dangerousness of NGRI defendants is difficult to determine, partly because it is often difficult to know how dangerous *anyone* might be. Assessing the public dangerousness of NGRI defendants is also complicated by the fact that most of them are immediately removed from public life and confined in a hospital, where they usually receive drugs and other treatment. Although people with serious mental disorders (including NGRI defendants) are somewhat more likely to be violent than people without such disorders, this relationship is typically found *only for people who are currently experiencing psychotic symptoms* (Link, Cullen, & Andrews, 1993; Monahan, 1992). If drugs or other treatments reduce these symptoms, the potential for violence is reduced as well.

Revisions and Reforms in the Insanity Defense

Of all the reforms introduced in insanity defense rules and procedures in the United States over the past few decades, three have received the most attention.

The Guilty But Mentally Ill Verdict For many decades, juries deliberating cases in which the insanity defense was raised could reach only verdicts of guilty, not guilty, or not guilty by reason of insanity. Since 1976, however, 13 states have passed laws giving juries a fourth possible verdict: **guilty but mentally ill (GBMI)**. The GBMI verdict is usually an additional alternative verdict to the three more standard options of guilty, not guilty, and NGRI (Costanzo & Krauss, 2010). Only Utah has adopted a GBMI verdict without also having an NGRI statute (Zapf, Golding, & Roesch, 2006). A defendant found GBMI is usually sentenced to the same period of confinement as any other defendant convicted of the same crime. Ideally, however, the GBMI prisoner's confinement begins in a treatment facility, and transfer to a prison occurs only after treatment is complete. The primary intent behind GBMI laws is to offer a compromise verdict that decreases the number of defendants found NGRI. It is unclear whether these laws are successful in this respect; there have been decreases in NGRI verdicts in some states using GBMI options but not in others (Callahan, McGreevey, Cirnicione, & Steadman, 1992; Roberts & Golding, 1991).

guilty but mentally ill (GBMI): A legal verdict that results in a defendant's conviction for a crime, even though the jury concludes that the defendant suffers from a mental disorder.

The Insanity Defense Reform Act In 1984, in the wake of the John Hinckley trial, Congress passed the *Insanity Defense Reform Act (IDRA)*. Its main purpose was to limit the number of defendants in federal courts who could successfully claim insanity as a defense. Although not abolishing the insanity defense, the IDRA changed its use in the federal courts in three important ways. First, it placed the burden on the defendant to prove insanity, rather than on the prosecution to prove sanity, which had previously been the case.

Second, it did away with the volitional section of the ALI rule. Lack of behavioral control because of mental disorders is no longer a basis for insanity in federal cases. Insanity is restricted to the cognitive part of the ALI rule—namely that, as a result of a mental disorder, the defendant could not appreciate the nature or wrongfulness of his or her acts. Removing the volitional section essentially makes the federal test of insanity the same as the McNaughton rule, although 22 states still include some form of the volitional prong in their insanity formulations (Costanzo & Krauss, 2010). The IDRA reform was introduced because of the view that (1) a person's ability to control his or her actions cannot be assessed reliably and (2) the issue of volition provided a loophole through which too many criminal offenders were walking to freedom. This change in federal insanity rules came about in spite of empirical research that tended to contradict both these claims.

Third, the IDRA prohibited mental health experts from giving *ultimate opinion* testimony about insanity. As a result of this change, experts may describe a defendant's mental condition and the effects it might have on behavior, but they may not state any conclusions about a defendant's insanity (Costanzo & Krauss, 2010). The reformers acted in the hope that this change would prohibit mental health experts from having too much control over verdicts, but there is some evidence that the prohibition might not have much effect on juries (Fulero & Finkel, 1991). Most mock jury studies of the IDRA have found that verdicts are little affected by whether jurors hear ALI instructions, IDRA instructions, or no instructions at all about the definition of insanity (Finkel, 1989). Jurors appear to depend on their own views about what constitutes insanity and interpret the evidence according to those views, regardless of the formal instructions that judges give them (Roberts & Golding, 1991).

Abolition of the Insanity Defense A few states, such as Idaho, Montana, Kansas, and Utah, have abolished the insanity defense (Costanzo & Krauss, 2010). Has this drastic step solved the problem of holding people with mental disorders responsible for criminal acts? Not really. Issues associated with insanity remain because, to be convicted of a crime in any state, one must have intended the illegal act. Defendants can be found guilty of theft, for example, only if it can be proved that they intended to steal. Accordingly, even states in which there is no insanity defense must allow evidence to be introduced at trial about a defendant's *mens rea*, or guilty mind, during specific types of alleged crimes. If, as a result of a mental disorder, defendants lack the *mens rea* for a crime, they should be found not guilty. And so, to help juries decide, experts continue to offer testimony about the effects of mental disorders on defendants' *mens rea*.

In short, a defendant's mental state can never be entirely eliminated from jurors' consideration, simply because it makes no sense to talk about guilt without knowing something about a person's state of mind at the time of the alleged crime. In one form or another, then, the issue of insanity is likely to remain a part of court decisions about criminal responsibility. Continuing tension between the desire to provide treatment for people with mental disorders and the desire to punish those same people when they commit terrible crimes will continue to shape debate about the insanity defense and the role of mental health professionals in the legal system.

Revisiting the Case of Justin

A weekend visit from Justin's mom prompted a long talk. After hearing about Justin's new job, Justin's mom shared how much she regretted not spending more time with him and how guilty she felt that he had never had a father figure. Justin appreciated the kind words and recalled how his teacher, Mr. Wallace, watched after him and how much he looked up to him. Justin's mom revealed to Justin that she had always had an uneasy feeling about Mr. Wallace that she could not quite put her finger on. She asked Justin frankly if Mr. Wallace had ever acted inappropriately toward him. Justin felt a mixture of shame and relief when he told his mom about his relationship with Mr. Wallace. Justin's mother told him that Mr. Wallace's actions were completely inappropriate and that Mr. Wallace never should have touched him or any other student in that way. She asked Justin if he had ever told anyone else or sought the help of a professional. When he informed his mother that he had not, she encouraged him to seek therapy. Justin was resistant at first and did not feel like he needed therapy of any kind, but he acknowledged to himself the sexual excitement he sometimes felt around his young students.

Because of these troubling feelings, should Justin be legally required to seek treatment to reduce the chances that he would ever act on his distressing urges? Current laws state that Justin is not required to get treatment if he has not done any illegal behavior (unlike the short story and film *Minority Report* in 2002, in which people were imprisoned for crimes that they were thinking about committing in the future!). However, with the help of his mom, Justin came to realize that it was in his own best interests to see a psychologist. He identified a psychotherapist, Dr. Joe, who specialized in sexual disorders. Dr. Joe used CBT to help Justin challenge his distorted beliefs about healthy relationships, and Justin developed an understanding that Mr. Wallace took advantage of him. He linked his ongoing difficulties in establishing romantic relationships to his history with Mr. Wallace. With the help of his therapist, Justin made the difficult decision that he should not work with children. He is currently working with college students in a GRE (graduate record examination) preparatory class and taking additional coursework to specialize in adult education. Justin has been able to live a relatively normal life without risk of hurting others the way he was hurt as a child.

Summary

Paraphilia Versus Paraphilic Disorder

By drawing a distinction between a paraphilia and a paraphilic disorder, the *DSM-5* recognizes that unusual sexual practices alone do not constitute a mental disorder. Intense and persistent sexual interest in fantasies or actions involving anomalous stimuli is considered a paraphilia. When such paraphilias cross a line to include (1) distress or impairment in social, occupational, or other important areas of functioning or (2) harm or risk of harm to others, then they are deemed paraphilic disorders.

Types of Paraphilic Disorders

The *DSM-5* describes eight paraphilic disorders. Voyeuristic disorder involves sexual arousal through the secret observation of others who are naked, disrobing, or engaging in sexual activity. Exhibitionistic disorder describes a

Brad Sagarin

Dr. Brad Sagarin is a professor of social and evolutionary psychology at Northern Illinois University, where he studies social influence, resistance to persuasion, deception, jealousy, infidelity, and human sexuality. Dr. Sagarin has been published in a variety of scholarly journals, has given radio interviews, has consulted for radio and television programs, and has delivered invited lectures to academic and nonacademic organizations. His research has been cited in newspapers and magazines, including The Economist *and* New Scientist. *He holds doctorate and master's degrees in social psychology from Arizona State University, as well as a baccalaureate degree in computer science from the Massachusetts Institute of Technology.*

Q *Do you think it makes sense that the DSM-5 distinguishes between paraphilias (unusual sexual practices) and paraphilic disorders (unusual sexual practices that cause distress or harm)?*

A The distinction between paraphilias and paraphilic disorders is critically important. Recent research on BDSM (bondage/discipline, dominance/submission, sadism/masochism), for example, suggests that con-

sensual sadomasochism is a relatively healthy social phenomenon performed by well-educated, psychologically healthy people with positive attitudes about themselves and their behaviors. So, although we should still seek to diagnose and treat individuals whose unusual sexual practices cause distress or harm, the evidence suggests that many people pursue unusual sexual practices with no harm to themselves or their sexual partners.

Q *As a researcher, what challenges have you had in assessing sexual behavior?*

A My colleagues and I study consensual sadomasochism, a set of activities that is still highly stigmatized. The two most important things that we do are to approach participants with an open mind and with procedures in place to protect their anonymity. For example, researchers usually obtain informed consent from participants using a signed *Informed Consent Form*, but we were concerned that a signed form could put our participants at risk. To avoid this, we have received permission from our IRB [institutional review board] to obtain informed consent verbally, ensuring that our participants' anonymity is protected.

Q *What does your research suggest about the function of paraphilic behaviors for couples?*

A One of the strongest findings from our research is that consensual BDSM has the potential to increase a couple's intimacy. The BDSM scenes we observed included bondage and painful stimuli, but they also included caring behavior before, during, and after the scenes. This caring behavior demonstrates the positive relationship context in which these activities typically take place, and it highlights the openness, communication, and trust that the activities can encourage in relationships.

---

pattern in which individuals gain sexual arousal by exposing their genitals to an unwilling observer. Frotteuristic disorder involves recurrent touching or rubbing against a nonconsenting person to become sexually aroused. In fetishistic disorder, individuals focus sexual interest on a nonliving object or specific nongenital body part to become aroused, whereas in transvestic disorder, individuals cross-dress to experience sexual arousal. Sexual sadism disorder describes when sexual arousal depends on the physical or psychological suffering of another person, and sexual masochism disorder describes when sexual arousal depends on being humiliated or made to suffer. In

pedophilic disorder, individuals who are at least 16 years of age engage in sexual activity with a child at least 5 years younger than them. All of the paraphilic disorders are more common in men than in women, and research suggests that individuals with only one paraphilic disorder are rare.

Causes of Paraphilias and Paraphilic Disorders

Whereas the causes of paraphilias and paraphilic disorders are unclear, they are likely due to a combination of biopsychosocial factors. Biological explanations focus on the brain differences between individuals with and without paraphilic interests. For example, temporal and parietal lobe abnormalities, elevated dopamine levels, abnormal androgen levels, and head trauma have all been linked to paraphilic behavior. Psychological explanations emphasize the role of early learning in the development of paraphilic interests. In particular, childhood experiences that lessen a person's ability to be aroused by consensual sexual stimulation, that increase the ability to be aroused by atypical stimuli, and that lower the capacity to empathize with victims may increase the likelihood of paraphilic interests. Social factors that overemphasize male sexual expression may help account for the higher rates of men with paraphilias and paraphilic disorders.

Treatment of Paraphilic Disorders

The results of treatments for paraphilic disorders are mixed. Whereas some studies indicate that specialized treatment programs can reduce the likelihood of recidivism, others suggest that treatment has no significant effects. Cognitive-behavioral therapy, combined with relapse prevention, social skills training, and the development of empathy for victims is the psychological treatment of choice. Behavioral methods involving aversive conditioning techniques have also been used, although with mixed evidence of long-term success. Biological methods are directed at lowering libido, either through surgical castration or antiandrogen medications.

Legal and Ethical Issues Involving People With Mental Disorders

The involuntary commitment of citizens with mental disorders illustrates one of the most fundamental controversies surrounding the treatment of abnormal behavior. Commitment procedures raise the question of how to balance the rights of individuals to be left alone with the rights of society to be protected from harm. In the United States, the rationale for involuntary commitment has been either *parens patriae* (deciding what is best for incapacitated people) or police power (protecting society against dangerous people). In the late 1960s and 1970s, commitment procedures were reformed throughout the United States, making it much more difficult to commit people with mental disorders on the basis of a *parens patriae* doctrine to this day. The populations of public mental hospitals declined throughout this period, although this deinstitutionalization process left many seriously disturbed patients without adequate treatment or protection. Beginning in the 1980s and continuing to the present, the procedures for involuntary commitments have attempted to balance concerns about patients' rights, while realizing that some people are so seriously disabled that society should insist on their treatment even if they pose no danger to others.

Other examples of the tension between individual and societal rights are revealed in questions about whether mental patients should have the right to refuse treatment.

As of now, the Supreme Court has not recognized such a right, but in many situations, patients are able to object to certain types of medication and thereby influence the kind of treatment they receive. American courts have established other basic rights for mental patients that guarantee treatment, fair housing, and professional assistance in criminal proceedings.

Mental Health Professionals in the Legal System

Two other psycholegal topics that have generated controversy involve forensic psychology—the interaction between psychological science and the legal system.

First, there are laws that affect mental health professionals' practice by placing limits on certain privileges, along with ethical obligations typically honored by these professions. For example, the right to confidential mental health treatment can be abridged in certain circumstances, such as when a therapy client threatens to harm a third party. This duty to warn is based on the famous *Tarasoff* case in the 1970s.

Second, there is the question of what the proper role is for mental health professionals who are asked to testify in court about a defendant's mental state as it relates to the insanity defense. *Insanity* is a legal term that has been defined in various ways over the past 2 centuries. The first way, still in use by most U.S. states today, is known as the McNaughton rule. This rule requires that, at the time the wrongful act was committed, the person accused was, as a result of a mental disorder, unable to know the nature and quality of the act or to know that the act was wrong. Many states use the ALI rule instead, though, which states that defendants are not criminally responsible if, as the result of mental disorder, they lack a substantial capacity either to appreciate the criminality of their conduct or to conform their conduct to the requirements of the law (i.e., control their behavior).

Although the public tends to believe that the insanity defense is used frequently in criminal cases, is often successful, and leads to large numbers of dangerous people being released from custody, the insanity defense is only rarely used and is seldom successful in setting defendants free. Most defendants found not guilty by reason of insanity (NGRI) serve lengthy periods of hospital confinement. Several reforms—such as the guilty-but-mentally-ill (GBMI) verdict—have been introduced in recent years, and four states have even abolished the insanity defense. None of these changes has been shown to substantially change the ways juries evaluate insanity defenses. Even states that have done away with the insanity defense still find it necessary to consider the effects that mental disorders might have had on defendants' capacity to understand the crimes with which they are charged.

Key Terms

Glossary

abnormal behavior: A pattern of behavioral, psychological, or physical functioning that is not culturally expected and that leads to psychological distress, behavioral disability, or impaired overall functioning.

absorption: A dimension of personality that describes a person's tendency to become caught up in private reveries, imaginings, or a current task, to the exclusion of surrounding stimuli; also known as fantasy proneness or imaginative involvement.

abstinence violation effect: A situation in which expectancies about using a drug may set off a chain of faulty decisions for an abuser that then increase the probability of resumed abuse.

acetylcholine (ACH): A neurotransmitter that is critical to movement, physiological arousal, memory, learning, and sleep.

achievement test: A measure of how much a person has learned about a specific area. One example is the Wide Range Achievement Test–Revised (WRAT-3).

acquired: A modifier used to describe a sexual dysfunction that develops after a period of normal sexual functioning.

active phase (of schizophrenia): The stage of schizophrenia during which one or more psychotic symptoms, such as delusions or hallucinations, appear.

activities of daily living (ADLs): A term used in health care to refer to daily self-care activities; health professionals routinely refer to the ability or inability to perform ADLs as a measurement of the functional status of a person, particularly in regard to people with disabilities and the elderly.

acute akathesia: An extrapyramidal side effect of some neuroleptics, involving uncontrollable restlessness and agitation.

acute dystonia: An extrapyramidal side effect of some neuroleptics, involving tics in the head, neck, and face.

acute stress disorder: A mental disorder in which a person who has undergone a traumatic event experiences trauma-related symptoms similar to PTSD that begin within 1 month of the trauma and last less than 1 month.

adaptive behavior: Behavior that enables an individual to meet the cultural expectations for independent functioning associated with a particular age.

adjustment disorder: Maladaptive behavioral and psychological reactions to a stressor occurring within 3 months of the stressor.

adolescent-onset conduct disorder: Children diagnosed with conduct disorder after age 10; these children are less likely to commit violent offenses or to persist in their antisocial behavior into adulthood.

adoption study: A method of systematically examining traits and disorders in persons who were separated from their biological parents at early ages; the method compares similarities between adopted individuals and their biological and adoptive parents.

adrenal corticosteroid: A chemical messenger, also known as a stress hormone, that intensifies alarm and prepares the body to cope with a stressor.

adrenocorticotrophic hormone (ACTH): A hormone that, in response to a stressor, directs the adrenal glands to release adrenal corticosteroids.

adverse childhood experiences: Stressful or traumatic experiences, including abuse, neglect, and a range of household dysfunction, such as witnessing domestic violence or growing up with substance abuse, mental disorders, parental discord, or crime in the home.

agoraphobia: A fear of open spaces or of being separated from a safe place.

alcohol expectancy: An individual's belief about the physical and psychological effects of alcohol.

alcoholic cirrhosis: A disease characterized by damaged liver cells, development of scar tissue, and the eventual inability of the liver to filter toxins from the blood.

alcoholism: A pattern of heavy drinking in which individuals lose control over drinking and become so dependent on alcohol that physical and mental health are jeopardized and social and occupational functioning are impaired.

ALI rule: A legal rule that holds that a defendant is not responsible for criminal conduct if he or she lacks substantial capacity to either appreciate the wrongfulness of the act or to control his or her conduct as required by law. ALI stands for American Law Institute.

alogia: A negative symptom of schizophrenia involving the failure to say much, if anything, in response to questions or comments.

alter personality (alter): In dissociative identity disorder, one of the different "personalities" that seems to assume control over the individual's functioning in different situations.

altruistic suicide: A suicide type proposed by Emile Durkheim, committed by people who choose suicide because they place a social goal or group ahead of personal survival.

Alzheimer's disease: The most frequent cause of dementia, characterized by memory loss, apathy, cognitive difficulties, language problems, and personality changes.

amenorrhea: The absence of menstruation.

amnesia: Loss or impairment of memory.

amnestic disorder: A disorder that involves primarily memory loss.

amniocentesis: The medical procedure of extracting amniotic fluid for the purpose of screening for potential fetal problems.

amniotic fluid: The fluid surrounding the fetus.

amotivational syndrome: A pattern of apathy and inability to meet personal or career goals that is linked to cannabis-induced alteration of brain functioning.

amphetamines: A class of drugs that stimulate the sympathetic nervous system, increasing alertness and reducing appetite.

amplifier hypothesis: A theory that explains how family stress may lead to aggressive, antisocial behavior in children and that suggests that stress in the family amplifies negative traits among parents, disturbs family functioning, and limits parents' ability to engage in effective, positive parenting behavior.

amygdala: A structure in the forebrain that is part of the limbic system and is linked to emotions.

amyloid (senile) plaque: A deposit found in large numbers in the brains of people who are likely to develop Alzheimer's disease.

amyloid precursor protein (APP): A form of protein produced by a gene on chromosome 21, thought to mutate in people with Alzheimer's disease.

anhedonia: Loss of the ability to enjoy activities central to a person's life.

anomic suicide: A suicide type proposed by Emile Durkheim; committed by people who feel lost or abandoned by society, often because of social upheaval such as divorce or job loss.

anorexia nervosa: A disorder whose main characteristics are an unreasonable fear of gaining weight, disturbances in the perception of one's body shape or size, and the relentless pursuit of thinness, leading to significantly low body weight.

anorexia nervosa, binge-eating/purging type: A subtype of anorexia in which an individual vomits or misuses laxatives, diuretics, or enemas after eating.

anorexia nervosa, restricting type: A subtype of anorexia in which an individual tries to reduce weight by extreme dieting, fasting, and/or excessive exercise.

antagonist: A drug that blocks the effects of neurotransmitters or other drugs.

anticonvulsants: A diverse group of pharmaceuticals used in the treatment of epileptic seizures. Anticonvulsant drugs are also increasingly being used in the treatment of bipolar disorders, since many seem to act as mood stabilizers, and for the treatment of neuropathic pain. Also commonly known as antiepileptic drugs or as antiseizure drugs.

antidepressants: A broad class of medications commonly used in the treatment of depressive and sometimes bipolar disorders; these drugs include monoamine oxidase inhibitors, tricyclics, and selective serotonin reuptake inhibitors (SSRIs), such as Prozac.

antisocial personality disorder: A personality disorder characterized by repeated rule breaking, chronic manipulativeness, a callous outlook toward the rights of others and society, and tendencies to behave impulsively, dishonestly, irresponsibly, and without remorse.

anxiety: A diffuse or vague sense of apprehension accompanied by fearful behavior and physiological arousal.

anxiety disorder: A group of mental disorders in which fear or anxiety and associated maladaptive behaviors are the core of the disturbance.

anxiety hierarchy: A graded list of fear-provoking stimuli or situations, ranging from the least to most threatening; used in systematic desensitization.

aphasia: A loss or impairment in language.

apolipoprotein E (ApoE): A protein that transports cholesterol in the blood.

applied behavior analysis: A behavioral modification intervention based on the principles of operant conditioning (i.e., learning theory) that is commonly used to teach new skills and enhance social functioning among children with autism spectrum disorder (ASD) and intellectual disability.

appraisal: An evaluation of our own behavior and the behavior of others.

aptitude test: A measure of the accumulated effects of educational or training experiences that attempts to forecast future performance. One example is the Scholastic Aptitude Test (SAT).

assertive community treatment (ACT): An intensive and highly integrated approach for community mental health service delivery, ACT programs serve outpatients whose mental disorders result in serious functioning difficulties in several major areas of life, often including work, social relationships, residential independence, money management, and physical health and wellness.

assessment: The collection of information for the purpose of making an informed decision.

attention-deficit/hyperactivity disorder (ADHD): A childhood mental disorder marked by inattention, impulsivity, and/or high motor activity.

attitude and interest tests: Tests that measure the range and strength of a person's interests, attitudes, preferences, and values.

attribution: An individual's explanation for behavior or other events.

atypical antipsychotics: Drugs that do not have the same biochemical or physiological effects as standard neuroleptics.

autism spectrum disorder (ASD): A broad category of neurodevelopmental disorders that are characterized by (1) deficits in social communication and interaction, and (2) restrictive, repetitive behaviors, interests, and activities.

aversion therapy: A behavioral treatment in which clients pair aversive events (e.g., foul smells or imagining friends watching them commit their paraphilic sex acts) with their preferred paraphilic stimuli in an attempt to reduce the sexual arousal conditioning to those stimuli.

avoidant personality disorder: A personality disorder characterized by constant feelings of inadequacy, especially in social situations.

avoidant/restrictive food intake disorder (ARFID): A problem with eating/feeding, not due to body image concerns, that results in inadequate nutrition or calorie consumption.

avolition: A negative symptom of schizophrenia in which patients may sit for hours making no attempt to do anything.

Axis I: In *DSM-IV*, the dimension that contained 16 general groupings of major mental disorders.

Axis II: In *DSM-IV*, the dimension that consisted of 10 personality disorders and intellectual disability. *DSM-5* now includes these 10 disorders with all the other (former Axis I) disorders on a single axis.

Axis III: In *DSM-IV*, the dimension where clinicians listed general medical conditions that could be relevant to understanding or treating a person's mental disorder. Using *DSM-5*, medical conditions are simply listed along with the mental disorders on the same axis.

Axis IV: In *DSM-IV*, the dimension where clinicians recorded psychosocial and environmental stressors that could affect the diagnosis, treatment, and course of a mental disorder. Using *DSM-5*, these factors may be listed along with the mental disorders on the same axis.

Axis V: In *DSM-IV*, the dimension on which clinicians rated a person's overall level of functioning at the time of the evaluation, giving a summary assessment of the person's general clinical status and providing a gauge for how well the person responded to treatment. *DSM-5* encourages use of the WHO-DAS system instead.

axon: A long fiber extension of a neuron from which neurotransmitters are released.

B

barbiturates: A class of drugs that are addictive and produce relaxation and mild euphoria at low levels, and have an effect similar to alcohol intoxication at higher levels.

basal ganglia: Clusters of brain cells (nuclei) that are situated at the base of the forebrain and that are associated with a variety of functions, including control of voluntary motor movements, procedural learning, routine behaviors or "habits," cognition, and emotion.

behavioral avoidance: A pervasive pattern of avoiding or withdrawing from social interactions; a defense mechanism by which individuals remove themselves from unpleasant situations.

behavioral genetics: A scientific field that examines genetic influences on behavior and their interaction with the environment.

behavioral health consultant (BHC): A mental health provider who offers supportive services and recommendations to an agency, physician, individual, or medical clinic.

behavioral theory: A theory of behavior that explains how normal and abnormal behaviors are shaped by people's experiences with the world, and how people learn to behave as a result of these experiences.

behavior modification (behavior therapy): Behavioral treatments based on learning theory that are aimed at helping people decrease specific maladaptive behaviors and increase adaptive behaviors.

benzodiazepines: A class of drugs derived from benzoic acid that are prescribed to alleviate anxiety and panic; includes Valium and Xanax.

bereavement: Feelings of sadness that follow the death of a loved one and are best characterized as normal grief reactions to loss.

beta-amyloid-4: An abnormal form of a common protein that is essential for life.

binge-eating disorder (BED): An eating disorder characterized by recurrent episodes of eating unusually large quantities of food.

biological model: A model of abnormal behavior that explains how biological factors influence thought and behavior, both normal and abnormal.

biopsychosocial model: A general model or approach positing that biological, psychological (which entails thoughts, emotions, and behaviors), and social (socioeconomic, environmental, and cultural) factors all play a significant role in human functioning in the context of disorder or disease.

bipolar disorders: Mood disorders marked by alternating periods of depression and mania.

bipolar I disorder: A mood disorder in which severe, full-blown manic symptoms are accompanied by one or more periods of major depression.

bipolar II disorder: A mood disorder in which a major depressive episode has occurred in addition to manic episodes that are mild, or hypomanic.

blood alcohol concentration (BAC): The amount of unmetabolized ethanol absorbed into the blood.

body dysmorphic disorder: A mental disorder in which individuals are preoccupied with one or more perceived defects in their physical appearance and perform repetitive behaviors or mental acts in response to these appearance-related concerns.

body mass index (BMI): A measure that uses weight and height to identify individuals who may be at risk for weight-related health problems.

borderline personality disorder: A personality disorder characterized by impulsivity and instability in several areas of functioning, including mood, behavior, self-image, and interpersonal relationships.

brief psychotic disorder: The sudden onset of psychotic symptoms marked by intense emotional turmoil and confusion.

Briquet's syndrome: First described in 1859 by Paul Briquet, this disorder involves patients who feel they have been sickly most of their lives and who complain of multiple symptoms related to numerous organ systems; the conviction of illness continues, despite negative medical testing, and patients continue to seek medical treatment and undergo procedures.

bulimia nervosa: An eating disorder characterized by recurrent binge eating in which large quantities of food are consumed in one sitting, followed by purging or other efforts to prevent weight gain.

C

cannabinoids: Psychoactive ingredients of cannabis, the most important of which is delta-9-tetrahydrocannabinol, or THC.

cannabis: A psychoactive drug derived from the hemp plant that causes a variety of intoxicating and hallucinatory effects.

Capgras syndrome: The delusion that impostors are posing as friends or relatives.

cataplexy: A period of muscle paralysis that causes the person to collapse and be immobile for several seconds to a few minutes.

catastrophizing: An exaggerated and irrational style of thought in which individuals assume the worst and may blow situations out of proportion.

catatonia: A dimension of disordered behavior ranging from immobility (where a person may maintain awkward body positions for hours at a time, appearing stuporous) to great excitement, extreme motor activity, repetitive gestures or mannerisms, and undirected violent behaviors.

catecholamine theory: The idea that low levels of norepinephrine lead to depression and high levels of norepinephrine lead to mania.

cerebral cortex: The outermost layered structure of neural tissue of the cerebrum (brain) in humans and other mammals. It is referred to as "gray matter" because it consists of cell bodies and capillaries and contrasts with the underlying white matter, which consists mainly of the white myelinated sheaths of neuronal axons.

cerebrum: Main part of human brain, covered by the cerebral cortex; responsible for integrative processes such as thought, language, and emotion. It is divided into two hemispheres, which are further divided into lobes.

chemical castration: The use of medication to suppress the male sex hormones such as androgen; sometimes used as treatment for sex offenders and people with paraphilic disorders.

childhood-onset conduct disorder: Children diagnosed with conduct disorder whose symptoms began prior to age 10; these children are more likely to be male, demonstrate more aggressive and illegal behavior, experience academic failure, and persist in their antisocial behavior over time.

circadian rhythm: An internally cued rhythmic schedule of biological activity that repeats roughly every 24 hours.

circadian rhythm sleep disorder: A sleep disturbance involving a mismatch between a person's natural circadian sleep/wake cycle and the demands of the environment.

civil commitment: The legal order by which an individual can be involuntarily committed to a psychiatric hospital.

classical conditioning: A form of learning in which a formerly neutral stimulus is able to elicit a new response. This learning occurs after repeated associations between the neutral stimulus and an unconditioned stimulus that automatically elicits a response that resembles the learned one.

classical method of classification: A method of classification in which every disorder is assumed to be a distinct and unique condition for which each and every attribute must be present for a diagnosis to be made.

clinical psychology: The branch of psychology devoted to studying, assessing, diagnosing, treating, and preventing abnormal behavior.

cocaine: A psychoactive, pain-reducing, stimulant drug.

codependent: A person who protects, monitors, or censures a person with a substance use disorder, becoming enmeshed in the user's problems and preventing change in the substance use pattern.

coercive cycle: Research suggests that the parent-child interactions in families of boys with aggression are characterized by cycles in which one person's aversive behavior is reinforced by termination of the other's aversive behavior.

cognition: Mental processes involved in an individual's capacity to learn, understand, retain, and use information.

cognitive-behavioral therapy (CBT): A psychotherapy that uses learning principles and rational thinking strategies to alter maladaptive thoughts and beliefs that accompany behavior problems.

cognitive processing therapy: A cognitive-behavioral treatment for PTSD that involves repeatedly exposing individuals to stimuli that remind them of their past trauma, in addition to having them process the meaning of their trauma through written exercises.

cognitive reappraisal: An attempt to reduce stress by thinking about a stressor in ways that make it less upsetting.

cognitive theory: A theory that explains behavior primarily in terms of the way people process information about the world—what they attend to, perceive, think about, and remember.

cognitive triad: Automatic, repetitive, and negative thoughts about the self, the world, and the future that are characteristic of depressed people.

community reinforcement: A treatment for substance use disorders in which social and environmental influences are used to help maintain sobriety.

comorbidity: The co-occurrence of two or more mental disorders in the same person.

competency to stand trial: A legal decision that an individual is mentally able to understand the nature of trial proceedings, participate meaningfully in the trial, and consult with an attorney at the time of the trial.

compulsion: A repetitive, nearly irresistible act that a person performs, often in response to some obsessive thought.

computerized tomography (CT): A neurodiagnostic procedure that provides computer-enhanced, three-dimensional pictures of the brain.

concordance rate: The rate at which a trait or disorder is shared with close relatives, such as a twin.

concussion: From the Latin *concutere* ("to shake violently"), concussion is the most common type of traumatic brain injury.

conduct disorder: A childhood mental disorder pattern of antisocial behavior at home or in the community, including significant physical aggression, property damage, deceitfulness, or rule violations.

confidentiality: The ethical obligation of a therapist to keep in confidence the information that is discussed with a client.

confounding variable: A variable that confuses or distorts research results, making it difficult to be sure whether the independent variable, confounding variable, or some combination of the two was responsible for observed effects on the dependent variable.

contingency management: Deliberately presenting or withdrawing reinforcers or aversive stimuli following change-worthy behaviors.

continuous amnesia: The loss of memory for events from a particular time or trauma up to the present.

control group: A group of subjects included in an experiment to control for some variable that could provide an alternative explanation for observed effects on a dependent variable.

conversion disorder: A *DSM-5* psychiatric disorder in which individuals experience problems with motor or sensory abilities that suggest a neurological impairment, but no recognized neurological condition exists to explain the symptoms; also called functional neurological symptom disorder.

coping: A person's efforts to modify, manage, or tolerate stressors.

coprolalia: The involuntary shouting or repeating of obscene words.

correlation: A measure of the degree to which one variable is related to another.

correlation coefficient: A number that quantifies the size of relationship between two variables, noted by the symbol *r*, and ranging from +1.00 to −1.00. The larger the absolute value of the correlation, the stronger the relationship between the variables.

corticotropin-releasing hormone (CRH): A hormone that starts a chain of coordinated physiological and biochemical defenses against a stressor, and signals the pituitary gland to secrete adrenocorticotrophic hormone (ACTH).

covert sensitization: A behavioral treatment in which clients imagine their preferred paraphilic stimuli and then substitute unpleasant, aversive images in an attempt to reduce the sexual arousal conditioning to their paraphilic stimuli.

culture-bound syndrome: A pattern of abnormal behavior that appears only in certain localities or cultures.

cyclothymic disorder: A mood disorder in which moods fluctuate over a long period, but neither the depressive nor the manic episodes are as severe as in bipolar I or II disorder.

D

dangerousness model: A model of civil commitment in which people with mental disorders can only be hospitalized against their will if they are an imminent danger to themselves or others.

default mode network: A set of remote, functionally connected cortical nodes in the brain that are less active during executive tasks than at rest; this network has functions that involve Theory of Mind, episodic memory, and other self-reflective processes.

defense mechanism: In psychoanalytic theory, psychological processes that operate unconsciously to minimize conflicts between the id, ego, and superego.

delayed ejaculation: A sexual dysfunction in which a man is unable to ejaculate or experiences an inordinately long delay before ejaculating during sexual activity.

delirium: A disturbance in consciousness involving impairments in attention, disorientation, memory and language problems, and hallucinations.

delirium tremens (DTs): A set of symptoms, including muscle tremors, hallucinations, and profuse sweating, that result from withdrawal from heavy alcohol use.

delta sleep: The most restorative period of sleep, in which slower brain waves called delta waves are predominant; it accounts for 10–20% of sleep time.

delusion: An extreme, false belief that is so firmly held that no evidence or argument can convince the person to give it up.

delusional disorder: A mental disorder in which the main symptom is the presence of at least one systematic delusional belief.

dendrite: A branchlike structure on a neuron that receives information from other neurons.

deoxyribonucleic acid (DNA): The substance that is the primary component of genes.

dependent personality disorder: A personality disorder characterized by excessive self-sacrifice, an inability to make decisions without exorbitant help, and a dread of being alone.

dependent variable (DV): The variable in an experiment that is observed in order to determine the effect of the independent variable.

depersonalization: A feeling that individuals have become detached from their real self, as if they are observing themselves from outside the body.

depersonalization/derealization disorder: A disorder in which individuals experience both depersonalization (detachment from others or themselves) and derealization (feeling that the world is not real) in the absence of other physical and mental disorders.

depersonalization disorder: A disorder in which a person experiences both depersonalization and derealization in the absence of other physical and mental disorders.

depression: An extremely low, miserably unhappy mood, along with other physical and cognitive symptoms.

depressive disorders: A group of emotional disturbances in which a person experiences a low, unhappy mood and has difficulty maintaining a more neutral or positive emotional state.

derealization: A feeling that objects or events are strange or unreal, or have suddenly changed shape, size, or location.

detoxification: A supervised period of "drying out" from an abused substance, often aided by drugs or other interventions to ease withdrawal symptoms and remedy nutritional deficits.

developmental psychopathology: A field of study that focuses on how problems that first appear in childhood or adolescence are linked to disorders occurring later in life.

developmental task: A psychological or cognitive task to be mastered during the course of development from infancy through adolescence; these tasks form a foundation for later learning and adjustment.

dexamethasone: A substance that temporarily suppresses the production of cortisol in healthy adults.

diagnosis: The classification of mental disorders by determining which of several possible descriptions best fits the nature of the problem(s).

dialectical behavior therapy (DBT): A comprehensive form of cognitive-behavioral therapy designed specifically for the treatment of borderline personality disorder. It focuses on increasing skills that allow individuals to accept current difficulties and work toward change.

diathesis: A biological or psychological predisposition for a disorder.

diathesis-stress model: A model that explains how a mental disorder can result from the interaction of a predisposition (diathesis) for a disorder with a trigger (stressor) that converts the predisposition into the actual disorder.

diffusion MRI (dMRI): Diffusion MRI, also known as diffusion tensor imaging, is a magnetic resonance imaging (MRI) method that allows the mapping of the diffusion process of molecules, mainly water, in biological tissues, in vivo and noninvasively; these water molecule diffusion patterns can reveal microscopic details about brain architecture.

dimensional approach: An approach to describing mental disorders in which disorders are portrayed along different personality dimensions that produce a profile summarizing the person's functioning.

disruptive mood dysregulation disorder: A mental disorder in children between 6 and 18 years old that involves persistent irritability and temper outbursts that are grossly out of proportion to the situation or developmental level.

dissociation: The process by which the normally integrated elements of consciousness, memory, and personal identity become splintered.

dissociative amnesia: Sudden loss of memory for personally important information that is not caused by a medical condition or other mental disorder, usually following a stressful event.

dissociative fugue: A dissociative state in which individuals travel to a new location without remembering their pre-fugue life, often also becoming confused about their identity.

dissociative identity disorder (DID): A mental disorder in which individuals experience a shattering of a unified identity into at least two separate but coexisting personalities with different memories, behavior patterns, and emotions; formerly called *multiple personality disorder*.

dopamine: A neurotransmitter that is prominent in several areas of the brain and is linked with several types of mental disorders.

double-bind hypothesis: An early theory suggesting that schizophrenia could arise from the confusion produced when a child was raised by parents who communicated incompatible messages to the child.

double-blind study: An experimental design in which only the director of the experiment knows which participants are in the experimental group and which are in the control group.

double depression: A condition in which both major depression and dysthymia are experienced.

Down syndrome: A form of intellectual disability caused by a genetic malfunction on chromosome 21.

duty to warn: An ethical and often legal obligation that requires a clinician who has reasonable grounds to believe that a client may be in imminent danger of harming himself or herself or others to warn the possible victims.

E

ecological model: Another name for the sociocultural model.

ego: One of the three structures in the psychoanalytic concept of personality; it seeks compromise between the id and the superego by following the reality principle.

ego analyst: A psychoanalytically oriented theorist who differs from Freud by assigning more importance to conscious personality factors.

ego-syntonic: Experiences that seem to be a natural part of the self.

electroconvulsive therapy (ECT): A treatment for severe depression that induces brief seizures through the use of an electric current.

electroencephalogram (EEG): A measure of changes in the electrical activity of the brain.

emotional dysregulation: A mental health term that refers to the inability of a person to control or regulate his or her emotional responses to provocative stimuli.

emotion-focused coping: Attempts to reduce stress by changing a person's emotional responses to a stressor.

empathizing-systemizing (E-S) theory: A theory postulating that the causes of autism spectrum disorder are deficits in empathizing (reading and responding appropriately to other people's emotions) and excesses in systemizing (a drive to understand and apply rules to a system).

empathy: The ability to appreciate and share the feelings of another person.

endocrine system: A network of glands that affects organs throughout the body by releasing hormones into the bloodstream.

endogenous opiate: A naturally occurring chemical, similar to an opioid drug, that produces a state of euphoria and reduces the experience of pain.

endorphin: An endogenous opioid that helps regulate cardiovascular activity, relieve pain, and facilitate psychological coping.

enuresis: A disorder involving repeated release of urine into bedding or clothes, after the age of five.

epidemiology: The scientific study of the onset and frequency of disorders in certain populations.

epigenetics: The study of heritable changes in gene activity that are not caused by changes in the actual DNA sequence. Epigenetics literally means "above" or "on top of" genetics and refers to external modifications to DNA that turn genes "on" or "off."

equifinality: Developmental psychopathology concept suggesting that different early experiences can result in the same outcome (or psychological disorder).

erectile disorder: A sexual dysfunction characterized by a recurrent failure to obtain or maintain an erection adequate for sexual activity.

etiological factor: A specific cause of disorders.

event-related potentials (ERPs): Measured brain responses that occur as the direct result of a specific sensory, cognitive, or motor event.

excoriation (skin-picking) disorder: A mental disorder that involves recurrent skin picking, resulting in distress and skin lesions, with repeated attempts to decrease or stop the picking.

executive functioning: The cognitive ability to attend to relevant information, plan or organize activities, and make good judgments about events in the environment.

exhibitionistic disorder: A paraphilic disorder in which a person gains sexual arousal by exposing his or her genitals to an unwilling observer.

experiment: A scientific process of determining cause and effect wherein subjects are randomly assigned to conditions manipulated by a researcher who measures the effect of this manipulation on other variables, while holding all other influences constant.

experimental group: The group that receives an active treatment or manipulation in an experiment.

exposure and response prevention: A behavioral treatment for obsessive-compulsive and related disorders that involves having individuals face (rather than avoid) their anxiety-provoking obsessions, material possessions, or body concerns without engaging in their usual compulsive or avoidant behavioral rituals.

expressed emotion (EE): A measure of the family environment describing criticism, hostility, and emotional overinvolvement with a person; a risk factor for relapse of mental disorders such as schizophrenia.

expressive language: Language that is used to communicate thoughts or needs.

externalizing problem: A disruptive childhood behavior that is a nuisance to others, such as aggression, hyperactivity, impulsivity, or inattention.

extinction: The decrease in a behavior caused by the absence of reinforcers for that behavior.

extrapyramidal symptoms: A group of side effects that result from neuroleptic drugs, consisting of movement abnormalities, such as tremors, rigidity, spasms, and agitation.

eye movement desensitization and reprocessing: A cognitive-behavioral treatment for PTSD that involves repeatedly exposing individuals to stimuli that remind them of their past trauma, while they engage in eye or other bilateral movements postulated to facilitate emotional processing.

F

factitious disorder: Pretending to have a physical illness or mental disorder, despite no obvious external rewards for having the disease.

family-focused treatment (FFT): A psychotherapy that provides families of people (often adolescents) with bipolar disorders with education and skills training relevant to the unique characteristics and developmental problems of teenagers. These problems include rapid onsets and offsets of irritable and/or depressed moods, disturbances in sleep/wake cycles, and high levels of family conflict (expressed emotion).

family heritability studies: Studies that examine the degree of risk for relatives to develop mental disorders experienced by other family members.

family study: A technique used by behavioral geneticists to examine patterns of a disorder in members of a family.

fantasy model (FM): The claim that dissociation makes individuals prone to fantasy, thereby engendering confabulated memories of trauma commonly seen in people with dissociative identity disorders.

Fast Track approach: A nationwide prevention project delivered to over 400 families of children at high risk for disruptive, aggressive, and antisocial behavior; the intervention was successful at preventing the development of ADHD, ODD, and CD for participants who were at highest initial risk (children who were rated by teachers and parents as exhibiting the highest frequency and severity of disruptive behavior). This work also highlighted the importance of early screening of children at risk for aggressive behavioral problems.

fatalistic suicide: A suicide type proposed by Durkheim, committed by people such as prisoners or slaves who experience severe isolation or rejection and who hold little hope for social integration.

fear: A set of emotional, behavioral, and physical responses to danger.

fear network: A memory network that connects fear stimuli and fearful responses.

feigning: To represent fictitiously; to put on an appearance of or to pretend.

female orgasmic disorder: A sexual dysfunction in which a woman cannot experience orgasm, takes an inordinately long time to reach orgasm, or experiences diminished intensity of orgasm.

female sexual interest/arousal disorder (FSI/AD): A sexual dysfunction in women marked by low or no sexual interest or arousal.

fetal alcohol syndrome (FAS): A pattern of abnormalities resulting from maternal ingestion of alcohol during pregnancy. FAS is associated with mild to severe intellectual disability, distinctive physical abnormalities, and social and emotional difficulties.

fetishistic disorder: A paraphilic disorder in which individuals focus sexual interest on a nonliving object or specific nongenital body part to become aroused.

field trial: A research study conducted in the natural environment.

fight-or-flight response: The immediate response to a stressor in which the individual's autonomic nervous system is activated to fight or to flee from the stressor.

fine motor skill: Involved in smaller movements that occur in the wrists, hands, fingers, feet and toes; fine motor skills coordinate actions such as picking up objects between the thumb and finger, writing carefully, and even blinking.

flat affect: Blunted emotionality, often consisting of minimal eye contact, an emotionless face, little or no tone in the voice, and a drab or listless demeanor.

flooding: A treatment technique to extinguish phobias or overcome anxiety by exposing persons to prolonged presentations of the most intense version of the feared stimulus.

forebrain: The largest of the three main parts of the brain, it includes structures that are responsible for processing sensory information, guiding body movements, and thinking.

forensic psychology: The use of psychological knowledge or research methods to advise, evaluate, or reform the legal system.

formal thought disorder: Symptoms involving disturbances in the way thinking is organized.

fragile X syndrome: A heritable genetic aberration involving chromosome 23 that results in moderate intellectual disability and physical anomalies.

frontal lobe: The area of the cerebral cortex that controls executive functions, such as planning and carrying out goal-directed activities.

frotteuristic disorder: A paraphilic disorder involving recurrent touching or rubbing against a nonconsenting person to become sexually aroused.

functional magnetic resonance imaging (fMRI): Functional magnetic resonance imaging or functional MRI (fMRI) is a functional neuroimaging procedure using magnetic resonance imaging (MRI) technology that measures brain activity by detecting associated changes in cerebral blood flow.

functional working memory model: A neurocognitive model that proposes that delayed cortical maturation and associated chronic cortical underarousal create working memory deficits that cause the symptoms of attention-deficit/hyperactivity disorder (ADHD).

G

gambling disorder: A new disorder in the *DSM-5* that involves persistent and recurrent problematic gambling behavior that leads to clinically significant impairment or distress.

gamma-aminobutyric acid (GABA): A neurotransmitter that inhibits postsynaptic activity.

gender dysphoria: A mental disorder that describes strong incongruence between one's assigned gender and one's experienced or expressed gender.

gender identity: Individuals' subjective sense of their own gender, often (but not always) male or female.

gene: Strands of DNA that are located along a chromosome and are the basic units of heredity.

general adaptation syndrome (GAS): A three-stage physiological reaction to a stressor, consisting of alarm, resistance, and exhaustion.

generalization: The process by which a learned behavior tends to occur in novel situations.

generalized: A modifier used to describe a sexual dysfunction that occurs in most or all sexual situations.

generalized amnesia: Loss of memory of a person's entire life.

generalized anxiety disorder (GAD): A mental disorder in which anxiety is experienced as "free floating" (not connected to any specific stimulus) and is pervasive enough to interfere with daily functioning.

genito-pelvic pain/penetration disorder (GPPD): A sexual dysfunction in women that describes tension or pain during intercourse or penetration, or fear of pain or penetration.

genotype: A person's genetic makeup.

glove anesthesia: Loss of sensation in an area that would be covered by a glove (e.g., one's entire hand up to the wrist).

glucocorticoid: A steroidal hormone the body uses to fight stress.

glutamate: The body's most prominent neurotransmitter; the brain's main excitatory neurotransmitter, and also the precursor for GABA, the brain's main inhibitory neurotransmitter.

graduated exposure: A treatment technique for extinguishing phobias in which an individual is exposed to progressively more frightening items from an anxiety hierarchy.

gross motor skill: The ability to control large muscle movements and body posture.

guilty but mentally ill (GBMI): A legal verdict that results in a defendant's conviction for a crime, even though the jury concludes that the defendant suffers from a mental disorder.

H

habit reversal training: A cognitive-behavioral treatment used for hair-pulling, skin-picking, tics, or other problem habits and that involves awareness training, competing response training, and social support.

habituation speed: The amount of time it takes to habituate, or lose interest in, a repetitively presented stimulus.

hallucination: A sensory experience that seems real but is not based on external stimulation of the relevant sensory organ.

hallucinogen: A drug that produces unusual perceptual experiences.

harm reduction: A range of public health policies designed to reduce the harmful consequences associated with various human behaviors, both legal and illegal. Harm reduction policies for alcohol use, for example, encourage drinking responsibly and try to reduce the harmful consequences often associated with excessive consumption.

heritability: The proportion of observable differences between individuals in a particular trait that is due to genetic differences.

heroin: A white, odorless powder derived from morphine; it is one of the most addictive and commonly abused opioids.

hindbrain: One of the three main parts of the brain, it includes structures such as the medulla, the reticular formation, and the cerebellum, which maintain activities essential to life.

histrionic personality disorder: A personality disorder characterized by extreme attention-getting behaviors, flamboyance, and suggestibility.

hoarding disorder: A mental disorder in which individuals have persistent difficulties discarding or parting with possessions, regardless of their actual value, leading to the severe cluttering of their personal living spaces.

hopelessness: A chronic tendency to view negative events as inevitable and positive events as unlikely, with no prospect for changing this pattern.

hormone: A chemical messenger secreted by the adrenal glands or other parts of the endocrine system.

hostile attributional bias: A cognitive distortion common among children with conduct disorder that results from the tendency to interpret neutral events as hostile or threatening.

host personality: In dissociative identity disorder, the primary identity that is in charge of the person's functioning most of the time.

humanistic model: Any of several theories of human behavior that explain how behavior is influenced by each person's unique perception of the world rather than instincts, conflicts, or environmental consequences.

Huntington's disease: A dementia involving progressive subcortical degeneration that leads to motor disturbances, changes in personality, and cognitive difficulties.

hypersomnolence disorder: A sleep disturbance in which an individual experiences excessive sleepiness and engages in prolonged sleep on an almost daily basis.

hypochondriasis: A significant concern about one's health, especially when accompanied by delusions of physical disease.

hypofrontality: Diminished activity in the frontal lobe of the brain.

hypomania: A mild form of mania.

hypothalamic-pituitary-adrenal (HPA) axis: A feedback loop that plays a critical role in the body's response to stress. In times of stress, the adrenal glands respond to messages from the hypothalamic-pituitary system by increasing their output of cortisol and adrenaline (epinephrine), hormones that help the body cope with stressors via "fight-or-flight" mechanisms.

hypothalamus: A key structure in the forebrain that aids in regulating hunger, thirst, sex drive, and other motivated behavior, as well as activity of various internal organs.

hypothesis: A theoretical proposition describing how two or more variables are related.

hysteria: A mental disorder in which patients with normal physical abilities appear unable to see or hear or walk.

I

id: One of three structures in the psychoanalytic conception of personality; it represents basic, unconscious instincts and provides the energy, or libido, to satisfy those instincts.

identity alteration: Behavioral patterns suggesting that individuals have assumed a new identity.

identity confusion: Individuals' uncertainty about the nature of their own identity, of who they are.

illness anxiety disorder (IAD): A *DSM-5* disorder defined by persistent concerns about having or acquiring a serious illness without the presence of strong somatic symptoms.

illusion: The misperception or misinterpretation of actual sensory experiences.

immunosuppression: A decrease in immune system effectiveness that sometimes follows sustained stress.

incidence: The number of people who develop a disorder in a specific time period, usually the previous six or twelve months.

independent variable (IDV): The variable in an experiment that is manipulated by the experimenter.

informed consent: Obtaining agreement from individuals to participate in research or receive treatment after they have been informed of the procedure's potential benefits and risks and the alternatives that are available.

insanity: A legal term that describes a state of mind and implies that a defendant cannot be held responsible for his or her illegal conduct.

insecure attachment: A pattern of infant-parent attachment in which infants show minimal separation distress, coupled with avoidance of the parent during reunions.

insistence on sameness: Also referred to as "preservation of sameness," this phenomenon is seen among children diagnosed with autism spectrum disorder (ASD) and involves a persistence that certain aspects of the environment be maintained across time. Since children with ASD often find the social environment to be puzzling, many believe that these "unspoken rules" may be a strategy that children use to make sense of the social world.

insomnia disorder: A condition in which a person experiences difficulty falling asleep, staying asleep, or waking up too early.

intellectual disability: Significantly subaverage intellectual functioning occurring before the age of 18 that is associated with significant limitations in adaptive functioning.

intelligence test: A measure of general mental ability and various specific intellectual abilities, such as verbal reasoning, quantitative skills, abstract thinking, visual recognition, and memory.

internalizing problem: A deficit in desired child behaviors, usually accompanied by subjective distress in the child.

interpersonal and social rhythm psychotherapy (IPSRT): A psychotherapy designed to help people with bipolar disorders improve their moods by understanding and working with their biological and social rhythms. The treatment emphasizes techniques to improve medication adherence, manage stressful life events, and reduce disruptions in social rhythms that may be involved in mood episodes.

interpersonal theory: A theory that explains personality as the result of consistent styles of interaction.

J

joint attention: The process of coordinating attention with another person.

L

la belle indifference: A naive, inappropriate lack of emotion or concern for the others' perceptions of one's disability; seen in people with conversion disorder.

lanugo: A downy layer of hair that grows on the body, including the neck and face.

learned helplessness: An explanation of depression suggesting that, if people feel chronically unable to control life events,

they learn a sense of helplessness that leads to depressive symptoms.

learning theories: Explanations of how new behaviors are acquired, retained, and used.

libido: In psychoanalytic theory, the energy that motivates people to satisfy their basic needs.

lifelong: A modifier used to describe a sexual dysfunction that has always occurred since one's first sexual experiences.

life records: Documents associated with important events and milestones in a person's life, such as school grades, court records, police reports, and medical histories.

light therapy: Exposing patients to a bright light source during the early morning hours to reduce symptoms of seasonal depression and to correct problems in body temperature or hormone output.

limbic system: A complex circuit of brain structures (including the thalamus, hippocampus, cingulate gyrus, hypothalamus, amygdala, septum, and parts of the cortex) that help regulate emotions, memory, and certain aspects of movement.

linkage analysis: A study of the linked occurrence of a disorder and some genetic marker across several generations.

lithium carbonate: A drug used to treat mania; commonly known as lithium.

localized amnesia: Loss of memory for a distinct period of time, usually the few hours immediately after a specific trauma.

locus coeruleus (LC): A small area of the brain stem in which abnormalities are associated with alarm or panic.

longitudinal study: A study in which an investigator repeatedly assesses the same individuals or variables over a period of time.

lysergic acid diethylamide (LSD): A hallucinogenic drug that excites the central nervous system.

M

magnetic resonance imaging (MRI): A neurodiagnostic procedure that tracks the activity of atoms in the body as they are "excited" by magnets in a chamber or coil placed around the patient.

mainstreaming: An educational policy in which children with disabilities spend part of their school time in regular classrooms.

maintenance: The persistence of a learned behavior.

major depressive disorder: One of the most severe forms of depression, characterized by constant sadness or despair, irritability, guilt, physical symptoms, insomnia, and lack of energy.

male hypoactive sexual desire disorder (MHSDD): A sexual disorder characterized by a man's lack of sexual thoughts and desire for sexual activity.

malingering: The purposeful production of false or grossly exaggerated complaints with the goal of receiving a benefit that may include money, an insurance settlement, drugs, or the avoidance of punishment, work, jury duty, the military, or some other kind of service or attention.

mania: An excited mood in which a person feels excessively and unrealistically positive and energetic.

masturbatory reconditioning: A behavioral treatment for paraphilic disorders that involves having clients use masturbation to modify their sexual preferences.

McNaughton rule: A legal definition of insanity requiring that at the time the wrongful act was committed, the person accused was, as a result of a mental disorder, unable to know the nature and quality of the act or to know that the act was wrong.

medically unexplained physical symptoms (MUPS): Symptoms that are present (experienced by the person) but that are not able to be accounted for by medical testing or investigation.

medical model: A model that explains abnormal behavior as symptoms resulting from an underlying illness.

melatonin: A hormone that affects the hypothalamus and helps prepare the body for sleep.

mental disorder: A behavioral or psychological syndrome that produces harmful dysfunction in an individual, causing objective impairment and/or subjective harm.

mental status examination (MSE): A brief, specialized, and focused interview designed to assess a person's memory, mood, orientation, thinking, and concentration.

mescaline: A hallucinogenic drug derived from the peyote cactus that causes effects similar to LSD.

meta-analysis: A statistical technique that combines the results of several studies into an overall average or estimate.

methadone maintenance therapy: A treatment designed to help opioid-dependent persons avoid relapses by giving them methadone until they can achieve complete opioid independence.

midbrain: One of the three main parts of the brain, it helps coordinate head and eye movements, controls gross body movements, and is involved in basic responses to visual, auditory, and tactile stimuli.

milieu program: A hospital program that intends to resocialize patients with severe mental disorders so that they can learn how to manage their lives better and engage in appropriate behavior in the community.

mindblindness: A cognitive deficit thought to underlie autism spectrum disorder wherein a person is not able to understand other people's behavior in terms of mental states.

model of abnormality: A comprehensive account of how and why abnormal behaviors develop and how best to treat them.

monoamine oxidase (MAO) inhibitor: A drug that blocks monoamine oxidase, an enzyme that breaks down neurotransmitters such as serotonin and norepinephrine, resulting in greater availability of these neurotransmitters at neural synapses.

mood disorders: A group of mental disorders associated with serious and persistent difficulty maintaining an even, productive emotional state.

morbidity risk: The risk of individuals developing a disorder over their lifetime.

MTA study (Multimodal Treatment Study of ADHD): A multi-site randomized controlled trial that was conducted over the course of 3 decades among children with ADHD; results indicated that children receiving either medication alone or the combination of medication plus behavioral therapy showed a greater reduction in ADHD symptoms over the first few years—but not after 6–8 years—compared to the groups receiving behavioral therapy alone or community care (which typically included medication).

multiaxial classification: A system for diagnosing mental disorders and describing a person along several dimensions, or axes, including physical health, psychosocial and environmental problems, and global functioning.

multifinality: A developmental psychopathology term referring to the fact that the same pathway (or early experiences) can lead to different outcomes (or different psychological disorders).

multisystemic treatment: A treatment method used in the context of childhood behavioral disorders that targets the child's maladaptive interactions with his or her family and community; this approach is supported by research and the positive effects are seen not only in child behaviors but also in child social relationships and overall family functioning.

Munchausen's syndrome by proxy (MSP): A type of factitious disorder in which people act as if an individual under their care has a physical or mental illness when the individual is not really sick; considered a form of abuse.

N

narcissistic personality disorder: A personality disorder characterized by an overinflated sense of self-importance and worth that leads to a sense of entitlement to special privileges and exemptions from the rules that apply to others.

narcolepsy: A sleep disturbance in which a person has sudden attacks of REM sleep, usually accompanied by temporary muscle paralysis and immobility.

natal sex assignment: One's sex assigned at birth based on physical genitalia.

negative affect: An emotional state that is a mixture of anxious and depressive symptoms.

negative affectivity: The experience of negative emotions and poor self-concept; includes a variety of negative emotions, such as anger, disgust, guilt, fear, and anxiety.

negative attributional style: A tendency to interpret successes in life as the result of external, temporary, and specific factors beyond a person's control, and to interpret failures in life as the result of internal, stable, and global factors within a person.

negative symptoms: Symptoms associated with schizophrenia, involving a diminution, absence, or loss of normal psychological functions; examples include apathy, flat emotions, lack of self-help skills, and social withdrawal.

neuritic plaque: The residue of dead neurons and cellular debris; found in patients diagnosed with Alzheimer's disease.

neurocognitive disorder (NCD): A mental disorder involving a loss of cognitive function in one or more key domains.

neurodevelopmental disorders: In the *DSM-5*, a category of disorders that affect children and adolescents and involve impairment in brain development or functioning. The neurodevelopmental disorders include intellectual disability, autism spectrum disorder, specific learning disorder, and attention-deficit/hyperactivity disorder.

neurofibrillary tangles: Twisted clumps of protein fibers found in dying brain cells.

neuroleptic: A drug that blocks the action of neurotransmitters in the brain, thereby relieving many positive symptoms of schizophrenia.

neuroleptic malignant syndrome (NMS): A rare side effect of neuroleptic drugs that is potentially fatal and involves extremely high fever, muscle rigidity, and irregular heart rate and blood pressure.

neuron: A nerve cell in the brain that specializes in transmitting information.

neuropsychological test: A psychological assessment tool that measures deficits in behavior, cognition, or emotion known to correlate with brain dysfunction and damage, and helps to determine whether a person is suffering from brain damage or deterioration.

neuroscience: A set of disciplines that study the structure, organization, functions, and chemistry of the nervous system, especially the brain.

neurotransmitter: A chemical released by neurons that acts on other neurons.

nicotine: A stimulant drug found in the leaves of the tobacco plant and usually ingested by smoking.

nightmare disorder: A parasomnia that involves repeated frightening dreams that interrupt sleep, usually during REM stages.

non-REM (NREM) sleep: Sleep stages 1 to 4, in which REM sleep is not experienced.

norepinephrine: A neurotransmitter involved in sleep and arousal, attention, mood, and eating.

norm: A score obtained from large numbers of people who have taken a test previously under similar conditions.

normalization: A social policy based on the idea that persons with intellectual disabilities should experience mainstream society in their everyday lives; associated with de-institutionalization and an emphasis on family care, community-based facilities, and public school education of children with disabilities.

nosology: A classification system containing categories of disorders and rules for categorizing disorders depending on observable signs and symptoms.

NREM sleep arousal disorders: Parasomnias in which a person experiences incomplete awakening from sleep, with either sleepwalking or sleep terrors.

nucleotide: Any of several biochemical compounds that make up DNA and contain sugar, phosphate, and a nitrogen base.

O

objective test: A personality test that requires answers or ratings to specific questions or statements that are scored quantitatively.

object relations theory: A modern variant of psychoanalytic theory that explains how adult personality is based on the nature and quality of early interactions between infants and their caregivers.

observational learning: In social learning theory, the view that behavior develops as a result of observing other people's behavior and its consequences.

obsession: An unwanted, disturbing, often irrational thought, feeling, or image that people cannot get out of their minds.

obsessive-compulsive disorder (OCD): An anxiety disorder that involves recurrent obsessions or compulsions that are serious enough to adversely affect a person's life.

obsessive-compulsive personality disorder: A personality disorder characterized by a preoccupation with rules, details, and organization in many aspects of life, so much so that the person is stubbornly perfectionistic.

obstructive sleep apnea hypopnea: A sleep disturbance involving repeated cessation of breathing during sleep.

operant conditioning: A form of learning in which the consequences of a behavior influence the probability of its being performed in the future.

operational definition: A statement that equates a concept with the exact methods used to represent or measure it.

opioid: An alkaloid containing opium or one of its derivatives, such as morphine, heroin, codeine, or methadone.

oppositional defiant disorder (ODD): A childhood mental disorder involving a pattern of negativistic, disobedient, and defiant behavior, usually shown at home and sometimes at school.

orgasm: The phase of sexual response when sexual pleasure peaks with involuntary rhythmic muscle contractions and a release of sexual tension; in males, this typically involves ejaculation, whereas in females, this involves contractions of the labia minora, vagina, and uterus.

other psychotic disorders: A group of mental disorders whose psychotic symptoms are usually more limited in duration and less intense than those of schizophrenia; includes schizophreniform disorder, schizoaffective disorder, delusional disorder, and brief psychotic disorder.

overpathologizing: A tendency to mistakenly construe some behavior as a symptom of a mental disorder when, in fact, the behavior is culturally appropriate.

oxidation: The process by which alcohol is converted to acetylaldehyde and metabolized.

P

pancreatitis: A condition in which cells in the pancreas are killed; commonly caused by heavy drinking.

panic: Fear when no actual danger is present.

panic attack: A period of unexpected, intense, terrifying anxiety that leaves victims feeling as if they are going crazy or are about to die.

panic disorder: An anxiety disorder marked by panic attacks, coupled with persistent anxiety that another attack will occur.

paranoid personality disorder: A personality disorder characterized by habitual suspicion, mistrust, irritability, and hostility.

paraphilia: A repetitive pattern of sexual behavior in which arousal and/or orgasm depends on atypical or socially inappropriate stimuli.

paraphilic disorder: A disorder in which a paraphilia causes (1) distress or impairment in social, occupational, or other important areas of functioning or (2) harm or risk of harm to others.

parasomnias: Sleep disturbances involving unusual behaviors or abnormal physiological events during sleep.

parasuicidal behavior: A behavior suggestive of suicide attempts, such as mild drug overdosing, mixing alcohol and other drugs, or minor cutting of the wrists.

parent management training: A treatment method used in the context of childhood behavioral disorders that involves teaching parents to change their child's behavior by using contingency management techniques; this strategy is effective for reducing aggressive and disruptive behavior.

Parkinsonism: An extrapyramidal side effect of some neuroleptic drugs, leading to symptoms that mimic Parkinson's disease, such as tremors, shuffling gait, blank facial expression, muscular weakness and rigidity, and slowed movement.

Parkinson's disease: A degenerative dementia characterized by tremor, difficulty in movement, and reduced production of dopamine.

participant modeling: A treatment technique in which a model demonstrates fearless behavior while a client is given increasingly close contact with the feared situation under protected circumstances.

pathological possession: The sense that another spirit or being has taken over one's behavior or mental processes.

pedophilic disorder: A paraphilic disorder involving sexual activity with a prepubescent child by a person who is at least 16 years of age and at least 5 years older than the child.

penetrance: The degree to which a genetic predisposition is actually expressed in behavior or physical features.

perseveration: Repeating the same answer over and over to different questions.

persistent depressive disorder: A depressive disorder in which depressed feelings and low self-esteem are present for at least 2 years but not as intensely as in major depressive disorder.

personality: The unique pattern of consistency in behavior that distinguishes each person from every other person.

personality disorder: An enduring pattern of inner experience and behavior that is inflexible, pervasive, and stable; deviates markedly from the expectations of a person's culture; and causes significant distress or impairment.

personality test: A standardized psychological assessment of an individual's predominant personality traits and characteristics.

personality trait: A psychological attribute that is relatively stable for an individual over time and across different situations.

pharmacogenetics: The study of inherited genetic differences in drug metabolic pathways that can affect individual responses to drugs, both in terms of therapeutic effects as well as adverse effects.

phenothiazines: A chemically similar group of neuroleptic drugs that act by blocking specific neurotransmitter receptors.

phenotype: The characteristics displayed by a person that result from the interaction of genetic makeup and the environment.

phenylketonuria (PKU): A genetic cause of intellectual disabilities that results from an abnormality in protein metabolism.

phobia: An irrational, excessive fear that causes intense emotional distress and interferes significantly with everyday life.

physiological dependence: Excessive or frequent consumption of a drug, resulting in drug tolerance or withdrawal.

pica: The ongoing consumption of nonnutritive, nonfood items that are inappropriate for an individual's developmental level.

pituitary gland: A structure in the forebrain that controls the endocrine system and plays a key role in physiological responses to stressful events.

placebo control group: In an experiment, a control group that receives an impressive, but inactive or theoretically inert, treatment.

placebo effect: Improvements that result from expectations or other psychological factors rather than from a treatment's active ingredients.

polysomnographic (PSG) assessment: A measurement process in which a person sleeps in a laboratory while sleep variables are observed and monitored.

polythetic approach: An approach to classification that requires a person to meet a particular number of criteria out of a larger set of criterion symptoms to be diagnosed with a specific mental disorder.

positive symptoms: Symptoms associated with schizophrenia, involving distorted or excess behaviors, such as hallucinations, delusions, bizarre behavior, confused thinking, and disorganized speech.

positron emission tomography (PET): A neurodiagnostic procedure that shows changes in the structure of the brain and in its metabolic functioning by tracking the rate at which brain cells consume injected radioactive glucose.

postconcussion syndrome: Also known as postconcussive syndrome or PCS, it is a set of symptoms that may continue for weeks, months, or a year or more after a concussion; a minor form of traumatic brain injury.

postpartum onset: Beginning of a disorder shortly after giving birth.

post-traumatic model (PTM): The claim that dissociative identity disorder is caused by childhood trauma, with which the person tries to cope by creating alternate personalities.

post-traumatic stress disorder (PTSD): An anxiety disorder in which a person experiences a pattern of intense, fear-related reactions after being exposed to a highly stressful event.

premature (early) ejaculation: A sexual dysfunction in which a man ejaculates after very little sexual stimulation, usually before or almost immediately after penetrating a partner.

premenstrual dysphoric disorder: A mental disorder that involves significant mood swings and irritability that occur during most menstrual cycles and then remit when menstruation occurs.

premorbid phase: The time period before the prodrome, in which it is possible to identify delays in early neurodevelopment (e.g., not meeting key pediatric milestones) that may suggest an increased risk of developing schizophrenia in the future.

preparedness theory: The hypothesis that people are biologically prepared to develop fears of certain classes of stimuli, such as snakes and spiders, that were potentially dangerous to our evolutionary ancestors.

prevalence: The total number of people who suffer from a disorder in a specific population.

primary appraisal: The evaluation of the significance of a stressor or threatening event.

privilege: The protection from being made to publicly disclose in court what individuals have said in confidence to certain other people (e.g., between a lawyer and client or doctor and patient).

problem-focused coping: An attempt to reduce stress by directly changing the stressor itself.

problem-solving skills training: A treatment method used in the context of childhood behavioral disorders that targets the social-cognitive deficits exhibited by children with conduct problems and teaches them to solve their problems differently; this method is effective for reducing aggressive, disruptive, and antisocial behavior.

prodromal phase: The usual first phase of schizophrenia in which there is an insidious onset of problems, suggesting psychological deterioration.

projective tests: Personality tests that require the person to respond to ambiguous stimuli, such as inkblots, incomplete sentences, or vague drawings. The responses are thought to reveal important characteristics about people by the way they project meaning onto the ambiguous stimuli.

prolonged exposure therapy: A cognitive-behavioral treatment for PTSD that involves repeatedly exposing individuals to stimuli that remind them of their past trauma in order to alter their fear networks.

psilocybin: Substances found in several species of Mexican mushrooms that produce visual illusions, distorted body image, and depersonalization.

psychiatrist: A medical doctor who specializes in the study and treatment of mental disorders.

psychoactive drugs: Drugs that alter cognitive, emotional, and behavioral processes.

psychoanalysis: A theory of human behavior and a therapeutic approach based on the idea that both normal and abnormal behaviors are influenced by conflicting unconscious forces, especially sexual and aggressive instincts.

psychoeducation: A key component of many psychotherapy treatments for a variety of mental disorders, this involves giving clients information regarding what is known about a specific disorder and how to identify and manage the symptoms.

psychological dependence: Intense desire for a drug and preoccupation with obtaining it.

psychological test: A systematic procedure for observing and describing a person's behavior in a standardized situation.

psychosis: A general term describing mental disorders that produce severe disorganization in behavior and gross impairment in the ability to comprehend and accurately perceive events.

psychosocial rehabilitation: A set of interventions focused on preventing unnecessary hospitalizations, reducing impairments in daily functioning, and strengthening independent living skills by teaching patients with severe mental disorders how to cope with these disorders.

psychotic disorder due to another medical condition: A mental disorder involving psychotic symptoms caused by a medical illness or condition.

punishment: The operant learning process that decreases the frequency of a preceding behavior.

R

random assignment: A method of assigning members to experimental and control groups such that they have an equal chance of being in either. Random assignment decreases the chance that variables other than the independent variable will influence the result of the experiment.

rapid eye movement (REM) sleep: A phase of sleep in which the eyes dart back and forth quickly under closed lids; often associated with dreaming.

rational emotive therapy (RET): Therapy developed by Albert Ellis based on the theory that psychological problems are caused by irrational thinking; the therapy challenges irrational beliefs and helps clients replace them with more logical beliefs.

reality principle: In psychoanalysis, a process used by the ego to reach rational compromises between the instincts of the id and the moral demands the superego.

receptive language: The understanding of language.

recidivism: Repeating an undesirable or illegal act that the person has been punished for in the past.

recovery movement: A movement that promotes the idea that individuals recovering from mental disorders should be able to successfully live and work in the community, enjoy active social lives, attend school, and maintain a healthy lifestyle, all while managing their own disorders with the supports that they may need.

reinforcement: The operant learning process that increases the frequency of a preceding behavior.

relapse: The return or worsening of a disorder after recovery.

relapse prevention: Part of the cognitive-behavioral treatment for many mental disorders, it focuses on identifying high-risk situations, stimuli, or stressors that lead to the unwanted behavior (drugs, alcohol, eating, paraphilias) and then teaching the client to avoid these triggers whenever possible.

reliability: Consistency or agreement among assessment data; includes test-retest reliability, internal consistency, and interrater reliability.

remission: When symptoms of a previously present disorder are no longer apparent, implying improvement or recovery.

replication: Repeating a research study with a new group of subjects and/or in a different situation to assess whether prior findings will be found under new circumstances.

representative sample: A sample in which participants are selected to represent levels of important subject variables such as age, gender, and ethnicity; a small group selected from a larger group in such a way that it approximates the characteristics of the larger group.

repression: A psychoanalytic defense mechanism that involves motivated forgetting of anxiety-arousing thoughts, images, or impulses.

residual phase (of schizophrenia): A stage of schizophrenia during which most psychotic symptoms have subsided in frequency and intensity; the affected person may still be withdrawn and apathetic, behave strangely at times, and continue to show social and occupational impairments.

resilience: The ability to solve problems effectively, cope with stressors, and overcome adversity.

retrospective research: Research done by asking respondents about past experiences.

reuptake: A process by which neurotransmitters are reabsorbed into the neurons that released them.

Ritalin: A drug that facilitates the release, and blocks the reuptake, of norepinephrine and dopamine, amplifying the impact of these neurotransmitters in the brain; commonly used to treat attention-deficit/hyperactivity disorder.

S

schizoaffective disorder: A mental disorder in which the person displays symptoms of both schizophrenia and a mood disorder without satisfying the full criteria for either diagnosis.

schizoid personality disorder: A personality disorder characterized by extreme indifference to social relationships and a pervasive emotional blandness.

schizophrenia: A psychotic mental disorder marked by serious impairments in basic psychological functions—attention, perception, thought, emotion, and behavior.

schizophreniform disorder: A disorder in which people experience symptoms of schizophrenia for only a few months.

schizophrenogenic mother: A formerly popular term for a type of mother thought to cause schizophrenia in her children by her domineering, overprotective, cold, and rigid manner and her discomfort with physical intimacy.

schizotypal personality disorder: A personality disorder characterized by odd ways of talking, thinking, acting, and dressing, as well as social isolation and a lack of close relationships.

scientific method: A systematic process of studying, observing, and recording data in order to assess the validity of hypotheses.

seasonal affective disorder: Mood disorders that are linked to a particular season of the year; probably caused by shifts in overall exposure to light.

season-of-birth effect: The finding that a greater proportion of people with schizophrenia are born in the winter or early spring months, when, in utero, they would presumably have been more likely to be exposed to viral infections that could affect brain development.

secondary gain: External rewards, including interpersonal or social advantages, gained indirectly from an illness.

secure attachment: A pattern of infant-parent attachment in which infants show moderate separation distress, coupled with a strong approach to the parent during reunions.

selective amnesia: Ability to remember only some of the events surrounding a trauma; the remainder are forgotten.

selective serotonin reuptake inhibitor (SSRI): A type of drug used to treat mental disorders such as depression that works by slowing the reuptake of serotonin.

self-efficacy: A person's belief that he or she can successfully perform a given behavior.

self-monitoring: A special form of observation in which people record the frequency, duration, intensity, or quality of their own behaviors, such as smoking, eating, moods, or thoughts.

self-schema: Core assumptions and beliefs about the self.

sensate focus: A method of increasing sensuality and the ability to experience physical pleasure by focusing on kissing, massage, or touch without attempting direct genital stimulation of a partner.

sensitivity: The probability that a person with a mental disorder is diagnosed as having that disorder.

serotonin: A neurotransmitter that influences emotion, sleep, and behavioral control.

sex: Physiological markers that indicate maleness or femaleness.

sex-linked chromosome: Chromosome 23 is known as the sex-linked chromosome because it consists of duplicate chromosomes in the female (designated XX) but not in the male (designated XY).

sexual dysfunctions: A category of disorders involving problems with sexual response or sexual pleasure. .

sexual masochism disorder: A paraphilic disorder describing when sexual arousal depends on being humiliated or made to suffer.

sexual response cycle: A sequence of psychological changes and physiological reactions, consisting of desire, excitement, orgasm, and resolution.

sexual sadism disorder: A paraphilic disorder describing when sexual arousal depends on the physical or psychological suffering of another person.

shaping: An operant learning technique in which successive approximations of a target behavior are reinforced until the final target behavior is performed or learned.

single photon emission computed tomography (SPECT): Similar to positron emission tomography (PET), a SPECT scan uses a radioactive chemical that allows pictures of the brain from several angles.

situational: A modifier used to describe a sexual dysfunction that occurs only in certain sexual situations.

sleep hygiene: A psychoeducational approach to sleep in which the person is taught how to develop and maintain effective sleep habits.

sleep paralysis: A symptom associated with panic disorder; it occurs when a person is waking up or falling asleep, and involves a brief inability to move.

social anxiety disorder (SAD): A mental disorder that involves intense fear or anxiety of social situations in which the individual may be scrutinized by others.

social causation theory: A theory suggesting that stress, poverty, racism, inferior education, unemployment, and social changes are sociocultural risk factors leading to mental disorders.

social drift hypothesis: Also called the *social selection hypothesis*, it explains higher rates of mental disorders among lower socioeconomic groups as the consequence of disordered people sinking to lower socioeconomic levels because of their disorders.

social history: Obtained as part of clinical interviews, it includes assessment of educational achievements, occupational positions, family history, marital status, physical health, and prior contacts with mental health professionals.

social learning theory: A theory that explains how behavior is learned through observation (vicarious learning), direct experiences, and cognitive processes such as expectancies.

social relativism: The idea that the same standards and definitions of abnormal behavior do not apply in all cultures.

social strain: Adverse social experiences (e.g., being criticized, ignored, overburdened) that could cause individuals to have a negative reaction to or concerns about their interpersonal relationships.

social support: The feeling that you are cared for by others or belong to a valued group.

sociocognitive model: The claim that dissociative identity disorder is a diagnosis given to people who have learned to enact a role that emphasizes multiple personalities, often in response to suggestions from therapists, media portrayals, or cultural influences; has been extended as the fantasy model.

sociocultural model: Explanations of mental disorders that emphasize external factors, such as harmful environments, unfortunate social policies, lack of personal power, and cultural traditions; also called the *ecological model*.

somaticizing: A tendency to express psychological problems through physical complaints.

somatic symptom disorder (SSD): A *DSM-5* disorder describing one or more somatic (physical) symptoms that are distressing or that disrupt a person's life, with a large amount of time spent thinking about or feeling anxiety about personal physical health or symptoms.

somatic symptom and related disorders: A group of *DSM-5* disorders sharing one common feature: the prominence of somatic (physical) symptoms or anxiety about these symptoms associated with significant distress and impairment.

somatization: Conversion of a mental state (such as depression or anxiety) into physical symptoms; also the existence of physical bodily complaints in the absence of a known medical condition.

somatoform disorders: The former name for the group of mental disorders in which individuals experience physical symptoms that are inconsistent with or cannot be fully explained by any underlying general medical or neurological condition.

specificity: The probability that a person without any mental disorder will be diagnosed as having no disorder.

specific learning disorder: A single overall diagnosis in the *DSM-5* incorporating deficits that impact academic achievement. The criteria describe general shortcomings in academic skills and allow for specifiers in areas such as reading, writing, and mathematics.

specific phobia: Intense, persistent fear of specific objects or situations that pose little or no actual threat.

specifier: A descriptor used in the *DSM-5* to indicate the likely course, severity, and specific symptom characteristics of certain mental disorders.

squeeze technique: A method of treating premature (early) ejaculation by firmly squeezing the head of the penis as sexual excitement begins to peak but before the point of ejaculatory inevitability, thus prolonging the time to ejaculation.

stage of exhaustion: The third stage of the general adaptation syndrome, in which organ systems break down.

stage of resistance: The second stage of the general adaptation syndrome, in which various coping mechanisms are used to defend against a stressor.

standardization: Administering and scoring a test using uniform procedures for all respondents.

stereotypic behavior: Behavior commonly seen among children diagnosed with autism spectrum disorder (ASD) and characterized by inflexible adherence to a specific routine, such as dressing in a particular order that never changes or lining up toys in an exact way at the end of every play period.

stimulant: A drug that has an excitatory effect on the central nervous system.

stimulus control: A treatment for insomnia in which individuals are instructed to get out of bed anytime they are not sleepy so that the association between bed and sleep is strengthened; this can be used on its own or in conjunction with a broader sleep hygiene approach.

stop-start technique: A method of treating premature (early) ejaculation by stopping sexual stimulation before ejaculatory inevitability and relaxing, thus prolonging the time to ejaculation.

Strange Situation: A laboratory assessment of infant-parent attachment that allows observation of how an infant responds to separations from parents.

stress: An ongoing process that occurs when environmental or social threats place demands on individuals.

stress hormone: A chemical messenger, also known as an adrenal corticosteroid, that intensifies alarm and prepares the body to cope with a stressor.

stressor: Any event that requires a person to adjust.

structured interview: An interview in which the interviewer asks questions in a predetermined sequence so that the procedure is essentially the same from one interview to another.

substance abuse: A maladaptive pattern of substance use resulting in repeated and significant adverse consequences and maladaptive behaviors.

substance dependence: A condition indicated by a set of behavioral, physiological, and cognitive symptoms and impairments caused by continued or excessive use of a substance.

substance/medication-induced psychotic disorder: A mental disorder in which a person experiences psychotic symptoms beyond what is expected from intoxication or withdrawal from a substance, and in which the person is not aware that the substance is producing the psychotic symptoms.

substance intoxication: A temporary condition in which, as a direct result of ingesting too much of a substance, individuals experience impaired judgment, altered thinking, pronounced mood changes, disturbed perception, or impaired motor behavior.

substance/medication-induced sleep disorder: Problems of sleep that are the direct physiological result of ingestion of medication or a drug of abuse.

substance use disorder: A new diagnosis in the *DSM-5* that combines substance abuse and substance dependence into one disorder; involves a problematic pattern of use of one of 10 categories of substances, leading to impairment or distress.

superego: One of the three components of the psychoanalytic conception of personality; it is the repository of cultural rules, models of ideal behavior, and moral values.

suprachiasmatic nucleus (SCN): A brain structure found in the hypothalamus that maintains the body's circadian rhythms.

switching: In dissociative identity disorder, the process of changing from one personality to another; thought to be stimulated by anxiety.

synapse: The tiny gap between neurons where neurotransmitters are released or received.

synesthesia: A drug-induced perceptual anomaly in which information from different senses is blended so that users "see" sounds or "feel" colors.

systematized amnesia: Loss of memory for certain classes of information.

T

tacrine: A drug treatment approved for Alzheimer's disease, it slows the breakdown of acetylcholine.

tardive dyskinesia (TD): An extrapyramidal side effect of some neuroleptic drugs, involving spasmodic jerks, tics, and twitches of the face, tongue, trunk, and limbs, as well as speech impairment.

tension reduction hypothesis: The idea that drinking alcohol is reinforced by its ability to reduce tension, anxiety, anger, depression, and other unpleasant emotions.

teratogen: A substance that crosses the placenta and damages the fetus.

thalamus: A key structure in the forebrain that receives, analyzes, and sends on information from all the senses except smell.

theory: A set of propositions used to predict and explain certain phenomena.

Theory of Mind: A cognitive process that allows an individual to infer the mental states of others.

thimerosal: An organomercury compound also known as thiomersal, it is a well-established antiseptic and antifungal agent used as a preservative in vaccines, ophthalmic and nasal products, and tattoo inks. Its use as a vaccine preservative was controversial, and it was phased out from routine childhood vaccines in the United States and many other countries in order to assuage popular but unfounded fears.

token economy: A procedure that uses operant reinforcement principles to alter the behaviors of individuals or groups by giving tokens (such as poker chips) that can be exchanged for other tangible rewards.

tolerance: A condition in which increasingly larger doses of a drug are required to achieve the same physical effect or subjective state.

Tourette's disorder: A disorder characterized by both repetitive vocal tics or vocalizations and motor acts and tics.

transactional process: Children with conduct disorder are thought to both influence and be influenced by their environment; for example, exposure to community violence is associated with conduct disorder, but it is also true that children who are predisposed to violence impact the neighborhood climate.

transference-focused psychotherapy: A treatment for borderline and other severe personality disorders that is based on psychoanalytic concepts and techniques that work with clients' early relationship templates to help clients construct a more stable adult identity.

transgender: People whose gender identity, gender expression, or behavior is different from what is typically associated with their natal sex.

transvestic disorder: A paraphilic disorder in which individuals cross-dress to become sexually aroused and experience distress or impairment as a result.

trichotillomania (TTM; hair-pulling disorder): A mental disorder that involves recurrent pulling out of one's hair, resulting in distress and hair loss, along with repeated attempts to decrease or stop the pulling.

tricyclics: Drugs used primarily to treat depression; they increase levels of neurotransmitters such as norepinephrine and serotonin by blocking their reuptake.

trisomy 21: Three chromosomes instead of the normal two on pair 21; another name for Down syndrome.

twin study: A method of systematically comparing the traits of monozygotic twins reared together or apart with the traits of dizygotic twins reared together or apart.

two-factor conditioning: A model that combines classical conditioning and operant conditioning to explain disorders such as PTSD and phobias.

U

underpathologizing: A tendency for clinicians to mistakenly construe some behavior as merely reflecting a cultural difference when, in fact, it is the symptom of a mental disorder.

V

validity: The degree to which an assessment instrument measures what it is supposed to measure, thereby providing an estimate of accuracy or meaning.

vasocongestion: An excessive accumulation of blood in tissue.

ventricle: A cavity in the center of the brain that is filled with cerebrospinal fluid.

visual-motor skills: The ability to control eye-hand coordination.

voyeuristic disorder: A paraphilic disorder in which individuals achieve sexual arousal through the clandestine observation of others who are naked, disrobing, or engaging in sexual activity.

W

Wernicke-Korsakoff syndrome: A rare, alcohol-induced memory disorder in which the affected individual becomes confused and unable to coordinate voluntary muscle movements, and then loses memory for personal experiences.

withdrawal: A pattern of physical symptoms that results from discontinuing drug use once individuals have become physically dependent on it.

References

A

Aaron, M. (2012). The pathways of problematic sexual behavior: A literature review of factors affecting adult sexual behavior in survivors of childhood sexual abuse. *Sexual Addiction & Compulsivity, 19*(3), 199–218.

Abbass, A., Kisely, S., & Kroenke, K. (2009). Short-term psychodynamic psychotherapy for somatic disorders: Systematic review and meta-analysis of clinical trials. *Psychotherapy and Psychosomatics, 78*, 265–274. doi:10.1159/000228247

Abbass, A. A., Rabung, S., Leichsenring, F., Refseth, J. S., & Midgley, N. (2013). Psychodynamic psychotherapy for children and adolescents: A meta-analysis of short-term psychodynamic models. *Journal of the American Academy of Child & Adolescent Psychiatry, 52*(8), 863–875. doi:10.1016/j.jaac.2013.05.014

Abel, G. G., Becker, J. V., Cunningham-Rather, J., Mittelman, M. & Rouleau, J. L. (1988). Multiple paraphilic diagnoses among sex offenders. *Bulletin of the American Academy of Psychiatry and the Law, 16*, 153–168.

Abel, G. G., & Rouleau, J. L. (1995). Sexual abuses. *Psychiatric Clinics of North America, 18*, 139–153.

Abies, B. S., & Brandsma, J. M. (1977). *Therapy for couples.* San Francisco: Jossey-Bass.

Abikoff, H., & Klein, R. G. (1992). Attention-deficit hyperactivity and conduct disorder: Comorbidity and implications for treatment. *Journal of Consulting and Clinical Psychology, 60*, 881–892.

Abikoff, H., Klein, R. G., Klass, E., & Ganeles, D. (1987, October). Methylphenidate in the treatment of conduct disordered children. In H. Abikoff (Chair), *Diagnosis and treatment issues in children with disruptive behavior disorders.* Symposium conducted at the annual meeting of the American Academy of Child and Adolescent Psychiatry, Washington, DC.

Abood, L. G. (1960). A chemical approach to the problem of mental illness. In D. D. Jackson (Ed.), *The etiology of schizophrenia* (pp. 91–119). New York: Basic Books.

Abraham, H. D., & Aldridge, A. M. (1993). Adverse consequences of lysergic acid diethylamide. *Addiction, 88*, 1327–1334.

Abraham, K. (1911). Notes on the psychoanalytic investigation and treatment of manic-depressive insanity and allied conditions. In *Selected papers on psychoanalysis.* New York: Basic Books (1960).

Abrahamson, D. J., Barlow, D. H., Beck, J. C., Sakheim, D. K., & Kelly, J. P. (1985). The effects of attentional focus and partner responsiveness on sexual responding: Replication and extension. *Archives of Sexual Behavior, 14*, 361–371.

Abram, K. M., & Teplin, L. A. (1991). Co-occuring disorders among mentally ill jail detainees: Implications for public policy. *American Psychologist, 46*, 1036-1045.

Abramowitz, J. S., Moore, E. L., Braddock, A. E., & Harrington, D. L. (2009). Self-help cognitive-behavioral therapy with minimal therapist contact for social phobia: A controlled trial. *Journal of Behavior Therapy and Experimental Psychiatry, 40*(1), 98–105. doi:10.1016/j.jbtep.2008.04.004

Abramowitz, J. S., Whiteside, S. P., & Deacon, B. J. (2005). The effectiveness of treatment for pediatric obsessive-compulsive disorder: A meta-analysis. *Behavior Therapy, 36*(1), 55–63. doi:10.1016/S0005-7894(05)80054-1

Abrams, D. B. (2014, January 8). Psychology's role in smoking decline continues 50 years after urgeon general's groundbreaking report. *American Psychological Association.* Retrieved on December 15, 2014 from http://www.apa.org/news/press/releases/2014/01/smoking-decline.aspx

Abrams, R. (1993). ECT technique: Electrode placement, stimulus type and treatment frequency. In C. E. Coffey, *The clinical science of electroconvulsive therapy* (pp. 17-28). Washington, DC: American Psychiatric Press.

Abramsky, S. (2004, August 19). Memory and manipulation: The trials of Elizabeth Loftus, defender of the wrongly accused. *LA Weekly.* Retrieved on December 7, 2014 from http://www.laweekly.com/2004-08-19/news/memory-and-manipulation/

Abramson, L. Y., Metalsky, G. I., & Alloy, L. B. (1989). Hopelessness depression: A theory-based subtype of depression. *Psychological Review, 96*(2), 358–372. doi:10.1037/0033-295X.96.2.358

Abramson, L. Y., Seligman, M. E. P., & Teasdale, J. D. (1978). Learned helplessness in humans: Critique and reformulation. *Journal of Abnormal Psychology, 87*, 49–74.

Achenbach, T. M. (1974). *Developmental psychopathology.* New York: Ronald Press.

Achenbach, T. M. (1997). *Empirically based assessment of child and adolescent psychopathology.* Thousand Oaks, CA.: Sage.

Achenbach, T. M., Howell, C. T., Quay, H. C., & Conners, C. K. (1991). National survey of problems and competencies among four- to sixteen-year-olds: Parents' reports for normative and clinical samples. *Monographs of the Society for Research in Child Development, 56*(3).

Ackerman, M. D., & Carey, M. P. (1995). Psychology's role in the assessment of erectile dysfunction: Historical precedents, current knowledge, and methods. *Journal of Clinical and Consulting Psychology, 63*, 862–876.

Adam, K. S. (1990). Environmental, psychosocial, and psychoanalytic aspects of suicidal behavior. In S. J. Blumenthal & D. J. Kupfer (Eds.), *Suicide over the life cycle: Risk factors, assessment, and treatment of suicidal patients* (pp. 39–96). Washington, DC: American Psychiatric Press.

Adams, M. L., & Cicero, T. J. (1991). Effects of alcohol on beta-endorphin and reproductive hormones in the male rat. *Alcoholism in Clinical and Experimental Research, 15*(4), 685–692.

Adams, R. E., & Boscarino, J. A. (2006). Predictors of PTSD and delayed PTSD after disaster: The impact of exposure and psychosocial resources. *Journal of Nervous and Mental Disease, 194*, 485–493.

Adamson, S. J., Heather, N., Morton, V., & Raistrick, D. (2010). Initial preference for drinking goal in the treatment of alcohol problems: II. Treatment outcomes. *Alcohol and Alcoholism, 45*(2), 136–142. doi:10.1093/alcalc/agq005

Adelstein, A. M. (1980). Life-style in occupational cancer. *Journal of Toxicology and Environmental Health, 6*, 953–962.

Ader, R. A., & Cohen, N. (1982). Behaviorally conditioned immunosuppression and murine systemic lupus erythematosus. *Science, 215*, 1534–1536.

Ader, R. A., & Cohen, N. (1993). Psychoneuroimmunology: Conditioning and stress. *Annual Review of Psychology, 44*, 53–85.

Adler, N. E., Boyce, T., Chesney, M. A., Cohen, S., Folk-man. S., Kahn, R. L., & Syme, S. L. (1994). Socioeconomic status and health: The challenge of the gradient. *American Psychologist, 49*, 15–24.

Adler, N. E., & Matthews, K. (1994). Health psychology: Why do some people get sick and some stay well. *Annual Review of Psychology, 45*, 229–259. Palo Alto, CA: Annual Reviews.

Afifi, T. O., Asmundson, G. G., Taylor, S., & Jang, K. L. (2010). The role of genes and environment on trauma exposure and posttraumatic stress disorder symptoms: A review of twin studies. *Clinical Psychology Review, 30*, 101–112. doi:10.1016/j.cpr.2009.10.002

Agaibi, C., & Wilson, J. (2005). Trauma, PTSD, and resilience: A review of the literature. *Trauma, Violence, & Abuse, 6*, 195–216.

Aggrawal, A. (2009). *Forensic and medico-legal aspects of sexual crimes and unusual sexual practices.* Boca Raton: CRC Press.

Agius, M., Goh, C., Ulhaq, S., & McGorry, P. (2010). The staging model in schizophrenia, and its clinical implications. *Psychiatria Danubina, 22*(2), 211–220.

Agostini, J. V., & Inouye, S. K. (2003). Delirium. In W. R. Hazzard, J. P. Blass, & J. B. Halter (Eds.), *Principles of geriatric medicine and gerontology,* 5th ed. (pp. 1503–1515). New York: McGraw-Hill.

Agras, W. S., Chapin, H., & Oliveau, D. (1972). The natural history of phobia. *Archives of General Psychiatry, 26*, 315–317.

Agras, W. S., Sylvester, D. & Oliveau, D. (1969). Epidemiology of common fears and phobias. *Comprehensive Psychiatry, 10*, 151–156.

Agrawal, A., Heath, A., & Lynskey, M. (2011). DSM-IV to DSM-5: The impact of proposed revisions on diagnosis of alcohol use disorders. *Addiction, 106*, 1935–1943.

Ahlers, C., Schaefer, G., Mundt, I., Roll, S., Englert, H., Willich, S. N., & Beier, K. (2011). How unusual are the contents of paraphilias? Paraphilia-associated sexual arousal patterns in a community-based sample of men. *Journal of Sexual Medicine, 8*(5), 1362–1370. doi:10.1111/j.1743-6109.2009.01597.x

Ahmed, N., & Lawn, S. (2012). Does starting with the behavioural component of cognitive behavioural therapy (CBT) increase patients' retention in therapy? *Behaviour Change, 29*(4), 238–257. doi:10.1017/bec.2012.23

Ainsworth, M. D. S., Blehar, M. C., Waters, E., & Wall, S. (1978). *Patterns of attachment.* Hillsdale, NJ: Erlbaum.

Ake v. Oklahoma, 105 S. Ct. 977 (1985).

Akhter, A., Fiedorowicz, J. G., Zhang, T., Potash, J. B., Cavanaugh, J., Solomon, D. A., & Coryell, W. H. (2013). Seasonal variation of manic and depressive symptoms in bipolar disorder. *Bipolar Disorders, 15*(4), 377–384. doi:10.1111/bdi.12072

Akintomide, G. S., & Rickards, H. (2011). Narcolepsy: A review. *Neuropsychiatric Disease and Treatment, 7,* 507–518. doi:10.2147/NDT.S23624

Akiskal, H. S. (1992). Delineating irritable and hyperthymic variants of the cyclothymic temperament. *Journal of Personality Disorders, 6,* 326–342.

AlAqeel, B., & Margolese, H. C. (2012). Remission in schizophrenia: Critical and systematic review. *Harvard Review of Psychiatry, 20*(6), 281–297.

Albee, G. (1959). *Mental health manpower trends.* New York: Basic Books.

Alberti, R. E., & Emmons, M. L. (1974). *Your perfect right: A guide to assertive behavior.* San Luis Obispo, CA: Impact.

Albright, D. L., & Thyer, B. (2010). EMDR is not an empirically supported treatment for combat-related PTSD. . .Yet: A response to Elisha C. Hurley, DMin, Colonel, USA (retired). *Behavioral Interventions, 25,* 355–360. doi:10.1002/bin.304

Alcohol, Drug Abuse, and Mental Health Administration. (1989). *Report of the Secretary's Task Force on Youth Suicide: Vols. I–IV.* (DHSS Publication No. ADM 89-1621-1624). Washington, DC: U.S. Government Printing Office.

Alden, L. (1989). Short-term structured treatment for avoidant personality disorder. *Journal of Consulting and Clinical Psychology, 57,* 756–764.

Alderson, R. M., Rapport, M. D., Hudec, K. L., Sarver, D. E., & Kofler, M. J. (2010). Competing core processes in ADHD: Do working memory deficiencies underlie behavioral inhibition deficits? *Journal of Abnormal Child Psychology, 38,* 497–507. doi:10.1007/s10802-010-9387-0

Alexander, A., Andersen, H., Heilman, P., Voeller, K., & Torgesen, J. (1991). Phonological awareness training and remediation of analytic decoding deficits in a group of severe dyslexics. *Annals of the Orton Society, 41,* 193–206.

Alexander, A. L., Lee, J. E., Lazar, M., & Field, A. S. (2007). Diffusion tensor imaging of the brain. *Neurotherapeutics, 4,* 316–329. doi:10.1016/j.nurt.2007.05.011

Alexander, B. K. (2010). *The globalization of addiction: A study in poverty of the spirit.* Oxford, UK: Oxford University Press.

Alexander, B. K. (2012). Addiction: The urgent need for a paradigm shift. *Substance Use & Misuse, 47*(13–14), 1475–1482. doi:10.3109/10826084.2012.705681

Alexander, F. M. (1950). *Psychosomatic medicine.* New York: W. W. Norton.

Alexander, F. M. (1956). *Psychoanalysis and psychotherapy.* New York: W. W. Norton.

Alexander, F. M., & French, T. M. (1946). *Psychoanalytic therapy.* New York: Ronald Press.

Alexander, J. F., Holtzworth-Monroe, A., & Jameson, P. B. (1994). The process and outcome of marital and family therapy: Research review and evaluation. In A. E. Bergin & S. L. Garfield (Eds.), *Handbook of psychotherapy and behavior change* (pp. 595–630). New York: John Wiley & Sons.

Alexander, J. F., & Parsons, B. V. (1973). Short-term behavioral intervention with delinquent families: Impact on family process and recidivism. *Journal of Abnormal Psychology, 81,* 219-225.

Alfrey, A. C. (1991). Aluminum intoxication, recognition and treatment. In M. Nicolini, P. F. Zatta, & B. Corain (Eds.), *Aluminum, in chemistry, biology, and medicine* (pp. 73–84). New York: Raven Press.

Alghobary, M., El-Bayoumy, Y., Mostafa, Y., Mahmoud, E. M., & Amr, M. (2010). Evaluation of tramadol on demand vs. daily paroxetine as a long-term treatment of lifelong premature ejaculation. *Journal of Sexual Medicine, 7*(8), 2860–2867. doi:10.1111/j.1743-6109.2010.01789.x

Ali, Z. (2001). Pica in people with intellectual disability: A literature review of aetiology, epidemiology and complications. *Journal of Intellectual and Developmental Disability, 26*(3), 205–215. doi: 10.1080/13668250020054486

Al-Issa, I. (1977). Social and cultural aspects of hallucinations. *Psychological Bulletin, 84,* 570–587.

Allan, A. M., &; Harris, R. A. (1987). Involvement of neuronal chloride channels in ethanol intoxication, tolerance, and dependence. In M. Galanter (Ed.), *Recent developments in alcoholism* (pp. 313–322). New York: Plenum.

Allemand, M., Steiger, A. E., & Hill, P. L. (2013). Stability of personality traits in adulthood: Mechanisms and implications. *GeroPsych, 26*(1), 5–13.

Allen, J. P., & Litten, R. Z. (1993). Psychometric and laboratory measures to assist in the treatment of alcoholism. *Clinical Psychology Review, 13,* 223–240.

Allen, L. S., & Gorski, R. A. (1992). Sexual orientation and the size of the anterior commissure in the human brain. *Proceedings of the National Academy of Science, USA, 89,* 7199–7202.

Allin, M., Streeruwitz, A., & Curtis, V. (2005). Progress in understanding conversion disorder. *Neuropsychiatric Disease and Treatment, 1*(3), 205–209.

Allison, R. (2010). Aligning bodies with minds: The case for medical and surgical treatment of gender dysphoria. *Journal of Gay & Lesbian Mental Health, 14,* 139–144.

Alloy, L. B., & Abramson, L. Y. (1979). Judgment of contingency in depressed and nondepressed students: Sadder but wiser? *Journal of Experimental Psychology: General, 108,* 441–485.

Alloy, L. B., & Abramson, L. Y. (1988). Depressive realism: Four theoretical perspectives. In L. B. Alloy (Ed.), *Cognitive processes in depression* (pp. 223–265). New York: Guilford Press.

Alloy, L. B., Abramson, L. Y., Grant, D., & Liu, R. (2009). Vulnerability to unipolar depression: Cognitive-behavioral mechanisms. In K. Salzinger & M.R. Serper (Eds.), *Behavioral mechanisms and psychopathology: Advancing the explanation of its nature, cause, and treatment* (pp. 107–140). Washington, DC: American Psychological Association. doi:10.1037/11884-004

Alloy, L. B., Urošević, S., Abramson, L. Y., Jager-Hyman, S., Nusslock, R., Whitehouse, W. G., & Hogan, M. (2012). Progression along the bipolar spectrum: A longitudinal study of predictors of conversion from bipolar spectrum conditions to bipolar I and II disorders. *Journal of Abnormal Psychology, 121*(1), 16–27. doi:10.1037/a0023973

Almedom, A. M., & Glandon, D. (2007). Resilience is not the absence of PTSD any more than health is the absence of disease. *Journal of Loss and Trauma, 12*(2), 127–143. doi:10.1080/15325020600945962

Alonso, P., Menchón, J. M., Mataix-Cols, D., Pifarré, J., Urretavizcaya, M., Crespo, J. M., . . . Vallejo, J. (2004). Perceived parental rearing style in obsessive-compulsive disorder: Relation to symptom dimensions. *Psychiatry Research, 127*(3), 267–278. doi:10.1016/j.psychres.2001.12.002

Alper, J. S., & Natowicz, M. R. (1993). On establishing the genetic basis of mental disease. *Trends in Neuroscience, 16,* 387–389.

Alphs, L. D., Summerfelt, A., Lann, H., Muller, R. J. (1989). The negative symptom assessment: A new instrument to assess negative symptoms of schizophrenia. *Psych op harmacology Bulletin, 25,* 159–163.

Althof, S. E. (1989). Psychogenic impotence: Treatment of men and couples. In S. R. Leiblum & R. C. Rosen (Eds.) *Principles and practice of sex therapy: Update for the 1990s* (pp 237–268). New York: Guilford Press.

Althof, S. E., Leiblum, S. R., Chevret-Measson, M., Hartmann, U., Levine, S. B., McCabe, M., . . . Wylie, K. (2005). Psychological and interpersonal dimensions of sexual function and dysfunction. Journal of Sexual Medicine, 2, 793–800

Althof, S. E., & Seftel, A. D. (1995). The evaluation and management of erectile dysfunction. *Psychiatric Clinics of North America, 18,* 171–192.

Alvarez, F. J., Del Rio, M. C., & Prada, R. (1995). Drinking and driving in Spain. *Journal of Studies on Alcohol, 56,* 403–407.

Álvarez, Y., Farré, M., Fonseca, F., & Torrens, M. (2010). Anticonvulsant drugs in cocaine dependence: A systematic review and meta-analysis. *Journal of Substance Abuse Treatment, 38*(1), 66–73. doi:10.1016/j.jsat.2009.07.001

Álvarez, Y., Pérez-Mañá, C., Torrens, M., & Farré, M. (2013). Antipsychotic drugs in cocaine dependence: A systematic review and meta-analysis. *Journal of Substance Abuse Treatment, 45*(1), 1–10. doi:10.1016/j.jsat.2012.12.013

Alvir, J., Lieberman, J., & Safferman, A. Z. (1994). The incidence of clozapine associated agranulocytosis in the United States. *Psychopharmacology Bulletin, 30,* 73.

Alzheimer, A. (1907). Uber eine eigenartige Erkrankungder Hirnrinde. *Allgemeine Zeitscrift fur Psychiatrie und Psychisch-Gerichtlich Medizine, 64,* 146–148.

Alzheimer's Association. (1994). Understanding the second leading cause of dementia. *Advances in Alzheimer Research, 3,* 1–4.

Alzheimer's Association. (1995a, summer). Researchers look to women for clues. *Advances in Alzheimer Research, 5,* 1A–4A.

Alzheimer's Association. (1995b, summer). Alzheimer's challenges couples' closest ties. *Alzheimer's Association National Newsletter, 15,* 1, 7.

Alzheimer's Association. (1995c, fall). Spirituality and Alzheimer's. *Alzheimer's Association National Newsletter, 15,* 3.

Alzheimer's Association (2013). Alzheimer's disease facts and figures. *Alzheimer's & Dementia, 9*(2), 208–245. doi: 10.1016/j.jalz.2013.02.003

Alzheimer's Society (n.d.). *Rarer causes of dementia.* Retrieved on December 4, 2014 from http://www.alzheimers.org.uk/site/scripts/documents_info.php?documentID=135

Amato, L., Minozzi, S., Davoli, M., & Vecchi, S. (2011). Psychosocial combined with agonist maintenance treatments versus agonist maintenance treatments alone for treatment of opioid dependence. *Cochrane Database of Systematic Reviews, 10.* Art. No.: CD004147. DOI: 10.1002/14651858.CD004147.pub4

Ambrosini, P. J., Bianchi, M. D., Rabinovich, H., & Elia, J. (1993). Antidepressant treatments in children and adolescents. I. Affective disorders. *Journal of the American Academy of Child Adolescent Psychiatry, 32,* 1–6.

American Academy of Child and Adolescent Psychiatry (2007). Practice parameter for the assessment and treatment of children and adolescents with oppositional defiant disorder. *Journal of the American Academy of Child and Adolescent Psychiatry, 46*, 127–141.

American Association of Suicidology (2014a). *Suicide in the USA*. Retrieved on August 12, 2014 from http://www.suicidology.org/c/document_library/get_file?-folderId=248&name=DLFE-800.pdf

American Association of Suicidology. (2014b). *Youth suicide fact sheet*. Retrieved on August 12, 2014 from http://www.suicidology.org/c/document_library/get_file?folderId=232&name=DLFE-161.pdf

American Foundation for Suicide Prevention (n.d.). *Facts and figures*. Retrieved July 25, 2014 from https://www.afsp.org/understanding-suicide/facts-and-figures

American Psychiatric Association. (1952). *Diagnostic and statistical manual of mental disorders*. Washington, DC: Author.

American Psychiatric Association. (1968). *Diagnostic and statistical manual of mental disorders* (2nd ed.). Washington, DC: Author.

American Psychiatric Association. (1980). *Diagnostic and statistical manual of mental disorders* (3rd ed.). Washington, DC: Author.

American Psychiatric Association. (1987). *Diagnostic and statistical manual of mental disorders* (3rd ed. Rev.). Washington, DC: Author.

American Psychiatric Association. (1993). Practice guide for major depressive disorder in adults. *American Journal of Psychiatry, 150* (Suppl. April), 1–26.

American Psychiatric Association. (1994). *Diagnostic and statistical manual of mental disorders* (4th ed.). Washington, DC: Author.

American Psychiatric Association. (2000). *Diagnostic and statistical manual of mental disorders* (4th ed., text revision). Washington, DC: American Psychiatric Association.

American Psychiatric Association. (2006). *Practice guideline for the treatment of patients with eating disorders* (3rd ed.). Washington, D.C.: American Psychiatric Association.

American Psychiatric Association. (2013a). *Diagnostic and statistical manual of mental disorders* (5th ed.). Arlington, VA: American Psychiatric Publishing.

American Psychiatric Association. (2013b). Personality disorders [Report]. Retrieved July 9, 2014 from http://www.dsm5.org/Documents/Personality%20Disorders%20Fact%20Sheet.pdf

American Psychiatric Association. (2013c, June 15). Online assessment measures: The Personality Inventory for *DSM-5* (PID-5)—Adults. Retrieved January 17, 2014, from http://www.psychiatry.org/practice/dsm/dsm5/online-assessment-measures#Personality.

American Psychological Association. (1992). Ethical principles of psychologists and code of conduct. *American Psychologist, 47*, 1597–1611.

American Psychological Association. (1995). Training in and dissemination of empirically-validated psychological procedures: Report and recommendations. *The Clinical Psychologist, 48*, 22–23.

American Psychological Association. (1995, October). Warning: Soccer can be harmful to your head's health. *The APA Monitor, 26*, 12–13.

American Psychological Association. (2010). *Ethical principles of psychologists and code of conduct*. Retrieved on October 31, 2014 from http://www.apa.org/ethics/code/principles.pdf

Amering, M., & Katschnig, H. (1990). Panic attacks and panic disorder in cross-cultural perspective. *Psychiatric Annals, 20*, 511–516.

Amrhein, P. C., Miller, W. R., Yahne, C., Palmer, M., & Fulcher, L. (2003). Client commitment language during motivational interviewing predicts drug use outcomes. *Journal of Consulting and Clinical Psychology, 71*, 862–878. doi:10.1037/0022-006X.71.5.862

Amundson, M. E., Hart, C. A., & Holmes, T. H. (1986). *Manual for the schedule of recent experience*. Seattle: University of Washington Press.

Anastasiow, N. J. (1990). Implications of the neurobiological model for early intervention. In S. J. Meisels & J. P. Shonkoff (Eds.), *Handbook of early childhood intervention* (pp. 196–216). New York: Cambridge University Press.

Anders, S., Tanaka, M., & Kinney, D. K. (2013). Depression as an evolutionary strategy for defense against infection. *Brain, Behavior, and Immunity, 31*, 9–22. doi:10.1016/j.bbi.2012.12.002

Andersen, B. L., & Cyranowski, J. M. (1995). Women's sexuality: Behaviors, responses, and individual differences. *Journal of Consulting and Clinical Psychology, 63*, 891–906.

Andersen, B. L., Kiecolt-Glaser, J. K., & Glaser, R. (1994). A biobehavioral model of cancer stress and disease course. *American Psychologist, 49*, 389–404.

Andersen, I., Thielen, K., Bech, P., Nygaard, E., & Diderichsen, F. (2011). Increasing prevalence of depression from 2000 to 2006. *Scandinavian Journal of Public Health, 39*(8), 857–863. doi:10.1177/1403494811424611

Anderson, A. (2014). A brief history of eating disorders in males. In L. Cohn & R. Lemberg (Eds.), *Current findings on males with eating disorders* (pp. 4–10). New York, NY: Routledge.

Anderson, D. M., & Rees, D. I. (2014). The legalization of recreational marijuana: How likely is the worst-case scenario? *Journal of Policy Analysis and Management, 33*(1), 221–232. doi:10.1002/pam.21727

Anderson, G. M., & Hosino, Y. (1987). Neurochemical studies of autism. In D. Cohen & A. Donnellan (Eds.), *Handbook of autism and pervasive developmental disorders* (pp. 166–191). New York: John Wiley & Sons.

Anderson, K. E., Lytton, H., & Romney, D. M. (1986). Mothers' interactions with normal and conduct-disordered boys: Who affects whom? *Developmental Psychology, 22*(5), 604–609.

Anderson, L. T., Campbell, M., Adams, P., Small, A. M., Perry, R., & Shell, J. (1989). The effects of haloperidol on discrimination learning and behavioral symptoms in autistic children. *Journal of Autism and Developmental Disorders, 19*, 227–239.

Anderson, N. B. (1989). Racial differences in stress-reduced cardiovascular reactivity and hypertension: Current status and substantive issues. *Psychological Bulletin, 105*, 89–105.

Andreasen, N. C. (1982). Negative symptoms in schizophrenia: Definition and reliability. *Archives of General Psychiatry, 39*, 784–788.

Andreasen, N. C. (1987). Creativity and mental illness: Prevalence rates in writers and their first-degree relatives. *American Journal of Psychiatry, 144*, 1288–1292.

Andreasen, N. C. (1988). Brain imaging: Applications in psychiatry. *Science, 239*, 1381–1388.

Andreasen, N. C., & Black, D. W. (1991). *Introductory textbook of psychiatry*. Washington, DC: American Psychiatric Press.

Andreasen, N. C., Arndt, S., Alliger, R., Miller, D., & Flaum, M. (1995). Symptoms of schizophrenia: Method, meaning and mechanisms. *Archives of General Psychiatry, 53*, 341–351.

Andreasen, N. C., Arndt, S., Swayze, V., Cozadlo, T., Flaum, M., O'Leary, D., Ehrhardt, J., & Yuh, W. T. C. (1994). Thalamic abnormalities in schizophrenia visualized through magnetic resonance imaging averaging. *Science, 266*, 294–298.

Andreasen, N. C., & Carpenter, N. T. (1993). Diagnosis and classification of schizophrenia. *Schizophrenia Bulletin, 19*, 199–214.

Andreasen, N. C., Erhardt, J, Swayze, V., Alliger, R., Yuh, W. T. C., Cohen, G., & Ziebell, S. (1990). Magnetic resonance imaging of the brain in schizophrenia. *Archives of General Psychiatry, 47*, 35–44.

Andreasen, N. C., Nasrullah, H., Dunn, V., Olson, S., Grove, W., Erhardt, J, Coffman, J., & Crosett, J. (1986). Structural abnormalities in the frontal system in schizophrenia. *Archives of General Psychiatry, 43*, 136–144.

Andreasen, N. C., Rezai, K., Alliger, R., Swayze, V., Flaum, M., Kirchner, P., Cohen, G., & O'Leary, D. (1992). Hypofrontality in neuroleptic-naive patients and in patients with chronic schizophrenia: Assessment with xenon-133 single proton emission computed tomography and the Tower of London. *Archives of General Psychiatry, 49*, 943–958.

Andreou, E., Alexopoulos, E. C., Lionis, C., Varvogli, L., Gnardellis, C., Chrousos, G. P., & Darviri, C. (2011). Perceived stress scale: Reliability and validity study in Greece. *International Journal of Environmental Research and Public Health, 8*, 3287–3298.

Andrews, D. A., & Bonta, J. (1994). *The psychology of criminal conduct*. Cincinnati, OH: Anderson Publishing.

Andrews, G., Cuijpers, P., Craske, M. G., McEvoy, P., & Titov, N. (2010). Computer therapy for the anxiety and depressive disorders is effective, acceptable, and practical health care: A meta-analysis. *Plos ONE, 5*(10). doi:10.1371/journal.pone.0013196

Andrews, G., & Harvey, R. (1981). Does psychotherapy benefit neurotic patients? A re-analysis of the Smith, Glass, and Miller data. *Archives of General Psychiatry, 38*, 1203–1208.

Andrulonis, P. A., Glueck, B. C., Stroebel, C. F., Vogel, N. G., Shapiro, A. L., & Aldridge, D. M. (1981). Organic brain dysfunctions and the borderline syndrome. *Psychiatric Clinics of North America, 4*, 47–66.

Andrykowski, M. A., & Redd, W. H. (1987). Longitudinal analysis of the development of anticipatory nausea, *journal of Consulting and Clinical Psychology, 55*, 36–41.

Anfag, S. A., & Appelbaum, P. S. (2009). Civil commitment—the American experience. *Israeli Journal of Psychiatry and Related Sciences, 43*(3): 209–218.

Angst, J., Felder, W., & Frey, R. (1979). The course of unipolar and bipolar affective disorders. In M. Schou & E. Stromgren (Eds.), *Origin, prevention, and treatment of affective disorders*. New York: Academic Press.

Anthony, W. A., Cohen, M. R., & Danley, K. S. (1988). The psychiatric rehabilitation model as applied to vocational rehabilitation. In J. A. Ciardiello & M. D. Bell (Eds.), *Vocational rehabilitation of persons with prolonged psychiatric disorders*. Baltimore: Johns Hopkins University Press.

Anton, R. F., O'Malley, S. S., Ciraulo, D. A., Cisler, R. A., Couper, D., Donovan, D. M., . . . Zweben, A. (2006). Combined pharmacotherapies and behavioral interventions for alcohol dependence: The COMBINE study: A randomized controlled trial. *JAMA: Journal of the American Medical Association, 295*(17), 2003–2017. doi:10.1001/jama.295.17.2003

Antoni, M. H., Baggett, L., Ironson, G., Laperriere, A., August, S., Klimas, N., Schneiderman, N., & Fletcher, M. A. (1991). Cognitive-behavioral stress management intervention buffers distress responses and immunologic changes following notification of HIV-1 seropositivity. *Journal of Consulting and Clinical Psychology, 59*, 906–915.

Antonuccio, D. O., Danton, W. G., & DeNelsky, G. Y. (1995). Psychotherapy versus medication for depression: Challenging the conventional wisdom with data. *Professional Psychology: Research and Practice, 6*, 574–585.

Apfelbaum, B. (2000) Retarded ejaculation: A much-misunderstood syndrome. In S. R. Leiblum & R. C. Rosen (Eds.), *Principles and practice of sex therapy*, (pp. 205–241). New York, NY: Guilford Press.

Appelbaum, P. S. (1986). Competence to be executed: Another conundrum for mental health professionals. *Hospital and Community Psychiatry, 37*, 682–684.

Appelbaum, P. S. (1988). The new preventive detention: Psychiatry's problematic responsibility for the control of violence. *The American Journal of Psychiatry, 145*(7), 779–785.

Appelbaum, P. S. (1994). *Almost a revolution: Mental health law and the limits of change*. New York: Oxford University Press.

Appelbaum, P. S., & Hoge, S. K. (1986). The right to refuse treatment: What the research reveals. *Behavioral Sciences and the Law, 4*, 279–292.

Appelbaum, P. S., Robbins, P. C., & Roth, L. H. (1999). Dimensional approach to delusions: Comparison across types and diagnoses. *American Journal of Psychiatry, 156*, 1938–1943.

Appels, A., & Otten, F. (1992). Exhaustion as precursor of cardiac death. *British Journal of Clinical Psychology, 31*, 351–356.

Appels, A., & Schouten, E. (1991). Burnout as a risk factor for coronary heart disease. *Behavioral Medicine, 17*, 53–59.

Arcelus, J., Mitchell, A. J., Wales, J., & Nielsen, S. (2011). Mortality rates in patients with anorexia nervosa and other eating disorders: A meta-analysis of 35 studies. *Archives of General Psychiatry, 68*(7): 724–731.

Arciniega, G. M., Anderson, T. C., Tovar-Blank, Z. G., & Tracey, T. J. G. (2008). Toward a fuller conception of machismo: Development of a traditional machismo and caballerismo scale. *Journal of Counseling Psychology, 55*(1), 19–33.

Arciniegas, D. B., & Wortzel, H. S. (2014). Emotional and behavioral dyscontrol after traumatic brain injury. *Psychiatric Clinics of North America, 37*(1), 31–53. doi:10.1016/j.psc.2013.12.001

Arguello, A., & Gogos, A. (2008). A signaling pathway AKTing up in schizophrenia. *The Journal of Clinical Investigation, 118*, 2018–2021.

Arieti, A., & Bemporad, J. (1978). *Severe and mild depression: A psychotherapeutic approach*. New York: Basic Books.

Arkowitz, H., & Burke, B. L. (2008). Motivational interviewing as an integrative framework for the treatment of depression. In H. Arkowitz, H. A. Westra, W. R. Miller, & S. Rollnick (Eds.), *Motivational interviewing in the treatment of psychological problems* (pp. 145–172). New York: Guilford Press.

Armor, D. J., Polich, J. M., & Stambul, H. B. (1976). *Alcoholism and treatment*. Prepared for the National Institute on Alcohol Abuse and Alcoholism. Santa Monica, CA: Rand Corp.

Arndt, J., Vail, K. I., Cox, C. R., Goldenberg, J. L., Piasecki, T. M., & Gibbons, F. X. (2013). The interactive effect of mortality reminders and tobacco craving on smoking topography. *Health Psychology, 32*(5), 525–532. doi:10.1037/a0029201

Arnold, L. D., Bachmann, G. A., Kelly, S., Rosen, R., & Rhoads, G. G. (2006). Vulvodynia: characteristics and associations with co-morbidities and quality of life. *Obstetrics and Gynecology, 107*(3), 617.

Arnold, L. M., Auchenbach, M. B., & McElroy, S. L. (2001). Psychogenic excoriation: Clinical features, proposed diagnostic criteria, epidemiology and approaches to treatment. *CNS Drugs, 15*(5), 351–359.

Arnold, L. M., McElroy, S. L., Mutasim, D. F., Dwight, M. M., Lamerson, C. L., & Morris, E. M. (1998). Characteristics of 34 adults with psychogenic excoriation. *Journal of Clinical Psychiatry, 59*(10), 509–514.

Arns, M., de Ridder, S., Strehl, U., Breteler, M., & Coenen, A. (2009). Efficacy of neurofeedback treatment in ADHD: The effects on inattention, impulsivity, and hyperactivity: A meta-analysis. *Clinical EEG and Neuroscience, 40*(3), 180–189. doi:10.1177/155005940904000311

Arrigo, B. A., & Purcell, C. E. (2001). Explaining paraphilias and lust murder: Toward an integrated model. *International Journal of Offender Therapy and Comparative Criminology, 45*(1), 6–31. doi:10.1177/0306624X01451002

Arrindell, W. A. (1993). The fear of fear concept: Stability, retest artifact, and predictive power. *Behaviour Research and Therapy, 31*, 139–148.

Arsenault-Lapierre, G., Kim, C., & Turecki, G. (2004). Psychiatric diagnoses in 3,275 suicides: A meta-analysis. *BMC Psychiatry, 4*, 37. doi:10.1186/1471-244X-4-37

Artiola i Fortuny, L., Garolera, M., Hermosillo Romo, D., Feldman, E., Fernandez Barillas, H., Keefe, R., . . . Verger Maestre, K. (2005). Research with Spanish-speaking populations in the United States: Lost in the translation. A commentary and a plea. *Journal of Clinical and Experimental Neuropsychology, 27*(5), 555–564. doi: 10.1080/13803390490918282

Asam, U., & Trager, S. E. (1973). Contribution to the etiology and pathogenesis of trichotillomania with special consideration of mother-child relations. *Praxis Der Kinderpsychologie Und Kinderpsychiatrie, 22*(8), 283–290.

Ashdown, H., Dumont, Y., Ng, M., Poole, S., Boksa, P., & Luheshi, G. N. (2006). The role of cytokines in mediating effects of prenatal infection on the fetus: Implications for schizophrenia. *Molecular Psychiatry, 11*, 47–55.

Ashton, H. (1991). Psychotropic-drug prescribing for women. *British Journal of Psychiatry, 158* (Suppl. 10). 30–35.

Asmundson, G. J., & Norton, G. R. (1993). Anxiety sensitivity and its relationship to spontaneous and cued panic attacks in college students. *Behaviour Research and Therapy, 31*, 199–201.

Asperger, H. (1944). Die autistischen Psychopathen im Kindesalter. *Archiv fur Psychiatrie und Nervenkrankheiten, 117*, 76–136.

Asplund, R. (1995). Sleep and hypnotics among the elderly in relation to body weight and somatic disease. *Journal of Internal Medicine, 238*(1), 65–70.

Associated Press (2006, October 24). Man with amnesia reunited with family, friends. *NBC News*. Retrieved on December 7, 2014 from http://www.nbcnews.com/id/15373503/ns/us_news-life/t/man-amnesia-reunited-family-friends/

Association of Reproductive Health Professionals. (2009). Talking with patients about sexuality and sexual health [online fact sheet]. Retrieved November 11, 2014 from http://www.arhp.org/Publications-and-Resources/Clinical-Fact-Sheets/SHF-Talking

Assumpção, A., Garcia, F., Garcia, H., Bradford, J. W., & Thibaut, F. (2014). Pharmacologic treatment of paraphilias. *Psychiatric Clinics of North America, 37*(2), 173–181. doi:10.1016/j.psc.2014.03.002

Aston, E. R., & Liguori, A. (2013). Self-estimation of blood alcohol concentration: A review. *Addictive Behaviors, 38*(4), 1944–1951. doi:10.1016/j.addbeh.2012.12.017

Aston-Jones, G., & Bloom, F. E. (1981). Activity of norepinephrine-containing neurons in behaving rats anticipates fluctuations in the sleep-waking cycle. *The Journal of Neuroscience, 1*, 876–886.

Astor, R., Cornell, D. G., Espelage, D. L., Furlong, M. J., Jimerson, S. R., Mayer, M. J., & . . . Sugai, G. (2013). December 2012 Connecticut school shooting position statement. *Journal of School Violence, 12*, 119–133. doi:10.1080/15388220.2012.762488

Athwal, B. S., Halligan, P., Fink, G. R., Marshall, J. C., & Frackowiak, R. S. (2001). Imaging hysterical paralysis. In P. Halligan, C .M. Bass, & J. C. Marshall (Eds.), *Contemporary approaches to the study of hysteria* (pp. 216–234). Oxford, UK: Oxford University Press.

Atkins, R., & Hawdon, J. E. (2007). Religiosity and participation in mutual-aid support groups for addictions. *Journal of Substance Abuse Treatment, 33*(3), 321–331. doi:10.1016/j.jsat.2007.07.001

Atladottir, H. O, Henricksen, T. B., Schendel, D. E., & Parner, E. T. (2012). Autism after infection, febrile episodes, and antibiotic use during pregnancy: An exploratory study. *Pediatrics, 130*, e1447–e1454.

Attarian, H. P. (2013). Epidemiology of sleep disorders in women. In H. P. Attarian & Viola-Saltzman, M. (Eds.), *Sleep disorders in women: A guide to practical management* (pp. 9–23). Totowa, NJ: Humana Press.

Atwood, G. E. (2011). *The Abyss of Madness*. New York: Routledge.

Aubin, S., Heiman, J. R., Berger, R. E., Murallo, A. V., & Yung-Wen, L. (2009). Comparing sildenafil alone vs. sildenafil plus brief couple sex therapy on erectile dysfunction and couples' sexual and marital quality of life: A pilot study. *Journal of Sex & Marital Therapy, 35*, 122–143.

Audenaert, K., Van Laere, K., Dumont, F., Slegers, G., Mertens, J., van Heeringen, C., & Dierckx, R. A. (2001). Decreased frontal serotonin 5-HT 2a receptor binding index in deliberate self-harm patients. *European Journal of Nuclear Medicine, 28*(2), 175–182.

Auerbach, R., & Kilmann, P. R. (1977). The effects of group systematic desensitization on secondary erectile failure. *Behavior Therapy, 8*, 330–339.

Auerbach, R. P., Webb, C. A., Gardiner, C. K., & Pechtel, P. (2013). Behavioral and neural mechanisms underlying cognitive vulnerability models of depression. *Journal of Psychotherapy Integration, 23*(3), 222–235. doi:10.1037/a0031417

Augustinavicius, J. S., Zanjani, A., Zakzanis, K. K., & Shapiro, C. M. (2014). Polysomnographic features of early-onset depression: A meta-analysis. *Journal of Affective Disorders, 158*, 11–18. doi:10.1016/j.jad.2013.12.009

Auquier, P., Lancon, C., Rouillon, F., & Lader, M. (2007). Mortality in schizophrenia. *Pharmacoepidemiology, 16*, 1308–1312.

Averill, J. R. (1973). Personal control over aversive stimuli and its relationship to stress. *Psychological Bulletin, 80*, 286-303.

Avery, D. H. (1993). Electroconvulsive therapy. In D. D. Dunner (Ed.), *Current psychiatric therapy* (pp. 524–528). Philadelphia: W. B. Saunders.

Avery, D. H., Bolte, M. A., Wolfson, J. K., & Kazaras, A. L. (1994). Dawn simulation compared with dim red signal in treatment of winter depression. *Biological Psychiatry, 36*, 180–188.

Avery, D. H., Dahl, D., Savage, M., Brengelmann, G., Larsen, L., Vitiello, M., & Prinz, P. (1990). Bright light treatment of winter depression: AM compared to PM light. *Acta Psychiatric Scandinavica, 82*, 335–338.

Avery, D. H., & Winoker, G. (1976). Mortality in depressed patients treated with electroconvulsive therapy and antidepressants. *Archives of General Psychiatry, 33,* 1029–1037.

Ayllon, T., & Azrin, N. H. (1965). The measurement and reinforcement of behavior of psychotics. *Journal of the Experimental Analysis of Behavior, 8,* 357-383.

Ayllon, T., & Azrin, N. H. (1968). *The token economy: A motivational system for therapy and rehabilitation.* New York: Appleton-Century-Crofts.

Azad, N.A., Al Bugami, M., & Loy-English, I. (2007). Gender differences in dementia risk factors. *Gender Medicine, 4*(2), 120–129.

Azevedo, F. C., Carvalho, L. B., Grinberg, L. T., Farfel, J., Ferretti, R. L., Leite, R. P., & . . . Herculano-Houzel, S. (2009). Equal numbers of neuronal and nonneuronal cells make the human brain an isometrically scaled-up primate brain. *The Journal of Comparative Neurology, 513,* 532–541. doi:10.1002/cne.21974

Azrin, N. H., Bersalel, A., Bechtel, R., Michalicek, A., Mancera, M., Carroll, D., Shuford, D., & Cox, J. (1980). Comparison of reciprocity and discussion-type counseling for marital problems. *American Journal of Family Therapy, 8,* 21–28.

Azrin, N. H., Hontos, P. T., & Besalel-Azrin, V, A. (1979). Elimination of enuresis without a conditioning apparatus: An extension by office instruction of the child and parents. *Behavior Therapy, 18,* 14–19.

Azrin, N. H., McMahon, P.T., Donohue, B., Besalel, V. A., & Lapinski, K. J. (1994). Behavior therapy for drug abuse: A controlled treatment outcome study. *Behaviour Research and Therapy, 32,* 857–866.

Azrin, N. H., & Nunn, R. G. (1973). Habit-reversal: A method of eliminating nervous habits and tics. *Behaviour Research and Therapy, 11*(4), 619–628. doi:10.1016/0005-7967(73)90119-8

Azrin, N. H., Nunn, R. G., & Frantz, S. E. (1980). Habit reversal vs. negative practice treatment of nailbiting. *Behaviour Research & Therapy, 18,* 281–285.

Azrin, N. H., Nunn, R. G., & Frantz-Renshaw, S. (1980). Habit reversal treatment of thumbsucking. *Behaviour Research and Therapy, 18,* 395–399.

Azrin, N. H., & Peterson, A. L. (1989). Reduction of an eye tic by controlled blinking. *Behavior Therapy, 20,* 467–473.

B

Baars, B. J. (2001). *In the theater of consciousness: The workspace of the mind.* New York: Oxford University Press.

Babor, T. F., Hofmann, M., DelBoca, F. K., Hesselbrock, V., Meyer, R. E., Dolinsky, Z. S., & Rounsaville, B. (1992). Types of alcoholics: I. Evidence for an empirically derived typology based on indicators of vulnerability and severity. *Archives of General Psychiatry, 49,* 599–608.

Babor, T. R (1994). Avoiding the horrid and beastly sin of drunkenness: Does dissuasion make a difference? *Journal of Consulting and Clinical Psychology, 62(6),* 1127–1140.

Bachmann, G. A., Leiblum, S. R., & Grill, J. (1989). Brief sexual inquiry in gynecologic practice. *Obstetrics and Gynecology, 73,* 425–427.

Baddeley, A. (2007). Working memory, thought, and action. New York: Oxford University Press. doi:10.1093/acprof:oso/9780198528012.001.0001

Baer, J. S., Marlatt, G. A., Kivlahan, D. R., Fromme, K., Larimer, M. E., & Williams, E. (1992). An experimental test of three methods of alcohol risk reduction with young adults. *Journal of Consulting and Clinical Psychology, 60*(6), 974–979.

Baer, L., Rauch, S. L., Ballantine, T., Martuza, R., Cosgrove, R., Cassem, E., Girunas, I., Manzo, P. A., Domino, C., & Jenike, M. A. (1995). Cingulotomy for intractable obsessive-compulsive disorder: Prospective long-term follow-up of 18 patients. *Archives of General Psychiatry, 52,* 384–392.

Baer, R. A., & Nietzel, M. T. (1991). Cognitive and behavioral treatment of impulsivity in children: A meta-analytic review of the outcome literature. *Journal of Clinical Child Psychology, 20*(4), 400–412.

Baethge, C., Baldessarini, R. J., Freudenthal, K., Streeruwitz, A., Bauer, M., & Bschor, T. (2005). Hallucinations in bipolar disorder: Characteristics and comparison to unipolar depression and schizophrenia. *Bipolar Disorders, 7*(2), 136–145. doi:10.1111/j.1399-5618.2004.00175.x

Baiano, M., David, A., Versace, A., Churchill, R., Balestrieri, M., & Brambilla, P. (2007). Anterior cingulate volumes in schizophrenia: A systematic review and a meta-analysis of MRI studies. *Schizophrenia Research, 93,* 1–12.

Bailey, J. M., & Pillard, R. C. (1991). A genetic study of male sexual orientation. *Archives of General Psychiatry, 48,* 1089–1091.

Bailey, J. M., Pillard, R. C., Neale, M. C., & Agyei, Y. (1993). Heritable factors influence sexual orientation in women. *Archives of General Psychiatry, 50,* 217–223.

Bailey, J. S. (1992). Gentle teaching: Trying to win friends and influence people with euphemism, metaphor, smoke, and mirrors. *Journal of Applied Behavior Analysis, 25,* 879–883.

Baillargeon, J., Binswanger, I. A., Penn, J. V., Williams, B. A., & Murray, O. J. (2009). Psychiatric disorders and repeat incarcerations: The revolving prison door. *The American Journal of Psychiatry, 166*(1), 103–109. doi:10.1176/appi.ajp.2008.08030416

Baker, C. A., & Morrison, A. P. (1998). Cognitive processes in auditory hallucinations: Attributional biases and metacognition. *Psychological Medicine, 28*(5), 1199–1208. doi:10.1017/S0033291798007314

Baker, L A., Jacobson, K. C., Raine, A. Lozano, D. I., & Bezdjian, S. (2007). Genetic and environmental bases of childhood antisocial behavior: A multi-informant twin study. *Journal of Abnormal Psychology, 116,* 219–235.

Bakker, P. R., van Harten, P. N., & van Os, J. (2006). Antipsychotic-induced tardive dyskinesia and the Ser9Gly polymorphism in the DRD3 gene: A meta analysis. *Schizophrenia Research, 83,* 185–192.

Baldessarini, R. J., Tondo, L. L., & Visioli, C. C. (2014). First-episode types in bipolar disorder: Predictive associations with later illness. *Acta Psychiatrica Scandinavica, 129*(5), 383–392. doi:10.1111/acps.12204

Baldwin, D. S., Ajel, K., Masdrakis, V. G., Nowak, M., & Rafiq, R. (2013). Pregabalin for the treatment of generalized anxiety disorder: An update. *Neuropsychiatric Disease and Treatment, 9,* 883–892.

Baldwin, J. D., & Baldwin, J. I. (1997). Gender differences in sexual interest. *Archives of Sexual Behavior, 26,* 181–210.

Balis, T., & Postolache, T. T. (2008). Ethnic differences in adolescent suicide in the United States. *International Journal of Child Health and Human Development, 1*(3, Special Issue), 281–296.

Ball, E., & Blackman, B. (1991). Does phoneme awareness training in kindergarten make a difference in early word recognition and developmental spelling? *Reading Research Quarterly, 26,* 49–66.

Ballenger, J., Burrows, G. D., DuPont, R., Lesser, I., Noyes, R., Pecknold, J., Rifkin, A., & Swinson, R. (1988). Alprazolam in panic disorder and agoraphobia: Results from a multicenter trial. *Archives of General Psychiatry, 45,* 413–422.

Balon, R. (2013). Controversies in the diagnosis and treatment of paraphilias. *Journal of Sex & Marital Therapy, 39*(1), 7–20. doi:10.1080/0092623X.2012.709219

Bandura, A. (1969). *Principles of behavior modification.* New York: Holt, Rinehart & Winston.

Bandura, A. (1977). Self-efficacy: Toward a unifying theory of behavioral change. *Psychological Review, 84,* 191–215.

Bandura, A. (1982). Self-efficacy mechanism in human agency. *American Psychologist, 33,* 344–358.

Bandura, A. (1986). *Social foundations of thought and action: A social cognitive theory.* Englewood Cliffs, NJ: Prentice Hall.

Bandura, A. (2011). But what about that gigantic elephant in the room? In R. M. Arkin (Ed.), *Most underappreciated: 50 prominent social psychologists describe their most unloved work* (pp. 51–59). New York: Oxford University Press.

Bandura, A. (2012). On the functional properties of perceived self-efficacy revisited. *Journal of Management, 38,* 9–44. doi:10.1177/0149206311410606

Bandura, A., Blanchard, E., and Ritter, B. (1969). Relative efficacy of desensitization and modeling approaches for inducting behavioral, affective, and attitudinal changes. *Journal of Personality and Social Psychology, 13,* 173–199.

Barbaree, H. E., Marshall, W. L. (1991). The role of male sexual arousal in rape: Six models. *Journal of Consulting and Clinical Psychology, 59,* 621–630.

Barbini, B., Colombo, C., Benedetti, F., Campori, E., Bellodi, L., & Smeraldi, E. (1998). The unipolar-bipolar dichotomy and the response to sleep deprivation. *Psychiatry Research, 79*(1), 43–50. doi:10.1016/S0165-1781(98)00020-1

Barker, S. L., Funk, S. C., & Houston, B. K. (1988). Psychological treatment versus nonspecific factors: A meta-analysis of conditions that engender comparable expectations for improvement. *Clinical Psychology Review, 8,* 579–594.

Barkley, R. A. (1990). A critique of current diagnostic criteria for attention deficit-hyperactive disorder: Clinical and research implications. *Developmental Behavioral Pediatrics, 11,* 343–352.

Barkley, R. A., DuPaul, G. J., & Costello, A. (1993). Stimulants. In J. S. Werry & M. G. Aman (Eds.), *Practitioner's guide to psychoactive drugs for children and adolescents* (pp. 205-237). New York: Plenum.

Barkley, R. A., DuPaul, G. J., & McMurray, M. B. (1990). Comprehensive evaluation of attention deficit disorder with and without hyperactivity as defined by research criteria. *Journal of Consulting and Clinical Psychology, 58,* 775–789.

Barkley, R. A., Guevremont, D. C., Anastopoulos, A. D., & Fletcher, K. E. (1992). A comparison of three family therapy programs for treating family conflicts in adolescents with attention-deficit hyperactivity disorder. *Journal of Consulting and Clinical Psychology, 60*(3), 450–462.

Barlow, D. H. (1986). Causes of sexual dysfunction: The role of anxiety and cognitive interference. *Journal of Consulting and Clinical Psychology, 54,* 140–148.

Barlow, D. H. (1988). *Anxiety and its disorders.* New York: Guilford Press.

Barlow, D. H. (1997). Anxiety disorders, comorbid substance abuse, and benzodiazepine discontinuation: Implications for treatment. *NIDA Research Monograph, 172,* 33–51.

Barlow, D. H. (2000). Unraveling the mysteries of anxiety and its disorders from the perspective of emotion theory. *American Psychologist, 55*(11), 1247–1263.

Barlow, D. H., Craske, M. G., Cerny, J. A., & Klosko, J. S. (1989). Behavior treatment of panic disorder. *Behavior Therapy, 20,* 261–282.

Barlow, D. H., & Durand, V. M. (2004). *Abnormal psychology: An integrative approach* (4th edition). New York: Thomson.

Barlow, D. H., Ellard, K. K., Fairholme, C. P., Farchione, T. J., Boisseau, C. L., Allen, L. B., & Ehrenreich-May, J. (2011). *Unified protocol for transdiagnostic* treatment of emotional disorders: Client workbook. New York: Oxford University Press.

Barlow, D. H., & Hersen, M. (1984). Single-case experimental designs: Strategies for studying behavior (2nd ed.). New York: Pergamon Press.

Barlow, D. H., Rapee, R. M., & Brown, T. A. (1992). Behavioral treatment of generalized anxiety disorder. Behavior Therapy, 23, 551–570.

Barlow, D. H., Reynolds, E. J., & Agras, W. S. (1973). Gender identity change in a transsexual. Archives of General Psychiatry, 28, 569–576.

Barlow, D. H., Sakheim, D. K., & Beck, J. G. (1983). Anxiety increases sexual arousal. Journal of Abnormal Psychology, 92, 49–54.

Barlow, J., & Kirby, N. (1991). Residential satisfaction of persons with an intellectual disability living in an institution or in the community. Australia and New Zealand Journal of Developmental Disabilities, 17(1), 7–23.

Barnard, E. A., Skolnick, P., Olsen, R. W., Mohler, H., Sieghart, W., Biggio, G., Braestrup, C., Bateson, A. N., & Langer, S. Z. (1998). International Union of Pharmacology. XV. Subtypes of gamma-aminobutyric acid A receptors: classification on the basis of subunit structure and receptor function. Pharmacology Review, 50(2), 291–313.

Barnard, K. E., Hammond, M. A., Booth, C. L., Bee, H. L., Mitchell, S. K., & Spieker, S. J. (in press). Measurement and meaning of parent-child interaction. In F. Morrison, C. Lord, & D. Keating (Eds.), Applied developmental psychology (Vol. 3). New York: Academic Press.

Barnard, K. E., & Kelly, J. F. (1990). Assessment of parent-child interaction. In S. J. Meisels & J. P. Shonkoff (Eds.), Handbook of early childhood intervention (pp. 278–302). New York: Cambridge University Press.

Barnes, D. E., Lui, L., & Yaffe, K. (2010). Physical activity over the life course and its association with cognitive performance and impairment in old age. Journal of the American Geriatrics Society, 58(7), 1322–1326. doi: 10.1111/j.1532-5415.2010.02903.x

Barnes, G. M., Farrell, M. P., & Cairns, A. L. (1986). Parental socialization factors and adolescent drinking behaviors. Journal of Marriage and the Family, 48, 27–36.

Barnes, J. (1986). Primary vaginismus (Part 2): Aetiological factors. Irish Medical Journal, 79, 62–65.

Barney, S. (2014). Making the world a better place, one abnormal psychology class at a time. Presidential Lecture given at Rocky Mountain Psychological Association Convention. Salt Lake City, UT (April 24–26).

Baron, M., Risch, N., Hamburger, R., Mandel, B., Kushner, S., Newman, M., Drumer, D., & Belmaker, R. H. (1987). Genetic linkage between X-chromosome markers and bipolar affective illness. Nature, 326, 289–292.

Baron-Cohen, S. (1989). Are autistic children "behaviorists"? An examination of their mental-physical and appearance-reality distinctions. Journal of Autism and Developmental Disorders, 19, 579–600.

Baron-Cohen, S. (1995). Mindblindness: An essay on autism and theory of mind. Cambridge, MA: MIT Press.

Baron-Cohen, S. (2004). The cognitive neuroscience of autism. Journal of Neurology, Neurosurgery & Psychiatry, 75(7), 945–948. doi:10.1136/jnnp.2003.018713.

Baron-Cohen, S. (2010). Empathizing, systemizing and the extreme male brain theory of autism. In I. Savic (Ed.), Progress in brain research: Sex differences in the human brain, their underpinnings and implications (Vol. 186, pp. 167–175). Cambridge, UK: Academic Press. doi:10.1016/B978-0-444-53630-3.00011-7

Baron-Cohen, S., Ring, H., Moriarity, J., Schmitz, B., Costa, D., & Ell, P. (1994). Recognition of mental state terms: Clinical findings in children with autism and a functional neuroimaging study of normal adults. British Journal of Psychiatry, 165, 640–649.

Baron-Cohen, S., & Wheelwright, S. (2004). The empathy quotient: An investigation of adults with Asperger syndrome or high-functioning autism, and normal sex differences. Journal of Autism and Developmental Disorders, 34, 163–175. doi:10.1023/B:JADD.0000022607.19833.00

Baron-Cohen, S., Wheelwright, S., Burtenshaw, A., & Hobson, E. (2007). Mathematical talent is linked to autism. Human Nature, 18(2), 125–131. doi:10.1007/s12110-007-9014-0

Barondes, S. H. (1993). Molecules and mental illness. Scientific American Library (p. 128). New York: Freeman.

Barone, J. J., & Roberts, H. R. (1996). Caffeine consumption. Food and Chemical Toxicology, 34(1), 119–129.

Barron, J. (2012, December 15). Children were all shot multiple times with a semiautomatic, officials say. The New York Times. Retrieved March 1, 2014 from http://www.nytimes.com/2012/12/16/nyregion/gunman-kills-20-children-at-school-in-connecticut-28-dead-in-all.html

Barron, J. (2013, May 29). Does DSM V represent progress for the LGBT community? [Speech]. Retrieved October 12, 2014, from http://www.communityaccess.org/storage/documents/ Discussion_on_Gender_and_Sexuality_in_DSM_5__Justin_Barron_.pdf

Barsky, A. J. (1989). Somatoform disorders. In H. I. Kaplan and B. J. Sadock (Eds.), Comprehensive textbook of psychiatry V (pp. 1009–1027). Baltimore: Williams & Wilkins.

Barsky, A. J. (1992). Amplification, somatization, and the somatoform disorders. Psychosomatics, 33, 28–34.

Barsky, A. J., Barnett, M. C., & Cleary, P. D. (1994). Hypochondriasis and panic disorder. Boundary and overlap. Archives of General Psychiatry, 51, 918–925.

Barsky, A. J., Wyshak, G., Klerman, G. L., & Latham, K. S. (1990). The prevalence of hypochondriasis in medical outpatients. Social Psychiatry and Psychiatric Epidemiology, 25, 89–94.

Barta, P., Pearlson, G., Powers, R., Richards, S., & Tune, L. (1990). Auditory hallucinations and smaller superior temporal gyral volume in schizophrenia. American Journal of Psychiatry, 147, 1457–1463.

Bartley, C. A., & Bloch, M. H. (2013). Meta-analysis: Pharmacological treatment of pathological gambling. Expert Review of Neurotherapeutics, 13(8), 887–894. doi:10.1586/14737175.2013.814938

Bartsch, D. (2007). Prevalence of body dysmorphic disorder symptoms and associated clinical features among Australian university students. Clinical Psychologist, 11(1), 16–23.

Bashir, N., Ahmed, N., Singh, A., Tang, Y. Z., Young, M., Abba, A., & Sampson, E. L. (2004). A precious case from Middle Earth. British Medical Journal, 329, 1435–1436. doi:10.1136/bmj.329.7480.1435

Bashore, T. R., & Rapp, P. E. (1993). Are there alternatives to traditional polygraph procedures? Psychological Bulletin, 113, 3–22.

Basic Behavioral Science Task Force of the National Advisory Mental Health Council (1996). Basic behavioral science research for mental health. American Psychologist, 51, 722–731.

Bass, E., & Davis, L. (1988). The courage to heal: A guide for women survivors of childhood sexual abuse. New York: Harper & Row.

Bassett, A. S., & Beiser, M. (1991). DSM-III: Use of the multiaxial diagnostic system in clinical practice. Canadian Journal of Psychiatry, 36, 270–274.

Bassman, R. (2005). Mental illness and the freedom to refuse treatment: Privilege or right. Professional Psychology: Research and Practice, 36(5), 488–497. doi:10.1037/0735-7028.36.5.488

Basson, R. (2005). Women's sexual dysfunction: Revised and expanded definitions. Canadian Medical Association Journal, 172(10), 1327–1333.

Basson, R., Rees, P., Wang, R., Montejo, A. L., & Incrocci, L. (2010). Sexual function in chronic illness. The Journal of Sexual Medicine, 7(1pt2), 374–388.

Bateson, G., Jackson, D. D., Haley, J., & Weakland, J. (1956). Toward a theory of schizophrenia. Behavioral Science, 1, 251–264.

Baucom, D. H., Epstein, N., Sayers, S., & Sher, T. G. (1989). The role of cognitions in marital relationships: Definitional, methodological, and conceptual issues. Journal of Consulting and Clinical Psychology, 57, 31–38.

Bauer, M. S., Grof, P., Rasgon, N., Bschor, T., Glenn, T., & Whybrow, P. C. (2006). Temporal relation between sleep and mood in patients with bipolar disorder. Bipolar Disorders, 8, 160–167.

Bauer, W. D., & Twentyman, C. T. (1985). Abusing, neglectful, and comparison mothers' responses to child-related and non-child stressors. Journal of Consulting and Clinical Psychology, 53, 335–343.

Baugh, C. M., Stamm, J. M., Riley, D. O., Gavett, B. W., Shenton, M. E., Lin, A., . . . Stern, R. A. (2012). Chronic traumatic encephalopathy: Neurodegeneration following repetitive concussive and subconcussive brain trauma. Brain Imaging and Behavior 6(2), 244–254.

Baum, A., & Fleming, I. (1993). Implications of psychological research on stress and technological accidents. American Psychologist, 48, 665–672.

Baum, A., Gatchel, R. J., & Schaeffer, M. A. (1983). Emotional, behavioral, and physiological effects of chronic stress at Three Mile Island. Journal of Consulting and Clinical Psychology, 51, 565–572.

Bauman, L. J., Stein, R. E. K., & Ireys, H. T. (1991). Reinventing fidelity: The transfer of social technology among settings. American Journal of Community Psychology, 19, 619–640.

Bauman, S., Toomey, R. B., & Walker, J. L. (2013). Associations among bullying, cyberbullying, and suicide in high school students. Journal of Adolescence, 36(2), 341–350. doi:10.1016/j.adolescence.2012.12.001

Baumeister, A. A., Kupstas, F. D., & Klindworth, L. M. (1991). The new morbidity: A national plan of action. American Behavioral Scientist, 34, 468–500.

Baumeister, R. F., & Leary, M. R. (1995). The need to belong: Desire for interpersonal attachments as a fundamental human motivation. Psychological Bulletin, 117, 497–529.

Baumrind, D. (1971). Current patterns of adult authority. Developmental Psychology Monograph, 4(1).

Baxter, A. J., Scott, K. M., Vos, T. T., & Whiteford, H. A. (2013). Global prevalence of anxiety disorders: A systematic review and meta-regression. Psychological Medicine, 43(5), 897–910. doi:10.1017/S003329171200147X

Baxter, L. M., Schwartz, J., Bergman, K., Szuba, M., Guze, B., Mazziotta, J. C., Alazaki, A., Selin, C., Ferng, H-G., Munford, P., & Phelps, M. (1992). Caudate glucose metabolic rate changes with both drug and behavior therapy for obsessive-compulsive disorder. Archives of General Psychiatry, 49, 681–689.

Beardsley, R. S., Gardocki, G. J., Larson, D., & Hidalgo, J. (1988). Prescribing of psychotropic medication by primary care physicians and psychiatrists. *Archives of General Psychiatry, 45*, 1117–1119.

Bearman, P. S., & Bruckner, H. (2001). Promising the future: Virginity pledges and first intercourse. *American Journal of Sociology, 106*(4), 859–912.

Beck, A. T. (1976). *Cognitive therapy and the emotional disorders.* New York: International Universities Press.

Beck, A. T. (1983). Cognitive therapy of depression: New Perspectives. In P. J. Clayton & J. E. Barrett (Eds.), *Treatment of depression: Old controversies and new approaches* (pp. 265–284). New York: Raven Press.

Beck, A. T. (1987). Cognitive models of depression. *Journal of Cognitive Psychotherapy: An International Journal, 1*, 5–37.

Beck, A. T., & Alford, B. A. (2009). *Depression: Causes and treatment* (2nd ed.). Baltimore, MD: University of Pennsylvania Press.

Beck, A. T., & Emery, G. (1985). *Anxiety disorders and phobias: A cognitive perspective.* New York: Basic Books.

Beck, A. T., Freeman, A., & Associates (1990). *Cognitive therapy of personality disorders.* New York: Guilford Press.

Beck, A. T., & Rector, N. A. (2003). A cognitive model of hallucinations. *Cognitive Therapy and Research, 27*(1), 19–52.

Beck, A. T., Rush, A. J., Shaw, B. F., & Emery, G. (1979). *Cognitive therapy of depression.* New York: Guilford Press.

Beck, A. T., Steer, R. A., & Brown, G. K. (1996). *Manual for the Beck Depression Inventory–II.* San Antonio, TX: Psychological Corporation.

Beck, H. (2014). *What can we really learn from the study of Little Albert?* Psi Chi Distinguished Lecture given at Rocky Mountain Psychological Association Convention. Salt Lake City, UT (April 24–26).

Beck, J. G. (1995). Hypoactive sexual desire disorder: An overview. *Journal of Consulting and Clinical Psychology, 63*, 919–927.

Becker, B., Klein, E. M., Striepens, N., Mihov, Y., Schlaepfer, T. E., Reul, J., & . . . Hurlemann, R. (2013). Nicotinic acetylcholine receptors contribute to learning-induced metaplasticity in the hippocampus. *Journal of Cognitive Neuroscience, 25*, 986–997. doi:10.1162/jocn_a_00383

Becker, J., & Schmaling, K. (1991). Interpersonal aspects of depression from psychodynamic and attachment perspectives. In J. Becker & A. Kleinman (Eds.), *Psychosocial aspects of depression* (pp. 131–138). Hillsdale, NJ: Erlbaum.

Becker, J. V., Johnson, B. R., & Perkins, A. (2014). Paraphilic disorders. In R. E. Hales, S. C. Yudofsky, & L. W. Robers (Eds.), *The American Psychiatric Publishing textbook of psychiatry* (pp. 895–925.) Arlington, VA: American Psychiatric Publishing.

Becker, J. V., Skinner, L., Abel, G., & Cichon, R. (1986). Level of postassault sexual functioning in rape and incest victims. *Archives of Sexual Behavior, 15*, 37–49.

Becker, M. H., & Maiman, L. A. (1975). Sociobehavioral determinants of compliance with health and medical care recommendations. *Medical Care, 13*, 10–24.

Becker-Blease, K. A., Deater-Deckard, K., Eley, T., Freyd, J. J., Stevenson, J., & Plomin, R. (2004). A genetic analysis of individual differences in dissociative behaviors in childhood and adolescence. *Journal of Child Psychology and Psychiatry and Allied Disciplines, 45*, 522–532.

Beckwith, L., & Parmelee, A. H. (1986). EEG patterns of preterm infants, home environment, and later IQ. *Child Development, 57*(3), 777–789.

Bednar, R. L., & Kaul, T. (1994). Experiential group research. In A. E. Bergin & S. L. Garfield (Eds.), *Handbook of psychotherapy and behavior change* (pp. 631–663). New York: John Wiley & Sons.

Beech, A. R., & Harkins, L. (2012). DSM-IV paraphilia: Descriptions, demographics and treatment interventions. *Aggression and Violent Behavior, 17*(6), 527–539. doi:10.1016/j.avb.2012.07.008

Beesdo, K., Höfler, M., Leibenluft, E., Lieb, R., Bauer, M., & Pfennig, A. (2009). Mood episodes and mood disorders: Patterns of incidence and conversion in the first three decades of life. *Bipolar Disorders, 11*(6), 637–649. doi:10.1111/j.1399-5618.2009.00738.x

Beesdo, K., Knappe, S., & Pine, D. S. (2009). Anxiety and anxiety disorders in children and adolescents: Developmental issues and implications for DSM-V. *Psychiatric Clinics of North America, 32*(3), 483–524.

Begleiter, H., Porjesz, B., Bihari, B., & Kissin, B. (1984). Event-related brain potentials in boys at risk for alcoholism. *Science, 225*(4669), 1493–1496.

Behkelfat, C., Murphy, D., Zohar, J., Hill, J., Grover, G., & Insel, T. (1989). Clomipramine in obsessive-compulsive disorder. *Archives of General Psychiatry, 46*, 23–28.

Beitchman, J. H., Inglis, A., & Schachter, D. (1992). Child psychiatry and early intervention: IV. The externalizing disorders. *Canadian Journal of Psychiatry, 37*, 245–249.

Beji, N. K., Yalçjn, Ö., & Erkan, H. A. (2002). The effect of pelvic floor training on sexual function. *Nursing Standard, 16*(19), 33–36.

Bellack, A. S., & Hersen, M. (Eds.). (1988). *Behavioral assessment: A practical handbook* (3rd ed.). New York: Pergamon Press.

Bellack, A. S., & Mueser, K. (1993). Psychosocial treatment for schizophrenia. *Schizophrenia Bulletin, 19*, 143–163.

Bellack, A. S., Hersen, M., & Kazdin, A. E. (1990). *International handbook of behavior modification and therapy* (2nd ed.). New York: Plenum Press.

Belsky, J. K. (1990). *The psychology of aging: Theory, research and interventions* (2nd ed.). Pacific Grove, CA: Brooks/Cole.

Benbow, S. (1989). The role of electroconvulsive therapy in the treatment of depressive illness in old age. *British Journal of Psychiatry, 155*, 147–152.

Benight, C. C., & Bandura, A. (2004). Social cognitive theory of posttraumatic recovery: The role of perceived self-efficacy. *Behaviour Research and Therapy, 42*, 1129–1148.

Ben-Itzhak, S., Bluvstein, I., Schreiber, S., Aharonov-Zaig, I., Maor, M., Lipnik, R., & Bloch, M. (2012). The effectiveness of brief versus intermediate duration psychodynamic psychotherapy in the treatment of adjustment disorder. *Journal of Contemporary Psychotherapy, 42*, 249–256. doi:10.1007/s10879-012-9208-6

Benjamin, L. S. (1993). *Interpersonal diagnosis and treatment of personality disorders.* New York: Guilford Press.

Benjamin, L. T. (2007). *A brief history of modern psychology.* Oxford, UK: Blackwell.

Bennett, C. C. (1965). Community psychology: Impressions of the Boston conference on the education of psychologists for community mental health. *American Psychologist, 20*, 832–835.

Bennett, J. M., Rodrigues, I. M., & Klein, L. C. (2013). Effects of caffeine and stress on biomarkers of cardiovascular disease in healthy men and women with a family history of hypertension. *Stress and Health: Journal of the International Society for the Investigation of Stress, 29*(5), 401–409. doi:10.1002/smi.2486

Bennett, L. A., & Wolin, S. J. (1990). Family culture and alcoholism transmission. In R. L. Collins, K. E. Leonard, & J. S. Searles (Eds.), *Alcohol and the family: Research and clinical perspectives* (pp. 194–219). New York: Guilford Press.

Ben-Porath, Y. S. (2012). *Interpreting the MMPI-2-RF.* Minneapolis, MN: University of Minnesota Press.

Ben-Porath, Y. S., Butcher, J. N., & Graham, J. R. (1991). Contribution of the MMPI-2 scales to the differential diagnosis of schizophrenia and major depression. *Psychological Assessment: A Journal of Consulting and Clinical Psychology, 3*, 634–640.

Ben-Porath, Y. S., & Tellegen, A. (2008/2011). *MMPI-2-RF (Minnesota Multiphasic Personality Inventory-2-Restructured Form): Manual for administration, scoring, and interpretation.* Minneapolis, MN: University of Minnesota Press.

Ben-Porath, Y. S., & Waller, N. G. (1992). "Normal" personality inventories in clinical assessment: General requirements and potential for using the NEO Personality Inventory. *Psychological Assessment, 4*, 14–19.

Bentall, R. P. (1990). The illusion of reality: A review and integration of psychological research on hallucinations. *Psychological Bulletin, 107*, 82–95.

Bentall, R. P., & Thompson, M. (1990). Emotional Stroop performance and the manic defence. *British Journal of Clinical Psychology, 29*(2), 235–237. doi:10.1111/j.2044-8260.1990.tb00877.x

Bentley, K. H., Gallagher, M. W., Boswell, J. F., Gorman, J. M., Shear, M., Woods, S. W., & Barlow, D. H. (2013). The interactive contributions of perceived control and anxiety sensitivity in panic disorder: A triple vulnerabilities perspective. *Journal of Psychopathology and Behavioral Assessment, 35*(1), 57–64. doi:10.1007/s10862-012-9311-8

Benton, M. K., & Schroeder, H. E. (1990). Social skills training with schizophrenics: A meta-analytic evaluation. *Journal of Consulting and Clinical Psychology, 58*, 741–747.

Berenbaum, H., & Oltmanns, T. F. (1992). Emotional experience and expression in schizophrenia and depression. *Journal of Abnormal Psychology, 101*, 37–44.

Berendt, J. (1994). *Midnight in the garden of good and evil.* New York: Random House.

Berg, L. (1988). The aging brain. In R. Strong, W. G. Wood, & W. J. Burke (Eds.), *Aging: Vol. 33. Central nervous system disorders of aging: Clinical interventions and research* (pp. 1–16). New York: Raven Press.

Berger, A., Edelsberg, J., Bollu, V., Alvir, J. J., Dugar, A., Joshi, A. V., & Oster, G. (2011). Healthcare utilization and costs in patients beginning pharmacotherapy for generalized anxiety disorder: A retrospective cohort study. *BMC Psychiatry, 11*, 193. doi:10.1186/1471-244X-11-193

Bergeron, S., Rosen, N. O., & Morin, M. (2011). Genital pain in women: Beyond interference with intercourse. *Pain, 152*(6), 1223–1225.

Bergin, A. E. (1971). The evaluation of therapeutic outcomes. In A. E. Bergin & S. L. Garfield (Eds.), *Handbook of psychotherapy and behavior change: An empirical analysis* (pp. 217–270). New York: John Wiley & Sons.

Bergin, A. E., & Lambert, M. J. (1978). The evaluation of therapeutic outcomes. In S. L. Garfield & A. E. Bergin (Eds.), *Handbook of psychotherapy and behavior change: An empirical analysis* (2nd ed., pp. 139–190). New York: John Wiley & Sons.

Bergink, V., Gibney, S. M., & Drexhage, H. A. (2014). Autoimmunity, inflammation, and psychosis: A search for peripheral markers. *Biological Psychiatry, 75*, 324–331. doi: 10.1016/j.biopsych.2013.09.037

Berglund, N., Vahlne, J., & Edman, Å. (2003). Family intervention in schizophrenia: Impact on family burden and attitude. *Social Psychiatry & Psychiatric Epidemiology, 38*, 116–121.

Bergmark, A. (2008). Interpretation of the outcome of the combine study: A response to the commentaries. *Addiction, 103*(5), 710.

Berk, L. E. (1991). *Child development* (2nd ed.). Boston: Allyn & Bacon.

Berkman, L. F. (1995). The role of social relations in health promotion. *Psychosomatic Medicine, 57*, 245–254.

Berlim, M. T., Neufeld, N. H., & Van den Eynde, F. (2013). Repetitive transcranial magnetic stimulation (rTMS) for obsessive-compulsive disorder (OCD): An exploratory meta-analysis of randomized and sham-controlled trials. *Journal of Psychiatric Research, 47*(8), 999–1006. doi:10.1016/j.jpsychires.2013.03.022

Berlim, M. T., Van den Eynde, F., & Daskalakis, Z. J. (2013). Efficacy and acceptability of high frequency repetitive transcranial magnetic stimulation (rTMS) versus electroconvulsive therapy (ECT) for major depression: A systematic review and meta-analysis of randomized trials. *Depression and Anxiety, 30*(7), 614–623. doi:10.1002/da.22060

Berman, J. S., & Norton, N. C. (1985). Does professional training make a therapist more effective? *Psychological Bulletin, 98*, 401–406.

Berman, K., & Meyer-Lindenberg, A. (2004). Functional brain imaging studies in schizophrenia, In D. S. Charney & E. J. Nestler (Eds.), *Neurobiology of mental illness* (2nd ed.), pp. 311–323. New York: Oxford University Press.

Berman, L., Berman, J., Felder, S., Pollets, D., Chhabra, S., Miles, M., & Powell, J. A. (2003). Seeking help for sexual function complaints: What gynecologists need to know about the female patient's experience. *Fertility and Sterility, 79*(3), 572–576.

Berney, T., Kolvin, I., Bhate, S. R., Garside, R. F., Jeans, J., Kay, B., & Scarth, L. (1981). School phobia: A therapeutic trial with clomipramine and short-term outcome. *British Journal of Psychiatry, 138*, 110–118.

Berninger, V. W. (1994). *Reading and writing acquisition: A developmental neuropsychological perspective.* Dubuque, IA: Wm. C. Brown Communications.

Bernstein, D. A. (2007). Promoting critical thinking and active learning in psychology courses. Keynote presentation given at the Mountain States Conference on the Teaching of Psychology. Durango, CO (October 6–7).

Bernstein, D. A., & Borkovec, T. D. (1973). *Progressive relaxation training.* Champaign, IL: Research Press.

Bernstein, D. P., Useda, D., & Siever, L. J. (1993). Paranoid personality disorder: Review of the literature and recommendations for DSM-IV. *Journal of Personality Disorders, 7*, 53–62.

Bernstein, G. A., & Borchardt, C. M. (1991). Anxiety disorders of childhood and adolescence: A critical review. *Journal of the American Academy of Child and Adolescent Psychiatry, 30*(4), 519–532.

Bernstein, G. A., Garfinkel, B. D., & Borchardt, C. M. (1990). Comparative studies of pharmacotherapy for school refusal. *Journal of the American Academy of Child and Adolescent Psychiatry, 29*(5), 773–781.

Berrendero, F., Robledo, P., Trigo, J. M., Martín-García, E., & Maldonado, R. (2010). Neurobiological mechanisms involved in nicotine dependence and reward: Participation of the endogenous opioid system. *Neuroscience and Biobehavioral Reviews, 35*(2), 220–231. doi:10.1016/j.neubiorev.2010.02.006

Berrios, D. C., Heart, N., & Perkins, L. L. (1992). HIV antibody testing in young, urban adults. *Archives of Internal Medicine, 152*, 397–402.

Berrios, G. E. (1994). Dementia and aging since the nineteenth century. In G. A. Huppert, C. Brayne, & D. W. O'Connor (Eds.), *Dementia and normal aging* (pp. 15–40). Cambridge: Cambridge University Press.

Berrios, G. E., & Freeman, H. (1991). *Alzheimer and the dementias.* London: Royal Society of Medicine.

Berry, C. A., Shaywitz, S. E., & Shaywitz, B. A. (1985). Girls with attention deficit disorder: A silent minority? A report on behavioral and cognitive characteristics. *Pediatrics, 76*, 801–809.

Berry, D. S., & Pennebaker, J. W. (1993). Nonverbal and verbal emotional expression and health. *Psychotherapy and Psychosomatics, 59*, 11–19. doi:10.1159/000288640

Bersoff, D. N. (2014). Protecting victims of violent patients while protecting confidentiality. *American Psychologist, 69*(5), 461–467. doi:10.1037/a0037198

Bertha, E. A., & Balázs, J. (2013). Subthreshold depression in adolescence: A systematic review. *European Child & Adolescent Psychiatry, 22*(10), 589–603. doi:10.1007/s00787-013-0411-0

Bertolote, J., Fleischmann, A., De Leo, D., & Wasserman, D. (2004). Psychiatric diagnoses and suicide: Revisiting the evidence. *Crisis: The Journal of Crisis Intervention and Suicide Prevention, 25*(4), 147–155. doi:10.1027/0227-5910.25.4.147

Bertschy, G. (1995). Methadone maintenance treatment: An update. *European Archives of Psychiatry and Clinical Neuroscience, 245*(2), 114–124.

Bespalov, A. Y., Zvartau, E. E., & Beardsley, P. M. (2001). Opioid–NMDA receptor interactions may clarify conditioned (associative) components of opioid analgesic tolerance. *Neurosciences and Biobehavioral Review, 25*, 343–353.

Beutler, L. E., & Crago, M. (Eds.) (1991). *Psychotherapy research: An international review of programmatic studies.* Washington, DC: American Psychological Association.

Beutler, L. E., Machado, P. P. P., & Neufeldt, S. A. (1994). Therapist variables. In A. E. Bergin, & S. L. Garfield (Eds.), *Handbook of psychotherapy and behavior change* (pp. 229–269). New York: John Wiley & Sons.

Beyreuther, K., & Masters, C. L. (1991). Amyloid precursor protein (APP) and beta-amyloid-4 amyloid in the etiology of Alzheimer's disease: Precursor-product relationships in the derangement of neuronal function. *Brain Pathology, 1*, 241–252.

Bhattacharya, A., Khess, C. J., Munda, S., Bakhla, A., Praharaj, S., & Kumar, M. (2011). Sex difference in symptomatology of manic episode. *Comprehensive Psychiatry, 52*(3), 288–292. doi:10.1016/j.comppsych.2010.06.010

Bhugra, D., Popelyuk, D., & McMullen, I. (2010). Paraphilias across cultures: Contexts and controversies. *Journal of Sex Research, 47*(2–3), 242–256. doi:10.1080/00224491003699833

Bieber, I., Dain, H. J., Dince, P. R., Orellich, M. G., Grand, H. C., Gundlach, R. H., Kremer, M. W., Rifkin, A. H., Wilbur, C. B., & Bieber, T. B. (1962). *Homosexuality: A psychoanalytic study.* New York: Random House.

Biederman, J., Milberger, S., Farone, S.V., Kiely, K., Guite, J., Mick, E., Ablon, J. S., Warburton, R., Reed, E. & Davis, S. G. (1995). Impact of adversity on functioning and comorbidity in children with attention-deficit hyperactivity disorder. *Journal of American Academy of Child and Adolescent Psychiatry, 34*, 1498–1502.

Biederman, J., Rosenbaum, J. F., Hirshfeld, D. R., Faraone, S. V., Bolduc, E. A., Gersten, M., Meminger, S. R., Kagan, J., Snidman, N., & Reznick, J. S. (1990). Psychiatric correlates of behavioral inhibition in young children of parents with and without psychiatric disorders. *Archives of General Psychiatry, 47*(1), 21–26.

Bigler, E. D. (2008). Neuropsychology and clinical neuroscience of persistent post-concussive syndrome. *Journal of the International Neuropsychological Society, 14*(1), 1–22. doi:10.1017/S135561770808017X

Biklen, D. (1990). Communication unbound: Autism and praxis. *Harvard Educational Review, 60*(3), 291–314.

Biklen, D., Morton, M. W., Gold, D., Berrigan, C., & Swaminathan, S. (1992). Facilitated communication: Implications for individuals with autism. *Topics in Language Disorders, 12*(4), 1–28.

Biklen, D., & Schubert, A. (1991). New words: The communication of students with autism. *Remedial and Special Education, 12*(6), 46–57.

Billings, A. G., & Moos, R. H. (1985). Children of parents with unipolar depression: A controlled 1-year follow-up. *Journal of Abnormal Child Psychology, 14*, 149.

Binder, R. L., & McNiel, D. E. (1996). Application of the *Tarasoff* ruling and its effect on the victim and the therapeutic relationship. *Psychiatric Services, 47*(11), 1212–1215.

Binks, E., & Ferguson, N. (2013). Religion, trauma and non-pathological dissociation in Northern Ireland. *Mental Health, Religion & Culture, 16*(2), 200–209.

Birmaher, B., Axelson, D., Goldstein, B., Strober, M., Gill, M. K., Hunt, J., . . . Keller, M. (2009). Four-year longitudinal course of children and adolescents with bipolar spectrum disorders: The course and outcome of bipolar youth (COBY) study. *American Journal of Psychiatry, 166*, 795–804.

Birmaher, B., Axelson, D., Strober, M., Gill, M. K., Valeri, S., Chiappetta, L., . . . Keller, M. (2006). Clinical course of children and adolescents with bipolar spectrum disorders. *Archives of General Psychiatry, 63*, 175–183.

Bittner, E. (1967). Police discretion in emergency apprehension of mentally ill persons. *Social Problems, 14*, 278–292.

Blacher, R. S. (1972). The hidden psychosis of open-heart surgery. *Journal of the American Medical Association, 222*, 305–308.

Black, D., Wesner, R., Bowers, W., & Gabel, J. (1993). A comparison of fluvoxamine, cognitive therapy, and placebo in the treatment of panic disorder. *Archives of General Psychiatry, 50*, 44–50.

Black, D. W. (2013). *Bad boys, bad men: Confronting antisocial personality disorder (sociopathy).* New York: Oxford University Press.

Black, D. W., & Blum, N. S. (2014). Antisocial personality disorder and other antisocial behavior. In J. M. Oldham, A. E. Skodol, & D. S. Bender (Eds.), *The American Psychiatric Publishing textbook of personality disorders* (pp. 429–453). Arlington, VA: American Psychiatric Association.

Black, D. W., Noyes, R., Goldstein, R., & Blum, N., (1992). A family study of obsessive-compulsive disorder. *Archives of General Psychiatry, 49*, 362–368.

Black, D. W., & Winokur, G. (1990). Suicide and psychiatric diagnosis. In S. J. Blumenthal & D. J. Kupfer (Eds.), *Suicide over the life cycle: Risk factors, assessment, and treatment of suicidal patients* (pp. 135–154). Washington, DC: American Psychiatric Press.

Black, F. W. (1973). Reversal and rotation errors by normal and retarded readers. *Perceptual and Motor Skills, 36*, 895–898.

Blackburn, H., Luepker, R. V., Kline, F. G., Bracht, N., Car-law, R., Jacobs, D., Mittelmark, M., Stauffer, L., & Taylor H. L. (1984). The Minnesota Heart Health Program: A research and demonstration project in cardiovascular disease prevention.

In J. D. Matarazzo (Ed.), *Behavioral health: A handbook of health enhancement and disease prevention* (pp. 1171–1178). New York: John Wiley & Sons.

Blackwell, B. (1973). Psychotropic drugs in use today. *Journal of the American Medical Association, 225,* 1637–1641.

Blader, J. C. (2011). Acute inpatient care for psychiatric disorders in the United States, 1996 through 2007. *Archives of General Psychiatry, 68*(12), 1276–1283. doi:10.1001/archgenpsychiatry.2011.84

Blair, K., Shaywitz, J., Smith, B. W., Rhodes, R., Geraci, M., Jones, M., . . . Pine, D. S. (2008). Response to emotional expressions in generalized social phobia and generalized anxiety disorder: Evidence for separate disorders. *The American Journal of Psychiatry, 165*(9), 1193–1202. doi:10.1176/appi.ajp.2008.07071060

Blair-West, G. W., & Mellsop, G. W. (2001). Major depression: Does a gender-based down-rating of suicide risk challenge its diagnostic validity? *Australian and New Zealand Journal of Psychiatry, 35*(3), 322–28. doi:10.1046/j.1440-1614.2001.00895.x

Blanchard, E. B. (1992). Psychological treatment of benign headache disorders. *Journal of Consulting and Clinical Psychology, 60,* 537–551.

Blanchard, E. B. (1994). Behavioral medicine and health psychology. In A. E. Bergin & S. L. Garfield (Eds.), *Handbook of psychotherapy and behavior change* (pp. 701–733). New York: John Wiley & Sons.

Blanchard, E. B., Andrasik, F., Ahles, T. A., Teders, S. J., & O'Keefe, D. (1980). Migraine and tension headache: A meta-analytic review. *Behavior Therapy, 11,* 613–631.

Blanchard, E. B., Hickling, E. J., Mitnick, N., Taylor, A. E., Loos, W. R., & Buckley, T. C. (1995). The impact of severity of physical injury and perception of life threat in the development of post-traumatic stress disorder in motor vehicle accident victims. *Behaviour Research and Therapy, 33,* 529–534. doi:10.1016/0005-7967(94)00079-Y

Blanchard, E. B., Schwarz, S. P., & Radnitz. CL. (1987). Psychological assessment and treatment of irritable bowel syndrome. *Behavior Modification, 11,* 348–372.

Blanchard, R., & Sheridan, R M. (1992). Sibship size, sibling sex ratio, birth order, and parental age in homosexual and nonhomosexual gender dysphorics. *Journal of Nervous and Mental Disease, 180,* 40–47.

Blanchard, R., Zucker, K. J., Bradley, S. J., & Hume, C. S. (1995). Birth order and sibling sex ratio in homosexual male adolescents and probably prehomosexual feminine boys. *Developmental Psychology, 31,* 22–30.

Blanchard, S. (1726). *The physical dictionary wherein the terms of anatomy, the names and causes of diseases, chirurgical instruments, and their use, are accurately described.* London: John & Benjamin Sprint.

Blanco, C., Okuda, M., Markowitz, J. C., Liu, S., Grant, B. F., & Hasin, D. S. (2010). The epidemiology of chronic major depressive disorder and dysthymic disorder: Results from the National Epidemiologic Survey on Alcohol and Related Conditions. *Journal of Clinical Psychiatry, 71*(12), 1645–1656. doi:10.4088/JCP.09m05663gry

Blatt, S. J. (1982). Depression and self criticism: Psychological dimensions of depression. *Journal of Clinical and Consulting Psychology, SO,* 113–124.

Blatt, S. J. (1995). The destructiveness of perfectionism. *American Psychologist, 5S0O,* 1003–1020.

Blatt, S. J., & Zuroff, D. C. (1992). Interpersonal relatedness and self-definition: Two prototypes for depression. *Clinical Psychology Review, 12,* 527–550.

Blatt, S. J., Quinlan, D. M., Pilkonis, P. A., & Shea, M. T. (1995). Impact of perfectionism and need for approval on the brief treatment of depression: The National Institute of Mental Health Depression Collaborative Research Program. *Journal of Clinical and Consulting Psychology, 63,* 125–132.

Blazer, D. G., Hughes, D., George, L. K., Swartz, M., & Boyer, R. (1991). Generalized anxiety disorder. In L. N. Robins & D. A. Regier (Eds.), *Psychiatric disorders in America: The epidemiologic catchment area study.* New York: Maxwell MacMillan International.

Bledsoe, K. L. (2003, March). Effectiveness of drug prevention programs designed for adolescents of color: A meta-analysis. *Dissertation Abstracts International, 63,* 4414.

Bleuler, E. (1911). *Dementia praecox or the group of schizophrenias* (J. Zinkin, Trans. 1950). New York: International Universities Press.

Bliss, E. L. (1986). *Multiple personality, allied disorders and hypnosis.* New York: Oxford University Press.

Bloch, M. H., Landeros-Weisenberger, A., Dombrowski, P., Kelmendi, B., Wegar, R., Nudel, J., . . . Coric, V. (2007). Systematic review: Pharmacological and behavioral treatment for trichotillomania. *Biological Psychiatry, 62,* 839–846. doi:10.1016/j.biopsych.2007.05.019

Bloch, M. H., Landeros-Weisenberger, A., Rosario, M. C., Pittenger, C., & Leckman, J. F. (2008). Meta-analysis of the symptom structure of obsessive-compulsive disorder. *The American Journal of Psychiatry, 165*(12), 1532–1542. doi:10.1176/appi.ajp.2008.08020320

Bloch, M. H., & Pittenger, C. (2010). The genetics of obsessive-compulsive disorder. *Current Psychiatry Reviews, 6*(2), 91–103. doi:10.2174/157340010791196439

Blum, K., Noble, E. P., Sheridan, P. J., Montgomery, A., Ritchie, T., Jagadeeswaran, P., Nogami, H., Briggs, A. H., & Cohn, J. B. (1990). Allelic association of human dopamine D2 receptor gene in alcoholism. *Journal of the American Medical Association, 263*(15), 2055–2060.

Blume, A. W. (2012). Seeking the middle way: G. Alan Marlatt and harm reduction. *Addiction Research & Theory, 20*(3), 218–226. doi:10.3109/16066359.2012.657281

Blume, E. S. (1990). *Secret survivors: Uncovering incest and its aftereffects in women.* New York: Ballantine.

Blumenthal, S. J. (1994). Introductory remarks. In S. J. Blumenthal, K. Matthews, & S. M. Weiss (Eds.), *New research frontiers in behavioral medicine* (pp. 9–15). Washington, DC: National Institute of Mental Health.

Blumenthal, S. J., Matthews, K., & Weiss, S. W. (Eds.). (1994). *New research frontiers in behavioral medicine.* Washington, DC: National Institute of Mental Health.

Blumer, D. (2002). The illness of Vincent van Gogh. *The American Journal of Psychiatry, 159*(4), 519–526. doi:10.1176/appi.ajp.159.4.519

Boals, A., Steward, J. M., & Schuettler, D. (2010). Advancing our understanding of posttraumatic growth by considering event centrality. *Journal of Loss & Trauma, 15,* 518–533. doi:10.1080/15325024.2010.519271

Bobes, J., Arango, C., Garcia-Garcia, M., & Rejas, J. (2010). Prevalence of negative symptoms in outpatients with schizophrenia spectrum disorders treated with antipsychotics in routine clinical practice: Findings from the CLAMORS study. *Journal of Clinical Psychiatry, 71*(3), 280–286. doi:10.4088/JCP.08m04250yel

Boddy, J. (1988). Spirits and selves in northern Sudan: The cultural therapeutics of possession and trance. *American Ethnologist, 15,* 4–27.

Bodkin, J. A., Zornberg, G. L., Lukas, S. E., & Cole, J. O. (1995). Buprenorphine treatment of refractory depression. *Journal of Clinical Psychopharmacology, 15*(1), 49–57.

Bodmer, W., & McKie, R. (1994). *The book of man: The human genome project and the quest to discover our genetic heritage.* New York: Scribner.

Boehnert, C. (1989). Characteristics of successful and unsuccessful insanity pleas. *Law and Human Behavior, 13,* 31-40.

Boettcher, J., Carlbring, P., Renneberg, B., & Berger, T. (2013). Internet-based interventions for social anxiety disorder—An overview. *Verhaltenstherapie, 23*(3), 160–168. doi:10.1159/000354747

Boffetta, P., & Garfinkel, L. (1990). Alcohol drinking and mortality among men enrolled in an American Cancer Society prospective study. *Epidemiology, 1*(5), 342–348.

Bohne, A., Keuthen, N., & Wilhelm, S. (2005). Pathologic hair pulling, skin picking, and nail biting. *Annals of Clinical Psychiatry, 17,* 227–232. doi:10.1080/10401230500295354

Bohne, A., Keuthen, N. J., Wilhelm, S., Deckersback, T., & Jenike, M. A. (2002). Prevalence of symptoms of body dysmorphic disorder and its correlates: A cross-cultural comparison. *Psychosomatics: Journal of Consultation and Liaison Psychiatry, 43*(6), 486–490. doi:10.1176/appi.psy.43.6.486

Bohne, A., Wilhelm, S., Keuthen, N. J., Florin, I., Baer, L., & Jenike, M. A. (2002). Prevalence of body dysmorphic disorder in a German college student sample. *Psychiatry Research, 109*(1), 101–104.

Bola, J. R. (2006). Medication-free research in early episode schizophrenia: Evidence of long-term harm? *Schizophrenia Bulletin, 32*(1): 288–296.

Bollini, A. M., & Walker, E. F. (2007). Schizotypal personality disorder. In W. O'Donohue, K. A. Fowler, & S. O. Lilienfeld (Eds.), *Personality disorders: Toward the DSM-V* (pp. 81–108). Los Angeles: Sage Publications.

Bombardier, C. H., Fann, J. R., Temkin, N. R., Esselman, P. C., Barber, J., & Dikmen, S. S. (2010). Rates of major depressive disorder and clinical outcomes following traumatic brain injury. *Journal of the American Medical Association, 303*(19), 1938–1945. doi: 10.1001/jama.2010.599

Bonanno, G. A. (2008). Loss, trauma, and human resilience: Have we underestimated the human capacity to thrive after extremely aversive events? *Psychological Trauma: Theory, Research, Practice, and Policy, S*(1), 101–113. doi:10.1037/1942-9681.S.1.101

Bonanno, G., Westfall, M., & Mancini, A. (2011). Resilience to loss and potential trauma. *Clinical Psychology, 7,* 511–535.

Bonanno, G. A., & Diminich, E. D. (2013). Annual research review: Positive adjustment to adversity—Trajectories of minimal-impact resilience and emergent resilience. *Journal of Child Psychology and Psychiatry, 54,* 378–401. doi:10.1111/jcpp.12021

Bond, G. R., Clark, R. E., & Drake, R. E. (1995, summer). Cost effectiveness of psychiatric rehabilitation. *Psychotherapy & Rehabilitation Research Bulletin,* 26–31.

Bond, G. R., Witheridge, T. F., Dincin, J., Wasmer, D., Webb, J., & Graff-Kaser, R. (1990). Assertive community treatment for frequent users of psychiatric hospitals in a large city: A controlled study. *American Journal of Community Psychology, 18,* 865–891.

Boney-McCoy, S., & Finkelhor, D. (1995). Psychosocial sequelae of violent victimization in a national youth sample. *Journal of Consulting and Clinical Psychology, 63,* 726–736.

Bongar, B. (1991). *The suicidal patient: Clinical and legal standards of care.* Washington, DC: American Psychological Association.

Boon, S., & Draijer, N. (1993). Multiple personality disorder in the Netherlands: A clinical investigation of 71 patients. *American Journal of Psychiatry, 150*(3), 489–491.

Boone, K. B., Victor, T. L., Wen, J., Razani, J., & Pontón, M. (2007). The association between neuropsychological scores and ethnicity, language, and acculturation variables in a large patient population. *Archives of Clinical Neuropsychology, 22*(3), 355–365. doi:10.1016/j.acn.2007.01.010

Boorsma, M., Joling, K. J., Frijters, D. H., Ribbe, M. E., Nijpels, G., & van Hout, H. P. (2012). The prevalence, incidence and risk factors for delirium in Dutch nursing homes and residential care homes. *International Journal of Geriatric Psychiatry 27,* 709–715.

Booth-Kewley, S., & Friedman, H. S. (1987). Psychological predictors of heart disease: A quantitative review. *Psychological Bulletin, 101,* 343–362.

Bootzin, R. R. (2013). Implementing stimulus control therapy for insomnia. In G. P. Koocher, J. C. Norcross, B. A. Greene (Eds.), *Psychologists' desk reference* (3rd ed.) (pp. 263–265). New York: Oxford University Press.

Borduin, C. M., Mann, B. J., Cone, L. T., Henggeler, S. W., Fucci, B. R., Blaske, D. M., & Williams, R. A. (1995). Multisystemic treatment of serious juvenile offenders: Long-term prevention of criminality and violence. *Journal of Consulting and Clinical Psychology, 63,* 569–578.

Boren, J., Leventhal, A., & Pigott, H. (2009). Just how effective are antidepressant medications? Results of a major new study. *Journal of Contemporary Psychotherapy, 39,* 93–100.

Borenstein, J., Dean, B., Leifke, E., Korner, P., & Yonkers, K. (2007). Differences in symptom scores and health outcomes in premenstrual syndrome. *Journal of Women's Health, 16*(8), 1139–1144.

Borkman, T., Kaskutas, L. A., & Owen, P. (2007). Contrasting and converging philosophies of three models of alcohol/other drugs treatment: Minnesota model, social model, and addiction therapeutic communities. *Alcoholism Treatment Quarterly, 25*(3), 21–38. doi:10.1300/J020v25n03_03

Borkovec, T. D., Abel, J. L., & Newman, H. (1995). Effects of psychotherapy on comorbid conditions in generalized anxiety disorder. *Journal of Consulting and Clinical Psychology, 63,* 479–483.

Borkovec, T. D., Alcaine, O. M., & Behar, E. (2004). Avoidance theory of worry and generalized anxiety disorder. In R. G. Heimberg, C. L. Turk, & D.S. Mennin (Eds.), *Generalized anxiety disorder: Advances in research and practice* (pp. 77–108). New York: Guilford Press.

Borkovec, T. D., & Costello, E. (1993). Efficiency of applied relaxation and cognitive behavioral theory in the treatment of generalized anxiety disorders. *Journal of Consulting and Clinical Psychology, 61,* 611–619.

Borkovec, T. D., Hopkins, M., Lyonfields, J., Lytle, R., Posa, S., Roemer, L., & Shadick, R. (1991, November). *Efficacy of nondirective therapy, applied relaxation, and combined cognitive behavioral therapy for generalized anxiety disorder.* Paper presented at the 25th annual convention of the Association for the Advancement of Behavior Therapy, New York.

Borkovec, T. D., & Hu, S. (1990). The effect of worry on cardiovascular response to phobic imagery. *Behaviour Research and Therapy, 28,* 69–73.

Borkovec, T. D., & Mathews, A. (1988). Treatment of non-phobic anxiety disorders: A comparison of nondirective, cognitive, and coping desensitization therapy. *Journal of Consulting and Clinical Psychology, 56,* 877–884.

Borkovec, T. D., Mathews, A. M., Chambers, A., Ebrahimi, S., Lytle, R., & Nelson, R. (1987). The effects of relaxation training with cognitive or nondirective therapy and the role of relaxation-induced anxiety in the treatment of generalized anxiety. *Journal of Consulting and Clinical Psychology, 55,* 883–888.

Borkovec, T. D., & Roemer, L. (1995). Perceived functions of worry among generalized anxiety disorder subjects: Distraction from more emotional topics? *Journal of Behavior Therapy and Experimental Psychiatry, 26,* 25–30. doi: 10.1016/0005-7916(94)00064-S

Bornstein, M. H., & Sigman, M. D. (1986). Continuity in mental development from infancy. *Child Development, 57*(2), 251–274.

Bornstein, M. H., Hahn, C., Bell, C., Haynes, O. M., Slater, A., Golding, J., . . . ALSPAC Study Team. (2006). Stability in cognition across early childhood: A developmental cascade. *Psychological Science, 17,* 151–158.

Bornstein, R. F., & Gold, S. H. (2008). Comorbidity of personality disorders and somatization disorder: A meta-analytic review. *Journal of Psychopathology and Behavioral Assessment, 30*(2), 154–161. doi:10.1007/s10862-007-9052-2

Boros, S., & Brubaker, L. C. (1992). Munchausen syndrome by proxy: Case accounts. *Federal Bureau of Investigation Law Enforcement Bulletin, 61*(6), 19.

Borum, R. (1996). Improving the clinical practice of violence risk assessment: Technology, guidelines, and training. *American Psychologist, 51,* 945–956.

Bosanac, P., Patton, G. C., & Castle, D. J. (2010). Early intervention in psychotic disorders: Faith before facts? *Psychological Medicine, 40*(3), 353–358. doi:10.1017/S0033291709990341

Bossini, L., Fagiolini, A., Valdagno, M., Polizzotto, N. R., & Castrogiovanni, P. (2007). Sexual disorders in subjects treated for mood and anxiety diseases. *Journal of Clinical Psychopharmacology, 27*(3), 310–312.

Botella, C., Villa, H. H., Baños, R. R., Perpiñá, C. C., & García-Palacios, A. A. (1999). The treatment of claustrophobia with virtual reality: Changes in other phobic behaviors not specifically treated. *Cyberpsychology & Behavior, 2*(2), 135–141. doi:10.1089/cpb.1999.2.135

Bottino, C. M. C., Carvalho, I. A. M., Alvarez, A. M. M. A., Avila, R., Zukauskas, P. R., Bustamante, S. E. Z., . . . Camargo, C. H. P. (2005). Cognitive rehabilitation combined with drug treatment in Alzheimer's disease patients: A pilot study. *Clinical Rehabilitation, 19*(8), 861–869.

Bouaboula, M., Rinaldi, M., Carayon, P., Carillon, C., Delpech, B., Shire, D., Le-Fur, G., & Casellas, P. (1993). Cannabinoid-receptor expression in human leukocytes. *European Journal of Biochemistry, 214*(1), 173–180.

Bouchard, T. J. (1984). Twins reared together and apart: What they tell us about human diversity. In S. W. Fox (Ed.), *Individuality and determinism.* New York: Plenum.

Bouchery, E. E., Harwood, H. J., Sacks, J. J., Simon, C. J., & Brewer, R. D. (2006). Economic costs of excessive alcohol consumption in the United States, 2006. *American Journal of Preventive Medicine, 41,* 516–524.

Boudin, H. (1972). Contingency contracting as a therapeutic tool in the deceleration of amphetamine use. *Behavior Therapy, 3,* 604–608.

Bouhoutsos, J. C., Holyrod, J., Lerman, H., Forer, B., & Greenberg, M. (1983). Sexual intimacies between therapists and patients. *Professional Psychology: Research and Practice, 14,* 185–196.

Bourdet, C., Brochard, R., Rouillon, F., & Drake, C. (2003). Auditory temporal processing in schizophrenia: High level rather than low level deficits? *Cognitive Neuropsychiatry, 8,* 89–106.

Bourdon, K. H., Boyd, J. H., Rae, D. S., Burns, B. J., Thompson, J. W., & Locke, B. Z. (1988). Gender differences in phobias: Results of the ECH community survey. *Journal of Anxiety Disorders, 2,* 227–241.

Bourgeois, M., Duhamel, P., & Verdoux, H. (1992). Delusional parasitosis: Folie a deux and attempted murder of a family doctor. *British Journal of Psychiatry, 161,* 709–711.

Bourne, E. J. (2005). *The anxiety & phobia workbook* (4th ed.). Oakland, CA: New Harbinger Publications.

Bourne, R. S., Tahir, T. A., Borthwick, M., & Sampson, E. L. (2008). Drug treatment of delirium: Past, present and future. *Journal of Psychosomatic Research, 65,* 273–282.

Bower, D. L., & Pettit, W. G. (2001). The Albuquerque Police Department's Crisis Intervention Team: A report card. *FBI Law Enforcement Bulletin, 70,* 1–6.

Bowers, K. S., & Farvolden, P. (1996). Revisiting a century-old Freudian slip—from suggestion disavowed to the truth repressed. *Psychological Bulletin, 119,* 355–380.

Bowers, T. G., & Al-Redha, M. R. (1990). A comparison of outcome with group/marital and standard/individual therapies with alcoholics. *Journal of Studies on Alcohol, 51,* 301–309.

Bowlby, J. (1980). *Attachment and loss. Vol. III: Loss, sadness and depression.* New York: Basic Books.

Bowlby, J. (1988a). *A secure base: Parent-child attachment and healthy human development.* New York: Basic Books.

Bowlby, J. (1988b). Developmental psychiatry comes of age. *American Journal of Psychiatry, 145,* 1–10.

Bowman, E. S., & Nurnberger, J. I. (1993). Genetics of psychiatry diagnosis and treatment. In D. L. Dunner (Ed.), *Current psychiatric therapy* (pp. 46–56). Philadelphia: W. B. Saunders.

Boyce, W. T., Jensen, E. W., Cassel, J. C., Collier, A. M., Smith, A. H., & Ramey, C. T. (1977). Influence of life events and family routines on childhood respiratory tract illness. *Pediatrics, 60,* 609–615.

Braaten, A. J., Parsons, T. D., McCue, R., Sellers, A., & Burns, W. J. (2006). Neurocognitive differential diagnosis of dementing diseases: Alzheimer's dementia, vascular dementia, frontotemporal dementia, and major depressive disorder. *International Journal of Neuroscience, 116*(11), 1271–1293. doi: 10.1080/00207450600920928

Bradbury, M. (2001). Classics revisited: Freud's mourning and melancholia. *Mortality, 6*(2), 212–219. doi:10.1080/13576270120051866

Bradbury, T., & Miller, G. A. (1985). Season of birth in schizophrenia: A review of evidence, methodology, and etiology. *Psychological Bulletin, 98,* 569–594.

Bradbury, T. N., & Fincham, F. D. (1990). Attributions in marriage: Review and critique. *Psychological Bulletin, 107,* 3–33.

Bradford, J. M., & McLean, D. (1984). Sexual offenders, violence and testosterone: A clinical study. *Canadian Journal of Psychiatry, 29,* 335–343.

Bradley, R., Conklin, C. Z., & Westen, D. (2007). Borderline personality disorder. In W. O'Donohue, K. A. Fowler, & S. O. Lilienfeld (Eds.), *Personality disorders: Toward the DSM-V* (pp. 167–201). Los Angeles: Sage Publications.

Brady et al v. Hopper, 570 F. Supp. 1333, 1339 (1983).

Brady, E. U., & Kendall, P. C. (1992). Comorbidity of anxiety and depression in children and adolescents. *Psychological Bulletin, 111(2)*, 244–255.

Brakoulias, V. (2013). Diagnostic subtyping of obsessive-compulsive disorder: Have we got it all wrong? *Australian and New Zealand Journal of Psychiatry, 47*(1), 23–25. doi:10.1177/0004867412455851

Brakoulias, V. (2014). DSM-5 bids farewell to hypochondriasis and welcomes somatic symptom disorder and illness anxiety disorder. *Australian and New Zealand Journal of Psychiatry, 48*(7), 688. doi:10.1177/0004867414525844

Brand, B. L., Classen, C., McNary, S. W., & Zaveri, P. (2009). A review of dissociative disorders treatment studies. *Journal of Nervous and Mental Disease, 197*, 646–654.

Brand, B. L., McNary, S. W., Myrick, A. C., Lowewenstein, R. J., Classen, C. C., Lanius, R. A., Pain, C., & Putnam, F. (2013). A longitudinal, naturalistic study of dissociative disorder patients treated by community clinicians. *Psychological Trauma: Theory, Research, Practice, and Policy, 5*, 301–308.

Brand, B. L., Myrick, A. C., Loewenstein, R. J., Classen, C. C., Lanius, R. A., Pain, C., & Putnam, F. W. (2012). A survey of practices and recommended treatment interventions among expert therapists treating patients with dissociative identity disorder and dissociative disorder not otherwise specified. *Psychological Trauma: Theory, Research, Practice, and Policy, 4*, 490–500.

Bratu, B. (2012, December 14). Connecticut school shooting is second worst in U.S. history. *NBC News.* Retrieved March 14, 2014 from http://usnews.nbcnews.com/_news/2012/12/14/15909827-connecticut-school-shooting-is-second-worst-in-us-history?lite

Braun, S. R., Gregor, B., & Tran, U. S. (2013). Comparing bona fide psychotherapies of depression in adults with two meta-analytical approaches. *Plos ONE, 8*(6), doi:10.1371/journal.pone.0068135

Bravo, I. M., & Roca, C. S. (2013). Assessing somatoform disorders with the Hispanic client. In L. T. Benuto (Ed.), *Guide to psychological assessment with Hispanics* (pp. 293–307). New York: Springer Science + Business Media. doi:10.1007/978-1-4614-4412-1_19

Brayne, C., & Calloway, P. (1988). Normal ageing, impaired cognitive function, and senile dementia of the Alzheimer's type: A continuum? *Lancet, ii*, 1265–1267.

Breggin, P. (1980). Brain disabling therapies. In E. S. Valenstein (Ed.), *The psychosurgery debate: Scientific, legal, and ethical perspectives.* San Francisco: Freeman.

Breggin, P. (1994). *Talking back to Prozac.* New York: Saint Martin's Press.

Breier, A. (1995). Serotonin, schizophrenia and antipsychotic drug action. *Schizophrenia Research, 14(3)*, 187–202.

Breier, A., Buchanan, R., Kirkpatrick, B., Davis, O., Irish, D., Summerfelt, A., & Carpenter, W. (1994). Effects of clozapine on positive and negative symptoms in outpatients with schizophrenia. *American Journal of Psychiatry, 151*, 20–26.

Breland, A. B., Spindle, T., Weaver, M., & Eissenberg, T. (2014). Science and electronic cigarettes: Current data, future needs. *Journal of Addiction Medicine, 8*(4), 223–233. doi:10.1097/ADM.0000000000000049

Bremner, J. P., Southwick, S. M., Darnell, A., & Charney, D. S. (1996). Chronic PTSD in Vietnam combat veterans: Course of illness and substance abuse. *American Journal of Psychiatry, 153*, 369–375.

Brems, C., Thevenin, D. M., & Routh, D. K. (1991). The history of clinical psychology. In C. E. Walker (Ed.), *Clinical psychology: Historical and research foundations* (pp. 3–36). New York: Plenum.

Brennan, P. A., Grekin, E. R., & Mednick, S. (2003). Prenatal and perinatal influences on conduct disorder and serious delinquency. In B. B. Lahey, T. E. Moffitt, & A. Caspi (Eds.), *Causes of conduct disorder and serious delinquency* (pp. 319–344). New York: Guilford Press.

Brensilver, M., & Shoptaw, S. (2013). Pharmacotherapy of cocaine dependence. In P. M. Miller, S. A. Ball, M. E. Bates, A. W. Blume, K. M. Kampman, D. J. Kavanagh, . . . P. De Witte (Eds.), *Comprehensive addictive behaviors and disorders, Vol. 3: Interventions for addiction* (pp. 439–448). San Diego, CA: Elsevier Academic Press. doi:10.1016/B978-0-12-398338-1.00046-4

Brent, D. A., & Silverstein, M. (2013). Shedding light on the long shadow of childhood adversity. *JAMA: Journal of the American Medical Association, 309*(17), 1777–1778. doi:10.1001/jama.2013.4220

Breslau, N., Kessler, R. C., Chilcoat, H. D., Schultz, L. R., Davis, G. C., & Andreski, P. (1998). Trauma and posttraumatic stress disorder in the community: The 1996 Detroit area survey of trauma. *Archives of General Psychiatry, 55*, 626–632.

Bretschneider, J. G., & McCoy, N. L. (1988). Sexual interest and behavior in healthy 80- to 102-year-olds. *Archives of Sexual Behavior, 17*, 109–129.

Brewerton, T. D. (1994). Hyperreligiosity in psychotic disorders. *Journal of Nervous and Mental Disease, 182*, 302–304.

Brewerton, T. D., & Costin, C. (2011). Long-term outcome of residential treatment for anorexia nervosa and bulimia nervosa. *Eating Disorders, 19*(2), 132–144.

Brewin, C. R., Andrews, B., & Valentine, J. D. (2000). Meta-analysis of risk factors for posttraumatic stress disorder in trauma-exposed adults. *Journal of Consulting and Clinical Psychology, 68*, 748–766.

Brick, J. (1990). Learning and motivational factors in alcohol consumption. In W. M. Cox (Ed.), *Why people drink: Parameters of alcohol as a reinforcer.* New York: Gardner Press.

Brickman, A. M., Cabo, R., & Manly, J. J. (2006). Ethical issues in cross-cultural neuropsychology. *Applied Neuropsychology, 13*(2), 91–100. doi: 10.1207/s15324826an1302_4

Bridge, J. A., Iyengar, S., Salary, C. B., Barbe, R., Birmaher, B., Pincus, H., . . . Brent, D. A. (2007). Clinical response and risk for reported suicidal ideation and suicide attempts in pediatric antidepressant treatment: A meta-analysis of randomized controlled trials. *JAMA: Journal of the American Medical Association, 297*(15), 1683–1696. doi:10.1001/jama.297.15.1683

Bridges, K. W., & Goldberg, D. P. (1985). Somatic presentation of DSM-III psychiatric disorders in primary care. *Journal of Psychosomatic Research, 29*, 563–569.

Bridges, P. K., Goktepe, E. O., Maratos, J., Browne, A., Young, L. (1973). A comparative review of patients with obsessional neurosis and depression treated by psychosurgery. *British Journal of Psychiatry, 123*, 663–674.

Briere, J. (1992). Methodological issues in the study of sexual abuse effects. *Journal of Consulting and Clinical Psychology, 60*, 196–203.

Briere, J. (2006). Dissociative symptoms and trauma exposure: Specificity, affect dysregulation and posttraumatic stress. *Journal of Nervous and Mental Disease, 194*, 78–82.

Briere, J., & Malamuth, N. M. (1983). Self-reported likelihood of sexually aggressive behaviors: Attitudinal versus sexual explanation. *Journal of Research in Personality, 17*, 315–323.

Brietzke, E., Kauer Sant'anna, M., Jackowski, A., Grassi-Oliveira, R., Bucker, J., Zugman, A., . . . Bressan, R. A. (2012). Impact of childhood stress on psychopathology. *Revista Brasileira de Psiquiatria, 34*(4), 480–488. doi:10.1016/j.rbp.2012.04.009. PMID 23429820.

Briggs, D. (1991). Preventing ICU psychosis. *Nursing Times, 87*, 30–31.

Briken, P., Hill, A., & Berner, W. (2003). Pharmacotherapy of paraphilias with long-acting agonists of luteinizing hormone-releasing hormone: A systematic review. *Journal of Clinical Psychiatry, 64*(8), 890–897. doi:10.4088/JCP.v64n0806

Brislin, R. (1991). *Understanding culture's influence on behavior.* Fort Worth, Texas: Harcourt, Brace, Jovanovich.

Brna, T. G., & Wilson, C. C. (1990). Psychogenic amnesia. *American Family Physician, 41*, 229–234.

Brockmeyer, T., Holtforth, M. G., Bents, H., Kämmerer, A., Herzog, W., & Friederich, H. (2012). Starvation and emotion regulation in anorexia nervosa. *Comprehensive Psychiatry, 53*(5), 496–501.

Broft, A., Berner, L. A., & Walsh, B. T. (2010). Pharmacotherapy for bulimia nervosa. In C. M. Grilo & J. E. Mitchell (Eds.), *The treatment of eating disorders: A clinical handbook.* New York: Guilford Press.

Bromberg, W. (1959). *The mind of man: A history of psychotherapy and psychoanalysis.* New York: Harper & Row.

Bromet, E., Andrade, L. H., Hwang, I., Sampson, N. A., Alonso, J., . . . Kessler, R. C. (2011). Cross-national epidemiology of *DSM-IV* major depressive episode. *BMC Medicine.* Retrieved on July 28, 2014 from http://www.biomedcentral.com/1741-7015/9/90

Bromet, E. J., Kotov, R., Fochtmann, L. J., Carlson, G. A., Tanenberg-Karant, M., Ruggero, C., & Chang, S. W. (2011). Diagnostic shifts during the decade following first admission for psychosis. *American Journal of Psychiatry, 168*, 1186–1194.

Bromet, E. J., Naz, B., Fochtmann, L. J., Carlson, G. A., & Tanenberg-Karant, M. (2005). Long-term diagnostic stability and outcome in recent first-episode cohort studies of schizophrenia. *Schizophrenia Bulletin, 31*, 639–649.

Brook, C. A., & Schmidt, L. A. (2008). Social anxiety disorder: A review of environmental risk factors. *Neuropsychiatric Disease and Treatment, 4*(1A), 123–143.

Brooker, R. (2011). *Genetics: Analysis and principles.* Columbus, OH: McGraw-Hill.

Brookmeyer, R., Johnson, E., Ziegler-Graham, K., & Arrighi, H. M. (2007). Forecasting the global burden of Alzheimer's disease. *Alzheimer's & Dementia, 3*(3), 186–191. doi: 10.1016/j.jalz.2007.04.381

Brotman, M. A., Schmajuk, M., Rich, B. A., Dickstein, D. P., Guyer, A. E., Costello, E., . . . Leibenluft, E. (2006). Prevalence, clinical correlates, and longitudinal course of severe mood dysregulation in children. *Biological Psychiatry, 60*(9), 991–997. doi:10.1016/j.biopsych.2006.08.042

Broussard, B., McGriff, J. A., Neubert, B. D., D'Orio, B., & Compton, M. T. (2010). Characteristics of patients referred to psychiatric emergency services by Crisis Intervention Team police officers. *Community Mental Health Journal, 46*(6), 579–584. doi:10.1007/s10597-010-9295-3

Brown, A. S., Cohen, P., Harkavy-Friedman, J., Babulas, V., Malaspina, D., Gorman, J. M., & Susser, E. S. (2001). Prenatal rubella, premorbid abnormalities, and adult schizophrenia. *Biological Psychiatry, 49*(6), 473–486. doi:10.1016/S0006-3223(01)01068-X

Brown, C. (2011). Schizophrenia. In C. Brown and V. C. Stoffel (Eds.), *Occupational therapy in mental health: A vision for participation* (pp. 179–191). Philadelphia, PA: F A Davis.

Brown, C. A., & Mehler, P. S. (2013). Medical complications of self-induced vomiting. *Eating Disorders: The Journal of Treatment & Prevention, 21*(4), 287–294. doi: 10.1080/10640266.2013.797317

Brown, E. S., & Lambert, M. T. (1995). Delusional electronic dental implants: Case reports and literature review. *Journal of Nervous and Mental Disease, 183,* 603–604.

Brown, G. L., Ebert, M. H., Goyer, P. F., Jimerson, D. C., Klein, W. J., Bunney, W. E., & Goodwin, F. K. (1982). Aggression, suicide, and serotonin: Relationships to CSF amine metabolites. *American Journal of Psychiatry, 139,* 741–746.

Brown, G. L., & Goodwin, F. K. (1986). Cerebrospinal fluid correlates of suicide attempts and aggression. *Annals of the New York Academy of Science, 487,* 175–188.

Brown, G. L., Goodwin, F. K., & Bunney, W. E. (1982). Human aggression and suicide: Their relationship to neuropsychiatric diagnoses and serotonin metabolism. *Advances in Biochemical Psychopharmacology, 34,* 287–307.

Brown, G. W., Adler, Z., & Bifulco, A. (1988). Life events, difficulties and recovery from chronic depression. *British Journal of Psychiatry, 152,* 487–498.

Brown, G. W., & Birley, J. L. T. (1968). Crises and life changes and the onset of schizophrenia. *Journal of Health and Social Behavior, 9,* 203–214.

Brown, G. W., Birley, J. L. T., & Wing, J. K. (1972). Influence of family life on the course of schizophrenic disorders: A replication. *British Journal of Psychiatry, 121,* 241–258.

Brown, G. W., & Harris, T. (1978). *Social origins of depression: A study of psychiatric disorder in women.* New York: The Free Press.

Brown, H., Pearson, N., Braithwaite, R. E., Brown, W. J., & Biddle, S. H. (2013). Physical activity interventions and depression in children and adolescents: A systematic review and meta-analysis. *Sports Medicine, 43*(3), 195–206. doi:10.1007/s40279-012-0015-8

Brown, J. (1987). A review of meta-analyses conducted on psychotherapy outcome research. *Clinical Psychology Review, 7,* 1–24.

Brown, R. J., & Lewis-Fernández, R. (2011). Culture and conversion disorder: Implications for *DSM-5. Psychiatry: Interpersonal and Biological Processes, 74*(3), 187–206. doi:10.1521/psyc.2011.74.3.187

Brown, S. A., Christiansen, B. A., & Goldman, M. S. (1987). The Alcohol Expectancy Questionnaire: An instrument for the assessment of adolescent and adult alcohol expectancies. *Journal of Studies on Alcohol, 48*(5), 483–491.

Brown, T. A., Antony, M. M., & Barlow, D. H. (1995). Diagnostic comorbidity in panic disorder: Effect on treatment outcome and course of comorbid diagnoses following treatment. *Journal of Consulting and Clinical Psychology, 63,* 408–418.

Brown, T. A., & Barlow, D. H. (1992). Comorbidity among anxiety disorders: Implications for treatment and DSM-IV. *Journal of Consulting and Clinical Psychology, 60,* 835–844.

Brown, T. A., & Barlow, D. H. (1995). Long-term outcome in cognitive-behavioral treatment of panic disorder: Clinical predictors and alternative strategies for assessment. *Journal of Consulting and Clinical Psychology, 63,* 754–765.

Brown, T. A., Moras, K., Zinbarg, R. E., & Barlow, D. H. (1993). Diagnostic and symptom distinguishability of generalized anxiety disorder and obsessive-compulsive disorder. *Behavior Therapy, 24,* 227–240.

Browne, H. A., Gair, S. L., Scharf, J. M., & Grice, D. E. (2014). Genetics of obsessive-compulsive disorder and related disorders. *Psychiatric Clinics of North America, 37*(3): 319–335. doi:10.1016/j.psc.2014.06.002

Brownell, K. D., & Foreyt, J. R (1985). Obesity. In D. H. Barlow (Ed.), *Clinical handbook of psychological disorders* (pp. 299–343). New York: Guilford Press.

Brownell, K. D., & Wadden, T. A. (1992). Etiology and treatment of obesity: Understanding a serious, prevalent, and refractory disorder. *Journal of Consulting and Clinical Psychology, 60,* 505–517.

Brownmiller, S. (1975). *Against our will: Men, women, and rape.* New York: Bantam Books.

Broz, D., & Ouellet, L. J. (2008). Racial and ethnic changes in heroin injection in the United States: Implications for the HIV/AIDS epidemic. *Drug and Alcohol Dependence, 94*(1–3), 221–233. doi:10.1016/j.drugalcdep.2007.11.020

Bruch, H. (1973). *Eating disorders: Obesity, anorexia nervosa, and the person within.* New York: Basic Books.

Bruchmüller, K., Margraf, J., Suppiger, A., & Schneider, S. (2011). Popular or unpopular? Therapists' use of structured interviews and their estimation of patient acceptance. *Behavior Therapy, 42,* 634–643. doi:10.1016/j.beth.2011.02.003

Brugge, K. L., Nichols, S. L., Salmon, D. P., Hill, L. R., Delis, D. C., Aaron, L., & Trauner, D. A. (1994). Cognitive impairment in adults with Down's syndrome: Similarities to early cognitive changes in Alzheimer's disease. *Neurology, 44*(2), 232–238.

Bruijnzeel, D., Suryadevara, U., & Tandon, R. (2014, in press). Antipsychotic treatment of schizophrenia: An update. *Asian Journal of Psychiatry.*

Brunet, A., Orr, S. P., Tremblay, J., Robertson, K., Nader, K., & Pitman, R. K. (2008). Effect of post-retrieval propranolol on psychophysiologic responding during subsequent script-driven traumatic imagery in post-traumatic stress. *Journal of Psychiatric Research, 42,* 503–506. doi:10.1016/j.jpsychires.2007.05.006

Brunet, A., Poundja, J., Tremblay, J., Bui, É., Thomas, É., Orr, S. P., . . . Pitman, R. K. (2011). Trauma reactivation under the influence of propranolol decreases post-traumatic stress symptoms and disorder: 3 open-label trials. *Journal of Clinical Psychopharmacology, 31,* 547–550. doi:10.1097/JCP.0b013e318222f360

Bruton, C., Crow, T. J., Firth, C. D., Johnson, E. C., Owens, D. G., & Roberts, G. W. (1990). Schizophrenia and the brain: A prospective clinico-neuropathological study. *Psychological Medicine, 20,* 285–304.

Bryant, R. (2011). Post-traumatic stress disorder vs. traumatic brain injury. *Dialogues in Clinical Neuroscience, 13*(3), 251–262.

Bryant, R. A., & McConkey, K. M. (1999). Functional blindness: A construction of cognitive social influences. *Cognitive Neuropsychiatry, 4*(3), 227–241. doi:10.1080/135468099395945

Bryant-Waugh, R. (2013). Avoidant restrictive food intake disorder: An illustrative case example. *International Journal of Eating Disorders, 46*(5), 420–423. doi:10.1002/eat.22093

Bschor, T., & Baethge, C. (2010). No evidence for switching the antidepressant: Systematic review and meta-analysis of RCTs of a common therapeutic strategy. *Acta Psychiatrica Scandinavica, 121*(3), 174–179. doi:10.1111/j.1600-0447.2009.01458.x. PMID 19703121

Buck, K. J., Milner, L. C., Denmark, D. L., Grant, S. N., & Kozell, L. B. (2012). Discovering genes involved in alcohol dependence and other alcohol responses. *Alcohol Research: Current Reviews, 34*(3), 367–374.

Buckner, F., & Firestone, M. (2000). "Where the public peril begins": 25 years after *Tarasoff. Journal of Legal Medicine, 21*(2), 187–222. doi:10.1080/01947640050074698

Budney, A. J., Moore, B. A., & Vandrey, R. (2004). Health consequences of marijuana use. In J. Brick (Ed.), *Handbook of the medical consequences of alcohol and drug abuse* (pp. 171–217). New York: Haworth Press.

Bugental, J. F. T. (1978). *Psychotherapy and process: The fundamentals of an existential-humanistic approach.* Reading, MA: Addison-Wesley.

Buhlmann, U., Marques, L. M., & Wilhelm, S. (2012). Traumatic experiences in individuals with body dysmorphic disorder. *Journal of Nervous and Mental Disease, 200*(1), 95–98. doi:10.1097/NMD.0b013e31823f6775

Bühringer, G., & Pfeiffer-Gerschel, T. (2008). COMBINE and Match: The final blow for large-scale black box randomized controlled trials. *Addiction, 103*(5), 708–710. doi:10.1111/j.1360-0443.2008.02162.x

Buhrmester, D., Whalen, C. K., Henker, B., MacDonald, V., & Hinshaw, S. P. (1992). Prosocial behavior in hyperactive boys: Effects of stimulant medication and comparison with normal boys. *Journal of Abnormal Child Psychology, 20,* 103–121.

Buka, S., Tsaung, M. T., & Lipsitt, L. (1993). Pregnancy/delivery complications and psychiatric diagnosis. *Archives of General Psychiatry, 50,* 151–156.

Bunney, W. E., & Garland, B. L. (1983). Possible receptor effects of chronic lithium administration. *Neuropharmacology, 22,* 367–372.

Buoli, M., Caldiroli, A., & Altamura, A. (2013). Psychotic versus nonpsychotic major depressive disorder: A comparative naturalistic study. *Asian Journal of Psychiatry, 6*(4), 333–337. doi:10.1016/j.ajp.2013.02.003

Burchard, J. D. (1967). Systematic socialization: A programmed environment for the habilitation of antisocial retardates. *Psychological Record, 17,* 461–476.

Burchard, S. N., Hasazi, J. S., Gordon, L. R., & Yoe, J. (1991). An examination of lifestyle and adjustment in three community residential alternatives. *Research in Developmental Disabilities, 12*(2), 127–142.

Burgess, G. C., Depue, B. E., Ruzic, L., Willcutt, E. G., Du, Y. P., & Banich, M. T. (2010). Attentional control activation relates to working memory in ADHD. *Biological Psychiatry, 67,* 632–640. doi:10.1016/j.biopsych.2009.10.036

Burish, T. G., & Carey, M. P. (1986). Conditioned aversive responses in cancer chemotherapy patients: Theoretical and developmental analysis. *Journal of Consulting and Clinical Psychology, 54,* 593–600.

Burish, T. G., Carey, M. P., Krozely, M. G., & Greco, F. A. (1987). Conditioned side effects induced by cancer chemotherapy: Prevention through behavioral treatment. *Journal of Consulting and Clinical Psychology, 55,* 42–48.

Burke, B. L., Martens, A., & Faucher, E. H. (2010). Two decades of terror management theory: A meta-analysis of mortality salience research. *Personality and Social Psychology Review, 14*(2), 155–195. doi:10.1177/1088868309352321

Burke, B. L., Sears, S. R., Kraus, S., & Roberts-Cady, S. (2014). Critical analysis: A comparison of critical thinking changes in psychology and philosophy classes. *Teaching of Psychology, 41,* 28–36.

Burkhouse, K., Uhrlass, D., Stone, L., Knopik, V., & Gibb, B. (2012). Expressed emotion-criticism and risk of depression onset in children. *Journal of Clinical Child and Adolescent Psychology, 41*(6), 771–777.

Burnam, M. A., Hough, R., Escobar, J. I., & Karno, M. (1987). Six months prevalence of specific psychiatric disorders among Mexican Americans and non-Hispanic whites in Los Angeles. *Archives of General Psychiatry, 44,* 687–694.

Burns, A., Gallagley, A., & Byrne, J. (2004). Delirium. *Journal of Neurology, Neurosurgery & Psychiatry, 75*, 362–367.

Burns, D. D. (1999). *The feeling good handbook* (revised ed.). New York: Plume/Penguin Books.

Burns, D. D., & Nolen-Hoeksema, S. (1991). Coping styles, homework compliance, and the effectiveness of cognitive-behavioral therapy. *Journal of Consulting and Clinical Psychology, 59*, 305–311.

Burstein, M., Georgiades, K., He, J., Schmitz, A., Feig, E., Khazanov, G., & Merikangas, K. (2012). Specific phobia among U.S. adolescents: Phenomenology and typology. *Depression and Anxiety, 29*(12), 1072–1082. doi:10.1002/da.22008

Burstein, M., He, J., Kattan, G., Albano, A., Avenevoli, S., & Merikangas, K. R. (2011). Social phobia and subtypes in the National Comorbidity Survey–Adolescent Supplement: Prevalence, correlates, and comorbidity. *Journal of the American Academy of Child & Adolescent Psychiatry, 50*(9), 870–880. doi:10.1016/j.jaac.2011.06.005

Burt, S. A. (2009). A mechanistic explanation of popularity: genes, rule breaking, and evocative gene-environment correlations. *Journal of Personality and Social Psychology, 96*(4), 783–794. doi: 10.1037/a0013702.

Burton, C. (2003). Beyond somatisation: A review of the understanding and treatment of medically unexplained physical symptoms (MUPS). *British Journal of General Practice, 53*(488), 231–239.

Burton, E. J., Mukaetova-Ladinska, E. B., Perry, R. H., Jaros, E., Barber, R., & O'Brien, J. T. (2012). Neuropathological correlates of volumetric MRI in autopsy-confirmed Lewy body dementia. *Neurobiology of Aging, 33*(7), 1228–1236. doi:10.1016/j.neurobiolaging.2010.12.015

Buschbaum, M., Haier, R., Potkin, S., Nuechterlein, K., Bracha, H., Katz, M., Lohr, J. M., Wu, J., Lottenberg, S., Jerabek, P., Trenary, M., Tafalla, R., Reynolds, C., & Bunney, W. (1992). Frontostriatal disorder of cerebral metabolism in never-medicated schizophrenics. *Archives of General Psychiatry, 49*, 935–942.

Buss, A. H. (1966). *Psychopathology.* New York: John Wiley & Sons.

Buss, D. M. (1995). Evolutionary psychology: A new paradigm for psychological science. *Psychological Inquiry, 6*, 1–30.

Busto, U., Sellers, E. M., Naranjo, C. A., Cappell, H. D., Sanchez-Craig, M., & Simpkins, J. (1986). Patterns of benzodiazepine abuse and dependence. *British Journal of Addiction, 81*(1), 87–94. doi:10.1111/j.1360-0443.1986.tb00299.x

Butcher, J. N., Dahlstron, W. G., Graham, J. R., Tellegen (1989). *Minnesota Multiphasic Personality Inventory-2 (MMPI-2): Manual for administration and scoring.* Minneapolis: University of Minnesota Press.

Butcher, J. N., Williams, C. L., Graham, J. R., Archer, R., Tellegen, A., Ben-Porath, Y. S., & Kaemmer, B. (1992). *MMPI-A: Manual for administration, scoring and interpretation.* Minneapolis: University of Minnesota Press.

Butler Hospital. (2008). More information on body dysmorphic disorder. The body dysmorphic disorder and body image program at Butler Hospital. Retrieved December 1, 2008, from http://www.butler.org/body.cfm?id=123.

Butler, A. C., Chapman, J. E., Forman, E. M., & Beck, A. T. (2006). The empirical status of cognitive-behavioral therapy: A review of meta-analyses. *Clinical Psychology Review, 26*(1), 17–31. doi:10.1016/j.cpr.2005.07.003

Butler, G., Fennell, M., Robson, P., & Gelder, M. (1991). Comparison of behavior therapy and cognitive behavior therapy in the treatment of generalized anxiety disorder. *Journal of Consulting and Clinical Psychology, 59*, 167–175.

Butler, L., Miezitis, S., Friedman, R., & Cole, E. (1980). The effect of two school-based intervention programs on depressive symptoms in preadolescents. *American Educational Research Journal, 17*, 111–119.

Butler, R., Wheeler, A., & Sheridan, J. (2010). Physical and psychological harms and health consequences of methamphetamine use amongst a group of New Zealand users. *International Journal of Mental Health & Addiction, 8*, 432–443.

Button, E., Aldridge, S., & Palmer, R. (2008). Males assessed by a specialized adult eating disorders service: Patterns over time and comparisons with females. *International Journal of Eating Disorders, 41*(8), 758–761.

Butzlaff, R. L., & Hooley, J. M. (1998). Expressed emotion and psychiatric relapse: A meta-analysis. *Archives of General Psychiatry, 55*, 547–552.

Buvat, J. (2011). Pathophysiology of premature ejaculation.,*The Journal of Sexual Medicine, 8*(Supplement 4), 316–327.

Buzsaki, G., & Gage, F. H. (1988). Mechanisms of action of neural grafts in the limbic system. *Canadian Journal of Neurological Sciences, 15*, 99–105.

Byne, W., & Parsons, B. (1993). Human sexual orientation: The biologic theories reappraised. *Archives of General Psychiatry, 50*, 228–239.

Byne, W., Bradley, S. J., Coleman, E., Evan Eyler, A., Green, R., Menvielle, E. J., . . . Tompkins, D.A. (2012). Report of the American Psychiatric Association task force on treatment of gender identity disorder. *Archives of Sexual Behavior, 41*, 759–796.

Byrne, M., Agerbo, E., Bennedsen, B., Eaton, W. W., & Mortensen, P. B. (2007). Obstetric conditions and risk of first admission with schizophrenia: A Danish national register based study. *Schizophrenia Research, 97*, 51–59.

C

Cabay, M. (1994). A controlled evaluation of facilitated communication using open-ended and fill-in questions. *Journal of Autism and Developmental Disorders, 24*(4), 517–527.

Čablová, L., Pazderková, K., & Miovský, M. (2014). Parenting styles and alcohol use among children and adolescents: A systematic review. *Drugs: Education, Prevention & Policy, 21*(1), 1–13. doi:10.3109/09687637.2013.817536

Cade, J. F. J. (1949). Lithium salts in the treatment of psychotic excitement. *Medical Journal of Australia, 36*, 349–352.

Cadoret, R. J. (1990). Genetics of alcoholism. In R. L. Collins, K. E. Leonard, & J. S. Searles (Eds.), *Alcohol and the family: Research and clinical perspectives* (pp. 39–78). New York: Guilford Press.

Caffeine Informer. (2014). *Caffeine content of drinks.* Retrieved on December 14, 2014 from http://www.caffeineinformer.com/the-caffeine-database

Cahill, K., Stevens, S., Perera, R., & Lancaster, T. (2013). Pharmacological interventions for smoking cessation: An overview and network meta-analysis. *Cochrane Database of Systematic Reviews, 5.* Art. No.: CD009329. DOI: 10.1002/14651858.CD009329.pub2.

Calamia, M., Markon, K., & Tranel, D. (2013). The robust reliability of neuropsychological measures: Meta-analyses of test–retest correlations. *The Clinical Neuropsychologist, 27*, 1077–1105.

Calati, R., Gressier, F., Balestri, M., & Serretti, A. (2013). Genetic modulation of borderline personality disorder: Systematic review and meta-analysis. *Journal of Psychiatric Research, 47*(10), 1275–1287. doi:10.1016/j.jpsychires.2013.06.002

Caldwell, C. B., & Gottesman, 1.1. (1990). Schizophrenics kill themselves too: A review of risk factors for suicide. *Schizophrenia Bulletin, 16*, 571–589.

Caldwell, M., Skeem, J., Salekin, R., & Van Rybroek, G. (2006). Treatment response of adolescent offenders with psychopathy features: A 2-year follow-up. *Criminal Justice and Behavior, 33*(5), 571–596. doi:10.1177/0093854806288176

Calev, A., Pass, H., Shapira, B., Fink, M., Tubi, N., & Lerer, B. (1993). In C. E. Coffey, (Ed.), *The clinical science of electroconvulsive therapy* (pp. 125–142). Washington, DC: American Psychiatric Press.

Calipari, E. S., & Ferris, M. J. (2013). Amphetamine mechanisms and actions at the dopamine terminal revisited. *Journal of Neuroscience, 33*(21), 8923–8925. doi:10.1523/JNEUROSCI.1033-13.2013

Callahan, V. A., McGreevey, M. A., Cirnicione, C., & Steadman, H. J. (1992). Measuring the effects of the guilty but mental ill (GBMI) verdict: Georgia's 1982 GBMI reform. *Law and Human Behavior, 16*, 447–462.

Cambor, R., & Millman, R. B. (1991). Alcohol and drug abuse in adolescents. In M. Lewis (Ed.), *Child and adolescent psychiatry: A comprehensive textbook* (pp. 736–754). Baltimore: Williams & Wilkins.

Camilleri, J. A., & Quinsey, V. L. (2008). Pedophilia: Assessment and treatment. In D. R. Laws & W. T. O'Donohue (Eds.), *Sexual deviance: Theory, assessment, and treatment* (pp. 183–212). New York, NY: Guilford Press.

Cammin-Nowak, S., Helbig-Lang, S., Lang, T., Gloster, A. T., Fehm, L., Gerlach, A. L., & . . . Wittchen, H. U. (2013). Specificity of homework compliance effects on treatment outcome in CBT: Evidence from a controlled trial on panic disorder and agoraphobia. *Journal of Clinical Psychology, 69*, 616–629. doi:10.1002/jclp.21975

Campbell, D. T., & Stanley, J. C. (1966). *Experimental and quasi-experimental designs for research.* Chicago: Rand McNally.

Campbell, F. A., Pungello, E. P., Burchinal, M., Kainz, K., Pan, Y., Wasik, B. H., & . . . Ramey, C. T. (2012). Adult outcomes as a function of an early childhood educational program: An Abecedarian Project follow-up. *Developmental Psychology, 48*, 1033–1043. doi:10.1037/a0026644

Campbell, F. A., Ramey, C. T., Pungello, E., Sparling, J., & Miller-Johnson, S. (2002). Early childhood education: Young adult outcomes from the Abecedarian Project. *Applied Developmental Science, 6*, 42–57. doi:10.1207/S1532480XADS0601_05

Campbell, J. L., Thomas, H. M., Gabrielli, W., Liskow, B. I., & Powell, B. J. (1994). Impact of desipramine or carbamazepine on patient retention in outpatient cocaine treatment: Preliminary findings. *Journal of Addictive Diseases, 13*(4), 191–199.

Campbell, M., Anderson, L. T., Small, A. M., Adams, P., Gonzalez, N. M., & Ernst, M. (1993). Naltrexone in autistic children: Behavioral symptoms and attentional learning. *Journal of the American Academy of Child and Adolescent Psychiatry, 32*(6), 1283–1291.

Campbell, S. B. (1990). *Behavior problems in preschool children: Clinical and developmental issues.* New York: Guilford Press.

Campbell, S. B., Ewing, L. J., Breaux, A. M., & Szumowski, E. K. (1986). Problem three-year-olds: Follow-up at school entry. *Journal of Child Psychology and Psychiatry, 27*, 473–488.

Camus, V., Gonthier, R., Dubos, G., Schwed, P., & Simeone, I. (2000). Etiologic and outcome profiles in hypoactive and hyperactive subtypes of delirium. *Journal of Geriatric Psychiatry & Neurology, 13*, 38–42.

Canino, G., Bird, H., Rubio-Stipec, M., & Bravo, M. (1997). The epidemiology of mental disorders in the adult population of Puerto Rico. *Puerto Rico Health Sciences Journal, 16*(2), 117-124.

Canino, G., Bird, H., Shrout, P., Rubio-Stipec, M., Bravo, M., Martinez, R., Sesman, M., & Guevara, L. (1987). The prevalence of specific psychiatric disorders in Puerto Rico. *Archives of General Psychiatry, 44,* 727–735.

Cannon, T., Mednick, S., Parnas, J. (1989). Genetic and perinatal determinants of structural brain deficits in schizophrenia. *Archives of General Psychiatry, 46,* 883–888.

Cannon, T., Mednick, S., Parnas, J., Schulsinger, F., Praestholm, J., & Vestergaard, A. (1993). Developmental brain abnormalities in the offspring of schizophrenic mothers. I: Contributions of genetic and perinatal factors. *Archives of General Psychiatry, 50,* 551–564.

Cannon, T., Mednick, S., Parnas, J., Schulsinger, F., Praestholm, J., & Vestergaard, A. (1994). Developmental brain abnormalities in the offspring of schizophrenic mothers: II: Structural brain characteristics of schizophrenia and schizotypal personality disorder. *Archives of General Psychiatry, 51,* 955-962.

Cansever, A., Uzun, O., Doenmez, E., & Ozsahin, A. (2003). The prevalence and clinical features of body dysmorphic disorder in college students: A study in a Turkish sample. *Comprehensive Psychiatry, 44*(1), 60–64.

Canton, J., Scott, K. M., & Glue, P. (2012). Optimal treatment of social phobia: Systematic review and meta-analysis. *Neuropsychiatric Disease and Treatment, 8,* 201–215.

Cantor, J. M., & Blanchard, R. (2012). White matter volumes in pedophiles, hebephiles, and teleiophiles. *Archives of Sexual Behavior, 41,* 749–752.

Cantor, J. M., Kabani, N., Christensen, B. K., Zipursky, R. B., Barberee, H. E., Dickey, R., . . . Blanchard, R. (2008). Cerebral white matter deficiencies in pedophilic men. *Journal of Psychiatric Research, 42,* 167–183.

Cantor-Graae, E., & Selten, J. P. (2005). Schizophrenia and migration: A meta-analysis and review. *American Journal of Psychiatry,* 162, 12–24.

Cantor-Graae, E., McNeil, T., Sjostrom, K., Nordstrom, L. G., & Rosenlund, T. (1994). Obstetric complications and their relationship to other etiological risk factors in schizophrenia. *Journal of Nervous and Mental Disease, 182,* 645–650.

Cantwell, D., Baker, L., & Rutter, M. (1978). Family factors. In M. Rutter & E. Schopler (Eds.), *Autism: A reappraisal of concepts and treatment* (pp. 269–296). New York: Plenum.

Cantwell, D. R, & Baker, L. (1989). Stability and natural history of DSM-III childhood diagnoses. *Journal of the American Academy of Child and Adolescent Psychiatry, 28,* 691–700.

Caplan, G. (1964). *An approach to community mental health.* New York: Grune & Stratton.

Caplan, G. (1964). *Principles of preventive psychiatry.* New York: Basic Books.

Caplehorn, J. R., & Ross, M. W. (1995). Methadone maintenance and the likelihood of risky needle-sharing. *International Journal of Addictions, 30,* 685–698.

Cappe, R. F., & Alden, L. E. (1986). A comparison of treatment strategies for clients functionally impaired by extreme shyness and social avoidance. *Journal of Consulting and Clinical Psychology, 54,* 796–801.

Cappell, H., & Greeley, J. (1987). Alcohol and tension reduction: An update on research and theory. In H. T. Blane & K. E. Leonard (Eds.), *Psychological theories of drinking* (pp. 15–51). New York: Guilford Press.

Capute, A. J., & Accardo, P. J. (1996). *Developmental disabilities in infancy and childhood* (2nd edition). Baltimore: Paul Brookes Publishing.

Cardeña, E., & Terhune, D. B. (2014). Hypnotizability, personality traits, and the propensity to experience alterations of consciousness. *Psychology of Consciousness: Theory, Research, and Practice, 1*(3), 292–307.

Cardno, A., Marshall, E. J., Coid, B., Macdonald, A. M., Ribchester, T. R., . . . Murray, R. M. (1999). Heritability estimates for psychotic disorders: The Maudsley twin psychosis series. *Archives of General Psychiatry, 56,* 162–168.

Cardon, L. R., Smith, S. D., Fulker, D. W., Kimberling, W. J., Pennington, B. F., & DeFries, J. C. (1994). Quantitative trait locus for reading disability on chromosome 6. *Science, 266,* 276–279.

Carey, K. B., Scott-Sheldon, L. J., Carey, M. P., & DeMartini, K. S. (2007). Individual-level interventions to reduce college student drinking: A meta-analytic review. *Addictive Behaviors, 32*(11), 2469–2494. doi:10.1016/j.addbeh.2007.05.004

Carey, M. P., & Burish, T. G. (1988). Etiology and treatment of the psychological side effects associated with cancer chemotherapy. *Psychological Bulletin, 104,* 307–325.

Carhart-Harris, R. L., & Nutt, D. J. (2010). User perceptions of the benefits and harms of hallucinogenic drug use: A web-based questionnaire study. *Journal of Substance Use, 15*(4), 283–300. doi:10.3109/14659890903271624

Carlbring, P., Gustafsson, H., Ekselius, L., & Andersson, G. (2002). 12-month prevalence of panic disorder with or without agoraphobia in the Swedish general population. *Social Psychiatry and Psychiatric Epidemiology, 37*(5), 207–211. doi:10.1007/s00127-002-0542-y

Carlson, C. L., Pelham, W. E., Jr., Milich, R., & Dixon, J. (1992). Single and combined effects of methylphenidate and behavior therapy on the classroom performance of children with attention-deficit hyperactivity disorder. *Journal of Abnormal Child Psychology, 20*(2), 213–232.

Carlson, E. A., Yates, T. M., & Sroufe, L. A. (2009). Dissociation and development of the self. In P. F. Dell & J. A. O'Neil (Eds.), *Dissociation and the dissociative disorders* (pp. 239–258). New York: Routledge/Taylor Francis.

Carlsten, A., Allebeck, P., & Brandt, L. (1996). Are suicide rates in Sweden associated with changes in the prescribing of medicines? *Acta Psychiatrica Scandinavica, 94*(2), 94–100. doi:10.1111/j.1600-0447.1996.tb09831.x

Carmiol, N. N., Peralta, J. M., Almasy, L. L., Contreras, J. J., Pacheco, A. A., Escamilla, M. A., . . . Glahn, D. C. (2014). Shared genetic factors influence risk for bipolar disorder and alcohol use disorders. *European Psychiatry, 29*(5), 282–287. doi:10.1016/j.eurpsy.2013.10.001

Carpenter W. T. (2001). Evidence-based treatment for first-episode schizophrenia? *American Journal of Psychiatry, 158,* 1771–1773.

Carpenter, L., & Chung, M. (2011). Childhood trauma in obsessive compulsive disorder: The roles of alexithymia and attachment. *Psychology and Psychotherapy: Theory, Research and Practice, 84*(4), 367–388. doi:10.1111/j.2044-8341.2010.02003.x

Carr, A. (2009). The effectiveness of family therapy and systemic interventions for child-focused problems. *Journal of Family Therapy, 31*(1), 3–45. doi:10.1111/j.1467-6427.2008.00451.x

Carr, C., Martins, C., Stingel, A., Lemgruber, V., & Juruena, M. (2013). The role of early life stress in adult psychiatric disorders: A systematic review according to childhood trauma subtypes. *Journal of Nervous and Mental Disease, 201,* 1007–1020. doi:10.1097/NMD.0000000000000049

Carroll, B. J. (1986). Informed use of the dexamethasone suppression test. *Journal of Clinical Psychiatry, 47* (Suppl. 1), 10–12.

Carroll, B. T. (2001). Kahlbaum's catatonia revisited. *Psychiatry and Clinical Neurosciences, 55*(5), 431–436. doi:10.1046/j.1440-1819.2001.00887.x

Carroll, J. L., Volk, K., & Hyde, J. (1985). Differences between males and females in motives for engaging in sexual intercourse. *Archives of Sexual Behavior, 14,* 131–139.

Carson, R. C. (1969). *Interaction concepts of personality.* Chicago: Aldine Publishing.

Carson, R. C. (1991). Dilemmas in the pathway of the *DSM-IV. Journal of Abnormal Psychology, 100,* 302–307.

Carta, M., Balestrieri, M., Murru, A., & Hardoy, M. (2009). Adjustment disorder: Epidemiology, diagnosis and treatment. *Clinical Practice and Epidemiology in Mental Health, 5.* doi:10.1186/1745-0179-5-15

Carter, C. S., MacDonald, A. W., Ross, L. L., & Stenger, V. A. (2001). Anterior cingulated cortex activity and impaired self-monitoring of performance in patients with schizophrenia: An event related fMRI study. *American Journal of Psychiatry, 158,* 1423–1428.

Carter, M. M., Hollon, S. D., Carson, R., & Shelton, R. C. (1995). Effects of a safe person on induced distress following a biological challenge in panic disorder with agoraphobia. *Journal of Abnormal Psychology, 104,* 156–163.

Carvalho, A. F., Dimellis, D., Gonda, X., Vieta, E., McIntyre, R. S., & Fountoulakis, K. N. (2014). Rapid cycling in bipolar disorder: A systematic review. *Journal of Clinical Psychiatry, 75*(6), e578–e586. doi:10.4088/JCP.13r08905

Carvalho, M. C., Santos, J. M., Bassi, G. S., & Brandão, M. L. (2013). Participation of NK1 receptors of the amygdala on the processing of different types of fear. *Neurobiology of Learning and Memory, 102,* 20–27. doi:10.1016/j.nlm.2013.03.004

Carvalho, M., Carmo, H., Costa, V. M., Capela, J. P., Pontes, H., Remião, F., . . . Bastos, M. L. (2012). Toxicity of amphetamines: An update. *Archives of Toxicology, 86*(8), 1167–1231. doi:10.1007/s00204-012-0815-5. PMID 22392347

Carver, C., & Scheier, M. (1981). *Attention and self-regulation.* New York: Springer-Verlag.

Casarett, D. J. (2003). Assessing decision-making capacity in the setting of palliative care research. *Journal of Pain Symptom Management, 25,* S6–S13.

Case, R. B., Moss, A. J., Case, N., McDermott, M., & Eberly, S. (1992). Living alone after myocardial infarction: Impact on prognosis. *Journal of the American Medical Association, 267,* 515–519.

Casellas-Grau, A., Font, A., & Vives, J. (2014). Positive psychology interventions in breast cancer. A systematic review. *Psycho-Oncology, 23,* 9–19. doi:10.1002/pon.3353

Casey, P. (2009). Adjustment disorder: Epidemiology, diagnosis and treatment. *CNS Drugs, 23*(11), 927–938. doi:10.2165/11311000-000000000-00000

Cassidy, J. (1988). Child-mother attachment and the self in six-year-olds. *Child Development, 59,* 121–134.

Castells, X., Casas, M., Vidal, X., Bosch, R., Roncero, C., Ramos-Quiroga, J. A., & Capellà, D. (2007). Efficacy of central nervous system stimulant treatment for cocaine dependence: A systematic review and meta-analysis of randomized controlled clinical trials. *Addiction, 102*(12), 1871–1887. doi:10.1111/j.1360-0443.2007.01943.x

Castillo, R. J. (2003). Trance, functional psychosis, and culture. *Psychiatry: Interpersonal & Biological Processes, 66*(1), 9–21.

Castle, D. J., & Murray, R. M.(1993). The epidemiology of late-onset schizophrenia. *Schizophrenia Bulletin, 19,* 691–700.

Cavanagh, J. O., Carson, A. J., Sharpe, M. M., & Lawrie, S. M. (2003). Psychological autopsy studies of suicide: A systematic review. *Psychological Medicine, 33*(3), 395–405. doi:10.1017/S0033291702006943

Ceccherini-Nelli, A., Bardellilni, L., Cur, A., Guazelli, M., Maggini, C., & Dilsaver, S. (1993). Antidepressant withdrawal: Prospective findings. *American Journal of Psychiatry, 150,* 165.

Centers for Disease Control and Prevention (n.d.). *Heads Up: Preventing Brain Injuries.* Retrieved on December 18, 2014 from http://www.cdc.gov/ncipc/pub-res/tbi_toolkit/patients/preventing.htm

Centers for Disease Control and Prevention (2007). *Methamphetamine use and risk for HIV/AIDS.* Retrieved on December 14, 2014 from http://www.cdc.gov/hiv/resources/factsheets/pdf/meth.pdf

Centers for Disease Control and Prevention (2011). *Suicide and self-inflicted injury.* Retrieved on August 12, 2014 from http://www.cdc.gov/nchs/fastats/suicide.htm

Centers for Disease Control and Prevention (2012). Vital signs: Binge drinking prevalence, frequency, and intensity among adults—U.S., 2010. *Morbidity and Mortality Weekly Reports, 61*(1), 14–19.

Centers for Disease Control and Prevention (2014). *Burden of mental illness.* Retrieved on November 5, 2014 from http://www.cdc.gov/mentalhealth/basics/burden.htm

Centers for Disease Control and Prevention (2014a). *Developmental milestones.* Retrieved on September 16, 2014 from http://www.cdc.gov/ncbddd/actearly/milestones

Centers for Disease Control and Prevention (2014b). *Fact sheets—Alcohol use and your health.* Retrieved on December 11, 2014 from http://www.cdc.gov/alcohol/fact-sheets/alcohol-use.htm

Centers for Disease Control and Prevention (2014c). *Fact sheets—Binge drinking.* Retrieved on December 11, 2014 http://www.cdc.gov/alcohol/fact-sheets/binge-drinking.htm

Centers for Disease Control and Prevention (2014d). *Suicide prevention: Youth suicide.* Retrieved on August 12, 2014 from http://www.cdc.gov/violenceprevention/pub/youth_suicide.html

Centers for Disease Control and Prevention (2014e). *Ten things to know about new autism data.* Retrieved on October 10, 2014 from http://www.cdc.gov/features/dsautismdata/

Centers for Disease Control Viet Nam Experience Survey (VES) (1988). Psychosocial Characteristics. *Journal of the American Medical Association, 259,* 2701-2707.

Cepeda-Benito, A. (1993). Meta-analytical review of the efficacy of nicotine chewing gum in smoking treatment programs. *Journal of Consulting and Clinical Psychology, 61*(5), 822–830.

Cerdá, M., Wall, M., Keyes, K. M., Galea, S., & Hasin, D. (2012). Medical marijuana laws in 50 states: Investigating the relationship between state legalization of medical marijuana and marijuana use, abuse and dependence. *Drug and Alcohol Dependence, 120*(1–3), 22–27. doi:10.1016/j.drugalcdep.2011.06.011

Cerletti, U., & Bini, L. (1938). Electroshock. *Archives of General Neurology, Psychiatry, and Psychoanalysis, 19,* 266–268.

Ceron-Litvoc, D., Soares, B., Geddes, J., Litvoc, J., & de Lima, M. (2009). Comparison of carbamazepine and lithium in treatment of bipolar disorder: A systematic review of randomized controlled trials. *Human Psychopharmacology: Clinical and Experimental, 24*(1), 19–28.

Chaleby, K., Jabbar, J. A., & Al-Sawaf, M. (1996). Psychotherapy of sexual dysfunction in Arab patients. *Arab Journal of Psychiatry, 7*(2), 99–110.

Chambers, M. J., & Keller, B. (1992). Alert insomniacs: Are they really sleep deprived? *Clinical Psychology Review, 13,* 649–666.

Chambless, D. L., Fydrich, T., & Rodebaugh, T. L. (2008). Generalized social phobia and avoidant personality disorder: Meaningful distinction or useless duplication? *Depression and Anxiety, 25,* 8–19.

Chambless, D. L., & Gillis, M. M. (1993). Cognitive therapy with anxiety disorders. *Journal of Consulting and Clinical Psychology, 61,* 248–260.

Chambless, D. L., Sultan, F. E., Stern, T. E., O'Neill, C., Garrison, S., & Jackson, A. (1984). Effect of pubococcygeal exercise on coital orgasm in women. *Journal of Consulting and Clinical Psychology, 52*(1), 114–118.

Champion, V. L. (1990). Breast self-examination in women 35 and older: A prospective study. *Journal of Behavioral Medicine, 13,* 523–538.

Chan, C. S., & Rhodes, J. E. (2014). Measuring exposure in Hurricane Katrina: A meta-analysis and an integrative data analysis. *PLoS ONE, 9*(4): e92899. doi:10.1371/journal.pone.0092899

Chandler, W., Schuster, J. W., & Stevens, K. B. (1993). Teaching employment skills to adolescents with mild and moderate disabilities using a constant time delay procedure. *Education and Training in Mental Retardation, 28(2),* 155–168.

Chaney, C. (1994). Language development, metalinguistic awareness, and emergent literacy skills of 3-year-old children in relation to social class. *Applied Psycholinguistics, 15*(3), 371–394.

Chang, B., Gitlin, D., & Patel, R. (2011). The depressed patient and suicidal patient in the emergency department: Evidence-based management and treatment strategies. *Emergency Medicine Practice, 13*(9), 1–23.

Chang, S. H., Klein, C., & Gorzalka, B. B. (2013). Perceived prevalence and definitions of sexual dysfunction as predictors of sexual function and satisfaction. *Journal of Sex Research, 50*(5), 502–512.

Chang, W., Hui, C. L., Tang, J. Y., Wong, G. H., Lam, M. M., Chan, S. K., & Chen, E. Y. (2011). Persistent negative symptoms in first-episode schizophrenia: A prospective three-year follow-up study. *Schizophrenia Research, 133*(1–3), 22–28. doi:10.1016/j.schres.2011.09.006

Chang, Y., Liu, S., Yu, H., & Lee, Y. (2012). Effect of acute exercise on executive function in children with attention deficit hyperactivity disorder. *Archives of Clinical Neuropsychology, 27*(2), 225–237. doi:10.1093/arclin/acr094

Chapman, L. J., & Chapman, J. P. (1980). Scales for rating psychotic and psychotic-like experiences as continua. *Schizophrenia Bulletin, 6,* 476–489.

Chapman, L. J., Chapman, J. P., Kwapil, T. R., Eckblad, M., & Zinser, M. C. (1994). Putatively psychosis-prone subjects 10 years later. *Journal of Abnormal Psychology, 103,* 171–183.

Charcot, J. M. (1881). *Clinical lectures on senile and chronic diseases.* London: New Sydenheim Society.

Chard, K. M., Schumm, J. A., Owens, G. P., & Cottingham, S. M. (2010). A comparison of OEF and OIF veterans and Vietnam veterans receiving cognitive processing therapy. *Journal of Traumatic Stress, 23*(1), 25–32.

Charlson, F. J., Ferrari, A. J., Flaxman, A. D., & Whiteford, H. A. (2013). The epidemiological modelling of dysthymia: Application for the Global Burden of Disease Study 2010. *Journal of Affective Disorders, 151*(1), 111–120. doi:10.1016/j.jad.2013.05.060

Charman, T. (2011). The highs and lows of counting autism. *American Journal of Psychiatry, 168,* 873–875.

Charney, D. S. (2004). Psychobiological mechanism of resilience and vulnerability: Implications for successful adaptation to extreme stress. *American Journal of Psychiatry, 161,* 195–216.

Chartier, M. J., Walker, J. R., & Stein, M. B. (2001). Social phobia and potential childhood risk factors in a community sample. *Psychological Medicine, 31,* 307–315.

Chassin, L., Pillow, D., Curran, P., Molina, B., & Barrera, M. (1993). Relation of parental alcoholism to early adolescent substance use: A test of three mediating mechanisms. *Journal of Abnormal Psychology, 102,* 3–19.

Chassin, L., Rogosch, F., & Barrera, M. (1991). Substance use and symptomatology among adolescent children of alcoholics. *Journal of Abnormal Psychology, 100(4),* 449–463.

Chauvin, C. D. (2012). Social norms and motivations associated with college binge drinking. *Sociological Inquiry, 82*(2), 257–281. doi:10.1111/j.1475-682X.2011.00400.x

Chavira, D. A., Garrido, H., Bagnarello, M., Azzam, A., Reus, V. I., & Mathews, C. A. (2008). A comparative study of obsessive-compulsive disorder in Costa Rica and the United States. *Depression and Anxiety, 25*(7), 609–619. doi:10.1002/da.20357

Chehil, S., & Kutcher, S. (2012). *Suicide risk management: A manual for health professionals* (2nd ed.). New York: Wiley-Blackwell.

Chekhov, A. (2000). *Stories of Anton Chekhov.* New York: Modern Library.

Chen, C. N., Wong, J., Lee, N., Chan-Ho, M. W., Lau, J., & Fung, M. (1993). The Shatin community mental health survey in Hong Kong. II. Major findings. *Archives of General Psychiatry, 50,* 125–132.

Cheng, J. Y., Ko, J. S., Chen, R. Y., & Ng, E. M. (2008). Meta-regression analysis using latitude as moderator of paternal age related schizophrenia risk. *Schizophrenia Research, 99,* 71–76.

Chin, A. L., Negash, S., & Hamilton, R. (2011). Diversity and disparity in dementia: The impact of ethnoracial differences in Alzheimer disease. *Alzheimer Disease and Associated Disorders, 25*(3), 187–195. doi: 10.1097/WAD.0b013e318211c6c9

Chiocca, E. A., & Martuza, R. (1990). Neurosurgical therapy of obsessive compulsive disorder. In M. A. Jenike, L. Baer, & W. Minichiello (Eds.) *Obsessive-compulsive disorders: Theory and management.* St. Louis: Mosby-Yearbook.

Choi, S. H., Lee, H., Chung, T. S., Park, K. M., Jung, Y. C., Kim, S. I., & Kim, J. J. (2012). Neural network functional connectivity during and after an episode of delirium. *American Journal of Psychiatry, 169*(5), 498–507.

Choo, E. K., Benz, M., Zaller, N., Warren, O., Rising, K. L., & McConnell, K. J. (2014). The impact of state medical marijuana legislation on adolescent marijuana use. *Journal of Adolescent Health, 55*(2), 160–166. doi:10.1016/j.jadohealth.2014.02.018

Chou, T. M., & Benowitz, N. L. (1994). Caffeine and coffee: Effects on health and cardiovascular disease. Comparative Biochemistry and Physiology. *Pharmacology, Toxicology and Endocrinology, 109*(2), 173–189.

Choy, Y. (2007). Managing side effects of anxiolytics. *Primary Psychiatry, 14*(7), 68–76.

Christiansen, B. A., Roehling, P. V., Smith, G. T., & Goldman, M. S. (1989). Using alcohol expectancies to predict adolescent drinking behavior after one year. *Journal of Consulting and Clinical Psychology, 57*(1), 93–99.

Chronis, A. M., Jones, H. A., & Raggi, V. L. (2006). Evidence-based psychosocial treatments for children and adolescents with attention-deficit/hyperactivity disorder. *Clinical Psychology Review, 26,* 486–502.

Chrousos, G. P., & Gold, P. W. (1992). The concepts of stress and stress system disorders. *Journal of the American Medical Association, 267,* 1244–1252.

Chughtai, B., Sciullo, D., Khan, S., Rehman, H., Mohan, E., & Rehman, J. (2009). Etiology, diagnosis, & management of hypersexuality: A review. *The Internet Journal of Urology, 6*(2).

Chung, R. C-Y., & Singer, M. K. (1995). Interpretation of symptom presentation and distress: A southeast Asian refugee example. *Journal of Nervous and Mental Disease, 183,* 639–648.

Chung, W. C. J., De Vries, G. J., & Swaab, D. F. (2002). Sexual differentiation of the bed nucleus of the stria terminalis in humans may extend into adulthood. *The Journal of Neuroscience, 22*(3), 1027–1033.

CIBA-GEIGY Corporation (1991). *OCD: When a habit isn't just a habit: A guide to obsessive-compulsive disorder.* Summit, NJ: Author.

Cicchetti, D., & Beeghly, M. (Eds.). (1990). *Children with Down syndrome: A developmental approach.* New York: Cambridge University Press.

Cicchetti, D., & Toth, S. L. (1991). A developmental perspective on internalizing and externalizing disorders. In D. Cicchetti & S. L. Toth (Eds.), *Internalizing and externalizing expressions of dysfunction: Rochester symposium on developmental psychopathology* (Vol. 2, pp. 1–19). Hillsdale, NJ: Erlbaum.

Cicchetti, D., & Toth, S. L. (2009). The past achievements and future promises of developmental psychopathology: The coming of age of a discipline. *Journal of Child Psychology and Psychiatry, 50,* 16–25.

Cinciripini, P. M., Lapitsky, L. G., Seay, S., Wallfisch, A., Kitchens, K., & Van Vunakis, H. (1995). The effects of smoking schedules on cessation outcome: Can we improve on common methods of gradual and abrupt nicotine withdrawal? *Journal of Consulting and Clinical Psychology, 63,* 388–399.

Cipriani, A., Hawton, K., Stockton, S., & Geddes, J. R. (2013). Lithium in the prevention of suicide in mood disorders: Updated systematic review and meta-analysis. *British Medical Journal, 346.*

Cipriani, A., Rendell, J., & Geddes, J. R. (2010). Olanzapine in the long-term treatment of bipolar disorder: A systematic review and meta-analysis. *Journal of Psychopharmacology, 24*(12), 1729–1738. doi:10.1177/0269881109106900

Clark, D. A., & Beck, A. T. (2010). *Cognitive therapy of anxiety disorders: Science and practice.* New York: Guilford Press.

Clark, D. M. (1986). A cognitive approach to panic. *Behavioral Research & Therapy, 24,* 461–470.

Clark, D. M. (2001). A cognitive perspective on social phobia. In W. Crozier & L.E. Alden (Eds.), *International handbook of social anxiety: Concepts, research and interventions relating to the self and shyness* (pp. 405–430). New York: Wiley.

Clark, D. M., Salkovskis, P. M., Hackman, A., Middleton, H., Anastasiades, P., & Gelder, M. (1994). A comparison of cognitive therapy, applied relaxation, and imipramine in the treatment of panic disorder. *British Journal of Psychiatry, 164,* 759–769.

Clark, L. A., Watson, D., &; Reynolds, S. (1995). Diagnosis and classification of psychopathology: Challenges to the current system and future directions. *Annual Review of Psychology, 46,* 121–153. Palo Alto, CA: Annual Reviews.

Clarke, D. E., Narrow, W. E., Regier, D. A., Kuramoto, J., Kupfer, D. J., Kuhl, E. A., Kraemer, H. C. (2013). *DSM-5* field trials in the United States and Canada, Part I: Study design, sampling strategy, implementation, and analytic approaches. *American Journal of Psychiatry, 170,* 43–58. doi:10.1176/appi.ajp.2012.12070998

Clarkin, J. F., & Kendall, P. C. (1992). Comorbidity and treatment planning: Summary and future directions. *Journal of Consulting and Clinical Psychology, 60,* 904–908.

Clarkin, J. F., Glick, I D., Haas, G. L., Spencer, J. H., Lewis, A. B., Peyser, J., Demane, N., Good-Ellis, M., Harris, E., & Lestelle, V. (1990). A randomized clinical trial of in-patient family intervention. V: Results for affective disorders. *Journal of Affective Disorders, 18,* 17–28.

Clay, R. A. (2014). From serious mental illness to recovery. *APA Monitor, 45*(8), 54.

Clay, R. A. (2014). Introducing the mental health action plan. *APA Monitor, 45,* 20.

Clayton, A. (2008). Symptoms related to the menstrual cycle: Diagnosis, prevalence, and treatment. *Journal of Psychiatric Practice, 14*(1), 13–21.

Clayton, A. H. (2012). Sexual arousal and lubrication problems in women with clinically diagnosed hypoactive sexual desire disorder: Preliminary findings from the Hypoactive Sexual Desire Disorder Registry for Women. *Journal of Sexual Medicine, 9*(7), 1738–1739.

Clayton, P. J. (1986). Bipolar illness. In G. Winokur & P. Clayton (Eds.), *The medical basis of psychiatry* (pp. 39–59). Philadelphia: W. B. Saunders.

Clayton, P. J., Herjanic, M., Murphy, G. E., Woodruff, R. (1974). Mourning and depression: Their similarities and differences. *Journal of the Canadian Psychiatric Association, 19,* 309–312.

Cleburne Living Center, Inc. v. City of Cleburne, Texas, 52 L. W. 2515, 726 F. 3d 191 (1985).

Cleckley, H. (1976). *The mask of sanity* (5th ed.). St. Louis: Mosby.

Clement, S., Singh, S. P., & Burns, T. (2003). Status of bipolar disorder research—bibliometric study. *The British Journal of Psychiatry, 182*(2), 148–152. doi:10.1192/bjp.182.2.148

Clementz, B. A., & Sweeney, J. A. (1990). Is eye movement dysfunction a biological marker for schizophrenia? A methodological review. *Psychological Bulletin, 108,* 77–92.

Cloninger, C. R. (1987). A systematic method for clinical description and classification of personality variants: A proposal. *Archives of General Psychiatry, 44,* 573–588.

Cloninger, C. R., Bohman, M., & Sigvardsson, S. (1981). Inheritance of alcohol abuse: Cross-fostering analysis of adopted men. *Archives of General Psychiatry, 38,* 861–868.

Cloninger, C. R., & Gottesman, I. (1987). Genetic and environmental factors in antisocial behavior disorders. In S. A. Mednick, T. E. Moffitt, & S. A. Stack (Eds.), *Causes of crime: New biological approaches.* Cambridge: Cambridge University Press.

Cloninger, C. R., Sigvardsson, S., & Bohman, M. (1988). Childhood personality predicts alcohol abuse in young adults. *Alcoholism in Clinical and Experimental Research, 12*(4), 494–505.

Cloninger, C. R., Sigvardsson, S., & Bohman, M. (1996). Type I and type II alcoholism: An update. *Alcohol Health & Research World, 20,* 18–23.

Close, H., & Garety, P. (1998). Cognitive assessment of voices: Further developments in understanding the emotional impact of voices. *British Journal of Clinical Psychology, 37*(2), 173–188. doi:10.1111/j.2044-8260.1998.tb01292.x

Clozapine Study Group (1993). The safety and efficacy of clozapine in severe treatment-resistant schizophrenics in the UK. *British Journal of Psychiatry, 163,* 150–155.

Clum, G. A., Clum, G. A., & Surls, R. (1993). A meta-analysis of treatments for panic disorder. *Journal of Consulting and Clinical Psychology, 61,* 317–326.

Coates, S. (1990). Ontogenesis of boyhood gender identity disorder. *Journal of the American Academy of Psychoanalysis, 18,* 414–438.

Coates, S., & Person, E. S. (1985). Extreme boyhood femininity: Isolated behavior or pervasive disorder? *Journal of the American Academy of Child Psychiatry, 24,* 702–709.

Coccaro, E. F. (1993). Psychopharmacological studies in patients with personality disorders: Review and perspective. *Journal of Personality Disorders, 7,* 181–192.

Coffey, C. E. (Ed.). (1993). *The clinical science of electro-convulsive therapy.* Washington DC: American Psychiatric Press.

Cohen, A. N., Hammen, C., Henry, R. M., & Daley, S. E. (2004). Effects of stress and social support on recurrence in bipolar disorder. *Journal of Affective Disorders, 82,* 143–147.

Cohen, C. I. (1993). Poverty and the course of schizophrenia: Implications for research and policy. *Hospital and Community Psychiatry, 44,* 951–958.

Cohen, H. L. (1968). Educational therapy: The design of learning environments. *Research in Psychotherapy, 3,* 21–58.

Cohen, J. B., & Reed, D. (1985). Type A behavior and coronary heart disease among Japanese men in Hawaii. *Journal of Behavioral Medicine, 8,* 343–352.

Cohen, J., & Servan-Schreiber, D. (1992). Context, cortex, and dopamine: A connectionist approach to behavior and biology in schizophrenia. *Psychological Review, 99,* 45–77.

Cohen, S., & Wills, T. A. (1985). Stress, social support, and the buffering hypothesis. *Psychological Bulletin, 98,* 310–357.

Cohen, S., Kamarck, T., & Mermelstein, R. (1983). A global measure of perceived stress. *Journal of Health and Social Behavior, 24,* 385–396.

Cohen, S., Tyrell, D. A. J., & Smith, A. P. (1991). Psychological stress and susceptibility to the common cold. *New England Journal of Medicine, 325,* 606–612.

Cohen-Kettenis, P., & Pfäfflin, F. (2009). The *DSM* diagnostic criteria for gender identity disorder in adolescents and adults. *Archives of Sexual Behavior,* 499–513.

Cohn, J. F., Campbell, S. B., Matias, R., & Hopkins, J. (1990). Face-to-face interactions of postpartum depressed and nondepressed mother-infant pairs at two months. *Developmental Psychology, 26,* 15–23.

Coie, J. D., Lochman, J. E., Terry, R., & Hyman, C. (1992). Predicting early adolescent disorder from childhood aggression and peer rejection. *Journal of Consulting and Clinical Psychology, 60,* 783-792.

Coie, J. D., Watt, N. F., West, S. G., Hawkins, J. D., Asarnow, J. R., Markman, H. J., Ramey, S. L., Shure, M. B., & Long, B. (1993). The science of prevention: A conceptual framework and some directions for a national research program. *American Psychologist, 48,* 1013–1022.

Cole, D. A., & White, K. (1993). Structure of peer impressions of children's competence: Validation of the peer nomination of multiple competencies. *Psychological Assessment, 5,* 449–456.

Cole, J. O., & Bodkin, J. A. (1990). Antidepressant drug side effects. *Journal of Clinical Psychiatry, 51* (Suppl.), 21–26.

Cole, M. G., McCusker, J., Dendukuri, N., & Han, L. (2002). Symptoms of delirium among elderly medical inpatients with or without dementia. *Journal of Neuropsychiatry & Clinical Neuroscience, 14*(2), 167–175.

Coleman, E., Bockting, W., Botzer, M., Cohen-Kettenis, P., DeCuypere, G., Feldman, J., . . . Zucker, K. (2011). Standards of care for the health of transsexual, transgender, and gender nonconforming people, version 7. *International Journal of Transgenderism, 13,* 165–232.

Coles, G. (1987). *The learning mystique: A critical look at "learning disabilities."* New York: Fawcett Columbine.

Coles, M. E., Frost, R. O., Heimberg, R. G., & Steketee, G. (2003). Hoarding behaviors in a large college sample. *Behaviour Research and Therapy, 41*(2), 179–194. doi: 10.1016/s0005-7967(01)00136-x

Collier, C. R., Czuchry, M., Dansereau, D. F., & Pitre, U. (2001). The use of node-link mapping in the chemical dependency treatment of adolescents. *Journal of Drug Education, 31*(3), 305–317. doi:10.2190/GMC2-K3XX-XLHF-K2J0

Colvin, C. R., & Block, J. (1994). Do positive illusions foster mental health? An examination of the Taylor and Brown formulation. *Psychological Bulletin, 116,* 3–20.

Combs, D. R., & Penn, D. L. (2004). The role of sub-clinical paranoia on social perception and behavior. *Schizophrenia Research, 69,* 93–104.

Comer, J. P. (1987). New Haven's school-community connection. *Educational Leadership, 44,* 13–16.

Comings, D. E., Comings, B. G., Muhleman, D., Dietz, G., Shahbahrami, B., Tast, D., Knell, E., Kocsis, P., Baum-garten, R., Kovacs, B. W., Levy, D. L., Smith, M., Borison, R. L., Evans, D. D., Klein, D. N., Macmurray, J., Tosk, J. M., Sverd, J., Gysin, R., & Flanagan, S. D. (1991). The dopamine D2 receptor locus as a modifying gene in neuropsychiatric disorders. *Journal of the American Medical Association, 266*(13), 1793–1800.

Compton, M. T., Bakeman, R., Broussard, B., Hankerson-Dyson, D., Husbands, L., Krishan, S., . . . Watson, A. C. (2014a). The police-based crisis intervention team (CIT) model: I. Effects on officers' knowledge, attitudes, and skills. *Psychiatric Services, 65*(4), 517–522. doi:10.1176/appi.ps.201300107

Compton, M. T., Bakeman, R., Broussard, B., Hankerson-Dyson, D., Husbands, L., Krishan, S., . . . Watson, A. C. (2014b). The police-based crisis intervention team (CIT) model: II. Effects on level of force and resolution, referral, and arrest. *Psychiatric Services, 65*(4), 523–529. doi:10.1176/appi.ps.201300108

Compton, M. T., Thompson, N. J., & Kaslow, N. J. (2005). Social environment factors associated with suicide attempt among low-income African Americans: The protective role of family relationships and social support. *Social Psychiatry and Psychiatric Epidemiology, 40*(3), 175–185. doi:10.1007/s00127-005-0865-6

Conde-Sala, J. L., Turró-Garriga, O., Calvó-Perxas, L., Vilalta-Franch, J., Lopez-Pousa, S., & Garre-Olmo, J. (2014). Three-year trajectories of caregiver burden in Alzheimer's disease. *Journal of Alzheimer's Disease, 42*(2), 623–633.

Conduct Problems Prevention Research Group (1994). A developmental and clinical model for the prevention of conduct disorder: The FAST Track Program. *Development and Psychopathology, 4,* 509–527.

Conduct Problems Prevention Research Group (2011). The effects of the fast-track preventative intervention on the development of conduct disorder across childhood. *Child Development, 82,* 331–345.

Conger, J. J. (1956). Alcoholism: Theory, problem and challenge: II. Reinforcement theory and the dynamics of alcoholism. *Quarterly Journal of Studies on Alcohol, 101* (1), 139–152.

Conger, R. D., Ge, X., Elder, G. H., Lorenz, F. O., & Simons, R. L. (1994). Economic stress, coercive family process, and developmental problems of adolescents. *Child Development, 65,* 541–561.

Conner, B. T., Noble, E. P., Berman, S. M., Ozkaragoz, T., Ritchie, T., Antolin, T., & Sheen, C. (2005). DRD2 genotypes and substance use in adolescent children of alcoholics. *Drug and Alcohol Dependence, 79*(3), 379–387. doi:10.1016/j.drugalcdep.2005.03.005

Conner, K. R., & Goldston, D. B. (2007). Rates of suicide among males increase steadily from age 11 to 21: Developmental framework and outline for prevention. *Aggression and Violent Behavior, 12*(2), 193–207. doi:10.1016/j.avb.2006.07.002

Connors, G. J., & Rychtarik, R. G. (1989). The Supreme Court VA/disease model case: Background and implications. *Psychology of Addictive Behaviors, 2,* 101–107.

Conoley, C. W., Conoley, J. C., McConnell, J. A., & Kimzey, C. E. (1983). The effect of the ABCs of rational emotive therapy and the empty-chair technique of Gestalt therapy on anger reduction. *Psychotherapy: Theory, Research, and Practice, 20,* 112–117.

Consensus Development Conference Statement (1985). *Electroconvulsive therapy.* National Institutes of Health OM-00-4018. vol 5, (11).

Conte, H. R., Plutchik, R., Wild, K., & Karasu, T. B. (1986). Combined psychotherapy and pharmacotherapy for depression: A systematic analysis of evidence. *Archives of General Psychiatry, 43,* 471–479.

"Conversion Disorder." (n.d.). Retrieved on December 5, 2014 from http://www.humanillnesses.com/Behavioral-Health-Br-Fe/Conversion-Disorder.html

Conway, J. B. (1988). Differences among clinical psychologists: Scientists, practitioners, and scientist-practitioners. *Professional Psychology: Research and Practice, 19,* 642–655.

Cook, C. C. H. (1988). The Minnesota model in the management of drug and alcohol dependency: Miracle, method or myth? Part II. Evidence and conclusions. *British Journal of Addictions, 83,* 735–748.

Cook, J. A. (1995, summer). Research on psychosocial rehabilitation services for persons with psychiatric disabilities. *Psychotherapy and Rehabilitation Research Bulletin,* 5–11.

Cook, M., & Mineka, S. (1987). Second-order conditioning and overshadowing in the observational conditioning of fear in monkeys. *Behaviour Research and Therapy, 25,* 349–364.

Cook, T. D., & Campbell, D. T. (1979). *Quasi-experimentation: Design and analysis issues for field settings.* Chicago: Rand-McNally.

Coolidge, F. L., & Segal, D. L. (2007). Was Saddam Hussein like Adolf Hitler? A personality disorder investigation. *Military Psychology, 19*(4), 289–299. doi:10.1080/08995600701548221

Coolidge, F. L., Thede, L. L., & Young, S. E. (2002). The heritability of gender identity disorder in a child and adolescent twin sample. *Behavior Genetics, 32*(4), 251–257. doi:10.1023/A:1019724712983

Cooney, N. L., Kadden, R. M., Litt, M. D., & Getter, H. (1991). Matching alcoholics to coping skills or interactional therapies: Two-year follow-up results. *Journal of Consulting and Clinical Psychology, 59*(4), 598–601.

Coons, P. M. (1986). Treatment progress in 20 patients with multiple personality disorder. *Journal of Nervous and Mental Disease, 174,* 715–721.

Coons, P. M., Milstein, V., & Marley, C. (1982). EEG studies of two multiple personalities and a control. *Archives of General Psychiatry, 39,* 823–825.

Cooper, G. L. (1988). The safety of fluoxetine—An update. *British Journal of Psychiatry, 153,* (Suppl. 3), 77–86.

Cooper, J. E., Kendell, R., Gurland, B., Sharpe, L., Copeland, J. R., & Simon, R. (1972). *Psychiatric diagnosis in New York and London.* London: Oxford University Press.

Cooper, M. L., Russell, M., Skinner, J. B., Frone, M. R., & Mudar, P. (1992). Stress and alcohol use: The moderating effects of gender, coping, and alcohol expectancies. *Journal of Abnormal Psychology, 101*(1), 139–152.

Coplan, J., Sharama, T., Rosenblum, L., Friedman, S., Bas-soff, T., Barbour, R., & Gorman, J. (1992). Effects of sodium lactate infusion on cisternal lactate and carbon dioxide levels in nonhuman primates. *American Journal of Psychiatry, 149,* 1369–1373.

Copolov, D. L., Mackinnon, A., & Trauer, T. (2004). Correlates of the affective impact of auditory hallucinations in psychotic disorders. *Schizophrenia Bulletin, 30*(1), 163–171.

Coppen, A., Mendelwicz, J., & Kielholz, P. (1986). *Pharmacotherapy of depressive disorders: A consensus statement.* Geneva: World Health Organization.

Corbett, R. W., Ryan, C., & Weinrich, S. P. (2003). Pica in pregnancy: Does it affect pregnancy outcomes? *The American Journal of Maternal/Child Nursing, 28*(3), 183–189.

Corbetta, M., & Shulman, G. L. (2002). Control of goal-directed and stimulus-driven attention in the brain. *Nature Reviews Neuroscience, 3,* 201–215.

Corder, B., Saunders, A. M., Strittmatter, W. J., Schmechel, D. E., Gaskell, P. C., & Small, G. N. (1993). Gene dose of apolipoprotein E type 4 allele and the risk of Alzheimer's disease in late onset families. *Science, 261,* 921–923.

Cordess, C. (2001). Munchausen syndrome by proxy abuse: A practical approach. *The British Journal of Psychiatry, 178*(5), 481–482. doi:10.1192/bjp.178.5.481

Corey, G., Corey, M. S., & Callahan, P. (2010). *Issues and ethics in the helping professions* (8th ed.). Pacific Grove, CA: Brooks Cole Publishing.

Corkin, S. (1980). A prospective study of cingulatomy. In E.S. Valenstein (Ed.), *The psychosurgery debate: Scientific, legal and ethical perspectives* (pp. 164–204). San Francisco: Freeman.

Corkum, P., Tannock, R., & Moldofsky, H. (1998). Sleep disturbances in children with attention-deficit/hyperactivity disorder. *Journal of the American Academy of Child and Adolescent Psychiatry, 37,* 637–646.

Cormier, J. F. (1997, March). Professional skepticism of multiple personality disorder. *Dissertation Abstracts International, 57,* 5911.

Corona, G., Petrone, L., Mannucci, E., Jannini, E. A., Mansani, R., Magini, A., . . . Maggi, M. (2004). Psychobiological correlates of rapid ejaculation in patients attending an andrologic unit for sexual dysfunctions. *European Urology, 46*(5), 615–622.

Corwin, D., & Olafson E. (1997). Videotaped discovery of a reportedly unrecallable memory of child sexual abuse: Comparison with a childhood interview videotaped 11 years before. *Child Maltreatment, 2*(2), 91–112. doi:10.1177/1077559597002002001

Coryell, W., Lavori, P., Endicott, J., Keller, M., & Van-Eerdewegh, M. (1984). Outcome in schizoaffective, psychotic and nonpsychotic depression. *Archives of General Psychiatry, 41,* 787–791.

Coryell, W., Leon, A. C., Turvey, C., Akiskal, H. S., Mueller, T., & Endicott, J. (2001). The significance of psychotic features in manic episodes: A report from the NIMH collaborative study. *Journal of Affective Disorders, 67*(1–3), 79–88. doi:10.1016/S0165-0327(99)00024-5

Cosgrove, G. R., Baer, L., Rauch, S., Ballantine, R., Cassem, E., Manzo, P., & Jenihy, M. (1995). Cingulotomy for intractable obsessive-compulsive disorder: A prospective long-term follow-up study. *Stereotactic and Functional Neurosurgery, 65*, 67–71.

Costa P. T., Jr., & McCrae, R. R. (1990). Personality disorders and the five-factor model of personality. *Journal of Personality Disorders, 4*, 362–371.

Costa, P. T., Jr., & McCrae, R. R. (1986). Personality stability and its implications for clinical psychology. *Clinical Psychology Review, 6*, 407–424.

Costa, P. T., Jr., & McCrae, R. R. (1992a). *Manual for the Revised NEO Personality Inventory (NEO-PIR) and the NEO Five-Factor Inventory (BEO-FFI)*. Odessa, FL: Psychological Assessment Resources.

Costa, P. T., Jr., & McCrae, R. R. (1992b). Normal personality assessment in clinical practice: The NEO Personality Inventory. *Psychological Assessment, 11*, 5–13.

Costa, P. T., Jr., & Widiger, T. A. (Eds.). (1994). *Personality disorders and the five-factor model of personality*. Washington, DC: American Psychological Association.

Costanzo, M., & Krauss, D. (2010). *Forensic and legal psychology*. New York: Worth Publishers.

Costello, E., Costello, A., Edelbrock, C., Burns, B., Dulcan, M., Brent, D., & Janiszewski, S. (1988). Psychiatric disorders in pediatric primary care. *Archives of General Psychiatry, 45*, 1107–1116.

Costello, R. M. (1975). Alcoholism treatment and evaluation: In search of methods. *International Journal of the Addictions, 10*, 251–275.

Coupey, S. M. (1997). Barbiturates. *Pediatric Review, 18*(8), 260–264. doi:10.1542/pir.18-8-260.

Courchesne, E., Yeung-Courchesne, R., Press, G. A., Hesselink, J. R., & Jernigan, T. L. (1988). Hypoplasia of cerebellar vermal lobules VI and VII in autism. *New England Journal of Medicine, 318*, 1349–1354.

Cowdry, R. W., & Gardner, D. L. (1988). Pharmacotherapy of borderline personality disorder: Alprazolam, carbamazepine, trifluoperazine, and tranylcypromine. *Archives of General Psychiatry, 45*, 111–119.

Cowen, E. L. (1994). The enhancement of psychological wellness: Challenges and opportunities. *American Journal of Community Psychology, 22*, 149–180.

Cowen, E. L., Gesten, E. L., & Wilson, A. B. (1979). The primary mental health project (PMHP): Evaluation of current program effectiveness. *American Journal of Community Psychology, 7*, 293–303.

Cowlishaw, S., Merkouris, S., Chapman, A., & Radermacher, H. (2014). Pathological and problem gambling in substance use treatment: A systematic review and meta-analysis. *Journal of Substance Abuse Treatment, 46*(2), 98–105. doi:10.1016/j.jsat.2013.08.019

Cox, W. M. (1987). Personality theory and research. In H. T. Blane & K. E. Leonard (Eds.), *Psychological theories of drinking and alcoholism: The Guilford Alcohol Studies Series G* (pp. 55-89). New York: Guilford Press.

Coyne, J. C. (1976). Toward an interactional description of depression. *Psychiatry, 39*, 28–40.

Coyne, J. C., & Downey, G. (1991). Social factors in psychopathology: Stress, social support, and coping processes. *Annual Review of Psychology, 42*, 401–425.

Coyne, J. C., Kessler, R. C., Tal, M., Turnbull, J., Wortman, C., & Greden, J. (1987). Living with a depressed person: Burden and psychological distress. *Journal of Clinical and Consulting Psychology, 55*, 347–352.

Craddock, N., & Jones, I. (2001). Molecular genetics of bipolar disorder. *The British Journal of Psychiatry, 178*(Suppl41), s128–s133. doi:10.1192/bjp.178.41.s128

Craig, T. K. J., Cox, A. D., & Klein, K. (2002). Intergenerational transmission of somatization behaviour: A study of chronic somatizers and their children. *Psychological Medicine, 32*(5), 805–816. doi:10.1017/S0033291702005846

Cramer, H., Lauche, R., Langhorst, J., & Dobos, G. (2013). Yoga for depression: A systematic review and meta-analysis. *Depression and Anxiety, 30*(11), 1068–1083. doi:10.1002/da.22166

Craner, J. R., Sigmon, S. T., Martinson, A. A., & McGillicuddy, M. L. (2014). Premenstrual disorders and rumination. *Journal of Clinical Psychology, 70*(1), 32–47. doi:10.1002/jclp.22007

Crapper-McLachlan, D. R., Dalton, A. J., Kruck, T. P. A., Bell, M. Y., Smith, W. L., Kalow, W., & Andrews, D. F. (1991). Intramuscular desferrioxamine in patients with Alzheimer's disease. *Lancet, 337*, 1304–1308.

Craske, M. G. (2003). *Origins of phobias and anxiety disorders: Why more women than men?* Kidlington, Oxon, UK: Elsevier.

Craske, M., & Barlow, D. H. (1993). Panic disorder and agoraphobia. In D. H. Barlow (Ed.), *Clinical handbook of psychological disorders: A step-by-step treatment manual* (2nd ed.). New York: Guilford Press.

Craske, M., Zarate, R., Burton, T., & Barlow, D. (1993). Specific fears and panic attacks: A survey of clinical and non-clinical samples. *Journal of Anxiety Disorders, 7*, 1–19.

Creamer, M., Burgess, P., & Pattison, P. (1992). Reactions to trauma: A cognitive processing model. *Journal of Abnormal Psychology, 101*, 452–459.

Creed, F. H., Davies, I., Jackson, J., Littlewood, A., Chew-Graham, C., Tomenson, B., . . . McBeth, J. (2012). The epidemiology of multiple somatic symptoms. *Journal of Psychosomatic Research, 72*(4), 311–317. doi:10.1016/j.jpsychores.2012.01.009

Creed, F. H., Tomenson, B., Chew-Graham, C., Macfarlane, G. J., Davies, I., Jackson, J., . . . McBeth, J. (2013). Multiple somatic symptoms predict impaired health status in functional somatic syndromes. *International Journal of Behavioral Medicine, 20*(2), 194–205. doi:10.1007/s12529-012-9257-y

Crews, F. (1994). *The memory wars: Freud's legacy in dispute.* New York: New York Review Imprints.

Crick, N. R., & Dodge, K. A. (1994). A review and reformulation of social-information-processing mechanisms in children's social adjustment. *Psychological Bulletin, 115*, 74–101.

Crisp, A. H., Norton, K., Gowers, S., Halek, C., Bowyer, C., Yeldham, D., Levett, G., & Bhat, A. (1991), A controlled study of the effect of therapies aimed at adolescent and family psychopathology in anorexia nervosa. *British Journal of Psychiatry, 159*, 325–333.

Critelli, J. W., & Neumann, K. R (1984). The placebo: Conceptual analysis of a construct in transition. *American Psychologist, 39*, 32–39.

Crnic, K. A., Greenberg, M. T., Ragozin, A. S., Robinson, N. M., & Basham, R. B. (1983). Effects of stress and social support on mothers and premature and full-term infants. *Child Development, 54*, 209–217.

Crockenberg, S., & Littman, C, (1990). Autonomy as competence in 2-year olds: Maternal correlates of child defiance, compliance, and self assertion. *Developmental Psychology, 26*, 961–971.

Cronbach, L. J., & Meehl, R E. (1955). Construct validity in psychology tests. *Psychological Bulletin, 52*, 281–302.

Cross, D. G., Sheehan, P. W., & Khan, J. A. (1980). Alternative advice and counsel in psychotherapy. *Journal of Consulting and Clinical Psychology, 48*, 615–625.

Cross-National Collaborative Group (1992). The changing rate of major depression: Cross-national comparisons. *Journal of the American Medical Association, 268*, 3098–3105.

Crow, T. (1980). Positive and negative schizophrenia symptoms and the role of dopamine. *British Journal of Psychiatry, 137*, 383–386.

Crow, T. (1985). The two-syndrome concept: Origins and current status. *Schizophrenia Bulletin, 11*, 471–486.

Crow, T. (2008). The "big bang" theory of the origin of psychosis and the faculty of language. *Schizophrenia Research, 102*, 31–52.

Crowe, M., Whitehead, L., Wilson, L., Carlyle, D., O'Brien, A., Inder, M., & Joyce, P. (2010). Disorder-specific psychosocial interventions for bipolar disorder—A systematic review of the evidence for mental health nursing practice. *International Journal of Nursing Studies, 47*(7), 896–908. doi:10.1016/j.ijnurstu.2010.02.012

Crowe, R., Noyes, R., Pauls, D., & Slyman, D. (1983). A family study of panic disorder. *Archives of General Psychiatry,. 40*, 1065–1069.

Crowell, J. A., Waters, E., Kring, A., & Riso, L. P. (1993). The psychosocial etiologies of personality disorders: What is the answer like? *Journal of Personality Disorders, 7*, 118–128.

Cryan, M. J., & Ganter, K. (1992). Childhood hallucinations in the context of parental psychopathology. *Irish Journal of Psychological Medicine, 9*, 120–122.

Crystal, H., Fuld, P., Masur, D., Scott, R., Mehler, M., Masdeu, J., Kawas, C., Aronson, M., & Wolfson, L. (1988). Clinico-pathological studies in dementia: Non-demented subjects with pathologically confirmed Alzheimer's disease. *Neurology, 38*, 1682–1687.

Cuijpers, P., Andersson, G., Donker, T., & van Straten, A. (2011). Psychological treatment of depression: Results of a series of meta-analyses. *Nordic Journal of Psychiatry, 65*(6), 354–364. doi:10.3109/08039488.2011.596570

Cuijpers, P., Donker, T., Johansson, R., Mohr, D. C., van Straten, A., & Andersson, G. (2011). Self-guided psychological treatment for depressive symptoms: A meta-analysis. *Plos ONE, 6*(6). doi:10.1371/journal.pone.0021274

Cuijpers, P., Geraedts, A. S., van Oppen, P., Andersson, G., Markowitz, J. C., & van Straten, A. (2011). Interpersonal psychotherapy for depression: A meta-analysis. *The American Journal of Psychiatry, 168*(6), 581–592. doi:10.1176/appi.ajp.2010.10101411

Cuijpers, P., Karyotaki, E., Weitz, E., Andersson, G., Hollon, S. D., & van Straten, A. (2014). The effects of psychotherapies for major depression in adults on remission, recovery, and improvement: A meta-analysis. *Journal of Affective Disorders, 159*, 118–126. doi:10.1016/j.jad.2014.02.026

Cuijpers, P., Sijbrandij, M., Koole, S., Huibers, M., Berking, M., & Andersson, G. (2014). Psychological treatment of generalized anxiety disorder: A meta-analysis. *Clinical Psychology Review, 34*(2), 130–140. doi:10.1016/j.cpr.2014.01.002

Cuijpers, P., van Straten, A., Andersson, G., & van Oppen, P. (2008). Psychotherapy for depression in adults: A meta-analysis of comparative outcome studies. *Journal of Consulting and Clinical Psychology, 76*(6), 909–922. doi:10.1037/a0013075

Cuijpers, P., van Straten, A., Hollon, S. D., & Andersson, G. (2010). The contribution of active medication to combined treatments of psychotherapy and pharmacotherapy for adult depression: A meta-analysis. *Acta Psychiatrica Scandinavica, 121*(6), 415–423.

Cuijpers, P., van Straten, A., Schuurmans, J., van Oppen, P., Hollon, S. D., & Andersson, G. (2010). Psychotherapy for chronic major depression and dysthymia: A meta-analysis. *Clinical Psychology Review, 30*(1), 51–62. doi:10.1016/j.cpr.2009.09.003

Cullen, B., Brown, C. H., Riddle, M. A., Grados, M., Bienvenu, O. J., Hoehn-Saric, R., . . . Nestadt, G. (2007). Factor analysis of the Yale-Brown Obsessive-Compulsive Scale in a family study of obsessive-compulsive disorder. *Depression and Anxiety, 24*, 130–138.

Cumins, R. A., Polzin, U., & Theobald, T. (1990). Deinstitutionalization of St. Nicholas Hospital. IV: A four-year follow-up of resident life-style. *Australia and New Zealand Journal of Developmental Disabilities, 16*(4), 305-321.

Cummings, C. M., Caporino, N. E., & Kendall, P. C. (2014). Comorbidity of anxiety and depression in children and adolescents: 20 years after. *Psychological Bulletin, 140*(3), 816–845. doi:10.1037/a0034733

Cummings, E. M., & Davies, P. T. (2002). Effects of marital conflict on children: Recent advances and emerging themes in process-oriented research. *Journal of Child Psychology, 43*, 31–63.

Cummings, J. L., & Coffey, C. E. (1994). Geriatric neuropsychiatry. In C. E. Coffey & J. L. Cummings (Eds.). *Textbook of geriatric neuropsychiatry* (pp. 3–15). Washington, DC: American Psychiatric Press.

Cunha, A. I., Relvas A. P., & Soares, I. (2009). Anorexia nervosa and family relationships: Perceived family functioning, coping strategies, beliefs, and attachment to parents and peers. *International Journal of Clinical and Health Psychology, 9*(2), 229–240.

Cunningham, J., Dockery, D. W., & Speizer, F. E. (1994). Maternal smoking during pregnancy as a predictor of lung function in children. *American Journal of Epidemiology, 139*(12), 1139–1152.

Cunningham, J., Yonkers, K. A., O'Brien, S., & Eriksson, E. (2009). Update on research and treatment of premenstrual dysphoric disorder. *Harvard Review of Psychiatry, 17*(2), 120–137.

Cunningham, N. K., Brown, P. M., Brooks, J., & Page, A. C. (2013). The structure of emotional symptoms in the postpartum period: Is it unique? *Journal of Affective Disorders, 151*(2), 686–694. doi:10.1016/j.jad.2013.08.002

Curran, C., Byrappa, N., & McBride, A. (2004). Stimulant psychosis: systematic review. *The British Journal of Psychiatry, 185*, 196–204.

Curran, S. L., Sherman, J. J., Cunningham, L. C., Okeson, J. P., Reid, K. I., & Carlson, C. R. (1995). Physical and sexual abuse among orofacial pain patients: Linkages with pain and psychologic distress. *Journal of Orofacial Pain, 9*, 340–346.

Cuzen, N. L., Andrew, C., Thomas, K. F., Stein, D. J., & Fein, G. (2013). Absence of P300 reduction in South African treatment-naïve adolescents with alcohol dependence. *Alcoholism: Clinical and Experimental Research, 37*(1), 40–48. doi:10.1111/j.1530-0277.2012.01837.x

D

Dahl, A. A. (1993). The personality disorders: A critical review of family, twin, and adoption studies. *Journal of Personality Disorders, 7*, 86–99.

Dalenberg, C. J., Brand, B. L., Gleaves, D. H., Dorahy, M. J., Loewenstein, R. J., Cardena, E., . . . Spiegel, D. (2012). Evaluation of the evidence for the trauma and fantasy models of dissociation. *Psychological Bulletin, 138*(3), 550–588.

Dalenberg, C. J., Brand, B. L., Loewenstein, R. J., Gleaves, D. H., Dorahy, M. J., Cardeña, E., . . . Spiegel, D. (2014). Reality versus fantasy: Reply to Lynn et al. (2014). *Psychological Bulletin, 140*(3), 911–920. doi:10.1037/a0036685

Dang, L. C., Samanez-Larkin, G. R., Young, J. S., Cowan, R. L., Kessler, R. M., & Zald, D. H. (2014). Caudate asymmetry is related to attentional impulsivity and an objective measure of ADHD-like attentional problems in healthy adults. *Brain Structure & Function*, doi:10.1007/s00429-014-0906-6

Danton, W. G., & Antonuccio, D. O. (1997). A focused empirical analysis of treatments for panic and anxiety. In S. Fisher & R.P. Greenberg (Eds.), *From placebo to panacea: Putting psychiatric drugs to the test* (pp. 229–280). Hoboken, NJ: John Wiley & Sons.

Dantzer, R., O'Connor, J. C., Freund, G. C., Johnson, R. W., & Kelley, K. W. (2008). From inflammation to sickness and depression: When the immune system subjugates the brain. *Nature Reviews Neuroscience, 9*(1), 46–57. doi:10.1038/nrn2297

Darcangelo, S. (2008). Fetishism: Psychopathology and theory. In D. R. Laws & W. T. O'Donohue (Eds.), *Sexual deviance: Theory, assessment, and treatment* (pp. 108–118). New York: Guilford Press.

Darke, S., Kaye, S., McKetin, R., & Duflou, J. (2008). Major physical and psychological harms of methamphetamine use. *Drug and Alcohol Reviews, 27*, 253–262.

Darke, S., Ross, J., & Cohen, J. (1994). The use of benzodiazepines among regular amphetamine users. *Addiction, 89*, 1683–1690.

Darke, S., Ross, J., Cohen, J., Hando, J., & Hall, W. (1995). Injecting and sexual risk-taking behaviour among regular amphetamine users. *AIDS Care, 7*, 19–26.

Darling, M. R., & Arendorf, T. M. (1993). Effects of cannabis smoking on oral soft tissues. *Community Denistry and Oral Epidemiology, 21*, 78–81.

Daubert v. Merrell Dow Pharmaceuticals, Inc., 509 U.S. 113 S. Ct. 2786 (1993).

Dauncey, K., Giggs, J., Baker, K., & Harrison, K. (1993). Schizophrenia in Nottingham: Lifelong residential mobility of a cohort. *British Journal of Psychiatry, 163*, 613–619.

Davanloo, H. L. (1994). *Basic principles and techniques in short-term dynamic psychotherapy*. Northdale, NJ: Jason Aronson.

Davidson, P. R., & Parker, K. H. (2001). Eye movement desensitization and reprocessing (EMDR): A meta-analysis. *Journal of Consulting and Clinical Psychology, 69*(2), 305–316. doi:10.1037/0022-006X.69.2.305

Davidson, R. J. (1991). Cerebral asymineUy and affective disorders: A developmental perspective. In D. Cicchetti & S. L. Toth (Eds.), *Internalizing and externalizing expressions of dysfunction: Rochester symposium on developmental psychopathology* (Vol. 2, pp. 123–154). Hillsdale, NJ: Erlbaum.

Davidson, R. J., & Fox, N. A. (1989). Frontal brain asymmetry predicts infants' response to maternal separation. *Journal of Abnormal Psychology, 98*, 127–131.

Davidson, R. J., Jackson, D. C., & Kalin, N. H. (2000). Emotion, plasticity, context, and regulation: Perspectives from affective neuroscience. *Psychological Bulletin, 126*, 890–909.

Davidson, W. S., Rappaport, J., Seidman, E., Berck, P., Rapp, C., Rhodes, W., & Herring, J. (1977). A diversion program for juvenile offenders. *Social Work Research and Abstracts, 1*, 47–56.

Davies, G., Welham, J., Chant, D., Torrey, E. F., & McGrath, J. (2003). A systematic review and meta-analysis of Northern Hemisphere season of birth studies in schizophrenia. *Schizophrenia Bulletin, 29*, 587–593.

Davila, J., Hammen, C., Burge, D., & Paley, B. (1995). Poor interpersonal problem solving as a mechanism of stress generation in depression among adolescent women. *Journal of Abnormal Psychology, 104*, 592–600.

Davis, A. S., Johnson, J. A., & D'Amato, R. (2005). Evaluating and using long-standing school neuropsychological batteries: The Halstead-Reitan and the Luria-Nebraska Neuropsychological Batteries. In R. D'Amato, E. Fletcher-Janzen, C. R. Reynolds (Eds.), *Handbook of school neuropsychology* (pp. 236–263). Hoboken, NJ: Wiley.

Davis, C., Levitan, R. D., Carter, J., Kaplan, A. S., Reid, C., Curtis, C., & Kennedy, J. L. (2008). Personality and eating behaviors: A case-control study of binge eating disorder. *International Journal of Eating Disorders, 41*(3), 243–250. doi:10.1002/eat.20499

Davis, D. (1993). Multiple personality, fugue, and amnesia. In D. L. Dunner (Ed.), *Current psychiatric therapy* (pp. 328–334). Philadelphia: W. B. Saunders.

Davis, J. M. (2010). The use of depot medications in the treatment of schizophrenia. *The American Journal of Psychiatry, 167*(2), 125–126. doi:10.1176/appi.ajp.2009.09111676

Davis, J. O., Phelps, J. A., & Bracha, H. S. (1995). Prenatal development of monozygotic twin and concordance in schizophrenia. *Schizophrenia Bulletin, 21*, 357–366.

Davis, K., Kahn, R., Ko, G., & Davidson, M. (1991). Dopamine in schizophrenia: A review and reconceptualization. *American Journal of Psychiatry, 148*, 1474–1486.

Davis, M. (1994). The role of the amygdala in emotion-learning. *International Review of Neuroscience, 36*, 225–266.

Davis, S. R., van der Mooren, M. J., van Lunsen, R. H. W., Lopes, P., Ribot, J., Rees, M., . . . Purdie, D. W. (2006). Efficacy and safety of a testosterone patch for the treatment of hypoactive sexual desire disorder in surgically menopausal women: A randomized, placebo-controlled trial. *Menopause: The Journal of the North American Menopause Society, 13*(3), 387–396.

Davison, G. C. (1978). Not can but ought: The treatment of homosexuality. *Journal of Clinical and Consulting Psychology, 46*, 170–172.

Dawes, R. M. (1994). *House of cards.* New York: The Free Press.

Dawes, R. M., Faust, D., & Meehl, P. (1989). Clinical versus actuarial judgment. *Science, 243*, 1668–1674.

Dawson, G., & Osterling, J. (1996). Early intervention in autism. In M. J. Guralnick (Ed.), *The effectiveness of early intervention*. Baltimore: Paul Brookes.

Dawson, G., & Lewy, A. (1989). Arousal, attention, and the socioemotional impairments of individuals with autism. In G. Dawson (Ed.), *Autism: Nature, diagnosis, and treatment*. New York: Guilford Press.

Day, N. L., Richardson, G. A., Geva, D., & Robles, N. (1994). Alcohol, marijuana, and tobacco: Effects of prenatal exposure on offspring growth and morphology at age six. *Alcoholism: Clinical and Experimental Research, 18*(4), 786–794.

Day, R., Nielsen, J. A., Kortcn, A., Ernberg, G., Dube, K. C., Gebhart, J., Jablensky, A., Leon, C., Marsella, A., Olatawura, M., Sartorius, N., Stromgren, E., Takahashi, R., Wig, N., Wynne, L. C. (1987). Stressful life events preceding the acute onset of schizophrenia: A cross-national study from the World Health Organization. *Cultural Medicine and Psychiatry, 11*, 123–205.

de Beurs, E., van Balkon, A. J., Lange, A., Koele, P., & van Dyke, R. (1995). Treatment of panic disorder with agoraphobia: Comparison of fluvoxamine, placebo, and psychological panic management combined with exposure and of exposure in vivo alone. *American Journal of Psychiatry, 152*, 683–691.

"Debunking the Amotivational Syndrome." (2006). *Drug Science.* Retrieved on December 16, 2014 from http://www.drugscience.org/Petition/C3F.html

de Carvalho, M., Dias, G., Cosci, F., de-Melo-Neto, V., do Nascimento Bevilaqua, M., Gardino, P., & Nardi, A. (2010). Current findings of fMRI in panic disorder: Contributions for the fear neurocircuitry and CBT effects. *Expert Review of Neurotherapeutics, 10*(2), 291–303. doi:10.1586/ern.09.161

de Greck, M., Scheidt, L., Bölter, A. F., Frommer, J., Ulrich, C., Stockum, E., . . . Northoff, G. (2012). Altered brain activity during emotional empathy in somatoform disorder. *Human Brain Mapping, 33*(11), 2666–2685. doi:10.1002/hbm.21392

de Leon, J. (2009). Pharmacogenomics: The promise of personalized medicine for CNS disorders. *Neuropsychopharmacology, 34*(1), 159–172. doi:10.1038/npp.2008.147

de Vries, A. L. C., & Cohen-Kettenis, P. T. (2012). Clinical management of gender dysphoria in children and adolescents: The Dutch approach. *Journal of Homosexuality, 59,* 301–320.

de Vries, A. L. C., Steensma, T. D., Doreleijers, T. A. H., & Cohen-Kettenis, P. T. (2011). Puberty suppression in adolescents with gender identity disorder: A prospective follow-up study. *Journal of Sexual Medicine, 8,* 2276–2283.

Deakins, S. A., Newmark, M., Dunne, E. J., Horen, B., & Toran, J. (1995). Multiple-family groups and psychoeducation in the treatment of schizophrenia. *Archives of General Psychiatry, 52,* 1, 679–687.

Deci, E. L., & Ryan, R. M. (1985). *Intrinsic motivation and self-determination in human behavior.* New York: Plenum Press.

DeCuypere, G., Knudson, G., & Bockting, W. (2011). Second response of the World Professional Association for Transgender Health to the proposed revision of the diagnosis of gender dysphoria for the *DSM 5. International Journal of Transgenderism, 13,* 51–53.

DeFries, J., Fulker, D., & LaBuda, M. (1987). Evidence for a genetic aetiology in reading disability of twins. *Nature, 329,* 537–539.

Deger, S. R., Strauss, W. L., Marro, K. I., Richards, T. L., Metzger, G. D., & Artru, A. A. (1995). Proton magnetic resonance spectroscopy investigation of hyperventilation in subjects with panic disorder and comparison subjects. *American Journal of Psychiatry, 152,* 666–672.

Dekker, J. M., Hendriksen, M., Kool, S., Bakker, L., Driessen, E., De Jonghe, F., . . . Van, H. L. (2014). Growing evidence for psychodynamic therapy for depression. *Contemporary Psychoanalysis, 50*(1–2), 131–155. doi:10.1080/00107530.2014.880312

Del Re, A. C., Maisel, N., Blodgett, J., & Finney, J. (2013). The declining efficacy of naltrexone pharmacotherapy for alcohol use disorders over time: A multivariate meta-analysis. *Alcoholism: Clinical and Experimental Research, 37*(6), 1064–1068. doi:10.1111/acer.12067

Del Re, A. C., Spielmans, G. I., Flückiger, C., & Wampold, B. E. (2013). Efficacy of new generation antidepressants: Differences seem illusory. *Plos ONE, 8*(6).

DelBello, M. P., Carlson, G. A., Tohen, M., Bromet, E. J., Schwiers, M., & Strakowski, S. M. (2003). Rates and predictors of developing a manic or hypomanic episode 1 to 2 years following a first hospitalization for major depression with psychotic features. *Journal of Child and Adolescent Psychopharmacology, 13*(2), 173–185. doi:10.1089/104454603322163899

Dell, P. F. (2006). A new model of dissociative identity disorder. *Psychiatric Clinics of North America, 29*(1), 1–26.

Dell, P. F. (2009). The phenomena of pathological dissociation. In P. F. Dell & J. A. O'Neil (Eds.), *Dissociation and the dissociative disorders: DSM-V and beyond* (pp 225–238). New York: Routledge.

Dell'osso, B., & Lader, M. (2013). Do benzodiazepines still deserve a major role in the treatment of psychiatric disorders? A critical reappraisal. *European Psychiatry, 28*(1), 7–20. doi:10.1016/j.eurpsy.2011.11.003

DeMartini, K. S., Devine, E. G., DiClemente, C. C., Martin, D. J., Ray, L. A., & O'Malley, S. S. (2014). Predictors of pretreatment commitment to abstinence: Results from the COMBINE study. *Journal of Studies on Alcohol and Drugs, 75*(3), 438–446.

Dembroski, T. M., MacDougall, J. M., Williams, R. B., Haney, T. L., & Blumenthal, J. A. (1985). Components of Type A, hostility, and anger-in: Relationship to angiographic findings. *Psychosomatic Medicine, 47,* 219-233.

Demerouti, E., Bakker, A. B., Nachreiner, F., & Schaufeli, W. B. (2001). The job demands-resources model of burnout. *Journal of Applied Psychology, 86,* 499–512.

Demirovic, J., Prineas, R., Loewenstein, D., Bean, J., Duara, R., Sevush, S., & Szapocznik, J. (2003). Prevalence of dementia in three ethnic groups: The South Florida program on aging and health. *Annals of Epidemiology, 13*(6), 472–478. doi: 10.1016/S1047-2797(02)00437-4

Denicola, J., & Sandler, J. (1980). Training abusive parents in child management and self-control skills. *Behavior Therapy, 11,* 263–270.

Denney, J. T. (2014). Families, resources, and suicide: Combined effects on mortality. *Journal of Marriage and Family, 76*(1), 218–231.

Dennis, M. L., Bray, R. M., Iachan, R., & Thornberry, J. (1999). Drug use and homelessness. In R. M. Bray, M. E. Marsden (Eds.), *Drug use in metropolitan America* (pp. 79–123). Thousand Oaks, CA: Sage Publications.

Deo, M. S., & Lymburner, J. A. (2011). Personality traits and psychological health concerns: The search for psychology student syndrome. *Teaching of Psychology, 38*(3), 155–157. doi:10.1177/0098628311411781

Depression Guideline Panel (1993). *Depression in primary care. Vol. 1: Detection and diagnosis.* Rockville, MD: U.S. Department of Health and Human Services.

DePrince, A. P., & Freyd, J. J. (2004). Forgetting trauma stimuli. *Psychological Science, 15,* 488–492.

Depue, R. A., & Iacono, W. G. (1989). Neurobehavioral aspects of affective disorders. *Annual Review of Psychology, 40,* 457–492.

Depue, R. A., Slater, J. R, Wolfstetter-Kausch, H., Klein, D., Goplerud, E., & Farr, D. (1981). A behavioral paradigm for identifying persons at risk for bipolar depressive disorder: A conceptual framework and five validation studies. *Journal of Abnormal Psychology Monograph, 90* (, 5), 381–437.

deRoon-Cassini, T., Mancini, A., Rusch, M., & Bonanno, G. (2010). Psychopathology and resilience following traumatic injury: A latent growth mixture model analysis. *Rehabilitation Psychology, 55,* 1–11.

deSilva, P., & Rachman, S. (1992). *Obsessive-compulsive disorder: The facts.* Oxford, UK: Oxford University Press.

Desrochers, G., Bergeron, S., Khalifé, S., Dupuis, M. J., & Jodoin, M. (2009). Fear avoidance and self-efficacy in relation to pain and sexual impairment in women with provoked vestibulodynia. *The Clinical Journal of Pain, 25*(6), 520–527.

Deutsch, A. R., Steinley, D., & Slutske, W. S. (2014). The role of gender and friends' gender on peer socialization of adolescent drinking: A prospective multilevel social network analysis. *Journal of Youth and Adolescence, 43*(9), 1421–1435. doi:10.1007/s10964-013-0048-9

Deutsch, J. A. (1983). The cholinergic synapse and the site of memory. In J. A. Deutsch (Ed.), *The physiological basis of memory.* New York: Academic Press.

Deutsch, R., & Strack, F. (2006). Reflective and impulsive determinants of addictive behavior. In R. W. Wiers & A. W. Stacy (Eds.), *The handbook of implicit cognition and addiction* (pp. 45–57). Thousand Oaks, CA: Sage Publishers.

Devanand, D. P., Pradhaban, G., Liu, X., Khandji, A., De Santi, S., Segal, S., . . . de Leon, M. J. (2007). Hippocampal and entorhinal atrophy in mild cognitive impairment: Prediction of Alzheimer disease. *Neurology, 68*(11), 828–836. doi: 10.1212/01.wnl.0000256697.20968.d7

Devilly, G. J., Ciorciari, J., Piesse, A., Sherwell, S., Zammit, S., Cook, F., & Turton, C. (2007). Dissociative tendencies and memory performance on directed-forgetting tasks. *Psychological Science, 18*(3), 212–217. doi:10.1111/j.1467-9280.2007.01875.x

Devor, E. J. (1994). A developmental-genetic model of alcoholism: Implications for genetic research. *Journal of Consulting and Clinical Psychology, 62*(6), 1108–1115.

Di Guilio, G., & Reissing, E. D. (2006). Premenstrual dysphoric disorder: Prevalence, diagnosis considerations, and controversies. *Journal of Psychosomatic Obstetrics and Gynecology, 27*(4), 201–210.

Diamond, M., & Sigmundson, H. K. (1997). Sex reassignment at birth: A long-term review and clinical implications. *Archives of Pediatrics and Adolescent Medicine, 151.* Retrieved October 20, 2014 from http://hawaii.edu/PCSS/biblio/articles/1961to1999/1997-sex-reassignment

Díaz-Caneja, C. M., Moreno, C., Llorente, C., Espliego, A., Arango, C., & Moreno, D. (2014). Practitioner review: Long-term pharmacological treatment of pediatric bipolar disorder. *Journal of Child Psychology and Psychiatry, 55*(9), 959–980. doi:10.1111/jcpp.12271

Dickstein, S. G., Bannon, K., Castellanos, F. X., & Milham, M. P. (2006). The neural correlates of ADHD: An ALE meta-analysis. *Journal of Child Psychology and Psychiatry, 47,* 1051–1062. doi:10.1111/j.1469-7610.2006.01671.x

Diefenbach, G., Mouton-Odum, S., & Stanley, M. (2002). Affective correlates of trichotillomania. *Behaviour Research and Therapy, 40,* 1305–1315.

Diefenbach, G. J., Reitman, D., & Williamson, D. A. (2000). Trichotillomania: A challenge to research and practice. *Clinical Psychology Review, 20*(3), 289–309. doi:10.1016/S0272-7358(98)00083-X

Diefenbach, G. J., Tolin, D. F., Meunier, S., & Worhunsky, P. (2008). Emotion regulation and trichotillomania: A comparison of clinical and nonclinical hair pulling. *Journal of Behavior Therapy and Experimental Psychiatry, 39,* 32–41. doi:10.1016/j.jbtep.2006.09.002

Diener, E. (1984). Subjective well-being. *Psychological Bulletin, 95,* 542–575.

Dierckx, B., Heijnen, W. T., van den Broek, W. W., & Birkenhäger, T. K. (2012). Efficacy of electroconvulsive therapy in bipolar versus unipolar major depression: A meta-analysis. *Bipolar Disorders, 14*(2), 146–150. doi:10.1111/j.1399-5618.2012.00997.x

Dietze, P., Jolley, D., Fry, C., & Bammer, G. (2005). Transient changes in behaviour lead to heroin overdose: Results from a case-crossover study of non-fatal overdose. *Addiction, 100*(5), 636–642.

Dikmen, S. S., Bombardier, C. H., Machamer, J. E., Fann, J. R., & Temkin, N. R. (2004). Natural history of depression in traumatic brain injury. *Archives of Physical Medicine and Rehabilitation, 85*(9), 1457–1464. doi: 10.1016/j.apmr.2003.12.041

DiLalla, D. L., & Gottesman, I. I. (1995). Normal personality characteristics in identical twins discordant for schizophrenia. *Journal of Abnormal Psychology, 104,* 490–499.

DiMascio, A., Weissman, M. M., Prusoff, B. A., Neu, C., Zwilling, M., & Klerman, G. L. (1979). Differential symptom reduction by drugs and psychotherapy in acute depression. *Archives of General Psychiatry, 36,* 1450–1456.

Dimeff, L. A., Baer, J. S., Kivlahan, D. R., & Marlatt, G. A. (1999). *Brief Alcohol Screening and Intervention for College Students (BASICS): A harm reduction approach.* New York: Guilford Press.

Dimidjian, S., Hollon, S. D., Dobson, K. S., Schmaling, K. B., Kohlenberg, R. J., Addis, M. E., . . . Jacobson, N. S. (2006). Randomized trial of behavioral activation, cognitive therapy, and antidepressant medication in the acute treatment of adults with major depression. *Journal of Consulting and Clinical Psychology, 74*(4), 658–670. doi:10.1037/0022-006X.74.4.658

Dimsdale, J. E., Creed, F., Escobar, J., Sharpe, M., Wulsin, L., Barsky, A., . . . Levenson, J. (2013). Somatic symptom disorder: An important change in the *DSM. Journal of Psychosomatic Research, 75*(3), 223–228. doi:10.1016/j. jpsychores.2013.06.033

Dishion, T. J., & Patterson, G. R. (1992). Age effects in parent training outcome. *Behavior Therapy, 23,* 719–729.

Dishion, T. J., & Patterson, G. R. (2006). The development and etiology of antisocial behavior in children and adolescents. In D. Cicchetti & D. J. Cohen (Eds.), *Developmental psychopathology: Vol. 3. Risk, disorder, and adaptation* (2nd ed., pp. 503–541). New York: Wiley.

Dixon, L. B., Dickerson, F., Bellack, A. S., Bennett, M., Dickinson, D., Goldberg, R. W., . . . Kreyenbuhl, J. (2010). The 2009 schizophrenia PORT psychosocial treatment recommendations and summary statements. *Schizophrenia Bulletin, 36,* 48–70.

Dixon, L. B., McFarlane, W., Lefley, H., Lucksted, A., Cohen, C., Falloon, I., . . . Sondheimer, D. (2001). Evidence-based practices for services to family members of people with psychiatric disabilities. *Psychiatric Services, 52,* 903–910.

Dobson, K. S. (1989). A meta-analysis of the efficacy of cognitive therapy for depression. *Journal of Consulting and Clinical Psychology, 57,* 414–419.

Dobson, K. S., Hollon, S. D., Dimidjian, S., Schmaling, K. B., Kohlenberg, R. J., Gallop, R. J., . . . Jacobson, N. S. (2008). Randomized trial of behavioral activation, cognitive therapy, and antidepressant medication in the prevention of relapse and recurrence in major depression. *Journal of Consulting and Clinical Psychology, 76*(3), 468–477. doi:10.1037/0022-006X.76.3.468

Docherty, N. M. (1995). Expressed emotion and language disturbances in parents of stable schizophrenic patients. *Schizophrenia Bulletin, 21,* 411–418.

Docherty, N. M., Cutting, L. P., & Bers, S. A. (1998). Expressed emotion and differentiation of self in the relatives of stable schizophrenic outpatients. *Psychiatry: Interpersonal and Biological Processes, 61*(4), 269–278.

Dodge, K. A., & Coie, J. D. (1987). Social information-processing factors in reactive and proactive aggression in children's peer groups. *Journal of Personality and Social Psychology, 53,* 389–409.

Dodge, K. A., McClaskey, C. L., & Feldman, E. (1985). Situational approach to the assessment of social competence in children. *Journal of Consulting and Clinical Psychology, 53,* 344–353.

Dodge, K. A., & Pettit, G. S. (2003). A biopsychosocial model of the development of chronic conduct problems in adolescence. *Developmental Psychology, 39,* 349–371.

Dodge, K. A., Pettit, G. S., McClaskey, C. L., & Brown, J. (1986). Social competence in children. *Monographs of the Society for Research in Child Development, 44* (2, Serial No. 213).

Doerfler, L. A., & Chaplin, W. F. (1985). Type III error in research on interpersonal models of depression. *Journal of Abnormal Psychology, 94,* 227–230.

Doherty, K., Kinnunen, T., Militello, F. S., & Garvey, A. J. (1995). Urges to smoke during the first month of abstinence: Relationship to relapse and predictors. *Psychopharmacology, 119*(2), 171–178.

Dohrenwend, B. P., Levav, I., Shrout, P. E., Schwartz, S., Naveh, G., Link, B. G., Skodol, A. E., & Stueve, A. (1992). Socioeconomic status and psychiatric disorders: The causation-selection issue. *Science, 255,* 946–952.

Dohrenwend, B. S. (1978). Social stress and community psychology. *American Journal of Community Psychology, 6,* 1–14.

Doman, R. J., Spitz, E. B., Zucman, E., Delacato, C. H., & Doman, G. (1960). Children with severe brain injuries. *Journal of the American Medical Association, 174,* 219–223.

Donnelly, D. A., & Murray, E. J. (1991). Emotional changes in written essays and therapy interviews. *Journal of Social and Clinical Psychology, 10,* 334–350.

Donnerstein, E. (1982). Erotica and human agression. In R. G. Green & E. Donnerstein (Eds.), *Aggression: Theoretical and empirical views.* Orlando, FL: Academic Press.

Donnerstein, E., & Berkowitz, L. (1981). Victim reactions in aggressive erotic films as a factor in violence against women. *Journal of Personality and Social Psychology, 41,* 710–724.

D'Onofrio, B., Singh, A. L., Iliadou, A., Lambe, M., Hultman, C. M., Grann, M., . . . Lichtenstein, P. (2010). Familial confounding of the association between maternal smoking during pregnancy and offspring criminality: A population-based study in Sweden. *Archives of General Psychiatry, 67,* 529–538.

D'Onofrio, B. M., Van Hulle, C. A., Waldman, I. D., Rodgers, J. L., Harden, K. P., Rathouz, P. J., . . . Lahey, B. B. (2008). Smoking during pregnancy and offspring externalizing problems: An exploration of genetic and environmental confounds. *Development and Psychopathology, 20,* 139–164.

Dorahy, M. J., & Lewis, C. A. (2002). Dissociative identity disorder in Northern Ireland: A survey of attitudes and experience among clinical psychologists and psychiatrists. *Journal of Nervous and Mental Disease, 190*(10), 707–710. doi:10.1097/00005053-200210000-00009

Dorahy, M. J., Brand, B. L., Şar, V., Krüger, C., Stavropoulos, P., Martínez-Taboas, A., . . . Middleton, W. (2014). Dissociative identity disorder: An empirical overview. *Australian and New Zealand Journal of Psychiatry, 48*(5), 402–417.

Doskoch, P. (2012). Youth have healthier sexual outcomes if their sex education classes discuss contraception. *Perspectives on Sexual and Reproductive Health, 44*(4), 270. doi:10.1363/4427012

Douglas, M. (1966). *Purity and danger: An analysis of concept of pollution and taboo.* New York, NY: Routledge.

Dowart, R. A., & Chartock, L. (1989). Suicide: A public health perspective. In D. G. Jacobs & H. N. Brown (Eds.), *Suicide: Understanding and responding: Harvard Medical School perspectives on suicide* (pp. 31-55). Madison, CT: International Universities Press.

Downey, G., & Coyne, J. C. (1990). Children of depressed parents: An integrative review. *Psychological Bulletin, 108,* 50–76.

Dozois, D. A. (2000). Influences on Freud's mourning and melancholia and its contextual validity. *Journal of Theoretical and Philosophical Psychology, 20*(2), 167–195. doi:10.1037/h0091208

Dozois, D. A. (2007). Stability of negative self-structures: A longitudinal comparison of depressed, remitted, and nonpsychiatric controls. *Journal of Clinical Psychology, 63*(4), 319–338. doi:10.1002/jclp.20349

Drescher, J., & Byne, J. (2012). Gender dysphoric/gender variant (GD/GV) children and adolescents: Summarizing what we know and what we have yet to learn. *Journal of Homosexuality, 59,* 501–510.

Driessen, E., & Hollon, S. D. (2010). Cognitive behavioral therapy for mood disorders: Efficacy, moderators and mediators. *Psychiatric Clinics of North America, 33*(3), 537–555. doi:10.1016/j.psc.2010.04.005

Drugwatch (n.d.). *Big Pharma.* Retrieved on August 8, 2014 from http://www. drugwatch.com/manufacturer/

Dryer, R., Kiernan, M. J., & Tyson, G. A. (2006). Implicit theories of the characteristics and causes of attention-deficit hyperactivity disorder held by parents and professionals in the psychological, educational, medical, and allied health fields. *Australian Journal of Psychology, 58*(2), 79–92. doi:10.1080/00049530600730443

Dube, K. C., Kumar, N., & Dube, S. (1984). Long term course and outcome of the Agra cases in the International Pilot Study of Schizophrenia. *Acta Psychiatrica Scandanavica, 70,* 170–179.

Dube, S. R., Fairweather, D., Pearson, W. S., Felitti, V. J., Anda, R. F., & Croft, J. B. (2009). Cumulative childhood stress and autoimmune disease. *Psychosomatic Medicine, 71,* 243–250.

Ducasse, D., Capdevielle, D., Attal, J., Larue, A., Macgregor, A., Brittner, M., & Fond, G. (2013). Blood-injection-injury phobia: Psychophysiological and therapeutic specificities. *Encephale, 39*(5): 326–331. doi: 10.1016/j.encep.2012.06.031

Duggan, C., Milton, J., Egan, V., McCarthy, L., Palmer, B., & Lee, A. (2003). Theories of general personality and mental disorder. *British Journal of Psychiatry, 182,* s19–s23.

Duke, A. A., Bègue, L., Bell, R., & Eisenlohr-Moul, T. (2013). Revisiting the serotonin-aggression relation in humans: A meta-analysis. *Psychological Bulletin, 139*(5), 1148–1172. doi:10.1037/a0031544

Duke, D. C., Keeley, M. L., Geffken, G. R., & Storch, E. A. (2010). Trichotillomania: A current review. *Clinical Psychology Review, 30,* 181–193. doi:10.1016/j. cpr.2009.10.008

Dumaguing, N. I., Singh, I., Sethi, M., & Devanand, D. P. (2003). Pica in the geriatric mentally ill: Unrelenting and potentially fatal. *Journal of Geriatric Psychiatry and Neurology, 16*(3), 189–191. doi: 10.1177/0891988703256049

Dunkell, S. (1994). *Goodbye insomnia, hello sleep.* New York: Dell.

Dunn, L. M. (1968). Special education for the mildly retarded: Is much of it justifiable? *Exceptional Children, 35,* 5–22.

DuPaul, G. J., & Barkley, R. A. (1990). Medication therapy. In R. A. Barkley (Ed.), *Attention deficit hyperactivity disorder: A handbook for diagnosis and treatment* (pp. 573–612). New York: Guilford Press.

DuPaul, G. J., & Rapport, M. D. (1993). Does methylphenidate normalize the classroom performance of children with attention deficit disorder? *Journal of the American Academy of Child and Adolescent Psychiatry, 32*(1), 190–198.

Dupont, R. L., & Saylor, K. E. (1992). Depressant substances in adolescent medicine. *Pediatrics in Review, 13*(10), 381–386.

Dupper, D. R. (2013). *School bullying: New perspectives on a growing problem.* New York: Oxford University Press. doi:10.1093/acprof:oso/9780199859597.001.0001

Durand, V. M., & Carr, E. G. (1987). Social influences on "self-stimulatory" behavior: Analysis and treatment application. *Journal of Applied Behavior Analysis, 20,* 119–132.

Durà-Vilà, G., & Hodes, M. (2012). Cross-cultural study of idioms of distress among Spanish nationals and Hispanic American migrants: Susto, nervios and ataque de nervios. *Social Psychiatry and Psychiatric Epidemiology, 47,* 1627–1637. doi:10.1007/s00127-011-0468-3

Durkheim, E. (1966). *Suicide: A study in sociology.* New York: Free Press.

Durlak, J. (1979). Comparative effectiveness of para-professional and professional helpers. *Psychological Bulletin, 86,* 80–92.

Dussias, P., Kalali, A. H., & Staud, R. M. (2010). Treatment of fibromyalgia. *Psychiatry, 7*(5), 15–18.

Dutra, L., Stathopoulou, G., Basden, S. L., Leyro, T. M., Powers, M. B., & Otto, M. W. (2008). A meta-analytic review of psychosocial interventions for substance use disorders. *The American Journal of Psychiatry, 165*(2), 179–187. doi:10.1176/appi.ajp.2007.06111851

Dworkin, R. H. (1994). Pain insensitivity in schizophrenia: A neglected phenomenon and some implications. *Schizophrenia Bulletin, 20,* 235–248.

Dworkin, S. F., & Wilson, L. (1993). Somatoform pain disorder and its treatment. In D. L. Dunner (Ed.), *Current psychiatric therapy* (pp. 320–328). Philadelphia: W. B. Saunders.

Dwosin, L. P., Rauhut, A. S., King-Pospisil, K. A., & Bardo, M. T. (2006). Review of the pharmacology and clinical profile of bupropion, an antidepressant and tobacco use cessation agent. *CNS Drug Reviews, 12*(3–4), 178–207. doi:10.1111/j.1527-3458.2006.00178.x

Dye, M. I., Rondeau, D., Guido, V., Mason, A., & O'Brien, R. (2013). Identification and management of factitious disorder by proxy. *The Journal for Nurse Practitioners, 9*(7), 435–442. doi:10.1016/j.nurpra.2013.04.006

Dykens, E. M, Hodapp, R. M., & Evans, D. W. (1994). Profiles and development of adaptive behavior in males with fragile X syndrome. *Journal of Autism and Developmental Disorders, 23,* 135–145.

Dykens, E. M., Hodapp, R. M., & Leckman, J. F. (1994). *Behavior and development in fragile X syndrome. Sage Series on developmental clinical psychology and psychiatry (No. 28).* Newbury Park, CA: Sage.

D'Zurilla, T. J., & Goldfried, M. R. (1971). Problem solving and behavior modification. *Journal of Abnormal Psychology, 78,* 107–126.

E

Eagle, M. (1984). *Recent developments in psychoanalysis: A critical evaluation.* New York: McGraw-Hill.

Eaker, E. D., Abbott, R. D., Kannel, W. B. (1989). Frequency of uncomplicated angina pectoris in Type A compared with Type B persons (the Framingham Study). *American Journal of Cardiology, 63,* 1042–1045.

Eaker, E. D., Pinsky, J., Castelli, W. P. (1992). Maintenance of safer sexual behaviors and predictors of risky sex: The San Francisco Men's Health Study. *American Journal of Public Health, 80,* 973–977.

Earls, F., Escobar, J. I., & Manson, S. M. (1990). Suicide in minority groups: Epidemiologic and cultural perspectives. In S. J. Blumenthal & D. J. Kupfer (Eds.), *Suicide over the life cycle: Risk factors, assessment, and treatment of suicide patients* (pp. 571–598). Washington, DC: American Psychiatric Press.

Eaton, D. K., McKnight-Eily, L. R., Lowry, R., Perry, G. S., Presley-Cantrell, L., & Croft, J. B. (2010). Prevalence of insufficient, borderline, and optimal hours of sleep among high school students—United States, 2007. *Journal of Adolescent Health, 46*(4), 399–401. doi:10.1016/j.jadohealth.2009.10.011

Eaton, W. W. (1986). Epidemiology of schizophrenia. *Epidemiology Review, 7,* 105–126.

Eaton, W. W., & Keyl, P. M. (1990). Risk factors for the onset of Diagnostic Interview Schedule/DSM-III agoraphobia in a prospective, population-based study. *Archives of General Psychiatry, 47,* 819–824.

Eaton, W. W., Alexandre, P., Bienvenu, O., Clarke, D., Martins, S. S., Nestadt, G., & Zablotsky, B. (2012). The burden of mental disorders. In W. W. Eaton (Ed.), *Public mental health* (pp. 3–30). New York: Oxford University Press.

Eaton, W. W., Kalaydjian, A. A., Scharfstein, D. O., Mezuk, B. B., & Ding, Y. Y. (2007). Prevalence and incidence of depressive disorder: The Baltimore ECA follow-up, 1981–2004. *Acta Psychiatrica Scandinavica, 116*(3), 182–188. doi:10.1111/j.1600-0447.2007.01017.x

Eaton, W. W., Martins, S. S., Nestadt, G., Bienvenu, O., Clarke, D., & Alexandre, P. (2008). The burden of mental disorders. *Epidemiologic Reviews, 30,* 1–14.

Eaton, W. W., Muntaner, C., & Sapag, J. C. (2010). Socioeconomic stratification and mental disorder. In T. L. Scheid and T. N. Brown (Eds.), *A handbook for the study of mental health: Social contexts, theories, and systems* (2nd ed.) (pp. 226–255). New York: Cambridge University Press.

Eaton, W. W., Weissman, M. M., Anthony, J. C., Robins, L. N., Blazer, D. G., & Karno, M. (1985). Problems in the definition and measurement of prevalence and incidence of psychiatric disorders. In W.W. Eaton & L.G. Kessler (Eds.), *Epidemiologic field methods in psychiatry: The NIMH epidemiologic catchment area program* (pp. 311–326). Orlando, FL: Academic Press.

Eberlin, M., McConnachie, G., Ibel, S., & Volpe, L. (1993). Facilitated communication: A failure to replicate the phenomenon. *Journal of Autism and Developmental Disorders, 23*(3), 507–530.

Ecker, C., Ginester, C., Feng, Y., Johnston, P., Lombardo, M. V., Lai, M.-C., . . . MRC AIMS Consortium. (2013). Brain surface anatomy in adults with autism: The relationship between surface area, cortical thickness, and autistic symptoms. *JAMA Psychiatry, 70,* 59–70.

Eckert, E. D., Bouchard, T. J., Bohlen, J., & Heston, L. L. (1986). Homosexuality in monozygotic twins reared apart. *British Journal of Psychiatry, 148,* 421–425.

Eddy, K. T., Dutra, L., Bradley, R., & Westen, D. (2004). A multidimensional meta-analysis of psychotherapy and pharmacotherapy for obsessive-compulsive disorder. *Clinical Psychology Review, 24*(8), 1011–1030. doi:10.1016/j.cpr.2004.08.004

Edelstein, B. A., & Michelson, L. (Eds.) (1986). *Handbook of prevention.* New York & London: Plenum.

Edlavitch, S. A., & Byrns, P. J. (2014). Primary prevention research in suicide. *Crisis: The Journal of Crisis Intervention and Suicide Prevention, 35*(2), 69–73. doi:10.1027/0227-5910/a000240

Edvardsen, J., Torgersen, S., Røysamb, E., Lygren, S., Skre, I., Onstad, S., & Øien, P. (2008). Heritability of bipolar spectrum disorders. Unity or heterogeneity? *Journal of Affective Disorders, 106*(3), 229–240. doi:10.1016/j.jad.2007.07.001

Edwards, A. C., Gillespie, N. A., Aggen, S. H., & Kendler, K. S. (2013). Assessment of a modified DSM-5 diagnosis of alcohol use disorder in a genetically informative population. *Alcoholism: Clinical and Experimental Research, 37*(3), 443–451.

Edwards, K. M., Burns V. E., Reynolds, T., Carroll, D., Drayson, M., & Ring, C. (2006). Acute stress exposure prior to influenza vaccination enhances antibody response in women. *Brain, Behavior, and Immunity, 20,* 159–168.

Edwards, S. J., & Sachmann, M. D. (2010). No-suicide contracts, no-suicide agreements, and no-suicide assurances: A study of their nature, utilization, perceived effectiveness, and potential to cause harm. *Crisis: The Journal of Crisis Intervention and Suicide Prevention, 31*(6), 290–302. doi:10.1027/0227-5910/a000048

Egbert, L., Battit, G., Welch, C., & Bartlett, M. (1964). Reduction of postoperative pain by encouragement and instruction of patients. *New England Journal of Medicine, 270,* 825–827.

Egel, A. L., & Powers, M. D. (1989). Behavioral parent training: A view of the past and suggestions for the future. In M. J. Begab (Ed.), *The treatment of severe behavior disorders: Behavior analysis approaches* (pp. 153–173). Washington, DC: American Association on Mental Retardation.

Egeland, J. A., Gerhard, D. S., Pauls, D. L., Susses, J. N., Kidd, K. K., Allen, C. R., Hostetter, A. M., & Housman, D. E. (1987). Bipolar affective disorders linked to DNA markers on chromosome 11. *Nature, 325,* 783–787.

Egger, J., Stolla, A., & McEwen, L. (1992). Controlled trial of hypersensitisation in children with food-induced hyperkinetic syndrome. *Lancet, 339,* 1150–1153.

Ehlers, C. L., & Schuckit, M. A. (1990). EEG fast frequency activity in sons of alcoholics. *Biological Psychiatry, 27*(6), 631–641.

Ehlers, C. L., Frank, E., & Kupfer, D. J. (1988). Social zeitgebers and biological rhythms: A unified approach to understanding the etiology of depression. *Archives of General Psychiatry, 45,* 948–952.

Ehlers, C. L., Liang, T., & Gizer, I. R. (2012). ADH and ALDH polymorphisms and alcohol dependence in Mexican and native Americans. *The American Journal of Drug and Alcohol Abuse, 38*(5), 389–394. doi:10.3109/00952990.2012.694526

Eidelman, P., Gershon, A., Kaplan, K., McGlinchey, E., & Harvey, A. G. (2012). Social support and social strain in inter-episode bipolar disorder. *Bipolar Disorders, 14*(6), 628–640. doi:10.1111/j.1399-5618.2012.01049.x

Eigenmann, P. A., & Haenggeli, C. A. (2004). Food colourings and preservatives—allergy and hyperactivity. *Lancet, 364*(9437), 823–824. doi:10.1016/S0140-6736(04)16996-1

Eilenberg, T., Kronstrand, L., Fink, P., & Frostholm, L. (2013). Acceptance and commitment group therapy for health anxiety—Results from a pilot study. *Journal of Anxiety Disorders, 27*(5), 461–468. doi:10.1016/j.janxdis.2013.06.001

Eiler, K., Schaefer, M. R., Salstrom, D., & Lowery, R. (1995). Double-blind comparison of bromocriptine and placebo in cocaine withdrawal. *American Journal of Drug and Alcohol Abuse, 21*(1), 65–79.

Eisler, I. (2009). Anorexia nervosa and the family. In J. H. Bray & M. Stanton (Eds.), *The Wiley-Blackwell handbook of family psychology* (pp. 551–563). Oxford, UK: Wiley-Blackwell.

Eker, C., Simsek, F., Yılmazer, E., Kitis, O., Cinar, C., Eker, O., . . . Gonul, A. (2014). Brain regions associated with risk and resistance for bipolar I disorder: A voxel-based MRI study of patients with bipolar disorder and their healthy siblings. *Bipolar Disorders, 16*(3), 249–261. doi:10.1111/bdi.12181

Ekstrand, M. L., & Coates, T. J. (1990). Maintenance of safer sexual behaviors and predictors of risky sex: The San Francisco Men's Health Study. *American Journal of Public Health, 80,* 973–977.

Eldevik, S., Hastings, R. P., Hughes, J. C., Jahr, E., Eikeseth, S., & Cross, S. (2009). Meta-analysis of early intensive behavioral intervention for children with autism. *Journal of Clinical Child and Adolescent Psychology, 38,* 439–450.

Elia, J., Gulotta, C., Rose, S. R., Marin, G., & Rapoport, J. L. (1994). Thyroid function and attention-deficit hyperactivity disorder. *Journal of the American Academy of Child and Adolescent Psychiatry, 33(2),* 169–172.

Elixhauser, A., & Steiner, C. (2013). Readmissions to U.S. hospitals by diagnosis, 2010. *HCUP Statistical Brief #153.* Rockville, MD: Agency for Healthcare Research and Quality. Retrieved on October 28, 2014 from http://www.hcup-us.ahrq.gov/reports/statbriefs/sb153.pdf.

Elkin, I. (1994). The NIMH treatment of depression collaborative research program: Where we began and where we are. In A. E. Bergin & S. L. Garfield (Eds.), *Handbook of psychotherapy and behavior change* (4th ed., pp. 114–139). New York: John Wiley and Sons.

Elkin, I., Gibbons, R. D., Shea, M. T., & Sotsky, S. M. (1995). Initial severity and different treatment outcomes in the National Institute of Mental Health Treatment of Depression Collaborative Research Program. *Journal of Clinical and Consulting Psychology, 63,* 841–847.

Elkin, I., Shea, M. T., Watkins, J. T., Imber, S. D., Sotsky, S. M., Collins, J. F., Glass, D. R., Pilkonis, P. A., Leber, W. R., Docherty, J. P., Fiester, S. J., & Parloff, M. B. (1989). National Institute of Mental Health Treatment of Depression Collaborative Research Program. General effectiveness of treatments. *Archives of General Psychiatry, 46,* 971–982.

Ellickson, P. L., Hays, R. D., & Bell, R. M. (1992). Stepping through the drug use sequence: Longitudinal scalogram analysis of initiation and regular use. *Journal of Abnormal Psychology, 101(3),* 441–451.

Ellinwood, E. H., Easier, M. E., Linnoila, M., Molter, D., Heatherly, D., & Bjornsson, T. (1983). Effects of oral contraceptives and diazepam-induced psychomotor impairment. *Clinical Pharmacology and Therapeutics, 35,* 360–366.

Elliott, D. S., Huizinga, D., & Menard, S. (1989). *Multiple problem youth: Delinquency, substance use, and mental health problems.* New York: Springer-Verlag.

Elliott, D., Huizinga, D., & Ageton, S.S. (1985). *Multiple problem youth: Delinquency, substance use, and mental health problems.* New York: Springer-Verlag.

Elliott, M., & Krivo, L. J. (1991). Structural determinants of homelessness in the United States. *Social Problems, 38(1).* doi:10.2307/800641.

Ellis, A. (1962). *Reason and emotion in psychotherapy.* New York: Lyle Stuart.

Ellis, A. (1973). Rational-emotive therapy. In R. Corsini (Ed.), *Current psychotherapies* (pp. 167–206). Itasca, IL: F. E. Peacock.

Ellis, A., & Ellis, D. (2014). Rational emotive behavior therapy. In G. R. VandenBos, E. Meidenbauer, and J. Frank-McNeil (Eds.), *Psychotherapy theories and techniques: A reader* (pp. 289–298). Washington, DC: American Psychological Association. doi:10.1037/14295-031

Ellis, J. G., Gehrman, P., Espie, C. A., Riemann, D., & Perlis, M. L. (2012). Acute insomnia: Current conceptualizations and future directions. *Sleep Medicine Reviews, 16(1),* 5–14.

El-Mallakh, R. S., & Hollifield, M. (2008). Comorbid anxiety in bipolar disorder alters treatment and prognosis. *Psychiatric Quarterly, 79(2),* 139–150. doi:10.1007/s11126-008-9071-5

Elzakkers, I. F., Danner, U. N., Hoek, H. W., Schmidt, U., & Elburg, A. A. (2014). Compulsory treatment in anorexia nervosa: A review. *International Journal of Eating Disorders,* doi:10.1002/eat.22330

Emerich, D. F., Cahill, D. W., and Sanberg, P. R. (1994). Excitotoxic lesions of the neostriatum as an animal model of Huntington's disease. In M. L. Woodruff & A. J. Nonneman (Eds.), *Neurotoxin-induced animal models of neurological disorders.* New York: Plenum.

Emilien, G., Maloteaux, J., Seghers, A. A., & Charles, G. (1996). Lithium compared to valproic acid and carbamazepine in the treatment of mania: A statistical meta-analysis. *European Neuropsychopharmacology, 6(3),* 245–252. doi:10.1016/0924-977X(96)00029-6

Emmelkamp, P. (1982). *Phobic and obsessive-compulsive disorders: theory, research and practice.* New York: Plenum.

Emmelkamp, P. M., Benner, A., Kuipers, A., Feiertag, G. A., Koster, H. C., & van Apeldoorn, F. J. (2006). Comparison of brief dynamic and cognitive-behavioural therapies in avoidant personality disorder. *British Journal of Psychiatry, 189,* 60–64.

Emmers-Sommer, T. M., Allen, M., Bourhis, J., Sahlstein, E., Laskowski, K., Falato, W. L., . . . Cashman, L. (2004). A meta-analysis of the relationship between social skills and sexual offenders. *Communication Reports, 17(1),* 1–10. doi:10.1080/08934210409389369

Emrick, C., Tonigan, J. S., Montgomery, H., & Little, L. (1993). Alcoholics Anonymous: What is currently known? In B. S. McCrady & W. R. Miller (Eds.), *Research on Alcoholics Anonymous: Opportunities and alternatives* (pp. 41–76). New Brunswick, NJ: Alcohol Research Documentation, Rutgers, The State University of New Jersey.

Endler, N. S. (1988). The origins of electroconvulsive therapy (ECT). *Convulsive Therapy, 4(1),* 5–23.

Engel, G. L. (1977). The need for a new medical model: A challenge for biomedicine. *Science, 196,* 129–136. doi:10.1126/science.847460

Epstein, E. E., & McCrady, B. S. (1994). Introduction to the special section: Research on the nature and treatment of alcoholism—Does one inform the other? *Journal of Consulting and Clinical Psychology, 62(6),* 1091–1095.

Ericksen, W., & Billick, S. (2012). Psychiatric issues in cosmetic plastic surgery. *Psychiatric Quarterly, 83(3),* 343–352. doi:10.1007/s11126-012-9204-8

Erickson, K. I., Weinstein, A. M., & Lopez, O. L. (2012). Physical activity, brain plasticity, and Alzheimer's disease. *Archives of Medical Research, 43(8),* 615–621. doi: 10.1016/j.arcmed.2012.09.008

Erikson, E. (1946). Ego development and historical change. *The psychoanalytic study of the child* (Vol. 2, pp. 359–396). New York: International Universities Press.

Erikson, E. (1982). *The life cycle completed.* New York: Norton.

Erlenmeyer-Kimling, L. E., & Cornblatt, B. (1987). The New York high-risk project: A follow-up report. *Schizophrenia Bulletin, 13,* 451–461.

Erlenmeyer-Kimling, L. E., Squires-Wheeler, E., Adamo, U., Bassett, A. S., Cornblatt, B., Kestenbaum, C. J., Rock, D., Roberts, S. A., & Gottesman, I. I. (1995). The New York High Risk Project: Psychoses and cluster A personality disorders in offspring of schizophrenic patients at 23 years of follow-up. *Archives of General Psychiatry, 52,* 857–865.

Ernst, N. D., & Harlan, W. R. (1991). Obesity and cardiovascular disease in minority populations: Executive summary. Conference highlights, conclusions, and recommendations. *American Journal of Clinical Nutrition, 53,* 1507S–1511S.

Escobar, J. I., Burnam, M. A., Karno, M., Burnam, M. A., & Wells, K. B. (1987). Somatization in the community. *Archives of General Psychiatry, 44,* 713–718.

Esterling, B. A., Antoni, M. H., Fletcher, M. A., Margulies, S., & Schneiderman, N. (1994). Emotional disclosure through writing or speaking modulates latent Epstein-Barr virus antibody titers. *Journal of Consulting and Clinical Psychology, 62,* 130–140.

Evans, D. A., Hebert, L. E., Beckett, L. A., Scherr, P. A., Albert, M. S., Chown, M. J., Pilgrim, D. M., & Taylor, J. O. (1997). Education and other measures of socioeconomic status and risk of incident Alzheimer disease in a defined population of older persons. *Archives of Neurology, 54(11),* 1399–1405. doi: 10.1001/archneur.1997.00550230066019

Evans, S. W., & Pelham, W. (1991). Psychostimulant effects on academic and behavioral measures of ADHD junior high school students in a lecture format classroom. *Journal of Abnormal Child Psychology, 19,* 537–552.

Excel at Life (2014, May). *Depression CBT self-help guide.* App for Android retrieved on August 11, 2014 from https://play.google.com/store/apps/details?id=com.excelatlife.depression&hl=en

Exner, J. E. (1993). *The Rorschach: A comprehensive system: Basic foundations* (3rd ed). New York: John Wiley & Sons.

Eyberg, S. (1988). Parent-child interaction therapy: Integration of traditional and behavioral concerns. *Child and Family Behavior Therapy, 10(1),* 33–46.

Eyeberg, S. M., Nelson, M. M., & Boggs, S. R. (2008). Evidence-based psychosocial treatments for children and adolescents with disruptive behavior. *Journal of Clinical Child and Adolescent Psychology, 37,* 215–237.

Eysenck, H. J. (1964). *Crime and personality.* Boston: Houghton Mifflin.

Eysenck, H. J., & Grossarth-Maticek, R. (1991). Creative novation behaviour therapy as a prophylactic treatment for cancer and coronary heart disease (Part II): Effects of treatment. *Behaviour Research & Therapy, 29,* 17–31.

Eysenck, H. J., & Rachman, S. (1965). *The causes and cures of neurosis.* San Diego, CA: Knapp.

Ezquiaga, E., Gutierrez, J. L. A., & Lopez, A. G. (1987). Psychosocial factors and episode number in depression. *Journal of Affective Disorders, 12,* 135–138.

F

Faber, R. (1994). Neuropsychiatric assessment. In C. E. Coffey & J. L. Cummings (Eds.). *Textbook of geriatric neuropsychiatry* (pp. 99–109). Washington, DC: American Psychiatric Press

Fabricatore, A. N., Wadden, T. A., Higginbotham, A. J., Faulconbridge, L. F., Nguyen, A. M., Heymsfield, S. B., & Faith, M. S. (2011). Intentional weight loss and changes in symptoms of depression: A systematic review and meta-analysis. *International Journal of Obesity, 35(11),* 1363–1376. doi:10.1038/ijo.2011.2

Faerna, J. M. (1995). *Munch.* New York: Harry N. Abrams.

Fagan, P. J., Wise, T. N., Schmidt, C. R., & Berlin, F. S. (2002). Pedophilia. *Journal of the American Medical Association, 288(19),* 2458–2465. doi:10.1001/jama.288.19.2458

Fahey, T. A., Abas, M., & Brown, J. C. (1989). Multiple personality: A symptom of psychiatric disorder. *British Journal of Psychiatry, 154,* 99–101.

Fairbairn, W. R. D. (1952). *Psychoanalytic studies of the personality.* London: Tavistock Publications/Routledge & Kegan Paul.

Fairbanks, J. A., & Brown, T. A. (1987). Current behavioral approaches to the treatment of post-traumatic stress disorder. *The Behavior Therapist, 3,* 57–64.

Fairburn, C. G., Jones, R., Peveler, R. C., Hope, R. A., & O'Connor, M. (1993). Psychotherapy and bulimia nervosa: Longer-term effects of interpersonal psychotherapy, behavior therapy, and cognitive behavior therapy. *Archives of General Psychiatry, 50*(6), 419–428.

Fairweather, G., Sanders, D., Maynard, H., Cressler, D. L., & Bleck, P. S. (1969). *Community life for the mentally ill: An alternative to institutional care.* Chicago: Aldine Publishing.

Falco, M. (2008, April 15). Herschel Walker reveals many sides of himself. *CNN Health.* Retrieved on December 7, 2014 from http://www.cnn.com/2008/HEALTH/conditions/04/15/herschel.walker.did/index.html?_s=PM%3AHEALTH

Fallon, A. E., & Rozin, P. (1985). Sex differences in perceptions of desirable body shape. *Journal of Abnormal Psychology, 94*(1), 102–105. doi:10.1037/0021-843X.94.1.102

Fallon, B. A., Qureshi, A. I., Laje, G., & Klein, B. (2000). Hypochondriasis and its relationship to obsessive-compulsive disorder. *The Psychiatric Clinics of North America, 23*(3), 605–616.

Falloon, I., Boyd, J., McGill, C., Williamson, M., Razani, J., Moss, H., Gilderman, A., & Simpson, G. (1985). Family management in the prevention of morbidity of schizophrenia: Clinical outcome of a two year longitudinal study. *Archives of General Psychiatry, 42,* 887–896.

Fals-Stewart, W., Marks, A., & Schafer, J. (1993). A comparison of behavioral group therapy and individual behavior therapy in treating obsessive-compulsive disorder. *Journal of Nervous and Mental Disease, 181,* 189–193.

"Famous People with ADHD" (2014). *Adult Attention Deficit Disorder Center of Maryland.* Retrieved on October 23, 2014 from http://www.addadult.com/add-education-center/famous-people-with-adhd/

Fann, J. R., Alfano, C. M., Roth-Roemer, S., Katon, W. J., & Syrjala, K. L. (2007). Impact of delirium on cognition, distress, and health-related quality of life after hematopoietic stem-cell transplantation. *Journal of Clinical Oncology, 25,* 1223–1231.

Faraone, S. V., Sergeant, J., Gillberg, C., & Biederman, J. (2003). The worldwide prevalence of ADHD: Is it an American condition? *World Psychiatry, 2,* 104–113.

Faravelli, C., Pallanti, S., Biondi, F., & Parerniti, S. (1992). Onset of panic disorder. *American Journal of Psychiatry, 149,* 827–828.

Faris, R. E. L., & Dunham, H. W. (1939). *Mental disorders in urban areas.* Chicago: University of Chicago Press.

Farley, A. C., Hajek, P., Lycett, D., & Aveyard, P. (2012). Interventions for preventing weight gain after smoking cessation. *Cochrane Database of Systematic Reviews, 1.* Art. No.: CD006219. DOI: 10.1002/14651858.CD006219.pub3

Farrington, D. P. (1991). Childhood aggression and adult violence: Early precursors and later-life outcomes. In D. J. Pepler & K. H. Rubin (Eds.), *The development of childhood aggression* (pp. 5–29). Hillsdale, NJ: Erlbaum.

Farrington, D. P. (2006). Family background and psychopathy. In C. J. Patrick (Ed.), *Handbook of psychopathy* (pp. 229–250). New York: Guilford Press.

Farrington, D. P., Jolliffe, D., Loeber, R., Stouthamer-Loeber, M., & Kalb, L. M. (2001). The concentration of offenders in families, and family criminality in the prediction of boys' delinquency. *Journal of Adolescence, 24,* 579–596.

Fauerbach, J. A., Lawrence, J. W., Schmidt, C. J., Munster, A. M., & Costa, P. J. (2000). Personality predictors of injury-related post-traumatic stress disorder. *Journal of Nervous and Mental Disease, 188*(8), 510–517. doi:10.1097/00005053-200008000-00006

Fauth, E. B., Schwartz, S., Tschanz, J. T., Østbye, T., Corcoran, C., & Norton, M. C. (2013). Baseline disability in activities of daily living predicts dementia risk even after controlling for baseline global cognitive ability and depressive symptoms. *International Journal of Geriatric Psychiatry, 28*(6), 597–606. doi: 10.1002/gps.3865

Fawzy, F. I., Cousins, N., Fawzy, N., Kemeny, M. E., Elashoff, R., & Morton, D. (1990). A structured psychiatric intervention for cancer patients. I: Changes over time in methods of coping and affective disturbance. *Archives of General Psychiatry, 47,* 720–725.

Fawzy, F. I., Fawzy, N. W., Arndt, L. A., & Pasnau, R. O. (1995). Critical review of psychosocial interventions in cancer care. *Archives of General Psychiatry, 52,* 100–113.

Fawzy, F. I., Fawzy, N. W., Hyun, C. S., Guthrie, D., Fahey, J. L., & Morton, D. (1993). Malignant melanoma: Effect of an early structured psychiatric intervention, coping and affective state on recurrence and survival 6 years later. *Archives of General Psychiatry, 50,* 681–689.

Federal Bureau of Investigation. (2010). *Crime in the United States.* Retrieved August 29, 2014 from http://www.fbi.gov/about-us/cjis/ucr/crime-in-the-u.s/2010/crime-in-the-u.s.-2010/tables/10tbl29.xls

Federal Task Force on Homelessness and Severe Mental Illness (1992). *Outcasts on Main Street.* Washington, DC: Interagency Council on the Homeless.

Feighner, J. (1987). The impact of anxiety therapy on patients' quality of life. *The American Journal of Medicine, 82,* (Suppl. 5A), 14–19.

Feighner, J., Merideth, C., & Hendrickson, G. (1982). A double blind comparison of buspirone and diazepam in outpatients with generalized anxiety disorder. *Journal of Clinical Psychiatry, 43,* 103–107.

Fein, D., Barton, M., Eigsti, I.-M., Kelley, E., Naigles, L., Schultz, R. T., . . . Tyson, K. (2013). Optimal outcome in individuals with a history of autism. *Journal of Child Psychology and Psychiatry, 54,* 195–205.

Feingold, B. F. (1975). Hyperkinesis and learning disabilities linked to artificial food flavors and colors. *American Journal of Nursing, 75,* 797–803.

Feldman, H. A., Goldstein, I., Hatzichristou, D. G. (1994). Impotence and its medical and psychosocial correlates: Results of the Massachusetts male aging study. *Journal of Urology, 151,* 54.

Feldman, H. A., Goldstein, I., Hatzichristou, D. G., Krane, R. J., & Mckinlay, J. (1994). Impotence and its medical and psychological correlates: Results of the Massachusetts Male Aging Study. *Journal of Urology, 151,* 54–61.

Feldman-Summers, S., & Jones, G. (1984). Psychological impacts of sexual contact between therapists and other health care professionals and their clients. *Journal of Consulting and Clinical Psychology, 52,* 1054–1061.

Felmingham, K., Kemp, A. H., Williams, L., Falconer, E., Olivieri, G.,Peduto, A., & Bryant, R. (2008). Dissociative responses to conscious and non-conscious fear impact underlying brain function in post-traumatic stress disorder. *Psychological Medicine, 38,* 1771–1780.

Felner, R. D., Farber, S. S., & Primavera, J. (1983). Transitions and stressful life events: A model for primary prevention. In R. D. Felner, L. A. Jason, J. N. Moritsugu, & S. S. Farber (Eds.), *Preventive psychology: Theory, research, and prevention* (pp. 191–215). New York: Pergamon Press.

Felner, R. D., Jason, L. A., Moritsugu, J. N., & Farber, S. S. (Eds.). (1983). *Preventive psychology: Theory, research and practice.* New York: Pergamon Press.

Feng, C., Chu, H., Chen, C., Chang, Y., Chen, T., Chou, Y., . . . Chou, K. (2012). The effect of cognitive behavioral group therapy for depression: A meta-analysis 2000–2010. *Worldviews on Evidence-Based Nursing, 9*(1), 2–17. doi:10.1111/j.1741-6787.2011.00229.x

Fenton, W., & McGlashan, T. (1991a) Natural history of schizophrenia subtypes: I. Longitudinal study of paranoid, hebephrenic, and undifferentiated schizophrenia. *Archives of General Psychiatry, 48,* 969–977.

Fenton, W., & McGlashan, T. (1991b) Natural history of schizophrenia subtypes II: Positive and negative symptoms and long term course. *Archives of General Psychiatry, 48,* 978–986.

Fergusson, D. M., Boden, J. M., & Horwood, L. J. (2006). Cannabis use and other illicit drug use: testing the cannabis gateway hypothesis. *Addiction, 101*(4), 556–569.

Fernández, A., Mendive, J. M., Salvador-Carulla, L., Rubio-Valera, M., Vicente Luciano, J., Pinto-Meza, A., . . . Serrano-Blanco, A. (2012). Adjustment disorders in primary care: Prevalence, recognition and use of services. *The British Journal of Psychiatry, 201,* 137–142. doi:10.1192/bjp.bp.111.096305

Fernandez, S. & Pritchard, M. (2012). Relationships between self-esteem, media influence, and drive for thinness. *Eating Behaviors, 13*(4), 321–325. doi: 10.1016/j.eatbeh.2012.05.004

Ferrarelli, F., Peterson, M. J., Sarasso, S., Riedner, B. A., Murphy, M. J., Benca, R. M., . . . Tononi, G. (2010). Thalamic dysfunction in schizophrenia suggested by whole-night deficits in slow and fast spindles. *The American Journal of Psychiatry, 167*(11), 1339–1348. doi:10.1176/appi.ajp.2010.09121731

Ferretti, R. P., Cavalier, A. R., Murphy, M. J., & Murphy, R. (1993). The self-management of skills by persons with mental retardation. *Research in Developmental Disabilities, 14*(3), 189–205.

Ferri, M., Amato, L., & Davoli, M. (2006). Alcoholics Anonymous and other 12-step programmes for alcohol dependence. *Cochrane Database of Systematic Reviews, 3,* 1–26. DOI: 10.1002/14651858.CD005032.pub2

Fervaha, G., Foussias, G., Agid, O., & Remington, G. (2014). Impact of primary negative symptoms on functional outcomes in schizophrenia. *European Psychiatry, 29*(7), 449–455. doi:10.1016/j.eurpsy.2014.01.007

Feske, U., & Chambless, D. L. (1995). Cognitive behavioral versus exposure only treatment for social phobia: A meta-analysis. *Behavior Therapy, 26*(4), 695–720. doi:10.1016/S0005-7894(05)80040-1

Feusner, J. D., Neziroglu, F., Wilhelm, S., Mancusi, L., & Bohon, C. (2010). What causes BDD: Research findings and a proposed model. *Psychiatric Annals, 40*(7), 349–355. doi:10.3928/00485713-20100701-08

Fichter, M. M., Leibl, K., Rief, W., Brunner, E., Schmidt-Auberger, S., & Engel, R. R. (1991). Fluoxetine versus placebo: A double-blind study with bulimic inpatients undergoing intensive psychotherapy. *Pharmacopsychiatry, 24*(1), 1–7.

Field, T. M., Schanberg, S. M., Scafidi, F., Bauer, C. R., Vega-Lahr, N., Garcia, R., Nystrom, J., & Kuhn, C. M. (1986). Tactile/kinesthetic stimulation effects on preterm neonates. *Pediatrics, 77*(5), 654–658.

Fielden, J. (2012). Management of adjustment disorder in the deployed setting. *Military Medicine, 177,* 1022–1027.

Filipek, P., & Kennedy, D. (1991). Magnetic resonance imaging: Its role in the developmental disorders. In D. Duane & D. Gray (Eds.), *The reading brain: The biological basis of dyslexia* (pp. 133–160). Parkton, MD: York Press.

Fine, S., Forth, A., Gilbert, M., Haley, G. (1991). Group therapy for adolescent depressive disorder: A comparison of social skills and therapeutic support. *Journal of American Academy of Child Adolescent Psychiatry, 30,* 79–85.

Fingarette, H. (1988). *Heavy drinking: The myth of alcoholism as a disease.* Berkeley, CA: University of California Press.

Fink, M. (1990). How does convulsive therapy work? *Neuropsychopharmacology, 3,* 73–82.

Fink, M. (1993). Who should get ECT? In C. E. Coffey (Ed.), *The clinical science of electroconvulsive therapy* (pp. 3–16). Washington, DC: American Psychiatric Press.

Fink, M. (1994). Indications for the use of ECT. *Psychopharmacology Bulletin, 30,* 269–275.

Fink, M. (2013). The mechanism of action of ECT. In N. Ghaziuddin & G. Walter (Eds.), *Electroconvulsive therapy in children and adolescents* (pp. 18–28). New York: Oxford University Press. doi:10.1093/med/9780199937899.003.0002

Fink, P., Rosendal, M., & Olesen, F. (2005). Classification of somatization and functional somatic symptoms in primary care. *Australian and New Zealand Journal of Psychiatry, 39*(9), 772–781. doi:10.1111/j.1440-1614.2005.01682.x

Finkel, N. J. (1989). The Insanity Defense Reform Act of 1984—Much ado about nothing. *Behavioral Sciences and the Law, 7,* 403–419.

Finkelhor, D. (1994). The international epidemiology of child sexual abuse. *Child Abuse and Neglect, 18,* 409–418.

Finkelhor, D., Hotaling, G., Lewis, I. A., & Smith, C. (1990). Sexual abuse in a national survey of adult men and women: Prevalence, characteristics, and risk factors. *Child Abuse and Neglect, 14,* 19–28.

Finkelhor, D., Turner, H., Shattuck, A., & Hamby, S. (2013). Violence, crime, and abuse exposure in a national sample of children and youth: An update. *JAMA Pediatrics, 167,* 614–621. doi:10.1001/jamapediatrics.2013.42

Finn, P. R., Zeitouni, N. C., & Pihl, R. O. (1990). Effects of alcohol on psychophysiological hyperreactivity to non-aversive and aversive stimuli in men at high risk for alcoholism. *Journal of Abnormal Psychology, 99*(1), 79–85.

First, M. B. (2010). Clinical utility in the revision of the *Diagnostic and Statistical Manual of Mental Disorders (DSM)*. *Professional Psychology: Research and Practice, 41,* 465-473. doi:10.1037/a0021511

First, M. B. (2014). *DSM-5* and paraphilic disorders. *Journal of the American Academy of Psychiatry and the Law, 42,* 191–201.

Fischer, C. T. (1989). A life-centered approach to psychodiagnostics: Attending to lifworld, ambiguity, and possibility. *Person-Centered Review, 4,* 163–170.

Fischer, M., Barkley, R. A., Fletcher, K. E., & Smallish, L. (1993). The adolescent outcome of hyperactive children: Predictors of psychiatric, academic, social, and emotional adjustment. *Journal of the American Academy of Child and Adolescent Psychiatry, 32*(2), 324–332.

Fisher, M. M., Rosen, D. S., Ornstein, R. M., Mammel, K. A., Katzman, D. K., Rome, E. S., . . . Walsh, B. T. (2014). Characteristics of avoidant/restrictive food intake disorder in children and adolescents: A "new disorder" in *DSM-5*. *Journal of Adolescent Health, 55*(1), 49–52. doi:10.1016/j.jadohealth.2013.11.013

Fishwick, D., Carroll, C., McGregor, M., Drury, M., Webster, J., Bradshaw, L., . . . Leaviss, J. (2013). Smoking cessation in the workplace. *Occupational Medicine, 63*(8), 526–536. doi:10.1093/occmed/kqt107

FitzGerald, S. (1995, August 22). Nuns find way to keep giving—after death. *The Philadelphia Inquirer,* pp. Al, A6.

Fitzpatrick, L. (2010, January 7). A brief history of antidepressants. *Time.* New York.

Fjorback, L. O., Arendt, M., Ørnbøl, E., Walach, H., Rehfeld, E., Schröder, A., & Fink, P. (2013). Mindfulness therapy for somatization disorder and functional somatic syndromes—randomized trial with one-year follow-up. *Journal of Psychosomatic Research, 74*(1), 31–40. doi:10.1016/j.jpsychores.2012.09.006

Flashman, L. A., & Green, M. F. (2004). Review of cognition and brain structure in schizophrenia: profiles, longitudinal course, and effects of treatment. *Psychiatric Clinics of North America, 27,* 1–18.

Flaskerud, J. H. (2012). Seasonal affective disorders. *Issues in Mental Health Nursing, 33*(4), 266–268. doi:10.3109/01612840.2011.617028

Fleming, I., Baum, A., Davidson, L. M., Rectanus, E., & McArdle, S. (1987). Chronic stress as a factor in psychologic reactivity to challenge. *Health Psychology, 6,* 221–238.

Flessner, C. A., Woods, D., Franklin, M., Keuthen, N., & Piacentini, J. (2008). Styles of pulling in youths with trichotillomania: Exploring differences in symptom severity, phenomenology, and comorbid psychiatric symptoms. *Behaviour Research and Therapy, 46,* 1055–1061. doi:10.1016/j.brat.2008.06.006

Flett, R. A., Kazantzis, N., Long, N. R., MacDonald, C., & Millar, M. (2002). Traumatic events and physical health in a New Zealand community sample. *Journal of Traumatic Stress, 15,* 303–312.

Fliege, H., Grimm, A., Eckhardt-Henn, A., Gieler, U., Martin, K., & Klapp, B. F. (2007). Frequency of ICD-10 factitious disorder: Survey of senior hospital consultants and physicians in private practice. *Psychosomatics, 48*(1), 60–64. doi:10.1176/appi.psy.48.1.60

Foa, E. B., & Kozak, M. J. (1986). Emotional processing of fear: Exposure to corrective information. *Psychological Bulletin, 99,* 20–35.

Foa, E. B., Hearst-Ikeda, D., & Perry, K. J. (1995). Evaluation of a brief cognitive-behavioral program for the prevention of chronic PTSD in recent assault victims. *Journal of Consulting and Clinical Psychology, 63,* 948–955. doi:10.1037/0022-006X.63.6.948

Foa, E. B., Riggs, D. S., Massie, E. D., & Yarczower, M. (1995). The impact of fear activation and anger on the efficacy of exposure treatment for posttraumatic stress disorder. *Behavior Therapy, 26,* 487–500.

Foa, E. B., Rothbaum, B. O., Riggs, D. S., & Murdock, T. B. (1991). Treatment of posttraumatic stress disorder in rape victims: A comparison between cognitive-behavioral procedures and counseling. *Journal of Consulting and Clinical Psychology, 59,* 715–723.

Foa, E. B., Steketee, G., & Olasov-Rothbaum, B. (1989). Behavioral/cognitive conceptualizations of post-traumatic stress disorder. *Behavior Therapy, 20,* 155–176.

Foa, E. B., Zinbarg, R., & Olasov-Rothbaum, B. (1992). Uncontrollability and unpredictability in post-traumatic stress disorder: An animal model. *Psychological Bulletin, 112,* 218–238.

Foley, J. M., & Heck, A. L. (2014). Neurocognitive disorders in aging: A primer on *DSM-5* changes and framework for application to practice. *Clinical Gerontologist, 37*(4), 317–346. doi: 10.1080/07317115.2014.907595

Folkman, S., & Lazarus, R. S. (1980). An analysis of coping in a middle-aged community sample. *Journal of Health & Social Behavior, 21,* 251–262.

Folstein, M. F., Folstein, S. E., & McHugh, P. R. (1975). "'Mini-mental state'": A practical method for grading the cognitive state of patients for the clinician. *Journal of Psychiatric Research, 12,* 189–198.

Folstein, S., & Rutter, M. (1977). Infantile autism: A genetic study of 21 twin pairs. *Journal of Child Psychology and Psychiatry, 18,* 297–321.

Folstein, S. E., & Piven, J. (1991). Etiology of autism: Genetic influences. *Pediatrics, 87,* 767–773.

Fombonne, E. (2008). Thimerosal disappears but autism remains. *Archives of General Psychiatry, 65,* 15–16.

Fonagy, P., Target. M., & Gergely, G. (2000). Attachment and borderline personality disorder: A theory of some evidence. *Psychiatric Clinics of North America, 23,* 103–122.

Fong, T. C., Tulebaev, S. R., & Inouye, S. K. (2009). Delirium in elderly adults: diagnosis, prevention, and treatment. *Nature Reviews Neurology, 5,* 210–220.

Fontaine, P., & Ansseau, M. (1995). Pharmaco-clinical aspects of methadone: Literature review of its importance in treatment of substance dependence. *Encephale, 21,* 167–179.

Ford v. Wainwright, 477 U.S. 399 (1986).

Ford, C. V. (1995). Dimensions of somatization and hypochondriasis. *Neurologic Clinics, 12,* 241–253.

Ford, D. E., & Kamerow, D. B. (1989). Epidemiologic study of sleep disturbances and psychiatric disorder: An opportunity for prevention? *Journal of the American Medical Association, 262,* 1479–1484.

Ford, M., & Widiger, T. (1989). Sex bias in the diagnosis of histrionic and antisocial personality disorders. *Journal of Consulting and Clinical Psychology, 57,* 301–305.

Forde, K. (2011, October 28). Top 10 famous hypochondriacs. *TopTenz.* Retrieved on December 5, 2014 from http://www.toptenz.net/top-10-famous-hypochondriacs.php

Fordyce, W. E. (1976). *Behavioral methods for chronic pain and illness.* Saint Louis, MO: Mosby.

Forehand, R. L., & McMahon, R. J. (1981). *Helping the noncompliant child: A clinician's guide to parent training.* New York: Guilford Press.

Forgas, J. P. (2013). Don't worry, be sad! On the cognitive, motivational, and interpersonal benefits of negative mood. *Current Directions in Psychological Science, 22*(3), 225–232. doi:10.1177/0963721412474458

Fortmann, S. P., &; Killen, J. D. (1995). Nicotine gum and self-help treatment for smoking relapse prevention: Results from a trial using population-based recruitment. *Journal of Consulting and Clinical Psychology, 63,* 460–468.

Fosse, R., & Read, J. (2013). Electroconvulsive treatment: Hypotheses about mechanisms of action. *Frontiers in Psychiatry, 4,* 94. doi:10.3389/fpsyt.2013.00094

Foster, G. D., & Kendall, P. C. (1994). The realistic treatment of obesity: Changing the scales of success. *Clinical Psychology Review, 11,* 701–736.

Foucha v. Louisiana, 112 S. Ct. 1780 (1992).

Foulks, F. F., Bland, I. J., & Shervington, D. (1995). Psychotherapy across cultures. *Review of Psychiatry, 14,* 511.

Fountoulakis, K. N., & Siamouli, M. (2009). Re: How well do psychosocial interventions work in bipolar disorder? *The Canadian Journal of Psychiatry, 54*(8), 578.

Fournier, J. C., DeRubeis, R. J., Hollon, S. D., Dimidjian, S., Amsterdam, J. D., Shelton, R. C., & Fawcett, J. (2010). Antidepressant drug effects and depression severity: A patient-level meta-analysis. *JAMA: Journal of the American Medical Association, 303*(1), 47–53. doi:10.1001/jama.2009.1943

Fournier, J. C., DeRubeis, R. J., Hollon, S. D., Gallop, R., Shelton, R. C., & Amsterdam, J. D. (2013). Differential change in specific depressive symptoms during antidepressant medication or cognitive therapy. *Behaviour Research and Therapy, 51*(7), 392–398. doi:10.1016/j.brat.2013.03.010

Fowler, A. (1988). Determinants of rate of language growth in children with Down syndrome. In L. Nadel (Ed.), *The psychobiology of Down syndrome* (pp. 217–245). Cambridge: MIT Press.

Foy, D., Sipprelle, R., Rueger, D., & Carroll, E. (1984). Etiology of post-traumatic stress disorder in Vietnam veterans: Analysis of premilitary, military, and combat exposure influences. *Journal of Consulting and Clinical Psychology, 52,* 79–87.

Fraboni, M., Cooper, D., Reed, T. L., & Saltstone, R. (1990). Offense type and two-point MMPI code profiles: Discriminating between violent and nonviolent offenders. *Journal of Clinical Psychology, 46,* 774–777.

Fraguas, D., Correll, C. U., Merchán-Naranjo, J., Rapado-Castro, M., Parellada, M., Moreno, C., & Arango, C. (2011). Efficacy and safety of second-generation antipsychotics in children and adolescents with psychotic and bipolar spectrum disorders: Comprehensive review of prospective head-to-head and placebo-controlled comparisons. *European Neuropsychopharmacology, 21*(8), 621–645.

France, C. M., Lysaker, P. H., & Robinson, R. P. (2007). The "chemical imbalance" explanation for depression: Origins, lay endorsement, and clinical implications. *Professional Psychology: Research and Practice, 38*(4), 411–420. doi:10.1037/0735-7028.38.4.411

France, K. G., & Hudson, S. M. (1992). Management of infant sleep disturbance: A review. *Clinical Psychology Review, 13,* 635–648.

Frances, A. (2010a, March 25). DSM-5 in distress: DSM5 "addiction" swallows substance abuse. *Psychology Today.* Retrieved on December 10, 2014 from http://www.psychologytoday.com/blog/dsm5-in-distress/201003/dsm5-addiction -swallows-substance-abuse

Frances, A. (2010b, March 24). DSM-5 in distress: DSM-5 suggests opening the door to behavioral addictions. *Psychology Today.* Retrieved on December 16, 2014 from http://www.psychologytoday.com/blog/dsm5-in-distress/201003/ dsm5-suggests-opening-the-door-behavioral-addictions

Frances, A. (2011, May 12). *DSM-5* rejects coercive paraphilia: Once again confirming that rape is not a mental disorder. *Couch in Crisis, Forensic Psychiatry, DSM-5.* Retrieved on October 7, 2014 from http://www.psychiatrictimes.com/ blogs/couch-crisis/dsm-5-rejects-coercive-paraphilia-once-again-confirming- rape-not-mental-disorder

Frances, A. (2012, December 8). Mislabeling medical illness as mental disorder. *Psychology Today.* Retrieved on November 17, 2014 from http://www.psychologytoday. com/blog/dsm5-in-distress/201212/mislabeling-medical-illness-mental-disorder

Frances, A. (2012a). *DSM 5* is guide not Bible—Ignore its ten worst changes [Web log post]. In *DSM-5 in Distress.* Retrieved May 20, 2013 from http://www .psychologytoday.com/blog/dsm5-in-distress/201212/dsm-5-is-guide-not-bible -ignore-its-ten-worst-changes

Frances, A. (2012b, November 20). Will *DSM-5* reduce rates of autism? [Blog post]. In *DSM-5 in Distress.* Retrieved on June 10, 2013 from http://www.psycholo- gytoday.com/blog/dsm5-in-distress/201211/will-the-dsm-5-reduce-rates-autism

Frances, A. (2013). *Essentials of psychiatric diagnosis: Responding to the challenge of* DSM-5. New York: Guilford Press.

Frances, A. (2013a, January 16). Bad news: *DSM-5* refuses to correct somatic symptom disorder. *Psychology Today.* Retrieved November 17, 2014 from http://www .psychologytoday.com/blog/dsm5-in-distress/201301/bad-news-dsm-5-refuses -correct-somatic-symptom-disorder

Frances, A. (2013b). The new somatic symptom disorder in *DSM-5* risks mislabeling many people as mentally ill. *British Medical Journal, 346,* f1580–f1580. doi:10.1136/bmj.f1580

Francis, J., Martin, D., & Kapoor, W. N. (1990). A prospective study of delirium in hospitalized elderly. *Journal of the American Medical Association, 263,* 1097–1101.

Franck, J. (2003). Pharmacotherapy for alcohol withdrawal syndrome. In M. Berglund, S. Thelander, & E. Jonsson (Eds.), *Treating alcohol and drug abuse: An evidence based review* (pp. 189–246). Weinheim, Germany: Wiley-VCH Verlag GmbH & Co KGaA. doi:10.1002/3527601465.ch3

Frank, E. (1981). How prevalent is lack of sexual desire in marriage? *Medical Aspects of Human Sexuality, 15,* 74–79.

Frank, E., & Swartz, H. A. (2004). Interpersonal and social rhythm therapy. In S.L. Johnson & R.L. Leahy (Eds.), *Psychological treatment of bipolar disorder* (pp. 162–183). New York: Guilford Press.

Frank, E., Kupfer, D. J., Thase, M. E., Mallinger, A. G., Swartz, H. A., & Fagiolini, A. (2005). Two-year outcomes for interpersonal and social rhythm therapy in individuals with bipolar I disorder. *Archives of General Psychiatry, 62,* 996–1004. doi: 10.1001/archpsyc.62.9.996

Frank, E., Kupfer, D., Perel, J., Cornes, C., Jarrett, D. Mallinger, A., Thase, M., McEachran, A., & Grochocin-ski, V. (1990). Three-year outcomes for maintenance therapies in recurrent depression. *Archives of General Psychiatry, 47,* 1093–1099.

Frank, E., Prien, R., Kupfer, D. & Alberts, L. (1985). Implications of noncompliance on research in affective disorders. *Psychopharmacology Bulletin, 21,* 37–42.

Frank, E., Swartz, H. A., & Kupfer, D. J. (2000). Interpersonal and social rhythm therapy: Managing the chaos of bipolar disorder. *Biological Psychiatry, 48,* 593–604.

Frank, J. D. (1957). Some determinants, manifestations, and effects of cohesiveness in therapy groups. *International Journal of Group Psychotherapy, 7,* 53–63.

Frank, J. D. (1973). *Persuasion and healing* (rev. ed.). Baltimore: Johns Hopkins University Press.

Frankl, V. (1967). *Psychotherapy and existentialism: Selected papers on logotherapy.* New York: Washington Square Press.

Franklin, J. E. (1989). Alcoholism among Blacks. *Hospital and Community Psychiatry, 40,* 1120–1127.

Frary, C. D., Johnson, R. K., & Wang, M. Q. (2005). Food sources and intakes of caffeine in the diets of persons in the United States. *Journal of the American Dietetic Association, 105*(1), 110–113.

Fraser, L., Karasic, D. H., Meyer, W. J., & Wylie, K. (2010). Recommendations for revision of the *DSM* diagnosis of gender identity disorder in adults. *International Journal of Transgenderism, 12,* 80–85.

Frassica, J. J., Orav, E. J., Walsh, E. P., & Lipshultz, S. E. (1994). Arrhythmias in children prenatally exposed to cocaine. *Archives of Pediatrics and Adolescent Medicine, 148*(11), 1163–1169.

Frattaroli, J. (2006). Experimental disclosure and its moderators: A meta-analysis. *Psychological Bulletin, 132*(6), 823–865. doi:10.1037/0033-2909.132.6.823

Frazer, A. A., & Benmansour, S. S. (2002). Delayed pharmacological effects of antidepressants. *Molecular Psychiatry, 7,* S23.

Frazier, P., & Esterly, E. (1990). Correlates of relationship beliefs: Gender, relationship experience and relationship satisfaction. *Journal of Social and Personal Relationships, 7,* 331–352.

Frazier, T. W., Thompson, L., Youngstrom, E. A., Law, P., Hardan, A. Y., Eng, C., & Morris, J. (2014). A twin study of heritable and shared environmental contributions to autism. *Journal of Autism and Developmental Disorders, 44*(8), 2013–2025. doi:10.1007/s10803-014-2081-2

Frazier, T. W., Youngstrom, E. A., Speer, L., Embacher, R., Law, P., Constantino, J., . . . Eng, C. (2012). Validation of proposed *DSM-5* criteria for autism spectrum disorder. *Journal of the American Academy of Child and Adolescent Psychiatry, 51,* 28–40.

Free, N., Winget, C., & Whitman, R. (1993). Separation anxiety in panic disorder. *American Journal of Psychiatry, 150,* 595–599.

Freedman, N. D., Park, Y., Abnet, C. C., Hollenbeck, A. R., & Sinha, R. (2012). Association of coffee drinking with total and cause-specific mortality. *The New England Journal of Medicine, 366*(20), 1891–1904. doi:10.1056/NEJMoa1112010

Freeman, H. (1994). Schizophrenia and city residence. *British Journal of Psychiatry, 164* (Suppl. 23), 39–50.

Freeman, T. (1971). Observations on mania. *International Journal of Psychoanalysis, 52,* 479–486.

Freitas-Ferrari, M., Hallak, J. C., Trzesniak, C., Filho, A., Machado-de-Sousa, J., Chagas, M. N., . . . Crippa, J. S. (2010). Neuroimaging in social anxiety disorder: A systematic review of the literature. *Progress in Neuro-Psychopharmacology & Biological Psychiatry, 34*(4), 565–580. doi:10.1016/j.pnpbp.2010.02.028

French, C. C., Richards, A., & Scholfield, E. C. (1996). Hypomania, anxiety and the emotional Stroop. *British Journal of Clinical Psychology, 35*(4), 617–626. doi:10.1111/j.2044-8260.1996.tb01217.x

Freud, A. (1946). *The ego and mechanisms of defense.* New York: International Universities Press.

Freud, S. (1901). *The psychopathology of everyday life.* New York: Macmillan.

Freud, S. (1917/1957). Mourning and melancholia. In J. Strachey (Ed.), *Collected works of Sigmund Freud: Third standard edition.* Vol. 14. London: Hogarth Press.

Freud, S. (1924). Neurosis and psychosis. In *The standard edition of the complete psychological works of Sigmund Freud, volume XIX (1923–1925): The ego and the id and other works* (pp. 147–154). London: Vintage.

Freud, S. (1933/1965). *New introductory lectures on psychoanalysis.* New York: W. W. Norton.

Freud, S. (1936/1963). *The problem of anxiety.* New York: W. W. Norton.

Freud, S. (1938). *The basic writings of Sigmund Freud.* New York: Modern Library.

Freud, S., & Breuer, J. (2004). *Studies in hysteria.* New York: Penguin Books.

Freund, B., Foa, E., Kozak, M., & Hembree, E. (1991, November). *Comparisons of OCD treatment outcome among clomipramine, fluvoxamine, placebo, and behavior therapy.* Presented at the 25th annual meeting of the Association for Advancement of Behavior Therapy, New York.

Frezza, M., Di Padova, C., Pozzato, G., Terpin, M., Baraona, E., & Lieber, C. S. (1990). High blood alcohol levels in women: The role of decreased gastric alcohol dehydrogenase activity and first-pass metabolism. *New England Journal of Medicine, 322*(2), 95–99.

Frick, P. J. (2000). A comprehensive and individualized treatment approach for children and adolescents with conduct disorders. *Cognitive and Behavioral Practice, 7,* 30–37.

Fridlund, A. J., Beck, H. P., Goldie, W. D., & Irons, G. (2012). Little Albert: A neurologically impaired child. *History of Psychology,* January, serial online. doi:10.1037/a0026720

Friederici, A. D. (2011). The brain basis of language processing: From structure to function. *Physiological Reviews, 91*(4), 1357–1392. doi: 10.1152/physrev.00006.2011

Friedman, H. S., & Booth-Kewley, S. (1987). The "disease-prone personality." *American Psychologist, 42,* 539–555.

Friedman, H. W., Tucker, J. S., Schwartz, J. E., Tomlinson-Keasey, C., Martin, L. R., Wingard, D. L., & Criqui, M. H. (1995). Psychosocial and behavioral predictors of longevity: The aging and death of the "Termites." *American Psychologist, 50,* 69–78.

Friedman, M., & Rosenman, R. H. (1974). *Type A behavior and your heart.* New York: Knopf.

Friedman, M., & Ulmer, D. (1984). *Treating type A behavior and your heart.* New York: Fawcett Crest.

Friedman, M., Thoresen, C. E., Gill, J., Ulmer, D., Powell, L. H., Price, V. A., Brown, B., Thompson, L., Rabin, D. D., Breall, W. S., Bourg, W., Levy, R., & Dixon, T. (1986). Alteration of Type A behavior and its effect on cardiac recurrences in post-myocardial infarction patients: Summary results on the Recurrent Coronary Prevention Project. *American Heart Journal, 112,* 653–665.

Friedrich, M. J. (2014). Researchers focus on recovery in schizophrenia. *JAMA, 312*(1), 16–18. doi:10.1001/jama.2014.7450.

Friedman, M. J., Resick, P. A., Bryant, R. A., & Brewin, C. R. (2011). Considering PTSD for *DSM-5. Depress Anxiety, 28*(9), 750–769.

Friedman, M. J., & Southwick, S. M. (1995). Towards pharmacotherapy for post-traumatic stress disorder. In M. J. Friedman, D. S. Charney, & A. Y. Deutch (Eds.), *Neurobiological and clinical consequences of stress: From normal adaptation to PTSD* (pp. 465–481). Philadelphia: Lippincott-Raven.

Friedman, R., Sandler, J., Hernandez, M., & Wolfe, D. (1981). Child abuse. In E. J. Marsh & L. G. Terdal (Eds.), *Behavioral assessment of childhood disorders* (pp. 221–255). New York: Guilford Press.

Friedrich, W. N., Beilke, R. L., & Urquiza, A. J. (1987). Children from sexually abusive families: A behavior comparison. *Journal of Interpersonal Violence, 2,* 391–402.

Friedrich, W. N., Beilke, R. L., & Urquiza, A. J. (1988). Behavior problems in young sexually abused boys: A comparison study. *Journal of Interpersonal Violence, 3,* 21–28.

Frischholz, E. J., Lipman, L. S., Braun, B. G., & Sachs, R. G. (1992). Psychopathology, hypnotizability, and dissociation. *American Journal of Psychiatry, 149,* 1521–1525.

Frisher, M. (2010). The science and politics of cannabis, drugs and schizophrenia—Commentary on: Cannabis causes schizophrenia? So does nicotine. *Addiction Research & Theory, 18*(6), 609–611. doi:10.3109/16066359.2010.490001

Fristad, M. A., & MacPherson, H. A. (2014). Evidence-based psychosocial treatments for child and adolescent bipolar spectrum disorders. *Journal of Clinical Child and Adolescent Psychology, 43*(3), 339–355. doi:10.1080/15374416.2013.822309

Fromme, K., Marlatt, G. A., Baer, J. S., & Kivlahan, D. R. (1994). The Alcohol Skills Training Program: A group intervention for young adult drinkers. *Journal of Substance Abuse Treatment, 11*(2), 143–154.

Fromm-Reichmann, F. (1948). Notes on the development of treatment of schizophrenics by psychoanalytic psychotherapy. *Psychiatry, 11,* 263–273.

Frost, R., & Gross, R. (1993). The hoarding of possessions. *Behaviour Research and Therapy, 31*(4), 367–381.

Frost, R., Hartl, T., Christian, R., & Williams, N. (1995). The value of possessions in compulsive hoarding: Patterns of use and attachment. *Behaviour Research and Therapy, 33*(8), 897–902.

Frost, R. O., & Hartl, T. L. (1996). A cognitive-behavioral model of compulsive hoarding. *Behaviour Research and Therapy, 34*(4), 341–350. doi:10.1016/0005-7967(95)00071-2

Frost, R. O., Patronek, G., & Rosenfield, E. (2011). Comparison of object and animal hoarding. *Depression and Anxiety, 28*(10), 885–891. doi:10.1002/da.20826

Frost, R. O., Steketee, G., & Williams, L. (2000). Hoarding: A community health problem. *Health and Social Care in the Community, 8*(4), 229–234. doi: 1156069210.1046/j.1365-2524.2000.00245.x

Frost, R. O., Steketee, G., Williams, L. F., & Warren, R. (2000). Mood, personality disorder symptoms and disability in obsessive-compulsive hoarders: A comparison with clinical and nonclinical controls. *Behaviour Research and Therapy, 38*(11), 1071–1081. doi:10.1016/S0005-7967(99)00137-0

Fuchs, D., & Fuchs, L. S. (1994). Inclusive schools movement and the radicalization of special education reform. *Exceptional Children, 60*(4), 294–309.

Fugl-Meyer, A., & Sjögren, K. (1999). Sexual disabilities, problems, and satisfaction in 18–74-year-old Swedes. *Scandinavian Journal of Sexology, 2,* 79.

Fulero, S., & Finkel, N. J. (1991). Barring ultimate issue testimony: An "insane" rule? *Law and Human Behavior, 15*(5), 495–508.

Fuller, R. K., Branchey, L., Brightwell, D. R., Derman, R. M., James, K. E., Lacoursiere, R. B., Lee, K. K., Lowenstam, I., Maany, I., Neiderheiser, D., Nocks, J. J., & Shaw, S. (1986). Disulfiram treatment of alcoholism: A Veterans Administra-

tion cooperative study. *Journal of the American Medical Association, 256*(11), 1449–1455.

Fuller, S. C. (1912). Alzheimer's disease (senium praecox): The report of a case and review of published cases. *Journal of Nervous and Mental Disease, 39,* 440–455; 536–557.

Fullerton, C. S., Ursano, R. J., & Wang, L. (2004). Acute stress disorder, posttraumatic stress disorder, and depression in disaster or rescue workers. *The American Journal of Psychiatry, 161,* 1370–1376.

Furby, L., Weinrott, M. R., & Blackshaw, L. (1989). Sex offender recidivism: A review. *Psychological Bulletin, 10S,* 3–30.

Furini, C. G., Myskiw, J. C., Benetti, F., & Izquierdo, I. (2013). New frontiers in the study of memory mechanisms. *Revista Brasileira De Psiquiatria, 35,* 173–177. doi:10.1590/1516-4446-2012-1046

Furnham, A., & Sen, R. (2013). Lay theories of gender identity disorder. *Journal of Homosexuality, 60*(10), 1434–1449. doi:10.1080/00918369.2013.819208

Furnham, A., Batey, M., Anand, K., & Manfield, J. (2008). Personality, hypomania, intelligence and creativity. *Personality and Individual Differences, 44,* 1060–1069. doi:10.1016/j.paid.2007.10.035

Fusar-Poli, P., Perez, J., Broome, M., Borgwardt, S., Placentino, A., Caverzasi, E., . . . McGuire, P. (2007). Neurofunctional correlates of vulnerability to psychosis: A systematic review and meta-analysis. *Neuroscience and Biobehavioral Reviews, 31,* 465–484.

Fustos, J., Gramann, K., Herbert, B. M., & Pollatos, O. (2013). On the embodiment of emotion regulation: Interoceptive awareness facilitates reappraisal. *Social Cognitive and Affective Neuroscience, 8,* 911–917.

Futon Critic, The (2009, May 4). *A&E premieres new original nonfiction series "Obsessed" profiling people suffering from extreme anxiety disorders and their efforts to overcome them.* Retrieved on September 23, 2014 from http://www.thefutoncritic.com/news/2009/05/04/a-and-e-premieres-new-original-nonfiction-series-obsessed-profiling-people-suffering-from-extreme-anxiety-disorders-and-their-efforts-to-overcome-them-31242/20090504aande01/

G

Gabrieli, J. D. E. (2009). Dyslexia: A new synergy between education and cognitive neuroscience. *Science, 325,* 280–283.

Gabrielli, W. F., Jr., Mednick, S. A., Volavka, J., Pollock, V. E., Schulsinger, F., & Itil, T. M. (1982). Electroencephalograms in children of alcoholic fathers. *Psychophysiology, 19*(4), 404–407.

Gadermann, A. M., Alonso, J., Vilagut, G., Zaslavsky, A. M., & Kessler, R. C. (2012). Comorbidity and disease burden in the National Comorbidity Survey Replication (NCS-R). *Depression and Anxiety, 29*(9), 797–806. doi:10.1002/da.21924

Gadow, K. D. (1992). Pediatric psychopharmacotherapy:. A review of recent research. *Journal of Child Psychology and Psychiatry and Allied Disciplines, 33*(1), 281–300.

Gadow, K. D. (1993). Prevalence of drug therapy. In J. S. Werry & M. G. Aman (Eds.), *Practitioner's guide to psychoactive drugs for children and adolescents* (pp. 57–74). New York: Plenum.

Gadow, K. D., Sverd, J., Sprafkin, J., Nolan, E. E., & Ezor, S. N. (1995). Efficacy of methylphenidate for attention-deficit hyperactivity disorder in children with tic disorder. *American Journal of Psychiatry, IS2,* 444–455.

Gadpaille, W. J. (1995). Homosexuality and homosexual behavior. In H. I. Kaplan & B. J. Sadock (Eds.), *Comprehensive textbook of psychiatry/VI* (pp. 1321–1333). Baltimore: Williams & Wilkins.

Gaffney, G. R., Kuperman, S., Tsai, L. Y., & Minchin, S. (1989). Forebrain structure in infantile autism. *Journal of the American Academy of Child and Adolescent Psychiatry, 28,* 534–537.

Gaissmaier, W., & Gigerenzer, G. (2012). 9/11, Act II: A fine-grained analysis of regional variations in traffic fatalities in the aftermath of the terrorist attacks. *Psychological Science, 23*(12), 1449–1454. doi:10.1177/0956797612447804

Galaburda, A. M., Menard, M. T., & Rosen, G. D. (1994). Evidence for aberrant auditory anatomy in developmental dyslexia. *Proceedings of the National Academy of Sciences of the United States of America, 91*(17), 8010–8013.

Galaburda, A. M., Wang, P. P., Bellugi, U., & Rossen, M. (1994). Cytoarchitectonic anomalies in a genetically based disorder: Williams syndrome. *Neuroreport, 5*(7), 753–757.

Galambos, N. L., Vargas Lascano, D. I., Howard, A. L., & Maggs, J. L. (2013). Who sleeps best? Longitudinal patterns and covariates of change in sleep quantity, quality, and timing across four university years. *Behavioral Sleep Medicine, 11*(1), 8–22. doi:10.1080/15402002.2011.596234

Galanter, M. (1988). Zealous self-help groups as adjuncts to psychiatric treatment: A study of Recovery, Inc. *American Journal of Psychiatry, 145,* 1248–1253.

Galenson, E., & Roiphe, H. (1974). The emergence of genital awareness during the second year of life. In R. C. Friedman, R. M. Richart, & R. L. V. Wiele (Eds.), *Sex differences in behavior: A conference* (pp. 223–231). New York: Wiley.

Galin, D., Diamond, R., & Braff, D. (1977). Lateralization of conversion symptoms: More frequent on the left. *American Journal of Psychiatry, 134,* 578–580.

Gallagher, H. L., & Frith, C. D. (2003). Functional imaging of "theory of mind." *Trends in cognitive sciences, 7*(2), 77–83.

Gallagher-Thompson, D., Hanley-Peterson, P., & Thompson, L. W. (1990). Maintenance of gains versus relapse following brief psychotherapy for depression. *Journal of Consulting and Clinical Psychology, 58,* 371–374.

Galloway, G. P., Newmeyer, J., Knapp, T., Stalcup, S. A., & Smith, D. (1994). Imipramine for the treatment of cocaine and methamphetamine dependence. *Journal of Addictive Diseases, 13(4),* 201–216.

Galluscio, E. H. (1990). *Biological psychology.* New York: Macmillan.

Gan, S. S., Zhong, C., Das, S., Gan, J. S., Willis, S., & Tully, E. (2014). The prevalence of bullying and cyberbullying in high school: A 2011 survey. *International Journal of Adolescent Medicine and Health, 26*(1), 27–31. doi:10.1515/ijamh-2012-0106

Gantt, L., & Tinnin, L. W. (2007). Intensive trauma therapy of PTSD and dissociation: An outcome study. *The Arts in Psychotherapy, 34*(1), 69–80. doi:10.1016/j.aip.2006.09.007

Gao, J., Pan, Z., Jiao, Z., Li, F., Zhao, G., Wei, Q., . . . Evangelou, E. (2012). TPH2 gene polymorphisms and major depression—A meta-analysis. *Plos ONE, 7*(5). doi:10.1371/journal.pone.0036721

Gapstur, S. M., Potter, J. D., Sellers, T. A., & Folsom, A. R. (1992). Increased risk of breast cancer with alcohol consumption in postmenopausal women. *American Journal of Epidemiology, 136,* 1221–1231.

Garber, J., Braafladt, N., & Zeman, J. (1991). The regulation of sad affect: An information-processing perspective. In J. Garber & K. A. Dodge (Eds.), *The development of emotion regulation and dysregulation* (pp. 208–242). New York: Cambridge University Press.

García-Campayo, J., Arevalo, E., Claraco, L. M., Alda, M., & Lopez del Hoyo, Y. (2010). A prevention programme for somatoform disorders is effective for affective disorders. *Journal of Affective Disorders, 122*(1–2), 124–132. doi:10.1016/j.jad.2009.06.031

Gardner, H. (1993). *Multiple intelligences: The theory in practice.* New York: Basic Books.

Gardner, H., Csikszentmihalyi, M., & Damon, W. (2001). *Good work: When excellence and ethics meet.* New York: Basic Books.

Gardner, W., Lidz, C. W., Mulvey, E. P., & Shaw, E. C. (1996). A comparison of actuarial methods for identifying repetitively violent patients. *Law and Human Behavior, 20,* 35–48.

Garety, P. A., & Freeman, D. (1999). Cognitive approaches to delusions: A critical review of theories and evidence. *British Journal of Clinical Psychology, 38,* 113–154

Garfield, S. L. (1994). Research on client variables in psychotherapy. In A. E. Bergin & S. L. Garfield, *Handbook of psychotherapy and behavior change* (pp. 190–228). New York: John Wiley & Sons.

Garfield, S. L., & Kurtz, R. (1976). Clinical psychologists in the 1970s. *American Psychologist, 31,* 1–9.

Garland, A. F., & Zigler, E. (1993). Adolescent suicide prevention: Current research and social policy implications. *American Psychologist, 48,* 169–182.

Garner, D. M., Garfinkel, P. E., Schwartz, D., & Thompson, M. (1980). Cultural expectations of thinness in women. *Psychological Reports, 47,* 483–491.

Garner, D. M., Olmstead, M. P., & Polivy, J. (1983). Development and validation of a multidimensional inventory for anorexia nervosa and bulimia. *International Journal of Eating Disorders, 2*(2), 15–34.

Garralda, M. E. (1996). Somatisation in children. *Child Psychology & Psychiatry & Allied Disciplines, 37*(1), 13–33. doi:10.1111/j.1469-7610.1996.tb01378.x

Gartner, J. D. (2011). *The hypomanic edge: The link between (a little) craziness and (a lot of) success in America.* New York: Simon & Schuster.

Gath, A. (1977). The impact of an abnormal child upon the parents. *British Journal of Psychiatry, 130,* 405–410.

Gatz, M., & Pearson, C. G. (1988). Ageism revised and the provision of psychological services. *American Psychologist, 43,* 184–188.

Gatzke-Kopp, L. M., Raine, A., Loeber, R., Stouthamer-Loeber, M., & Steinhauer, S. R. (2002). Serious delinquent behavior, sensation seeking, and electrodermal arousal. *Journal of Abnormal Child Psychology, 30*(5), 477–486.

Gay, P. (2006). *Freud: A life for our time.* New York: Norton.

Geddes, J. R., & Miklowitz, D. J. (2013). Treatment of bipolar disorder. *Lancet, 381*(9878), 1672–1682. doi:10.1016/S0140-6736(13)60857-0. PMID 23663953.

Geller, B., Fox, L. W., & Fletcher, M. (1993). Effect of tricyclic antidepressants on switching to mania and on the onset of bipolarity in depressed 6- to 12-year-olds. *Journal of American Academy Child Adolescent Psychiatry, 32,* 43–50.

Geller, B., Luby, J. L., Joshi, P., Wagner, K., Emslie, G., Walkup, J. T., . . . Lavori, P. (2012). A randomized controlled trial of risperidone, lithium, or divalproex sodium for initial treatment of bipolar I disorder, manic or mixed phase, in children and adolescents. *JAMA Psychiatry, 69*(5), 515–528.

Gelles, R. (1980). A profile of violence toward children in the United States. In G. Gerbner, C. J. Ross, & E. Ligler (Eds.), *Child abuse: An agenda for action* (pp. 82–105). New York: Oxford University Press.

Gelles, R. J., & Straus, M. A. (1988). *Intimate violence.* New York: Simon & Schuster.

Gendlin, E. T. (1981). *Focusing* (2nd ed.). New York: Bantam Books.

Geoffroy, P., Bellivier, F., Scott, J., Boudebesse, C., Lajnef, M., Gard, S., . . . Etain, B. (2013). Bipolar disorder with seasonal pattern: Clinical characteristics and gender influences. *Chronobiology International, 30*(9), 1101–1107. doi:10.3109/07420528.2013.800091

George, M., Trimble, M., Ring, H., Sallee, F., & Robertson, M. (1993). Obsessions in obsessive-compulsive disorder with and without Gilles de la Tourette's syndrome. *American Journal of Psychiatry, 150*(1), 93–97.

George, M. S., & Post, R. M. (2011). Daily left prefrontal repetitive transcranial magnetic stimulation for acute treatment of medication-resistant depression. *American Journal of Psychiatry, 168*(4), 356–364.

German, L., Gidron, Y., Shahar, A., Yirmiyahu, T., Castel, H., Harman-Boehm, I., & Shahar, D. R. (2006). Depressive symptoms are associated with both immune suppression and leucocytosis among elderly with acute hospitalization. *Geriatrics & Gerontology International, 6*(1), 53–59. doi:10.1111/j.1447-0594.2006.00318.x

Gershon, E. S., Berretini, W. H., & Goldin, L. R. (1989). Mood disorders: Genetic aspects. In H. I. Kaplan & B. J. Sadock (Eds.), *Comprehensive textbook of psychiatry V* (pp. 879–887). Baltimore: Williams & Wilkins.

Gershon, E. S., Hamovit, J. H., Guroff, J. J., & Nurnberger, J. I. (1987). Birth-cohort changes in manic and depressive disorders in relatives of bipolar and schizoaffective patients. *Archives of General Psychiatry, 44,* 314–319.

Gershuny, B. S., Keuthen, N. J., Gentes, E. L., Russo, A. R., Emmott, E. C., Jameson, M., . . . Jenike, M. A. (2006). Current posttraumatic stress disorder and history of trauma in trichotillomania. *Journal of Clinical Psychology, 62*(12), 1521–1529. doi:10.1002/jclp.20303

Geschwind, N., & Levitsky, W. (1968). Human brain: Left-right asymmetries in temporal speech region. *Science, 161,* 186–187.

Ghaemi, S. N. (2008). Why antidepressants are not antidepressants: STEP-BD, STAR*D, and the return of neurotic depression. *Bipolar Disorders, 10*(8), 957–968. doi: 10.1111/j.1399-5618.2008.00639.x.

Ghahramanlou-Holloway, M. M., Bhar, S. S., Brown, G. K., Olsen, C. C., & Beck, A. T. (2012). Changes in problem-solving appraisal after cognitive therapy for the prevention of suicide. *Psychological Medicine, 42,* 1185–1193. doi:10.1017/S0033291711002169

Ghahramanlou-Holloway, M., Wenzel, A., Lou, K., & Beck, A. T. (2007). Differentiating cognitive content between depressed and anxious outpatients. *Cognitive Behaviour Therapy, 36,* 170–178. doi:10.1080/16506070701374256

Ghosh, K., Agarwal, P., & Haggerty, G. (2011). Alzheimer's disease—Not an exaggeration of healthy aging. *Indian Journal of Psychological Medicine, 33*(2), 106–114. doi: 10.4103/0253-7176.92047

Gianotten, W. L., Bender, J. L., Post, M. W., & Höing, M. (2006). Training in sexology for medical and paramedical professionals: A model for the rehabilitation setting. *Sexual and Relationship Therapy, 21*(3), 303–317.

Gibbons, F. X. (1986). Social comparison and depression: Company's effect on misery. *Journal of Personality and Social Psychology, 51,* 140–149.

Gibbons, J. L. (1969). Corticosteroid metabolism in depressive illness. *Psychiatria, Neurologia, Neurochirurgia, 72*(2), 195–199.

Gibbs, C. J., Gajdusek, D. C., Asher, D. M., Alpers, M. P., Beck, E., Daniel, P. M., & Matthews, W. B. (1968). Creutzfeldt-Jacob disease (spongiform encephalopathy): Transmission to the chimpanzee. *Science, 161,* 388–389.

Giblin, P. (1986). Research and assessment in marriage and family enrichment: A meta-analysis study. *Journal of Psychotherapy and the Family, 2,* 79–96.

Giesbrecht, T., Lynn, S. J., Lilienfeld, S. O., & Merckelbach, H. (2008). Cognitive processes in dissociation: An analysis of core theoretical assumptions. *Psychological Bulletin, 134*(5), 617–647. doi:10.1037/0033-2909.134.5.617

Gil, P., Carrillo, F., & Meca, J. (2001). Effectiveness of cognitive-behavioural treatment in social phobia: A meta-analytic review. *Psychology in Spain, 5*(1), 17–25.

Gil, S., & Caspi, Y. (2006). Personality traits, coping style, and perceived threat as predictors of posttraumatic stress disorder after exposure to a terrorist attack: A prospective study. *Psychosomatic Medicine, 68,* 904–909.

Gilbert, D. (2006). *Stumbling on happiness.* New York: Alfred A. Knopf.

Gilbert, P. (1992). *Depression: The evaluation of powerlessness.* New York: Guilford Press.

Gilbert, P. L., Harris, M. J., McAdams, L. A., & Jeste, D. (1995). Neuroleptic withdrawal in schizophrenic patients. *Archives of General Psychiatry, 52,* 173–187.

Giles, P., Elliston, L., Higgs, G. V., Brooks, S. P., Dunnett, S. B., & Jones, L. (2012). Longitudinal analysis of gene expression and behaviour in the HdhQ150 mouse model of Huntington's disease. *Brain Research Bulletin, 88,* 199–209. doi:10.1016/j.brainresbull.2011.10.001

Gillespie, N. A., Zhu, G., Heath, A. C., Hickie, I. B., & Martin, N. G. (2000). The genetic aetiology of somatic distress. *Psychological Medicine, 30*(5), 1051–1061.

Gillig, P. M. (2009). Dissociative identity disorder: A controversial diagnosis. *Psychiatry, 6,* 24–29.

Giordano, M., Dominguez, L. J., Vitrano, T., Curatolo, M., Ferlisi, A., Di Prima, A., . . . Barbagallo, M. (2010). Combination of intensive cognitive rehabilitation and donepezil therapy in Alzheimer's disease (AD). *Archives of Gerontology and Geriatrics, 51*(3), 245–249. doi: 10.1016/j.archger.2009.11.008

Giovino, G. A. (2002). Epidemiology of tobacco use in the United States. *Oncogene, 21*, 7326–7340.

Gislason, I. L. (1988). Eating disorders in childhood (ages 4 through 11 years). In B. J. Blinder, B. F. Chaitin, & R. Goldstein (Eds.), *The eating disorders* (pp. 285–293). PMA Publishing Corporation.

Gittelman, R., & Klein, D. F. (1980). Separation anxiety in school refusal and its treatment with drugs. In L. Hersov & I. Berg (Eds.), *Out of school.* New York: John Wiley & Sons.

Gittelman, R. & Klein, D. F. (1985). Childhood separation anxiety and adult agoraphobia. In A. Tuma & J. Maser (Eds.), *Anxiety and the anxiety disorders.* Hillsdale, NJ: Erlbaum.

Givelber, D. J., Bowers, W. J., & Blitch, C. L. (1984). *Tarasoff,* myth and reality: An empirical study of private law reaction. *Wisconsin Law Review, 1984*, 443–497.

Givens, B. S., & Breese, G. R. (1990). Electrophysiological evidence that ethanol alters function of medial septal area without affecting lateral septal function. *Journal of Pharmacology and Experimental Therapeutics, 253* (1), 95–103.

Gjerde, L. C., Czajkowski, N. N., Røysamb, E. E., Ørstavik, R. E., Knudsen, G. P., Østby, K. K., & . . . Reichborn-Kjennerud, T. T. (2012). The heritability of avoidant and dependent personality disorder assessed by personal interview and questionnaire. *Acta Psychiatrica Scandinavica, 126*, 448–457. doi:10.1111/j.1600-0447.2012.01862.x

Glaser, R., Rice, J., Sheridan, J., Fertel, R., Stout, J. C., Speicher, C. E., Pinsky, D., Kotur, M., Post, A., Beck, M., & Kiecolt-Glaser, J. K. (1987). Stress-related immune suppression: Health implications. *Brain, Behavior, and Immunity, 1*, 7–20.

Glaser, R., Robles, T. F., Malarkey, W. B., Sheridan, J. F., & Kiecolt-Glaser, J. K. (2003). Mild depressive symptoms are associated with amplified and prolonged inflammatory responses following influenza vaccination in older adults. *Archives of General Psychiatry, 60*, 1009–1014.

Glasofer, D. R., & Devlin, M. J. (2013). Cognitive behavioral therapy for bulimia nervosa. *Psychotherapy, 50*(4), 537–542.

Glatt, A. E., Zinner, S. H. & McCormack, W. M. (1990). The prevalence of dyspareunia. *Obstetrics and Gynecology, 75*, 433–436.

Glazener, C. M., Evans, J. H., & Peto, R. E. (2000). Tricyclic and related drugs for nocturnal enuresis in children. *Cochrane Database Systems Review, 3*, CD002117.

Glazer, W., Moore, D., Schooler, N., Brenner, L., & Morgenstern, H. (1984). Tardive dyskinesia: A discontinuation study. *Archives of General Psychiatry, 41*, 623–627.

Gleaves, D. H. (1996). The sociocognitive model of dissociative identity disorder: A reexamination of the evidence. *Psychological Bulletin, 120*, 42–59.

Gleaves, D. H., May, M. C., & Cardeña, E. (2001). An examination of the diagnostic validity of dissociative identity disorder. *Clinical Psychology Review, 21*(4), 577–608.

Gleeson, J. F., Alvarez-Jimenez, M., Cotton, S. M., Parker, A. G., & Hetrick, S. (2010). A systematic review of relapse measurement in randomized controlled trials of relapse prevention in first-episode psychosis. *Schizophrenia Research, 119*, 79–88.

Gleick, J. (1978, August 21). Getting away with murder. *New Times*, 21–27.

Glue, P., & Nutt, D. (1990). Overexcitement and disinhibition. Dynamic neurotransmitter interactions in alcohol withdrawal. *British Journal of Psychiatry, 157*, 491–499.

Goddard, A. W., & Charney, D. S. (1997). Toward an integrated neurobiology of panic disorder. *Journal of Clinical Psychiatry, 58*(Suppl 2), 4–12.

Goetz, R., Klein, D., Gully, R., Kahn, J., Leibowitz, M., Fyer, A., & Gorman, J. (1993). Panic attacks during placebo procedures in the laboratory. *Archives of General Psychiatry, 50*, 280–295.

Goghari, V. M., Harrow, M., Grossman, L. S., & Rosen, C. (2013). A 20-year multi-follow-up of hallucinations in schizophrenia, other psychotic, and mood disorders. *Psychological Medicine, 43*(6), 1151–1160. doi:10.1017/S0033291712002206

Goisman, R. M., Warshaw, M. G., Steketee, G. S., Fierman, E. J., Rogers, M. P., Goldenberg, I., Weinshenker, N. J., Vasile, R. G., & Keller, M. B. (1995). *DSM-IV* and the disappearance of agoraphobia without a history of panic disorder: New data on a controversial diagnosis. *American Journal of Psychiatry, 152*, 1438–1443.

Gold, N. (1993). Depression and social adjustment in siblings of boys with autism. *Journal of Autism and Developmental Disorders, 23*, 147–164.

Goldberg, C. (2011, September 13). New drug and alcohol prevention program proven successful in helping parents talk with their kids. *Partnership for Drug-Free Kids.* Retrieved on December 13, 2014 from http://www.drugfree.org/newsroom/new-drug-and-alcohol-prevention-program-proven-successful-in-helping-parents-talk-with-their-kids/

Goldbloom, D. S., & Olmsted, M. P. (1993). Pharmacotherapy of bulimia nervosa with fluoxetine: Assessment of clinically significant attitudinal change. *American Journal of Psychiatry, 150*(5), 770–774.

Golden, C. J. (2004). The Adult Luria-Nebraska Neuropsychological Battery. In G. Goldstein, S. R. Beers, M. Hersen (Eds.), *Comprehensive handbook of psychological assessment, Vol. 1: Intellectual and neuropsychological assessment* (pp. 133–146). Hoboken, NJ: Wiley.

Golden, C. J. (2011). The Luria-Nebraska Neuropsychological Children's Battery. In A. S. Davis (Ed.), *Handbook of pediatric neuropsychology* (pp. 367–378). New York: Springer.

Golden, C. J., Purisch, A. D., & Hammeke, T. A. (1985). *Luria-Nebraska Neuropsychological Battery: Forms I and II Manual.* Los Angeles: Western Psychological Services.

Golden, C. J., Purisch, A. D., & Hammeke, T. A. (1985). *Luria-Nebraska Neuropsychological Battery: Forms I and II Manual.* Los Angeles: Western Psychological Services.

Golden, D. (1994, July). Building a better brain. *Life*, 63–70.

Golden, G. (1987). Neurological functioning. In D. Cohen & A. Donnellan (Eds.), *Handbook of autism and pervasive developmental disorders* (pp. 133–147). New York: John Wiley & Sons.

Golden, G. S. (2008). Review of "Dyslexia, learning, and the brain." *New England Journal of Medicine, 359*, 2737.

Golden, R. N., Gaynes, B. N., Ekstrom, R., Hamer, R. M., Jacobsen, F. M., Suppes, T., . . . Nemeroff, C. B. (2005). The efficacy of light therapy in the treatment of mood disorders: A review and meta-analysis of the evidence. *The American Journal of Psychiatry, 162*(4), 656–662. doi:10.1176/appi.ajp.162.4.656

Goldfried, M. R. (1980). Toward the delineation of therapeutic change principles. *American Psychologist, 24*, 991–999.

Goldman, M. S., Brown, S. A., & Christiansen, B. A. (1987). Expectancy theory: Thinking about drinking. In H. T. Blane & K. E. Leonard (Eds.), *Psychological theories of drinking and alcoholism* (pp. 181–226). New York: Guilford Press.

Goldner, E. M., Hsu, L., Waraich, P., & Somers, J. M. (2002). Prevalence and incidence studies of schizophrenic disorders: A systematic review of the literature. *Canadian Journal of Psychiatry, 47*, 833–843.

Goldsmith, S. J., Fyer, M., & Frances, A. (1990). Personality and suicide. In S. J. Blumenthal & D. J. Kupfer (Eds.), *Suicide over the life cycle: Risk factors, assessment, and treatment of suicidal patients* (pp. 155–176). Washington, DC: American Psychiatric Press.

Goldstein, A., & Chambless, D. (1978). A reanalysis of agoraphobia. *Behavior Therapy, 9*, 47–59.

Goldstein, B. I., Abela, J. Z., Buchanan, G. M., & Seligman, M. P. (2000). Attributional style and life events: A diathesis-stress theory of alcohol consumption. *Psychological Reports, 87*(3, Pt 1), 949–955. doi:10.2466/PR0.87.7.949-955

Goldstein, G. (2012). Delirium, dementia, and amnestic and other cognitive disorders (neurocognitive disorders). In M. Hersen & D. C. Beidel (Eds.), *Adult psychopathology and diagnosis*, 6th ed. (pp. 149–196). Hoboken, NJ: John Wiley & Sons.

Goldstein, J. (2009). Geel, Belgium: A model of "community recovery." *Samford University Psychology Department.* Retrieved on November 16, 2014 from http://faculty.samford.edu/~jlgoldst

Goldstein, M. J. (1985). Family factors that antedate the onset of schizophrenia and related disorders: The results of a 15-year prospective longitudinal study. *Acta Psychiatrica Scandinavica Suppl.um, 319*, 7–18.

Goldstein, M. J. (1988). Gender differences in the course of schizophrenia. *American Journal of Psychiatry, 145*, 684–689.

Goldstein, M. J., & Rodnick, E. (1975). The family's contribution to the etiology of schizophrenia: Current status. *Schizophrenia Bulletin, 14*, 48-63.

Goldstein, T. R., Fersch-Podrat, R., Axelson, D. A., Gilbert, A., Hlastala, S. A., Birmaher, B., & Frank, E. (2014). Early intervention for adolescents at high risk for the development of bipolar disorder: Pilot study of interpersonal and social rhythm therapy (IPSRT). *Psychotherapy, 51*(1), 180–189. doi:10.1037/a0034396

Golombok, S., & Tasker, F. (1996). Do parents influence the sexual orientation of their children? Findings from a longitudinal study of lesbian families. *Developmental Psychology, 32*, 3–11.

Gonsiorek, J. C., Sell, R. L., & Weinrich, J. D. (1995). Definition and measurement of sexual orientation. *Suicide and Life Threatening Behavior* (Suppl. 25), 40–51.

González, H. M., Tarraf, W., Whitfield, K. E., & Vega, W. A. (2010). The epidemiology of major depression and ethnicity in the United States. *Journal of Psychiatric Research, 44*(15), 1043–1051. doi:10.1016/j.jpsychires.2010.03.017

González-Pardo, H., & Álvarez, M. (2013). Epigenetics and its implications for psychology. *Psicothema, 25*, 3–12.

Goodheart, C. A. (2014). *A primer for ICD-10-CM users: Psychological and behavioral conditions.* Washington, D.C.: American Psychological Association.

Goodman, G., & Poillion, M. J. (1992). ADD: Acronym for any dysfunction or difficulty. *The Journal of Special Education, 26*(1), 37–56.

Goodman, L. S., & Gilman, A. G. (2001). *The pharmacological basis of therapeutics.* New York: McGraw-Hill, pp. 1649–1678.

Goodwin, F. K., & Jamison, K. R. (1990). *Manic-depressive illness.* New York: Oxford University Press.

Goodyear, R, & Hynd, G. W. (1992). Attention-deficit disorder with (ADD/H) and without (ADD/WO) hyperactivity: Behavioral and neuropsychological differentiation. *Journal of Clinical Child Psychology, 21*(3), 273–305.

Gordon, A. J., Conley, J. W., & Gordon, J. M. (2013). Medical consequences of marijuana use: A review of current literature. *Current Psychiatry Reports, 15*(12), 419. doi:10.1007/s11920-013-0419-7

Gore, W. L., & Widiger, T. A. (2013). The DSM-5 dimensional trait model and five-factor models of general personality. *Journal of Abnormal Psychology, 122*(3), 816–821. doi:10.1037/a0032822

Gorelick, R B., & Mangone, C. A. (1991). Vascular dementias in the elderly. In J. Biller (Ed.), *Clinics in geriatric medicine: Cerebrovascular disorders in the 1990s,* 599–615. Philadelphia: W. B. Saunders.

Gorenstein, E. E., & Newman, J. P. (1980). Disinhibitory psychopathology: A new perspective and a model for research. *Psychological Review, 87,* 301–315.

Gorman, J., Leibowitz, M., Fryer, A., & Stein, J. (1989). A neuroanatomical hypothesis for panic disorder. *American Journal of Psychiatry, 146,* 148–161.

Gotlib, I. H., & Hammen, C. L. (2002). *Handbook of depression.* New York: The Guilford Press.

Gotlib, I. H., Joormann, J., & Foland-Ross, L. C. (2014). Understanding familial risk for depression: A 25-year perspective. *Perspectives on Psychological Science, 9*(1), 94–108. doi:10.1177/1745691613513469

Gottesman, 1.1., & Bertelsen, A. (1989). Confirming unexpressed genotypes for schizophrenia: Risks in the offspring of Fischer's Danish identical and fraternal discordant twins. *Archives of General Psychiatry, 46,* 867–872.

Gottesman, I. I. (1991). *Schizophrenia genesis: The origins of madness.* New York: Freeman.

Gottesman, I. I. (2001). Psychopathology through a lifespan genetic prism. *American Psychologist, 56,* 867–878.

Gottesman, I. I., & Shields, J. (1972). *Schizophrenia and genetics: A twin study vantage point.* New York: Academic Press.

Gottfredson, L. S. (1994). The science and politics of race-norming. *American Psychologist, 49,* 955–963.

Gottlieb, B. H., & Peters, L. (1991). A national demographic portrait of mutual aid group participants in Canada. *American Journal of Community Psychology, 19,* 651–666.

Gough, H. (1987). *California Psychological Inventory: Administrator's guide.* Palo Alto, CA: Consulting Psychologists Press.

Gould, M., Jamieson, P., & Romer, D. (2003). Media contagion and suicide among the young. *American Behavioral Scientist, 46*(9), 1269–1284. doi:10.1177/0002764202250670

Gould, M. A., Otto, M. W., & Pollack, M. H. (1995). A meta-analysis of treatment outcome for panic disorder. *Clinical Psychology Review, 15*(8), 819–844.

Gould, M. S. (1990). Suicide clusters and medial exposure. In S. J. Blumenthal & D. J. Kupfer (Eds.), *Suicide over the life cycle: Risk factors, assessment, and treatment of suicidal patients* (pp. 517–532). Washington, DC: American Psychiatric Press.

Gould, M. S., Kalafat, J., Munfakh, J., & Kleinman, M. (2007). An evaluation of crisis hotline outcomes: Part 2: Suicidal callers. *Suicide and Life-Threatening Behavior, 37*(3), 338–352. doi:10.1521/suli.2007.37.3.338

Gould, R. A., & Clum, G. A. (1995). Self-help plus minimal therapist contact in the treatment of panic disorder: A replication and extension. *Behavior Therapy, 26,* 533–546.

Gould, R. A., & Johnson, M. W. (2001). Comparative effectiveness of cognitive-behavioral treatment and pharmacotherapy for social phobia: Meta-analytic outcome. In S.G. Hofmann & P. DiBartolo (Eds.), *From social anxiety to social phobia: Multiple perspectives* (pp. 379–390). Needham Heights, MA: Allyn & Bacon.

Graden, J., Thurlow, M., & Ysseldyke, J. (1983). Instructional ecology and academic responding time for students at three levels of teacher-perceived behavioral competence. *Journal of Experimental Child Psychology, 36,* 241–256.

Grady, C. L., McIntosh, A. R., Horwitz, B., Maisog, J. M., Ungerleider, L. G., Mentis, M. J., Pietrini, P., Schapiro, M. B., & Haxby, J. V. (1995). Age-related education in human recognition memory due to impaired encoding. *Science, 269,* 218–221.

Graham, C. A., Sanders, S. A., Milhausen, R. R., & McBride, K. R. (2004). Turning on and turning off: A focus group study of the factors that affect women's sexual arousal. *Archives of Sexual Behavior, 33*(6), 527–538.

Graham, N., Kimonis, E. R., Wasserman, A. L., & Kline, S. M. (2012). Associations among childhood abuse and psychopathy facets in male sexual offenders. *Personality Disorders: Theory, Research, and Treatment, 3*(1), 66–75.

Grammaticos, P. C., & Diamantis, A. (2008). Useful known and unknown views of the father of modern medicine, Hippocrates, and his teacher Democritus. *Hellenic Journal of Nuclear Medicine, 11,* 2–4.

Grande, I., Bernardo, M., Bobes, J., Saiz-Ruiz, J., Álamo, C., & Vieta, E. (2014). Antipsychotic switching in bipolar disorders: A systematic review. *International Journal of Neuropsychopharmacology, 17*(3), 497–507. doi:10.1017/S1461145713001168

Grandin, T. (2008). *The way i see it: A personal look at Autism & Asperger's.* Arlington, TX: Future Horizons.

Grandjean, E., & Aubry, J. (2009). Lithium: Updated human knowledge using an evidence-based approach: Part I: Clinical efficacy in bipolar disorder. *CNS Drugs, 23*(3), 225–240. doi:10.2165/00023210-200923030-00004

Grann, M., Långström, N., Tengström, A., & Kullgren, G. (1999). Psychopathy (PCL-R) predicts violent recidivism among criminal offenders with personality disorders in Sweden. *Law and Human Behavior, 23*(2), 205–217.

Grant, B. F., & Dawson, D. A. (2005). Introduction to the National Epidemiologic Survey on alcohol and related conditions. *Alcohol Research & Health, 29*(2), 74–78.

Grant, B. F., DeBakey, S., & Zobeck, T. S. (1991). *Liver cirrhosis mortality in the United States, 1973–1988.* (NIAAA Surveillance Report No. 18. DHHS Pub. No. (ADM) 281-89-0001.) Washington, DC: Superintendent of Documents, U.S. Government Printing Office.

Grant, B. F., Harford, T. C., Dawson, D. A., Chou, P., Dufour, M., & Pickering, R. (1994). Prevalence of DSM-IV alcohol abuse and dependence: United States, 1992. *NIAAA's Epidemiologic Bulletin No. 35, 18(3),* 243–248.

Grant, B. F., Stinson, F. S., Dawson, D. A., Chou, S. P., Ruan, W. J., & Pickering, R. P. (2004). Co-occurrence of 12-month alcohol and drug use disorders and personality disorders in the United States: Results from the National Epidemiologic Survey on Alcohol and Related Conditions. *Archives of General Psychiatry, 61,* 361–368.

Grant, B. F., Stinson, F. S., Dawson, D. A., Chou, S., Dufour, M. C., Compton, W., . . . Kaplan, K. (2006). Prevalence and co-occurrence of substance use disorders and independent mood and anxiety disorders: Results from the National Epidemiologic Survey on Alcohol and Related Conditions. *Alcohol Research & Health, 29*(2), 107–120.

Grant, J. E., Odlaug, B. L., & Won Kim, S. (2010). A clinical comparison of pathologic skin picking and obsessive-compulsive disorder. *Comprehensive Psychiatry, 51*(4), 347–352. doi:10.1016/j.comppsych.2009.10.006

Grant, J. E., Stein, D. J., Woods, D. W., & Keuthen, N. J. (2012). *Trichotillomania, skin picking, and other body-focused repetitive behaviors.* Arlington, VA: American Psychiatric Publishing.

Grant, P. M., Reisweber, J., Luther, L., Brinen, A. P., & Beck, A. T. (2013). Successfully breaking a 20-year cycle of hospitalizations with recovery-oriented cognitive therapy for schizophrenia. *Psychological Services,* Sept. 30, online ahead of print. doi:10.1037/a0033912

Gray, J. (1981). A critique of Eysenck's theory of personality. In H. Eysenck (Ed.), *A model for personality* (pp. 246–276). New York: Springer-Verlag.

Graybiel, A. M., & Rauch, S. L. (2000). Toward a neurobiology of obsessive-compulsive disorder. *Neuron, 28*(2), 343–347.

Grayson, A. D., & De Luca, R. V. (1999). Female perpetrators of child sexual abuse: A review of the clinical and empirical literature. *Aggression and Violent Behavior, 4*(1), 93–106.

Greco, L. A., & Morris, T. L. (2002). Paternal child-rearing style and child social anxiety: Investigation of child perceptions and actual father behavior. *Journal of Psychopathology and Behavioral Assessment, 24,* 259–267.

Green, A. R., Cross, A. J., & Goodwin, G. M. (1995). Review of the pharmacology and clinical pharmacology of 3,4-methylenedioxymethamphetamine (MDMA or "Ecstasy"). *Psychopharmacology, 119*(3), 247–260.

Green, B., Grace, M., Lindy, J., Gleser, G., & Leonard, A. C. (1990). Risk factors for PTSD and other diagnoses in a general sample of Vietnam vVeterans. *American Journal of Psychiatry, 147,* 729–733.

Green, B. L., Grace, M. C., & Lindy, J. D., Titchener, J. L., & Lindy, J. G. (19.83). Levels of functional impairment following a civilian disaster: The Beverly Hills Supper Club fire. *Journal of Consulting and Clinical Psychology, 51,* 573–580.

Green, R. (1974). *Sexual identity conflict in children and adults.* New York: Basic Books.

Green, R. (1987). *The "sissy boy syndrome" and the development of homosexuality.* New Haven, CT: Yale University Press.

Green, R., & Blanchard (1995). Gender identity disorders. In H. I. Kaplan & B. J. Sadock (Eds.), *Comprehensive textbook of psychiatry/VI* (pp. 1345–1360). Baltimore: Williams & Wilkins.

Green, R. & Fleming, D. T. (1990). Transsexual surgery follow-up: Status in the 1990s. *Annual Review of Sex Research, 1,* 163–174.

Greenberg, L. S. (1986). Change process research. *Journal of Consulting and Clinical Psychology, 54,* 4–9.

Greenberg, L. S., Elliott, R. K., & Lietaer, G. (1994). Research on experiential psychotherapies. In A. E. Bergin & S. L. Garfield (Eds.), *Handbook of psychotherapy and behavior change* (pp. 509–539). New York: John Wiley & Sons.

Greenberg, L. S., & Johnson, S. M. (1988). *Emotionally focused couples therapy.* New York: Guilford Press.

Greenberg, M. T., Speltz, M. L., & DeKlyen, M. (1993). The role of attachment in the early development of disruptive behavior problems. *Development and Psychopathology, 5,* 191–213.

Greenberg, M. T., Speltz, M. L., DeKlyen, M., & Endriga, M. C. (1991). Attachment security in preschoolers with and without externalizing problems: A replication. *Developmental Psychopathology, 3,* 413–430.

Greenberg, S. T., & Schoen, E. G. (2008). Males and eating disorders: Gender-based therapy for eating disorder recovery. *Professional Psychology: Research and Practice, 39*(4), 464–471.

Greenberg, W. M., Shah, P. J., & Seide, M. (1993). Recidivism on an acute psychiatric forensic service. *Hospital & Community Psychiatry, 44,* 583–585.

Greenblatt, D., Harmatz, J., & Shader, R. I. (1993). Plasma alprazolam concentrations: Relation to efficacy and side effects in the treatment of panic disorder. *Archives of General Psychiatry, 50,* 715–732.

Greenwood, T. A., Badner, J. A., Byerley, W., Keck, P. E., McElroy, S. L., Remick, R. A., . . . Kelsoe, J. R. (2013). Heritability and linkage analysis of personality in bipolar disorder. *Journal of Affective Disorders, 151*(2), 748–755. doi:10.1016/j.jad.2013.06.015

Greer, A., & Buss, D. (1994). Tactics for promoting sexual encounters. *Journal of Sex Research, 31,* 185–201.

Greeven, A., van Balkom, A. M., van der Leeden, R., Merkelbach, J. W., van den Heuvel, O. A., & Spinhoven, P. (2009). Cognitive behavioral therapy versus paroxetine in the treatment of hypochondriasis: An 18-month naturalistic follow-up. *Journal of Behavior Therapy and Experimental Psychiatry, 40*(3), 487–496. doi:10.1016/j.jbtep.2009.06.005

Grenier, S., Schuurmans, J., Goldfarb, M., Préville, M., Boyer, R., O'Connor, K., . . . Hudon, C. (2011). The epidemiology of specific phobia and subthreshold fear subtypes in a community-based sample of older adults. *Depression and Anxiety, 28*(6), 456–463. doi:10.1002/da.20812

Grey, S. (2011). Vincent van Gogh, a formal and psychological analysis of the final years at Arles, Saint-Rémy, and Auvers. *Dissertation Abstracts International Section A, 71,* 2259.

Griffiths, R. R., Richards, W. A., McCann, U. D., & Jesse, R. (2007). Psilocybin can occasion mystical-type experiences having substantial and sustained personal meaning and spiritual significance. In M. J. Winkelman & T. B. Roberts (Eds.), *Psychedelic medicine: New evidence for hallucinogenic substances as treatments (Vol. 2)* (pp. 227–254). Westport, CT: Praeger Publishers/Greenwood Publishing Group.

Grilo, C. M., White, M. A., & Masheb, R. M. (2009). *DSM-IV* psychiatric disorder comorbidity and its correlates in binge eating disorder. *International Journal of Eating Disorders, 42*(3), 228–234. doi:10.1002/eat.20599

Grimes, K., & Walker, E. F. (1994). Childhood emotional expressions, educational attainment, and age at onset of illness in schizophrenia. *Journal of Abnormal Psychology, 103,* 784–790.

Grisham, J., Norberg, M., Williams, A., Certoma, S., & Kadib, R. (2010). Categorization and cognitive deficits in compulsive hoarding. *Behaviour Research and Therapy, 48*(9), 866–872.

Groch, S. S., Wilhelm, I. I., Diekelmann, S. S., & Born, J. J. (2013). The role of REM sleep in the processing of emotional memories: Evidence from behavior and event-related potentials. *Neurobiology of Learning and Memory, 99,* 1–9. doi:10.1016/j.nlm.2012.10.006

Grof, P., Angst, J., & Haines, T. (1974). The clinical course of depression: Practical issues. In J. Angst (Ed.), *Classification and prediction of outcome of depression.* New York Symposia Medical Hoeschst 8, F. K. Schattauer Verlag.

Groneman, C. (1994). Nymphomania: The historical construction of female sexuality. *Signs, 19*(2), 337–367.

Gross, A. M., & Hersen, M. (2008). *Handbook of clinical psychology, adults* (Vol. 1). Hoboken, NJ: Wiley.

Grossarth-Maticek, R., & Eysenck, H. J. (1991). Creative novation behaviour therapy as a prophylactic treatment for cancer and coronary heart disease. Part I: Description of treatment. *Behaviour Research & Therapy, 29,* 1–16.

Grossberg, G. T., & Nakra, R. (1988). The diagnostic dilemma of depressive pseudodementia. In R. Strong, W. G., Wood & W. J. Burke (Eds.), *Aging:* Vol. 33. *Central nervous system disorders of aging: Clinical intervention and research,* (pp. 107–115). New York: Raven Press.

Grossman, H. J. (Ed.). (1973). *Manual on terminology and classification in mental retardation.* Washington, DC: American Association on Mental Deficiency.

Grossman, L. S., Harrow, M., Rosen, C., Faull, R., & Strauss, G. P. (2008). Sex differences in schizophrenia and other psychotic disorders: A 20-year longitudinal study of psychosis and recovery. *Comprehensive Psychiatry, 49,* 523–529.

Grossman, P. B., & Hughes, J. N. (1992). Self-control interventions with internalizing disorders: A review and analysis. *School Psychology Review, 21*(2), 229–245.

Groth-Marnat, G., & Edkins, G. (1996). Professional psychologists in general health care settings: A review of the financial efficacy of direct treatment interventions. *Professional Psychology: Research and Practice, 27,* 161–174.

Grove, R., Baillie, A., Allison, C., Baron-Cohen, S., & Hoekstra, R. A. (2013). Empathizing, systemizing, and autistic traits: Latent structure in individuals with autism, their parents, and general population controls. *Journal of Abnormal Psychology, 122*(2), 600–609. doi:10.1037/a0031919

Gruber, R. (2014). ADHD, anxiety and sleep: A window to understanding the interplay between sleep, emotional regulation, and attention in children? *Behavioral Sleep Medicine, 12*(1), 84–87. doi:10.1080/15402002.2014.862089

Grucza, R. A., Przybeck, T. R., & Cloninger, C. R. (2007). Prevalence and correlates of binge eating disorder in a community sample. *Comprehensive Psychiatry, 48*(2), 124–131. doi: 10.1016/j.comppsych.2006.08.002

Grunhaus, L., & Pande, A. C. (1994). Electroconvulsive therapy for severe depressive disorder. In L. Grunhaus & J. F. Greden (Eds.), *Severe depressive disorders* (pp. 297–330). Washington, DC: American Psychiatric Press.

Guay, D. P. (2009). Drug treatment of paraphilic and nonparaphilic sexual disorders. *Clinical Therapeutics: The International Peer-Reviewed Journal of Drug Therapy, 31*(1), 1–31.

Gueguen, J., Godart, N., Chambry, J., Brun-Eberentz, A., Foulon, C., Divac, S. M., . . . Huas, C. (2012). Severe anorexia nervosa in men: Comparison with severe AN in women and analysis of mortality. *International Journal of Eating Disorders, 45*(4), 537–545.

Guerra, N. G., Huesmann, L. R., Tolan, R. H., Acker, R. V., Eron, L. D. (1995). Stressful events and individual beliefs as correlates of economic disadvantage and aggression among urban children. *Journal of Consulting and Clinical Psychology, 63,* 518–528.

Guirguis-Blake, J., Wright, A., & Rich, J. (2008). Which drugs are most effective for moderate to severe depression in adolescents? *The Journal of Family Practice, 57*(5), 330–332.

Guller, Y., Ferrarelli, F., Shackman, A. J., Sarasso, S., Peterson, M. J., Langheim, F. J., . . . Postle, B. R. (2012). New probing thalamic integrity in schizophrenia using concurrent transcranial magnetic stimulation and functional magnetic resonance imaging. *JAMA Psychiatry, 69*(7), 662–671.

Gunderson, J. G., & Sabo, A. N. (1993). "Borderline personality disorder and PTSD": Reply. *American Journal of Psychiatry, 150*(12), 1906–1907.

Gunderson, J. G., Stout, R. L., McGlashan, T. H., Shea, M., Morey, L. C., Grilo, C. M., . . . Skodol, A. E. (2011). Ten-year course of borderline personality disorder: Psychopathology and function from the collaborative longitudinal personality disorders study. *Archives of General Psychiatry, 68*(8), 827–837. doi:10.1001/archgenpsychiatry.2011.37

Günzler, C., & Berner, M. M. (2012). Efficacy of psychosocial interventions in men and women with sexual dysfunctions—A systematic review of controlled clinical trials: Part 2—The efficacy of psychosocial interventions for female sexual dysfunction. *Journal of Sexual Medicine, 9,* 3108–3125. doi:10.1111/j.1743-6109.2012.02965.x

Gur, R. C., & Gur, R. E. (1995). Hypofrontality in schizophrenia: RIR. *The Lancet, 345,* 1383–1384.

Gur, R. E., Kohler, C. G., Ragland, J. D., Siegel, S. J., Lesko, K., Bilker, W. B., & Gur, R. C. (2006). Flat affect in schizophrenia: Relation in emotion processing and neurocognitive measures. *Schizophrenia Bulletin, 32,* 279–287.

Gur, R. E., & Pearlson, G. D. (1993). Neuroimaging in schizophrenia research. *Schizophrenia Bulletin, 19,* 337–353.

Gusella, J. F., Wexler, N. S., Conneally, P. M., Naylor, S. L., Anderson, M. A. . . . Sakaguchi, A. Y. (1983). A polymorphic DNA marker genetically linked to Huntington's disease. *Nature, 306,* 234–238.

Guy, L. S., & Douglas, K. S. (2006). Examining the utility of the PCL: SV as a screening measure using competing factor models of psychopathy. *Psychological Assessment, 18*(2), 225–230. doi:10.1037/1040-3590.18.2.225

Guze, S. B. (1993). Genetics of Briquet's syndrome and somatization disorder. A review of family, adoption, and twin studies. *Annals of Clinical Psychiatry, 5,* 225-230.

H

Haaga, D. A., Dyck, M. J., & Ernst, D. (1991). Empirical status of cognitive theory of depression. *Psychological Bulletin, 110,* 215–236.

Hacker, D., Birchwood, M., Tudway, J., Meaden, A., & Amphlett, C. (2008). Acting on voices: Omnipotence, sources of threat, and safety-seeking behaviours. *British Journal of Clinical Psychology, 47*(2), 201–213. doi:10.1348/014466507X249093

Häfner, H., Heiden, W. A., Behrens, S., Gattaz, W. F., Hambrecht, M., Löffler, W., . . . Stein, A. (1998). Causes and consequences of the gender difference in age at onset of schizophrenia. *Schizophrenia Bulletin, 24,* 99–113.

Hafner, H., Maurer, K., Fatkenheuer, B., An Der Heiden, W., Riecher-Rossler, A., Behrens, S., & Gattz, W. (1994). The epidemiology of early schizophrenia: Influence of age and gender on onset and early course. *British Journal of Psychiatry, 164* (Suppl.), 29–38.

Hagmann, P., Jonasson, L., Maeder, P., Thiran, J., Wedeen, V. J., & Meuli, R. (2006). Understanding diffusion MR imaging techniques: From scalar diffusion-weighted imaging to diffusion tensor imaging and beyond. *RadioGraphics, 26,* S205–S223.

Hagopian, L. P., Rooker, G. W., & Rolider, N. U. (2011). Identifying empirically supported treatments for pica in individuals with intellectual disabilities. *Research in Developmental Disabilities, 32*(6), 2114–2120. doi: 10.1016/j.ridd.2011.07.042

Haidt, J. (2006). *The happiness hypothesis: Finding modern truth in ancient wisdom.* New York: Basic Books.

Haile, C. N., Kosten, T. R., & Kosten, T. A. (2009). Pharmacogenic treatments for drug addiction: Cocaine, amphetamine, and methamphetamine. *The American Journal of Drug and Alcohol Abuse, 35*(3), 161–177. doi:10.1080/00952990902825447

Hajek, P., Etter, J., Benowitz, N., Eissenberg, T., & McRobbie, H. (2014). Electronic cigarettes: Review of use, content, safety, effects on smokers and potential for harm and benefit. *Addiction, 109*(11), 1801–1810. doi:10.1111/add.12659

Hakala, M., Vahlberg, T., Niemi, P. M., & Karlsson, H. (2006). Brain glucose metabolism and temperament in relation to severe somatization. *Psychiatry and Clinical Neurosciences, 60*(6), 669–675. doi:10.1111/j.1440-1819.2006.01581.x

Halikas, J. A. (1993). Treatment of drug abuse syndromes. *Psychiatric Clinics of North America, 16*(4), 693–702.

Halikas, J. A., Meller, J., Morse, C., & Lyttle, M. D. (1990). Predicting substance abuse in juvenile offenders: Deficit disorder versus aggressivity. *Child Psychiatry & Human Development, 21,* 49–55.

Hall, G. C. (1990). Prediction of sexual aggression. *Clinical Psychology Review, 10,* 229–245.

Hall, G. C., & Hirschman, R. (1991). Toward a theory of sexual aggression: A quadripartite model. *Journal of Consulting and Clinical Psychology, 59,* 662–669.

Hall, G. C., & Proctor, W. C. (1987). Criminological predictors of recidivism in a sexual offender population. *Journal of Consulting and Clinical Psychology, 55,* 111–112.

Hall, G. C., Shondrick, D. D., & Hirschman, R. (1993). The role of sexual arousal in sexually aggressive behavior: A meta-analysis. *Journal of Consulting and Clinical Psychology, 61,* 1091–1095.

Halperin, J. M., & Healey, D. M. (2011). The influences of environmental enrichment, cognitive enhancement, and physical exercise on brain development: Can we alter the developmental trajectory of ADHD? *Neuroscience and Biobehavioral Reviews, 35*(3), 621–634. doi:10.1016/j.neubiorev.2010.07.006

Halvorsen, J. G., & Metz, M. E. (1992). Sexual dysfunction. Part I: Classification, etiology, and pathogenesis. *Journal of the American Board of Family Practitioners, 5,* 51–61.

Halvorsen, M., Wang, C. E., Eisemann, M., & Waterloo, K. (2010). Dysfunctional attitudes and early maladaptive schemas as predictors of depression: A 9-year follow-up study. *Cognitive Therapy and Research, 34*(4), 368–379. doi:10.1007/s10608-009-9259-5

Halweg, K., & Markman, H. J. (1988). Effectiveness of behavioral marital therapy: Empirical status of behavioral techniques in preventing and alleviating marital distress. *Journal of Consulting and Clinical Psychology, 56*(3), 440–447.

Hamelin, J. P., Frijters, J., Griffiths, D., Condillac, R., & Owen, F. (2011). Meta-analysis of deinstitutionalisation adaptive behaviour outcomes: Research and clinical implications. *Journal of Intellectual and Developmental Disability, 36*(1), 61–72. doi:10.3109/13668250.2010.544034

Hamer, D. H., Hu, S., Magnuson, V. L., Hu, N., & Pattatucci, A. M. L. (1993). A linkage between DNA markers on the X chromosome and the male sexual orientation. *Science, 261,* 321–327.

Hamer, M., & Chida, Y. (2009). Physical activity and risk of neurodegenerative disease: A systematic review of prospective evidence. *Psychological Medicine, 39*(01), 3–11. doi: 10.1017/S0033291708003681

Hamilton, M. (1989). Mood disorders: Clinical features. In H. I. Kaplan and B. J. Sadock (Eds.), *Comprehensive textbook of psychiatry V* (Vol. 1). Baltimore: Williams & Wilkins.

Hamm, J. A., Hasson-Ohayon, I., Kukla, M., & Lysaker, P. H. (2013). Individual psychotherapy for schizophrenia: Trends and developments in the wake of the recovery movement. *Psychology Research and Behavior Management, 6,* 45–54.

Hammen, C. (1992). Cognitive, life stress, and interpersonal approaches to a developmental psychopathology model of depression. *Development and Psychopathology, 4,* 189–206.

Hammen, C., & Goodman-Brown, T. (1990). Self-schemas and vulnerability to specific life stress in children at risk for depression. *Cognitive Therapy and Research, 14,* 215–227.

Hammen, C., Marks, T., Mayol, A., & deMayo, T. (1985). Depressive self-schemas, life stress, and vulnerability to depression. *Journal of Abnormal Psychology, 94,* 308–319.

Hammill, D. D., Leigh, J. E., McNutt, G., & Larsen, S. C. (1981). A new definition of learning disabilities. *Learning Disabilities Quarterly, 4,* 336–342.

Handelsman, M. M., & Galvin, M. D. (1988). Facilitating informed consent for outpatient psychotherapy: A suggested written format. *Professional Psychology: Research and Therapy, 19,* 223–225.

Hansen, A., Heath, M., Williams, M., Fox, J., Hudnall, G. A., & Bledsoe, C. (2012). No-suicide contracts with suicidal youth: Mental health professionals' perceptions and current practice. *Contemporary School Psychology, 16,* 145–159.

Hansen, D. J., St. Lawrence, J. S., & & Christoff, K. A. (1989). Group conversational-skills training with inpatient children and adolescents. *Behavior Modification, 3,* 4–31.

Hansen, L., Salmon, D., Mashliah, F.,, Katzman, R., De-Teresa, R., Thai, L., Pay, M., Hoffstetter, R., Klauber, M., Rice, V., Butters, N. & Alford, M. (1990). The Lewy body variant of Alzheimer's disease: A clinical and pathological entity. *Neurology, 40,* 1–8.

Hansen, W. B. (1994). School-based substance abuse prevention: A review of the state of the art in curriculum. *Health Education Research, 7*(3), 403–430.

Hansen, W. B., & Graham, J. W. (1991). Preventing alcohol, marijuana, and cigarette use among adolescents: Peer pressure resistance training versus establishing conservative norms. *Preventive Medicine, 20*(13), 414–430.

Hanson, D. (2009). Marijuana withdrawal: A survey of symptoms. In A. Browne-Miller (Ed.), *The Praeger international collection on addictions, Vol. 2: Psychobiological profiles* (pp. 111–124). Santa Barbara, CA: Praeger/ABC-CLIO.

Hanson, K. A., & Gidycz, C. A. (1993). Evaluation of a sexual assault prevention program. *Journal of Consulting and Clinical Psychology, 61,* 1046–1052.

Hanson, R. K., Steffy, R. A., & Gauthier, R. (1993). Long-term recidivism of child molesters. *Journal of Consulting and Clinical Psychology, 61,* 646–652.

Hansson, P., Murison, R., Lund, A., & Hammar, Å. (2013). Cognitive functioning and cortisol suppression in recurrent major depression. *Psych Journal, 2*(3), 167–174. doi:10.1002/pchj.29

Hapke, U. L., Schumann, A., Rumpf, H. J., John, U., & Meyer, C. (2006). Post-traumatic stress disorder: The role of trauma, pre-existing psychiatric disorders, and gender. *European Archives of Psychiatry and Clinical Neuroscience, 256,* 299–306.

Haraldsen, I., Ehrbar, R. D., Gorton, R. N., & Menvielle, E. (2010). Recommendations for revision of the *DSM* diagnosis of gender identity disorder in adolescents. *International Journal of Transgenderism, 12,* 75–79.

Harbin, T. J. (1989). The relationship between the Type A behavior pattern and physiological responsivity: A quantitative review. *Psychophysiology, 26,* 110–119.

Harburg, E., Davis, D. R., & Caplan, R. (1982). Parent and offspring alcohol use. *Journal of Studies on Alcohol, 43,* 497–516.

Hardy, J., & Selkoe, D. J. (2002). The amyloid hypothesis of Alzheimer's disease: Progress and problems on the road to therapeutics. *Science, 297*(5580), 353–356. doi: 10.1126/science.1072994

Hardy, M. S., & Calhoun, L. G. (1997). Psychological distress and the "medical student syndrome" in abnormal psychology students. *Teaching of Psychology, 24*(3), 192–193. doi:10.1207/s15328023top2403_10

Hare, R. D. (2003). *The psychopathy checklist—revised* (2nd edition). Toronto: Multi-Health Systems.

Hare, R. D., Hart, S. D., & Harpur, T. J. (1991). Psychopathy and the *DSM-IV* criteria for antisocial personality disorder. *Journal of Abnormal Psychology, 100,* 391–398.

Hare, R. D., & McPherson, L. M. (1984). Psychopathy and perceptual asymmetry during verbal dichotic listening. *Journal of Abnormal Psychology, 93,* 141–149.

Hare, R. D., McPherson, L. M., & Forth, A. E. (1988). Male psychopaths and their criminal careers. *Journal of Consulting and Clinical Psychology, 56,* 710–714.

Harkness, K. L., Alavi, N., Monroe, S. M., Slavich, G. M., Gotlib, I. H., & Bagby, R. (2010). Gender differences in life events prior to onset of major depressive disorder: The moderating effect of age. *Journal of Abnormal Psychology, 119*(4), 791–803. doi:10.1037/a0020629

Harkness, K. L., Theriault, J. E., Stewart, J. G., & Bagby, R. (2014). Acute and chronic stress exposure predicts 1-year recurrence in adult outpatients with residual depression symptoms following response to treatment. *Depression and Anxiety, 31*(1), 1–8. doi:10.1002/da.22177

Harmer, C. J., Goodwin, G. M., & Cowen, P. J. (2009). Why do antidepressants take so long to work? A cognitive neuropsychological model of antidepressant drug action. *The British Journal of Psychiatry, 195*(2), 102–108. doi:10.1192/bjp.bp.108.051193

Haro, J. M., Novick, D., Bertsch, J., Karaqianis, J., Dossenbach, M., & Jones, P. B. (2011). Cross-national clinical and functional remission rates: Worldwide schizophrenia outpatient health outcomes (W-SOHO) study. *British Journal of Psychiatry, 199,* 194–201.

Harpur, T. J., & Hare, R. D. (1994). Assessment of psychopathy as a function of age. *Journal of Abnormal Psychology, 103,* 604–609.

Harrington, R. (1992). Annotation: The natural history and treatment of child and adolescent affective disorders. *Journal of Child Psychology and Psychiatry, 33*(8), 1287–1302.

Harris, G. T., Rice, M. E., & Cormier, C. A. (1991). Length of detention in matched groups of insanity acquittees and convicted offenders. *International Journal of Law and Psychiatry, 14*(3), 223–236. doi:10.1016/0160-2527(91)90004-7

Harris, K. B., & Miller, W. R. (1990). Behavioral self-control training for problem drinkers: Components of efficacy. *Psychology of Addictive Behaviors, 4*(2), 82–90.

Harris, M. J., & Jeste, D. V. (1988). Late-onset schizophrenia: An overview. *Schizophrenia Bulletin, 14,* 39–55.

Harrison, G., Hopper, K., Craig, T., Laska, E., Siegel, C., Wanderling, J., . . . Wiersma, D. (2001). Recovery from psychotic illness: A 15- and 25-year international follow-up study. *The British Journal of Psychiatry, 178,* 506–517. doi:10.1192/bjp.178.6.506

Harrison, K. (2011, January). PCP. *3DChem*. Retrieved on December 16, 2014 from http://www.3dchem.com/moremolecules.asp?ID=473&othername=PCP

Harrison, P. J., Law, A. J., & Eastwood, S. L. (2003). Glutamate receptors and transporters in the hippocampus in schizophrenia. In B. Moghaddam & M. E. Wolf (Eds.), *Glutamate and disorders of cognition and motivation* (pp. 94–101). New York: New York Academy of Sciences.

Harry Benjamin International Gender Dysphoria Association (1998, June 15). RetrievedOctober 19, 2014, from http://www.tc.umn.edu/~colem001/hbigda/hstn-drd.htm

Hart, H., Radua, J., Nakao, T., Mataix-Cols, D., & Rubia, K. (2013). Meta-analysis of functional magnetic resonance imaging studies of inhibition and attention in attention-deficit/hyperactivity disorder. *JAMA Psychiatry, 709*, 185–198.

Hart, S. D., Kropp, P. R., & Hare, R. D. (1988). Performance of male psychopaths following conditional release from prison. *Journal of Consulting and Clinical Psychology, 56*, 227–232.

Hartl, T., Duffany, S., Allen, G., Steketee, G., & Frost, R. (2005). Relationships among compulsive hoarding, trauma, and attention-deficit/-hyperactivity disorder. *Behaviour Research and Therapy, 43*(2), 269–276.

Hartley, T. R., Lovallo, W. R., Whitsett, T. L., Sung, B. H., & Wilson, M. F. (2001). Caffeine and stress: Implications for risk, assessment, and management of hypertension. *Journal of Clinical Hypertension, 3*, 354–361.

Hartman, H. (1958). *Ego psychology and the problem of adaptation*. New York: International Universities Press.

Hartmann, U., & Waldinger, M. D. (2007). Treatment of delayed ejaculataion. In S. R. Leiblum & R. C. Rosen (Eds.), *Principles and practice of sex therapy* (pp. 241–276). New York, NY: Guilford Press.

Hartmann, U., Heiser, K., Rüffer-Hesse, C., & Kloth, G. (2002). Female sexual desire disorders: Subtypes, classification, personality factors and new directions for treatment. *World Journal of Urology, 20*(2), 79–88.

Hartnoll, R. L. (1994). Opiates: Prevalence and demographic factors. *Addiction, 89*(11), 1377–1383.

Hartung, D. M., McCarty, D., Fu, R., Wiest, K., Chalk, M., & Gastfriend, D. R. (2014). Extended-release naltrexone for alcohol and opioid dependence: A meta-analysis of healthcare utilization studies. *Journal of Substance Abuse Treatment, 47*(2), 113–121. doi:10.1016/j.jsat.2014.03.007

Harvard Medical School. (1995, February, March). Update on Alzheimer's disease. Part I, Part II. *The Harvard Mental Health Letter, 11*, 1–5.

Harvey, A. G., Schmidt, D. A., Scarna, A., Semler, C.N., & Goodwin, G. M. (2005). Sleep-related functioning in euthymic patients with bipolar disorder, patients with insomnia, and subjects without sleep problems. *American Journal of Psychiatry, 162*, 50–57.

Harvey, P. D., Mohs, R., & Davidson, M. (1993). Leukotomy and aging in chronic schizophrenia: A follow-up study 40 years after psychosurgery. *Schizophrenia Bulletin, 19*, 723-732.

Harvey, S. B., Stanton, B. R., & David, A. S. (2006). Conversion disorder: towards a neurobiological understanding. *Neuropsychiatric Disease and Treatment, 2*(1), 13–20.

Haskell, S. G., Gordon, K. S., Mattocks, K., Duggal, M., Erdos, J., Justice, A., & Brandt, C. A. (2010). Gender differences in rates of depression, PTSD, pain, obesity, and military sexual trauma among Connecticut war veterans of Iraq and Afghanistan. *Journal of Women's Health, 19*, 267–271. doi:10.1089/jwh.2008.1262

Hassan, R. (1998). One hundred years of Emile Durkheim's *Suicide: A Study in Sociology*. *Australian and New Zealand Journal of Psychiatry, 32*(2), 168–171. doi:10.3109/00048679809062725

Hattie, J. A., Sharpley, C. F., & Rogers, H. J. (1984). Comparative effectiveness of professional and paraprofessional helpers. *Psychological Bulletin, 95*, 534–541.

Hautzinger, S., & Scandlyn, J. (2013). *Beyond post-traumatic stress: Homefront struggles with the wars on terror*. Walnut Creek, CA: Left Coast Press.

Havassy, B. E., Wasserman, D. A., & Hall, S. M. (1995). Social relationships and abstinence from cocaine in an American treatment sample. *Addiction, 90*(5), 699–710.

Havens, L. L., & Ghaemi, S. N. (2005). Existential despair and bipolar disorder: The therapeutic alliance as a mood stabilizer. *American Journal of Psychotherapy, 59*(2), 137–147.

Hawkins, E. J., Malte, C. A., Imel, Z. E., Saxon, A. J., & Kivlahan, D. R. (2012). Prevalence and trends of benzodiazepine use among Veterans Affairs patients with posttraumatic stress disorder, 2003–2010. *Drug and Alcohol Dependence, 124*(1–2), 154–161. doi:10.1016/j.drugalcdep.2012.01.003

Hawkins-Gilligan, J., Dygdon, J. A., & Conger, A. J. (2011). Examining the nature of fear of flying. *Aviation, Space, and Environmental Medicine, 82*(10), 964–971. doi:10.3357/ASEM.3062.2011

Hawton, K., Comabella, C. I., Haw, C., & Saunders, K. (2013). Risk factors for suicide in individuals with depression: A systematic review. *Journal of Affective Disorders, 147*(1–3), 17–28. doi:10.1016/j.jad.2013.01.004

Hayes, R. D., Dennerstein, L., Bennett, C. M., & Fairley, C. K. (2008). What is the "true" prevalence of female sexual dysfunctions, and does the way we assess these conditions have an impact?. *The Journal of Sexual Medicine, 5*(4), 777–787.

Hayes, S. L., Storch, E. A., & Berlanga, L. (2009). Skin picking behaviors: An examination of the prevalence and severity in a community sample. *Journal of Anxiety Disorders, 23*(3), 314–319. doi:10.1016/j.janxdis.2009.01.008

Haynes, S. G., Feinleib, M., & Kannel, W. B. (1980). The relationahip of psychosocial factors to coronary heart disease in the Framingham study: III. Eight-year incidence of coronary heart disease. *American Journal of Epidemiology, 111*, 37–58.

Hazan, C. (1992, July). *Transitions and transformations in attachment*. Paper presented at the meeting of the International Society for the Study of Personal Relationships, Orono, ME.

Hazan, C., & Shaver, P. (1987). Romantic love conceptualized as an attachment process. *Journal of Personality and Social Psychology, 52*(3), 511–524. doi:10.1037/0022-3514.52.3.511

Hazel, N. A., Oppenheimer, C. W., Technow, J. R., Young, J. F., & Hankin, B. L. (2014). Parent relationship quality buffers against the effect of peer stressors on depressive symptoms from middle childhood to adolescence. *Developmental Psychology, 50*(8), 2115–2123. doi:10.1037/a0037192

Hazelrigg, M. D., Cooper, H. M., & Boudin, C. M. (1987). Evaluating the effectiveness of family therapies: An integrative review and analysis. *Psychological Bulletin, 101*, 428–442.

Hazlett, E. A., Dawson, M. E., Buchsbaum, M. S., & Nuechterlein, K. H. (1993). Reduced regional brain glucose metabolism assessed by positron emission tomography in electrodermal nonresponder schizophrenics: A pilot study. *Journal of Abnormal Psychology, 102*, 39–46.

Health Research Funding (2014, January 8). Famous people with body dysmorphic disorder. Retrieved on September 15, 2014 from http://healthresearchfunding.org/famous-people-body-dysmorphic-disorder/

Healy, D. (2004). *Let them eat prozac: The unhealthy relationship between the pharmaceutical industry and depression*. New York: New York University Press.

Heasley, S. (2014, April 9). Autism-vaccine concerns remain widespread. *Disability Scoop*. Retrieved on October 10, 2014 from http://www.disabilityscoop.com/2014/04/09/autism-vaccine-widespread/19267/

Heather, N. (2010). Breaking new ground in the study and practice of alcohol brief interventions. *Drug and Alcohol Review, 29*(6), 584–588. doi:10.1111/j.1465-3362.2010.00204.x

Heaton, R. K., Gladsjo, J. A., Palmer, B. W., Kuck, J., Marcotte, T. D., & Jeste, D. V. (2001). Stability and course of neurpsychological deficits in schizophrenia. *Archives of General Psychiatry, 58*, 24–32.

Heber, R. (1961). Modifications in the manual on terminology and classification in mental retardation. *American Journal on Mental Deficiency, 65*, 499–500.

Heckler, S. (1994). Facilitated communication: A response by Child Protection. *Child Abuse and Neglect: The International Journal, 18*(6), 495–503.

Heckman, C. J., Egleston, B. L., & Hofmann, M. T. (2010). Efficacy of motivational interviewing for smoking cessation: A systematic review and meta-analysis. *Tobacco Control: An International Journal, 19*(5), 410–416. doi:10.1136/tc.2009.033175

Hedden, T., & Gabrieli, J. D. E. (2004). Insights into the ageing mind: A view from cognitive neuroscience. *Nature Reviews Neuroscience, 5*(2), 87–96. doi: 10.1038/nrm1323

Hedrick, A. N., & Berlin, H. A. (2012). Implicit self-esteem in borderline personality and depersonalization disorder. *Frontiers in Psychology, 3*, 91. doi:10.3389/fpsyg.2012.00091

Heijnen, W. T., Birkenhäger, T. K., Wierdsma, A. I., & van den Broek, W. W. (2010). Antidepressant pharmacotherapy failure and response to subsequent electroconvulsive therapy: A meta-analysis. *Journal of Clinical Psychopharmacology, 30*(5), 616–619. doi:10.1097/JCP.0b013e3181ee0f5f

Heilbrun, A. B. (1993). Multifactorial theories of hallucinations. In C. G. Costello (Ed.), *Symptoms of schizophrenia* (pp. 56–91). New York: John Wiley & Sons.

Heilbrun, K. S. (1987). The assessment of competence for execution: An overview. *Behavioral Sciences and the Law, 5*, 383–396.

Heim, C., & Binder, E. B. (2012). Current research trends in early life stress and depression: review of human studies on sensitive periods, gene-environment interactions, and epigenetics. *Experimental Neurology, 233*(1), 102–111. doi:10.1016/j.expneurol.2011.10.032.

Heiman J., & LoPiccolo, J. (1988). *Becoming orgasmic: A sexual and personal growth program for women* (2nd ed.). New York: Prentice Hall.

Heiman, J. (1993). Sexual dysfunctions. In D. L. Dunner (Ed.), *Current psychiatric therapy* (pp. 346–353). Philadelphia, PA: W. B. Saunders.

Heiman, J. R. (2002). Sexual dysfunction: Overview of prevalence, etiological factors, and treatments. *The Journal of Sex Research, 39* (1), 73–78.

Heiman J. R. (2007). Orgasmic disorders in women. In S. R. Leiblum & R. C. Rosen (Eds.), *Principles and practice of sex therapy* (pp. 84–123). New York, NY: Guilford Press.

Heiman, J., & Grafton-Becker, V. (1989). Orgasmic disorders in women. In S. R. Leiblum & R. C. Rosen (Eds), *Principles and practice of sex therapy: Update for the 1990s* (pp. 51–88). New York: Guilford Press.

Heimberg, R. G., Dodge, C. S., Hope, D. A., Kennedy, C. R., & Zollo, I. J. (1990). Cognitive behavioral group treatment for social phobia: Comparison with a credible placebo control. *Cognitive Therapy & Research, 14,* 1–23.

Heinrichs, M., Wagner, D., Schoch, W., Soravia, L. M., Hellhammer, D. H., & Ehlert, U. (2005). Predicting posttraumatic stress symptoms from pretraumatic risk factors: A 2-year prospective follow-up study in firefighters. *American Journal of Psychiatry, 162,* 2276–2286.

Heinrichs, R. W. (2005). The primacy of cognition in schizophrenia. *American Psychologist, 60,* 229–242.

Heinssen, R. K., Levendusky, P. G., & Hunter, R. H. (1995). Client as colleague: Therapeutic contracting with the seriously mentally ill. *American Psychologist, 50,* 522–532.

Helgeson, V. S., Reynolds, K. A., & Tomich, P. L. (2006). A meta-analytic review of benefit finding and growth. *Journal of Consulting and Clinical Psychology, 74,* 797–816.

Heller, K. A., Holtzman, W. H., & Messick, S. (Eds.). (1982). *Placing children in special education: A strategy for equity.* Washington, DC: National Academy Press.

Heller, K. A., Swindle, R. W., Jr., & Dusenbury, L. (1986). Component social support processes: Comments and integration. *Journal of Consulting and Clinical Psychology, 54,* 466–470.

Hellerstein, D., Yanowitch, P., Rosenthal, J., Samstag, L. W., Maurer, M., Kasch, K., Burrows, L., Poster, M., Cantillon, M., & Winston, R. (1993). A randomized double-blind study of fluoxetine versus placebo in the treatment of dysthymia. *American Journal of Psychiatry, 150,* 1169–1175.

Helmes, E., & Landmark, J. (2003). Subtypes of schizophrenia: a cluster analytic approach. *Canadian Journal of Psychiatry, 48,* 702–708.

Helmes, E., & Reddon, J. R. (1993). A perspective on developments in assessing psychopathology: A critical review of the MMPI and MMPI-2. *Psychological Bulletin, 113,* 453–471.

Helzer, J. E., Canino, G. J., Yeh, E. K., Bland, R. C., Lee, C. K., Hwu, H. G., & Newman, S. (1990). Alcoholism—North America and Asia: A comparison of population surveys with the Diagnostic Interview Schedule. *Archives of General Psychiatry, 47,* 313–319.

Helzer, J. E., Robins, L. N., & McEvoy, L. (1987). Post-traumatic stress disorder in the general population. *New England Journal of Medicine, 317,* 1630–1634.

Henggeler, S. W., & Lee, T. (2003). Multi-systemic treatment of serious clinical problems. In A. E. Kazdin & J. R. Weisz (Eds.), *Evidence-based psychotherapies for children and adolescents* (pp. 301–322). New York: Guilford Press.

Henggeler, S. W., Sheidow, A. J., & Lee, T. (2007). Multisystemic treatment of serious clinical problems in youth and their families. In D.W. Springer & A.R. Roberts (Eds.), *Handbook of forensic mental health with victims and offenders: Assessment, treatment and research* (pp. 315–345). New York: Springer.

Henker, B., & Whalen, C. (1989). Hyperactivity and attention deficits. *American Psychologist, 44,* 216–223.

Henn, F. A. (1986). The neurobiologic basis of psychiatric illness. In G. Winokur and P. Clayton (Eds.), *The Medical Basis of Psychiatry* (pp. 461–485). Philadelphia: W. B. Saunders.

Hennessy, E. A., & Tanner-Smith, E. E. (2014). Effectiveness of brief school-based interventions for adolescents: A meta-analysis of alcohol use prevention programs. *Prevention Science, 16*(3), 463–474. doi:10.1007/s11121-014-0512-0

Henry, W. P., Strupp, H. H., Butler, S. F., Schacht, T. E., & Binder, J. L. (1993). Effects of training in time-limited dynamic psychotherapy: Changes in therapist behavior. *Journal of Consulting and Clinical Psychology, 61,* 434–440.

Hepp, U., Spindler, A., & Milos, G. (2005). Eating disorder symptomology and gender role orientation. *International Journal of Eating Disorders, 37*(3), 227–233. doi: 10.1002/eat.20087

Herba, C. M., Hodgins, S., Blackwood, N., Kumari, V., Naudts, K. H., Phillips, M. L. (2007). The neurobiology of psychopathy: A focus on emotion processing. In H. Herve & J. C. Yuille (Eds.), *The psychopath: Theory, research and practice* (pp. 253–283). Mahwah, NJ: Lawrence Erlbaum.

Herbert, B. M., & Pollatos, O. (2012). The body in the mind: On the relationship between interoception and embodiment. *Topics in Cognitive Science, 4,* 692–704.

Herbert, J. D., Hope, D. A., & Bellack, A. S. (1992). Validity of the distinction between generalized social phobia and avoidant personality disorder. *Journal of Abnormal Psychology, 101,* 332–339.

Herbert, T. B., & Cohen, S. (1993a). Stress and immunity in humans: A meta-analytic review. *Psychosomatic Medicine, 55,* 364–379.

Herbert, T. B., & Cohen, S. (1993b). Depression and immunity: A meta-analytic review. *Psychological Bulletin, 113,* 472–486.

Herd, D. (1989). The epidemiology of drinking patterns and alcohol-related problems among U.S. blacks. In D. Spiegler, D. Tate, S. Aitken, & C. Christian (Eds.), *Alcohol use among U.S. ethnic minorities: Proceedings of a conference on the epidemiology of alcohol use and abuse among ethnic minority groups* (NIAAA Research Monograph No. 18, DHHS Pub. No. (ADM) 89-1435, pp. 3–50). Washington, DC: Supt. of Docs., U.S. Government Printing Office.

Hergenhahn, B. R., & Henley, T. (2013). *An introduction to the history of psychology.* Belmont, CA: Wadsworth.

Herguner, S., Ozyildirim, I., & Tanidir, C. (2008). Is pica an eating disorder or an obsessive-compulsive spectrum disorder? *Progress in Neuro-psychopharmacology & Biological Psychiatry, 32*(8), 2010–2011. doi:10.1016/j.pnpbp.2008.09.011

Herman, J. L., Perry, J. C., & Van der Kolk, B. A. (1989). Childhood trauma in borderline personality disorder. *American Journal of Psychiatry, 146*(4), 490–495.

Hermann, E. C., Dorwart, R. A., Hoover, C. W. & Brody, J. (1995). Variation in ECT use in the United States. *American Journal of Psychiatry, 152,* 869–875.

Herndon, R., & Iacono, W. G. (2005). Psychiatric disorder in the children of antisocial parents. *Psychological Bulletin, 35,* 1815–1824.

Herning, R. I., Glover, B. J., Koeppl, B., Phillips, R. L., & London, E. D. (1994). Cocaine-induced increases in EEG alpha and beta activity: Evidence for reduced cortical processing. *Neuropsychopharmacology, 11*(1), 1–9.

Herrnstein, R. J., & Murray, C. (1994). *The bell curve: Intelligence and class structure in American life.* New York: Free Press.

Hersen, M., & Bellack, A. S. (1976). Social skills training for chronic psychiatric patients: Rationale, research findings, and future directions. *Comprehensive Psychiatry, 17,* 559–580.

Herz, M. I., & Melville, C. (1980). Relapse in schizophrenia. *American Journal of Psychiatry, 137,* 801–805.

Hess, R. D., & McDevitt, T. M. (1984). Some cognitive consequences of maternal intervention techniques: A longitudinal study. *Child Development, 55*(6), 2017–2030.

Heston, L. L. (1966). Psychiatric disorders in foster home reared children of schizophrenic mothers. *British Journal of Psychiatry, 112,* 819–825.

Heston, L. L., & White, J. A. (1983). *Dementia: A practical guide to Alzheimer's disease and related illnesses.* New York: W. H. Freeman.

Hettema, J. M., Neale, M. C., & Kendler, K. S. (2001). A review and meta-analysis of the genetic epidemiology of anxiety disorders. *The American Journal of Psychiatry, 158*(10), 1568–1578. doi:10.1176/appi.ajp.158.10.1568

Hetzel, C. J., & Mann, K. (2014, August 10). Passing through the looking glass: The social psychological dynamics of transgender identity- A qualitative study. Unpublished manuscript, Cardinal Stritch University, Milwaukee, WI.

Heuzenroeder, L., Donnelly, M., Haby, M. M., Mihalopoulos, C., Rossell, R., Carter, R., & Vos, T. (2004). Cost-effectiveness of psychological and pharmacological interventions for generalized anxiety disorder and panic disorder. *Australian and New Zealand Journal of Psychiatry, 38,* 602–612. doi:10.1111/j.1440-1614.2004.01423.x

Hibbard, J., & Pope, C. (1993). The quality of social roles as predictors of morbidity and mortality. *Social Science and Medicine, 36,* 217–225.

Hickey, E. W. (2010). *Serial murderers and their victims* (5th ed.). Belmont, CA: Wadsworth/Cengage Learning.

Hickie, I., Kirk, K., & Martin, N. (1999). Unique genetic and environmental determinants of prolonged fatigue: A twin study. *Psychological Medicine, 29*(2), 259–268.

Hickie, I. B. (2014). Evidence for separate inheritance of mania and depression challenges current concepts of bipolar mood disorder. *Molecular Psychiatry, 19*(2), 153–155.

Higgins, S. T., Budney, A. J., Bickel, W. K., Foerg, F. E., & Badger, G. J. (1994). Alcohol dependence and simultaneous cocaine and alcohol use in cocaine-dependent patients. *Journal of Addictive Diseases, 13*(4), 177–189.

Higgins, S. T., Budney, A. J., Bickel, W. K., Hughes, J. R., Foerg, F., & Badger, G. (1993). Achieving cocaine abstinence with a behavioral approach. *American Journal of Psychiatry, 150,* 763–769.

Higgins, S. T., Delaney, D. D., Budney, A. J., Bickel, W. K., Hughes, J. R., Foerg, F., & Fenwick, J. W. (1991). A behavioral approach to achieving initial cocaine abstinence. *American Journal of Psychiatry, 148*(9), 1218–1224.

Hilbert, K., Lueken, U., & Beesdo-Baum, K. (2014). Neural structures, functioning and connectivity in generalized anxiety disorder and interaction with neuroendocrine systems: A systematic review. *Journal of Affective Disorders, 158,* 114–126. doi:10.1016/j.jad.2014.01.022

Hill, K., Mann, L., Laws, K. R., Stephenson, C. M., Nimmo-Smith, I., & McKenna, P. J. (2004). Hypofrontality in schizophrenia: A meta-analysis of functional imaging studies. *Acta Psychiatrica Scandinavica, 110,* 243–256.

Hill, S. Y. (1992). Absence of paternal sociopathy in the etiology of severe alcoholism: Is there a Type III alcoholism? *Journal of Studies on Alcohol, 53*(2), 161–169.

Himle, M. B., Hayes, L. P., Mouton-Odum, S., & Golomb, R. (2014). Trichotillomania (hair pulling disorder). In L. Grossman & S. Walfish (Eds.), *Translating psychological research into practice* (pp. 283–288). New York: Springer.

Hinshaw, S. P., Lahey, B. B., & Hart, E. L. (1993). Issues of taxonomy and comorbidity in the development of conduct disorder. *Development and Psychopathology, 5,* 31–49.

Hinshaw, S. P. (1987). On the distinction between attentional deficits/hyperactivity and conduct problems/aggression in child psychopathology. *Psychological Bulletin, 101,* 443–463.

Hinton, D. E., & Lewis-Fernández, R. (2011). The cross-cultural validity of post-traumatic stress disorder: Implications for DSM-5. *Depression and Anxiety, 28*(9), 783–801. doi:10.1002/da.20753

Hiroto, D. S., & Seligman, M. E. P. (1975). Generality of learned helplessness in man. *Journal of Personality and Social Psychology, 31,* 311–327.

Hirsch, C. R., Clark, D. M., & Mathews, A. (2006). Imagery and interpretations in social phobia: Support for the combined cognitive biases hypothesis. *Behavior Therapy, 37*(3), 223–236. doi:10.1016/j.beth.2006.02.001

Hirsch, C. R., Hayes, S., Mathews, A., Perman, G., & Borkovec, T. (2012). The extent and nature of imagery during worry and positive thinking in generalized anxiety disorder. *Journal of Abnormal Psychology, 121*(1), 238–243. doi:10.1037/a0024947

Hirschfeld, R. M. A. (2001). The comorbidity of major depression and anxiety disorders: Recognition and management in primary care. *Primary Care Companion Journal of Clinical Psychiatry, 3*(6), 244–254.

Hirshfeld, D. R., Rosenbaum, J. F., Biederman, J., Bolduc, E. A., Faraone, S. V., Snidman, N., Reznick, F. S., & Kagan, J. (1992). Stable behavioral inhibition and its association with anxiety disorder. *Journal of the American Academy of Adolescent Psychiatry, 31*(1), 103–111.

Hirshfeld, R. M., & Goodwin, F. K. (1988). Mood disorders. In J. A. Talbot, R. E. Hales, & S. C. Yudofsky (Eds.), *Textbook of psychiatry.* Washington, DC: American Psychiatric Press.

Hite, S. (1976). *Hite report: A nationwide study on female sexuality.* New York: Macmillan.

Hlavaty, C. (2014, June 20). 13 years later, the Andrea Yates drownings still haunt. *The Houston Chronicle.* Retrieved July 30, 2014 from http://www.chron.com/neighborhood/bayarea/crime-courts/article/Andrea-Yates-Rusty-Yates-5567726.php

Hobbs, S., & Goswick, R. (1977). Behavioral treatment of self-stimulation: An examination of alternatives to physical punishment. *Journal of Clinical Child Psychology, 6,* 20–23.

Hobson, R. P. (1989). On sharing experiences. *Development and Psychopathology, 1,* 197–205.

Hodapp, R. M. (1994). Cultural-familial mental retardation. In R. Sternberg (Ed.), *Encyclopedia of intelligence* (pp. 711–717). New York: Macmillan.

Hodapp, R. M., & Dykens, E. M. (1994). The two cultures of behavioral research in mental retardation. *American Journal on Mental Retardation, 97,* 675–687.

Hodapp, R. M., & Krasner, D. V. (1995). Families of children with disablties: Findings from a national sample of eighth-grade students. *Exceptionality, 5*(2), 71–81.

Hodapp, R. M., Burack, J. A., & Zigler, E. (Eds.). (1990). *Issues in the developmental approach to mental retardation.* New York: Cambridge University Press.

Hodapp, R. M., Leckman, J. F., Dykens, E. M., Sparrow, S. S., Zelinsky, D. G., & Ort, S. I. (1992). K-ABC profiles in children with fragile X syndrome, Down syndrome, and nonspecific mental retardation. *American Journal on Mental Retardation, 97,* 39–46.

Hodges, J. R. (1993). Pick's disease. In A. Burns & R. Levy (Eds.). *Dementia* (pp. 737–750). London: Chapman and Hall.

Hodges, J. R. (1994). Neurological aspects of dementia and normal aging. In F. A. Huppert, C. Brayne, & D. W. O'Connor (Eds.), *Dementia and normal aging* (pp. 118–129). Cambridge: Cambridge University Press.

Hodgins, G., Creamer, M., & Bell, R. (2001). Risk factors for posttrauma reactions in police officers: A longitudinal study. *Journal of Nervous & Mental Disease, 189,* 541–547.

Hodgkinson, S., Sherrington, R., Gurling, H., Marchbanks, R., Reeders, S., Mallet, J., McInnis, M., Perursson, H., & Brynjolfsson, J. (1987). Molecular genetic evidence for heterogeneity in manic depression. *Nature, 325,* 805–806.

Hodgson, K., Hutchinson, A. D., & Denson, L. (2014). Nonpharmacological treatments for ADHD: A meta-analytic review. *Journal of Attention Disorders, 18*(4), 275–282. doi:10.1177/1087054712444732

Hodiamont, P. (1991). How normal are anxiety and fear? *International Journal of Sociological Psychiatry, 37*(1), 43–50.

Hoekstra, P. J., & Minderaa, R. B. (2005). Tic disorders and obsessive-compulsive disorder: Is autoimmunity involved? *International Review of Psychiatry, 17*(6), 497–502. doi:10.1080/02646830500382003

Hoelscher, T. J., Lichstein, K. L., & Rosenthal, T. L. (1986). Home relaxation practice in hypertension treatment: Objective assessment and compliance induction. *Journal of Consulting and Clinical Psychology, 54,* 217–221.

Hoffmann, J. P., & Bahr, S. J. (2014). Parenting style, religiosity, peer alcohol use, and adolescent heavy drinking. *Journal of Studies on Alcohol and Drugs, 75*(2), 222–227.

Hofmann, S. G., & Smits, J. J. (2008). Cognitive-behavioral therapy for adult anxiety disorders: A meta-analysis of randomized placebo-controlled trials. *Journal of Clinical Psychiatry, 69*(4), 621–632. doi:10.4088/JCP.v69n0415

Hofmann, S. G., Asnaani, A., & Hinton, D. E. (2010). Cultural aspects in social anxiety and social anxiety disorder. *Depression and Anxiety, 27*(12), 1117–1127. doi:10.1002/da.20759

Hofmann, S. G., Asnaani, A., Vonk, I. J., Sawyer, A. T., & Fang, A. (2012). The efficacy of cognitive behavioral therapy: A review of meta-analyses. *Cognitive Therapy and Research, 36,* 427–440. doi:10.1007/s10608-012-9476-1

Hogarty, G. E., Kornblith, S. J., Greenwald, D., DiBarry, A. L., Cooley, S., Flesher, S., Reiss, D., Carter, M., & Ulrich, R. (1995). Personal therapy: A disorder-relevant psychotherapy for schizophrenia. *Schizophrenia Bulletin, 21,* 379–393.

Hogarty, G., Anderson, C., Reiss, D., Kornblith, S., Greenwald, D., Javna, C., & Madonia, M. (1986). Family psychoeducation, social skills training, and maintenance chemotherapy in the aftercare treatment of schizophrenia. I: One-year effects of a controlled study on relapse and expressed emotion. *Archives of General Psychiatry, 43,* 633–642.

Hoge, C. W., McGurk, D., Thomas, J. J., Cox, A. L., Engel, C. C., & Castro, C. A. (2008). Mild traumatic brain injury in the U.S. soldiers returning from Iraq. *New England Journal of Medicine, 358,* 453–463.

Hoien, T., Lundberg, I., Larsen, J., & Tonnessen, F. (1989). Profiles of reading related skills in dyslexic families. *Reading and Writing. An Interdisciplinary Journal, 1,* 381–392.

Holbrook, T., Hoyt, D., Stein, M., & Sieber, W. (2002). Gender differences in long-term posttraumatic stress disorder outcomes after major trauma: women are at higher risk of adverse outcomes than men. *Journal of Trauma, 53,* 882–888.

Holland, J. (2013, December 16). Land of the free? US has 25 percent of the world's prisoners. *Moyers and Company.* Retrieved October 29, 2014 from http://billmoyers.com/2013/12/16/land-of-the-free-us-has-5-of-the-worlds-population-and-25-of-its-prisoners/

Hollander, E. & McCarley, A. (1992). Yohimbine treatment of sexual side effects induced by serotonin reuptake blockers. *Journal of Clinical Psychiatry, 53,* 207–209.

Hollifield, M., Tuttle, L., Paine, S., & Kellner, R. (1999). Hypochondriasis and somatization related to personality and attitudes toward self. *Psychosomatics, 40*(5), 387–395. doi:10.1016/S0033-3182(99)71203-X

Hollister, L. E., & Csernansky, J. G. (1990). *Clinical pharmacology of psychotherapeutic drugs* (3rd ed.). New York: Churchill Livingstone.

Hollon, S. D. (1993). Review of psychosocial treatments for mood disorders. In D. D. Dunner (Ed.), *Current psychiatric therapy* (pp. 240–246). Philadelphia: W. B. Saunders.

Hollon, S. D., Shelton, R. C., & Davis, D. D. (1993). Cognitive therapy for depression: Conceptual issues and clinical efficacy. *Journal of Clinical and Consulting Psychology, 61,* 270–275.

Hollon, S. D., Shelton, R. C., & Loosen, P. T. (1991). Cognitive therapy and pharmacotherapy for depression. *Journal of Consulting and Clinical Psychology, 59,* 88–99.

Hollon, S.D., Thase, M.E., & Markowitz, J.C. (2002). Treatment and prevention of depression. *Psychological Science in the Public Interest, 3*(2), 39–77.

Holma, K., Melartin, T. K., Haukka, J., Holma, I. K., Sokero, T., & Isometsä, E. T. (2010). Incidence and predictors of suicide attempts in *DSM-IV* major depressive disorder: A five-year prospective study. *The American Journal of Psychiatry, 167*(7), 801–808. doi:10.1176/appi.ajp.2010.09050627

Holmes, R., & Holmes, S. (2010). *Serial murder* (3rd ed.). Thousand Oaks, CA: Sage Publications.

Holmes, T. H., & Rahe, R. H. (1967). The social readjustment rating scale. *Journal of Psychosomatic Research, 11,* 213–218.

Holroyd, J., & Brodsky, A. M. (1977). Psychologists' attitudes and practices regarding erotic and nonerotic physical contact with patients. *American Psychologist, 32,* 843–849.

Holroyd, S., Rabins, P., Finkelstein, D., and Lavrisha, M. (1994). Visual hallucinations in patients from an ophthalmology clinic and medical clinic population. *Journal of Nervous and Mental Disease, 182,* 273–276.

Holtzman, P. S., Kringlen, E., Matthysse, S., Flanagan, S. D., Lipton, R. B., Cramer, S., Levin, S., Lange, K., & Levy, D. L. (1988). A single dominant gene can account for eye tracking dysfunctions and schizophrenia in offspring of discordant twins. *Archives of General Psychiatry, 45,* 641–647.

Holzer, C. E., Shae, B. M., Swanson, J. W. (1986). The increased risk for specific psychiatric disorders among persons of low socioeconomic status. *American Journal of Social Psychiatry, 4,* 259–271.

Homan, S., Lachenbruch, P., Winokur, G., Clayton, P. (1982). An efficacy study of electroconvulsive therapy and antidepressants in treatment of primary depression. *Psychological Medicine, 12,* 615–624.

Honyashiki, M., Furukawa, T. A., Noma, H., Tanaka, S., Chen, P., Ichikawa, K., . . . Caldwell, D. M. (2014). Specificity of CBT for depression: A contribution from multiple treatments meta-analyses. *Cognitive Therapy and Research, 38*(3), 249–260. doi:10.1007/s10608-014-9599-7

Hooley, J. M. (1987). The nature and origins of expressed emotion. In K. Hahlweg & M. J. Goldstein (Eds.), *Understanding major mental disorder: The contribution of family interaction research* (pp. 176–194). New York: Family Process.

Hooley, J. M. (1998). Expressed emotion and locus of control. *Journal of Nervous and Mental Disease, 186*(6), 374–378. doi:10.1097/00005053-199806000-00009

Hooley, J. M., & Gotlib, I. H. (2000). A diathesis-stress conceptualization of expressed emotion and clinical outcome. *Applied and Preventive Psychology, 32*, 1091–1099.

Hooley, J. M., & Hiller, J. B. (2000). Expressed emotion and personality. *Journal of Abnormal Psychology, 109*, 40–44.

Hopper, J. W., Frewen, P. A., Sack, M., Lanius, R. A., & Van der Kolk, B. A. (2007). The Responses to Script-Driven Imagery Scale (RSDI): Assessment of state post-traumatic symptoms for psychobiological and treatment research. *Journal of Psychopathology and Behavioral Assessment, 29*, 249–268.

Hopper, K., Harrison, G., Janca, A., & Sartorius, N. (2007). *Recovery from schizophrenia: An international perspective: A report from the WHO Collaborative Project, the international study of schizophrenia.* New York: Oxford University Press.

Hor, K., & Taylor, M. (2010). Suicide and schizophrenia: A systematic review of rates and risk factors. *Journal of Psychopharmacology, 24*, 81–90.

Hori, H., Teraishi, T., Ota, M., Hattori, K., Matsuo, J., Kinoshita, Y., . . . Kunugi, H. (2014). Psychological coping in depressed outpatients: Association with cortisol response to the combined dexamethasone/CRH test. *Journal of Affective Disorders, 152–154*, 441–447. doi:10.1016/j.jad.2013.10.013

Horn, W. E., Ialongo, N. S., Pascoe, J. M., Greenberg, G., Packard, T., Lopez, M., Wagner, A., & Puttier, L. (1991). Additive effects of psychostimulants, parent training, and self-control therapy with ADHD children. *Journal of the American Academy of Child and Adolescent Psychiatry, 30*(2), 233–240.

Horvath, A. O., & Luborsky, L. (1993). The role of the therapeutic alliance in psychotherapy. *Journal of Consulting and Clinical Psychology, 61*, 561–573.

Horvath, A. T., & Yeterian, J. (2012). Smart recovery: Self-empowering, science-based addiction recovery support. *Journal of Groups in Addiction & Recovery, 7*(2–4), 102–117. doi:10.1080/1556035X.2012.705651

Horwath, E., Johnson, J., & Hornig, C. (1993). Epidemiology of panic disorder in African-Americans. *American Journal of Psychiatry, 150*, 465–469.

Horwitz, A., & Wakefield, J. (2007). *The loss of sadness: How psychiatry transformed normal sorrow into depressive disorder.* New York: Oxford University Press.

Houben, K., & Wiers, R. W. (2007). Are drinkers implicitly positive about drinking alcohol? Personalizing the alcohol-IAT to reduce negative extrapersonal contamination. *Alcohol & Alcoholism, 42*, 301–307.

House, J. S., Landis, K. R., & Umberson, D. (1988). Social relationships and health. *Science, 241*, 540–545.

House, J. S., Robbins, C., & Metzner, H. L. (1982). The association of social relationships and activities with mortality: Prospective evidence from the Tecumseh Community Health Study. *American Journal of Epidemiology, 116*, 123–140.

Houts, A. C. (1991). Nocturnal enuresis as a biobehavioral problem. *Behavior Therapy, 22*, 133–151.

Houts, A. C., Peterson, J. K., & Whelan, J. P. (1986). Prevention of relapse in full-spectrum home training for primary enuresis: A components analysis. *Behavior Therapy, 17*, 462–469.

Howard, A., Pion, G. M., Gottfredson, G. D., Flattau, P. E., Oskamp, S., Pfafflin, S. M., Bray, D. W. (1986). The changing face of American psychology: A report from the Committee on Employment and Human Resources. *American Psychologist, 41*, 1311–1327.

Howard, K. I., Lueger, R. J., Maling, M. S., & Martinovich, Z. (1993). A phase model of psychotherapy outcome: Causal mediation of change. *Journal of Consulting and Clinical Psychology, 61*, 678–685.

Howard, R. (1992). Folie a deux involving a dog. *American Journal of Psychiatry, 149*, 414.

Howard, R., Rabins, P. V., Seeman, M. V., & Jeste, D. V. (2000). Late-onset schizophrenia and very-late-onset schizophrenia-like psychosis. *American Journal of Psychiatry, 157*, 172–178.

Howard, R. C., & Clark, C. R. (1985). When courts and experts disagree: Discordance between insanity recommendations and adjudications. *Law and Human Behavior, 9*, 385–395.

"How does heroin work?" (2012, November 30). *Addiction Blog.* Retrieved on December 15, 2014 from http://drug.addictionblog.org/how-does-heroin-work/

Hsiao, M., Lin, K., Liu, C., Tzen, K., & Yen, T. (2003). Dopamine transporter change in drug-naïve schizophrenia: An imaging study with ⁹⁹mTc-TRODAT-1. *Schizophrenia Research, 65*(1), 39–46. doi:10.1016/S0920-9964(03)00006-9

Hsii, A., & Golden, N. H. (2013). Eating disorders. In P. J. A. Hillard (Ed.), *Practical pediatric and adolescent gynecology* (pp. 131–137). Hoboken, NJ: John Wiley & Sons.

Hsu, L. K. G. (1988). The etiology of anorexia nervosa. In B. J. Blinder, B. F. Chaitin, & R. Goldstein (Eds.), *The eating disorders* (pp. 239–246). Rockford, IL: PMA Publishing Corporation.

Hsu, L. K. G. (1990). *Eating disorders.* New York: Guildford Press.

Hu, J., Henry, S., Gallezot, J., Ropchan, J., Neumaier, J. F., Potenza, M. N., . . . Neumeister, A. (2010). Serotonin 1B receptor imaging in alcohol dependence. *Biological Psychiatry, 67*(9), 800–803. doi:10.1016/j.biopsych.2009.12.028

Hu, Y., Xie, G., & Yang, K. (2010). Sleep ectroencephalogram physiological characteristics in patients with depression and insomnia. *Chinese Journal of Clinical Psychology, 18*(1), 53–55.

Huang, F., Li, Z., Han, H., Xiong, H., & Ma, Y. (2013). Cognitive-behavioral therapy combined with pharmacotherapy for obsessive-compulsive disorder: A meta-analysis. *Chinese Mental Health Journal, 27*(9), 643–649.

Huang, F., Qian, Q., & Wang, Y. (2013). Psychological treatment for adults with attention-deficit/hyperactivity disorder: A review. *Chinese Mental Health Journal, 27*(9), 659–664.

Huber, H., Karlin, R., & Nathan, P. E. (1976). Blood alcohol level discrimination by nonalcoholics: The role of internal and external cues. *Journal of Studies on Alcohol, 37*, 27–39.

Huberman, B. K., & Berne, L. A. (1995). Sexuality education: Sorting fact from fiction. *Phi Delta Kappan, 77*, 229–232.

Hucker, S. J. & Bain, J. (1990). Androgenic hormones and sexual assault. In W. L. Marshall, D. R. Laws, & H. E. Barbaree (Eds.), *Handbook of sexual assault* (pp. 93–102). New York: Plenum.

Hudson, A., Melita, B., & Arnold, N. (1993). A case study assessing the validity of facilitated communication. *Journal of Autism and Developmental Disorders, 23*(1), 165–173.

Hudson, J. I., Hiripi. E., Pope Jr., H. G., & Kessler, R. C. (2007). The prevalence and correlates of eating disorders in the National Comorbidity Survey Replication. *Biological Psychiatry, 61*(3), 348–358.

Huerta, M., Bishop, S. L., Duncan, A., Hus, V., & Lord, C. (2012). Application of *DSM-5* criteria for autism spectrum disorder to three samples of children with *DSM-IV* diagnoses of pervasive developmental disorders. *American Journal of Psychiatry, 169*, 1056–1064.

Huettel, S. A., Song, A. W., & McCarthy, G. (2009). *Functional magnetic resonance imaging* (2nd ed.). Sunderland, MA: Sinauer.

Hughes, J. R., & Carpenter, M. J. (2005). The feasibility of smoking reduction: An update. *Addiction, 100*(8), 1074–1089. doi:10.1111/j.1360-0443.2005.01174.x

Hughes, P. H., Coletti, S. D., Neri, R. L., Urmann, C. F., Stahl, S., Sicilian, D. M., & Anthony, J. C. (1995). Retaining cocaine-abusing women in a therapeutic community: The effect of a child live-in program. *American Journal of Public Health, 5*(8), 1149–1152.

Hughlings-Jackson, J. (1875). A lecture on softening of the brain. *Lancet, ii*, 335–339.

Human Capital Initiative Coordinating Committee (1996). Reducing mental disorders: A behavioral science research plan for psychopathology. *American Psychological Society Observer,* February special issue.

Hunsley, J., & Bailey, J. (1999). The clinical utility of the Rorschach: Unfulfilled promises and an uncertain future. *Psychological Assessment, 11*, 266–277. doi:10.1037/1040-3590.11.3.266

Hunt, G. M., & Azrin, N. H. (1973). A community-reinforcement approach to alcoholism. *Behaviour Research and Therapy, 11*(1), 91–104. doi:10.1016/0005-7967(73)90072-7

Hunt, I. M., Kapur, N., Windfuhr, K., Robinson, J., Bickley, H., Flynn, S., . . . Appleby, L. (2006). Suicide in schizophrenia: Findings from a national clinical survey. *Journal of Psychiatric Practice, 12*(3), 139–147. doi:10.1097/00131746-200605000-00002

Hunt, T. J., Thienhaus, O., & Ellwood, A. (2008). The mirror lies: Body dysmorphic disorder. *American Family Physician, 78*(2), 217–222.

Hunter, C. L., Goodie, J. L., Oordt, M. S., & Dobmeyer, A. C. (2009). *Integrated behavioral health in primary care: Step-by-step guidance for assessment and intervention.* Washington, DC: American Psychological Association.

Hunter, D. (2007). *Antidepressants and advertising: Marketing happiness.* Broomall, PA: Mason Crest Publishers.

Hunter, E. C., Baker, D., Phillips, M. L., Sierra, M., & David, A. S. (2005). Cognitive behavior therapy for depersonalization disorder: An open study. *Behaviour Research and Therapy, 43*, 1121–1130.

Hunter, E. C., Salkovskis, P. M., & David, A. S. (2014). Attributions, appraisals and attention for symptoms in depersonalisation disorder. *Behaviour Research and Therapy, 53*, 20–29. doi:10.1016/j.brat.2013.11.005

Hunter, E. C., Sierra, M., & David, A. S. (2004). The epidemiology of depersonalisation and derealisation: A systematic review. *Social Psychiatry and Psychiatric Epidemiology, 39*(1), 9–18.

Hunter, J., & Schaecher, R. (1995). Gay and lesbian adolescents. In R. L. Edwards & J. G. Hopps (Eds.), *Encyclopedia of Social Work, 19th Ed.* (pp. 1055–1063). Washington, DC: National Association of Social Workers.

Hunter, R. H. (1995). Benefits of competency-based treatment programs. *American Psychologist, 50*, 509–513.

Huppert, F. A. (2010). Psychological well-being: Evidence regarding its causes and consequences. In C. L. Cooper, J. Field, U. Goswami, R. Jenkins, & B. J. Sahakian (Eds.), *Mental capital and well-being* (pp. 907–925). Hoboken, NJ: Wiley-Blackwell.

Huppert, F. A., & Brayne, C. (1994). What is the relationship between dementia and normal aging? In F. A. Huppert, C. Brayne, & D. W. O'Connor (Eds.), *Dementia and normal aging* (pp. 3–14). Cambridge: Cambridge University Press.

Hurlbert, D. F. (1993). A comparative study using orgasm consistency training in the treatment of women reporting hypoactive sexual desire. *Journal of Sex and Marital Therapy, 19,* 41–55.

Hurlburt, M. S., Nguyen, K., Reid, J., Webster-Stratton, C., & Zhang, J. (2013). Efficacy of the Incredible Years group parent program with families in Head Start who self-reported a history of child maltreatment. *Child Abuse & Neglect, 37,* 531–543. doi:10.1016/j.chiabu.2012.10.008

Hürlimann, F., Kupferschmid, S., & Simon, A. E. (2012). Cannabis-induced depersonalization disorder in adolescence. *Neuropsychobiology, 65*(3), 141–146. doi:10.1159/000334605

Hurt, H., Brodsky, N. L., Betancourt, L., Braitman, L. E., Malmud, E., & Giannetta, J. (1995). Cocaine-exposed children: Follow-up through 30 months. *Developmental and Behavioral Pediatrics, 16*(1), 29–35.

Hustad, J. P., Barnett, N. P., Borsari, B., & Jackson, K. M. (2010). Web-based alcohol prevention for incoming college students: A randomized controlled trial. *Addictive Behaviors, 35*(3), 183–189. doi:10.1016/j.addbeh.2009.10.012

Hutton, P., Weinmann, S., Bola, J., & Read, J. (2013). Antipsychotic drugs. In J. Read & J. Dillon (Eds.), *Models of madness: Psychological, social and biological approaches to psychosis* (2nd ed.) (pp. 105–124). New York: Routledge/Taylor & Francis Group.

Hwu, H., Yeh, E. K., Chang, L. Y., & Yeh, Y. L. (1986). Chinese diagnostic interview schedule: II. A validity study on estimation of lifetime prevalence. *Acta Psychiatrica Scandinavica, 73*(4), 348–357. doi:10.1111/j.1600-0447.1986.tb02695.x

Hyland, A., Borland, R., Li, Q., Yong, H., McNeill, A., Fong, G., O'Connor, R. J., & Cummings, K. M. (2006). Individual level predictors of cessation behaviors among participants in the International Tobacco Control (ITC) Four Country Survey. *Tobacco Control, 15*(suppl 3), 83–94.

Hyler, S. E. (1998). DSM III at the cinema: Madness in the movies. *Comprehensive Psychiatry, 29,* 195–206.

Hynd, G. W., & Semrud-Clikeman, M. (1989). Dyslexia and brain morphology. *Psychological Bulletin, 106,* 447–482.

Hynd, G. W., Hern, K. L., Voeller, K. K., & Marshall, R. M. (1991). Neurobiological basis of attention-deficit hyperactivity disorder (ADHD). *School Psychology Review, 20*(2), 174–186.

Hynd, G. W., Semrud-Clikeman, M., Lorys, A. R., Novey, E. S., & Eliopulos, D. (1990). Brain morphology in developmental dyslexia, attention deficit disorder/hyperactivity. *Archives of Neurology, 47,* 919–926.

Hynd, G. W., Semrud-Clikeman, M., & Lyytinen, H. (1991). Brain imaging in learning disabilities. In J. E. Obrzut & G. W. Hynd (Eds.), *Neuropsychological foundations of learning disabilities: A handbook of issues, methods and practice* (pp. 475–511). New York: Academic Press.

I

Iacono, W. G. (1988). Eye movement abnormalities in schizophrenic and affective disorders. In C. W. Jhohnson & F. J. Pirozzolo (Eds.), *Neuropsychology of eye movements* (pp. 115–145). Hillsdale, NJ: Erlbaum.

Iacono, W. G., Moreau, M., Beiser, M., Fleming, J. A. E., & Lin, T. Y. (1992). Smooth-pursuit eye movement dysfunction and liability for schizophrenia: Implications for genetic modeling. *Journal of Abnormal Psychology, 101,* 104–116.

Iacovino, J. M., Gredysa, D. M., Altman, M., & Wilfley, D. E. (2012). Psychological treatments for binge eating disorder. *Current Psychiatry Reports, 14*(4), 432–446.

Iavarone, A., Ziello, A. R., Pastore, F., Fasanaro, A. M., & Poderico, C. (2014). Caregiver burden and coping strategies in caregivers of patients with Alzheimer's disease. *Neuropsychiatric Disease and Treatment, 10,* 1407–1413.

Iervolino, A. C., Perroud, N., Fullana, M., Guipponi, M., Cherkas, L., Collier, D. A., & Mataix-Cols, D. (2009). Prevalence and heritability of compulsive hoarding: A twin study. *The American Journal of Psychiatry, 166*(10), 1156–1161. doi:10.1176/appi.ajp.2009.08121789

Igreja, V., Dias-Lambranca, B., Hershey, D. A., Racin, L., Richters, A., & Reis, R. (2010). The epidemiology of spirit possession in the aftermath of mass political violence in Mozambique. *Social Science & Medicine, 71*(3), 592–599.

Ilardi, S. S. (2009). *The depression cure: The 6-step program to beat depression without drugs.* Cambridge, MA: Da Capo Press.

Ilardi, S. S. (2013, May). Depression is a disease of civilization. *TEDxEmory presentation.* Atlanta, GA. Retrieved on August 6, 2014 from https://www.youtube.com/watch?v=drv3BP0Fdi8

Imabayashi, E., Matsuda, H., Tabira, T., Arima, K., Araki, N., . . . Ishii, K. (2013). Comparison between brain CT and MRI for voxel-based morphometry of Alzheimer's disease. *Brain and Behavior, 3,* 487–493. doi: 10.1002/brb3.146.

Inglehart, R. (1990). *Culture shift in advanced industrial society.* Princeton, NJ: Princeton University Press.

Ingram, R. E. (1990). Self-focused attention in clinical disorders: Review and a conceptual model. *Psychological Bulletin, 107,* 156–176.

Ingram, R. E., & Luxton, D. D. (2005). Vulnerability-stress models. In B.L. Hankin & J. R. Z. Abela (Eds.), *Development of psychopathology: A vulnerability stress perspective* (pp. 32–46). Thousand Oaks, CA: Sage.

Inouye, S. K. (1998). Delirium in hospitalized older patients. *Clinical Geriatric Medicine, 14,* 745–764.

Inouye, S. K. (2006). Delirium in older persons. *New England Journal of Medicine, 354*(11), 1157–1165.

Inouye, S., & Marcantonio, E. (2007). Delirium. In J. Growdon & M. Rossor (Eds.), *The dementias* (pp. 285–312). Philadelphia: Butterworth-Heinemann Elsevier.

Insel, T. (2010). Rethinking schizophrenia. *Nature, 468,* 187–193.

Insel, T. R. (1992). Toward a neuroanatomy of obsessive-compulsive disorder. *Archives of General Psychiatry, 49,* 739–744.

Insel, T. R., & Wang, P. S. (2009). The STARD trial: Revealing the need for better treatments. *Psychiatric Services, 60*(11), 1466–1467. doi:10.1176/appi.ps.60.11.1466

Institute of Medicine. (1989). *Prevention and treatment of alcohol problems: Research opportunities.* Washington, DC: National Academy of Sciences.

Institute of Medicine (1994). *Reducing risks for mental disorders: Frontiers for prevention.* Washington, DC: National Academy Press.

Institute of Medicine (2008). Long-term consequences of traumatic brain injury. *Gulf War and Health,* Vol 7. Washington, DC: Institute of Medicine.

Institute of Medicine. (2014). *Treatment for posttraumatic stress disorder in military and veteran populations: Final assessment.* Retrieved on September 11, 2014 from http://www.iom.edu/Reports/2014/Treatment-for-Posttraumatic-Stress-Disorder-in-Military-and-Veteran-Populations-Final-Assessment.aspx

International OCD Foundation (2014). *Hoarding fact sheet.* Retrieved on September 15, 2014 from http://www.ocfoundation.org/uploadedFiles/Hoarding%20Fact%20Sheet.pdf?n=3557.

Irle, E., Lange, C., Sachsse, U., & Weniger, G. (2009). Further evidence that post-traumatic stress disorder but not dissociative disorders are related to amygdala and hippocampal size reduction in trauma-exposed individuals. *Acta Psychiatrica Scandinavica, 119,* 330–331.

Irvin, J. E., Bowers, C. A., Dunn, M. E., & Wang, M. C. (1999). Efficacy of relapse prevention: A meta-analytic review. *Journal of Consulting and Clinical Psychology, 67*(4), 563–570. doi:10.1037/0022-006X.67.4.563

Isen, A. M., Daubman, K. A., & Nowicki, G. P. (1987). Positive affect facilitates creative problem solving. *Journal of Personality and Social Psychology, 52,* 1122–1131.

Isenberg-Grzeda, E., Kutner, H. E., & Nicolson, S. E. (2012). Wernicke-Korsakoff-syndrome: Under-recognized and under-treated. *Psychosomatics: Journal of Consultation and Liaison Psychiatry, 53*(6), 507–516. doi:10.1016/j.psym.2012.04.008

Ito, T. A., Miller, N., & Pollock, V. E. (1996). Alcohol and aggression: A meta-analysis on the moderating effects of inhibitory cues, triggering events, and self-focused attention. *Psychological Bulletin, 120,* 60–82.

Ivanov, I., Bansal, R., Hao, X., Zhu, H., Kellndonk, C., Miller, L., . . . Peterson, B. S. (2010). Morphological abnormalities of the thalamus in youths with attention deficit hyperactivity disorder. *American Journal of Psychiatry, 167,* 397–408.

J

Jabbar, F., Leonard, M., Meehan, K., O'Connor, M., Cronin, C., Reynolds, P., . . . Meagher, D. (2011). Neuropsychiatric and cognitive profile of patients with *DSM-IV* delirium referred to an old age psychiatry consultation-liaison service. *International Psychogeriatrics, 23*(7), 1167–1174.

Jablensky, A. (1999). Schizophrenia: Epidemiology. *Current Opinion in Psychiatry, 12,* 19–28.

Jablensky, A., Sartorius, N., Ernberg, G., Anker, M., Korten, A., & Cooper, J. E. (1992). Schizophrenia: Manifestations, incidence, and course in different cultures. A World Health Organization ten country study. *Psychological Medical Monograph Supplement, 20,* 1–97.

Jackson, A. (2003). A systematic review of manic and depressive prodromes. *Journal of Affective Disorders, 74,* 209–217.

Jackson, A. C., Dowling, N. A., Honigman, R. J., Francis, K. L., & Kalus, A. M. (2012). The experience of teasing in elective cosmetic surgery patients. *Behavioral Medicine, 38*(4), 129–137. doi:10.1080/08964289.2012.703976

Jackson, C. L., Hanson, R. F., Amstadter, A. B., Saunders, B. E., & Kilpatrick, D. G. (2013). The longitudinal relation between peer violent victimization and delinquency: Results from a national representative sample of U.S. adolescents. *Journal of Interpersonal Violence, 28,* 1596–1616.

Jackson, D. N. (1989). *Basic Personality Inventory manual.* Port Huron, MI: Sigma Assessment Systems.

Jacobs, G. A. (1995). The development of a national plan for disaster mental health. *Professional Psychology: Research and Practice, 26,* 543–549.

Jacobs, M. (2013, April 4). Celebrity drug confessions: 20 stars reveal their partying ways. *The Huffington Post.* Retrieved on December 13, 2014 from http://www.huffingtonpost.com/2013/04/03/celebrity-drug-confessions_n_3009497.html

Jacobs, M. K., & Goodman, G. (1989). Psychology and self-help groups: Predictions on a partnership. *American Psychologist, 44,* 536–545.

Jacobson, J. W., Mulick, J. A., & Schwartz, A. A. (1995). A history of facilitated communication: Science, pseudoscience, and antiscience. Science working group on facilitated communication. *American Psychologist, 50*(9), 750–765.

Jacobson, N. S. (1991). Behavioral versus insight-oriented marital therapy: Labels can be misleading. *Journal of Consulting and Clinical Psychology, 59*(1), 142–145.

Jacobson, N. S., & Follette, W. C. (1985). Clinical significance of improvement resulting from two behavioral marital therapy components. *Behavior Therapy, 16,* 249–262.

Jacobson, N. S., Holtzworth-Monroe, A., & Schmaling, K. B. (1989). Marital therapy and spouse involvement in the treatment of depression, agoraphobia, and alcoholism. *Journal of Consulting and Clinical Psychology, 57,* 5–10.

Jacobson, N. S., Schmaling, K. B., & Holtzworth-Munroe, A. (1987). Component analysis of behavioral marital therapy: 2-year follow-up and prediction of relapse. *Journal of Marital and Family Therapy, 13*(2), 187–195.

Jacobson, R. (2014). Should children take antipsychotic drugs? Prescriptions are on the rise, but evidence for the drugs' safety and effectiveness is mixed. *Scientific American Mind, 25*(2). Retrieved on October 15, 2014 from http://www.scientificamerican.com/article/should-children-take-antipsychotic-drugs/

Jacobvitz, D., & Sroufe, L. A. (1987). The early caregiver-child relationship and attention-deficit disorder with hyperactivity in kindergarten: A prospective study. *Child Development, 58,* 1488–1495.

Jaffee v. Redmond, 133 L. 2d 758 (1996).

Jakobsen, J., Hansen, J., Simonsen, E., & Gluud, C. (2011). The effect of interpersonal psychotherapy and other psychodynamic therapies versus "treatment as usual" in patients with major depressive disorder. *Plos ONE, 6*(4). doi:10.1371/journal.pone.0019044

Jakobsen, K. D., Frederiksen, J. N., Parnas, J., & Werge, T. (2006). Diagnostic agreement of schizophrenia spectrum disorders among chronic patients with functional psychoses. *Psychopathology, 39,* 269–276.

James, J. E. (1994). Chronic effects of habitual caffeine consumption on laboratory and ambulatory blood pressure levels. *Journal of Cardiovascular Risk, 1*(2), 159–164.

Jamison, K. (1996). *An unquiet mind.* New York: Crown Publishing Group/Random House.

Jamison, K. R. (1989). Mood disorders and patterns of creativity in British writers and artists. *Psychiatry, 52,* 125–134.

Janet Kuramoto, S. S., Wilcox, H. C., & Latkin, C. A. (2013). Social integration and suicide-related ideation from a social network perspective: A longitudinal study among inner-city African Americans. *Suicide and Life-Threatening Behavior, 43*(4), 366–378. doi:10.1111/sltb.12023

Jang, K. L., Paris, J., Zweig-Frank, H., & Livesley, W. J. (1998). Twin study of dissociative experiences. *Journal of Abnormal Psychology, 186,* 345–351.

Janicak, P., Sharma, R., Israni, T., Dowd, S., Altman, E., & Davis, J. (1991). Effects of unilateral-non-dominant vs. bilateral ECT on memory and depression: A preliminary report. *Psychopharmacology Bulletin, 27,* 353–357.

Janis, I. (1958). *Psychological stress: Psychoanalytic and behavioral studies of surgical patients.* New York: John Wiley & Sons.

Jann, M., Lam, T. W., & Chang, W. H. (1993). Haloperidol and reduced haloperidol plasma concentrations in different ethnic populations and interindividual variabilities in haloperidol metabolism. In K. M. Lin, R. Poland, & G. Nakasaki (Eds.), *Psychopharmacology and psychobiology of ethnicity.* Washington, DC: American Psychiatric Association Press.

Jarvis, E. (1844). Insanity among the coloured population of the free states. *American Journal of Mental Science, 7,* 71–83.

Jauhar, S., McKenna, P. J., Radua, J., Fung, E., Salvador, R., & Laws, K. R. (2014). Cognitive-behavioural therapy for the symptoms of schizophrenia: Systematic review and meta-analysis with examination of potential bias. *The British Journal of Psychiatry, 204*(1), 20–29. doi:10.1192/bjp.bp.112.116285

Jauregui-Garrido, B., & Jauregui-Lobera, I. (2012). Sudden death in eating disorders. *Vascular Health Risk Management, 8,* 91–98. doi:10.2147/VHRM.S28652

Jeffers, H. P. (1991). *Who killed Precious.* New York: Pharos Books.

Jeffery, R. W. (1988). Dietary risk factors and their modification in cardiovascular disease. *Journal of Consulting and Clinical Psychology, 56,* 350–357.

Jellesma, F. C., Rieffe, C., Terwogt, M. M., & Westenberg, P. M. (2008). Do parents reinforce somatic complaints in their children? *Health Psychology, 27*(2), 280–285. doi:10.1037/0278-6133.27.2.280

Jellinek, E. M. (1946). The problem of alcohol. In Yale Studies on Alcohol (Ed.), *Alcohol, science, and society* (pp. 13–30). Westport, CT: Greenwood Press.

Jellinger, K. A., & Attems, J. (2010). Prevalence of dementia disorders in the oldest-old: An autopsy study. *Acta Neuropathologica, 119*(4), 421–433. doi: 10.1007/s00401-010-0654-5

Jelovac, A., Kolshus, E., & McLoughlin, D. M. (2013). Relapse following successful electroconvulsive therapy for major depression: A meta-analysis. *Neuropsychopharmacology, 38*(12), 2467–2474. doi:10.1038/npp.2013.149

Jenike, M. A., Baer, L., Ballentine, T., Martuza, R., Tynes, S., Giriunas, I., Buttolph, M., & Cassem, N. (1991). Cingulotomy for refractory obsessive-compulsive disorder: A long-term follow-up of 33 cases. *Archives of General Psychiatry, 48,* 548–555.

Jenike, M. A., Hyman, S., Baer, L., Holland, A., Minichiello, W., Buttolph, L., Summergrad, P., Seymour, J. & Ricciardi, J. (1990). A controlled trial of fluvoxamine in obsessive-compulsive disorder: Implications for a serotonergic theory. *American Journal of Psychiatry, 147,* 1209–1215.

Jenkins, C. D., Zyzanski, S., & Rosenman, R. H. (1979). *The Jenkins Activity Survey.* New York: Psychological Corporation.

Jensen, J. P., Bergin, A. E., & Greaves, D. W. (1990). The meaning of eclecticism: New survey and analysis of components. *Professional Psychology: Research and Practice, 21,* 124–130.

Jeong, S., & Lee, B. H. (2013). A multilevel examination of peer victimization and bullying preventions in schools. *Journal of Criminology, 2013.* doi:10.1155/2013/735397

Jespersen, A. F., Lalumiere, M. L., & Seto, M. C. (2009). Sexual abuse history among adult sex offenders and non-sex offenders: A meta-analysis. *Child Abuse & Neglect, 33*(3), 179–192.

Jesse, D., Kim, E., & Herndon, C. (2014). Social support and self-esteem as mediators between stress and antepartum depressive symptoms in rural pregnant women. *Research in Nursing & Health, 37,* 241–252.

Jessor, R., & Jessor, S. L. (1977). *Problem behavior and psychosocial development: A longitudinal study of youth.* San Diego: Academic Press.

Jha, P., Ramasundarahettige, C., Landsman, V., Rostron, B., Thun, M., Anderson, R. N., McAfee, T., & Peto, R. (2013). 21st century hazards of smoking and benefits of cessation in the United States. *New England Journal of Medicine, 368,* 341–350.

Joe, G. W., Dansereau, D. F., & Simpson, D. D. (1994)= Node-link mapping for counseling cocaine users in methadone treatment. *Journal of Substance Abuse, 6*(4), 393–406.

Johnson, B. H. (1973). *The alcohol movement in America: A study in cultural innovation.* Unpublished doctoral dissertation, University of Illinois at Urbana–Champaign. (University Microfilms No. 74-5603).

Johnson, J. G., Cohen, P., Kasen, S., & Brook, J. S. (2006). Dissociative disorders among adults in the community, impaired functioning, and axis I and II comorbidity. *Journal of Psychiatric Research, 40*(2), 131–140.

Johnson, M. A. (2014). Fed-up judge delays James Holmes' Theater shooting trial to January. *NBC News.* Retrieved on November 1, 2014 from http://www.nbcnews.com/news/us-news/fed-judge-delays-james-holmes-theater-shooting-trial-january-n235136

Johnson, M. R., Marazziti, D., Brawman-Mintzer, O., Emmanuel, N. P., Ware, M. R., Morton, W., . . . Lydiard, R. (1998). Abnormal peripheral benzodiazepine receptor density associated with generalized social phobia. *Biological Psychiatry, 43*(4), 306–309. doi:10.1016/S0006-3223(97)00390-9

Johnson, S. L., & Roberts, J. E. (1995). Life events and bipolar disorder: Implications from biological theories. *Psychological Bulletin, 117,* 434–449.

Johnson, S. L., Fulford, D., & Eisner, L. (2009). Psychosocial mechanisms in bipolar disorder. In K. Salzinger and M. R. Serper (Eds.), *Behavioral mechanisms and psychopathology: Advancing the explanation of its nature, cause, and treatment* (pp. 77–106). Washington, DC: American Psychological Association. doi:10.1037/11884-003

Johnson, S. L., Ruggero, C. J., & Carver, C. S. (2005). Cognitive, behavioral, and affective responses to reward: Links with hypomanic symptoms. *Journal of Social and Clinical Psychology, 24*(6), 894–906. doi:10.1521/jscp.2005.24.6.894

Johnson, S. L., Winett, C. A., Meyer, B., Greenhouse, W. J., & Miller, I. (1999). Social support and the course of bipolar disorder. *Journal of Abnormal Psychology, 108,* 558–566.

Johnson, S. M., & Greenberg, L. S. (1985). Differential effects of experiential and problem-solving interventions in resolving marital conflict. *Journal of Consulting and Clinical Psychology, 53,* 175–184.

Joinson, C., Heron, J., Butler, U., von Gontard, A., & The Avon Longitudinal Study of Parents and Children Study Team (2006). Psychological differences between children with and without soiling problems. *Pediatrics, 117,* 1575–1584.

Jonas, D. E., Amick, H. R., Feltner, C., Bobashev, G., Thomas, K., Wines, R., . . . Garbutt, J. C. (2014). Pharmacotherapy for adults with alcohol use disorders in outpatient settings: A systematic review and meta-analysis. *JAMA: Journal of the American Medical Association, 311*(18), 1889–1900.

Jones, M. C. (1924). A laboratory study of fear. The case of Peter. *Pedagogical Seminary, 31,* 308–315.

Jones, P. B., Barnes, T. E., Davies, L., Dunn, G., Lloyd, H., Hayhurst, K. P., . . . Lewis, S. W. (2006). Randomized controlled trial of the effect on quality of life of second- vs first-generation antipsychotic drugs in schizophrenia. *Archives of General Psychiatry, 63*(10), 1079–1087. doi:10.1001/archpsyc.63.10.1079

Jones, S. H., Sellwood, W., & McGovern, J. (2005). Psychological therapies for bipolar disorder: The role of model-driven approaches to therapy integration. *Bipolar Disorders, 7*(1), 22–32. doi:10.1111/j.1399-5618.2004.00157.x

Jones, W. R., & Morgan, J. F. (2010). Eating disorders in men: A review of the literature. *Journal of Public Mental Health, 9*(2), 23–31.

Jónsson, H. H., & Hougaard, E. E. (2009). Group cognitive-behavioural therapy for obsessive-compulsive disorder: A systematic review and meta-analysis. *Acta Psychiatrica Scandinavica, 119*(2), 98–106. doi:10.1111/j.1600-0447.2008.01270.x

Jordaan, G. P., & Emsley, R. (2014). Alcohol-induced psychotic disorder: A review. *Metabolic Brain Disease, 29*(2), 231–243. doi:10.1007/s11011-013-9457-4

Jørgensen, C. H., Pedersen, B., & Tønnesen, H. (2011). The efficacy of disulfiram for the treatment of alcohol use disorder. *Alcoholism: Clinical and Experimental Research, 35*(10), 1749–1758. doi:10.1111/j.1530-0277.2011.01523.x

Jorm, A. F. (1994). A method for measuring dementia as a continuum in community surveys. In F. A. Huppert, C. Brayne, & D. W. O'Connor (Eds.), *Dementia and normal aging* (pp. 244–253). Cambridge: Cambridge University Press.

Josefsson, T. T., Lindwall, M. M., & Archer, T. T. (2014). Physical exercise intervention in depressive disorders: Meta-analysis and systematic review. *Scandinavian Journal of Medicine & Science in Sports, 24*(2), 259–272. doi:10.1111/sms.12050

Joseph, J., & Leo, J. (2006). Genetic relatedness and the lifetime risk for being diagnosed with schizophrenia: Gottesman's 1991 figure 10 reconsidered. *Journal of Mind and Behavior, 27*(1), 73–90.

Joseph, S., Williams, R., & Yule, W. (1995). Psychosocial perspectives on post-traumatic stress. *Clinical Psychology Review, 15*, 515–544.

Joshi, D., Koirala, S., Lamichhane, S., Paladugu, A., Johal, R., & Lippmann, S. (2010). Capgras syndrome in postictal delirium. *Psychiatry, 7*, 37–39.

Joy, D., Probert, R., Bisson, J, & Shepherd, J. (2000). Posttraumatic stress reactions after injury. *Journal of Trauma, 48*, 490–494.

Joyce, J. N., Shane, A., Lexow, N., Winokur, A., Casanova, M. F., & Kleinman, J. E. (1993). Serotonin uptake sites and serotonin receptors are altered in the limbic system of schizophrenics. *Neuropsychopharmacology, 5*(4), 315–336.

Judd, L. L. (2012). Dimensional paradigm of the long-term course of unipolar major depressive disorder. *Depression and Anxiety, 29*(3), 167–171. doi:10.1002/da.21934\

Juliano, L. M., Evatt, D. P., Richards, B. D., & Griffiths, R. R. (2012). Characterization of individuals seeking treatment for caffeine dependence. *Psychology of Addictive Behaviors, 26*(4), 948–954. doi:10.1037/a0027246

Julien, R. (1992). *A primer of drug action* (6th ed.). New York: Freeman.

Julien, R. (1995). *A primer of drug action* (7th ed.). New York: Freeman.

K

Kabat-Zinn, J. (1990). *Full catastrophe living: Using the wisdom of your body and mind to face stress, pain, and illness.* New York: Delacorte Press.

Kafka, M. P. (1994). Sertraline pharmacotherapy for paraphilias and paraphilia-related disorders: An open trial. *Annals of Clinical Psychiatry, 3*, 189–195.

Kagan, J. (1989). Temperamental contributions to social behavior. *American Psychologist, 44*, 668–674.

Kahn, A., Mirolo, H., Lai, H., Claypoole, K., Bierut, L., Malik, R., & Bhang, J. (1993). ECT and TRH: Cholinergic involvement in a cognitive deficit stale. *Psychopharmacology Bulletin, 29*, 345–352.

Kahn, E. (1985). Heinz Kohut and Carl Rogers: A timely comparison. *American Psychologist, 40*, 893–904.

Kahn, J. S., Kehle, T. J., Jenson, W. R., & Clark, E. (1990). Comparison of cognitive-behavioral, relaxation and self-modeling interventions for depression among middle-school students. *School Psychology Review, 19*, 196–211.

Kahn, R. J., McNair, D., Lipman, R., Covi, L., Rickels, K., Fisher, S., & Frankenthaler, L. (1986). Imipramine and chlordiazepoxide in depressive and anxiety disorders. II: Efficacy in anxious outpatients. *Archives of General Psychiatry, 43*, 79–85.

Kahn, R., Jampala, V. C., Dong, K., & Vedak, C. (1994). Speech abnormalities in tardive dyskinesia. *American Journal of Psychiatry, 151*, 760–762.

Kahneman, D., Diener, E., & Schwarz, N. (Eds.). (1999). *Well-being: The foundations of hedonic psychology.* New York: Russell Sage Foundation.

Kalaria, R. N., Maestre, G. E., Arizaga, R., Friedland, R. P., Galasko, D., Hall, K., . . . Antuono, P. (2008). Alzheimer's disease and vascular dementia in developing countries: prevalence, management, and risk factors. *The Lancet Neurology, 7*(9), 812–826. doi: 10.1016/S1474-4422(08)70169-8

Kaler, S. R., & Freeman, B. J. (1994). Analysis of environmental deprivation: Cognitive and social development in Romanian orphans. *Journal of Child Psychology and Psychiatry and Allied Disciplines, 35*(4), 769–781.

Kalra, G., Bhugra, D., & Shah, N. (2012). Cultural aspects of schizophrenia. *International Review of Psychiatry, 24*(5), 441–449. doi:10.3109/09540261.2012.708649

Kandel, D. B., & Andrews, K. (1987). Processes of adolescent socialization by parents and peers. *International Journal of Addiction, 22*(4), 319–342.

Kandel, D. B., Kessler, R. C., & Marguiles, R. Z. (1978). Antecedents of adolescent initiation into stages of drug use: A developmental analysis. In D. B. Kandel (Ed.), *Longitudinal research on drug use.* Washington, DC: Hemisphere.

Kandel, E. R., Schwartz, J. H., & Jessell, J. M. (1995). *Essentials of neural science and behavior.* Norwalk, CT: Prentice Hall.

Kane, J. M., & Lieberman, J. A. (1992). *Adverse effects of psychotropic drugs.* New York: Guilford Press.

Kane, J. M., Honigfeld, G., Singer, J. & Melzer, H., (1988). Clozapine for the treatment-resistant schizophrenic: A double-blind comparison with chlorpromazine. *Archives of General Psychiatry, 45*, 789–796.

Kaner, E. S., Dickinson, H. O., Beyer, F., Pienaar, E., Schlesinger, C., Campbell, F., . . . Heather, N. (2009). The effectiveness of brief alcohol interventions in primary care settings: A systematic review. *Drug and Alcohol Review, 28*(3), 301–323. doi:10.1111/j.1465-3362.2009.00071.x

Kanner, A. D., Coyne, J. C., Schaefer, C., & Lazarus, R. S. (1981). Comparison of two modes of stress measurement: Daily hassles and uplifts versus major life events. *Journal of Behavioral Medicine, 14*, 1–39.

Kanner, L. (1943). Autistic disturbances of affective contact. *Nervous Child, 2*, 217–230.

Kanner, L., & Lesser, L. (1958). *Early infantile autism: The pediatric clinics of North America.* Philadelphia: W. B. Saunders.

Kaplan, A. S., Garfinkel, P. E., Darby, P. L., & Garner, D. M. (1983). Carbamazepine in the treatment of bulimia. *American Journal of Psychiatry, 140*, 1225–1226.

Kaplan, H., Wamboldt, R., & Barnhardt, R. (1986). Behavioral effects of dietary sucrose in disturbed children. *American Journal of Psychology, 7*, 143.

Kaplan, H. I., Saddock, B. J., & Grebb, J. A. (1994). *Synopsis of psychiatry: Behavioral sciences, clinical psychiatry.* Baltimore: Williams & Wilkins.

Kaplan, H. S. (1974). *Disorders of sexual desire.* New York, NY: Simon & Schuster

Kaplan, H. S. (1974, October). Fiction and fantasy: No-nonsense therapy for six sexual malfunctions. *Psychology Today*, 77–86.

Kaplan, H. S. (1977). Hypoactive sexual desire. *Journal of Sex and Marital Therapy, 3*, 3–9.

Kaplan, H. S. (1979). *Disorders of sexual desire.* New York: Brunner/Mazel.

Kaplan, H. S. (1988). Intimacy disorders and sexual panic states. *Journal of Sex and Marital Therapy, 14*, 3–12.

Kaplan, H. S., & Owett, T. (1993). The female androgen deficiency syndrome. *Journal of Sex & Marital Therapy, 19*, 3–24.

Kaplan, K., Talbot, L., Gruber, J., & Harvey, A. (2012). Evaluating sleep in bipolar disorder: Comparison between actigraphy, polysomnography, and sleep diary. *Bipolar Disorders, 14*(8), 870–879. doi:10.1111/bdi.1202

Kaplan, M. (1983). A woman's view of *DSM-III. American Psychologist, 38*, 786–792.

Kaplan, R M. (1994). The use of serotonergic uptake inhibitors in the treatment of premature ejaculation. *Journal of Sex and Marital Therapy, 20*, 321–324.

Kapur, S., & Mann, J. J. (1993). Antidepressant action and the neurobiologic effects of ECT: Human studies. In C. E. Coffey (Ed.), *The clinical science of electroconvulsive therapy* (pp. 235–250). Washington, DC: American Psychiatric Press.

Karasek, R. A. (1979). Job demands, job decision latitude and mental strain: Implications for job redesign. *Administrative Science Quarterly, 24*, 285–308.

Karasu, T. B. (1990). Toward a clinical model of psychotherapy for depression. I: Systematic comparison of three psychotherapies. *American Journal of Psychiatry, 147*, 133–147.

Kardener, S. H., Fuller, M., & Mensch, I. N. (1973). A survey of physicians' attitudes and practices regarding erotic and noneroetic contact with patients. *American Journal of Psychiatry, 130*, 1077–1081.

Karg, K., Burmeister, M., Shedden, K., & Sen, S. (2011). The serotonin transporter promoter variant (5-HTTLPR), stress, and depression meta-analysis revisited: Evidence of genetic moderation. *Archives of General Psychiatry, 68*(5), 444–454. doi:10.1001/archgenpsychiatry.2010.189. Epub 2011 Jan 3.

Kartsounis, L. D., Poynton, A., Bridges, P. K., & Bartlett, J. R. (1991). Neuropsychological correlates of stereotaxic subcaudate tractotomy. *Brain, 114*, 2657–2673.

Karwoski, L. (2008). Therapeutic lifestyle change: Piloting a novel group-based intervention for depression. *Dissertation Abstracts International, 68*, 4828.

Karyadi, K., Coskunpinar, A., Dir, A. L., & Cyders, M. A. (2013). The interactive effects of affect lability, negative urgency, and sensation seeking on young adult problematic drinking. *Journal of Addiction, 2013*, 1–7.

Kasper, L. J., Alderson, R. M., & Hudec, K. L. (2012). Moderators of working memory deficits in children with attention-deficit/hyperactivity disorder (ADHD): A meta-analytic review. *Clinical Psychology Review, 32*, 605–617.

Katerberg, H., Delucchi, K. L., Stewart, S., Lochner, C., Denys, D. P., Stack, D. E., . . . Cath, D. C. (2010). Symptom dimensions in OCD: Item-level factor analysis and heritability estimates. *Behavior Genetics, 40*(4), 505–517. doi:10.1007/s10519-010-9339-z

Katerndahl, D. A., & Realini, J. P. (1993). Lifetime prevalence of panic states. *American Journal of Psychiatry, 150*(2), 246–249.

Kato, K., Sullivan, P. F., Evengård, B., & Pedersen, N. L. (2009). A population-based twin study of functional somatic syndromes. *Psychological Medicine, 39*(3), 497–505. doi:10.1017/S0033291708003784

Katon, W. (1993). Somatization disorder, hypochondriasis, and conversion disorder. In D. L. Dunner (Ed.), *Current psychiatric therapy* (pp. 314–320). Philadelphia: W. B. Saunders.

Katon, W., & Russo, J. (1989). Somatic symptoms and depression. *Journal of Family Practice, 29*, 65–69.

Katon, W., Ries, R. K., & Kleinman, A. (1984). The prevalence of somatization in primary care. *Comprehensive Psychiatry, 25*(2), 208–215. doi:10.1016/0010-440X(84)90009-9

Katon, W., Von Korff, M., Lin, E., Liscomb, P., Russo, J., Wagner, E., & Polk, E. (1990). Distressed high utilizers of medical care. DSM-III-R diagnosis and treatment needs. *General Hospital Psychiatry, 12,* 355–362.

Katz, I. R., Curyto, K. J., TenHave, T., Mossey, J., Sands, L., & Kallan, M. J. (2001). Validating the diagnosis of delirium and evaluating its association with deterioration over a one-year period. *American Journal of Geriatric Psychiatry, 9,* 148–159.

Katz, J. L., Boyar, R., Roffwarg, H., Hellman, L., & Weiner, H. (1978). Weight and circadian luteinizing hormone secretory pattern in anorexia nervosa. *Psychosomatic Medicine, 40,* 549–567.

Katz, M. M., Bowden, C. L., Berman, N., & Frazer, A. (2006). Resolving the onset of antidepressants' clinical actions: Critical for clinical practice and new drug development. *Journal of Clinical Psychopharmacology, 26*(6), 549–553. doi:10.1097/01.jcp.0000246220.04422.de

Katz-Bearnot, S. (2010). Menopause, depression, and loss of sexual desire: A psychodynamic contribution. *Journal of the American Academy of Psychoanalysis & Dynamic Psychiatry, 38*(1), 99–116.

Katzman, R., & Kawas, C. (1994). The epidemiology of dementia and Alzheimer's disease. In R. D. Terry, R. Katz-man, & K. L. Bick (Eds.), *Alzheimer's disease* (pp. 105–121). New York: Raven Press.

Katzman, R., & Saitoh, T. (1991). Advances in Alzheimer's disease. *FASEB Journal, 5,* 278–286.

Kaufman, H. S., & Biren, P. L. (1977). Persistent reversers: Poor readers, writers, spellers? *Academic Therapy, 12,* 209–217.

Kavanagh, D. J. (1992). Recent developments in expressed emotion in schizophrenia. *British Journal of Psychiatry, 148,* 601–620.

Kawachi, I., Colditz, G. A., Ascherio, A., Rimm, E. B., Giovannucci, E., Stampfer, M. J., & Willett, W. C. (1993). Prospective study of phobic anxiety and risk of coronary heart disease in men. *Circulation, 89,* 1992–1997.

Kaye, W. H., & Weltzin, T. E. (1991). Neurochemistry of bulimia nervosa. *Journal of Clinical Psychiatry, 52,* 21–28.

Kaye, W. H., Bulik, C. M., Thornton, L., Barbarich, N., & Masters, K. (2004). Comorbidity of anxiety disorders with anorexia and bulimia nervosa. *American Journal of Psychiatry, 161*(12), 2215–2221.

Kazdin, A. E. (1973). Covert modeling and reduction of avoidance behavior. *Journal of Abnormal Psychology, 81,* 87–95.

Kazdin, A. E. (1994a). Psychotherapy for children and adolescents. In A. E. Bergin & S. L. Garfield (Eds.), *Handbook of psychotherapy and behavior change* (pp. 543–594). New York: John Wiley & Sons.

Kazdin, A. E. (1994b). Methodology, design, and evaluation in psychotherapy research. In A. E. Bergin & S. L. Garfield (Eds.), *Handbook of psychotherapy and behavior change* (pp. 19–71). New York: John Wiley & Sons.

Kazdin, A. E. (2003). Problem-solving skills training and parent management training for conduct disorder. In A. E. Kazdin & J. R. Weisz (Eds.), *Evidence-based psychotherapies for children and adolescents* (pp. 241–262). New York: Guilford.

Kazdin, A. E. (2007). Psychosocial treatments for conduct disorder in children and adolescents. In P.E. Nathan & J.M. Gorman (Eds.), *A guide to treatments that work* (3rd ed., pp. 71–104). New York: Oxford University Press.

Kazdin, A. E., Bass, D., Siegel, T., & Thomas, C. (1989). Cognitive-behavioral therapy and relationship therapy in the treatment of children referred for antisocial behavior. *Journal of Consulting and Clinical Psychology, 26,* 57, 522–535.

Kazdin, A. E., Esveldt-Dawson, K., French, N. H., & Unis, A. S. (1987). Problem-solving skills training and relationship therapy in the treatment of antisocial child behavior. *Journal of Consulting and Clinical Psychology, 55,* 76–85.

Kazdin, A. E., & Wassell, G. (2000). Therapeutic changes in children, parents, and families resulting from treatment of children with conduct problems. *Journal of the American Academy of Child and Adolescent Psychology, 39,* 414–420.

Kazdin, A. E., & Wilcoxin, L. A. (1976). Systematic desensitization and nonspecific treatment effects: A methodological evaluation. *Psychological Bulletin, 83,* 729–758.

Kazdin, A. E., & Wilson, G. T. (1978). *Evaluation of behavior therapy: Issues, evidence and research strategies.* Cambridge, MA: Ballinger.

Keane, T. M., Fairbank, J. A., Caddell, J. M., & Zimering, R. T. (1989). Implosive (flooding) therapy reduces symptoms of PTSD in Vietnam combat veterans. *Behavior Therapy, 20,* 245–260.

Keane, T. M., Kolb, L. C., Kaloupek, D. G., Orr, S. P., Blanchard, E. B., Thomas, R. G., . . . Lavori, P. W. (1998). Utility of psychophysiology measurement in the diagnosis of posttraumatic stress disorder: Results from a department of Veteran's Affairs cooperative study. *Journal of Consulting and Clinical Psychology, 66,* 914–923. doi:10.1037/0022-006X.66.6.914

Keane, T. M., Zimering, R. T., & Caddell, J. (1985). A behavioral formulation of post-traumatic stress disorder in Vietnam veterans. *The Behavior Therapist, 8,* 9–12.

Kearns, M. C., Ressler, K. J., Zatzick, D., & Rothbaum, B. (2012). Early interventions for PTSD: A review. *Depression and Anxiety, 29,* 833–842. doi:10.1002/da.21997

Keefe, F. J., Dunsmore, J., & Burnett, R. (1992). Behavioral and cognitive-behavioral approaches to chronic pain: Recent advances and future directions. *Journal of Consulting and Clinical Psychology, 60,* 528–536.

Keeley, R. D., Brody, D., Engel, M., Moralez, M., Nordstrom, K., Burke, B. L., Dickinson, M., & Emsermann, C. (2015). *Clinical effectiveness of training primary care providers to use motivational interviewing when treating major depression: A cluster randomized trial.* Manuscript in preparation.

Keeley, R. D., Burke, B. L., Brody, D., Dimidjian, S., Engel, M., . . . Kaplan, J. (2014, in press). Training to use motivational interviewing techniques for depression: A cluster randomized trial. *Journal of the American Board of Family Medicine, 27*(5).

Keen, L., Khan, M., Clifford, L., Harrell, P. T., & Latimer, W. W. (2014). Injection and noninjection drug use and infectious disease in Baltimore city: Differences by race. *Addictive Behaviors, 39*(9), 1325–1328. doi:10.1016/j.addbeh.2014.04.020

Keller, L. S., & Butcher, J. N. (1991). *Assessment of chronic pain patients with the MMPI-2.* Minneapolis: University of Minnesota Press.

Keller, M. B., Baker, L. A., & Russell, C. W. (1993). Classification and treatment of dysthymia. In D. D. Dunner (Ed.), *Current psychiatric therapy* (pp. 210–214). Philadelphia: W. B. Saunders.

Keller, M. B., Lavori, P. W., Mueller, T. I., Endicott, J., Coryell, W., Hirschfeld, R. M. A., & Shea, T. (1992). Time to recovery, chronicity, and levels of psychopathology in major depression. A 5-year prospective follow-up of 431 subjects. *Archives of General Psychiatry, 49,* 809–816.

Kellner, C., Nixon, D., & Bernstein, H. (1991). ECT-drug interactions: A review. *Psychopharmacology Bulletin, 27,* 595–609.

Kelly, J. A., & Murphy, D. A. (1992). Psychological interventions with AIDS and HIV: Prevention and treatment. *Journal of Consulting and Clinical Psychology, 60,* 576–585.

Kelly, J. A., St. Lawrence, J. S., Hood, H. V., & Brashfield, T. L. (1989). Behavioral intervention to reduce AIDS risk activities. *Journal of Consulting and Clinical Psychology, 57,* 60–67.

Kelly, M. P., Strassberg, D. S., & Turner, C. M. (2006). Behavioral assessment of couples' communication in female orgasmic disorder. *Journal of Sex & Marital Therapy, 32*(2), 81–95.

Keltner, B. (1994). Home environments of mothers with mental retardation. *Mental Retardation, 32,* 123–127.

Kendall, P. C. (1994). Treating anxiety disorders in children: Results of a randomized clinical trial. *Journal of Consulting and Clinial Psychology, 62,* 100–110.

Kendall, P. C., & Braswell, L. (1985). *Cognitive behavioral modification with impulsive children.* New York: Guilford Press.

Kendall, P. C., & Clarkin, J. F. (1992). Introduction to special section: Comorbidity and treatment implications. *Journal of Consulting and Clinical Psychology, 60,* 833–834.

Kendall, P. C., & Watson, D. (1989). *Anxiety and depression: Distinctive and overlapping features.* San Diego: Academic Press.

Kendall, T. (2011). The rise and fall of the atypical antipsychotics. *The British Journal of Psychiatry, 199*(4), 266–268. doi:10.1192/bjp.bp.110.083766

Kendler, K. S., & Diehl, S. R. (1993). The genetics of schizophrenia: A current genetic-epidemiologic perspective. *Schizophrenia Bulletin, 19,* 87–112.

Kendler, K. S., Gatz, M., Gardner, C. O., & Pedersen, N. (2006). A Swedish national twin study of lifetime major depression. *The American Journal of Psychiatry, 163*(1), 109–114. doi:10.1176/appi.ajp.163.1.109

Kendler, K. S., Gruenberg, A. M., & Strauss, J. S. (1981). An independent analysis of the Copenhagen sample of the Danish adoption study of schizophrenia. *Archives of General Psychiatry, 38,* 982–974.

Kendler, K. S., Karkowski, L. M., & Prescott, C. A. (1999). Causal relationship between stressful life events and the onset of major depression. *The American Journal of Psychiatry, 156*(6), 837–841.

Kendler, K. S., McGuire, M., Gruenberg, A., O'Hare, A., Spellman, M., & Walsh, D. (1993a). The Roscommon family study. I: Methods, diagnosis of probands, and risk of schizophrenia in relatives. *Archives of General Psychiatry, 50,* 527–540.

Kendler, K. S., McGuire, M., Gruenberg, A., O'Hare, A., Spellman, M., & Walsh, D. (1993b). The Roscommon family study. III: Schizophrenia-related personality disorders in relatives. *Archives of General Psychiatry, 50,* 781–788.

Kendler, K. S., McGuire, M., Gruenberg, A., O'Hare, A., Spellman, M., & Walsh, D. (1993c). The Roscommon family study. IV: Affective illness, anxiety disorders, and alcoholism in relatives. *Archives of General Psychiatry, 50,* 952–960.

Kendler, K. S., Neale, M., Kessler, R. C., Heath, A., & Eaves, L. (1992a). The genetic epidemiology of phobias in women: The interrelationship of agoraphobia, social phobia, situational phobia, and simple phobia. *Archives of General Psychiatry, 49,* 273–281.

Kendler, K. S., Neale, M., Kessler, R. C., Heath, A., & Eaves, L. (1992b). Major depression and generalized anxiety disorder: Same genes, (partly) different environments. *Archives of General Psychiatry, 49,* 716–725.

Kendler, K. S., Neale, M., Kessler, R. C., Heath, A., & Eaves, L. (1992c). Generalized anxiety disorder in women: A population-based twin study. *Archives of General Psychiatry, 49,* 267–272.

Kendler, K. S., Walters, E. E., Neale, M. C., Kessler, R. C., Heath, A. C., & Eaves, L. J. (1995). The structure of the genetic and environmental risk factors for six major psychiatric disorders in women: Phobia, generalized anxiety disorder, panic disorder, bulimia, major depression, and alcoholism. *Archives of General Psychiatry, 52,* 374–383.

Kendurkar, A. (2008). Presentation of catatonia in mood disorder vs. schizophrenia. *German Journal of Psychiatry, 11*(1), 32–33.

Kennard, C. (2014). *Clock drawing test.* Retrieved on December 4, 2014 from http://alzheimers.about.com/od/diagnosisissues/a/clock_test.htm

Kent, D. A., Tomasson, K., & Coryell, W. (1995). Course and outcome of conversion and somatization disorders. A four-year follow-up. *Psychosomatics, 36*(2), 138–144. doi:10.1016/S0033-3182(95)71683-8

Keough, M. E., Timpano, K. R., & Schmidt, N. B. (2009). Ataques de nervios: Culturally bound and distinct from panic attacks? *Depression and Anxiety, 26*(1), 16–21. doi:10.1002/da.20498

Kernberg, O. (1967). Borderline personality organization. *Journal of the American Psychoanalytic Association, 15,* 641–685.

Kernberg, O. F. (1976). *Object relations, theory and clinical psychoanalysis.* New York: Jason Aaronson.

Kernberg, O. F. (1984). *Severe personality disorders.* New Haven, CT: Yale University Press.

Kernberg, O. F., Selzer, M. A., Koenigsberg, H. W., Carr, A. C., & Appelbaum, A. H. (1989). *Psychodynamic psychotherapy of borderline patients.* New York: Basic Books.

Kerner, B. (2014). Genetics of bipolar disorder. *Applied Clinical Genetics, 7,* 33–42. doi:10.2147/tacg.s39297. PMID 24683306

Keshavan, M. S., Tandon, R., Boutros, N. N., & Naasrallah, H. A. (2008). Schizophrenia, just the facts: What we know in 2008. Part 3: Neurobiology. *Schizophrenia Research, 106,* 89–107.

Keso, L., & Salaspuro, M. (1990). Inpatient treatment of employed alcoholics: A randomized clinical trial on Hazelden-type and traditional treatment. *Alcoholism in Clinical and Experimental Research, 14*(4), 584–589.

Kessler, R. C., Angermeyer, M., Anthony, J. C., De Graaf, R., Demyttenaere, K., . . . Gasquet, I. (2007). Lifetime prevalence and age-of-onset distributions of mental disorders in the World Health Organization's World Mental Health Survey Initiative. *World Psychiatry, 6,* 168–176.

Kessler, R. C., Berglund, P., Demler, O., Jin, R., Koretz, D., Merikangas, K. R., . . . Wang, P. S. (2003). The epidemiology of major depressive disorder: Results from the National Comorbidity Survey Replication (NCS-R). *JAMA: Journal of the American Medical Association, 289*(23), 3095–3105. doi:10.1001/jama.289.23.3095

Kessler, R. C., Berglund, P., Demler, O., Jin, R., Merikangas, K. R., & Walters, E. E. (2005). Lifetime prevalence and age-of-onset distributions of DSM-IV disorders in the National Comorbidity Survey Replication. *Archives of General Psychiatry, 62,* 593–602.

Kessler, R. C., & Bromet, E. J. (2013). The epidemiology of depression across cultures. *Annual Review of Public Health, 34,* 119–138. doi:10.1146/annurev-publhealth-031912-114409

Kessler, R. C., Chiu, W., Demler, O., & Walters, E. E. (2005). Prevalence, severity, and comorbidity of 12-month *DSM-IV* disorders in the National Comorbidity Survey Replication. *Archives of General Psychiatry, 62*(6), 617–627. doi:10.1001/archpsyc.62.6.617

Kessler, R. C., Gruber, M., Hettema, J. M., Hwang, I., Sampson, N., & Yonkers, K. A. (2008). Co-morbid major depression and generalized anxiety disorders in the National Comorbidity Survey follow-up. *Psychological Medicine, 38*(3), 365–374.

Kessler, R. C., McGonagle, K. A., Zhao, S., Nelson, C. B., . . . Hughes, M. (1994). Lifetime and 12-month prevalence of *DSM-III-R* psychiatric disorders in the United States: Results from the National Comorbidity Study. *Archives of General Psychiatry, 51,* 8–19.

Kessler, R. C., Petukhova, M., Sampson, N. A., Zaslavsky, A. M., & Wittchen, H. (2012). Twelve-month and lifetime prevalence and lifetime morbid risk of anxiety and mood disorders in the United States. *International Journal of Methods in Psychiatric Research, 21,* 169–184. doi:10.1002/mpr.1359

Kessler, R. C., Sonnega, A., Bromet, E., Hughes, M., & Nelson, C. B. (1995). Posttraumatic stress disorder in the National Comorbidity Survey. *Archives of General Psychiatry, 52,* 1048–1060.

Kessler, R. C., & Ustun, T. B. (2004). The World Mental Health (WMH) survey initiative version of the World Health Organization (WHO) Composite International Diagnostic Interview (CIDI). *International Journal of Methods in Psychiatric Research, 13,* 93–121.

Kettlewell, P. W., Mizes, J. S., & Wasylyshyn, N. A. (1992). A cognitive-behavioral group treatment of bulimia. *Behavior Therapy, 23,* 657–670.

Kety, S. S. (1990). Genetics factors in suicide: Family, twin, and adoption studies. In S. J. Blumenthal & D. J. Kupfer (Eds.), *Suicide over the life cycle: Risk factors, assessment, and treatment of suicidal patients* (pp. 127–134). Washington, DC: American Psychiatric Press.

Keuthen, N. J., Koran, L. M., Aboujaoude, E., Large, M. D., & Serpe, R. T. (2010). The prevalence of pathologic skin picking in U.S. adults. *Comprehensive Psychiatry, 51*(2), 183–186. doi:10.1016/j.comppsych.2009.04.003

Keyes, D. (1981). *The minds of Billy Milligan.* New York: Random House.

Khachaturian, Z. S., Phelps, C. H., & Buckholtz, N. S. (1994). The prospect for developing treatments for Alzheimer's disease. In R. D. Terry, R. Katzman, & K. L. Bick (Eds.). *Alzheimer's disease* (pp. 445–454). New York: Raven Press.

Kiecolt-Glaser, J. K., & Glaser, R. (1987). Chronic stress and immunity in family caregivers of Alzheimer's disease victims. *Psychosomatic Medicine, 49,* 523–535.

Kiecolt-Glaser, J. K., & Glaser, R. (1992). Psychoneuroimmunology: Can psychological interventions modulate immunity? *Journal of Consulting and Clinical Psychology, 60,* 569–575.

Kiecolt-Glaser, J. K., Malarkey, W. B., Chee, M. A., Newton, T., Cacioppo, J. T., Mao, H.-Y, & Glaser, R. (1993). Negative behavior during marital conflict is associated with immunological down-regulation. *Psychosomatic Medicine, 55,* 395–409.

Kiecolt-Glaser, J. K., McGuire, L., Robles, T., & Glaser, R. (2002). Psychoneuroimmunology: Psychological influences on immune function and health. *Journal of Consulting and Clinical Psychology, 70,* 537–547.

Kiehl, K. A., Smith, A. M., Hare, R. D., Mendrek, A., Forster, B. B., Brink, J., & Liddle, P. F. (2001). Limbic abnormalities in affective processing by criminal psychopaths as revealed by functional magnetic resonance imaging. *Biological Psychiatry, 50,* 677–684.

Kierlin, L. (2008). Sleeping without a pill: Nonpharmacologic treatments for insomnia. *Journal of Psychiatric Practice, 14*(6), 403–407. doi:10.1097/01.pra.0000341896.73926.6c

Kiesler, C. (1991). Changes in general hospital psychiatric care, 1980–1985. *American Psychologist, 46,* 416–421.

Kiesler, C., & Simpkins, C. (1991). The de facto national system of psychiatric inpatient care: Piecing together the national puzzle. *American Psychologist, 46,* 579–584.

Kiesler, C. A. (1993). Mental health policy and mental hospitalization. *Current directions in psychological science, 2*(3), 93–95. doi:10.1111/1467-8721.ep10770950

Kiesler, C. A., & Sibulkin, A. E. (1987). *Mental hospitalization: Myths and facts about a national crisis.* Beverly Hills, CA: Sage.

Kiesler, D. J. (1986). Interpersonal methods of diagnosis and treatment. In J. O. Cavenar, Jr. (Ed.), *Psychiatry* (Vol. 1, pp. 1–23). Philadelphia: J. B. Lippincott.

Kikuchi, H., Fujii, T., Abe, N., Suzuki, M., Takagi, M., Mugikura, S., . . . Mori, E. (2010). Memory repression: Brain mechanisms underlying dissociative amnesia. *Journal of Cognitive Neuroscience, 22*(3), 602–613. doi:10.1162/jocn.2009.21212

Kikuchi, M., Komuro, R., Oka, H., Kidani, T., Hanaoka, A., & Koshino, Y. (2005). Panic disorder with and without agoraphobia: Comorbidity within a half-year of the onset of panic disorder. *Psychiatry and Clinical Neurosciences, 59*(6), 639–643. doi:10.1111/j.1440-1819.2005.01430.x

Kilian, R., Lauber, C., Kalkan, R., Dorn, W., Rössler, W., Wiersma, D., . . . Becker, T. (2012). The relationships between employment, clinical status, and psychiatric hospitalization in patients with schizophrenia receiving either IPS or a conventional vocational rehabilitation program. *Social Psychiatry & Psychiatric Epidemiology, 47,* 1381–1389.

Kilmann, P. R., Boland, J. P., & Norton, S. C. (1986). Perspectives on sex therapy outcome: A survey of AASECT providers. *Journal of Sex and Marital Therapy, 12,* 116–138.

Kilpatrick, D., Saunders, B., Amick-McMullan, A., Best, C., Vernonen, L., & Resnick, H. (1989). Victim and crime factors associated with the development of crime-related post-traumatic stress disorder. *Behavior Therapy, 20,* 199–214.

Kim, B., Kim, J., Cummins, T. R., Bellgrove, M. A., Hawi, Z., Hong, S., . . . Han, D. (2013). Norepinephrine genes predict response time variability and methylphenidate-induced changes in neuropsychological function in attention deficit hyperactivity disorder. *Journal of Clinical Psychopharmacology, 33,* 356–362.

Kim, E., Lauterbach, E. C., Reeve, A., Arciniegas, D. B., Coburn, K. L., Mendez, M. F., . . . Coffey, E.C. (2007). Neuropsychiatric complications of traumatic brain injury: A critical review of the literature (a report by the ANPA Committee on Research). *Journal of Neuropsychiatry and Clinical Neuroscience, 19,* 106–127.

Kim, H., Steketee, G., & Frost, R. O. (2001). Hoarding by elderly people. *Health & Social Work, 26*(3), 176–184. doi:10.1093/hsw/26.3.176

Kim, W., Tateno, A., Arakawa, R., Sakayori, T., Ikeda, Y., Suzuki, H., & Okubo, Y. (2014). In vivo activity of modafinil on dopamine transporter measured with positron emission tomography and [18F]FE-PE2I. *International Journal of Neuropsychopharmacology, 22,* 1–7.

Kim, Y., Chen, L., McCarley, R. W., & Strecker, R. E. (2013). Sleep allostasis in chronic sleep restriction: The role of the norepinephrine system. *Brain Research, 1531,* 9–16. doi:10.1016/j.brainres.2013.07.048

Kim, Y. S., Leventhal, B. L., Koh, Y.-J., Fombonne, E., Laska, E., Lim, E.-C., . . . Grinker, R. R. (2011). Prevalence of autism spectrum disorders in a total population sample. *American Journal of Psychiatry, 168,* 904–912.

King, D. A., & Heller, K. (1984). Depression and the response of others. A reevaluation. *Journal of Abnormal Psychology, 93,* 477–480.

King, M., & McDonald, E. (1992). Homosexuals who are twins: A study of 46 probands. *British Journal of Psychiatry, 160,* 407–409.

King, N. J., & Ollendick, T. H. (1989). Children's anxiety and phobic disorders in school settings: Classification, assessment, and intervention issues. *Review of Educational Research, 59*(4), 431–470.

King, N. S. (2003). Post-concussion syndrome: Clarity amid the controversy? *The British Journal of Psychiatry, 183*(4), 276–278. doi:10.1192/bjp.183.4.276

Kinsey, A. C., Pomeroy, W. B., & Martin, C. E. (1948). *Sexual behavior in the human male.* Philadelphia: W. B. Saunders.

Kinsey, A. C., Pomeroy, W. B., Martin, C. E., & Gebhardt, P. H. (1953). *Sexual behavior in the human female.* Philadelphia: W. B. Saunders.

Kirch, D. G. (1993). Infection and autoimmunity as etiologic factors in schizophrenia: A review and reappraisal. *Schizophrenia Bulletin, 19,* 181–255.

Kircher, T. T., Rapp, A., Grodd, W., Buchkremer, G., Weiskopf, N., Lutzenberger, W., . . . Mathiak, K. (2004). Mismatch negativity responses in schizophrenia: A combined fMRI and whole-head MEG study. *The American Journal of Psychiatry, 161,* 294–304.

Kirkbride, J. B., Fearon, P., Morgan, C., Dazzan, P., Morgan, K., Tarrant, J., . . . Jones, P. B. (2006). Heterogeneity in incidence rates of schizophrenia and other psychotic syndromes: Findings from the 3-center ÆSOP study. *Archives of General Psychiatry, 63*(3), 250–258. doi:10.1001/archpsyc.63.3.250

Kirmayer, L. (1991). The place of culture in psychiatric nosology: *Taijin Kyofusho* and DSM-III-R. *The Journal of Nervous and Mental Disease, 179,* 19–28.

Kirmayer, L. J. (1994). Pacing the void: Social and cultural dimensions of dissociation. In D. Spiegel (Ed.), *Dissociation: Culture, mind, and body* (pp. 91–122). Washington DC: American Psychiatric Press.

Kirmayer, L. J., Groleau, D., Looper, K. J., & Dao, M. D. (2004). Explaining medically unexplained symptoms. *Canadian Journal of Psychiatry, 49*(10), 663–672.

Kirmayer, L. J., & Young, A. (1998). Culture and somatization: Clinical, epidemiological, and ethnographic perspectives. *Psychosomatic Medicine, 60*(4), 420–430.

Kirsch, I. (2009). Antidepressants and the placebo response. *Epidemiology and Psychiatric Sciences, 18*(4), 318–322.

Kirschenbaum, D. S., & Fitzgibbon, M. L. (1995). Controversy about the treatment of obesity: Criticisms or challenges? *Behavior Therapy, 26,* 43–68.

Kisely, S., Campbell, L. A., & Preston, N. (2005). Compulsory community and involuntary outpatient treatment for people with severe mental disorders. *Cochrane Database of Systematic Reviews* (3), CD004408. doi:10.1002/14651858.CD004408.pub2

Kisely, S., Morkell, D., Allbrook, B., Briggs, P., & Jovanovic, J. (2002). Factors associated with dysmorphic concern and psychiatric morbidity in plastic surgery outpatients. *Australian & New Zealand Journal of Psychiatry, 36*(1), 121–126. doi:10.1046/j.1440-1614.2002.00981.x

Kissen, D. M., & Eysenck, H. J. (1962). Personality in male lung cancer patients. *Journal of Psychosomatic Research, 6,* 123–127.

Kitagawa, E. M., & Hauser, P. M. (Eds.) (1973). *Differential mortality in the United States: A study in socioeconomic epidemiology.* Cambridge: Harvard University Press.

Kivlahan, D. R., Marlatt, G. A., Fromme, K., Coppel, D. B., & Williams, E. (1990). Secondary prevention with college drinkers: Evaluation of an alcohol skills training program. *Journal of Consulting and Clinical Psychology, 58,* 805–810.

Klahr, A. M., & Burt, S. (2014). Elucidating the etiology of individual differences in parenting: A meta-analysis of behavioral genetic research. *Psychological Bulletin, 140,* 544–586. doi:10.1037/a0034205

Klanecky, A. K., & McChargue, D. E. (2013). Vulnerability to alcohol use disorders following early sexual abuse: The role of effortful control. *Addiction Research & Theory, 21*(2), 160–180. doi:10.3109/16066359.2012.703269

Klassen, D., & O'Connor, W. A. (1988). A prospective study of predictors of violence in adult male mental health admissions. *Law and Human Behavior, 12,* 143–158.

Kleber, H. D. (2003). Pharmacologic treatments for heroin and cocaine dependence. *The American Journal on Addictions, 12*(Suppl2), S5–S18. doi:10.1080/10550490390210083

Kleim, B., Ehlers, A., & Glucksman, E. (2007). Early predictors of chronic post-traumatic stress disorder in assault survivors. *Psychological Medicine, 37,* 1457–1467.

Klein, A. A., & Ross, B. L. (2014). Substance use and mental health severity among LGBTQ individuals attending Minnesota model-based residential treatment. *Journal of Gay & Lesbian Social Services: The Quarterly Journal of Community & Clinical Practice, 26*(3), 303–317. doi:10.1080/10538720.2014.924459

Klein, D., Ross, D., & Cohen, R (1987). Panic and avoidance in agoraphobia: Application of path analysis to treatment studies. *Archives of General Psychiatry, 44,* 377–385.

Klein, D. F. (1990). NIMH collaborative research on the treatment of depression. *Archives of General Psychiatry, 47,* 682–688.

Klein, D. F. (1993). False suffocation alarms, spontaneous panics, and related conditions: An integrative hypothesis. *Archives of General Psychiatry, 50*(4), 306–317. doi:10.1001/archpsyc.1993.01820160076009

Klein, D. N., Shankman, S. A., & Rose, S. (2006). Ten-year prospective follow-up study of the naturalistic course of dysthymic disorder and double depression. *The American Journal of Psychiatry, 163*(5), 872–880. doi:10.1176/appi.ajp.163.5.872

Klein, M. (1975). *The writings of Melanie Klein* (Vol. III). London: Hogarth Press.

Klein, M. H. (1993). Issues in the assessment of personality disorders. *Journal of Personality Disorders,* (Suppl.), 18–33.

Klein, R., & Mannuzza, S. (1988). Hyperactive boys almost grown up III: Methylphenidate effects on ultimate height. *Archives of General Psychiatry, 45,* 1131–1134.

Klein, R. G. (1988). Hyperactive boys almost grown-up. Ill: Methylphenidate effects on ultimate height. *Archives of General Psychiatry, 45,* 1131–1134.

Klein, R. G., & Mannuzza, S. (1991). Long-term outcome of hyperactive children: A review. *Journal of the American Academy of Child and Adolescent Psychiatry, 30*(3), 383–387.

Kleindienst, N., Bohus, M., Ludascher, P., Limberger, M. F., Kuenkele, K., Ebner-Priemer, U. W., . . . Schmahl, C. (2008). Motives for nonsuicidal self-injury among women with borderline personality disorder. *Journal of Nervous and Mental Disease, 196*(3), 230–236.

Kleindienst, N., Engel, R. R., & Greil, W. (2005). Psychosocial and demographic factors associated with response to prophylactic lithium. A systematic review for bipolar disorders. *Psychological Medicine, 35,* 1685–1694.

Kleinhaus, K., Harlap, S., Perrin, M. C., Manor, O., Weiser, M., Harkavy-Friedman, J. M., . . . Malaspina, D. (2012). Catatonic schizophrenia: A cohort prospective study. *Schizophrenia Bulletin, 38*(2), 331–337. doi:10.1093/schbul/sbq087

Kleinknecht, R. A., (1991). *Mastering anxiety: The nature and treatment of anxious conditions.* New York: Plenum.

Kleinknecht, R. A. (1993). Rapid treatment of blood and injection phobia with eye movement desensitization. *Journal of Behavior Therapy and Experimental Psychiatry, 24,* 2211–2217.

Kleinknecht, R. A., & Lenz, J. (1989). Blood/injury fear, fainting and avoidance of medical treatment: A family correspondence study. *Behaviour Research and Therapy, 27,* 537–547.

Kleinknecht, R. A., & Morgan, M. (1992). Treatment of posttraumatic stress disorder using eye movement desensitization. *Journal of Behavior Therapy and Experimental Psychiatry, 23,* 43–49.

Kleinman, A. (1981). Culture and patient care: Psychiatry among the Chinese. *Drug Therapy, 11,* 134–140.

Klenowski, P. M., Bell, K. J., & Dodson, K. D. (2010). An empirical evaluation of juvenile awareness programs in the United States: Can juveniles be "scared straight"? *Journal of Offender Rehabilitation, 49,* 254–272. doi:10.1080/10509671003716068

Klerman, G. L. (1988). The current age of youthful melancholia: Evidence for increase in depression among adolescents and young adults. *British Journal of Psychiatry, 152,* 4–7.

Klerman, G. L., Weissman, M. M., Rounsaville, B. J. & Chevron, E. S. (1984). *Interpersonal psychotherapy of depression.* New York: Basic Books.

Klin, A. (1993). Asperger syndrome. *Child and Adolescent Psychiatric Clinics of North America, 3*(1), 131–148.

Klin, A., Volkmar, F. R., Naylor, S., Sparrow, S. S., & Rourke, B. P. (1993, October). *Asperger syndrome: Diagnosis, neuropsychological aspects, and interventions.* Poster presented at the 40th Annual Meeting of the American Academy of Child and Adolescent Psychiatry, San Antonio, TX.

Klosko, J. S., Barlow, D. H., Tassinari, R., & Cerny, J. A. (1990). A comparison of alprazolam and behavior therapy in the treatment of panic disorder. *Journal of Consulting and Clinical Psychology, 58,* 77–84.

Klott, J. (2012). *DSM-5: Revolutionizing diagnosis and treatment* [DVD]. Eau Claire, WI: CMI Education Institute.

Kluft, R. P. (1984). Multiple personality in childhood. *Psychiatric Clinics of North America, 7,* 121–134.

Kluft, R. P. (1995). Current controversies surrounding dissociative identity disorder. In L. M. Cohen, J. N. Berzoff, & M. R. Elin (Eds.), *Dissociative identity disorder: Theoretical and treatment controversies* (pp. 347–437). Northvale, NJ: Jason Aronson.

Kluft, R. P. (2012). Hypnosis in the treatment of dissociative identity disorder and allied state: An overview and case study. *South African Journal of Psychology, 42*(2), 146–155. doi:10.1177/008124631204200202

Klump, K. L., Burt, S., McGue, M., & Iacono, W. G. (2007). Changes in genetic and environmental influences on disordered eating across adolescence: A longitudinal twin study. *Archives of General Psychiatry, 64,* 1409–1415. doi:10.1001/archpsyc.64.12.1409

Klump, K. L., Suisman, J. L., Burt, S., McGue, M., & Iacono, W. G. (2009). Genetic and environmental influences on disordered eating: An adoption study. *Journal of Abnormal Psychology, 118*, 797–805. doi:10.1037/a0017204

Klunk, W. E., Engler, H., Nordberg, A., Wang, Y., Blomqvist, G., Holt, D. P., . . . Langstrom, B. (2004). Imaging brain amyloid in Alzheimer's disease with Pittsburgh Compound-B. *Annals of Neurology, 55*(3), 306–319. doi: 10.1002/ana.20009

Knaus, W. J. (2008). *The cognitive behavioral workbook for anxiety: A step-by-step program.* Oakland, CA: New Harbinger Publications. Retrieved on November 1, 2014 from http://public.eblib.com/choice/publicfullrecord.aspx?p=776079

Knorr, U., Vinberg, M., Kessing, L. V., & Wetterslev, J. (2010). Salivary cortisol in depressed patients versus control persons: A systematic review and meta-analysis. *Psychoneuroendocrinology, 35*(9), 1275–1286. doi:10.1016/j.psyneuen.2010.04.001

Kobak, R. R., & Sceery, A. (1988). Attachment in late adolescence: Working models, affect regulation, and representations of self and others. *Child Development, 59,* 135–146.

Kocalevent, R.-D., Fliege, H., Rose, M., Walter, M., Danzer, G., & Klapp, B. F. (2005). Autodestructive syndromes. *Psychotherapy and Psychosomatics, 74*(4), 202–211. doi:10.1159/000085143

Kochanek, T. T., Kabacoff, R. I., & Lipsitt, L. P. (1990). Early identification of developmentally disabled and at-risk preschool children. *Exceptional Children, 56*, 528–538.

Kochman, F. J., Hantouche, E. G., Ferrari, P., Lancrenon, S., Bayart, D., & Akiskal, H. S. (2005). Cyclothymic temperament as a prospective predictor of bipolarity and suicidality in children and adolescents with major depressive disorder. *Journal of Affective Disorders, 85*, 181–189.

Kocsis, R. N. (2013). Review of *Diagnostic and Statistical Manual of Mental Disorders: Fifth edition (DSM-5). International Journal of Offender Therapy and Comparative Criminology, 57*, 1546–1548. doi:10.1177/0306624X13511040

Koegel, R. L., & Koegel, L. K. (1989). Community-referenced research on self-stimulation. In M. J. Begab (Ed.), *The treatment of severe behavior disorders: Behavior analysis approaches* (pp. 129–149). Washington, DC: American Association on Mental Retardation.

Koelen, J. A., Houtveen, J. H., Abbass, A., Luyten, P., Eurelings-Bontekoe, E. M., Van Broeckhuysen-Kloth, M., . . . Geenen, R. (2014). Effectiveness of psychotherapy for severe somatoform disorder: Meta analysis. *The British Journal of Psychiatry, 204*(1), 12–19. doi:10.1192/bjp.bp.112.121830

Koenders, M. A., Giltay, E. J., Spijker, A. T., Hoencamp, E. E., Spinhoven, P. P., & Elzinga, B. M. (2014). Stressful life events in bipolar I and II disorder: Cause or consequence of mood symptoms? *Journal of Affective Disorders, 161*, 55–64. doi:10.1016/j.jad.2014.02.036

Koenen, K. C. (2007). Genetics of posttraumatic stress disorder: Review and recommendations for future studies. *Journal of Traumatic Stress, 20*, 737–750. doi:10.1002/jts.20205

Koenen, K. C., Harley, R., Lyons, M. J., Wolfe, J., Simpson, J. C., Goldberg, J., . . . Tsuang, M. (2002). A twin registry study of familial and individual risk factors for trauma exposure and posttraumatic stress disorder. *Journal of Nervous and Mental Disease, 190*, 209–218.

Koenigsberg, H., & Handley, R. (1986). Expressed emotion: From predictive index to clinical construct. *American Journal of Psychiatry, 143,* 1361–1373.

Koffinke, C. (1991). Family recovery issues and treatment resources. In D. C. Daley & M. S. Raskin (Eds.), *Treating the chemically dependent and their families.* Newbury Park, CA: Sage.

Kofler, M. J., Alderson, R., Raiker, J. S., Bolden, J., Sarver, D. E., & Rapport, M. D. (2014). Working memory and intraindividual variability as neurocognitive indicators in ADHD: Examining competing model predictions. *Neuropsychology, 28*(3), 459–471. doi:10.1037/neu0000050

Kofler, M. J., Rapport, M. D., Bolden, J., Sarver, D. E., & Raiker, J. S. (2010). ADHD and working memory: The impact of central executive deficits and exceeding storage/rehearsal capacity on observed inattentive behavior. *Journal of Abnormal Child Psychology, 38*, 149–161. doi:10.1007/s10802-009-9357-6

Kofler, M. J., Rapport, M. D., Bolden, J., Sarver, D. E., Raiker, J. S., & Alderson, R. M. (2011). Working memory deficits and social problems in children with ADHD. *Journal of Abnormal Child Psychology, 39*, 805–817. doi:10.1007/s10802-011-9492-8

Kohlenberg, R. J. (1973). Behavioristic approach to multiple personality: A case study. *Behavior Therapy, 4,* 137–140.

Kohut, H. (1977). *The restoration of the self.* New York: International Universities Press.

Kojima, T., Matsushima, E., Ohta, K., Toru, M., Han, Y. H., Shen, Y.C., . . . Prilipko, L. (2001). Stability of exploratory eye movements as a marker of schizophrenia—a WHO multi-center study. *Schizophrenia Research, 52*, 203–213.

Kolata, G. (1987). Manic-depression gene tied to chromosome 11. *Science, 235,* 1139–1140.

Kolb, L. (1968). *Noyes' modern clinical psychiatry* (7th ed.). Philadelphia: W. B. Saunders.

Kolko, D. J., Loar, L. L., & Sturnick, D. (1990). Inpatient social-cognitive skills training groups with conduct disordered and attention deficit disordered children. *Journal of Child Psychology and Psychiatry, 31,* 737–748.

Kong, A., Frigge, M. L., Masson, G., Besenbacher, S., Sulem, P., Magnusson, G., . . . Stegansson, K. (2012). Rate of de novo mutations and the importance of father's age to disease risk. *Nature, 488*, 471–475.

Konick, L. C., & Friedman, L. (2001). Meta-analysis of thalamic size in schizophrenia. *Biological Psychiatry, 49*, 28–38.

Konopka, A., Pełka-Wysiecka, J., Grzywacz, A., & Samochowiec, J. (2013). Psychosocial characteristics of benzodiazepine addicts compared to not addicted benzodiazepine users. *Progress in Neuro-Psychopharmacology & Biological Psychiatry, 40*, 229–235. doi:10.1016/j.pnpbp.2012.09.001

Kontula, O., & Haavio-Mannila, E. (2009). The impact of aging on human sexual activity and sexual desire. *Journal of Sex Research, 46*(1), 46–56.

Koponen, S., Taiminen, T., Portin, R., Himanen, L., Isoniemi, H., Heinonen, H., Hinkka, S., & Tenovuo, O. (2002). Axis I and II psychiatric disorders after traumatic brain injury: A 30-year follow-up study. *The American Journal of Psychiatry, 159*(8), 1315–1321. doi: 10.1176/appi.ajp.159.8.1315

Korolenko, C., Minevich, V., & Segal, B. (1994). The politicalization of alcohol in the USSR and its impact on the study and treatment of alcoholism. *International Journal of the Addictions, 29*, 1269–1285.

Koss, M. P., Gidycz, C. A., & Wisniewski, N. (1987). The scope of rape: Incidence and prevalence of sexual aggression and victimization in a national sample of higher education students. *Journal of Consulting and Clinical Psychology, 55,* 162–170.

Koss, M. P. & Shiang, J. (1994). Research on brief psychotherapy. In A. E. Bergin & S. L. Garfield (Eds.), *Handbook of psychotherapy and behavior change* (pp. 664–700). New York: John Wiley & Sons.

Koster, A., Lajer, M., & Lindhardt, A. (2008). Gender differences in first episode psychosis (FEP). *European Psychiatry, 43*, 940–946.

Kotsaftis, A., & Neale, J. M. (1993). Schizotypal personality disorder. I: The clinical syndrome. *Clinical Psychology Review, 13,* 451–472.

Kovacs, M., Gatsonis, C., Paulauskas, S. L., & Richards, C. (1989). Depressive disorders in childhood. IV. A longitudinal study of comorbidity with and risk for anxiety disorders. *Archives of General Psychiatry, 46*, 776–782.

Kovacs, M., Goldston, D., & Gatsonis, C. (1993). Suicidal behaviors and childhood-onset depressive disorders: A longitudinal investigation. *Journal of the American Academy of Child and Adolescent Psychiatry, 32*, 8–20.

Kovalenko, I. L., Galyamina, A. G., Smagin, D. A., Michurina, T. V., Kudryavtseva, N. N., & Enikolopov, G. (2014). Extended effect of chronic social defeat stress in childhood on behaviors in adulthood. *PLoS ONE, 9*, e91762.

Kowalski, R. M., Giumetti, G. W., Schroeder, A. N., & Lattanner, M. R. (2014). Bullying in the digital age: A critical review and meta-analysis of cyberbullying research among youth. *Psychological Bulletin, 140*(4), 1073–1137. doi:10.1037/a0035618

Kownacki, R. J., & Shadish, W. R. (1999). Does Alcoholics Anonymous work? The results from a meta-analysis of controlled experiments. *Substance Use & Misuse, 34*(13), 1897–1916. doi:10.3109/10826089909039431

Kposowa, A. J. (2013). Association of suicide rates, gun ownership, conservatism, and individual suicide risk. *Social Psychiatry and Psychiatric Epidemiology, 48*(9), 1467–1479. doi:10.1007/s00127-013-0664-4

Kraemer, H., Stice, E., Kazdin, A., Offord, D., & Kupfer, D. (2001). How do risk factors work together? Mediators, moderators, and independent, overlapping, and proxy risk factors. *The American Journal of Psychiatry, 158*, 848–856.

Kraepelin, E. (1910). *Dementia praecox and paraphrenia* (R. M. Barclay & G. M. Robertson, trans.). Edinburgh: E. & S. Livingstone (1971).

Krahn, L. E., Li, H., & O'Connor, M. K. (2003). Patients who strive to be ill: Factitious disorder with physical symptoms. *The American Journal of Psychiatry, 160*(6), 1163–1168.

Kramer, P. (1993). *Listening to Prozac.* New York: Penguin Books.

Krantz, D. S., & Manuck, S. B. (1984). Acute psychophysiologic reactivity and risk of cardiovascular disease—A review and methodologic critique. *Psychological Bulletin, 96*, 435–464.

Krentzman, A. R. (2013). Review of the application of positive psychology to substance use, addiction, and recovery research. *Psychology of Addictive Behaviors, 27*, 151–165. doi:10.1037/a0029897

Kroenke, K. (1992). Symptoms in medical patients: An untended field. *The American Journal of Medicine, 92*(1A), 3S–6S.

Kroenke, K. (2007). Efficacy of treatment for somatoform disorders: A review of randomized controlled trials. *Psychosomatic Medicine, 69*(9), 881–888. doi:10.1097/PSY.0b013e31815b00c4

Kroenke, K., Spitzer, R. L., & Williams, J. W. (2003). The Patient Health Questionnaire-2: Validity of a two-item depression screener. *Medical Care, 41*(11), 1284–1292. doi:10.1097/01.MLR.0000093487.78664.3C

Kroft, C., & Cole, J. (1992). Adverse behavioral effects of psychostimulants. In J. M. Kane & J. A. Lieberman (Eds.), *Adverse effects of psychotropic drugs.* New York: Guilford Press.

Krogh, J., Nordentoft, M., Sterne, J. C., & Lawlor, D. A. (2011). The effect of exercise in clinically depressed adults: Systematic review and meta-analysis of randomized controlled trials. *Journal of Clinical Psychiatry, 72*(4), 529–538. doi:10.4088/JCP.08r04913blu

Krueger, P. M. & Friedman, E. M. (2009). Sleep duration in the United States: A cross-sectional population-based study. *American Journal of Epidemiology, 169*(9), 1052–1063.

Kruesi, M. J., Hibbs, E. D., Zahn, T. P., Keysor, C. S., Hamburger, S., Bartko, J. J., & Rapoport, J. L. (1992). A 2-year prospective follow-up study of children and adolescents with disruptive behavior disorders. *Archives of General Psychiatry, 49,* 429–435.

Krupnick, J. L., Sotsky, S. M., Simmens, S., Moyer, J., Elkin, I., Watkins, J., & Pilkonis, P. A. (1996). The role of the therapeutic alliance in psychotherapy and pharmacotherapy outcome: Findings in the National Institute of Mental Health Treatment of Depression Collaborative Research Program. *Journal of Consulting and Clinical Psychology, 64,* 532–539.

Kuechler, J., & Hampton, R. (1988). Learning and behavioral approaches to the treatment of anorexia nervosa and bulimia. In B. J. Blinder, B. F. Chaitin, & R. Goldstein (Eds.), *The eating disorders* (pp. 423–431). PMA Publishing Corporation.

Kuehn, B. M. (2012). Data on autism prevalence, trajectories, illuminate socioeconomic disparities. *Journal of the American Medical Association, 307,* 2137–2138.

Kukull, W. A., Higdon, R., Bowen, J. D., McCormick, W. C., Teri, L., Schellenberg, G. D., van Belle, G., Jolley, L., & Larson, E. B. (2002). Dementia and Alzheimer disease incidence: A prospective cohort study. *Archives of Neurology, 59*(11), 1737–1746. doi: 10.1001/archneur.59.11.1737.

Kulik, J. A., & Mahler, H. I. (1989). Social support and recovery from surgery. *Health Psychology, 8,* 221–238.

Kumar, R. N., Chambers, W. A., & Pertwee, R. G. (2001). Pharmacological actions and therapeutic uses of cannabis and cannabinoids. *Anaesthesia, 56*(11), 1059–1068. doi: 10.1111/j.1365-2044.2001.02269.x

Kunitoh, N. (2013). From hospital to the community: The influence of deinstitutionalization on discharged long-stay psychiatric patients. *Psychiatry and Clinical Neurosciences, 67*(6), 384–396. doi:10.1111/pcn.12071

Kuokkanen, M., & Heljala, L. (2005). Early identification and brief intervention for risky drinkers in Finnish occupational health services. *Scandinavian Journal of Work and Environmental Health, 1,* 35–37.

Kupfersmid, J. (1989). Treatment of nocturnal enuresis: A status report. *The Psychiatric Forum, 14,* 37–46.

Kurtz, M. M., & Mueser, K. T. (2008). A meta-analysis of controlled research on social skills training for schizophrenia. *Journal of Consulting and Clinical Psychology, 76,* 491–504.

Kushner, M., Riggs, D., Foa, E., & Miller, S. (1992). Perceived controllability and the development of posttraumatic stress disorder (PTSD) in crime victims. *Behaviour Research and Therapy, 31,* 105–110.

Kushner, M., Sher, K., & Beitman, B. (1990). The relation between alcohol and the anxiety disorders. *American Journal of Psychiatry, 147,* 685–695.

Kutcher, S., Malkin, D., Silverberg, J., Marton, P., Williamson, P., Malkin, A., Szalai, J., & Katie, M. (1991). Nocturnal cortisol, thyroid stimulating hormone, and growth hormone secretory profiles in depressed adolescents. *Journal of the American Academy of Child Psychiatry, 30,* 407–414.

Kyaga, S., Landén, M., Boman, M., Hultman, C. M., Långström, N., & Lichtenstein, P. (2013). Mental illness, suicide and creativity: 40-year prospective total population study. *Journal of Psychiatric Research, 47,* 83–90.

Kyaga, S., Lichtenstein, P., Boman, M., Hultman, C. M., Långström, N., & Landén, M. (2011). Creativity and mental disorder: Family study of 300,000 people with severe mental disorder. *The British Journal of Psychiatry, 199,* 373–379. doi:10.1192/bjp.bp.110.085316

L

LaBrie, J. W., Kenney, S. R., Napper, L. E., & Miller, K. (2014). Impulsivity and alcohol-related risk among college students: Examining urgency, sensation seeking, and the moderating influence of beliefs about alcohol's role in the college experience. *Addictive Behaviors, 39*(1), 159–164. doi:10.1016/j.addbeh.2013.09.018

Lacks, P., & Morin, C. M. (1992). Recent advances in the assessment and treatment of insomnia. *Journal of Consulting and Clinical Psychology, 60,* 586–594.

Lacourse, E., Côté, S., Nagin, D. S., Vitaro, F., Brendgen, M., & Tremblay, R. E. (2002). A longitudinal-experimental approach to testing theories of antisocial behavior development. *Development and Psychopathology, 14,* 909–924.

Ladouceur, R., Freeston, M. H., Rhéaume, J., Dugas, M. J., Gagnon, F., Thibodeau, N., & Fournier, S. (2000). Strategies used with intrusive thoughts: A comparison of OCD patients with anxious and community controls. *Journal of Abnormal Psychology, 109*(2), 179–187. doi:10.1037/0021-843X.109.2.179

Lago, J. A., & Kosten, T. R. (1994). Stimulant withdrawal. *Addiction, 89 (*11), 1477–1481.

Lahey, B. B. (2008). Oppositional defiant disorder, conduct disorder, and juvenile delinquency. In T.P. Beauchaine & S.P. Hinshaw (Eds.), *Child and adolescent psychopathology* (pp. 335–369). Hoboken, NJ: Wiley.

Lahey, B. B., Goodman, S. H., Waldman, I. D., Bird, H. Canino, G., Jensen, P., . . . Applegate, B. (1999). Relation of age of onset to type and severity of child and adolescent conduct problems. *Journal of Abnormal Child Psychology, 27,* 247–260.

Lahey, B. B., Loeber, R., Burke, J. D., & Applegate, B. (2005). Predicting future antisocial personality disorder in males from a clinical assessment in childhood. *Journal of Consulting and Clinical Psychology, 73,* 389–399.

Lahey, B. B., & Waldman, I. D., (2003). A developmental propensity model of the origins of conduct problems during childhood and adolescents. In B. B. Lahey, T. E. Moffitt, & A. Caspi (Eds.), *Causes of conduct disorder and juvenile delinquency* (pp. 76–117). New York: Guilford Press.

Lai, M.-C., Lombardo, M. V., Pasco, G., Ruigrok, A. N. V., Wheelwright, S. J., Sadek, S. A., & Baron-Cohen, S. (2011). A behavioral comparison of male and female adults with high-functioning autism spectrum conditions. *PLoS ONE, 6,* e20835. doi:10.1371/journal.pone.0020835

Lakdawalla, Z., Hankin, B. L., & Mermelstein, R. (2007). Cognitive theories of depression in children and adolescents: A conceptual and quantitative review. *Clinical Child and Family Psychology Review, 10*(1), 1–24. doi:10.1007/s10567-006-0013-1

Lalkhen, A. G., & McCluskey, A. (2008). Clinical tests: Sensitivity and specificity. *Continuing Educaton in Anaesthesia, Critical Care, & Pain, 8*(6), 221–223. doi:10.1093/bjaceaccp/mkn041

Lam, D., & Wong, G. (1997). Prodromes, coping strategies, insight and social functioning in bipolar affective disorders. *Psychological Medicine, 27*(5), 1091–1100. doi:10.1017/S0033291797005540

Lam, D. H. (1991). Psychosocial family intervention in schizophrenia: A review of empirical studies. *Psychological Medicine, 21,* 423–441.

Lam, D. H., Burbeck, R., Wright, K., & Pilling, S. (2009). Psychological therapies in bipolar disorder: The effect of illness history on relapse prevention—A systematic review. *Bipolar Disorders, 11*(5), 474–482. doi:10.1111/j.1399-5618.2009.00724.x

Lamb, H. R. (1992). Is it time for a moratorium on deinstitutionalization? *Hospital and Community Psychiatry, 43,* 669.

Lambe, S. (2013, October 3). Paris Hilton names her 35 pets. *Vh1 Celebrity.* Retrieved on September 16, 2015 from http://www.vh1.com/celebrity/2013-10-03/paris-hilton-names-her-35-pets/

Lambert, M. C., Weisz, J. R., & Knight, F. (1989). Over- and undercontrolled clinic referral problems of Jamaican and American children and adolescents: The culture general and the culture specific. *Journal of Consulting and Clinical Psychology, 57,* 467–472.

Lambert, M. J., & Bergin, A. E. (1994). The effectiveness of psychotherapy. In A. E. Bergin & S. L. Garfield (Eds.), *Handbook of psychotherapy and behavior change* (pp. 143-189). New York: John Wiley & Sons.

Lamy, P. P. (1985). Patterns of prescribing and drug use. In R. N. Butler & A. D. Beard (Eds.), *The aging process: Therapeutic implications* (pp. 53–82). New York: Raven Press.

Landman, J. T., & Dawes, R. (1982). Experimental outcome: Smith and Glass' conclusions stand up under scrutiny. *American Psychologist, 37,* 504–516.

Landolt, H. P., Werth, E., Borb'ely, A. A., & Dijk, D. J. (1995). Caffeine intake (200 mg) in the morning affects human sleep and EEG power spectra at night. *Brain Research, 675*(1–2), 67–74.

Landry, T., & Bergeron, S. (2011). Biopsychosocial factors associated with dyspareunia in a community sample of adolescent girls. *Archives of Sexual Behavior, 40*(5), 877–889.

Lang, F. U., Kösters, M., Lang, S., Becker, T., & Jäger, M. (2013). Psychopathological long-term outcome of schizophrenia—A review. *Acta Psychiatrica Scandinavica, 127*(3), 173–182. doi:10.1111/acps.12030

Lang, P. J. (1985). The cognitive psychophysiology of emotion: Fear and anxiety. In A. H. Tuma & J. D. Maser (Eds.), *Anxiety and the anxiety disorders* (pp. 131–170). Hillsdale, NJ: Erlbaum.

Lang, R., Didden, R., Machalicek, W., Rispoli, M., Sigafoos, J., Lancioni, G., . . . Kang, S. (2010). Behavioral treatment of chronic skin-picking in individuals with developmental disabilities: A systematic review. *Research in Developmental Disabilities, 31*(2), 304–315. doi:10.1016/j.ridd.2009.10.017

Lang, S., af Klinteberg, B., & Alm, P.-O. (2002). Adult psychopathy and violent behavior in males with early neglect and abuse. *Acta Psychiatrica Scandinavica, 106*(Suppl. 412), 93–100.

Langdon, R., McGuire, J., Stevenson, R., & Catts, S. V. (2011). Clinical correlates of olfactory hallucinations in schizophrenia. *British Journal of Clinical Psychology, 50*(2), 145–163. doi:10.1348/014466510X500837

Langevin, R. (1993). A comparison of neuroendocrine and genetic factors in homosexuality and in pedophilia. *Annals of Sex Research, 1,* 67–76.

Lanius, R. A., Brand, B., Vermetten, E., Frewen, P. A., & Spiegel, D. (2012). The dissociative subtype of PTSD: Rationale, clinical and neurobiological evidence and implications. *Depression and Anxiety, 29,* 701–708.

Lanius, R. A., Vermetten, E., Loewenstein, R. J., Brand, B., Schmahl, C., Bremner, J. D., & Spiegel, D. (2010). Emotion modulation in PTSD: Clinical and neurobiological evidence for a dissociative subtype. *American Journal of Psychiatry, 167,* 640–647.

LaPerriere, A. R., Antoni, M. H., Schneiderman, N., Iron-son, G., Klimas, N., Caralis, P., & Fletcher, M. A. (1990). Exercise intervention attenuates emotional distress and natural killer cell decrements following notification of positive serologic status for HIV-1. *Biofeedback and Self-Regulation, 15,* 229–242.

Laria, A. J., & Lewis-Fernández, R. (2001). The professional fragmentation of experience in the study of dissociation, somatization and culture. *Journal of Trauma and Dissociation, 2,* 17–47.

Larimer, M. E., & Cronce, J. M. (2007). Identification, prevention, and treatment revisited: Individual-focused college drinking prevention strategies 1999–2006. *Addictive Behaviors, 32*(11), 2439–2468. doi:10.1016/j.addbeh.2007.05.006

Laruelle, M., Ai-Dargham, A., Casanova, M., Toti, R., Weinberger, D., & Kleinman, J. (1993). Selective abnormalities of prefrontal serotonergic receptors in schizophrenia. *Archives of General Psychiatry, 50,* 810–818.

Last, C. G., Barlow, D. H., & O'Brien, G. (1984). Precipitants of agoraphobia: Role of stressful life events. *Psychological Reports, 54,* 567–570.

Last, C. G., Francis, G , Hersen, M., Kazdin, A. E., & Strauss, C. C. (1987). Separation anxiety and school phobia: A comparison using DSM-III criteria. *American Journal of Psychiatry, 144,* 653–657.

Last, C. G., & Strauss, C. C. (1990). School refusal in anxiety-disordered children and adolescents. *Journal of the American Academy of Child and Adolescent Psychiatry, 29,* 31–35.

Latagliata, E., Patrono, E., Puglisi-Allegra, S., & Ventura, R. (2010). Food seeking in spite of harmful consequences is under prefrontal cortical noradrenergic control. *BMC Neuroscience, 11,* 15. doi:10.1186/1471-2202-11-15

Lau, M. A., Segal, Z., & Williams, J. M. G. (2004). Teasdale's differential activation hypothesis: Implications for mechanisms of depressive relapse and suicidal behaviour. *Behaviour Research and Therapy, 42,* 1001–1017. doi:10.1016/j.brat.2004.03.003

Laufer, N., Maayan, R., Hermesh, H., Marom, S., Gilad, R., Strous, R., & Weizman, A. (2005). Involvement of GABAA receptor modulating neuroactive steroids in patients with social phobia. *Psychiatry Research, 137*(1–2), 131–136. doi:10.1016/j.psychres.2005.07.003

Laughman, E., Gagnon, J. H., Michael, R., & Michaels, S. (1994). *Sex in America.* Chicago: University of Chicago Press.

Laumann, E. O., Paik, A., & Rosen, R. C. (1999). Sexual dysfunction in the United States: Prevalence and predictors. *Journal of the American Medical Association, 281*(6), 537–544.

Lautenschlager, N. T., Cox, K. L., Flicker, L., Foster, J. K., van Bockxmeer, F. M., Xiao, J., . . . Almeida, O. P. (2008). Effect of physical activity on cognitive function in older adults at risk for Alzheimer disease: A randomized trial. *Journal of the American Medical Association, 300*(9), 1027–1037. doi: 10.1001/jama.300.9.1027

Lavender, J. M., Wonderlich, S. A., Crosby, R. D., Engel, S. G., Mitchell, J. E., Crow, S. J., . . . Le Grange, D. (2013). Personality-based subtypes of anorexia nervosa: Examining validity and utility using baseline clinical variables and ecological momentary assessment. *Behaviour Research and Therapy, 51*(8), 512–517.

Laws, D. R., & Marshall, W. L. (1991). Masturbatory reconditioning with sexual deviates: An evaluative review. *Advances in Behaviour Research & Therapy, 13*(1), 13–25. doi:10.1016/0146-6402(91)90012-Y

Lawson, G., Peterson, J. S., & Lawson, A. (1983). *Alcoholism and the family: A guide to treatment and prevention.* Rockville, MD: Aspen.

Lawson, J., Baron-Cohen, S., & Wheelwright, S. (2004). Empathising and systemising in adults with and without Asperger syndrome. *Journal of Autism and Developmental Disorders, 34,* 301–310. doi:10.1023/B:JADD.0000029552.42724.1b

Lazarus, A. A. (1989). Dyspareunia: A multimodal psychotherapeutic perspective. In S. R. Leiblum & S. R. Rosen (Eds.), *Principles and practices of sex therapy* (2nd ed., pp. 89–112). New York: Guilford Press.

Lazarus, R. S. (1993). From psychological stress to the emotions: A history of changing outlooks. *Annual Review of Psychology, 44,* 1–21.

Lazarus, R. S., & Folkman, S. (1984). *Stress, appraisal, and coping.* New York: Springer-Verlag.

Leahey, T. H. (1992). *History of psychology* (3rd ed.). Englewood Cliffs, NJ: Prentice Hall.

Leary, T. (1957). *Interpersonal diagnosis of personality. A functional theory and methodology for personality evaluation.* New York: Ronald Press.

Lecci, L., Karoly, P., Ruehlman, L. S., & Lanyon, R. I. (1996). Goal-relevant dimensions of hypochondriacal tendencies and their relation to symptom manifestation and psychological distress. *Journal of Abnormal Psychology, 105,* 42–52.

Lecendreux, M., & Córtese, S. (2007). Sleep problems associated with ADHD: A review of current therapeutic options and recommendations for the future. *Expert Review of Neurotherapeutics, 7,* 1799–1806.

Leckman, J. F. (2002). Tourette's syndrome. *Lancet, 360,* 1577–1586.

Leckman, J. F., & Cohen, D. J. (1994). Tic disorders. In M. Rutter, E. Taylor, & L. Hersou (Eds.), *Child and adolescent psychiatry.* Oxford, UK: Blackwell Scientific Publications.

Leckman, J. F., Denys, D., Simpson, H., Mataix-Cols, D., Hollander, E., Saxena, S., . . . Stein, D. J. (2010). Obsessive-compulsive disorder: A review of the diagnostic criteria and possible subtypes and dimensional specifiers for *DSM-V. Depression and Anxiety, 27*(6), 507–527. doi:10.1002/da.20669

Leckman, J. F., Grice, D. E., Boardman, J., & Zhang, H. (1997). Symptoms of obsessive-compulsive disorder. *The American Journal of Psychiatry, 154*(7), 911–917.

Leclair-Visonneau, L., Oudiette, D., Gaymard, B., Leu-Semenescu, S., & Arnulf, I. (2010). Do the eyes scan dream images during rapid eye movement sleep? Evidence from the rapid eye movement sleep behaviour disorder model. *Brain: A Journal of Neurology, 133*(6), 1737–1746. doi:10.1093/brain/awq110

LeDoux, J. (2003). The emotional brain, fear, and the amygdala. *Cellular and Molecular Neurobiology, 23*(4–5), 727–738.

Lee, B., & Tyler, K. (2010). The new homelessness revisited. *Annual Review of Sociology, 36,* 501–521. doi:10.1146/annurev-soc-070308-115940

Lee, D., Riccio, C. A., & Hynd, G. W. (2004). The role of executive functions in ADHD: Testing predictions from two models. *Canadian Journal of School Psychology, 19,* 167–189. doi:10.1177/082957350401900109

Lee, S., Chen, S., Chang, Y., Chu, C., Huang, S., Tzeng, N., . . . Lu, R. (2012). The ALDH2 and 5-HT2A genes interacted in bipolar-I but not bipolar-II disorder. *Progress in Neuro-Psychopharmacology & Biological Psychiatry, 38*(2), 247–251. doi:10.1016/j.pnpbp.2012.04.005

Leekam, S., & Perner, J. (1991). Does the autistic child have a theory of representation? *Cognition, 40,* 203–218.

Leff, J. (1994). Working with families of schizophrenic patients. *British Journal of Psychiatry, 164,* (Suppl. 23), 71–76.

Legarda, J. J., & Gossop, M. (1994). A 24-hour inpatient detoxification treatment for heroin addicts: A preliminary investigation. *Drug and Alcohol Dependence, 35*(1), 91–93.

Lehman, E. J., Hein, M. J., Baron, S. L., & Gersic, C. M. (2012). Neurodegenerative causes of death among retired National Football League players. *Neurology, 79*(19), 1970–1974. doi: 10.1212/WNL.0b013e31826daf50

Lehti, A., Johansson, E. E., Bergs, C., Danielsson, U., & Hammarstrom, A. (2010). "The western gaze"—an analysis of medical research publications concerning the expressions of depression, focusing on ethnicity and gender. *Health Care for Women International, 31*(2), 100–112. doi:10.1080/07399330903067861

Leibowitz, S. F., Weiss, G. F., Yee, F., and Tretter, J. B. (1985). Noradrenergic innervation of the paraventricular nucleus: Specific role in control of carbohydrate ingestions. *Brain Research Bulletin, 14,* 561–567.

Leichner, P., & Gertler, A. (1988). Prevalence and incidence studies of anorexia nervosa. In B. J. Blinder, B. F. Chaitin, & R. Goldstein (Eds.), *The eating disorders* (pp. 131-149). PMA Publishing Corporation.

Leitenberg, H., & Henning, K. (1995). Sexual fantasy. *Psychological Bulletin, 117,* 469-496.

Lejonclou, A., Nilsson, D., & Holmqvist, R. (2013). Variants of potentially traumatizing life events in eating disorder patients. *Psychological Trauma: Theory, Research, Practice, and Policy,* December 30. doi:10.1037/a0034926

Lenz, A. S., Taylor, R., Fleming, M., & Serman, N. (2014). Effectiveness of dialectical behavior therapy for treating eating disorders. *Journal of Counseling & Development, 92*(1), 26–35.

Lenzenweger, M. F., Lane, M. C., Loranger, A. W., & Kessler, R. C. (2007). *DSM-IV* personality disorders in the National Comorbidity Survey Replication. *Biological Psychiatry, 62*(6), 553–564.

Leonard, C., Voeller, K., Lombardino, L., Alexander, A., Andersen, H., Morris, M., Garofalakis, M., Hynd, G., Honeyman, J., Mao, J., Agee, F., & Staab, E. (1993). Anomalous cerebral structure in dyslexia revealed with magnetic resonance imaging. *Archives of Neurology, 50,* 461–469.

Leonard, H., Swedo, S., Rapoport, J., Koby, E., Lenane, M., Cheslow, D., & Hamberger, S. (1989). Treatment of obsessive-compulsive disorder with clomipramine and desipramine in children and adolescents. *Archives of General Psychiatry, 46,* 1088–1092.

Leonard, K. E. (1990). Marital functioning among episodic and steady alcoholics. In R. L. Collins, K. E. Leonard, & J. S. Searles (Eds.), *Alcohol and the family: Research and clinical perspectives* (pp. 220–243). New York: Guilford Press.

Leonardi, R. C., & Riemann, B. C. (2012). The co-occurrence of obsessions and compulsions in OCD. *Journal of Obsessive-Compulsive and Related Disorders, 1*(3), 211–215.

Leonardi-Bee, J., Britton, J., & Venn, A. (2011). Secondhand smoke and adverse fetal outcomes in nonsmoking pregnant women: A meta-analysis. *Pediatrics, 127*(4), 734–741. doi:10.1542/peds.2010-3041

Lerner, A. G., Gelkopf, M., Skladman, I., Rudinski, D., Nachshon, H., & Bleich, A. (2003). Clonazepam treatment of lysergic acid diethylamide-induced hallucinogen persisting perception disorder with anxiety features. *International Clinical Psychopharmacology, 18*(2), 101–105. doi:10.1097/00004850-200303000-00007

Leroux, E., Delcroix, N., Alary, M., Razafimandimby, A., Brazo, P., Delamillieure, P., & Dollfus, S. (2013). Functional and white matter abnormalities in the language network in patients with schizophrenia: A combined study with diffusion tensor imaging and functional magnetic resonance imaging. *Schizophrenia Research, 150,* 93–100. doi:10.1016/j.schres.2013.07.016

Lesage, F. X., Berjot, S., & Deschamps, F. (2012). Clinical stress assessment using a visual analogue scale. *Occupational Medicine, 62,* 600–605.

Lesser, I., Lydiard, R. B., Antal, A., Rubin, R., Ballenger, J., & DuPont, R. (1992). Alprazolam plasma concentrations and treatment response in panic disorder and agoraphobia. *American Journal of Psychiatry, 149,* 1556–1562.

Lester, D. (1988). Gun control, gun ownership, and suicide prevention. *Suicide and Life-Threatening Behavior, 18,* 176–180.

Lester, D. (1993). The effectiveness of suicide prevention centers. *Suicide and Life-Threatening Behavior, 23,* 263–267.

Lester, D. (1995). The concentration of neurotransmitter metabolites in the cerebrospinal fluid of suicidal individuals: A meta-analysis. *Pharmacopsychiatry, 28*(2), 45–50. doi:10.1055/s-2007-979587

Lester, D. (2006). Sex differences in completed suicide by schizophrenic patients: A meta-analysis. *Suicide and Life-Threatening Behavior, 36,* 50–56.

Lester, D., & Murrell, M. E. (1980). The influence of gun control laws on suicidal behavior. *American Journal of Psychiatry, 137,* 121–122.

Letourneau, E. J., Resnick, H. S., Kilpatrick, D. G., Saunders, B. E., & Best, C. L. (1996). Comorbidity of sexual problems and post-traumatic stress disorder in female crime victims. *Behavior Therapy, 27,* 321–336.

Leucht, S., Corves, C., Arbter, D., Engel, R. R., Li, C., & Davis, J. M. (2009). Second-generation versus first-generation antipsychotic drugs for schizophrenia: A meta-analysis. *Lancet, 373*(9657), 31–41. doi:10.1016/S0140-6736(08)61764-X

Leung, D., Lam, T., & Chan, S. (2010).Three versions of Perceived Stress Scale: Validation in a sample of Chinese cardiac patients who smoke. *BMC Public Health, 10,* 513.

LeVay, S. (1991). A difference in hypothalamic structure between heterosexual and homosexual men. *Science, 253,* 1034–1037.

Leventhal, A. M., & Antonuccio, D. O. (2009). On chemical imbalances, antidepressants, and the diagnosis of depression. *Ethical Human Psychology and Psychiatry: An International Journal of Critical Inquiry, 11*(3), 199–214. doi:10.1891/1559-4343.11.3.199

Levin, J., & Fox, J. A. (1985). *Mass murder: America's growing menace.* New York: Plenum.

Levin, R. (2008). Critically revisiting aspects of the human sexual response cycle of Masters and Johnson: Correcting errors and suggesting modifications. *Sexual and Relationship Therapy, 23*(4), 393–399.

Levin, R., Sirof, B., Simeon, D., & Guralnik, O. (2004). Role of fantasy proneness, imaginative involvement, and psychological absorption in depersonalization disorder. *Journal of Nervous and Mental Disease, 192*(1), 69–71.

Levine, A. G., & Stone, R. A. (1986). Threats to people and what they value: Residents' perceptions of the hazards of Love Canal. In A. H. Lebovits, A. Baum, & J. E. Singer (Eds.), *Advances in environmental psychology: Vol. 6. Exposure to hazardous substances: Psychological parameters* (pp. 109–130). Hillsdale, NJ: Erlbaum.

Levine, B. E. (2013, August). How our society breeds anxiety, depression and dysfunction. *Salon.* Retrieved on August 8, 2014 from http://www.salon.com/2013/08/26/how_our_society_breeds_anxiety_depression_and_dysfunction_partner/

Levine, K., Shane, H. C., & Wharton, R. H. (1994). What if . . . : A plea to professionals to consider the risk-benefit ratio of facilitated communication. *Mental Retardation, 32*(4), 300–304.

Levine, S. B. (1995). What is clinical sexuality? *Psychiatric Clinics of North America, 18,* 1–6.

Levitt, A. J., Boyle, M. H., Joffe, R. T., & Baumal, Z. (2000). Estimated prevalence of the seasonal subtype of major depression in a Canadian community sample. *The Canadian Journal of Psychiatry/La Revue Canadienne de Psychiatrie, 45*(7), 650–654.

Levy, K. N., Meehan, K. B., & Yeomans, F. E. (2012). An update and overview of the empirical evidence for transference-focused psychotherapy and other psychotherapies for borderline personality disorder. In R. A. Levy, J. Ablon, & H. Kächele (Eds.), *Psychodynamic psychotherapy research: Evidence-based practice and practice-based evidence* (pp. 139–167). Totowa, NJ: Humana Press.

Levy-Lahad, E., Wasco, W., Poorkaj, P., Romano, D. M., Oshima, J., Pettingell, W., Yu, Chang-en, Jondro, P. D., Schmidt, S. D., Wang, K., Crowley, A. C., Fu, Ying-Hui, Guenette, S., Galas, D., Nemens, E., Wijsman, E. M., Bird, T. D., Schellenberg, G. D., & Tanzi, R. E. (1995a). Candidate gene for the chromosome I familial Alzheimer's disease locus. *Science, 269,* 973–977.

Levy-Lahad, E., Wijsman, E. M., Nemens, E., Anderson, L., Goddard, K. A. B., Weber, J. L., Bird, T. D. & Schellenberg, G. D. (1995b). A familial Alzheimer's disease locus on chromosome 1. *Science, 269,* 970–973.

Lewinsohn, P. M. (1974). A behavioral approach to depression. In R. J. Freidman & M. M. Katz (Eds.), *The psychology of depression: Contemporary theory and research* (pp. 157–170). Washington, DC: Winston-Wiley.

Lewinsohn, P. M., & Clarke, G. N. (1984). Group treatment of depressed individuals: The "coping with depression" course. *Advances in Behavior Research and Therapy, 6,* 99–114.

Lewinsohn, P. M., Clarke, G. N., Hops, H., & Andrews, J. (1990). Cognitive-behavioral treatment for depressed adolescents. *Behavior Therapy, 21,* 385–401.

Lewinsohn, P. M., Hoberman, H. M., & Clarke, G. N. (1989). The Coping with Depression Course: Review and future directions. *Canadian Journal of Behavioural Science, 21,* 470–493.

Lewinsohn, P. M., Rohde, P., & Seeley, J. R. (1993). Psychosocial characteristics of adolescents with a history of suicide attempt. *Journal of the American Academy of Child and Adolescent Psychiatry, 31,* 60–68.

Lewinsohn, P. M., Rohde, P., & Seeley, J. R. (1996). Adolescent suicidal ideation and attempts: Prevalence, risk factors, and clinical implications. *Clinical Psychology: Science and Practice, 3,* 25–46.

Lewinsohn, P. M., Youngren, M. A., & Grosscup, S. J. (1979). Reinforcement and depression. In R. A. Depue (Ed.), *The psychobiology of depressive disorders: Implications for the effects of stress.* New York: Academic Press.

Lewinsohn, P. M., Zinbarg, R., Seeley, J. R., Lewinsohn, M., & Sack, W. H. (1997). Lifetime comorbidity among anxiety disorders and between anxiety disorders and other mental disorders in adolescents. *Journal of Anxiety Disorders, 11*(4), 377–394.

Lewis, D. O., Yeager, C. A., Swica, Y., Pincus, J. H., & Lewis, M. (1997). Objective documentation of child abuse and dissociation in 12 murderers with dissociative identity disorder. *American Journal of Psychiatry, 154*(12), 1703–1710.

Lewis, G., Davis, A., Andreason, S., & Allebek, P. (1992). Schizophrenia and city life. *The Lancet, 340,* 137–140.

Lewis, J. A., Dana, R. Q., & Blevins, G. A. (1988). *Substance abuse counseling: An individualized approach.* Pacific Grove, CA: Brooks/Cole.

Lewis, M. A., & Neighbors, C. (2006). Social norms approaches using descriptive drinking norms education: A review of the research on personalized normative feedback. *Journal of American College Health, 54*(4), 213–218. doi:10.3200/JACH.54.4.213-218

Lewis, M. J., Perry, L. B., June, H. L., Garnett, M. L., & Porrino, L. J. (1990). Regional changes in functional brain activity with ethanol stimulant and depressant effects. *Soc Neurosci Abstracts, 16*(1), 459.

Lewis, R. W., Fugl-Meyer, K. S., Corona, G., Hayes, R. D., Laumann, E. O., Moreira Jr, E. D., ... Segraves, T. (2010). Definitions/epidemiology/risk factors for sexual dysfunction. *The Journal of Sexual Medicine, 7*(4pt2), 1598–1607.

Lewis-Fernandez, R. (1994). Culture and dissociation: A comparison of Ataque de Nervios among Pureto Ricans and possession syndrome in India. In D. Spiegel (Ed.), *Dissociation: Culture, mind, and body* (pp. 123–170). Washington DC: American Psychiatric Press.

Lewis-Fernández, R., Guarnaccia, P. J., Martínez, I. E., Salmán, E., Schmidt, A., & Liebowitz, M. (2002). Comparative phenomenology of ataques de nervios, panic attacks, and panic disorder. *Culture, Medicine and Psychiatry, 26*(2), 199–223. doi:10.1023/A:1016349624867

Lewis-Fernández, R., Hinton, D. E., Laria, A. J., Patterson, E. H., Hofmann, S. G., Craske, M. G., . . . Liao, B. (2010). Culture and the anxiety disorders: Recommendations for *DSM-V. Depression and Anxiety, 27*(2), 212–229. doi:10.1002/da.20647

Lewontin, R. C., Rose, S., & Kamin, L. J. (1984). *Not in our genes.* New York: Pantheon.

Lewy, A. J. (1993). Seasonal mood disorders. In D. D. Dunner (Ed.), *Current psychiatric therapy* (pp. 220–225). Philadelphia: W. B. Saunders.

Lewy, A. J., Sack, R. L., Miller, S., Hoban, T. M. (1987). Antidepressant and circadian phase-shifting effects of light. *Science, 235,* 352–354.

Ley, R. (1985). Blood, breathe, and fears: A hyperventilation theory of panic attacks and agoraphobia. *Clinical Psychology Review, 5,* 171–285.

Leyton, E. (1986). *Compulsive killers: The story of modern multiple murder.* New York: New York University Press.

Lezak, M. (1995). *Neuropsychological assessment* (3rd ed.). New York: Oxford University Press.

Li, C., Friedman, B., Conwell, Y., & Fiscella, K. (2007). Validity of the Patient Health Questionnaire 2 (PHQ-2) in identifying major depression in older people. *Journal of the American Geriatrics Society, 55*(4), 596–602. doi:10.1111/j.1532-5415.2007.01103.x

Li, D., Sulovari, A., Cheng, C., Zhao, H., Kranzler, H. R., & Gelernter, J. (2014). Association of gamma-aminobutyric acid A receptor α2 gene (GABRA 2) with alcohol use disorder. *Neuropsychopharmacology, 39*(4), 907–918. doi:10.1038/npp.2013.291

Liberman, R. P. (1972). Behavioral modification of schizophrenia: A review. *Schizophrenia Bulletin, 1,* 37–48.

Lichtenstein, E., & Glasgow, R. E. (1992). Smoking cessation: What have we learned over the past decade? *Journal of Consulting and Clinical Psychlogy, 60*(4), 518–527.

Lichtigfeld, F. J., & Gilman, M. A. (1991). Combination therapy with carbamazepine/benzodiazepine for polydrug analgesic/depressant withdrawal. *Journal of Substance Abuse Treatment, 8*(4), 293–295.

Lickey, M., & Gordon, B. (1991). *Medicine and mental illness: The use of drugs in psychiatry.* New York: W. H. Freeman.

Liddle, P. F., Friston, K., Frith, C., Hirsh, S., Jones, T., & Frackowiak, S. J. (1992). Patterns of blood flow in schizophrenia. *British Journal of Psychiatry, 160,* 179–186.

Lidz, C., Mulvey, E., & Gardner, W. (1993). The accuracy of predictions of violence to others. *Journal of the American Medical Association, 269,* 1007–1011.

Lidz, R. W., & Lidz, T. (1949). The family environment of schizophrenic patients. *American Journal of Psychiatry, 106,* 332–345.

Lieb, K., Vollm, B., Rucker, G., Timmer, A., & Stoffers, J. M. (2010). Pharmacotherapy for borderline personality disorder: Cochrane systematic review of randomised trials. *British Journal of Psychiatry, 196*(1), 4–12.

Lieberman, J. A. (1993). Understanding the mechanism of action of atypical antipsychotic drugs: A review of compounds in use and development. *British Journal of Psychiatry, 63,* 7–18.

Lieberman, J. A., & Koreen, A. R. (1993). Neurochemistry and neuroendocrinology of schizophrenia. *Schizophrenia Bulletin, 19,* 197–256.

Lieberman, J. A., Kinon, B. J., & Loebel, A. D. (1990). Dopaminergic mechanisms in idiopathic and drug-induced psychoses. *Schizophrenia Bulletin, 16*(1), 97–110.

Lieberman, J. A., Stroup, T. S., McEvoy, J. P., Rosenheck, R. A., Perkins, D. O., . . . Hsiao, J. K. (2005). Effectiveness of antipsychotic drugs in patients with chronic schizophrenia, Clinical Antipsychotic Trials of Intervention Effectiveness (CATIE) investigators. *New England Journal of Medicine, 353,* 1209–1223.

Liebrenz, M., Boesch, L., Stohler, R., & Caflisch, C. (2010). Agonist substitution—A treatment alternative for high-dose benzodiazepine-dependent patients? *Addiction, 105*(11), 1870–1874. doi:10.1111/j.1360-0443.2010.02933.x

Lilienfeld, S. O. (1992). The association between antisocial personality and somatization disorders: A review and integration of theoretical models. *Clinical Psychology Review, 12,* 641–662.

Lilienfeld, S. O., & Arkowitz, H. (2011, February 17). Does Alcoholics Anonymous work? For some heavy drinkers, the answer is a tentative yes. *Scientific American.*

Lilienfeld, S. O., & Lynn, S. J. (2003). Dissociative identity disorder: Multiple personalities, multiple controversies. In S. O. Lilienfeld, S. J. Lynn, & J. M. Lohr (Eds.), *Science and pseudoscience in clinical psychology* (pp. 109–142). New York: Guilford Press.

Lilienfeld, S. O., & Lynn, S. J. (2015). Dissociative identity disorder: A contemporary scientific perspective. In S. O. Lilienfeld, S. J. Lynn, & J. M. Lohr (Eds.), *Science and pseudoscience in clinical psychology*, 2nd ed. (pp. 113–154). New York: Guilford Press.

Lilienfeld, S. O., & Marino, L. (1995). Mental disorder as a Roschian concept: A critique of Wakefield's "harmful dysfunction" analysis. *Journal of Abnormal Psychology, 104,* 411–420.

Lilienfeld, S. O., & Waldman, I. D. (1990). The relationship between childhood attention-deficit hyperactivity disorder and adult antisocial behavior reexamined: The problem of heterogeneity. *Clinical Psychology Review, 10,* 699–725.

Lilienfeld, S. O., Wood, J. M., & Garb, H. N. (2000). The scientific status of projective techniques. *Psychological Science in the Public Interest, 1,* 27–66. doi:10.1111/1529-1006.002

Lin, K. L., & Kleinman, A. M. (1988). Psychopathology and course of schizophrenia: A cross-cultural perspective. *Schizophrenia Bulletin, 14,* 555–567.

Lin, K. M., Poland, R., & Fleishaker, J. (1993). Ethnicity and differential response to benzodiazepines. In K. M. Lin, R. Poland, & G. Nakasaki (Eds.), *Psychopharmacology and psychobiology of ethnicity.* Washington, DC: American Psychiatric Press.

Lin, K. M., Poland, R., & Nakasaki, G. (1993). Introduction: Psychopharmacology, psychobiology, and ethnicity. In K. M. Lin, R. Poland, & G. Nakasaki (Eds.), *Psychopharmacology and psychobiology of ethnicity.* Washington, DC: American Psychiatric Press.

Lin, K. M., Poland, R., & Nakasaki, G. (Eds.). (1993). *Psychopharmacology and psychobiology of ethnicity.* Washington, DC: American Psychiatric Press.

Lin, P., Huang, S., & Su, K. (2010). A meta-analytic review of polyunsaturated fatty acid compositions in patients with depression. *Biological Psychiatry, 68*(2), 140–147. doi:10.1016/j.biopsych.2010.03.018

Linares, I. P., Trzesniak, C., Chagas, M. N., Hallak, J. C., Nardi, A. E., & Crippa, J. S. (2012). Neuroimaging in specific phobia disorder: A systematic review of the literature. *Revista Brasileira De Psiquiatria, 34*(1), 101–111. doi:10.1016/S1516-4446(12)70017-X

Linde, K., Berner, M., Egger, M., & Mulrow, C. (2005). St John's wort for depression: Meta-analysis of randomised controlled trials. *The British Journal of Psychiatry, 186*(2), 99–107. doi:10.1192/bjp.186.2.99

Lindesay, J., Macdonald, A. & Starke, I. (1990). *Delirium in the elderly.* Oxford, UK: Oxford University Press.

Lindqvist, D. D., Janelidze, S. S., Erhardt, S. S., Träskman-Bendz, L. L., Engström, G. G., & Brundin, L. L. (2011). CSF biomarkers in suicide attempters—a principal component analysis. *Acta Psychiatrica Scandinavica, 124*(1), 52–61. doi:10.1111/j.1600-0447.2010.01655.x

Lindsay, D. & Read, J. (1995). Memory work and recovered memories of childhood sexual abuse: Scientific evidence and public, professional, and personal issues. *Psychology, Public Policy, and Law, 1,* 846–908.

Lindsey, K. P., & Paul, G. L. (1989). Involuntary commitments to public mental institutions: Issues involving the overrepresentation of Blacks and assessment of relevant functioning. *Psychological Bulletin, 106,* 171–183.

Lindsley, O. R., Skinner, B. F., & Solomon, H. C. (1953). *Studies in behavior therapy. Status report 1.* Waltham, MA: Metropolitan State Hospital.

Linehan, M. M. (1993). *Cognitive-behavioral treatment of borderline personality disorder.* New York: Guilford Press.

Linehan, M. M., Armstrong, H. E., Suarez, A., Allmon, D., & Heard, H. L. (1991). Cognitive-behavioral treatment of chronically parasuicidal borderline patients. *Archives of General Psychiatry, 48,* 1060–1064.

Linehan, M. M., Comtois, K. A., Murray, A. M., Brown, M. Z., Gallop, R. J., Heard, H. L., . . . Lindenboim, N. (2006). Two-year randomized controlled trial and follow-up of dialectical behavior therapy vs. therapy by experts for suicidal behaviors and borderline personality disorder. *Archives of General Psychiatry, 63*(7), 757–766.

Linehan, M. M., & Kehrer, C. A. (1993). Borderline personality disorder. In D. H. Barlow (Ed.), *Clinical handbook of psychological disorders* (pp. 396–441). New York: Guilford Press.

Linehan, M. M., Tutek, D., & Heard, H. L. (1992, November). *Interpersonal and social treatment outcomes for borderline personality disorder.* Poster presented at the annual meeting of the Association for the Advancement of Behavior Therapy, Boston, MA.

Link, B. G., Phelan, J. C., Bresnahan, M., Stueve, A., & Pescosolido, B. A. (1999). Public conceptions of mental illness: Labels, causes, dangerousness, and social distance. *American Journal of Public Health, 89*(9), 1328–1333. doi:10.2105/AJPH.89.9.1328

Link, B., Cullen, E, & Andrews, H. (1993). Reconsidering the violent and illegal behavior of mental patients. *American Sociological Review, 57,* 1229–1236.

Linnoila, M., Virkkunen, M., Scheinin, M., Nuutila, A., Rimon, R., & Goodwin, F. K. (1983). Low cerebrospinal fluid 5-hydroxindoleacetic acid concentration differentiates impulsive from nonimpulsive violent behavior. *Life Sciences, 33,* 2609–2614.

Linz, D., Donnerstein, E., & Penrod, S. (1984). The effects of long-term exposure to filmed violence against women. *Journal of Communication, 34,* 130–147.

Linz, D., Donnerstein, E., & Penrod, S. (1987a). Sexual violence in the news media: Social psychological implications. In P. Shaver & C. Hendrick (Eds.), *Sex and gender.* Newbury, CA: Sage.

Linz, D., Donnerstein, E., & Penrod, S. (1987b). The findings and recommendations of the Attorney General's Commission on Pornography: Do the psychological facts fit the political fury. *American Psychologist, 42,* 946–953.

Linz, D., Donnerstein, E., & Penrod, S. (1988). Effects of long-term exposure to violent and sexually degrading depictions of women. *Journal of Personality & Social Psychology, 55,* 758–768.

Lipowski, Z. J. (1990). *Delirium: Acute confusional states.* New York: Oxford University Press.

Lipp, A. (2011). Universal school-based prevention programmes for alcohol misuse in young people. *International Journal of Evidence-Based Healthcare, 9*(4), 452–453. doi:10.1111/j.1744-1609.2011.00244.x

Lips, W., Mascayano, F., & Lanfranco, R. (2014). Diagnostic indicators of dissociative amnesia: A case report. *Psychiatria Danubina, 26*(1), 70–73.

Lipsey, M. W., & Wilson, D. B. (1993). The efficacy of psychological, educational, and behavioral treatment: Confirmation from meta-analysis. *American Psychologist, 48,* 1181–1209.

Lishman, W. A. (1994). The history of research into dementia and its relationship to current concepts. In F. A. Huppert, C. Brayne, & D. W. O'Connor (Eds.), *Dementia and normal aging* (pp. 41–56). Cambridge: Cambridge University Press.

Lisman, J. (2012). Excitation, inhibition, local oscillations, or large-scale loops: What causes the symptoms of schizophrenia? *Current Opinion in Neurobiology, 22*(3), 537–544. doi:10.1016/j.conb.2011.10.018

List, S. M., & Cleghorn, J. M. (1993). Implications of positron emission tomography research for the investigation of the action of antipsychotic drugs. *British Journal of Psychiatry, 163,* 25–30.

Litt, M. D., Babor, T. F., DelBoca, F. K., Kadden, R. M., & Cooney, N. (1992). Types of alcoholics: II. Application of an empirically derived typology to treatment matching. *Archives of General Psychiatry, 49,* 609–614.

Little, L. M., & Curren, J. P. (1978). Covert sensitization: A clinical procedure in need of some explanation. *Psychological Bulletin, 85,* 513–531.

Litwack, T. R., & Schlesinger, L. B. (1987). Assessing and predicting violence: Research, law and applications. In I. B. Weiner & A. K. Hess (Eds.), *Handbook of forensic psychology.* New York: John Wiley & Sons.

Litz, B. T., & Keane, T. M. (1989). Information processing in anxiety disorders: Application to the understanding of post-traumatic stress disorder. *Clinical Psychology Review, 12,* 417–432.

Liu, T., Wang, X., Hao, W., & Zeng, W. (2000). Frequency of withdrawal symptoms of natural detoxification in heroin addicts. *Chinese Mental Health Journal, 14*(2), 114–116.

Lobo, R. A., Rosen, R. C., Yang, H. M., Block, B., & Van Der Hoop, R. G. (2003). Comparative effects of oral esterified estrogens with and without methyltestosterone on endocrine profiles and dimensions of sexual function in postmenopausal women with hypoactive sexual desire. *Fertility and Sterility, 79*(6), 1341–1352.

Lochman, J. E., & Dodge, K. A. (1994). Social-cognitive processes of severely violent, moderately aggressive and nonaggressive boys. *Journal of Consulting and Clinical Psychology, 62,* 366–374.

Lochman, J. E., & Lenhart, L. A. (1993). Anger coping intervention for aggressive children: Conceptual models and outcome effects: Disinhibition disorders in childhood [Special issue]. *Clinical Psychology Review, 13*(8), 785–805.

Loeb, T. B., Williams, J. K., Carmona, J. V., Rivkin, I., Wyatt, G. E., Chin, D., & Asuan-O'Brien, A. (2002). Child sexual abuse: Associations with the sexual functioning of adolescents and adults. *Annual Review of Sex Research, 13,* 307–345.

Loeber, R. (1990). Development and risk factors of juvenile antisocial behavior and delinquency. *Clinical Psychology Review, 10,* 1–42.

Loeber, R., & Dishion, T. (1983). Early predictors of male delinquency: A review. *Psychological Bulletin, 94,* 68–99.

Loeber, R., & Stouthamer-Loeber, M. (1986). Family factors as correlates and predictors of juvenile conduct problems and delinquency. In M. Tonry & N. Morris (Eds.), *Crime and justice: An annual review of research* (Vol. 7, pp. 29–149). Chicago, IL: University of Chicago Press.

Loeffler, W. (2012, May 19). Faces of Alzheimer's: Celebrities bring visibility to disease. *Trib Live.* Retrieved on December 3, 2014 from http://triblive.com/lifestyles/1826101-74/alzheimer-disease-says-plan-care-diagnosed-families-already-patients-association

Loehlin, J. C. (1989). Partitioning environmental and genetic contributions to behavioral development. *American Psychologist, 44,* 1285–1292.

Loening-Baucke, V. A. (1990). Modulation of abnormal defecation dynamics by biofeedback treatment in chronically constipated children with encopresis. *Journal of Pediatrics, 116,* 214–221.

Loening-Baucke, V. A., & Cruikshank, B. M. (1986). Abnormal defecation dynamics in chronically constipated children with encopresis. *Journal of Pediatrics, 108,* 562-566.

Loewenstein, R. J. (1991). Rational psychopharmacology in the treatment of multiple personality disorder. *Psychiatric Clinics of North America, 14*(3), 721–740.

Loewenstein, R. J. (1996). Dissociative amnesia and dissociative fugue. In W. Michaelson & H. R. Ray (Eds.), *Handbook of dissociation* (pp. 307–336). New York: Plenum.

LoFrisco, B. M. (2011). Female sexual pain disorders and cognitive behavioral therapy. *Journal of Sex Research, 48*(6), 573–579. doi:10.1080/00224499.2010.540682

Loftus, E. (1993). The reality of repressed memories. *American Psychologist, 48,* 518–537.

Loftus, E. (2011). *Manufacturing memories.* Psi Chi Distinguished Lecture. Rocky Mountain Psychological Association Annual Convention. Salt Lake City, UT (April 15).

Loftus, E. F. (1994). The repressed memory controversy. *American Psychologist, 49*(5), 443–445. doi:10.1037/0003-066X.49.5.443.b

Loftus, E. F. (2000). Remembering what never happened. In E. Tulving (Ed.), *Memory, consciousness, and the brain: The Tallinn Conference* (pp. 106–118). New York: Psychology Press.

Loftus, E. F., & Ketcham, K. (1994). *The myth of repressed memory.* New York: St. Martin's Press.

Longnecker, M. P. (1994). Alcohol consumption and the risk of cancer in humans: An overview. *Alcohol, 12*(2), 87–96.

Long-term outcome for children with autism who received early intensive behavioral treatment. *American Journal on Mental Retardation, 97*(4), 359–372.

Lopez, S. R. (1989). Patient variable biases in clinical judgement: Conceptual overview and methodological considerations. *Psychological Bulletin, 106,* 184–203.

López-Figueroa, A. L., Norton, C. S., López-Figueroa, M. O., Armellini-Dodel, D., Burke, S., Akil, H., López, J. F., & Watson S. J. (2004). Serotonin 5-HT1A, 5-HT1B, and 5-HT2A receptor mRNA expression in subjects with major depression, bipolar disorder, and schizophrenia. *Biological Psychiatry, 55,* 225–233.

LoPiccolo, J. (1993). Paraphilias. In D. L. Dunner (Ed.), *Current psychiatric therapy* (pp. 339–346). Philadelphia: W. B. Saunders.

LoPiccolo, J. (1994). The evolution of sex therapy. *Sexual and Marital Therapy, 9,* 5–7.

LoPiccolo, J., & Friedman, J. M. (1989). Broad-spectrum treatment of low sexual desire: Integration of cognitive, behavioral, and systemic therapy. In S. R. Leiblum & R. C. Rosen (Eds), *Principles and practice of sex therapy: Update for the 1990s* (pp. 107–144). New York: Guilford Press.

LoPiccolo, J., & Stock, W. E. (1986). Treatment of sexual dysfunction. *Journal of Consulting and Clinical Psychology, 54,* 158–167.

Lorber, M. (2004). Psychophysiology of aggression, psychopathy, and conduct problems. *Psychological Bulletin, 130,* 531–552.

Lord, J., & Pedlar, A. (1991). Life in the community: Four years after the closure of an institution. *Mental Retardation, 29*(4), 213–221.

Lorion, R. (1978). Research on psychotherapy and behavior change with the disadvantaged. In A. E. Bergin & S. L. Garfield (Eds.), *Handbook of psychotherapy and behavior change.* New York: John Wiley & Sons.

Losel, F., & Schmucker, M. (2005). The effectiveness of treatment for sexual offenders: A comprehensive meta-analysis. *Journal of Experimental Criminology, 1,* 117–146.

Lou, H. C., Henrikson, L., & Bruhn, P. (1984). Focal cerebral hypoperfusion in children with dysphasia and/or attention deficit disorders. *Archives of Neurology, 41,* 825–829.

Lovaas, O. I. (1987). Behavioral treatment and normal educational and intellectual functioning in young autistic children. *Journal of Consulting and Clinical Psychology, 55,* 3–9.

Lovaas, O. I., & Smith, T. (1989). Intensive behavioral treatment with young autistic children. In B. B. Lahey & A. E. Kazdin (Eds.), *Advances in clinical child psychology* (Vol. 11, pp. 285–324). New York: Plenum.

Lovato, L., Ferrão, Y., Stein, D. J., Shavitt, R. G., Fontenelle, L. F., Vivan, A., . . . Cordioli, A. (2012). Skin picking and trichotillomania in adults with obsessive-compulsive disorder. *Comprehensive Psychiatry, 53*(5), 562–568. doi:10.1016/j.comppsych.2011.06.008

Lovejoy, M. C., & Steuerwald, B. L. (1992). Psychological characteristics associated with subsyndromal affective disorder. *Personality and Individual Differences, 13,* 303–308.

Lovejoy, M. C., & Steuerwald, B. L. (1995). Subsyndromal unipolar and bipolar disorders: Comparisons on positive and negative affect. *Journal of Abnormal Psychology, 104*(2), 381–384.

Loveland, K. A., Tunali-Kotoski, B., Pearson, D. A., Brelsford, K. A., Ortegon, J., & Chen, R. (1994). Imitation and expression of facial affect in autism. *Development and Psychopathology, 6,* 433–444.

Lovell, M. R., & Nussbaum, P. D. (1994). Neuropsychological assessment. In C. E. Coffey & J. L. Cummings (Eds.), *Textbook of geriatric neuropsychiatry* (pp. 129–144). Washington, DC: American Psychiatric Press.

Lovibond S. H., & Caddy, G. (1970). Discriminated aversive control in the moderation of alcoholics' drinking behavior. *Behavior Therapy, 1,* 437–444.

Luborsky, L. (1984). *Principles of psychoanalytic psychotherapy: A manual for supportive-expressive treatment.* New York: Basic Books.

Luborsky, L., Singer, B., & Luborsky, L. (1975). Comparative studies of psychotherapies: Is it true that "Everyone has won and all must have prizes" ? *Archives of General Psychiatry, 32,* 995–1008.

Luchsinger, J. A., Reitz, C., Honig, L. S., Tang, M. X., Shea, S., & Mayeux, R. (2005). Aggregation of vascular risk factors and risk of incident Alzheimer disease. *Neurology, 65*(4), 545–551. doi: 10.1212/01.wnl.0000172914.08967.dc

Luck, S. J. (2005). *An introduction to the event-related potential technique.* Boston: The MIT Press.

Luckasson, R., Coulter, D. L., Polloway, E A., Reiss, S., Schalock, R. L., Snell, M. E., Spitalnik, D. M., & Stark, J. A. (1992). *Mental retardation: Definition, classification, and systems of supports.* Washington, DC: American Association on Mental Retardation.

Luczak, S. E., Glatt, S. J., & Wall, T. J. (2006). Meta-analyses of ALDH2 and ADH1B with alcohol dependence in Asians. *Psychological Bulletin, 132*(4), 607–621. doi:10.1037/0033-2909.132.4.607

Ludwig, A. M. (1995). *The price of greatness: Resolving the creativity and madness controversy.* New York: Guilford Press.

Lundahl, B., & Burke, B. L. (2009). The effectiveness and applicability of motivational interviewing: A practice-friendly review of four meta-analyses. *Journal of Clinical Psychology, 65*(11), 1232–1245. doi:10.1002/jclp.20638

Lundahl, B., Moleni, T., Burke, B. L., Butters, R., Tollefson, D., Butler, C., & Rollnick, S. (2013). Motivational interviewing in medical care settings: A systematic review and meta-analysis of randomized controlled trials. *Patient Education and Counseling, 93*(2), 157–168. doi:10.1016/j.pec.2013.07.012

Lundahl, B. W., & Burke, B. L. (2009). The effectiveness and applicability of motivational interviewing: A practice-friendly review of four meta-analyses. *Journal of Clinical Psychology: In session, 65,* 1232–1245.

Lundahl, B. W., Kunz, C., Brownell, C., Tollefson, D., & Burke, B. L. (2010). A meta-analysis of motivational interviewing: Twenty-five years of empirical studies. *Research on Social Work Practice, 20*(2), 137–160. doi:10.1177/1049731509347850

Lunner, K., Wertheim, E. H., Thompson, J. K., Paxton, S. J., McDonald, F., & Halvaarson, K. S. (2000). A cross-cultural examination of weight-related teasing, body image, and eating disturbance in Swedish and Australian samples. *International Journal of Eating Disorders, 28,* 430–435.

Lusignan, F., Godbout, R., Dubuc, M., Daoust, A., Mottard, J., & Zadra, A. (2010). NonREM sleep mentation in chronically treated persons with schizophrenia. *Consciousness and Cognition: An International Journal, 19*(4), 977–985. doi:10.1016/j.concog.2010.09.021

Lykken, D. T. (1957). A study of anxiety in the sociopathic personality. *Journal of Abnormal and Social Psychology, 55,* 6–10.

Lynam, D., Moffitt, T., & Stouthamer-Loeber, M. (1993). Explaining the relation between IQ and delinquency: Class, race, test motivation, school failure, or self-control? *Journal of Abnormal Psychology, 102,* 187–196.

Lynam, D. R., & Widiger, T. A. (2001). Using the five-factor model to represent *DSM-IV* personality disorders: An expert consensus approach. *Journal of Abnormal Psychology, 110*(3), 401–412.

Lyness, S. A. (1993). Predictors of differences between Type A and B individuals in heart rate and blood pressure reactivity. *Psychological Bulletin, 114,* 266–295.

Lynn, S. J., Berg, J., Lilienfeld, S., Merckelbach, H., Biesbrecht, T., Accardi, M., & Cleere, C. (2012). Dissociative disorders. In M. Hersen & D. C. Beidel, *Adult psychopathology and diagnosis* (pp. 497–537). New Jersey: Wiley & Sons.

Lynn, S. J., Condon, L., & Colletti, G. (2013). The treatment of dissociative identity disorder: Questions and considerations. In W. O'Donohue & S. O. Lilienfeld (Eds.), *Case studies in clinical psychological science: Bridging the gap from science to practice* (pp. 329–351). New York: Oxford University Press.

Lynn, S. J., Lilienfeld, S. O., Merckelbach, H., Giesbrecht, T., McNally, R. J., Loftus, E. F., . . . Malaktaris, A. (2014). The trauma model of dissociation: Inconvenient truths and stubborn fictions. Comment on Dalenberg et al. (2012). *Psychological Bulletin, 140*(3), 896–910. doi:10.1037/a0035570

Lynn, S. J., & Pintar, J. (1997). A social narrative model of dissociative identity disorder. *Australian Journal of Clinical and Experimental Hypnosis, 25,* 1–7.

Lynn, S. J., & Ruhe, J. W. (1986). The fantasy-prone person: Hypnosis, imagination, and creativity. *Journal of Personality and Social Psychology, 51,* 404–408.

Lynskey, M., & Hall, W. (2000). The effects of adolescent cannabis use on educational attainment: A review. *Addiction, 95*(11), 1621–1630. doi:10.1046/j.1360-0443.2000.951116213.x

Lyon, G. R. (1985). Identification and remediation of learning disability subtypes: Preliminary findings. *Learning Disabilities Focus, 1,* 21–35.

Lyonfields, J. D., Borkovec, T. D., & Thayer, J. F. (1995). Vagal tone in generalized anxiety disorders and the effects of aversive imagery and worrisome thinking. *Behavior Therapy, 26,* 457–465.

M

Machlin, A., Pirkis, J., & Spittal, M. J. (2013). Which suicides are reported in the media—and what makes them "newsworthy"? *Crisis: The Journal of Crisis, Intervention and Suicide Prevention, 34*(5), 305–313. doi:10.1027/0227-5910/a000177

MacHovek, F. J. (1981). Hypnosis to facilitate recall in psychogenic amnesia and fugue states: Treatment variables. *American Journal of Clinical Hypnosis, 24*(1), 7–13. doi:10.1080/00029157.1981.10403278

Mackie, K., & Hille, B. (1992). Cannabinoids inhibit N-type calcium channels in neuroblastomaglioma cells. *Proceedings of the National Academy of Sciences USA, 89*(9), 3825–3829.

MacMillan, D. L., Gresham, F. M., & Siperstein, G. N. (1993). Conceptual and psychometric concerns about the 1992 AAMR definition of mental retardation. *American Journal on Mental Retardation, 98*(3), 325–335.

Macmilan, M. (1991). *Freud evaluated: The completed arc.* Amersterdam: North-Holland.

MacPhee, D. C., Johnson, S. M., & Van Der Veer, M. M. (1995). Low sexual desire in women: The effects of marital therapy. *Journal of Sex and Marital Therapy, 21,* 159–182.

Madakasira, S., & O'Brien, K. F. (1987). Acute post-traumatic stress disorder in victims of a natural disaster. *Journal of Nervous and Mental Disease, 175,* 286–290.

Maercker, A., Forstmeier, S., Enzler, A., Krüsi, G., Hörler, E., Maier, C., & Ehlert, U. (2008). Adjustment disorders, posttraumatic stress disorder, and depressive disorders in old age: Findings from a community survey. *Comprehensive Psychiatry, 49,* 113–120. doi:10.1016/j.comppsych.2007.07.002

Maercker, A., Forstmeier, S., Pielmaier, L., Spangenberg, L., Brähler, E., & Glaesmer, H. (2012). Adjustment disorders: Prevalence in a representative nationwide survey in Germany. *Social Psychiatry and Psychiatric Epidemiology, 47,* 1745–1752. doi:10.1007/s00127-012-0493-x

Magaletta, P. R., Diamond, P. M., Faust, E., Daggett, D. M., & Camp, S. D. (2009). Estimating the mental illness component of service need in corrections: Results from the Mental Health Prevalence Project. *Criminal Justice and Behavior, 36*(3), 229–244. doi:10.1177/0093854808330390

Magill, M., Gaume, J., Apodaca, T. R., Walthers, J., Mastroleo, N. R., Borsari, B., & Longabaugh, R. (2014). The technical hypothesis of motivational interviewing: A meta-analysis of MI's key causal model. *Journal of Consulting and Clinical Psychology, 82*(6), 973–983. doi:10.1037/a0036833

Magrab, P., & Papadopoulou, Z. L. (1977). The effect of a token economy on dietary compliance for children on hemodialysis. *Journal of Applied Behavioral Analysis, 10,* 573–578.

Magruder, K. M., & Yeager, D. E. (2009). The prevalence of PTSD across war eras and the effect of deployment on PTSD: A systematic review and meta-analysis. *Psychiatric Annals, 39,* 778–788. doi:10.3928/00485713-20090728-04

Magura, S., Rosenblum, A., Lovejoy, M., Handelsman, L., Foote, J., & Stimmel, B. (1994). Neurobehavioral treatment for cocaine-using methadone patients: A preliminary report. *Journal of Addictive Diseases, 13*(4), 143–160.

Maher, B. (1968). *Abnormal psychology.* New York: McGraw-Hill.

Maher, B., & Spitzer, M. (1993). Delusions. In C. G. Costello (Ed.), *Symptoms of schizophrenia* (pp. 92–120). New York: John Wiley & Sons.

Mahler, M. S., Pine, F., & Bergman, A. (1975). *The psychological birth of the human infant.* New York: Basic Books.

Mahoney, M. J. (1993). Introduction to Special Section: Theoretical developments in the cognitive psychotherapies. *Journal of Consulting and Clinical Psychology, 61,* 187–193.

Mahrer, A. R. (1988). Discovery-oriented psychotherapy research: Rationale, aims, and methods. *American Psychologist, 43,* 694–702.

Maier, S. F., Watkins, L. R., & Fleshner, M. (1994). Psychoneuroimmunology: The interface between behavior, brain, and immunity. *American Psychologist, 49,* 1004–1017.

Maier, W., Lichtermann, D., Klingler, T., Heun, R., & Hallmayer, J. (1992). Prevalences of personality disorders (DSM-III-R) in the community. *Journal of Personality Disorders, 6,* 187–196.

Main, M., & Hesse, E. (1990). Parents' unresolved traumatic experiences are related to infant disorganized attachment status: Is frightened and/or frightening parental behavior the linking mechanism? In M. T. Greenberg, D. Cicchetti, & M. Cummings (Eds.), *Attachment in the preschool years: Theory, research, and intervention* (pp. 161–182). Chicago, IL: The University of Chicago Press.

Maj, M. (2012). Bereavement-related depression in the *DSM-5* and *ICD-11. World Psychiatry, 11*(1), 1–2.

Mäkinen, J., Miettunen, J., Isohanni, M., & Koponen, H. (2008). Negative symptoms in schizophrenia—A review. *Nordic Journal of Psychiatry, 62*(5), 334–341. doi:10.1080/08039480801959307

Makino, M., Tsuboi, K., Yasushi, M., & Dennerstein, L. (2004). Prevalence of eating disorders: A comparison of Western and non-Western countries. *Medscape General Medicine, 6*(3), 49.

Makman, M. H. (1994). Morphine receptors in immunocytes and neurons. *Advances in Neuroimmunology, 4*(2), 69–82.

Malamuth, N. M. (1981). Rape proclivity among males. *Journal of Social Issues, 37,* 138–157.

Malamuth, N. M., & Donnerstein, E. (1982). The effects of aggressive-pornographic mass media stimuli. In L. Berkowitz (Ed.), *Advances in experimental social psychology.* Orlando, FL: Academic Press.

Maldonado, J. R., Butler, L. D., & Spiegel, D. (2002). Treatments for dissociative disorders. In P. E. Nathan & J. M. Gorman (Eds.), *A guide to treatments that work* (2nd ed.) (pp. 463–496). New York: Oxford University Press.

Maletsky, B. M. (1973). "Assisted" covert sensitization: A preliminary report. *Behavior Therapy, 4,* 117–119.

Maletsky, B. M. (1991). *Treating the sexual offender.* Newbury Park, CA: Sage.

Maletzky, B. M. (2002). The paraphilias: Research and treatment. In P. E. Nathan & J. M. Gorman (Eds.), *A guide to treatments that work* (2nd ed.) (pp. 525–557). New York: Oxford University Press.

Malhi, G. S., Green, M., Fagiolini, A., Peselow, E. D., & Kumari., V. (2008). Schizoaffective disorder: Diagnostic issues and future recommendations. *Bipolar Disorders, 10,* 215–230.

Mallan, K. M., Lipp, O. V., & Cochrane, B. (2013). Slithering snakes, angry men and out-group members: What and whom are we evolved to fear? *Cognition and Emotion, 27*(7), 1168–1180. doi:10.1080/02699931.2013.778195

Mallick, B. N., & Singh, A. (2011). REM sleep loss increases brain excitability: Role of noradrenalin and its mechanism of action. *Sleep Medicine Reviews, 15*(3), 165–178. doi:10.1016/j.smrv.2010.11.001

Mallinckrodt, C. H., Watkin, J. G., Liu, C., Wohlreich, M. M., & Raskin, J. (2005). Duloxetine in the treatment of major depressive disorder: A comparison of efficacy in patients with and without melancholic features. *BMC Psychiatry, 5,* 1. doi:10.1186/1471-244X-5-1

Mallon, G. P. (1995). *Suicide and the gay and lesbian adolescent.* Workshop presentation. Western Regional Meeting on Youth Suicide, Salt Lake City, UT.

Malta, L. S., Blanchard, E. B., Taylor, A. E., Hickling, E. J., & Freidenberg, B. M. (2002). Personality disorders and post-traumatic stress disorder in motor vehicle accident survivors. *Journal of Nervous and Mental Disease, 190,* 767–774.

Manderscheid, R. W., Atay, J. E., & Crider, R. A. (2009). Changing trends in state psychiatric hospital use from 2002 to 2005. *Psychiatric Services, 60*(1), 29–34. doi:10.1176/appi.ps.60.1.29

Manderscheid, R. W., & Sonnenschein, M. A. (1990). *Mental health, United States 1990.* Rockville, MD: National Institute of Mental Health.

Mangialasche, F., Solomon, A., Winblad, B., Mecocci, P., & Kivipelto, M. (2010). Alzheimer's disease: Clinical trials and drug development. *The Lancet Neurology, 9*(7), 702–716. doi: 10.1016/S1474-4422(10)70119-8

Mangweth-Matzek, B., Rupp, C. I., Hausmann, A., Gusmerotti, S., Kemmler, G., & Biebl, W. (2010). Eating disorders in men: Current features and childhood factors. *Eating and Weight Disorders, 15,* 15–22.

Manly, J. J. (2005). Advantages and disadvantages of separate norms for African Americans. *The Clinical Neuropsychologist, 19*(2), 270–275. doi: 10.1080/13854040590945346

Manly, J. J., & Echemendia, R. J. (2007). Race-specific norms: Using the model of hypertension to understand issues of race, culture, and education in neuropsychology. *Archives of Clinical Neuropsychology, 22*(3), 319–325. doi: 10.1016/j.acn.2007.01.006

Mann, J., & Currier, D. (2011). Evidence-based suicide prevention strategies: An overview. In M. Pompili & R. Tatarelli (Eds.), *Evidence-based practice in suicidology: A source book* (pp. 67–87). Cambridge, MA: Hogrefe Publishing.

Mann, J. J., & Kapur, S. (1991). The emergence of suicidal ideation and behavior during antidepressant pharmacotherapy. *Archives of General Psychiatry, 48,* 1027–1033.

Mannuzza, S., Klein, R. G., Bonagura, N., Malloy, P., Giampino, T. L., & Addalli, K. A. (1991). Hyperactive boys almost grownup: V. Replication of psychiatric status. *Archives of General Psychiatry, 48,* 77–83.

Manschreck, T. C. (1993). Psychomotor abnormalities. In C. G. Costello (Ed.), *Symptoms of schizophrenia* (pp. 261–290). New York: John Wiley & Sons.

Manuck, S. B., Kaplan, J. R., & Clarkson, T. B. (1983). Behaviorally induced heart rate reactivity and atheroslerosis in cynomolgus monkeys. *Psychosomatic Medicine, 49,* 95–108.

Manuck, S. B., Kaplan, J. R., Adams, M. R., & Clarkson, T. B. (1988). Effects of stress and the sympathetic nervous system on coronary artery atherosclerosis in the cynomolgus macaque. *American Heart Journal, 116,* 328–333.

Marar, M., McIlvain, N. M., Fields, S. K., & Comstock, R. D. (2012). Epidemiology of concussions among United States high school athletes in 20 sports. *The American Journal of Sports Medicine, 40,* 747–755.

Marchi, M., & Cohen, R (1990). Early childhood eating behaviors and adolescent eating disorders. *Journal of the American Academy of Child and Adolescent Psychiatry, 29*(1), 112–117.

Marcus, J., Hans, S. L., Nagier, S., Auerbach, J. G., Mirsky, A. F., & Aubrey, A. (1987). Review of the NIMH Israeli Kibbutz-City and the Jerusalem infant development study. *Schizophrenia Bulletin, 13,* 425–438.

Marcus, P. (2014). Teenage marijuana use down nationally. *The Durango Herald.* Retrieved on December 17, 2014 from http://www.durangoherald.com/article/20141216/NEWS01/141219659/0/News/Teenage-marijuana-use-down-nationally

Marengo, J., Harrow, M., & Edell, W. S. (1993). Thought disorder. In C. G. Costello (Ed.), *Symptoms of schizophrenia* (pp. 56–91). New York: John Wiley & Sons.

Margoshes, R (1995a, May). For many, old age is the prime of life. *The APA Monitor, 26,* 36–37.

Margoshes, R (1995b, May). Creative spark lives on, can increase with age. *The APA Monitor, 26,* 37.

Margraf, J., Barlow, D., Clark, D., & Telch, M. (1993). Psychological treatment of panic: Work in progress on outcome, active ingredients, and follow-up. *Behaviour Research and Therapy, 31,* 1–8.

Markesbery, W. R., & Ehmann, W. D. (1994). Brain trace elements in Alzheimer's disease. In R. D. Terry, R. Katzman, & K. L. Bick (Eds.). *Alzheimer's disease* (pp. 353–367). New York: Raven Press.

Markowitz, F. E. (2006). Psychiatric hospital capacity, homelessness, and crime and arrest rates. *Criminology: An Interdisciplinary Journal, 44*(1), 45–72. doi:10.1111/j.1745-9125.2006.00042.x

Markowitz, J., Weissman, M., Ouellette, R., Lish, J., & Klerman, G. (1989). Quality of life in panic disorder. *Archives of General Psychiatry, 46,* 984–992.

Markowitz, J. H., Matthews, K. A., Wing, R. R., Kuller, L. H., & Meilahn, E. (1991). Psychological, biological and health behavior predictors of blood pressure changes in middle-aged women. *Journal of Hypertension, 9,* 399–406.

Marks, I. M. (1987). *Fears, phobias, and rituals.* Oxford, UK: Oxford University Press.

Marks, I. M., & O'Sullivan, G. (1988). Drugs and psychological treatments for agoraphobia/panic and obsessive-compulsive disorders: A review. *British Journal of Psychiatry, 153,* 650–658.

Marks, I. M., Swinson, R. P., Basoglu, M., Kuch, K., Noshirvani, H., O'Sullivan, G., Lelliot, P. T., Kirby, M., McNamee, G., Sengun, S., & Wickwire, K. (1993). Alprazolam and exposure alone and combined in panic disorder with agoraphobia. *British Journal of Psychiatry, 162,* 776–787.

Marlatt, G. A. (1987). Alcohol, the magic elixir: Stress, expectancy, and the transformation of emotional states. In E. Gottheil, K. A. Druly, S. Pashko, S. P. Weinstein (Eds.) *Stress and addiction,* (pp. 302–322). New York: Brunner/Mazel.

Marlatt, G. A., Demming, B., & Reid, J. B. (1973). Loss of control drinking in alcoholics: An experimental analogue. *Journal of Abnormal Psychology, 81,* 223–241.

Marlatt, G. A., & Gordon, J. R. (Eds.). (1985). *Relapse prevention maintenance strategies in the treatment of addictive behaviors.* New York: Guilford Press.

Marlatt, G. A., & Witkiewitz, K. (2005). Relapse prevention for alcohol and drug problems. In G. A. Marlatt & D. M. Donovan (Eds.), *Relapse prevention: Maintenance strategies in the treatment of addictive behaviors* (2nd ed.) (pp. 1–44). New York: Guilford Press.

Marmol, F. (2008). Lithium: Bipolar disorder and neurodegenerative diseases possible cellular mechanisms of the therapeutic effects of lithium. *Progress in Neuro-Psychopharmacology & Biological Psychiatry, 32*(8), 1761–1771. doi:10.1016/j.pnpbp.2008.08.012

Marmorstein, N. R., Iacono, W. G., & McGue, M. (2012). Associations between substance use disorders and major depression in parents and late adolescent–emerging adult offspring: An adoption study. *Addiction, 107*(11), 1965–1973. doi:10.1111/j.1360-0443.2012.03934.x

Maroda, K. J. (2010). *Psychodynamic techniques: Working with emotion in the therapeutic relationship.* New York: Guilford Press.

Maron, E. E., Hettema, J. M., & Shlik, J. J. (2010). Advances in molecular genetics of panic disorder. *Molecular Psychiatry, 15*(7), 681–701. doi:10.1038/mp.2009.145

Marona-Lewicka, D., Nichols, C. D., & Nichols, D. E. (2011). An animal model of schizophrenia based on chronic LSD administration: Old idea, new results. *Neuropharmacology, 61*(3), 503–512. doi:10.1016/j.neuropharm.2011.02.006

Marques, J., Nelson, C., West, M. A., & Day, D. M. (1994). The relationship between treatment goals and recidivism among child molesters. *Behaviour Research and Therapy, 32,* 577–588.

Marques, J. K., Wiederanders, M., Day, D. M., Nelson, C., & van Ommeren, A. (2005). Effects of a relapse prevention program on sexual recidivism: Final results from California's Sex Offender Treatment and Evaluation Project (SOTEP). *Sexual Abuse, 17,* 79–107.

Marques, L., Alegria, M., Becker, A. E., Chen, C.N., Fang, A., Chosak, A., & Diniz, J. B. (2011). Comparative prevalence, correlates of impairment, and service utilization for eating disorders across U.S. ethnic groups: Implications for reducing ethnic disparities in health care access for eating disorders. *International Journal of Eating Disorders, 44*(5), 412–420.

Mars, B., Harold, G. T., Elam, K. K., Sellers, R., Owen, M. J., Craddock, N., . . . Thapar, A. (2013). Specific parental depression symptoms as risk markers for new-onset depression in high-risk offspring. *Journal of Clinical Psychiatry, 74*(9), 925–931.

Marsh, P. J., Odlaug, B. L., Thomarios, N., Davis, A. A., Buchanan, S. N., Meyer, C. S., & Grant, J. E. (2010). Paraphilias in adult psychiatric inpatients. *Annals of Clinical Psychiatry, 22*(2), 129–134.

Marshall, B., & Katz, S. (2002). Forever functional: Sexual fitness and the aging male body. *Body and Society, 8*(4), 43–70.

Marshall, R. D., Beebe, K. L., Oldham, M., & Zaninelli, R. (2001). Efficacy and safety of paroxetine treatment for chronic PTSD: A fixed-dose, placebo-controlled study. *American Journal of Psychiatry, 158,* 1982–1988.

Marshall, R. D., & Pierce, D. (2000). Implications of recent findings in posttraumatic stress disorder and the role of pharmacotherapy. *Harvard Review of Psychiatry, 7,* 247–256.

Marshall, W. L. (2006). Olfactory aversion and directed masturbation in the modification of deviant preferences: A case study of a child molester. *Clinical Case Studies, 5*(1), 3–14.

Marshall, W. L., & Eccles, A. (1996). Cognitive-behavioral treatment of sex offenders. In V. B. Van Hasselt & M. Hersen (Eds.), *Sourcebook of psychological treatment manuals for adult disorders* (pp. 295–332). New York: Plenum.

Marshall, W. L., Eccles, A., & Barbaree, H. E. (1990). The treatment of exhibitionists: A focus on sexual deviance versus cognitive and relationship features. *Behaviour Research and Therapy, 29,* 129–135.

Marshall, W. L., & Fernandez, Y. M. (1998). Cognitive-behavioral approaches to the treatment of the paraphilias: Sexual offenders. In V.E. Caballo (Ed.), *International handbook of cognitive and behavioural treatments for psychological disorders* (pp. 281–312). Oxford, England: Pergamon/Elsevier Science Ltd. doi:10.1016/B978-008043433-9/50012-2

Marshall, W. L., Jones, R., Ward, T., Johnston, P., & Barbaree, H. E. (1991). Treatment outcome with sex offenders. *Clinical Psychology Review, 11,* 465–485.

Martin, A. D. (1982). Learning to hide: The socialization of the gay adolescent. In J. G. Looney, A. Z. Schwartburg & A. D. Sorosky (Eds), *Adolescent psychiatry* (Vol. 10, pp. 52–65). Chicago: University of Chicago Press.

Martin, J. L., Sainz-Pardo, M., Furukawa, T. A., Martín-Sánchez, E., Seoane, T., & Galán, C. (2007). Benzodiazepines in generalized anxiety disorder: Heterogeneity of outcomes based on a systematic review and meta-analysis of clinical trials. *Journal of Psychopharmacology, 21*(7), 774–782. doi:10.1177/0269881107077355

Martin, L. A., Neighbors, H. W., & Griffith, D. M. (2013). The experience of symptoms of depression in men vs women analysis of the national comorbidity survey replication. *JAMA Psychiatry, 70*(10), 1100–1106. doi:10.1001/jamapsychiatry.2013.1985

Martin, P. R. (2007). Understanding alcohol-induced brain disorders through neuroimaging studies. *Alcoologie Et Addictologie, 29*(Suppl 4), 2S–12S.

Martin, R. (1994). *Out of silence: A journey into language.* New York: Holt.

Martínez-Arán, A., Vieta, E., Colom, F., Reinares, M., Benabarre, A., Gastó, C., & Salamero, M. (2000). Cognitive dysfunctions in bipolar disorder: Evidence of neuropsychological disturbances. *Psychotherapy & Psychosomatics, 69,* 2–18.

Marvez, A. (2014, October 30). NFL can do better job following concussion protocols, experts say. *Fox Sports.* Retrieved on December 3, 2014 from http://

www.foxsports.com/nfl/story/nfl-can-do-better-job-with-concussion-protocols-experts-say-103014

Marziali, E. A., & Munroe-Blum, H. (1987). A group approach: The management of projective identification in group treatment of self-destructive borderline patients. *Journal of Personality Disorders, 1*, 340–343.

Masho, S. W., & Ahmed, G. (2007). Age at sexual assault and posttraumatic stress disorder among women: Prevalence, correlates, and implications for prevention. *Journal of Women's Health, 16*, 262–271. doi:10.1089/jwh.2006.M076

Maslow, A. H. (1954). *Motivation and personality.* New York: Harper.

Maslow, A. H. (1962). *Toward a psychology of being.* Princeton, NJ: Van Nostrand.

Massachusetts General Hospital. (2008). *Massachusetts General Hospital comprehensive clinical psychiatry.* (T. A. Stern, Ed.) (1st ed.). Philadelphia, PA: Mosby/Elsevier.

Massion, A., Warshaw, M., & Keller, M. (1993). Quality of life and psychiatric morbidity in panic disorder and generalized anxiety disorder. *American Journal of Psychiatry, 150*, 600–607.

Masson, J. M. (1983). *The assault on the truth: Freud's suppression of the seduction theory.* New York: Farrar, Straus & Giroux.

Mast, R. C., & Smith, A. B. (2012). Elimination disorders: Enuresis and encopresis. In W. M. Klykyo & J. Kay (Eds.), *Clinical child psychiatry* (pp. 305–328). New York: Wiley.

Masters, W. H., & Johnson, V. E. (1966). *Human sexual response.* Boston, MA: Little, Brown and Company.

Masters, W. H. & Johnson, V. E. (1970). *Human sexual inadequacy.* Boston: Little, Brown and Company.

Masur, F. T. (1981). Adherence to health care regimens. In C. K. Prokop & L. A. Bradley (Eds.), *Medical psychology: Contributions to behavioral medicine* (pp. 442–470). New York: Academic Press.

Mathews, D. C., Richards, E. M., Niciu, M. J., Ionescu, D. F., Rasimas, J. J., & Zarate, C. A. Jr. (2013). Neurobiological aspects of suicide and suicide attempts in bipolar disorder. *Translational Neuroscience, 4*, 203–216. doi:10.2478/s13380-013-0120-7

Matson, J. L., Hattier, M. A., Belva, B., & Matson, M. L. (2013). Pica in persons with developmental disabilities: Approaches to treatment. *Research in Developmental Disabilities, 34*(9), 2564–2571. doi: 10.1016/j.ridd.2013.05.018

Matteson, L. K., McGue, M., & Iacono, W. G. (2013). Shared environmental influences on personality: A combined twin and adoption approach. *Behavior Genetics, 43*, 491–504. doi:10.1007/s10519-013-9616-8

Matthews, B. A., Kish, S. J., Xu, X., Boileau, I., Rusjan, P. M., Wilson, A. A., . . . Meyer, J. H. (2014). Greater monoamine oxidase A binding in alcohol dependence. *Biological Psychiatry, 75*(10), 756–764. doi:10.1016/j.biopsych.2013.10.010

Matthews, K. A. (1982). Psychological perspectives on the Type A behavior pattern. *Psychological Bulletin, 91*, 293–323.

Matthews, K. A. (1988). Coronary heart disease and Type A behavior: Update on and alternative to the Booth-Kewley and Friedman (1987) quantitative review. *Psychological Bulletin, 104*, 373–380.

Matthews, K. A., & Haynes, S. G. (1986). Type A behavior pattern and coronary risk: Update and critical evaluation. *American Journal of Epidemiology, 123*, 923–960.

Mattick, R. P., Andrews, G., Hadzi-Pavlovic, D., & Christensen, H. (1990). Treatment of panic and agoraphobia: An integrative review. *Journal of Nervous and Mental Disease, 178*, 567–576.

Mattick, R. P., Breen, C., Kimber, J., & Davoli, M. (2009). Methadone maintenance therapy versus no opioid replacement therapy for opioid dependence. *Cochrane Database of Systematic Reviews, 3*. Art. No.: CD002209. DOI: 10.1002/14651858.CD002209.pub2

Mattick, R. P., Breen, C., Kimber, J., & Davoli, M. (2014). Buprenorphine maintenance versus placebo or methadone maintenance for opioid dependence. *Cochrane Database of Systematic Reviews, 2*. Art. No.: CD002207. DOI: 10.1002/14651858.CD002207.pub4

Mattick, R. P., & Peters, L. (1988). Treatment of severe social phobia: Effects of guided exposure with and without cognitive restructuring. *Journal of Consulting and Clinical Psychology, 56*, 251–260.

Mattila, M., Aranko, K., & Seppala, T. (1982). Acute effects of buspirone and alcohol on psychomotor skills. *Journal of Clinical Psychiatry, 43*, 56–61.

Mattison, A. M. & McWhirter, D. P. (1995). Lesbians, gay males, and their families: Some therapeutic issues. *Psychiatric Clinics of North America, 18*, 123–137.

Mattson, M. E., & Allen, J. P. (1991). Research on matching alcoholic patients to treatments: Findings, issues, and implications. *Journal of Addictive Diseases, 11*(12), 33–49.

Matz, P. A., Altepeter, T. S., & Perlman, B. (1992). MMPI-2 reliability with college students. *Journal of Clinical Psychology, 48*, 330–334.

Mavissakalian, M. R. (1989). Imipramine dose-response relationship in panic disorder with agoraphobia: Preliminary findings. *Archives of General Psychiatry, 46*, 127–131.

Mavissakalian, M. R. (1990). Differential efficacy between tricyclic antidepressants and behavior therapy of panic disorder. In J. Ballenger (Ed.), *Clinical aspects of panic disorder* (pp. 195–209). New York: Wiley-Liss.

Mavissakalian, M. R., & Michelson, L. (1986). Agoraphobia: Relative and combined effectiveness of therapist-assisted in vivo exposure and imipramine. *Journal of Clinical Psychiatry, 47*, 117–122.

Mavissakalian, M. R., & Perel, J. M. (1995). Imipramine treatment of panic disorder with agoraphobia: Dose ranging and plasma level-response relationships. *American Journal of Psychiatry, 152*, 673–682.

Max, W., Sung, H. Y., & Shi, Y. (2012). Deaths from environmental tobacco smoke exposure in the United States: Economic implications. *American Journal of Public Health, 102*, 2173–2180. doi:10.2105/AJPH.2012.300805

Maxwell, H., Tasca, G. A., Ritchie, K., Balfour, L., & Bissada, H. (2014). Change in attachment insecurity is related to improved outcomes 1-year post group therapy in women with binge eating disorder. *Psychotherapy, 51*, 57–65.

May, R. (1969). *Love and will.* New York: W. W. Norton.

Mayberg, H. S., Liotti, M., Brannan, S. K., McGinnis, S., Mahurin, R. K., Jerabek, P. A., . . . Fox, P. T. (1999). Reciprocal limbic-cortical function and negative mood: Converging PET findings in depression and normal sadness. *The American Journal of Psychiatry, 156*(5), 675–682.

Mayhew, S. L., & Gilbert, P. (2008). Compassionate mind training with people who hear malevolent voices: A case series report. *Clinical Psychology & Psychotherapy, 15*(2), 113–138. doi:10.1002/cpp.566

Mayo Clinic (2012). Kegel exercises for men: Understand the benefits. Retrieved October 5, 2014 from http://www.mayoclinic.org/healthy-living/mens-health/in-depth/kegel-exercises-for-men/art-20045074

Mayville, S., Katz, R. C., Gipson, M. T., & Cabral, K. (1999). Assessing the prevalence of body dysmorphic disorder in an ethnically diverse group of adolescents. *Journal of Child and Family Studies, 8*, 357–362.

Mazzucchelli, T., Kane, R., & Rees, C. (2009). Behavioral activation treatments for depression in adults: A meta-analysis and review. *Clinical Psychology: Science and Practice, 16*(4), 383–411. doi:10.1111/j.1468-2850.2009.01178.x

McAdoo, W., & DeMeyer, M. (1978). Personality characteristics of parents. In M. Rutter & E. Schopler (Eds.), *Autism: A reappraisal of concepts and treatment* (pp. 251–267). New York: Plenum.

McAllister, T. W., Flashman, L. A., Maerlender, A., Greenwald, R. M., Beckwith, J. G., Tosteson, T. D., . . . Turco, J. H. (2012). Cognitive effects of one season of head impacts in a cohort of collegiate contact sport athletes. *Neurology, 78*(22), 1777–1784.

McBride, W. J., Murphy, J. M., Lumeng, L., & Li, T.-K. (1990). Serotonin, dopamine, and GABA involvement in alcohol drinking of selectively bred rats. *Alcohol, 7*, 199–205.

McCabe, M. P. (2001). Evaluation of a cognitive behavior therapy program for people with sexual dysfunction. *Journal of Sex & Marital Therapy, 27*, 259–271.

McCarney, R., Schulz, J., & Grey, A. (2012). Effectiveness of mindfulness-based therapies in reducing symptoms of depression: A meta-analysis. *European Journal of Psychotherapy and Counselling, 14*(3), 279–299.

McCarthy, B. (1988). *Male sexual awareness.* New York: Carroll and Graf.

McCarthy, B. (1993). Relapse prevention strategies and techniques in sex therapy. *Journal of Sex and Marital Therapy, 19*, 142–146.

McCartney, K., Harris, M. J., & Bernieri, F. (1990). Growing up and growing apart: A developmental meta-analysis of twin studies. *Psychological Bulletin, 107*, 226–237.

McCarty, C. A., & Weisz, J. R. (2007). Effects of psychotherapy for depression in children and adolescents: What we can (and can't) learn from meta-analysis and component profiling. *Journal of the American Academy of Child & Adolescent Psychiatry, 46*(7), 879–886. doi:10.1097/chi.0b013e31805467b3

McCauley, E., & Myers, K. (1992). The longitudinal clinical course of depression in children and adolescents. *Child and Adolescent Psychiatric Clinics of North America, 1*(1), 183–196.

McCauley, E., Pavlidis, K., & Kendall, K. (2001). Developmental precursors of depression: The child and the social environment. In I.M. Goodyer (Ed.), *The depressed child and adolescent* (2nd ed.) (pp. 46–78). New York: Cambridge University Press. doi:10.1017/CBO9780511543821.004

McCauley, E., Reid, M., Kerns, K., & Calderon, R. (1991, April). *Perceptions of parent and peer relationships in depressed youth.* Paper presented at the meeting of the Society for Research in Child Development, Seattle, WA.

McCave, E. L. (2007). Comprehensive sexuality education vs. abstinence-only sexuality education: The need for evidence-based research and practice. *School Social Work Journal, 32*(1), 14–28.

McConaghy, N. (1990). Assessment and treatment of sex offenders: The Prince of Wales Programme. *Australian and New Zealand Journal of Psychiatry, 24*, 175–181.

McConaghy, N. (1996). Treatment of sexual dysfunctions. In V. B. Van Hasselt & M. Hersen (Eds.), *Sourcebook of psychological treatment manuals for adult disorders.* New York: Plenum.

McCord, J. (1979). Some child rearing antecedents of criminal behavior in adult men. *Journal of Personality and Social Psychology, 9*, 1477-1486.

McCrady, B. S. (1994). Alcoholics Anonymous and behavior therapy: Can habits be treated as diseases? Can diseases be treated as habits? *Journal of Consulting and Clinical Psychology, 62(6)*, 1159–1156.

McCrady, B. S., Stout, R., Noel, N., Abrams, D., & Nelson, H. F. (1991). Effectiveness of three types of spouse-involved behavioral alcoholism treatments. *British Journal of the Addictions, 86*(11), 1415–1424.

McCrae, R. R., & Costa, P. T., Jr. (1994). The stability of personality: Observations and evaluations. *Current Directions in Psychological Science, 3*, 173–175.

McCraw, S., Parker, G., Fletcher, K., & Friend, P. (2013). Self-reported creativity in bipolar disorder: Prevalence, types and associated outcomes in mania versus hypomania. *Journal of Affective Disorders, 151*(3), 831–836. doi:10.1016/j.jad.2013.07.016

McCubbin, J. A. (1993). Stress and endogenous opioids: Behavioral and circulatory interventions. *Biological Psychology, 35*, 91–122.

McCusker, J., Cole, M., Dendukuri, N., Belzile, E., & Primeau, F. (2001). Delirium in older medical inpatients and subsequent cognitive and functional status: A prospective study. *Canadian Medical Association Journal, 165*, 575–583.

McDonald, K. (2012). Trichotillomania: Identification and treatment. *Journal of Counseling & Development, 90*(4), 421–426. doi:10.1002/j.1556-6676.2012.00053.x

McDougle, C. J., Scahill, L., Amana, M. G., McCracken, J. T., Tierney, E., Davies, M., . . . Vitiello, B. (2005). Risperidone for the core symptom domains of autism: Results from the study by the autism network of the research units on pediatric psychopharmacology. *American Journal of Psychiatry, 162*, 1142–1148.

McDowell, J. A., Mion, L. C., Lydon, T. J., & Inouye, S. K. (1998). A nonpharmacologic sleep protocol for hospitalized older patients. *Journal of the American Geriatric Society, 46*, 700–705.

McEachin, J. J., Smith, T., & Lovaas, O. I. (1993). Long-term outcome for children with autism who received early intensive behavioral treatment. *American Journal on Mental Retardation, 97*(4), 359–372.

McEwen, B. S. (1991). Sex differences in the brain: What are they and how do they arise? In M. T. Notman & C. C. Nadelson (Eds.), W*omen and men: New perspectives on gender differences*, (pp. 35–41). Washington, DC: American Psychiatric Press.

McEwen, B. S. (1994). How do sex and stress hormones affect nerve cells? In V. N. Luine & C. F. Harding (Eds.), *Hormonal restructuring of the adult brain: Basic and clinical perspectives*. New York: Annals of the New York Academy of Sciences.

McGee, J. J. (1992). Gentle teaching's assumptions and paradigm. *Journal of Applied Behavior Analysis, 25*, 869-872.

McGlashan, T., & Fenton, W. (1991). Classical subtypes for schizophrenia: Literature review for DSM-IV. *Schizophrenia Bulletin, 17*, 610–632.

McGrath, J., Saha, S., Welham, J., El Saadi, O., MacCauley, C., & Chant, D. (2004). A systematic review of the incidence of schizophrenia: The distribution and the influence of sex, urbanicity, migrant status, and methodology. *BMC Medicine, 2*, 13.

McGrath, M. J., & Cohen, D. B. (1978). REM sleep facilitation of adaptive waking behavior: A review of the literature. *Psychological Bulletin, 85*, 24–57.

McGue, M., Gottesman, I. I., & Rao, D. C. (1983). The transmission of schizophrenia under a multifactorial threshold model. *American Journal of Human Genetics, 55*(6), 1161.

McGue, M., Pickens, R. W., & Svikis, D. S. (1992). Sex and age effects on the inheritance of alcohol problems: A twin study. *Journal of Abnormal Psychology, 101*(3), 3–17.

McGuffin, P., Rijsdijk, F., Andrew, M., Sham, P., Katz, R., & Cardno, A. (2003). The heritability of bipolar affective disorder and the genetic relationship to unipolar depression. *Archives of General Psychiatry, 60*(5), 497–502. doi:10.1001/archpsyc.60.5.497

McGuigan, F. J. (1994). *Biological psychology: A cybernetic science.* Englewood Cliffs, NJ: Prentice Hall.

McGuinness, D. (1985). *When children don't learn: Understanding the biology and psychology of learning disabilities.* New York: Basic Books.

McGuire, J. F., Ung, D., Selles, R. R., Rahman, O., Lewin, A. B., Murphy, T. K., & Storch, E. A. (2014). Treating trichotillomania: A meta-analysis of treatment effects and moderators for behavior therapy and serotonin reuptake inhibitors. *Journal of Psychiatric Research, 58*:76–83. doi:10.1016/j.jpsychires.2014.07.015

McGuire, P. K., Shah, G. M. S., & Murray, R. M. (1993). Increased blood flow in Broca's area during auditory hallucinations in schizophrenia. *Lancet, 342*, 703–706.

McIntyre, R. S., Tohen, M. M., Berk, M. M., Zhao, J. J., & Weiller, E. E. (2013). DSM-5 mixed specifier for manic episodes: Evaluating the effect of depressive features on severity and treatment outcome using asenapine clinical trial data. *Journal of Affective Disorders, 150*(2), 378–383. doi:10.1016/j.jad.2013.04.025

McKeon, R. (Ed.) (1941). *The basic works of Aristotle.* New York: Random House.

McKey, R. H., Condelli, L., Ganson, H., Barrett, B., Mc-Conkey, C., & Plantz, M. (1985). *The impact of Head Start on children, family, and communities: Final report of the Head Start Evaluation, Synthesis and Utilization Project* (DHHS Publication No. OHDS 85-31193). Washington, DC: U.S. Government Printing Office.

McKim, W. A. (1991). *Drugs and behaviors: An introduction to behavioral pharmacology.* Upper Saddle River, NJ: Prentice Hall.

McKinnon, W., Weisse, C. S., Reynolds, C. P., Bowles, C. A., & Baum, A. (1989). Chronic stress, leukocyte sub-populations, and hormonal response to latent viruses. *Health Psychology, 8*, 399–402.

McKowen, J. W., Tompson, M. C., Brown, T. A., & Asarnow, J. R. (2013). Longitudinal associations between depression and problematic substance use in the Youth Partners in Care study. *Journal of Clinical Child and Adolescent Psychology, 42*(5), 669–680. doi:10.1080/15374416.2012.759226

McLean, C. P., & Anderson, E. R. (2009). Brave men and timid women? A review of the gender differences in fear and anxiety. *Clinical Psychology Review, 29*(6), 496–505. doi:10.1016/j.cpr.2009.05.003

McLellan, A. T., Alterman, A. I., Metzger, D. S., Grissom, G. R., Woody, G. E., Luborsky, L., & O'Brien, C. P. (1994). Similarity of outcome predictors across opiate, cocaine, and alcohol treatments: Role of treatment services. *Journal of Consulting and Clinical Psychology, 62*, 1141–1158.

McLeod, J. D., & Kessler, R. C. (1990). Socioeconomic status differences in vulnerability to undesirable life events. *Journal of Health and Social Behavior, 31*, 162–172.

McLeskey, J., & Pacchiano, D. P. (1994). Mainstreaming students with learning disabilities: Are we making progress? *Exceptional Children, 60*, 508–517.

McMahon, R. J., Wells, K. C., & Kotler, J. S. (2006). Conduct problems. In E. J. Mash & R. A. Barkley (Eds.), *Treatment of childhood disorders* (3rd ed., pp. 137–268). New York: Guilford.

McManus, M. A., Hargreaves, P., Rainbow, L., & Alison, L. J. (2013). Paraphilias: definition, diagnosis and treatment. *F1000Prime Rep, 5*, 36. doi: 10.12703/P5-36

McMyler, C. C., & Pryjmachuk, S. S. (2008). Do "no-suicide" contracts work? *Journal of Psychiatric and Mental Health Nursing, 15*(6), 512–522. doi:10.1111/j.1365-2850.2008.01286.x

McNally, R. (1987). Preparedness and phobias: A review. *Psychological Bulletin, 101*, 283–303.

McNally, R. (1994). *Panic disorder: A critical analysis.* New York: Guilford.

McNally, R. J. (2012). Searching for repressed memory. In R. F. Belli (Ed.), *True and false recovered memories: Toward a reconciliation of the debate* (pp. 121–147). New York: Springer Science + Business Media. doi:10.1007/978-1-4614-1195-6_4

McNally, R. J., Hornig, C. D., & Donnell, C. D. (1995). Clinical versus nonclinical panic: A test of suffocation false alarm theory. *Behaviour Research and Therapy, 33*(2), 127–131. doi:10.1016/0005-7967(94)00037-K

McNeal, E. T., & Cimbolic, P. (1986). Antidepressants and biochemical theories of depression. *Psychological Bulletin, 99*, 361–374.

McNeil, D. W., Vrana, S. R., Melamed, B. G., Cuthbert, B. N., & Lang, P. J. (1993). Emotional imagery in simple and social phobia: Fear versus anxiety. *Journal of Abnormal Psychology, 102*, 212–225.

McReynolds, P. (1989). Diagnosis and clinical assessment: Current status and major issues. In M. R. Rosenzweig & L. W. Porter (Eds.), *Annual Review of Psychology* (pp. 83–108). Palo Alto, CA: Annual Reviews.

McWilliams, N. (1994). *Psychoanalytic diagnosis: Understanding personality structure in the clinical process.* New York: Guilford Press.

Meador, B. D., & Rogers, C. R. (1973). Client-centered therapy. In R. Corsini (Ed.), *Current psychotherapies* (pp. 119–165). Itasca, IL: F. E Peacock.

Medawar, C., & Hardon, A. (2004). *Medicines out of control? Antidepressants and the conspiracy of goodwill.* Amsterdam, Netherlands: Aksant Academic Publishers.

Medley, A. N., Capron, D. W., Korte, K. J., & Schmidt, N. B. (2013). Anxiety sensitivity: A potential vulnerability factor for compulsive hoarding. *Cognitive Behaviour Therapy, 42*(1), 45–55. doi:10.1080/16506073.2012.738242

Mednick, S., Gabrielli, W., & Hutchings, B. (1987). Genetic influences in the etiology of criminal behavior. In S. A. Mednick, T. Moffit, & S. Stack (Eds.), *The causes of crime: New biological approaches* (pp. 74–91). Cambridge: Cambridge University Press.

Mednick, S. A., Gabrielli, W. F., & Hutchings, B. (1984). Genetic influences in criminal convictions: Evidence from an adoption cohort. *Science, 224*, 891–894.

Mednick, S. A., Machon, R. A., & Huttunen, M. O. (1990). An update 011 the Helsinki influenza project [Letter to the editor]. *Archives of General Psychiatry, 47*, 292.

Mednick, S. A., Machon, R. A., Huttunen, M. O., & Bonett, D. (1988). Adult schizophrenia following prenatal exposure to an influenza epidemic. *Archives of General Psychiatry, 45*, 189–192.

Mednick, S. A., & Schulsinger, R (1968). Some premorbid characteristics related to breakdown in children with schizophrenic mothers. In D. Rosenthal & S. S. Kety (Eds.), *The transmission of schizophrenia* (pp. 267–291). Oxford, UK: Pergamon Press.Meehan, K. (1998). The myth of beauty. In *Jargonline.* Retrieved August 28, 2014 from http://schools.tdsb.on.ca/jarvisci/jargonline/myth.html

Meehl, P. (1962). Schizophrenia, schizotypy and schizophrenia. *American Psychologist, 17*, 827–838.

Meehl, P. (1990). Toward an integrated theory of schizotaxia, schizotypy, and schizophrenia. *Journal of Personality Disorders, 4,* 1–99.

Meeus, W., Iedema, J., Maassen, G., & Engels, R. (2005). Separation-individuation revisited: On the interplay of parent-adolescent relations, identity, and emotional adjustment in adolescence. *Journal of Adolescence, 28,* 89–106.

Megargee, E. I. (2009). The California Psychological Inventory. In J. N. Butcher (Ed.), *Oxford handbook of personality assessment* (pp. 323–335). New York: Oxford University Press. doi:10.1093/oxfordhb/9780195366877.013.0017

Mehler, P. S. (2011). Medical complications of bulimia nervosa and their treatments. *International Journal of Eating Disorders, 44*(2), 95–104.

Meichenbaum, D. (1971). Examination of model characteristics in reducing avoidance behavior. *Journal of Personality and Social Psychology, 17,* 298–307.

Meier-Tackmann, D., Leonhardt, R. A., Agarwal, D. P., & Goedde, H. W. (1990). Effect of acute ethanol drinking on alcohol metabolism in subjects with different ADH and ALDH genotypes. *Alcohol, 7*(5), 413–418.

Melartin, T., Leskelä, U., Rytsälä, H., Sokero, P., Lestelä-Mielonen, P., & Isometsä, E. (2004). Co-morbidity and stability of melancholic features in *DSM-IV* major depressive disorder. *Psychological Medicine, 34*(8), 1443–1452. doi:10.1017/S0033291704002806

Melloni, R. H., Delville, Y., & Ferris, C. E. (1995). Vaso-suppression/serotonin interactions in the anterior hypothalamus control aggressive behavior in golden hamsters. *Society for Neuroscience Abstracts,* p. 1695.

Melton, G., Petrila, J., Poythress, N., & Slobogin, C. (1987). *Psychological evaluation for the courts.* New York: Guilford Press.

Melton, G. B., Petrila, J., Poythress, N. G., Slobogin, C., Lyons Jr., P. M., & Otto, R. K. (2007). *Psychological evaluations for the courts, third edition: A handbook for mental health professionals and lawyers.* New York: Guilford Press.

Meltzoff, A. N., & Gopnik, A. (1993). The role of imitation in understanding persons and developing a theory of mind. In S. Baron-Cohen, H. Tager-Flusberg, & D. Cohen (Eds.), *Understanding other minds: Perspectives from autism* (pp. 335–366). New York: Oxford University Press.

Meltzoff, J., & Kornreich, M. (1970). *Research in psychotherapy.* New York: Atherton Press.

Mendelson, W. B., & Rich, C. L. (1993). Sedatives and suicide: The San Diego study. *Acta Psychiatrica Scandinavica, 88*(5), 337–341.

Mendelwicz, J., & Rainer, J. D. (1977). Adoption study supporting genetic transmission in manic-depressive illness. *Nature, 268,* 327–329.

Mendez-Bustos, P., de Leon-Martinez, V., Miret, M., Baca-Garcia, E., & Lopez-Castroman, J. (2013). Suicide reattempters: A systematic review. *Harvard Review of Psychiatry, 21*(6), 285–295. doi:10.1097/HRP.0000000000000001

Mendoza, L., Navinés, R., Crippa, J. A., Fagundo, A. B., Gutierrez, F., Nardi, A. E., . . . Martín-Santos, R. (2011). Depersonalization and personality in panic disorder. *Comprehensive Psychiatry, 52*(4), 413–419. doi:10.1016/j.comppsych.2010.09.002

Menezes, N. M., Arenovich, T., & Zipursky, R. B. (2006). A systematic review of longitudinal outcome studies of first-episode psychosis. *Psychological Medicine, 36*(10), 1349–1362. doi:10.1017/S0033291706007951

Menting, A. A., de Castro, B., & Matthys, W. (2013). Effectiveness of The Incredible Years parent training to modify disruptive and prosocial child behavior: A meta-analytic review. *Clinical Psychology Review, 33*(8), 901–913. doi:10.1016/j.cpr.2013.07.006

Menzies, R. G., & Clarke, J. C. (1995). The etiology of phobias: A nonassociative account. *Clinical Psychology Review, 15,* 23–48.

Merckelbach, H., Dejong, P. J., Muris, P., & van den Hout, M. A. (1996). The etiology of specific phobias: A review. *Clinical Psychology Review, 16,* 337–361.

Merckelbach, H., Horselenberg, R., & Schmidt, H. (2002). Modeling the connection between self-reported trauma and dissociation in a student sample. *Personality and Individual Differences, 32*(4), 695–705. doi:10.1016/S0191-8869(01)00070-8

Merckelbach, H., & Muris, P. (2001). The causal link between self-reported trauma and dissociation: A critical review. *Behaviour Research and Therapy, 39,* 245–254.

Mergl, R., Seidscheck, I., Allgaier, A.-K., Möller, H.-J., Hegerl, U., & Henkel, V. (2007). Depressive, anxiety, and somatoform disorders in primary care: Prevalence and recognition. *Depression and Anxiety, 24*(3), 185–195. doi:10.1002/da.20192

Merikangas, K. R. (1990). The genetic epidemiology of alcoholism. *Psychological Medicine, 20,* 11–22.

Merikangas, K. R., Cui, L. L., Heaton, L. L., Nakamura, E. E., Roca, C. C., Ding, J. J., . . . Angst, J. J. (2014). Independence of familial transmission of mania and depression: Results of the NIMH family study of affective spectrum disorders. *Molecular Psychiatry, 19*(2), 214–219. doi:10.1038/mp.2013.116

Merikangas, K. R., Jin, R., He, J., Kessler, R. C., Lee, S., Sampson, N. A., . . . Zarkov, Z. (2011). Prevalence and correlates of bipolar spectrum disorder in the World Mental Health Survey Initiative. *Archives of General Psychiatry, 68*(3), 241–251. doi:10.1001/archgenpsychiatry.2011.12

Merlotti, E., Mucci, A., Volpe, U., Montefusco, V., Monteleone, P., Bucci, P., & Galderisi, S. (2013). Impulsiveness in patients with bulimia nervosa: Electro-physiological evidence of reduced inhibitory control. *Neuropsychobiology, 68*(2), 116–123.

Mersky, H. (1995). The manufacture of personalities: The production of multiple personality disorder. In L. M. Cohen, J. N. Berzoff, & M. R. Elin (Eds.), *Dissociative identity disorder: Theoretical and treatment controversies* (pp. 3–32). Northvale, NJ: Jason Aronson.

Merwood, A. A., Greven, C. U., Price, T. S., Rijsdijk, F. F., Kuntsi, J. J., McLoughlin, G. G., . . . Asherson, P. J. (2013). Different heritabilities but shared etiological influences for parent, teacher, and self-ratings of ADHD symptoms: An adolescent twin study. *Psychological Medicine, 43*(9), 1973–1984.

Messer, K., Pierce, J. P., Zhu, S.-H., Hartman, A. M., Al-Delaimy, W. K., Trinidad, D. R., & Gilpin, E. A. (2007). The California Tobacco Control Programs effect on adult smokers: (1) Smoking cessation. *Tobacco Control, 16*(2), 85–90. 2007-08676-00310.1136/tc.2006.016873. http://0-dx.doi.org.opac.fortlewis.edu/10.1136/tc.2006.016873

Metalsky, G. I., Joiner, T. E., Hardin, T. S., & Abramson, L. Y. (1993). Depressive reactions to failure in a naturalistic setting: A test of the hopelessness and self-esteem theories of depression. *Journal of Abnormal Psychology, 103,* 101–109.

"Methamphetamine and cocaine" (n.d.). *University of Arizona.* Retrieved on December 14, 2014 from http://methoide.fcm.arizona.edu/infocenter/index.cfm?stid=173

Meuwly, N., Bodenmann, G., & Coyne, J. C. (2012). The association between partners' expressed emotion and depression: Mediated by patients' dysfunctional attitudes? *Journal of Social and Clinical Psychology, 31*(7), 690–706. doi:10.1521/jscp.2012.31.7.690

Mewton, L., Slade, T., & Teesson, M. (2013). An evaluation of the proposed *DSM-5* cannabis use disorder criteria using Australian National Survey data. *Journal of Studies on Alcohol and Drugs, 74*(4), 614–621.

Mewton, L., Slade, T., McBride, O., Grove, R., & Teesson, M. (2011). An evaluation of the proposed DSM-5 alcohol use disorder criteria using Australian national data. *Addiction, 106,* 941–950.

Meyer, A., Wapp, M., Strik, W., & Moggi, F. (2014). Association between drinking goal and alcohol use one year after residential treatment: A multicenter study. *Journal of Addictive Diseases, 33*(3), 234–242. doi:10.1080/10550887.2014.950025

Meyer, A. J., Nash, J. D., McAlister, A. L., Maccoby, N., & Farquhar, J. W. (1980). Skills training in a cardiovascular education campaign. *Journal of Consulting and Clinical Psychology, 48,* 129–142.

Meyer, J. (1995). Paraphilias. In H. I. Kaplan & B. J. Sadock (Eds.), *Comprehensive textbook of psychiatry/VI* (pp. 1334–1346). Baltimore: Williams & Wilkins.

Meyer, P. T., Rijntjes, M., & Weiller, C. (2012). Neuroimaging: Functional neuroimaging. In R. B. Daroff, G. M. Fenichel, J. Jankovic, & J. C. Mazziotta (Eds.), *Bradley's neurology in clinical practice,* 6th ed. (Chapter 33C). Philadelphia, PA: Elsevier Saunders.

Meyer, R. B. (1993). *The clinician's handbook: Integrated diagnostics, assessment, and intervention in adult and adolescent psychopathology.* Boston: Allyn & Bacon.

Meyer-Bahlburg, H. F. L. (1993). Psychobiologic research on homosexuality. *Child and Adolescent Psychiatric Clinics of North America, 2,* 489–500.

Meyer-Lindenberg, A., Miletich, R. S., Kohn, P. D., Esposito, G., Carson, R. E., Quarantelli, M., . . . Berman, K. F. (2002). Reduced prefrontal activity predicts exaggerated striatal dopaminergic function in schizophrenia. *Nature Neuroscience, 5,* 267–271.

Meyerowitz, B. E., Heinrich, R. L., & Schag, C. C. (1983). A competency-based approach to coping with cancer. In T. G. Burish & L. A. Bradley (Eds.), *Coping with chronic disease* (pp. 137–158). New York: Academic Press.

Meyler, A., Keller, T. A., Cherkassky, V. L., Gabrieli, J. D. E, & Just, M. A. (2008). Modifying the brain activation of poor readers during sentence comprehension with extended remedial instruction: A longitudinal study of neuroplasticity. *Neuropsychologia, 46,* 2580–2592.

Mezuk, B., Rafferty, J. A., Kershaw, K. N., Hudson, D., Abdou, C. M., Lee, H., . . . Jackson, J. S. (2010). Reconsidering the role of social disadvantage in physical and mental health: Stressful life events, health behaviors, race, and depression. *American Journal of Epidemiology, 172,* 1238–1249.

Mezzich, A., Tarter, R., Kirisci, L., Clark, D., Bukstein, O., & Martin, C. (1993). Subtypes of early age onset alcoholism. *Alcoholism in Clinical and Experimental Research, 17,* 767–770.

Mezzich, J. A., & von Cranach, M. (Eds.). (1988). *International classificaion in psychiatry.* Cambridge: Cambridge University Press.

Mezzich, J. E., Fabrega, H., Coffman, G. A., & Haley, R. (1989). DSM-III disorders in a large sample of psychiatric patients: Frequency and specificity of diagnoses. *American Journal of Psychiatry, 146,* 212–219.

Michael, R. I., Gagnon, J. H., Laumann, E. O., & Kolata, G. (1994). *Sex in America: A definitive survey.* Boston, MA: Little, Brown and Company.

Michal, M., Reuchlein, B., Adler, J., Reiner, I., Beutel, M. E., Vögele, C., . . . Schulz, A. (2014). Striking discrepancy of anomalous body experiences with normal interoceptive accuracy in depersonalization-derealization disorder. *Plos ONE, 9*(2), e89823. doi:10.1371/journal.pone.0089823

Michetti, P. M., Rossi, R., Bonanno, D., De Dominicis, C., Iorl, F., & Simonelli, C. (2007). Dysregulation of emotions and premature ejaculation (PE): Alexithymia in 100 outpatients. *Journal of Sexual Medicine, 4*(5), 1462–1467.

Middleton, L. E., Barnes, D. E., Lui, L., & Yaffe, K. (2010). Physical activity over the life course and its association with cognitive performance and impairment in old age. *Journal of the American Geriatrics Society, 58*(7), 1322–1326. doi:10.1111/j.1532-5415.2010.02903.x

Mihura, J. L., Meyer, G. J., Dumitrascu, N., & Bombel, G. (2013). The validity of individual Rorschach variables: Systematic reviews and meta-analyses of the comprehensive system. *Psychological Bulletin, 139*, 548–605. doi:10.1037/a0029406

Mikita, N., & Stringaris, A. (2013). Mood dysregulation. *European Child & Adolescent Psychiatry, 22*(Suppl 1), 11–16. doi:10.1007/s00787-012-0355-9

Miklowitz, D. J. (2012). Family treatment for bipolar disorder and substance abuse in late adolescence. *Journal of Clinical Psychology, 68*(5), 502–513. doi:10.1002/jclp.21855

Miklowitz, D. J., Axelson, D. A., Birmaher, B., George, E. L., Taylor, D. O., Schneck, C. D., . . . Brent, D. A. (2008). Family-focused treatment for adolescents with bipolar disorder: Results of a 2-year randomized trial. *Archives of General Psychiatry, 65*(9), 1053–1061. doi:10.1001/archpsyc.65.9.1053

Miklowitz, D. J., & Chang, K. D. (2008). Prevention of bipolar disorder in at-risk children: Theoretical assumptions and empirical foundations. *Development and Psychopathology, 20*(3), 881–897. doi:10.1017/S0954579408000424

Miklowitz, D. J., & Goldstein, M. J. (1997). *Bipolar disorder: A family-focused treatment approach.* New York: Guilford Press.

Miklowitz, D. J., Goodwin, G. M., Bauer, M. S., & Geddes, J. R. (2008). Common and specific elements of psychosocial treatments for bipolar disorder: A survey of clinicians participating in randomized trials. *Journal of Psychiatric Practice, 14*(2), 77–85. doi:10.1097/01.pra.0000314314.94791.c9

Miklowitz, D. J., Goldstein, M. J., Nuechterlein, K. H., Snyder, K. S., & Mintz, J. (1988). Family factors and the course of bipolar affective disorder. *Archives of General Psychiatry, 45*, 225–231.

Miklowitz, D. J., Otto, M. W., Frank, E., Reilly-Harrington, N. A., Wisniewski, S. R., Kogan, J. N., . . .Sachs, G. S. (2007). Psychosocial treatments for bipolar depression: A 1-year randomized trial from the systematic treatment enhancement program. *Archives of General Psychiatry, 64*, 419–426. doi: 10.1001/archpsyc.64.4.419

Miklowitz, D. J., Schneck, C. D., George, E. L., Taylor, D. O., Sugar, C. A., Birmaher, B., . . . Axelson, D. A. (2014). Pharmacotherapy and family-focused treatment for adolescents with bipolar I and II disorders: A 2-year randomized trial. *The American Journal of Psychiatry, 171*(6), 658–667. doi:10.1176/appi.ajp.2014.13081130

Miklowitz, D. J., & Scott, J. (2009). Psychosocial treatments for bipolar disorder: Cost-effectiveness, mediating mechanisms, and future directions. *Bipolar Disorders, 11*(Suppl2), 110–122. doi:10.1111/j.1399-5618.2009.00715.x

Milam, J. R., & Ketcham, K. (1983). *Under the influence: A guide to the myths and realities of alcoholism.* New York: Bantam.

Milaniak, I., & Widom, C. S. (2014). Does child abuse and neglect increase risk for perpetration of violence inside and outside the home? *Psychology of Violence.* doi:10.1037/a0037956

Miles, S. W., Sheridan, J., Russell, B., Kydd, R., Wheeler, A., Walters, C., . . . Tiihonen, J. (2013). Extended-release methylphenidate for treatment of amphetamine/methamphetamine dependence: A randomized, double-blind, placebo-controlled trial. *Addiction, 108*(7), 1279–1286. doi:10.1111/add.12109

Miller, B. L., Chang, L., Oropilla, G., & Mena, I. (1994). Alzheimer's disease and frontal lobe dementias. In C. E. Coffey & J. L. Cummings (Eds.). *Textbook of geriatric neuropsychiatry,* (pp. 389–404). Washington, DC: American Psychiatric Press.

Miller, H. L., Combs, D. W., Leeper, J. D., & Bartan, S. N. (1984). An analysis of the effects of suicide prevention facilities on suicide rates in the United States. *American Journal of Public Health, 74,* 340–343.

Miller, I. W., Keitner, G. E., Whisman, M. A., Ryan, C. E., Epstein, N. B., & Bishop, D. S. (1992). Depressed patients with dysfunctional families: Description and course of illness. *Journal of Abnormal Psychology, 101,* 637–646.

Miller, L. K., & Miller, O. (1970). Reinforcing self-help group activities of welfare recipients. *Journal of Applied Behavior Analysis, 3,* 57–64.

Miller, M. (2013). When depression doesn't lead with depression. *JAMA Psychiatry, 70*(11), 1131–1132. doi:10.1001/jamapsychiatry.2013.3493

Miller, N. E. (1969). Learning of visceral and glandular responses. *Science, 163,* 434–445.

Miller, N. S., Gold, M. S., & Pottash, A. C. (1989). A 12-step treatment approach for marijuana (cannabis) dependence. *Journal of Substance Abuse Treatment, 6,* 241–250.

Miller, T. Q., Turner, C. W., Tindale, R. S., Posavac, E. J., & Dugoni, B. L. (1991). Reasons for the trend toward null findings in research on Type A behavior. *Psychological Bulletin, 110,* 469–485.

Miller, W. R. (1983). Motivational interviewing with problem drinkers. *Behavioral Psychotherapy, 11,* 147–172.

Miller, W. R., Benefield, R. G., & Tonigan, J. S. (2001). Enhancing motivation for change in problem drinking: A controlled comparison of two therapist styles. In C. E. Hill (Ed.), *Helping skills: The empirical foundation* (pp. 243–255). Washington, DC: American Psychological Association. doi:10.1037/10412-014

Miller, W. R., & Kurtz, E. (1999). Models of alcoholism used in treatment: Contrasting A.A. and other models with which it is often confused. In *The Collected Ernie Kurtz* (pp. 91–108). Wheeling, WV: The Bishop of Books.

Miller, W. R., Meyers, R. J., & Tonigan, J. S. (1999). Engaging the unmotivated in treatment for alcohol problems: A comparison of three strategies for intervention through family members. *Journal of Consulting and Clinical Psychology, 67*(5), 688–697. doi:10.1037/0022-006X.67.5.688

Miller, W. R., & Munoz, R. F. (1982). *How to control your drinking* (2nd ed.). Albuquerque: University of New Mexico Press.

Miller, W. R., & Rollnick, S. (2013). *Motivational interviewing: Helping people change* (3rd edition). New York: Guilford Press.

Miller, W. R., & Rose, G. S. (2009). Toward a theory of motivational interviewing. *American Psychologist, 64*(6), 527–537. doi:10.1037/a0016830Millman, R. B., & Sbriglio, R. (1986). Patterns of use and psychopathology in chronic marijuana users. *Psychiatric Clinics of North America, 9,* 533–545.

Millon, T. (1987). *Manual for the MCMI-II* (2nd ed.). Minneapolis: National Computer Systems.

Millon, T. (1990). *Toward a new personology.* New York: John Wiley & Sons.

Millon, T. (1991). Classification in psychopathology: Rationale, alternatives, and standards. *Journal of Abnormal Psychology, 100,* 245–261.

Millon, T., & Klerman, G. L. (Eds.). (1986). *Contemporary directions in psychopathology: Toward the DSM-IV.* New York: Guilford Press.

Millon, T., & Meagher, S. E. (2004). The Millon Clinical Multiaxial Inventory-III (MCMI-III). In M. J. Hilsenroth & D. L. Segal (Eds.), *Comprehensive handbook of psychological assessment, Vol. 2: Personality assessment* (pp. 109–121). Hoboken, NJ: Wiley.

Milner, A., Page, A., & LaMontagn, A. D. (2013). Duration of unemployment and suicide in Australia over the period 1985–2006: An ecological investigation by sex and age during rising versus declining national unemployment rates. *Journal of Epidemiology and Community Health, 67*(3), 237–244. doi:10.1136/jech-2012-201594

Milner, J. S. (1994). Assessing physical child abuse risk: The child abuse potential inventory. *Clinical Psychology Review, 14,* 547–583.

Mineka, S., & Cook, M. (1986). Immunization against the observational conditioning of snake fear in Rhesus monkeys. *Journal of Abnormal Psychology, 95,* 307–318.

Mineka, S., Davison, M., Cook, M., & Keir, R. (1984). Observational conditioning of snake fear in Rhesus monkeys. *Journal of Abnormal Psychology, 93,* 355–372.

Minichiello, W., Baer, L., Jenike, M. A., & Holland, A. (1990). Age of onset and major subtypes of obsessive-compulsive disorder. *Journal of Anxiety Disorders, 4,* 147–150.

Minuchin, S. (1974). *Families and family therapy.* Cambridge: Harvard University Press.

Minuchin, S., Rosman, R., & Baker, L. (1978). *Psychosomatic families: Anorexia nervosa in context.* Cambridge: Harvard University Press.

Miquel, L., Usall, J., Reed, C., Bertsch, J., Vieta, E., González-Pinto, A., . . . Haro, J. (2011). Gender differences in outcomes of acute mania: A 12-month follow-up study. *Archives of Women's Mental Health, 14*(2), 107–113. doi:10.1007/s00737-010-0185-z

Mirsky, A., & Orzack, M. H. (1980). Two retrospective studies of psychosurgery. In E. S. Valenstein (Ed), *The psychosurgery debate: Scientific, legal and ethical perspectives* (pp. 205–244). San Francisco: W. C. Freeman.

Mirsky, A., Kugelmass, S., Ingraham, L. J., Frenkel, E., & Nathan, M. (1995). Overview and summary: Twenty-five years follow-up of high-risk children. *Schizophrenia Bulletin, 21,* 227–239.

Mitchell, J., McCauley, E., Burke, P. M., & Moss, S. J. (1988). Phenomenology of depression in children and adolescents. *Journal of American Academy of Child Adolescence Psychiatry, 27,* 12–20.

Mitchell, J. E., Pyle, R. L., Eckert, E. D., Hatsukami, D., Pomeroy, C., & Zimmerman, R. (1990). A comparison study of antidepressants and structured intensive group psychotherapy in the treatment of bulimia nervosa. *Archives in General Psychiatry, 47*(2), 149–157.

Mitchell, R. E., Billings, A. G., & Moos, R. H. (1982). Social support and well-being: Implications for prevention programs. *Journal of Primary Prevention, 3,* 77–98.

Mitchell, S. H., deWit, H., & Zancy, J. P. (1995). Caffeine withdrawal symptoms and self-administration following caffeine deprivation. *Pharmacology, Biochemistry and Behavior, 51*(4), 941–945.

Mittenberg, W., & Strauman, S. (2000). Diagnosis of mild head injury and the postconcussion syndrome. *Journal of Head Trauma Rehabilitation, 15*(2), 783–791.

Miyake, A, Friedman, N. P., Emerson, M. J., Witzki, A. H., Howerter, A., & Wager, T. D. (2000). The unity and diversity of executive functions and their contributions to complex "frontal lobe" tasks: A latent variable analysis. *Cognitive Psychology, 41*(1), 49–100. doi: 10.1006/cogp.1999.0734

Miyamoto, S., Miyake, N., Jarskog, L., Fleischhacker, W., & Lieberman, J. (2012). Pharmacological treatment of schizophrenia: A critical review of the pharmacology and clinical effects of current and future therapeutic agents. *Molecular Psychiatry, 17*, 1206–1227.

Modestin, J. (1992). Multiple personality disorders in Switzerland. *American Journal of Psychiatry, 149*, 88–91.

Moffitt, T. E. (1990). Juvenile delinquency and attention-deficit disorder: Developmental trajectories from age 3 to 15. *Child Development, 61*, 893–910.

Moffitt, T. E. (1993). Adolescence-limited and life-course persistent antisocial behavior: A developmental taxonomy. *Psychological Review, 100*, 674–701.

Moffitt, T. E., Caspi, A., Harrington, H., Milne, B., Melchior, M., Goldberg, D., & Poulton, R. (2010). Generalized anxiety disorder and depression: Childhood risk factors in a birth cohort followed to age 32 years. In D. Goldberg, K. S. Kendler, & P. J. Sirovatka (Eds.), *Diagnostic issues in depression and generalized anxiety disorder: Refining the research agenda for DSM-V* (pp. 217–239). Arlington, VA: American Psychiatric Association.

Moffitt, T. E., Caspi, A., Taylor, A., Kokaua, J., Milne, B. J., Polanczyk, G., & Poulton, R. (2010). How common are common mental disorders? Evidence that lifetime prevalence rates are doubled by prospective versus retrospective ascertainment. *Psychological Medicine, 40*(6), 899–909. doi: 10.1017/S0033291709991036.

Moffitt, T. E., & Lynam, D. R. (1994). The neuro-psychology of conduct disorder and delinquency: Implications for understanding antisocial behavior. In D. Fowles, P. Sutker, & S. Goodman (Eds.), *Psychopathy and antisocial personality: A developmental perspective* (pp. 233–262). New York: Springer.

Mohs, R. C., Breitner, J. C. S., Silverman, J. M., & Davis, K. L. (1987). Alzheimer's disease. Morbid risk among first-degree relatives approximates 50 percent by 90 years of age. *Archives of General Psychiatry, 44*, 405–408.

Moitra, E., Herbert, J. D., & Forman, E. M. (2008). Behavioral avoidance mediates the relationship between anxiety and depressive symptoms among social anxiety disorder patients. *Journal of Anxiety Disorders, 22*(7), 1205–1213. doi:10.1016/j.janxdis.2008.01.002

Mokdad, A. H., Marks, J. S., Stroup, D. F., & Gerberding, J. L. (2004). Actual causes of death in the United States, 2000. *Journal of the American Medical Association, 291*(10), 1238–1245.

Molina, B. S. G., Hinshaw, S. P., Swanson, J. M., Arnold, E. A., Vitiello, B., Jensen, P. S., . . . MTA Cooperative Group. (2009). The MTA at 8 years: Prospective follow-up of children treated for combination type ADHD in a multisite study. *Journal of the American Academy of Child and Adolescent Psychiatry, 48*, 484–500.

Monahan, J. (1981). *The clinical prediction of violent behavior.* Washington, DC: National Institutes of Health.

Monahan, J. (1984). The prediction of violent behavior: Toward a second generation of theory and practice. *American Journal of Psychiatry, 141*, 10–15.

Monahan, J. (1992). Mental disorder and violent behavior: Perceptions and evidence. *American Psychologist, 47*, 511–521.

Mond, J. M., Myers, T. C., Crosby, R. D., Hay, P. J., & Mitchell, J. E. (2010). Bulimic eating disorders in primary care: Hidden morbidity still? *Journal of Clinical Psychology in Medical Settings, 17*(1), 56–63. doi: 10.1007/s10880-009-9180-9

Mondimore, F. M., Zandi, P. P., MacKinnon, D. F., McInnis, M. G., Miller, E. B., Crowe, R. P., . . . Potash, J. B. (2006). Familial aggregation of illness chronicity in recurrent, early-onset major depression pedigrees. *The American Journal of Psychiatry, 163*(9), 1554–1560. doi:10.1176/appi.ajp.163.9.1554

Money, J., & Pranzarone, R. (1993). Development of paraphilia in childhood and adolescence. *Child and Adolescent Psychiatric Clinics of North America, 2*, 463–476.

Moniz, E. (1948). *How I came to perform prefrontal leucotomy* (pp. 7–18). Proceedings of the First International Congress of Psychosurgery, Lisboa, Edicoes Atica.

Monroe, S. M., & Depue, R. A. (1991). Life stress and depression. In J. Becker & A. Kleinman (Eds.), *Psychosocial aspects of depression* (pp. 101–130). Hillsdale, NJ: Erlbaum.

Montgomery, S. A. (2006). Guidelines in major depressive disorder, and their limitations. *International Journal of Psychiatry in Clinical Practice, 10*(Suppl3), 3–9. doi:10.1080/13651500600940492

Monzani, B., Rijsdijk, F., Harris, J., & Mataix-Cols, D. (2014). The structure of genetic and environmental risk factors for dimensional representations of *DSM-5* obsessive-compulsive spectrum disorders. *JAMA Psychiatry, 71*(2), 182–189. doi:10.1001/jamapsychiatry.2013.3524

Monzani, B. B., Rijsdijk, F. F., Anson, M. M., Iervolino, A. C., Cherkas, L. L., Spector, T. T., & Mataix-Cols, D. D. (2012). A twin study of body dysmorphic concerns. *Psychological Medicine, 42*(9), 1949–1955. doi:10.1017/S0033291711002741

Morasco, B. (2013). Psychological treatments for pathological gambling. In P. M. Miller, S. A. Ball, M. E. Bates, A. W. Blume, K. M. Kampman, D. J. Kavanagh, . . . P. De Witte (Eds.), *Comprehensive addictive behaviors and disorders, Vol. 3: Interventions for addiction* (pp. 227–233). San Diego, CA: Elsevier Academic Press. doi:10.1016/B978-0-12-398338-1.00024-5

Moretti, M. (2013). *Natural-born delinquents or psychopathology untreated?* Keynote presentation at the 4th International Conference on the Teaching of Psychology. Vancouver, BC, Canada.

Morey, L. (1991). *Personality Assessment Inventory manual.* Odessa, FL: Psychological Assessment Resources.

Morgan, A. B., & Lilienfeld, S. O. (2000). A meta-analytic review of the relation between antisocial behavior and neuropsychological measures of executive function. *Clinical Psychology Review, 20*, 113–136.

Morgenstern, H., & Glazer, W. (1993). Identifying risk factors for tardive dyskinesia among long-term outpatients maintained with neuroleptic medications: Results of the Yale Tardive Dyskinesia Study. *Archives of General Psychiatry, 50*, 723–733.

Morokoff, P. J. (1978). Determinants of female orgasm. In J. LoPiccolo & L. LoPiccolo (Eds.), *Handbook of sex therapy.* New York: Plenum.

Morokoff, P. J., & Heiman, J. (1980). Effects of erotic stimuli on sexually functional and dysfunctional women: Multiple measures before and after sex therapy. *Behaviour Research and Therapy, 18*, 127–137.

Morris, J. (1974). *Conundrum.* New York, NY: Harcourt Brace Jovanovich, Inc.

Morris, J. G., Grattan, L. M., Mayer, B., & Blackburn, J. K. (2013). Psychological responses and resilience of people and communities impacted by the Deepwater Horizon Oil Spill. *Transactions of the American Clinical and Climatological Association, 124*, 191–201.

Morris, M. C., Ciesla, J. A., & Garber, J. (2008). A prospective study of the cognitive-stress model of depressive symptoms in adolescents. *Journal of Abnormal Psychology, 117*(4), 719–734. doi:10.1037/a0013741

Morrison, J. (1989). Childhood sexual histories of women with somatization disorder. *The American Journal of Psychiatry, 146*(2), 239–241.

Morrow, J., & Nolen-Hoeksema, S. (1990). Effects of responses to depression on the remediation of depressive affect. *Journal of Personality and Social Psychology, 58*, 519–527.

Mortensen, P. B., Pedersen, C. B., Westergaard, T., Wohlfahrt, J., Ewald, H., Mors, O., Andersen, P. K., & Melbye, M. (1999). Effects of family history and place and season of birth on the risk of schizophrenia. *New England Journal of Medicine, 340*, 603–608.

Mortimer, J. A. (1994). What are the risk factors for dementia? In F. A. Huppert, C. Brayne, & D. W. O'Connor (Eds.). *Dementia and normal aging* (pp. 208–229). Cambridge: Cambridge University Press.

Mortimer, J. A., Snowdon, D. A., & Markesbery, W. R. (2003). Head circumference, education and risk of dementia: Findings from the Nun Study. *Journal of Clinical and Experimental Neuropsychology, 25* (5), 671–679. doi: 10.1076/jcen.25.5.671.14584

Moscarelli, M., & Capri, S. (1992). The cost of schizophrenia: Editors' introduction. *Schizophrenia Bulletin, 17*, 367–369.

Moseley, J. B., O'Malley, K., Petersen, N. J., Menke, T. J., Brody, B. A., Kuykendall, D. H., & . . . Wray, N. P. (2002). A controlled trial of arthroscopic surgery for osteoarthritis of the knee. *New England Journal of Medicine, 347*, 81–88.

Mosing, M. A., Gordon, S. D., Medland, S. E., Statham, D. J., Nelson, E. C., Heath, A. C., . . . Wray, N. R. (2009). Genetic and environmental influences on the co-morbidity between depression, panic disorder, agoraphobia, and social phobia: A twin study. *Depression and Anxiety, 26*(11), 1004–1011. doi:10.1002/da.20611

Moskowitz, H., & Smiley, A. (1982). Effects of chronically administered buspirone and diazepam on driving-related skills performance. *Journal of Clinical Psychiatry, 43*, 45–55.

Mossman, K. (1994). Assessing predictions of violence: Being accurate about accuracy. *Journal of Consulting and Clinical Psychology, 62*, 783–792.

Mouridsen, S. (2012). Current status of research on autism spectrum disorders and offending. *Research in Autism Spectrum Disorders, 6*, 79–86. doi:10.1016/j.rasd.2011.09.003

Mowrer, O. H. (1939). A stimulus-response analysis of anxiety and its role as a reinforcing agent. *Psychological Review, 46*, 553–565.

Mrazek, P. J., & Haggerty, R. J. (Eds.). (1994). *Reducing risks for mental disorders: Frontiers for preventive intervention research.* Washington, DC: National Academy Press.

MRFIT (Multiple Risk Factors Intervention Trial Research Group). (1982). Multiple risk factor intervention trial: Risk factor changes and mortality results. *Journal of the American Medical Association, 248*, 1465–1477.

MTA Cooperative Group. (1999). A 14-month randomized clinical trial of treatment strategies for attention-deficit/hyperactivity disorder. *Archives of General Psychiatry, 56*(12), 1073–1086. doi:10.1001/archpsyc.56.12.1073

MTA Cooperative Group (2004a). National Institute of Mental Health multimodal treatment study of ADHD follow-up: 24-month outcomes of treatment strategies for attention-deficit/hyperactivity disorder. *Pediatrics, 113*, 754–761.

MTA Cooperative Group (2004b). National Institute of Mental Health multimodal treatment study of ADHD follow-up: Changes in effectiveness and growth after the end of treatment. *Pediatrics 113*, 762–769.

Mukerjee, M. (1995). Hidden scares: Sexual and other abuse may alter a brain region. *Scientific American,* October, 14–15.

Mukherjee, S., Sackeim, H., & Schnur, D. (1994). Electroconvulsive therapy of acute manic episodes: A review of 50 years experience. *American Journal of Psychiatry, 151,* 169–176.

Mulhall, J., King, R., Glina, S., & Hvidsten, K. (2008). Importance of and satisfaction with sex among men and women worldwide: Results of the Global Better Sex Survey. *Journal of Sexual Medicine, 5*(4), 788–795. doi:10.1111/j.1743-6109.2007.00765.x

Mullen, B., & Suls, J. (1982). The effectiveness of attention and rejection as coping styles. *Journal of Psychosomatic Research, 26,* 43–49.

Mulligan, K., Jones, N., Davies, M., McAllister, P., Fear, N. T., Wessely, S., & Greenberg, N. (2012). Effects of home on the mental health of British forces serving in Iraq and Afghanistan. *The British Journal of Psychiatry, 201,* 193–198. doi:10.1192/bjp.bp.111.097527

Mulvey, E. P., & Lidz, C. W. (1984). Clinical considerations in the prediction of dangerousness in mental patients. *Clinical Psychology Review, 4,* 379–401.

Mundy, P., Sigman, M., & Kasari, C. (1994). Joint attention, developmental level, and symptom presentation in autism. *Development and Psychopathology, 6,* 389–401.

Munn-Chernoff, M. A., Duncan, A. E., Grant, J. D., Wade, T. D., Agrawal, A., Bucholz, K. K., . . . Heath, A. C. (2013). A twin study of alcohol dependence, binge eating, and compensatory behaviors. *Journal of Studies on Alcohol and Drugs, 74*(5), 664–673.

Munoz, R. F., Hollon, S. D., McGrath, E., Rehm, L. P., & VandenBos, G. R. (1994). On the AHCPR *Depression in Primary Care Guidelines:* Further considerations for practitioners. *American Psychologist, 49,* 42–61.

Munro A. (2000). Persistent delusional symptoms and disorders. In M. G. Gelder, J. J. Lopez-Ibor, and N. Andreasen (Eds.), *Oxford textbook of psychiatry* (pp. 651–676). Oxford, UK: New Oxford University Press.

Munroe, R. (1955). *Schools of psychoanalytic thought.* New York: Dryden Press.

Muroff, J., Bratiotis, C., & Steketee, G. (2011). Treatment for hoarding behaviors: A review of the evidence. *Clinical Social Work Journal, 39*(4), 406–423. doi:10.1007/s10615-010-0311-4

Murphy, J. M. (1976). Psychiatric labeling in cross-cultural perspective. *Science, 191,* 1019–1028.

Murphy, W. D., & Page, I. J. (2008). Exhibitionism: Psychopathology and theory. In D. R. Laws & W. T. O'Donohue (Eds.), *Sexual deviance: Theory, assessment, and treatment* (pp. 61–75). New York: Guilford Press.

Murray, C. J. L., & Lopez, A. D. (1996). *The global burden of disease: A comprehensive assessment of mortality and disability from diseases, injuries, and risk factors in 1990 and projected to 2020.* Geneva, Switzerland: World Health Organization.

Murray, C. J. L., & Lopez, A. D. (eds.) (1996). *The global burden of disease and injury series, volume 1: A comprehensive assessment of mortality and disability from diseases, injuries, and risk factors in 1990 and projected to 2020.* Cambridge, MA: Harvard University Press.

Murray, C., & Healy, O. (2013). Increasing response variability in children with autism spectrum disorder using lag schedules of reinforcement. *Research in Autism Spectrum Disorders, 7,* 1481–1488. doi:10.1016/j.rasd.2013.08.004

Murray, S. B., Rieger, E., Touyz, S. W., & De la Garza García, Y. (2010). Muscle dysmorphia and the *DSM-V* conundrum: Where does it belong? A review paper. *International Journal of Eating Disorders, 43*(6), 483–491. doi:10.1002/eat.20828

Musty, R. E., & Kaback, L. (1995). Relationships between motivation and depression in chronic marijuana users. *Life Sciences, 56,* 2151–2155.

Mychailyszyn, M. P., Brodman, D. M., Read, K. L., & Kendall, P. C. (2012). Cognitive-behavioral school-based interventions for anxious and depressed youth: A meta-analysis of outcomes. *Clinical Psychology: Science and Practice, 19*(2), 129–153. doi:10.1111/j.1468-2850.2012.01279.x

Myers, D. G. (2011). *Psychology, 10th edition.* New York: Worth.

Myers, D. G., & Diener, E. (1995). Who is happy? *Psychological Science, 6,* 10–19.

Myers, J., Weissman, M., Tischler, G., Holzer, C. E., Leaf, P., Oravaschel, H., Anthony, J., Boyd, J., Burke, J., Kramer, M., & Stoltzman, R. (1984). Six-month prevalence of psychiatric disorders in three communities. *Archives of General Psychiatry, 41,* 959–967.

Myers, W. C, Bukhanovskiy, A., Justen, E., Morton, R. J., Tilley, J., Adams, K., Vandagriff, V. L., & Hazelwood, R. R. (2008). The relationship between serial sexual murder and autoerotic asphyxiation. *Forensic Science International, 176*(2–3), 187–195.

N

Nabeta, H., Mizoguchi, Y., Matsushima, J., Imamura, Y., Watanabe, I., Tateishi, T., . . . Monji, A. (2014). Association of salivary cortisol levels and later depressive state in elderly people living in a rural community: A 3-year follow-up study. *Journal of Affective Disorders, 158,* 85–89. doi:10.1016/j.jad.2014.02.003

Nabi, R. L., Prestin, A., & So, J. (2013). Facebook friends with (health) benefits? Exploring social network site use and perceptions of social support, stress, and well-being. *Cyberpsychology, Behavior, and Social Networking, 16,* 721–727. doi:10.1089/cyber.2012.0521

Nadel, L., & Jacobs, W. (1998). Traumatic memory is special. *Current Directions in Psychological Science, 7,* 154–157. doi:10.1111/1467-8721.ep10836842

Nahum, L., Pignat, J., Bouzerda-Wahlen, A., Gabriel, D., Liverani, M. C., Lazeyras, F., . . . Schnider, A. (2014). Neural correlate of anterograde amnesia in Wernicke–Korsakoff syndrome. *Brain Topography*, August 23. doi:10.1007/s10548-014-0391-5

Naimi, T. S., Brewer, R. D., Mokdad, A., Clark, D., Serdula, M. K., & Marks, J. S. (2003). Binge drinking among U.S. adults. *JAMA, 289*(1), 70–75.

Nakane, Y., Jorm, A., Yoshioka, K., Christensen, H., Nakane, H., & Griffiths, K. (2005). Public beliefs about causes and risk factors for mental disorders: A comparison of Japan and Australia. *BMC Psychiatry, 5,* 33. doi:10.1186/1471-244X-5-33

Nanda, S. (1990). *Neither man nor woman: The hijras of India.* New York, NY: Wadsworth.

Nandagopal, J. J., & DelBello, M. P. (2010). Pharmacotherapy for pediatric bipolar disorder. *Psychiatric Annals, 40*(4), 221–230. doi:10.3928/00485713-20100330-07

Narrow, W. E., Clarke, D. E., Kuramoto, J., Kraemer, H. C., Kupfer, D. J., Greiner, L., & Regier, D. A. (2013). *DSM-5* field trials in the United States and Canada, part III: Development and reliability testing of a cross-cutting symptom assessment for *DSM-5*. *American Journal of Psychiatry, 170,* 71–82. doi:10.1176/appi.ajp.2012.12071000

Narrow, W. E., Rae, D. S., Robins, L. N., & Regier, D. A. (2002). Revised prevalence estimates of mental disorders in the United States. *Archives of General Psychiatry, 59,* 115–123.

Nathan, D. (2011). *Sybil exposed.* New York: Simon and Schuster.

Nathan, P. E. (1987a). DSM-III-R and the behavior therapist. *Behavior Therapy, 10,* 203–205.

Nathan, P. E. (1987b). What do behavioral scientists know and what can they do about alcoholism? In C. P. Rivers (Ed.), *Alcohol and addictive behavior: Vol. 34. Nebraska Symposium on Motivation.* Lincoln: University of Nebraska Press.

Nathan, S. (1986). The epidemiology of the DSM-III psy-chosexual dysfunctions. *Journal of Sex and Marital Therapy, 12,* 267–281.

National Center for Health Statistics. (1992). *Vital statistics of the United States, 1992.* Washington, DC: U.S. Government Printing Office.

National Center for Transgender Equality. (2014, January). Retrieved November 7, 2014, from http://transequality.org/Resources/TransTerminology_2014.pdf

National Collaborating Centre for Mental Health (London) (2009). Attention deficit hyperactivity disorder: Diagnosis and management of ADHD in children, young people and adults. *Attention deficit hyperactivity disorder National Clinical Practice Guideline Number 72.* Leicester: British Psychological Society.

National Eating Disorders Association. (n.d.). *Athletes and eating disorders.* Retrieved June 9, 2014 from http://www.nationaleatingdisorders.org/athletes-and-eating-disorders

National Eating Disorders Association. (n.d.). *Health consequences of eating disorders.* Retrieved June 24, 2014 from https://www.nationaleatingdisorders.org/health-consequences-eating-disorders

National Heart, Lung, and Blood Institute. (2011). *Your guide to healthy sleep.* (NIH Publication No. 11-5271). Washington, DC: U.S. Government Printing Office.

National Institute for Health and Care Excellence, NICE (2011). *Generalised anxiety disorder and panic disorder (with or without agoraphobia) in adults: Management in primary, secondary and community care.* Retrieved on August 28, 2014 from http://www.nice.org.uk/guidance/cg113/chapter/guidance

National Institute of Mental Health. (1985). *Consensus development conference statement on electroconvulsive therapy,* Vol. 5 (11, pp. 1–8). Bethesda, MD: Author.

National Institute of Mental Health (2011, September 28). *Prescribed stimulant use for ADHD continues to rise steadily.* Retrieved on October 11, 2014 from http://www.nimh.nih.gov/news/science-news/2011/prescribed-stimulant-use-for-adhd-continues-to-rise-steadily.shtml

National Institute on Alcohol Abuse and Alcoholism. (1990). *Alcohol and health: Seventh special report to the U.S. Congress* (DHHS Publication No. ADM 90-1656). Washington, DC: U.S. Government Printing Office.

National Institute on Alcohol Abuse and Alcoholism. (2014). *Alcohol use disorder.* Retrieved on December 11, 2014 from http://niaaa.nih.gov/alcohol-health/overview-alcohol-consumption/alcohol-use-disorders

National Institute on Drug Abuse (1991). *National household survey on drug abuse. Populations estimates 1990.* Rockville, MD: U.S. Department of Health and Human Services.

National Institutes of Health. (1987). Differential diagnosis of dementing diseases. *Journal of the American Medical Association, 258,* 3411–3416.

National Law Center on Homelessness and Poverty (2011). *Simply unacceptable: homelessness and the human right to housing in the United States 2011.* Retrieved on October 29, 2014 from http://www.nlchp.org/Simply_Unacceptable

Nawrot, P., Jordan, S., Eastwood, J., Rotstein, J., Hugenholtz, A. & Feeley, M. (2003). Effects of caffeine on human health. *Food Additives and Contaminants, 20*(1), 1–30.

Nay, W., Brown, R., & Roberson-Nay, R. (2013). Longitudinal course of panic disorder with and without agoraphobia using the National Epidemiologic Survey on Alcohol and Related Conditions (NESARC). *Psychiatry Research, 208*(1), 54–61. doi:10.1016/j.psychres.2013.03.006

Ndetei, D. M., & Vadher, A. (1984). A comparative cross-cultural study of the frequencies of hallucination in schizophrenia. *Acta Psychiatrica Scandinavica, 70*(6), 545–549. doi:10.1111/j.1600-0447.1984.tb01247.x

Neal, A. M., & Turner, S. M. (1991). Anxiety disorders research with African Americans: Current status. *Psychological Bulletin, 109*, 400–410.

Neal-Barnett, A., Flessner, C., Franklin, M. E., Woods, D. W., Keuthen, N. J., & Stein, D. J. (2010). Ethnic differences in trichotillomania: Phenomenology, interference, impairment, and treatment efficacy. *Journal of Anxiety Disorders, 24*, 553–558.

Nelson, S. (2014). *Hallucinogens: Unreal visions.* Broomall, PA: Mason Crest.

Nemeroff, C. B., & Schatzberg, A. F. (2007). Pharmacological treatments for unipolar depression. In P.E. Nathan & J.M. Gorman (Eds.), *A guide to treatments that work* (3rd ed.) (pp. 271–287). New York: Oxford University Press.

Nemzer, E. D. (1996). Psychopharmacologic interventions for children and adolescents with dissociative disorders. In J. L. Silberg (Ed.), *The dissociative child: Diagnosis, treatment, and management* (2nd ed.) (pp. 235–270). Baltimore, MD: The Sidran Press.

Nestler, E. J. (2014). Epigenetic mechanisms of drug addiction. *Neuropharmacology, 76* (Part B), 259–268. doi:10.1016/j.neuropharm.2013.04.004

New Freedom Commission on Mental Health. (2003). *Achieving the promise: Transforming mental health care in America.* Rockville, MD: President's New Freedom Commission on Mental Health.

New Health Guide (2014). *Famous people with OCD.* Retrieved on September 15, 2014 from http://www.newhealthguide.org/Famous-People-With-Ocd.html

Newcorn, J. H., Kratochvil, C. J., Allen, A. J., Casat, C. D., Ruff, D. D., Moore, R. J, & Michelson, D. (2008). Atomoxetine and osmotically released methylphenidate for the treatment of attention deficit/hyperactivity disorder: Acute comparison and differential response. *American Journal of Psychiatry, 165*, 721–730.

Newman, D. (2011). Special issue on neuroscience: The autism enigma. *Nature, 479*, 21. doi:10.1038/479021a

Newman, D. L., Moffitt, T. E., Caspi, A., Magdol, L., Silva, P., & Stanton, W. R. (1996). Psychiatric disorder in a birth cohort of young adults: Prevalence, comorbidity, clinical significance, and new case incidence from ages 11 to 21. *Journal of Consulting and Clinical Psychology, 64*, 552–562.

Newman, E., Orsillo, S. M., Herman, D. S., Niles, B. L., & Litz, B. T. (1995). Clinical presentation of disorders of extreme stress in combat veterans. *Journal of Nervous and Mental Disease, 183*, 628–632.

Newman, S. C., & Bland, R. C. (2006). A population-based family study of DSM-III generalized anxiety disorder. *Psychological Medicine, 36*(9), 1275–1281. doi:10.1017/S0033291706007732

Newman, S. C., & Bland, R. C. (2009). A population-based family study of minor depression. *Depression and Anxiety, 26*(4), 389–392. doi:10.1002/da.20560

Newton-Howes, G., & Wood, R. (2013). Cognitive behavioural therapy and the psychopathology of schizophrenia: Systematic review and meta-analysis. *Psychology and Psychotherapy: Theory, Research and Practice, 86*(2), 127–138. doi:10.1111/j.2044-8341.2011.02048.x

Newton-Howes, G., Tyrer, P., & Johnson, T. (2006). Personality disorder and the outcome of depression: Meta-analysis of published studies. *British Journal of Psychiatry, 188*, 13–20.

Neziroglu, F., Anemone, R., & Yaryura-Tobias, Jj. A. (1992). Onset of obsessive-compulsive disorder in pregnancy. *American Journal of Psychiatry, 149*, 947–950.

Neziroglu, F., McKay, D., Fodaro, J., & Yaryura-Tobias, J. A. (1996). Effect of cognitive behavior therapy on persons with body dysmorphic disorder and co-morbid Axis II diagnoses. *Behavior Therapy, 27*, 67–68.

Nichols, D. S. (2006). Tell me a story: MMPI responses and personal biography in the case of a serial killer. *Journal of Personality Assessment, 86*, 242–262.

Nicholson, R. A., & Berman, J. S. (1983). Is follow-up necessary in evaluating psychotherapy? *Psychological Bulletin, 93*, 261–278.

Nicholson, R. A., & Kugler, K. E. (1991). Competent and incompetent criminal defendants: A quantitative review of comparative research. *Psychological Bulletin, 109*, 355–370.

Nicholson, R. A., Norwood, S., & Enyart, C. (1991). Characteristics and outcomes of insanity acquitees in Oklahoma. *Behavioral Sciences and the Law, 9*, 487–500.

Nicolosi, J. (1991). *Reparative therapy of male homosexuality.* Northvale, NJ: Aronson.

Nicolosi, J. (1994). Objections to AAP statement on homosexuality and adolescence (letter). *Pediatrics, 92*, 631–634.

Nicolosi, S., Buvat, J., Glasser, D. B., Hartmann, U., Laumann, E. O., & Gingell, C. (2006). Sexual behaviour, sexual dysfunctions and related help seeking patterns in middle-aged and elderly Europeans: The global study of sexual attitudes and behaviors. *World Journal of Urology, 24*, 423–428.

Nicolson, R. I., & Fawcett, A. J. (2008). *Dyslexia, learning, and the brain.* Cambridge, MA: MIT Press.

Niederkrotenthaler, T., Fu, K., Yip, P. F., Fong, D. T., Stack, S., Cheng, Q., & Pirkis, J. (2012). Changes in suicide rates following media reports on celebrity suicide: A meta-analysis. *Journal of Epidemiology and Community Health, 66*(11), 1037–1042. doi:10.1136/jech-2011-200707

Nietzel, M. T. (1979). *Crime and its modification: A social learning perspective.* New York: Pergamon Press.

Nietzel, M. T., Bernstein, D. A., & Milich, R. (1998). *Introduction to clinical psychology* (4th ed.). Englewood Cliffs, NJ: Prentice Hall.

Nietzel, M. T., & Dillehay, R. C. (1986). *Psychological consultation in the courtroom.* New York: Pergamon Press.

Nietzel, M. T., & Fisher, S. G. (1981). Effectiveness of professional and paraprofessional helpers. A reply to Durlak. *Psychological Bulletin, 89*, 555–565.

Nietzel, M. T., Guthrie, P. R., & Susman, D. T. (1991). Utilization of community and social support services. In F. H. Kanfer & A. P. Goldstein (Eds.), *Helping people change* (4th ed., pp. 396–421). New York: Pergamon Press.

Nietzel, M. T., & Harris, M. (1990). Relationship of dependency and achievement/autonomy to depression. *Clinical Psychology Review, 10*, 279–297.

Nietzel, M. T., Hasemann, D. M., & Lynam, D. R. (1999). Behavioral perspectives on violent behavior. In V. B. Van Hasselt & M. Hersen (Eds.), *Handbook of psychological approaches with violent offenders: Contemporary strategies and issues* (pp. 39–66). New York: Plenum.

Nietzel, M. T., & Himelein, M. (1986). Prevention of crime and delinquency. In L. Michelson & B. Edelstein (Eds.), *Handbook of prevention* (pp. 195–221). New York: Plenum.

Nietzel, M. T., Russell, R. L., Hemmings, K. A., &; Gretter, M. L. (1987). The clinical significance of psychotherapy for unipolar depression: A meta-analytic approach to social comparison. *Journal of Consulting and Clinical Psychology, 55*, 156–161.

Nietzel, M. T., & Trull, T. J. (1988). Meta-analytic approaches to social comparisons: A method for measuring clinical significance. *Behavioral Assessment, 10*, 159–169.

Nietzel, M. T., Winett, R. A., Macdonald, M. L., & Davidson, W. S. (1977). *Behavioral approaches to community psychology.* New York: Pergamon Press.

Nigg, J. (2008). ADHD, lead exposure and prevention: How much lead or how much evidence is needed? *Expert Review of Neurotherapeutics, 8*, 519–521.

Nigg, J. T., & Goldsmith, H. H. (1994). Genetics of personality disorders: Perspectives from personality and psychopathology research. *Psychological Bulletin, 115*, 346–380.

Nigg, J. T., Lewis, K., Edinger, T., & Falk, M. (2012). Meta-analysis of attention-deficit/hyperactivity disorder or attention-deficit/hyperactivity disorder symptoms, restriction diet, and synthetic food color additives. *Journal of the American Academy of Child & Adolescent Psychiatry, 51*(1), 86–97. doi:10.1016/j.jaac.2011.10.015

Nihira, K., Leland, H., & Lambert, N. (1993). *Adaptive behavior scales: Residential and community.* Austin, Texas: Pro-Ed.

Nijenhuis, E. S. (2009). Somatoform dissociation and somatoform dissociative disorders. In P. F. Dell & J. A. O'Neil (Eds.), *Dissociation and the dissociative disorders: DSM-V and beyond* (pp. 259–275). New York: Routledge/Taylor & Francis Group.

Nijenhuis, E. S. (2014). Ten reasons for conceiving and classifying post-traumatic stress disorder as a dissociative disorder. *Psichiatria E Psicoterapia, 33*(1), 74–106.

Nikkelen, S. C., Valkenburg, P. M., Huizinga, M., & Bushman, B. J. (2014). Media use and ADHD-related behaviors in children and adolescents: A meta-analysis. *Developmental Psychology, 50*(9), 2228–2241. doi:10.1037/a0037318

Nikolaus, S., Hautzel, H., Heinzel, A., & Müller, H. (2012). Key players in major and bipolar depression—A retrospective analysis of in vivo imaging studies. *Behavioural Brain Research, 232*(2), 358–390. doi:10.1016/j.bbr.2012.03.021

Nilsson, K. W., Wargelius, H., Sjöberg, R. L., Leppert, J., & Oreland, L. (2008). The MAO-A gene, platelet MAO-B activity and psychosocial environment in adolescent female alcohol-related problem behaviour. *Drug and Alcohol Dependence, 93*(1–2), 51–62. doi:10.1016/j.drugalcdep.2007.08.022

Nimnuan, C., Hotopf, M., & Wessely, S. (2001). Medically unexplained symptoms: An epidemiological study in seven specialties. *Journal of Psychosomatic Research, 51*(1), 361–367. doi:10.1016/S0022-3999(01)00223-9. PMID 11448704.

Nobel Media AB (2013). *The Nobel Prize in physiology or medicine 2013.* Retrieved January 2, 2014, from http://www.nobelprize.org.

Noble, R. N., Heath, N. L., & Toste, J. R. (2011). Positive illusions in adolescents: The relationship between academic self-enhancement and depressive symptomatology. *Child Psychiatry and Human Development, 42*(6), 650–665. doi:10.1007/s10578-011-0242-5

Nobler, M., & Sackeim, H. (1993). ECT stimulus dosing: Relations to efficacy and adverse effects. In C. E. Coffey (Ed.), *The clinical science of electroconvulsive therapy* (pp. 29–52). Washington, DC: American Psychiatric Press.

Nobler, M. S., Sackeim, H. A., Prohovnik, I., Moeller, J. R., Schnur, D. B., Prudic, J., & Devanand, D. P. (1994). Regional cerebral blood flow in mood disorders. III: Treatment and clinical response. *Archives of General Psychiatry, 51*, 884–897.

Nobre, P. J., & Pinto-Gouveia, J. (2006). Dysfunctional sexual beliefs as vulnerability factors for sexual dysfunction. *Journal of Sex Research, 43*(1), 68–75. doi:10.1080/00224490609552300

Nock, M. K., Deming, C. A., Fullerton, C. S., Gilman, S. E., Goldenberg, M., Kessler, R. C., . . . Ursano, R. J. (2013). Suicide among soldiers: A review of psychosocial risk and protective factors. *Psychiatry: Interpersonal and Biological Processes, 76*(2), 97–125. doi:10.1521/psyc.2013.76.2.97

Nock, M. K., Kazdin, A. E., Hiripi, E., & Kessler, R. C. (2007). Lifetime prevalence, correlates, and persistence of oppositional defiant disorder: Results from the National Comorbidity Survey Replication. *Journal of Child Psychology and Psychiatry, 48*, 703–713.

Nolen-Hoeksema, S. (1987). Sex differences in unipolar depression: Evidence and theory. *Psychological Bulletin, 101*, 259–282.

Nolen-Hoeksema, S. (1991). Responses to depression and their effects on the duration of depressive episodes. *Journal of Abnormal Psychology, 100*, 569–582. doi:10.1037/0021-843X.100.4.569

Nolen-Hoeksema, S., Morrow, J., & Fredrickson, B. (1993). Response styles and the duration of episodes of depressed mood. *Journal of Abnormal Psychology, 102*, 20–28.

Nolen-Hoeksema, S., Wisco, B. E., & Lyubomirsky, S. (2008). Rethinking rumination. *Perspectives on Psychological Science, 3*(5), 400–424.

Noll, R. B., Zucker R. A., & Greenberg, G. S. (1990). Identification of alcohol by smell among preschoolers: Evidence for early socialization about drugs occurring in the home. *Child Development, 61*(5), 1520–1527.

Norcross, J. C. (2002). *Psychotherapy relationships that work: Therapist contributions and responsiveness to patients.* New York: Oxford University Press.

Nordentoft, M., Mortensen, P. B., & Pedersen, C. B. (2011). Absolute risk of suicide after first hospital contact in mental disorder. *Archives of General Psychiatry, 68*, 1058–1064.

Nordsletten, A. E., Reichenberg, A., Hatch, S. L., de la Cruz, L., Pertusa, A., Hotopf, M., & Mataix-Cols, D. (2013). Epidemiology of hoarding disorder. *The British Journal of Psychiatry, 203*(6), 445–452. doi:10.1192/bjp.bp.113.130195

Nordstrom, B. R., & Levin, F. R. (2007). Treatment of cannabis use disorders: A review of the literature. *The American Journal on Addictions, 16*(5), 331–342. doi:10.1080/10550490701525665

North, C. S., Ryall, J. E. M., Ricci, D. A., & Wetzsel, R. D. (1993). *Multiple personalities, multiple disorders: Psychiatric classification and media influence.* New York: Oxford University Press.

Norton, P. J., & Philipp, L. M. (2008). Transdiagnostic approaches to the treatment of anxiety disorders: A quantitative review. *Psychotherapy: Theory, Research, Practice, Training, 45*, 214–226. doi:10.1037/0033-3204.45.2.214

Novella, S. (2010, February 3). The *Lancet* retracts Andrew Wakefield's article. *Science-Based Medicine.* Retrieved on October 10, 2014 from http://www.science-basedmedicine.org/lancet-retracts-wakefield-article/

Novotney, A. (2013). Five major psychiatric disorders share genetic links. *APA Monitor on Psychology, 44*, 10.

Novotney, A. (2014). Students under pressure: College and university counseling centers are examining how best to serve the growing number of students seeking their services. *APA Monitor on Psychology, 45*(8), 36.

Noyes, R., Crowe, R. R., Harris, E. L., Hamra, B. J., McChesney, C. M., & Chandry, D. R. (1986). Relationship between panic disorder and agoraphobia: A family study. *Archives of General Psychiatry, 43*, 227–232.

Noyes, R., Garvey, M., & Cook, B. (1990). Benzodiazepines other than alprazolam in the treatment of panic disorder. In J. Ballenger (Ed.), *Clinical aspects of panic disorder* (pp. 251–258). New York: Wiley-Liss.

Noyes, R., Garvey, M., Cook, B., & Sulzer, M. (1991). Controlled discontinuation of benzodiazepine treatment for patients with panic disorder. *American Journal of Psychiatry, 148*, 517–523.

Noyes, R., Kathol, R. G., Fisher, M. M., Phillips, B. M., Suelzer, M. T., Woodman, C. L. (1994). One-year follow-up of medical outpatients with hypochondriasis. *Psychosomatics, 35*, 533–545.

Noyes, R., Stuart, S., Watson, D. B., & Langbehn, D. R. (2006). Distinguishing between hypochondriasis and somatization disorder: A review of the existing literature. *Psychotherapy and Psychosomatics, 75*(5), 270–281. doi:10.1159/000093948

Noyes, R., Woodman, C., Garvey, M., Cook, B., Sulzer, M., Clancy, J., & Anderson, D. (1992). Generalized anxiety disorder *vs.* panic disorder: Distinguishing characteristics and patterns of comorbidity. *Journal of Nervous and Mental Diseases, 180*, 369–379.

Nugent, N. R., Christopher, N. C., & Delahanty, D. L. (2006). Emergency medical service and in-hospital vital signs as predictors of subsequent PTSD symptom severity in pediatric injury patients. *Journal of Child Psychology and Psychiatry, 47*, 919–926. doi:10.1111/j.1469-7610.2006.01648.x

Nunes, E. V., Frank, K. A., & Kornfeld, S. D. (1987). Psychologic treatment for Type A behavior pattern and for coronary heart disease: A meta-analysis of the literature. *Psychosomatic Medicine, 48*, 159–173.

Núñez-Navarro, A., Agüera, Z., Krug, I., Jiménez-Murcia, S., Sánchez, I., Araguz, N., . . . Fernández-Aranda, F. (2012). Do men with eating disorders differ from women in clinics, psychopathology and personality? *European Eating Disorders Review. 20*(1), 23–31.

Nurnberger, J. I., & Gershon, E. S. (1992). Genetics. In E. S. Paykel (Ed.), *Handbook of affective disorders.* New York: Guilford Press.

Nutt, D., King, L. A., Saulsbury, W., & Blakemore, C. (2007). Development of a rational scale to assess the harm of drugs of potential misuse. *The Lancet, 369*, 1047–1053.

Nutt, D., Wilson, S., & Paterson, L. (2008). Sleep disorders as core symptoms of depression. *Dialogues in Clinical Neuroscience, 10*(3), 329–336.

Nye, C. L., Zucker, R. A., & Fitzgerald, H. E. (1995). Early intervention in the path to alcohol problems through conduct problems: Treatment involvement and child behavior change. *Journal of Consulting and Clinical Psychology, 63*(5), 831–840.

O

Oakes, M., & Bor, R. (2010). The psychology of fear of flying (part II): A critical evaluation of current perspectives on approaches to treatment. *Travel Medicine and Infectious Disease, 8*, 339–363.

O'Brien, C. P. (2005). Benzodiazepine use, abuse, and dependence. *Journal of Clinical Psychiatry, 66*(Suppl 2), 28–33.

O'Brien, J. T. (2007). Role of imaging techniques in the diagnosis of dementia. *The British Journal of Radiology, 80*, S71–S77. doi: 10.1259/bjr/33117326

Obrist, P. (1981). *Cardiovascular psychophysiology: A perspective.* New York: Plenum.

O'Conner, S., Hesselbrock, V., Tasman, A., & DePalma, N. (1987). P3 amplitude in two distinct tasks are decreased in young men with a history of paternal alcoholism. *Alcohol, 4*, 323–330.

O'Connor v. Donaldson, 422 U.S. 563 (1975).

O'Connor, D. W. (1994). Mild dementia: A clinical perspective. In F. A. Huppert, C. Brayne, &; D. W. O'Connor (Eds.), *Dementia and normal aging* (pp. 91–117). Cambridge: Cambridge University Press.

O'Connor, M., Sales, B. D., & Shuman, D. (1996). Mental health professional expertise in the courtroom. In B. D. Sales & D. W. Shuman (Eds.), *Law, mental health, and mental disorder.* Pacific Grove, CA: Brooks/Cole.

O'Connor, T. G., & Rutter, M. (2000). Attachment disorder behavior following early severe deprivation: Extension and longitudinal follow-up. English and Romanian adoptees study team. *Journal of the American Academy of Child and Adolescent Psychiatry, 39*, 703–712.

Odlaug, B. L., & Grant, J. E. (2008a). Clinical characteristics and medical complications of pathologic skin picking. *General Hospital Psychiatry, 30*(1), 61–66. doi:10.1016/j.genhosppsych.2007.07.009

Odlaug, B. L., & Grant, J. E. (2008b). Trichotillomania and pathologic skin picking: Clinical comparison with an examination of comorbidity. *Annals of Clinical Psychiatry, 20*, 57–63. doi:10.1080/10401230802017027

Odom, S. L., Jenkins, J. R., Speltz, M. L., & DeKlyen, M. (1982). Promoting social integration of young children at risk for learning disabilities. *Learning Disability Quarterly, 5*(4), 379–387.

Offer, D., & Sabshin, M. (1991). *The diversity of normal behavior.* New York: Basic Books.

Office of Juvenile Justice and Delinquency Prevention. (2005). *Drinking in America: Myths, realities, and prevention policy.* Washington, DC: U.S. Department of Justice, Office of Justice Programs, Office of Juvenile Justice and Delinquency Prevention.

Office of the Surgeon General (U.S.). (2001). Section 1: Overweight and obesity as public health problems in America. In *The Surgeon General's call to action to prevent and decrease overweight and obesity.* Retrieved June 3, 2014 from http://www.ncbi.nlm.nih.gov/books/NBK44210/

Offidani, E., Guidi, J., Tomba, E., & Fava, G. (2013). Efficacy and tolerability of benzodiazepines versus antidepressants in anxiety disorders: A systematic review and meta-analysis. *Psychotherapy and Psychosomatics, 82*(6), 355–362. doi:10.1159/000353198

Ofshe, R., & Watters, E. (1993, March/April). Making monsters. *Society,* 4–16.

Ogawa, J. R., Sroufe, L. A., Weinfield, N. S., Carlson, E. A., & Egeland, B. (1997). Development and the fragmented self: Longitudinal study of dissociative symptomatology in a nonclinical sample. *Development and Psychopathology, 9*(4), 855–879. doi:10.1017/S0954579497001478

Ogloff, J. P. (2006). Psychopathy/antisocial personality disorder conundrum. *Australian and New Zealand Journal of Psychiatry, 40*(6–7), 519–528. doi:10.1111/j.1440-1614.2006.01834.x

O'Hara, M. W., Zekoski, E. M., Phillipps, L. H., & Wright, E. J. (1990). Controlled prospective study of postpartum mood disorders: Comparison of childbearing and non-childbearing women. *Journal of Abnormal Psychology, 99*, 3–15.

Ohman, A. (1985). Face the beast and fear the face: Animal and social phobia as prototypes for evolutionary analyses of emotion. *Psychophysiology, 23*, 123–145.

Ohnishi, T., Matsuda, H., Tabira, T., Asada, T., & Uno, M. (2001). Changes in brain morphology in Alzheimer disease and normal aging: Is Alzheimer disease an exaggerated aging process? *American Journal of Neuroradiology, 22*(9), 1680–1685.

OJJDP Statistical Briefing Book. (2013). Retrieved January 17, 2010, from http://www.ojjdp.gov/ojstatbb/court/qa06206.asp?qaDate=2010.

Okazaki, S., & Sue, S. (1995). Methodological issues in assessment research with ethnic minorities. *Psychological Assessment, 7,* 367–375.

O'Kearney, R., & Pech, M. (2014). General and sleep-specific worry in insomnia. *Sleep and Biological Rhythms, 12*(3), 212–215. doi: 10.1111/sbr.12054

Olatunji, B. O., Davis, M. L., Powers, M. B., & Smits, J. A. J. (2013). Cognitive-behavioral therapy for obsessive-compulsive disorder: A meta-analysis of treatment outcome and moderators. *Journal of Psychiatric Research, 47,* 33–41. doi:10.1016/j.jpsychires.2012.08.020

Olatunji, B. O., Deacon, B. J., & Abramowitz, J. S. (2009). Is hypochondriasis an anxiety disorder? *The British Journal of Psychiatry, 194*(6), 481–482. doi:10.1192/bjp.bp.108.061085

Olatunji, B. O., Etzel, E. N., Tomarken, A. J., Ciesielski, B. G., & Deacon, B. (2011). The effects of safety behaviors on health anxiety: An experimental investigation. *Behaviour Research and Therapy, 49*(11), 719–728. doi:10.1016/j.brat.2011.07.008

Olds, J., & Milner, P. (1954). Positive reinforcement produced by electrical stimulation of septal area and other regions of rat brain. *Journal of Comparative and Physiological Psychology, 47*(6), 419–427. doi:10.1037/h0058775

O'Leary, A. (1990). Stress, emotion, and human immune function. *Psychological Bulletin, 108,* 363–382.

O'Leary, K. D., & Becker, W. C. (1967). Behavior modification of an adjustment class: A token reinforcement program. *Exceptional Children, 33,* 637–642.

Olfson, M. (1990). Assertive community treatment: An evaluation of the experimental evidence. *Hospital and Community Psychiatry, 41,* 634–641.

Olfson, M., & Marcus, S. C. (2009). National patterns in antidepressant medication treatment. *Archives of General Psychiatry, 66*(8), 848–856. doi: 10.1001/archgenpsychiatry.2009.81.

Olfson, M., Pincus, H., & Sabshin, M. (1994). Pharmacotherapy in outpatient psychiatric practice. *American Journal of Psychiatry, 151,* 580–585.

Olgiati, P., Bajo, E., Bigelli, M., Montgomery, S., & Serretti, A. (2013). Challenging sequential approach to treatment resistant depression: Cost-utility analysis based on the Sequenced Treatment Alternatives to Relieve Depression (STAR*D) trial. *European Neuropsychopharmacology, 23*(12), 1739–1746. doi:10.1016/j.euroneuro.2013.08.008

Olin, J. T., & Zelinski, E. M. (1991). The 12-month reliability of the Mini-Mental State Examination. *Psychological Assessment: A Journal of Consulting and Clinical Psychology, 3,* 427–432.

Ollendick, T. H., & Davis, T. (2013). One-session treatment for specific phobias: A review of Öst's single-session exposure with children and adolescents. *Cognitive Behaviour Therapy, 42*(4), 275–283. doi:10.1080/16506073.2013.773062

Olson, R., Wise, B., Conners, F., Rack, J., & Fulker, D. (1989). Specific deficits in component reading and language skills: Genetic and environmental influences. *Journal of Learning Disabilities, 22,* 339–348.

Olweus, D. (1995). Bullying or peer abuse at school: Facts and intervention. *Current Directions in Psychological Science, 4,* 196–200.

O'Malley, S. S., Jaffe, A., Chang, G., Witte, G., Schotten-feld, R. S., & Rounsaville, B. J. (1992). Naltrexone in the treatment of alcohol dependence: Preliminary findings. In C. A. Naranjo & E. M. Sellars (Eds.), *Novel pharmacological interventions for alcoholism* (pp. 148–157). New York: Springer-Verlag.

Omer, H., & Alon, N. (1994). The continuity principle: A unified approach to disaster and trauma. *American Journal of Community Psychology, 22,* 273–287.

Onken, S. J., Dumont, J. M., Ridgeway, P., Dornan, D. H., & Ralph, R. O. (2002). *Mental health recovery: What helps and what hinders?* Alexandria, VA: National Association of State Mental Health Program Directors. Retrieved on October 29, 2014 from http://www.nasmhpd.org/docs/publications/archiveDocs/2002/MH-SIPReport.pdf

Onstad, S., Skre, I., Torgersen, S., & Kringlen, E. (1991). Twin concordance for DSM-III-R schizophrenia. *Acta Psychiatrica Scandinavica, 83,* 395–401.

Oquendo, M. A., Bongiovi-Garcia, M. E., & Galfalvy, H. (2007). Sex differences in clinical predictors of suicidal acts after major depression: A prospective study. *The American Journal of Psychiatry, 164*(1): 134–141. doi:10.1176/appi.ajp.164.1.134

O'Reilly, E., McNeill, K. G., Mavor, K. I., & Anderson, K. (2014). Looking beyond personal stressors: An examination of how academic stressors contribute to depression in Australian graduate medical students. *Teaching and Learning in Medicine, 26*(1), 56–63. doi:10.1080/10401334.2013.857330

Orlinsky, D. E., & Howard, K. I. (1987). A generic model of psychotherapy. *Journal of Integrative and Eclectic Psychotherapy, 6,* 6–27.

Orlinsky, D. E., Grawe, K., & Parks, B. K. (1994). Process and outcome in psychotherapy—Noch Einmal. In A. E. Bergin & S. L. Garfield, *Handbook of psychotherapy and behavior change* (pp. 270–376). New York: John Wiley & Sons.

Orr, S. P., Lasko, N. B., Shalev, A. Y., & Pittman, R. (1995). Physiological responses to loud tones in Vietnam veterans with posttraumatic stress disorder. *Journal of Abnormal Psychology, 104,* 75–82.

Osborne, G. B., & Fogel, C. (2008). Understanding the motivations for recreational marijuana use among adult Canadians. *Substance Use & Misuse, 43*(3–4), 539–572. doi:10.1080/10826080701884911

Osgood, N. J., & Thielman, S. (1990). Geriatric suicidal behavior: Assessment and treatment. In S. J. Blumenthal & D. J. Kupfer (Eds.), *Suicide over the life cycle: Risk factors, assessment, and treatment of suicidal patients* (pp. 341–379). Washington, DC: American Psychiatric Press.

Osiezagha, K., Ali, S., Freeman, C., Barker, N. C., Jabeen, S., Maitra, S., . . . Bailey, R. K. (2013). Thiamine deficiency and delirium. *Innovations in Clinical Neuroscience, 10*(4), 26–32.

Osman, O. T., & Loschen, E. L. (1992). Self-injurious behavior in the developmentally disabled: Pharmacologic treatment. *Psychopharmacology Bulletin, 28*(4), 439–449.

Osofsky, J. D. (1995). The effects of exposure to violence on young children. *American Psychologist, 50,* 782–788.

Ossorio, P., & Duster, T. (2005). Race and genetics: Controversies in biomedical, behavioral, and forensic sciences. *American Psychologist, 60,* 115–128. doi:10.1037/0003-066X.60.1.115

Ost, L. (2012). One-session treatment: Principles and procedures with adults. In T. Davis, T. H. Ollendick, & L. Ost (Eds.), *Intensive one-session treatment of specific phobias* (pp. 59–95). New York: Springer Science + Business Media. doi:10.1007/978-1-4614-3253-1_4

Ost, L-G.(1987). Age of onset in different phobias. *Journal of Abnormal Psychology, 96,* 223-229.

Ost, L-G. (1988). Applied relaxation vs. progressive relaxation in the treatment of panic disorder. *Behaviour Research and Therapy, 26,* 13–22.

Ost, L-G. (1992). Blood and injection phobia: Background and cognitive, physiological, and behavioral variables. *Journal of Abnormal Psychology, 101,* 68–74.

Ost, L-G., & Hugdahl, K. (1984). Acquisition of blood and dental phobia and anxiety response patterns in clinical patients. *Behaviour Research and Therapy, 23,* 27–34.

Ost, L-G., & Westling, B. E. (1991). *Treatment of panic disorder by applied relaxation versus cognitive therapy.* Paper presented at the meeting of the European Association of Behaviour Therapy, Oslo.

Osterling, J., & Dawson, G. (1994). Early recognition of children with autism: A study of first birthday home videotapes. *Journal of Autism and Developmental Disorders, 24,* 247–257.

O'Sullivan, K. (1979). Observations on vaginismus in Irish women. *Archives of General Psychiatry, 36,* 824–826.

Otto, M., Pollack, M., Sachs, G., Reiter, S., Meltzer-Brody, B. S., & Rosenbaum, J. (1993). Discontinuation of benzodiazepine treatment: Efficacy of cognitive-behavioral therapy for patients with panic disorder. *American Journal of Psychiatry, 150,* 1485–1490.

Otto, M. W., Teachman, B. A., Cohen, L. S., Soares, C. N., Vitonis, A. F., & Harlow, B. L. (2007). Dysfunctional attitudes and episodes of major depression: Predictive validity and temporal stability in never-depressed, depressed, and recovered women. *Journal of Abnormal Psychology, 116*(3), 475–483. doi:10.1037/0021-843X.116.3.475

Otto, M. W., Tuby, K. S., Gould, R. A., McLean, R. S., & Pollack, M. H. (2001). An effect-size analysis of the relative efficacy and tolerability of serotonin selective reuptake inhibitors for panic disorder. *The American Journal of Psychiatry, 158*(12), 1989–1992. doi:10.1176/appi.ajp.158.12.1989

Oude Voshaar, R. C., Couveé, J. E., Van Balkom, A. M., Mulder, P. H., & Zitman, F. G. (2006). Strategies for discontinuing long-term benzodiazepine use: Meta-analysis. *The British Journal of Psychiatry, 189*(3), 213–220. doi:10.1192/bjp.189.3.213

Outcasts on Main Street: Report of the Federal Task Force on Homelessness and Severe Mental Illness. (1992). Washington, DC: Interagency Council on the Homeless.

Owens, J., Sangal, R., Sutton, V. K., Bakken, R., Allen, A. J., & Kelsey, D. (2009). Subjective and objective measures of sleep in children with attention-deficit/hyperactivity disorder. *Sleep Medicine, 10*(4), 446–456. doi:10.1016/j.sleep.2008.03.0139

Ozbay, F., Johnson, D. C., Dimoulas, E., Morgan, C. A., Charney, D., & Southwick, S. (2007). *Psychiatry, 4,* 35–40.

Ozer, E. J., Best, S. R., Lipsey, T. L., & Weiss, D. S. (2003). Predictors of posttraumatic stress disorder and symptoms in adults: A meta-analysis. *Psychological Trauma: Theory, Research, Practice, and Policy, 5*(1), 3–36.

Ozguven, H. D., Oner, O., Baskak, B., Oktem, F., Olmez, S., & Munir, K. (2010). Theory of mind in schizophrenia and Asperger's syndrome: Relationship with negative symptoms. *Bulletin of Clinical Psychopharmacology, 20*(1), 5–13.

Ozonoff, S., & McEvoy, R. E. (1994). A longitudinal study of executive function and theory of mind development in autism. *Development and Psychopathology, 6,* 415–431.

Ozonoff, S., Strayer, D. L., McMahon, W. M., & Filloux, F. (1994). Executive function abilities in autism and Tourette syndrome: An information processing approach. *Journal of Child Psychology and Psychiatry and Allied Disciplines, 35(6),* 1015–1032.

Özyildirim, İ. İ., Çakir, S. S., & Yazici, O. O. (2010). Impact of psychotic features on morbidity and course of illness in patients with bipolar disorder. *European Psychiatry, 25*(1), 47–51. doi:10.1016/j.eurpsy.2009.08.004

P

Pacchiarotti, I., Bond, D. J., Baldessarini, R. J., Nolen, W. A., Grunze, H., Licht, R. W., . . . Vieta, E. (2013). The International Society for Bipolar Disorders (ISBD) task force report on antidepressant use in bipolar disorders. *The American Journal of Psychiatry, 170*(11), 1249–1262. doi:10.1176/appi.ajp.2013.13020185

Pae, C., Tharwani, H., Marks, D. M., Masand, P. S., & Patkar, A. A. (2009). Atypical depression: A comprehensive review. *CNS Drugs, 23*(12), 1023–1037. doi:10.2165/11310990-000000000-00000

Pagani, S., Boulerice, B., Vitaro, F., & Tremblay, R. E. (1999). Effects of poverty on academic failure and delinquency in boys: A change and process model approach. *Journal of Child Psychology and Psychiatry, 40,* 1209–1219.

Palazzoli, M. S. (1985). *Self-starvation.* New York: Aronson.

Paliast, E., Jongbloet, P., Straatman, H., & Zielhuis, G. (1994). Excess seasonality of births among patients with schizophrenia and seasonal ovopathy. *Schizophrenia Bulletin, 20,* 269–276.

Palmer, C. S., Kleinman, L., Taylor, L. A., & Revicki, D. A. (1998). Pharmacoeconomics of antidepressant drug overdose. *CNS Drugs, 10*(3), 223–231. doi:10.2165/00023210-199810030-00006

Palmstierna, T. (2001). A model for predicting alcohol withdrawal delirium. *Psychiatric Services, 52*(6), 820–823. doi:10.1176/appi.ps.52.6.820

Pandey, G. N. (2013). Biological basis of suicide and suicidal behavior. *Bipolar Disorders, 15*(5), 524–541. doi:10.1111/bdi.12089

Pandey, G. N., & Dwivedi, Y. (2009). Peripheral biological markers for mood disorders. In M.S. Ritsner (Ed.), *The handbook of neuropsychiatric biomarkers, endophenotypes and genes, Vol 3: Metabolic and peripheral biomarkers* (pp. 121–149). New York: Springer Science & Business Media. doi:10.1007/978-1-4020-9838-3_9

Pangalos, M. N., Malizia, A. L., Francis, P. T., Lowe, S., Bertolucci, P., Procter, A., Bridges, P., Bartlett, J., Bowen, D. (1992). Effect of psychotropic drugs on excitatory amino acids in patients undergoing psychosurgery for depression. *British Journal of Psychiatry, 160,* 638–642.

Panos, P. T., Jackson, J. W., Hasan, O., & Panos, A. (2014). Meta-analysis and systematic review assessing the efficacy of dialectical behavior therapy (DBT). *Research on Social Work Practice, 24*(2), 213–223. doi:10.1177/1049731513503047

Papadopoulos, F. C., Ekbom, A., Brandt, L., & Ekselius, L. (2009). Excess mortality, causes of death and prognostic factors in anorexia nervosa. *The British Journal of Psychiatry, 194,* 10–17.

Papp, L., Klein, D., Martinez, J., Schneier, F., Cole, R., Liebowitz, M., Hollander, E., Fryer, A., Jordan, F., & Gorman, J. (1993). Diagnostic and substance specificity of carbondioxide-induced panic. *American Journal of Psychiatry, 150,* 250–257.

Paquette, K. (2011). Current statistics on the prevalence and characteristics of people experiencing homelessness in the United States. *Homelessness Resource Center.* Retrieved on October 29, 2014 from http://homeless.samhsa.gov/ResourceFiles/hrc_factsheet.pdf

Paracchini, S., Steer, C. D., Buckingham, L.-L., Morris, A. P, Ring, S., Scerri, T., . . . Monaco, A. P.(2008). Association of the KIAA0319 dyslexia susceptibility gene with reading skills in the general population. *American Journal of Psychiatry, 165,* 1576–1584.

Pariante, C. M. (2003). Depression, stress and the adrenal axis. *Journal of Neuroendocrinology, 15*(8), 811–812.

Parikh, S. V., Hawke, L. D., Zaretsky, A., Beaulieu, S., Patelis-Siotis, I., MacQueen, G., . . . Cervantes, P. (2013). Psychosocial interventions for bipolar disorder and coping style modification: Similar clinical outcomes, similar mechanisms? *The Canadian Journal of Psychiatry, 58*(8), 482–486.

Paris, J. (2011). Pharmacological treatments for personality disorders. *International Review of Psychiatry, 23*(3), 303–309. doi:10.3109/09540261.2011.586993

Paris, J. (2012). The rise and fall of dissociative identity disorder. *Journal of Nervous and Mental Disease, 200*(12), 1076–1079. doi:10.1097/NMD.0b013e318275d285

Paris, J. (2013). *The intelligent clinician's guide to the DSM-5.* New York: Oxford University Press.

Paris, J. (2014). Modernity and narcissistic personality disorder. *Personality Disorders: Theory, Research, and Treatment, 5*(2), 220–226. doi:10.1037/a0028580

Park, E., Tudiver, F., Schultz, J. K., & Campbell, T. (2004). Does enhancing partner support and interaction improve smoking cessation? A meta-analysis. *Annals of Family Medicine, 2*(2), 170–174. doi:10.1370/afm.64

Parker, G. (2007). Is depression overdiagnosed? Yes. *British Medical Journal, 335*(7615), 328. doi:10.1136/bmj.39268.475799.AD

Parker, G., McCraw, S., & Fletcher, K. (2012). Cyclothymia. *Depression and Anxiety, 29*(6), 487–494. doi:10.1002/da.21950

Parkin, A. J. (1987). *Memory and amnesia: An introduction.* New York: Blackwell.

Parks, J., Svendsen, D., Singer, P., & Foti, M. E. (2006). Morbidity and mortality in people with serious mental illness. *National Association of State Mental Health Program Directors (NASMHPD) Medical Directors Council.* Alexandria, Virginia. Retrieved on November 5, 2014 from www.nasmhpd.org/publications/technical reports.

Parmar, R. S., Cawley, J. F., & Miller, J. H. (1994). Differences in mathematics performance between students with learning disabilities and students with mild retardation. *Exceptional Children, 60,* 549–563.

Parnas, J., Cannon, T., Jacobsen, B., Schulsinger, H., Schulsinger, F., & Mednick, S. (1993). Lifetime DSM-III-R diagnostic outcomes in the offspring of schizophrenic mothers: Results of the Copenhagen high-risk study. *Archives of General Psychiatry, 50,* 707–714.

Parr, J. M., Kavanagh, D. J., Cahill, L., Mitchell, G., & Young, R. M. (2009). Effectiveness of current treatment approaches for benzodiazepine discontinuation: A meta-analysis. *Addiction, 104*(1), 13–24. doi:10.1111/j.1360-0443.2008.02364.x

Parrott, A. C. (2007). Drug-related harm: A complex and difficult concept to scale. *Human Psychopharmacology: Clinical and Experimental, 22*(7), 423–425. doi:10.1002/hup.874

Parsons, O. A., Butters, N., & Nathan, P. E. (Eds.). (1987). *Neuropsychology of alcoholism: Implications for diagnosis and treatment.* New York: Guilford Press.

Parsons, T. D., & Rizzo, A. A. (2008). Affective outcomes of virtual reality exposure therapy for anxiety and specific phobias: A meta-analysis. *Journal of Behavior Therapy and Experimental Psychiatry, 39*(3), 250–261. doi:10.1016/j.jbtep.2007.07.007

Pascual, R., Fernandez, V., Ruiz, S., & Kuljis, R. O. (1993). Environmental deprivation delays the maturation of motor pyramids during the early postnatal period. *Early Human Development, 33,* 145–155.

Pasewark, R. A., & Pantle, M. L. (1981). Opinions about the insanity plea. *Journal of Forensic Psychology, 8,* 63.

Pasewark, R. A., Bieber, S., Bosten, K. J., Kiser, M., & Steadman, H. J. (1982). Criminal recidivism among insanity acquitees. *International Journal of Law and Psychiatry, 5,* 365–374.

Patrick, C. J. (2007). Antisocial personality disorder and psychopathy. In W. O'Donohue, K. A. Fowler, & S. O. Lilienfeld (Eds.), *Personality disorders: Toward the DSM-V* (pp. 109–166). Los Angeles, CA: Sage Publications.

Patten, S. B. (2013). Childhood and adult stressors and major depression risk: Interpreting interactions with the sufficient-component cause model. *Social Psychiatry and Psychiatric Epidemiology, 48*(6), 927–933. doi:10.1007/s00127-012-0603-9

Patterson, D. R. (2005). Behavioral methods for chronic pain and illness: A reconsideration and appreciation. *Rehabilitation Psychology, 50*(3), 312–315. doi:10.1037/0090-5550.50.3.312

Patterson, E. B. (1996). Poverty, income inequality, and community crime rates. In D. G. Rojet & G. F. Jensen (Eds.), *Exploring delinquency: Causes and control* (pp. 142–149). Los Angeles, CA: Roxbury Publishing.

Patterson, G. R. (1982). *A social learning approach to family intervention: III. Coercive family process.* Eugene, OR: Castalia.

Patterson, G. R. (1986). Performance models for antisocial boys. *American Psychologist, 41,* 432–444.

Patterson, G. R., Chamberlain, P., & Reid, J. B. (1982). A comparative evaluation of a parent training program. *Behavior Therapy, 13,* 638–650.

Patterson, G. R., DeBaryshe, E., & Ramsey, E. (1989). A developmental perspective on antisocial behaviour. *American Psychologist, 44,* 329–335.

Patterson, G. R., Reid, J. B., & Dishion, T. J. (1992). *Antisocial boys.* Eugene, OR: Castalia.

Paul, G. L., & Lentz, R. J. (1977). *Psychosocial treatment of chronic mental patients: Milieu versus social-learning programs.* Cambridge: Harvard University Press.

Paulozzi, L. J., Mack, K. A., & Hockenberry, J. M. (2014). Vital signs: Variation among states in prescribing of opioid pain relievers and benzodiazepines—United States, 2012. *CDC Morbidity and Mortality Weekly Report, 63*(26), 563–568. Retrieved on December 13, 2014 from http://www.cdc.gov/mmwr/preview/mmwrhtml/mm6326a2.htm?mobile=nocontent

Pauls, D. L., Raymond, C. L., & Robertson, M. (1991). The genetics of obsessive-compulsive disorder: A review. In J. Zohar, I. Insel, & S. Rasmussen (Eds.), *The psychobiology of obsessive-compulsive disorder.* New York: Springer.

Paulson, G. W. (2012). *Closing the asylums: Causes and consequences of the deinstitutionalization movement.* Jefferson, NC: McFarland.

Pavan, C., Vindigni, V., Semenzin, M., Mazzoleni, F., Gardiolo, M., Simonato, P., & Marini, M. (2006). Personality, temperament and clinical scales in an Italian plastic surgery setting: What about body dysmorphic disorder? *International Journal of Psychiatry in Clinical Practice, 10*(2), 91–96. doi:10.1080/13651500500487677

Pedersen, C. B., & Mortensen, P. B. (2001). Evidence of a dose-response relationship between urbanicity during upbringing and schizophrenia risk. *Archives of General Psychiatry, 58,* 1039–1046.

Pelham, W. E., & Murphy, H. A. (1986). Behavioral and psychopharmacological treatment of attention deficit and conduct disorders. In M. Hersen (Ed.), *Pharmacological and behavioral treatment: An integrative approach* (pp. 108–148). New York: John Wiley & Sons.

Pelham, W. E., Murphy, D. A., Vannatta, K., Milich, R., Licht, B. G., Gnagy, E. M., Greenslade, K. E., Greiner, A. R., & Vodde-Hamilton, M. (1992). Methylphenidate and attributions in boys with attention-deficit hyperactivity disorder. *Journal of Consulting and Clinical Psychology, 60*, 282–292.

Pellman, E. J., Lovell, M. R., Viano, D. C., & Casson, I. R. (2006). Concussion in professional football: Recovery of NFL and high school athletes assessed by computerized neuropsychological testing—Part 12. *Neurosurgery, 58*(2), 263–274.

Peñas-Lledó, E., Vaz Leal F. J., & Waller, G. (2002). Excessive exercise in anorexia nervosa and bulimia nervosa: Relation to eating characteristics and general psychopathology. *International Journal of Eating Disorders, 31*(4), 370–375. doi:10.1002/eat.10042

Pendery, M. L., Maltzman, I. M., & West, L. J. (1982). Controlled drinking by alcoholics?: New findings and reevaluation of a major affirmative study. *Science, 217*, 169–174.

Pennebaker, J., & Beall, S. (1986). Confronting a traumatic event: Toward an understanding of inhibition and disease. *Journal of Abnormal Psychology, 95*, 274–281.

Pennebaker, J., Kiecolt-Glaser, J. K., & Glaser, R. (1988). Disclosure of traumas and immune function: Health implications for psychotherapy. *Journal of Consulting and Clinical Psychology, 56*, 239–245.

Pennebaker, J. W., Barger, S. D., & Tiebout, J. (1989). Disclosure of traumas and health among Holocaust survivors. *Psychosomatic Medicine, 51*, 577–589.

Peplau, L. A. (2003). Human sexuality: How do men and women differ? *Current Directions in Psychological Science, 12*(2), 37–40.

Perelman, M. A. (2009) Understanding and treating retarded ejaculation: A sex therapist's perspective. *Newsletter of the International Society of Sexual Medicine, 27*, 17–20.

Pérès, K., Helmer, C., Amieva, H., Orgogozo, J., Rouch, I., Dartigues, J., & Barberger-Gateau, P. (2008). Natural history of decline in instrumental activities of daily living performance over the 10 years preceding the clinical diagnosis of dementia: A prospective population-based study. *Journal of the American Geriatrics Society, 56*(1), 37–44. doi: 10.1111/j.1532-5415.2007.01499.x

Perilla, J. L., Norris, F. H., & Lavizzo, E. A. (2002). Ethnicity, culture, and disaster response: Identifying and explaining ethnic differences in PTSD six months after Hurricane Andrew. *Journal of Social and Clinical Psychology, 21*, 20–45.

Peris, F. S. (1969). *Gestalt therapy verbatim.* Lafayette, CA: Real People Press.

Perkins, K. A. (1993). Weight gain following smoking cessation. *Journal of Consulting and Clinical Psychology, 61*(5), 768–777.

Perlin, M. (1989). *Mental disability law: Civil and criminal.* Charlottesville, VA: Michie.

Perlin, M. L. (2013). *Mental disability and the death penalty: The shame of the states.* Washington, DC: Rowman & Littlefield Publishers.

Perlis, M. L., Smith, L. J., Lyness, J. M., Matteson, S. R., Pigeon, W. R., Jungquist, C. R., & Tu, X. (2006). Insomnia as a risk factor for onset of depression in the elderly. *Behavioral Sleep Medicine, 4*(2), 104–113. doi:10.1207/s15402010bsm0402_3

Perner, J., Frith, U., Leslie, A. M., & Leekam, S. R. (1989). Exploration of the autistic child's theory of mind: Knowledge, belief and communication. *Child Development, 60*, 689–700.

Perry, C. L., Klepp, K., & Schultz, J. M. (1988). Primary prevention of cardiovascular disease: Community-wide strategies for youth. *Journal of Consulting and Clinical Psychology, 56*, 358–364.

Perry, J. C. (1993). Longitudinal studies of personality disorders. *Journal of Personality Disorders, 7*, 63–85.

Perry, S., Difede, J., Musngi, G., Frances, A., & Jacobsberg, L. (1992). Predictors of posttraumatic stress disorder after burn injury. *American Journal of Psychiatry, 149*, 931–935.

Persons, J. B. (1991). Psychotherapy outcome studies do not accurately represent current models of psychotherapy: A proposed remedy. *American Psychologist, 46*, 99–106.

Pertusa, A., Frost, R., Fullana, M., Samuels, J., Steketee, G., Tolin, D., . . . Mataix-Cols, D. (2010). Refining the diagnostic boundaries of compulsive hoarding: A critical review. *Clinical Psychology Review, 30*(4), 371–386.

Peters, J. (2013). When ice cream sales rise, so do homicides. coincidence, or will your next cone murder you? *Slate.* Retrieved March 7, 2014 from http://www.slate.com/blogs/crime/2013/07/09/warm_weather_homicide_rates_when_ice_cream_sales_rise_homicides_rise_coincidence.html

Petersen, L., Sørensen, T. A., Andersen, P., Mortensen, P., & Hawton, K. (2014). Genetic and familial environmental effects on suicide attempts: A study of Danish adoptees and their biological and adoptive siblings. *Journal of Affective Disorders, 155*, 273–277. doi:10.1016/j.jad.2013.11.012

Petersen, R. C., Caracciolo, B., Brayne, C., Gauthier, S., Jelic, V., & Fratiglioni, L. (2014). Mild cognitive impairment: A concept in evolution. *Journal of Internal Medicine, 275*(3), 214–228. doi: 10.1111/joim.12190

Peterson v. State, 100 Wn2d 421, 671 P.2d 320 (1983).

Peterson, C. (2006). *A primer in positive psychology.* New York: Oxford University Press.

Peterson, C. B., Thuras, P., Ackard, D. M., Mitchell, J. E., Berg, K., Sandager, N., . . . Crow, S. J. (2010). Personality dimensions in bulimia nervosa, binge eating disorder, and obesity. *Comprehensive Psychiatry, 51*(1), 31–36.

Peterson, C. C., & Palermo, T. M. (2004). Parental reinforcement of recurrent pain: The moderating impact of child depression and anxiety on functional disability. *Journal of Pediatric Psychology, 29*(5), 331–341.

Peterson, C., & Park, N. (2003). Positive psychology as the even-handed positive psychologist views it. *Psychological Inquiry, 14*(2), 143–147.

Peterson, C., Seligman, M. E. P., & Vaillant, G. E. (1988). Pessimistic explanatory style is a risk factor for physical illness: A thirty-five-year longitudinal study. *Journal of Personality and Social Psychology, 55*, 23–27.

Peterson, K. (2004). Biomarkers for alcohol use and abuse: A summary. *Alcohol Research & Health, 28*(1), 30–37.

Peterson, L., & Brown, D. (1994). Integrating child injury and abuse-neglect research: Common histories, etiologies, and solutions. *Psychological Bulletin, 116*, 293–315.

Petraitis, J., Flay, B. R., & Miller, T. Q. (1995). Reviewing theories of adolescent substance use: Organizing pieces in the puzzle. *Psychological Bulletin, 117*, 67–86.

Petrie, J., Bunn, F., & Byrne, G. (2007). Parenting programmes for preventing tobacco, alcohol or drugs misuse in children: A systematic review. *Health Education Research, 22*(2), 177–191. doi:10.1093/her/cyl061

Petrie, K. J., Booth, R. J., Pennebaker, J. W., & Davison, K. P. (1995). Disclosure of trauma and immune response to a hepatitis B vaccination program. *Journal of Consulting and Clinical Psychology, 63*, 787–792.

Pettinati, H. M., Tamburello, T. A., Ruetsch, C., & Kaplan, F. (1994). Patient attitudes toward electroconvulsive therapy. *Psychopharmacology Bulletin, 30*, 471–475.

Pettit, G. S., & Bates, J. E. (1989). Family interaction patterns and children's behavior problems from infancy to 4 years. *Developmental Psychology, 25*, 413–420.

Peugh, J., & Belenko, S. (2001). Alcohol, drugs and sexual function: A review. *Journal of Psychoactive Drugs, 33*(3), 223–232.

Pharoah, F., Mari, J., Rathbone, J., & Wong, W. (2010). Family intervention for schizophrenia. *The Cochrane Database of Systematic Reviews, 12*, CD000088. doi:10.1002/14651858.CD 000088.pub2

Phelps, L., Cox, D., & Bajorek, E. (1992). School phobia and separation anxiety: Diagnostic and treatment comparisons. *Psychology in the Schools, 29*, 384–394.

Philliber, S., & Allen, J. P. (1992). Life options and community services: Teen Outreach Program. In B. C. Miller, J. J. Card, R. L. Paikoff, & J. L. Peterson (Eds.), *Preventing adolescent pregnancy: Model programs and evaluation* (pp. 139–155). Newbury Park, CA: Sage.

Phillips, K. A. (2005). *The broken mirror: Understanding and treating body dysmorphic disorder* (revised and expanded edition). New York: Oxford University Press.

Phillips, K. A., McElroy, S. L., Keck, P. E., Pope, H. G., & Hudson, J. I. (1993). Body dysmorphic disorder: 30 cases of imagined ugliness. *Amercian Journal of Psychiatry, 150*, 302–308.

Phillips, K. A., Wilhelm, S., Koran, L. M., Didie, E. R., Fallon, B. A., Feusner, J., & Stein, D. J. (2010). Body dysmorphic disorder: Some key issues for *DSM-V. Depression and Anxiety, 27*(6), 573–591. doi:10.1002/da.20709

Phillips, S. D., Burns, B. J., Edgar, E. R., Mueser, K. T., Linkins, K. W., Rosenheck, R. A., . . . McDonel Herr, E. C. (2001). Moving assertive community treatment into standard practice. *Psychiatric Services, 52*(6), 771–779. doi:10.1176/appi.ps.52.6.771

Pickar, D., Owen, R., Litman, R., Konicki, P., Guiterrez, R., & Rapaport, M. (1992). Clinical and biologic response to clozapine in patients with schizophrenia. *Archives of General Psychiatry, 49*, 345–353.

Pickens, R. W., Svikis, D. S., McGue, M., Lykken, D. T., Hesten, L. L., & Clayton, P. J. (1991). Heterogeneity in the inheritance of alcoholism. *Archives of General Psychiatry, 48*(1), 19–28.

Pickles, A. A., Aglan, A. A., Collishaw, S. S., Messer, J. J., Rutter, M. M., & Maughan, B. B. (2010). Predictors of suicidality across the life span: The Isle of Wight study. *Psychological Medicine, 40*(9), 1453–1466. doi:10.1017/S0033291709991905

Pierce, K. A., & Kirkpatrick, D. R. (1992). Do men lie on fear surveys? *Behavior Research and Therapy, 30*, 415–418.

Pigott, H. (2011). STARD: A tale and trail of bias. *Ethical Human Psychology and Psychiatry: An International Journal of Critical Inquiry, 13*(1), 6–28. doi:10.1891/1559-4343.13.1.6

Pigott, T., Pato, M., Bernstein, S., Grover, G., Hill, J., Tolliver, T., & Murphy, D. (1990). Controlled comparisons of clomipramine and fluoxetine in treatment of obsessive-compulsive disorder. *Archives of General Psychiatry, 47*, 926–932.

Pihl, R. O., & Peterson, J. B. (1991). Attention-deficit hyperactivity disorders, childhood conduct disorder and alcoholism: Is there an association? *Alcohol Health Research World, 15*, 25–31.

Pike, K. M., Hilbert, A., Wilfley, D. E., Fairburn, C. G., Dohm, F. A., Walsh, B. T., & Striegel-Moore, R. (2008). Toward an understanding of risk factors for anorexia nervosa: A case-control study. *Psychological Medicine, 38*(10), 1443–1453. doi:10.1017/S0033291707002310

Pillard, R. C. & Bailey, J. M. (1995). A biologic perspective on sexual orientation. *Psychiatric Clinics of North America, 18,* 71–84.

Pillard, R. C. (1988). Sexual orientation and mental disorder. *Psychiatric Annals, 18,* 52-56.

Pilling, S., Bebbington, P. P., Kuipers, E. E., Garety, P. P., Geddes, J. J., Orbach, G. G., & Morgan, C. C. (2002). Psychological treatments in schizophrenia: I. Meta-analysis of family intervention and cognitive behaviour therapy. *Psychological Medicine, 32,* 763–782.

Pilver, C. E., Libby, D. J., Hoff, R. A., & Potenza, M. N. (2013). Gender differences in the relationship between gambling problems and the incidence of substance-use disorders in a nationally representative population sample. *Drug and Alcohol Dependence, 133*(1), 204–211. doi:10.1016/j.drugalcdep.2013.05.002

Pincus, D. B., May, J., Whitton, S. W., Mattis, S. G., & Barlow, D. H. (2010). Cognitive-behavioral treatment of panic disorder in adolescence. *Journal of Clinical Child and Adolescent Psychology, 39*(5), 638–649. doi:10.1080/15374416.2010.501288

Pinder-Amaker, S. (2014). Identifying the unmet needs of college students on the autism spectrum. *Harvard Review of Psychiatry, 22*(2), 125–137. doi:10.1097/HRP.0000000000000032

Pion, G. M. (1991). A national human resources agenda for psychology: The need for a broader perspective. *Professional Psychology: Research and Practice, 22,* 449–455.

Piper, A. (1994). Multiple personality disorder. *British Journal of Psychiatry, 164,* 600–612.

Piper, A., & Merskey, H. (2004). The persistence of folly: Critical examination of dissociative identity disorder Part II. *Canadian Journal of Psychiatry, 49,* 678–683.

Piper, W. E., Azim, H. F., McCallum, M., & Joyce, A. S. (1990). Patient suitability and outcome in short-term individual psychotherapy. *Journal of Consulting and Clinical Psychology, 58,* 475–481.

Pisani, M. A., Inouye, S. K., McNicoll, L., & Redlich, C. A. (2003). Screening for preexisting cognitive impairment in older intensive care unit patients: Use of proxy assessment. *Journal of the American Geriatrics Society, 51*(5), 689–693. doi:10.1034/j.1600-0579.2003.00215.x

Pitman, R. K. (1989). Post-traumatic stress disorder, hormones, and memory. *Biological Psychiatry, 26,* 221–223.

Pitman, R. K., Orr, S. P., Forgue, D. F., de Jong, J., & Claiborn, J. M. (1987). Psychophysiologic assessment of posttraumatic stress disorder imagery in Vietnam combat veterans. *Archives of General Psychiatry, 44*(11), 970–975. doi:10.1001/archpsyc.1987.01800230050009

Pitman, R. K., Rasmusson, A. M., Koenen, K. C., Shin, L. M., Orr, S. P., Gilbertson, M. W., & Liberzon, I. (2012). Biological studies of post-traumatic stress disorder. *Nature Reviews Neuroscience, 13*(11), 769–787. doi:10.1038/nrn3339

Pitschel-Walz, G., Leucht, S., Bauml, J., Kissling, W., & Engel, R.R. (2001). The effect of family interventions on relapse and rehospitalization in schizophrenia: A meta-analysis. *Schizophrenia Bulletin, 27,* 73–92.

Piven, J., Simon, J., Chase, G. A., Wzorek, M., Landa, R., Gayle, J., & Folstein, S. (1993). The etiology of autism: Pre-, peri- and neonatal factors. *Journal of the American Academy of Child and Adolescent Psychiatry, 32,* 1256–1263.

Plassman, B. L., Havlik, R. J., Steffens, D. C., Helms, M. J., Newman, T. N., Drosdick, D., . . . Breitner, J. C. (2000). Documented head injury in early adulthood and risk of Alzheimer's disease and other dementias. *Neurology, 55*(8), 1158–1166. doi:10.1212/WNL.55.8.1158

Platt, B., & Riedel, G. (2011). The cholinergic system, EEG and sleep. *Behavioural Brain Research, 221,* 499–504. doi:10.1016/j.bbr.2011.01.017

Pliszka, S., & AACAP Work Group on Quality Issues (2007). Practice parameter for the assessment and treatment of children and adolescents with attention-deficit/hyperactivity disorder. *Journal of the American Academy of Child and Adolescent Psychiatry, 46*(7), 894–921. doi:10.1097/chi.0b013e318054e724

Plomin, R. (1989). Environment and genes: Determinants of behavior. *American Psychologist, 44,* 105–111.

Poikolainen, K. (1999). Effectiveness of brief interventions to reduce alcohol intake in primary health care populations: A meta-analysis. *Preventive Medicine: An International Journal Devoted to Practice and Theory, 28*(5), 503–509. doi:10.1006/pmed.1999.0467

Polanczyk, G., de Lima, M. S., Horta, B. L., Biederman, J., & Rohde, L. A. (2007). The worldwide prevalence of ADHD: A systematic review and meta-regression analysis. *American Journal of Psychiatry, 164,* 942–948.

Polich, J. M., Armor, D. J., & Braiker, H. B. (1981). Stability and change in drinking patterns. In J. M. Polich (Ed.), *The course of alcoholism: Four years after treatment* (pp. 159–200). New York: John Wiley & Sons.

Polich, J., & Bloom, F. E. (1988). Event-related brain potentials in individuals at high and low risk for developing alcoholism: Failure to replicate. *Alcoholism in Clinical and Experimental Research, 12,* 368–373.

Polich, J., & Ochoa, C. J. (2004). Alcoholism risk, tobacco smoking, and P300 event-related potential. *Clinical Neurophysiology, 115,* 1374–1383.

Polich, J., Pollock, V. E., & Bloom, F. E. (1994). Meta-analysis of P300 amplitude from males at risk for alcoholism. *Psychological Bulletin, 115*(1), 55–73. doi:10.1037/0033-2909.115.1.55

Polisois-Keating, A., & Joyal, C. C. (2013). Functional neuroimaging of sexual arousal: A preliminary meta-analysis comparing pedophilic to non-pedophilic men. *Archives of Sexual Behavior, 42*(7), 1111–1113. doi:10.1007/s10508-013-0198-6

Polivy, J., & Herman, C. P. (2002).Causes of eating disorders. *Annual Review of Psychology, 53,* 187–213.

Pollan, M. (2015). The trip treatment. *The New Yorker*, Feb. 9 issue. Retrieved on February 13, 2015 from http://www.newyorker.com/magazine/2015/02/09/trip-treatment

Pollard, C. A., Detrick, P., Flynn, T., & Frank, M. (1990). Panic attacks and related disorders in alcohol-dependent, depressed, and non-clinical samples. *Journal of Nervous and Mental Disease, 178,* 180–185.

Pollock, B., Perel, J. M., Paradis, C. F., Fasiczka, A. L., & Reynolds, C. F. (1994). Metabolic and physiologic consequences of nortriptyline treatment in the elderly. *Psychopharmacology Bulletin, 30,* 80.

Pollock, I., & Warner, J. O. (1990). Effect of artificial food colours on childhood behaviour. *Archives of Disease in Childhood, 65,* 74–77.

Pomerleau, O. F., Collins, A. C., Shiffman, S., & Sanderson, C. S. (1993). Why some poeple smoke and others do not: New perspectives. *Journal of Consulting and Clinical Psychology, 61,* 723–731.

Pompili, M., Innamorati, M., Girardi, P., Tatarelli, R., & Lester, D. (2011). Evidence-based interventions for preventing suicide in youths. In M. Pompili & R. Tatarelli (Eds.), *Evidence-based practice in suicidology: A source book* (pp. 171–209). Cambridge, MA: Hogrefe Publishing.

Pompili, M., Lester, D., Innamorati, M., Tatarelli, R., & Girardi, P. (2008). Assessment and treatment of suicide risk in schizophrenia. *Expert Review of Neurotherapeutics, 8,* 51–74.

Pontifex, M. (2013). Transient modulations of inhibitory control in children with ADHD: The effect of a single bout of physical activity. *Dissertation Abstracts International, 73.*

Pope, C. G., Pope, H. G., Menard, W., Fay, C., Olivardia, R., & Phillips, K. A. (2005). Clinical features of muscle dysmorphia among males with body dysmorphic disorder. *Body Image, 2*(4), 395–400. doi:10.1016/j.bodyim.2005.09.001

Pope, H. G., Gruber, A. J., Choi, P., Olivardia, R., & Phillips, K. A. (1997). Muscle dysmorphia: An under-recognized form of body dysmorphic disorder. *Psychosomatics: Journal of Consultation and Liaison Psychiatry, 38*(6), 548–557. doi:10.1016/S0033-3182(97)71400-2

Pope, H. G., Jr., Gruber, A. J., & Yurgelun-Todd, D. (1995). The residual neuropsychological effects of cannabis: The current status of research. *Drug and Alcohol Dependence, 38*(1), 25–34.

Pope, H. G., Jr., McElroy, S. L., Keck, P. E., & Hudson, J. I. (1991). Valproate in the treatment of acute mania. A placebo-controlled study. *Archives of General Psychiatry, 48,* 62–68.

Pope, H. G., Phillips, K. A., & Olivardia, R. (2000). *The Adonis complex: The secret crisis of male body obsession.* New York: The Free Press.

Pope, H. J., Poliakoff, M. B., Parker, M. P., Boynes, M., & Hudson, J. I. (2007). Is dissociative amnesia a culture-bound syndrome? Findings from a survey of historical literature. *Psychological Medicine, 37*(2), 225–233. doi:10.1017/S0033291706009500

Pope, K. S., & Feldman-Summers, S. (1992). National survey of psychologists' sexual and physical abuse history and their evaluation of training and competence in these areas. *Professional Psychology: Research and Practice, 23,* 353–361.

Pope, K. S., & Tabachnick, B. G. (1994). Therapists as patients: A national survey of psychologists' experiences, problems, and beliefs. *Professional Psychology: Research and Practice, 25,* 247–258.

Pope, K. S., & Vasquez, M. J. T. (1991). *Ethics in psychotherapy and counseling: A practical guide for psychologists.* San Francisco, CA: Jossey-Bass.

Pope, K. S., & Vetter, V. A. (1992). Ethical dilemmas encountered by members of the American Psychological Association: A national survey. *American Psychologist, 47,* 397–411.

Pope, K. S., Levenson, H., & Schover, L. R. (1979). Sexual intimacy in psychology training: Results and implication of a national survey. *American Psychologist, 34,* 682–689.

Pope, K. S., Tabachnick, B. G., & Keith-Spiegel, P. (1987). Ethics of practice: The beliefs and behaviors of psychologists as therapists. *American Psychologist, 42,* 993–1006.

Porcelli, S., Fabbri, C., & Serretti, A. (2012). Meta-analysis of serotonin transporter gene promoter polymorphism (5-HTTLPR) association with antidepressant efficacy. *European Neuropsychopharmacology, 22*(4), 239–258. doi:10.1016/j.euroneuro.2011.10.003

Posner, M. I., & Raichle, M. C. (1994). *Images of mind.* New York: Scientific American Library.

Post, C. G. (1963). *An introduction to the law.* Englewood Cliffs, NJ: Prentice Hall.

Post, R. M. (1990). Non-lithium treatment for bipolar disorder. *Journal of Clinical Psychiatry, 51,* (Suppl.), 9–16.

Post, R. M. (1992). Transdirection of psychosocial stress into the neurobiology of recurrent affective disorder. *American Journal of Psychiatry, 149,* 999–1010.

Post, R. M. (1993). Mood disorders: Acute mania. In D. D. Dunner (Ed.), *Current psychiatric therapy* (pp. 204–210). Philadelphia: W. B. Saunders.

Posternak, M. A., & Zimmerman, M. (2005). Is there a delay in the antidepressant effect? A meta-analysis. *Journal of Clinical Psychiatry, 66*(2), 148–158. doi:10.4088/JCP.v66n0201

Potts, A., Grace, V. M., Vares, T., & Gavey, N. (2006). "Sex for life"? Men's counter-stories on "erectile dysfunction," male sexuality and ageing. *Sociology of Health & Illness, 28*(3), 306–329.

Pouba, K., & Tianen, A. (2006). Lunacy in the 19th Century: Women's admission to asylums in United States of America. *Oshkosh Scholar, 1,* 95–103.

Powell, R. A., & Gee, T. L. (1999). The effects of hypnosis on dissociative identity disorder: A re-examination of the evidence. *Canadian Journal of Psychiatry, 44,* 914–916.

Powell, T. J. (1987). *Self-help organizations and professional practice.* Silver Springs, MD: National Association of Social Workers.

Power, K. G., Simpson, R., Swanson, V., & Wallace, L. (1990). A controlled comparison of cognitive-behavioral therapy, diazepam, and placebo, alone and in combination for the treatment of generalized anxiety disorder. *Journal of Anxiety Disorders, 4,* 267–292.

Powers, M. B., Halpern, J. M., Ferenschak, M. P., Gillihan, S. J., & Foa, E. B. (2010). A meta-analytic review of prolonged exposure for posttraumatic stress disorder. *Clinical Psychology Review, 30*(6), 635–641. doi:10.1016/j.cpr.2010.04.007

Powers, M. B., Vedel, E., & Emmelkamp, P. G. (2008). Behavioral couples therapy (BCT) for alcohol and drug use disorders: A meta-analysis. *Clinical Psychology Review, 28*(6), 952–962. doi:10.1016/j.cpr.2008.02.002

Prat, S., Rérolle, C., & Saint-Martin, P. (2013). Suicide pacts: Six cases and literature review. *Journal of Forensic Sciences, 58*(4), 1092–1098. doi:10.1111/1556-4029.12056

Prati, G., & Pietrantoni, L. (2009). Optimism, social support, and coping strategies as factors contributing to posttraumatic growth: A meta-analysis. *Journal of Loss and Trauma, 14*(5), 364–388. doi:10.1080/15325020902724271

Prazeres, A. M., Nascimento, A. L., & Fontenelle, L. F. (2013). Cognitive-behavioral therapy for body dysmorphic disorder: A review of its efficacy. *Neuropsychiatric Disease and Treatment, 9,* 307–316.

Prendergast, M., Podus, D., Finney, J., Greenwell, L., & Roll, J. (2006). Contingency management for treatment of substance use disorders: A meta-analysis. *Addiction, 101*(11), 1546–1560.

Pressman, S. D., Cohen, S., Miller, G. E., Barkin, A., Rabin, B. S., & Treanor, J. J. (2005). *Loneliness, social network size and immune response to influenza vaccination in college freshmen. Health Psychology, 24*(30), 297–306.

Preston, R. (1994). *The hot zone.* London: Doubleday.

Preter, M., & Klein, D. F. (2014). Lifelong opioidergic vulnerability through early life separation: A recent extension of the false suffocation alarm theory of panic disorder. *Neuroscience and Biobehavioral Reviews.* doi:10.1016/j.neubiorev.2014.03.025

Price, R. H., Cowen, E. L., Lorion, R. L., & Ramos-McKay, J. (1988). *Fourteen ounces of prevention: A casebook for practitioners.* Washington, DC: American Psychological Association.

Prickaerts, J., van Goethem, N. P., Chesworth, R., Shapiro, G., Boess, F. G., Methfessel, C., & . . . König, G. (2012). EVP-6124, a novel and selective α7 nicotinic acetylcholine receptor partial agonist, improves memory performance by potentiating the acetylcholine response of α7 nicotinic acetylcholine receptors. *Neuropharmacology, 62,* 1099–1110. doi:10.1016/j.neuropharm.2011.10.024

Prien, R. F., & Potter, W. Z. (1993). Maintenance treatment for mood disorders. In D. L. Dunner (Ed.), *Current psychiatric treatments* (pp. 255–260). Philadelphia: W. B. Saunders.

Prigatano, G. P., Parsons, O. A., & Bortz, J. J. (1995). Methodological considerations in clinical neuropsycho-logical research: 17 years later. *Psychological Assessment, 7,* 396–403.

Prince, M., Bryce, R., Albanese, E., Wimo, A., Ribeiro, W., & Ferri, C. P. (2013). The global prevalence of dementia: A systematic review and metaanalysis. *Alzheimer's & Dementia, 9*(1), 63–75. doi:10.1016/j.jalz.2012.11.007

Prinz, R. J., Sanders, M. R., Shapiro, C. J., Whitaker, D. J., & Lutzker, J. R. (2009). Population-based prevention of child maltreatment: The U.S. triple P system population trial. *Prevention Science, 10*(1), 1–12. doi:10.1007/s11121-009-0123-3

Prochaska, J. O., DiClemente, C. C., & Norcross, J. C. (1992). In search of how people change: Applications to addictive behaviors. *American Psychologist, 47,* 1102–1114.

Project MATCH Research Group (1997). Matching alcoholism treatments to client heterogeneity: Project MATCH posttreatment drinking outcomes. *Journal of Studies on Alcohol, 58,* 7–29.

Project MATCH Research Group. (1998). Matching patients with alcohol disorders to treatments: Clinical implications from project MATCH. *Journal of Mental Health, 7*(6), 589–602. doi:10.1080/09638239817743

Przeworski, A., Cain, N., & Dunbeck, K. (2014). Traumatic life events in individuals with hoarding symptoms, obsessive-compulsive symptoms, and comorbid obsessive-compulsive and hoarding symptoms. *Journal of Obsessive-Compulsive and Related Disorders, 3*(1), 52–59. doi:10.1016/j.jocrd.2013.12.002

Pueschel, S. M., Gallagher, P. L., Zartler, A. S., & Pezzullo, J. C. (1987). Cognitive and learning processes in children with Down syndrome. *Research in Developmental Disabilities, 8,* 21–37.

Pull, C. B., & Damsa, C. (2008). Pharmacotherapy of panic disorder. *Neuropsychiatric Disease and Treatment, 4*(4), 779–795. doi:10.2147/NDT.S1224

Pum, M., Carey, R. J., Huston, J. P., & Müller, C. P. (2007). Dissociating effects of cocaine and d-amphetamine on dopamine and serotonin in the perirhinal, etorhinal, and prefrontal cortex of freely moving rats. *Psychopharmacology, 193*(3), 375–390. doi:10.1007/s00213-007-0791-2

Punjabi, N. M. (2008). The epidemiology of adult obstructive sleep apnea. *Proceedings of the American Thoracic Society, 5*(2), 136–143. doi:10.1513/pats.200709-155MG.

Purcell, C. (2001, September). An investigation of paraphilias, lust murder, and the case of Jeffrey Dahmer: An integrative theoretical model (Jeffrey Dahmer). *Dissertation Abstracts International, 62,* 1594.

Purisch, A. D. (2001). Misconceptions about the Luria-Nebraska Neuropsychological Battery. *Neurorehabilitation, 16,* 275–280.

Putnam, F. W. (1988). The switch process in multiple personality disorder and other state-change disorders. *Dissociation, 1,* 24–32.

Putnam, F. W. (1989). *Diagnosis and treatment of multiple personality disorder.* New York: Guilford Press.

Putnam, F. W. (1995). Development of dissociative disorders. In D. Cicchetti & D. J. Cohen (Eds.), *Developmental psychopathology, Vol. 2: Risk, disorder, and adaptation* (pp. 581–608). Oxford, England: John Wiley & Sons.

Putnam, F. W., Helmers, K., Horowitz, L. A., & Trickett, P. K. (1995). Hypnotizability and dissociativity in sexually abused girls. *Child Abuse and Neglect, 19,* 645–655.

Pyzczynski, T., & Greenberg, J. (1987). Self-regulatory perservation and the depressive self-focusing style: A self-awareness theory of reactive depression. *Psychological Bulletin, 102,* 122–138.

Q

Qin, P., Agerbo, E., & Mortensen, P. (2003). Suicide risk in relation to socioeconomic, demographic, psychiatric, and familial factors: A national register-based study of all suicides in Denmark, 1981–1997. *The American Journal of Psychiatry, 160*(4), 765–772. doi:10.1176/appi.ajp.160.4.765

Quarfordt, S. D., Kalmus, G. W., & Myers, R. D. (1991). Ethanol drinking following 6-OHDA lesions of nucleus accumbens and tuberculum olfactorium of the rat. *Alcohol, 8*(3), 211–217.

Quay, H. C. (1965). Psychopathic personality as pathological stimulation-seeking. *American Journal of Psychiatry, 122,* 180–183.

Quintana, D. S., Guastella, A. J., McGregor, I. S., Hickie, I. B., & Kemp, A. H. (2013). Heart rate variability predicts alcohol craving in alcohol dependent outpatients: Further evidence for HRV as a psychophysiological marker of self-regulation. *Drug and Alcohol Dependence, 132*(1–2), 395–398. doi:10.1016/j.drugalcdep.2013.02.025

Qureshi, I. A., & Mehler, M. F. (2013). Understanding neurological disease mechanisms in the era of epigenetics. *JAMA Neurology, 70,* 703–710.

R

Rachman, S. J. (1990). *Fear and courage* (2nd ed.) New York: W. F. Freeman.

Rachman, S. J. (1993). Obsessions, responsibility, and guilt. *Behavior Research and Therapy, 31,* 149–154.

Rachman, S. J., & Hodgson, R. (1968). Experimentally induced "sexual fetishism": Replication and development. *Psychological Record, 18,* 25–27.

Rachman, S. J., & Hodgson, R. (1980). *Obsessions and compulsions.* Englewood Cliffs, NJ: Prentice Hall.

Rachman, S. J., & Wilson, G. T. (1980). *The effects of psychological therapy.* Oxford, UK: Pergamon Press.

Ragland, D. R., & Brand, R. J. (1988). Type A behavior and mortality from coronary heart disease. *New England Journal of Medicine, 318,* 65–69.

Ragland, J. D., Yoon, J., Minzenberg, M. J., & Carter, C. S. (2007). Neuroimaging of cognitive disability in schizophrenia: Search for a pathophysiological mechanism. *International Review of Psychiatry, 19,* 417–427.

Rahimi, R., Nikfar, S., & Abdollahi, M. (2009). Efficacy and tolerability of *Hypericum perforatum* in major depressive disorder in comparison with selective serotonin reuptake inhibitors: A meta-analysis. *Progress in Neuro-Psychopharmacology & Biological Psychiatry, 33*(1), 118–127. doi:10.1016/j.pnpbp.2008.10.018

Raiker, J. S., Rapport, M. D., Kofler, M. J., & Sarver, D. E. (2012). Objectively measured impulsivity and ADHD: Testing competing predictions from the working memory and behavioral inhibition models. *Journal of Abnormal Child Psychology, 40,* 699–713. doi:10.1007/s10802-011-9607-2

Raine, A. (2002). Biosocial studies of antisocial and violent behavior in children and adults: A review. *Journal of Abnormal Child Psychology, 30* (311–326.)

Raine, A. (2002). The role of prefrontal deficits, low autonomic arousal, and early health factors in the development of antisocial and aggressive behavior in children. *Journal of Child Psychology and Psychiatry, 43,* 417–434.

Raine, A., & Jones, F. (1987). Attention, autonomic arousal, and personality in behaviorally disordered children. *Journal of Abnormal Child Psychology, IS,* 583–599.

Raine, A., Venebles, P. H., & Williams, M. (1990). Relationships between central and autonomic measures of arousal at age 15 years and criminality at age 24 years. *Archives of General Psychiatry, 47,* 1003–1007.

Rajan, K. B., Hebert, L. E., Scherr, P. A., Mendes de Leon, C. F., & Evans, D. A. (2012). Disability in basic and instrumental activities of daily living is associated with faster rate of decline in cognitive function of older adults. *The Journals of Gerontology Series A: Biological Sciences and Medical Sciences, 68*(5), 624–630. doi: 10.1093/gerona/gls208

Rajji, T. K., Ismail, Z., & Mulsant, B. H. (2009). Age at onset and cognitive in schizophrenia: Meta-analysis. *British Journal of Psychiatry, 195,* 286–293.

Rak, N., Bellebaum, C., & Thoma, P. (2013). Empathy and feedback processing in active and observational learning. *Cognitive, Affective & Behavioral Neuroscience, 13,* 869–884. doi:10.3758/s13415-013-0187-1

Ramey, C. T. (1993). High-risk children and IQ: Altering intergenerational patterns. *Intelligence, 16,* 239–256.

Ramey, C. T., & Ramey, S. L. (1992). Effective early intervention. *Mental Retardation, 30,* 337–345.

Ramey, C. T., & Smith, B. J. (1977). Assessing the intellectual consequences of early intervention with high-risk infants. *American Journal of Mental Deficiency, 81,* 318–324.

Ramsland, K. (2007). When women kill together. *The Forensic Examiner, 16*(1), 64.

Rangasamy, S., D'Mello, S. R., & Narayanan, V. (2013). Epigenetics, autism spectrum, and neurodevelopmental disorders. *Neurotherapeutics, 10,* 742–756. doi:10.1007/s13311-013-0227-0

Rao, D. C., Morton, N. E., Gottesman, I. I., & Lew, R. (1981). Path analysis of qualitative data on pairs of relatives: Application to schizophrenia. *Human Heredity, 31,* 325–333.

Rapee, R., Brown, T., Antony, M., & Barlow, D. (1992). Response to hyperventilation and inhalation of 5.5% carbon dioxide-enriched air across the DSM-III-R anxiety disorders. *Journal of Abnormal Psychology, 101,* 538–552.

Raphael, S., & Stoll, M. (2013). Assessing the contribution of the deinstitutionalization of the mentally ill to growth in the U.S. incarceration rate. *The Journal of Legal Studies, 42*(1).

Rapoport, J. (1989). The biology of obsessions and compulsions. *Scientific American, 260,* (3), 83–89.

Rapoport, J., Elkins, R., Langer, D. H., Sceery, W., Buschbaum, M. S., Gillin, J. C., Murphy, D., Zahn, T. P., Ludlow, C., & Mendelson, W. (1981). Childhood obsessive compulsive disorder. *American Journal of Psychiatry, 138,* 1545–1554.

Rapoport, J., Ryland, D. H., & Kriete, M. (1992). Drug treatment of canine acral lick: An animal model of obsessive-compulsive disorder. *Archives of General Psychiatry, 49,* 517–521.

Rappaport, J. (1977). *Community psychology: Values, research and action.* New York: Holt, Rinehart & Winston.

Rappaport, J. (1981). In praise of paradox: A social policy of empowerment over prevention. *American Journal of Community Psychology, 9,* 1–25.

Rappaport, J. (1987). Terms of empowerment/exemplars of prevention: Toward a theory for community psychology. *American Journal of Community Psychology, IS,* 121–148.

Rappaport, J., Seidman, E., Toro, P., McFadden, L., Reischel, T., Roberts, L., Salem, D., & Zimmerman, M. (1985). Collaborative research with a mutual help organization. *Social Policy, IS,* 12–24.

Rapport, M. D., Alderson, R. M., Kofler, M. J., Sarver, D. E., Bolden, J., & Sims, V. (2008). Working memory deficits in boys with ADHD: The contribution of central executive and subsystem processes. *Journal of Abnormal Child Psychology, 36,* 825–837. doi:10.1007/s10802-008-9215-y

Rapport, M. D., Bolden, J., Kofler, M. J., Sarver, D. E., Raiker, J. S., & Alderson, R. M. (2009). Hyperactivity in boys with ADHD: A ubiquitous core symptom or manifestation of working memory deficits? *Journal of Abnormal Child Psychology, 37,* 521–534. doi:10.1007/s10802-008-9287-8

Raschle, N., Chang, M., & Gaab, N. (2011). Structural brain alterations associated with dyslexia predate reading onset. *Neuroimage, 57*(3), 742–749. doi:10.1016/j.neuroimage.2010.09.055

Rasmussen, K. G. (2011). Electroconvulsive therapy and melancholia: Review of the literature and suggestions for further study. *The Journal of ECT, 27*(4), 315–322.

Ratcliff, G., & Saxton, J. (1994). Age-associated memory impairment. In C. E. Coffey & J. L. Cummings (Eds.), *Textbook of geriatric neuropsychiatry* (pp. 145–158). Washington, DC: American Psychiatric Press.

Rauch, S. A. M., & Foa, E. B. (2003). Post-traumatic stress disorder. In D. Nutt & J. Ballenger (Eds.), *Anxiety disorders* (pp. 65–81). Malden, MA: Blackwell Science.

Rauschenberger, S. L., & Lynn, S. J. (1995). Fantasy proneness, DSM-II-R Axis 1 psychopathology, and dissociation. *Journal of Abnormal Psychology, 104,* 373–380.

Raymond, M. J. (1956). Case of fetishism treated by aversion therapy. *British Medical Journal 2,* 854–857.

Raymond, N. C., Coleman, E., Ohlerking, F., Christenson, G. A., & Miner, M. (1999). Psychiatric comorbidity in pedophilic sex offenders. *The American Journal of Psychiatry, 156*(5), 786–788.

Raz, S., & Raz, N. (1990). Structural brain abnormalities in the major psychoses: A quantitative review of the evidence from computerized imaging. *Psychological Bulletin, 89,* 93–108.

Razay, G., Heaton, K. W., Bolton, C. H., & Hughes, A. O. (1992). Alcohol consumption and its relation to cardiovascular risk factors in British Women. *British Medical Journal, 304*(6819), 80–82.

Read, J., Magliano, L., & Beavan, V. (2013). Public beliefs about the causes of "schizophrenia": Bad things happen and can drive you crazy. In J. Read & J. Dillon (Eds.), *Models of madness: Psychological, social and biological approaches to psychosis* (2nd ed.) (pp. 143–156). New York: Routledge/Taylor & Francis Group.

Reas, D. L., Ro, O., Karterud, S., Hummelen, B. & Pedersen, G. (2013). Eating disorders in a large clinical sample of men and women with personality disorders. *International Journal of Eating Disorders, 46,* 801–809.

Rebok, G. W., & Folstein, M. F. (1993). Dementia. *Journal of Neuropsychiatry and Clinical Neurosciences, 5,* 265–276.

Reck, C. C., Struben, K. K., Backenstrass, M. M., Stefenelli, U. U., Reinig, K. K., Fuchs, T. T., . . . Mundt, C. C. (2008). Prevalence, onset and comorbidity of postpartum anxiety and depressive disorders. *Acta Psychiatrica Scandinavica, 118*(6), 459–468. doi:10.1111/j.1600-0447.2008.01264.x

Rector, N. A., & Beck, A. T. (2012). Cognitive behavioral therapy for schizophrenia: An empirical review. *Journal of Nervous and Mental Disease, 200*(10), 832–839. doi:10.1097/NMD.0b013e31826dd9af

Reed, S. D., Katkin, E. S., & Goldband, S. (1986). Biofeed-back and behavioral medicine. In F. H. Kanfer & A. P. Goldstein (Eds.), *Helping people change: A textbook of methods* (3rd ed., pp. 381–436). New York: Pergamon Press.

Rees, C. S., & Pritchard, R. (2013). Brief cognitive therapy for avoidant personality disorder. *Psychotherapy.* Advance online publication.

Regal, R. A., Rooney, J. R., & Wandas, T. (1994). Facilitated communication: An experimental evaluation. *Journal of Autism and Developmental Disorders, 24*(3), 345–355.

Regier, D. A. (2007). Time for a fresh start? Rethinking psychosis in DSM-V. *Schizophrenia Bulletin, 33,* 843–845.

Regier, D. A., Boyd, J. H., Burke, J. D., Rae, D. S., Myers, J. K., Kramer, M., Robins, L. N., George, L. K., Karno, M., & Locke, B. Z. (1988). One-month prevalence of mental disorders in the United States. *Archives of General Psychiatry, 45,* 977–986.

Regier, D. A., Farmer, M. E., Rae, D. S., Locke, B. Z., Keith, S. J., Judd, L. J., & Goodwin, F. K. (1990). Comorbidity of mental disorders with alcohol and other drug abuse. *Journal of the American Medical Association, 264*(19), 2511–2518.

Regier, D. A., Hirschfeld, R. M. A., Goodwin, F. K., Burke, J. D. Jr., Lazar, J. B., & Judd, L. L. (1988). The NIMH Depression Awareness, Recognition, and Treatment program: Structure, aims and scientific basis. *American Journal of Psychiatry, 145,* 1351–1357.

Rehm, L. P. (1977). A self-control model of depression. *Behavior Therapy, 8,* 787–804.

Rehm, L. P. (1984). Self-management therapy for depression. *Advances in Behavior Research and Therapy, 6,* 83–98.

Reich, R. R., Below, M. C., & Goldman, M. S. (2010). Explicit and implicit measures of expectancy and related alcohol cognitions: A meta-analytic comparison. *Psychology of Addictive Behaviors, 24,* 13–25.

Reichborn-Kjennerud, T., Czajkowski, N., Neale, M. C., Orstavik, R. E., Torgersen, S., Tambs, K., . . . Kendler, K. S. (2007). Genetic and environmental influences on dimensional representations of *DSM-IV* cluster C personality disorders: A population-based multivariate twin study. *Psychological Medicine, 37,* 645–653.

Reid, R. C., Carpenter, B. N., Hook, J. N., Garos, S., Manning, J. C., Gilliland, R., . . . Fong, T. (2012). Report of findings in a *DSM-5* field trial for hypersexual disorder. *Journal of Sexual Medicine, 9*(11), 2868–2877.jsm_

Reifman, A., & Windle, M. (1995). Adolescent suicidal behaviors as a function of depression, hopelessness, alcohol use, and social support: A longitudinal investigation. *American Journal of Community Psychology, 23,* 329–354.

Reilly, M., Klima, E., & Bellugi, U. (1990). Once more with feeling: Affect and language in atypical populations. *Development and Psychopathology, 2,* 367–391.

Reinders, A. A., Nijenhuis, E. R., Paans, A. M., Korf, J., Willemsen, A. T., & den Boer, J. A. (2003). One brain, two selves. *Neuroimage, 20,* 2119–2125.

Reinders, A. S., Nijenhuis, E. S., Quak, J., Korf, J., Haaksma, J., Paans, A. J., . . . den Boer, J. A. (2006). Psychobiological characteristics of dissociative identity disorder: A symptom provocation study. *Biological Psychiatry, 60*(7), 730–740. doi:10.1016/j.biopsych.2005.12.019

Reinders, A. S., Willemsen, A. M., Vos, H. J., den Boer, J. A., & Nijenhuis, E. S. (2012). Fact or factitious? A psychobiological study of authentic and simulated dissociative identity states. *Plos ONE, 7*(6), e39279.

Reisberg, B., Ferris, S. H., DeLeon, M. J., & Crook, T. (1982). The global deterioration scale for assessment of primary degenerative dementia. *American Journal of Psychiatry, 139,* 1136–1139.

Reissing, E. D., Binik, Y. M., Khalifé, S., Cohen, D., & Amsel, R. (2004). Vaginal spasm, pain, and behavior: An empirical investigation of the diagnosis of vaginismus. *Archives of Sexual Behavior, 33*(1), 5–17.

Reitan, R. M., & Wolfson, D. (2009). The Halstead-Reitan Neuropsychological Test Battery for Adults—Theoretical, methodological, and validational bases. In I. Grant & K. M. Adams (Eds.), *Neuropsychological assessment of neuropsychiatric and neuromedical disorders* (3rd ed.) (pp. 3–24). New York: Oxford University Press.

Rekers, G. A., Kilgus, M., & Rosen, A. C. (1990). Long-term effect of treatment for gender identity disorder of childhood. *Journal of Psychology and Human Sexuality, 3,* 121–153.

Relkin, N. R. (2007). Beyond symptomatic therapy: A re-examination of acetylcholinesterase inhibitors in Alzheimer's disease. *Expert Review of Neurotherapeutics, 7*(6), 735–748. doi: 10.1586/14737175.7.6.735

Rellini, A., & Meston, C. (2007). Sexual function and satisfaction in adults based on the definition of child sexual abuse. *The Journal of Sexual Medicine, 4*(5), 1312–1321.

Remafedi, G., Farrow, J., & Deisher, R. (1991). Risk factors for attempted suicide in gay and bisexual youth. *Pediatrics, 87,* 869–876.

Remafedi, G., Resnick, M., Blum, R., & Harris, L. (1993). Demography of sexual orientation in adolescents. *Pediatrics, 89,* 714–721.

Remschimdt, H., Schulz, E., Martin, M., Warnke, A., & Trott, G. E. (1994). Childhood onset schizophrenia: History of the concept and recent studies. *Schizophrenia Bulletin, 20,* 727–745.

Rennie v. Klein, 462 F. Supp. 1131 (D. N.J. 1978).

Renouf, A. G. & Harter, S. (1990). Low self-worth and anger as components of the depressive experience in young adolescents. *Development and Psychopathology, 2,* 293–310.

Renshaw, D. C. (1988). Profile of 2376 patients treated at Loyola Sex Clinic between 1972 and 1987. *Social and Marital Therapy, 3,* 111–117.

Resick, P. & Schnicke, M. (1992). Cognitive processing therapy for sexual assault victims. *Journal of Consulting and Clinical Psychology, 60,* 748–756.

Resick, P. A., Nishith, P., Weaver, T. L., Astin, M. C., & Feuer, C. A. (2002). A comparison of cognitive processing therapy with prolonged exposure therapy and a waiting list condition for the treatment of chronic posttraumatic stress disorder in female rape victims. *Journal of Consulting and Clinical Psychology, 70,* 867–879.

Resick, P. A., & Schnicke, M. K. (1993). *Cognitive processing therapy for rape victims: A treatment manual.* Newbury Park, CA: Sage.

Resnick, G. (2010). Project Head Start: Quality and links to child outcomes. In A. J. Reynolds, A. J. Rolnick, M. M. Englund, & J. A. Temple (Eds.), *Childhood programs and practices in the first decade of life: A human capital integration* (pp. 121–156). New York: Cambridge University Press. doi:10.1017/CBO9780511762666.007

Resnick, H. S., Kilpatrick, D. G., Dansky,, B. S., Saunders, B., & Best, C. L. (1993). Prevalence of civilian trauma and posttraumatic stress disorder in a representative national sample of women. *Journal of Consulting and Clinical Psychology, 61,* 984–991.

Restak, R. (2000). *Mysteries of the mind.* Washington, DC: National Geographic Society.

Rettew, D. C., Zanarini, M. C., Yen, S., Grilo, C. M., Skodol, A. E., Shea, M. T., . . . Gunderson, J. G. (2003). Childhood antecedents of avoidant personality disorder: A retrospective study. *Journal of the American Academy of Child & Adolescent Psychiatry, 42*(9), 1122–1130.

Rettner, R. (2013, June 24). Epigenetics: Definition and examples. *Live Science.* Retrieved April 18, 2014 from http://www.livescience.com/37703-epigenetics.html

Reveley, M., Reveley, A., & Baldy, R. (1987). Left cerebral hemisphere hypodensity in discordant schizophrenic twins. *Archives of General Psychiatry, 44,* 625–632.

Revenson, T. A., & Felton, B. J. (1989). Disability and coping as predictors of psychological adjustment to rheumatoid arthritis. *Journal of Consulting and Clinical Psychology, 57,* 344–348.

Rey, J. M., Bashir, M. R., Schwarz, M., Richards, I. N., Plapp, J. M., & Stewart, G. W. (1988). Oppositional disorder: Fact or fiction? *Journal of the American Academy of Child and Adolescent Psychiatry, 27,* 157–162.

Reyes, A. C., & Amador, A. A. (2009). Qualitative and quantitative EEG abnormalities in violent offenders with antisocial personality disorder. *Journal of Forensic and Legal Medicine, 16,* 59–63.

Reynolds, C. R. (2000). Why is psychometric research on bias in mental testing so often ignored? *Psychology, Public Policy, and Law, 6,* 144–150.

Reynolds, M. R., Floyd, R. G., & Niileksela, C. R. (2013). How well is psychometric g indexed by global composites? Evidence from three popular intelligence tests. *Psychological Assessment, 25,* 1314–1321. doi:10.1037/a0034102

Reynolds, S. (1999). *Generation ecstasy: Into the world of techno and rave culture.* New York: Routledge.

Reynolds, W. M., & Coats, K. I. (1986). A comparison of cognitive-behavioral therapy and relaxation training for the treatment of depression in adolescents. *Journal of Consulting and Clinical Psychology, 54,* 653–660.

Rhebergen, D., & Graham, R. (2014). The re-labelling of dysthymic disorder to persistent depressive disorder in *DSM-5:* Old wine in new bottles? *Current Opinion in Psychiatry, 27*(1), 27–31. doi:10.1097/YCO.0000000000000022

Rhebergen, D., Beekman, A. F., de Graaf, R., Nolen, W. A., Spijker, J., Hoogendijk, W. J., & Penninx, B. H. (2009). The three-year naturalistic course of major depressive disorder, dysthymic disorder, and double depression. *Journal of Affective Disorders, 115*(3), 450–459. doi:10.1016/j.jad.2008.10.018

Ribeiro, L. A., Target, M., Chiesa, M., Bateman, A., Stein, H., & Fonagy, P. (2010). The problematic object representation scales (PORS): A preliminary study to assess object relations in personality disorder through the AAI protocol. *Bulletin of the Menninger Clinic, 74*(4), 328–352.

Rice, F., Harold, G., Boivin, J., van den Bree, M. B., & Thapar, A. (2009). Disentangling prenatal and inherited influences in humans with an experimental design. *Proceedings of the National Academy of Sciences in the USA, 106,* 2464–2467.

Richards, S. J., & VanBroeckoven, C. (1994). Genetic linkage in Alzheimer's disease. In F. A. Huppert, C. Brayne, & D. W. O'Connor (Eds.), *Dementia and normal aging* (pp. 492–518). Cambridge: Cambridge University Press.

Richelson, E. (1993). Treatment of acute depression. *Psychiatric Clinics of North America, 16,* 461–478.

Richters, J. E., Arnold, L. E., Jensen, P. S., Abikoff, H., Conners, C. K., Greenhill, L. L., Hechtman, L., Hinshaw, S. P., Pelham, W. E., and Swanson, J. M. (1995). NIMH collaborative multisite multimodal treatment study of children with ADHD: I. Background and rationale. *Journal of the American Academy of Child and Adolescent Psychiatry, 34,* 987–1000.

Rickels, K., Chung, H., Csanalosi, I., Hurowitz, A., London, J., Wiseman, K., Kaplan, M., & Amsterdam, J. (1987). Alprazolam, diazepam, imipramine, and placebo in outpatients with major depression. *Archives of General Psychiatry, 44,* 862–866.

Rickels, K., Schweizer, E., Weiss, S., & Zavodnick, S. (1993). Maintenance drug treatment of panic disorder. II: Short- and long-term outcome after drug taper. *Archives of General Psychiatry, 50,* 61–68.

Ridenour, J., & Moehringer, J. (2014). *Psychodynamic theories of schizophrenia.* Manuscript in preparation.

Riedel, G., & Davies, S. N. (2005). Cannabinoid function in learning, memory and plasticity. *Handbook of Experimental Pharmacology, 168,* 445–477. doi:10.1007/3-540-26573-2_15

Riether, A. M., & Stoudemire, A. (1988). Psychogenic fugue states: A review. *Southern Medical Journal, 82,* 568–571.

Riggins v. Nevada, 112 S. Ct. 1810 (1992).

Riggs, S. A., & Han, G. (2009). Predictors of anxiety and depression in emerging adulthood. *Journal of Adult Development, 16*(1), 39–52. doi:10.1007/s10804-009-9051-5

Riihimäki, K. K., Vuorilehto, M. M., Melartin, T. T., Haukka, J. J., & Isometsä, E. E. (2014). Incidence and predictors of suicide attempts among primary-care patients with depressive disorders: A 5-year prospective study. *Psychological Medicine, 44*(2), 291–302. doi:10.1017/S0033291713000706

Riley, K. P., Snowdon, D. A., Desrosiers, M. F., & Markesbery, W. R. (2005). Early life linguistic ability, late life cognitive function, and neuropathology: Findings from the Nun Study. *Neurobiology of Aging, 26*(3), 341–347. doi: 10.1016/j.neurobiolaging.2004.06.019

Risby, W., Hsiao, J., Manji, H., Bitran, J., Moses, F., Zhou, D., & Potter, W. (1991). The mechanism of action of lithium II: Effects of adenylate cyclase activity and beta-adrenergic receptor binding in normal subjects. *Archives of General Psychiatry, 48,* 513–523.

Riskind, J. H., Kleiman, E. M., & Schafer, K. E. (2013). "Undoing" effects of positive affect: Does it buffer the effects of negative affect in predicting changes in depression? *Journal of Social and Clinical Psychology, 32*(4), 363–380. doi:10.1521/jscp.2013.32.4.363

Ritenbaugh, C., Shisslak, C., Teufal, N., & Leonard-Green, T. K. (1996). A cross-cultural review of eating disorders in regard to DSM-IV. In J. E. Mezzich, A. Kleinman, H. Fabrega, & D. L. Parron (Eds.), *Culture and psychiatric diagnosis: A DSM-IV perspective.* Washington, DC: American Psychiatric Press.

Ritsner, M., Ponizovsky, A., Kurs, R., & Modai, I. (2000). Somatization in an immigrant population in Israel: A community survey of prevalence, risk factors, and help-seeking behavior. *The American Journal of Psychiatry, 157*(3), 385–392.

Rivara, F. P., Booth, C. L., Bergman, A. B., Rogers, L. W., & Weiss, J. (1991). Prevention of pedestrian injuries to children: Effectiveness of a school training program. *Pediatrics, 88*(4), 770–775.

Rivera, R., & Borda, T. (2001). The etiology of body dysmorphic disorder. *Psychiatric Annals, 31*(9), 559–563.

Rivers, P. C. (1994). *Alcohol and human behavior: Theory, research, and practice.* Englewood Cliffs, NJ: Prentice Hall.

Roback, A. A. (1961). *History of psychology and psychiatry.* New York: Philosophical Library.

Roberts, C. F., & Golding, S. (1991). The social construction of criminal responsibility and insanity. *Law and Human Behavior, 15,* 349–376.

Roberts, G. (1991). Delusional belief systems and meaning in life: A preferred reality? *The British Journal of Psychiatry, 159*(Suppl 14), 19–28.

Roberts, N. P., Kitchiner, N. J., Kenardy, J., & Bisson, J. I. (2009). Systematic review and meta-analysis of multiple-session early interventions following traumatic events. *American Journal of Psychiatry, 166*(3), 293–301.

Roberts, Y., Mitchell, M. J., Witman, M., & Taffaro, C. (2010). Mental health symptoms in youth affected by Hurricane Katrina. *Professional Psychology: Research and Practice, 41*(1), 10–18. doi:10.1037/a0018339

Robiner, W. N. (1991). How many psychologists are needed? A call for a national psychology human resource agenda. *Professional Psychology: Research and Practice, 22,* 427–440.

Robins, C. J., & Hayes, A. M. (1993). An appraisal of cognitive therapy. *Journal of Consulting and Clinical Psychology, 61,* 205–214.

Robins, L. N. (1966). *Deviant children grown up: A sociological and psychiatric study of sociopathic personality.* Baltimore: Williams & Wilkins.

Robins, L. N. (1991). Conduct disorder. *Journal of Child Psychology and Psychiatry, 32*(1), 193–212.

Robins, L. N., Helzer, J. E., Weissman, M. M., Orvaschel, H., Gruenberg, E., Burke, J. K., & Regier, D. H. (1984). Lifetime prevalance of specific psychiatric disorders in three cities. *Archives of General Psychiatry, 41,* 949–958.

Robins, L. N., & Regier, D. A. (1991). *Psychiatric disorders in America: The epidemiological catchment area study.* New York: The Free Press.

Robins, L. N., & Rutter, M. (1990). Childhood prediction of psychiatric status in the young adulthood of hyperactive boys: A study controlling for chance associations. In L. Robins & M. Rutter (Eds.), *Straight and deviant pathways from childhood to adulthood* (pp. 279–299). Cambridge, MA.: Cambridge University Press.

Robins, L. N., Tipp, J., & Przybeck, T. (1991). Antisocial personality. In L. N. Robins & D. A. Regier (Eds.), *Psychiatric disorders in America* (pp. 258–290). New York: Free Press.

Robins, R. W., & Beer, J. S. (2001). Positive illusions about the self: Short-term benefits and long-term costs. *Journal of Personality and Social Psychology, 80,* 340–352.

Robinson, D. G., Woerner, M. G., McMeniman, M., Mendelowitz, A., & Bilder, R. M. (2004). Symptomatic and functional recovery from a first episode of schizophrenia or schizoaffective disorder. *American Journal of Psychiatry, 161,* 473–479.

Robinson, L. A., Berman, J. S., & Neimeyer, R. A. (1990). Psychotherapy for the treatment of depression: A comprehensive review of controlled outcome research. *Psychological Bulletin, 108,* 30–49.

Rocket, J. R., Regier, M. D., Kapusta, N. D., Coben, J. H., Miller, T. R., Hanzlick, R. L., . . . Smith, G. S. (2012). Leading causes of unintentional and intentional injury mortality: United States 2000–2009. *American Journal of Public Health, 102*(11), 84–92.

Rockwell, E., Lam, E. R., & Zisook, S. (1988). Antidepressant drug studies in the elderly. *Psychiatric Clinics of North America, 11,* 215–321.

Rodewald, F., Wilhelm-Gobling, C., Emrich, H. M., Reddemann, L., & Gast, U. (2011). Axis 1 comorbidity in female patients with dissociative identity disorder and dissociative identity disorder not otherwise specified. *Journal of Nervous and Mental Disease, 199,* 122–131.

Rodin, J., & Salovey, P. (1989). Health psychology. *Annual Review of Psychology, 40,* 533–579.

Rodricks, D. (1992, March 2). Jackson's silence sends a message. *The Baltimore Sun.* Retrieved on November 3, 2014 from http://articles.baltimoresun.com/1992-03-02/news/1992062147_1_jackson-tom-harkin-shiloh 682877

Rodrigues, E. E., Wenzel, A. A., Ribeiro, M. P., Quarantini, L. C., Miranda-Scippa, A. A., de Sena, E. P., & de Oliveira, I. R. (2011). Hippocampal volume in borderline personality disorder with and without comorbid posttraumatic stress disorder: A meta-analysis. *European Psychiatry, 26*(7), 452–456. doi:10.1016/j.eurpsy.2010.07.005

Rodriguez, C. I., Simpson, H., Liu, S., Levinson, A., & Blanco, C. (2013). Prevalence and correlates of difficulty discarding: Results from a national sample of the U.S. population. *Journal of Nervous and Mental Disease, 201*(9), 795–801.

Rodriguez, J. G. (1990). Childhood injuries in the United States: A priority issue. *American Journal of Diseases of Children, 144,* 625–626.

Rodriquez, C. M., & Richardson, M. J. (2007). Stress and anger as contextual factors and preexisting cognitive schemas: Predicting parental child maltreatment risk. *Child Maltreatment, 12,* 325–337.

Rodriquez, C. M., & Tucker, M. C. (2014). Predicting maternal physical child abuse risk beyond distress and social support: Additive role of cognitive processes. *Journal of Family & Community Studies.* doi:10.1007/s10826-014-9981-9

Roe, D., Mashiach-Eisenberg, M., & Lysaker, P. H. (2011). The relation between objective and subjective domains of recovery among persons with schizophrenia-related disorders. *Schizophrenia Research, 131,* 133–138.

Roelofs, K., Spinhoven, P., Sandijck, P., Moene, F. C., & Hoogduin, K. A. L. (2005). The impact of early trauma and recent life-events on symptom severity in patients with conversion disorder. *The Journal of Nervous and Mental Disease, 193*(8), 508–514.

Roepke, A. (2014, May 19). Psychosocial interventions and posttraumatic growth: A meta-Analysis. *Journal of Consulting and Clinical Psychology.* doi:10.1037/a0036872

Roerig, J. L., Steffen, K. J., Mitchell, J. E., & Zunker, C. (2010). Laxative abuse: Epidemiology, diagnosis, and management. *Drugs, 70*(12), 1487–1503.

Roffwarg, H. P., Muzio, J. N., & Dement, W. C. (1966). Ontogenetic development of the human sleep-dream cycle. *Science, 152,* 604–619.

Rogeness, G. A., Javors, M. A., & Pliszka, S. R. (1992). Neurochemistry and child and adolescent psychiatry. *Journal of the American Academy of Child and Adolescent Psychiatry, 31,* 765–781.

Roger, R. (2001). *Handbook of diagnostic and structured interviewing.* New York: Guilford Press.

Rogers v. Okin, 478 F. Supp. 1342, 1369 (Mass. 1979).

Rogers, C. R. (1942). *Counseling and psychotherapy.* Boston: Houghton Mifflin.

Rogers, C. R. (1951). *Client-centered therapy: Its current practice, implications, and theory.* Boston: Houghton Mifflin.

Rogers, C. R. (1954). *Psychotherapy and personality change.* Chicago: University of Chicago Press.

Rogers, C. R. (1962). Toward becoming a fully functioning person. In A. W. Combs (Ed.), *Perceiving, behaving, becoming: A new focus for education* (pp. 21–33). Washington, DC: National Education Association. doi:10.1037/14325-003

Rogers, C. R. (2007). The necessary and sufficient conditions of therapeutic personality change. *Psychotherapy: Theory, research, practice, training, 44,* 240–248. doi:10.1037/0033-3204.44.3.240

Rogers, R. (1995). *Diagnostic and structured interviewing: A handbook for psychologists.* New York: Psychological Assessment Resources.

Rogers, R. (2003). Standardizing *DSM-IV* diagnoses: The clinical applications of structured interviews. *Journal of Personality Assessment, 81,* 220–225. doi:10.1207/S15327752JPA8103_04

Rogers, R., & Ewing, C. P. (1989). Ultimate opinion proscriptions: A cosmetic fix and a plea for empiricism. *Law and Human Behavior, 13,* 357–374.

Rogers, S., & Vismara, L. (2008). Evidence-based comprehensive treatments for early autism. *Journal of Clinical Child and Adolescent Psychology, 37,* 8–38.

Rogers, S. J., Ozonoff, S., & Maslin-Cole, C. (1991). A comparative study of attachment behavior in children with autism and children with other disorders of behavior and development. *Journal of the American Academy of Child and Adolescent Psychiatry, 30,* 433–438.

Rogoff, B., & Chavajay, P. (1995). What's become of research on the cultural basis of cognitive development? *American Psychologist, 50,* 859–877.

Rohling, M. L., Binder, L. M., Demakis, G. J., Larrabee, G. J., Ploetz, D. M., & Langhinrichsen-Rohling, J. (2011). A meta-analysis of neuropsychological outcome after mild traumatic brain injury: Re-analyses and reconsiderations of Binder et al. (1997), Frencham et al. (2005), and Pertab et al. (2009). *The Clinical Neuropsychologist, 25*(4), 608–623.

Rohrbaugh, M. J., & Shoham, V. (2002). Couple treatment for alcohol abuse: A systemic family-consultation model. In S.G. Hofmann & M.C. Tompson (Eds.), *Treating chronic and severe mental disorders: A handbook of empirically supported interventions* (pp. 277–295). New York: Guilford Press.

Roid, G., & Barram, R. (2004). *Essentials of Stanford-Binet intelligence scales (sb5) assessment.* Hoboken, NJ: Wiley.

Rokeach, M. (1964). *The three Christs of Ypsilanti.* New York: Knopf.

Romano, J. M., Turner, J. A., Friedman, L. S., Bulcroft, R. A., Jensen, M. P., Hops, H., & Wright, S. F. (1992). Sequential analysis of chronic pain behaviors and spouse responses. *Journal of Consulting and Clinical Psychology, 60*(5), 777–782.

Romanos, G. E., Javed, F., Romanos, E. B., & Williams, R. C. (2012). Oro-facial manifestations in patients with eating disorders. *Appetite, 59*(2), 499–504. doi:10.1016/j.appet.2012.06.016

Rombouts, S. A. R. B., Barkhof, F., & Sheltens, P. (2007). *Clinical applications of functional brain MRI.* Oxford, UK: Oxford University Press.

Romme, M., & Escher, D. (1989). Hearing voices. *Schizophrenia Bulletin, 15,* 209–216.

Ronson, J. (2011). *The psychopath test: A journey through the madness industry.* New York: Penguin Group, Inc.

Rook, K. S. (1990). Parallels in the study of social support and social strain. *Journal of Social & Clinical Psychology, 9,* 118–132.

Rooke, S. E., Hine, D. W., & Thorsteinsson, E. B. (2008). Implicit cognition and substance use: A meta-analysis. *Addictive Behaviors, 33*, 1314–1328.

Rooth, F. G., & Marks, I. M. (1974). Persistent exhibitionism: Short-term response to aversion, self-regulation, and relaxation treatments. *Archives of Sexual Behavior, 3*, 227–248.

Ropper, A. H., & Gorson, K. C. (2007). Clinical practice: Concussion. *New England Journal of Medicine, 356*, 166–172.

Rorty, M., & Yager, J. (1996). Histories of childhood trauma and complex post-traumatic sequelae in women with eating disorders. *Psychiatry Clinics of North America, 19*(4), 773–791.

Rosa-Alcázar, A. I., Sánchez-Meca, J., Gómez-Conesa, A., & Marín-Martínez, F. (2008). Psychological treatment of obsessive-compulsive disorder: A meta-analysis. *Clinical Psychology Review, 28*(8), 1310–1325. doi:10.1016/j.cpr.2008.07.001

Rose, D., Wykes, T., Leese, M., Bindman, J., & Fleischmann, P. (2003). Patients' perspectives on electroconvulsive therapy: Systematic review. *BMJ: British Medical Journal, 326*(7403), 1363–1368. doi:10.1136/bmj.326.7403.1363

Rose, S. D., & LeCroy, C. W. (1991). Group methods. In F. H. Kanfer & A. P. Goldstein (Eds.), *Helping people change* (4th ed., pp. 422–453). New York: Pergamon Press.

Rosen, N. O., Bergeron, S., Leclerc, B., Lambert, B., & Steben, M. (2010). Woman and partner-perceived partner responses predict pain and sexual satisfaction in provoked vestibulodynia (PVD) couples. *The Journal of Sexual Medicine, 7*(11), 3715–3724.

Rosen, R. C., & Leiblum, S. R. (1988). A sexual scripting approach to inhibited sexual desire. In S. R. Leiblum & R. C. Rosen (Eds.), *Sexual desire disorders* (pp. 168–191). New York: Guilford Press.

Rosen, R. C. & Leiblum, S. R. (1995a). Hypoactive sexual desire. *Psychiatric Clinics of North America, 18*, 107–121.

Rosen, R. C., & Leiblum, S. R. (1995b). Treatment of sexual disorders in the 1990s: An integrated approach. *Journal of Consulting and Clinical Psychiatry, 63*, 877–890.

Rosen, R. C., Taylor, J. F., Leiblum, S. R., & Bachmann, G. A. (1993). Prevalence of sexual dysfunction in women: Results of a survey study of 329 women in an outpatient gynecological clinic. *Journal of Sex and Marital Therapy, 19*, 171–188.

Rosenbach, A., & Hunot, V. (1995). The introduction of a methadone prescribing programme to a drug-free treatment service: Implications for harm reduction. *Addiction, 90*, 815–821.

Rosenbaum, D. A., Carlson, R. A., & Gilmore, R. O. (2001). Acquisition of intellectual and perceptual-motor skills. *Annual Review of Psychology, 52*, 453–470. doi: 10.1146/annurev.psych.52.1.453

Rosenbaum, J. F., Biederman, J., Hirshfeld, D. R., Bolduc, E. A., & Chaloff, J. (1991). Behavioral inhibition in children: A possible precursor to panic disorder or social phobia. *Journal of Clinical Psychiatry, 52* (Suppl.), 5–9.

Rosenbaum, M. S., & Ayllon, T. (1981). The behavioral treatment of neurodermatitis through habit-reversal. *Behavioral Research and Therapy, 19*, 313–318.

Rosenbaum, T. Y. (2007). Pelvic floor involvement in male and female sexual dysfunction and the role of pelvic floor rehabilitation in treatment: A literature review. *The Journal of Sexual Medicine, 4*(1), 4–13.

Rosenberg, M. L., Smith, J. C., & Davidson, L. E. (1987). The emergence of youth suicide: An epidemiologic analysis and public health perspective. *Annual Review Public Health, 8*, 417–440.

Rosenfarb, I. S., Goldstein, M.J., Mintz, J., & Nuechterlein, K. H. (1995). Expressed emotion and subclinical psychopathology observable within transactions between schizophrenia patients and their family members. *Journal of Abnormal Psychology, 104*, 259–267.

Rosenhan, D. L. (1973). On being sane in insane places. *Science, 179*, 250–258.

Rosenman, R. H. (1978). ihe interview method of assessment of the coronary-prone behavior pattern. In T. M. Dembroski, S. M. Weiss, J. L. Shields, S. G. Haynes, & M. Feinleib (Eds.), *Coronary-prone behavior* (pp. 55–69). New York: Springer-Verlag.

Rosenman, R. H., Brand, R. J., Jenkins, D. D., Friedman, M., Straus, R., & Wurm, M. (1975). Coronary heart disease in the Western Collaborative Group Study: Final follow-up experiences after 8V2 years. *Journal of The American Medical Association, 233*, 872–877.

Rosenstock, I. M. (1966). Why people use health services. *Milbank Memorial Fund Quarterly, 44*, 94–127.

Rosenthal, T. L. (1982). Social learning theory. In G. T. Wison & C. M. Franks (Eds.), *Contemporary behavior therapy: Conceptual and empirical foundations* (pp. 339–363). New York: Guilford Press.

Rosenthal, T. L., & Steffek, B. D. (1991). Modeling methods. In F. H. Kanfer & A. P. Goldstein (Eds.), *Helping people change* (4th ed. pp. 70–121). New York: Pergamon Press.

Rosenzweig, S., Greeson, J. M., Reibel, D. K., Green, J. S., Jasser, S. A., & Beasley, D. (2010). Mindfulness-based stress reduction for chronic pain conditions: Variation in treatment outcomes and role of home meditation practice. *Journal of Psychosomatic Research, 68*(1), 29–36.

Roshanaei-Moghaddam, B., Pauly, M. C., Atkins, D. C., Baldwin, S. A., Stein, M. B., & Roy-Byrne, P. (2011). Relative effects of CBT and pharmacotherapy in depression versus anxiety: Is medication somewhat better for depression, and CBT somewhat better for anxiety? *Depression and Anxiety, 28*(7), 560–567. doi:10.1002/da.20829

Ross, C., & Read, J. (2004). Antipsychotic medications: Myth and facts. In J. Read et al. (Eds.), *Models of madness.* London: Routledge.

Ross, C. A. (1989). *Multiple personality disorder: Diagnosis, clinical features, and treatment.* New York: John Wiley & Sons.

Ross, C. A. (1991). Epidemiology of multiple personality disorder and dissociation. *Psychiatric Clinics of North America, 14*, 596–600.

Ross, C. A. (1995). Current treatment of dissociative identity disorder. In L. M. Cohen, J. N. Berzoff, & M. R. Elin (Eds.), *Dissociative identity disorder: Theoretical and treatment controversies* (pp. 413–434). Northvale, NJ: Jason Aronson.

Ross, C. A. (1997). *Dissociative identity disorder: Diagnosis, clinical features, and treatment of multiple personality.* Hoboken, NJ: Wiley & Sons.

Ross, C. A. (2011). Possession experiences in dissociative identity disorder: A preliminary study. *Journal of Trauma & Dissociation, 12*, 393–400.

Ross, C. A., Anderson, G., Fleisher, W. P., & Norton, G. R. (1991). The frequency of multiple personality disorder among psychiatric inpatients. *American Journal of Psychiatry, 148*, 1717–1720.

Ross, C. A., Duffy, C. M. M., & Ellason, J. W. (2002). Prevalence, reliability, and validity of dissociative disorders in an inpatient setting. *Journal of Trauma & Dissociation, 3*, 7–17.

Ross, C. A., & Ness, L. (2010). Symptom patterns in dissociative identity disorder patients and the general population. *Journal of Trauma & Dissociation, 11*, 458–468.

Ross, H. E., Glaser, F. B., & Germanson, T. (1988). The prevalence of psychiatric disorders in patients with alcohol and other drug problems. *Archives of General Psychiatry, 45*(11), 1023–1031.

Ross, R. T., Begab, M. J., Dondis, E. H., Giampiccolo, J., & Meyers, C. E. (1985). *Lives of the retarded: A forty-year follow-up study.* Stanford, CA: Stanford University Press.

Rostron, B. (2013). Mortality risks associated with environmental tobacco smoke exposure in the United States. *Nicotine & Tobacco Research, 15*(10), 1722–1728.

Roth, M. (1994). The relationship between dementia and normal aging of the brain. In F. A. Huppert, C. Brayne, & D. W. O'Connor (Eds.), *Dementia and normal aging* (pp. 57–78). Cambridge: Cambridge University Press.

Roth, M., Huppert, F. A., Tym, E., & Mountjoy, C. Q. (1988). *CAMD EX: The Cambridge Examination for Mental Disorders in the Elderly.* Cambridge: Cambridge University Press.

Roth, M., Tym, E., Mountjoy, C. Q., Huppert, F. A., Hendrie, H., Verma, S., & Goddard, R. (1986). CAMDEX: A standardized instrument for the diagnosis of mental disorder in the elderly with special reference to the early detection of dementia. *British Journal of Psychiatry, 149*, 698–709.

Rothbaum, B. O., Hodges, L. F., Kooper, R., Opdyke, D., Wilford, J. S., & North, M. (1995). Virtual reality graded exposure in the treatment of acrophobia: A case report. *Behavior Therapy, 26*, 547–554.

Rotheram-Borus, M. J., Hunter, J., & Rosario, M. (1994). Suicidal behavior and gay-related stress among gay and bisexual male adolescents. *Journal of Adolescent Research, 9*, 498–508.

Rotheram-Borus, M. J., Hunter, J., & Rosario, M. (1995). Coming out as lesbian or gay in the era of AIDS. In G. M. Herek & B. Greene (Eds.), *AIDS, identity, and community: The HIV epidemic and lesbians and gay men: Psychological perspectives on lesbian and gay issues* (Vol. 2, pp. 150–168). Thousand Oaks, CA: Sage.

Rottenberg, J. (2014). *The depths: The evolutionary origins of the depression epidemic.* New York: Basic Books.

Rotter, J. (1954). *Social learning and clinical psychology.* New Jersey: Prentice Hall.

Rottwarg, H. P., Rottwarg, Muzio, J. N., & Dement, W. C. (1966). Ontogenetic development of the human sleep-dream cycle. *Science, 152*, 604–619.

Rouse v. Cameron, 373 F. 2d 451 (1966).

Rovio, S., Kåreholt, I., Helkala, E.-L., Viitanen, M., Winblad, B., Tuomilehto, J., . . . Kivipelto, M. (2005). Leisure-time physical activity at midlife and the risk of dementia and Alzheimer's disease. *The Lancet Neurology, 4*(11), 705–711. doi: 10.1016/S1474-4422(05) 70198-8

Rowland, D. L. (2011). Psychological impact of premature ejaculation and barriers to its recognition and treatment. *Current Medical Research and Opinion, 27*(8), 1509–1518.

Rowland, D. L. (2012). *Sexual dysfunction in men.* Cambridge, MA: Hogrefe Publishing.

Rowland, D. L., Cooper, S. E., & Slob, A. K. (1996). Genital and psychoaffective response to erotic stimulation in sexually functional and dysfunctional men. *Journal of Abnormal Psychology, 105*, 194–203.

Rowland, D. L., McMahon, C. G., Abdo, C., Chen, J., Jannini, E., Waldinger, M. D., & Ahn, T. (2010). Disorders of orgasm and ejaculation in men. *Journal of Sexual Medicine, 7*, 1668–1686.

Rowland, D. L., Tai, W. L., & Slob, A. K. (2003). An exploration of emotional response to erotic stimulation in men with premature ejaculation: Effects of treatment with clomipramine. *Archives of Sexual Behavior, 32*(2), 145–153.

Rowling, J. K. (2004). *Harry Potter and the order of the phoenix.* New York: Scholastic Paperbacks.

Roy, A. K., Klein, R. G., Angelosante, A., Bar-Haim, Y., Leibenluft, E., Hulvershorn, L., . . . Spindel, C. (2013). Clinical features of young children referred for impairing temper outbursts. *Journal of Child and Adolescent Psychopharmacology, 23*(9), 588–596. doi:10.1089/cap.2013.0005

Rubin, K. H., Hymel, S., Mills, R. S. L., & Rose-Krasnor, L. (1991). In D. Cicchetti & S. L. Toth (Eds.), *Internalizing and externalizing expressions of dysfunction: Rochester symposium on developmental psychopathology* (Vol. 2, pp. 91–122). Hillsdale, NJ: Erlbaum.

Rubin, L. J. (1996). Childhood sexual abuse: False accusations of "false memory"? *Professional Psychology: Research and Practice, 27,* 447–451.

Ruderman, M. A., Stifel, S. F., O'Malley, M., & Jimerson, S. R. (2013). The school psychologist's primer on childhood depression: A review of research regarding epidemiology, etiology, assessment, and treatment. *Contemporary School Psychology, 17*(1), 35–49.

Rueter, M. A., Scaramella, L., Wallace, L. E., & Conger, R. D. (1999). First onset of depressive or anxiety disorders predicted by the longitudinal course of internalizing symptoms and parent-adolescent disagreements. *Archives of General Psychiatry, 56*(8), 726–732.

Ruhé, H. G., Huyser, J., Swinkels, J. A., & Schene, A. H. (2006). Switching antidepressants after a first selective serotonin reuptake inhibitor in major depressive disorder: A systematic review. *Journal of Clinical Psychiatry, 67*(12), 1836–1855. doi:10.4088/JCP.v67n1203

Ruhé, H. G., Mason, N. S., & Schene, A. H. (2007). Mood is indirectly related to serotonin, norepinephrine, and dopamine levels in humans: A meta-analysis of monoamine depletion studies. *Molecular Psychiatry, 12*(4), 331–359. doi:10.1038/sj.mp.4001949

Rumble, B., Retallack, R., Hilbich, C., Simms, G., Multhaup, G., Martins, R., Hockey, A., Montgomery, P., Beyreuther, K., & Masters, C. L. (1989). Amyloid A4 protein and its precursor in Down's syndrome and Alzheimer's disease. *New England Journal of Medicine, 320,* 1446–1452.

Ruscio, A. M., Stein, D. J., Chiu, W. T., & Kessler, R. C. (2010). The epidemiology of obsessive-compulsive disorder in the National Comorbidity Survey Replication. *Molecular Psychiatry, 15*(1), 53–63. doi:10.1038/mp.2008.94

Rush, A. J. (1993). Mood disorders in DSM-IV. In D. L. Dunner (Ed.), *Current psychiatric treatments* (pp. 189–195). Philadelphia: W. B. Saunders.

Russell, C. J., & Keel, P. K. (2002). Homosexuality as a specific risk factor for eating disorders in men. *International Journal of Eating Disorders, 31*(3), 300–306.

Russell, J., Mauthner, N., Sharpe, S., & Tidswell, T. (1991). The "windows task" as a measure of strategic deception in preschoolers and autistic children. *British Journal of Developmental Psychology, 9,* 331–349.

Russo, J., Katon, K., Sullivan, M., Clark, M., & Buchwald, D. (1994). Severity of somatization and its relationship to psychiatric disorders and personality. *Psychosomatics, 35,* 546–556.

Rutter, M. (1970). Autistic children: Infancy to adulthood. *Seminal Psychiatry, 2,* 435–450.

Rutter, M., & Quinton, D. (1984). Parental psychiatric disorder: Effects on children. *Psychological Medicine, 14,* 853.

Rutter, M., & Schopler, E. (1992). Classification of pervasive developmental disorders: Some concepts and practical considerations. *Journal of Autism and Developmental Disorders, 22,* 459–482.

Rutter, M., & Sroufe, L. A. (2000). Developmental psychopathology: Concepts and challenges. *Development and Psychopathology, 12,* 265–296.

Rutter, M., Beckett, C., Castle, J., Colvert, E., Kreppner, J., Mehta, M., . . . Sonuga-Barke, E. (2007). Effects of profound early institutional deprivation: An overview of findings from a UK longitudinal study of Romanian adoptees. *European Journal of Developmental Psychology, 4,* 332–350.

Rutter, M., Caspi, A., Fergusson, D., Horwood, L. J., Goodman, R., Maaughan, B., . . . Carroll, J. (2004). Sex differences in developmental reading disability: New findings from 4 epidemiological studies. *Journal of the American Medical Association, 291,* 2007–2012.

Rutter, M., Macdonald, H., Le Couteur, A., Harrington, R., Bolton, P., & Bailey, A. (1990). Genetic factors in child psychiatric disorders. II: Empirical findings. *Journal of Child Psychology and Psychiatry, 31,* 39–83.

Rutter, M., Tizard, J., & Whitmore, K. (1970). *Education, health, and behavior.* London: Longman.

Ryan, N. D. (1992). The pharmacologic treatment of child and adolescent depression. *Psychiatric Clinics of North America, IS,* 29–40.

Ryan, L. M., & Warden, D. L. (2003). Post concussion syndrome. *International Review of Psychiatry, 15*(4), 310–316. doi:10.1080/09540260310001606692

Rybakowski, J. K., Borkowska, A., Czerski, P. M., & Hauser, J. (2001). Dopamine D3 receptor (DRD3) gene polymorphism is associated with the intensity of eye movement disturbances in schizophrenic patients and healthy subjects. *Molecular Psychiatry, 6,* 718–724.

Rydelius, P. A. (1988). The development of antisocial behavior and sudden violent death. *Acta Psychiatrica Scandinavica, 77,* 398–403.

Ryff, C. D., & Singer, B. (1996). Psychological well-being: Meaning, measurement, and implications for psychotherapy research. *Psychotherapy and Psychosomatics, 65,* 14–23.

S

Sachar, E. J., Heilman, L., Roffwarg, H. P. Halpern, F. S., Fukushima, D. K., Gallagher, T. F. (1973). Disrupted 24-hour patterns of cortisol secretion in psychotic depression. *Archives of General Psychiatry, 28,* 19–24.

Sachdev, P. & Hay, P. (1995). Does neurosurgery for obsessive-compulsive disorder produce personality changes? *Journal of Nervous and Mental Disease, 183,* 408-413.

Sachdev, P., Hay, P., & Cumming, S. (1992). Psychosurgical treatment of obsessive-compulsive disorder. *Archives of General Psychiatry, 49,* 582–583.

Sachdev, P. S. (2000). The current status of tardive dyskinesia. *Australian & New Zealand Journal of Psychiatry, 34,* 355–369.

Sachdev, P. S., Blacker, D., Blazer, D. G., Ganguli, M., Jeste, D. V., Paulsen, J. S., & Petersen, R.C. (2014). Classifying neurocognitive disorders: The *DSM-5* approach. *Nature Reviews Neurology, 10,* 634–642.

Sachs-Ericsson, N., & Blazer, D. G. (2015). The new *DSM-5* diagnosis of mild neurocognitive disorder and its relation to research in mild cognitive impairment. *Aging & Mental Health, 19*(1), 2–12. doi: 10.1080/13607863.2014.920303.

Sachs-Ericsson, N., Cromer, K., Hernandez, A., & Kendall-Tackett, K. (2009). A review of childhood abuse, health, and pain-related problems: The role of psychiatric disorders and current life stress. *Journal of Trauma & Dissociation, 10*(2), 170–188. doi:10.1080/15299730802624585

Sack, R. L., Lewy, A. J., White, D. M., Singer, C. M., Fireman, M. J., & Vandiver, R. (1990). Morning vs. evening light treatment for winter depression: Evidence that the therapeutic effects of light are mediated by circadian phase shifts. *Archives of General Psychiatry, 47,* 343–351.

Saczynski, J. S., Pfeifer, L. A., Masaki, K., Korf, E. S. C., Laurin, D., White, L., & Launer, L. J. (2006). The effect of social engagement on incident dementia: The Honolulu-Asia aging study. *American Journal of Epidemiology, 163*(5), 433–440.

Sadock, V. A. (1995). Normal human sexuality. In H. I. Kaplan & B. J. Sadock (Eds.), *Comprehensive textbook of psychiatry/VI* (pp. 1295–1321). Baltimore, MD: Williams & Wilkins.

Safer, D. J., & Krager, J. M. (1984). Trends in medication therapy for hyperactivity: National and international perspectives. *Advances in Learning & Behavioral Disabilities, 3,* 125–149.

Safer, D. J., & Krager, J. M. (1988). A survey of medication treatment for hyperactive/inattentive students. *Journal of the American Medical Association, 260,* 2256–2258.

Sagan, C. (1977). *The dragons of Eden.* New York: Random House.

Saha, S., Chant, D., Welham, J., & McGrath, J. (2005). A systematic review of the prevalence of schizophrenia. *Public Library of Science, 2,* e141.

Saha, T. D., Chou, S. P., & Grant, B. F. (2006). Toward an alcohol use disorder continuum using item response theory: Results from the National Epidemiologic Survey on Alcohol and Related Conditions. *Psychological Medicine, 36*(7), 931–941. doi:10.1017/S003329170600746X

Sales, B., & Hafemeister, T. (1984). Empiricism and legal policy on the insanity defense. In L. A. Teplin (Ed.), *Mental health and criminal justice.* Newbury Park, CA: Sage.

Salinger, J. D. (1951/1985). *The catcher in the rye.* New York: Bantam.

Salzman, C. (1991). The APA task force report on benzodiazepine dependence, toxicity, and abuse. *American Journal of Psychiatry, 148,* 151–152.

Sameroff, A. J., Seifer, R., Zax, M., & Barocas, R. (1987). Early indicators of developmental risk: Rochester longitudinal study. *Schizophrenia Bulletin, 13,* 383–394.

Samuel, D. B., & Widiger, T. A. (2006). Differentiating normal and abnormal personality from the perspective of the *DSM.* In S. Strack (Ed.), *Differentiating normal and abnormal personality* (2nd ed., pp. 165–183). New York: Springer.

Samuel, D. B., Sanislow, C. A., Hopwood, C. J., Shea, M., Skodol, A. E., Morey, L. C., & Grilo, C. M. (2013). Convergent and incremental predictive validity of clinician, self-report, and structured interview diagnoses for personality disorders over 5 years. *Journal of Consulting and Clinical Psychology, 81,* 650–659. doi:10.1037/a0032813

Samuels, A. (1995). Somatization disorder: A major public health issue. *The Medical Journal of Australia, 163,* 147–149.

Samuels, J. F., Bienvenu, O., Grados, M. A., Cullen, B., Riddle, M. A., Liang, K., . . . Nestadt, G. (2008). Prevalence and correlates of hoarding behavior in a community-based sample. *Behaviour Research and Therapy, 46*(7), 836–844. doi:10.1016/j.brat.2008.04.004

Samuels, J., Eaton, W. W., Bienvenu, O. J., Brown, C. H., Costa Jr., P. T., & Nestadt, G. (2002). Prevalence and correlates of personality disorders in a community sample. *British Journal of Psychiatry, 180,* 536–542.

Sanchez, M. M., Heyn, S. N., Das, D., Moghadam, S., Martin, K. J., & Salehi, A. (2012). Neurobiological elements of cognitive dysfunction in Down syndrome: Exploring the role of APP. *Biological Psychiatry, 71*, 403.

Sandberg, D. E., Meyer-Bahlburg, H. F. L., Ehrhardt, A. A., & Yager, T. J. (1993). The prevalence of gender-atypical behavior in elementary school children. *Journal of the American Academy of Child and Adolescent Psychiatry, 32*, 306–314.

Sander, D. (2013). Models of emotion: The affective neuroscience approach. In J. Armony & P. Vuilleumier (Eds.), *The Cambridge handbook of human affective neuroscience* (pp. 5–53). New York: Cambridge University Press.

Sanders, M. R., Cann, W., & Markie-Dadds, C. (2003). The triple p-positive programme: A universal population-level approach to the prevention of child abuse. *Child Abuse Review, 12*, 155–171.

Sanderson, C. A. (2010). *Social psychology.* Hoboken, NJ: Wiley.

Sanderson, W., Rapee, R., & Barlow, D. (1989). The influence of perceived control on panic attacks induced via inhalation of 5.5% CO_2-enriched air. *Archives of General Psychiatry, 46*, 157–162.

Sandin, S., Lichtenstein, P., Kuja-Halkola, R., Larsson, H., Hultman, C. M., & Reichenberg, A. (2014). The familial risk of autism. *JAMA: Journal of the American Medical Association, 311*(17), 1770–1777. doi:10.1001/jama.2014.4144

Sandler, I., Wolchik, S., Braver, S., & Fogas, B. (1991). Stability and quality of life events and psychological symptomatology in children of divorce. *American Journal of Community Psychology, 19*, 501–520.

Sar, V., Tutkun, H., Alyanak, B., Bakim, B., & Barai, I. (2000). Frequency of dissociative disorders among psychiatric outpatient in Turkey. *Comprehensive Psychiatry, 41*, 216–222.

Sarason, I. G., Johnson, J. H., & Siegel, J. M. (1978). Assessing the impact of life changes: Development of the life experiences survey. *Journal of Consulting and Clinical Psychology, 46*, 932–946.

Sarbin, T. R. (1969). The scientific status of the mental illness metaphor. In S. G. Plog & R. B. Edgerton (Eds.), *Changing perspectives in mental illness.* New York: Holt, Rinehart, & Winston.

Sartorius, N., Ustiin, T. B., Korten, A., Cooper, J. E., & van Drimmelen, J. (1995). Progress toward achieving a common language in psychiatry. II: Results from the international field trials of the I CD-10 diagnostic criteria for research for mental and behavioral disorders. *The American Journal of Psychiatry, 152*(10), 1427–1437.

Satir, V. (1967). *Conjoint family therapy* (rev. ed.). Palo Alto, CA: Science and Behavior Books.

Satterfield, J. H., & Dawson, M. E. (1971). Electrodermal correlates of hyperactivity in children. *Psychophysiology, 8*, 191–197.

Sauer-Zavala, S., Burris, J. L., & Carlson, C. R. (2014). Understanding the relationship between religiousness, spirituality, and underage drinking: The role of positive alcohol expectancies. *Journal of Religion and Health, 53*(1), 68–78.

Saxena, S. (2011). Pharmacotherapy of compulsive hoarding. *Journal of Clinical Psychology, 67*(5), 477–484. doi:10.1002/jclp.20792

Saxena, S., Brody, A. L., Maidment, K. M., & Baxter, L. R. (2007). Paroxetine treatment of compulsive hoarding. *Journal of Psychiatric Research, 41*(6), 481–487. doi:10.1016/j.jpsychires.2006.05.001

Sayegh, A. A., & Reid, D. (2010). Prevalence of catatonic signs in acute psychiatric patients in Scotland. *The Psychiatrist, 34*(11), 479–484. doi:10.1192/pb.bp.109.025908

Scahill, L, McDougle, C. J., Aman, M. G., Johnson, C., Handen, B., Bearss, K., . . . Vitiello, B. (2012). Effects of risperidone and parent training on adaptive functioning in children with pervasive developmental disorder sand serious behavioral problems. *Journal of the American Academy of Child and Adolescent Psychiatry, 51*, 136. doi: 10.1016/j.jaac.2011.11.010

Scarpini, E., Scheltens, P., & Feldman, H. (2003). Treatment of Alzheimer's disease: Current status and new perspectives. *The Lancet Neurology, 2*(9), 539–547. doi: 10.1016/S1474-4422(03)00502-7

Schachter, S., & Latane, B. (1964). Crime, cognition, and the autonomic nervous system. In D. Levine (Ed.), *Nebraska Symposium on motivation* (Vol. 12, pp. 221–273). Lincoln: University of Nebraska Press.

Schaie, K. W. (1994). The course of adult intellectual development. *American Psychologist, 49*, 304–313.

Scharfstein, L. A., Beidel, D. C., Finnell, L., Distler, A., & Carter, N. T. (2011). Do pharmacological and behavioral interventions differentially affect treatment outcome for children with social phobia? *Behavior Modification, 35*(5), 451–467. doi:10.1177/0145445511408590

Schatz, P. (2011). Computerized neuropsychological assessment in sport. In F. M. Webbe (Ed.), *The handbook of sport neuropsychology* (pp. 173–186). New York: Springer Publishing Co.

Scheff, T. J. (1966). *Being mentally ill.* Chicago: Aldine.

Scheier, M. F., & Carver, C. S. (1985). Optimism, coping, and health: Assessment and implications of generalized outcome expectancies. *Health Psychology, 4*, 219–247.

Scherwitz, L. W., Perkins, L. L., Chesny, M. A., Hughes, G. H., & Sidney, S. (1992). Hostility and health behaviors in young adults: The CARDIA Study. *American Journal of Epidemiology, 136*, 136–145.

Schiavi, R. C., Schreiner-Engel, P., Mandeli, J., Schanzer, H., & Cohen, E. (1990). Healthy aging and male sexual function. *American Journal of Psychiatry, 174*, 766–771.

Schiavi, R. C., Schreiner-Engel, P., White, D., & Mandeli, J. (1988). Pituitary-gonadal function during sleep in men with hypoactive sexual desire and in normal controls. *Psychosomatic Medicine, SO*, 304–318.

Schifano, F. (2004). A bitter pill. Overview of ecstasy (MDMA, MDA) related fatalities. *Psychopharmacology, 173*, 242–248.

Schmalleger, F. (2001). *Criminal justice: A brief introduction.* Upper Saddle River, NJ: Prentice Hall.

Schmand, B., Eikelenboom, P., & van Gool, W. A. (2011). Value of neuropsychological tests, neuroimaging, and biomarkers for diagnosing Alzheimer's disease in younger and older age cohorts. *Journal of the American Geriatrics Society, 59*(9), 1705–1710. doi:10.1111/j.1532-5415.2011.03539.x

Schmauck, F. J. (1970). Punishment, arousal, and avoidance learning in sociopaths. *Journal of Abnormal Psychology, 76*, 443–453.

Schnabel, T. (1987). Evaluations of the safety and side effects of antianxiety agents. *The American Journal of Medicine, 82*, (Suppl. 5A), 7–13.

Schneider, H., & Eisenberg, D. (2006). Who receives a diagnosis of attention-deficit/hyperactivity disorder in the United States elementary school population? *Pediatrics, 117*, e601–e609.

Schneider, K. (1959). *Clinical psychopathology.* New York: Grune & Stratton.

Schneider, S. F. (1991). No fluoride in our future. *Professional Psychology: Research and Practice, 22*, 456–460.

Schnurr, P., Friedman, M. J., & Rosenberg, S. D. (1993). Preliminary MMPI scores as predictors of combat-related PTSD symptoms. *American Journal of Psychiatry, 150*(3), 479–483.

Schoepf, D., Heun, R., Weiffenbach, O., Herrmann, S., & Maier, W. (2003). The 4-week prevalence of somatoform disorders and associated psychosocial impairment. *Der Nervenarzt, 74*(3), 245–251. doi:10.1007/s00115-001-1241-8

Schoepf, D., Uppal, H., Potluri, R., Chandran, S., & Heun, R. (2014). Comorbidity and its relevance on general hospital-based mortality in major depressive disorder: A naturalistic 12-year follow-up in general hospital admissions. *Journal of Psychiatric Research, 52*, 28–35. doi:10.1016/j.jpsychires.2014.01.010

Schooler, N. R., & Keith, S. J. (1993). The clinical research base for the treatment of schizophrenia. *Psychopharmacology Bulletin, 29*, 431–446.

Schöttle, D., Schimmelmann, B. G., Karow, A., Ruppelt, F., Sauerbier, A. L., Bussopulos, A. . . . Lambert, M. (2014). Effectiveness of integrated care including therapeutic assertive community treatment in severe schizophrenia spectrum and bipolar I disorders: The 24-month follow-up ACCESS II study. *Journal of Clinical Psychiatry.* DOI: http://dx.doi.org/10.4088/JCP.13m08817

Schradle, S. B., & Dougher, M. J. (1985). Social support as a mediator of stress: Theoretical and empirical issues. *Clinical Psychology Review, S*, 641–662.

Schreiber, F. R. (1973). *Sybil.* Chicago: Henry Regnery.

Schreiner-Engel, P., & Schiavi, R. C. (1986). Lifetime psychopathology in individuals with low sexual desire. *Journal of Nervous and Mental Diseases, 174*, 646–651.

Schukit, M. A., Goodwin, D. W., & Winokur, G. (1972). Biological vulnerability to alcoholism. *American Journal of Psychiatry, 128*, 1132–1136.

Schuckit, M. A., Smith, T. L., Danko, G. P., Reich, T., Bucholz, K. K., & Bierut, L. J. (2002). Similarities in the clinical characteristics related to alcohol dependence in two populations. *American Journal of Addiction, 11*, 1–9.

Schulz, P. M., Resick, P. A., Huber, L. C., & Griffin, M. G. (2006). The effectiveness of cognitive processing therapy for PTSD with refugees in a community setting. *Cognitive and Behavioral Practice, 13*, 322–331.

Schumacher, J. E., Milby, J. B., Wallace, D., Meehan, D., Kertesz, S., Vuchinich, R., . . . Usdan, S. (2007). Meta-analysis of day treatment and contingency-management dismantling research: Birmingham Homeless Cocaine Studies (1990–2006). *Journal of Consulting and Clinical Psychology, 75*(5), 823–828. doi:10.1037/0022-006X.75.5.823

Schwartz, M. F., & Masters, W. H. (1984). The Masters and Johnson treatment program for dissatisfied homosexual men. *American Journal of Psychiatry, 141*, 173–181.

Schwartz, R. H. (1995). LSD: Its rise, fall, and renewed popularity among high school students. *Pediatric Clinics of North America, 42*(2), 403–413.

Schwartz, S., & Johnson, J. H. (1985). *Psychopathology of childhood: A clinical-experimental approach* (2nd ed.). New York: Pergamon Press.

Schwarz, A., & Cohen, S. (2013, April 1). More diagnoses of hyperactivity in new C.D.C. data. *The New York Times*, pp. A1–A11.

Schwarzwald, J., Weisenberg, M., Waysman, M., Solomon, Z., & Klingman, A. (1993). Stress reaction of school-age children to the bombardment by SCUD missiles. *Journal of Abnormal Psychology, 102*, 404–410.

Schweinhart, L. J., Weikart, D. P., & Larner, M. B. (1986). Consequences of three preschool curriculum models through age 15. *Early Childhood Research Quarterly, 1*(1), 15–45.

Schweinhart, L. L., Barnes, H. V., & Weikhart, D. R (1993). *Significant benefits. The High/Scope Perry School Study through age 27.* Ypsilanti, MI: High/Scope Press.

Schweitzer, I. (1989). The psychiatric assessment of the patient requesting facial surgery. *Australian and New Zealand Journal of Psychiatry, 23,* 249–254.

Schweizer, E., Rickels, K., Weiss, S., & Zavodnick, S. (1993). Maintenance drug treatment of panic disorder: I. Results of a prospective, placebo-controlled comparison of alprazolam and imipramine. *Archives of General Psychiatry, 50,* 51–60.

Scinto, L. F. M., Daffner, K. R., Dressier, D., Ransil, B. I., Rentz, D., Weintraub, S., Mesulam, M., & Potter, H. (1994). A potential noninvasive neurobiological test for Alzheimer's disease. *Science, 266,* 1051–1054.

Scott, A. (1989). Which depressed patients will respond to electroconvulsive therapy? The search for biological predictors of recovery. *British Journal of Psychiatry, 154,* 8–17.

Scott, A. M., & Poon, A. M. T. (2004). PET imaging of brain tumors. In P. J. Ell & S. S. Gambhir (Eds.), *Nuclear medicine in clinical diagnosis and treatment,* 3rd ed. (Chapter 26). Philadelphia, PA: Elsevier Churchill-Livingstone.

Scott, C. L., & Holmberg, T. (2003). Castration of sex offenders: Prisoners' rights versus public safety. *Journal of the American Academy of Psychiatry and the Law, 31,* 502–509.

Scotti, J. R., Evans, I. M., Meyer, L. H., & Walker, P. (1991). A meta-analysis of intervention research with problem behavior: Treatment validity and standards of practice. *American Journal on Mental Retardation, 96,* 233–256.

Scott-Sheldon, L. J., Carey, K. B., Elliott, J. C., Garey, L., & Carey, M. P. (2014). Efficacy of alcohol interventions for first-year college students: A meta-analytic review of randomized controlled trials. *Journal of Consulting and Clinical Psychology, 82*(2), 177–188. doi:10.1037/a0035192

Scott-Sheldon, L. J., Demartini, K. S., Carey, K. B., & Carey, M. P. (2009). Alcohol interventions for college students improves antecedents of behavioral change: Results from a meta-analysis of 34 randomized controlled trials. *Journal of Social and Clinical Psychology, 28*(7), 799–823. doi:10.1521/jscp.2009.28.7.799

Searight, H. R. (2013). Deinstitutionalization of people with mental illness: A failed policy that could have succeeded. *Psyccritiques, 58*(27). doi:10.1037/a0032865

Sedensky, S. J., III. (2013). *State's attorney report of the state's attorney for the judicial district of Danbury on the shootings at Sandy Hook Elementary School and 36 Yogananda Street, Newtown, Connecticut on December 14, 2012.* Retrieved March 14, 2014 from http://www.nytimes.com/interactive/2013/11/26/nyregion/26newtown-report.html?ref=nyregion

Seeman, P. (1987). Dopamine receptors and the dopamine hypothesis of schizophrenia. *Synapse, 1,* 133–152.

Segal, R., & Smith, M. (2014). Treatment for adult ADD/ADHD: A guide to finding treatments that work. *Helpguide.org.* Retrieved on October 23, 2014 from http://www.helpguide.org/articles/add-adhd/adult-adhd-attention-deficit-disorder-treatment.htm

Segal, Z. V., Williams, J. M. G., & Teasdale, J. D. (2002). *Mindfulness-based cognitive therapy for depression: A new approach to preventing relapse.* New York: Guilford Press.

Segerstrom, S. C., & Miller, G. E. (2004). Psychological stress and the human immune system: A meta-analytic study of 30 years of inquiry. *Psychological Bulletin, 130,* 601–630. doi:10.1037/0033-2909.130.4.601

Segraves, K. B., & Segraves, R. T. (1991). Hypoactive sexual desire disorder: Prevalence and comorbidity in 906 subjects. *Journal of Sex and Marital Therapy, 17,* 55–58.

Segraves, R. T. (1988). Drugs and desire. In S. R. Leiblum & R. C. Rosen (Eds.), *Sexual desire disorders* (pp. 313–347). New York: Guilford Press.

Segraves, R. T., Clayton, A., Croft, H., Wolf, A., & Warnock, J. (2004). Bupropion sustained release for the treatment of hypoactive sexual desire disorder in premenopausal women. *Journal of Clinical Psychopharmacology, 24*(3), 339–342.

Seidman, E. (1988). Back to the future, community psychology: Unfolding a theory of social intervention. *American Journal of Community Psychology, 16,* 3–24.

Seidman, E., Allen, L., Aber, J. L., Mitchell, C., & Feinman, J. (1994). The impact of school transitions in early adolescence on the self-system and perceived social context of poor urban youth. *Child Development, 65,* 507–522.

Seidman, S. N., & Rieder, R. O. (1994). A review of sexual behavior in the United States. *The American Journal of Psychiatry, 151,* 330–341.

Seki, M., Yoshida, K., & Okamura, Y. (1991). A study on hyperprolactinemia in female patients with alcoholism. *Arukoru Kenkyu-to Yakubutsu Ison, 26*(1), 49–89.

Seligman, M. E. P. (1971).Phobias and preparedness. *Behavior Therapy, 2,* 307–320.

Seligman, M. E. P. (1975). *Helplessnesss: On depression, development, and death.* San Francisco: Freeman.

Seligman, M. E. P. (1995). The effectiveness of psychotherapy: The *Consumer Reports* study. *American Psychologist, 50,* 965–974.

Seligman, M. E. P., & Maier, S. F. (1967). Failure to escape traumatic shock. *Journal of Experimental Psychology, 74,* 1–9.

Seligman, M. P. (1990). Why is there so much depression today? The waxing of the individual and the waning of the commons. In R.E. Ingram (Ed.), *Contemporary psychological approaches to depression: Theory, research, and treatment* (pp. 1–9). New York: Plenum Press. doi:10.1007/978-1-4613-0649-8_1

Seligman, M. P. (1998, September). American Psychological Association Presidential Address. *National Press Club: Morning Newsmaker.* Washington, DC.

Seligman, M. P. (2011). *Flourish: A visionary new understanding of happiness and well-being.* New York: Free Press.

Seligman, M. P., & Fowler, R. D. (2011). Comprehensive soldier fitness and the future of psychology. *American Psychologist, 66,* 82–86. doi:10.1037/a0021898

Seligman, M. P., & Nolen-Hoeksema, S. (1987). Explanatory style and depression. In D. Magnusson & A. Ohman, *Psychopathology: An Interactional Perspective* (pp. 125–139). New York: Academic Press.

Seligman, M. P., Steen, T. A., Park, N., & Peterson, C. (2005). Positive psychology progress: Empirical Validation of interventions. *American Psychologist, 60,* 410–421. doi:10.1037/0003-066X.60.5.410

Seligman, R., & Kirmayer, L. J. (2008). Dissociative experience and cultural neuroscience: Narrative, metaphor and mechanism. *Culture, Medicine and Psychiatry, 32*(1), 31–64.

Selle, V. V., Schalkwijk, S. S., Vázquez, G. H., & Baldessarini, R. J. (2014). Treatments for acute bipolar depression: Meta-analyses of placebo-controlled, monotherapy trials of anticonvulsants, lithium and antipsychotics. *Pharmacopsychiatry, 47*(2), 43–52. doi:10.1055/s-0033-1363258

Selman, R., Beardslee, W., Schultz, L., Krupa, M., & Podorefsky, D. (1986). Assessing adolescent interpersonal negotiation strategies: Toward the integration of structural and functional models. *Developmental Psychology, 22*(4), 450–459.

Selten, J., Wiersma, D., & van den Bosch, R. J. (2000). Distress attributed to negative symptoms in schizophrenia. *Schizophrenia Bulletin, 26*(3), 737–744.

Selvin, E., Burnett, A. L., & Platz, E. A. (2007). Prevalence and risk factors for erectile dysfunction in the US. *American Journal of Medicine, 120*(2), 151–157.

Selye, H. (1936). A syndrome produced by diverse noxious agents. *Nature, 38,* 32–36.

Selye, H. (1982). History and present status of the stress concept. In L. Goldberger and S. Breznitz (Eds.), *Handbook of stress: Theoretical and clinical aspects* (pp. 7–17). New York: The Free Press.

Semrud-Clikeman, M., & Hynd, G. W. (1991). Specific nonverbal and social-skills deficits in children with learning disabilities. In J. E. Obrzut & G. W. Hynd (Eds.), *Neuropsychological foundations of learning disabilities: A handbook of issues, methods and practice* (pp. 603–629). New York: Academic Press.

Serpell, R. (1979). How specific are perceptual skills? A cross-cultural study of pattern reproduction. *British Journal of Psychology, 70,* 365–380.

Serrano, N. (2013). *The behavioral health consultant: Helping you do what you already do better.* Webinar given for Oregon Rural Health Centers. Portland, OR (January 16).

Seto, M. C., Cantor, J. M. & Blanchard, R. (2006). Child pornography offenses are a valid diagnostic indicator of pedophilia. *Journal of Abnormal Psychology, 115*(3), 610–615.

Sewell, K. W. (2005). The experience cycle and the sexual response cycle: Conceptualization and application to sexual dysfunctions. *Journal of Constructivist Psychology, 18*(1), 3–13.

Sexton, M. M. (1979). Behavioral epidemiology. In O. F. Pomerleau & J. P. Brady (Eds.), *Behavioral medicine: Theory and practice* (pp. 3–22). Baltimore: Williams & Wilkins.

Shadish, W. R., Jr., Matt, G. E., Navarro, A. M., Liegle, G., Crits-Christoph, P., Hazelrigg, M., Jorm, A., Lyons, L. S., Nietzel, M. T., Prout, H. T., Robinson, L., Smith, M. L., Svartberg, M., & Weiss, B. (in press). The generalization of psychotherapy research to clinically representative conditions. *Journal of Consulting and Clinical Psychology.*

Shadish, W. R., Jr., & Sweeney, R. B. (1991). Mediators and moderators in meta-analysis: There's a reason we don't let dodo birds tell us which psychotherapies should have prizes. *Journal of Consulting and Clinical Psychology, 59,* 763–765.

Shaffer, D. (1988). The epidemiology of teen suicide: An examination of risk factors. *Journal of Clinical Psychiatry, 49*(9, Suppl), 36–41.

Shaffer, D. (1990). Adolescent suicide. Presentation at the ADAMHOL clinical training meetings, Reston, VA.

Shaffer, D., Garland, A., Gould, M., Fisher, P., & Trautman, P. (1988). Preventing teenage suicide: A critical review. *Journal of the American Academy of Child and Adolescent Psychiatry, 27,* 675–687.

Shager, H. M., Schindler, H. S., Magnuson, K. A., Duncan, G. J., Yoshikawa, H., & Hart, C. D. (2013). Can research design explain variation in Head Start research results? A meta-analysis of cognitive and achievement outcomes. *Educational Evaluation and Policy Analysis, 35,* 76–95.

Shapiro, D. (1984). *Psychological evaluation and expert testimony: A practical guide to forensic work.* New York: Van Nostrand Reinhold.

Shapiro, D. A., & Shapiro, D. (1982). Meta-analysis of comparative therapy outcome research: A critical appraisal. *Behavioral Psychotherapy, 10,* 4–25.

Shapiro, F. (1995). *Eye movement desensitization and reprocessing: Basic principles, protocols and procedures.* New York: Guilford Press.

Shapiro, M. A., Chang Y. L., Munson S. K., Okun, M. S., & Fernandez, H. H. (2006). Hypersexuality and paraphilia induced by selegiline in Parkinson's disease: Report of 2 cases. *Parkinsonism & Related Disorders, 12*(6), 392–395.

Shariat, M. (2003, March). Examination of the interactive effects of expectancies of tension reduction and trait anxiety in the prediction of alcohol consumption. *Dissertation Abstracts International, 63,* 3938.

Shariff, H. (1995). Mother-child tilV transmission: Prevention options for women in developing countries. *AIDcaptions,* 25–27.

Sharma, M., & Branscum, P. (2010). Is Alcoholics Anonymous effective? *Journal of Alcohol and Drug Education, 54*(3), 3–6.

Sharpley, C. F., Palanisamy, S. A., & McFarlane, J. R. (2013). Differing models of association between childhood events, recent life stressors, psychological resilience and depression across three alleles of the serotonin transporter 5-HTTLPR. *German Journal of Psychiatry, 16*(3), 103–111.

Shaw, P., Eckstrand, K., Sharp, W., Blumenthal, J., Lerch, J. P., Greenstein, D., . . . Rapoport, J. L. (2007). ADHD is characterized by a delay in cortical maturation. *Proceedings of the National Academy of Sciences, USA, 104,* 19649–19654. doi:10.1073/pnas.0707741104

Shaw, P., Gilliam, M., Liverpool, M., Weddle, C., Malek, M., Sharp, W., . . . Giedd, J. (2011). Cortical development in typically developing children with symptoms of hyperactivity and impulsivity: Support for a dimension view of attention deficit hyperactivity disorder. *American Journal of Psychiatry, 168,* 143–151.

Shefler, G., & Dasberg, H. (1989, June). *A randomized controlled outcome and follow-up study of James Mann's time-limited psychotherapy in a Jerusalem community mental health center.* Paper presented at the meeting of the Society for Psychotherapy Research, Toronto.

Sheline, Y. I., Barch, D. M., Donnelly, J. M., Ollinger, J. M., Snyder, A. Z., & Mintun, M. A. (2001). Increased amygdala response to masked emotional faces in depressed subjects resolves with antidepressant treatment: An fMRI study. *Biological Psychiatry, 50*(9), 651–658. doi:10.1016/S0006-3223(01)01263-X

Shelley, P. B. (1813). *Queen Mab.* New York: Thomas Y. Crowell.

Sher, K. J. (1991). *Children of alcoholics: A critical appraisal of theory and research.* Chicago: University of Chicago Press

Sher, K. J., Walitzer, K. S., Wood, P. K., & Brent, E. F. (1991). Characteristics of children of alcoholics: Putative risk factors, substance use and abuse, and psychopathology. *Journal of Abnormal Psychology, 100,* 427–448.

Shergill, S. S., Brammer, M. J., Williams, S. C., Murray, R. M., & McGuire, P. K. (2000). Mapping auditory hallucinations in schizophrenia using functional magnetic resonance imaging. *Archives of General Psychiatry, 57,* 1033–1038.

Sherman, J. A. (2001). Evolutionary origin of bipolar disorder (EOBD). *Psycoloquy, 12*(28).

Sherman, J. A. (2012). Evolutionary origin of bipolar disorder-revised: EOBD-R. *Medical Hypotheses, 78*(1), 113–122. doi:10.1016/j.mehy.2011.10.005

Sherman, S. (1992, June). *Epidemiology and screening.* Paper presented at the Third International Fragile X Conference, Snowmass Resort, CO.

Sherrington, R., Rogaev, E. I., Liang, Y, Rogaev, E. A., Levesque, G., Ikeda, M., Chi, H., Lin, C., Li, G., Holman, K., Tsuda, T., Mar, L., Foncin, J.-F., Bruni, A. C., Montesi, M. P., Sorbi, S., Rainero, I., Pinessi, L., Nee, L., Chumakov, I., Pollen, D., Brookes, A., Sanseau, P., Polinsky, R. J., Wasco, W., Da Silva, H. A. R., Haines, J. L., Pericak-Vance, M. A., Tanzi, R. E., Roses, A. D., Fraser, P. E., Rommens, J. M., & St. George-Hyslop, P. H. (1995). Cloning of a gene bearing missense mutations in early-onset familial Alzheimer's disease. *Nature, 375,* 754–760.

Sherwin, B. B. (1985). Changes in sexual behavior as a function of plasma sex steroid levels in post-menopausal women. *Maturity, 7,* 225–233.

Sherwin, B. B., & Gelfand, M. M. (1987). The role of androgen in the maintenance of sexual functioning in oophorectomized women. *Psychosomatic Medicine, 49,* 397–409.

Sherwin, B. B., Gelfand, M. M., & Brender, W. (1985). Androgen enhances sexual motivation in females: A prospective, crossover study of sex steroid administration in the surgical menopause. *Psychosomatic Medicine, 47,* 339–351.

Shields, D., & Salerno, S. (2013). *Salinger.* New York: Simon & Schuster.

Shiffman, S. (1993). Smoking cessation treatment: Any progress? *Journal of Consulting and Clinical Psychology, 61*(5), 718–722.

Shifren, J. L., Braunstein, G. D., Simon, J. A., Casson, P. R., Buster, J. E., Redmond, G. P., . . . Mazer, N. A. (2000). Transdermal testosterone treatment in women with impaired sexual function after oophorectomy. *New England Journal of Medicine, 343*(10), 682–688.

Shifren, J. L., Monz, B. U., Russo, P. A., Segreti, A., & Johannes, C. B. (2008). Sexual problems and distress in United States women: Prevalence and correlates. *Obstetrics & Gynecology, 112*(5), 970–978.

Shim, I., Woo, Y., Jun, T., & Bahk, W. (2014). A reevaluation of the possibility and characteristics in bipolar mania with mixed features: A retrospective chart review. *Psychiatry Research, 215*(2), 335–340. doi:10.1016/j.psychres.2013.11.002

Shin, S. H., Hong, H. G., & Jeon, S. (2012). Personality and alcohol use: The role of impulsivity. *Addictive Behaviors, 37*(1), 102–107. doi:10.1016/j.addbeh.2011.09.006

Shiraev, E. B. (2010). *A History of psychology: A global perspective.* Thousand Oaks, CA: Sage.

Shoham, V., Bootzin, R. R., Rohrbaugh, M. J., & Urry, H. (1996). Paradoxical versus relaxation treatment for insomnia: The moderating role of reactance. *Sleep Research, 24a,* 365.

Shonkoff, J. P., & Marshall, P. C. (1990). Biological bases on developmental dysfunction. In S. J. Meisels &; J. P. Shonkoff (Eds.), *Handbook of early childhood intervention* (pp. 35–52). New York: Cambridge University Press.

Shorter, E. (1994). *From the mind into the body: The cultural origins of psychosomatic symptoms.* New York: Free Press.

Shukla, G. D. (1989). Electroconvulsive therapy: A review. *Indian Journal of Psychiatry, 31,* 97–115.

Shulman, C., Yirmiya, N., & Greenbaum, C. W. (1995). From categorization to classification. A comparison among individuals with autism, mental retardation, and normal development. *Journal of Abnormal Psychology, 104,* 601–609.

Shulman, I., Cox, B., Swinson, R., Kuch, K., & Reichman, J. (1994). Precipitating events, locations, and reactions associated with initial unexpected panic attacks. *Behaviour Research and Therapy, 32,* 17–20.

Shulman, K. I., Shedletsky, R., & Silver, I. L. (1986). The challenge of time: Clock-drawing and cognitive functions in the elderly. *International Journal of Geriatric Psychiatry, 1,* 135–140.

Shumaker, S. A., & Czajkowski, S. M. (1994). *Social support and cardiovascular disease.* New York: Plenum.

Shusterman, A., Feld, L., Baer, L., & Keuthen, N. (2009). Affective regulation in trichotillomania: Evidence from a large-scale Internet survey. *Behaviour Research and Therapy, 47,* 637–644. doi:10.1016/j.brat.2009.04.004

Siegel, J. M., & Kuykendall, D. H. (1990). Loss, widowhood, and psychological distress among the elderly. *Journal of Consulting and Clinical Psychology, 58,* 519–524.

Siegel, S. (1982). Drug dissociation in the nineteenth century. In F. C. Colpaert & J. L. Slangen (Eds.), *Drug discrimination: Applications in CNS pharmacology.* Amsterdam: Elsevier.

Sierra, M. (2009). *Depersonalization: A new look at a neglected syndrome.* New York: Cambridge University Press.

Sierra, M., & Berrios, G. E. (2000). Conversion hysteria: The relevance of attentional awareness. In P. Halligan, C. M. Bass, & J. C. Marshall (Eds.), *Contemporary approaches to the study of hysteria* (pp. 192–202). Oxford, UK: Oxford University Press.

Sierra, M., & David, A. S. (2011). Depersonalization: A selective impairment of self-awareness. *Consciousness and Cognition, 20,* 99–108.

Sierra, M., Medford, N., Wyatt, G., & David, A. S. (2012). Depersonalization disorder and anxiety: A special relationship? *Psychiatry Research, 197*(1–2), 123–127. doi:10.1016/j.psychres.2011.12.017

Sierra, M., Senior, C., Dalton, J., McDonough, M., & Bond, A. (2002). Autonomic response in depersonalization disorder. *Archives in General Psychiatry, 59*(9), 833–838.

Sifneos, P. E. (1979). *Short-term dynamic psychotherapy: Evaluation and technique.* New York: Plenum.

Sigmon, S. T., Craner, J. R., Yoon, K. L., & Thorpe, G. L. (2012). Premenstrual syndrome. In V. S. Ramachandran (Ed.), *Encyclopedia of human behavior.* New York: Elsevier.

Sikkes, S. A. M., Visser, P. J., Knol, D. L., de Lange-de Klerk, E. S. M., Tsolaki, M., Frisoni, G. B., . . . Uitdehaag (2011). Do instrumental activities of daily living predict dementia at 1- and 2-year follow-up? Findings from the development of screening guidelines and diagnostic criteria for predementia Alzheimer's disease study. *Journal of the American Geriatrics Society, 59*(12), 2273–2281. doi:10.1111/j.1532-5415.2011.03732.x

Silk, J. S., Ziegler, M. L., Whalen, D. J., Dahl, R. E., Ryan, N. D., Dietz, L. J., . . . Williamson, D. E. (2009). Expressed emotion in mothers of currently depressed, remitted, high-risk, and low-risk youth: Links to child depression status and longitudinal course. *Journal of Clinical Child and Adolescent Psychology, 38*(1), 36–47. doi:10.1080/15374410802575339

Silveira, H., Moraes, H., Oliveira, N., Coutinho, E., Laks, J., & Deslandes, A. (2013). Physical exercise and clinically depressed patients: A systematic review and meta-analysis. *Neuropsychobiology, 67*(2), 61–68. doi:10.1159/000345160

Silver, B., Poland, R., & Lin, K. M. (1993). Ethnicity and pharmacology of tricyclic antidepressants. In K. M. Lin, R. Poland, & G. Nakasaki (Eds.), *Psychopharmacology and psychobiology of ethnicity.* Washington, DC: American Psychiatric Press.

Silver, E. (1995). Punishment or treatment? Comparing the lengths of confinement of successful and unsuccessful insanity defendants. *Law and Human Behavior, 19*(4), 375–388. doi:10.1007/BF01499138

Silver, L. B. (1992). Psychological and family problems associated with learning disabilities: Assessment and intervention. *Journal of the American Academy of Child and Adolescent Psychiatry, 28*(3), 319–325.

Silverstein, C. (2009). The implications of removing homosexuality from the *DSM* as a mental disorder. *Archives of Sexual Behavior, 38*, 161–163. doi:10.1007/s10508-008-9442-x

Simeon, D. (2004). Depersonalization disorder: A contemporary overview. *CNS Drugs, 18*, 343–354.

Simeon, D., & Knutelska, M. (2005). An open trial of naltrexone in the treatment of depersonalization disorder. *Journal of Clinical Psychopharmacology, 25*(3), 267–270. doi:10.1097/01.jcp.0000162803.61700.4f

Simeon, D., Guralnik, O., Hazlett, E. A., Spiegel-Cohen, J., Hollander, E., & Buchsbaum, M. S. (2000). Feeling unreal: A PET study of depersonalization disorder. *American Journal of Psychiatry, 157*, 1782–1788.

Simeon, D., Guralnik, O., Knutelska, M., Yehuda, R., & Schmeidler, J. (2003). Basal norepinephrine in depersonalization disorder. *Psychiatry Research, 121*, 93–97.

Simeon, D., Knutelska, M., Nelson, D., & Guralnik, O. (2003). Feeling unreal: A depersonalization disorder update of 117 cases. *The Journal of Clinical Psychiatry, 64*, 990–997.

Simon, N. M. (2009). Generalized anxiety disorder and psychiatric comorbidities such as depression, bipolar disorder, and substance abuse. *Journal of Clinical Psychiatry, 70*, 4–10.

Simone, S., & Fulero, S. M. (2005). *Tarasoff* and the duty to protect. *Journal of Aggression, Maltreatment & Trauma, 11*(1–2), 145–168. doi:10.1300/J146v11n01_12

Simpson, H. B., Neria, Y., Lewis-Fernández, R., & Schneier, F. (2010). *Anxiety disorders: Theory, research and clinical perspectives*. New York: Cambridge University Press.

Singer, M., Mirhej, G., Shaw, S., Saleheen, H., & Vivian, J. (2005). When the drug of choice is a drug of confusion: Embalming fluid use in inner-city Hartford, CT. *Journal of Ethnicity in Substance Abuse, 4*(2), 73–96. doi:10.1300/J233v04n02_04

Singh, I. (2014, August 27). Adam Duritz opens up about depersonalization disorder. The Huffington Post. Retrieved on December 7, 2014 from http://www.huffingtonpost.com/2014/08/27/adam-duritz-depersonalization-disorder_n_5725220.html

Sinyor, M., Schaffer, A., & Levitt, A. (2010). The Sequenced Treatment Alternatives to Relieve Depression (STARD) trial: A review. *The Canadian Journal of Psychiatry / La Revue Canadienne De Psychiatrie, 55*(3), 126–135.

Sirkin, M. I. (1992). The role of network therapy in the treatment of relational disorders: Cults and Folie a deux. *Contemporary Family Therapy, 14*, 211–224.

Sirri, L., & Fava, G. A. (2013). Diagnostic criteria for psychosomatic research and somatic symptom disorders. *International Review of Psychiatry, 25*(1), 19–30. doi:10.3109/09540261.2012.726923

Sitaram, N., Moore, A. M., and Gillin, J. C. (1978). Experimental acceleration and slowing of REM ultradian rhythm by cholinergic agonist and antagonist. *Nature, 274*, 490–492.

Sitzer, D. I., Twamley, E. W., & Jeste, D. V. (2006). Cognitive training in Alzheimer's disease: A meta-analysis of the literature. *Acta Psychiatrica Scandinavica, 114*(2), 75–90. doi: 10.1111/j.1600-0447.2006.00789.x

Skinner, M. D., Lahmek, P., Pham, H., & Aubin, H. (2014). Disulfram efficacy in the treatment of alcohol dependence: A meta-analysis. *Plos ONE, 9*(2). doi:10.1371/journal.pone.0087366

Skodol, A. E., Bender, D. S., Morey, L. C., Clark, L. A., Oldham, J. M., Alarcon, R. D., . . . Siever, L. J. (2011). Personality disorder types proposed for *DSM-5*. *Journal of Personality Disorders (25)*2, 136–169.

Skre, I., Onstad, S., Torgersen, S., Lygren, S., & Kringlen, E. (2000). The heritability of common phobic fear: A twin study of a clinical sample. *Journal of Anxiety Disorders, 14*(6), 549–562. doi:10.1016/S0887-6185(00)00049-9

Slade, P. D. & Bentall, R. P. (1988). *Sensory deception: A scientific analysis of hallucination*. Baltimore: Johns Hopkins University Press.

Slater, L. (1996). *Welcome to my country*. New York: Random House.

Slavich, G. M., & Irwin, M. R. (2014). From stress to inflammation and major depressive disorder: A social signal transduction theory of depression. *Psychological Bulletin 140*(3), 774–815. doi: 10.1037/a0035302

Slipp, S. (Ed.). (1981). *Curative factors in psycho dynamic therapy*. New York: McGraw-Hill.

Slutske, W. S. (2005). Alcohol use disorders among U.S. college students and their non–college-attending peers. *Archives of General Psychiatry, 62*(3), 321–327. doi:10.1001/archpsyc.62.3.321.

Slutske, W. S., Ellingson, J. M., Richmond-Rakerd, L. S., Zhu, G., & Martin, N. G. (2013). Shared genetic vulnerability for disordered gambling and alcohol use disorder in men and women: Evidence from a national community-based Australian twin study. *Twin Research and Human Genetics, 16*(2), 525–534. doi:10.1017/thg.2013.11

Small, G. W., Mazziotta, J. C., Collins, M. T., Baxter, L. R., Phelps, M. E., Mandelkern, M. A., Kaplan, A., LaRue, A., Adamson, C. F., & Chang, L. (1995). Apolipoprotein E type 4 allele and cerebral glucose metabolism in relatives at risk for familial Alzheimer's disease. *Journal of the American Medical Association, 273*, 942–947.

Small, G. W., Siddarth, P., Kepe, V., Ercoli, L. M., Burggren, A. C., Bookheimer, S. Y., . . . Barrio, J. R. (2012). Prediction of cognitive decline by positron emission tomography of brain amyloid and tau. *Archives of Neurology, 69*(2), 215–222. doi: 10.1001/archneurol.2011.559

Small, J. (1990). Anticonvulsants in affective disorders. *Psychopharmacology Bulletin, 26*, 25–36.

Small, J., Klapper, M., Kellams, J., Miller, M., Milstein, V., Sharpley, P., & Small, I. (1988). Electroconvulsive treatment compared with lithium in the management of manic states. *Archives of General Psychiatry, 45*, 727–732.

Smalley, S. L., Asarnow, R. F., & Spence, M. A. (1988). Autism and genetics: Decade of research. *Archives of General Psychiatry, 45*, 953–961.

Smink, F. R., van Hoeken, D., & Hoek, H. W. (2013). Epidemiology, course, and outcome of eating disorders. *Current Opinion in Psychiatry, 26*(6), 543–548.

Smith, D. M., & Atkinson, R. M. (1997). Alcoholism and dementia. In A. M. Gurnack (Ed.), *Older adults' misuse of alcohol, medicines, and other drugs: Research and practice issues* (pp. 132–157). New York: Springer.

Smith, D. W., & Wilson, A. A. (1973). *The child with Down's syndrome (mongolism)*. Philadelphia: W. B. Saunders.

Smith, E. G. (2009). Association between antidepressant half-life and the risk of suicidal ideation or behavior among children and adolescents: Confirmatory analysis and research implications. *Journal of Affective Disorders, 114*(1–3), 143–148. doi:10.1016/j.jad.2008.06.018

Smith, E. M., North, C. S., & Price, P. C. (1988). Response to technological accidents. In M. Lystad (Ed.), *Mental health response to mass emergencies* (pp. 52–95). New York: Brunner/Mazel.

Smith, G. T., Goldman, M., Greenbaum, P. E., Christiansen, B. A. (1995). Expectancy for social facilitation from drinking: The divergent paths of high-expectancy and low-expectancy adolescents. *Journal of Abnormal Psychology, 104*, 32–40.

Smith, J., Frawley, P. J., & Polissar, L. (1991). Six- and twelve-month abstinence rates in inpatient alcoholics treated with aversion therapy compared with matched in-patients from a treatment registry. *Alcoholism in Clinical and Experimenta Research, 15*(5), 862–870.

Smith, J. C., Nielson, K. A., Woodard, J. L., Seidenberg, M., Durgerian, S., Antuono, P., . . . Rao, S. M. (2011). Interactive effects of physical activity and APOE-epsilon4 on BOLD semantic memory activation in healthy elders. *Neuroimage, 54*(1), 635–644. doi: 10.1016/j.neuroimage.2010.07.070

Smith, J. C., Nielson, K. A., Woodard, J. L., Seidenberg, M., Durgerian, S., Hazlett, K. E., . . . Rao, S. M. (2014). Physical activity reduces hippocampal atrophy in elders at genetic risk for Alzheimer's disease. *Frontiers in Aging Neuroscience, 6*, 61. doi: 10.3389/fnagi.2014.00061

Smith, J. E., Meyers, R. J., & Miller, W. R. (2001). The community reinforcement approach to the treatment of substance use disorders. *The American Journal on Addictions, 10*(Suppl), 51–59. doi:10.1080/10550490150504137

Smith, L. A., Cornelius, V., Warnock, A., Tacchi, M., & Taylor, D. (2007). Pharmacological interventions for acute bipolar mania: A systematic review of randomized placebo-controlled trials. *Bipolar Disorders, 9*, 551–560. doi:10.1111/j.1399-5618.2007.00468.x

Smith, W., & Dimsdale, J. E. (1989). Postcardiotomy delirium: Conclusions after 25 years? *American Journal of Psychiatry, 146*, 452–458.

Smith, M., Lin, K. M., & Mendoza, R. (1993). Non-biological issues affecting psychopharmacotherapy: Cultural considerations. In K. M. Lin, R. Poland, & G. Nakasaki (Eds.), *Psychopharmacology and psychobiology of ethnicity*. Washington, DC: American Psychiatric Press.

Smith, M. D., & Belcher, R. G. (1993). Facilitated communication with adults with autism. *Journal of Autism and Developmental Disorders, 23*(1), 175–183.

Smith, M. L., & Glass, G. V. (1977). Meta-analysis of psychotherapy outcome studies. *American Psychologist, 32*, 752–777.

Smith, M. L., Glass, G. V., & Miller, T. I. (1980). *The benefits of psychotherapy*. Baltimore: Johns Hopkins University Press.

Smith, R. E., & Winokur, G. (1991). Mood disorders (bipolar). In M. Hersen & S. M. Turner (Eds.), *Adult psychopathology and diagnosis*. New York: John Wiley & Sons.

Smith, S. R. (1996). Malpractice liability of mental health professionals and institutions. In B. D. Sales & D. W. Shuman (Eds.), *Law, mental health, and mental disorders*. Pacific Grove, CA: Brooks/Cole.

Smolak, L., & Chun-Kennedy, C. (2013). Sociocultural influences on the development of eating disorders and obesity. In L. H. Choate (Ed.), *Eating disorders and obesity: A counselor's guide to prevention and treatment* (pp. 3–20). Alexandria, VA: American Counseling Association.

Snaith, P., Tarsh, M. J., & Reid, R. (1993). Sex reassignment surgery. A study of 141 Dutch transsexuals. *British Journal of Psychiatry, 162*, 681–685.

Snell, L. D., Ramchandani, V. A., Saba, L., Herion, D., Heilig, M., George, D. T. . . . Tabakoff, B. (2012). The biometric measurement of alcohol consumption. *Alcoholism Clinical and Experimental Research, 36*, 332–341. doi: 10.1111/j.1530-0277.2011.01605.x

Snorrason, I. I., Stein, D. J., & Woods, D. W. (2013). Classification of excoriation (skin picking) disorder: Current status and future directions. *Acta Psychiatrica Scandinavica, 128*(5), 406–407. doi:10.1111/acps.12153

Snowdon, D. A., Greiner, L. H., & Markesbery, W. R. (2000). Linguistic ability in early life and the neuropathology of Alzheimer's disease and cerebrovascular disease. Findings from the Nun Study. *Annals of the New York Academy of Sciences 903*, 34–38.

Snowdon, D. A., Kemper, S. J., Mortimer, J., Greiner, L., Wekstein, D., & Markesbery, W. R. (1996). Linguistic ability in early life and cognitive function and Alzheimer's disease in later life. *Journal of the American Medical Association, 275*, 528–532.

Snowdon, D. A., Ostwald, S. K., & Kane, R. L. (1989). Education, survival, and independence of elderly Catholic sisters, 1936–1988. *American Journal of Epidemiology, 42*, 1055–1066.

Snyder, D. K., & Wills, R. M. (1989). Behavioral versus insight-oriented marital therapy: Effects on individual and interspousal functioning. *Journal of Consulting and Clinical Psychology, 57*, 39–46.

Snyder, D. K., Wills, R. M., & Grady-Fletcher, A. (1991). Long-term effectiveness of behavioral versus insight-oriented marital therapy: A 4-year follow-up study. *Journal of Consulting and Clinical Psychology, 59*, 138–141.

Snyder, H., & Sickmund, M. (1999). *Juvenile offenders and victims: 1999 national report*. Washington, DC: Office of Juvenile Justice and Delinquency Prevention.

So, J. K. (2008). Somatization as cultural idiom of distress: Rethinking mind and body in a multicultural society. *Counselling Psychology Quarterly, 21*(2), 167–174. doi:10.1080/09515070802066854

So, S. H., Freeman, D., Dunn, G., Kapur, S., Kuipers, E., Bebbington, P., . . . Garety, P. A. (2012). Jumping to conclusions, a lack of belief flexibility and delusional conviction in psychosis: A longitudinal investigation of the structure, frequency, and relatedness of reasoning biases. *Journal of Abnormal Psychology, 121*(1), 129–139. doi:10.1037/a0025297

Sobel, E., Davanipour, Z., Sulkava, R., Erkinjuntti, T., Wikstrom, J., Henderson, V. W., Buckwalter, G., Bowman, J. D., & Lee, P. J. (1995). Occupations with exposure to electromagnetic fields: A possible risk factor for Alzheimer's disease. *American Journal of Epidemiology, 142*, 515–519.

Sobell, L. C., Toneatto, T., & Sobell, M. B. (1994). Behavioral assessment and treatment planning for alcohol, tobacco, and other drug problems: Current status with an emphasis on clinical applications. *Behavior Therapy, 25*, 533–580

Sobell, M. B., & Sobell, L. C. (1973). Alcoholics treated by individualized behavior therapy: One year treatment outcome. *Behavior Research and Therapy, 11*, 599–618.

Sobell, M. B., & Sobell, L. C. (1976). Second- year treatment outcome of alcoholics treated by individualized behavior therapy: Results. *Behaviour Research and Therapy, 14*, 195–215.

Sobin, C., Sackeim, H., Prudic, J., Devanand, D. P., Moody, B. J., & McElhiney, M. C. (1995). Predictors of retrograde amnesia following ECT. *American Journal of Psychiatry, 152*, 995–1001.

Soderstrom, C. A., Dischinger, P. C., Kerns, T. J., & Trifillis, A. L. (1995). Marijuana and other drug use among automobile and motorcycle drivers treated at a trauma center. *Accident Analysis and Prevention, 27*(1), 131–135.

Sodian, B., & Frith, U. (1992). Deception and sabotage in autistic, retarded and normal children. *Journal of Child Psychology and Psychiatry and Allied Disciplines, 33*(3), 591–605.

Soldz, S., Budman, S., Demby, A., & Merry, J. (1993). Representation of personality disorders in circumplex and five-factor space: Explorations with a clinical sample. *Psychological Assessment, 5*, 41–52.

Solhaug, H., Romuld, E., Romild, U., & Stordal, E. (2012). Increased prevalence of depression in cohorts of the elderly: An 11-year follow-up in the general population—The HUNT study. *International Psychogeriatrics, 24*(1), 151–158. doi:10.1017/S1041610211001141

Soloff, P., George, A., Nathan, R. S., Schulz, P. M., Cornelius, J. R., Herring, J., & Perel, J. M. (1989). Amitriptyline versus haloperidol in borderlines: Final outcomes and predictors of response. *Journal of Clinical Psychopharmacology, 9*, 238–246.

Solomon, S., Greenberg, J., & Pyszczynski, T. (2015). *The worm at the core: On the role of death in life*. New York: Random House.

Solursh, D. S., Ernst, J. L., Lewis, R. W., Prisant, L. M., Mills, T. M., . . . Solursh, L. P. (2003). The human sexuality education of physicians in North American medical schools. *International Journal of Impotence Research, 15*(5), S41.

Somashekar, B., Jainer, A., & Wuntakal, B. (2013). Psychopharmacotherapy of somatic symptoms disorders. *International Review of Psychiatry, 25*(1), 107–115. doi:10.3109/09540261.2012.729758

Sommers-Flanagan, J., & Sommers-Flanagan, R. (1996). Efficacy of antidepressant medication with depressed youth: What psychologists should know. *Professional Psychology: Research and Practice, 27*, 145–153.

Sonuga-Barke, E. S., Brandeis, D., Cortese, S., Daley, D., Ferrin, M., Holtmann, M., . . . Sergeant, J. (2013). Nonpharmalogical interventions for ADHD: Systematic review and meta-analyses of randomized controlled trials of dietary and psychological treatments. *The American Journal of Psychiatry, 170*(3), 275–289.

Soreca, I., Frank, E., & Kupfer, D. J. (2009). The phenomenology of bipolar disorder: What drives the high rate of medical burden and determines long-term prognosis? *Depression and Anxiety, 26*(1), 73–82. doi:10.1002/da.20521

Southard, E. E. (1910). Anatomical findings in "senile dementia" : A diagnostic study bearing especially on the group of cerebral atrophies. *American Journal of Insanity, 61*, 673–708.

Southwick, S. M., Vythilingam, M., & Charney, D. S. (2005). The psychobiology of depression and resilience to stress: Implications for prevention and treatment. *Annual Review of Clinical Psychology, 1*, 255–291.

Southwick, S. M., Yehuda, R., & Morgan, C. A. (1995). Clinical studies of neurotransmitter alterations in posttraumatic stress disorder. In M. J. Friedman, D. S. Charney, & A. Y. Deutch (Eds.), *Neurobiological and clinical consequences of stress: FProm normal adaptation to PTSD* (pp. 335–349). Philadelphia: Lippincott-Raven.

Spake, A. (1992). Breaking the silence. *Teacher Magazine, 3*(9), 14–21.

Spanos, N. (1994). Multiple identity enactments and multiple personality disorder. *Psychological Bulletin, 116*, 143–165.

Spanos, N. P. (1978). Witchcraft in histories of psychiatry: A critical analysis and an alternative conceptualization. *Psychological Bulletin, 85*, 417–439.

Spanos, N. P., Weekes, J. R., Bertrand, L. D. (1985). Multiple personality: A social psychological perspective. *Journal of Abnormal Psychology, 94*, 362–376.

Spanos, N. P., Weekes, J. R., Menary, E., & Bertrand, L. D. (1986). Hypnotic interview and age regression procedures in the elicitation of multiple personality symptoms: A simulation study. *Psychiatry, 49*, 298–311.

Sparks, G. M., Axelson, D. A., Yu, H., Ha, W., Ballester, J., Diler, R. S., . . . Birmaher, B. (2014). Disruptive mood dysregulation disorder and chronic irritability in youth at familial risk for bipolar disorder. *Journal of the American Academy of Child & Adolescent Psychiatry, 53*(4), 408–416. doi:10.1016/j.jaac.2013.12.026

Sparrow, S., & Zigler, E. (1978). Evaluation of patterning treatment for retarded children. *Pediatrics, 62*, 137–150.

Sparrow, S. S., Balia, D. A., & Cicchetti, D. V. (1984). *Vineland adaptive behavior scales*. Circle Pines, MN: American Guidance Service.

Speltz, M. L. (1990). The treatment of preschool conduct problems: An integration of behavioral and attachment concepts. In M. T. Greenberg, D. Cicchetti, & M. Cummings (Eds.), *Attachment in the preschool years: Theory, research, and intervention* (pp. 399–426). Chicago, IL: University of Chicago Press.

Speltz, M. L., Shimimura, J., & McReynolds, W. T. (1982). Procedural variations in group contingencies: Effects on children's academic and social behavior. *Journal of Applied Behavior Analysis, 15*, 533–544.

Spencer, T. (1996). Pharmacotherapy of attention-deficit hyperactivity disorder across the life cycle. *Journal of the American Academy of Child and Adolescent Psychiatry, 35*, 409–432.

Speranza, M. M. (2013). Borderline personality disorders: The central role of emotional dysregulation. *European Psychiatry, 28*(8, Suppl), 61. doi:10.1016/j.eurpsy.2013.09.160

Sperling, R. A., Aisen, P. S., Beckett, L. A., Bennett, D. A., Craft, S., Fagan, A. M., . . . Phelps, C. H. (2011). Toward defining the preclinical stages of Alzheimer's disease: Recommendations from the National Institute on Aging-Alzheimer's Association workgroups on diagnostic guidelines for Alzheimer's disease. *Alzheimer's & Dementia, 7*(3), 280–292. doi: 10.1016/j.jalz.2011.03.003

Spiegel, D., & Bloom, J. R. (1983). Group therapy and hypnosis reduce metastatic breast carcinoma pain. *Psychosomatic Medicine, 45*, 333–339.

Spiegel, D., Bloom, J. R., Kraemer, H. C., & Gottheil, E. (1989, October 14). Effect of psychosocial treatment on survival of patients with metastatic breast cancer. *Lancet, 14*, 888–891.

Spiegel, D., Bloom, J. R., & Yalom, I. (1981). Group support for patients with metastatic cancer: A randomized outcome study. *Archives of General Psychiatry, 38*, 527–533.

Spiegel, D., Lewis-Fernández, R., Lanius, R., Vermetten, E., Simeon, D., & Friedman, M. (2013). Dissociative disorders in *DSM-5. Annual Review of Clinical Psychology, 9*, 299–326.

Spiegel, D., & Vermutten, E. (1994). Physiological correlates of hypnosis and dissociation. In D. Spiegel (Ed.), *Dissociation: Culture, mind, and body* (pp. 185–210). Washington DC: American Psychiatric Press.

Spiegler, M. D., & Guevremont, D. C. (1993). *Contemporary behavior therapy* (2nd ed.). Belmont, CA: Brooks/Cole.

Spielmans, G. I., Berman, M. I., & Usitalo, A. N. (2011). Psychotherapy versus second-generation antidepressants in the treatment of depression: A meta-analysis. *Journal of Nervous and Mental Disease, 199*(3), 142–149. doi:10.1097/NMD.0b013e31820caefb

Spierings, C., Poels, P. J., Sijben, N., Babreels, F. J., & Renier, W. O. (1990). Conversion disorders in childhood: A retrospective follow-up study of 84 inpatients. *Developmental Medicine and Child Neurology, 32*, 865–871.

Spitzer, R. L. (1975). On pseudoscience in science, logic in remission and psychiatric diagnosis: A critique of Rosenhan's " On being sane in insane places." *Journal of Abnormal Psychology, 84,* 442–452.

Spitzer, R. L., Gibbon, M., Skodol, A. E., Williams, J. B. W., & First, M. B. (Eds.). (1994). DSM-IV *casebook: A learning companion to the* Diagnostic and Statistical Manual of Mental Disorders (4th ed.). Washington, DC: American Psychiatric Press.

Spivack, G., & Shure, M. B. (1974). *Social adjustment of young children: A cognitive approach to solving real-life problems.* San Francisco: Jossey-Bass.

Squire, L. R. (2004). Memory systems of the brain: A brief history and current perspective. *Neurobiology of Learning and Memory, 82*(3), 171–177. doi: 10.1016/j.nlm.2004.06.005

Srole, L., Langner, T. S., Michael, S. T., Opler, M. K., & Rennie, T. A. C. (1962). *Mental health in the metropolis: The midtown Manhattan study.* New York: McGraw-Hill.

Sroufe, L. A. (2005). Attachment and development: A prospective, longitudinal study from birth to adulthood. *Attachment and Human Development, 7,* 349–367.

Sroufe, L. A., Egeland, B., Carlson, E., & Collins, W. A. (2005). *The development of the person: The Minnesota study of risk and adaptation from birth to adulthood.* New York: Guilford.

Sroufe, L. A., & Fleeson, J. (1986). Attachment and the construction of relationships. In W. Hartup & Z. Rubin (Eds.), *Relationships and development* (pp. 51–71). Hillsdale, NJ: Erlbaum.

Sroufe, L. A., & Rutter, M. (1984). The domain of developmental psychopathology. *Child Development, 55,* 17–29.

St. Lawrence, J. S., Brasfield, T. L., Jefferson, K. W., Alleyne, E., & O'Bannon, R. E., Ill (1995). Cognitive-behavioral intervention to reduce African American adolescents' risk for HIV infection. *Journal of Consulting and Clinical Psychology, 63,* 221–237.

Stacy, A. W., Ames, S. L., Sussman, S., & Dent, C. W. (1996). Implicit cognition in adolescent drug use. *Psychology of Addictive Behaviors, 10,* 190–203.

Stacy, A. W., Widaman, K. F., & Marlatt, G. A. (1990). Expectancy models of alcohol use. *Journal of Personality and Social Psychology, 58,* 918–928.

Stahre, M., Roeber, J., Kanny, D., Brewer, R. D., & Zhang, X. (2014). Contribution of excessive alcohol consumption to deaths and years of potential life lost in the United States. *Preventing Chronic Disease, 11,* 130293.

Stainback, S., & Stainback, W. (1992). *Curriculum considerations in inclusive classrooms: Facilitating learning for all students.* Baltimore: Paul Brookes.

Stampfer, M. J. (2006). Cardiovascular disease and Alzheimer's disease: Common links. *Journal of Internal Medicine, 260*(3), 211–223. doi: 10.1111/j.1365-2796.2006.01687.x

Stange, J. P., Sylvia, L. G., da Silva Magalhães, P., Frank, E., Otto, M. W., Miklowitz, D. J., & . . . Deckersbach, T. (2013). Extreme attributions predict transition from depression to mania or hypomania in bipolar disorder. *Journal of Psychiatric Research, 47,* 1329–1336. doi:10.1016/j.jpsychires.2013.05.009

Staniloiu, A., Markowitsch, H. J., & Brand, M. (2010). Psychogenic amnesia—a malady of the constricted self. *Consciousness and Cognition, 19*(3), 778–801.

Starcević, V. (1990). Relationship between hypochondriasis and obsessive-compulsive personality disorder: Close relatives separated by nosological schemes? *American Journal of Psychotherapy, 44*(3), 340–347.

Staring, A. B., ter Huurne, M. B., & van der Gaag, M. (2013). Cognitive-behavioral therapy for negative symptoms (CBT-n) in psychotic disorders: A pilot study. *Journal of Behavior Therapy and Experimental Psychiatry, 44*(3), 300–306. doi:10.1016/j.jbtep.2013.01.004

Stark, K. D., Reynolds, W., & Kaslow, N. J. (1987). A comparison of the relative efficacy of self-control therapy and a behavioral problem-solving therapy for depression in children. *Journal of Abnormal Child Psychology, 15,* 91–113.

Starr, E. (1994). Facilitated communication: A response by Child Protection: Commentary. *Child Abuse and Neglect: The International Journal, 18,* 515–527.

Starr, L. R., & Davila, J. (2008). Excessive reassurance seeking, depression, and interpersonal rejection: A meta-analytic review. *Journal of Abnormal Psychology, 117*(4), 762–775. doi:10.1037/a0013866

Stead, L. F., & Lancaster, T. (2012). Combined pharmacotherapy and behavioural interventions for smoking cessation. *Cochrane Database of Systematic Reviews, 10.* Art. No.: CD008286. DOI: 10.1002/14651858.CD008286.pub2.

Steadman, H. J., & Braff, J. (1983). Defendants not guilty by reason of insanity. In J. Monahan & H. Steadman (Eds.), *Mentally disordered offenders: Perspectives from law and social science.* New York: Plenum.

Steadman, H. J., Keitner, L., Braff, J., & Arvanites, T. M. (1983). Factors associated with a successful insanity plea. *American Journal of Psychiatry, 140,* 401–405.

Steel, C. (2013). *CBT for schizophrenia: Evidence-based interventions and future directions.* Hoboken, NJ: Wiley-Blackwell.

Steele, K., van der Hart, O., & Nijenhuis, E. (2009). The trauma-related structural dissociation of personality. In P. F. Dell & J. A. O'Neil (Eds.), *Dissociation and the dissociative disorders* (pp. 239–258). New York: Routledge/Taylor Francis.

Stevenson, Robert Lewis (1886). *The strange case of Dr. Jekyll and Mr. Hyde.*

Steen, R. G., Mull, C., McClure, R., Hamer, R. M., & Lieberman, J. A. (2006). Brain volume in first-episode schizophrenia: Systematic review and meta-analysis of magnetic resonance imaging studies. *British Journal of Psychiatry, 188,* 510–518.

Steensma, T. D., Kreukels, B. P., de Vries, A. L., & Cohen-Kettenis, P. T. (2013). Gender identity development in adolescence. *Hormones and Behavior, 64*(2), 288–297.

Stein, D. M., & Lambert, M. J. (1984). On the relationship between therapist experience and psychotherapy outcome. *Clinical Psychology Review, 4,* 127–142.

Stein, D. M., & Lambert, M. J. (1995). Graduate training in psychotherapy: Are therapy outcomes enhanced? *Journal of Consulting and Clinical Psychology, 63,* 182–196.

Stein, M. B., Jang, K. L., & Livesley, W. (2002). Heritability of social anxiety-related concerns and personality characteristics: A twin study. *Journal of Nervous and Mental Disease, 190*(4), 219–224. doi:10.1097/00005053-200204000-00002

Stein, M. B., Walker, J. R., Anderson, G., Hazen, A. L. Ross, C. A., Eldridge, G., & Forde, D. R. (1996). Childhood physical and sexual abuse in patients with anxiety disorders and in a community sample. *American Journal of Psychiatry, 153,* 275–277.

Stein, R. E. K., Bauman, L. J., & Ireys, H. T. (1991). Who enrolls in prevention trials? Discordance in perception of risk by professionals and participants. *American Journal of Community Psychology, 19,* 603–618.

Steinberg, M. (1994). Systematizing dissociation: Symptomatology and diagnostic assessment. In D. Spiegel (Ed.), *Dissociation: Culture, mind, and body* (pp. 59–90). Washington, DC: American Psychiatric Press.

Steiner, L. (2002, November). Plastic surgeons' awareness of body dysmorphic disorder. *Dissertation Abstracts International, 63,* 2606.

Steinglass, P., Bennett, L. A., Wolin, S. J., & Reiss, D. (1987). *The alcoholic family.* New York: Basic Books.

Steketee, G., Foa, E. B., & Grayson, J. B. (1982). Recent advances in the behavioral treatment of obsessive-compulsives. *Archives of General Psychiatry, 39,* 1365–1371.

Steketee, G., & Frost, R. O. (2007). *Compulsive hoarding and acquiring: A therapist guide.* New York: Oxford University Press.

Steketee, G., & White, K. (1990). *When once is not enough: Help for obsessive compulsives.* Oakland, CA: New Harbinger Press.

Steketee, M., Junger, M., & Junger-Tas, J. (2013). Sex differences in the predictors of juvenile delinquency: Females are more susceptible to poor environments; males are influenced more by low self-control. *Journal of Contemporary Criminal Justice, 29,* 88–105. doi:10.1177/1043986212470888

Stengel, E. (1943). Further studies on pathological wanderings. *Journal of Mental Science, 89,* 224–241.

Stengler-Wenzke, K., Müller, U., Angermeyer, M. C., Sabri, O., & Hesse, S. (2004). Reduced serotonin transporter-availability in obsessive-compulsive disorder (OCD). *European Archives of Psychiatry and Clinical Neuroscience, 254*(4), 252–255. doi:10.1007/s00406-004-0489-y

Stephens, R. S., Roffman, R. A., & Simpson, E. E. (1994). Treating adult marijuana dependence: A test of the relapse prevention model. *Journal of Consulting and Clinical Psychology, 62,* 92–99.

Stevenson, J., Buitelaar, J., Cortese, S., Ferrin, M., Konofal, E., Lecendreux, M., ... Sonuga-Barke, E. (2014). Research review: The role of diet in the treatment of attention-deficit/hyperactivity disorder—An appraisal of the evidence on efficacy and recommendations on the design of future studies. *Journal of Child Psychology and Psychiatry, 55*(5), 416–427. doi:10.1111/jcpp.12215

Stewart, J. G., Mazurka, R., Bond, L., Wynne-Edwards, K. E., & Harkness, K. L. (2013). Rumination and impaired cortisol recovery following a social stressor in adolescent depression. *Journal of Abnormal Child Psychology, 41*(7), 1015–1026. doi:10.1007/s10802-013-9740-1

Stewart, J. W., McGrath, P. J., Quitkin, F. M., & Klein, D. F. (2007). Atypical depression: Current status and relevance to melancholia. *Acta Psychiatrica Scandinavica, 115*(Suppl 433), 58–71. doi:10.1111/j.1600-0447.2007.00964.x

Stewart, J. W., Rabkin, J. G., Quitkin, F. M., McGrath, P. J., & Klein, D. F. (1993). Atypical depression. In D. L. Dunner (Ed.), *Current psychiatric therapy* (pp. 215–220). Philadelphia: W. B. Saunders.

Stice, E., Becker, C., & Yokum, S. (2013). Eating disorder prevention: Current evidence-base and future directions. *International Journal of Eating Disorders, 46*(5), 478–485.

Stice, E., Butryn, M. L., Rohde, P., Shaw, H., & Marti, C. (2013). An effectiveness trial of a new enhanced dissonance eating disorder prevention program among female college students. *Behaviour Research and Therapy, 51*(12), 862–871. doi:10.1016/j.brat.2013.10.003

Stice, E., Marti, C., & Cheng, Z. (2014). Effectiveness of a dissonance-based eating disorder prevention program for ethnic groups in two randomized controlled trials. *Behaviour Research and Therapy, 55,* 54–64. doi:10.1016/j.brat.2014.02.002

Stice, E., Marti, C. N., & Durant, S. (2011). Risk factors for onset of eating disorders: Evidence of multiple risk pathways from an 8-year prospective study. *Behaviour Research and Therapy, 49*(10), 622–627. doi: 10.1016/j.brat.2011.06.009

Stice, E., Marti, C., Spoor, S., Presnell, K., & Shaw, H. (2008). Dissonance and healthy weight eating disorder prevention programs: Long-term effects from a randomized efficacy trial. *Journal of Consulting and Clinical Psychology, 76*(2), 329–340. doi:10.1037/0022-006X.76.2.329

Stice, E., Rohde, P., Shaw, H., & Gau, J. (2011). An effectiveness trial of a selected dissonance-based eating disorder prevention program for female high school students: Long-term effects. *Journal of Consulting and Clinical Psychology, 79*(4), 500–508. doi:10.1037/a0024351

Stice, E., Rohde, P., Shaw, H., & Marti, C. (2013). Efficacy trial of a selective prevention program targeting both eating disorders and obesity among female college students: 1- and 2-year follow-up effects. *Journal of Consulting and Clinical Psychology, 81*(1), 183–189. doi:10.1037/a0031235

Stice, E., Spangler, D., & Agras, W. S. (2001). Exposure to media-portrayed thin-ideal images adversely affects vulnerable girls: A longitudinal experiment. *Journal of Social & Clinical Psychology, 20*(3), 270–288.

Stiegler, L. N. (2005). Understanding pica behavior: A review for clinical and education professionals. *Focus on Autism and Other Developmental Disabilities, 20*(1), 27–38. doi:10.1177/10883576050200010301

Stiles, W. A., Shapiro, D. A., & Elliott, R. (1986). Are all psychotherapies equivalent? *American Psychologist, 41,* 165–180.

Stitzer, M. L., Iguchi, M. Y., & Felch, L. J. (1992). Contingent take-home incentives: Effects on drug use of methadone maintenance patients. *Journal of Consulting and Clinical Psychology, 60*(6), 927–934.

Stitzer, M. L., Jones, H. E., Tuten, M., & Wong, C. (2011). Community reinforcement approach and contingency management interventions for substance abuse. In W. M. Cox & E. Klinger (Eds.), *Handbook of motivational counseling: Goal-based approaches to assessment and intervention with addiction and other problems* (2nd ed.) (pp. 549–569). New York: Wiley-Blackwell. doi:10.1002/9780470979952.ch23

Stoeber, J., & Janssen, D.P. (2011). Perfectionism and coping with daily failures: Positive reframing helps achieve satisfaction at the end of the day. *Anxiety, Stress, & Coping, 24,* 477–497.

Stokes, C., & Hirsch, C. R. (2010). Engaging in imagery versus verbal processing of worry: Impact on negative intrusions in high worriers. *Behaviour Research and Therapy, 48,* 418–423. doi: 10.1016/j.brat.2009.12.011

Stoller, R. J. (1968). Male childhood transsexualism. *Journal of the American Academy of Child Psychiatry, 7,* 193–209.

Stoller, R. J. (1975). *Sex and gender: Vol. 2. The transsexual experiment.* London: Hogarth Press.

Stompe, T., Ortwein-Soboda, G., Ritter, K., Schanda, H., & Friedmann, A. (2002). Are we witnessing the disappearance of catatonic schizophrenia? *Comprehensive Psychiatry, 43,* 167–174.

Stone, A. (1976). The *Tarasoff* decision: Suing psychotherapists to safeguard society. *Harvard Law Review, 90,* 358–378.

Stone, A. A., & Neale, J. M. (1984). New measures of daily coping: Developments and preliminary results. *Journal of Personality and Social Psychology, 46,* 892–906.

Stone, J. (2002). Functional weakness and sensory disturbance. *Journal of Neurology, Neurosurgery & Psychiatry, 73*(3), 241–245. doi:10.1136/jnnp.73.3.241

Stone, J. (2006). La belle indifference in conversion symptoms and hysteria: Systematic review. *The British Journal of Psychiatry, 188*(3), 204–209. doi:10.1192/bjp.188.3.204

Stone, M. H. (1986). Exploratory psychotherapy in schizophrenia-spectrum patients: A reevaluation in the light of long-term follow-up of schizophrenic and borderline patients. *Bulletin of the Menninger Clinic, 50,* 287–306.

Stonnington, C. M., Locke, D. C., Hsu, C., Ritenbaugh, C., & Lane, R. D. (2013). Somatization is associated with deficits in affective theory of mind. *Journal of Psychosomatic Research, 74*(6), 479–485. doi:10.1016/j.jpsychores.2013.04.004

Stoving, R. K., Andries, A., Brixen, K. T., Bilenberg, N., Lichtenstein, M. B., & Horder, K. (2012). Purging behavior in anorexia nervosa and eating disorders not otherwise specified: A retrospective cohort study. *Psychiatry Research, 198*(2), 253–258. doi:10.1016/j.psychres.2011.10.009

Strachan, A. (1986). Family intervention for the rehabilitation of schizophrenia: Toward protection and coping. *Schizophrenia Bulletin, 12,* 678–698.

Strakowski, S. M., Adler, C. M., Almeida, J., Altshuler, L. L., Blumberg, H. P., Chang, K. D., . . . Townsend, J. D. (2012). The functional neuroanatomy of bipolar disorder: A consensus model. *Bipolar Disorders, 14*(4), 313–325. doi:10.1111/j.1399-5618.2012.01022.x

Strang, J. F., Kenworth, L., Dominska, A., Sokoloff, J., Kenealy, L. E., Madison, B., . . . Wallace, G. L. (2014). Increased gender variance in autism spectrum disorders and attention deficit hyperactivity disorder. *Archives of Sexual Behavior. 43*(8), 1525–1533.

Strassberg, D. S., Kelly, M. P., Carroll, C., & Kircher, J. C. (1987). The psychophysiological nature of premature ejaculation. *Archives of Sexual Behavior, 16,* 327–336.

Strassberg, D. S., Perelman, M. A., & Watter, D. N. (2014). Sexual dysfunction in males. In L. Grossman, S. Walfish (Eds.), *Translating psychological research into practice* (pp. 435–442). New York, NY: Springer Publishing.

Strasser, H. C., Lilyestrom, J., Ashby, E. R., Honeycutt, N. A., Schretlen, D. J., Pulver, A. E., . . . Pearlson, G. D. (2005). Hippocampal and ventricular volumes in psychotic and nonpsychotic bipolar patients compared with schizophrenia patients and community control subjects: A pilot study. *Biological Psychiatry, 57,* 633–639.

Strauss, C. C. (1990). Anxiety disorders of childhood and adolescence. *School Psychology Review, 19*(2), 142–157.

Strauss, M. E. (1993). Relations of symptoms to cognitive deficit in schizophrenia. *Schizophrenia Bulletin, 19,* 41–57.

Strawn, J., Keck, P., & Caroff, S. (2007). Neuroleptic malignant syndrome. *American Journal of Psychiatry, 164,* 870–876.

Streissguth, A. P. (1994). A long-term perspective of FAS. *Alcohol Health and Research World, 18,* 74–81.

Streissguth, A. P., Barr, H. M., & Sampson, P. D. (1990). Moderate prenatal alcohol exposure: Effects on child IQ and learning problems at age 7-1/2 years. *Alcoholism: Clinical and Experimental Research, 14,* 662–669.

Strickland, T., Ranganath, V., Lin, K. M., Poland, R., Mendoza, R., & Smith, M. (1991). Psychopharmacologic considerations in the treatment of Black American populations. *Psychopharmacology Bulletin, 27,* 441–448.

Striegel-Moore, R. H., Dohm, F., Pike, K. M., Wilfley, D. E., & Fairburn, C. G. (2002). Abuse, bullying, and discrimination as risk factors for binge eating disorder. *American Journal of Psychiatry, 159,* 1902–1907.

Stringaris, A. (2011). Irritability in children and adolescents: A challenge for *DSM-5. European Child and Adolescent Psychiatry, 20*(2), 61–66.

Strober, M., & Bulik, C. M. (2002) Genetic epidemiology of eating disorders. In C. G. Fairburn & K. D. Brownell (Eds.), *Eating disorders and obesity: A comprehensive handbook.* New York: Guilford.

Strober, M., Freeman, F., & Rigali, J. (1990). The pharmacotherapy of depressive illness in adolescence: I. An open label trial of imipramine. *Psychopharmacology Bulletin, 26,* 80–84.

Strober, M., Lampert, C., Schmidt, S., & Morrell, W. (1993). The course of major depressive disorder in adolescents: I. Recovery and risk of manic switching in a follow-up of psychotic and nonpsychotic subtypes. *Journal of the American Academy of Child and Adolescent Psychiatry, 32,* 34–42.

Strober, M., Morrell, W., Burroughs, J., Lampert, C., Danforth, H., & Freeman, R. (1988). A family study of bipolar I disorder in adolescence: Early onset of symptoms linked to increased familial loading and lithium resistance: Childhood affective disorders [Special Issue]. *Journal of Affective Disorders, 15,* 255–268.

Strohmeier, D., & Noam, G. G. (2012). *Evidence-based bullying prevention programs for children and youth.* San Francisco, CA: Jossey-Bass.

Stroman, D., Young, C., Rubano, A. R., & Pinkhasov, A. (2011). Adult-onset pica leading to acute intestinal obstruction. *Psychosomatics, 52*(4), 393–394. doi: 10.1016/j.psym.2011.01.031

Strother, E., Lemberg, R., Stanford, S. C., & Turberville, D. (2014). Eating disorders in men: Underdiagnosed, undertreated, and misunderstood. In L. Cohn & R. Lemberg (Eds.), *Current findings on males with eating disorders* (pp. 13–22). New York: Routledge.

Stroul, B. (1993). *Psychiatric crisis response systems: A descriptive study.* Rockville, MD: Substance Abuse and Mental Health Services Administration.

Strupp, H. H. (1989). Psychotherapy: Can the practitioner learn from the researcher? *American Psychologist, 44,* 717–724.

Strupp, H. H., & Binder, J. L. (1984). *Psychotherapy in a new key: A guide to time-limited dynamic psychotherapy.* New York: Basic Books.

Strupp, H. H., & Hadley, S. W. (1977). A tripartite model of mental health and therapeutic outcomes. *American Psychologist, 32,* 187–196.

Stuart, M., & Masterson, J. (1992). Patterns of reading and spelling in 10-year-old children related to prereading phonological abilities. *Journal of Experimental Child Psychology, 54,* 168–187.

Stunkard, A., Sorensen, T., & Shulsinger, F. (1980). Use of the Danish adoption register for the study of obesity and thinness. In S. Kety (Ed.), *The genetics of neurological and psychiatric disorders.* New York: Raven Press.

Sturgeon, J. A. (2014). Psychological therapies for the management of chronic pain. *Psychology Research & Behavior Management, 7,* 115–124. doi:10.2147/PRBM. S44762

Sturgess, J. E., George, T. P., Kennedy, J. L., Heinz, A., & Müller, D. J. (2011). Pharmacogenetics of alcohol, nicotine, and drug addiction treatments. *Addiction Biology, 16*(3), 357–376. doi:10.1111/j.1369-1600.2010.00287.x

Sturgis, E. T., & Adams, H. E. (1978). The right to treatment: Issues in the treatment of homosexuality. *Journal of Consulting and Clinical Psychology, 46,* 165–169.

Styron, W. (1990). *Darkness visible: A memoir of madness.* New York: Random House.

Substance Abuse and Mental Health Services Administration [SAMHSA]. (2014). *Results from the 2013 National Survey on Drug Use and Health: Summary of national findings*, NSDUH Series H-48, HHS Publication No. (SMA) 14-4863. Rockville, MD: Substance Abuse and Mental Health Services Administration. Retrieved on December 10, 2014 from http://www.samhsa.gov/data/sites/default/files/NSDUHresultsPDFWHTML2013/Web/NSDUHresults2013.pdf

Suddath, R. L., Christison, G. W., Torrey, E. F., Casanova, M. F., & Weinberger, D. (1990). Anatomical abnormalities in the brains of monozygotic twins discordant for schizophrenia. *New England Journal of Medicine, 322,* 789–794.

Sue, S., Fujino, D. C., Hu, L. T., Takeuchi, D. T., & Zane, N. W. S. (1991). Community mental health services for ethnic minority groups: A test of the cultural responsiveness hypothesis. *Journal of Counseling Psychology, 59,* 533–540.

Sue, S., Zane, N., & Young, K. (1994). Research on psychotherapy with culturally diverse populations. In A. E. Bergin & S. L. Garfield (Eds.), *Handbook of psychotherapy and behavior change* (pp. 783–820). New York: John Wiley & Sons.

Sukhai, R. N., Mol, J., & Harris, A. S. (1989). Combined therapy of enuresis alarm and desmopressin in the treatment of nocturnal enuresis. *European Journal of Pediatrics, 148,* 465–467.

Sullivan, H. S. (1953). *The interpersonal theory of psychiatry.* New York: W. W. Norton.

Sullivan, J. (2007). *Jeans: A cultural history of an American icon.* London: Gotham Books.

Sullivan, L. E., Tetrault, J. M., Braithwaite, R. S., Turner, B. J., & Fiellin, D. A. (2011). A meta-analysis of the efficacy of nonphysician brief interventions for unhealthy alcohol use: Implications for the patient-centered medical home. *The American Journal on Addictions, 20*(4), 343–356. doi:10.1111/j.1521-0391.2011.00143.x

Suls, J., & Wang, C. K. (1993). The relationship between trait hostility and cardiovascular reactivity: A quantitative review and analysis. *Psychophysiology, 30,* 1–12.

Suls, J. M., Luger, T. M., Curry, S. J., Mermelstein, R. J., Sporer, A. K., & An, L. C. (2012). Efficacy of smoking-cessation interventions for young adults: A meta-analysis. *American Journal of Preventive Medicine, 42*(6), 655–662. doi:10.1016/j.amepre.2012.02.013

Sulser, F., & Sanders-Bush, E. (1989). From neurochemical to molecular pharmacology of antidepressants. In E. Costa (Ed.), *Tribute to B. B. Brodie.* New York: Raven Press.

Sundberg, N. (1977). *Assessment of persons.* Englewood Cliffs, NJ: Prentice Hall.

Sundgot-Borgen, J., & Torstveit, M. K. (2004). Prevalence of eating disorders in elite athletes is higher than in the general population. *Clinical Journal of Sports Medicine, 14,* 25–32.

Sung, V., Hiscock, H., Sciberras, E., & Efron D. (2008). Sleep problems in children with attention-deficit/hyperactivity disorder: Prevalence and the effect on the child and family. *Archives of Pediatrics and Adolescent Medicine, 162,* 336–342.

Suokas, J. T., Suvisaari, J. M., Grainger, M., Raevuori, A., Gissler, M., & Haukka, J. (2014). Suicide attempts and mortality in eating disorders: A follow-up study of eating disorder patients. *General Hospital Psychiatry, 36*(3), 355–357.

Suomi, S. J. (1991). Early stress and adult emotional reactivity in rhesus monkeys. *CIBA Foundation Symposium, 156,* 171–183.

Suppes, T., Baldessarini, R. J., Faedda, G. L., & Tohen, M. (1991). Risk of recurrence following discontinuation of lithium in treatment of bipolar disorder. *Archives of General Psychiatry, 48,* 82–88.

Suppiger, A., In-Albon, T., Hendriksen, S., Hermann, E., Margraf, J., & Schneider, S. (2009). Acceptance of structured diagnostic interviews for mental disorders in clinical practice and research settings. *Behavior Therapy, 40,* 272–279. doi:10.1016/j.beth.2008.07.002

Susser, E., & Wanderling, J. (1994). Epidemiology of nonaffective remitting psychosis vs schizophrenia: Sex and sociocultural setting. *Archives of General Psychiatry, 51,* 294–301.

Sutherland, N. S. (1976). *Breakdown.* New York: Signet.

Sutker, P., Davis, J. M., Uddo, M., & Ditta, S. (1995). War zone stresses, personal resources, and PTSD in Persian Gulf returnees. *Journal of Abnormal Psychology, 104,* 444–452.

Svartberg, M., & Stiles, T. C. (1991). Comparative effects of short-term psychotherapy: A metaanalysis. *Journal of Consulting and Clinical Psychology, 59,* 704–714.

Sveinsson, I. S. (1975). Postoperative psychosis after heart surgery. *The Journal of Thoracic and Cardiovascular Surgery, 70,* 717–726.

Svenaeus, F. (2013). Anorexia nervosa and the body uncanny: A phenomenological approach. *Philosophy, Psychiatry, & Psychology, 20*(1), 81–91.

Swaab, D. F., Gooren, L. J. G., & Hofman, M. A. (1995). Brain research, gender, and sexual orientation. *Journal of Homosexuality, 28*(3/4), 283–301.

Swaab, D. F., Hofman, M. A., Lucasen, P. D., Purba, J. S., Raadsheer, F. L., & van der Nas, J. A. P. (1993). Functional neuroanatomy and neuropathology of the human hypothalamus. *Anatomical Embryology, 187,* 317–330.

Swaim, R. C., Oetting, E. R., Edwards, R. W., & Beauvais, F. (1989). Links from emotional distress to adolescent drug use: A path model. *Journal of Consulting and Clinical Psychology, 57,* 227–231.

Swain, M. A., & Steckel, S. B. (1981). Influencing adherence among hypertensives. *Research Nursing and Health, 4,* 213–218.

Swann, A. C., Lijffijt, M., Lane, S. D., Steinberg, J. L., & Moeller, F. G. (2009). Trait impulsivity and response inhibition in antisocial personality disorder. *Journal of Psychiatric Research, 43*(12), 1057–1063.

Swanson, J. M., Elliott, G. R., Greenhill, L. L., Wigal, T., Arnold, L. E., Vitiello, B., . . . Volkow, N. D. (2007). Effects of stimulant medication on growth rates across 3 years in the MTA follow-up. *Journal of the American Academy of Child & Adolescent Psychiatry, 46*(8), 1015–1027. doi:10.1097/chi.0b013e3180686d7e

Swartz, H. A. (2014). Family-focused therapy study raises new questions. *The American Journal of Psychiatry, 171*(6), 603–606. doi:10.1176/appi.ajp.2014.14020217

Swedo, S., Pietrini, P., Leonard, H., Schapiro, M., Rettew, D., Goldberger, E., Rapoport, J., & Grady, C. (1992). Cerebral glucose metabolism in childhood-onset obsessive-compulsive disorder: Revisualization during pharmacotherapy. *Archives of General Psychiatry, 49,* 690–694.

Swift, J. (1704). *A tale of a tub.* London: J. Nutt.

Swift, R., Oslin, D. W., Alexander, M., & Forman, R. (2011). Adherence monitoring in naltrexone pharmacotherapy trials: A systematic review. *Journal of Studies on Alcohol and Drugs, 72*(6), 1012–1018.

Sylvia, L. G., Tilley, C. A., Lund, H. G., & Sachs, G. S. (2008). Psychosocial interventions: Empirically derived treatments for bipolar disorder. *Current Psychiatry Reviews, 4*(2), 108–113. doi:10.2174/157340008784529278

Syvalahti, E. K. G. (1994). Biological factors in schizophrenia: Structural and functional aspects. *British Journal of Psychiatry, 164* (Suppl. 23), 9–14.

Szab'o, G., Tabakoff, B., & Hoffman, P. L. (1994). The NMDA receptor antagonist dizocilpine differentially affects enviromnent-dependent and environment-independent ethanol tolerance. *Psychopharmacology, 113(3-4),* 511–517.

Szapocznik, J., Kurtines, W. M., Foote, F., Perez-Vidal, A., & Hervis, O. (1986). Conjoint versus one-person family therapy: Further evidence for the effectiveness of conducting family therapy through one person with drug-abusing adolescents. *Journal of Consulting and Clinical Psychology, 54,* 395–397.

Szapocznik, J., Kurtines, W., Santisteban, D. A., & Rio, A. T. (1990). Interplay of advances between theory, research, and application in treatment interventions aimed at behavior problem children and adolescents. *Journal of Consulting and Clinical Psychology, 58,* 696–703.

Szasz, T. S. (1961). *The myth of mental illness: Foundations of a theory of personal conduct.* New York: Hoeber-Harper.

Szasz, T. S. (1986). The case against suicide. *American Psychologist, 41,* 806–812.

Szatmari, P., Jones, M. B., Tuff, L., Bartolucci, G., Fisman, S., & Mahoney, W. (1993). Lack of cognitive impairment in first-degree relatives of children with pervasive developmental disorders. *Journal of the American Academy of Child and Adolescent Psychiatry, 32,* 1264–1273.

Szatmari, P., Offord, D., & Boyle, M. H. (1989). Ontario Health Study: Prevalence of attention deficit disorders with hyperactivity. *Journal of Child Psychology and Psychiatry, 30,* 219–230.

Szentagotai, A., & David, D. (2010). The efficacy of cognitive-behavioral therapy in bipolar disorder: A quantitative meta-analysis. *Journal of Clinical Psychiatry, 71*(1), 66–72. doi:10.4088/JCP.08r04559yel

Szpakowicz, M., & Herd, A. (2008). "Medically cleared": How well are patients with psychiatric presentations examined by emergency physicians? *Journal of Emergency Medicine, 35,* 369–372.

T

Tabakoff, B., & Hoffman, P. L. (1991). Neurochemical effects of alcohol. In R. J. Frances & S. I. Muller (Eds.), *Clinical textbook of addictive disorders* (pp. 501–525). New York: Guilford Press.

Tabakoff, B., Whelan, J. P., & Hoffman, P. L. (1990). Two biological markers of alcoholism. In C. R. Cloninger & H. Begleiter (Eds.), *Genetics and biology of alcoholism* (pp. 195–204). Cold Spring Harbor, NY: Cold Spring Harbor Laboratory Press.

Tabert, M. H., Manly, J. J., Liu, X., Pelton, G. H., Rosenblum, S., Jacobs, M., . . . Devanand, D. P. (2006). Neuropsychological prediction of conversion to Alzheimer disease in patients with mild cognitive impairment. *Archives of General Psychiatry, 63*(8), 916–924. doi: 10.1001/archpsyc.63.8.916

Takahashi, T. (1989). Social phobia syndrome in Japan. *Comprehensive Psychiatry, 30,* 45–52.

Takahashi, Y. (1990). Is multiple personality disorder really rare in Japan? *Dissociation, 3,* 57–59.

Talcott, G. W., Fiedler, E. R., Pascale, R. W., Klesges, R. C., Peterson, A. L., & Johnson, R. S. (1995). Is weight gain after smoking cessation inevitable? *Journal of Consulting and Clinical Psychology, 63,* 313–316.

Tanaka, M., & Kinney, D. K. (2011). Does the immune system regulate mood to defend against infection? Evidence from studies of immune factors, depression, and antidepressants. *Current Psychiatry Reviews, 7*(1), 57–66. doi:10.2174/157340011795945829

Tandon, R., Gaebel, W., Barch, D. M., Bustillo, J., Gur, R. E., Heckers, S., . . . Carpenter, W. (2013). Definition and description of schizophrenia in the *DSM-5. Schizophrenia Research, 150*(1), 3–10. doi:10.1016/j.schres.2013.05.028

Tandon, R., & Kane, J. M. (1993). Neuropharmacologic basis for clozapine's unique profile. *Archives of General Psychiatry, 50*, 158–159.

Tandon, R., Keshavan, M., & Nasrallah, H. A. (2008). Schizophrenia, just the facts: What we know in 2008. 2. Epidemiology and etiology. *Schizophrenia Research, 102*, 1–18.

Tandon, R., & Maj, M. (2008). Nosological status and definition of schizophrenia: Some considerations for *DSM-V* and *ICD-11*. *Asian Journal of Psychiatry, 1*(2), 22–27. doi:10.1016/j.ajp.2008.10.002

Tandon, R., Nasrallah, H. A. & Keshavan, M. (2009). Schizophrenia, just the facts: Clinical features and conceptualization. *Schizophrenia Research, 110*, 1–23.

Tang, M. X., Cross, P., Andrews, H., Jacobs, D. M., Small, S., Bell, K., . . . Mayeux, R. (2001). Incidence of AD in African-Americans, Caribbean Hispanics, and Caucasians in northern Manhattan. *Neurology, 56*(1), 49–56. doi: 10.1212/WNL.56.1.49

Tarasoff v. Regents of the University of California (Tarasoff II). (2008). In D.N. Bersoff, *Ethical conflicts in psychology* (4th ed.) (pp. 171–174). Washington, DC: American Psychological Association.

Tarasoff v. Regents of the University of California, 17 Cal. 3d 425,551 P.2d 334, 131 Cal. Reptr. 14 (1976).

Tarrier, N., Barrowclough, C., Porceddu, K. & Watts, S. (1988). The assessment of psychophysiological reactivity to expressed emotion of relatives of schizophrenic patients. *British Journal of Psychiatry, 152*, 618–624.

Tarrier, N., Taylor, K., & Gooding, P. (2008). Cognitive-behavioral interventions to reduce suicide behavior: A systematic review and meta-analysis. *Behavior Modification, 32*(1), 77–108. doi:10.1177/0145445507304728

Tartakovsky, M. (2009). Media's damaging depictions of mental illness. *Psych Central*. Retrieved on November 30, 2014 from http://psychcentral.com/lib/medias-damaging-depictions-of-mental-illness/0002220

Tarter, R., Blackson, T., Martin, C., Seilhamer, R., Pelham, W., & Loeber, R. (1993). Mutual dissatisfaction between mother and son in substance abuse and normal families: Association with child behavior problems. *American Journal on Addiction, 2*, 1–10.

Tarterre, R. E., Kabene, M., Escallier, E. A., Laird, S. B., & Jacob, T. (1990). Temperament deviation and risk for alcoholism. *Alcoholism in Clinical and Experimental Research, 14*, 380–382.

Tarterre, R. E., & Vanyukov, M. (1994). Alcoholism: A developmental disorder. *Journal of Consulting and Clinical Psychology, 62*, 1096–1107.

Tartre, R., Blackson, T., Martin, C., Seilhamer, R., Pelham, W., & Loeber, R. (1993). Mutual dissatisfaction between mother and son in substance abuse and normal families: Association with child behavior problems. *American Journal on Addiction, 2*, 1–10.

Tartre, R. E., Kabene, M., Escallier, E. A., Laird, S. B., & Jacob, T. (1990). Temperament deviation and risk for alcoholism. *Alcoholism in Clinical and Experimental Research, 14*, 380–382.

Tavris, C., & Sadd, S. (1977). *The Redbook report on female sexuality: 100,000 married women disclose the good news about sex*. New York: Delacorte Press.

Taylor, A., & Wang, K. (2014). Association between DPYSL2 gene polymorphisms and alcohol dependence in Caucasian samples. *Journal of Neural Transmission, 121*(1), 105–111. doi:10.1007/s00702-013-1065-2

Taylor, C. B., Ironson, G., & Burnett, K. (1990). Adult medical disorders. In A. S. Bellack, M. Hersen, & A. E. Kazdin (Eds.), *International handbook of behavior modification and therapy* (pp. 371–398). New York: Plenum.

Taylor, D. J., Vatthauer, K. E., Bramoweth, A. D., Ruggero, C., & Roane, B. (2013). The role of sleep in predicting college academic performance: Is it a unique predictor? *Behavioral Sleep Medicine, 11*(3), 159–172. doi:10.1080/15402002.2011.602776

Taylor, M.A., & Fink, M. (2003). Catatonia in psychiatric classification: A home of its own. *American Journal of Psychiatry, 160*, 1233–1241.

Taylor, P. J., & Kopelman, M. D. (1984). Amnesia for criminal offenses. *Psychological Medicine, 14*, 581–588.

Taylor, S., Koch, W. J., & McNally, R. J. (1992). How does anxiety sensitivity vary across the anxiety disorders? *Journal of Anxiety Disorders, 6*(3), 249–259.

Taylor, S., Thordarson, D. S., Jang, K. L., & Asmundson, G. J. G. (2006). Genetic and environmental origins of health anxiety: A twin study. *World Psychiatry: Official Journal of the World Psychiatric Association (WPA), 5*(1), 47–50.

Taylor, S. E. (1983). Adjustment to threatening events: A theory of cognitive adaptation. *American Psychologist, 38*, 1161–1173.

Taylor, S. E. (1989). *Positive illusions: Creative self-deception and the healthy mind*. New York: Basic Books.

Taylor, S. E. (1994). Asymmetrical effects of positive and negative events: The mobilization-minimization hypothesis. *Psychological Bulletin, 110*, 67–85.

Taylor, S. E. (1995). *Health psychology*. New York: McGraw-Hill.

Taylor, S. E., & Brown, J. D. (1988). Illusion and well-being: A social psychological perspective on mental health. *Psychological Bulletin, 103*, 193–210.

Tazaki, M., & Landlaw, K. (2006). Behavioural mechanisms and cognitive-behavioural interventions of somatoform disorders. *International Review of Psychiatry, 18*(1), 67–73. doi:10.1080/09540260500467046

Teasdale, G., & Jennett, B. (1974). Assessment of coma and impaired consciousness. A practical scale. *Lancet, 13*, 81–84.

Tedeschi, R., & Calhoun, L. (1996). The posttraumatic growth inventory: Measuring the positive legacy of trauma. *Journal of Traumatic Stress, 9*, 455–471.

Telch, M., Lucus, J., Schmidt, N., Hanna, H., Jaimez, T., & Lucas, R. (1993). Group cognitive-behavioral treatment of panic disorder. *Behaviour Research and Therapy, 31*, 279–287.

Tellegen, A., Ben-Porath, Y. S., McNulty, J. L., Arbisi, P. A., Graham, J. R., & Kaemmer, B. (2003). *MMPI-2 restructured clinical (RC) scales: Development, validation, and interpretation*. Minneapolis, MN: University of Minnesota Press.

Tellegen, A., Ben-Porath, Y. S., & Sellbom, M. (2009). Construct validity of the MMPI-2 restructured clinical (RC) scales: Reply to Rouse, Greene, Butcher, Nichols, and Williams. *Journal of Personality Assessment, 91*, 211–221. doi:10.1080/00223890902794192

Tellegen, A., Lykken, D. T., Bouchard, T. J., Jr., Wilcox, K. J., Segal, N. L., & Rich, S. (1988). Personality similarity in twins reared apart and reared together. *Journal of Personality and Social Psychology, 54*, 1031–1039.

Tendolkar, I., van Beek, M., van Oostrom, I., Mulder, M., Janzing, J., Voshaar, R., & van Eijndhoven, P. (2013). Electroconvulsive therapy increases hippocampal and amygdala volume in therapy refractory depression: A longitudinal pilot study. *Psychiatry Research: Neuroimaging, 214*(3), 197–203. doi:10.1016/j.pscychresns.2013.09.004

Tennant, F., & Shannon, J. (1995). Cocaine abuse in methadone maintenance patients is associated with low serum methadone concentrations. *Journal of Addictive Disorders, 14*, 67–74.

Tennen, H., & Affleck, G. (1990). Blaming others for threatening events. *Psychological Bulletin, 108*, 209–232.

Teplin, L. (1984). The criminalization of the mentally ill: Speculation in search of data. In L. A. Teplin (Ed.), *Mental health and criminal justice*. Newbury Park, CA: Sage.

Teri, L, & Gallagher, T. D. (1991). Cognitive therapy and depression in Alzheimer's patients. *Gerontologist, 31*, 413-416.

Terman, L. M., & Oden, M. H. (1947). *Genetic studies of genius: The gifted child grows up* (Vol. 4). Stanford, CA: Stanford University Press.

Tessler, R. C., & Dennis, D. L. (1989). *A synthesis of NIMH-funded research concerning persons who are homeless and mentally ill*. Rockville, MD: National Institute of Mental Health.

Testa, M., & West, S. G. (2010). Civil commitment in the United States. *Psychiatry, 7*(10), 30–40.

Teusch, L., Bohme, H., Finke, J., & Gastpar, M. (2001). Effects of client-centered psychotherapy for personality disorders alone in combination with psychopharmacological treatment. *Psychotherapy and Psychosomatics, 70*, 328–336.

Thaker, G. K., Cassady, S., Adami, H., Moran, M., & Ross, D. E. (1996). Eye movements in spectrum personality disorders: Comparison of community subjects and relatives of schizophrenic patients. *The American Journal of Psychiatry, 153*, 362–368.

Thapar, A., Cooper, M., Eyre, O., & Langley, K. (2013). Practitioner review: What have we learnt about the causes of ADHD? *Journal of Child Psychology and Psychiatry, 54*(1), 3–16. doi:10.1111/j.1469-7610.2012.02611.x

Thapar, A., Davies, G., Jones, T., & Rivett, M. (1992). Treatment of childhood encopresis—A review. *Child: Care, Health and Development, 18*, 343–353.

Thapar, A., Rice, F., Hay, D., Boivin, J., Langley, K., van den Bree, M., . . . Harold, G. (2009). Prenatal smoking might not cause attention-deficity/hyperactivity disorder: Evidence from a novel design. *Biological Psychiatry, 66*, 722–72.

Thara, R. (2004). Twenty-year course of schizophrenia: The Madras longitudinal study. *Canadian Journal of Psychiatry, 49*, 564–569.

Thase, M. E. (2007). Recognition and diagnosis of atypical depression. *Journal of Clinical Psychiatry, 68*(Suppl8), 11–16.

Thibaut, F., De LaBarra, F., Gordon, H., Cosyns, P., & Bradford, J. W. (2010). The World Federation of Societies of Biological Psychiatry (WFSBP) guidelines for the biological treatment of paraphilias. *The World Journal of Biological Psychiatry, 11*(3–4), 604–655.

Thigpen, C. H., & Cleckley, H. (1957). *The three faces of Eve*. New York: McGraw-Hill.

Thihalolipavan, S., Candalla, B. M., & Ehrlich, J. (2013). Examining pica in NYC pregnant women with elevated blood lead levels. *Maternal and Child Health Journal, 17*(1), 49–55. doi: 10.1007/s10995-012-0947-5

Thoits, P. A. (1986). Social support as coping assistance. *Journal of Consulting and Clinical Psychology, 54*, 416–423.

Thomas, H. V., Dalman, C., David, A. S., Gentz, J., Lewis, G., & Allebeck, P. (2001). Obstetric complications and risk of schizophrenia: Effect of gender, age at diagnosis, and maternal history of psychosis. *British Journal of Psychiatry, 179*, 409–414.

Thomas, J. J., & Bentall, R. P. (2002). Hypomanic traits and response styles to depression. *British Journal of Clinical Psychology, 41*, 309–313.

Thomas, P., Mathur, P., Gottesman, I. I., Nagpal, R., Nimgaonkar, V. L., & Deshpande, S. N. (2007). Correlates of hallucinations in schizophrenia: A cross-cultural evaluation. *Schizophrenia Research, 92*(1–3), 41–49. doi:10.1016/j.schres.2007.01.017

Thomasson, H. R., Edenberg, H. J., Crabb, D. W., Mai, X. L., Jerome, R. E., Li, T.-K., Wang, S.-P., Lin, Y.-T., Lu, R.-B., & Yin, S.-J. (1991). Alcohol and aldehyde dehydrogenase genotypes and alcoholism in Chinese men. *American Journal of Human Genetics, 48,* 677–681.

Thombs, D. L. (1993). The differentially discriminating properties of alcohol expectancies for female and male drinkers. *Journal of Counseling and Development, 71,* 321–325.

Thombs, D. L. (1994). *Introduction to addictive behaviors.* New York: Guilford Press.

Thompson, J. W., Weiner, R. D., & Myers, C. P. (1994). Use of ECT in the United States in 1976, 1980, and 1986. *American Journal of Psychiatry, 151,* 1657–1661.

Thompson, L. W., Gallagher, D., & Breckenridge, J. S. (1987). Comparative effectiveness of psychotherapies for depressed elders. *Journal of Consulting and Clinical Psychology, 55,* 385–390.

Thompson, T., Hackenberg, T., Cerutti, D., Baker, D., & Axtell, S. (1994). Opioid antagonist effects on self-injury in adults with mental retardation: Response form and location as determinants of medication effects. *American Journal on Mental Retardation, 99*(1), 85–102.

Thompson-Hollands, J., Edson, A., Tompson, M. C., & Comer, J. S. (2014). Family involvement in the psychological treatment of obsessive-compulsive disorder: A meta-analysis. *Journal of Family Psychology, 28*(3), 287–298. doi:10.1037/a0036709

Thoresen, C. E., & Powell, L. H. (1992). Type A behavior pattern: New perspectives on theory, assessment and intervention. Special issue: Behavioral medicine: An update for the 1990s. *Journal of Consulting and Clinical Psychology, 60,* 595–604.

Thorndike, R. L., Hagen, E. P., & Sattler, J. M. (1986). *The Stanford-Binet Intelligence Scale: Fourth Edition, Guide for administering and scoring.* Chicago: Riverside Publishing.

Thriveport (2011). *MoodKit.* App for iPhone retrieved on August 11, 2014 from http://www.thriveport.com/

Thush, C., & Wiers R. W. (2007). Explicit and implicit alcohol-related cognitions and the prediction of future drinking in adolescents. *Addictive Behaviors, 32,* 1367–1383.

Thyer, B. A. (1991). Diagnosis and treatment of child and adolescent anxiety disorders. *Behavior Modification, 15*(3), 310–325.

Thyer, B., Nesse, R., Curtis, G., & Cameron, O. (1986). Panic disorder: A test of the separation anxiety hypothesis. *Behaviour Research and Therapy, 24,* 209–211.

Tidemalm, D. D., Runeson, B. B., Waern, M. M., Frisell, T. T., Carlström, E. E., Lichtenstein, P. P., & Långström, N. N. (2011). Familial clustering of suicide risk: A total population study of 11.4 million individuals. *Psychological Medicine, 41*(12), 2527–2534. doi:10.1017/S0033291711000833

Tiefer, L. (1991). Historical, scientific, clinical and feminist criticisms of the human sexual response cycle model. *Annual Review of Sex Research,* 21–23.

Tiefer, L., & Melman, A. (1989). Comprehensive evaluation of erectile dysfunction and medical treatments. In S. R. Leiblum & R. C. Rosen (Eds.), *Principles and practice of sex therapy: Update for the 1990s* (pp. 207–236). New York: Guilford Press.

Tienari, P. (1991). Interaction between genetic vulnerability and family environment: The Finnish adoptive family study of schizophrenia. *Acta Psychiatrica Scandanavica, 84,* 460–465.

Tienari, P., Sorri, A., Lahti, I., Naarala, M., Wahlberg, K., . . . Wynne., L. C. (1987). Genetic and psychosocial factors in schizophrenia spectrum disorder: The Finnish adoptive family study. *Schizophrenia Bulletin, 13,* 477–484.

Tienari, P., Wynne, L. C., Sorri, A., Lahti, I., Laksy, K., . . . Wahlberg, K. (2004). Genotype-environment interaction in schizophrenia spectrum disorder. *British Journal of Psychiatry, 184,* 216–222.

Tiet, Q. Q., Bird, H. R., Hoven, C. W., Moore, R., Wu, P., Wicks, J., . . . Cohen, P. (2001). Relationship between specific adverse life events and psychiatric disorders. *Journal of Abnormal Child Psychology, 29*(2), 153–164. doi:10.1023/A:1005288130494

Timbrook, R. E., & Graham, J. R. (1994). Ethnic differences on the MMPI-2? *Psychological Assessment, 6,* 212–217.

Timpano, K. R., Keough, M. E., Mahaffey, B., Schmidt, N. B., & Abramowitz, J. (2010). Parenting and obsessive-compulsive symptoms: Implications of authoritarian parenting. *Journal of Cognitive Psychotherapy, 24*(3), 151–164. doi:10.1891/0889-8391.24.3.151

Tipton, L., & Blacher, J. (2014). Brief report: Autism awareness: Views from a campus community. *Journal of Autism and Developmental Disorders, 44*(2), 477–483. doi:10.1007/s10803-013-1893-9

Tisdelle, D. A., & St. Lawrence, J. S. (1988). Adolescent interpersonal problem-solving skill training: Social validation and generalization. *Behavior Therapy, 19,* 171–182.

Toh, S. (2006). Datapoints: Trends in ADHD and stimulant use among children, 1993–2003. *Psychiatric Services, 57,* 1091.

Tohen, M., Strakowski, S. M., Zarate, C., Hennen, J., Stoll, A. L., Suppes, T., . . . Baldessarini, R. J. (2000). The McLean-Harvard First-Episode Project: 6-month symptomatic and functional outcome in affective and nonaffective psychosis. *Biological Psychiatry, 48*(6), 467–476. doi:10.1016/S0006-3223(00)00915-X

Tohen, M., Zarate, C., Hennen, J., Khalsa, H., Strakowski, S. M., Gebre-Medhin, P., . . . Baldessarini, R. J. (2003). The McLean-Harvard First-Episode Mania Study: Prediction of recovery and first recurrence. *The American Journal of Psychiatry, 160*(12), 2099–2107. doi:10.1176/appi.ajp.160.12.2099

Tolan, P. H., Guerra, N. G., & Kendall, P. C. (1995). A developmental-ecological perspective on antisocial behavior in children and adolescents: Toward a unified risk and intervention framework. *Journal of Consulting and Clinical Psychology, 63,* 579–584.

Tolin, D. F., Frost, R. O., Steketee, G., Gray, K. D., & Fitch, K. E. (2008). The economic and social burden of compulsive hoarding. *Psychiatry Research, 160*(2), 200–211. doi:10.1016/j.psychres.2007.08.008

Tolin, D. F., Meunier, S. A., Frost, R. O., & Steketee, G. (2010). Course of compulsive hoarding and its relationship to life events. *Depression and Anxiety, 27*(9), 829–838. doi:10.1002/da.20684

Tollefson, G. D. (1993). Major depression. In D. L. Dunner (Ed.), *Current psychiatric practice* (pp. 196–204). Philadelphia: W. B. Saunders.

Tollefson, G. D., Rampey, A. H., & Genduso, L. A., (1994). A fixed-dose, placebo-controlled trial in OCD. *Psych opharmacology Bulletin, 30,* 84.

Tollefson, G. D., Rampey, A. H., Potvin, J., Jenike, M. A., Rush, J., Dominguez, R. A., Koran, L. M., Shear, K., Goodman, W., & Genduso, L. A. (1994). A multicenter investigation of a fixed-dose fluoxetine in the treatment of obsessive-compulsive disorder. *Archives of General Psychiatry, 51,* 559–563.

Tomarken, A. J. (1995). A psychometric perspective on psychophysiological measures. *Psychological Assessment, 7,* 387–395.

Tomasson, K., Kent, D., & Coryell, W. (1991). Somatization and conversion disorders: comorbidity and demographics at presentation. *Acta Psychiatrica Scandinavica, 84*(3), 288–293.

Torgersen, S. (1986). Genetics of somatoform disorders. *Archives of General Psychiatry, 43*(5), 502–505.

Torgersen, S., Kringlen, E., & Cramer, V. (2001). The prevalence of personality disorders in a community sample. *Archives of General Psychiatry, 58*(6), 590–596.

Torgersen, S., Lygren, S., Øien, P. A., Skre, I., Onstad, S., Edvardsen, J., . . . Kringlen, E. (2000). A twin study of personality disorders. *Comprehensive Psychiatry, 41*(6), 416–425.

Torgersen, S. G. (1983). Genetic factors in anxiety disorders. *Archives of General Psychiatry, 40,* 1065–1069.

Torgersen, S. G. (1984). Genetic and nosological aspects of schizotypal and borderline personality disorders. *Archives of General Psychiatry, 41,* 546–554.

Torgersen, S. G. (1986). Genetics of somatoform disorder. *Archives of General Psychiatry, 43,* 502–505.

Torrey, E. F. (1987). Prevalence studies of schizophrenia. *British Journal of Psychiatry, 164,* 589–608.

Torrey, E. F. (1988). *Nowhere to go: The tragic odyssey of the homeless mentally ill.* New York: Harper & Row.

Torrey, E. F. (2001). *Surviving schizophrenia* (4th ed.). New York: HarperCollins.

Torrey, E. F., & Bowler, A. (1990). Geographical distribution of insanity in America: Evidence for an urban factor. *Schizophrenia Bulletin, 16,* 591–604.

Torrey, E. F., Bowler, A. E., Rawlings, R., & Terrazas, A. (1993). Seasonality of schizophrenia and stillbirths. *Schizophrenic Bulletin, 19,* 557–562.

Torrey, E. F. Taylor, E. H. J., Bracha, H., Bowler, A., McNeil, T., Rawlings, R., Quinn, P., Biglow, L., Rickler, K., Sjostrom, K., Higgins, E., & Gottesman, I. (1994). Prenatal origin of schizophrenia in a subgroup of discordant monozygotic twins. *Schizophrenia Bulletin, 20,* 423–431.

Torrey, E. F., & Yolkin, R. H. (1995). Could schizophrenia be a viral zoonosis transmitted from house cats? *Schizophrenia Bulletin, 21,* 167–171.

Town, M., Naimi, T. S., Mokdad, A. H., & Brewer, R. D. (2006). Health care access among U.S. adults who drink alcohol excessively: Missed opportunities for prevention. *Preventing Chronic Disease* [serial online], April. Available from http://www.cdc.gov/pcd/issues/2006/apr/05_0182.htm.

Tranter, R., O'Donovan, C., Chandarana, P., & Kennedy, S. (2002). Prevalence and outcome of partial remission in depression. *Journal of Psychiatry & Neuroscience, 27*(4), 241–247.

Trapnell, P. D., & Campbell, J. D. (1999). Private self-consciousness and the five-factor model of personality distinguishing rumination from reflection. *Journal of Personality and Social Psychology, 76,* 284–304. doi:10.1037/0022-3514.76.2.284

Tremblay, R. E., Masse, B., Perron, D., Leblanc, M., Schwartzman, A. E., & Ledingham, J. E. (1992). Early disruptive behavior, poor school achievement, delinquent behavior, and delinquent personality: Longitudinal analyses. *Journal of Consulting and Clinical Psychology, 60,* 64–72.

Tremblay, R. E., Pagani-Kurtz, L., Masse, L. C., Vitaro, F., & Pihl, R. O. (1995). A bimodal preventive intervention for disruptive kindergarten boys: Its impact through mid-adolescence. *Journal of Consulting and Clinical Psychology, 63,* 560–568.

Treneman, A. (2000, June 30). J.K. Rowling, the interview. *The Times (UK)*. Retrieved from http://www.accio-quote.org/articles/2000/0600-times-treneman.html

Trickett, E. J., Dahiyal, C., & Selby, P. M. (1994). *Primary prevention in mental health: An annotated bibliography 1983–1991*. Rockville, MD: National Institute of Mental Health.

Trickett, P. K., & Putnam, F. W. (1993). Impact of child sexual abuse on females: Toward a developmental, psychobiological integration. *Psychological Science, 4*, 81–87.

Troop, N. A., Holbrey, A., & Treasure, J. L. (1998). Stress, coping, and crisis support in eating disorders. *International Journal of Eating Disorders, 24*(2), 157–166.

Trost, S. E., Burke, B. L., & Schoenfeld, J. (2014). *DSM-5*: Using key changes to highlight critical teaching points for undergraduate psychology instructors. *Society for the Teaching of Psychology's Office of Teaching Resources*. Retrieved on October 10, 2014 from http://teachpsych.org/Resources/Documents/otrp/resources/trost14.pdf

Trudel, G., Marchand, A., Ravart, M., Aubin, S., Turgeon, L., & Fortier, P. (2001). The effect of a cognitive-behavioral group treatment program on hypoactive sexual desire in women. *Sexual and Relationship Therapy, 16*(2), 145–164.

True, W. R., Rice, J., Eisen, S. A., Heath, A. C., Goldberg, J. Lyons, M. J., & Nowak, J. (1993). A twin study of genetic and environmental contributions to liability for posttraumatic stress symptoms. *Archives of General Psychiatry, 50*, 257–264.

Trujillo, K. A., & Akil, H. (1995). Excitatory amino acids and drugs of abuse: A role for N-methyl-D-aspartate receptors in drug tolerance, sensitization and physical dependence. *Drug and Alcohol Dependence, 38*, 139–154.

Trull, T. J. (1992). DSM-III-R personality disorders and the five-factor model of personality: An empirical comparison. *Journal of Abnormal Psychology, 101*, 553–560.

Trull, T. J., Nietzel, M. T., & Main, A. (1988). The use of meta-analysis to assess the clinical significance of behavior therapy for agoraphobia. *Behavior Therapy, 19*, 527–538.

Tsai, L. Y. (1987). Pre-, peri-, and neonatal factors in autism. In E. Schopler & G. G. Mesibov (Eds.), *Neurobiological issues in autism* (pp. 180–187). New York: Plenum.

Tsao, J. C. I., Allen, L. B., Evans, S., Lu, Q., Myers, C. D., & Zeltzer, L. K. (2009). Anxiety sensitivity and catastrophizing: Associations with pain and somatization in non-clinical children. *Journal of Health Psychology, 14*(8), 1085–1094. doi:10.1177/1359105309342306

Tsoi, W. F. (1993). Follow-up study of transsexuals after sex-reassignment surgery. *Singapore Medical Journal, 34*, 515–517.

Tsuang, D. & Coryell, W. (1993). An 8-year follow-up of patients with DSM-III-R psychotic depression, schizoaffective disorder and schizophrenia. *American Journal of Psychiatry, 150*(8), 1182–1188.

Tully, E. C., Iacono, W. G., & McGue, M. (2008). An adoption study of parental depression as an environmental liability for adolescent depression and childhood disruptive disorders. *The American Journal of Psychiatry, 165*(9), 1148–1154. doi:10.1176/appi.ajp.2008.07091438

Tune, L., & Ross, C. (1994). Delirium. In C. E. Coffey & J. L. Cummings (Eds.), *Textbook of geriatric neuropsychiatry* (pp. 351–365). Washington, DC: American Psychiatric Press.

Turk, D. C. (2002). Clinical effectiveness and cost-effectiveness of treatments for patients with chronic pain. *The Clinical Journal of Pain, 18*(6), 355–365. doi:10.1097/00002508-200211000-00003

Turk, D. C., & Rudy, T. E. (1990). Pain. In A. S. Bellack, M. Hersen, & A. E. Kazdin (Eds), *International handbook of behavior modification and therapy*. New York: Plenum.

Turkheimer, E., & Parry, C. D. H. (1992). Why the gap? Practice and policy in civil commitment hearings. *American Psychologist, 47*, 646–655.

Turner, E., Ewing, J., Shilling, P., Smith, T. L., Irwin, M., Schuckit, M., & Kelsoe, J. R. (1992). Lack of association between an RFLP near the D2 dopamine receptor gene and severe alcoholism. *Biological Psychiatry, 31*, 285–290.

Turner, J. B., Kessler, R. C., & House, J. S. (1991). Factors facilitating adjustment to unemployment: Implications for intervention. *American Journal of Community Psychology, 19*, 521–542.

Turner, M. J. (1995). Homosexuality, Type 1: An Xq28 phenomenon. *Archives of Sexual Behavior, 24*, 109–134.

Turner, S. M., Beidel, D. C., & Jacob, R. G. (1994). Social phobia: A comparison of behavior therapy and atenolol. *Journal of Consulting and Clinical Psychology, 62*, 350–358.

Turrisi, R., & Wiersma, K. (1999). Examination of judgments of drunkenness, binge drinking, and drunk-driving tendencies in teens with and without a family history of alcohol abuse. *Alcoholism: Clinical and Experimental Research, 23*(7), 1191–1198. doi:10.1097/00000374-199907000-00008

Twamley, E. W., Ropacki, S. L., & Bondi, M. W. (2006). Neuropsychological and neuroimaging changes in preclinical Alzheimer's disease. *Journal of the International Neuropsychological Society, 12*(5), 707–735. doi:10.1017/S1355617706060863

Tyrer, P., Fowler-Dixon, R., Ferguson, B., & Kelemen, A. (1990). A plea for the diagnosis of hypochondriacal personality disorder. *Journal of Psychosomatic Research, 34*(6), 637–642. doi:10.1016/0022-3999(90)90107-F

Tyrer, P., & Kendall, T. (2009). The spurious advance of antipsychotic drug therapy. *Lancet, 373*, 4–5.

Tyrka, A. R., Cannon, T. D., Haslam, N., Mednick, S. A., Schulsinger, F., Schulsinger, H., & Parnas, J. (1995). The latent structure of schizotypy. I: Premorbid indicators of a taxon of individuals at risk for schizophrenia-spectrum disorders. *Journal of Abnormal Psychology, 104*, 173–183.

U

U.S. Department of Health and Human Services (HHS) Office of the Surgeon General and National Action Alliance for Suicide Prevention. (2012). *2012 National strategy for suicide prevention: Goals and objectives for action*. Washington, DC: HHS.

U.S. Department of Health and Human Services. (1987). *National Center for Health Statistics: Detailed diagnoses and procedures for patients discharged from short-stay hospitals: United States, 1985*. Hyattsville, MD: Author.

U.S. Department of Health and Human Services. (1990). *The health benefits of smoking cessation: A report of the Surgeon General* (DHHS Publication No. CDC 90-8416). Washington, DC: U.S. Government Printing Office.

U.S. Department of Health and Human Services. (2008). *Treating tobacco use and dependence: 2008 update*. Rockville, MD: U.S. Public Health Service.

U.S. Department of Health and Human Services. (2014). *The health consequences of smoking—50 Years of progress: A report of the surgeon general*. Atlanta, GA: U.S. Department of Health and Human Services, Centers for Disease Control and Prevention, National Center for Chronic Disease Prevention and Health Promotion, and Office on Smoking and Health. Retrieved on December 14, 2014 from http://www.cdc.gov/tobacco/data_statistics/sgr/50th-anniversary/index.htm

U.S. Department of Housing and Urban Development. (2014, October 30). *Annual Homeless Assessment Report to Congress*. Retrieved on December 17, 2014 from https://www.hudexchange.info/resources/documents/2014-AHAR-Part1.pdf

U.S. Department of Transportation, National Highway Traffic Safety Administration. (1991). *Fatal accident reporting system (FARS) 1990: A review of information on fatal traffic crashes in the United States*. (DOT HS 807 794). Washington, DC: Supt. of Docs., U.S. Government Printing Office.

U.S. Food and Drug Administration (2004). *Relationship between psychotropic drugs and pediatric suicidality: Review and evaluation of clinical data*. Retrieved on August 7, 2014 from http://www.fda.gov/ohrms/dockets/ac/04/briefing/2004-4065b1-10-TAB08-Hammads-Review.pdf

U.S. Food and Drug Administration (2007). Revisions to product labeling. *Antidepressant Use in Children, Adolescents, and Adults*. Retrieved on August 11, 2014 from http://www.fda.gov/downloads/Drugs/DrugSafety/InformationbyDrugClass/UCM173233.pdf

U.S. General Accounting Office (1990). *Methadone maintenance: Some treatment programs are not effective; greater federal oversight needed*. Washington, DC: U.S. General Accounting Office.

U.S. Interagency Council on Homelessness. (2010). *Opening doors: The federal strategic plan to prevent and end homelessness*. Retrieved on October 29, 2014 from http://usich.gov/PDF/OpeningDoors_2010_FSPPreventEndHomeless.pdf

Uddin, L. Q., Menon, V., Young, C. B., Ryali, S., Chen, T., Khouzam, A., . . . Hardan, A. Y. (2011). Multivariate searchlight classification of structural magnetic resonance imaging in children and adolescents with autism. *Biological Psychiatry, 70*, 833–841.

Uher, R. (2014). Gene–environment interactions in severe mental illness. *Frontiers in Psychiatry, 5*, 48. doi:10.3389/fpsyt.2014.00048

UK ECT Review Group. (2003). Efficacy and safety of electroconvulsive therapy in depressive disorders: A systematic review and meta-analysis. *Lancet, 361*(9360), 799–808.

Ullmann, L. P., & Krasner, L. (1975). *A psychological approach to abnormal behavior*. Englewood Cliffs, NJ: Prentice Hall.

Unger, K. V., & Anthony, W. A. (1992). A supported education program for young adults with long-term mental illness. *Hospital and Community Psychiatry, 42*, 838–842.

Ungur, L. A., Neuner, B., John, S., Wernecke, K., & Spies, C. (2013). Prevention and therapy of alcohol withdrawal on intensive care units: Systematic review of controlled trials. *Alcoholism: Clinical and Experimental Research, 37*(4), 675–686. doi:10.1111/acer.12002

Urban, J., Carlson, E., Egeland, B., & Sroufe, A. L. (1991). Patterns of individual adaptation across childhood: Attachment and developmental psychopathology [Special Issue]. *Developmental Psychology, 3*, 445–460.

Ussher, M., Taylor, A. H., & Faulkner, G. (2012). Exercise for smoking cessation. *Mental Health and Physical Activity, 5*(1), 99–100. doi:10.1016/j.mhpa.2011.12.001

V

Vaillant, G. E. (1984). The disadvantages of DSM-III outweigh its advantages. *American Journal of Psychiatry, 141*, 542–545.

Vaillant, G. E. (1994a). Ego mechanisms of defense and personality psychopathology. *Journal of Abnormal Psychology, 103*, 44–50.

Vaillant, G. E. (1994b). Behavioral medicine over the life span. In S. J. Blumenthal, K. Mathews, & S. M. Weiss (Eds.), *New research frontiers in behavioral medicine: Proceedings of the national conference*. Washington, DC: National Institutes of Health.

Valenstein, E. S. (1986). *Great and desperate cures: The rise and decline of psychosurgery and other radical treatments for mental illness*. New York: Basic Books.

Valenstein, E. S. (Ed.). (1980). *The psychosurgery debate: Scientific, legal and ethical perspectives*. San Francisco: Freeman.

van Amsterdam, J., & van den Brink, W. (2013). Reduced-risk drinking as a viable treatment goal in problematic alcohol use and alcohol dependence. *Journal of Psychopharmacology, 27*(11), 987–997. doi:10.1177/0269881113495320

VandenBos, G. R., & Stapp, J. (1983). Service providers in psychology: Results of the 1982 APA human resources survey. *American Psychologist, 38*, 1330–1352.

van de Nes, J. P., Nafe, R., & Schlote, W. (2008). Non-tau based neuronal degeneration in Alzheimer's disease—An immunocytochemical and quantitative study in the supragranular layers of the middle temporal neocortex. *Brain Research, 1213*, 152–165. doi:10.1016/j.brainres.2008.03.043

van der Heiden, C., & Melchior, K. (2012). Cognitive-behavioral therapy for adjustment disorder: A preliminary study. *The Behavior Therapist, 35*(3), 57–60.

van der Heijden, K. B., Smits, M. G., & Gunning, W. B. (2005). Sleep-related disorders in ADHD: A review. *Clinical Pediatrics, 44*, 201–210.

van der Heijden, P. T., Egger, J. M., & Derksen, J. L. (2008). Psychometric evaluation of the MMPI-2 restructured clinical scales in two Dutch samples. *Journal of Personality Assessment, 90*, 456–464. doi:10.1080/00223890802248745

van der Heijden, P. T., Egger, J. I. M., Rossi, G. M. P., Grundel, G., & Derksen, J. J. L. (2013). The MMPI-2-restructured form and the standard MMPI-2 clinical scales in relation to *DSM-IV. European Journal of Psychological Assessment, 29*, 182–188.

van der Klink, J. J., Blonk, R. W., Schene, A. H., & van Dijk, F. J. (2003). Reducing long term sickness absence by an activating intervention in adjustment disorders: A cluster randomised controlled design. *Occupational and Environmental Medicine, 60*(6), 429–437.

VanderLaan, D. P., Gothreau, L. M., Bartlett, N. H., & Vasey, P. L. (2010). Separation anxiety in feminine boys: Pathological or prosocial? *Journal of Gay & Lesbian Mental Health, 15*(1), 30–45. doi:10.1080/19359705.2011.530570

van der Oord, S., Bögels, S. M., & Peijnenburg, D. (2012). The effectiveness of mindfulness training for children with ADHD and mindful parenting for their parents. *Journal of Child and Family Studies, 21*(1), 139–147. doi:10.1007/s10826-011-9457-0

van der Oord, S., Prins, P. J. M., Oosterlaan, J., & Emmelkamp, P. M. G. (2008). Efficacy of methylphenidate, psychosocial treatments and their combination in school-aged children with ADHD: A meta-analysis. *Clinical Psychology Review, 28*, 783–800.

van Dessel, N., den Boeft, M., van der Wouden, J. C., Kleinstäuber, M., Leone, S. S., Terluin, B., . . . van Marwijk, H. (2014). Non-pharmacological interventions for somatoform disorders and medically unexplained physical symptoms (MUPS) in adults. In The Cochrane Collaboration (Ed.), *Cochrane database of systematic reviews*. Chichester, UK: John Wiley & Sons. Retrieved on November 1, 2014 from http://doi.wiley.com/10.1002/14651858.CD011142.pub2

Vangeli, E., Stapleton, J., Smit, E. S., Borland, R., & West, R. (2011).Predictors of attempts to stop smoking and their success in adult general population samples: A systematic review. *Addiction, 16*, 2110–2121. doi: 10.1111/j.1360-0443.2011.03565.x.2011-25715-01110.1111/j.1360-0443.2011.03565.x

Van Hoesen, G. W., & Damasio, A. R. (1987). Neural correlates of cognitive impairment in Alzheimer's disease. In F. Blum (Ed.), *Handbook of physiology: Section I. The nervous system: Vol. V. Higher functions of the brain*, Bethesda, MD: American Physiological Society.

Van Houtem, C. H., Laine, M. L., Boomsma, D. I., Ligthart, L. L., van Wijk, A. J., & De Jongh, A. A. (2013). A review and meta-analysis of the heritability of specific phobia subtypes and corresponding fears. *Journal of Anxiety Disorders, 27*(4), 379–388. doi:10.1016/j.janxdis.2013.04.007

van Ijzendoorn, M. H., & Kroonenberg P. M. (1988). Cross-cultural patterns of attachment: A meta-analysis of the strange situation. *Child Development, 59*, 147–156.

Van Meter, A., Youngstrom, E. A., Demeter, C., & Findling, R. L. (2013). Examining the validity of cyclothymic disorder in a youth sample: Replication and extension. *Journal of Abnormal Child Psychology, 41*(3), 367–378. doi:10.1007/s10802-012-9680-1

Van Meter, A. R., Youngstrom, E. A., & Findling, R. L. (2012). Cyclothymic disorder: A critical review. *Clinical Psychology Review, 32*(4), 229–243. doi:10.1016/j.cpr.2012.02.001

van Ours, J. C. (2012). The long and winding road to cannabis legalization. *Addiction, 107*(5), 872–873. doi:10.1111/j.1360-0443.2011.03625.x

Van Overwalle, F. (2009). Social cognition and the brain: A meta-analysis. *Human Brain Mapping, 30*(3), 829–858. doi: 10.1002/hbm.20547

van Reekum, R., Cohen, T., & Wong, J. (2000). Can traumatic brain injury cause psychiatric disorders? *The Journal of Neuropsychiatry and Clinical Neurosciences, 12*(3), 316–327. doi: 10.1176/appi.neuropsych.12.3.316

van Reekum, R., Conway, C. A., Gansler, D., White, R., & Bachman, D. L. (1993). Neurobehavioral study of borderline personality disorder. *Journal of Psychiatry and Neuroscience, 18*(3): 121–129.

Varadaraj, R., Norman, R. C., Caroff, S. N., Mann, S., Sullivan, K., & Antelo, E. (1994). Progression of symptoms in neuroleptic malignant syndrome. *Journal of Nervous and Mental Disease, 182*, 168–173.

Vaughan, E. (1993). Individual and cutural differences in adaptation to environmental risks. *American Psychologist, 48*, 673–680.

Vaughn, C., & Leff, J. (1976). Measurement of expressed emotion in the families of psychiatric patients. *British Journal of Social and Clinical Psychology, 15*, 157–165.

Vaughn, C., Sorenson, K., Jones, S., Freeman, W, & Falloon, I. (1984). Family factors in schizophrenia relapse: Replication in California of British research on expressed emotion. *Archives of General Psychiatry, 41*, 1169–1177.

Vedantam, S. (2005, June 27). Social network's healing power is borne out in poorer nations. *The Washington Post*. Retrieved on November 6, 2014 from http://www.washingtonpost.com/wp-dyn/content/article/2005/06/26/AR2005062601091.html

Velamoor, V. R., Norman, R. M., Caroff, S. N., Mann, S. C., Sullivan, K., & Antelo, R. E. (1994). Progression of symptoms in neuromalignant syndrome. *The Journal of Nervous and Mental Disease, 182*, 168–173.

Veling, W., Susser, E., Os, J. V., Mackenbach, J. P., Selten, J., & Hoek, H. W. (2008). Ethnic density of neighborhoods and incidence of psychotic disorders among immigrants. *The American Journal of Psychiatry, 165*, 66–73.

Vellutino, F., & Scanlon, D. (1985). Verbal memory in poor and normal readers: Developmental differences in the use of linguistic codes. In D. B. Gray & J. F. Kavanagh (Eds.), *Biobehavioral measures of dyslexia* (pp. 117–214). Parkton, MD: York Press.

Venables, P. H. (1996). Schizotypy and maternal exposure to influenza and to cold temperature: The Mauritius study. *Journal of Abnormal Psychology, 105*, 53–60.

Venkatesh, B. K., Thrithalli, J., Naveen, M. N., Kishorekumar, K., Arunachala U., Venkatasubramanian, G., . . . Gangadhar, B. (2008). Sex difference in age of onset of schizophrenia: Findings from a community-based study in India. *World Psychiatry, 7*, 173–176.

Venner, K. L., & Feldstein, S. W. (2006). Natural history of alcohol dependence and remission events for a Native American sample. *Journal of Studies on Alcohol, 67*(5), 675–684.

Venner, K. L., & Miller, W. R. (2001). Progression of alcohol problems in a Navajo sample. *Journal of Studies on Alcohol, 62*(2), 158–165.

Ventura, J., Nuechterlein, K. H., Lukoff, D., & Hardesty, J. P. (1989). A prospective study of stressful life events and schizophrenic relapse. *Journal of Abnormal Psychology, 98*, 407–411.

Verhaeghen, P., Joorman, J., & Khan, R. (2005). Why we sing the blues: The relation between self-reflective rumination, mood, and creativity. *Emotion, 5*(2), 226–232. doi:10.1037/1528-3542.5.2.226

Verhaeghen, P., Joormann, J., & Aikman, S. N. (2014). Creativity, mood, and the examined life: Self-reflective rumination boosts creativity, brooding breeds dysphoria. *Psychology of Aesthetics, Creativity, and the Arts, 8*(2), 211–218. doi:10.1037/a0035594

Verheul, R., & Herbrink, M. (2007). The efficacy of various modalities of psychotherapy for personality disorders: A systematic review of the evidence and clinical recommendations. *International Review of Psychiatry, 19*(1), 25–38. doi:10.1080/09540260601095399

Verhulst, F. C., Eussen, M. L. J. M., Berden, G. F. M. G., Sanders-Woudstra, J., & Van Der Ende, J. (1993). Pathways of problem behaviors from childhood to adolescence. *Journal of the American Academy of Child Adolescence Psychiatry, 32*, 388–396.

Verhulst, J., & Heiman, J. (1988). A systems perspective on sexual desire. In S. R. Leiblum & R. C. Rosen (Eds.), *Perspectives on sexual desire* (pp. 168–191). New York: Guilford Press.

Vermetten, E., Schmahl, C., Lindner, S., Loewenstein, R. J., & Bremner, J. D. (2006). Hippocampal and amygdalar volumes in dissociative identity disorder. *American Journal of Psychiatry, 163*, 630–636.

Vernberg, E. M., La Greca, A. M., Silverman, W. K., & Prinstein, M. J. (1996). Prediction of posttraumatic stress symptoms in children after Hurricane Andrew. *Journal of Abnormal Psychology', 105*, 237–248.

Videbech, P. (2000). PET measurements of brain glucose metabolism and blood flow in major depressive disorder: A critical review. *Acta Psychiatrica Scandinavica, 101*(1), 11–20. doi:10.1034/j.1600-0447.2000.101001011.x

Vieta, E., Grunze, H., Azorin, J., & Fagiolini, A. (2014). Phenomenology of manic episodes according to the presence or absence of depressive features as defined in *DSM-5*: Results from the IMPACT self-reported online survey. *Journal of Affective Disorders, 156*, 206–213. doi:10.1016/j.jad.2013.12.031

Vieta, E., Günther, O., Locklear, J., Ekman, M., Miltenburger, C., Chatterton, M., . . . Paulsson, B. (2011). Effectiveness of psychotropic medications in the maintenance phase of bipolar disorder: A meta-analysis of randomized controlled trials. *International Journal of Neuropsychopharmacology, 14*(8), 1029–1049. doi:10.1017/S1461145711000885

Vik, P. W., Islam-Zwart, K. A., & Ruge, L. N. (2008). Application of the PTSD-alcohol expectancy questionnaire (P-AEQ) to sexually assaulted college women. *Addiction Research & Theory, 16*(6), 585–594. doi:10.1080/16066350701867273

Viken, R. J., & McFall, R. M. (1994). Paradox lost: Implications of contemporary reinforcement theory for behavior therapy. *Current Directions in Psychological Science, 3*, 121–125.

Virkkunen, M., & Narvanen, S. (1987). Plasma insulin, tryptophan and serotonin levels during the glucose tolerance test among habitually violent and impulsive offenders. *Neuropsychobiology, 17*, 19–23.

Vishnevsky, T., Cann, A., Calhoun, L. G., Tedeschi, R. G., & Demakis, G. J. (2010). Gender differences in self-reported posttraumatic growth: A meta-analysis. *Psychology of Women Quarterly, 34*(1), 110–120. doi:10.1111/j.1471-6402.2009.01546.x

Vismara, L. A., & Rogers, S. J. (2010). Behavioral treatments in autism spectrum disorder: What do we know? *Annual Review of Clinical Psychology, 6*, 447–468.

Visser, L., de Winter, A. F., Veenstra, R., Verhulst, F. C., & Reijneveld, S. A. (2013). Alcohol use and abuse in young adulthood: Do self-control and parents' perceptions of friends during adolescence modify peer influence? The TRAILS study. *Addictive Behaviors, 38*(12), 2841–2846. doi:10.1016/j.addbeh.2013.08.013

Visser, L., de Winter, A. F., Vollebergh, W. M., Verhulst, F. C., & Reijneveld, S. A. (2013). The impact of parenting styles on adolescent alcohol use: The TRAILS study. *European Addiction Research, 19*(4), 165–172.

Visser, S., & Bouman, T. K. (2001). The treatment of hypochondriasis: Exposure plus response prevention vs cognitive therapy. *Behaviour Research and Therapy, 39*(4), 423–442. doi:10.1016/S0005-7967(00)00022-X

Vitiello, B. (2013). How effective are the current treatments for children diagnosed with manic/mixed bipolar disorder? *CNS Drugs, 27*(5), 331–333. doi:10.1007/s40263-013-0060-3

Vlachos, F., Andreou, E., & Delliou, A. (2013). Brain hemisphericity and developmental dyslexia. *Research in Developmental Disabilities, 34*(5), 1536–1540. doi:10.1016/j.ridd.2013.01.027

Vocks, S., Tuschen-Caffier, B., Pietrowsky, R., Rustenbach, S. J., Kersting, A., & Herpertz, S. (2010). Meta-analysis of the effectiveness of psychological and pharmacological treatments for binge eating disorder. *International Journal of Eating Disorders, 43*(3), 205–217.

Vogt, D. S., King, D. W., & King, L. A. (2007). Risk pathways for PTSD. In M.J. Friedman, T.M. Keane, & P.A. Resick (Eds.), *Handbook of PTSD: Science and practice* (pp. 99–113). New York: KluwerAcademic/Plenum.

Vohs, K. D., Bardone, A. M., Joiner Jr., T. E., Abramson, L. Y., & Heatherton, T. F. (1999). Perfectionism, perceived weight status, and self-esteem interact to predict bulimic symptoms: A model of bulimic symptom development, *Journal of Abnormal Psychology, 108*(4), 695–700.

Volkmar, F. R. (1992). Autism and the pervasive developmental disorders. In M. Lewis (Ed.), *Child and adolescent psychiatry: A comprehensive textbook* (pp. 499–508). Baltimore: Williams & Wilkins.

Volpicelli, J. R., Alterman, A. I., Hayashida, M., & O'Brien, C. P. (1992). Naltrexone in the treatment of alcohol dependence. *Archives of General Psychiatry, 49*, 876–880.

Volpp, S. (2012). Adjustment disorder: Queer stressors: Adjustment disorder in a lesbian mother. In P. Levounis, J. Drescher, & M. E. Barber (Eds.), *The LGBT casebook* (pp. 195–203). Arlington, VA: American Psychiatric Publishing, Inc.

von Bertalanffy, L. (1968). *General systems theory.* New York: Braziller.

Von Knorring, A. L., Cloninger, C. R., Boham, M., & Sigvardsson, S. (1983). An adoption study of depressive disorders and substance abuse. *Archives of General Psychiatry, 40*, 943–950.

Von Korff, M., Dworkin, S. F., & LeResche, L. (1990). Graded chronic pain status: An epidemiologic evaluation. *Pain, 40*, 2791.

von Wolff, A. A., Hölzel, L. P., Westphal, A. A., Härter, M. M., & Kriston, L. L. (2013). Selective serotonin reuptake inhibitors and tricyclic antidepressants in the acute treatment of chronic depression and dysthymia: A systematic review and meta-analysis. *Journal of Affective Disorders, 144*(1–2), 7–15. doi:10.1016/j.jad.2012.06.007

Vreeburg, S. A., Hoogendijk, W. G., Pelt, J., DeRijk, R. H., Verhagen, J. M., van Dyck, R., . . . Penninx, B. H. (2009). Major depressive disorder and hypothalamic-pituitary-adrenal axis activity: Results from a large cohort study. *Archives of General Psychiatry, 66*(6), 617–626. doi:10.1001/archgenpsychiatry.2009.50

W

Wager, T. D., & Smith, E. E. (2003). Neuroimaging studies of working memory: A meta-analysis. *Cognitive, Affective, & Behavioral Neuroscience, 3*, 255–274. doi:10.3758/CABN.3.4.255

Wagner, K., Redden, L., Kowatch, R. A., Wilens, T. E., Segal, S., Chang, K., . . . Saltarelli, M. (2009). A double-blind, randomized, placebo-controlled trial of divalproex extended-release in the treatment of bipolar disorder in children and adolescents. *Journal of the American Academy of Child & Adolescent Psychiatry, 48*(5), 519–532. doi:10.1097/CHI.0b013e31819c55ec

Waite, L. J., & Joyner, K. (2001). Emotional satisfaction and physical pleasure in sexual unions: Time horizon, sexual behavior, and sexual exclusivity. *Journal of Marriage and the Family. 63*, 247–264.

Wakefield, A. J., Murch, S. H., Anthony, A., Linnell, J., Casson, D. M., . . . Walker-Smith, J. A. (1998). Ileal-lymphoid-nodular hyperplasia, nonspecific colitis, and pervasive developmental disorder in children. *Lancet, 351*(9103), 637–641.

Wakefield, H., & Underwager, R. (1992). Recovered memories of alleged sexual abuse: Lawsuits against parents. *Behavioral Sciences and the Law, 10*, 483–507.

Wakefield, J. C. (1992). The concept of mental disorder: On the boundary between biological facts and social values. *American Psychology, 47*, 373–388.

Wakefield, J. C. (2011). *DSM-5* proposed diagnostic criteria for sexual paraphilias: Tensions between diagnostic validity and forensic utility. *International Journal of Law & Psychiatry, 34*, 195–209. doi: 10.1016/j.ijlp.2011.04.012.

Walach, H., & Kirsch, I. (2003). Herbal treatments and antidepressant medication: Similar data, divergent conclusions. In S.O. Lilienfeld, S. Lynn, & J. M. Lohr (Eds.), *Science and pseudoscience in clinical psychology* (pp. 306–330). New York: Guilford Press.

Waldman, I. D., & Gizer, I. R. (2006). The genetics of attention deficit/hyperactivity disorder. *Clinical Psychology Review, 26*(4), 396–432. doi:10.1016/j.cpr.2006.01.007

Waldman, I. D., & Rhee, S. H. (2006). Genetic and environmental influences on psychopathy and antisocial behavior. In C. J. Patrick (Ed.), *Handbook of psychopathy* (pp. 205–228). New York: Guilford Press.

Walker, C. E., Hedberg, A., Clement, P. W., & Wright, L. (1981). *Clinical procedures for behavior therapy.* Engle-wood Cliffs, NJ: Prentice Hall.

Walker, D., Greenwood, C. R., Hart, B., & Carta, J. (1994). Prediction of school outcomes based on early language production and socioeconomic factors: Children and poverty [Special Issue]. *Child Development, 65*, 606–621.

Walker, E. F., Grimes, K. E., Davis, D., & Smith, A. (1993). Childhood precursors of schizophrenia: Facial expressions of emotion. *American Journal of Psychiatry, 150*, 1654–1660.

Walker, H. (2008). *Breaking free: My life with dissociative identity disorder.* Austin, TX: Touchstone.

Walker, L. S., Garber, J., & Greene, J. W. (1994). Somatic complaints in pediatric patients: A prospective study of the role of negative life events, child social and academic competence, and parental somatic symptoms. *Journal of Consulting and Clinical Psychology, 62*, 1213–1221.

Wallace, C. J. (1993). Psychiatric rehabilitation. *Psychopharmacology Bulletin, 29*, 537–548.

Waller, N. G., & Ross, C. A. (1997). The prevalence of biometric structure of pathological dissociation in the general population: Taxometric and behavior genetic findings. *Journal of Abnormal Psychology, 106*, 499–510.

Walsh, B. T. (1988). Pharmacotherapy of eating disorders. In B. J. Blinder, B. F. Chaitin, & R. Goldstein (Eds.), *The eating disorders* (pp. 469–476). PMA Publishing Corporation.

Walsh, S. L., June, H. L., Schuh, K. J., Preston, K. L., Bigelow, G. E., & Stitzer, M. L. (1995). Effects of buprenorphine and methadone in methadone-maintained subjects. *Psychopharmacology, 119*, 268–276.

Walter, H. I., & Gilmore, S. K. (1973). Placebo versus social learning effects in parent training procedures designed to alter the behavior of aggressive boys. *Behavior Therapy, 4*, 361–377.

Walters, S. T., & Neighbors, C. (2005). Feedback interventions for college alcohol misuse: What, why and for whom? *Addictive Behaviors, 30*(6), 1168–1182. doi:10.1016/j.addbeh.2004.12.005

Walther, M., Ricketts, E., Conelea, C., & Woods, D. (2010). Recent advances in the understanding and treatment of trichotillomania. *Journal of Cognitive Psychotherapy, 24*, 46–64. doi:10.1891/0889-8391.24.1.46

Wang, H. H., Wu, S.Z., & Liu, Y.Y. (2003). Association between social support and health outcomes: A meta-analysis. *Kaohsiung Journal of Medical Science, 19*, 345–351.

Wang, K., Liu, X., Zhang, Q., Pan, Y., Aragam, N., & Zeng, M. (2011). A meta-analysis of two genome-wide association studies identifies 3 new loci for alcohol dependence. *Journal of Psychiatric Research, 45*(11), 1419–1425. doi:10.1016/j.jpsychires.2011.06.005

Wang, Y., & Watson, R. R. (1995). Is alcohol consumption a cofactor in the development of acquired immunodeficiency syndrome? *Alcohol, 12*, 105–109.

Warburton, D. M. (1995). Effects of caffeine on cognition and mood without caffeine abstinence. *Psychopharmacology, 119,* 66–70.

Warden, D. (2006). Military TBI during Iraq and Afghanistan wars. *Journal of Head Trauma and Rehabilitation, 21,* 398–402.

Wark, D. M. (2008). What we can do with hypnosis: A brief note. *American Journal of Clinical Hypnosis, 51*(1), 29–36. doi:10.1080/00029157.2008.10401640

Warneke, L. B. (1991). Benzodiazepines: Abuse and new use. *Canadian Journal of Psychiatry, 36,* 194–205.

Warner, J. O. (1993). Food and behaviour: allergy, intolerance or aversion. *Pediatric Allergy and Immunology, 4,* 112–116.

Warner, L. A., Kessler, R. C., Hughes, M., Anthony, J. C., & Nelson, C. B. (1995). Prevalence and correlates of drug use and dependence in the United States. *Archives of General Psychiatry, 52,* 219–229.

Warner, M. D., Peabody, C., Boutros, N., & Whiteford, H. (1990). Alprazolam and withdrawal seizures. *Journal of Nervous and Mental Disease, 178,* 208–209.

Warren, J., Murrie, D. C., Stejskal, W., Colwell, L. H., Morris, J., Chauhan, P., & Dietz, P. (2006). Opinion formation in evaluating the adjudicative competence and restorability of criminal defendants: A review of 8,000 evaluations. *Behavioral Sciences & the Law, 24*(2), 113–132.

Wartenberg, A. A., Nirenberg, T. D., Liepman, M. R., Silvia, L. Y., Begin, A. M., & Monti, P. M. (1990). Detoxification of alcoholics: Improving care by symptom-triggered sedation. *Alcoholism in Clinical and Experimental Research, 14,* 71–75.

Washington v. Harper, 494 U.S. 210 (1990).

Washington, S. D., Gordon, E. M., Brar, J., Warburton, S., Sawyer, A. T., Wolfe, A., . . . VanMeter, J. W. (2014). Dysmaturation of the default mode network in autism. *Human Brain Mapping, 35*(4), 1284–1296. doi:10.1002/hbm.22252

Watanabe, N., Churchill, R., & Furukawa, T. A. (2007). Combination of psychotherapy and benzodiazepines versus either therapy alone for panic disorder: A systematic review. *BMC Psychiatry, 7,* 18. doi:10.1186/1471-244X-7-18

Waterhouse, B. D., Sessler, F. M., Cheng, J. G., Woodward, D. J., Azizi, S. A., and Moises, H. C. (1988). New evidence for a gating action of norepinephrine in central neuronal circuits of mammalian brain. *Brain Research Bulletin, 1,* 425–432.

Waterman, B., & Lewandowski, L. (1993). Phonologic and semantic processing in reading-disabled and nondisabled males at two age levels. *Journal of Experimental Child Psychology, 55,* 87–103.

Watkins, J. (1984). The Bianchi (L. A. Hillside Strangler) case: Sociopath or multiple personality? *The International Journal of Clinical and Experimental Hypnosis, 2,* 67–101.

Watson, A. C., Morabito, M. S., Draine, J., & Ottati, V. (2008). Improving police response to persons with mental illness: A multi-level conceptualization of CIT. *International Journal of Law and Psychiatry, 31*(4), 359–368. doi:10.1016/j.ijlp.2008.06.004

Watson, C., Quilty, L. C., & Bagby, R. (2011). Differentiating bipolar disorder from major depressive disorder using the MMPI-2-RF: A receiver operating characteristics (ROC) analysis. *Journal of Psychopathology and Behavioral Assessment, 33*(3), 368–374. doi:10.1007/s10862-010-9212-7

Watson, C. G., Anderson, P., Gearhart, L. P. (1995). Post-traumatic stress disorder (PTSD) symptoms in PTSD patients' families of origin. *Journal of Nervous and Mental Disease, 183,* 633–638.

Watson, D., Clark, L. A., & Harkness, A. R. (1994). Structures of personality and their relevance to psychopathology. *Journal of Abnormal Psychology, 103,* 18–31.

Watson, D., & Kendall, P. C. (1989). Understanding anxiety and depression: Their relation to negative and positive affective states. In P. C. Kendall & D. Watson (Eds.), *Anxiety and depression: Distinctive and overlapping features* (pp. 3–26). San Diego: Academic Press.

Watson, H. J., & Bulik, C. M. (2013). Update on the treatment of anorexia nervosa: Review of clinical trials, practice guidelines and emerging interventions. *Psychological Medicine, 43*(12), 2477–2500.

Watson, H. J., & Rees, C. S. (2008). Meta-analysis of randomized, controlled treatment trials for pediatric obsessive-compulsive disorder. *Journal of Child Psychology and Psychiatry, 49,* 489–498. doi:10.1111/j.1469-7610.2007.01875.x

Watson, J. B., & Rayner, R. (1920). Conditioned emotional reaction. *Journal of Experimental Psychology, 3,* 1–14.

Watt, N. F., & Saiz, C. (1991). Longitudinal studies of premorbid development of adult schizophrenics. In P. F. Walker (Ed.), *Schizophrenia: A life-course in developmental perspective.* San Diego: Academic Press.

Webb, C., Pfeiffere, M., Mueser, K. T., Mensch, E., DeGirolomo, J., & Levenson, D. F. (1998). Burden and well-being of caregivers for the severely mentally ill: The role of coping style and social support. *Schizophrenia Research, 34,* 169–180.

Webster-Stratton, C. (1984). Randomized trial of two parent training programs for families with conduct disordered children. *Journal of Consulting and Clinical Psychology, 52,* 666–678.

Wechsler, D. (1981). *Wechsler Adult Intelligence Scale-Revised.* New York: Psychological Corporation.

Wechsler, D. (1991). *WISC-III: Manual.* San Antonio, TX: Psychological Corporation.

Wechsler, D. (2003). *The Wechsler Intelligence Scale for Children—Fourth edition.* San Antonio, TX: Psychological Corporation.

Wechsler, D. (2008). *WAIS-IV administration and scoring manual.* San Antonio, TX: Psychological Corporation.

Wechsler, H., Lee, J. E., Kuo, M., & Lee, H. (2000). College binge drinking in the 1990s: A continuing problem. *Journal of American College Health, 48,* 199–210.

Wehr, T. A., & Sack, D. A. (1987). Sleep disruption: A treatment for depression and a cause of mania. *Psychiatric Annals, 17*(10), 654–663.

Wei, C. C., Wan, L., Lin, W.-Y., & Tsai, F.-J. (2010). Rs 6313 polymorphism in 5-hydroxytryptamine receptor 2A gene association with polysymptomatic primary nocturnal enuresis. *Journal of Clinical Laboratory Analysis, 24,* 371–375.

Wei, Y., Szumilas, M., & Kutcher, S. (2010). Effectiveness on mental health of psychological debriefing for crisis intervention in schools. *Educational Psychology Review, 22*(3), 339–347. doi:10.1007/s10648-010-9139-2

Weiler, B. L., & Widom, C. S. (1996). Psychopathy and violent behaviour in abused and neglected young adults. *Criminal Behavior and Mental Health, 6,* 253–271.

Weinberger, D., Berman, K., & Torrey, E. F. (1992). Evidence of dysfunction of a prefrontal-limbic network in schizophrenia: A magnetic resonance imaging and blood flow study of discordant monozygotic twins. *American Journal of Psychiatry, 149,* 890–897.

Weinberger, L. E., Sreenivasan, S., Garrick, T., & Osran, H. (2005). The impact of surgical castration on sexual recidivism risk among sexually violent predatory offenders. *Journal of the American Academy of Psychiatry and the Law, 33*(1), 16–36.

Weiner, A., Weiner, Z., & Leonard, M. A. (1977). Bipolar manic-depressive disorder: A reassessment of course and outcome. *Comprehensive Psychiatry, 18,* 327–332.

Weintraub, K. (2011). The autism enigma. *Nature, 479,* 21–24.

Weintraub, S., Wicklund, A. H., & Salmon, D. P. (2012). The neuropsychological profile of Alzheimer disease. *Cold Spring Harbor Perspectives in Medicine, 2*(4), a006171. doi: 10.1101/cshperspect.a006171

Weisberg, R. B., Brown, T. A., Wincze, J. P., & Barlow, D. H. (2001). Causal attributions and male sexual arousal: The impact of attributions for a bogus erectile difficulty on sexual arousal, cognitions, and affect. *Journal of Abnormal Psychology, 110*(2), 324–334.

Weisenberg, M., Schwarzwald,, J., Waysman, M., Solomon, Z., & Klingman, A. (1993). Coping of school-age children in the sealed room during scud missile bombardment and postwar stress reactions. *Journal of Consulting and Clinical Psychology, 61,* 462–467.

Weishaar, M. E., & Beck, A. T. (1990). Cognitive approaches to understanding and treating suicidal behavior. In S. J. Blumenthal & D. J. Kupfer (Eds.), *Suicide over the life cycle: Risk factors, assessment, and treatment of suicidal patients* (pp. 469–498). Washington, DC: American Psychiatric Press.

Weiss, M. D., & Salpekar, J. (2010). Sleep problems in the child with attention-deficit/hyperactivity disorder: Defining aetiology and appropriate treatments. *CNS Drugs, 24*(10), 811–828. doi:10.2165/11538990-000000000-00000

Weiss, R. E., Stein, M. A., Trommer, B., & Refetoff, S. (1993). Attention-deficit hyperactivity disorder and thyroid function. *Journal of Pediatrics, 123,* 539–545.

Weisse, C. S. (1992). Depression and immunocompetence: A review of the literature. *Psychological Bulletin, 111,* 475–489.

Weissman, M. M. (1993). The epidemiology of personality disorders: A 1990 update. *Journal of Personality Disorders* (Suppl.), 44-62.

Weissman, M. M., Bruce, M. L., Leaf, P. J., Florio, L., & Holzer, C. (1991). Affective disorders. In L. N. Robins & D. A. Regier (Eds.), *Psychiatric disorders in America* (pp. 53–80). New York: The Free Press.

Weissman, M. M., Klerman, G. L., Markowitz^ J. S., & Ouellette, R. (1989). Suicidal ideation and suicide attempts in panic disorder and attacks. *New England Journal of Medicine, 321,* 1209–1214.

Weisz, J. R., Suwanlert, S., Chaiyasit, W., & Walter, B. R. (1987). Over- and undercontrolled clinic-referral problems among Thai and American children and adolescents: The *wat* and *wai* of cultural differences. *Journal of Consulting and Clinical Psychology, 55,* 719–726.

Weisz, J. R., Weiss, B., & Donenberg, G. R. (1992). The lab versus the clinic: Effects of child and adolescent psychotherapy. *American Psychologist, 47,* 1578–1585.

Weisz, J. R., Weiss, B., Suwanlert, S., & Chaiyasit, W. (2006). Culture and youth psychopathology: Testing the syndromal sensitivity model in Thai and American adolescents. *Journal of Consulting and Clinical Psychology, 74,* 1098–1107. doi:10.1037/0022-006X.74.6.1098

Wells, K., Katon, W., Rogers, B., & Camp, P. (1994). Use of minor tranquilizers and antidepressant medications by depressed outpatients: Results from the medical outcome studies. *American Journal of Psychiatry, 151,* 694–700.

Wells, K. B., Burnam, A., Rogers, W., Flays, R., & Camp, P. (1992). The course of depression in adult outpatients: Results from the Medical Outcome Study. *Archives of General Psychiatry, 49,* 788–794.

Wells, K. C., & Egan, J. (1988). Social learning and systems family therapy for childhood oppositional disorder: Comparative treatment outcome. *Comprehensive Psychiatry, 29,* 138–146.

Weltzin, T. E., Cornella-Carlson, T., Fitzpatrick, M. E., Kennington, B., Bean, P., & Jefferies, C. (2014). Treatment issues and outcomes for males with eating disorders. In L. Cohn & R. Lemberg (Eds.), *Current findings on males with eating disorders* (pp.151–167). New York, NY: Routledge.

Weltzin, T. E., Weisensel, N., Franczyk, D., Burnett, K., Klitz, C., & Bean, P. (2005). Eating disorders in men: Update. *The Journal of Men's Health & Gender, 2*(2), 186–193. doi: 10.1016/j.jmhg.2005.04.008

Wender, P. H., Kety, S. S., Rosenthal, D., Schulsinger, F., Ortmann, J., & Lunde, I. (1986). Psychiatric disorders in the biological and adoptive families of adopted individuals with affective disorders. *Archives of General Psychiatry, 43,* 923–929.

Wenk, G. L. (2014, November 21). Amotivational syndrome and marijuana use: Why does this syndrome only develop in some long-term users? *Psychology Today.* Retrieved on December 16, 2014 from http://www.psychologytoday.com/blog/your-brain-food/201411/amotivational-syndrome-and-marijuana-use

Wersebe, H., Sijbrandij, M., & Cuijpers, P. (2013). Psychological group-treatments of social anxiety disorder: A meta-analysis. *Plos ONE, 8*(11). doi:10.1371/journal.pone.0079034

Wesolowski, M. D., & Zawlocki, R. J. (1982). The differential effects of procedures to eliminate an injurious self-stimulating behavior (digito-ocular sign) in blind retarded twins. *Behavior Therapy, 13,* 334–345.

West Virginia Alcohol Beverage Control Administration (2014). *Blood alcohol chart.* Retrieved on December 11, 2014 from http://www.abca.wv.gov/enforcement/Documents/BAC%20Chart.pdf

Westermeyer, J. (1987). Cultural factors in clinical assessment. *Journal of Consulting and Clinical Psychology, 55,* 472–478.

Wetherill, L., Kapoor, M., Agrawal, A., Bucholz, K., Koller, D., Bertelsen, S. E., . . . Foroud, T. (2014). Family-based association analysis of alcohol dependence criteria and severity. *Alcoholism: Clinical and Experimental Research, 38*(2), 354–366. doi:10.1111/acer.12251

Wetzel, R. D., Guze, S. B., Cloninger, R., Martin, R. L., & Clayton, P. J. (1994). Briquet's syndrome (hysteria) is both a somatoform and a "psychoform" illness: A Minnesota Multiphasic Personality Inventory Study. *Psychosomatic Medicine, 56,* 564–569.

Wexler, B. E., & Cicchetti, D. V. (1992). The outpatient treatment of depression. Implications of outcome research for clinical practice. *Journal of Nervous and Mental Diseases, 180,* 277–286.

Wexler, D., & Winnick, B. J. (1991). *Essays in therapeutic jurisprudence.* Durham, NC: Carolina Academic Press.

Whalen, C. K., & Henker, B. (1991). Therapies for hyperactive children: Comparisons, combinations, and compromises. *Journal of Consulting and Clinical Psychology, 59,* 126–137.

Whalen, C. K., Henker, B., & Hinshaw, S. P. (1985). Cognitive-behavior therapies for hyperactive children: Premises, problems, and prospects. *Journal of Abnormal Child Psychology, 13,* 391–410.

Whalley, H. C., Mowatt, L., Standfield, A. C., Hall, J., Johnstone, E. C., Laurie, S. M., & McIntosh, A. M. (2007). Hypofrontality in subjects at increased risk of schizophrenia with depressive symptoms. *Journal of Affective Disorders, 109,* 99–106.

Whelan-Goodinson, R., Ponsford, J., Johnston, L., & Grant, F. (2009). Psychiatric disorders following traumatic brain injury: Their nature and frequency. *The Journal of Head Trauma Rehabilitation, 24*(5), 324–332. doi: 10.1097/HTR.0b013e3181a712aa

Whiffen, V. E. (1992). Is postpartum depression a distinct diagnosis? *Clinical Psychology Review, 12,* 485–508.

Whiffen, V. E., & Gotlib, I. H. (1993). Comparison of post-partum and nonpostpartum depression: Clinical presentation, psychiatric history, and psychosocial functioning. *Journal of Clinical and Consulting Psychology, 61,* 485–494.

Whitam, F. L., Diamond, M., & Martin, J. (1993). Homosexual orientation in twins: A report on 61 pairs and three triplet sets. *Archives of Sexual Behavior, 22,* 187–206.

White, J., Moffitt, T. E., Earls, F., Robins, L., & Silva, P. (1990). How early can we tell? Preschool predictors of conduct disease. *Criminology, 28,* 507–533.

White, K. S., & Barlow, D. H. (2002). Panic disorder and agoraphobia. In D.H. Barlow (Ed.), *Anxiety and its disorders* (2nd ed.). New York: Guilford Press.

Whitehead, B. S. (2004). *Winter seasonal affective disorder: A global biocultural perspective.* Retrieved on July 30, 2014 from http://www.as.ua.edu/ant/bindon/ant570/Papers/Whitehead.pdf

Wible, C. G., Kubicki, M., Yoo, S. S., Kacher, D. F., Salisbury, D. F., Anderson, M. C., . . . McCarley, R.W. (2001). A functional magnetic resonance imaging study of auditory mismatch in schizophrenia. *The American Journal of Psychiatry, 158,* 938–943.

Wichmann, T., & DeLong, M. R. (1996). Functional and pathophysiological models of the basal ganglia. *Current Opinions in Neurobiology, 6*(6), 751–758. doi:10.1016/S0959-4388(96)80024-9.

Widiger, T., & Frances, A. (1989). Epidemiology, diagnosis, and comorbidity of borderline personality disorder. In A. Tasman, R. Hales, & A. Frances (Eds.), *American Psychiatric Press Review of Psychiatry* (Vol. 8, pp. 8–24). Washington, DC: American Psychiatric Press.

Widiger, T., Frances, A., & Trull, T. (1987). A psychometric analysis of the social-interpersonal and cognitive-perceptual items for the schizoptypal personality disorder. *Archives of General Psychiatry, 44,* 741–745.

Widiger, T., Miele, G., & Tilly, S. (1992). Alternative perspectives on the diagnosis of borderline personality disorder. In J. Clarkin, E. Marziali, & H. Munroe-Blum (Eds.), *Borderline personality disorder: Clinical and empirical perspectives* (pp. 89–115). New York: Guilford Press.

Widiger, T., & Spitzer, R. (1991). Sex bias in the diagnosis of personality disorders. *Clinical Psychology Review, 11,* 1–22.

Widiger, T., & Trull, T. (1991). Diagnosis and clinical assessment. *Annual Review of Psychology, 42,* 109–133.

Widiger, T., & Weissman, M. (1991). Epidemiology of borderline personality disorder. *Hospital and Community Psychiatry, 42,* 1015–1021.

Widiger, T. A., & Costa, P. T., Jr. (1994). Personality and personality disorders. *Journal of Abnormal Psychology, 103,* 78–91.

Widiger, T. A., Frances, A. J., Pincus, H. A., Davis, W. W., & First, M. B. (1991). Toward an empirical classification for the DSM-IV. *Journal of Abnormal Psychology, 100,* 280–288.

Widiger, T. A., Frances, A. J., Pincus, H. A., First, M., Ross, R., & Davis, W. (Eds.). (1994). *DSM-IV Sourcebook* (Vol 1). Washington, DC: American Psychiatric Press.

Widiger, T. A., Livesley, W. J., & Clark, L. A. (2009). An integrative dimensional classification of personality disorder. *Psychological Assessment, 21*(3), 243–255.

Widiger, T. A., Mangine, S., Corbitt, E. M., Ellis, C. G., & Thomas, G. V. (1995). *Personality disorder interview-IV: A semistructured interview for the assessment of personality disorders.* Odessa, FL: Psychological Assessment Resources.

Widiger, T. A., & Mullins-Sweatt, S. N. (2009). Five-factor model of personality disorder: A proposal for *DSM-V. Annual Review of Clinical Psychology, 5,* 197–220.

Widiger, T. A., & Rogers, J. H. (1989). Prevalence and comorbidity of personality disorders. *Psychiatric Annals, 19,* 132–136.

Widiger, T. A., & Trull, T. J. (1991). Diagnosis and clinical assessment. *Annual Review of Psychology, 42,* 109–133.

Widiger, T. A., & Trull, T. J. (2007). Plate tectonics in the classification of personality disorder: Shifting to a dimensional model. *American Psychologist, 62,* 71–83.

Widiger, T. A., Trull, T. J., Hurt, S. W., Clarkin, J., & Frances, A. (1987). A multidimensional scaling of the DSM-III personality disorders. *Archives of General Psychiatry, 44,* 557–563.

Widom, C. S. (1989). Child abuse, neglect, and adult behavior: Research design and findings on criminality, violence, and child abuse. *American Journal of Orthopsychiatry, 59,* 355–367.

Widom, C. S. (1992). The cycle of violence. *National Institute of Justice Research in Brief.* Washington, DC: U.S. Department of Justice.

Wiederhold, B. K., & Wiederhold, M. D. (2005). Claustrophobia. In *Virtual reality therapy for anxiety disorders: Advances in evaluation and treatment* (pp. 165–171). Washington, DC: American Psychological Association. doi:10.1037/10858-015

Wiers, R. W., van Woerden N., Smulders, F. T., & De Jong, P. J. (2002). Implicit and explicit alcohol-related cognitions in heavy and light drinkers. *Journal of Abnormal Psychology, 111,* 648–658.

Wiggins, J. S., & Pincus, A. L. (1989). Conceptions of personality disorders and dimensions of personality. *Psychological Assessment: A Journal of Consulting and Clinical Psychology, 1,* 305–316.

Wiggins, J. S., & Pincus. L. (1992). Personality: Structure and assessment. *Annual Review of Psychology, 43,* 473–504.

Wikipedia (n.d.). *Cedillo v. Secretary of Health and Human Services.* Retrieved on October 10, 2014 from http://en.wikipedia.org/wiki/Cedillo_v._Secretary_of_Health_and_Human_Services

Wilde, A. A., Chan, H. N., Rahman, B. B., Meiser, B. B., Mitchell, P. B., Schofield, P. R., & Green, M. J. (2014). A meta-analysis of the risk of major affective disorder in relatives of individuals affected by major depressive disorder or bipolar disorder. *Journal of Affective Disorders, 158,* 37–47. doi:10.1016/j.jad.2014.01.014

Wilfley, D. E., Agras, W. S., Telch, C. F., Rossiter, E. M., Schneider, J. A., Cole, A. G., Sifford, L., & Raeburn, S. D. (1993). Group cognitive-behavioral therapy and group interpersonal psychotherapy for the nonpurging bulimic individual: A controlled comparison. *Journal of Consulting and Clinical Psychology, 61,* 296–305.

Wilhelm, S., Phillips, K. A., & Steketee, G. (2013). *Cognitive-behavioral therapy for body dysmorphic disorder: A treatment manual.* New York: Guilford Press.

Williams, C. L, Arnold, C. B., & Wynder, E. L. (1977). Primary prevention of chronic disease beginning in childhood: The Know Your Body Program: Design of study. *Preventive Medicine, 6,* 344–357.

Williams, D. E., & McAdam, D. (2012). Assessment, behavioral treatment, and prevention of pica: Clinical guidelines and recommendations for practitioners. *Research in Developmental Disabilities, 33*(6), 2050–2057. doi: 10.1016/j.ridd.2012.04.001

Williams, J., Hadjistavropoulos, T., & Sharpe, D. (2006). A meta-analysis of psychological and pharmacological treatments for body dysmorphic disorder. *Behaviour Research and Therapy, 44*(1), 99–111. doi:10.1016/j.brat.2004.12.006

Williams, J. G., Crane, C., Barnhofer, T., Brennan, K., Duggan, D. S., Fennell, M. V., . . . Russell, I. T. (2014). Mindfulness-based cognitive therapy for preventing relapse in recurrent depression: A randomized dismantling trial. *Journal of Consulting and Clinical Psychology, 82*(2), 275–286. doi:10.1037/a0035036

Williams, L. M. (1994). Recall of childhood trauma: A prospective study of women's memories of child sexual abuse. *Journal of Consulting and Clinical Psychology, 62,* 1167–1176.

Williams, R. B., Jr., & Barefoot, J. C. (1988). Coronary-prone behavior: The emerging role of the hostility complex. In B. K. Houston & C. R. Snyder (Eds.), *Type A behavior pattern: Research, theory, and intervention* (pp. 189–211). New York: John Wiley & Sons.

Williams, S. L., & Zane, G. (1989). Guided mastery and stimulus exposure treatments for severe performance anxiety in agoraphobics. *Behaviour Research and Therapy, 27,* 237–246.

Wills, R. M., Faitler, S. L., & Snyder, D. K. (1987). Distinctiveness of behavioral versus insight-oriented marital therapy: An empirical analysis. *Journal of Consulting and Clinical Psychology, 55,* 685–690.

Wills, T. A., McNamara, G., Vaccaro, D, & Hirky, A. E. (1996). Escalated substance abuse: A longitudinal grouping analysis from early to middle adolescence. *Journal of Abnormal Psychology, 105,* 166–180.

Wilson, C. P. (1988). The psychoanalytic treatment of anorexia nervosa and bulimia. In B. J. Blinder, B. F. Chaitin, & R. Goldstein (Eds.), *The eating disorders* (pp. 433–446). Rockford, IL: PMA Publishing Corporation.

Wilson, H. A. (2014). Can antisocial personality disorder be treated? A meta-analysis examining the effectiveness of treatment in reducing recidivism for individuals diagnosed with ASPD. *The International Journal of Forensic Mental Health, 13*(1), 36–46. doi:10.1080/14999013.2014.890682

Wilson, W. H., Ellinwood, E. H., Mathew, R. J., & Johnson, K. (1994). Effects of marijuana on performance of a computerized cognitive-neuromotor test battery. *Psychiatry Research, 51,* 115–125.

Winchel, R. M., Stanley, B., & Stanley, M. (1990). Biochemical aspects of suicide. In S. J. Blumenthal & D. J. Kupfer (Eds.), *Suicide over the life cycle: Risk factors, assessment, and treatment of suicide patients* (pp. 96–127). Washington, DC: American Psychiatric Press.

Wincze, J., Steketee, G., & Frost, R. (2007). Categorization in compulsive hoarding. *Behaviour Research and Therapy, 45*(1), 63–72.

Wincze, J. P., & Carey, M. P. (2001). *Sexual dysfunctions: A guide for assessment and treatment.* New York, NY: Guilford Press.

Wincze, J. P., Bansal, S., & Malamud, M. (1986). Effects of medroxyprogesterone acetate on subjective arousal, arousal to erotic stimulation, and nocturnal penile tumescence in male sex offenders. *Archives of Sexual Behavior, 15,* 293–305.

Windle, M., & Windle, R. C. (1993). The continuity of behavioral expression among disinhibited and inhibited childhood subtypes. *Clinical Psychology Review, 13,* 741–762.

Winerman, L. (2005). Figuring out phobia. *Monitor on Psychology, 36*(7), 96.

Winett, R. A. (1995). A framework for health promotion and disease prevention programs. *American Psychologist, 50,* 341–350.

Winnicott, D. W. (1965). *The maturational processes and the facilitating environment.* New York: International Universities Press.

Winokur, G. (1986). Unipolar depression. In G. Winokur & P. Clayton (Eds.), *The medical basis of psychiatry* (pp. 60–79). Philadelphia: W. B. Saunders.

Winokur, G., Scharfetter, C. H., & Angst, J. J. (1985). The diagnostic value in assessing mood congruence in delusions and hallucinations and their relationship to the affective state. *European Archives of Psychiatry & Neurological Sciences, 234*(5), 299–302. doi:10.1007/BF00381040

Winston, A., Pollack, J., McCullough, L., Flegenheimer, W., Kestenbaum, R., & Trujillo, M. (1991). Brief dynamic psychotherapy of personality disorders. *Journal of Nervous and Mental Disease, 179,* 188–193.

Winter, D., Bradshaw, S., Bunn, F., & Wellsted, D. (2013). A systematic review of the literature on counselling and psychotherapy for the prevention of suicide: 1. Quantitative outcome and process studies. *Counselling & Psychotherapy Research, 13*(3), 164–183. doi:10.1080/14733145.2012.761717

Winthorst, W. H., Post, W. J., Meesters, Y., Penninx, B. J., & Nolen, W. A. (2011). Seasonality in depressive and anxiety symptoms among primary care patients and in patients with depressive and anxiety disorders; Results from the Netherlands Study of Depression and Anxiety. *BMC Psychiatry, 11,* 198. doi:10.1186/1471-244X-11-198

Wise, E. A. (2009). Selected MMPI-2 scores of forensic offenders in a community setting. *Journal of Forensic Psychology Practice, 9,* 299–309.

Wise, R. A., & Bozarth, M. A. (1987). A psychomotor stimulant theory of addiction. *Psychological Review, 94,* 469–492.

Wise, T. (1978). Where the public peril begins: A survey of psychotherapists to determine the effect of *Tarasoff. Stanford Law Review, 31,* 165–190.

Wisner, K. L., Moses-Kolko, E. L., & Sit, D. Y. (2010). Postpartum depression: A disorder in search of a definition. *Archives of Women's Mental Health, 13*(1), 37–40. doi:10.1007/s00737-009-0119-9

Wittchen, H., & Hoyer, J. (2001). Generalized anxiety disorder: Nature and course. *Journal of Clinical Psychiatry, 62*(Suppl11), 15–19.

Witztum, E., Margalit, H., & van der Hart, O. (2002). Combat-induced dissociative amnesia: Review and case example of generalized dissociative amnesia. *Journal of Trauma & Dissociation 3*(2), 35–55.

Wohl, M., & Gorwood, P. (2007). Paternal ages below or above 35 years old are associated with a different risk of schizophrenia in the offspring. *European Psychiatry, 22,* 22–26.

Wojakiewicz, A., Januel, D., Braha, S., Prkachin, K., Danziger, N., & Bouhassira, D. (2013). Alteration of pain recognition in schizophrenia. *European Journal of Pain, 17,* 1385–1392.

Wolf, E. J., Lunney, C. A., Miller, M. W., Resick, P. A., Friedman, M. J., & Schnurr, P. P. (2012). The dissociative subtype of PTSD: A replication and extension. *Depression and Anxiety, 29*(8), 679–688. doi:10.1002/da.21946

Wolf, E. M., & Crowther, J. H. (1992). An evaluation of behavioral and cognitive-behavioral group interventions for the treatment of bulimia nervosa in women. *International Journal of Eating Disorders, 11,* 3–15.

Wolfensberger, W. (1972). *Normalization: The principle of normalization in human services.* Toronto, Canada: National Institute of Mental Retardation.

Wolkin, A., Sanfilpo, M., Wolf, A., Angrist, B., Brodie, J., & Rotrosen, J. (1992). Negative symptoms and hypofrontality chronic schizophrenia. *Archives of General Psychiatry, 49,* 959–965.

Wolpe, J. (1958). *Psychotherapy by reciprocal inhibition.* Stanford, CA: Stanford University Press.

Wolpe, J., & Lazarus, A. A. (1966). *Behavior therapy techniques: A guide to the treatment of neuroses.* New York: Pergamon Press.

Wolraich, M. L., Lindgren, S. D., Stumbo, P. J., Stegink, L. D., Appelbaum, M. I., Kiritsy, M. C. (1994). Effects of diets high in sucrose or aspartame on the behavior and cognitive performance of children. *New England Journal of Medicine, 330,* 301–307.

Wolrich, M. K. (2011). Body dysmorphic disorder and its significance to social work. *Clinical Social Work Journal, 39*(1), 101–110. doi:10.1007/s10615-010-0289-y

Wolsk, B. (n.d.). *Working toward compassion and moderation.* Anxiety and Depression Association of America. Retrieved on September 23, 2014 from http://www.adaa.org/living-with-anxiety/personal-stories/working-toward-compassion-and-moderation

Wonderlich, S. A., Gordon, K. H., Mitchell, J. E., Crosby, R. D., & Engel, S. G. (2009). The validity and clinical utility of binge eating disorder. *International Journal of Eating Disorders, 42*(8), 687–705. doi:10.1002/eat.20719

Wood, J. A., Bootzin, R. R., Rosenhan, D., Nolen-Hoek-sema, S., & Jourden, F. (1992). Effects of the 1989 San Francisco earthquake on frequency and content of nightmares. *Journal of Abnormal Psychology, 101,* 219–224.

Wood, J. M., Nezworski, M. T., & Stejskal, W. J. (1996). The comprehensive system for the Rorschach: A critical examination. *Psychological Science, 7,* 3–10.

Wood, K., Harris, M. J., Morreale, A., & Rizos, A. (1988). Drug-induced psychosis and depression in the elderly. *Psychiatric Clinics of North America, 11,* 167–191.

Wood, L., Birtel, M., Alsawy, S., Pyle, M., & Morrison, A. (2014). Public perceptions of stigma towards people with schizophrenia, depression, and anxiety. *Psychiatry Research, 220*(1–2), 604–608. doi:10.1016/j.psychres.2014.07.012

Wood, L. F., & Jacobson, N. S. (1985). Marital distress. In D. Barlow (Ed.), *Clinical handbook of psychological disorders* (pp. 344–416). New York: Guilford Press.

Wood, R. L., Williams, C., & Kalyani, T. (2009). The impact of alexithymia on somatization after traumatic brain injury. *Brain Injury, 23*(7–8), 649–654. doi:10.1080/02699050902970786

Woods, P. A., Higson, P. J., & Tannahill, M. M. (1984). Token-economy programmes with chronic psychotic patients: The importance of direct measurement and objective evaluation for long-term maintenance. *Behaviour Research and Therapy, 22,* 41–51.

Woody, G. E., Luborsky, L., McLellan, A. T., & O'Brien, C. P. (1990). Corrections and revised analyses for psychotherapy in methadone maintenance patients. *Archives of General Psychiatry, 47,* 788–789.

Woody, G. E., McLellan, A. T., Luborsky, L., & O'Brien, C. P. (1995). Psychotherapy in community methadone programs: A validation study. *American Journal of Psychiatry, 152,* 1302–1308.

Workman, E. A., & LaVia, M. F. (1987). T-lymphocyte polyclonal proliferation: Effects of stress and stress response style on medical students taking national board examinations. *Clinical Immunology and Immunopathology, 43,* 308–313.

World Health Organization (WHO) (1968). *Manual of the international statistical classification of diseases, injuries, and causes of death (ICD-8).* Geneva, Switzerland: Author.

World Health Organization (WHO) (1978). *Schizophrenia: An international follow-up study.* London: John Wiley & Sons.

World Health Organization (WHO) (1992). *The ICD-10 classification of mental disorders: Clinical descriptions and diagnostic guide.* Geneva, Switzerland: Author.

World Health Organization (WHO) (1993). *The ICD-10 chapter V: Mental and behavioral disorders: Diagnostic criteria for research.* Geneva, Switzerland: Author.

World Health Organization. (2006) *Defining sexual health: Report of a technical consultation on sexual health,* 28–31 January 2002, Geneva, Switzerland: Author.

World Health Organization (WHO) (2008). *The global burden of disease: 2004 update.* Geneva, Switzerland: Author. Retrieved on July 28, 2104 from http://www.who.int/healthinfo/global_burden_disease/2004_report_update/en/index.html

World Health Organization (WHO) (2011). *WHO report on the global tobacco epidemic, 2011.* Geneva: World Health Organization. Retrieved on December 14, 2014 from http://www.who.int/tobacco/global_report/2011/en/

World Health Organization (WHO) (2013). *Comprehensive mental health action plan 2013–2020.* Retrieved January 19, 2014, from http://www.who.int/mental_health/action_plan_2013/en/

World Health Organization (WHO) (2013, January 27). *Guidelines for the psychosocially assisted pharmacological treatment of opioid dependence.* Retrieved on December 16, 2014 from http://findings.org.uk/count/downloads/download.php?file=WHO_5.txt

World Health Organization (WHO) (2014). *Suicide prevention: WHO mortality database.* Geneva, Switzerland: Author. Retrieved on August 12, 2104 from http://apps.who.int/healthinfo/statistics/mortality/whodpms/

World Health Organization (WHO) (2014a). *Global status report on alcohol and health 2014.* Retrieved on December 10, 2014 from http://www.who.int/substance_abuse/publications/global_alcohol_report/msb_gsr_2014_1.pdf

World Health Organization (WHO) (2014b). *Global Health Observatory (GHO): Prevalence of alcohol use disorders.* Retrieved on December 11, 2014 from http://gamapserver.who.int/gho/interactive_charts/substance_abuse/bod_alcohol_prevalence/atlas.html

Worling, J. R. (1995). Sexual abuse histories of adolescent male sex offenders: Differences on the basis of the age and gender of their victims. *Journal of Abnormal Psychology, 104,* 610–613.

Wortman, C. B., & Lehman, D. R. (1985). Reactions to victims of life crises: Support attempts that fail. In I. G. Sarason & B. R. Sarason (Eds.), *Social support: Theory, research, and applications* (pp. 463–489). Dordrecht, The Netherlands: Martinus Nijhoff.

Wortmann, F. (2013). "Why Monk stunk," in Triggered: Exploring the psychological landscape of OCD. *Psychology Today.* Retrieved on September 22, 2014 from http://www.psychologytoday.com/blog/triggered/201305/why-monk-stunk

Wozniak, K. M., Pert, A., & Linnoila, M. (1990). Antagonism of 5-HT3 receptors attenuates the effects of ethanol on extracellular dopamine. *European Journal of Pharmacology, 187,* 287–289.

Wright, L. (1994). *Remembering Satan: A case of recovered memory and the shattering of an American family.* New York: Knopf.

Wright, L. M., Holborn, S. W., & Rezutek, P. E. (2002). An experimental test of stimulus estimation theory: Danger and safety with snake phobic stimuli. *Behaviour Research and Therapy, 40*(8), 911–922. doi:10.1016/S0005-7967(01)00078-X

Wright, L., & Walker, C. E. (1978). A simple behavioral treatment program for psychogenic encopresis. *Behaviour Research and Therapy, 16,* 209–212.

Wright, R, Nobrega, J., Langevin, R., & Wortzman, G. (1990). Brain density and symmetry in pedophilic and sexually aggressive offenders. *Annals of Sex Research, 3,* 319–328.

Wright, R. H. (2010). Is attention-deficit hyperactivity disorder (ADHD) a real disorder? In B. Slife (Ed.), *Clashing views on psychological issues* (16th ed.) (pp. 250–271). New York: McGraw-Hill.

Wrightsman, L. S., Nietzel, M. T., & Fortune, W. H. (1994). *Psychology and the legal system* (3rd ed.). Pacific Grove, CA: Brooks/Cole.

Wu, K. D., & Watson, D. (2005). Hoarding and its relation to obsessive-compulsive disorder. *Behaviour Research and Therapy, 43*(7), 897–921. doi: 10.1016/j.brat.2004.06.013

Wu, K., Hanna, G. L., Rosenberg, D. R., & Arnold, P. D. (2012). The role of glutamate signaling in the pathogenesis and treatment of obsessive-compulsive disorder. *Pharmacology, Biochemistry and Behavior, 100*(4), 726–735. doi:10.1016/j.pbb.2011.10.007

Wurtzel, E. (1995), *Prozac nation.* Boston: Houghton-Mifflin.

Wyatt v. Stickney, 325 F. Supp. 781 (1971).

Wyatt, G. E., Guthrie, D., & Notgrass, C. M. (1991). Differential effects of women's child sexual abuse and subsequent sexual revictimization. *Journal of Consulting and Clinical Psychology, 60,* 167–173.

Wygant, D. B., Anderson, J. L., Sellbom, M., Rapier, J. L., Allgeier, L. M., & Granacher, R. P. (2011). Association of the MMPI-2 restructured form (MMPI-2-RF) validity scales with structured malingering criteria. *Psychological Injury and Law, 4,* 13–23. doi:10.1007/s12207-011-9098-z

X

Xu, Z., Zhang, Z., Shi, Y., Pu, M., Yuan, Y., Zhang, X., & Li, L. (2011). Influence and interaction of genetic polymorphisms in catecholamine neurotransmitter systems and early life stress on antidepressant drug response. *Journal of Affective Disorders, 133*(1–2), 165–173. doi:10.1016/j.jad.2011.04.011

Y

Yalom, I. D. (1985). *The theory and practice of group psychotherapy* (3rd ed.). New York: Basic Books.

Yang, M., Kim, B., Lee, E., Lee, D., Yu, B., Jeon, H., & Kim, J. (2014). Diagnostic utility of worry and rumination: A comparison between generalized anxiety disorder and major depressive disorder. *Psychiatry and Clinical Neurosciences, 68*(9),712–720. doi:10.1111/pcn.12193

Yang, M., Wong, S. P., & Coid, J. (2010). The efficacy of violence prediction: A meta-analytic comparison of nine risk assessment tools. *Psychological Bulletin, 136*(5), 740–767. doi:10.1037/a0020473

Yassa, R., Nastase, C., Dupont, D., & Thibeau, M. (1992). Tardive dyskinesia in elderly psychiatric patients: A 5-year study. *American Journal of Psychiatry, 149,* 1209–1211.

Yates, A. (1993). Sexually inhibited children. *Child and Adolescent Psychiatric Clinics of North America, 2,* 451–461.

Yee, A. H., Fairchild, FI. H., Weizmann, F., & Wyatt, G. E. (1993). Addressing psychology's problems with race. *American Psychologist, 48,* 1132–1140.

Yiend, J., Paykel, E., Merritt, R., Lester, K., Doll, H., & Burns, T. (2009). Long-term outcome of primary care depression. *Journal of Affective Disorders, 118*(1–3), 79–86. doi:10.1016/j.jad.2009.01.026

Ying, Y. (1989). Nonresponse on the Center for Epidemiological Studies-Depression scale in Chinese Americans. *International Journal of Social Psychiatry, 35,* 156–163.

Yong, H., Borland, R., Hyland, A., & Siahpush, M. (2008). How does a failed quit attempt among regular smokers affect their cigarette consumption? Findings from the International Tobacco Control Four-Country Survey (ITC-4). *Nicotine & Tobacco Research, 10*(5), 897–905. doi:10.1080/14622200802023841

Yonkers, K., Kando, J., Cole, J., & Blumenthal, S. (1992). Gender differences in pharmacokinetics and pharmacodynamics of psychotropic medication. *The American Journal of Psychiatry, 149,* 587–595.

Yoshikawa, H. (1994). Prevention as cumulative protection: Effects of early family support and education on chronic delinquency and its risks. *Psychological Bulletin, 115,* 28–54.

You, S., & Conner, K. R. (2009). Stressful life events and depressive symptoms: Influences of gender, event severity, and depression history. *The Journal of Nervous and Mental Disease, 197*(11), 829–833. doi:10.1097/NMD.0b013e3181be7841

Youn, G. (2013). Challenges facing sex therapy in Korea. In K. K. Hall & C. A. Graham (Eds.), *The cultural context of sexual pleasure and problems: Psychotherapy with diverse clients* (pp. 160–169). New York: Routledge/Taylor & Francis Group.

Young, L. D. (1992). Psychological factors in rheumatoid arthritis. *Journal of Consulting and Clinical Psychology, 60,* 619–643.

Youngberg v. Romeo, 457 U.S. 307 (1982).

Ysseldyke, J. E., Algozzine, B., & Epps, S. (1983). A logical and empirical analysis of current practice in classifying students as handicapped. *Exceptional Children, 50,* 160–166.

Yu, C. (2014). Toward 100% dream retrieval by rapid-eye-movement sleep awakening: A high-density electroencephalographic study. *Dreaming, 24*(1), 1–17. doi:10.1037/a0035792

Yufik, A. (2005). Revisiting the *Tarasoff* decision: Risk assessment and liability in clinical and forensic practice. *American Journal of Forensic Psychology, 23*(4), 5–21.

Yüksel, C., McCarthy, J., Shinn, A., Pfaff, D. L., Baker, J. T., Heckers, S., . . . Öngür, D. (2012). Gray matter volume in schizophrenia and bipolar disorder with psychotic features. *Schizophrenia Research, 138*(2–3), 177–182. doi:10.1016/j.schres.2012.03.003

Yung, C. R. (2011) Symposium: Preventative detention: Sex offender exceptionalism and preventive detention. *Journal of Criminal Law and Criminology, 101*(3).

Yur'yev, A., Värnik, P., Sisask, M., Leppik, L., Lumiste, K., & Värnik, A. (2013). Some aspects of social exclusion: Do they influence suicide mortality? *International Journal of Social Psychiatry, 59*(3), 232–238. doi:10.1177/0020764011431792

Yury, C. A., Fisher, J. E., Antonuccio, D. O., Valenstein, M., & Matuszak, J. (2009). Meta-analysis of antidepressant augmentation: Piling on in the absence of evidence. *Ethical Human Psychology and Psychiatry: An International Journal of Critical Inquiry, 11*(3), 171–182. doi:10.1891/1559-4343.11.3.171

Z

Zager, D. (2013). Positive psychology and autism spectrum disorders. In M. L. Wehmeyer (Ed.), *The Oxford handbook of positive psychology and disability* (pp. 494–505). New York: Oxford University Press.

Zaiontz, C. A., Arduini, A., Buren, D., & Fungi, G. (2012). Migration fluxes and adjustment disorder: An examination of a native English-speaking population in Milan. *Journal of Social, Evolutionary, and Cultural Psychology, 6*(1), 66–81. doi:10.1037/h0099224

Zanarini, M. C., Gunderson, J. G., Frankenburg, F. R., & Chauncey, D. L. (1989). The revised diagnostic interview for borderlines: Discriminating BPD from other axis II disorders. *Journal of Personality Disorders, 3,* 10–18.

Zanetti, T., Santonastaso, P., Sgaravatti, E., Degortes, D., & Favaro, A. (2013). Clinical and temperamental correlates of body image disturbance in eating disorders. *European Eating Disorders Review, 21*(1), 32–37. doi:10.1002/erv.2190

Zapf, P. A., Golding, S. L., & Roesch, R. (2006). Criminal responsibility and the insanity defense. In I.B. Weiner & A.K. Hess (Eds.), *The handbook of forensic psychology,* 3rd edition (pp. 332–363). Hoboken, NJ: John Wiley & Sons.

Zara, G., & Farrington, D. P. (2013). Assessment of risk for juvenile compared with adult criminal onset implications for policy, prevention, and intervention. *Psychology, Public Policy, and Law, 19,* 235–249. doi:10.1037/a0029050

Zaretsky, A. E., Rizvi, S., & Parikh, S. V. (2007). How well do psychosocial interventions work in bipolar disorder? *Canadian Journal of Psychiatry, 52*(1), 14–21.

Zatzick, D., Rivara, F., Nathens, A., Jurkovich, G., Wang, J., Fan, M., . . . Mackenzie, E. (2007). A nationwide U.S. study of post-traumatic stress after hospitalization for physical injury. *Psychological Medicine, 37*(10), 1469–1480.

Zelkowitz, P., Paris, J., Guzder, J., & Feldman, R. (2001). Diathesis and stressors in borderline pathology of childhood: The role of neuropsychological risk and trauma. *Journal of the American Academy of Child & Adolescent Psychiatry, 40*(1), 100–105.

Zellner, D. A., Harner, D. E., & Adler, R. L. (1989). Effects of eating abnormalities and gender on perceptions of desirable body shape. *Journal of Abnormal Psychology, 98*(1), 93–96. doi:10.1037/0021-843X.98.1.93

Zhou, J., Hofman, M. A., Gooren, L. G., & Swaab, D. F. (1995). A sex difference in the human brain and its relation to transsexuality. *Nature, 378,* 68–70.

Zhou, X., Nonnemaker, J., Sherrill, B., Gilsenan, A. W., Coste, F., & West, R. (2009). Attempts to quit smoking and relapse: Factors associated with success or failure from the ATTEMPTS cohort study. *Addictive Behaviors, 34*(4), 365–373. doi:10.1016/j.addbeh.2008.11.013

Zigler, E., & Hodapp, R. M. (1986). *Understanding mental retardation.* New York: Cambridge University Press.

Zigler, E., Levine, I., & Zigler, B. (1976). The relation between premorbid competence and paranoid-nonparanoid status in schizophrenia. *Psychological Bulletin, 83,* 303–313.

Zigler, E., & Styfco, S. J. (1993). Head Start: Criticisms in a constructive context. *American Psychologist, 49,* 127–132.

Zigler, E., Taussig, C., & Black, K. (1992). Early childhood intervention: A promising preventative for juvenile delinquency. *American Psychologist, 47,* 997–1006.

Zimmerman, M. (1983). Melhudological issues in the assessment of life events: A review of issues and research. *Clinical Psychology Review, 3,* 339–370.

Zimmerman, M., & Coryell, W. (1989). DSM-III personality disorder diagnoses in a non-patient sample. *Archives of General Psychiatry, 46,* 682–689.

Zimmerman, M., & Galione, J. (2010). Psychiatrists' and nonpsychiatrist physicians' reported use of the *DSM-IV* criteria for major depressive disorder. *Journal of Clinical Psychiatry, 71,* 235–238.

Zimmerman, M., Martinez, J. H., Dalrymple, K., Chelminski, I., & Young, D. (2013). Is the distinction between adjustment disorder with depressed mood and adjustment disorder with mixed anxious and depressed mood valid? *Annals of Clinical Psychiatry, 25*(4), 257–265.

Zimmerman, M., Rothschild, L., & Chelminski, I. (2005). The prevalence of *DSM-IV* personality disorders in psychiatric outpatients. *The American Journal of Psychiatry, 162*(10), 1911–1918. doi:10.1176/appi.ajp.162.10.1911

Zinbarg, R., Barlow, D., Brown, T., & Hertz, R. (1992). Cognitive-behavioral approaches to the nature and treatment of anxiety disorders. *Annual Review of Psychology, 43,* 235–267.

Zinbarg, R. E., & Mineka, S. (1991). Animal models of psychopathology: II. Simple phobia. *Behavior Therapy, 14,* 61–65.

Ziskin J., & Faust, D. (1988). *Coping with psychiatric and psychological testimony.* Marina del Rey, CA: Law and Psychology Press.

Zisook, S., Paulus, M., & Shuchter, S. R. (1997). The many faces of depression following spousal bereavement. *Journal of Affective Disorders, 45,* 85–95.

Zitrin, C. M., Klein, D. F., & Woerner, M. G. (1980). Treatment of agoraphobia with group exposure in vivo and imipramine. *Archives of General Psychiatry, 37,* 63–72.

Zohar, J., Yahalom, H., Kozlovsky, N., Cwikel-Hamzany, S., Matar, M. A., Kaplan, Z., . . . Cohen, H. (2011). High dose hydrocortisone immediately after trauma may alter the trajectory of PTSD: Interplay between clinical and animal studies. *European Neuropsychopharmacology, 21*(11), 796–809. doi:10.1016/j.euroneuro.2011.06.001

Zook, A. H., & Walton, J. M. (1989). Theoretical orientations and work settings of clinical and counseling psychologists: A current perspective. *Professional Psychology: Research and Practice, 20,* 23–31.

Zubin, J., & Spring, B. (1977). Vulnerability: A new view of schizophrenia. *Journal of Abnormal Psychology, 86,* 103–126.

Zucker, K. J. (2004). Gender identity development and issues. *Child and Adolescent Psychiatric, 13*(3), 551–568.

Zucker, K. J. & Bradley, S. J. (1995). *Gender identity disorder and psychosexual problems in children and adolescents.* New York: Guilford Press.

Zucker, K. J. & Green, R. (1992). Psychosexual disorders in children and adolescents. *Journal of Child Psychology and Psychiatry and Allied Disciplines, 33,* 107–151.

Zucker, K. J., & Green, R. (1993). Psychological and familial aspects of gender identity disorder. In A. Yates (Ed.), Sexual and gender identity disorders, *Child and Adolescent Psychiatric Clinics of North America, 2,* 513–542.

Zucker, K. J., Wild, J., Bradley, S. J., & Lowry, C. B. (1993). Physical attractiveness of boys with gender identity disorder. *Archives of Sexual Behavior, 22,* 23–34.

Zucker, R. A. (1987). The four alcoholisms: A developmental account of the etiologic process. In P. C. Rivers (Ed.), *Nebraska symposium on motivation, 1986: Vol. 34, Alcohol and addictive behaviors.* Lincoln: University of Nebraska Press.

Zucker, R. A., & Fitzgerald, H. E. (1991). Early developmental factors and risk for alcohol problems. *Alcohol Health Research World, 15,* 18–24.

Zuger, B. (1989). Homosexuality in families of boys with early effeminate behavior: An epidemiological study. *Archives of Sexual Behavior, 18,* 155–166.

Zuvekas, S. H., & Vitiello, B. (2012). Stimulant medication use in children: A 12-year perspective. *The American Journal of Psychiatry, 169*(2), 160–166. doi:10.1176/appi.ajp.2011.11030387

Zuvekas, S. H., Vitiello, B., & Norquist, G. S. (2006). Recent trends in stimulant medication use among U.S. children. *American Journal of Psychiatry, 163,* 579–585.

Name Index

Subject Index